GEN Z EDITION
HOLY BIBLE

Disclaimer:
This modern translation is intended for educational and personal study purposes. While every effort has been made to ensure accuracy and clarity, interpretations of religious texts can vary, and readers are encouraged to consult multiple sources and translations to gain a comprehensive understanding.

Dedication:
To all the young souls seeking wisdom, guidance, and inspiration in the digital age.

Acknowledgements:
We extend our heartfelt gratitude to the many scholars, linguists, and cultural advisors who contributed their expertise and insight to this project. Special thanks to the original authors and translators of the King James Version, whose work has inspired generations.

Book Original Title: Holy Bible (includes Old & New Testament books)
Book Original Version: King James Version
Book New Version Translator: Nathanael Ross
Book Genre / Category: Christian Bible; Spiritual, Religious Books;

First Edition.

Book Contents:

- Includes 39 books of the Old Testament and the 27 books of the New Testament.

THE OLD
TESTAMENT

Contents

+++

Genesis..*1*

Exodus...16

Leviticus...31

Numbers...41

Deuteronomy..54

Joshua...68

Judges...75

Ruth..82

1 Samuel...84

2 Samuel...93

1 Kings..100

2 Kings..111

1 Chronicles..120

2 Chronicles..131

Ezra...143

Nehemiah..147

Esther..153

Job...156

Psalms...166

Proverbs..198

Ecclesiastes...210

Song of Songs...213

Isaiah...215

Jeremiah..234

Lamentations..253

Ezekiel..255

Daniel..274

Hosea..280

Joel..284

Amos...286

Obadiah...289

Jonah...290

Micah...291

Nahum...293

Habakkuk..294

Zephaniah..295

Haggai...296

Zechariah...297

Malachi..301

Genesis

✦✦✦

{1:1} Yo, in the beginning, God created the sky and the earth. {1:2} The earth was like a total blank slate, all dark and empty, with water everywhere. God's Spirit was just chilling over the waters. {1:3} Then God was like, "Let there be light!" Boom, there was light. {1:4} God checked out the light, thought it was dope, and split it from the darkness. {1:5} He named the light "Day" and the darkness "Night." That was the first day, fam. {1:6} Next up, God was like, "Let's have a sky in the middle of these waters, dividing them." {1:7} So God made the sky and separated the waters below from those above. It was lit. {1:8} He called this sky "Heaven." That was day two. {1:9} Then God was like, "Let the waters come together, and let dry land appear." And it happened, bro. {1:10} God called the dry land "Earth" and the waters "Seas." God thought it was all good. {1:11} God was like, "Yo Earth, grow some grass, herbs, and fruit trees with seeds in 'em." And just like that, it happened. {1:12} The Earth did its thing and grew all kinds of plants, trees, and fruit. God was impressed. {1:13} That's day three, yo. {1:14} Then God was like, "Let's put lights in the sky to tell day from night, and mark seasons, days, and years." {1:15} So, God made the sun, moon, and stars to light up the Earth. It was a vibe. {1:16} The sun ruled the day, the moon the night, and God threw in the stars too. {1:17} They were there to light up the Earth and set the rhythm of day and night. God approved. {1:18} That was day four. {1:19} Next up, God was like, "Time for sea creatures and birds to pop up." And they did—whales, fish, birds—doing their thing. {1:20} God blessed them to multiply and fill the waters and the sky. {1:21} He was vibing with what he made. {1:22} That was day five. {1:23} Then God was like, "Let the Earth bring forth all sorts of creatures—cattle, bugs, beasts." And it happened just like that. {1:24} God made all kinds of animals, and he thought it was all good. {1:25} That's day six, my dude. {1:26} Finally, God was like, "Let's create humans in our image, to rule over everything on Earth." {1:27} So God created humans, male and female, reflecting his own image. {1:28} He blessed them, telling them to multiply and take charge of the Earth and all its creatures. {1:29} God said, "Yo, I've given you all these plants and trees for food." {1:30} And he hooked up the animals with greenery too. {1:31} God looked at everything and was like, "Yo, this is all lit!" That was the end of day six.

{2:1} So, like, everything in the heavens and on earth was done and set up, all complete. {2:2} Then on the seventh day, God wrapped up all his work and chilled out from all the creating. {2:3} He blessed that day and made it special because he took a break from making everything. {2:4} These are the deets on how the heavens and earth came to be, when the LORD God made everything. {2:5} Before plants were even poppin' up and growing, there wasn't any rain and no one was farming the land yet. {2:6} But there was this mist coming up from the earth and watering everything. {2:7} Then the LORD God crafted man out of the dust and breathed life into him. Boom, man was alive. {2:8} The LORD God planted a garden in Eden and put the man he made there. {2:9} He grew all sorts of good-looking and tasty trees, including the tree of life and the tree of knowing good and bad. {2:10} A river flowed out of Eden to water the garden, splitting into four rivers. {2:11} One was called Pison, running through Havilah where there's gold. {2:12} Gold in that land is top-notch, along with bdellium and onyx stones. {2:13} Another river was Gihon, winding through Ethiopia. {2:14} The third river was Hiddekel, flowing east of Assyria. And the fourth was the Euphrates. {2:15} The LORD God put man in the garden of Eden to care for it. {2:16} He told him, "Eat from any tree here, except the one that gives knowledge of good and bad. Don't touch that or you're out." {2:17-18} Then the LORD God was like, "It ain't cool for man to be alone. Let's find him a partner." {2:19-20} So, the LORD God made all the beasts and birds and brought them to Adam to see what he'd call them. Whatever Adam named them became their name. {2:20} Adam named all the animals, but there wasn't a suitable partner for him. {2:21-22} So, the LORD God made Adam sleep, took a rib, and made a woman from it, bringing her to Adam. {2:23} Adam was like, "Yo, she's bone of my bones and flesh of my flesh. Let's call her Woman, 'cause she came from Man." {2:24} That's why a man leaves his fam and sticks with his wife, and they're like one unit. {2:25} They were both naked and not feeling embarrassed about it.

{3:1} Yo, this sneaky serpent was slicker than any other creature God made. He goes to the woman and asks, "Did God really say you can't eat from any tree in the garden?" {3:2} The woman's like, "Nah, we can eat from any tree except the one in the middle. God said we'd die if we mess with it." {3:4} Then the serpent's all, "You won't die! God knows that if you eat it, you'll be woke, like gods, knowing good and evil." {3:6} The woman checks out the tree, sees it's tasty and looks dope, and decides to eat some. She gives some to her man, and he eats it too. {3:7} Suddenly, they realize they're naked and make some leaf aprons. {3:8} Later, they hear God walking in the garden and hide because they're ashamed of being naked. {3:9} God calls out to Adam, like, "Where you at?" {3:10} Adam admits he was scared 'cause he was naked, so he hid. {3:11} God's like, "Who told you that? Did you eat from that tree I warned you about?" {3:12} Adam blames Eve and indirectly throws God under the bus for giving him Eve. {3:13} Then God asks Eve what she did, and she's like, "The snake tricked me, so I ate it." {3:14} God curses the serpent, making it crawl on its belly and eat dust forever. {3:15} He also predicts conflict between the serpent's descendants and the woman's, with her offspring crushing its head. {3:16} To the woman, God says childbirth will be painful, and she'll desire her man, who will rule over her. {3:17} Then to Adam, God's like, "Because you listened to your wife and ate the fruit, the ground's cursed for you. {3:18} You'll deal with thorns and thistles, and farming will be tough." {3:19} Adam's gonna sweat to eat bread until he's dust again. {3:20} Adam names his wife Eve 'cause she's the mom of all living. {3:21} God makes them clothes from animal skins. {3:22} God's like, "Now they're like us, knowing good and evil.

Gotta keep 'em away from the tree of life so they don't live forever." {3:23} So, God kicks them out of Eden to work the ground they came from. {3:24} He sets up cherubim and a flaming sword to guard the way back to the tree of life.

{4:1} So, Adam and Eve did their thing, and Eve got pregnant and had Cain, saying, "I got a man from the LORD." {4:2} Then she had another son, Abel. Abel was into sheep, but Cain was all about farming. {4:3} One day, Cain brought some fruits from his farm as an offering to the LORD. {4:4} Abel also brought the firstborn of his flock and the best parts. God liked Abel's offering but not Cain's, which made Cain mad and bummed out. {4:6} God asks Cain why he's upset and warns him that sin's knocking at the door, but if he does right, he'll be accepted. {4:8} Later, Cain chats with Abel, and then out of nowhere, Cain kills his brother in the field. {4:9} God asks Cain where Abel is, and Cain's like, "I dunno, am I supposed to watch him?" {4:10} God's like, "Your brother's blood is crying out from the ground." {4:11} Cain's cursed from the earth, which won't yield good crops for him anymore, and he'll be a wanderer. {4:13} Cain complains to God that his punishment is too much to handle. {4:14} God banishes Cain, who worries that anyone who finds him will kill him. {4:15} God says anyone who kills Cain will face sevenfold vengeance and puts a mark on Cain for protection. {4:16} So Cain leaves God's presence and lives in Nod, east of Eden. {4:17} Cain marries and has a son named Enoch, who builds a city named after him. {4:18} Enoch has a son named Irad, who has descendants like Mehujael, Methusael, and Lamech. {4:19} Lamech takes two wives, Adah and Zillah. {4:20} Adah has a son named Jabal, who's into tents and raising livestock. {4:21} Jabal's brother Jubal is into music, playing the harp and organ. {4:22} Zillah has a son named Tubal-cain, skilled in metalwork, and a daughter named Naamah. {4:23} Lamech brags to his wives about killing someone and warns that if Cain's avenged sevenfold, he'd be avenged seventy-sevenfold. {4:25} Adam and Eve have another son named Seth, saying God replaced Abel, who Cain killed. {4:26} Seth has a son named Enos, and people start calling on the name of the LORD.

{5:1} Yo, this is the rundown of Adam's crew. When God made humans, he made them in his image, both male and female, and called them Adam back in the day they were created. {5:3} Adam lived 130 years and had a son named Seth in his own likeness. {5:4} After Seth was born, Adam lived a total of 800 years and had more kids. {5:5} Adam's whole life was 930 years before he kicked the bucket. {5:6} Seth lived 105 years and had a son named Enos. {5:7} After Enos, Seth lived another 807 years, having more children. {5:8} Seth lived to be 912 years old before he passed away. {5:9} Enos lived 90 years and had a son named Cainan. {5:10} After Cainan, Enos lived another 815 years, continuing to expand the family. {5:11} Enos's lifespan was 905 years before he died. {5:12} Cainan lived 70 years and became a dad to Mahalaleel. {5:13} Cainan lived another 840 years after Mahalaleel's birth, having more kids. {5:14} Cainan lived for a total of 910 years. {5:15} Mahalaleel lived 65 years and had a son named Jared. {5:16} After Jared, Mahalaleel lived another 830 years, having a large family. {5:17} Mahalaleel's life lasted 895 years. {5:18} Jared was 162 years old when he became a father to Enoch. {5:19} Jared lived another 800 years after Enoch's birth, having more children. {5:20} Jared's total lifespan was 962 years. {5:21} Enoch was 65 years old when he had Methuselah. {5:22} Enoch spent the next 300 years walking with God and having a family. {5:23} Enoch lived for 365 years before God took him. {5:25} Methuselah was 187 years old when he became a dad to Lamech. {5:26} Methuselah lived another 782 years after Lamech's birth, continuing his legacy. {5:27} Methuselah's life spanned 969 years. {5:28} Lamech was 182 years old when he had a son. {5:30} Lamech lived for another 595 years after Noah's birth, having more children. {5:31} Lamech lived to be 777 years old. {5:32} Noah was 500 years old when he became a father to Shem, Ham, and Japheth.

{6:1} So, when people started multiplying like crazy on earth and having daughters, {6:2} the sons of God noticed how beautiful these daughters of men were, and they chose them as wives. {6:3} Then God was like, "I'm not gonna keep dealing with humans forever; they're just flesh after all, and their lifespan is gonna cap at 120 years." {6:4} Back then, there were these giants roaming around, especially when the sons of God hooked up with human women and had mighty offspring, known as legendary figures of old. {6:5} God saw how wicked everyone had become on earth, with every thought being nothing but evil all the time. {6:6} It actually made God feel regretful about creating humans and broke his heart. {6:7} So God decided to wipe out all humans, along with animals, creepy-crawlies, and birds—basically everything he made—because he regretted making them. {6:8} But Noah was an exception; he found favor in God's eyes. {6:9} Now, here's the scoop on Noah: he was a righteous dude, perfect in his generation, and he walked with God. {6:10} Noah had three sons: Shem, Ham, and Japheth. {6:11} The earth was totally messed up in God's eyes, filled with violence everywhere. {6:12} God looked down and saw the earth was corrupted, with everyone going astray. {6:13} God told Noah, "The end is near; the whole world is full of violence because of them. I'm going to wipe them all out along with the earth." {6:14} "Build yourself an ark out of gopher wood; make rooms and seal it inside and out with pitch. {6:15} The dimensions? It's gonna be huge—300 cubits long, 50 cubits wide, and 30 cubits high. {6:16} There'll be a window and a door, and three stories inside. {6:17} I'm bringing a massive flood to wipe out everything on earth, every living creature that breathes air; they're all gonna die. {6:18} But you, Noah, I'll make a covenant with; you, your sons, your wife, and their wives will enter the ark. {6:19} And bring pairs of every living creature, male and female, to keep them alive with you. {6:20} Birds, livestock, and every crawling creature—bring them all. {6:21} Also, gather enough food for yourselves and them. {6:22} Noah followed God's instructions exactly as he was told.

{7:1} Then God said to Noah, "Gather your whole crew and get into the ark; I've seen how righteous you are in this messed-up generation." {7:2} For the clean animals, take them in pairs of seven—male and female; for the unclean ones, just two—male and female. {7:3} Also, bring in birds by sevens—male and female—to keep their kind alive all over the earth. {7:4} It's gonna start raining in seven days, and it won't stop for forty days and nights; everything I created will be wiped out from the face of the earth. {7:5} Noah did everything just as the LORD commanded him. {7:6} Noah was six hundred years old when the floodwaters came. {7:7} So Noah, his sons, his wife, and his sons' wives entered the ark to escape the flood. {7:8} They took in all kinds of animals—clean and unclean—and birds, and every creeping thing on earth. {7:9} They all went in pairs as God had commanded Noah. {7:10} After seven days, the floodwaters covered the earth. {7:11} It happened in the six hundredth year of Noah's life, on the seventeenth day of the second month; that's when the great deep broke open and the windows of heaven poured rain. {7:12} The rain continued for forty days and nights. {7:13} On that same day, Noah, Shem, Ham, Japheth, and their wives entered the ark, along with every kind of animal, cattle, creeping thing, and bird. {7:14} They all entered the ark in pairs, male and female, just as God commanded. {7:15} Then the LORD closed the door behind them. {7:16} For forty days, the flood covered the earth, lifting up the ark above the ground. {7:17} The waters continued to rise, covering even the highest hills under the whole sky. {7:18} They kept rising until the ark was afloat. {7:19} The floodwaters rose above the earth, covering even the mountains by fifteen cubits. {7:20} Every living thing on earth—birds, cattle, beasts, and creeping things—died, along with all humans. {7:21} Everything that breathed air on dry land perished. {7:22} Only Noah and those with him in the ark survived, {7:23} as the flood wiped out every living creature from the face of the earth—humans, animals, creeping things, and birds of the sky. {7:24} The floodwaters prevailed on the earth for a hundred and fifty days.

{8:1} Then God was like, "Oh yeah, Noah and all the living things and animals with him in the ark—time to calm things down." So God made a wind blow over the earth, and the waters started going down. {8:2} The deep fountains and the windows of heaven shut, and the rain stopped. {8:3} The waters slowly receded from the earth. After one hundred fifty days, things started to settle down. {8:4} The ark finally rested on the mountains of Ararat in the seventh month, on the seventeenth day of the month. {8:5} The water kept going down until the tenth month. On the first day of the tenth month, the mountain tops started showing. {8:6} After forty days, Noah opened the window he had made in the ark. {8:7} He sent out a raven, which flew back and forth until the waters dried up. {8:8} Then he sent out a dove to see if the waters were gone from the ground. {8:9} But the dove couldn't find a place to rest and came back to Noah in the ark. Noah reached out and brought the dove back inside. {8:10} He waited another seven days and sent out the dove again. {8:11} This time, the dove returned in the evening with an olive leaf in its mouth, showing that the waters were going down. {8:12} Noah waited another seven days and sent out the dove again, and this time it didn't come back. {8:13} In the six hundred and first year, on the first day of the first month, the earth was dry. Noah took off the ark's covering and saw that the ground was dry. {8:14} By the twenty-seventh day of the second month, the earth was completely dry. {8:15} Then God spoke to Noah, saying, {8:16} "Go out of the ark with your wife, your sons, and their wives." {8:17} Bring out all the living creatures—birds, cattle, and creeping things—to breed and multiply on the earth. {8:18-19} So Noah, his sons, and their wives all left the ark along with every living creature. {8:20} Noah built an altar to the LORD and took clean animals and birds to offer burnt offerings. {8:21} The LORD was pleased with the sacrifice and said, "I won't curse the ground again because of humans. People are messed up from the start, but I won't destroy everything like this again." {8:22} "As long as the earth remains, there will be planting and harvesting, cold and heat, summer and winter, day and night—no stopping that."

{9:1} So God blessed Noah and his sons, telling them, "Go forth, multiply, and fill up the earth." {9:2} Animals will fear and respect you—all creatures, birds, and fish are under your authority. {9:3} You can eat meat now, just like you eat plants. {9:4} But don't eat meat with its lifeblood; that's a no-go. {9:5} If anyone sheds human blood, they'll answer for it—whether it's an animal or another human. {9:6} Whoever takes a life will pay with their own, because humans are made in God's image. {9:7} And you guys, keep multiplying and filling up the earth. {9:8} Then God spoke to Noah and his sons, saying, {9:9} "I'm making a covenant with you and your descendants, and with every living creature on earth—birds, cattle, and all animals." {9:10} This covenant includes all creatures that came out of the ark. {9:11} From now on, there won't be another flood to wipe out all life. {9:12} The sign of this covenant is the rainbow—I'll set it in the clouds as a reminder. {9:13} When I bring clouds over the earth, the rainbow will appear. {9:14} It's a sign of the covenant between me and the earth. {9:15} The rainbow signifies that I'll never again destroy all life with a flood. {9:16} Every time I see the rainbow, I'll remember this everlasting covenant. {9:17} So, this rainbow is the sign of the covenant I've made with all living creatures on earth. {9:18} Noah's sons who left the ark were Shem, Ham, and Japheth; Ham was Canaan's father. {9:19} These three sons of Noah repopulated the whole earth. {9:20} Noah started farming and planted a vineyard. {9:21} He drank wine and got drunk, ending up uncovered in his tent. {9:22} Ham saw his father naked and told his brothers outside. {9:23} Shem and Japheth covered their father's nakedness respectfully. {9:24} When Noah woke up and realized what Ham had done, he cursed Canaan. {9:25} Canaan would serve his brothers as a servant. {9:26} Noah blessed the God of Shem, making Canaan his servant. {9:27} Japheth would be enlarged and dwell in Shem's tents, with Canaan also serving him. {9:28} Noah lived for three hundred and fifty years after the flood. {9:29} In total, Noah lived nine hundred and fifty years before passing away.

{10:1} So here's the rundown on Noah's sons—Shem, Ham, and Japheth—along with their post-flood offspring. {10:2} Japheth's crew included Gomer, Magog, Madai, Javan, Tubal, Meshech, and Tiras. {10:3} Gomer's sons were Ashkenaz, Riphath, and Togarmah. {10:4} Javan's crew included Elishah, Tarshish, Kittim, and Dodanim. {10:5} These guys populated different areas, each with their own language, families, and nations. {10:6} Now onto Ham's descendants—Cush, Mizraim, Phut, and Canaan. {10:7} Cush's sons were Seba, Havilah, Sabtah, Raamah, Sabtechah, with Raamah's sons being Sheba and Dedan. {10:8} Cush was the dad of Nimrod, a real powerhouse on Earth, known as a mighty hunter. {10:9} His kingdom kicked off in Babel, Erech, Accad, and Calneh in Shinar. {10:10-12} From there, Asshur headed out and built Nineveh, Rehoboth-Ir, Calah, and Resen. {10:13-14} Mizraim's descendants were Ludim, Anamim, Lehabim, Naphtuhim, Pathrusim, Casluhim (who gave rise to the Philistines), and Caphtorim. {10:15-18} Canaan's firstborn was Sidon, followed by Heth and others like the Jebusites, Amorites, Girgasites, Hivites, Arkites, Sinites, Arvadites,

Zemarites, Hamathites, and the rest of the Canaanite families. {10:19} Their territory stretched from Sidon to Gaza, then all the way to Sodom, Gomorrah, Admah, Zeboim, and Lasha. {10:20} This was Ham's clan—spread out in different nations with their own languages and lands. {10:21} Shem, the older brother of Japheth, was the ancestor of the Hebrews. {10:22} Shem's descendants included Elam, Asshur, Arphaxad, Lud, and Aram. {10:23} Aram's kids were Uz, Hul, Gether, and Mash. {10:24} Arphaxad had a son named Salah, who later had Eber. {10:25} Eber had two sons—Peleg, named because the earth was divided in his time, and Joktan. {10:26-29} Joktan's sons were Almodad, Sheleph, Hazar-maveth, Jerah, Hadoram, Uzal, Diklah, Obal, Abimael, Sheba, Ophir, Havilah, and Jobab. {10:30} They lived eastward from Mesha towards Sephar, a mountain. {10:31} These were Shem's descendants, each with their own families, languages, lands, and nations. {10:32} These were Noah's sons who spread out and formed nations after the flood..

{11:1} So back in the day, everyone on Earth spoke the same language. {11:2} As they moved eastward, they found a spot in Shinar and settled down. {11:3} They decided, "Let's make bricks and build a city with a tower that reaches the sky, so we'll be famous and won't be scattered across the world." {11:5} The LORD checked out what they were up to. {11:6} Seeing they were united and capable of anything they imagined, God said, "Let's mix up their language so they can't understand each other." {11:8} That's when God scattered them across the earth, and they stopped building the city. {11:9} That's why it's called Babel—because God mixed up everyone's language and scattered them across the globe. {11:10} Now let's talk about Shem's family tree. Shem was a hundred when Arphaxad was born, two years post-flood. {11:11} Shem lived five hundred more years, having more kids. {11:12} Arphaxad was thirty-five when Salah was born. {11:13} Arphaxad lived four hundred and three years afterward, having more kids. {11:14} Salah was thirty when Eber was born. {11:15} Salah lived four hundred and three years more, having more kids. {11:16} Eber was thirty-four when Peleg was born. {11:17} Eber lived four hundred and thirty more years, having more kids. {11:18} Peleg was thirty when Reu was born. {11:19} Peleg lived two hundred and nine years more, having more kids. {11:20} Reu was thirty-two when Serug was born. {11:21} Reu lived two hundred and seven years more, having more kids. {11:22} Serug was thirty when Nahor was born. {11:23} Serug lived two hundred years more, having more kids. {11:24} Nahor was twenty-nine when Terah was born. {11:25} Nahor lived a hundred and nineteen years more, having more kids. {11:26} Terah was seventy when he had Abram, Nahor, and Haran. {11:27} Now let's look at Terah's family line. Terah had Abram, Nahor, and Haran; Haran had Lot. {11:28} Haran passed away in Ur of the Chaldees, before Terah. {11:29} Abram and Nahor got married—Abram to Sarai and Nahor to Milcah. {11:30} Sarai couldn't have kids. {11:31} Terah took Abram, Sarai, and Lot from Ur to Canaan, settling in Haran. {11:32} Terah lived to be two hundred and five before passing away in Haran.

{12:1} So God told Abram, "Leave your hometown and family and head to a new land that I'll show you. {12:2} I'll make you a big deal, bless you, and make your name famous. You'll be a blessing to others. {12:3} Anyone who blesses you will be blessed, and anyone who curses you will get cursed. Through you, all families on Earth will be blessed. {12:4} So Abram dipped, just as God told him, and took his nephew Lot with him. Abram was seventy-five when he left Haran. {12:5} He took Sarai, Lot, all their stuff, and the people they picked up in Haran, and they headed to Canaan, where they settled. {12:6} They passed through Sichem to Moreh's plain, but the Canaanites were already there. {12:7} God appeared to Abram and promised him the land for his descendants. So Abram built an altar to the LORD who appeared to him. {12:8} He then moved east toward Bethel, pitching his tent between Bethel and Hai. Abram built another altar to the LORD and called on his name. {12:9} Abram kept heading south. {12:10} But then a famine hit, so Abram went to Egypt to chill because things were rough in Canaan. {12:11} As they approached Egypt, Abram told Sarai, "You're a knockout. When the Egyptians see you, they'll want to marry you and kill me." {12:13} "Tell them you're my sister, so things go well for me and I stay alive because of you." {12:14} When they reached Egypt, everyone noticed Sarai's beauty. {12:15} Pharaoh's officials praised her to him, and she ended up in Pharaoh's house. {12:16} Pharaoh treated Abram well because of Sarai, hooking him up with livestock and servants. {12:17} But then God hit Pharaoh and his house with serious plagues because of Sarai, Abram's wife. {12:18} Pharaoh confronted Abram, asking why he didn't say Sarai was his wife. {12:19} "You could've caused trouble by saying she's your sister!" Pharaoh said, giving Sarai back to Abram and telling them to leave with all their stuff.

{13:1} So Abram bounced out of Egypt with his wife, Lot, and all his stuff, heading south. {13:2} Abram was loaded, with tons of cattle, silver, and gold. {13:3} He traveled back from the south to Bethel, where he had set up camp before, between Bethel and Hai. {13:4} He returned to the altar he'd built there before and called on the LORD. {13:5} Lot, who was rolling with Abram, also had flocks, herds, and tents. {13:6} But the land couldn't handle both of them living together because their stuff was too much. {13:7} This caused tension between Abram's herdsmen and Lot's herdsmen, and the Canaanites and Perizzites were around too. {13:8} Abram told Lot, "Let's not beef with each other, man. We're family. {13:9} Look around and pick where you wanna go. If you go left, I'll go right. If you go right, I'll head left." {13:10} Lot checked out the whole Jordan plain, which was lush like a paradise, before the LORD took out Sodom and Gomorrah. It was as sweet as Egypt, all the way to Zoar. {13:11} Lot picked the Jordan plain and moved east, separating from Abram. {13:12} Abram chilled in Canaan, but Lot moved into the cities of the plain and set up camp toward Sodom. {13:13} Now, the people of Sodom were straight-up wicked sinners in the eyes of the LORD. {13:14} Then the LORD told Abram, after Lot split, "Look around—north, south, east, west. {13:15} All this land you see, I'm giving it to you and your descendants forever. {13:16} Your descendants will be too many to count, like dust on the ground. {13:17} Go check out the whole land, because I'm giving it to you." {13:18} So Abram packed up, settled in the plain of Mamre near Hebron, and built an altar to the LORD there.

{14:1} Back in the day when Amraphel was king of Shinar, Arioch was king of Ellasar, Chedorlaomer ruled Elam, and Tidal was king over nations; {14:2} These dudes went to war against Bera, king of Sodom, and Birsha, king of Gomorrah, along with Shinab, king of

Admah, Shemeber, king of Zeboiim, and the king of Bela (aka Zoar). {14:3} They all teamed up in the valley of Siddim, near the salt sea. {14:4} For twelve years, they were under Chedorlaomer's thumb, but in the thirteenth year, they rebelled. {14:5} Then in the fourteenth year, Chedorlaomer and his crew attacked the Rephaim in Ashteroth Karnaim, the Zuzim in Ham, and the Emim in Shaveh Kiriathaim. {14:6} They also took on the Horites in Mount Seir all the way to El-paran in the wilderness. {14:7} After that, they hit up En-mishpat (Kadesh) and wrecked the Amalekites and Amorites in Hazezon-tamar. {14:8} The kings of Sodom, Gomorrah, Admah, Zeboiim, and Bela (Zoar) geared up and went to battle against Chedorlaomer, king of Elam, Tidal, king of nations, Amraphel, king of Shinar, and Arioch, king of Ellasar; four kings against five. {14:10} The valley of Siddim was full of tar pits, and the kings of Sodom and Gomorrah fled, with some falling into the pits; the rest escaped to the mountains. {14:11} Chedorlaomer's crew took all the goods from Sodom and Gomorrah and bounced. {14:12} They even took Lot, Abram's nephew, who was living in Sodom, along with his stuff, and split. {14:13} One dude managed to escape and told Abram the Hebrew, who was chilling in Mamre's plain, a bro of the Amorites, hanging with Eshcol and Aner. {14:14} When Abram found out his nephew got nabbed, he geared up his trained servants, 318 in total, and chased after them all the way to Dan. {14:15} He split his crew and attacked them by night, chasing them to Hobah near Damascus. {14:16} Abram brought back all the goods, rescued Lot and his stuff, along with the women and the people. {14:17} The king of Sodom met Abram after he wiped out Chedorlaomer and his crew at the Valley of Shaveh, aka the King's Valley. {14:18} Then Melchizedek, king of Salem, brought out bread and wine; he was a priest of the Most High God. {14:19} He blessed Abram, saying, "Blessed be Abram by the Most High God, the possessor of heaven and earth. {14:20} And blessed be God Most High, who handed your enemies over to you." Abram gave him a tenth of everything. {14:21} The king of Sodom told Abram, "Give me the people and take the goods for yourself." {14:22} Abram swore to the king of Sodom, "I've raised my hand to the LORD, the Most High God, the possessor of heaven and earth, {14:23} and I won't take a thing from you, not even a thread or shoelace, so you can't say you made me rich. {14:24} Let Aner, Eshcol, and Mamre take their share of what my crew has consumed."

{15:1} So one day, God hit up Abram with a vision, saying, "Chill out, Abram. I got your back, and I'm hooking you up big time." {15:2} Abram was like, "Yo, Lord GOD, what's the deal? I'm out here with no kids, and the dude running my place is Eliezer from Damascus." {15:3} Abram was like, "Look, I don't have any descendants of my own. This dude in my house is all I got." {15:4} Then God was like, "Nah, that's not gonna cut it. Your heir will be your own flesh and blood." {15:5} God took Abram outside and said, "Check out the stars, man. Can you count 'em? That's how many descendants you're gonna have." {15:6} Abram was all in, believing God, and God was like, "That's what's up. I'm counting you as righteous." {15:7} Then God reminded Abram, "I'm the one who brought you out of Ur of the Chaldees to give you this land." {15:8} Abram was like, "Lord GOD, how do I know this land will be mine?" {15:9} So God told him, "Bring me a three-year-old heifer, she-goat, and ram, plus a turtledove and young pigeon." {15:10} Abram did as God said, dividing the animals but not the birds. {15:11} When the birds came down, Abram scared 'em off. {15:12} As the sun set, a deep sleep and darkness fell over Abram. {15:13} God then told Abram, "Your descendants will be strangers in a foreign land, enslaved and mistreated for four hundred years." {15:14} "But I'll judge the nation that enslaves them, and they'll leave with great wealth," God said. {15:15} "You'll kick it with your ancestors in peace, living to a ripe old age." {15:16} "After four generations, your descendants will come back here, once the Amorites' wickedness hits full tilt." {15:17} As the sun set and darkness fell, Abram saw a smoking furnace and a burning lamp pass between the animal pieces. {15:18} That same day, God cut a deal with Abram, saying, "I'm giving this land to your descendants, from the river of Egypt to the Euphrates." {15:19} "It'll be home to the Kenites, Kenizzites, Kadmonites, Hittites, Perizzites, Rephaims, Amorites, Canaanites, Girgashites, and Jebusites."

{16:1} So Sarai, Abram's wife, couldn't have kids, but she had this Egyptian handmaid named Hagar. {16:2} Sarai was like, "Yo, Abram, the LORD isn't letting me have kids. Why don't you go hook up with Hagar and maybe I'll get kids through her." And Abram was down with Sarai's plan. {16:3} After Abram had been in Canaan for ten years, Sarai gave Hagar to him as his wife. {16:4} Abram went for it, and Hagar got pregnant. But when Hagar saw she was expecting, she started acting all high and mighty toward Sarai. {16:5} Sarai was like, "This is all your fault, Abram. I gave you my maid, and now she disrespects me. May the LORD judge between us." {16:6} Abram told Sarai, "She's your maid; do whatever you want with her." So Sarai treated Hagar harshly, and Hagar took off. {16:7} Then an angel found Hagar by a water fountain in the wilderness on the way to Shur. {16:8} The angel asked, "Hagar, where did you come from, and where are you going?" She replied, "I'm running from my mistress Sarai." {16:9} The angel told her, "Go back to Sarai and submit to her." {16:10} The angel promised, "I'll make sure your descendants are so numerous they can't be counted." {16:11} The angel continued, "You're gonna have a son and name him Ishmael because the LORD heard your suffering." {16:12} "He'll be a wild man, always fighting with everyone, and they'll fight back. He'll live near all his relatives." {16:13} Hagar called the LORD who spoke to her "The God who sees me" because she realized she'd seen the One who saw her. {16:14} That's why the well was called Beer-lahai-roi; it's between Kadesh and Bered. {16:15} Hagar had Abram's son, and Abram named him Ishmael. {16:16} Abram was eighty-six years old when Ishmael was born.

{17:1} When Abram hit ninety-nine, the LORD showed up and was like, "I'm the Almighty God; walk with me and be legit." {17:2} Then God promised Abram a huge covenant and said he'd multiply him like crazy. {17:3} Abram was so moved he fell on his face, and God kept talking, saying, {17:4} "I'm making a covenant with you, and you're gonna be the father of many nations." {17:5} "From now on, you're not just Abram; you're Abraham, 'cause I'm making you a father of nations." {17:6} "You're gonna have tons of descendants, and kings will come from you." {17:7} "I'm setting up this everlasting covenant with you and your descendants to be your God and theirs." {17:8} "I'm giving you and your descendants the land of Canaan forever, and I'll be their God." {17:9} Then God told Abraham to keep the covenant, him and his descendants forever. {17:10} "Here's the deal: every male among you has gotta be circumcised; it's our covenant thing." {17:11} "You gotta circumcise everyone's foreskin; it's a sign of our deal." {17:12} "Every boy when he's eight days old, whether born in your house or bought with money, has to be circumcised." {17:13} "It's an everlasting covenant marked in your flesh." {17:14} "Any uncircumcised dude is out; he's broken the covenant." {17:15} Then God changed Sarai's name to Sarah and promised to bless her with a son, who'd become the mother of nations with kings from her. {17:16} When Abraham heard this, he laughed and thought, "I'm a hundred, and Sarah's ninety; how can we have a kid?" {17:18} He was like, "God, just let Ishmael live before you." {17:19} But God was clear: Sarah would have a son named Isaac, and God's covenant would be with him and his descendants forever. {17:20} God blessed Ishmael too, promising he'd be fruitful with twelve princes and a great nation. {17:21} But God emphasized that the covenant was with Isaac, whom Sarah would bear the next year. {17:22} After that, God finished talking and left. {17:23} So Abraham circumcised Ishmael and all the males in his household, as God had instructed. {17:24} Abraham himself was ninety-nine when he got circumcised. {17:25} Ishmael was thirteen when he was circumcised along with Abraham. {17:26} They both got circumcised on the same day, along with all the other males in Abraham's household, whether born in the house or bought with money from foreigners.

{18:1} So one day, the LORD showed up to Abram in Mamre, and Abram was chilling at his tent door in the heat of the day; {18:2} he looked up and saw three dudes standing nearby. When he spotted them, he hustled over, bowed down, and welcomed them, asking them not to leave. {18:3} He was like, "Hey, if you think I'm cool, hang out with me for a bit." {18:4} Then he offered them some water to wash their feet and rest under the tree, {18:5} promising to bring them bread to fill their hearts. They were totally down with that plan. {18:6} So Abram rushed into the tent to Sarah and said, "Quick, whip up three measures of fine meal and bake some cakes." {18:7} Then he hurried to the herd, picked out a tender calf, and had it prepared. {18:8} He served them butter, milk, and the cooked calf, standing by them under the tree as they ate. {18:9} They asked him, "Where's Sarah, your wife?" He said, "She's in the tent." {18:10} Then one of the dudes said, "I'll come back next year, and Sarah will have a son." Sarah heard this and laughed to herself in the tent behind him. {18:11} Both Abraham and Sarah were pretty old by then, and she wasn't having kids anymore. {18:12} Sarah laughed inside, thinking, "Can I really have pleasure when I'm old, and my husband's ancient?" {18:13} The LORD asked Abraham, "Why did Sarah laugh and doubt she could have a child at her age?" {18:14} "Is anything too hard for the LORD? Next year, Sarah will have a son." {18:15} Sarah denied laughing, afraid she'd been caught, but the LORD was like, "Nah, I heard you laugh." {18:16} After that, the dudes looked toward Sodom, and Abraham walked with them part of the way. {18:17} Then the LORD said, "Should I hide from Abraham what I'm about to do? {18:18} Abraham's gonna be a big deal, and everyone will be blessed through him." {18:19} "I know he'll raise his kids and household right, following the LORD's ways for justice and righteousness, bringing about what the LORD promised him." {18:20} The LORD said, "The cry of Sodom and Gomorrah is serious because of their sin; {18:21} I'm gonna check it out and see if things are as bad as I've heard." {18:22} Then the dudes headed toward Sodom, but Abraham stayed with the LORD. {18:23} Abraham approached the LORD and asked, "Are you gonna wipe out the righteous along with the wicked?" {18:24} "What if there are fifty righteous people in the city? Will you still destroy it?" {18:25} "It wouldn't be right to treat the righteous like the wicked; the Judge of all the earth should do what's fair." {18:26} The LORD said, "If I find fifty righteous, I'll spare the whole place." {18:27} Abraham bargained, "What if there are forty-five righteous?" The LORD agreed not to destroy it for forty-five. {18:28} Abraham kept negotiating, "What about forty?" The LORD said he'd spare it for forty's sake. {18:29} Abraham persisted, "Let's say there are thirty." The LORD agreed again not to destroy it for thirty. {18:30} Abraham tried again, "What if there are twenty?" The LORD said he wouldn't destroy it for twenty's sake. {18:31} Once more, Abraham said, "What if only ten are found?" The LORD promised not to destroy it for ten's sake. {18:33} After that, the LORD left, and Abraham returned to his place.

{19:1} So, like, two angels rolled into Sodom in the evening, and Lot was posted up at the city gate. When Lot spotted them, he jumped up, bowed down, and welcomed them, asking them to crash at his place for the night and wash up. {19:2} But the angels were like, "Nah, we'll just crash outside." {19:3} Lot insisted, so they finally caved and went with him, chowing down on a feast of unleavened bread. {19:4} Before they could crash, though, the guys of Sodom—old and young—surrounded Lot's house, demanding to see the visitors. {19:5} They wanted to, you know, "get to know them." {19:6} Lot tried to reason with them, offering his daughters instead, which was messed up. {19:7} He was like, "Come on, guys, don't be so wicked." {19:8} The mob wasn't having it and started pressuring Lot. {19:9} They accused Lot of trying to judge them since he was just a foreigner, and they threatened to break down the door. {19:10} The angels inside grabbed Lot and pulled him back, shutting the door. {19:11} The angels struck the mob outside with blindness, and they struggled to find the door. {19:12} Then the angels told Lot to gather anyone else from his family because they were gonna destroy the city. {19:13} So Lot warned his sons-in-law, but they didn't take him seriously. {19:15} The next morning, the angels hurried Lot, his wife, and daughters out of the city before it got wrecked. {19:16} Lot hesitated, so the angels grabbed him and his family and led them out of the city. {19:17} Once they were out, the angels warned them to run to the mountains without looking back or stopping in the plain. {19:18} Lot was like, "Nah, let's go to this smaller city instead." {19:19} He pleaded for mercy, grateful for the angels saving his life. {19:20} The angels agreed not to destroy that city. {19:21} Lot was told to hurry to Zoar. {19:22} So Lot fled to Zoar, and the city was spared. {19:23} The sun was up when Lot reached Zoar. {19:24} Then the LORD rained down brimstone and fire on Sodom and Gomorrah, destroying the cities and everything in the plain. {19:25-26} Lot's wife looked back and turned into a pillar of salt. {19:27-28} Abraham woke up and saw the smoke rising from the cities. {19:29} God remembered Abraham and rescued Lot from the destruction. {19:30} Lot left Zoar and lived in the mountains with his daughters because he was scared to stay in Zoar. {19:31-35} The daughters, thinking there were no other men around, got their dad drunk and slept with him to have kids. {19:36} Both daughters ended up pregnant by their father. {19:37} The firstborn named her son Moab, who became the father of the Moabites. {19:38} The younger daughter named her son Ben-ammi, who became the father of the Ammonites.

{20:1} Abraham bounced south toward Gerar and crashed there for a bit. {20:2} He pulls the old "she's my sister" move with Sarah, and the king of Gerar, Abimelech, hears about it and snags Sarah. {20:3} But God drops a dream bomb on Abimelech, warning him he's as good as dead for messing with Abraham's wife. {20:4} Abimelech's like, "Hold up, I didn't touch her! You gonna wipe out a whole nation for this?" {20:5} He insists they both claimed Sarah was Abraham's sister, so it was an innocent mistake. {20:6} God's like, "I know you thought you were in the clear, but I stopped you from going there." {20:7} God tells Abimelech to return Sarah pronto since Abraham's a prophet who can pray for him. {20:8} Abimelech freaks out and spreads the word to his peeps. {20:9} He confronts Abraham, asking why he brought this mess upon them. {20:10} Abimelech wants to know what Abraham was thinking. {20:11} Abraham's excuse is that he thought nobody feared God in Gerar and figured they'd off him for Sarah. {20:12} Abraham admits Sarah's his half-sister but married her anyway. {20:13} He explains that they agreed to call each other siblings wherever they went. {20:14} Abimelech makes things right by giving Abraham livestock and servants and returns Sarah. {20:15} Abimelech offers Abraham free reign in his land. {20:16} He gives Sarah silver, thinking he's doing her a favor. {20:17} Abraham prays, and God lifts the infertility curse from Abimelech's household because of Sarah.

{21:1} So, like, God finally hooked up Sarah as He said He would, and everything went down exactly as He had said. {21:2} Sarah got pregnant and gave birth to Abraham's son, Isaac, just as God had promised, even though Abraham was ancient by then. {21:3} Abraham named his son Isaac, born to him by Sarah. {21:4} When Isaac was eight days old, Abraham circumcised him like God told him to. {21:5} Abraham was a hundred years old when Isaac was born. {21:6} Sarah was all like, "God totally made me laugh with this! Everyone's gonna be laughing with me." {21:7} She was like, "Who would've thought I'd be nursing a baby at my age? I mean, I gave birth to a son in Abraham's old age!" {21:8} Isaac grew up and was weaned, and Abraham threw this epic feast on the same day Isaac was weaned. {21:9} Then Sarah saw Ishmael (the son of her servant Hagar) mocking Isaac. {21:10} So she told Abraham to kick out Hagar and Ishmael, 'cause Isaac was the real heir, and Ishmael wasn't gonna share that. {21:11} Abraham was bummed 'cause of Ishmael, but God told him to listen to Sarah and send them away. {21:12} God promised to make a nation out of Ishmael too 'cause he was Abraham's seed. {21:13} Early the next morning, Abraham gave Hagar and Ishmael some provisions and sent them off into the wilderness. {21:14} They ran out of water, and Hagar thought Ishmael was gonna die, but God heard him crying. {21:15} An angel assured Hagar that God was gonna make Ishmael into a great nation. {21:16} God showed Hagar a well, and she gave Ishmael water to drink. {21:17} Ishmael grew up in the wilderness and became skilled with a bow. {21:18} He settled in Paran, and his mom got him a wife from Egypt. {21:22} Meanwhile, Abimelech and his chief dude Phichol spoke to Abraham, recognizing God's favor on him. {21:23} They made a deal not to mess each other over, and Abraham swore to it. {21:24} Abraham called out Abimelech for his servants taking Abraham's well by force. {21:25} Abimelech was clueless about it until then. {21:26} Abraham gave Abimelech livestock, and they made a covenant. {21:27} Abraham set aside seven ewe lambs as proof of his ownership of a well. {21:28} So they named the place Beersheba after making their oath. {21:29} Abraham set up a place to worship God in Beersheba, where he stayed for a while in Philistine territory.

{22:1} So, like, after all that stuff, God decides to test Abraham. He's like, "Yo, Abraham!" And Abraham's like, "Here I am." {22:2} Then God drops a bomb on him, saying, "Take your only son Isaac, whom you love, and head to Moriah. Sacrifice him as a burnt offering on a mountain I'll show you." {22:3} Abraham's up at the crack of dawn, saddles his donkey, takes two dudes with him, plus Isaac, and gets the wood ready for the sacrifice. They head to the spot God told him about. {22:4} Three days later, Abraham spots the place from afar. {22:5} He tells his boys to chill with the donkey while he and Isaac go worship and then come back. {22:6} Abraham puts the wood on Isaac's back, takes the fire and a knife, and they head out together. {22:7} Isaac's like, "Dad, where's the lamb for the offering?" {22:8} Abraham's smooth, saying, "God will provide the lamb, my son." So off they go. {22:9} They reach the spot, and Abraham builds the altar, arranges the wood, binds Isaac, and lays him on the altar. {22:10} Abraham's about to do the deed when an angel calls out, "Abraham, stop!" {22:12} The angel's like, "Don't lay a finger on the boy. I know you fear God 'cause you didn't hold back your son." {22:13} Abraham looks around and sees a ram caught in a thicket. He sacrifices the ram instead of Isaac. {22:14} He names the place Jehovah-jireh, saying, "This is where God provides." {22:15} The angel calls out again, {22:16} promising blessings and multiplication for Abraham's obedience. {22:17-18} Abraham's descendants will be as numerous as stars, inheriting their enemies' gates, and blessing all nations. {22:19} Abraham heads back to his crew, and they head to Beer-sheba where he settles. {22:20} Later, Abraham finds out about Nahor's family tree, including his grandkid Rebekah.

{23:1} Sarah was like, a hundred and twenty-seven years old when she kicked it. {23:2} She passed away in Kirjath-arba (aka Hebron), and Abraham was devastated, mourning and crying for her. {23:3} After Sarah's death, Abraham got up and talked to the locals, the sons of Heth. {23:4} He's like, "I'm just a visitor here, and I need a burial plot for my wife. Can you hook me up with some land to bury her?" {23:5} The sons of Heth were like, "Yo, mighty prince, pick any of our tombs to bury your dead. No one's gonna stop you." {23:7} Abraham shows respect, bowing to the people of the land. {23:8} He then negotiates with them, asking them to help him get the cave of Machpelah from Ephron the son of Zohar. {23:9} Abraham offers to pay for the cave, fair and square. {23:10} Ephron, who was there, tells Abraham publicly that he'll just give him the whole field and cave for free. {23:11-12} But Abraham insists on paying for it. {23:13-15} He tells Ephron, "Take the money and let me bury my wife there." {23:16} So Abraham pays Ephron four hundred shekels of silver, as agreed. {23:17-18} The field, cave, and all its trees became Abraham's property, witnessed by the sons of Heth. {23:19} Abraham laid Sarah to rest in the cave at Machpelah near Mamre (Hebron) in Canaan. {23:20} The field and cave were confirmed as Abraham's burial site by the sons of Heth.

{24:1} So Abraham was getting up there in age, and God had blessed him big time. {24:2-4} Abraham tells his head servant, who manages everything, "Yo, put your hand under my thigh and swear by God that you won't let my son marry any Canaanite girl. Go back to my homeland and find a wife for Isaac there." {24:5} The servant's like, "What if she won't come back with me? Should I take Isaac there instead?" {24:6} Abraham's like, "No way, don't bring my son back there." {24:7-9} Abraham reminds the servant that God promised to give him this land for his descendants, so an angel will help find a wife for Isaac there. {24:10} The servant loads up ten camels with Abraham's stuff and heads to Nahor in Mesopotamia. {24:11} He stops outside the city by a well in the evening, when the ladies come out to draw water. {24:12-14} He prays, asking God to hook him up and show kindness to Abraham. {24:15} Before he's done praying, Rebekah shows up, looking fine, with a pitcher on her shoulder. {24:16} She's a total catch—beautiful and untouched. {24:17-18} The servant asks for a sip of water, and she's like, "Sure, drink!" {24:19-21} Then she offers to water all his camels too. {24:22} The servant's amazed, wondering if God's making his trip successful. {24:23-27} He gives Rebekah some bling and asks about her family and a place to stay. {24:28} The servant thanks God for leading him to Rebekah. {24:29-30} Rebekah's brother Laban rushes out to greet the servant. {24:31-33} Laban invites him in, offering a place to stay for him and his camels. {24:34-49} The servant explains his mission, praising Abraham and all his blessings. {24:50-56} Laban and Bethuel agree that Rebekah should marry Isaac as God planned. {24:57-58} They ask Rebekah if she wants to go, and she's like, "I'm in." {24:59-60} So they send Rebekah off with blessings. {24:61} Rebekah and her crew ride off on camels with the servant. {24:62} Meanwhile, Isaac's chilling by the well Lahai-roi in the south. {24:63-65} He's out there meditating when he spots the camels approaching. {24:65} Rebekah asks the servant about Isaac, and when she finds out it's him, she covers up. {24:66} The servant fills Isaac in on everything. {24:67} Isaac welcomes Rebekah into Sarah's tent, they get hitched, and Isaac finds comfort after Sarah's passing.

{25:1} Abraham found himself a new wife named Keturah. {25:2} She had a bunch of kids for him: Zimran, Jokshan, Medan, Midian, Ishbak, and Shuah. {25:3} Jokshan had Sheba and Dedan. Dedan's sons were Asshurim, Letushim, and Leummim. {25:4} Midian had Ephah, Epher, Hanoch, Abidah, and Eldaah. These were all Keturah's children. {25:5} Abraham left everything to Isaac. {25:6} He gave gifts to his other sons and sent them away while he was still alive, off to the east. {25:7} Abraham lived for 175 years. {25:8} Eventually, Abraham passed away at a ripe old age, and his sons Isaac and Ishmael buried him in the cave of Machpelah next to Sarah. {25:11} After Abraham's death, God blessed Isaac, and he settled near the well Lahai-roi. {25:12} Now let's talk about Ishmael, Abraham's son by Hagar the Egyptian. {25:13} Ishmael had Nebajoth, Kedar, Adbeel, Mibsam, Mishma, Dumah, Massa, Hadar, Tema, Jetur, Naphish, and Kedemah. {25:17} Ishmael lived for 137 years and passed away, joining his ancestors. {25:18} His descendants settled from Havilah to Shur, towards Egypt, and died among their kin. {25:19} Now let's get into Isaac's story. {25:20} Isaac was 40 when he married Rebekah, Laban's sister from Padan-aram. {25:21} Rebekah couldn't conceive, so Isaac prayed, and God answered by letting her get pregnant. {25:22} The twins in her belly struggled, and she asked God what was up. {25:23} God told her that two nations were coming from her sons, and the younger would rule over the older. {25:24} Rebekah gave birth to twins. {25:25} The first one, red and hairy, was named Esau. {25:26} The second one, holding onto Esau's heel, was named Jacob. Isaac was 60 when they were born. {25:27} The boys grew up different: Esau was outdoorsy, while Jacob liked staying home. {25:28} Isaac favored Esau for his venison, but Rebekah favored Jacob. {25:29} One day, Esau was starving, so Jacob made stew. {25:30} Esau begged for some, giving him the nickname "Edom." {25:31} Jacob seized the opportunity and asked Esau to sell his birthright. {25:32} Esau agreed, thinking he was going to die anyway. {25:33} They made a deal, and Esau gave up his birthright to Jacob. {25:34} Jacob fed Esau, who then left, not valuing his birthright.

{26:1} There was this famine in the land, the second one after Abraham's time. Isaac decided to head to Gerar, to Abimelech king of the Philistines. {26:2} Then God showed up and told Isaac, "Don't go to Egypt. Stay here in this land that I'll point out to you. {26:3} Hang out here, and I'll stick with you and bless you. All this land will be yours and your descendants', just like I promised your dad Abraham. {26:4} Your family will multiply like the stars in the sky, and through your line, all nations will get blessed. {26:5} All because Abraham was obedient and followed my rules, commands, and laws." {26:6} Isaac set up shop in Gerar. {26:7} People there asked about his wife, and he said, "She's my sister," scared they'd kill him for Rebekah's looks if they knew she was his wife. {26:8} After a while, Abimelech looked out and saw Isaac hanging out with Rebekah, his wife. {26:9} Abimelech called Isaac out, saying, "That's definitely your wife! Why'd you say she's your sister?" Isaac's like, "I thought I'd get killed over her." {26:10} Abimelech's like, "Dude, you could've caused serious trouble for us if someone took her." {26:11} So, Abimelech told everyone not to mess with Isaac or Rebekah, or else. {26:12} Isaac planted crops, and that year, he got a hundred times what he sowed, thanks to God's blessing. {26:13} Isaac kept getting bigger and better until he was seriously huge, owning flocks, herds, and lots of servants. The Philistines were jealous. {26:15} The Philistines had filled in all the wells Abraham's servants had dug, so Isaac had to redig them. {26:16} Abimelech told Isaac to move on because he was too powerful. {26:17} So Isaac left for the valley of Gerar and settled there. {26:18} He reopened the wells his dad had dug and named them after Abraham had named them. {26:19} Isaac's crew found a new well with fresh water. {26:20} The locals claimed the water was theirs, so Isaac named the well Esek ('contention') because they argued with him. {26:21} They dug another well, and there was more drama, so he named it Sitnah ('enmity'). {26:22} Isaac moved on and dug a well without trouble, calling it Rehoboth ('spacious'), saying, "God's made room for us, and we'll thrive here." {26:23} Then he went to Beer-sheba.

{26:24} God appeared to him that night and reassured him, saying, "I'm the God of your dad Abraham. Don't worry; I'm with you and will bless you for Abraham's sake." {26:25} Isaac built an altar, called on God, and set up camp there while his crew dug another well. {26:26} Abimelech and his crew came from Gerar to meet Isaac. {26:27} Isaac asked them why they showed up when they'd kicked him out. {26:28} They said they knew God was with Isaac and wanted to make peace. {26:29} So, they made an oath not to hurt each other, recognizing Isaac as blessed by God. {26:30} They celebrated together. {26:31} The next morning, they swore oaths to each other again and parted ways peacefully. {26:32} Isaac's servants then told him they'd found water at the well, calling it Shebah, and Beer-sheba has been its name since. {26:34} Esau was 40 when he married Judith and Bashemath, causing Isaac and Rebekah a lot of grief.

{27:1} Isaac was getting old, couldn't see well, and called his oldest son, Esau, like, "Hey, son." And Esau's like, "Yeah, what's up?" {27:2} Isaac's all like, "Dude, I'm old, and I have no idea when I'm gonna kick the bucket." {27:3} "So, grab your gear, your bow, and arrow, head out to the field, and hunt some venison for me," he says. {27:4} "Cook it just how I like it, bring it to me, and I'll bless you before I croak," he adds. {27:5} Meanwhile, Rebekah overhears and tells Jacob, "Listen up, I overheard your dad telling Esau to get him some venison for a blessing before he dies." {27:6} Rebekah then tells Jacob to get two goats so she can cook them up for Isaac. {27:7} "Then take it to your dad, and he'll bless you," she says. {27:8} She's like, "Do as I say, son." {27:9} "Head to the flock, grab two good goats, and I'll cook them up just like your dad likes," she instructs. {27:10} "Then take it to him for the blessing," she adds. {27:11} Jacob's like, "But dad will know I'm not Esau because he's all hairy, and I'm not." {27:12} "If he figures it out, I'm toast," Jacob worries. {27:13} Rebekah's like, "If there's any blame, it's on me. Just do as I say and get the goats." {27:14} So, Jacob does as he's told, brings the cooked meat to his mom, and she prepares it. {27:15} She then dresses Jacob in Esau's clothes and covers his hands and neck with goat skins. {27:16} Jacob takes the food and heads to Isaac. {27:17} He presents the meal to his dad. {27:18} Isaac's like, "Who's there?" And Jacob's like, "It's me, Esau, your firstborn. I did what you asked. Sit and eat, so you can bless me." {27:19} Isaac's confused, like, "How'd you do this so fast?" And Jacob's like, "God hooked me up, Dad." {27:20} Isaac wants to check if it's really Esau, so he asks Jacob to come closer. {27:21} After feeling him, Isaac's like, "Your voice sounds like Jacob, but you feel like Esau." {27:22} Since Jacob's hands are all hairy, Isaac's convinced and blesses him. {27:23} He's still not sure, but since Jacob's hands are hairy like Esau's, he blesses him anyway. {27:24} Isaac asks again if he's really Esau, and Jacob lies again, saying he is. {27:25} So, Isaac eats, drinks, and blesses him. {27:26} Then he wants a hug from Esau, or so he thinks. {27:27} He smells Esau's clothes and blesses Jacob, saying he smells like a blessed field. {27:28} Isaac prays for God to give Jacob abundant blessings. {27:29} He prays for people to serve Jacob and nations to bow down to him. {27:30} Just as Isaac finishes blessing Jacob, Esau walks in with his venison. {27:31} He's like, "Dad, eat my food and bless me too!" {27:32} Isaac's confused and asks who he is. {27:33} Realizing what happened, Isaac trembles but acknowledges Jacob's blessing. {27:34} Esau's heartbroken and begs for a blessing too. {27:35} Isaac explains that Jacob outsmarted him and took Esau's blessing. {27:36} Esau's bitter, saying Jacob took everything from him, including his birthright. {27:37} Isaac confirms that Jacob's in charge and Esau's his servant. {27:38} Esau desperately asks for at least one blessing, and Isaac blesses him. {27:39-40} Isaac predicts Esau's future and tells him he'll live by the sword and serve his brother until he breaks free. {27:41} Esau's furious and plots to kill Jacob after Isaac dies. {27:42} Rebekah hears and warns Jacob to flee to her brother Laban in Haran. {27:43} She tells him to chill there until Esau calms down. {27:44} Rebekah plans to bring Jacob back once things settle. {27:45} She doesn't want to lose both her sons in one day. {27:46} Rebekah complains to Isaac about Esau's Hittite wives and worries about Jacob marrying a local girl.

{28:1} So, Isaac calls Jacob, blesses him, and gives him some serious instructions: "Don't marry a Canaanite girl, bro." {28:2} He's like, "Get up, go to Padanaram, to Grandpa Bethuel's house, and find a wife from Uncle Laban's daughters." {28:3} Isaac's praying for Jacob, like, "May God bless you big time, make you super fruitful, and give you the land promised to Abraham." {28:4} He wants Jacob to get the whole Abraham blessing package. {28:5} Then Isaac sends Jacob off to Padanaram to find a wife from Laban's crew, Rebekah's brother. {28:6} Esau, seeing Jacob getting all blessed up and sent away to find a wife from Padanaram and not Canaan, decides to make his parents happy too. {28:7} Jacob listens to his folks and heads to Padanaram. {28:8} Esau figures out that Canaanite girls aren't cutting it for Isaac, so he heads off to find a wife among Ishmael's descendants. {28:9-10} Jacob leaves Beer-sheba and heads towards Haran. {28:11} He finds a spot to crash for the night, grabs some rocks for pillows, and goes to sleep. {28:12} Then he has this wild dream about a ladder going up to heaven with angels doing their thing. {28:13-15} God shows up and reaffirms the promise to Jacob. {28:16} Jacob wakes up, like, "Whoa, God's here and I didn't even know!" {28:17} He's freaked out, calling the place God's house and the gate to heaven. {28:18-19} Early the next day, Jacob turns his rock pillow into a pillar, pours oil on it, and renames the place Bethel. {28:20} Jacob makes a vow to God, like, "If you watch over me, keep me safe, and bring me back home in one piece, then you're my God, and I'll give you a tenth of everything.

{29:1} Jacob rolls into the land of the east and spots this well with three flocks chilling nearby, waiting to water up. {29:2-3} The well's got a huge stone on it, but when all the flocks gather, they roll it away, water up, then put it back. {29:4} Jacob's like, "Yo, where you guys from?" They're like, "Haran, bro." {29:5} Jacob asks if they know Laban, Nahor's son, and they're like, "Yeah, we know him." {29:6} They confirm Laban's good, and boom, Rachel shows up with her dad's sheep. {29:7-9} Jacob's like, "It's still early—water the sheep and go feed 'em." {29:10} When Jacob sees Rachel, Laban's daughter, he's all in, rolls the stone, and waters Laban's flock. {29:11} Then Jacob kisses Rachel and gets emotional. {29:12-14} He spills the beans about being Rebekah's son and Laban's nephew, and Rachel runs to tell her dad. {29:15} Laban's like, "Since you're family, what do you wanna get paid, bro?" {29:16-17} Laban's got two daughters: Leah's not so hot, but Rachel's a knockout. {29:18-19} Jacob's all about Rachel, offering to work seven years for her. {29:20} Those years fly by 'cause he's smitten. {29:21} After seven years, Jacob's ready to marry Rachel. {29:22} Laban throws a big party. {29:23-24} But plot twist: Jacob ends up with Leah instead of Rachel. {29:25-27} Jacob's like, "Dude, I worked for Rachel!" Laban's like, "Our custom's oldest first; work another seven years, and you'll get her too." {29:28-30} Jacob does it, and finally gets Rachel as his wife. {29:31} God sees Leah's struggle, blesses her with sons while Rachel's barren. {29:32} Leah names her first son Reuben, thinking Jacob will love her now. {29:33} She has another son, Simeon, feeling heard 'cause she was hated. {29:34} Then she has Levi, hoping Jacob will be all in now that she's given him three sons. {29:35} When she has Judah, she praises the Lord and stops having babies.

{30:1} Rachel's feeling left out 'cause she ain't having kids, and she's like, "Give me kids or I'm out." {30:2} Jacob's not happy, saying he ain't God, and it's not up to him. {30:3} Rachel's like, "Take my maid Bilhah; she'll have kids for me." {30:4-5} So Rachel gives Bilhah to Jacob, and they have a son. {30:6} Rachel's all grateful, names him Dan, thinking God's heard her. {30:7-8} Bilhah has another son, and Rachel names him Naphtali, feeling victorious. {30:9} When Leah stops having babies, she gives Jacob her maid Zilpah. {30:10} Zilpah has a son for Jacob. {30:11} Leah names him Gad, expecting a troop of kids. {30:12} Zilpah has another son for Jacob. {30:13} Leah's happy and names him Asher. {30:14-16} Reuben finds mandrakes and gives them to Leah, causing drama with Rachel. {30:17-18} God blesses Leah with another son, and she names him Issachar, grateful for her maid. {30:19-21} Leah has another son, naming him Zebulun, hoping Jacob will stick around. {30:22-24} God remembers Rachel and opens her womb, and she has a son, Joseph. {30:25-27} After Joseph, Jacob wants out, asking Laban to let him leave with his fam. {30:28-30} They talk wages, and Jacob suggests a deal. {30:31} Jacob wants the speckled and spotted animals as his payment. {30:32} Laban agrees, and Jacob separates the flocks. {30:33} Jacob uses some trickery with rods to get the stronger cattle for himself. {30:34} Jacob's doing well, stacking up cattle, servants, and livestock like crazy.

{31:1} Laban's sons are talking smack, saying Jacob's taken everything from their dad and gotten all the credit. {31:2} Jacob notices Laban's attitude change. {31:3} Then God tells Jacob to go back home, promising to be with him. {31:4-5} Jacob gathers Rachel and Leah, telling them how Laban's treating him different now that God's been on his side. {31:6} Jacob reminds them he worked hard for their dad. {31:7-9} Laban kept changing Jacob's wages, but God protected Jacob. {31:10-11} Jacob has a dream about the sheep having speckled and spotted rams. {31:12-13} God tells Jacob to leave Laban's place and go back to his homeland. {31:14-16} Rachel and Leah agree, saying they're not getting any inheritance from their dad. {31:17-18} Jacob loads up his family and belongings on camels to leave. {31:19-20} While Laban's away, Rachel steals her dad's idols. {31:21-22} Jacob secretly leaves with everything he has. {31:23-24} Laban hears and chases after Jacob. {31:25-26} Laban catches up and confronts Jacob. {31:27-28} Laban's mad Jacob left without a big farewell. {31:29-30} Laban says he could've hurt Jacob but God warned him not to. {31:31} Jacob defends himself, saying he left in fear. {31:32} Jacob and Laban argue about Jacob leaving secretly. {31:33} Laban claims everything Jacob has belongs to him. {31:34} They make a covenant and set up a stone pillar. {31:35} They name the place and the pillar to mark their agreement. {31:36} Laban and Jacob set boundaries, swearing not to harm each other. {31:55} Laban kisses his family goodbye and goes back home.

{32:1} Jacob was on his way when he met God's crew of angels. {32:2} When he saw them, he was like, "This is a divine squad," and named the place Mahanaim. {32:3} Jacob sent messengers ahead to Esau in Seir, Edom's land. {32:4} He told them to say to Esau, "Your boy Jacob has been chilling with Laban till now. {32:5} I've got oxen, donkeys, flocks, and a whole entourage. I'm hoping to get on your good side." {32:6} The messengers returned, saying Esau's rolling up with four hundred men. {32:7} Jacob got scared and split his crew and livestock into two groups, thinking if Esau attacks one, at least the other might escape. {32:8} Jacob prayed to God of Abraham and Isaac for protection, acknowledging he started with nothing and now he's big-time. {32:9} He asked God to save him from Esau's wrath. {32:10} Jacob prepared a gift for Esau—sheep, goats, camels, cattle, and donkeys. {32:11} That night, Jacob took his family across the Jabbok River. {32:12} Jacob wrestled with a man until dawn. {32:13} The man injured Jacob's thigh, but Jacob wouldn't let him go until he blessed him. {32:14} The man renamed Jacob to Israel, saying he's got power with God and humans. {32:15} Jacob named the place Peniel, saying he saw God face to face and lived.

{33:1} Jacob scoped out Esau rolling in with his crew of four hundred. He split up the kids between Leah, Rachel, and the two maids. {33:2} The maids and their kids went first, then Leah and her crew, and finally Rachel and Joseph in the back. {33:3} Jacob led the way, bowing down seven times as he approached his brother. {33:4} When they met, Esau ran up and hugged him, crying and all. {33:5} Esau checked out the women and kids and asked who they were. Jacob said they were his family, given by God. {33:6} The maids and their kids bowed down too. {33:7} Then Leah and her crew bowed, followed by Joseph and Rachel. {33:8} Esau asked about all the animals Jacob sent ahead, and Jacob said it was to win favor. {33:9} Esau was like, "I'm good, bro. Keep your stuff." {33:10} Jacob insisted Esau take the gifts as a sign of goodwill. {33:11} Esau accepted the gifts and suggested they travel together. {33:12} Jacob was concerned the journey might be tough for the kids and livestock, so he wanted to take it slow. {33:13} Esau offered to leave some of his people to help, but Jacob declined. {33:14} Esau headed back to Seir, and Jacob moved to Succoth, setting up camp and making shelters for his animals. {33:15} Jacob arrived at Shechem in Canaan, pitching his tent near the city. {33:16} He bought land from Hamor for a hundred pieces of money. {33:17} Jacob built an altar there and named it El-elohe-Israel.

{34:1} So Dinah, Leah's daughter, decided to hang out with the local girls. {34:2} Then Shechem, Hamor's son, who was a big shot around there, spotted her and ended up sleeping with her. {34:3} Shechem really fell for Dinah and started speaking kindly to her. {34:4} He went to his dad Hamor and said, "I want to marry this girl." {34:5} When Jacob found out Dinah had been defiled, his sons were out in the fields with the livestock, so he kept quiet until they got back. {34:6} Hamor, Shechem's dad, went to talk to Jacob about it. {34:7} Jacob's sons heard about it and were furious that Shechem had done this to their sister Dinah, something totally not cool. {34:8} Hamor tried to smooth things over, saying that Shechem really liked Dinah and wanted to marry her. {34:9} He suggested they intermarry and make alliances. {34:10} Hamor said they could live together, trade, and get rich in the land. {34:11} Shechem pleaded with them to agree to his proposal. {34:12} He was willing to pay any dowry they asked for Dinah. {34:13} Jacob's sons, though, responded deceitfully, saying Shechem had to get circumcised along with all the other guys in the city. {34:14} They said they couldn't give Dinah to an uncircumcised man—it would be a disgrace. {34:15} But if all the guys got circumcised, they could intermarry and live as one people. {34:16} Shechem and Hamor agreed, and Shechem wasted no time getting circumcised because he was so into Dinah. {34:17} The city leaders also decided to go along with it and got circumcised. {34:18} Three days later, while the men were in pain from the circumcision, Simeon and Levi, Dinah's brothers, attacked the city and killed all the males. {34:19} They took Dinah out of Shechem's house and left. {34:20} Jacob's sons then looted the city, taking livestock, possessions, and captives, all to avenge their sister's honor. {34:21} Jacob was worried about the consequences, fearing reprisal from neighboring peoples. {34:22} Simeon and Levi argued that Shechem shouldn't have treated their sister like that.

{35:1} God was like, "Yo Jacob, get up and head to Bethel, and stay there. Build an altar to God, the one who showed up when you were running from Esau." {35:2} So Jacob told everyone in his crew, "Get rid of all those weird idols and stuff, clean yourselves up, and change your clothes." {35:3} Then they packed up and headed to Bethel to make that altar to God, who had come through for Jacob when he was in trouble. {35:4} They handed over all their idols and earrings to Jacob, who buried them under an oak tree near Shechem. {35:5} As they traveled, the nearby cities were too scared to mess with Jacob's crew, so they left them alone. {35:6} Jacob and his crew arrived in Luz (Bethel) in Canaan. {35:7} He built an altar there and named the place El-beth-el because that's where God had appeared to him before. {35:8} Meanwhile, Deborah, Rebekah's nurse, passed away and was buried under an oak tree near Bethel, called Allon-bachuth. {35:9} God appeared to Jacob again after he left Padan-aram and blessed him. {35:10} God told Jacob, "Your name isn't Jacob anymore; it's Israel." {35:11} God promised that Israel would become a great nation with kings coming from his descendants. {35:12} God also promised to give the land of Canaan to Israel and his descendants. {35:13} After talking with Jacob, God left. {35:14} Jacob set up a stone pillar where he talked with God, poured a drink offering and oil on it. {35:15} He named the place Bethel. {35:16} They left Bethel, and Rachel went into labor near Ephrath. {35:17} During a difficult labor, the midwife assured Rachel she would have another son. {35:18} Sadly, Rachel died giving birth; she named her son Ben-oni, but Jacob called him Benjamin. {35:19} Rachel was buried on the way to Ephrath, which is Bethlehem. {35:20} Jacob set up a pillar at Rachel's grave. {35:21} They moved on to Edar. {35:22} While living there, Reuben slept with Bilhah, his father's concubine, which Jacob found out about. {35:23-26} Jacob had twelve sons: Reuben, Simeon, Levi, Judah, Issachar, Zebulun (from Leah); Joseph and Benjamin (from Rachel); Dan and Naphtali (from Rachel's servant Bilhah); Gad and Asher (from Leah's servant Zilpah). {35:27} Jacob later reunited with his father Isaac at Mamre near Hebron, where Abraham and Isaac had lived. {35:28} Isaac lived to be 180 years old. {35:29} Isaac passed away and was buried by his sons Esau and Jacob.

{36:1} So, like, here's the rundown on Esau's crew, aka Edom. {36:2} Esau hooked up with some Canaanite ladies: Adah (Elon the Hittite's daughter), Aholibamah (Anah's daughter, granddaughter of Zibeon the Hivite), and Bashemath (Ishmael's daughter, Nebajoth's sister). {36:3-4} Adah had Eliphaz, and Bashemath had Reuel. {36:5} Aholibamah had Jeush, Jaalam, and Korah while they were living in Canaan. {36:6-8} Esau peaced out from Jacob's hood 'cause their crews were too big for the same turf, so he bounced to Mount Seir, reppin' as Edom. {36:9} Esau's Edomite legacy started there. {36:10-11} Eliphaz (from Adah) had sons: Teman, Omar, Zepho, Gatam, and Kenaz. {36:12} Eliphaz's concubine, Timna, had Amalek. {36:13} Reuel (from Bashemath) had Nahath, Zerah, Shammah, and Mizzah. {36:14} Aholibamah (Anah's daughter) had Jeush, Jaalam, and Korah. {36:15-16} These were the Edomite chiefs: Teman, Omar, Zepho, Kenaz, Korah, Gatam, and Amalek from Eliphaz's crew. {36:17-19} Reuel's sons included Nahath, Zerah, Shammah, and Mizzah. {36:18} Aholibamah's crew featured Jeush, Jaalam, and Korah. {36:20-21} Now, check out Seir the Horite's fam: Lotan, Shobal, Zibeon, Anah, Dishon, Ezer, and Dishan. {36:22-24} Lotan had Hori and Hemam, with Timna as his sis. {36:25-30} Anah's kids were Dishon and Aholibamah. {36:31} Before Israel had kings, these were the rulers in Edom. {36:32-34} Bela was king in Dinhabah, then Jobab took over. {36:35} Hadad, who wrecked Midian, ruled from Avith. {36:36} Hadar ruled in Pau, married to Mehetabel. {36:40} These dukes of Esau's crew were named Timnah, Alvah, Jetheth, Aholibamah, Elah, Pinon, Kenaz, Teman, Mibzar, Magdiel, and Iram, repping Edom.

{37:1} So, like, Jacob was chilling in Canaan, where his dad had been kicking it. {37:2} Now, let's talk about Jacob's crew. Joseph, who was seventeen, was out there with his brothers, the sons of Bilhah and Zilpah (his dad's wives), and he straight-up snitched on them to his dad. {37:3} Jacob was all about Joseph, especially since he was the old man's favorite, and even hooked him up with a sick multicolored coat. {37:4} But when his brothers peeped the favoritism, they couldn't stand him and wouldn't even talk nicely to him. {37:5} Joseph had these dreams and, of course, bragged to his brothers about it, which just made them hate him even more. {37:6} He's like, "Listen up, fam, I had this wild dream where our sheaves bowed down to mine." {37:7-8} His brothers were like, "You really think you're gonna boss us around?" and got even more ticked off. {37:9} Then he drops another bomb: "The sun, moon, and stars were bowing to me." {37:10-11} Joseph told his dad and brothers, and Jacob was like, "Are you saying we're all gonna bow to you?" His brothers were seething with jealousy, but Jacob was low-key pondering it. {37:12-13} One day, Jacob's sons were in Shechem tending the flock, and he sent Joseph to check up on them. {37:14} So, Joseph heads out and finds them in Dothan. {37:15} When his brothers see him from afar, they plot to kill him, calling him "the dreamer." {37:16} Reuben tries to be the voice of reason, suggesting they toss him in a pit instead of straight-up murking him. {37:17} They snatch his multicolored coat and chuck him in an empty pit. {37:18} While they're chowing down, a caravan of Ishmaelites rolls by, and they decide to sell Joseph to them. {37:19} Reuben returns to the pit, finds it empty, and freaks out. {37:20} They dip Joseph's coat in goat blood, then show it to Jacob, claiming he got wrecked by a beast. {37:21} Jacob loses it, mourning for his son, convinced he's gone. {37:22} His other kids try to comfort him, but he's like, "Nah, I'm mourning till I die." {37:23} Meanwhile, Joseph gets sold to Potiphar in Egypt by the Midianites.

{38:1} So, like, at that time Judah bounced from his crew and linked up with this Adullamite dude named Hirah. {38:2} Judah spotted a Canaanite girl named Shuah and hooked up with her. {38:3} She got pregnant and had a son named Er. {38:4-5} Then she had another son named Onan. {38:5} After that, she had a third son named Shelah, who was born in Chezib. {38:6} Judah set up Er with a wife named Tamar. {38:7} But Er was a bad dude, and the Lord took him out. {38:8} Judah told Onan to marry Tamar and have kids to carry on Er's line. {38:9-10} But Onan knew the kids wouldn't be his, so he didn't do what he was supposed to, and that didn't fly with the Lord, so he got taken out too. {38:11} Judah told Tamar to chill until Shelah grew up, but he was worried Shelah might end up like his brothers. So Tamar went back to her dad's place. {38:12} Eventually, Shuah (Judah's wife) died, and after mourning, Judah went to Timnath with his buddy Hirah to shear sheep. {38:13} When Tamar heard about this, she got an idea. {38:14} She changed out of her mourning clothes, covered herself with a veil, and posted up by the road to Timnath because Shelah had grown up, but Judah hadn't given him to her as a husband. {38:15} When Judah saw her, he thought she was a prostitute because of the veil. {38:16} So he rolls up to her and offers to pay for some action, not knowing she was actually his daughter-in-law. {38:17-18} They agree on a goat as payment, but she wants a guarantee, so he gives her his signet, bracelets, and staff. They do their thing, and she ends up pregnant. {38:19} Afterward, Tamar goes back to her mourning clothes. {38:20-23} Judah sends his buddy with a goat to get back his stuff, but Tamar is nowhere to be found. {38:24} A few months later, word gets to Judah that Tamar is pregnant from harlotry, and he calls for her to be punished. {38:25} When she's brought out, she reveals Judah as the father by showing his stuff. {38:26} Judah admits his mistake and acknowledges Tamar's righteousness. {38:27} Tamar gives birth to twins, and the firstborn's hand is marked, earning him the name Pharez.

{39:1} So Joseph ended up in Egypt after the Ishmeelites sold him to Potiphar, who was like Pharaoh's top guard. {39:2} The Lord was totally on Joseph's side, and everything he did was successful while he was working for Potiphar. {39:3} Potiphar saw that Joseph had that divine favor, and he put Joseph in charge of everything. {39:4} Joseph was so well-liked that Potiphar made him the overseer of his whole house. {39:5} The Lord blessed Potiphar's house because of Joseph, and everything was going great, both inside and outside. {39:6} Potiphar trusted Joseph with everything, only worrying about what food he was eating. Joseph was a good-looking guy, no doubt about it. {39:7} But then Potiphar's wife got eyes for Joseph and straight-up asked him to hook up with her. {39:8-9} Joseph shut her down, saying that he couldn't betray Potiphar's trust or sin against God. {39:10} She kept pushing him every day, but Joseph wasn't having it. {39:11} One day, Joseph was doing his thing in the house, and no one else was around. {39:12} Potiphar's wife grabbed him by his clothes, but Joseph slipped out of them and ran off. {39:13-19} When she saw Joseph had left his clothes, she accused him of trying to hook up with her and made a scene. {39:20} Potiphar believed his wife's story and threw Joseph in prison. {39:21} But even in prison, the Lord had Joseph's back and showed him kindness. {39:22} The prison warden put Joseph in charge of all the other prisoners because he saw that Joseph was legit. {39:23} The warden didn't have to worry about anything under Joseph's watch because the Lord was blessing Joseph's work.

{40:1} So, after all that drama, the king of Egypt got ticked off at his butler and baker. {40:2} Pharaoh was seriously mad at these two top dudes. {40:3} He threw them in the same slammer where Joseph was locked up. {40:4} Joseph ended up looking after them for a while. {40:5} Then one night, both the butler and baker had dreams. {40:6} Joseph noticed they were down in the dumps the next morning. {40:7} He asked them why they were so gloomy. {40:8} They told him about their dreams, wishing they had someone to interpret them. Joseph was like, "Isn't interpreting dreams God's thing? Tell me your dreams." {40:9} The butler spilled his dream to Joseph about a vine and stuff. {40:12} Joseph interpreted it, saying the three branches meant three days. {40:13} He told the butler he'd be back in Pharaoh's good books in three days, handing him the cup again. {40:14} Joseph asked the butler to put in a good word for him when things turned around. {40:15} He reminded the butler that he was kidnapped and didn't deserve to be in prison. {40:16} The baker saw the good news and shared his dream about baskets on his head. {40:18} Joseph told him the three baskets meant three days too. {40:19} But the bad news was, the baker would be executed and birds would eat his flesh. {40:20} Three days later was Pharaoh's birthday bash. {40:21} He pardoned the butler and put him back on duty, just like Joseph said. {40:22} Unfortunately, he hanged the baker. {40:23} But the butler totally forgot about Joseph after he got out.

{41:1} So, after two full years, Pharaoh had a wild dream where he was chilling by the river. {41:2} In this dream, seven good-looking, fat cows came out of the river and started grazing. {41:3-4} Then seven ugly, skinny cows came out and ate up the first ones. Pharaoh woke up shook. {41:5} He fell back asleep and dreamed again about seven healthy ears of corn on one stalk. {41:6-7} Then seven thin, withered ears sprouted up and swallowed the good ones. Pharaoh was tripping when he woke up. {41:8} The next morning, he was stressed, so he called all the magicians and wise folks to interpret his dreams, but no one could. {41:9-13} Then the butler remembered Joseph and spilled the tea about Joseph interpreting dreams. {41:14} Pharaoh brought Joseph out of the dungeon ASAP, cleaned him up, and brought him to the palace. {41:15} Pharaoh told Joseph about his dream, hoping Joseph could decode it. {41:16} Joseph was humble, saying only God could provide the answer. {41:17} Pharaoh described the dream: fat cows eaten by skinny cows and healthy corn devoured by withered ones. {41:18} Joseph explained that the dream meant seven years of plenty followed by seven years of famine. {41:19} Joseph suggested finding a wise dude to manage during the good times and prepare for the famine. {41:20} Pharaoh and his crew liked Joseph's plan. {41:21} Pharaoh recognized Joseph's connection with God. {41:22} Pharaoh put Joseph in charge, making him second only to himself. {41:23} Pharaoh appointed Joseph as ruler over all Egypt. {41:24} He decked Joseph out and gave him authority. {41:25} Joseph married Asenath, the daughter of a priest. {41:26} Joseph was 30 when he started his role. {41:27} Egypt boomed during the good years, and Joseph stored up food like crazy. {41:28} Before the famine hit, Joseph had two sons with Asenath. {41:29} The years of plenty ended, and the famine began just as Joseph predicted. {41:30} When Egypt faced famine, Pharaoh directed everyone to Joseph for food. {41:31} People from everywhere came to Egypt for food because of the severe famine.

{42:1} When Jacob peeped that there was food in Egypt, he was like, "Why y'all just staring at each other?" {42:2} He heard there was corn in Egypt, so he told his sons to go down there, buy some, and save their lives. {42:3} Joseph's ten brothers went to Egypt to cop some corn. {42:4} Jacob didn't send Benjamin, Joseph's brother, 'cause he was worried something bad might happen to him. {42:5} The sons of Israel went to buy corn since there was a famine in Canaan. {42:6} Joseph, who was running the show, sold corn to everyone. When his brothers showed up, they bowed down to him without knowing who he was. {42:7} Joseph recognized his brothers but acted like he didn't and spoke harshly to them, asking where they came from. {42:8} His brothers didn't recognize him. {42:9} Joseph remembered his dreams about them and accused them of being spies. {42:10} They denied it, saying they just came for food. {42:11} They reassured him they were all brothers and honest guys, not spies. {42:12} Joseph didn't buy it and accused them again. {42:13} They explained they were twelve brothers from Canaan, with one back home and one no longer around. {42:14} Joseph insisted they prove themselves by bringing their youngest brother. {42:15} He demanded they stay in prison until they returned with him. {42:16-20} Joseph ordered them to send one brother to fetch the youngest and kept the rest in prison. {42:21} The brothers felt guilty about their past treatment of Joseph. {42:22} Reuben reminded them how he had warned them not to harm Joseph. {42:23} They didn't realize Joseph understood them because he spoke through an interpreter. {42:24} Joseph wept in private upon hearing this. {42:25} He filled their sacks with corn, returned their money, and provided them with provisions. {42:26} They loaded up their donkeys and left. {42:27} One brother discovered his money in his sack at an inn. {42:28} They were shocked and afraid, wondering what was happening. {42:29} When they returned to Canaan, they told Jacob everything, including being accused of spying. {42:30} They assured Jacob they were innocent. {42:31} They were told to bring their youngest brother back to prove they were telling the truth. {42:32} When they discovered their money in their sacks, they were terrified.

{43:1} The famine was hitting hard. {43:2} After they finished the corn from Egypt, their dad was like, "Go get more food." {43:3} Judah reminded him about the deal the man made, saying they couldn't go back without their brother. {43:4} Judah promised they'd go back if Benjamin came with them. {43:5} They insisted that without Benjamin, they couldn't go back to see the man. {43:6} Israel was upset, wondering why they had to spill the beans about having another brother. {43:7} They explained that the man asked about their family, and they couldn't predict he'd ask for their brother. {43:8} Judah convinced Israel to send Benjamin so they could survive. {43:9} He guaranteed Benjamin's safety, saying he'd take the blame forever if anything happened to him. {43:10} Otherwise, they would have been back by now. {43:11-14} Israel told them to take a gift for the man, including the best fruits and double the money they found in their sacks, in case it was a mistake. {43:15} The men took the gifts, double money, and Benjamin, and headed to Egypt. {43:16} When Joseph saw Benjamin, he ordered his house ruler to prepare for a feast. {43:17} They were brought into Joseph's house, which scared them. {43:18} They worried the money in their sacks might be used against them. {43:19} They explained the situation to Joseph's steward. {43:20} They recounted how they found their money in their sacks. {43:21-22} The steward reassured them, saying their God gave them treasure. {43:23} Simeon was released to them. {43:24-25} They were taken care of and prepared for Joseph's arrival. {43:26} When Joseph arrived, they presented their gifts and bowed to him. {43:27} Joseph asked about their father's well-being. {43:28} They assured him their father was well. {43:29} Joseph saw Benjamin and blessed him. {43:30} Overcome with emotion, Joseph had to step away to compose himself. {43:31} He returned and ordered a meal. {43:32} They ate separately because Egyptians found eating with Hebrews disgusting. {43:33} They were seated according to birthright, and everyone was amazed. {43:34} Joseph sent them generous portions, especially to Benjamin, and they all enjoyed the meal together.

{44:1} Joseph told his house steward, "Load up their sacks with as much food as they can carry, and put each man's money back in his sack." {44:2} He sneaked in his own silver cup into Benjamin's sack along with his money. The steward followed Joseph's orders. {44:3} Early in the morning, they were sent off with their donkeys. {44:4} Joseph instructed his steward to chase after them and accuse them of repaying evil for good. {44:5} Joseph's cup was what he used for divination and they messed up big time. {44:6} The steward caught up to them and dropped the bomb. {44:7} They were shocked and denied it, swearing they'd never steal. {44:8} They insisted they returned the money and would accept any punishment if the cup was found with them. {44:9-10} Joseph agreed that the one with the cup would be his servant, and the rest could go. {44:11} They opened their sacks to prove their innocence. {44:12} Benjamin's sack was the guilty one. {44:13} They were devastated and headed back to the city. {44:14} Judah and his bros faced Joseph and fell to the ground. {44:15} Joseph confronted them about the cup. {44:16} Judah admitted they were caught red-handed. {44:17} Joseph decided only Benjamin would stay while the others returned home in peace. {44:18} Judah pleaded with Joseph, explaining their dad's feelings. {44:19} He recounted how Joseph had asked about their family. {44:20} They shared their family story, especially about their beloved younger brother. {44:21} Joseph wanted to see him. {44:22} They couldn't bring him because it would crush their dad. {44:23} Joseph insisted they couldn't return without the youngest brother. {44:24} They explained to their dad everything that happened. {44:25} Their dad asked them to get more food. {44:26} They couldn't go without Benjamin. {44:27} Their dad feared losing another son. {44:28} He was still mourning the loss of one son. {44:29} Losing Benjamin would devastate him. {44:30} Judah pleaded for Benjamin's life, knowing it was tied to their dad's happiness. {44:31} If Benjamin didn't return, their dad would die from sorrow. {44:32} Judah took responsibility for Benjamin's safety. {44:33} He offered himself as a servant instead of Benjamin. {44:34} He couldn't face his dad without Benjamin.

{45:1} Joseph couldn't hold it in anymore with all the people around, so he told everyone to leave the room. No one else was there when Joseph revealed himself to his brothers. {45:2} He broke down crying loudly, and even the Egyptians and Pharaoh's household heard him. {45:3} Joseph said to his brothers, "Hey, I'm Joseph! Is Dad still alive?" They were speechless and stunned. {45:4} Joseph told them to come closer and said, "I'm Joseph, your brother, the one you sold into Egypt." {45:5} He comforted them, saying not to be upset with themselves because God sent him there to save lives. {45:6} There's been a famine for two years, and there are five more to go with no crops. {45:7} God sent Joseph ahead to save them and their descendants. {45:8} Joseph explained that it wasn't their doing but God's plan. He became a big shot in Egypt. {45:9} Joseph urged them to hurry back to Dad and tell him Joseph is in charge and to move to Egypt ASAP. {45:10} They would settle in the land of Goshen with all their stuff. {45:11} Joseph promised to take care of them during the remaining famine years. {45:12} They realized it was really Joseph talking. {45:13} Joseph wanted them to tell Dad about his status and bring him to Egypt quickly. {45:14} He hugged Benjamin and cried, and Benjamin cried on his shoulder. {45:15} Joseph hugged all his brothers and wept with them. After that, they talked. {45:16} News spread in Pharaoh's palace that Joseph's brothers were there, and Pharaoh was thrilled. {45:17} Pharaoh told Joseph's brothers to load up and bring everyone back to Canaan with their families. {45:18} They were invited to live well in Egypt. {45:19} They were instructed to take wagons for their kids and wives and bring Dad. {45:20} Joseph assured them not to worry about their possessions; they'd get the best in Egypt. {45:21} The Israelites followed the plan, and Joseph hooked them up with wagons and supplies. {45:22} Everyone got new clothes, but Benjamin scored 300 pieces of silver and five outfits. {45:23} Joseph sent Dad tons of gifts for the journey. {45:24} Joseph warned them not to argue along the way. {45:25} They left Egypt and returned to Canaan to Jacob, their dad. {45:26} They shared the incredible news that Joseph was alive and ruling Egypt. Jacob was in shock and didn't believe them at first. {45:27} They recounted everything Joseph said and showed Jacob the wagons Joseph sent. {45:28} Jacob, overjoyed to learn Joseph was alive, decided to see him before he died.

{46:1} So, Israel packed up everything he had and headed to Beer-sheba, where he offered sacrifices to God like his dad Isaac used to do. {46:2} That night, God appeared to Israel in a dream and called out, "Jacob, Jacob." Jacob was like, "Yo, I'm here." {46:3} God reassured him, saying, "I'm God, the God of your dad. Don't trip about going to Egypt; I'm gonna make a great nation out of you there." {46:4} God promised to go with Jacob to Egypt and bring him back, and Joseph would be there when Jacob passed away. {46:5} Jacob left Beer-sheba, and his sons helped carry him along with their families in the wagons Pharaoh sent. {46:6} They brought all their stuff from Canaan and settled in Egypt, Jacob and his whole crew. {46:7} He brought his sons, grandsons, daughters, and granddaughters—everyone went to Egypt. {46:8} Here are the names of the Israelite kids who went to Egypt with Jacob: Reuben was the oldest. {46:9} Reuben's sons were Hanoch, Phallu, Hezron, and Carmi. {46:10} Simeon's sons were Jemuel, Jamin, Ohad, Jachin, Zohar, and Shaul (his mom was Canaanite). {46:11} Levi's sons were Gershon, Kohath, and Merari. {46:12} Judah's sons were Er, Onan, Shelah, Pharez, and Zarah (Er and Onan died in Canaan, and Pharez had Hezron and Hamul). {46:13} Issachar's sons were Tola, Phuvah, Job, and Shimron. {46:14} Zebulun's sons were Sered, Elon, and Jahleel. {46:15} Leah had all these kids with Jacob in Padan-aram, including Dinah. In total, Jacob's sons and daughters numbered thirty-three. {46:16} Gad's sons were Ziphion, Haggi, Shuni, Ezbon, Eri, Arodi, and Areli. {46:17} Asher's sons were Jimnah, Ishuah, Isui, Beriah, and their sister Serah, whose sons were Heber and Malchiel. {46:18} These were Zilpah's sixteen kids that Laban gave to Leah. {46:19} Rachel had two sons with Jacob: Joseph and Benjamin. {46:20} Joseph had two sons in Egypt with Asenath, Potipherah's daughter: Manasseh and Ephraim. {46:21} Benjamin's sons were Belah, Becher, Ashbel, Gera, Naaman, Ehi, Rosh, Muppim, Huppim, and Ard. {46:22} Rachel had a total of fourteen kids with Jacob. {46:23} Dan's only son mentioned was Hushim. {46:24} Naphtali's sons were Jahzeel, Guni, Jezer, and Shillem. {46:25} These were the seven sons of Bilhah that Laban gave to Rachel. {46:26} In total, all the people who came with Jacob to Egypt, not counting his sons' wives, were sixty-six. {46:27} Joseph had two sons in Egypt, making the total seventy people from Jacob's household who came to Egypt. {46:28} Judah went ahead to lead them to Goshen, and they arrived there. {46:29} Joseph prepared his chariot and went to meet his dad in Goshen. He hugged and cried with his dad for a long time. {46:30} Jacob was relieved and felt ready to pass away now that he'd seen Joseph alive. {46:31} Joseph told Pharaoh that his family from Canaan was there, and they were shepherds who'd brought their flocks and herds. {46:32} He explained that they've been shepherds all their lives, just like their ancestors, and asked if they could settle in Goshen since Egyptians don't dig shepherds.

{47:1} So, Joseph went to Pharaoh and was like, "Yo, my dad, my bros, their animals, and all their stuff rolled in from Canaan, and they're chilling in Goshen." {47:2} Then he brought five of his brothers to Pharaoh. {47:3} Pharaoh was like, "What do you guys do for a living?" They replied, "We're shepherds, just like our ancestors." {47:4} They explained that they came to Egypt because of the famine in Canaan, and they needed good pasture for their flocks, so they asked to settle in Goshen. {47:5} Pharaoh said to Joseph, "Your family is here; choose the best land in Egypt for them to live in Goshen. And if any of them are skilled, put them in charge of my livestock." {47:7} Joseph brought his dad Jacob to Pharaoh, and Jacob blessed him. {47:8} Pharaoh asked Jacob how old he was. {47:9} Jacob replied, "I'm 130 years old, and my life has been tough, not as long as my ancestors' lives." {47:10} Jacob blessed Pharaoh and left.

{47:11} Joseph settled his family in the best part of Egypt, as Pharaoh instructed. {47:12} Joseph provided bread for his family according to their needs. {47:13} The famine was severe, affecting both Egypt and Canaan. {47:14} Joseph collected all the money from Egypt and Canaan for the grain they bought and brought it to Pharaoh's house. {47:15} When money ran out, the Egyptians came to Joseph asking for bread. {47:16} Joseph told them to trade their livestock for food. {47:17} They traded their animals for food that year. {47:18} The next year, they admitted they had no money left except themselves and their land, offering to sell everything to Pharaoh for food. {47:20} Joseph bought all the land of Egypt for Pharaoh due to the famine. {47:21} He relocated the people to cities across Egypt. {47:22} He exempted the land of the priests, who received rations from Pharaoh and didn't sell their land. {47:23} Joseph told the people that Pharaoh owned them and their land, giving them seed to sow. {47:24} They agreed to give Pharaoh one-fifth of their produce, keeping the rest for themselves and their households. {47:25} They thanked Joseph for saving their lives and agreed to be Pharaoh's servants. {47:26} Joseph established this policy, except for the priests' land. {47:27} Jacob and his family settled in Goshen, where they thrived and multiplied greatly. {47:28} Jacob lived in Egypt for 17 years and reached the age of 147. {47:29} As Jacob's end approached, he asked Joseph not to bury him in Egypt but with his ancestors. {47:30} Joseph promised to fulfill his father's wishes.

{48:1} So, someone came to Joseph and was like, "Hey, your dad is sick," so Joseph took his two sons, Manasseh and Ephraim. {48:2} They told Jacob, "Joseph is coming to see you," so Jacob gathered his strength and sat up in bed. {48:3} Jacob told Joseph how God Almighty appeared to him and blessed him in Canaan. {48:4} God promised to make Jacob fruitful, multiply him, and give Canaan to his descendants forever. {48:5} Jacob claimed Joseph's sons, Ephraim and Manasseh, as his own, just like Reuben and Simeon. {48:6} Any children Joseph has after them will be his, named after their uncles in their inheritance. {48:7} Jacob recounted Rachel's death in Canaan and her burial in Bethlehem. {48:8} When Israel saw Joseph's sons, he asked who they were. {48:9} Joseph introduced them and asked Israel to bless them. {48:10} Israel's eyesight was poor due to age, so he brought the boys close, kissed them, and embraced them. {48:11} Israel marveled at seeing Joseph's descendants. {48:12} Joseph brought his sons out and bowed before his father. {48:13} He positioned Ephraim and Manasseh so that Jacob's hands were on their heads correctly. {48:14} Jacob intentionally blessed Ephraim over Manasseh, despite Manasseh being the firstborn. {48:15} He blessed Joseph and invoked God's favor on the boys. {48:16} Jacob prayed for them to carry on the legacy of Abraham and Isaac. {48:17} When Joseph saw Jacob favoring Ephraim, he tried to correct him, but Jacob persisted. {48:18} Joseph insisted that Manasseh, the firstborn, should receive the greater blessing, but Jacob refused, foreseeing Ephraim's greatness. {48:19} Jacob affirmed Ephraim's future greatness and multitude of descendants. {48:20} He blessed them, saying, "May others be blessed as Ephraim and Manasseh." {48:21} Israel acknowledged his impending death but predicted God's return of Joseph's descendants to Canaan. {48:22} Jacob also gave Joseph an extra portion of land acquired with his sword and bow from the Amorites.

{49:1} Jacob called his sons together and was like, "Listen up, I'm about to tell you what's gonna go down in the future." {49:2} He gathered them around to hear his words. {49:3} He started with Reuben, his firstborn, saying he had potential but was unreliable because of what he did with his father's bed. {49:4-7} Then he talked about Simeon and Levi, calling them violent and cursing their anger. {49:8} Next up was Judah, whom he praised, saying he'd rule over his enemies and be honored by his family. {49:9-12} Jacob compared Judah to a lion, strong and respected. {49:13} Zebulun was told he'd dwell by the sea and become a port. {49:14-15} Issachar was described as strong but choosing a life of servitude. {49:16-18} Dan would judge his people like any other tribe. {49:19} Gad would face challenges but ultimately prevail. {49:20} Asher's bread would be rich and he'd provide royal delicacies. {49:21} Naphtali was free-spirited and spoke beautifully. {49:22-26} Joseph was blessed as a fruitful vine, hated by many but strong and blessed by God. {49:27} Benjamin was compared to a wolf, fierce in battle. {49:28} Jacob blessed each son according to his character. {49:29} Then he told them to bury him with his ancestors in Canaan. {49:30} After sharing these words, Jacob passed away peacefully.

{50:1} Joseph was devastated when his father died, crying and kissing him. {50:2} He told his servants, the doctors, to embalm his father, and they did so. {50:3} They spent forty days embalming him, and then the Egyptians mourned for him for seventy days. {50:4} After the mourning period, Joseph asked Pharaoh's household to let him fulfill his father's dying wish to be buried in Canaan. {50:5-6} Joseph explained how his father made him promise to bury him there, and Pharaoh granted his request. {50:7-9} Joseph, accompanied by Pharaoh's servants and many others, went to bury his father in Canaan. {50:10-11} They mourned for Jacob for seven days at the threshingfloor of Atad. {50:12-13} Jacob's sons carried out his instructions and buried him in the cave at Machpelah. {50:14} After burying his father, Joseph returned to Egypt with his brothers. {50:15} When Joseph's brothers saw that their father was gone, they worried that Joseph might retaliate against them for their past actions. {50:16-18} They sent a message to Joseph, claiming their father's dying wish was for Joseph to forgive them. {50:19} Joseph reassured them, saying he wouldn't take the place of God in judging them. {50:20-21} He explained that even though they intended harm, God turned it into good to save many lives. {50:22-23} Joseph lived to be a hundred and ten years old, seeing his grandchildren grow up. {50:24} Before his death, Joseph told his brothers that God would fulfill His promise to bring them out of Egypt to the land He swore to Abraham, Isaac, and Jacob. {50:25} Joseph made the Israelites promise to carry his bones with them when they left Egypt. {50:26} Joseph died at the age of one hundred and ten, and they embalmed him and placed him in a coffin in Egypt.

Exodus

+++

{1:1} So, here's the squad of Israelites who rolled into Egypt with Jacob and their fams. {1:2} We got Reuben, Simeon, Levi, Judah, {1:3} Issachar, Zebulun, Benjamin, {1:4} Dan, Naphtali, Gad, Asher. {1:5} The whole crew that came from Jacob's line was 70 strong, 'cause Joseph was already in Egypt. {1:6} Then Joseph and all his crew passed on, along with that whole generation. {1:7} The Israelites started blowing up in numbers, getting real mighty, and filling up the land. {1:8} But a new pharaoh took charge who didn't know Joseph. {1:9} He saw how deep our squad was getting and got worried. {1:10} So, he schemed to put the pressure on us, 'cause he was scared we'd join forces with enemies if a war broke out, and bounce from Egypt. {1:11} They made us slave away, building Pharaoh's cities like Pithom and Raamses. {1:12} But the more they tried to keep us down, the more we came up. They were not happy about it. {1:13} Egypt had us grinding with harsh labor, laying bricks, farming – the whole nine yards, all under intense pressure. {1:14} Then Pharaoh laid down the law to the Hebrew midwives, Shiphrah and Puah. {1:16} Pharaoh said, if it's a boy, snuff him out; if it's a girl, let her ride. {1:17} But those midwives feared God more than Pharaoh, so they let the boys live. {1:18} Pharaoh called them out for saving the boys. {1:19} They told Pharaoh the Hebrew women are quick on the draw, popping out babies before they can even get there. {1:20} God blessed the midwives, and the Israelites kept booming. {1:21} The midwives got rewarded 'cause they respected God. {1:22} Then Pharaoh orders everyone: drown the boys, but keep the girls alive.

{2:1} Now, a Levite guy married a Levite gal. {2:2} She had a son, and she hid him for three months 'cause he was a looker. {2:3} When she couldn't hide him no more, she floated him down the river in a makeshift crib. {2:4} His sis kept watch from afar. {2:5} Pharaoh's daughter found the baby and took pity, knowing he was Hebrew. {2:6} The sis suggested a Hebrew nurse for the baby. {2:7} Pharaoh's daughter said, "Do it." {2:8-9} The sis brought the baby's mom, and Pharaoh's daughter paid her to nurse the baby. {2:10} The kid grew up as Pharaoh's daughter's son, named Moses 'cause she pulled him from the water. {2:11} When Moses was grown, he checked on his Hebrew fam and saw an Egyptian beating one of them. {2:12} He made sure no one was watching, then took out the Egyptian and buried him. {2:13} The next day, he tried to stop a fight between two Hebrew dudes. {2:14} They called him out for offing the Egyptian, and Moses got nervous. {2:15} Pharaoh found out and wanted Moses dead, so Moses skedaddled to Midian and hung out by a well. {2:16-17} The priest of Midian's daughters came to water their flock, but some shepherds hassled them. Moses helped out, and they told their dad what happened. {2:18} Reuel, their dad, asked why they came home early. {2:19-20} They told him about Moses, and Reuel wanted to meet him. {2:21} Moses kicked it with Reuel and married his daughter Zipporah. {2:22} Zipporah had a son named Gershom, 'cause Moses felt like a stranger in a foreign land. {2:23} Eventually, Pharaoh bit the dust. {2:24} The Israelites moaned about their tough grind, and God heard their cries, remembering the covenant with Abraham, Isaac, and Jacob. {2:25} God peeped the Israelites and showed them respect.

{3:1} Moses was chilling, taking care of Jethro's flock out in the desert, and he ended up at God's mountain, Horeb. {3:2} Then an angel of the Lord showed up in a burning bush that didn't burn up. {3:3} Moses was like, "Let me check out this wild sight and see why the bush isn't toast." {3:4} When God saw Moses peeping, He called out to him from the bush, saying, "Moses, Moses." And Moses was like, "Here I am." {3:5} God told him to take off his shoes 'cause he was standing on holy ground. {3:6} Then God said, "I'm the God of your ancestors—Abraham, Isaac, and Jacob." Moses got shook and covered his face. {3:7} God said, "I've seen how rough it is for my people in Egypt, heard their cries from their slave drivers. I know their pain. {3:8} I'm coming down to rescue them from Egypt, bringing them to a good land, flowing with milk and honey—the land of the Canaanites, Hittites, Amorites, Perizzites, Hivites, and Jebusites. {3:9} So now the cries of the Israelites have reached me, and I've seen how the Egyptians are treating them. {3:10} Now, I'm sending you to Pharaoh to lead my people out of Egypt." {3:11} Moses was like, "Who am I to go to Pharaoh and bring the Israelites out of Egypt?" {3:12} God said, "I'll be with you. And when you've brought the people out, you'll worship God on this mountain as a sign." {3:13} Moses was like, "When I tell the Israelites that their ancestors' God sent me, and they ask His name, what do I say?" {3:14} God said, "Tell them 'I AM WHO I AM' sent you." {3:15} Also, tell them, "The Lord, God of your ancestors—Abraham, Isaac, and Jacob—sent me. This is my name forever." {3:16} Go gather the elders and tell them God appeared to you and has seen what's going on in Egypt. {3:17} God said, "I'm bringing you out of Egypt to the land of the Canaanites, Hittites, Amorites, Perizzites, Hivites, and Jebusites—a land flowing with milk and honey." {3:18} They'll listen to you. Then go with the elders to Pharaoh and tell him, "The God of the Hebrews met with us. Let us go three days into the wilderness to sacrifice to the Lord our God." {3:19} God said, "Pharaoh won't let you go easily, even with a strong hand. {3:20} So, I'll use my power and work wonders in Egypt, and then he'll let you go. {3:21} I'll make sure the Egyptians look kindly on you when you leave. You won't leave empty-handed; {3:22} every woman will ask her neighbor and any guests for silver, gold, and clothing to give to their kids. You'll plunder the Egyptians."

{4:1} So like, Moses was all, "Bro, they ain't gonna believe me or listen to me, 'cause they gonna be like, 'Nah, God didn't show up to you.'" {4:2} Then God was like, "Dude, what's that in your hand?" And Moses was like, "Just a rod, man." {4:3} And God was like, "Chuck it on the ground." So he did, and it turned into a snake, freaking Moses out. {4:4} Then God was all, "Grab it by the tail." And when Moses did, it turned back into a rod. God was like, "See? They gotta believe you now." {4:5} This is all so they know it's the God of their ancestors who's talking to Moses. {4:6} Then God was like, "Stick your hand in your shirt." So Moses did, and when he pulled it out, it was all leprous. {4:7} God was like, "Shove it back in." So he did, and when he pulled it out again, it was back to normal. {4:8} God was like, "If they don't believe these signs, pour some river water on the ground; it'll turn to blood." {4:9} Moses was like, "Bro, I'm not smooth with words." {4:10} God was like, "Who do you think made mouths? I got you, man. I'll tell you what to say." {4:11} Then Moses was like, "Please, send someone else." {4:12} God got ticked at Moses but was like, "Fine, your bro Aaron can do the talking." {4:13} Moses was like, "Cool, send him then." {4:14} God was mad but sent Aaron anyway. {4:15} God was like, "Aaron will talk for you, and I'll guide both of you." {4:16} Aaron's basically your mouthpiece, and you're like a mini-god to him. {4:17} Oh, and take that rod with you for the signs. {4:18} So Moses went back to his father-in-law and was like, "Can I bounce and check on my peeps in Egypt?" {4:19} God told him it was cool 'cause all the guys who wanted to kill him were dead. {4:20} Moses packed up his fam and went back to Egypt with his God rod. {4:21} God was like, "When you get there, show Pharaoh some crazy stuff, but I'll make him stubborn." {4:22} Tell Pharaoh Israel's like my firstborn son; let him go or I'll off his kid. {4:23} So Moses was ready to roll. {4:24} But then God was about to zap Moses for some reason. {4:25} So Zipporah, his wife, was like, "Hold up, let me circumcise our kid." She threw the foreskin at Moses' feet and called him a bloody man. {4:26} Then God was cool with Moses again. Weird. {4:27} God told Aaron to go meet Moses, so he did and they had a bro moment. {4:28} Moses filled Aaron in on all the God stuff. {4:29} They gathered the elders of Israel. {4:30} Aaron told them everything and did the signs. {4:31} The people were like, "Okay, we're down; God's got our back."

{5:1} So Moses and Aaron went to Pharaoh like, "Yo, let our people bounce to worship God." {5:2} But Pharaoh was clueless, like, "Who's this God guy? Nah, they ain't leaving." {5:3} Moses and Aaron were like, "God's met with us; let us peace out for three days to worship, or else." {5:4} Pharaoh was like, "Stop distracting my workers, get back to work." {5:5} Pharaoh made things harder for the Israelites, saying they're lazy. {5:6} He told them to get their own straw but still make the same number of bricks. {5:7} The taskmasters were harsh. {5:8} They were like, "No more freebies; make your own bricks." {5:9} Pharaoh was like, "Make them work harder and ignore their complaints." {5:10} The taskmasters were jerks, telling the Israelites they had to find their own straw. {5:11} So they had to scrounge for stubble. {5:12} They were rushed to make the same amount of bricks without straw. {5:13} The Israelite officers got beaten for not meeting quotas. {5:14} They were like, "Why you beating us? We ain't got no straw!" {5:15} The officers pleaded with Pharaoh, but he blamed them for being lazy. {5:16} The officers told Moses and Aaron what was up. {5:17} Pharaoh was harsh, saying they just wanted to slack off. {5:18} He told them to get back to work without straw but still make bricks. {5:19} The officers saw they were in deep trouble. {5:20} So they ran into Moses and Aaron, blaming them for making things worse with Pharaoh. {5:21} Moses was like, "God, seriously, why'd you make things worse for us?" {5:22} Moses went to God, questioning why things went south since he showed up. {5:23} He was like, "Ever since we talked to Pharaoh, things got worse. You haven't helped us at all."

{6:1} Then God was like, "Moses, get ready to witness what I'm about to do to Pharaoh. He'll let the Israelites go, but it won't be easy." {6:2} God told Moses, "I'm the LORD. {6:3} I appeared to Abraham, Isaac, and Jacob as God Almighty, but they didn't know me by the name JEHOVAH. {6:4} I made a covenant with them to give them the land of Canaan, where they lived as foreigners. {6:5} I've heard the Israelites' cries under Egyptian oppression, and I remember my covenant. {6:6} So tell the Israelites that I am the LORD, and I'll free them from Egyptian burdens and bondage with a strong hand and great judgments. {6:7} They'll be my people, and I'll be their God. They'll know that I'm the one who rescued them from Egypt's oppression. {6:8} I'll bring them into the promised land, just like I swore to Abraham, Isaac, and Jacob. I am the LORD. {6:9} Moses delivered this message to the Israelites, but they were too beaten down and crushed to listen. {6:10} Then the LORD told Moses, {6:11} "Go and tell Pharaoh, 'Let my people go.'" {6:12} Moses was like, "But the Israelites won't even listen to me. How will Pharaoh listen to someone with such awkward speaking skills?" {6:13} So the LORD instructed Moses and Aaron, charging them to bring the Israelites out of Egypt. {6:14} Here are the heads of the Israelite clans: Reuben's sons were Hanoch, Pallu, Hezron, and Carmi—these were Reuben's families. {6:15} Simeon's sons were Jemuel, Jamin, Ohad, Jachin, Zohar, and Shaul (born to a Canaanite woman)—these were Simeon's families. {6:16} Levi's descendants were Gershon, Kohath, and Merari; Levi lived for 137 years. {6:17} Gershon's sons were Libni and Shimi, with their families. {6:18} Kohath's sons were Amram, Izhar, Hebron, and Uzziel; Kohath lived for 133 years. {6:19} Merari's sons were Mahali and Mushi—these were Levi's families. {6:20} Amram married Jochebed, his father's sister, and they had Aaron and Moses; Amram lived for 137 years. {6:21} Izhar's sons were Korah, Nepheg, and Zichri. {6:22} Uzziel's sons were Mishael, Elzaphan, and Zithri. {6:23} Aaron married Elisheba, Amminadab's daughter and Naashon's sister; they had Nadab, Abihu, Eleazar, and Ithamar. {6:24} Korah's sons were Assir, Elkanah, and Abiasaph—these were the Korhite families. {6:25} Eleazar (Aaron's son) married one of Putiel's daughters, and they had Phinehas; these were the heads of the Levite families. {6:26} This Moses and Aaron were the ones whom the LORD commanded to lead the Israelites out of Egypt in their military formations. {6:27} They spoke to Pharaoh to release the Israelites from Egypt—Moses and Aaron. {6:28} One day, when the LORD spoke to Moses in Egypt, {6:29} the LORD said, "I am the LORD. Speak everything I tell you to Pharaoh." {6:30} Moses responded, "But I struggle to speak clearly. How will Pharaoh listen to me?"

{7:1} So like, God was telling Moses, "Check it out, I'm making you a big deal to Pharaoh, and Aaron's gonna back you up." {7:2} God was like, "You tell Aaron what's up, and he'll lay it down to Pharaoh to let Israel bounce." {7:3} God was saying He'd make Pharaoh stubborn but would show off with signs and wonders in Egypt. {7:4} But Pharaoh ain't gonna listen, so God's gonna bring the heat with plagues to free the Israelites. {7:5} Then Egypt's gonna be like, "Oh snap, this is the real deal." {7:6} Moses and Aaron did everything God said, just like He told them. {7:7} Oh, and Moses was eighty, and Aaron was eighty-three when they talked to Pharaoh.

{7:8} Then God hit up Moses and Aaron again, saying, {7:9} "When Pharaoh asks for a magic show, tell Aaron to whip out his rod; it'll turn into a snake." {7:10} So they rolled up to Pharaoh and did their thing, and Aaron's rod turned into a snake. {7:11} Then Pharaoh brought in his crew of magicians, who did the same trick. {7:12} But Aaron's snake ate up theirs. {7:13} And Pharaoh kept being stubborn, just like God said. {7:14} God was like, "Pharaoh ain't budging; he won't let the people go." {7:15} So God told Moses to catch Pharaoh by the river in the morning with the snake-rod. {7:16} Moses was supposed to tell Pharaoh that God's calling the shots and to let the people go, but Pharaoh ain't been listening. {7:17} God was like, "This is how Pharaoh's gonna know I'm the real deal: I'm gonna turn this river into blood." {7:18} The fish died, the river stank, and the Egyptians were grossed out by the water. {7:19} Then God told Moses to tell Aaron to do his thing with the rod again, but this time, turn all the water in Egypt into blood. {7:20} So Moses and Aaron did it, and boom, all the water turned to blood. {7:21} The river was nasty, the fish were dead, and nobody could drink the water. {7:22} But the Egyptian magicians pulled the same stunt with their tricks, and Pharaoh was still stubborn. {7:23} Then Pharaoh went back home, still ignoring the whole situation. {7:24} The Egyptians were digging around for water, desperate to find something clean. {7:25} And for a whole week, the river stayed jacked up after God messed with it.

{8:1} So, God tells Moses, "Yo, go to Pharaoh and tell him, 'Let my people bounce so they can worship me.'" {8:2} And if Pharaoh acts all stubborn, I'mma hit up his whole turf with a frog invasion. {8:3} These frogs gonna be everywhere, in his crib, on his bed, in the kitchen—everywhere! {8:4} Pharaoh and his crew gonna be covered in frogs, no escaping it. {8:5} Then God's like, "Yo, Aaron, use your rod and summon more frogs on Egypt." {8:6} Aaron does it, and bam! Frogs are all over Egypt. {8:7} Even the magicians try to pull off the same trick, but it's a no-go. {8:8} So Pharaoh's like, "Moses and Aaron, get rid of these frogs and I'll let your people bounce to worship." {8:9} Moses is like, "Sure thing, just let me know when you want these frogs gone." {8:10} Pharaoh's like, "Tomorrow, do your thing, so I know you ain't playin'." {8:11} So, Moses hits up God, and the frogs dip out. {8:12} After that, Moses and Aaron bounce, and Moses prays to God to get rid of the frogs. {8:13} God listens to Moses, and the frogs vanish, leaving a nasty smell. {8:14} But Pharaoh, he sees the relief and gets all stubborn again, just like God said he would. {8:16} Next up, God tells Moses, "Yo, tell Aaron to smack the ground with his rod, and it's gonna rain lice all over Egypt." {8:17} Aaron does it, and boom! Lice everywhere, on people and animals, straight-up infestation. {8:18} Even the magicians try, but they can't pull it off, so they're dealing with lice too. {8:19} The magicians admit it's some divine stuff, but Pharaoh's still acting hard-headed, just like God said he would. {8:20} Then God's like, "Moses, catch Pharaoh early in the morning by the water and tell him, 'Let my people go or I'm sending swarms of flies everywhere.'" {8:21} And if Pharaoh keeps acting up, flies are gonna swarm all over Egypt, except in Goshen where the Israelites chill. {8:22} This is gonna show Pharaoh who's boss in this land. {8:23} It's going down tomorrow. {8:24} Next day, bam! Flies infest Egypt, even Pharaoh's crib. {8:25} Pharaoh's like, "Okay, fine, you can do your sacrifices here." {8:26} But Moses ain't having it, saying they can't worship like that 'cause it's not cool with the Egyptians. {8:27} He insists they gotta dip for a three-day worship sesh. {8:28} Pharaoh's like, "Okay, go worship, but don't go too far and pray for me." {8:29} Moses is like, "Sure, I'll ask God to get rid of the flies tomorrow, but don't try any tricks." {8:30} So, Moses bounces and prays to God. {8:31} God listens and clears out the flies. {8:32} But Pharaoh's still acting tough, just like before.

{9:1} So God tells Moses, "Yo, hit up Pharaoh again and say, 'Let my people bounce so they can worship me.'" {9:2} God warns that if Pharaoh keeps acting stubborn, bad stuff is coming for his livestock. {9:3} Cue a serious livestock disease—cows, horses, donkeys, camels, oxen, sheep—all hit hard. {9:4} But God's like, "Israelite animals? They're off-limits." {9:5} God sets a date: Tomorrow, Egypt's gonna see this go down. {9:6} True to his word, next day all of Egypt's livestock drops dead, but not a single Israelite animal. {9:7} Pharaoh checks, and sure enough, Israel's livestock is untouched. But Pharaoh's heart stays hard, and he won't let the people go. {9:8} Then God's like, "Moses, Aaron, grab some furnace ashes and throw it up in front of Pharaoh." {9:9} Those ashes turn into painful boils on everyone in Egypt—humans and animals alike. {9:10} Moses does it, and bam! Boils break out all over the place. {9:11} The magicians can't even front this time because they're covered in boils too. {9:12} Pharaoh's heart stays hard, just like God said. {9:13} God's not done, though. He tells Moses, "Hit up Pharaoh again and tell him, 'Let my people bounce so they can worship me.'" {9:14} God's about to unleash all the plagues on Pharaoh, his crew, and the people to show who's boss. {9:15} God's gonna bring down a serious pestilence on Pharaoh, wiping him out. {9:16} It's all to show God's power and make sure everyone knows who's running the show. {9:17} God's like, "Pharaoh, seriously, still not letting my people go?" {9:18} Tomorrow, get ready for some crazy hail like Egypt's never seen. {9:19} Pharaoh's warned: Get your people and animals inside, or they're gonna get wrecked by this hail. {9:20} Some of Pharaoh's crew listen and shelter their stuff, but others blow it off. {9:21} Hail comes down hard, smashing everything in the fields. {9:22} God's like, "Moses, stretch out your hand and bring on the hail—people, animals, plants, everything's getting hit." {9:23} Moses does it, and boom! Thunder, fire, and hail hit Egypt hard. {9:24} Hail and fire mix it up, the worst Egypt's ever seen. {9:25} Everything in the fields gets wrecked by hail, including people, animals, and plants. {9:26} But Goshen, where the Israelites are, stays safe. {9:27} Pharaoh's like, "Okay, I messed up. Make this stop, and I'll let your people go." {9:28} Moses agrees, but he knows Pharaoh's not really getting it yet. {9:29} As soon as Moses leaves the city, he prays, and the storm stops. {9:30} Moses knows Pharaoh's crew still isn't fearing God. {9:31} The barley and flax are wrecked, but wheat and rye survive 'cause they weren't grown yet. {9:32-33} Moses prays, and the storm stops. {9:34} Pharaoh, seeing the calm, reverts to his old ways, hardening his heart and refusing to let the Israelites go.

{10:1} God hit up Moses, like, "Yo, go talk to Pharaoh; I've made him and his crew stubborn so I can flex my powers in front of them. {10:2} Then you can tell your kids and grandkids about the epic stuff I did in Egypt, so they know I'm the real deal." {10:3} So Moses and Aaron rolled up on Pharaoh, dropping truth bombs like, "How long you gonna act all high and mighty? Let my people bounce so they can worship me." {10:4} And they warned him, "If you keep tripping, tomorrow we're unleashing locusts on your turf." {10:5} These locusts were gonna cover everything and chomp up whatever the hail didn't wreck, even your backyard trees. {10:6} They'd swarm into your houses, your servants' cribs, and everywhere, like nothing Egypt's ever seen before. Then Moses dipped. {10:7} Pharaoh's crew was like, "Bruh, how long we gotta deal with this? Let the Israelites go before Egypt gets wrecked." {10:8} So Pharaoh called Moses and Aaron back and was like, "Fine, go worship your God, but who's tagging along?" {10:9} Moses was like, "We're taking everyone, young and old, sons and daughters, and all our livestock. We gotta throw down a party for God." {10:10} Pharaoh was like, "Alright, but watch yourselves; trouble's coming." {10:11} Then he was like, "Nah, only the guys can go worship; you've been asking for it." And he kicked them out. {10:12} Then God was like, "Moses, wave your hand and summon locusts to munch on Egypt's crops, everything left after the hailstorm." {10:13} So Moses did his thing, and a strong east wind blew in the locusts. {10:14} These locusts went crazy, wrecking Egypt like nobody's business. {10:15} They devoured all the plants, leaving Egypt in darkness with nothing green left. {10:16} Pharaoh was shook and called Moses and Aaron, admitting he messed up against their God. {10:17} He begged them to pray for God to stop the locust plague. {10:18} Moses dipped to talk to God. {10:19} God sent a fierce west wind to sweep away the locusts into the Red Sea, leaving no trace in Egypt. {10:20} But God made Pharaoh stubborn again, so he wouldn't let the Israelites bounce. {10:21} Then God was like, "Moses, stretch your hand toward the sky, and let there be darkness over Egypt, thick darkness you can feel." {10:22} So Moses did it, and darkness hit Egypt for three days. {10:23} It was pitch black; nobody could see a thing or even move from where they were, but the Israelites had light in their homes. {10:24} Pharaoh called Moses and was like, "Alright, you can worship your God, but leave your animals behind." {10:25} Moses was like, "Nah, we're taking everything, and we need sacrifices to offer God." {10:26} He was like, "Not a single hoof stays behind; we gotta serve our God right." {10:27} But God made Pharaoh stubborn again, and he wouldn't let them go. {10:28} Pharaoh was fed up and told Moses to scram, warning him not to show his face again, or else. {10:29} Moses was like, "You got it; I won't bother you anymore."

{11:1} God tells Moses, "I'm about to drop one more crazy plague on Pharaoh and Egypt. After this, Pharaoh's gonna be begging you all to leave, no doubt." {11:2} Moses tells the people to hit up their neighbors for some bling—silver and gold. {11:3} The Egyptians are feeling generous towards the Israelites, especially Moses, who's like a big deal in Egypt, even with Pharaoh's crew and the locals. {11:4} Moses tells them, "Around midnight, I'm stepping out into Egypt." {11:5} Here's the deal: Every firstborn in Egypt, from Pharaoh's heir to the lowest servant's child and even animals, is gonna bite it. {11:6} There's gonna be a massive cry across Egypt like never before or ever again. {11:7} But not a peep from any dog against the Israelites—God's making it clear who's who. {11:8} After this, Pharaoh's people are gonna be all about kicking out Moses and the Israelites. Moses storms out from Pharaoh, totally ticked off. {11:9} God tells Moses straight up: Pharaoh ain't gonna listen, 'cause I'm gonna show off my wonders big-time in Egypt. {11:10} Moses and Aaron keep throwing down these miracles, but God keeps Pharaoh's heart stubborn so he won't let the Israelites go.

{12:1} So, God hit up Moses and Aaron in Egypt, saying, {12:2} "This month is your new start, like, the first month of your year. {12:3} Tell everyone in Israel that on the 10th day of this month, each fam's gotta snag a lamb, one per household. {12:4} If a fam's too small for a whole lamb, they should team up with their neighbor. Everyone needs to have enough lamb to go around. {12:5} Make sure the lamb is flawless, a year-old male, and you can use either sheep or goats. {12:6} Keep it until the 14th day, then everyone in Israel has to kill it at twilight. {12:7} Take the blood and splash it on the sides and top of the doorframes where you're gonna eat it. {12:8} That night, roast the lamb with fire, eat it with unleavened bread and bitter herbs. {12:9} Don't eat it raw or boiled, only roasted with its head, legs, and innards. {12:10} Don't leave any leftovers until morning; if there's anything left, burn it. {12:11} Eat it ready to go: belt fastened, shoes on, staff in hand, and chow down fast. It's the LORD's Passover. {12:12} I'll roll through Egypt tonight and take out all the firstborn, humans and animals, and flex on all the gods of Egypt. I am the LORD. {12:13} The blood on your houses will be a sign for you; when I see it, I'll pass over you, and no plague will hit you when I smack Egypt. {12:14} This day is a memorial for you; keep it as a feast to the LORD forever. {12:15} For seven days, eat unleavened bread. On the first day, ditch all the yeast from your houses. Anyone eating yeast from the first to the seventh day will get cut off from Israel. {12:16} The first and seventh days are sacred assemblies; no work is allowed except preparing food. {12:17} Keep the Feast of Unleavened Bread because on this very day I brought your divisions out of Egypt. Keep it forever in your generations. {12:18} From the evening of the 14th day of the first month to the evening of the 21st day, eat unleavened bread. {12:19} For seven days, no yeast should be found in your houses. Anyone, native or foreign, eating anything with yeast gets cut off from the community of Israel. {12:20} Eat nothing with yeast; in all your homes, eat unleavened bread." {12:21} Moses gathered all the elders of Israel and said, "Pick out and take lambs for your families and kill the Passover lamb. {12:22} Take a bunch of hyssop, dip it in the blood in the basin, and hit the top and sides of the doorframe with the blood. No one should go out until morning. {12:23} When the LORD passes through to strike down the Egyptians, He'll see the blood on the top and sides of the doorframe and pass over that door, not letting the destroyer hit you. {12:24} Keep this command as a law for you and your kids forever. {12:25} When you enter the land the LORD will give you, keep this ceremony. {12:26} When your kids ask, 'What does this mean?' {12:27} say, 'It's the Passover sacrifice to the LORD, who passed over the houses of the Israelites in Egypt and spared our homes when He struck down the Egyptians.' Then the people bowed down and worshipped. {12:28} The Israelites did just as the LORD commanded Moses and Aaron. {12:29} At midnight, the LORD struck down all the firstborn in Egypt, from Pharaoh's firstborn to the firstborn of the prisoner in the dungeon, and all the firstborn of the livestock. {12:30} Pharaoh and all his officials and all the Egyptians got up during the night, and there was loud wailing in Egypt, for there wasn't a house without someone dead. {12:31} Pharaoh called Moses and Aaron and said, "Get out, you and the Israelites! Go worship the LORD as you requested. {12:32} Take your flocks and herds and leave, and bless me too." {12:33} The Egyptians urged the people to hurry and leave the country, saying, "If you don't, we're all dead." {12:34} The Israelites took their dough before the yeast was added, carried it on their shoulders in kneading troughs wrapped in clothing. {12:35} The Israelites did as Moses instructed and asked the Egyptians for silver, gold, and clothing. {12:36} The LORD made the Egyptians favorably disposed toward the people, and they gave them what they asked for; so they plundered the Egyptians. {12:37} The Israelites traveled from Rameses to Succoth, about six hundred thousand men on foot, plus women and children. {12:38} Many other people went up with them, along with flocks, herds, and a lot of livestock. {12:39} They baked unleavened cakes of the dough they had brought from Egypt. The dough was without yeast because they had been driven out of Egypt and did not have time to prepare food for themselves. {12:40} The Israelites had lived in Egypt for 430 years. {12:41} At the end of the 430 years, to the very day, all the LORD's divisions left Egypt. {12:42} Because the LORD kept vigil that night to bring them out of Egypt, all the Israelites are to keep vigil to honor the LORD for the generations to come. {12:43} The LORD said to Moses and Aaron, "These are the regulations for the Passover: No foreigner may eat it. {12:44} Any slave you have bought may eat it after you have circumcised him. {12:45} But temporary residents and hired workers may not eat it. {12:46} It must be eaten inside the house; take none of the meat outside the house. Do not break any of the bones. {12:47} The whole community of Israel must celebrate it. {12:48} Any foreigner residing among you who wants to celebrate the LORD's Passover must have all the males in his household circumcised; then he may take part like one born in the land. No uncircumcised male may eat it. {12:49} The same law applies both to the native-born and to the foreigner residing among you." {12:50} All the Israelites did just what the LORD had commanded Moses and Aaron. {12:51} And on that very day, the LORD brought the Israelites out of Egypt by their divisions.

{13:1} The LORD hollered at Moses, saying, {13:2} "Set apart all the firstborn for me, both human and animal, they're mine." {13:3} Moses told the squad, "Remember this day when you bounced from Egypt, from the house of slavery; the LORD flexed his power to get you out. No yeast in your bread. {13:4} You left today in the month of Abib. {13:5} When the LORD brings you into the land of the Canaanites, Hittites, Amorites, Hivites, and Jebusites, the land he promised your ancestors, a land flowing with milk and honey, you gotta keep this ritual this month. {13:6} For seven days, munch on unleavened bread, and on the seventh day, throw a feast for the LORD. {13:7} For seven days, eat unleavened bread; no leavened bread should be seen anywhere in your hood. {13:8} Tell your kid that day, 'We do this because of what the LORD did for me when I bounced from Egypt.' {13:9} It'll be like a sign on your hand and a reminder on your forehead that the LORD's law is in your mouth: the LORD flexed his power to get you out of Egypt. {13:10} So, keep this ordinance every year. {13:11} When the LORD brings you into the land of the Canaanites, as he promised you and your ancestors, and gives it to you, {13:12} you gotta set apart all the firstborn for the LORD, both humans and animals; the males belong to the LORD. {13:13} For a firstborn donkey, redeem it with a lamb; if you don't, break its neck. All firstborn boys must be redeemed. {13:14} When your kid asks in the future, 'What's this about?' say, 'The LORD flexed his power to get us out of Egypt, out of the house of slavery. {13:15} When Pharaoh was stubborn about letting us go, the LORD killed all the firstborn in Egypt, both human and animal. That's why I sacrifice all firstborn males to the LORD, but I redeem all my firstborn sons.' {13:16} It'll be like a sign on your hand and a reminder on your forehead that the LORD flexed his power to get us out of Egypt. {13:17} When Pharaoh let the squad go, God didn't lead them through the Philistine country, though it was shorter, because God thought they might freak out if they see war and bounce back to Egypt. {13:18} So God led the people around by the desert road toward the Red Sea, and the Israelites left Egypt ready for battle. {13:19} Moses took Joseph's bones with him, because Joseph had made the Israelites swear to carry his bones with them when God came to their rescue. {13:20} They left Succoth and camped at Etham on the edge of the wilderness. {13:21} The LORD led them by day in a pillar of cloud and by night in a pillar of fire, so they could travel day and night. {13:22} The LORD didn't take away the pillar of cloud by day or the pillar of fire by night from in front of the squad.

{14:1} The LORD hit up Moses, saying, {14:2} "Tell the Israelites to turn and camp out by Pi-hahiroth, between Migdol and the sea, across from Baal-zephon. Camp by the sea." {14:3} "Pharaoh will think the Israelites are lost in the desert." {14:4} "I'll harden Pharaoh's heart so he'll chase after them, and I'll get my glory through Pharaoh and all his army. Then the Egyptians will know I am the LORD." And they did it. {14:5} The king of Egypt got the news that the people had fled, and Pharaoh and his officials changed their minds about them and said, "Why did we let them go? Now we have no one to serve us." {14:6} So Pharaoh got his chariot ready and took his army with him. {14:7} He took six hundred of his best chariots along with all the other chariots of Egypt, with officers over all of them. {14:8} The LORD hardened Pharaoh's heart, and he pursued the Israelites, who were marching out boldly. {14:9} The Egyptians chased them with all Pharaoh's horses, chariots, horsemen, and troops, and caught up with them as they camped by the sea near Pi-hahiroth, opposite Baal-zephon. {14:10} As Pharaoh approached, the Israelites looked up and saw the Egyptians coming after them. They freaked out and cried out to the LORD. {14:11} They said to Moses, "Were there no graves in Egypt that you brought us here to die in the desert? Why did you bring us out of Egypt?" {14:12} "Didn't we tell you in Egypt, 'Leave us alone; let us serve the Egyptians?' It would have been better for us to serve the Egyptians than to die in the desert!" {14:13} Moses answered, "Don't be afraid. Stand firm and you'll see the LORD's salvation today. The Egyptians you see today you'll never see again." {14:14} "The LORD will fight for you, just chill." {14:15} Then the LORD said to Moses, "Why are you crying out to me? Tell the Israelites to move forward." {14:16} "Raise your staff and stretch out your hand over the sea to divide the water so the Israelites can go through the sea on dry ground." {14:17} "I'll harden the hearts of the Egyptians so they'll go in after them. I'll gain glory through Pharaoh and all his army, through his chariots and horsemen." {14:18} "The Egyptians will know I am the LORD when I gain glory through Pharaoh, his chariots, and horsemen." {14:19} Then the angel of God, who had been leading the Israelites, moved and went behind them. The pillar of cloud also moved from in front and stood behind them, {14:20} coming between the armies of Egypt and Israel. Throughout the night, the cloud brought darkness to one side and light to the other, so neither went near the other all night long. {14:21} Then Moses stretched out his hand over the sea, and all that night the LORD drove the sea back with a strong east wind and turned it into dry land. The waters were divided. {14:22} The Israelites went through the sea on dry ground, with a wall of water on their right and on their left. {14:23} The Egyptians pursued them, and all Pharaoh's horses, chariots, and horsemen followed them into the sea. {14:24} During the last watch of the night, the LORD looked down from the pillar of fire and cloud at the Egyptian army and threw it into confusion. {14:25} He jammed the wheels of their chariots so that they had difficulty driving. The Egyptians said, "Let's get away from the Israelites! The LORD is fighting for them against Egypt." {14:26} Then the LORD said to Moses, "Stretch out your hand over the sea so that the waters may flow back over the Egyptians and their chariots and horsemen." {14:27} Moses stretched out his hand over the sea, and at daybreak the sea went back to its place. The Egyptians were fleeing toward it, and the LORD swept them into the sea. {14:28} The water flowed back and covered the chariots and horsemen—the entire army of Pharaoh that had followed the Israelites into the sea. Not one of them survived. {14:29} But the Israelites went through the sea on dry ground, with a wall of water on their right and on their left. {14:30} That day the LORD saved Israel from the hands of the Egyptians, and Israel saw the Egyptians lying dead on the shore. {14:31} When the Israelites saw the mighty hand of the LORD displayed against the Egyptians, they feared the LORD and put their trust in him and in Moses his servant.

{15:1} Moses and the Israelites dropped a sick beat for the LORD, singing, "I'll sing to the LORD, 'cause He's awesome: He yeeted the horse and rider into the sea. {15:2} The LORD is my strength and my jam, He's my savior: He's my God, and I'll build Him a spot; my dad's God, and I'll hype Him up. {15:3} The LORD's a warrior; His name's the LORD. {15:4} Pharaoh's chariots and army, He tossed into the sea: His top guys got dunked in the Red Sea. {15:5} The depths covered them: they sank like a stone. {15:6} Your right hand, LORD, is lit in power: your right hand, LORD, smashed the enemy. {15:7} In your epicness, you crushed those who came at you: you unleashed your wrath, which burned them up like straw. {15:8} With the blast of your nostrils, the waters piled up, the waves stood tall like a heap, the depths froze in the heart of the sea. {15:9} The enemy said, 'I'll chase them, catch them, split the loot; I'll flex on them; I'll draw my sword, my hand will wreck them.' {15:10} But you blew with your wind, and the sea covered them: they sank like lead in the mighty waters. {15:11} Who's like you, LORD, among the gods? Who's like you, awesome in holiness, majestic in praise, working wonders? {15:12} You stretched out your right hand, and the earth swallowed them. {15:13} In your love, you led the people you saved; you guided them in your strength to your holy place. {15:14} The nations heard and freaked out: trembling gripped the people of Philistia. {15:15} The chiefs of Edom were shocked; the mighty men of Moab were shaking; all the people of Canaan melted away. {15:16} Terror and dread fell on them; by the power of your arm, they stood still as a rock until your people passed by, LORD, until the people you bought passed by. {15:17} You'll bring them in and plant them on the mountain you own, the place you made for your crib, LORD, the sanctuary, Lord, that your hands set up. {15:18} The LORD will reign forever and ever. {15:19} When Pharaoh's horses, chariots, and horsemen went into the sea, the LORD brought the waters back over them, but the Israelites walked on dry land through the sea. {15:20} Then Miriam the prophetess, Aaron's sister, grabbed a timbrel, and all the women followed her with timbrels and dancing. {15:21} And Miriam sang back to them, 'Sing to the LORD, 'cause He's awesome; He yeeted the horse and rider into the sea.' {15:22} Moses led Israel from the Red Sea into the wilderness of Shur; they traveled three days without finding water. {15:23} When they got to Marah, they couldn't drink the water there 'cause it was bitter. That's why it's called Marah. {15:24} The people complained to Moses, 'What are we gonna drink?' {15:25} Moses cried out to the LORD, and the LORD showed him a piece of wood. He threw it into the water, and it became sweet. There, the LORD made a rule and tested them. {15:26} He said, 'If you listen carefully to the LORD your God, do what's right in His eyes, pay attention to His commands, and keep all His decrees, I won't bring on you any of the diseases I brought on the Egyptians; for I am the LORD who heals you.' {15:27} Then they came to Elim, where there were twelve springs and seventy palm trees, and they camped there by the water.

{16:1} They bounced from Elim, and the whole squad of the Israelites rolled up to the wilderness of Sin, between Elim and Sinai, on the fifteenth day of the second month after ditching Egypt. {16:2} The whole crew started whining to Moses and Aaron in the wild: {16:3} The Israelites said, "Bro, we wish God had just let us die in Egypt, where we had meat and bread all day; you dragged us out here to starve us all to death." {16:4} Then the LORD told Moses, "I'm gonna rain bread from heaven for you; let the people gather just enough each day to test if they'll follow my rules or not. {16:5} On the sixth day, they need to prep what they bring in, and it'll be double what they gather every other day." {16:6} Moses and Aaron told the Israelites, "By evening, you'll know it was the LORD who brought you out of Egypt: {16:7} And in the morning, you'll see the LORD's glory; He hears your whining against Him: we're just the messengers." {16:8} Moses added, "When the LORD gives you meat in the evening and all the bread you want in the morning, it's because He hears your complaints against Him. Who are we? You're not griping at us, but at the LORD." {16:9} Moses told Aaron, "Tell everyone to come before the LORD; He's heard your whining." {16:10} While Aaron was speaking, they all looked towards the wilderness and saw the LORD's glory in a cloud. {16:11} The LORD told Moses, {16:12} "I've heard the Israelites' complaints. Tell them, 'In the evening you'll eat meat, and in the morning you'll be full of bread. Then you'll know I am the LORD your God.'" {16:13} That evening, quails covered the camp, and in the morning there was dew around the camp. {16:14} When the dew dried up, there was a small round thing on the ground, like frost. {16:15} When the Israelites saw it, they were like, "What is it?" Moses said, "This is the bread the LORD's given you to eat. {16:16} Here's what the LORD commands: gather as much as each person needs, an omer per person, for everyone in your tent." {16:17} The Israelites did so, some gathering more, some less. {16:18} When they measured it, those who gathered much didn't have too much, and those who gathered little had enough; each person gathered as much as they needed. {16:19} Moses said, "Don't keep any of it till morning." {16:20} But they didn't listen, and some kept it till morning, and it bred worms and stank: and Moses was mad at them. {16:21} They gathered it every morning, each person as much as they needed: and when the sun got hot, it melted. {16:22} On the sixth day, they gathered twice as much, two omers per person: and the leaders reported this to Moses. {16:23} Moses told them, "This is what the LORD said: Tomorrow is a holy sabbath to the LORD. Bake what you want and boil what you want; save whatever's left till morning." {16:24} They saved it till morning as Moses commanded, and it didn't stink or get worms. {16:25} Moses said, "Eat it today, because today is a sabbath to the LORD. You won't find any in the field today. {16:26} Gather it for six days, but the seventh day is the sabbath; there won't be any." {16:27} Some people went out on the seventh day to gather, but found none. {16:28} The LORD said to Moses, "How long will you refuse to follow my commands and laws? {16:29} Look, the LORD gave you the sabbath; that's why He gives you bread for two days on the sixth day. Stay where you are; don't go out on the seventh day." {16:30} So the people chilled on the seventh day. {16:31} The Israelites called it Manna: it was like coriander seed, white, and tasted like wafers with honey. {16:32} Moses said, "This is what the LORD commands: Fill an omer of it to be kept for future generations, so they can see the bread I fed you in the wilderness when I brought you out of Egypt." {16:33} Moses told Aaron, "Take a jar and put an omer of manna in it, and place it before the LORD to be kept for generations." {16:34} As the LORD commanded, Aaron placed it before the Testimony to be kept. {16:35} The Israelites ate manna for forty years until they reached the inhabited land; they ate manna until they reached the borders of Canaan. {16:36} An omer is a tenth of an ephah.

{17:1} The whole squad of Israelites bounced from the wilderness of Sin, following the LORD's command, and camped at Rephidim, but there was no water for them to drink. {17:2} So the people beefed with Moses, saying, "Give us water to drink." Moses was like, "Why are you beefing with me? Why are you testing the LORD?" {17:3} The people were thirsty and kept whining to Moses, saying, "Why did you bring us out of Egypt just to kill us and our kids and cattle with thirst?" {17:4} Moses cried out to the LORD, "What am I supposed to do with these people? They're about to stone me!" {17:5} The LORD told Moses, "Go ahead of the people, take some of the elders, and bring your rod that you used to strike the river. {17:6} I'll be there on the rock at Horeb; strike the rock, and water will come out for everyone to drink." Moses did this in front of the elders of Israel. {17:7} He called the place Massah and Meribah because the Israelites were beefing and testing the LORD, asking, "Is the LORD with us or not?" {17:8} Then Amalek rolled up and started beefing with Israel at Rephidim. {17:9} Moses told Joshua, "Pick some men and go fight Amalek. Tomorrow, I'll be on the hilltop with God's rod in my hand." {17:10} Joshua did what Moses said and fought Amalek while Moses, Aaron, and Hur went up the hill. {17:11} As long as Moses held up his hand, Israel was winning; when he dropped it, Amalek started winning. {17:12} But Moses' hands got heavy, so they took a stone for him to sit on, and Aaron and Hur held up his hands, one on each side, keeping them steady until sunset. {17:13} Joshua defeated Amalek and his people with the sword. {17:14} The LORD told Moses, "Write this down as a reminder and tell Joshua: I will wipe out Amalek's memory from under heaven." {17:15} Moses built an altar and called it Jehovah-nissi: {17:16} because he said, "The LORD has sworn to have war with Amalek from generation to generation."

{18:1} So Jethro, the priest of Midian and Moses' father-in-law, heard about all the epic stuff God did for Moses and Israel, like bringing them out of Egypt. {18:2} Jethro then took Zipporah, Moses' wife, after Moses had sent her back, {18:3} along with her two sons. One was named Gershom, because Moses said, "I've been a stranger in a foreign land." {18:4} The other was Eliezer, meaning "God of my father was my help and saved me from Pharaoh's sword." {18:5} Jethro came with Moses' wife and sons to meet him in the wilderness, near the mountain of God. {18:6} He sent word to Moses, "Yo, it's Jethro, your father-in-law, coming to see you with your wife and her two sons." {18:7} Moses went out to meet Jethro, bowed down, and kissed him. They asked each other how they were doing and went into the tent. {18:8} Moses told Jethro all about what the LORD had done to Pharaoh and the Egyptians for Israel, and about all their struggles along the way, and how the LORD had saved them. {18:9} Jethro was hyped about all the good things the LORD had done for Israel, saving them from the Egyptians. {18:10} Jethro said, "Blessed be the LORD, who saved you from the Egyptians and Pharaoh, and rescued the people from their oppressors. {18:11} Now I know that the LORD is the greatest, because he showed up and owned those who tried to act all proud." {18:12} Jethro then offered a burnt offering and sacrifices to God, and Aaron and all the elders of Israel came to eat bread with Jethro before God. {18:13} The next day, Moses sat down to judge the people, and they stood around him from morning till evening. {18:14} When Jethro saw what Moses was doing, he said, "What is this you're doing for the people? Why are you sitting alone with everyone standing around you from morning till night?" {18:15} Moses replied, "Because the people come to me to seek God's guidance. {18:16} When they have issues, they come to me, and I decide between them and teach them God's laws and instructions." {18:17} Jethro said, "What you're doing is not good. {18:18} You'll wear yourself out, and the people too. This job is too heavy for you; you can't handle it alone. {18:19} Listen to me now, I'll give you some advice, and may God be with you: Be the people's representative before God, and bring their issues to him. {18:20} Teach them the decrees and laws, show them the way to live and the work they must do. {18:21} But also, pick capable men from all the people—men who respect God, are trustworthy, and hate dishonest gain. Appoint them as officials over thousands, hundreds, fifties, and tens. {18:22} Let these guys judge the people at all times. Have them bring the big issues to you, but they can handle the small stuff themselves. It'll make your load lighter because they'll share it with you. {18:23} If you do this, and God so commands, you'll be able to endure, and all these people will go home satisfied." {18:24} Moses listened to his father-in-law and did everything he said. {18:25} He chose capable men from all Israel and made them leaders of the people—officials over thousands, hundreds, fifties, and tens. {18:26} They judged the people at all times, handling the difficult cases themselves, but bringing the big ones to Moses. {18:27} Then Moses let his father-in-law leave, and he went back to his own land.

{19:1} So in the third month after the Israelites bounced from Egypt, they rolled up into the wilderness of Sinai. {19:2} They left Rephidim, hit the Sinai desert, and set up camp there in front of the mountain. {19:3} Moses went up to God, and the LORD called out to him from the mountain, saying, "Tell the house of Jacob, the children of Israel this: {19:4} You've seen what I did to the Egyptians, and how I carried you on eagles' wings and brought you to me. {19:5} So, if you listen to my voice and keep my covenant, you'll be my special treasure above all people, because the whole earth is mine. {19:6} You'll be a kingdom of priests and a holy nation. These are the words you must tell the Israelites." {19:7} Moses came back, called the elders, and laid out everything the LORD told him. {19:8} All the people answered together, "We'll do everything the LORD said." Moses took their words back to the LORD. {19:9} The LORD said to Moses, "I'll come to you in a thick cloud so the people can hear me talking to you and always believe you." Moses relayed this to the LORD. {19:10} The LORD told Moses, "Go to the people, consecrate them today and tomorrow, and have them wash their clothes. {19:11} Get them ready by the third day, because on that day, the LORD will come down on Mount Sinai in sight of everyone. {19:12} Set boundaries for the people around the mountain, telling them not to go up or touch its edge. Whoever touches the mountain will surely die. {19:13} No hand shall touch it, but the offender will be stoned or shot with arrows; whether beast or human, they shall not live. When the trumpet sounds long, they can come up to the mountain." {19:14} Moses went down from the mountain, consecrated the people, and they washed their clothes. {19:15} He told them, "Get ready for the third day; don't go near your wives." {19:16} On the third day in the morning, there were thunders, lightnings, a thick cloud on the mountain, and a very loud trumpet sound, making everyone in the camp tremble. {19:17} Moses brought the people out of the camp to meet God, and they stood at the foot of the mountain. {19:18} Mount Sinai was smoking all over because the LORD came down on it in fire. The smoke rose like from a furnace, and the whole mountain shook. {19:19} The trumpet sound grew louder and louder. Moses spoke, and God answered him with a voice. {19:20} The LORD came down on Mount Sinai, on the top of the mountain, and called Moses up to the top. Moses went up. {19:21} The LORD told Moses, "Go down and warn the people not to break through to look at the LORD, or many of them will die. {19:22} Even the priests who come near the LORD must consecrate themselves, or the LORD will break out against them." {19:23} Moses said to the LORD, "The people can't come up Mount Sinai because you warned us, setting boundaries around the mountain and making it holy." {19:24} The LORD said, "Go down and bring Aaron back up with you. But the priests and the people must not force their way through to come up to the LORD, or he will break out against them." {19:25} So Moses went down to the people and told them.

{20:1} And God dropped all these words, saying, {20:2} "I am the LORD your God who brought you out of Egypt, out of the house of slavery. {20:3} Don't have any other gods before me. {20:4} Don't make any carved idols or any images of what's in the sky, on the earth, or in the water. {20:5} Don't bow down or serve them, because I, the LORD your God, am a jealous God, punishing the kids for their parents' sins to the third and fourth generation of those who hate me, {20:6} but showing love to thousands who love me and keep my commandments. {20:7} Don't misuse the name of the LORD your God, because the LORD won't let anyone go unpunished who misuses his name. {20:8} Remember the Sabbath day and keep it holy. {20:9} Work for six days and get all your stuff done, {20:10} but the seventh day is the Sabbath of the LORD your God. Don't do any work, neither you, your kids, your servants, your animals, nor any foreigner living with you. {20:11} For in six days, the LORD made the heavens, the earth, the sea, and everything in them, but rested on the seventh day. That's why the LORD blessed the Sabbath day and made it holy. {20:12} Respect your parents so you'll live long in the land the LORD your God is giving you. {20:13} Don't murder. {20:14} Don't cheat on your partner. {20:15} Don't steal. {20:16} Don't lie about others. {20:17} Don't be jealous of your neighbor's house, wife, servants, animals, or anything else that belongs to them. {20:18} When all the people saw the thunder, lightning, trumpet sounds, and the smoking mountain, they freaked out and stood at a distance. {20:19} They told Moses, "You speak to us, and we'll listen, but don't let God speak to us, or we'll die." {20:20} Moses said, "Don't be scared. God's testing you so you'll fear him and not sin." {20:21} The people stayed at a distance while Moses approached the thick darkness where God was. {20:22} The LORD told Moses, "Tell the Israelites this: You've seen that I've spoken to you from heaven. {20:23} Don't make gods of silver or gold to worship alongside me. {20:24} Make an altar of earth for me and sacrifice your burnt and peace offerings, your sheep, and your oxen on it. Wherever I make my name known, I'll come to you and bless you. {20:25} If you make an altar of stone, don't use cut stones, because using tools on it makes it unholy. {20:26} Don't use steps to go up to my altar, so your nakedness isn't exposed."

{21:1} So here's the deal with these rules you gotta lay down for them. {21:2} If you buy a Hebrew servant, he's gotta serve you for six years, and on the seventh year, he's outta there, no strings attached. {21:3} If he came in alone, he leaves alone; if he was married when he came in, his wife goes with him when he leaves. {21:4} But if his master gave him a wife and they have kids, the wife and kids belong to the master, and the servant can leave by himself. {21:5} Now, if the servant straight up says, "I love my master, my wife, and my kids; I don't wanna go free," {21:6} then his master brings him to the judges, and they pierce his ear against the doorpost, and he stays on as a servant forever. {21:7} If a guy sells his daughter as a maidservant, she doesn't get to leave like the male servants do. {21:8} If she doesn't please her master who promised to marry her, he can let her be redeemed; he can't sell her to a foreign nation after deceiving her. {21:9} But if he betroths her to his son, she gets the same treatment as his daughters. {21:10} If he takes another wife, he can't slack off on providing food, clothing, or marital rights to the first wife. {21:11} If he doesn't do these three things, she goes free without paying a dime. {21:12} Whoever kills a person intentionally must be put to death. {21:13} But if it was unintentional and God allows it, then there's a designated place where the killer can flee. {21:14} But if someone intentionally kills someone else, drag them away even from the altar so they can be put to death. {21:15} Anyone who attacks their parents must be put to death. {21:16} Kidnapping someone, whether you sell them or keep them, results in the death penalty. {21:17} Cursing your parents also leads to the death penalty. {21:18} If two guys get into a fight and one hurts the other but not fatally, {21:19} and the injured person recovers and can walk around with a staff, then the guy who hurt him is off the hook, but he has to pay for the guy's lost work time and medical expenses. {21:20} If a man hits his servant or maid with a rod and they die, he's in big trouble. {21:21} But if the servant survives a day or two, there's no punishment because the servant is the master's property. {21:22} If men are fighting and accidentally hurt a pregnant woman so she loses the baby but isn't seriously harmed, they have to pay a fine as determined by the woman's husband and the judges. {21:23} But if there's serious harm, it's a life for a life, {21:24} eye for eye, tooth for tooth, hand for hand, foot for foot, {21:25} burn for burn, wound for wound, and bruise for bruise. {21:26} If a man blinds his servant's eye or knocks out a tooth, the servant must be set free as compensation for the eye or tooth. {21:27} If the man knocks out his servant's tooth, the servant must also be set free as compensation for the tooth. {21:28} If an ox gores a man or woman and they die, the ox must be stoned and not eaten, and the owner is off the hook. {21:29} But if the ox was known to be dangerous and the owner didn't take precautions, and it kills someone, both the ox and the owner are put to death. {21:30} If the owner is fined, they must pay whatever is demanded to spare their own life. {21:31} The same rules apply if the ox gores a son or daughter. {21:32} If the ox gores a manservant or maidservant, the owner has to pay thirty shekels of silver to the servant's master, and the ox must be stoned. {21:33} If someone digs a pit and doesn't cover it, and an ox or donkey falls into it, {21:34} the pit's owner has to compensate for the loss and keep the dead animal. {21:35} If one person's ox injures another's and it dies, they must sell the live ox and split the proceeds, as well as dividing the dead animal. {21:36} But if the ox was previously known to be dangerous and the owner didn't control it, they must pay ox for ox, and the dead animal becomes theirs.

{22:1} Here's the deal with stealing livestock: if someone steals an ox or sheep and kills or sells it, they gotta pay back five oxen for an ox and four sheep for a sheep. {22:2} If a thief is caught breaking in and gets killed, no one's gonna be charged for his death. {22:3} But if it happens after sunrise, then there's gonna be consequences; he'll have to pay back what he stole, and if he can't, he'll have to work off his debt. {22:4} If stolen property is found alive with a thief—whether it's an ox, donkey, or sheep—he's gotta give back double. {22:5} If a guy's animal eats someone else's field or vineyard, he's gotta make up for it with the best of his own field or vineyard. {22:6} If a fire breaks out and destroys someone's crops, the one who started the fire has to make restitution. {22:7} If someone gives money or goods to their neighbor to hold onto, and it gets stolen from the neighbor's house, the thief has to pay double if caught. {22:8} If the thief isn't caught, the neighbor has to go before the judges to prove they didn't take the goods. {22:9} For any kind of stolen property, whether it's an ox, donkey, sheep, clothing, or anything else disputed, both parties will go before the judges, and whoever is found guilty will have to pay double to their neighbor. {22:10} If someone entrusts an animal to their neighbor to take care of, and it dies, gets hurt, or is taken away without anyone seeing, they'll take an oath and the owner won't be held responsible. {22:12} But if it's stolen, the owner must make restitution to the owner. {22:13} If the animal is torn apart, he has to bring it as evidence and won't be responsible for what was torn. {22:14} If someone borrows something from their neighbor and it gets damaged or dies while the owner isn't around, they have to make it right. {22:15} But if the owner is there, they don't have to make restitution if it's rented. {22:16} If a guy seduces an unmarried woman and sleeps with her, he has to marry her and pay her dowry. {22:17} If her father refuses to give her to him, he still has to pay according to the customary dowry. {22:18} You can't allow a witch to live. {22:19} Anyone who has sexual relations with an animal will be put to death. {22:20} If someone sacrifices to any god other than the LORD, they'll be utterly destroyed. {22:21} Don't mistreat strangers or oppress them, 'cause you were once strangers in Egypt. {22:22} Don't mess with widows or orphans. {22:23} If you do and they cry out to God, He'll hear them and take action against you. {22:24} His wrath will come down, and you'll be killed, leaving your wives widows and your children fatherless. {22:25} If you lend money to a poor person, don't charge interest. {22:26} If you take your neighbor's cloak as collateral, give it back before sunset; it's their only covering. {22:27} When they cry out to God, He'll listen, 'cause He's compassionate. {22:28} Don't insult the gods or curse the ruler of your people. {22:29} Offer the first of your crops and drinks without delay; give the firstborn of your sons to God. {22:30} Same goes for your oxen and sheep; let them stay with their mother for seven days, then dedicate them to God on the eighth day. {22:31} Be holy and don't eat meat from an animal torn by wild beasts; give that to the dogs.

{23:1} Don't spread fake rumors or team up with bad people to lie about others. {23:2} Don't just follow the crowd into doing wrong, and don't twist the truth to win a case, no matter how many people are pressuring you. {23:3} Treat everyone equally in court, whether they're rich or poor. {23:4} If you come across your enemy's lost ox or donkey, return it to him. {23:5} Even if you see your enemy's donkey struggling under a heavy load, don't ignore it—help them out. {23:6} Always be fair to the poor when they're in court. {23:7} Stay far away from lies and don't let innocent people be harmed, 'cause I won't let the guilty get away with it. {23:8} Don't accept bribes, 'cause they can blind even wise people and twist the words of the righteous. {23:9} Don't mistreat strangers, 'cause you know what it's like to be a stranger in Egypt. {23:10} Plant and harvest your crops for six years, but let the land rest on the seventh year so the poor can eat, and let the wild animals benefit too. {23:11} Same goes for your vineyards and olive groves. {23:12} Work six days a week, but rest on the seventh day so even your animals and servants can take a break. {23:13} Always be careful to follow what I've told you, and don't even mention the names of other gods. {23:14} Celebrate three feasts each year in my honor. {23:15} Keep the Feast of Unleavened Bread for seven days in the month of Abib to remember how you came out of Egypt; don't come empty-handed. {23:16} Also celebrate the Feast of Harvest with the firstfruits of your labor from the fields, and the Feast of Ingathering at the end of the year. {23:17} All males must appear before the Lord GOD three times a year. {23:18} Don't offer sacrifices with leavened bread, and don't let any sacrifice's fat remain until morning. {23:19} Bring the first of your firstfruits to the house of the LORD your God, and don't cook a young goat in its mother's milk. {23:20} I'm sending an Angel ahead of you to guide you and lead you to the place I've prepared. {23:21} Listen to Him and don't rebel against His instructions, 'cause He won't overlook your disobedience; He carries my authority. {23:22} But if you obey Him and do what I say, I'll be your protector against your enemies. {23:23} My Angel will go before you to conquer the Amorites, Hittites, Perizzites, Canaanites, Hivites, and Jebusites—I'll wipe them out. {23:24} Don't worship their gods, destroy their idols completely. {23:25} Serve the LORD your God, and He'll bless your food and water and keep sickness away. {23:26} There won't be any miscarriages or infertility in your land; I'll ensure you live a long life. {23:27} I'll send terror ahead of you and make your enemies retreat. {23:28} I'll even send hornets to drive out your enemies like the Hivites, Canaanites, and Hittites. {23:29} I won't force them out all at once, or else the land will become desolate and overrun with wild animals. {23:30} I'll drive them out little by little until your population grows and you inherit the land. {23:31} I'll establish your borders from the Red Sea to the Mediterranean and from the desert to the Euphrates River; I'll hand over the inhabitants of the land to you and drive them out. {23:32} Don't make any treaties with them or their gods. {23:33} Don't let them live in your land, or else they'll lead you into sin with their gods—it'll be a trap for you.

{24:1} So Moses was like, "Hey, come up to the LORD—bring Aaron, Nadab, Abihu, and seventy elders of Israel, but worship from a distance. {24:2} Only Moses gets to go near the LORD; the others and the people gotta stay back. {24:3} So Moses goes down and tells everyone what the LORD said, and all the people are like, "Yeah, we'll do everything the LORD said." {24:4} Then Moses writes down everything the LORD said, builds an altar with twelve pillars representing the twelve tribes of Israel. {24:5} He sends young Israelite dudes to offer burnt offerings and peace offerings to the LORD. {24:6} Moses takes half the blood and puts it in bowls and sprinkles the other half on the altar. {24:7} Then he reads the book of the covenant to the people, and they're like, "We'll do everything the LORD said." {24:8} Moses takes the blood and sprinkles it on the people, saying, "This is the blood of the covenant the LORD made with you based on these words." {24:9} Then Moses, Aaron, Nadab, Abihu, and seventy elders go up to see the God of Israel. {24:10} They see God, and there's this cool sapphire-like pavement under His feet, kind of like clear sky. {24:11} God doesn't mess with the nobles of Israel, and they even get to eat and drink while seeing God. {24:12} God tells Moses, "Come up to the mountain, and I'll give you stone tablets with laws and commandments for you to teach." {24:13} So Moses and Joshua head up the mountain. {24:14} Moses tells the elders to chill there with Aaron and Hur, and if anyone has issues, they can go to them. {24:15} Moses goes up the mountain, and a cloud covers it. {24:16} The glory of the LORD stays on Mount Sinai, covered by a cloud for six days, and on the seventh day, God calls to Moses from the cloud. {24:17} The Israelites see the glory of the LORD like a devouring fire on the mountaintop. {24:18} Moses enters the cloud and goes up the mountain, where he stays for forty days and forty nights.

{25:1} So God was like, "Yo, Moses, listen up. Tell the Israelites to bring me offerings from their hearts—whatever they're cool with giving willingly. {25:2} Here's what I want them to bring: gold, silver, brass, {25:3} along with blue, purple, and scarlet yarn, fine linen, goat hair, {25:4} and red-dyed ram skins, badger skins, and acacia wood. {25:5} Also, oil for lamps, spices for anointing oil and incense, {25:6} onyx stones, and gems for the ephod and breastplate. {25:8} They're gonna make me a sanctuary so I can hang out with them. {25:9} Build it exactly like I showed you—just copy the tabernacle design and all its gear. {25:10} They'll start with an ark made of acacia wood: two and a half cubits long, one and a half cubits wide and high. {25:11} Cover it inside and out with pure gold and put a gold rim around it. {25:12} Make four gold rings for it, two on each side, and attach poles covered in gold. {25:13} Use the poles to carry the ark; they stay in the rings all the time. {25:16} Inside the ark, put the testimony I give you. {25:17} Make a pure gold mercy seat: two and a half cubits long and one and a half cubits wide. {25:18} Then craft two gold cherubim for the mercy seat's ends. {25:19} Position them with wings outstretched, covering the mercy seat and facing each other. {25:21} Place the mercy seat on top of the ark and keep the testimony inside. {25:23} Next up, make a table of acacia wood: two cubits long, one cubit wide, and one and a half cubits high. {25:24} Cover it with pure gold and add a gold rim around it. {25:25} Make a border and a gold rim for it. {25:26} Attach four gold rings to it for carrying with poles. {25:29} Also, make gold dishes, spoons, covers, and bowls for the table. {25:30} Keep setting showbread on the table before me. {25:31} Now, make a pure gold lampstand: hammered out with a central shaft, branches, bowls, knobs, and flowers all in one piece. {25:32} Six branches should extend from its sides—three on each side. {25:34} The lampstand will have four almond-shaped bowls with their knobs and flowers. {25:37} Include seven lamps to light up the area. {25:38} And the tongs and snuff dishes for it should be pure gold. {25:39} Use a talent of pure gold to make it all, including the vessels. {25:40} Build everything exactly like I showed you on the mountain.

{26:1} So, like, God was telling Moses, "Yo, you gotta make the tabernacle with ten curtains, ya know? They gotta be made of fine linen, blue, purple, and scarlet, with some dope cherubim designs on 'em. {26:2} Each curtain's gotta be twenty-eight cubits long and four cubits wide, all the same size, ya feel? {26:3} Then, ya gotta connect five curtains together and another five curtains together. {26:4} Put loops on one curtain's edge and match 'em up with loops on another curtain's edge. {26:5} Fifty loops on each curtain, bro, so they can hook together. {26:6} Then use fifty gold clasps to connect 'em all, and bam, you got one sick tabernacle. {26:7} Oh, and don't forget to make curtains out of goat hair to cover it all up—eleven curtains should do the trick. {26:8} They gotta be thirty cubits long and four cubits wide, all the same size, ya know? {26:9} Mix it up by joining five curtains together and six curtains together, doubling up the sixth one at the front. {26:10} Attach fifty loops on the edge of one curtain, and fifty more on the edge of the curtain next to it. {26:11} Then, use fifty bronze clasps to hook 'em all up and make it one seamless tent. {26:12} Let the leftover bit hang over the back of the tabernacle. {26:13} And let some hang over the sides too, like, a cubit on each side, covering it up nice. {26:14} Moses, make sure you get some rad red-dyed ram skins and badger skins to cover the tent up. {26:15} And for the structure, use shittim wood boards, ten cubits long and a cubit and a half wide. {26:16} Each board's gotta have two tenons to fit together snugly. {26:18} You'll need twenty boards for the south side, held up by forty silver sockets. {26:20} Same deal for the north side, bro. {26:22} And six boards for the west side, with two more for the corners. {26:25} Eight boards total, each with two silver sockets underneath. {26:26} Craft some bars out of shittim wood, five for each side of the tabernacle. {26:27} In the middle, put a gold-covered bar stretching from end to end. {26:29} Overlay the boards with gold and attach gold rings for the bars. {26:30} Set up the tabernacle just like I showed you on the mountain, dude. {26:31} Oh, and don't forget a vail made of blue, purple, and scarlet, with some sick cherubim art. {26:32} Hang it on four gold-covered pillars with gold hooks, resting on silver sockets. {26:33} Put the vail under some clasps so you can bring the ark of the testimony into the most holy place. {26:34} Stick the mercy seat on top of the ark in there too. {26:35} Outside the vail, put the table on the north side and the candlestick on the south side. {26:36} And for the tent door, make a fly hanging of blue, purple, scarlet, and fine linen, with some tight needlework. {26:37} Use five shittim wood pillars for support, covered in gold, with brass sockets for stability.

{27:1} Alright, so Moses, you gotta build an altar out of shittim wood—make it five cubits long, five cubits wide, and three cubits high. {27:2} Put horns on each of the four corners, all covered in brass. {27:3} You'll need pans, shovels, basins, fleshhooks, and firepans—all made of brass. {27:4} And don't forget a brass grate with four rings for the corners. {27:5} Hang the grate under the altar to reach halfway up. {27:6} Make some brass-covered staves out of shittim wood to carry it. {27:7} The staves go through the rings on the sides of the altar. {27:8} Build it hollow with boards, just like I showed you on the mountain. {27:9} Next up, build the courtyard of the tabernacle. {27:9} On the south side, use fine linen hangings—each a hundred cubits long. {27:10} Support them with twenty brass pillars and sockets, with silver hooks and fillets. {27:11} Same deal on the north side—hundred cubits of hangings, twenty brass pillars with silver hooks and fillets. {27:12} The west side gets fifty cubits of hangings, ten pillars, and sockets. {27:13} East side, fifty cubits too. {27:14} Gate hangings are fifteen cubits each, with three pillars and sockets. {27:15} Same on the other side. {27:16} The gate gets a twenty-cubit hanging of blue, purple, scarlet, and fine linen—real needlework. {27:17} All the courtyard pillars are silver-filleted with silver hooks and brass sockets. {27:18} Courtyard's length is a hundred cubits, width fifty cubits, and height five cubits—lined with fine linen and brass sockets. {27:19} Everything—the tabernacle vessels, service pins, and courtyard pins—are all brass. {27:20} Oh, and tell the Israelites to bring you pure olive oil for the lamp, so it burns continuously. {27:21} Aaron and his sons gotta keep that lamp burning in the tabernacle from evening to morning, forever, in front of the LORD.

{28:1} Yo, Moses, grab your bro Aaron and his crew—Nadab, Abihu, Eleazar, and Ithamar—from the Israelites. They're gonna be priests, especially Aaron. {28:2} Time to make some lit holy garments for Aaron, decked out for glory and style. {28:3} Find some skilled folks filled with wisdom and the spirit, and get them to craft Aaron's gear to set him apart for priestly duty. {28:4} Here's the gear list: a breastplate, ephod, robe, embroidered coat, mitre, and girdle—all holy swag for Aaron and his crew to do their priest thing. {28:5} Grab gold, blue, purple, scarlet, and fine linen for the job. {28:6} The ephod's gotta be gold, blue, purple, scarlet, and fine linen—super intricate. {28:7} Shoulderpieces gotta be on point, joined together just right. {28:8} The ephod's gotta have a dope girdle, matching the outfit with gold, blue, purple, scarlet, and fine linen. {28:9} Get two onyx stones and carve the names of Israel's kids on them. {28:10} Six names on each stone, representing the tribes. {28:11} Skilled engraving, like a pro, and set them in gold settings. {28:12} Place these stones on the ephod's shoulders as a memorial for Israel, carried by Aaron before the LORD. {28:13} Make gold settings for sure. {28:14} Craft two pure gold chains with sick designs and attach them to the settings. {28:15} The breastplate's key—it's all about judgment, matching the ephod's style with gold, blue, purple, scarlet, and fine linen. {28:16} It's gotta be square and doubled up, with each side a span long and wide. {28:17} Set it with stones in four rows: sardius, topaz, carbuncle; emerald, sapphire, diamond; ligure, agate, amethyst; beryl, onyx, jasper—all in gold. {28:21} The stones rep the twelve tribes of Israel, engraved with names like a signet. {28:22} Make gold chains for the breastplate's ends. {28:23} Add two gold rings to the breastplate's ends. {28:24} Connect the gold chains to the rings on the breastplate. {28:25} Fasten the ends of the chains to the ephod's shoulderpieces in front. {28:26} Attach two gold rings to the breastplate's border on the ephod's side. {28:27} Two more rings underneath the ephod's shoulders, facing the front, over the ephod's girdle. {28:28} Connect the breastplate to the ephod with a blue lace to keep it secure above the girdle, not falling off. {28:29} Aaron's gonna rep Israel's tribes on his heart with the breastplate when he goes into the holy place before the LORD—a constant reminder. {28:30} Don't forget the Urim and Thummim in the breastplate for judgment, always close to Aaron's heart before the LORD. {28:31} The ephod's robe? Keep it all blue. {28:32} Add a woven binding around the top hole, strong like armor to prevent tearing. {28:33} Decorate the robe's hem with blue, purple, scarlet pomegranates and gold bells in between. {28:34} Gold bells and pomegranates all around the hem. {28:35} Aaron's gotta wear this when he ministers—those bells make sure he's heard in the holy place and doesn't die. {28:36} Make a pure gold plate and engrave it with "HOLINESS TO THE LORD" like a signet. {28:37} Attach it to a blue lace on the mitre's front. {28:38} This plate stays on Aaron's forehead to cover Israel's holy gifts and keep them accepted by the LORD. {28:39} Don't forget the fine linen coat, mitre, and needlework girdle. {28:40} Aaron's sons get coats, girdles, and bonnets too, all for style and glory. {28:41} Get Aaron and his crew suited up, anointed, consecrated, and sanctified to serve as priests. {28:42} They need linen breeches too, covering from waist to thighs, for protection and to avoid death when they minister in the holy place. {28:43} This gear's a forever thing for Aaron and his descendants.

{29:1} Alright, here's the plan to set them up as priests so they can do their thing: grab a young bullock and two spotless rams. {29:2} Also, get some unleavened bread, oil-tempered cakes, and oil-anointed wafers—make them with wheat flour. {29:3} Toss all these in a basket with the bullock and rams. {29:4} Take Aaron and his sons to the tabernacle door, and give them a good wash with water. {29:5} Then dress Aaron up: coat, ephod robe, breastplate, and that fancy ephod girdle. {29:6} Pop the mitre on his head and crown it with the holy crown. {29:7} Time for the anointing oil—pour it on Aaron's head to consecrate him. {29:8} Outfit Aaron's sons in their coats, gird them up, and pop on their bonnets. {29:9} The priest gig is theirs forever; this is how you consecrate Aaron and his sons.

{29:10} Now bring a bullock before the tabernacle, and Aaron and his sons lay hands on it. {29:11} Slay the bullock by the tabernacle door. {29:12} Take the bullock's blood, dab it on the altar horns, and pour the rest at the base. {29:13} Burn the fat and inner organs on the altar, but the rest—flesh, skin, dung—burn outside the camp; it's a sin offering. {29:15} Next, grab a ram; Aaron and his sons lay hands on it. {29:16} Slay the ram and sprinkle its blood around the altar. {29:17} Cut up the ram, wash the parts, and burn it all on the altar—it's a burnt offering, a sweet fragrance to the LORD. {29:19} Now take the other ram; Aaron and his sons lay hands on it. {29:20} Slay it and dab its blood on Aaron's right ear, thumb, and toe, then sprinkle the blood on the altar. {29:21} Mix the altar blood with anointing oil, sprinkle it on Aaron, his garments, and his sons' garments. {29:22} Set aside the ram's fat, rump, inwards, and other parts—it's a ram of consecration. {29:23} Add a loaf, oiled bread, and a wafer from the unleavened basket that's before the LORD. {29:24} Put it all in Aaron's and his sons' hands, wave them as an offering before the LORD. {29:25} Receive them back and burn them on the altar—a sweet offering to the LORD by fire. {29:26} Wave the ram's breast for a wave offering before the LORD; it's your portion. {29:27} Sanctify the breast and shoulder as heave offerings; they're for Aaron and his sons, a perpetual statute from Israel as their heave offering to the LORD. {29:29} Aaron's holy garments will pass to his sons after him, used for anointing and consecration. {29:30} The new priest, Aaron's son, wears them for seven days when ministering in the holy place. {29:31} Boil the ram's flesh in the holy place for their consecration meal. {29:32} Aaron and his sons eat the ram's flesh and the bread at the tabernacle door. {29:33} Only they can eat it—it's consecrated and holy. {29:34} Burn any leftovers by morning if there's any; it's too holy to eat. {29:35} Follow these instructions for seven days to consecrate Aaron and his sons. {29:36} Offer a daily sin offering, cleanse the altar, and anoint it to make it holy. {29:37} Spend seven days making atonement and sanctifying the altar—it'll be most holy; anything touching it becomes holy. {29:38} Now, for the daily altar offering: two year-old lambs, one in the morning and one at twilight. {29:39} With each lamb, add flour, oil, and wine for a drink offering. {29:41} Do this every evening as a sweet offering by fire to the LORD. {29:42} This is a continual burnt offering at the tabernacle door before the LORD, where I'll meet you to speak. {29:43} That's where I'll meet the Israelites, and the tabernacle will be sanctified by my glory. {29:44} I'll sanctify the tabernacle and altar, and Aaron and his sons, for their priestly service. {29:45} I'll dwell among the Israelites and be their God. {29:46} They'll know I'm the LORD who brought them out of Egypt to dwell among them—I'm their God.

{30:1} So, you gotta craft an altar for burning incense using acacia wood. {30:2} It's gonna be a cubit in length, a cubit in width, and two cubits tall—square-shaped with horns on the corners. {30:3} Cover it all in pure gold: top, sides, and horns, and add a gold rim around it. {30:4} Make two gold rings for it under the rim, on opposite sides, to hold the carrying poles. {30:5} Craft carrying poles from acacia wood and overlay them with gold. {30:6} Place this altar in front of the veil near the Ark of the Testimony and the mercy seat where I'll meet you. {30:7} Aaron's job is to burn sweet incense on it every morning when he's tending the lamps. {30:8} At twilight, when Aaron lights the lamps, he'll burn incense on it—an ongoing offering before the LORD for generations. {30:9} No weird incense, burnt sacrifices, grain offerings, or drink offerings on this altar. {30:10} Once a year, Aaron will atone on its horns with blood from the sin offering—a most holy thing to the LORD. {30:11} Then the LORD said to Moses, {30:12} When you count the Israelites, each one must give a ransom for their life to the LORD to prevent a plague during the census. {30:13} Everyone counted must give half a shekel, according to the sanctuary shekel (which equals twenty gerahs), as an offering to the LORD. {30:14} Anyone twenty years old and up, rich or poor, must give this offering to the LORD as atonement for their souls. {30:15} The rich shouldn't give more, and the poor shouldn't give less than half a shekel when making this offering to the LORD. {30:16} Take this atonement money from the Israelites and use it for the service of the tabernacle as a reminder before the LORD to atone for their souls. {30:17} Then the LORD told Moses, {30:18} Make a bronze basin and stand for washing, and place it between the tabernacle and the altar, filling it with water. {30:19} Aaron and his sons must wash their hands and feet from it before entering the tabernacle or approaching the altar to serve the LORD with fire offerings. {30:20} Washing is essential to avoid death when they enter the tabernacle or approach the altar—it's a perpetual statute for Aaron and his descendants. {30:22} The LORD continued, {30:23} Take the finest spices: five hundred shekels of myrrh, two hundred and fifty shekels of cinnamon, two hundred and fifty shekels of sweet calamus, {30:24} five hundred shekels of cassia, and a hin of olive oil. {30:25} Use these to make a holy anointing oil, blended like a perfumer's work. {30:26} Anoint the tabernacle, the Ark of the Testimony, {30:27} the table and its utensils, the lampstand and its accessories, the altar of incense, {30:28} the altar of burnt offering and its utensils, and the bronze basin and its stand. {30:29} By anointing them, they become most holy, and anything touching them becomes holy. {30:30} Anoint Aaron and his sons to consecrate them for priestly service. {30:31} This anointing oil is holy throughout your generations and must not be used on ordinary people or recreated—it's sacred and reserved for the LORD. {30:33} Anyone who duplicates this oil or uses it on someone else will be cut off from the community. {30:34} Then the LORD said to Moses, {30:34} Take sweet spices: stacte, onycha, galbanum, and pure frankincense in equal amounts. {30:35} Blend them into a fragrant incense, a perfumer's masterpiece, pure and sacred. {30:36} Crush some to place before the Ark in the tabernacle where I'll meet you—it's most holy. {30:37} Don't replicate this perfume for personal use; it's holy, dedicated to the LORD. {30:38} Anyone who recreates this fragrance to enjoy its scent will be cut off from the community.

{31:1} So, the LORD was talking to Moses, like, "Check it out," {31:2} "I've chosen this dude Bezaleel, son of Uri, son of Hur, from the tribe of Judah. {31:3} I filled him with God's spirit, giving him wisdom, understanding, and mad skills in all kinds of craftsmanship. {31:4} He's gonna design cool stuff in gold, silver, and brass, {31:5} also cutting stones and carving wood—basically, he can do anything crafty. {31:6} Plus, I've hooked him up with Aholiab, son of Ahisamach from the tribe of Dan, and all the skilled people I've given wisdom to, so they can build everything you need: {31:7} the tabernacle, the Ark of the Testimony, the mercy seat, and all the tabernacle furniture; {31:8} the table, candlestick, and altar of incense; {31:9} also the altar of burnt offering and the laver with its stand; {31:10} and all the priestly clothes for Aaron and his sons, plus the anointing oil and sweet incense for the holy place—basically, they'll do it all as I've instructed you." {31:12} Then the LORD said to Moses again, {31:13} "Tell the Israelites to keep my sabbaths as a sign between us throughout generations, so they know I'm the LORD who makes them holy. {31:14} The sabbath is sacred; anyone who messes with it gets the boot—don't work on the sabbath or you're out. {31:15} Six days are for work, but the seventh is a chill day for the LORD; if you work on the sabbath, you're done. {31:16} The Israelites gotta keep the sabbath forever as a lasting deal with me. {31:17} It's a forever thing, a sign that I made heaven and earth in six days and chilled on the seventh. {31:18} So, when Moses finished talking with the LORD on Mount Sinai, he got two stone tablets written by God's own finger.

{32:1} So, when the people peeped that Moses was taking forever to come down from the mountain, they all huddled up to Aaron like, "Yo, do something! Make us some gods to lead us. We don't know what happened to Moses, the dude who brought us out of Egypt." {32:2} Aaron was like, "Alright, bring me all your bling—your wives', sons', and daughters' earrings." {32:3} So everyone handed over their golden earrings to Aaron. {32:4} Aaron took the earrings, used a tool to carve a golden calf, and they were like, "These are our gods, Israel, who brought us out of Egypt!" {32:5} When Aaron saw the calf, he built an altar and announced, "Tomorrow we party for the LORD!" {32:6} The next day, they offered burnt offerings, peace offerings, ate, drank, and got down to partying. {32:7} Meanwhile, the LORD told Moses, "Get down there quick! Your people have messed up big time. {32:8} They turned away fast from what I told them, made a golden calf, worshipped it, and said, 'These are your gods, Israel, who brought you out of Egypt!'" {32:9} The LORD told Moses, "These people are stubborn. {32:10} Leave me alone so I can unleash my anger and wipe them out. I'll make a new nation out of you." {32:11} But Moses begged the LORD, "Why are you so mad at your people? You brought them out of Egypt with power and a strong hand." {32:12} "Think about your reputation," Moses said, "Don't let the Egyptians think you brought them out to destroy them in the mountains! Cool down and don't bring disaster on your people." {32:13} "Remember your promises to Abraham, Isaac, and Israel," Moses pleaded. "You swore to make their descendants as countless as the stars and give them this land forever." {32:14} The LORD changed his mind about punishing the people. {32:15} Moses came down the mountain carrying the two stone tablets inscribed on both sides by God's hand. {32:16} These tablets were God's work, with God's writing engraved on them. {32:17} Joshua thought they were at war because of the noise, but it was actually singing and dancing. {32:18} When Moses saw the calf and the partying, he got so mad he smashed the tablets. {32:20} Then he burned the calf, ground it into powder, scattered it in the water, and made the Israelites drink it. {32:21} Moses confronted Aaron, "What did these people do to you that you let them commit such a great sin?" {32:22} Aaron replied, "Don't be mad. You know these people are troublemakers." {32:23} "They demanded gods," Aaron explained, "because they didn't know what happened to Moses." {32:25} Moses saw the people were out of control—Aaron had let them get wild, embarrassing them in front of their enemies. {32:26} Moses stood at the camp gate and shouted, "Who's with the LORD?" All the Levites joined him. {32:27} Moses commanded them, "Grab your swords and go through the camp, killing anyone—brother, friend, or neighbor—who worshipped the calf." {32:28} The Levites followed Moses' orders and about three thousand people died that day. {32:29} Moses told them, "Today you've consecrated yourselves to the LORD, and he will bless you." {32:30} The next day, Moses said to the people, "You messed up big time. I'll talk to the LORD and see if I can fix this." {32:31} Moses returned to the LORD, saying, "These people sinned big time, making themselves golden gods." {32:32} "If you won't forgive them," Moses pleaded, "then erase me from your book." {32:33} The LORD replied, "Those who sinned against me will be erased from my book." {32:34} "Now lead the people to the place I told you," the LORD instructed Moses. "My Angel will guide you, but when the time comes, I'll punish them for their sin." {32:35} So the LORD punished the people for making the calf Aaron made.

{33:1} So, the LORD was like, "Yo, Moses, take your crew and bounce from here—go to that land I promised Abraham, Isaac, and Jacob, saying I'd give it to your descendants. {33:2} I'll send an angel ahead to clear out the Canaanites, Amorites, Hittites, Perizzites, Hivites, and Jebusites. {33:3} It's a land flowing with milk and honey, but I'm not rolling with you guys because you're stubborn. I might end up wiping you out along the way." {33:4} When the people heard this bad news, they mourned and ditched their bling. {33:5} The LORD told Moses to tell the Israelites, "You're a stubborn bunch. I could come down there and wipe you out in a flash. So take off your jewelry, and let me figure out what to do with you." {33:6} So, the Israelites stripped off their ornaments at Mount Horeb. {33:7} Moses set up the tabernacle outside the camp and called it the Tabernacle of the Congregation. Anyone seeking the LORD would go to this tent outside the camp. {33:8} Whenever Moses went to the tabernacle, everyone would stand at their tent doors, watching until he entered. {33:9} As Moses went into the tabernacle, the cloudy pillar descended and stood at the door, and the LORD talked with Moses. {33:10} Seeing this, all the people worshipped at their tent doors. {33:11} The LORD spoke to Moses face to face, like a friend, and then Moses returned to camp. Joshua, however, stayed in the tabernacle. {33:12} Moses said to the LORD, "You told me to lead these people, but you haven't told me who's coming with us. You know my name and you've shown me favor. {33:13} Now, if I've found favor, show me your way so I know you better and consider that these people are yours." {33:14} The LORD replied, "My presence will go with you, and I'll give you rest." {33:15} Moses said, "If your presence doesn't go with us, don't bother taking us from here. {33:16} How will anyone know we're favored unless you go with us? That's what separates us from everyone else on earth." {33:17} The LORD agreed, saying Moses had found favor and the LORD knew him by name. {33:18} Moses asked to see the LORD's glory. {33:19} The LORD said he would reveal his goodness and proclaim his name, showing mercy and grace to whom he chooses. {33:20} The LORD explained that Moses couldn't see his face and live, but offered to let Moses see his back parts. {33:21} The LORD told Moses to stand on a rock while his glory passed by. {33:22} He would shield Moses with his hand as he passed, letting Moses see his back.

{34:1} So the LORD told Moses, "Yo, carve out two stone tablets like the first ones I wrote on, the ones you smashed. {34:2} Be ready in the morning, head up to Mount Sinai, and meet me at the top. {34:3} No one else is coming with you, and no one should be seen anywhere on the mountain, not even animals grazing nearby." {34:4} Moses got up early the next morning, went to Mount Sinai as instructed, and took the two stone tablets with him. {34:5} The LORD descended in a cloud and stood with Moses, proclaiming His name. {34:6} As the LORD passed by, He declared, "The LORD, the LORD God, merciful and gracious, patient, overflowing with goodness and truth, {34:7} showing mercy to thousands, forgiving all kinds of wrongdoing and sin, yet not letting the guilty go unpunished, visiting the sins of the fathers on the children and grandchildren, to the third and fourth generations." {34:8} Moses bowed down, worshiping the LORD in haste. {34:9} He said, "If I've found favor in Your sight, O Lord, please go among us. We're a stubborn bunch—forgive our sins and adopt us as Your own." {34:10} The LORD agreed, saying, "I'm making a covenant. Before your people, I'll perform wonders never seen before in all the earth. {34:11} Obey what I command you today—I'll drive out the Amorites, Canaanites, Hittites, Perizzites, Hivites, and Jebusites before you. {34:12} Don't make agreements with the people in the land you're entering, or it'll trap you. {34:13} Tear down their altars, smash their idols, and cut down their sacred poles. {34:14} Worship no other gods because the LORD, whose name is Jealous, is a jealous God. {34:15} If you make a pact with them, they'll lead you astray to worship their gods and offer sacrifices, tempting you to join in. {34:16} They'll marry your sons and daughters, leading them astray too. {34:17} Don't make idols. {34:18} Celebrate the Feast of Unleavened Bread for seven days, as I commanded, during the month of Abib, when you came out of Egypt. {34:19} Every firstborn among your livestock belongs to Me, whether ox or sheep. {34:20} Redeem your firstborn donkey with a lamb; if not, break its neck. Redeem all your firstborn sons—no one should come before Me empty-handed. {34:21} Work for six days, but rest on the seventh day, even during planting and harvest seasons. {34:22} Celebrate the Feast of Weeks and the Feast of Ingathering at the end of the year. {34:23} All your males must appear before the Lord GOD three times a year. {34:24} I'll drive out the nations before you, expanding your territory, and no one will covet your land when you go up to appear before the LORD three times a year. {34:25} Don't offer the Passover sacrifice with leaven, and don't leave any of it until morning. {34:26} Bring the firstfruits of your land to the house of the LORD your God. Don't cook a young goat in its mother's milk. {34:27} The LORD told Moses to write down these words, making a covenant with him and Israel. {34:28} Moses stayed with the LORD for forty days and nights, without eating or drinking, and wrote the words of the covenant on the tablets—the Ten Commandments. {34:29} When Moses came down from Mount Sinai with the tablets, he didn't realize his face was radiant because he'd been talking with the LORD. {34:30} When Aaron and the Israelites saw Moses, they were afraid to approach him because of his shining face. {34:31} Moses called to them, and Aaron and the leaders of the community came back to him, and Moses talked with them. {34:32} After that, all the Israelites gathered around, and Moses gave them the LORD's commands he'd received on Mount Sinai. {34:33} While Moses spoke to them, he covered his face with a veil. {34:34} But when he went before the LORD, he removed the veil until he left the LORD's presence, then he covered his face again.

{35:1} So Moses gathered all the crew of Israel together and laid it out: "Here's the deal straight from the LORD—these are the tasks you gotta handle. {35:2} You grind for six days, but on the seventh, it's chill time, a sacred day off for the LORD. Anyone pulling a shift gets a one-way ticket to oblivion. {35:3} No fire in your homes on the Sabbath—keep it cool." {35:4} Then Moses broke it down for everyone, saying, "Here's what the LORD wants: {35:5} Bring offerings—whatever your heart feels cool with—gold, silver, brass, {35:6} blue, purple, scarlet, fine linen, goat hair, {35:7} red-dyed ram skins, badger skins, acacia wood, {35:8} oil for lighting, spices for anointing, and sweet incense, {35:9} plus onyx stones and stones for the ephod and breastplate. {35:10} Any skilled craftsperson among you, step up and make what the LORD's laid out. {35:11} Build the tabernacle, its tent, coverings, fasteners, boards, bars, pillars, sockets, {35:12} the ark with its poles and mercy seat, and the curtain. {35:13} Also, the table with its accessories and showbread, {35:14} the lampstand, its furniture, lamps, and oil, {35:15} the incense altar, its tools, anointing oil, sweet incense, and the door curtain. {35:16} The altar of burnt offering with its bronze grate, poles, and tools, and the basin with its stand. {35:17} Make the courtyard curtains, pillars, sockets, and door curtain. {35:18} Secure the tabernacle and courtyard with pegs and cords, {35:19} and craft the priestly garments for Aaron and his sons for their sacred duties. {35:20} After Moses laid it down, the Israelites bounced. {35:21} Everyone with a willing heart brought offerings for the tabernacle's work and the priestly garments. {35:22} Both men and women, feeling it, brought gold jewelry—bracelets, earrings, rings, and gold stuff—everyone pitching in for the LORD. {35:23} Those with materials like blue, purple, scarlet, fine linen, goat hair, and animal skins came through. {35:24} Anyone with silver, brass, or acacia wood for the work also brought it. {35:25} Skilled women spun yarn and contributed blue, purple, scarlet, and fine linen. {35:26} Wise-hearted women spun goat hair too. {35:27} The leaders pitched in with onyx stones and stones for the ephod and breastplate, spices, and oils. {35:28} The Israelites willingly offered whatever the LORD had commanded through Moses. {35:30} Moses then announced, "Check it—the LORD's tapped Bezalel, son of Uri, grandson of Hur, from Judah, with divine skills and wisdom for the job. {35:31} He's filled with the spirit, wisdom, understanding, and craftiness. {35:32} He's got the skills for gold, silver, and brass work, {35:33} stone cutting, setting, and wood carving—any crafty task. {35:34} And he'll teach others, along with Aholiab from Dan, to be skilled in engraving, craftiness, and embroidery—experts in all kinds of cool work and design.

{36:1} So Bezaleel, Aholiab, and all the skilled crew, blessed by the LORD with wisdom and understanding for the sanctuary work, got down to business, doing everything just as the LORD commanded. {36:2-3} Moses gathered them, including those with stirred-up hearts ready to work, and they received all the offerings from the Israelites for the sanctuary work, with additional freebies pouring in daily. {36:4-5} All the skilled workers took a break from their tasks to address Moses, saying, "The people are bringing way more than we need for this job the LORD's assigned." {36:6-7} Moses ordered a camp-wide announcement to stop any more offerings for the sanctuary. The people were told to chill with their contributions, as they had plenty to get the job done and then some. {36:8} Each skilled worker made ten curtains of fancy linen, blue, purple, and scarlet, embroidered with cherubim. {36:9} Each curtain was 28 cubits long and 4 cubits wide, all the same size. {36:10-13} They coupled five curtains together and another set of five, making loops and taches to hold them together as one tabernacle. {36:14-19} They also crafted goat hair curtains for the tent above the tabernacle, making eleven curtains of 30 cubits long and 4 cubits wide each. {36:20} Shittim wood boards were made for the tabernacle, standing upright. {36:21} Each board was 10 cubits long and 1.5 cubits wide, with two tenons to fit together. {36:22} They made twenty boards for the south side, each with two sockets. {36:23} Bars of shittim wood were made, five for each side of the tabernacle, including the west side, with a middle bar running through. {36:24} A veil of blue, purple, scarlet, and linen with embroidered cherubim was crafted skillfully.

{37:1} Bezaleel whipped up the ark out of shittim wood, sizing it up at two and a half cubits long, a cubit and a half wide, and a cubit and a half high. {37:2} He blinged it out with pure gold inside and out, even adding a gold crown all around. {37:3} Four gold rings were cast for it, two on each side, and he made gold-covered staves to carry it. {37:4} Then he crafted the mercy seat, two and a half cubits long and a cubit and a half wide, topped with two golden cherubim. {37:5} The table came next, made of shittim wood, two cubits long, a cubit wide, and a cubit and a half high, decked out in pure gold with a gold crown and a gold border. {37:6} He also made all the bling for the table out of pure gold: dishes, spoons, bowls, and covers. {37:7} The candlestick was pure gold, intricately beaten into shape with its shaft, branches, bowls, knops, and flowers. {37:8} The incense altar, made of shittim wood, was a cubit long, a cubit wide, and two cubits high, with gold plating all over, including a gold crown.

{38:1} So, Bezaleel whipped up the altar of burnt offering using shittim wood, measuring it at five cubits long and wide, and three cubits high. {38:2} He put horns on each of the four corners and covered them with brass. {38:3} All the altar's gear—pots, shovels, basins, fleshhooks, and firepans—were made of brass. {38:4} Underneath, he added a brass grate and cast rings and staves for carrying. {38:4} Then came the laver made of brass, using the women's mirrors for the metal. {38:5} The court was set up with fine twined linen hangings on the south, supported by twenty pillars and sockets, all silver-hooked. {38:6} The gate's hanging was needlework of blue, purple, scarlet, and linen, twenty cubits long and five cubits high. {38:7} All the gold used was twenty-nine talents and seven hundred thirty shekels, and the silver was a hundred talents and one thousand seven hundred seventy-five shekels. {38:8} Every man gave a bekah, half a shekel, for the sanctuary count—six hundred three thousand five hundred fifty men.

{39:1} They whipped up some snazzy cloths for doing holy service and made cool outfits for Aaron, just like Moses said. {39:2} The ephod was made with gold, blue, purple, scarlet, and fine linen, all fancy and skillfully crafted. {39:3} They hammered gold into thin sheets and made wires to work into the fabric with blue, purple, scarlet, and linen. {39:4} Shoulderpieces were added to hold it all together. {39:5} The ephod's curious girdle matched, made of gold, blue, purple, scarlet, and fine linen. {39:6} Onyx stones were engraved with the names of the Israelites and placed on the ephod's shoulders as a reminder. {39:7} The breastplate was made with gold, blue, purple, scarlet, and fine linen, with stones representing the tribes of Israel. {39:8} It was square and doubled up, with rows of precious stones. {39:9} The breastplate had twelve stones, each engraved with a tribe's name. {39:10} Chains of gold were added to the breastplate, as per Moses' command. {39:11} The robe for the ephod was woven and all blue. {39:12} They added pomegranates and bells to the hem of the robe. {39:13} Fine linen coats, mitres, bonnets, breeches, and girdles were made as instructed. {39:14} The holy crown plate was made of pure gold with "HOLINESS TO THE LORD" engraved on it. {39:15} Everything was finished according to Moses' commands, and they presented it all to him.

{40:1} So God hit up Moses and said, "Yo, on the first day of the first month, set up the tabernacle of the congregation." {40:2} Moses was to put the ark of the testimony inside and cover it with a curtain. {40:3-4} He'd bring in the table, set it up, and arrange everything on it. Then light the lamps of the candlestick. {40:5} The golden altar for incense would go before the ark, with a door hanging on the tabernacle. {40:6-7} The burnt offering altar was to be set up at the tabernacle door. {40:7} Place the laver between the tent and the altar, filling it with water. {40:8} Then set up the courtyard with its gate hanging. {40:9} Use the anointing oil to make everything holy—the tabernacle and all its stuff. {40:10} Anoint the burnt offering altar and all its gear; it's gotta be super holy. {40:11} Do the same with the laver; make it all sacred. {40:12} Moses was to bring Aaron and his sons to the tabernacle door, wash them with water. {40:13} Dress Aaron up in his holy garments, anoint him, and set him apart for priestly duties. {40:14-16} Then do the same with Aaron's sons, outfitting them for their priestly gig. {40:17-19} The tabernacle was set up on the first day of the second year. {40:20} Moses placed the testimony in the ark, set the staves, and put the mercy seat on top. {40:21} He brought the ark inside and covered it with a curtain. {40:22} The table was set up north of the tabernacle, outside the curtain. {40:23-24} The candlestick went south of the tabernacle, across from the table. {40:25-26} The golden altar was placed before the curtain, and incense was burned. {40:27-28} The gate hanging was set up at the tabernacle door. {40:29} The burnt offering altar was placed by the door, and Moses did the offerings. {40:30} The laver was set up between the tent and the altar for washing. {40:31} Then a cloud covered the tent, and God's glory filled the tabernacle.

Leviticus

✦✦✦

{1:1} So, like, God hit up Moses, talking from the tent, like, "Yo, Moses, tell the Israelites if they wanna flex with an offering for the Big G, it's gotta be from the farm, ya know, like, cattle or sheep, no scuffed up ones though. {1:2} If it's a cow, it gotta be a primo dude without any flaws, and they gotta willingly drop it off at the tent door for God. {1:3} Then they gotta lay hands on it, like, giving it props or something, and it's cool with God. {1:4} Then they gotta off it, and Aaron's boys splash its blood around the altar. {1:5} After that, they gotta skin it and chop it up. {1:6} Aaron's boys stack the wood and light it up, and then put the meat and fat on there. {1:7} They gotta wash its guts and legs, then the priest burns everything on the altar, making it smell good for God. {1:8} Same drill for sheep and goats. {1:9} If it's birds, just doves or pigeons, heads off, blood out, feathers off, and straight to the flames. {1:10} Now, if you're rolling up with a grain offering, it's gotta be top-notch flour with oil and incense. {1:11} Hand it over to Aaron's crew, they burn a bit on the altar, and the rest is theirs, sacred stuff, ya feel? {1:12} If it's baked, no yeast, just flour and oil, whether it's cakes or wafers. {1:13} Pan-fried? Same deal, but in chunks, with oil. {1:14-15} Fryer action? Fine flour and oil again. {1:15} Offer it up to God, and the priest takes a piece for the altar, making it smell good. {1:16} Whatever's left is for Aaron and his squad, holy leftovers. {1:17} And remember, no leaven or honey in God's offerings, and always season with salt.

{2:1} Oh, and firstfruits? Offer 'em, but not for burning, just like, show 'em some love to God. {2:2} Add salt to everything, and no skipping it, it's a covenant thing. {2:3} Firstfruits get the fire treatment with oil and incense. {2:4} The priest burns some and keeps the rest, again, holy stuff. {2:5} Alright, no leaven, just fire-dried corn and oil, with incense. {2:6} Burn some of it, and what's left is Aaron's crew's treat. {2:7} And that's the scoop on offerings, yo!

{3:1} If someone wants to throw down a chill peace offering from their cattle—whether it's a dude or a lady cow—it's gotta be top-notch, no flaws, presented to God. {3:2} They gotta lay hands on it, then off it goes at the tent entrance, where Aaron's crew sprinkles the blood on the altar. {3:3} They burn the choice fats and parts on the altar, giving that sweet aroma to the Big G. {3:4} This includes the kidneys, the fat by the flanks, and the liver stuff. {3:5} Aaron's sons handle the BBQ duties, making it a savory offering for God. {3:6} Now, if the offering's from the flock—a flawless dude or lady sheep—they present it to God. {3:7} Same deal, hands-on-head action, then off with its head at the tent, with blood sprinkling by Aaron's sons. {3:8} They offer up the fats and choice rump parts for the fire, again making it a tasty treat for God. {3:9} This includes the rump and inner fat. {3:10} The priest handles the burning on the altar, ensuring that sweet smell reaches God. {3:11} If it's a goat, same process as with the sheep. {3:12} Off it goes at the tent entrance, blood sprinkled, and the fats burned on the altar. {3:13} All the fats go to God. {3:14} These rules are forever—no eating fat or blood.

{4:1-2} Then God told Moses, "Yo, if someone messes up and doesn't even know it, but breaks one of my rules—like a priest slipping up—bring a young flawless bull for a 'my bad' offering." {4:3-4} The priest lays hands on the bull's head, then off with its head at the tent entrance. {4:5-7} The priest dips fingers in the blood, sprinkling it seven times in front of God's digs. {4:7} Blood goes on the altar and gets poured at its base. {4:8} The priest collects the fat for burning. {4:9} This includes the kidneys and liver fat. {4:10} It's burnt as a sin offering. {4:11-12} The bull's entire body is taken outside camp and burned. {4:13-16} Now, if the whole crew of Israel messes up, and it's hidden from the masses but comes to light, they bring a young bull as an apology offering. The elders lay hands on the bull, then off with its head before God. {4:17-18} Blood's sprinkled seven times, and the altar horns get a blood dab. {4:18} Blood's poured at the altar base. {4:19} The fat's burned on the altar as a sweet treat for God. {4:20-21} The priest sorts them out, and they're forgiven. {4:22-23} If a ruler goofs up unknowingly, they bring a flawless male goat as an apology. {4:24-26} Lay hands, then off with the goat's head, blood on the altar horns, and fat burned as an apology. {4:27-28} If an everyday person messes up unknowingly, they bring a flawless female goat for their oops. {4:29} Lay hands, then off with the goat's head, blood on the altar horns, and fat burned as an apology.

{5:1} So if someone messes up but didn't even realize it, they're forgiven. {5:2} But if they know about some sketchy stuff, like touching gross dead animals or other unclean stuff, and didn't clean up, they're unclean and guilty. {5:3} Or if they get defiled by some human uncleanliness and didn't know, they're still guilty once they find out. {5:4} Same goes for swearing to do bad or good stuff and not remembering—it's still on them once they realize. {5:5} When they realize they messed up, they gotta own it and confess. {5:6} Then they gotta bring a lamb or goat to the LORD as a sorry offering, and the priest will sort them out. {5:7} If they're broke, they can bring doves or pigeons instead—one for the oops and one for a burnt offering. {5:8} The priest does the sin offering first, cuts the head off one bird, sprinkles blood, and burns it. {5:9} Then it's burnt offering time. {5:10} The priest sorts them out, and they're forgiven. {5:11} If they can't even afford birds, they can bring fine flour with no oil or incense—just straight-up sorry flour. {5:12} The priest burns a bit on the altar, and the rest is theirs. {5:13} The priest sorts them out, and they're forgiven, with the rest going to the priest. {5:14-15} Then God told Moses, "Yo, if someone messes up unknowingly with holy stuff, they gotta bring a perfect ram and some cash for the trouble." {5:16} They make up for it plus an extra, and the priest sorts them out with the ram, and they're forgiven. {5:17} If someone breaks a rule without knowing, they're still guilty once they find out. {5:18} They bring a ram, sort things out with the priest, and they're forgiven—it's a serious deal.

{6:1} So, God tells Moses, "Listen up!" {6:2} If someone messes up and does wrong against the Lord, like lying to their neighbor about something they were supposed to keep safe, or in a business deal, or by stealing, or straight-up lying about finding something, and swearing falsely about it—basically, if they break the rules this way: {6:4} They gotta make things right—return what they stole, or what they deceitfully gained, or what was entrusted to them, or what they found and lied about. {6:5} Plus, they gotta pay back what they swore falsely about, adding an extra fifth to it, and give it back on the day they bring their offering for messing up. {6:6} Then they bring a flawless ram as their apology offering to the Lord, {6:7} and the priest sorts it out before God, and they're forgiven for all their screw-ups. {6:8} God's like, "Yo, Aaron and the crew, here's the deal with burnt offerings: it's gotta burn on the altar all night till morning, and that fire's gotta keep going." {6:10} The priest wears specific clothes to scoop up the burnt offering ashes and puts them by the altar. {6:11} After that, they change clothes and take the ashes outside camp to a clean spot. {6:12} The fire on the altar keeps burning, and every morning, they burn the offering and the fat of the peace offerings. {6:13} That fire never goes out. {6:14} Then there's the lowdown on the grain offering: Aaron's sons present it before the Lord at the altar. {6:15} They take a handful of the flour, oil, and frankincense, burning it on the altar for God—a sweet scent for the Lord. {6:16} The rest, Aaron and his sons chow down on in the holy place, without leaven, as their portion of the fire offerings. {6:17-18} Only dudes from Aaron's fam can eat it—forever rule. {6:19-21} God's back like, "Now, Aaron and the crew, when you're anointed, you bring this grain offering: fine flour, a tenth in the morning and a tenth at night, mixed with oil and baked for a sweet scent to the Lord." {6:22-23} The priest or his anointed sons offer it up—it's gotta be fully burnt for the Lord. {6:24-25} Then there's the rundown on the sin offering: where the burnt offering goes down, the sin offering goes down too—super holy. {6:26} The priest who offers it eats it in the holy place, within the tabernacle court. {6:27} Anything that touches its flesh becomes holy; if its blood gets on clothing, they gotta wash it in a holy place. {6:28} Vessels used to cook it gotta be destroyed if they're clay; if they're bronze, they gotta be cleaned. {6:29} Only the dudes from the priest crew can eat it—it's super holy. {6:30} No sin offering whose blood is brought into the tabernacle can be eaten; it's gotta be burnt up.

{7:1} So, this is the deal with the trespass offering—it's super holy. {7:2} Where they sacrifice the burnt offering, that's where they do the trespass offering too, sprinkling its blood all around the altar. {7:3} They offer up all the fat of it—the rump, the fat around the organs, {7:4} the kidneys, the fat on them, around the flanks, the liver's caul, and the kidneys—they take it all out. {7:5} The priest burns it all on the altar as a fire offering to the Lord—it's the trespass offering. {7:6} All the male priests chow down on it in the holy place—it's that sacred. {7:7} Just like with the sin offering, it's the same deal with the trespass offering—one law for them. The priest who makes atonement with it gets to have it. {7:8} Also, any priest who offers someone's burnt offering gets to keep the skin of the burnt offering for themselves. {7:9} All the baked and pan-cooked meat offerings belong to the priest who offers them. {7:10} Every meat offering mixed with oil belongs to all the sons of Aaron equally. {7:11} Now, for the peace offerings, here's how it goes down when you offer them to the Lord. {7:12} If it's a thanksgiving offering, you gotta bring it with unleavened cakes and wafers, anointed with oil, and fried fine flour cakes. {7:13} Along with that, you offer leavened bread with your thanksgiving peace offerings. {7:14} From the whole offering, a portion is offered as a heave offering to the Lord, and it's for the priest who sprinkles the blood of the peace offerings. {7:15} The meat from the thanksgiving peace offerings must be eaten the same day it's offered—none left till morning. {7:16} But if it's a vow or voluntary offering, you can eat it the same day you offer it, and the next day too; anything left on the third day must be burnt up. {7:17} Eating any of the sacrifice's flesh on the third day is a no-go—it's an abomination. {7:18} If anyone eats it, they're guilty. {7:19} Any flesh that touches something unclean can't be eaten—it's gotta be burnt up. {7:20} Anyone who eats the flesh of the peace offerings but is unclean will be cut off from their people. {7:21} Anyone who touches something unclean and then eats the peace offerings is also cut off. {7:22-223} God tells Moses to remind the Israelites: don't eat any fat from oxen, sheep, or goats. {7:24} You can use the fat from animals that die naturally or are torn by beasts for other things, but don't eat it. {7:25} Eating the fat of animals offered as fire offerings to the Lord means being cut off. {7:26} And don't eat any blood, whether from birds or beasts, in your dwellings. {7:27-28} Anyone who does eat blood is also cut off. {7:29} When offering peace offerings to the Lord, bring them to the altar as your offering. {7:30} You bring the offerings made by fire with your own hands—the fat with the breast, which is waved as a gesture before the Lord. {7:31} The priest burns the fat on the altar, but the breast belongs to Aaron and his sons. {7:32} The right shoulder is given to the priest as a heave offering from your peace offerings. {7:33} The priest who offers the blood and fat gets the right shoulder. {7:34} These portions have been given to Aaron and his sons forever as part of the peace offerings from the Israelites. {7:35} This was given to them when they were anointed to serve as priests. {7:36} It's a commandment from God for all generations. {7:37} This covers the laws of burnt offerings, meat offerings, sin offerings, trespass offerings, consecrations, and peace offerings. {7:38} God gave these commands to Moses on Mount Sinai when he instructed the Israelites about their offerings in the wilderness.

{8:1} So, God hit up Moses, saying, {8:2} "Grab Aaron and his crew, along with their swag, some anointing oil, a sin-offering bull, two rams, and a basket of unleavened bread. {8:3} Gather everyone at the door of the tent. {8:4} Moses did his thing, and the whole crew assembled at the tent door. {8:5} Moses told them, "This is what God wants us to do." {8:6} Then Moses washed up Aaron and his boys. {8:7} He suited Aaron up—coat, belt, robe, ephod, and the blingy ephod's special belt, and then the breastplate with the Urim and Thummim. {8:9} Topped it off with the holy crown on Aaron's head, just as God told Moses. {8:10} Moses used the anointing oil on the tent and everything in it, making it holy. {8:11} Sprinkled oil on the altar and all its gear—the washbasin and stand—to make them holy. {8:12} Poured oil on Aaron's head, setting him apart. {8:13} Then Moses decked out Aaron's sons, following God's orders. {8:14}

They brought the sin-offering bull, and Aaron and his sons laid hands on it. {8:15} Moses spilled its blood on the altar's horns, purifying it, then poured the rest at the base to reconcile it. {8:16} Moses burned the fat and innards on the altar, but the rest he burned outside the camp, as God told him. {8:18} Then they brought a ram for the burnt offering, and Aaron and his sons laid hands on it. {8:19} After Moses spilled its blood on the altar, he chopped up the ram, burning the head, pieces, and fat. {8:21} He washed the innards and legs, burning the whole ram on the altar—a sweet-smelling fire offering to God, just like He commanded Moses. {8:22} Next, they brought another ram for consecration, and Aaron and his sons laid hands on it. {8:23} After Moses spilled its blood, he dabbed some on Aaron's right ear, thumb, and big toe. {8:24} He did the same for Aaron's sons and sprinkled blood on the altar. {8:25} Moses took the fat, rump, innards, liver's caul, kidneys, fat, and right shoulder. {8:26} Using unleavened bread from the Lord's basket, Moses put it all on the fat and right shoulder. {8:27} He placed it in Aaron's and his sons' hands, waving them before the Lord as a gesture. {8:28} Moses took it back and burned it on the altar with the burnt offering—it was consecrated and smelled good to God. {8:29} Moses took the ram's breast, waved it before the Lord, claiming his share from the consecration ram, as God commanded Moses. {8:30} Using anointing oil and blood from the altar, Moses sprinkled it on Aaron, his sons, and their garments, setting them apart. {8:31} Moses instructed Aaron and his sons to boil the flesh at the tent door and eat it with the consecration bread, just as God commanded. {8:32} Anything left over they burned. {8:33} For seven days, they stayed at the tent door, consecrating themselves as God commanded, so they could atone. {8:35} They stayed at the tent door day and night, keeping God's charge, as commanded, to stay alive. {8:36} Aaron and his sons followed every detail of God's command through Moses.

{9:1} So, on the eighth day, Moses hit up Aaron, his crew, and the elders of Israel. {9:2} He told Aaron, "Grab a young calf for a sin-offering and a spotless ram for a burnt offering, and present them to the LORD. {9:3} Tell the Israelites to bring a goat kid for a sin-offering, along with a calf and a lamb (both first-year and flawless) for a burnt offering. {9:4} Also, bring a bull and a ram for peace offerings, along with a grain offering mixed with oil. Today, the LORD will show up for you. {9:5} They did what Moses said before the tent, and everyone gathered before the LORD. {9:6} Moses laid out what the LORD commanded and said, "Get ready to see the glory of the LORD." {9:7} Moses told Aaron, "Head to the altar, offer your sin-offering and burnt offering, and make atonement for yourself and the people. {9:8} Aaron went to the altar and sacrificed the calf for his sin-offering. {9:9} His sons brought him the blood, and he dabbed it on the altar's horns and poured the rest at the base, as Moses commanded. {9:10} He burned the fat, kidneys, and liver caul on the altar, just as the LORD told Moses. {9:11} The flesh and hide were burned outside the camp. {9:12} Then he sacrificed the burnt offering; his sons brought him the blood, which he sprinkled around the altar. {9:13} They offered the burnt offering with its pieces and head, burning them on the altar. {9:14} Aaron washed the innards and legs and burned them with the burnt offering. {9:15} Then he took the goat for the people's sin offering, slaughtered it, and presented it for sin. {9:16} He offered the burnt offering according to the procedure. {9:17} Then he brought the grain offering, took a handful, and burned it on the altar alongside the morning burnt sacrifice. {9:18} He also sacrificed the bull and ram for the people's peace offerings; his sons brought him the blood, which he sprinkled around the altar. {9:19} He burned the fat of the bull and ram, including the rump, innards' covering, kidneys, and liver caul. {9:20} They placed the fat on the breasts, and he burned it on the altar. {9:21} Aaron waved the breasts and right shoulder as a wave offering before the LORD, as Moses commanded. {9:22} Aaron blessed the people, finished offering the sin, burnt, and peace offerings, and came down. {9:23} Moses and Aaron went into the tent, came out, and blessed the people; then the glory of the LORD appeared to everyone. {9:24} Fire came from the LORD and consumed the burnt offering and fat on the altar. When the people saw this, they shouted and fell on their faces.

{10:1} So Nadab and Abihu, Aaron's sons, each grabbed their censer, put fire and incense on it, and offered unauthorized fire before the LORD, which they weren't supposed to do. {10:2} Instantly, fire from the LORD consumed them, and they died before the LORD. {10:3} Moses then told Aaron, "This is what the LORD meant when He said, 'I will be honored by those who come near me, and before all the people I will be glorified.'" Aaron stayed quiet. {10:4} Moses called Mishael and Elzaphan, Uzziel's sons (Aaron's cousins), and said, "Come, carry your brothers away from the sanctuary out of the camp." {10:5} They did as Moses instructed, carrying them out of camp in their coats. {10:6} Moses warned Aaron, Eleazar, and Ithamar, "Don't uncover your heads or tear your clothes, or you'll die, and wrath will come upon the people. Let all the Israelites mourn the burning caused by the LORD." {10:7} "Stay inside the tabernacle; the anointing oil is upon you." They obeyed Moses. {10:8} Then the LORD told Aaron, "Don't drink wine or strong drink when you enter the tabernacle, or you and your sons will die. This is a rule forever. {10:9} It'll help you differentiate between holy and unholy, clean and unclean, teaching the Israelites all the LORD's statutes through Moses. {10:10} Moses told Aaron, Eleazar, and Ithamar, "Take the remaining meat offering from the fire offerings and eat it unleavened beside the altar; it's most holy. {10:13} Eat it in the holy place, as commanded. {10:14} The wave breast and heave shoulder you shall eat in a clean place, you, your sons, and daughters, given from the peace offerings of the Israelites. {10:15} These are forever statutes commanded by the LORD. {10:16} Moses found the goat of the sin offering burnt, and he was angry with Eleazar and Ithamar, Aaron's remaining sons, asking why they hadn't eaten it in the holy place. {10:17} "You should've eaten it to bear the congregation's iniquity and make atonement before the LORD, as I commanded." {10:18} Aaron responded, explaining that they had offered their sin and burnt offerings before the LORD, leading to these circumstances. If they had eaten the sin offering today, would the LORD have accepted it? {10:20} When Moses heard this, he was satisfied.

{11:1} So the LORD hit up Moses and Aaron, telling them, {11:2} "Tell the Israelites what's up with the animals you can munch on among all the creatures on earth. {11:3} If an animal has split hooves, chews its cud, it's good to go. {11:4} But check this—don't chow down on camels even if they chew cud but don't split hooves; they're a no-go. {11:5} Same deal with coney and hare, chewing cud but no split hooves—they're out. {11:6} Oh, and swine? They've got split hooves but skip the cud; they're a no-eat zone. {11:7-8} Don't touch their flesh or carcasses; they're unclean. {11:9} Now for water creatures: if it's got fins and scales—go ahead and dig in. {11:10} But anything in the water without fins and scales? Total abomination, don't even think about it. {11:11} They're a big nope, not for eating, just avoid them. {11:12} Anything without fins and scales in water? Big nope again. {11:13-19} And here's the deal with birds: eagles, vultures, ospreys, kites, ravens, owls, hawks, storks—they're off-limits. {11:20} No eating birds that creep on all fours; they're a no-go. {11:21} But you can chow down on locusts, bald locusts, beetles, and grasshoppers. {11:22} Other flying crawling critters with legs for hopping? Eat those locusts and such. {11:23} But any other crawling thing with four feet? Nope, they're off-limits. {11:24} If you touch their carcasses, you're unclean until evening. {11:25-28} Same if you carry their carcasses; wash up and wait till evening. {11:29-30} These creeping things are a no-go: weasels, mice, tortoises, ferrets, chameleons, lizards, snails, and moles. {11:31} Touching these dead critters? Unclean till evening. {11:32-33} If their dead bodies touch anything—clothing, utensils, whatever—wash it up; it's unclean till evening. {11:34} If you've got meat touched by unclean water, it's unclean; and any drink from an unclean vessel? Also unclean. {11:35} If a carcass touches anything, like an oven or pot, smash it; it's unclean and stays that way. {11:36-38} But a clean fountain or pit? Totally fine; only the stuff touching the carcass is unclean. {11:39} If an eatable beast kicks the bucket, anyone touching it is unclean till evening. {11:40} Eating it? Wash up and wait till evening; same if you carry its carcass. {11:41} Any crawling critter? Off-limits; no munching on those. {11:42} Don't make yourself nasty with these critters; stay clean and holy. {11:43} The LORD brought you out of Egypt to be holy; so stay that way, avoid creepy-crawlies. {11:44} This is the lowdown on animals, birds, water creatures, and crawlers—to know clean from unclean, edible from inedible.

{12:1} So the LORD dropped some knowledge on Moses, saying, {12:2} "Yo, tell the Israelites this: if a woman has a baby boy, she's unclean for a week, just like when she's on her period. {12:3} Then on the eighth day, the baby's gotta get circumcised. {12:4} After that, she's gotta stay pure for 33 days; no touching holy stuff or going to the sanctuary until then. {12:5} But if she has a girl, double the time—two weeks of uncleanness and 66 days of purification. {12:6} When her time's up, whether boy or girl, she's gotta bring a lamb for a burnt offering and a pigeon or turtledove for a sin offering to the tabernacle, to the priest. {12:7} The priest hooks her up, makes atonement, and she's cleansed from her blood flow. That's the law for new moms. {12:8} And if she can't afford a lamb, two turtles or pigeons will do; one for burning, the other for sin. The priest sorts her out, and she's good to go.

{13:1} Then the LORD hit up Moses and Aaron, saying, {13:2} "Listen up, if someone's got a weird rash, scab, or funky spot on their skin, like leprosy, bring 'em to Aaron the priest or one of his crew. {13:3} The priest checks it out; if the hair turns white and it's deeper than the skin, it's leprosy, and they're unclean. {13:4} If it's just a white spot and not deep, they're quarantined for a week. {13:5} If it stays put after a week, another week's quarantine. {13:6} If it's getting better, just a scab; wash up and you're good. {13:7} But if it spreads after getting checked, it's leprosy. {13:8} And if it's getting worse, definitely leprosy. {13:9} Bring 'em to the priest; if it's bad, they're unclean. {13:10} If it's white and the hair's white, and there's raw flesh, it's old leprosy—definitely unclean. {13:11} If it's spreading, it's leprosy. {13:12} If it covers the skin, it's clean. {13:13} But if raw flesh shows up, they're unclean. {13:14} The priest checks; if there's raw flesh, they're unclean. {13:15} If it's getting better, it's clean. {13:16-17} If it turns white again, they're clean. {13:18} If a healed boil leaves a white spot, it's leprosy. {13:19} If there's a white or reddish spot, show it to the priest. {13:20} If it's deeper than the skin, it's leprosy. {13:21} If it's not, quarantine for a week. {13:22} If it spreads, it's leprosy. {13:23} If it stays, it's just a boil. {13:24} If there's a hot, bright spot after a burn heals, it's leprosy. {13:25} If it's deeper and the hair's white, it's leprosy. {13:26} Quarantine for a week if not sure. {13:27} If it spreads, it's leprosy. {13:28} If it doesn't spread, it's just an inflammation. {13:29} If there's a weird spot on the head or beard, check with the priest. {13:30} If it's deeper than the skin with yellow hair, it's a dry scall, also leprosy. {13:31} Quarantine for a week if unsure. {13:32} If it doesn't spread after a week, quarantine again. {13:33} Shave, but don't touch the scall. {13:34} If it stays put, wash up and you're clean. {13:35} If it spreads after getting clean, it's unclean. {13:36} If it stays, it's just a burn. {13:37} If the spot's chill and there's black hair, it's healed—clean. {13:38} If there are white spots on the skin, check with the priest. {13:39} If they're not deep and a different color, they're cool. {13:40} Bald? No prob, still clean. {13:41} Even forehead bald's all good. {13:42} But if there's a sore, check it out; if it's reddish-white, it's leprosy. {13:43} If it's the same as leprosy, you're unclean. {13:44-45} Lepers gotta dress rough and cover their lips, shouting "Unclean!" {13:46} Lepers stay away from everyone; they're unclean. {13:47} If leprosy's in clothes, they're unclean. {13:48} Burn anything with leprosy, cloth or skin. {13:49} Greenish or reddish plague? Show the priest. {13:50} Quarantine for a week. {13:51} If it spreads, burn it; it's unclean. {13:52} Burn it all if it doesn't clear up. {13:53} Wash and quarantine for a week. {13:54} If it's still there, burn it. {13:55} If it hasn't changed, it's unclean. {13:56} Burn it if it's dark after washing. {13:57} If it stays, burn it. {13:58} Wash again if it clears up. {13:59} That's the deal with leprosy in clothes—clean or unclean.

{14:1} So, God hits up Moses like, "Yo, listen up." {14:2} This is the deal when someone with leprosy gets cleaned up: They bring 'em to the priest. {14:3} The priest checks it out, and if the leprosy's gone, here's the plan. {14:4} Get two clean birds, some cedar wood, scarlet thread, and hyssop. {14:5} Kill one bird over running water in a clay pot. {14:6} Then take the living bird, cedar, scarlet, and hyssop, dip 'em in the dead bird's blood and water. {14:7} Sprinkle the mixture on the cleansed person seven times, declare 'em clean, and set the live bird free. {14:8} The person cleansed shaves, washes their clothes, and stays outside the camp for seven days. {14:9} On the seventh day, shave again, wash clothes and body, and boom—clean. {14:10} On the eighth day, bring two perfect lambs, a ewe lamb, fine flour mixed with oil for an offering, and oil. {14:11} The priest presents the person and these offerings at the tabernacle. {14:12} The priest waves a lamb as a trespass offering and pours oil, waving them before God. {14:13} Then he kills the lamb in the holy place. {14:14}

Dabs blood on the person's ear, thumb, and toe. {14:15} Pours oil in his hand. {14:16} Sprinkles oil seven times before God. {14:17} Puts oil on the person's ear, thumb, toe, and head. {14:18} More oil on the head for atonement. {14:19} Offers a sin offering, making atonement for the cleanse. {14:20} Offers a burnt offering and meal offering. {14:21} If broke, bring a lamb, flour mixed with oil, and birds for sin and burnt offerings. {14:22} All presented on the eighth day at the tabernacle. {14:23} The priest waves a lamb and oil before God. {14:24} Kills the lamb and dabs blood on the person's ear, thumb, toe. {14:25} Pours oil in his hand. {14:26} Sprinkles oil seven times before God. {14:27} Puts oil on the person's ear, thumb, toe, and head. {14:28} More oil on the head for atonement. {14:29} Offers a bird for sin and burnt offerings. {14:30} Makes atonement for the person. {14:31} This covers the law for leprosy cases.

{15:1} So, God hits up Moses and Aaron, like, "Listen up." {15:2} Tell the Israelites this: if a dude's got some kind of running issue from his flesh, he's unclean because of it. {15:3} Here's how it works: if his flesh is leaking or if it stops leaking, he's unclean either way. {15:4} Any bed he lies on while he's got the issue is unclean, and anything he sits on becomes unclean too. {15:5} Anyone who touches his bed has to wash their clothes, bathe, and they're unclean until evening. {15:6} Same goes for anyone who sits on something he sat on—wash up and stay unclean until evening. {15:7} If you touch the guy's flesh with the issue, wash your clothes, bathe, and stay unclean until evening. {15:8} Even if he spits on a clean person, that person has to wash up and stay unclean until evening. {15:9} Oh, and any saddle he rides on becomes unclean. {15:10} Anyone who touches something he sat on is unclean until evening, and whoever carries those things has to wash up and stay unclean until evening. {15:11} If he touches someone without washing his hands, that person has to wash up and stay unclean until evening. {15:12} If he touches an earthen vessel, it's gotta be destroyed, and wooden vessels need a good rinse. {15:13} When the guy gets rid of his issue, he takes seven days to cleanse himself: wash clothes, bathe, and then he's clean. {15:14} On the eighth day, he brings two turtledoves or pigeons to the tabernacle as offerings. {15:15} The priest does his thing—offering one as a sin offering and the other as a burnt offering—to make atonement for the guy before the Lord. {15:16} If a guy's "seed" comes out, he washes up and stays unclean until evening. {15:17} Any garment with his "seed" on it needs a wash and stays unclean until evening. {15:18} Same goes if a guy sleeps with a woman and there's "seed" involved—they both bathe and stay unclean until evening. {15:19} If a woman's issue is blood, she's separated for seven days, and anyone who touches her is unclean until evening. {15:20} Anything she lies on during her separation is unclean, as is anything she sits on. {15:21} If you touch her bed, wash your clothes, bathe, and stay unclean until evening. {15:22} Same goes for anything she sat on—wash up and stay unclean until evening. {15:23} If you touch her bed or anything she sat on, you're unclean until evening. {15:24} If a guy sleeps with her during her period, he's unclean for seven days, and the bed is unclean too. {15:25} If her issue continues beyond the normal time, she's unclean as long as it lasts. {15:26} Anything she lies on during her issue is like her period bed—unclean. {15:27} If you touch any of these things, wash up and stay unclean until evening. {15:28} Once she's done with her issue, she takes seven days to cleanse herself. {15:29} On the eighth day, she brings two turtles or pigeons to the tabernacle for offerings. {15:30} The priest does his thing—sin offering and burnt offering—to make atonement for her uncleanness before the Lord. {15:31} This is to keep the Israelites clean so they don't defile God's tabernacle and die in their uncleanness. {15:32} These rules apply to guys with issues, those whose seed comes out, women with period problems, and anyone involved with them.

{16:1} So, God hits up Moses after Aaron's two sons die for messing up their offering. {16:2} God tells Moses to warn Aaron not to go into the holy place behind the curtain whenever he feels like it, or he'll end up dead, because God appears in a cloud on the mercy seat. {16:3} Here's the plan: Aaron comes into the holy place with a young bull for a sin offering and a ram for a burnt offering. {16:4} He puts on special linen clothes, washes up, and gets dressed in these holy threads. {16:5} Then he grabs two goats from the Israelites for a sin offering and another ram for a burnt offering. {16:6} Aaron starts by offering the bull as a sin offering for himself and his family. {16:7} Next, he presents the two goats before the Lord at the tabernacle entrance. {16:8} Aaron flips a coin for the goats—one is for the Lord, and the other is the scapegoat. {16:9} He sacrifices the goat chosen for the Lord as a sin offering. {16:10} The scapegoat, chosen by lot, is kept alive to take away the people's sins into the wilderness. {16:11} Aaron then offers the bull for his own sin and makes atonement for himself and his family. {16:12} He takes coals from the altar and incense inside the curtain to the mercy seat. {16:13} The incense smoke covers the mercy seat so Aaron doesn't die. {16:14} He sprinkles the bull's blood on the mercy seat eastward seven times. {16:15} Afterward, he sacrifices the goat for the people's sin, bringing its blood inside the curtain and doing the same as with the bull's blood. {16:16} This whole process makes atonement for the holy place and the tabernacle among the Israelites' uncleanness and sins. {16:17} No one is allowed inside while Aaron does this until he's done atoning for himself, his family, and all the people. {16:18} Aaron then goes to the altar and atones for it using the blood of the bull and goat. {16:19} He sprinkles the blood on the altar seven times to cleanse it from Israel's uncleanness. {16:20} After reconciling everything, Aaron brings out the live scapegoat. {16:21} He confesses all the people's sins over the scapegoat's head and sends it into the wilderness with a designated person. {16:22} The scapegoat carries away all the sins to an uninhabited land. {16:23} Aaron changes out of his linen clothes in the tabernacle and leaves them there. {16:24} He washes up, puts on his regular clothes, and offers burnt offerings for himself and the people. {16:25} He burns the fat of the sin offering on the altar. {16:26} The person who leads the scapegoat away washes up before returning to camp. {16:27} The bull and goat's carcasses, whose blood was used in the atonement, are taken outside the camp and burned. {16:28} The person who burns them washes up before returning to camp. {16:29} God sets a rule: on the tenth day of the seventh month, everyone must rest, afflict their souls, and do no work—whether native Israelite or foreigner among them. {16:30} The priest atones for everyone to cleanse them from their sins before the Lord. {16:31} It's a day of rest and affliction as an everlasting rule. {16:32} The anointed priest does the atonement work, wearing the holy clothes. {16:33} He atones for the sanctuary, tabernacle, altar, and all the people. {16:34} This yearly atonement is an everlasting rule for the sins of Israel, as God commanded Moses.

{17:1} So, God hits up Moses and says, {17:2} "Tell Aaron, his sons, and all the Israelites this: If any Israelite kills an ox, lamb, or goat in or out of camp {17:3} and doesn't bring it to the tabernacle to offer as a sacrifice to the Lord, that's a big no-no. Blood's on his hands, and he's out of the community. {17:4} This rule ensures sacrifices are done properly at the tabernacle, offered by the priests for peace with the Lord. {17:5} No more sacrificing to demons like they did before—this is the forever law for all generations. {17:8} Also, if anyone—Israelite or foreigner—offers a burnt offering and doesn't bring it to the tabernacle, they're cut off. {17:10} And eating blood? Not cool. I'll be against anyone who does it and they'll be cut off. {17:11} Blood's for atonement; it's sacred. {17:12} So, no eating blood for anyone—Israelite or foreigner. {17:13} When hunting, drain the blood, cover it, and respect the life. {17:14} Blood's the life force; don't eat it. {17:15} If you eat an animal that died on its own or was killed by another animal, wash up and be unclean until evening. {17:16} Don't wash? That's on you.

{18:1} Then God tells Moses, {18:2} "Tell the Israelites this: I'm your God. {18:3} Don't act like the Egyptians or Canaanites—I'm taking you somewhere new with different rules. {18:4} Follow my laws, don't copy theirs. {18:5} If you do, you'll thrive. {18:6} No getting with close relatives; that's off-limits. {18:7} Don't uncover your parents' nakedness; that's just wrong. {18:8} Stepmoms are off-limits too. {18:9} Sisters, daughters, granddaughters—none of their nakedness either. {18:10} Same goes for daughters-in-law. {18:11} Your dad's wife's daughter? Nope, she's like a sister. {18:12} Also, don't uncover your aunt's nakedness—she's family. {18:13} And your mom's sister? No way. {18:14} Uncles' wives are off-limits too. {18:15} And don't mess with a woman and her daughter or granddaughter. {18:18} Don't marry sisters while one's alive; that's just asking for trouble. {18:19} Don't mess with a woman during her time of uncleanness. {18:20} Cheating with your neighbor's wife? Absolutely not. {18:21} No sacrificing children to Molech—it's a disgrace. {18:22} Don't be with a guy like you're with a girl; that's messed up. {18:23} And definitely no relations with animals. {18:24} Keep away from these things; that's why the old nations were kicked out. {18:25} The land was defiled, and it'll do the same to you. {18:26} Obey my rules to stay clean—Israelite or foreigner among you. {18:27} The old nations did these sins, and they got booted. {18:28} Keep the land clean, or you'll be out too. {18:29} Anyone who does these things will be cut off from their people. {18:30} Follow my rules and avoid these gross practices—I'm your God."

{19:1} God hits up Moses again, saying, {19:2} "Tell all the Israelites this: You gotta be cool because I'm your God and I'm cool. {19:3} Respect your parents and keep my sabbaths; I'm your God. {19:4} Don't mess with idols or make your own gods; I'm your God. {19:5} If you offer a peace offering to me, do it willingly. {19:6} Eat it up the same day or the next, and anything left over by the third day gets burned. {19:7} Eating it on the third day? Gross—it won't be accepted, and you'll carry the guilt. {19:8} Anyone who eats it late will be cut off from the community. {19:9} When harvesting, leave some behind for the poor and strangers. {19:10} Don't be greedy; leave some in the vineyard too. {19:11} No stealing, lying, or cheating. {19:12} Don't swear falsely or disrespect my name. {19:13} Treat your neighbor fairly; don't cheat them of their wages. {19:14} Don't mock the deaf or trip up the blind; show respect—I'm your God. {19:15} Be just in judgment; don't favor the rich or disrespect the poor. {19:16} No spreading rumors or standing by while someone is in danger. {19:17} Don't hold grudges or hate secretly; speak up and help each other. {19:18} Don't seek revenge; love your neighbor like yourself—I'm your God. {19:19} Follow my rules: no mixing animals, seeds, or fabrics. {19:20} If a man sleeps with a bondmaid promised to another, he'll face consequences, but not death if she wasn't free. {19:21} Bring a trespass offering to the tabernacle if you mess up. {19:22} The priest will make atonement, and you'll be forgiven. {19:23} Don't eat from newly planted trees for the first three years. {19:24} In the fourth year, the fruit is holy, and from the fifth year, eat freely. {19:26} No eating blood, practicing magic, or fortune-telling. {19:27} Don't mess with your hair or body; keep it natural. {19:28} No cutting or marking your body for the dead—I'm your God. {19:29} Don't allow your daughter to become a prostitute; it's bad for the land. {19:30} Keep my sabbaths and respect my sanctuary. {19:31} Stay away from mediums and wizards; don't get defiled. {19:32} Respect the elderly and fear God. {19:33} Treat strangers well; they're like locals to you. {19:34} Love them as yourself because you were strangers in Egypt—I'm your God. {19:35} Be fair in judgment, in measuring things—keep it honest. {19:36} Use fair weights and measures; I brought you out of Egypt—I'm your God. {19:37} Follow all my rules and judgments; I'm your God."

{20:1} So God talks to Moses again, saying, {20:2} "Tell the Israelites this: If anyone—Israelite or stranger living among them—sacrifices their children to Molech, they're done for. The people will stone them to death. {20:3} I'll turn against that person and cut them off from the community because they defiled my sanctuary and disrespected my name. {20:4} If anyone sees this happening and ignores it, {20:5} I'll be against them too, along with their family, for following after such wickedness. {20:6} Also, anyone messing with mediums or wizards, looking for trouble, I'm coming after them too—cutting them off from the community. {20:7} So stay pure and holy, because I'm your God. {20:8} Follow my rules and do them—I'm the one who makes you special. {20:9} Anyone who curses their parents is in big trouble and deserves what they get. {20:10} If a man sleeps with another man's wife, both the cheaters will be put to death. {20:11} Sleeping with your father's wife is a no-go—both will face death. {20:12} If a man sleeps with his daughter-in-law, they're both done for. {20:13} Same goes for men sleeping with men—it's an abomination, and they'll be put to death. {20:14} Taking a wife and her mother? Both burn. {20:15} Sleeping with animals? Death for the person and the animal. {20:16} If a woman gets it on with an animal, they both get the axe. {20:17} Incest with close family? No way—it's wicked, and they'll be cut off from the community. {20:18} Sleeping with a woman during her period? Both are out. {20:19} No messing with your mother's or father's sisters—it's off-limits. {20:20} If a man sleeps with his uncle's wife, they're out too, and no kids for them. {20:21} Marrying your brother's wife? Unclean. {20:22} Follow all my rules and judgments to stay in this land I'm giving you. {20:23} Don't act like the nations I kicked out before you—they did all this nasty stuff, and that's why I got rid of them. {20:24} But I promised you their land—a land flowing with milk and honey. I'm your God, and I've set you apart. {20:25} Keep clean and don't mix up clean and unclean animals or birds. {20:26} Be holy because I'm holy, and I've set you apart from others. {20:27} Anyone with a familiar spirit or practicing magic gets stoned to death—it's on them."

{21:1} So God tells Moses to talk to Aaron's priestly crew, saying they can't mess with dead bodies except for close family like mom, dad, son, daughter, or sister who's still a virgin. {21:2} But they gotta stay clean because they're VIPs in the community. {21:3} No shaving their heads bald or trimming their beards weird or cutting themselves up. {21:4} They're set apart for God, so they better act like it. {21:5} No marrying loose women or divorced ladies—gotta keep it holy. {21:6} They gotta stay pure for the Lord because they handle the holy stuff. {21:7} If a priest's daughter goes wild and gets with random guys, she's in big trouble—burnt with fire. {21:8} Priests gotta be sanctified because they serve God's bread—holy business. {21:9} Any priest's daughter who acts up brings shame on her dad and gets torched. {21:10} High priests can't mess up their anointed look or touch dead bodies, even for family. {21:11} They're all about keeping the sanctuary clean—holy crown and all. {21:12} High priests gotta marry virgins and keep their seed pure. {21:13} No messing with widows, divorced women, or loose ladies for high priests. {21:14} Priests with blemishes can't offer God's bread—no blind, lame, or broken allowed. {21:15} Only the best without blemishes can serve up the sacrifices. {21:16} Blemished priests can eat the holy food but can't get too close to the altar. {21:17} Any blemished priest can't serve up God's offerings—no blind, lame, or deformed. {21:18} God wants the best sacrifices—no blemishes or defects allowed. {21:19} Only perfect offerings for the Lord—no messed-up animals. {21:20} Blemished sacrifices won't cut it—God wants the best. {21:21} Moses tells Aaron and the crew what's up.

{22:1} God tells Moses to let Aaron know to keep the holy things sacred and not to mess up. {22:2} Don't mess with God's name when handling sacred stuff. {22:3} If anyone's unclean and touches the holy things, they're cut off. {22:4} No lepers or anyone unclean can eat the holy stuff. {22:5} Stay clean—no touching dead things or creepy crawlies. {22:6} If you're unclean, wash up before chowing down on the holy stuff. {22:7} Wait till sunset to eat the holy food if you've been unclean. {22:8} Don't eat animals that died on their own or got mauled by beasts. {22:9} Follow the rules or face the consequences—God keeps them holy. {22:10} Only priests and their families can eat the holy stuff—no strangers allowed. {22:11} Priests can share their food with their households. {22:12} Priest's daughters can't eat the holy offerings if they're married to non-priests. {22:13} If a priest's daughter becomes a widow or gets divorced and returns home childless, she can eat her dad's food, but no one else can. {22:14} If someone accidentally eats the holy food, they gotta make it right with the priest. {22:15} Don't disrespect the holy offerings—God keeps them sacred. {22:16} Don't let others take on your sins by eating the holy things. {22:17} God tells Moses to remind Aaron and the crew about offerings and vows. {22:18} Don't offer messed-up sacrifices—only the best for God. {22:19} Offer male animals without blemish for burnt offerings. {22:20} No blemished offerings allowed—gotta be perfect for God. {22:21} Perfect sacrifices for thanksgiving or freewill offerings. {22:22} Don't offer up the flawed animals as sacrifices. {22:23} You can offer flawed animals as freewill offerings but not for vows. {22:24} Don't offer bruised, crushed, or broken animals to God. {22:25} No foreigner can offer God's bread if the animals are flawed. {22:26} Newborn animals gotta stay with their moms for a week before they can be offered to God. {22:27} Don't kill a cow and its young on the same day. {22:28} Offerings must be eaten the same day they're made. {22:29} Keep God's commandments—He's the one who makes you special. {22:30} Don't disrespect God's name—He's holy among the Israelites.

{23:1} So God hits up Moses and says, "Tell the Israelites about my lit feasts that are totally sacred." {23:2} He's all about these special events. {23:3} Chill on the seventh day—no work allowed; it's a total sabbath vibe for the Lord wherever you're at. {23:4} Here's the rundown of God's epic feasts to announce at the right times. {23:5} Passover kicks off on the 14th day of the first month at night. {23:6} Then it's the Feast of Unleavened Bread on the 15th day for a whole week—strictly unleavened bread. {23:7} First day is all about rest and no work. {23:8} Offer stuff to the Lord for a week, and the seventh day is another chill sabbath. {23:9} God's like, "Yo, Moses!" {23:10} When you finally settle in the promised land and start reaping, bring the firstfruits to the priest. {23:11} He waves it to God the day after the sabbath. {23:12} Offer a spotless lamb and some fine flour mixed with oil. {23:13} Add in some wine for good measure—it's all for God. {23:14} Don't eat bread, parched corn, or green ears until you offer to God; it's a forever rule. {23:15} Count seven sabbaths plus one day after the seventh sabbath for a total of fifty days, then bring a new offering to the Lord. {23:16} Bake two loaves with leaven as firstfruits to God. {23:17} Alongside that, bring seven lambs, a young bull, and two rams for offerings. {23:18} Sacrifice a goat kid for sin and two lambs for peace. {23:19} The priest waves it all with the bread before the Lord—it's holy. {23:20} Make this day a sacred gathering with no work, forever. {23:21} Don't forget to leave the corners of your field and gleanings for the poor and strangers—that's God's rule. {23:23} God talks to Moses again. {23:24} On the first day of the seventh month, have a sabbath with trumpets blasting—a special day. {23:25} No work, but offer stuff to the Lord. {23:26} God keeps chatting with Moses. {23:27} Tenth day of the seventh month is a big day of atonement—everyone needs to be there and offer to the Lord. {23:28} No work allowed—it's all about making things right with God. {23:29} Anyone who doesn't take it seriously gets cut off; anyone who works gets destroyed by God. {23:30} Seriously, no work allowed—it's a forever rule. {23:32} This is a serious sabbath day of rest and soul-searching. {23:33} God talks to Moses again. {23:34} Fifteenth day of the seventh month is the Feast of Tabernacles for a week. {23:35} First day is a holy convocation—no work allowed. {23:36} Offerings every day for seven days, and on the eighth day, another holy convocation with offerings—no work. {23:37} These are the feasts—sacred gatherings with offerings to the Lord. {23:39} On the fifteenth day of the seventh month, celebrate with a sabbath, and again on the eighth day. {23:40} Get some branches and celebrate before the Lord for seven days. {23:41} Keep this feast forever to remember God's goodness. {23:42} Stay in booths for seven days—everyone born in Israel should join in. {23:43} This is to remember when God had Israel dwell in booths after leaving Egypt—God's the real deal.

{24:1} So God hollered at Moses, saying, {24:2} "Tell the Israelites to bring you some top-tier olive oil to keep the lamps lit 24/7. {24:3} Outside the testimony curtain in the meeting tent, Aaron's got to keep it going from dusk till dawn before the Lord, forever and ever. {24:4} He's gotta keep the lamps on the pure candlestick shining non-stop for God. {24:5} Take some premium flour and bake twelve cakes: each one needs to be made with two-tenths of an ephah. {24:6} Arrange them in two stacks, six per stack, on the pure table before the Lord. {24:7} Put pure frankincense on each stack, making it a fire offering to the Lord as a memorial. {24:8} Every Sabbath, Aaron's got to set it in order before the Lord, taken from the Israelites as a forever deal. {24:9} Aaron and his sons will eat it in the holy place; it's super holy, part of the fire offerings to the Lord, a forever rule. {24:10} An Israelite woman's son, whose dad was Egyptian, got into a fight with an Israelite dude in the camp; {24:11} the woman's son cursed God. They brought him to Moses (his mom was Shelomith, daughter of Dibri from the tribe of Dan). {24:12} They held him until they could hear from God. {24:13} God told Moses, {24:14} "Take the curser outside the camp; everyone who heard him must lay their hands on his head, and the whole assembly must stone him. {24:15} Tell the Israelites: Whoever curses their God will bear the sin. {24:16} Anyone who blasphemes God's name must be put to death; the entire community must stone them, whether they're a foreigner or native-born. {24:17} Anyone who kills a person must be put to death. {24:18} Whoever kills an animal must make it good; life for life. {24:19} If someone injures their neighbor, whatever they did must be done to them: {24:20} fracture for fracture, eye for eye, tooth for tooth. As they've caused injury, so it will be done to them. {24:21} Whoever kills an animal must make it good, but whoever kills a person must be put to death. {24:22} The same law applies to both foreigners and native-born: I am the Lord your God." {24:23} Moses told the Israelites to take the curser outside the camp and stone him. They did as God commanded Moses.

{25:1} God spoke to Moses on Mount Sinai, saying, {25:2} "Tell the Israelites: When you enter the land I give you, let the land have a Sabbath rest for God. {25:3} For six years, sow your fields and prune your vineyards and gather their crops; {25:4} but the seventh year is a Sabbath of rest for the land, a Sabbath for the Lord. Don't sow your fields or prune your vineyards. {25:5} Don't reap what grows of itself or harvest the grapes of your untended vines; it's a year of rest for the land. {25:6} The Sabbath of the land will provide food for you, your servants, hired workers, and temporary residents living among you, {25:7} as well as for your livestock and the wild animals in your land. Whatever the land produces may be eaten. {25:8} Count off seven Sabbath years—seven times seven years—so that the seven Sabbath years amount to forty-nine years. {25:9} Then sound the trumpet everywhere on the tenth day of the seventh month; on the Day of Atonement, sound the trumpet throughout the land. {25:10} Consecrate the fiftieth year and proclaim liberty throughout the land to all its inhabitants. It will be a jubilee for you; each of you is to return to your family property and your clan. {25:11} The fiftieth year will be a jubilee for you; don't sow or reap what grows of itself or harvest the untended vines. {25:12} For it's a jubilee and is to be holy for you; eat only what is taken directly from the fields. {25:13} In this Year of Jubilee, everyone is to return to their own property. {25:14} If you sell land to any of your own people or buy land from them, don't take advantage of each other. {25:15} You are to buy from your own people on the basis of the number of years since the Jubilee. {25:16} Increase or decrease the price according to the number of years left for harvesting crops. {25:17} Don't take advantage of each other, but fear your God. I am the Lord your God. {25:18} Follow my decrees and be careful to obey my laws, and you will live safely in the land. {25:19} The land will yield its fruit, and you will eat your fill and live there in safety. {25:20} You may ask, 'What will we eat in the seventh year if we do not plant or harvest our crops?' {25:21} I will send you such a blessing in the sixth year that the land will yield enough for three years. {25:22} While you plant during the eighth year, you will eat from the old crop and will continue to eat from it until the harvest of the ninth year comes in. {25:23} The land must not be sold permanently, because the land is mine and you reside in my land as foreigners and strangers. {25:24} Throughout the land that you hold as a possession, you must provide for the redemption of the land. {25:25} If one of your fellow Israelites becomes poor and sells some of their property, their nearest relative is to come and redeem what they have sold. {25:26} If, however, there is no one to redeem it for them but later on they prosper and acquire sufficient means to redeem it themselves, {25:27} they are to determine the value for the years since they sold it and refund the balance to the one to whom they sold it; they can then go back to their own property. {25:28} But if they do not acquire the means to repay, what was sold will remain in the possession of the buyer until the Year of Jubilee. It will be returned in the Jubilee, and they can then go back to their property. {25:29} Anyone who sells a house in a walled city retains the right of redemption a full year after its sale. During that time, the seller may redeem it. {25:30} If it is not redeemed before a full year has passed, the house in the walled city shall belong permanently to the buyer and the buyer's descendants. It is not to be returned in the Jubilee. {25:31} But houses in villages without walls are to be considered as belonging to the open country. They can be redeemed, and they are to be returned in the Jubilee. {25:32} The Levites always have the right to redeem their houses in the Levitical towns, which they possess. {25:33} So the property of the Levites is redeemable—that is, a house sold in any town they hold—and is to be returned in the Jubilee, because the houses in the towns of the Levites are their property among the Israelites. {25:34} But the pastureland belonging to their towns must not be sold; it is their permanent possession. {25:35} If any of your fellow Israelites become poor and are unable to support themselves among you, help them as you would a foreigner and stranger, so they can continue to live among you. {25:36} Do not take interest or any profit from them, but fear your God, so that they may continue to live among you. {25:37} You must not lend them money at interest or sell them food at a profit. {25:38} I am the Lord your God, who brought you out of Egypt to give you the land of Canaan and to be your God. {25:39} If any of your fellow Israelites become poor and sell themselves to you, do not make them work as slaves. {25:40} They are to be treated as hired workers or temporary residents among you; they are to work for you until the Year of Jubilee. {25:41} Then they and their children are to be released, and they will go back to their own clans and to the property of their ancestors. {25:42} Because the Israelites are my servants, whom I brought out of Egypt, they must not be sold as slaves. {25:43} Do not rule over them ruthlessly, but fear your God. {25:44} Your male and female slaves are to come from the nations around you; from them you may buy slaves. {25:45} You may also buy some of the temporary residents living among you and members of their clans born in your country, and they will become your property. {25:46} You can bequeath them to your children as inherited property and can make them slaves for life, but you must not rule over your fellow Israelites ruthlessly. {25:47} If a foreigner residing among you becomes rich and any of your fellow Israelites become poor and sell themselves to the foreigner or to a member of the foreigner's clan, {25:48} they retain the right of redemption after they have sold themselves. One of their relatives may redeem them: {25:49} An uncle or a cousin or any blood relative in their clan may redeem them. Or if they prosper, they may redeem themselves. {25:50} They and their buyer are to count the time from the year they sold themselves up to the Year of Jubilee. The price for their release is to be based on the rate paid to a hired worker for that number of years. {25:51} If many years remain, they must pay for their redemption a larger share of the price paid for them. {25:52} If only a few years remain until the Year of Jubilee, they are to compute that and pay for their redemption accordingly. {25:53} They are to be treated as workers hired from year to year; you must see to it that those who own them do not rule over them ruthlessly. {25:54} Even if someone is not redeemed in any of these ways, they and their children are to be released in the Year of Jubilee, {25:55} for the Israelites belong to me as servants. They are my servants, brought out of Egypt. I am your God.

{26:1} Don't make idols, carved images, or set up stone images to worship in your land, 'cause I'm the LORD your God. {26:2} Keep my sabbaths and respect my sanctuary; I'm the LORD. {26:3} If you follow my rules and keep my commandments, {26:4} then I'll give you rain at the right times, the land will produce crops, and the trees will bear fruit. {26:5} Your harvesting will last till the grape harvest, and the grape harvest will last till planting; you'll eat your fill and live safely in your land. {26:6} I'll bring peace to the land, and you'll lie down without fear; I'll remove dangerous animals and prevent wars in your land. {26:7} You'll chase your enemies, and they'll fall by your sword. {26:8} Five of you will chase a hundred, and a hundred of you will chase ten thousand, and your enemies will fall by the sword. {26:9} I'll favor you, make you fruitful, multiply you, and uphold my covenant with you. {26:10} You'll still be eating old stored goods when you need to make room for the new. {26:11} I'll make my dwelling among you, and I won't despise you. {26:12} I'll walk among you and be your God, and you'll be my people. {26:13} I'm the LORD your God, who brought you out of Egypt so you wouldn't be slaves; I broke the bars of your yoke and made you walk upright. {26:14} But if you won't listen to me and don't follow these commandments, {26:15} and if you reject my decrees and despise my laws, breaking my covenant, {26:16} then I'll bring terror, diseases, and fevers that destroy your eyesight and drain your life away. You'll plant seeds in vain, 'cause your enemies will eat them. {26:17} I'll turn against you, and you'll be defeated by your enemies. Those who hate you will rule over you, and you'll flee when no one's chasing you. {26:18} If after all this you still don't listen, I'll punish you seven times over for your sins. {26:19} I'll break your stubborn pride and make the sky like iron and the ground like bronze. {26:20} Your efforts will be for nothing, 'cause the land won't yield crops, nor will the trees bear fruit. {26:21} If you keep going against me and won't listen, I'll bring seven times more plagues on you for your sins. {26:22} I'll send wild animals to rob you of your children, destroy your livestock, and reduce your numbers until your roads are deserted. {26:23} If you still don't reform and continue to oppose me, {26:24} then I'll oppose you and punish you seven times over for your sins. {26:25} I'll bring a sword to avenge the breaking of my covenant. When you gather in your cities, I'll send a plague among you, and you'll be handed over to your enemies. {26:26} When I cut off your food supply, ten women will bake your bread in one oven and dole it out by weight. You'll eat but not be satisfied. {26:27} If you still don't listen and go against me, {26:28} then I'll go against you in anger and punish you seven times over for your sins. {26:29} You'll eat the flesh of your sons and daughters. {26:30} I'll destroy your high places, smash your idols, and pile your dead bodies on the remains of your idols, and I'll despise you. {26:31} I'll lay waste to your cities and make your sanctuaries desolate, and I won't take pleasure in your offerings. {26:32} I'll make the land desolate, and your enemies living there will be appalled. {26:33} I'll scatter you among the nations and draw my sword against you. Your land will be desolate and your cities in ruins. {26:34} Then the land will enjoy its sabbath years as it lies desolate while you're in your enemies' land. {26:35} As long as it lies desolate, the land will have the rest it didn't get while you lived on it. {26:36} For those of you who survive, I'll make their hearts weak in their enemies' lands. The sound of a windblown leaf will scare them, and they'll flee as if from a sword, and they'll fall even though no one is chasing them. {26:37} They'll stumble over each other as if fleeing a sword, even though no one's pursuing them. You won't be able to stand against your enemies. {26:38} You'll perish among the nations, and your enemies' land will devour you. {26:39} Those of you who remain will waste away in your enemies' lands because of their sins and the sins of their ancestors. {26:40} But if they confess their sins and the sins of their ancestors—their unfaithfulness and hostility toward me, {26:41} which made me hostile toward them and sent them into their enemies' land—then if their uncircumcised hearts are humbled and they accept their guilt, {26:42} I'll remember my covenant with Jacob, Isaac, and Abraham, and I'll remember the land. {26:43} The land will be deserted by them and enjoy its sabbaths while it lies desolate without them. They'll pay for their sins because they rejected my laws and abhorred my decrees. {26:44} Yet despite all this, while they're in their enemies' land, I won't reject or abhor them to destroy them completely or break my covenant with them, 'cause I'm the LORD their God. {26:45} For their sake, I'll remember the covenant with their ancestors, whom I brought out of Egypt in the sight of the nations to be their God. I'm the LORD. {26:46} These are the decrees, laws, and regulations the LORD established between himself and the Israelites through Moses on Mount Sinai.

{27:1} And God told Moses, {27:2} "Yo, tell the Israelites: When someone makes a unique vow, people should be evaluated for God based on your judgment. {27:3} For a dude between 20 and 60 years old, the price is fifty shekels of silver, using the sanctuary shekel.

{27:4} For a chick, it's thirty shekels. {27:5} For kids between 5 and 20 years old, a boy's worth twenty shekels, and a girl's worth ten shekels. {27:6} For babies from one month to 5 years old, a boy's value is five shekels of silver, and a girl's value is three shekels of silver. {27:7} For anyone 60 and above, a guy's value is fifteen shekels, and a girl's is ten shekels. {27:8} If the person is broke, he should go to the priest who will set a value based on what he can afford. {27:9} If it's an animal fit for offering to God, it's holy once given. {27:10} Don't swap it, good for bad or bad for good; if you do, both animals become holy. {27:11} If it's an unclean animal not fit for offering, present it to the priest. {27:12} The priest will set its value, whether it's good or bad; what he says goes. {27:13} If the owner wants to buy it back, he adds a fifth to the set value. {27:14} When someone dedicates their house as holy to God, the priest will assess its value, good or bad; that's its set value. {27:15} If the owner wants to redeem the house, they add a fifth to the valuation price, and it's theirs. {27:16} If someone dedicates part of their field to God, the value is set based on the seed: a homer of barley is worth fifty shekels of silver. {27:17} If they dedicate it in the Jubilee year, the full valuation stands. {27:18} If after the Jubilee, the priest will adjust the value based on years left till the next Jubilee, reducing the set value. {27:19} If the owner wants to redeem the field, they add a fifth to the set price, and it's assured to them. {27:20} If they don't redeem it or sell it to someone else, it can't be redeemed anymore. {27:21} In the Jubilee, the field becomes holy to God like a devoted field, belonging to the priests. {27:22} If someone dedicates a bought field not part of their original property, {27:23} the priest will assess its value up to the Jubilee year, and it becomes holy to God. {27:24} In the Jubilee year, the field returns to the original owner from whom it was bought. {27:25} All valuations must use the sanctuary shekel, which is twenty gerahs per shekel. {27:26} The firstborn of animals, which are already God's, can't be dedicated; whether ox or sheep, it's already God's. {27:27} If it's an unclean animal, it can be redeemed at its set value plus a fifth; if not redeemed, it's sold at the valuation. {27:28} Anything a person devotes to God, whether human, animal, or field, can't be sold or redeemed; everything devoted is super holy to God. {27:29} No one devoted to destruction can be redeemed; they must be put to death. {27:30} A tithe of everything from the land, seed, or fruit, is holy to God. {27:31} If someone wants to redeem part of their tithe, they add a fifth to its value. {27:32} The tithe of the herd or flock, every tenth animal that passes under the rod, is holy to God. {27:33} Don't check if it's good or bad or swap it; if swapped, both it and its substitute become holy and can't be redeemed. {27:34} These are the commands God gave Moses for the Israelites on Mount Sinai.

Numbers

✦✦✦

{1:1} So, the LORD hit up Moses in the Sinai desert, in the tent of meeting, on the first day of the second month, in the second year after they bounced out of Egypt, saying, {1:2} "Yo, take a headcount of all the Israelites by their families and clans, listing every dude by name; {1:3} every male twenty years old and up, who can serve in the army in Israel. You and Aaron will count them by their divisions. {1:4} And you'll have one dude from each tribe helping out, each the head of his family. {1:5} Here are the names of the dudes who will help: from Reuben, Elizur son of Shedeur; {1:6} from Simeon, Shelumiel son of Zurishaddai; {1:7} from Judah, Nahshon son of Amminadab; {1:8} from Issachar, Nethaneel son of Zuar; {1:9} from Zebulun, Eliab son of Helon; {1:10} from the sons of Joseph: from Ephraim, Elishama son of Ammihud; from Manasseh, Gamaliel son of Pedahzur; {1:11} from Benjamin, Abidan son of Gideoni; {1:12} from Dan, Ahiezer son of Ammishaddai; {1:13} from Asher, Pagiel son of Ocran; {1:14} from Gad, Eliasaph son of Deuel; {1:15} from Naphtali, Ahira son of Enan. {1:16} These were the famous dudes of the community, leaders of their ancestral tribes, heads of the clans of Israel. {1:17} So Moses and Aaron took these men who had been named, {1:18} and on the first day of the second month, they gathered everyone together and listed them by their clans and families, with the names of all the men twenty years old and up, {1:19} just as the LORD commanded Moses. So he counted them in the Sinai desert. {1:20} From the tribe of Reuben, Israel's firstborn, all the men twenty years old and up who could serve in the army were numbered by name, one by one; {1:21} the number from the tribe of Reuben was 46,500. {1:22} From the tribe of Simeon, all the men twenty years old and up who could serve in the army were numbered by name, one by one; {1:23} the number from the tribe of Simeon was 59,300. {1:24} From the tribe of Gad, all the men twenty years old and up who could serve in the army were listed by name, one by one; {1:25} the number from the tribe of Gad was 45,650. {1:26} From the tribe of Judah, all the men twenty years old and up who could serve in the army were listed by name, one by one; {1:27} the number from the tribe of Judah was 74,600. {1:28} From the tribe of Issachar, all the men twenty years old and up who could serve in the army were listed by name, one by one; {1:29} the number from the tribe of Issachar was 54,400. {1:30} From the tribe of Zebulun, all the men twenty years old and up who could serve in the army were listed by name, one by one; {1:31} the number from the tribe of Zebulun was 57,400. {1:32} From the sons of Joseph: from the tribe of Ephraim, all the men twenty years old and up who could serve in the army were listed by name, one by one; {1:33} the number from the tribe of Ephraim was 40,500. {1:34} From the tribe of Manasseh, all the men twenty years old and up who could serve in the army were listed by name, one by one; {1:35} the number from the tribe of Manasseh was 32,200. {1:36} From the tribe of Benjamin, all the men twenty years old and up who could serve in the army were listed by name, one by one; {1:37} the number from the tribe of Benjamin was 35,400. {1:38} From the tribe of Dan, all the men twenty years old and up who could serve in the army were listed by name, one by one; {1:39} the number from the tribe of Dan was 62,700. {1:40} From the tribe of Asher, all the men twenty years old and up who could serve in the army were listed by name, one by one; {1:41} the number from the tribe of Asher was 41,500. {1:42} From the tribe of Naphtali, all the men twenty years old and up who could serve in the army were listed by name, one by one; {1:43} the number from the tribe of Naphtali was 53,400. {1:44} These were the dudes counted by Moses and Aaron and the leaders of Israel, twelve men, one from each family. {1:45} So all the Israelites twenty years old and up who could serve in Israel's army were counted by their families; {1:46} the total number was 603,550. {1:47} But the Levites weren't counted along with the other Israelites, {1:48} 'cause the LORD had told Moses, {1:49} "Don't count the tribe of Levi or include them in the census of the other Israelites. {1:50} Instead, put the Levites in charge of the tabernacle of the covenant law, all its equipment, and everything that belongs to it. They are to carry the tabernacle and all its furnishings; they are to take care of it and camp around it. {1:51} Whenever the tabernacle is to move, the Levites are to take it down, and whenever the tabernacle is to be set up, the Levites shall do it. Anyone else who approaches it is to be put to death. {1:52} The rest of the Israelites are to set up their tents by divisions, each of them in their own camp under their standard. {1:53} The Levites, however, are to set up their tents around the tabernacle of the covenant law so that my wrath will not fall on the Israelite community. The Levites are to be responsible for the care of the tabernacle of the covenant law." {1:54} The Israelites did all this just as the LORD commanded Moses.

{2:1} The LORD spoke to Moses and Aaron, saying, {2:2} "Each dude of the Israelites should set up camp under their own flag, by their family signs, around the tent of meeting but at a distance. {2:3} On the east side, where the sun rises, the camp of Judah will set up with their army, and Nahshon, son of Amminadab, will be the captain. {2:4} His crew numbered 74,600. {2:5} Next to him will be the tribe of Issachar, with Nethaneel, son of Zuar, as their captain. {2:6} His crew numbered 54,400. {2:7} Then the tribe of Zebulun, with Eliab, son of Helon, as their captain. {2:8} His crew numbered 57,400. {2:9} All together, the camp of Judah had 186,400. They'll move out first. {2:10} On the south side will be the camp of Reuben with their army, and Elizur, son of Shedeur, will be the captain. {2:11} His crew numbered 46,500. {2:12} Next to him will be the tribe of Simeon, with Shelumiel, son of Zurishaddai, as their captain. {2:13} His crew numbered 59,300. {2:14} Then the tribe of Gad, with Eliasaph, son of Reuel, as their captain. {2:15} His crew numbered 45,650. {2:16} All together, the camp of Reuben had 151,450. They'll move out second. {2:17} Then the tent of meeting with the camp of the Levites will move out in the middle of the camps, as they camp, so they'll move, each in their place under their flags. {2:18} On the west side will be the camp of Ephraim with their army, and Elishama, son of Ammihud, will be the captain. {2:19} His crew numbered 40,500. {2:20} Next to him will be the tribe of Manasseh, with Gamaliel, son of Pedahzur, as their captain. {2:21} His crew numbered 32,200. {2:22} Then the tribe of Benjamin, with Abidan, son of Gideoni, as their captain. {2:23} His crew numbered 35,400. {2:24} All together, the camp of Ephraim had 108,100. They'll move out third. {2:25} On the north side will be the camp of Dan with their army, and Ahiezer, son of Ammishaddai, will be the captain. {2:26} His crew numbered 62,700. {2:27} Next to him will be the tribe of Asher, with Pagiel, son of Ocran, as their captain. {2:28} His crew numbered 41,500. {2:29} Then the tribe of Naphtali, with Ahira, son of Enan, as their captain. {2:30} His crew numbered 53,400. {2:31} All together, the camp of Dan had 157,600. They'll move out last, under their flags. {2:32} So all those numbered among the Israelites by their families were 603,550. {2:33} But the Levites weren't counted among the Israelites, as the LORD commanded Moses. {2:34} The Israelites did everything the LORD commanded Moses: they camped under their flags and moved out, each by their family and their clan.

{3:1} These are the fam histories of Aaron and Moses when the LORD chatted with Moses on Mount Sinai. {3:2} Here are the names of Aaron's sons: Nadab the firstborn, Abihu, Eleazar, and Ithamar. {3:3} These are the names of Aaron's sons, the priests who got anointed and consecrated to serve in the priest's office. {3:4} Nadab and Abihu died before the LORD when they brought some sus fire before Him in the Sinai wilderness, and they had no kids. So Eleazar and Ithamar served as priests under their dad Aaron. {3:5} The LORD spoke to Moses, saying, {3:6} "Bring the Levi squad close, present them to Aaron the priest, so they can serve him. {3:7} They'll handle his duties and the duties of the whole congregation before the tent of meeting, doing the tent service. {3:8} They'll keep all the tools of the tent and the responsibilities of the Israelites, doing the tent service. {3:9} Give the Levites to Aaron and his sons; they're fully given to him from among the Israelites. {3:10} Appoint Aaron and his sons to attend to the priest's office, and any outsider who comes near must be put to death." {3:11} The LORD spoke to Moses, saying, {3:12} "Look, I've taken the Levites from among the Israelites instead of all the firstborns who open the womb among the Israelites, so the Levites are mine; {3:13} Because all the firstborns are mine. On the day I struck down all the firstborns in Egypt, I consecrated all the firstborns in Israel, both humans and animals, to myself. They are mine. I am the LORD." {3:14} The LORD spoke to Moses in the Sinai wilderness, saying, {3:15} "Count the Levites by their families and clans, every male from a month old and up." {3:16} Moses counted them according to the LORD's command. {3:17} These were Levi's sons by their names: Gershon, Kohath, and Merari. {3:18} Here are the names of Gershon's sons by their families: Libni and Shimei. {3:19} Kohath's sons by their families: Amram, Izehar, Hebron, and Uzziel. {3:20} Merari's sons by their families: Mahli and Mushi. These are the Levite families by their fathers' houses. {3:21} From Gershon came the Libnite family and the Shimite family. These are the Gershonite families. {3:22} Those counted of them, all the males a month old and up, were 7,500. {3:23} The Gershonite families camped behind the tent, westward. {3:24} Eliasaph, son of Lael, was the chief of the Gershonites. {3:25} The Gershonites were responsible for the tent, its coverings, the curtain at the entrance of the meeting tent, {3:26} the hangings of the courtyard, the curtain for the courtyard entrance, around the tent and altar, and its cords for all the service. {3:27} From Kohath came the Amramite, Izeharite, Hebronite, and Uzzielite families. These are the Kohathite families. {3:28} All the males a month old and up were 8,600, responsible for the sanctuary duties. {3:29} The Kohathite families camped south of the tent. {3:30} Elizaphan, son of Uzziel, was the chief of the Kohathite families. {3:31} They were responsible for the ark, the table, the lampstand, the altars, the sanctuary vessels, the curtain, and all the service. {3:32} Eleazar, son of Aaron the priest, was chief over the leaders of the Levites and oversaw those responsible for the sanctuary duties. {3:33} From Merari came the Mahlite and Mushite families. These are the Merarite families. {3:34} Those counted of them, all the males a month old and up, were 6,200. {3:35} Zuriel, son of Abihail, was the chief of the Merarite families, who camped north of the tent. {3:36} The Merarites were responsible for the tent boards, bars, pillars, bases, and all its equipment and service items, {3:37} and the surrounding courtyard pillars, bases, pegs, and cords. {3:38} Those camping in front of the tent, eastward, were Moses, Aaron, and his sons, responsible for the sanctuary duties for the Israelites. Any outsider coming near was to be put to death. {3:39} All the Levites counted by Moses and Aaron at the LORD's command, by their families, all the males a month old and up, were 22,000. {3:40} The LORD told Moses, "Count all the firstborn Israelite males a month old and up, and take their names. {3:41} Take the Levites for me (I am the LORD) instead of all the firstborn Israelites, and the Levites' cattle instead of their cattle." {3:42} Moses counted all the firstborn Israelites as the LORD commanded. {3:43} All the firstborn males a month old and up were 22,273. {3:44} The LORD spoke to Moses, saying, {3:45} "Take the Levites instead of all the firstborn Israelites, and the Levites' cattle instead of their cattle; the Levites are mine. I am the LORD. {3:46} To redeem the 273 firstborn Israelites who outnumber the Levites, {3:47} take five shekels each, by the sanctuary shekel (20 gerahs per shekel), {3:48} and give the redemption money to Aaron and his sons." {3:49} Moses collected the redemption money from those who were over and above the redeemed by the Levites. {3:50} From the firstborn Israelites, he collected 1,365 shekels, by the sanctuary shekel. {3:51} Moses gave the redemption money to Aaron and his sons, according to the LORD's command.

{4:1} And the LORD spoke to Moses and Aaron, saying, {4:2} "Count the Kohath boys from Levi's squad, by families, by dads' houses, {4:3} from 30 to 50 years old, everyone who can squad up to work in the congregation's tent. {4:4} This is the job of the Kohath squad in the congregation tent, dealing with the holy stuff: {4:5} When the camp moves, Aaron and his sons will come and take down the veil and cover the Ark of the Testimony with it, {4:6} then throw a badger skin cover over it and a blue cloth on top, and put the poles in place. {4:7} On the shewbread table, spread a blue cloth, set the dishes, spoons, bowls, and covers, and the continuous bread will be on it; {4:8} spread a scarlet cloth, cover it with badger skins, and put in the poles. {4:9} Take a blue cloth and cover the lampstand, lamps, tongs, snuffdishes, and oil vessels used with it, {4:10} put all this stuff in a badger skin cover on a bar. {4:11} Spread a blue cloth on the golden altar, cover it with badger skins, and put the poles in place. {4:12} Take all the ministry tools used in the sanctuary, wrap them in a blue cloth, cover them with badger skins, and put them on a bar. {4:13} Remove the ashes from the altar and spread a purple cloth over it, {4:14} place all the altar tools—censers, fleshhooks, shovels, basins, and vessels—and cover with badger skins, then put the poles in place. {4:15} When Aaron and his sons finish covering the sanctuary and tools as the camp moves, the Kohath boys will come to carry them, but they can't touch any holy stuff, or they'll die. This is the load of the Kohath boys in the congregation tent. {4:16} Eleazar, Aaron's son, is in charge of the oil for the light, the sweet incense, the daily offering, the anointing oil, and the oversight of the whole tabernacle and its tools. {4:17} The LORD spoke to Moses and Aaron, saying, {4:18} "Don't let the Kohathite families be cut off from the Levites, {4:19} do this so they live and not die when approaching the holy stuff: Aaron and his sons will assign each person their service and load, {4:20} but they can't go in to see the holy stuff being wrapped, or they'll die." {4:21} The LORD spoke to Moses, saying, {4:22} "Count the Gershon boys by families and dads' houses; {4:23} from 30 to 50 years old, everyone who can serve in the congregation's tent. {4:24} This is the Gershonites' service and load: {4:25} they'll carry the curtains of the tabernacle, the congregation tent, its covering, the badger skin cover, and the entrance curtain, {4:26} the court hangings, the gate curtain, the altar, and all the service tools. {4:27} Aaron and his sons will oversee all their service and load, assigning each task. {4:28} This is the Gershonites' job under Ithamar, Aaron's son. {4:29} Count the Merari boys by families and dads' houses; {4:30} from 30 to 50 years old, everyone who can serve in the congregation's tent. {4:31} Their load is the tabernacle's boards, bars, pillars, and sockets, {4:32} the court pillars, sockets, pins, cords, and all their tools. {4:33} This is the service of the Merari families under Ithamar, Aaron's son. {4:34} Moses, Aaron, and the chiefs counted the Kohathites by families and dads' houses, {4:35} from 30 to 50 years old, everyone who could serve in the congregation's tent; {4:36} there were 2,750 of them. {4:37} These are the Kohathites counted for service in the congregation's tent, as Moses and Aaron numbered them by the LORD's command. {4:38} The Gershon boys were also numbered by families and dads' houses, {4:39} from 30 to 50 years old, everyone who could serve in the congregation's tent; {4:40} there were 2,630 of them. {4:41} These are the Gershonites counted for service in the congregation's tent, as Moses and Aaron numbered them by the LORD's command. {4:42} The Merari boys were numbered by families and dads' houses, {4:43} from 30 to 50 years who could serve in the congregation's tent; {4:44} there were 3,200 of them. {4:45} These are the Merarites counted for service in the congregation's tent, as Moses and Aaron numbered them by the LORD's command. {4:46} All the Levites were numbered by families and dads' houses, {4:47} from 30 to 50 years old, everyone who could serve in the ministry and the congregation's tent; {4:48} there were 8,580 of them. {4:49} They were numbered by Moses as commanded by the LORD, each assigned to their service and load.

{5:1} The LORD spoke to Moses, saying, {5:2} "Tell the Israelites to kick out every leper, everyone with a discharge, and anyone unclean from touching a dead body, {5:3} whether male or female, out of the camp so they don't make the camp, where I live, unclean." {5:4} So the Israelites did as the LORD told Moses and kicked them out of the camp. {5:5} Then the LORD spoke to Moses, saying, {5:6} "Tell the Israelites, when anyone commits a sin against the LORD and feels guilty, {5:7} they must confess their sin, repay what they owe, add a fifth more, and give it to the person they wronged. {5:8} If the person has no relative to repay, give the restitution to the LORD, for the priest, along with a ram for atonement. {5:9} Every holy offering brought by the Israelites to the priest belongs to him. {5:10} Each man's sacred gifts are his; whatever anyone gives the priest is his." {5:11} The LORD spoke to Moses, saying, {5:12} "Tell the Israelites, if a man's wife cheats on him, {5:13} and sleeps with another man without her husband knowing, and there's no witness, {5:14} but her husband gets jealous and suspects her, whether she's guilty or not, {5:15} he must bring his wife to the priest with a barley flour offering, no oil or incense, as it's a jealousy offering, a reminder of guilt. {5:16} The priest will bring her before the LORD, {5:17} take holy water in a clay jar, add some tabernacle floor dust, {5:18} set the woman before the LORD, uncover her head, put the jealousy offering in her hands, and hold the bitter water that brings a curse. {5:19} The priest will make her swear, "If no man has slept with you and you haven't cheated, be free from this bitter water. {5:20} But if you've cheated, {5:21} the priest will make her swear an oath with a curse: "May the LORD make you a curse among your people, causing your thigh to rot and belly to swell; {5:22} may this water curse your insides, making your belly swell and thigh rot." The woman will say, "Amen, amen." {5:23} The priest will write the curses and wash them off into the bitter water, {5:24} and make the woman drink it. {5:25} The priest will take the jealousy offering from her hands, wave it before the LORD, and burn it on the altar, {5:26} take a handful as a memorial, burn it, and make her drink the water. {5:27} If she's guilty, the water will curse her, making her belly swell and thigh rot, and she will be a curse among her people. {5:28} If she's innocent, she will be free and can have children. {5:29} This is the law of jealousy for a wife who cheats, {5:30} or if a husband gets jealous and suspects his wife. He will bring her before the LORD, and the priest will do all this. {5:31} The man will be free from guilt, but the woman will bear her sin.

{6:1} And the LORD spoke to Moses, saying, {6:2} "Tell the Israelites, if anyone wants to take a Nazarite vow to get closer to the LORD, {6:3} they gotta avoid wine, strong drinks, vinegar, and anything made from grapes, no fresh or dried grapes either. {6:4} During their vow, they can't eat anything from the vine, not even the seeds or skin. {6:5} They can't cut their hair until the vow is over, letting it grow to show they're dedicated to the LORD. {6:6} They can't go near any dead body the whole time, {6:7} not even for family members if they die, because they're set apart for God. {6:8} They're holy to the LORD all the days of their vow. {6:9} If someone dies suddenly next to them and makes them unclean, they must shave their head on the seventh day for cleansing. {6:10} On the eighth day, they bring two doves or pigeons to the priest at the tabernacle entrance, {6:11} and the priest offers one as a sin offering and the other as a burnt offering to make atonement and rededicate their head. {6:12} They then restart their vow days and bring a year-old lamb for a guilt offering, but the previous days don't count because they were defiled. {6:13} When their vow period ends, they come to the tabernacle entrance, {6:14} bringing a year-old male lamb without blemish for a burnt offering, a year-old female lamb for a sin offering, and a blemish-free ram for a peace offering, {6:15} plus a basket of unleavened bread, cakes mixed with oil, and wafers anointed with oil, along with grain and drink offerings. {6:16} The priest will present these before the LORD, offering the sin and burnt offerings, {6:17} and then the ram for the peace offering with the unleavened bread basket, plus the grain and drink offerings. {6:18} The Nazarite then shaves their head at the tabernacle entrance and puts the hair into the fire under the peace offering sacrifice. {6:19} The priest will take the boiled ram shoulder, an unleavened cake, and an unleavened wafer, and place them in the Nazarite's hands after the hair is shaved. {6:20} The priest will wave these before the LORD as a wave offering, which is holy for the priest along with the waved breast and the heaved shoulder. After this, the Nazarite can drink wine. {6:21} This is the law for Nazarites who take vows and their offerings to the LORD for their separation, besides whatever else they can afford, according to their vow of separation. {6:22} The LORD spoke to Moses, saying, {6:23} "Tell Aaron and his sons to bless the Israelites like this: {6:24} 'The LORD bless you and keep you; {6:25} the LORD make his face shine on you and be gracious to you; {6:26} the LORD lift up his countenance on you and give you peace.' {6:27} They shall put my name on the Israelites, and I will bless them."

{7:1} So, like, when Moses finished setting up the tabernacle all legit, anointed it, and made it all holy, including all the stuff like the altar and the vessels, he gave them a makeover and made them holy too. {7:2} Then the big shots of Israel, heads of their fams and leaders of the tribes, brought their game: six fancy wagons and twelve oxen. One wagon for every two leaders and an ox for each one, and they rolled up to the tabernacle. {7:3} The Lord told Moses, "Yo, take these wheels and oxen to handle the tabernacle work and give 'em to the Levites according to their gigs." {7:4} So Moses hooked up the wagons and oxen to the Levites. {7:5} Two wagons and four oxen went to the Gershon crew, as per their job. {7:6} Four wagons and eight oxen were given to the Merari crew, under Ithamar, Aaron's son, the priest. {7:7} But the Kohath crew got no wheels 'cause their job was carrying stuff on their shoulders. {7:8} The big shots made offerings to dedicate the altar when it was anointed. Each prince gave their offering at the altar. {7:9} The first prince to step up was Nahshon, from team Judah. {7:10} He brought a silver charger weighing 130 shekels, a silver bowl of 70 shekels, and a gold spoon of 10 shekels, all filled with fine flour and oil for a feast. Plus, a young bullock, ram, and lamb for burnt offerings, and a goat kid for sinning, and loads more for peace offerings. {7:11} This was Nahshon's deal, straight up. {7:12} Next in line was Nethaneel from Issachar, bringing the same swag but repping his tribe. {7:13} Then Eliab from Zebulun stepped up with his offering. {7:14} Following him was Elizur from Reuben, with the same package. {7:15} Shelumiel from Simeon kept the vibe going on his day. {7:16} Eliasaph from Gad rolled in with his offering. {7:17} Elishama from Ephraim brought his flavor to the altar. {7:18} Then came Gamaliel from Manasseh with his contribution. {7:19} Abidan from Benjamin kept the offerings flowing. {7:20} Ahiezer from Dan was next up on his day. {7:21} Pagiel from Asher followed suit. {7:22} Finally, Ahira from Naphtali closed out the dedication with his offering. {7:23} This whole deal with the altar dedication was straight-up legit, done by the Israel princes. Twelve silver chargers, bowls, and gold spoons, each weighing right, for real. {7:24} Each silver charger was 130 shekels, and each bowl was 70 shekels, adding up to 2,400 shekels in total, all legit. {7:25} Twelve gold spoons, each weighing ten shekels, all in tune with the sanctuary scale. {7:26-29} So Eliab, son of Helon, came through with his offering: a golden spoon with ten shekels of incense, a young bullock, a ram, and a lamb (all first-year), for a burnt offering, and a kid of the goats for a sin offering. Plus, he threw down two oxen, five rams, five he-goats, and five yearling lambs for peace offerings. {7:30-35} Then on the fourth day, Elizur (son of Shedeur) from Reuben brought his game: a silver charger weighing 130 shekels, a silver bowl of 70 shekels, both filled with fine flour and oil. He also had a golden spoon with ten shekels of incense, a young bullock, a ram, and a lamb (all first-year) for burnt offerings, and a kid of the goats for sinning. Plus, two oxen, five rams, five he-goats, and five yearling lambs for peace offerings. {7:36-41} Shelumiel (son of Zurishaddai) from Simeon then stepped up on the fifth day with his offering: a silver charger of 130 shekels, a silver bowl of 70 shekels, both filled with fine flour and oil. He also had a golden spoon with ten shekels of incense, a young bullock, a ram, and a lamb (all first-year) for burnt offerings, and a kid of the goats for a sin offering. Plus, two oxen, five rams, five he-goats, and five yearling lambs for peace offerings. {7:42-47} On the sixth day, Eliasaph (son of Deuel) from Gad made his move: a silver charger of 130 shekels, a silver bowl of 70 shekels, both with fine flour and oil. He also had a golden spoon with ten shekels of incense, a young bullock, a ram, and a lamb (all first-year) for burnt offerings, and a kid of the goats for a sin offering. Plus, two oxen, five rams, five he-goats, and five yearling lambs for peace offerings. {7:48-53} Finally, on the seventh day, Elishama (son of Ammihud) from Ephraim brought his offering: a silver charger of 130 shekels, a silver bowl of 70 shekels, both filled with fine flour and oil. He also had a golden spoon with ten shekels of incense, a young bullock, a ram, and a lamb (all first-year) for burnt offerings, and a kid of the goats for a sin offering. Plus, two oxen, five rams, five he-goats, and five yearling lambs for peace offerings. {7:54-59} On the eighth day, Gamaliel, the boss of the Manasseh crew, came through: he dropped one silver charger weighing a hundred and thirty shekels, plus one silver bowl of seventy shekels, both packed with fine flour and oil for a meat offering. Also, he had a lit golden spoon with ten shekels of incense, along with a young bullock, a ram, and a first-year lamb for a burnt offering, and a goat kid for a sin offering. Not to forget, two oxen, five rams, five he-goats, and five yearling lambs for peace offerings—straight from Gamaliel, son of Pedahzur. {7:60-66} Then on the ninth day, Abidan from Benjamin stepped up: his offering included a silver charger weighing a hundred and thirty shekels, and a silver bowl of seventy shekels, both filled with fine flour and oil. He also brought a golden spoon with ten shekels of incense, a young bullock, a ram, and a first-year lamb for a burnt offering, and a goat kid for a sin offering. Additionally, he presented two oxen, five rams, five he-goats, and five yearling lambs for peace offerings—Abidan, son of Gideoni, representing. {7:66-71} Next up, on the tenth day, Ahiezer from Dan made his move: his offering was a silver charger weighing a hundred and thirty shekels, and a silver bowl of seventy shekels, both filled with fine flour and oil. He also had a golden spoon with ten shekels of incense, a young bullock, a ram, and a first-year lamb for a burnt offering, and a goat kid for a sin offering. Plus, two oxen, five rams, five he-goats, and five yearling lambs for peace offerings—Ahiezer, son of Ammishaddai, stepping up. {7:72-76} Then on the eleventh day, Pagiel from Asher came through: he dropped a silver charger weighing a hundred and thirty shekels, and a silver bowl of seventy shekels, both filled with fine flour and oil. He also brought a golden spoon with ten shekels of incense, a young bullock, a ram, and a first-year lamb for a burnt offering, and a goat kid for a sin offering. Not to mention, two oxen, five rams, five he-goats, and five yearling lambs for peace offerings—Pagiel, son of Ocran, representing Asher. {7:78} Finally, on the twelfth day, Ahira from Naphtali came through: his offering included a silver charger weighing a hundred and thirty shekels, and a silver bowl of seventy shekels, both filled with fine flour and oil. He also brought a golden spoon with ten shekels of incense, a young bullock, a ram, and a first-year lamb for a burnt offering, and a goat kid for a sin offering. Alongside, two oxen, five rams, five he-goats, and five yearling lambs for peace offerings—Ahira, son of Enan, representing Naphtali. This was the dedication of the altar, lit up after it got anointed. When Moses went into the tabernacle to chat, he heard a voice from the mercy seat on the ark of testimony, between the two cherubims, speaking to him.

{8:1} So God told Moses, "Yo, talk to Aaron. When you light up those lamps, make sure all seven are shining toward the lampstand." {8:2-6} Aaron did exactly that, lighting the lamps as Moses was told. The candlestick was all gold, crafted according to God's design shown to Moses. {8:6} Then God said, "Grab the Levites from Israel and purify them. {8:7} Sprinkle purifying water on them, have them shave everything, wash their clothes—get them clean. {8:8} Then bring a young bull with a grain offering and another bull for a sin offering. {8:9-10} Bring the Levites before the tabernacle along with the whole Israelite crew. {8:11} Aaron's gonna present the Levites as an offering from Israel to serve the LORD. {8:12} Separate the Levites from the rest of Israel; they belong to me. {8:13} They're mine instead of all the firstborn of Israel, both people and animals. {8:14} I've taken the Levites instead of the firstborn. {8:15} Here's the deal for Levites: from 25 years old and up, they start their service at the tabernacle; {8:16} and at 50, they retire from service and just assist without doing the heavy lifting. This is how you handle the Levites' duties."

{9:1} So, like, God hit up Moses in the Sinai wilderness, in the first month of the second year post-Egypt exodus, saying, "Tell the Israel crew to keep the Passover at the right time." {9:2} It's gotta go down on the fourteenth day of this month, starting in the evening, like all the proper rites and rituals—keep it legit. {9:3} Moses told the Israelites to get on it and keep the Passover as instructed. {9:4} They did it too, on the fourteenth day of the first month, in the evening out in the Sinai wilderness, just like God told Moses. {9:6} Now, some dudes were unclean 'cause they touched a dead body, so they couldn't do the Passover. {9:7} They came to Moses and Aaron like, "Yo, we're defiled, why can't we join in the Lord's offering party with the Israel fam?" {9:8} Moses was like, "Hold up, let me see what God says about this." {9:9} Then God told Moses, "Tell the Israelites that if anyone's unclean 'cause of a dead body or is far away on a journey, they can still do the Passover for the Lord." {9:10} They gotta do it on the fourteenth day of the second month in the evening, chowin' down on unleavened bread and bitter herbs. {9:12} Don't leave any leftovers till morning and don't break any bones—stick to the Passover rules. {9:13} But if someone's clean and around and skips the Passover, they're outta the crew 'cause they didn't bring the Lord's offering at the right time. {9:14} Even if a stranger's chillin' with the Israelites and wants to do the Passover, they gotta follow the same rules—everyone's gotta play by the same Passover playbook, whether native or newbie. {9:15} The day the tabernacle went up, a cloud covered it—the tent of testimony. {9:16} During the day, the cloud was there, and at night, it glowed like fire. {9:17} Whenever the cloud lifted, the Israelites moved out; wherever it settled, they camped. {9:18} They rolled when God said roll, and they chilled when God said chill—just followed the cloud's lead. {9:19} When the cloud stuck around for a while, the Israelites stayed put, followin' God's orders. {9:20} If the cloud hung around for a few days, they'd chill in their tents; when it moved, they moved, all by God's command. {9:21} Day or night, if the cloud moved, they moved too. {9:22} Whether the cloud stayed a couple days, a month, or even a year on the tabernacle, the Israelites stayed put until it moved again, following God's lead. {9:23} They were all about that resting and moving life, strictly following God's orders delivered through Moses.

{10:1} So, the LORD hits up Moses with a message, saying, {10:2} "Yo, make two silver trumpets, carve 'em outta one piece. You'll use 'em to call the crew together and signal when it's time to move camp. {10:3} Blow those bad boys, and the whole squad rolls up to the tabernacle door. {10:4} If you hit one trumpet, just the big shots, the leaders of Israel's thousands, gather to you. {10:5} When you blast an alarm, the camps on the east side move out. {10:6} Second blast, the southern camps hit the road, and they keep blasting as they roll. {10:7} But when it's assembly time, blow, but no alarm vibe. {10:8} Aaron's boys, the priests, handle the trumpet duty. This setup's forever, for all your descendants. {10:9} And if you're up against enemies in your land, trumpet it up; the LORD will notice, and you'll get saved. {10:10} Also, when you're celebrating, at your festivals, and kicking off each month, give those trumpets a blast over your sacrifices to remember your God. I'm the LORD your God. {10:11} Fast forward to the twentieth day of the second month in the second year; the cloud bounced from the tabernacle. {10:12} Israelites packed up from the Sinai desert, and the cloud chilled in Paran. {10:13} They rolled out following Moses' orders. {10:14} Judah's camp led the way, with Nahshon leading. {10:15} Issachar had Nethaneel; Zebulun, Eliab. {10:16-17} The tabernacle got packed up, with Gershon and Merari hauling it. {10:18-20} Reuben's camp followed, led by Elizur; Simeon had Shelumiel, and Gad, Eliasaph. {10:21} The Kohathites carried the sanctuary, setting it up when they stopped. {10:22-24} Ephraim's camp went next, with Elishama; Manasseh had Gamaliel, and Benjamin, Abidan. {10:25-28} Dan's camp brought up the rear, led by Ahiezer; Asher had Pagiel, and Naphtali, Ahira. {10:28} That's how the Israelite squads rolled out, organized by their armies. {10:29} Moses hits up Hobab, his Midianite father-in-law, saying, "We're heading to the spot the LORD promised us. Roll with us, and we'll hook you up; the LORD's got good plans for Israel." {10:30} But Hobab's like, "Nah, I'll pass; I'm heading back home to my peeps." {10:31} Moses pleads, "Don't bail on us; you know this wilderness inside out, you'll be our eyes." {10:32} "Stick with us, and whatever blessings the LORD brings, you'll get a piece." {10:33} They dip from the LORD's mountain, three days out. The ark of the covenant led the way, scouting out their resting spots. {10:34} LORD's cloud was on them during the day as they marched. {10:35} When the ark moved, Moses called out, "Yo, LORD, scatter our enemies and make those who hate you run!" {10:36} And when they stopped, he's like, "Come back to us, LORD, we're rolling deep."

{11:1} So, when the people started whining, it seriously ticked off the LORD. He heard their gripes, got super heated, and bam—LORD's fire went down and toasted those on the edges of the camp. {11:2} The people freaked and cried to Moses, and when Moses prayed, the fire chilled out. {11:3} They named the place Taberah 'cause of the LORD's fire show. {11:4} Then the mixed crowd got hungry, and the Israelites were like, "Where's the meat at?" {11:5} They started reminiscing about the good old days in Egypt, when they had fish, cucumbers, melons, leeks, onions, and garlic, no sweat. {11:6} But now it's all about that manna, and they're over it. {11:7} Manna looked like coriander seed and had that bdellium vibe. {11:8} People went around gathering it up, grinding it, baking cakes—tasted like olive oil. {11:9} Dew brought the manna at night. {11:10} Moses heard the crying everywhere, and it ticked off the LORD big time. Even Moses was over it. {11:11} He's like, "Why you putting this on me, LORD?" {11:12} "Did I birth these people? Am I their nanny, carrying them like a father with a baby?" {11:13} "Where am I gonna get meat for all these crybabies?" {11:14} "I can't handle this alone; it's too much." {11:15} "Just end it for me if you're cool with me, so I don't have to deal." {11:16} Then the LORD tells Moses to gather seventy elders who are the real OGs of Israel, and bring them to the tabernacle to stand with him. {11:17} LORD's gonna come down, take Moses' vibe, and pass it to them so they can help carry the load. {11:18} Moses tells the people to get ready for tomorrow, 'cause they're getting meat—LORD heard their whining about Egypt and is serving it up. {11:19} Not just one day, two days, or even five days—try a whole month 'til it's coming out your nose and you're sick of it. {11:20} 'Cause you dissed the LORD and complained about leaving Egypt. {11:21} Moses is like, "We got six hundred thousand foot soldiers; you really gonna give them meat for a month?" {11:22} "You gonna slaughter all the animals or haul in all the fish?" {11:23} LORD's like, "Is my power too weak for you?" {11:24} Moses tells the people, gathers the seventy elders around the tabernacle. {11:25} LORD shows up in a cloud, gives the elders a piece of Moses' vibe, and they start prophesying non-stop. {11:26} Two dudes, Eldad and Medad, start prophesying in the camp; they weren't at the tabernacle meet-up. {11:27} Someone runs to Moses saying Eldad and Medad are prophesying. {11:28} Joshua's like, "Moses, tell them to chill." {11:29} Moses wishes everyone was a prophet with the LORD's spirit. {11:30} Then Moses and the elders head back to camp. {11:31} Then a wind from the LORD blows in quail from the sea, dropping them around the camp—like a day's walk in each direction, two cubits high all over. {11:32} People spent a day and night gathering quail; the least anyone gathered was ten homers. {11:33} But before they could even chew, LORD's wrath hit hard, striking them with a bad plague. {11:34} They called that place Kibroth-hattaavah 'cause that's where they buried those craving meat. {11:35} Then they left Kibroth-hattaavah for Hazeroth and stayed there.

{12:1} So, Miriam and Aaron start gossiping about Moses because of his Ethiopian wife—he really went and married one. {12:2} They're like, "Does the LORD only talk through Moses? Doesn't he speak through us too?" And the LORD heard it. {12:3} (By the way, Moses was the chillest dude on the planet.) {12:4} Then suddenly, the LORD calls out Moses, Aaron, and Miriam to the tabernacle. They all show up. {12:5} The LORD drops in with the cloud, stands at the tabernacle door, and calls Aaron and Miriam out. They step forward. {12:6} The LORD lays it down, saying, "Listen up. When there's a prophet among you, I give them visions and dreams to talk to them. {12:7} But Moses? He's my homie, faithful in everything I'm about. {12:8} I talk to him face to face, clearly—not in riddles. And he sees the LORD's form. So why'd you diss my boy Moses?" {12:9} The LORD gets mad at them and peaces out. {12:10} The cloud bails from the tabernacle, and boom—Miriam's leprous, white as snow. Aaron sees it. {12:11} Aaron's like, "Oh no, Moses, please don't blame us for this foolishness and sin." {12:12} "Don't let her be like a dead person, all messed up." {12:13} Moses cries out to the LORD, "Please heal her, God." {12:14} The LORD tells Moses, "If her dad had spit in her face, wouldn't she be ashamed for seven days? She's out of the camp for seven days, then she can come back in." {12:15} Miriam's out of the camp for seven days, and the crew waits until she's back. {12:16} After that, they bounce from Hazeroth and set up camp in the wilderness of Paran.

{13:1} Then the LORD talks to Moses, saying, {13:2} "Send some dudes to check out the land of Canaan, the land I'm giving to Israel. Each tribe sends a representative." {13:3} Moses follows orders, sending these leaders from the wilderness of Paran—they're heads of Israel's tribes. {13:4-6} Here are their names: from Reuben, Shammua; from Simeon, Shaphat; from Judah, Caleb; {13:7-8} from Issachar, Igal; from Ephraim, Oshea; {13:9-11} from Benjamin, Palti; from Zebulun, Gaddiel; {13:12-14} from Dan, Ammiel; from Asher, Sethur; {13:15} from Gad, Geuel. {13:16} These are the dudes Moses sent to spy out the land. Moses renames Oshea to Jehoshua. {13:17-18} He sends them to Canaan, saying, "Check it out, head south into the mountains, scope the land, peep the people—strong or weak, few or many." {13:19-20} "Check if it's a good land, what kind of cities they have—tents or forts, and how the land is—fat or lean, with trees or not. And be brave, bring back fruit; it's grape season." {13:21} They go up, scouting from Zin to Rehob, like heading to Hamath. {13:22} They hit up Hebron, where giants Anak's kids dwell (Hebron was built seven years before Egypt's Zoan). {13:23-24} They reach Eshcol, grab a giant cluster of grapes, carried by two dudes on a stick, plus pomegranates and figs. {13:25-26} They're back after forty days, reporting to Moses, Aaron, and the crew in Paran, showing them the fruits of Canaan. {13:27} They're like, "It's totally flowing with milk and honey, look at this fruit!" {13:28-31} But—they add—the folks there are strong, cities are walled, giants like Anak are there. {13:32} They give a scary report, saying the land eats up its people; they felt tiny like grasshoppers compared to the giants.

{14:1} So, the whole crew starts bawling their eyes out, crying all night long. {14:2} And then they start trash-talking Moses and Aaron, saying, "Man, we should've died in Egypt or out here in the desert!" {14:3} They're like, "Why'd the LORD bring us here just to get slaughtered? Wouldn't it be better to go back to Egypt?" {14:4} And they're like, "Let's pick a new leader and head back to Egypt." {14:5} Meanwhile, Moses and Aaron hit the ground, face down in front of everyone. {14:6} Joshua and Caleb, the same dudes who scoped out the land, rip their clothes in frustration. {14:7} They're like, "Yo, the land is dope! It's lit!" {14:8} They're like, "If the LORD vibes with us, he'll hook us up with this land, flowing with milk and honey." {14:9} "Just don't rebel against the LORD, and don't be scared of the people there. They're easy pickings for us; their protection is gone, and the LORD's got our backs. Don't even trip." {14:10} But the whole crew wants to stone them. Suddenly, the glory of the LORD shows up in the tabernacle. {14:11} The LORD's fed up, asking Moses, "How long are these people gonna test me? When will they finally trust me, after all the miracles I've shown them?" {14:12} "I'm gonna hit them with a plague, disown them, and make a new nation out of you, Moses." {14:13} Moses is like, "Hold up, if you wipe them out, the Egyptians will hear about it." {14:14} "They'll tell everyone how you're with us, appearing face to face, leading us with a cloud and fire. {14:15-16} If you wipe them out, people will think you couldn't handle bringing us to the promised land." {14:17-19} Moses is like, "Show off your power, forgive their mess, like you always do." {14:20} The LORD's like, "Alright, I'll forgive them as you asked." {14:21} "But trust me, everyone's gonna see my glory everywhere." {14:22-24} "Those who saw my miracles but still messed up—none of them will see the promised land, except Caleb. He's got the right attitude, so he's in. {14:25} Now, head back to the wilderness tomorrow, toward the Red Sea." {14:26} Then the LORD talks to Moses and Aaron, saying, {14:27} "How long do I have to deal with these whiners? I've heard enough of their complaining." {14:28} "Tell them, as they spoke in my ears, that's what's gonna happen to them." {14:29} "Their bodies will drop in this desert, all of them over twenty who whined against me." {14:30} "None of them will see the promised land except Caleb and Joshua." {14:31} "But the kids they were so scared for, I'll bring them in—they'll see the land these fools despised." {14:32} "But as for these whiners, their bodies will drop in this desert." {14:33} "Their kids will wander for forty years, paying for their parents' mistakes, until they drop dead too." {14:34} "Each day they spent scoping the land, they'll pay for it with a year of wandering—forty years for forty days—so they'll know I keep my word." {14:35} "This whole rebellious crew will die out here in the desert." {14:36-37} "Those dudes who gave the bad report about the land, they died from the plague before the LORD." {14:38} But Joshua and Caleb are still kicking. {14:39} Moses spills all this to the Israelites, and they're all super bummed out. {14:40} Early next morning, they try to go up the mountain, saying, "We messed up, let's go to the promised land!" {14:41} Moses is like, "Why are you disobeying the LORD? It won't end well." {14:42} "The LORD isn't with you; you'll get wrecked by your enemies." {14:43} "The Amalekites and Canaanites are waiting to destroy you because you turned away from the LORD." {14:44} But they still try to go up the hill. Meanwhile, Moses and the ark of the covenant stay put in camp. {14:45} Then the Amalekites and Canaanites come down and crush them, wiping them out until Hormah.

{15:1} So, the LORD hits up Moses, like, "Yo, tell the Israelites when they finally settle in the land I'm hooking them up with," {15:2-3} "They gotta make fire offerings, burnt offerings, sacrifices for vows, freewill offerings, and feasts—all to give off that sweet scent to the LORD, using animals from their herds or flocks." {15:4} "Whoever brings an offering to the LORD needs to include a tenth of flour mixed with oil." {15:5} "And don't forget the wine for the drink offering with each lamb." {15:6-7} "For a ram, double the flour with oil, and the wine increases too." {15:8} "If it's a bull for a burnt offering, vow, or peace offering, bring three tenths of flour with half a hin of oil." {15:9-10} "And half a hin of wine for the drink offering—makes that sweet scent for the LORD." {15:11} "Same deal whether it's a bull, ram, lamb, or goat." {15:12} "Do this according to the number of offerings you bring." {15:13} "All Israelites must follow these rules when offering fire offerings." {15:14-16} "Even strangers living among you must follow the same rules when making offerings to the LORD." {15:17-18} Then the LORD tells Moses again, like, "When you get to the land I'm bringing you to," {15:19} "Whenever you eat bread from the land, give a portion to the LORD as a heave offering." {15:20-21} "Offer the first of your dough as a heave offering, just like you do with grain from the threshing floor." {15:22-23} "If you mess up and forget any of these commands, and the congregation doesn't know," {15:24-25} "Everyone offers a young bull as a burnt offering and a goat as a sin offering." {15:26} "The priest atones for everyone's ignorance with these offerings, and they're forgiven." {15:27} "If anyone sins unintentionally, they bring a one-year-old she-goat as a sin offering." {15:28-31} "The priest atones for their ignorance before the LORD, and they're forgiven." {15:32-34} "But anyone who intentionally disobeys, Israelite or stranger, disrespects the LORD and gets cut off from the people." {15:36} "Oh, and by the way, when the Israelites found a dude gathering sticks on the Sabbath," {15:35} "The LORD said, 'Stone him outside the camp,' so the whole congregation did just that." {15:37} Then the LORD tells Moses to tell the Israelites to add fringes with a blue thread on their garments as a reminder to obey all his commandments and not follow their own hearts and desires, but to stay dedicated to God, the one who brought them out of Egypt.

{16:1} So there's this guy Korah, son of Izhar, a Levi, and Dathan and Abiram, sons of Eliab, along with On, son of Peleth from the tribe of Reuben, got together {16:2-3} with two hundred and fifty big shots from Israel, all famous dudes in the community, and they confront Moses and Aaron saying, "Why are you acting so high and mighty? We're all holy, and the LORD is among us. Who made you the rulers over us?" {16:4} When Moses hears this, he hits the ground face-first. {16:5-7} Then he tells Korah and his crew, "Tomorrow the LORD will reveal who's really chosen and holy. Let's do this: each of you take a censer with fire and incense before the LORD." {16:8-11} Moses tells Korah, "Seriously? God chose you Levi dudes to serve in the tabernacle, and now you're going after the priesthood too?" {16:12-14} Moses sends for Dathan and Abiram, but they refuse to come, saying, "You led us out here to die in the desert instead of a land flowing with milk and honey. Now you want to boss us around like princes?" {16:15} Moses is ticked off and tells the LORD not to accept their offering, because he hasn't taken anything from them or wronged them. {16:16-18} Then Moses tells Korah and his crew, "Tomorrow you, Aaron, and I will bring our censers before the LORD." {16:19-20} Korah gathers everyone against Moses and Aaron at the tabernacle, and boom, the glory of the LORD shows up. {16:21} The LORD tells Moses and Aaron, "Step away from this group so I can wipe them out in an instant." {16:22-23} Moses and Aaron fall on their faces and plead with God not to punish the whole congregation for one guy's sin. {16:24-25} Moses tells everyone to move away from Korah, Dathan, and Abiram's tents. {16:26-30} The people back up, and Dathan and Abiram come out with their families. {16:31} As soon as Moses finishes talking, the ground opens up and swallows Korah, Dathan, Abiram, and their families. {16:32} Then fire comes out from the LORD and takes out the two hundred and fifty dudes with their incense. {16:33} Next day, the Israelites start blaming Moses and Aaron for killing the LORD's people. {16:34} Moses tells Aaron to grab a censer, put incense in it, and make atonement for the people because a plague has started. {16:35} Aaron stands between the dead and the living, and the plague stops. {16:36} Fourteen thousand seven hundred people die from the plague, not counting those from Korah's crew.

{17:1-2} So God tells Moses, "Yo, speak to the Israelites and have each of them grab a rod representing their family house, twelve in total, with each prince's name on it." {17:3} Aaron's rod is tagged for Levi's house, the top dog. {17:4} These rods are stashed in the tabernacle as a sign of God's meeting place. {17:5} God's like, "Watch this: the rod of the guy I choose will blossom, shutting down the Israelites' complaints against you." {17:6} Moses tells the Israelite leaders to hand over their rods, including Aaron's. {17:7} Moses puts the rods before the LORD in the tabernacle. {17:8-9} Next day, Aaron's rod representing Levi has blossomed with buds, flowers, and almonds. {17:10-11} God tells Moses to keep Aaron's rod as proof against the complainers, so they stop griping and dying. {17:12} The Israelites freak out, thinking they'll all perish. {17:13} They're scared to even go near the tabernacle, fearing death.

{18:1} Then God tells Aaron, "You and your sons will bear the responsibility for the sanctuary and priesthood." {18:2} Other Levites will assist you, but only you and your sons will serve before the tabernacle. {18:4} They'll take care of the tabernacle service but must stay away from the sacred items to avoid death. {18:7} God assigns the Levites to assist Aaron and his sons in their priestly duties; anyone else who gets too close will be killed. {18:8} God also gives Aaron the charge over offerings from the Israelites forever. {18:11} All the best offerings belong to Aaron and his family, a perpetual statute. {18:20} God tells Aaron he won't inherit land among the Israelites; God is his inheritance. {18:21} Instead, God gives the Levites the tithes from Israel as their inheritance for their service at the tabernacle. {18:24} The tithes are the Levites' inheritance since they can't own land. {18:26} Moses tells the Levites to give a tenth of their tithes as an offering to the LORD, like grain and wine. {18:30} After giving their best portion, the Levites can enjoy it with their families as a reward for their service.

{19:1} So God hits up Moses and Aaron, saying, "Here's the law: tell the Israelites to bring a flawless red heifer that's never been used for work. {19:3} Give it to Eleazar the priest outside the camp to slaughter. {19:4} Eleazar will sprinkle its blood toward the tabernacle seven times. {19:5} Then burn the whole heifer—skin, flesh, blood, and dung—right before him. {19:6} Toss in cedar wood, hyssop, and scarlet into the burning heifer. {19:7} After that, the priest has to wash his clothes and bathe, but he's unclean until evening. {19:8} The guy who burns the heifer also has to wash up and is unclean until evening. {19:9} Someone clean collects the ashes and stores them outside the camp in a clean spot for a water of purification—it's for sin. {19:10} The guy who gathers the ashes has to wash his clothes and is unclean until evening. {19:11} If you touch a dead body, you're unclean for seven days. {19:12} You gotta purify yourself with this stuff on the third and seventh day to be clean. {19:13} If you don't, you're defiling the tabernacle and get cut off from Israel. {19:14} If someone dies in a tent, everyone and everything inside is unclean for seven days. {19:15} Any open container is also unclean. {19:16} If you touch a dead body, bone, or grave, you're unclean for seven days. {19:17} Use the ashes from the red heifer and mix them with running water in a vessel for purification. {19:18} Sprinkle the water on the tent, vessels, and people who touched bones, dead bodies, or graves. {19:19} On the third and seventh day, sprinkle them again. {19:20} If you don't purify yourself, you're cut off from the congregation for defiling the sanctuary. {19:21} This rule's forever: anyone handling the water of purification has to wash up, and touching it makes you unclean until evening. {19:22} Whatever an unclean person touches becomes unclean, and they stay unclean until evening.

{20:1} So the whole crew of Israel rolled into the desert of Zin in the first month and camped at Kadesh. Miriam passed away and was buried there. {20:2} But then they hit a major issue—no water at all for the crew. So they started grumbling against Moses and Aaron. {20:3} People were beefing with Moses, saying, "Man, we wish we had just died like our brothers before the Lord!" {20:4} They were like, "Why'd you drag us out here into this desert to die, us and our livestock?" {20:5} "And why'd you drag us out of Egypt to this awful place? No crops, no fruit, no water—what's the deal?" {20:6} So Moses and Aaron dipped out from the assembly and went to the tabernacle door, falling on their faces. That's when the Lord showed up. {20:7-8} God told Moses, "Grab your rod, gather the crew, and speak to the rock in front of everyone. Water will flow from it, and you'll give the people and their animals a drink." {20:9} Moses grabbed the rod as God commanded. {20:10} So Moses and Aaron gathered the crew in front of the rock. Moses said to them, "Listen up, you rebels! Do we really have to get water from this rock for you?" {20:11} Then Moses struck the rock twice with his rod, and water gushed out. The whole crew and their animals drank. {20:12} But because they didn't trust God enough to honor Him before the Israelites, God said Moses and Aaron wouldn't lead the people into the promised land. {20:13} This place was named Meribah, where Israel challenged the Lord and He was honored. {20:14-15} After that, Moses sent messengers from Kadesh to the king of Edom, saying, "Look, our fam has been through a lot in Egypt and we've been there a while. The Egyptians treated us and our ancestors badly. {20:16} But when we cried out to the Lord, He heard us and brought us out of Egypt. Now we're in Kadesh, on your border. {20:17} Let us pass through your land. We won't go through your fields or vineyards or drink your water. We'll stick to the highway until we're out of your territory." {20:18} But Edom refused and threatened to come out against them with swords. {20:19} So Israel offered to pay for any water they drank and promised to only pass through on foot. {20:20} Edom still said no and came out against them with a big crew. {20:21} So Israel had to turn away. {20:22-23} Then the whole crew of Israel left Kadesh and arrived at Mount Hor. {20:24} God told Moses and Aaron at Mount Hor that Aaron would die because they rebelled against God's command at Meribah. {20:25} Moses was to take Aaron and Eleazar up Mount Hor, where Aaron would pass away. {20:26-27} Moses was to transfer Aaron's garments to Eleazar, and Aaron would die there. {20:28} Moses did as God commanded, and Aaron passed away on top of the mountain. Moses and Eleazar came down afterward. {20:29} When the whole crew saw Aaron was gone, they mourned for him for thirty days.

{21:1} So, like, when King Arad the Canaanite, who lived in the south, heard that Israel had come through the spy route, he straight up attacked Israel and captured some of them. {21:2} Then Israel made a promise to the Lord, saying, "If you deliver these people into my hands, I'll totally wipe out their cities." {21:3} The Lord listened to Israel and handed over the Canaanites; they totally destroyed them and their cities, and the place was named Hormah. {21:4} After leaving Mount Hor by the Red Sea route to circle around Edom, the people's spirits were totally down because of the journey. {21:5} Then the people started complaining against God and Moses, like, "Why'd you bring us out of Egypt to die in this wilderness? There's no bread, no water, and we're sick of this bland food." {21:6} So the Lord sent fiery serpents among them, and many Israelites died from their bites. {21:7} The people then came to Moses, admitting they'd sinned against the Lord and him, asking Moses to pray and remove the serpents. {21:8-9} The Lord told Moses to make a bronze serpent and put it on a pole. When anyone was bitten and looked at the serpent, they'd live. {21:10} The Israelites moved on and camped in Oboth. {21:11} They left Oboth and camped at Ije Abarim, in the wilderness facing Moab to the east. {21:12} From there they moved to the Zared Valley. {21:13} Then they moved across the Arnon and camped in the wilderness that extends into Amorite territory. {21:14} This area is known for what the Lord did in the Red Sea and the Arnon River, {21:15} and at the streams flowing down to the settlement of Ar, on the Moabite border. {21:16} From there they went to Beer, where the Lord told Moses to gather the people for water. {21:17} So Israel sang, "Spring up, O well! Sing about it!" {21:18-19} The leaders dug the well, guided by the lawgiver, using their staffs. Then they moved on to Mattanah, Nahaliel, and Bamoth. {21:20} From Bamoth in the Moabite valley, they went to the top of Pisgah, overlooking Jeshimon. {21:21-22} Israel sent messengers to Sihon, king of the Amorites, asking to pass through peacefully. {21:23} But Sihon refused and attacked Israel in the wilderness, reaching Jahaz. {21:24} Israel defeated Sihon and took his land from Arnon to Jabbok, to the Ammonite border. {21:25} They captured all the Amorite cities, settling in Heshbon and its villages. {21:26} Heshbon was the former city of Sihon, who fought against Moab and took its land up to Arnon. {21:27-28} There's a saying: "Come to Heshbon; let Sihon's city be rebuilt and established." {21:29} Woe to Moab! They're undone, given over to Sihon by Chemosh. {21:30} They attacked Heshbon, destroying it as far as Dibon and Nophah, up to Medeba. {21:31} So Israel settled in the land of the Amorites. {21:32} Moses sent spies to Jazer, capturing its villages and driving out the Amorites there. {21:33} They went up through Bashan, where King Og of Bashan and his people came out to fight at Edrei. {21:34} The Lord told Moses not to fear, for He'd delivered Og and his land into their hands, just like Sihon. {21:35} So they defeated Og, his sons, and all his people, possessing his land completely.

{22:1} So the Israelites moved and camped in the plains of Moab near Jericho. {22:2} Balak, Zippor's son, peeped all the action against the Amorites by Israel. {22:3} Moab got shook because there were so many Israelites, and they were stressed out. {22:4} Moab told the Midian elders, "This crew is gonna devour everything around us like an ox munches on grass. Balak's the Moab king RN." {22:5} Balak hit up Balaam, Beor's son in Pethor, saying, "Yo, these Egypt escapees are deep; they're all up in my face. {22:6} Curse 'em for me; they're too strong. If you bless, it's blessed; if you curse, it's cursed." {22:7} So the Moab and Midian elders rolled up to Balaam with their divination rewards, delivering Balak's message. {22:8} Balaam was like, "Crash here tonight; I'll hit you back after I hear from the LORD." {22:9} God hit up Balaam, "Who's with you?" {22:10} Balaam spilled, "Balak wants me to curse these Egypt escapees, hoping we can beat 'em down and kick 'em out." {22:12} God was like, "Nah, don't go or curse 'em; they're blessed." {22:13} Balaam told Balak's crew the LORD said no go. {22:14} Moab's princes went back to Balak with the news. {22:15} Balak sent more VIP princes like, "Come thru; I'll hook you up big time if you curse these folks." {22:16} They told Balaam, "Balak's like, no excuses; just come and curse 'em." {22:18} Balaam's reply was, "Even if Balak paid me in gold and silver, I can't go against the LORD's word." {22:19} "Stay over, I need to hear more from the LORD," he said to them. {22:20} God got at Balaam that night, saying if the men come calling, go but only speak His word. {22:21} Balaam got up, saddled up, and rode out with Moab's VIPs. {22:22} God got mad Balaam went, so the LORD's angel blocked their path. Balaam was riding his donkey with two homies. {22:23} The donkey saw the angel, turned off the road into a field, and Balaam got mad, hitting the donkey to steer her back. {22:24} The angel moved to a vineyard path with walls; the donkey squished Balaam's foot against a wall. {22:25} When the donkey saw the angel again, she jammed Balaam's foot into a wall; he hit her again. {22:26} The angel moved to a narrow spot, nowhere to go left or right; the donkey lay down, and Balaam got even angrier, hitting her with a stick. {22:28} Then the LORD made the donkey talk, asking Balaam why he hit her three times. {22:29} Balaam was like, "You're mocking me; I'd kill you if I had a sword." {22:30} The donkey reminded him they'd been tight since forever and never acted like this before. {22:31} God opened Balaam's eyes; he saw the angel, bowed, and fell flat on his face. {22:32} The angel asked, "Why'd you hit your donkey? I was here to stop you; your path's messed up." {22:33} The angel said if the donkey hadn't stopped, he would've offed Balaam instead. {22:34} Balaam owned up, admitting he messed up, and offered to turn back if it bugged the angel. {22:35} The angel said go with the men, but only speak His words. So Balaam rolled with Balak's crew. {22:36} Balak caught wind and met Balaam at a Moab city by the Arnon border. {22:37} Balak was like, "I called you; why didn't you come? I could hook you up." {22:38} Balaam was like, "I'm here, but I can only speak what God tells me." {22:39} Balaam rolled with Balak to Kirjathhuzoth. {22:40} Balak splurged on oxen and sheep for Balaam and the VIPs. {22:41} Next day, Balak took Balaam to Baal's high spots to peep the Israelite situation.

{23:1} So Balaam hits up Balak like, "Yo, build me seven altars here, and round up seven oxen and seven rams." {23:2} Balak's like, "Word," and they both drop a bullock and a ram on each altar. {23:3} Then Balaam's like, "Yo, chill by your burnt offering, I'm gonna bounce up high, maybe the Big Guy will show and tell me something." {23:4} God vibes with Balaam, telling him He's set up seven altars and offerings. {23:5} God puts words in Balaam's mouth, saying, "Go back to Balak and spill the tea." {23:6} Balaam comes back, and he's all up in his burnt offering zone, with Balak and his Moab crew. {23:7} Then he starts spitting bars, talking about how Balak brought him over to curse Jacob and diss Israel. {23:8} But Balaam's like, "How can I curse when God ain't cursed them? And how can I diss when the Big Guy ain't dissed them?" {23:9} He's like, "From the mountain tops, I peep them, and they're on their own vibe, not blending in with other nations." {23:10} Then he's like, "Who can even count the dust of Jacob? Let me vibe like the righteous and have a dope ending like theirs." {23:11} Balak's shook, like, "Bro, I brought you to curse my enemies, and now you're blessing them?" {23:12} Balaam's just like, "Hey, I gotta speak what God's putting in my mouth, you know?" {23:13} So Balak's like, "Alright, let's try another spot, maybe you can curse them from there." {23:14} They roll to a new spot, build seven more altars, and drop more offerings. {23:15} Balaam's like, "Stay here by your offering, I'm gonna vibe with the Big Guy." {23:16} God meets him again, giving him more to say to Balak. {23:17} When he comes back, Balak's still posted by his burnt offering, with his Moab squad. He's like, "What's the word from the Big Guy?" {23:18} Balaam's back with another message, telling Balak to listen up. {23:19} He's like, "God ain't human, He don't lie or change His mind. What He says, He does." {23:20} Balaam's like, "I got the blessing vibe from Him, and I can't flip it." {23:21} He's like, "No sin in Jacob, no dirt in Israel, 'cause the Big Guy's got their back, and they're shouting like kings." {23:22} He's like, "God led them out of Egypt, and He's got the strength of a unicorn, straight up." {23:23} Balaam's like, "Ain't no magic or divination working against Jacob and Israel. People are gonna be like, 'Dang, look at what God's doing!'" {23:24} He's like, "These people rise up like lions, ready to feast on their enemies." {23:25} Balak's like, "Bro, don't bless or curse them, just chill." {23:26} But Balaam's like, "Didn't I tell you? I gotta do what God says." {23:27} So Balak's like, "Alright, let's try another spot, maybe God will let you curse them from there." {23:28} They roll to a new spot, and Balaam's like, "Build me seven more altars, and round up more bullocks and rams." {23:29} Balak's like, "Done," and they drop more offerings. {23:30} And that's the vibe, fam.

{24:1} When Balaam peeped that God was vibing with blessing Israel, he didn't even bother with his usual enchantment-seeking vibe. He just turned towards the wilderness. {24:2} Checking out Israel doing their tent life thing by their tribes, he gets hit with the divine spirit. {24:3} So he's like, "Listen up, I'm Balaam, and I got some real talk to spit." {24:4} He's like, "I'm tuned in to God's words, caught a glimpse of the Almighty's vision while in a trance but with eyes wide open." {24:5} He's feeling the vibes of Jacob's dope tents and Israel's chill tabernacles, spreading out like valleys, lush like riverside gardens, and planted by the Lord like cedar trees by water. {24:6-7} He's predicting showers of blessings, abundant offspring, and a king who's next level, towering over Agag, with a kingdom on the rise. {24:8} Remembering the Egypt exodus, he's comparing Israel's strength to a unicorn, ready to conquer and crush enemies with arrows. {24:9} He's laying down lion vibes, daring anyone to mess with them. Blessed are those who bless Israel, and cursed are those who curse them. {24:10} Balak's not feeling the blessing spree and gets heated, like, "Bro, I brought you here to curse my enemies, but you've been blessing them non-stop!" {24:11} So he's like, "Time for you to bounce. I thought I'd hook you up, but clearly, the Big Guy's not feeling it." {24:12-13} But Balaam's like, "Didn't I tell your messengers that even if you loaded me up with cash, I can't go against God's command? I only speak His word." {24:14} Now he's dipping back to his crew, but he's like, "Hit me up later, and I'll give you the 411 on what's going down between our peoples in the future." {24:15-16} Again, he's spitting truth, reminding everyone who he is and how he's got the divine scoop. {24:17} Talking future visions, he sees a star rising from Jacob, a scepter from Israel, bringing down Moab and the sons of Sheth. {24:18} Edom and Seir will fall under Israel's dominance, and they'll be flexing their bravery. {24:19} The ultimate ruler will come from Jacob, taking out any stragglers from the city. {24:20} Gazing at Amalek, he predicts their downfall, despite once being top dog among nations. {24:21-22} He peeps at the Kenites, acknowledging their strength but seeing their future capture by Asshur. {24:23} Reflecting on God's power, he's like, "Who's gonna survive when He's in action?" {24:24} Ships from Chittim will bring trouble to Asshur and Eber, leading to their demise. {24:25} Balaam dips out and heads home, and Balak does the same, maybe to cool off.

{25:1} So, Israel's kicking it in Shittim, but things start getting wild when they start hooking up with Moabite girls. {25:2} Next thing you know, they're getting invited to worship Moab's gods, chowing down on sacrifices, and bowing down to idols. {25:3} They even start vibing with Baal-peor, ticking off the Big Guy big time. {25:4} The Lord's like, "Moses, grab the leaders, hang them up in the sun to cool down my anger." {25:5} Moses tells the judges to straight-up execute anyone getting cozy with Baal-peor. {25:6} But then, one dude brings a Midianite girl right in front of everyone, and they're all bawling outside the tent. {25:7-8} Phinehas, Aaron's grandson, sees this and goes full action hero, jabbing them both with a javelin. Plague over. {25:9} But not before 24,000 people bite the dust. {25:10} The Lord's like, "Yo, Moses, props to Phinehas for shutting down my rage. He's real zealous for me." {25:11-13} So God's like, "Phinehas gets the peace treaty from me, and his family gets the priesthood forever for repping me so hard." {25:14} The guy who got skewered was Zimri, a Simeonite big shot, and the girl was Cozbi, daughter of Midian's head honcho. {25:15} God's like, "Time to mess with Midian. They've been playing games and causing trouble, especially with that whole Peor scandal."

{26:1-3} After the plague calms down, God's like, "Moses, Eleazar, let's do a headcount of the Israelite troops, 20 and up, ready for war." {26:4} So they count everyone, just like God told Moses and the Exodus crew. {26:5} Reuben's fam, 43,730 strong. {26:6} Simeon's got 22,200 troops. {26:7} Gad's rolling with 40,500 fighters. {26:8} Judah's packing 76,500 soldiers. {26:9} Issachar's got 64,300 warriors. {26:10} Zebulun's flexing with 60,500 troops. {26:11} Manasseh's got 52,700 soldiers in the mix. {26:12} Ephraim's bringing 32,500 fighters to the table. {26:13} Benjamin's got 45,600 troops ready to roll. {26:14} Dan's got 64,400 soldiers suited up. {26:15} Asher's got 53,400 troops on standby. {26:16} Naphtali's got 45,400 fighters ready to go. {26:17} So, in total, Israel's got a force of 601,730 troops. {26:18} And don't forget the Levites: Gershonites, Kohathites, and Merarites, with a total of 23,000 peeps. {26:19} So, that's how many Moses and Eleazar counted up in the plains of Moab, just as God said. {26:20} Except for Caleb and Joshua, everyone else from the first headcount in the desert ended up biting the dust. Tough break.

{27:1-3} So these five sisters from Manasseh, Mahlah, Noah, Hoglah, Milcah, and Tirzah, approached Moses, Eleazar the priest, the leaders, and the whole crew at the tabernacle, explaining that their dad, Zelophehad, died in the wilderness without siding with Korah's rebellion and left no sons. {27:4} They asked why their dad's name should be wiped out from the family line just because he had no sons. They wanted an inheritance among their dad's relatives. {27:5} Moses took their case to the LORD. {27:6-7} The LORD told Moses that the daughters of Zelophehad were right and should indeed inherit their dad's portion among his relatives. {27:8-9} He instructed Moses to tell the Israelites that if a man dies without sons, his inheritance should go to his daughters. {27:10} If he has no daughters, then to his brothers. {27:11} If no brothers, then to his nearest relative. These rules were to be a standard in Israel. {27:12-13} The LORD then told Moses to climb Mount Abarim to see the land given to Israel before being gathered to his people, like Aaron. {27:14} This was because Moses disobeyed at the waters of Meribah in Kadesh. {27:15} Moses pleaded with the LORD, asking Him to appoint a leader over the congregation. {27:16} The LORD chose Joshua, son of Nun, a man filled with His spirit, and told Moses to commission him before Eleazar and the people. {27:17} Moses was to share his authority with Joshua so the Israelites would obey him. {27:18} Joshua would consult Eleazar using the Urim before the LORD, leading the people in and out as commanded. {27:19} Moses followed the LORD's instructions, setting Joshua before Eleazar and the congregation, laying hands on him and giving him authority.

{28:1} Yo, the LORD hit up Moses with a message, saying, {28:2} "Tell the Israelites that they gotta bring me my offerings and sacrifices on point, just how I like 'em, at the right times. {28:3} Here's the deal: offer two spotless year-old lambs every day as a burnt offering to keep the good vibes going. {28:4-5} One lamb in the morning, and the other at sundown, along with a tenth of an ephah of flour mixed with a quarter hin of beaten oil. {28:6} This burnt offering is non-stop, set up back at Mount Sinai to please me with that sweet smell of fire." {28:7} Plus, pour a quarter hin of strong wine as a drink offering with each lamb in the holy place for me. {28:8} Repeat the same setup with the other lamb at sundown, along with the morning meat and drink offering, all pleasing to the LORD. {28:9} Now, on the Sabbath, bring two spotless year-old lambs, two tenths of an ephah of flour mixed with oil, and their drink offering. {28:10} This is on top of the regular burnt offering and its drink. {28:11} At the start of each month, offer up two young bulls, one ram, and seven spotless year-old lambs. {28:12} For the bulls, mix three tenths of flour with oil, and for the ram, two tenths. {28:13} Also, offer a tenth of flour with oil for each lamb, all as a burnt offering that pleases the LORD. {28:14} And don't forget the drink offerings: half hin of wine for the bulls, a third hin for the ram, and a quarter hin for each lamb, every month, a pleasing burnt offering. {28:15} Throw in a goat as a sin offering to the LORD, alongside the regular burnt offering and its drink offering. {28:16} On the fourteenth day of the first month is the LORD's Passover, {28:17} followed by a seven-day feast of eating unleavened bread from the fifteenth day. {28:18-19} The first day is a holy day with no work, offering two young bulls, one ram, and seven year-old lambs without blemish. {28:20-21} Mix their flour offerings with oil: three tenths for each bull and two tenths for the ram. {28:22} Plus, one goat for a sin offering to make things right. {28:23} These offerings are in addition to the daily burnt offering. {28:24} Repeat this daily setup throughout the feast days, keeping the sweet-scented fire offerings coming, alongside the regular burnt offering and drink. {28:25} On the seventh day, have another holy day with no work. {28:26-27} On the day of firstfruits, after counting seven weeks, have another holy day with no work, offering two bulls, one ram, and seven year-old lambs. {28:28-29} For these, use flour mixed with oil: three tenths for each bull, two tenths for the ram, and a tenth for each lamb. {28:30} Plus, offer a goat for atonement. {28:31} These are in addition to the regular burnt offering and its meal and drink, all spotless and pleasing to the LORD.

{29:1} So, when the seventh month rolls in on the first day, it's time for a lit gathering; no work allowed, just trumpet vibes all day. {29:2} You gotta bring the offerings: one young bullock, one ram, and seven flawless lambs. {29:3-4} Mix up that flour and oil, three-tenths for the bullock, two-tenths for the ram, and one-tenth for each lamb. {29:5-6} Plus, toss in a goat for a sin offering to make things right. {29:7} Fast forward to the tenth day, another holy day where you chill out and offer up the same lineup of animals without any flaws. {29:8} Then, on the fifteenth day, it's time for a major feast to the Lord, with 13 bullocks, two rams, and 14 flawless lambs. {29:9} Day two's menu: 12 bullocks, two rams, and 14 lambs. {29:10} Day three, it's 11 bullocks, two rams, and 14 lambs again. {29:11} On the fourth day, it's 10 bullocks, two rams, and 14 lambs. {29:12} Day five, nine bullocks, two rams, and 14 flawless lambs. {29:13} Sixth day, eight bullocks, two rams, and 14 flawless lambs. {29:14} And on the seventh day, seven bullocks, two rams, and 14 flawless lambs once more. {29:15} Finally, on the eighth day, it's another big bash, with one bullock, one ram, and seven flawless lambs. {29:16} These are the rules for the Lord's parties, alongside your regular offerings. And Moses breaks it down for the crew just like the Lord said.

{30:1} So Moses gathered the tribal leaders of Israel and laid down what the LORD had commanded. {30:2} Basically, if anyone—guy or girl—makes a vow to the LORD or swears an oath, they gotta stick to their word and do exactly what they promised. {30:3-4} Now, if a woman in her dad's house makes a vow when she's young and her dad hears it and doesn't object, she's locked in; her vows stand. {30:5} But if her dad hears it and says nope, then her vows are off the table, and the LORD lets it slide because her dad nixed it. {30:6-7} If she's married and makes a vow and her husband hears it but doesn't say anything, her vows hold up. {30:8} But if her husband steps in and says nope, her vow is null and void, and the LORD forgives her. {30:9} Widows and divorced women, though, are on their own with their vows—they gotta stick to 'em. {30:10-11} If a married woman makes a vow in her husband's house and he hears but doesn't say anything, she's good to go. {30:12} But if he decides later that her vow is off, then it's off, and the LORD lets it slide. {30:13-14} Ultimately, it's up to the husband to decide if his wife's vows stick or not; if he stays quiet, they're all good. {30:15} But if he changes his mind later, he's the one taking the blame. {30:16} These are the rules straight from the LORD through Moses, governing vows between spouses and fathers and daughters, especially when the daughters are still under their dad's roof.

{31:1-2} So the LORD hit up Moses and was like, "Yo, time to get payback on the Midianites. Once that's done, you'll be joining your ancestors." {31:3} Moses rallied the crew and was like, "Get ready for war, fam. We're taking on the Midianites to show the LORD what's up." {31:4} Each tribe sent a thousand soldiers, making it twelve thousand troops ready to roll. {31:5} So, they suited up twelve thousand warriors from all the tribes of Israel. {31:6} Moses sent them out with Phinehas, the priest's son, and holy gear, including trumpets to blow. {31:7} They went to war against the Midianites, doing exactly what the LORD told Moses. They wiped out all the dudes. {31:8} They took down the Midianite kings, including Evi, Rekem, Zur, Hur, and Reba, plus Balaam, the son of Beor. {31:9} The Israelites took the Midianite women and kids captive, along with their livestock and goods. {31:10} They burned down all the Midianite cities and forts. {31:11} Then they grabbed all the loot, both people and animals. {31:12-15} Moses and Eleazar met them outside camp, and Moses wasn't happy with the commanders who spared the women. {31:16} He was like, "These women caused Israel to stray thanks to Balaam's advice, which led to a plague among the LORD's people." {31:17} So Moses ordered them to kill all the male kids and every woman who had been with a man. {31:18} Only the virgin girls were spared for the Israelites to keep. {31:19-20} After the battle, they had to chill outside camp for seven days to purify themselves and their captives. {31:21} Eleazar laid down the law to the warriors on how to handle the spoils as the LORD commanded.{31:22} Then the officers in charge of thousands and hundreds came to Moses and said, "Moses, we've counted all our troops, and not a single man is missing. {31:23} So, we've brought an offering to the LORD from what each of us gathered—gold jewelry, chains, bracelets, rings, earrings, and tablets—as a way to atone for our souls before the LORD." {31:24} Moses and Eleazar accepted their gold and jewelry as an offering to the LORD. {31:25} The total gold collected from the commanders of thousands and hundreds amounted to sixteen thousand seven hundred and fifty shekels. {31:26} (Each soldier had taken spoil for themselves.) {31:27} Moses and Eleazar brought this gold into the tabernacle as a reminder before the LORD on behalf of the Israelites.

{32:1} So, like, the Reubenites and Gadites had a ton of cattle, and when they scoped out the land of Jazer and Gilead, they were like, "Yo, this place is perfect for our herds." {32:2} They hit up Moses, Eleazar, and the squad, saying, "Check it, Ataroth, Dibon, Jazer, Nimrah, Heshbon, Elealeh, Shebam, Nebo, and Beon—all prime spots for us." {32:3-5} They were like, "The land the Lord wrecked is all set for cattle, and we're loaded. So, can we just chill here and not cross the Jordan?" {32:6-9} But Moses was like, "Hold up, you guys cool with your bros fighting while you kick back here?" {32:10} God was seriously ticked and swore none of the adults from Egypt would see the Promised Land. {32:11-13} Except Caleb and Joshua, 'cause they were legit. {32:14-19} Moses was like, "You're just like your ancestors, fueling God's rage against Israel." {32:20-22} Moses was like, "If you guys suit up and fight first, then you can chill here after." {32:23} But if not, you're gonna regret it. {32:24} "You promised to build cities and folds, so do it." {32:25-28} And the Gadites and Reubenites were like, "We're in, whatever Moses says." {32:29-33} So Moses was like, "If they fight, they get Gilead." {32:33} And Moses hooked them up with the kingdoms of Sihon and Og. {32:34-35} The Gadites were on building duty in Dibon, Ataroth, and Aroer, while the Reubenites were handling Heshbon and Elealeh. {32:36-38} They also built Beth-nimrah and Beth-haran as fortified cities and sheepfolds. {32:39} Meanwhile, the Manassites took over Gilead and booted out the Amorites. {32:40} Moses gave Gilead to Machir, and he set up shop there. {32:41} Jair, another Manassite, snagged some small towns and named them Havoth-jair. {32:42} Nobah claimed Kenath and renamed it after himself.

{33:1} So, like, these are the trips the Israelites took after they bounced from Egypt, led by Moses and Aaron. {33:2} Moses kept track of their moves, as ordered by the big man upstairs. {33:3} They peaced out of Rameses on the fifteenth of the first month, right after Passover, flexing in front of the Egyptians. {33:4} 'Cause, you know, the Egyptians were burying their firstborn and dealing with divine smackdowns. {33:5} First stop: Succoth. {33:6} Then Etham, on the edge of the wilderness. {33:7} Back to Pi-hahiroth near Baal-zephon and Migdol. {33:8} They split the sea, marched three days into the Etham desert, and crashed in Marah. {33:9} Next up: Elim, with a bunch of water fountains and palm trees. {33:10} Then they camped by the Red Sea. {33:11} Desert of Sin, here they come. {33:12} Out of Sin, into Dophkah. {33:13} After Dophkah, they hit Alush. {33:14} Rephidim, where the water situation was dire. {33:15} From Rephidim, they headed to the Sinai wilderness. {33:16} Then Kibroth-hattaavah. {33:17} Bye-bye Kibroth-hattaavah, hello Hazeroth. {33:18} Hazeroth to Rithmah. {33:19} Rithmah to Rimmon-parez. {33:20} Rimmon-parez to Libnah. {33:21} Libnah to Rissah. {33:22} Rissah to Kehelathah. {33:23} Kehelathah to Mount Shapher. {33:24} Mount Shapher to Haradah. {33:25} Haradah to Makheloth. {33:26} Makheloth to Tahath. {33:27} Tahath to Tarah. {33:28} Tarah to Mithcah. {33:29} Mithcah to Hashmonah. {33:30} Hashmonah to Moseroth. {33:31} Moseroth to Bene-jaakan. {33:32} Bene-jaakan to Hor-hagidgad. {33:33} Hor-hagidgad to Jotbathah. {33:34} Jotbathah to Ebronah. {33:35} Ebronah to Ezion-gaber. {33:36} Ezion-gaber to the Zin wilderness, aka Kadesh. {33:37} Out of Kadesh to Mount Hor, where Aaron kicked the bucket. {33:38} Aaron died at 123, in the first month of the fortieth year post-Egyptian exodus. {33:39} RIP Aaron. {33:40} Meanwhile, King Arad of Canaan heard about the Israelites. {33:41} So, they left Mount Hor and camped in Zalmonah. {33:42} Then it was on to Punon. {33:43} And from Punon to Oboth. {33:44} Oboth to Ije-abarim, on the Moab border. {33:45} Iim to Dibon-gad. {33:46} Dibon-gad to Almon-diblathaim. {33:47} Almon-diblathaim to the Abarim mountains, near Nebo.

{33:48} From the Abarim mountains to the plains of Moab, near Jericho. {33:49} And they camped by the Jordan, from Beth-jesimoth to Abel-shittim in the Moab plains. {33:50} Then God hit up Moses in Moab and laid down some rules. {33:51} Moses relayed the message: clear out Canaan and wreck their stuff. {33:52} Kick out the locals and tear down their high places. {33:53} The land is yours for the taking. {33:54} Divide it up by lot, big families get more, small families less, and everyone chills where they land. {33:55} But if you slack, those left behind will be a pain in the butt. {33:56} You snooze, you lose, just like they did.

{34:1} So God was like, "Moses, listen up!" {34:2} "Tell the Israelites when they hit up Canaan, that's their spot, like their inheritance, the whole Canaan area and its borders. {34:3} The southern boundary starts at the Zin wilderness, goes along Edom's coast, and hits the Dead Sea's east coast. {34:4} It runs from the south to Akrabbim Pass, then to Zin, and keeps going to Kadesh-barnea, Hazar-addar, and Azmon. {34:5} It curves from Azmon to the Egyptian River and ends at the sea. {34:6} The west border is the Great Sea. That's it, your west boundary. {34:7} The north border starts at the Great Sea to Mount Hor. {34:8} From Mount Hor, it extends to the entrance of Hamath and goes to Zedad. {34:9} Then it goes to Ziphron and ends at Hazar-enan. That's your north border. {34:10} The east border runs from Hazar-enan to Shepham. {34:11} It goes down to Riblah east of Ain and reaches the Sea of Galilee's eastern shore. {34:12} From there, it heads to the Jordan River and ends at the Dead Sea. That's your land and its borders. {34:13} Moses told the Israelites, "This is the land you'll get by lot, as the LORD commanded, for the nine and a half tribes. {34:14} Reuben's tribe, Gad's tribe, and half of Manasseh have already got their spots east of the Jordan by Jericho. {34:16} Then God was like, "Eleazar the priest and Joshua son of Nun are the ones who will divide up the land for you. {34:18} Get a prince from each tribe to do the dividing." {34:19} Here are the names: For Judah, Caleb son of Jephunneh. {34:20} For Simeon, Shemuel son of Ammihud. {34:21} For Benjamin, Elidad son of Chislon. {34:22} For Dan, Bukki son of Jogli. {34:23} For Manasseh, Hanniel son of Ephod. {34:24} For Ephraim, Kemuel son of Shiphtan. {34:25} For Zebulun, Elizaphan son of Parnach. {34:26} For Issachar, Paltiel son of Azzan. {34:27} For Asher, Ahihud son of Shelomi. {34:28} For Naphtali, Pedahel son of Ammihud. {34:29} These are the ones the LORD told to divide up the land of Canaan for the Israelites.

{35:1} So, like, God was chatting with Moses in Moab, near Jericho, and He's like, "Yo, tell the Israelites to hook up the Levites with some cities and suburbs to chill in." {35:2} "These cities are their pads, and the suburbs are for their stuff and their pets." {35:3} "The Levites need space for their cattle, goods, and beasts, ya know?" {35:4} "The suburbs gotta be about a thousand cubits out from the city walls, all around." {35:5} "Measure two thousand cubits on each side, and the city goes in the middle, making those the suburbs." {35:6} "Oh, and six of these cities gotta be safe havens for accidental killers, with forty-two more on top of that." {35:7} "So, 48 cities total, along with their suburbs, go to the Levites." {35:8} "These cities are from the Israelites' land, so give more to those with lots and fewer to those with less. It's all about fairness based on their inheritance." {35:9} Then God's like, "Moses, listen up again." {35:10} "When you cross the Jordan into Canaan, designate some cities as safe havens for accidental killers." {35:11} "These cities are where someone can flee if they accidentally off someone." {35:12} "The cities are there to protect them from revenge until they stand trial." {35:13} "You'll need six of these cities for refuge." {35:14} "Three on each side of the Jordan, making six total in Canaan." {35:15} "These six cities are open to all, Israelite or foreigner, for anyone who accidentally takes a life." {35:16} "But if they murder someone with intent, like with a weapon, they're toast." {35:17} "Same goes if they chuck a stone or use a wooden weapon." {35:18} "If they're caught red-handed, the avenger of blood gets 'em." {35:19} "But if it's an accident without malice, there's a trial to sort it out." {35:20} "If it's a premeditated hit or they're caught in the act, they're done." {35:21} "But if it's a sudden, unintended thing, there's room for debate." {35:22} "Once they're safe in the city, they gotta stay there until the high priest dies." {35:23} "If they leave the city and get nabbed by the avenger of blood, they're fair game." {35:24} "But if they're judged innocent, they can return to their land after the high priest dies." {35:25-29} "These rules are for generations to come in all the Israelite territories." {35:30} "And if someone kills another person, they get the death penalty, but only if there are witnesses." {35:31} "No bribes or deals for murderers; they get what's coming to 'em." {35:32} "And if someone flees to a city of refuge, they can't leave until the high priest dies." {35:33} "Keep the land clean of bloodshed, 'cause it's a big deal to God who's living among you."

{36:1} "Now, the leaders of the Gileadite families approached Moses." {36:2} "They're like, 'God told you to give land to the Israelites by lot, and now you gotta give Zelophehad's daughters their piece too.'" {36:3} "But if they marry outside their tribe, their inheritance is gone from our tribe's lot." {36:4} "Same goes for the jubilee; their land switches tribes." {36:5} "Moses was like, 'Yeah, that makes sense.'" {36:6} "God said it's cool for them to marry who they want, as long as it's in their dad's tribe." {36:7} "Can't be shifting inheritances around; everyone sticks to their tribe." {36:8} "So, every daughter keeps it in the family to keep the land in the tribe." {36:9} "No tribe-hopping; everyone stays in their lane." {36:10} "And the daughters of Zelophehad did just that, marrying their cousins in the tribe of Manasseh." {36:11} "Their land stayed put in their dad's tribe." {36:12} "Mahlah, Tirzah, Hoglah, Milcah, and Noah all married within their tribe, keeping the inheritance in the family." {36:13} "And that's the Word of the Lord, delivered by Moses in Moab, near Jericho."

Deuteronomy

✛✛✛

{1:1} So here's what Moses said to all of Israel while they were still chillin' on the east side of the Jordan River, in the desert near the Red Sea, between Paran, Tophel, Laban, Hazeroth, and Dizahab. {1:2}(It's like an eleven-day road trip from Horeb via Mount Seir to Kadesh-barnea. {1:3} So, in the 40th year, on the first day of the eleventh month, Moses gave the squad all the commands from the LORD. {1:4} This was after he had taken down Sihon, king of the Amorites in Heshbon, and Og, king of Bashan, who lived in Astaroth at Edrei. {1:5} On the east side of the Jordan in Moab, Moses started explaining the laws, saying, {1:6} "The LORD our God told us at Horeb, 'You've stayed at this mountain long enough. {1:7} Pack up and head to the hill country of the Amorites and all the nearby places: the plains, hills, valleys, the southern area, the coast, the land of the Canaanites, and all the way to Lebanon and the Euphrates River. {1:8} Look, I've given you this land. Go take it, just like the LORD promised your ancestors, Abraham, Isaac, and Jacob, and their descendants.' {1:9} Back then, I told y'all, 'I can't handle all this on my own. {1:10} The LORD your God has made you as many as the stars in the sky. {1:11} (May the LORD, the God of your ancestors, make you a thousand times more and bless you as promised!) {1:12} How can I handle all your problems, burdens, and arguments by myself? {1:13} Pick wise, understanding, and respected men from each tribe, and I'll appoint them as your leaders.' {1:14} You agreed, saying it was a good idea. {1:15} So I took the top guys from your tribes, wise and respected men, and made them leaders over you: commanders of thousands, hundreds, fifties, and tens, and officers for your tribes. {1:16} I told your judges, 'Hear disputes between your people fairly, whether it's between Israelites or foreigners. {1:17} Don't show favoritism; judge everyone equally. Don't be afraid, because judgment belongs to God. If a case is too hard, bring it to me, and I'll handle it.' {1:18} And I gave you all the commands you needed to follow. {1:19} So we left Horeb and trekked through that vast and scary desert, like the LORD commanded, and we reached Kadesh-barnea. {1:20} I told you, 'You've reached the mountain of the Amorites, which the LORD our God is giving us. {1:21} Look, the LORD your God has given you the land. Go take it, just like the LORD, the God of your ancestors, told you. Don't be afraid or discouraged.' {1:22} But you all came to me and said, 'Let's send some scouts to check out the land and bring back info on the best route and the cities we'll hit.' {1:23} I thought it was a good plan, so I picked twelve men, one from each tribe. {1:24} They went up the hills, reached the Valley of Eshcol, and scouted it out. {1:25} They brought back some fruit and said, 'The land the LORD our God is giving us is legit!' {1:26} But you refused to go up and rebelled against the LORD's command. {1:27} You complained in your tents, saying, 'The LORD hates us! He brought us out of Egypt to hand us over to the Amorites and destroy us. {1:28} Where can we go? Our brothers have made us lose heart, saying the people there are bigger and taller, with cities fortified up to the sky, and they've seen giants there.' {1:29} Then I told you, 'Don't be scared or freak out. {1:30} The LORD your God, who goes ahead of you, will fight for you, just like He did in Egypt. {1:31} In the wilderness, you saw how the LORD your God carried you, like a father carries his son, all the way until you reached this place.' {1:32} But even after all this, you didn't trust the LORD your God, {1:33} who went ahead of you, finding places for you to camp, with fire by night and a cloud by day to show you the way. {1:34} When the LORD heard what you said, He got mad and swore, {1:35} 'Not one of these evil people will see the good land I promised to your ancestors, {1:36} except Caleb son of Jephunneh. He'll see it, and I'll give him and his descendants the land he walked on because he followed the LORD wholeheartedly.' {1:37} The LORD was also mad at me because of you, and said, 'You're not going in either. {1:38} But your assistant Joshua son of Nun will enter it. Encourage him, because he will lead Israel to inherit it. {1:39} And your little ones, who you said would be captured, and your kids who don't know right from wrong yet, they will enter the land. I'll give it to them, and they'll take it. {1:40} But you, turn around and head back into the desert toward the Red Sea.' {1:41} Then you answered, 'We've sinned against the LORD. We'll go up and fight like He commanded.' So you got your weapons ready, thinking it'd be easy to go up into the hill country. {1:42} But the LORD told me, 'Tell them not to go up and fight because I'm not with them. They'll be defeated by their enemies.' {1:43} I told you, but you didn't listen. You rebelled against the LORD's command and arrogantly went up into the hill country. {1:44} The Amorites who lived there came out, attacked you, chased you like a swarm of bees, and beat you down all the way to Hormah. {1:45} You came back and wept before the LORD, but He didn't listen to you. {1:46} So you stayed in Kadesh for a long time, much longer than you expected.

{2:1} So we turned and headed into the wilderness towards the Red Sea, like the LORD told me, and we circled around Mount Seir for a long time. {2:2} Then the LORD spoke to me, saying, {2:3} 'You've been circling this mountain long enough, turn north. {2:4} Tell the people they're about to pass through the land of their relatives, the descendants of Esau, who live in Seir. They'll be scared of you, so be super careful. {2:5} Don't mess with them, because I'm not giving you even a foot of their land; I've given Mount Seir to Esau. {2:6} Buy food and water from them with money so you can eat and drink. {2:7} The LORD your God has blessed you in everything you've done; He knows your journey through this huge wilderness. These forty years the LORD your God has been with you, and you haven't lacked anything.' {2:8} So we passed by our relatives, the descendants of Esau in Seir, through the plain from Elath and Ezion-geber, then we turned and went through the wilderness of Moab. {2:9} The LORD told me, 'Don't bother the Moabites or fight them, because I'm not giving you any of their land; I've given Ar to the descendants of Lot. {2:10} The Emims used to live there, a great, numerous, and tall people, like the Anakims. {2:11} They were also considered giants, but the Moabites called them Emims. {2:12} The Horites used to live in Seir, but the descendants of Esau took over after destroying them, just like Israel did in their land that the LORD gave them. {2:13} Now get up and cross the Zered Valley.' So we crossed the Zered Valley. {2:14} The time it took for us to come from Kadesh-barnea until we crossed the Zered Valley was thirty-eight years, until all the men of war from that generation had died, as the LORD had sworn to them. {2:15} Indeed, the LORD's hand was against them, to destroy them until they were all gone. {2:16} When all the men of war had died from among the people, {2:17} the LORD spoke to me, saying, {2:18} 'Today you're going to pass through Ar, the region of Moab. {2:19} When you approach the Ammonites, don't harass or provoke them, because I'm not giving you any of their land; I've given it to the descendants of Lot.' {2:20} (This land was also considered the land of giants; giants used to live there, called Zamzummims by the Ammonites. {2:21} They were a great and numerous people, as tall as the Anakims. The LORD destroyed them so the Ammonites could take over and live there, {2:22} just like He did for the descendants of Esau in Seir, when He destroyed the Horites for them. They took over and have lived there to this day. {2:23} And the Avims, who lived in villages as far as Gaza, were destroyed by the Caphtorims from Caphtor, who then lived in their place.) {2:24} 'Get up, set out, and cross the Arnon Valley. Look, I've given Sihon the Amorite, king of Heshbon, and his land into your hands. Start taking possession and engage him in battle. {2:25} Today I'll start to put the fear and dread of you on all the nations under heaven. When they hear reports about you, they'll tremble and be in anguish because of you.' {2:26} From the Kedemoth Desert, I sent messengers to Sihon, king of Heshbon, with words of peace, saying, {2:27} 'Let us pass through your land. We'll stay on the main road and won't turn to the right or the left. {2:28} Sell us food and water for money, so we can eat and drink. Just let us pass through on foot, {2:29} as the descendants of Esau in Seir and the Moabites in Ar did for us, until we cross the Jordan into the land the LORD our God is giving us.' {2:30} But Sihon, king of Heshbon, refused to let us pass because the LORD your God had hardened his spirit and made his heart obstinate, so He could deliver him into your hands, as you see today. {2:31} The LORD said to me, 'Look, I've begun to deliver Sihon and his land over to you. Start taking possession so you can inherit his land.' {2:32} Sihon and all his people came out to fight us at Jahaz. {2:33} The LORD our God delivered him to us, and we defeated him, his sons, and all his people. {2:34} We captured all his cities at that time and completely destroyed every city—men, women, and children. We left no survivors. {2:35} We only took the livestock and the plunder from the cities. {2:36} From Aroer on the edge of the Arnon Valley, and the city in the valley, even to Gilead, no city was too strong for us; the LORD our God gave them all to us. {2:37} But you didn't go near the land of the Ammonites, all along the Jabbok River, or the cities in the mountains, or any place the LORD our God had forbidden.

{3:1} So we turned and headed up to Bashan, and Og, the king of Bashan, rolled up with his crew to battle us at Edrei. {3:2} But the LORD was like, "Don't sweat it; I've got this. I'll hand him, his people, and his land over to you. Do to him what you did to Sihon, king of the Amorites, from Heshbon." {3:3} So, the LORD our God handed Og, king of Bashan, and his people to us, and we wiped them out until no one was left. {3:4} We took all his cities—like, sixty of them—from the whole region of Argob, Og's kingdom in Bashan. {3:5} These cities had mad high walls, gates, and bars; and there were a bunch of unwalled towns too. {3:6} We destroyed them all, just like with Sihon, completely wiping out men, women, and kids in every city. {3:7} But we snagged all the cattle and the loot from the cities for ourselves. {3:8} At that time, we took the land from the two Amorite kings east of the Jordan, from the Arnon River to Mount Hermon; {3:9} (Hermon, which the Sidonians call Sirion, and the Amorites call Shenir). {3:10} We took all the cities of the plain, Gilead, and Bashan, right up to Salchah and Edrei—cities of Og's kingdom in Bashan. {3:11} Og was the last of the giants, and his iron bed is still in Rabbah of the Ammonites—nine cubits long and four cubits wide. {3:12} We took this land at that time, from Aroer by the Arnon River and half of Mount Gilead with its cities, and I gave it to the Reubenites and Gadites. {3:13} The rest of Gilead and all of Bashan, Og's kingdom, I gave to half the tribe of Manasseh—the whole region of Argob and all Bashan, which is known as the land of giants. {3:14} Jair, son of Manasseh, took the whole region of Argob to the borders of Geshuri and Maachathi and named it Bashan-havoth-jair after himself, which is still its name today. {3:15} I gave Gilead to Machir. {3:16} To the Reubenites and Gadites, I gave the land from Gilead to the Arnon River—the middle of the valley is the boundary—and up to the Jabbok River, the border of the Ammonites. {3:17} I also gave them the Arabah, from the Sea of Galilee to the Dead Sea, below the slopes of Pisgah to the east. {3:18} At that time, I told you, "The LORD your God has given you this land. All your warriors must cross over, armed, ahead of your fellow Israelites. {3:19} But your wives, kids, and livestock (I know you have a lot of livestock) can stay in the cities I've given you {3:20} until the LORD gives rest to your fellow Israelites as He has to you, and they too take over the land the LORD your God is giving them across the Jordan. Then you can all head back to your own land." {3:21} I commanded Joshua at that time, "You've seen everything the LORD your God has done to these two kings. He'll do the same to all the kingdoms where you're going. {3:22} Don't be afraid of them; the LORD your God will fight for you." {3:23} At that time, I pleaded with the LORD, {3:24} "O Lord GOD, you've started to show your servant your greatness and your strong hand. What god in heaven or on earth can do the deeds and mighty works you do? {3:25} Please let me cross over and see the good land beyond the Jordan—that fine hill country and Lebanon." {3:26} But the LORD was angry with me because of you and wouldn't listen. The LORD said, "That's enough! Don't talk to me about this again. {3:27} Go up to the top of Pisgah and look west, north, south, and east. Take a good look, because you're not going to cross this Jordan. {3:28} But commission Joshua, encourage him, and strengthen him, for he will lead these people across and cause them to inherit the land you see." {3:29} So we stayed in the valley near Beth-peor.

{4:1} So listen up, Israel, to the rules and judgments I'm teaching you to follow so you can live and take over the land the LORD, the God of your ancestors, is giving you. {4:2} Don't add or take away from what I command you, just keep the LORD's commandments as I tell you. {4:3} You saw what the LORD did at Baal-peor; He wiped out everyone who followed Baal-peor. {4:4} But all of you who stuck with the LORD are alive today. {4:5} Look, I've taught you statutes and judgments just as the LORD my God commanded, so you can follow them in the land you're going to possess. {4:6} So keep and do them, because this is your wisdom and understanding in the eyes of other nations, who will hear about these laws and say, "This great nation is truly wise and understanding." {4:7} What other nation is so great that they have their god near them like the LORD our God is whenever we call on Him? {4:8} And what other nation is so great to have such righteous statutes and judgments as this law I'm giving you today? {4:9} Just be careful and watch yourselves closely so you don't forget what you've seen or let it fade from your heart. Teach these things to your kids and grandkids, {4:10} especially about the day you stood before the LORD your God at Horeb. The LORD said to me, "Assemble the people so they can hear my words and learn to fear me for as long as they live on earth and so they can teach their children." {4:11} You came near and stood at the base of the mountain, and the mountain was ablaze with fire up to the heavens, with darkness, clouds, and thick gloom. {4:12} Then the LORD spoke to you out of the fire. You heard the sound of words but saw no form, just a voice. {4:13} He proclaimed His covenant to you, which He commanded you to follow—the Ten Commandments—and He wrote them on two stone tablets. {4:14} The LORD commanded me at that time to teach you statutes and judgments so you could follow them in the land you're crossing over to possess. {4:15} So watch yourselves closely since you didn't see any form on the day the LORD spoke to you at Horeb out of the fire. {4:16} Don't corrupt yourselves by making an idol in any form, whether in the shape of a man or a woman, {4:17} or any animal on the earth, or any bird that flies in the sky, {4:18} or any creature that moves along the ground, or any fish in the waters below. {4:19} And when you look up to the sky and see see the sun, moon, and stars—all the heavenly array—don't be enticed to bow down to them and worship things the LORD your God has apportioned to all the nations under heaven. {4:20} But the LORD took you and brought you out of the iron furnace, out of Egypt, to be His people of inheritance, as you are today. {4:21} The LORD was angry with me because of you and swore that I would not cross the Jordan and enter the good land the LORD your God is giving you as your inheritance. {4:22} I will die in this land; I will not cross the Jordan. But you are about to cross over and take possession of that good land. {4:23} So be careful not to forget the covenant of the LORD your God that He made with you, and don't make for yourselves an idol in any form the LORD your God has forbidden. {4:24} For the LORD your God is a consuming fire, a jealous God. {4:25} After you have had children and grandchildren and have lived in the land a long time—if you then become corrupt and make any kind of idol, doing evil in the eyes of the LORD your God and arousing His anger, {4:26} I call the heavens and the earth to witness against you this day that you will quickly perish from the land you are crossing the Jordan to possess. You will not live there long but will be utterly destroyed. {4:27} The LORD will scatter you among the nations, and only a few of you will survive among the nations to which the LORD will drive you. {4:28} There you will worship man-made gods of wood and stone, which cannot see or hear or eat or smell. {4:29} But if from there you seek the LORD your God, you will find Him if you seek Him with all your heart and all your soul. {4:30} When you are in distress and all these things have happened to you, then in later days you will return to the LORD your God and obey Him. {4:31} For the LORD your God is a merciful God; He will not abandon or destroy you or forget the covenant with your ancestors, which He confirmed to them by oath. {4:32} Ask now about the former days, long before your time, from the day God created human beings on the earth; ask from one end of the heavens to the other. Has anything so great as this ever happened, or has anything like it ever been heard of? {4:33} Has any other people heard the voice of God speaking out of fire, as you have, and lived? {4:34} Has any god ever tried to take for himself one nation out of another nation, by testings, by signs and wonders, by war, by a mighty hand and an outstretched arm, or by great and awesome deeds, like all the things the LORD your God did for you in Egypt before your very eyes? {4:35} You were shown these things so that you might know that the LORD is God; besides Him there is no other. {4:36} From heaven He made you hear His voice to discipline you. On earth He showed you His great fire, and you heard His words from out of the fire. {4:37} Because He loved your ancestors and chose their descendants after them, He brought you out of Egypt by His Presence and His great strength, {4:38} to drive out before you nations greater and stronger than you and to bring you into their land to give it to you for your inheritance, as it is today. {4:39} Acknowledge and take to heart this day that the LORD is God in heaven above and on the earth below. There is no other. {4:40} Keep His decrees and commands, which I am giving you today, so that it may go well with you and your children after you and that you may live long in the land the LORD your God gives you for all time. {4:41} Then Moses set aside three cities east of the Jordan, {4:42} to which anyone who had killed a person could flee if they had unintentionally killed a neighbor without malice aforethought. They could flee into one of these cities and save their life. {4:43} The cities were Bezer in the wilderness plateau, for the Reubenites; Ramoth in Gilead, for the Gadites; and Golan in Bashan, for the Manassites. {4:44} This is the law Moses set before the Israelites. {4:45} These are the stipulations, decrees, and laws Moses gave them when they came out of Egypt {4:46} and were in the valley near Beth Peor east of the Jordan, in the land of Sihon king of the Amorites, who reigned in Heshbon and was defeated by Moses and the Israelites as they came out of Egypt. {4:47} They took possession of his land and the land of Og king of Bashan, the two Amorite kings east of the Jordan. {4:48} This land extended from Aroer on the rim of the Arnon Gorge to Mount Siyon (that is, Hermon), {4:49} and included all the Arabah east of the Jordan, as far as the Dead Sea below the slopes of Pisgah.

{5:1} So Moses called everyone in Israel and said, "Listen up, fam, to the rules and judgments I'm dropping today so you can learn them, keep them, and do them. {5:2} The LORD our God made a pact with us at Horeb. {5:3} This covenant wasn't just with our ancestors but with all of us who are alive today. {5:4} The LORD talked to you face to face at the mountain out of the fire, {5:5} (I was the middleman between the LORD and you at that time because you were scared of the fire and didn't go up the mountain) and said, {5:6} "I'm the LORD your God who brought you out of Egypt, out of the house of bondage. {5:7} Don't have any other gods before me. {5:8} Don't make any idols or images of anything in the sky, on the earth, or in the waters. {5:9} Don't bow down or serve them, because I, the LORD your God, am a jealous God, punishing the kids for the sins of the parents to the third and fourth generation of those who hate me, {5:10} but showing love to thousands who love me and keep my commandments. {5:11} Don't misuse the name of the LORD your God, because the LORD won't hold anyone guiltless who takes His name in vain. {5:12} Keep the Sabbath day holy, as the LORD your God commanded you. {5:13} Work for six days and do all your tasks, {5:14} but the seventh day is a Sabbath to the LORD your God. On it, don't do any work—neither you, your kids, your servants, your animals, nor any foreigner living among you—so your servants can rest just like you. {5:15} Remember you were slaves in Egypt and the LORD your God brought you out with a mighty hand and outstretched arm. That's why He commanded you to keep the Sabbath day. {5:16} Respect your parents as the LORD your God commanded so you can live long and it goes well with you in the land the LORD your God is giving you. {5:17} Don't murder. {5:18} Don't cheat. {5:19} Don't steal. {5:20} Don't lie about your neighbor. {5:21} Don't crave your neighbor's wife, house, field, servants, ox, donkey, or anything that belongs to them. {5:22} These are the words the LORD spoke to your entire assembly at the mountain out of the fire, cloud, and thick darkness, with a loud voice. He added nothing more and wrote them on two stone tablets and gave them to me. {5:23} When you heard the voice from the darkness while the mountain was on fire, all the leaders and elders came to me. {5:24} You said, "The LORD our God has shown us His glory and greatness, and we've heard His voice from the fire. We've seen that God can talk to us, and we can live. {5:25} But now, why should we risk dying? This great fire will consume us, and if we keep hearing the voice of the LORD our God, we'll die. {5:26} For who among all flesh has heard the voice of the living God speaking out of the fire, as we have, and lived? {5:27} Go near and listen to all the LORD our God says. Then tell us everything He tells you, and we'll listen and obey." {5:28} The LORD heard what you said and told me, "I've heard what these people said. They did well in all they spoke. {5:29} Oh, that their hearts would always fear me and keep all my commands so it might go well with them and their children forever! {5:30} Go tell them to return to their tents. {5:31} But you stay here with me so I can give you all the commands, decrees, and laws to teach them, so they can follow them in the land I'm giving them to possess." {5:32} So be careful to do what the LORD your God has commanded you; don't turn to the right or left. {5:33} Walk in all the ways the LORD your God has commanded you so you may live, prosper, and prolong your days in the land you will possess.

{6:1} So here are the commands, rules, and judgments the LORD your God told me to teach you so you can follow them in the land you're about to take over: {6:2} Do this so you, your kids, and your grandkids can respect the LORD your God, keep all His rules and commands, and live a long life. {6:3} Listen up, Israel, and do these things so you can thrive and grow strong, just as the LORD God of your ancestors promised, in this land flowing with milk and honey. {6:4} Listen, Israel: The LORD our God is the only LORD: {6:5} Love the LORD your God with all your heart, soul, and strength. {6:6} Keep these words I'm commanding you today in your heart: {6:7} Teach them to your kids, talk about them at home, when you're out, when you lie down, and when you get up. {6:8} Tie them as symbols on your hands and wear them on your forehead. {6:9} Write them on your house's doorframes and on your gates. {6:10} When the LORD your God brings you into the land He promised to your ancestors—Abraham, Isaac, and Jacob—with cities you didn't build, {6:11} houses full of good stuff you didn't fill, wells you didn't dig, and vineyards and olive groves you didn't plant, and you eat and are satisfied, {6:12} be careful not to forget the LORD who brought you out of slavery in Egypt. {6:13} Respect the LORD your God, serve Him, and take oaths in His name. {6:14} Don't chase after other gods from the people around you, {6:15} because the LORD your God is a jealous God and His anger will burn against you and destroy you from the earth. {6:16} Don't test the LORD your God as you did at Massah. {6:17} Carefully keep the commands, testimonies, and statutes He gave you. {6:18} Do what is right and good in the LORD's eyes so it will go well with you, and you'll take over the good land the LORD promised your ancestors, {6:19} driving out all your enemies before you, as the LORD said. {6:20} When your kids ask in the future, "What's up with these testimonies, statutes, and judgments the LORD our God commanded you?" {6:21} tell them, "We were slaves in Egypt, but the LORD brought us out with a mighty hand. {6:22} The LORD did awesome signs and wonders against Egypt, Pharaoh, and his household before our eyes. {6:23} He brought us out to give us the land He promised our ancestors. {6:24} The LORD commanded us to follow all these statutes and respect Him for our own good, to keep us alive, as we are today. {6:25} It will be our righteousness if we carefully follow all these commands before the LORD our God, as He commanded us."

{7:1} When the LORD your God brings you into the land you're about to take over and kicks out a bunch of nations ahead of you—the Hittites, Girgashites, Amorites, Canaanites, Perizzites, Hivites, and Jebusites, seven nations way stronger than you; {7:2} And when the LORD your God hands them over to you, you gotta defeat them and completely wipe them out; no making deals with them or showing mercy: {7:3} Don't marry them either; don't give your daughter to their sons or take their daughters for your sons. {7:4} They'll turn your kids away from following me to serve other gods, and the LORD's anger will burn against you and destroy you fast. {7:5} Here's how to deal with them: tear down their altars, smash their sacred stones, cut down their Asherah poles, and burn their idols. {7:6} You're a holy people to the LORD your God; He chose you to be His special people above all others on earth. {7:7} The LORD didn't love you or choose you because you were the most numerous, but actually, you were the fewest: {7:8} He loved you and kept the oath He made to your ancestors, so He brought you out with a powerful hand and saved you from slavery in Egypt. {7:9} So know that the LORD your God is God, the faithful God, keeping His covenant of love to a thousand generations of those who love Him and keep His commandments; {7:10} But He repays those who hate Him to their face, destroying them: He won't hesitate to repay anyone who hates Him. {7:11} So keep the commands, rules, and judgments I'm giving you today, and do them. {7:12} If you listen to these judgments and keep them, the LORD your God will keep His covenant of love with you, just like He swore to your ancestors: {7:13} He'll love you, bless you, and multiply you; He'll bless your kids, your crops, your grain, new wine, and olive oil, the calves of your herds, and the lambs of your flocks in the land He swore to your ancestors to give you. {7:14} You'll be more blessed than any other people; none of you or your livestock will be childless. {7:15} The LORD will keep you free from disease, not inflicting on you the horrible diseases you knew in Egypt, but instead, He'll bring them upon all who hate you. {7:16} You must destroy all the people the LORD your God hands over to you; don't look on them with pity and don't serve their gods, for that'll be a trap for you.

{7:17} If you think, "These nations are stronger than we are; how can we drive them out?" {7:18} Don't be scared; remember what the LORD your God did to Pharaoh and all Egypt: {7:19} The great trials, signs, wonders, and mighty hand and outstretched arm by which He brought you out. The LORD your God will do the same to all the people you now fear. {7:20} Moreover, the LORD your God will send the hornet against them until even the survivors who hide from you are destroyed. {7:21} Don't be terrified of them, for the LORD your God, who is among you, is a great and awesome God. {7:22} The LORD your God will drive out those nations before you, little by little; you won't be allowed to eliminate them all at once, or the wild animals will multiply around you. {7:23} But the LORD your God will deliver them over to you, throwing them into great confusion until they're destroyed. {7:24} He will hand their kings over to you, and you'll wipe out their names from under heaven; no one will be able to stand against you until you destroy them. {7:25} Burn the images of their gods in the fire; don't covet the silver and gold on them, don't take it for yourselves, or you'll be trapped by it, for it's detestable to the LORD your God. {7:26} Don't bring any detestable thing into your house, or you, like it, will be set apart for destruction. Regard it as vile and utterly detest it, for it is set apart for destruction.

{8:1} Follow all the commands I'm giving you today so you can live, thrive, and take over the land the LORD promised your ancestors. {8:2} Remember how the LORD your God led you through the wilderness for forty years, humbling you and testing your heart to see if you'd keep His commands. {8:3} He made you experience hunger and then fed you with manna, something you and your ancestors had never seen, to show you that life's not just about bread but about every word from the LORD. {8:4} Your clothes didn't wear out, and your feet didn't swell for those forty years. {8:5} Think about it: just like a dad disciplines his kid, the LORD your God disciplines you. {8:6} So, keep the commands of the LORD your God, walk in His ways, and respect Him. {8:7} The LORD your God is bringing you into a good land, full of streams, springs, and rivers flowing from valleys and hills; {8:8} A land with wheat, barley, vines, fig trees, pomegranates, olive oil, and honey; {8:9} A place where you'll always have food and won't lack anything; a land with iron and copper in its hills. {8:10} When you've eaten and are satisfied, praise the LORD your God for the good land He's given you. {8:11} Don't forget the LORD your God by not keeping His commands, laws, and decrees I'm giving you today: {8:12} Otherwise, when you've eaten and are full, and have built fine houses and live in them; {8:13} And when your herds and flocks grow large, and your silver and gold increase, and everything you have multiplies; {8:14} Your heart might become proud, and you'll forget the LORD your God who brought you out of Egypt, out of the land of slavery; {8:15} Who led you through the vast and dreadful wilderness, with its fiery serpents, scorpions, and thirsty ground where there was no water; who brought water out of a hard rock; {8:16} Who fed you with manna in the wilderness, something your ancestors had never known, to humble and test you so that in the end it might go well with you; {8:17} You might say in your heart, "My power and my own strength have made me this wealthy." {8:18} But remember the LORD your God, for it's He who gives you the ability to produce wealth, confirming His covenant, which He swore to your ancestors, as it is today. {8:19} If you ever forget the LORD your God and follow other gods, worshiping and bowing down to them, I testify against you today that you will surely be destroyed. {8:20} Like the nations the LORD is about to destroy before you, so will you be destroyed for not obeying the LORD your God.

{9:1} Listen up, Israel: Today you're crossing the Jordan to take over nations way bigger and stronger than you, with massive cities walled up to the sky. {9:2} These are some huge people, the Anakims, who you know and have heard about. People say, "Who can stand up to the Anak?" {9:3} But know this: the LORD your God is going ahead of you like a blazing fire. He'll wipe them out and make them fall before you. You'll kick them out and destroy them quickly, just as the LORD promised. {9:4} Don't think, "The LORD brought me here because I'm so righteous." Nah, it's because those nations are super wicked that the LORD is getting rid of them. {9:5} It's not because you're righteous or have a pure heart that you're taking their land. It's because they're wicked and to keep the promise He made to your ancestors, Abraham, Isaac, and Jacob. {9:6} So, remember, it's not because you're all that righteous; you're actually pretty stubborn. {9:7} Don't forget how you made the LORD mad in the wilderness. From the day you left Egypt until now, you've been rebelling against the LORD. {9:8} At Horeb, you ticked off the LORD so much He wanted to destroy you. {9:9} When I went up the mountain to get the stone tablets, the ones with the covenant the LORD made with you, I stayed there forty days and nights, not eating or drinking. {9:10} The LORD gave me the two stone tablets written by His finger, with all the words He spoke to you from the fire on the mountain. {9:11} After forty days and nights, the LORD handed me the two stone tablets, the covenant tables. {9:12} Then the LORD said, "Go down quickly because your people, the ones you brought out of Egypt, have messed up. They've quickly turned away from what I commanded and made a molten image." {9:13} The LORD said, "I see this people, and they're so stubborn. {9:14} Leave me alone so I can destroy them and erase their name from under heaven. I'll make you into a stronger and greater nation." {9:15} So I went down the mountain, which was burning with fire, with the two tablets of the covenant in my hands. {9:16} I saw that you had sinned against the LORD your God by making a molten calf and quickly turning from His commands. {9:17} I took the two tablets and smashed them before your eyes. {9:18} Then I lay down before the LORD for another forty days and nights, not eating or drinking, because of your sinning and wickedness, provoking the LORD. {9:19} I was scared of the LORD's fierce anger that threatened to destroy you, but He listened to me that time too. {9:20} The LORD was super mad at Aaron, ready to destroy him, but I also prayed for Aaron. {9:21} I took that calf you made, burned it, crushed it into dust, and threw the dust into the brook flowing down the mountain. {9:22} At Taberah, Massah, and Kibroth-hattaavah, you made the LORD angry. {9:23} When the LORD sent you from Kadesh-barnea, saying, "Go take the land I've given you," you rebelled against the LORD's command, didn't trust Him, or listen to His voice. {9:24} You've been rebelling against the LORD since I've known you. {9:25} So I lay down before the LORD for forty days and nights because He said He would destroy you. {9:26} I prayed to the LORD, "Lord GOD, don't destroy your people, your inheritance, whom you redeemed with your greatness, whom you brought out of Egypt with a mighty hand. {9:27} Remember your servants, Abraham, Isaac, and Jacob. Don't look at the stubbornness, wickedness, and sin of these people. {9:28} Otherwise, the land you brought us from will say, 'The LORD couldn't bring them into the promised land and hated them, so He killed them in the wilderness.' {9:29} But they are your people, your inheritance, brought out by your mighty power and stretched-out arm.

{10:1} So, at that time, the LORD told me, "Cut out two stone tablets like the first ones and come up the mountain to me, and make a wooden ark. {10:2} I'll write on these tablets the same words that were on the ones you broke, and you'll put them in the ark." {10:3} So I made an ark of acacia wood, cut out two stone tablets like the first ones, and went up the mountain with the two tablets in my hands. {10:4} The LORD wrote the same ten commandments on the tablets that He had spoken to you from the fire on the mountain during the assembly, and He gave them to me. {10:5} I turned and came down the mountain and put the tablets in the ark I had made, just as the LORD commanded me, and they are there now. {10:6} The Israelites traveled from Beeroth of the children of Jaakan to Mosera, where Aaron died and was buried. His son Eleazar took over as priest. {10:7} From there, they traveled to Gudgodah, and from Gudgodah to Jotbath, a land with rivers of water. {10:8} At that time, the LORD set apart the tribe of Levi to carry the ark of the covenant, to stand before the LORD to minister and to bless in His name, which they still do today. {10:9} That's why the Levites don't have a share of the inheritance with the other tribes; the LORD is their inheritance, just as He promised them. {10:10} I stayed on the mountain for forty days and forty nights, like the first time, and the LORD listened to me again and didn't destroy you. {10:11} The LORD told me, "Get up, lead the people so they can enter and take possession of the land I promised their ancestors." {10:12} Now, Israel, what does the LORD your God ask of you but to fear Him, walk in His ways, love Him, and serve Him with all your heart and soul, {10:13} and to keep the LORD's commandments and decrees that I'm giving you today for your own good? {10:14} Look, the heavens, even the highest heavens, belong to the LORD your God, along with the earth and everything in it. {10:15} Yet the LORD set His affection on your ancestors and loved them, and He chose you, their descendants, above all nations, as it is today. {10:16} So, cut away the stubbornness of your heart and stop being so hard-headed. {10:17} For the LORD your God is the God of gods and Lord of lords, the great, mighty, and awesome God, who shows no partiality and accepts no bribes. {10:18} He defends the cause of the fatherless and widow, and loves the foreigner, giving him food and clothing. {10:19} So you must love the foreigner, for you were foreigners in Egypt. {10:20} Fear the LORD your God and serve Him. Hold fast to Him and take your oaths in His name. {10:21} He is your praise, He is your God, who performed for you those great and awesome wonders you saw with your own eyes. {10:22} Your ancestors went down into Egypt with seventy people, and now the LORD your God has made you as numerous as the stars in the sky.

{11:1} So, like, you gotta love the LORD your God and keep all His rules and stuff, always. {11:2} And, like, remember this, okay? 'Cause I'm not talking to your kids who haven't seen all the crazy things the LORD did, His power, His mighty hand, and how He showed up in Egypt to Pharaoh and everyone there; {11:3} and all the miracles and stuff He did, like with the army of Egypt, their horses, and chariots, drowning them in the Red Sea while they chased after you—like, the LORD totally wiped them out. {11:4} And don't forget what He did for you in the wilderness till you got here; {11:6} and remember what He did to Dathan and Abiram, how the ground swallowed them up with their families and everything they owned right in front of everyone. {11:7} But you saw it all go down, all the amazing things the LORD did. {11:8} So, make sure you keep all these rules I'm giving you today so you can be strong and take over the land you're going to. {11:9} And so you can live long in the land the LORD promised your ancestors—a land flowing with milk and honey. {11:10} 'Cause the land you're heading to isn't like Egypt, where you planted and watered everything with your feet, like a garden; {11:11} it's a land of hills and valleys, depending on rain from heaven. {11:12} The LORD takes care of this land; His eyes are always on it, from the beginning of the year to the end. {11:13} If you really listen to my rules today and love the LORD your God and serve Him with all your heart and soul, {11:14} He'll give you rain at the right time, so you'll have plenty of crops—corn, wine, and oil. {11:15} He'll make sure your fields have grass for your animals so you can eat and be full. {11:16} Just make sure you don't get tricked and start worshiping other gods; {11:17} 'cause if you do, the LORD will get mad, shut off the rain, and your land won't produce any fruit, and you'll be kicked off the good land He gave you. {11:18} So, keep my words in your heart and soul, and carry them with you as a sign on your hand and between your eyes. {11:19} Teach these rules to your kids, talk about them at home, when you're out, when you lie down, and when you get up. {11:20} Write them on your doorposts and gates. {11:21} This way, you and your kids will have long, blessed days in the land the LORD promised your ancestors. {11:22} 'Cause if you really keep all these rules, loving the LORD, walking in His ways, and sticking with Him, {11:23} the LORD will kick out all those nations in front of you, and you'll take over lands of nations bigger and stronger than you. {11:24} Everywhere you go, that land will be yours—from the wilderness to Lebanon, from the Euphrates River to the Mediterranean Sea. {11:25} No one will be able to stand up against you; the LORD your God will make sure everyone is scared of you, just like He said. {11:26} So, check this out: I'm putting before you today a blessing and a curse; {11:27} a blessing if you obey the LORD your God's rules that I'm giving you today, {11:28} and a curse if you don't obey and start following other gods you don't even know. {11:29} When the LORD brings you into the land you're going to, mark my words: put the blessing on Mount Gerizim and the curse on Mount Ebal. {11:30} They're on the other side of the Jordan, where the sun sets, in the land of the Canaanites, near Gilgal, by the plains of Moreh. {11:31} You're crossing the Jordan to take over the land the LORD your God is giving you and live there. {11:32} Follow all these rules and laws I'm giving you today.

{12:1} So, like, these are the rules and judgments you gotta follow once you're in the land that the LORD God of your ancestors is giving you to live on all your days. {12:2} You gotta totally wipe out all the places where the nations you're taking over worshiped their gods—on high mountains, hills, and under every green tree. {12:3} Tear down their altars, break their pillars, burn their groves with fire, smash their idols, and erase their names from those places. {12:4} But don't treat the LORD your God like that. {12:5} Instead, go to the place the LORD chooses to put His name among your tribes; that's where you bring your offerings, sacrifices, tithes, and other offerings. {12:6} Bring your offerings and chill there before the LORD your God, celebrating with everything you've been blessed with. {12:8} Don't just do whatever you think is right; {12:9} you're not settled in the land yet that the LORD is giving you as an inheritance. {12:10} But when you cross the Jordan and settle in the land the LORD gives you, and you're safe from enemies, {12:11} there will be a place the LORD chooses for His name; that's where you bring all your offerings, sacrifices, tithes, and vows. {12:12} Celebrate before the LORD your God—everyone in your household, including the Levites who don't have their own inheritance. {12:13} Don't offer your sacrifices everywhere you see. {12:14} Only offer them where the LORD chooses, in one of your tribes. {12:15} You can eat meat in any of your cities as you like, whether you're clean or unclean, like eating deer or gazelle. {12:16} Just don't eat the blood; pour it out on the ground like water. {12:17} Don't eat your tithes or offerings at home; eat them before the LORD your God at the place He chooses, and rejoice in everything you do. {12:19} Make sure you don't neglect the Levites as long as you live on this earth. {12:20} When the LORD enlarges your territory as promised, and you crave meat, {12:21} and if the place the LORD chooses is too far, you can slaughter animals for food in your cities as I commanded, just like deer or gazelle. {12:22} Both clean and unclean can eat them. {12:23} But never eat the blood; it's life, and don't mix that with your meat. {12:24} Pour it out on the ground like water. {12:25} This is for your own good and for your children's, if you do what's right in the LORD's sight. {12:26} Only bring your holy offerings and vows to the place the LORD chooses. {12:27} Offer your sacrifices on the LORD's altar; pour the blood on it and eat the meat. {12:28} Make sure you listen and follow all these commands, so things go well for you and your kids forever when you do what's right in the LORD's sight. {12:29} When the LORD wipes out the nations before you and you take over their land, {12:30} be careful not to be trapped by imitating their practices after they're gone—don't ask about their gods, saying, "How did they worship?" {12:31} Don't do those things to the LORD your God; they did awful stuff He hates, even sacrificing their children in fire to their gods. {12:32} Just do exactly what I command you; don't add or take away from it.

{13:1} Yo, if there's some prophet or dreamer among you who pulls off a crazy sign or wonder, {13:2} and then tries to get you to follow other gods you never heard of, saying, "Let's worship them," {13:3} don't listen to them! The LORD is testing you to see if you really love Him with all your heart and soul. {13:4} Stick with the LORD your God, fear Him, keep His commandments, obey His voice, serve Him, and hold tight to Him. {13:5} That prophet or dreamer has gotta go—straight up! They're trying to lead you away from the God who rescued you from Egypt and set you free from slavery. Get rid of that evil influence among you. {13:6} Even if it's your own family—your brother, son, daughter, wife, or best friend—secretly trying to get you to worship other gods you never knew about, {13:7} from all over the place, near or far, don't give in. {13:8} Don't sympathize, spare, or hide them; {13:9} you gotta be the first to deal with them, and then everyone else. {13:10} Stone them to death! They're trying to turn you away from the LORD your God who brought you out of Egypt. This is serious business. {13:11} This needs to be a lesson for all Israel—no more of this wickedness! {13:12} If word gets around in one of your cities that troublemakers are trying to get everyone to worship other gods, {13:13} you better investigate. {13:14} If it's true and they've really led people astray, {13:15} wipe out that city, everyone and everything in it, with the edge of the sword. {13:16} Burn it all down, including the loot, as an offering to the LORD your God. Let it be a desolate heap forever. {13:17} Don't keep anything cursed; you want the LORD to chill out and bless you, right? {13:18} So, do what's right in the eyes of the LORD your God by following His commands.

{14:1} Yo, you're the LORD's crew, so don't go cutting yourselves or shaving your heads for the dead. {14:2} You're special to the LORD your God; He picked you out above all the nations on earth. {14:3} Don't eat any nasty stuff. {14:4} Here's the deal on the animals you can eat: oxen, sheep, goats, {14:5} deer, roebuck, fallow deer, wild goat, pygarg, wild ox, chamois. {14:6} Any animal that chews the cud and has a split hoof, you can munch on it. {14:7} But don't eat animals that only chew the cud or only have split hooves like camels, hares, and coneys—they're a no-go. {14:8} And pork? Nope, it's unclean for you. Don't eat it or even touch its carcass. {14:9} Seafood's cool if it has fins and scales; if not, it's off-limits. {14:10} Clean birds are fair game. {14:11-18} But don't eat eagles, ossifrages, ospreys, glede, kite, vulture, ravens, owls, night hawks, cuckoos, or any other unclean birds. {14:19} Insects that fly? Nope, they're off the menu too. {14:20} Stick to clean birds for eating. {14:21} Don't eat animals that died on their own; give them to foreigners or sell them, but don't eat them. And don't boil a baby goat in its mother's milk. {14:22} Always give a tenth of your produce to the LORD every year. {14:23} Eat your tithes in the place the LORD chooses, to show respect and fear for Him. {14:24-26} If it's too far to carry your tithe, exchange it for money and buy whatever you want to feast on before the LORD, celebrating with your family and the Levites. {14:27} Don't forget the Levites in your town; they don't have land like you do. {14:28} Every three years, bring out all your tithes and share them with the Levites, strangers, orphans, and widows in your town so the LORD can bless your work.

{15:1} Every seven years, it's release time. {15:2} Here's the deal: Any lender among you should release the debts of their neighbors without pushing them; it's called the LORD'S release. {15:3} But if it's a foreigner, you can collect. {15:4} Especially when there are no more poor among you, 'cause the LORD's blessing you in the land He gave you. {15:5} Just keep rocking those commandments. {15:6} The LORD's hooking you up; you'll be lending to many nations and not borrowing, ruling over them but not the other way around. {15:7} If there's a poor dude among your crew, don't be cold-hearted or stingy. {15:8} Be generous and help them out with what they need. {15:9} Don't start thinking, "Oh, it's almost the seventh year, time for release," and then stiff your bro. {15:10} Give willingly; don't hold back, and the LORD will bless everything you do. {15:11} There will always be poor peeps around, so keep sharing the love with your bros and those in need. {15:12} Now, if one of your Hebrew homies gets sold to you and serves for six years, let them go free in the seventh year. {15:13} Send them off well-equipped; don't let them leave empty-handed. {15:14} Hook them up from your flock, your crops, your wine—share the blessings the LORD's given you. {15:15} Remember, you were slaves in Egypt, and the LORD set you free; that's why I'm telling you this today. {15:16} If they choose to stay 'cause they love you and your crib, you can mark them with an awl at the door to be your lifelong servant. Same goes for maidservants. {15:18} Don't sweat it when you set them free; they've been worth double the work. The LORD's gonna bless everything you do. {15:19} All firstborn males from your herds and flocks belong to the LORD; don't use them for work or shear them. {15:20} Feast on them before the LORD each year in the chosen place with your fam. {15:21} But if they're blemished—lame, blind, or sick—don't sacrifice them to the LORD. {15:22} Eat them in your town, clean or unclean, like you would a roebuck or a deer. {15:23} Just don't eat the blood; pour it out like water.

{16:1} Remember Abib month and celebrate the passover for the LORD your God; that's when He brought you out of Egypt at night. {16:2} Sacrifice the passover to the LORD your God from your flocks and herds at the chosen place where His name dwells. {16:3} No leavened bread during this—seven days of eating unleavened bread to remember your quick exit from Egypt. {16:4} No leavened bread should be seen around during these seven days, and don't let any meat from the first day's sacrifice stay overnight until morning. {16:5} Don't hold the passover in your local spots; it's gotta be at the place the LORD chooses, at sunset, just like when you left Egypt. {16:6} Roast and eat it there, then head back to your tents in the morning. {16:8} Feast for six days with unleavened bread; on the seventh, have a serious assembly for the LORD—no work allowed. {16:9} Count seven weeks from when you start harvesting, then celebrate the feast of weeks, giving a freewill offering as a tribute to the LORD. {16:11} Rejoice together with everyone—family, servants, Levites, strangers, orphans, widows—at the chosen place where the LORD's name is. {16:12} Remember your time in Egypt and keep these statutes. {16:13} Celebrate the feast of tabernacles for seven days after harvesting your crops and wine. {16:14} It's a joyful feast for everyone—family, servants, Levites, strangers, orphans, and widows, all in your town. {16:15} Keep a weeklong solemn feast to the LORD at His chosen place; He'll bless your hard work, so celebrate big time. {16:16} Every male must appear before the LORD three times a year at His chosen place—during the feast of unleavened bread, weeks, and tabernacles—and don't show up empty-handed; bring an offering according to what you can give. {16:18} Make sure you appoint judges and officers in all your towns; they gotta judge the people fairly. {16:19} No playing favorites or taking bribes; that messes up justice. {16:20} Stick to what's right so you can live long and inherit the land the LORD's giving you. {16:21} Don't plant trees near the LORD's altar to make a grove, and don't set up any idols, which the LORD hates.

{17:1} Don't offer up any messed-up animals to the LORD—blemishes or weird stuff are a big no-go. {17:2} If someone in your community does something super messed up, like worshipping other gods, especially sun, moon, or stars which God never told us to do, {17:3} and it turns out to be true after checking, {17:4} then bring that person out and stone them to death—yep, serious consequences. {17:6} You need at least two or three witnesses to take someone down like that; one witness isn't enough. {17:7} The witnesses throw the first stones, then everyone else follows. Got to clean up that evil from among us. {17:8} If you've got a tough situation to figure out—like a big disagreement or fight—take it to the place the LORD chooses. {17:9} Talk to the Levite priests and the judges; they'll give you the verdict. {17:10} Whatever they decide, you've gotta stick to it—no going against their judgment. {17:11} Follow the law and don't veer off course. {17:12} Anyone who refuses to listen to the priests or judges deserves to be cut off from Israel. {17:14} When you settle in the land and decide you want a king like other nations, {17:15} pick someone God chooses from your own people—no outsiders. {17:16} The king shouldn't pile up horses or send people back to Egypt just to get more horses; God said no way to that. {17:17} And no collecting a bunch of wives or hoarding silver and gold. {17:18-19} The king must copy down the law, keep it close, and read it every day to stay humble and follow God's rules. {17:20} By doing that, he'll stay level-headed and ensure a long reign for himself and his family within Israel.

{18:1} So, the Levite priests—they don't get any land in Israel like the other tribes. Instead, they live off the offerings made to the LORD, which is basically their paycheck. {18:2} Their inheritance is the LORD himself, as he promised. {18:3} When people bring sacrifices—like oxen or sheep—the priests get a cut: the shoulder, cheeks, and stomach. {18:4} Plus, they get the first of your crops, wine, oil, and wool. {18:5} The LORD picked them out from all the tribes to serve him forever. {18:6} If a Levite leaves his home anywhere in Israel and wants to serve at the place the LORD chose, {18:7} he can minister to the LORD just like the other Levites who are already there. {18:8} They all share the same perks, aside from whatever they get from selling their own property. {18:9} When you settle in the land, don't copy the disgusting practices of other nations. {18:10} No sacrificing your kids, practicing divination, fortune-telling, enchanting, witchcraft, {18:11} casting spells, consulting spirits, wizardry, or summoning the dead. {18:12} These things are disgusting to the LORD, and that's why he kicked out those nations before you. {18:13} Stay true to the LORD your God. {18:14} The nations you're replacing listened to fortune-tellers and diviners, but that's not your vibe. {18:15} The LORD will send you a Prophet from among your own people—listen to him. {18:16} Remember back at Horeb when you were like, "I can't handle hearing God's voice or seeing fire"? {18:17} God agreed with you, saying you made a good call. {18:18} He'll send a Prophet like Moses, speaking only God's words. {18:19} If anyone ignores this Prophet, God's gonna hold them accountable. {18:20} But if a prophet speaks on his own or in the name of other gods—yeah, that prophet's in trouble. {18:21} If you wonder how to spot a fake, just wait and see if what they predict actually happens. {18:22} If their predictions flop, they're not speaking for God—don't stress about them.

{19:1} So, when God wipes out the nations in the land he's giving you, and you take over their cities and houses; {19:2} set aside three cities in your land as safe havens. {19:3} Make sure there are good roads and divide the land into three parts so anyone who accidentally kills someone can flee there. {19:4} Here's the deal with accidental killings: If you're chopping wood with a friend and the axe head flies off, hitting and killing your buddy, head to one of those cities to stay alive. {19:6} This way, the victim's family won't come after you in anger, thinking you did it on purpose. {19:7} That's why I'm telling you to set up these cities. {19:8} And if God expands your territory, like he promised your ancestors, {19:9} and if you keep all his commands, loving and following him; add three more cities to the list. {19:10} We don't want innocent bloodshed in the land God gave you, or you'll be responsible. {19:11} Now, if someone hates their neighbor, plans to kill them, and actually does it—then heads to one of those cities; {19:12} the elders will hand them over to the victim's family to be put to death. {19:13} Don't show pity; getting rid of innocent blood is crucial for your well-being. {19:14} Don't mess with your neighbor's property lines that were set by their ancestors in the land you're inheriting. {19:15} You can't convict someone of a crime based on one person's word alone; you need two or three witnesses to make it stick. {19:16} If someone lies about another person's wrongdoing; {19:17} both parties will stand trial before God, the priests, and judges. {19:18} The judges will thoroughly investigate, and if the accuser is lying, {19:19} whatever they planned to happen to the accused should happen to them—get rid of the evil in your midst. {19:20} This will make everyone think twice about doing wrong. {19:21} Remember, it's an eye for an eye, tooth for a tooth—life for life.

{20:1} So, when you're about to face off against your enemies—maybe they've got horses, chariots, and seem like a big deal—don't stress; God's got your back, just like when he brought you out of Egypt. {20:2} When you're getting close to battle, the priest steps up and says, {20:3} "Listen up, Israel! Don't get scared or tremble in fear of them; {20:4} God's the one fighting for you against your enemies, ready to save you. {20:5} Here's the drill from the officers: If anyone just built a new house but hasn't dedicated it, they better go back home or they might not make it back from battle, and someone else will dedicate it. {20:6} Same goes for anyone who planted a vineyard but hasn't tasted the fruit—they should head home too, or they might not get the chance. {20:7} And if anyone recently got engaged but hasn't married yet, they should go home, or someone else might swoop in while they're away. {20:8} And if anyone's feeling too scared or unsure, they should go home too; we don't want them bringing down the morale of the crew. {20:9} Once the officers finish, they'll appoint army captains to lead the way. {20:10} Now, when you approach a city to fight, offer peace first. {20:11} If they accept and open their gates, they become your subjects and serve you. {20:12} But if they refuse and choose war, then prepare for a siege. {20:13-14} Once you've taken the city, take out all the men, but spare the women, children, and livestock—take the spoils as your reward from God. {20:15} This is how you handle cities far away that aren't part of these nations. {20:16-18} But for the cities of these nations that God gives you, wipe them out completely—the Hittites, Amorites, Canaanites, Perizzites, Hivites, and Jebusites—as God commanded, so they don't corrupt you with their practices. {20:19} When you've been besieging a city for a while, don't chop down all the trees; they're useful for food and shouldn't be destroyed recklessly. {20:20} Only cut down the trees that aren't good for food to build your siege works against the city until it falls.

{21:1} If someone is found dead in the land that God gave you, and no one knows who did it, {21:2} the elders and judges will figure out which city is closest to the scene. {21:3} Then, the elders of that city will take a young cow that hasn't been used for work, {21:4} bring it to a rough valley, and chop off its head there. {21:5} The priests, chosen by God, will handle the legal stuff, settling every dispute and case. {21:6} The elders of that city will wash their hands over the cow to show they're innocent. {21:7} They'll declare, "We didn't do this; we didn't even see it happen." {21:8} They'll pray for mercy, asking God not to blame the people for innocent blood. {21:9} This clears the guilt of innocent blood when you do what's right in God's eyes. {21:10} Now, when you're off to war and God gives you victory, and you capture prisoners, {21:11} if you see a beautiful woman among them and want to marry her, {21:12} bring her home, shave her head, and let her mourn her family for a month. {21:13} After that, you can marry her, but if it doesn't work out, don't treat her like property; let her go free. {21:15} If a man has two wives—one loved and one not so much—and both have children, {21:16} he can't play favorites with the inheritance, especially favoring the child of the loved wife over the firstborn of the unloved one. {21:17} The firstborn of the unloved wife gets a double portion; that's the rule. {21:18} Now, if a man has a rebellious son who won't listen to his parents and is a troublemaker, {21:19} the parents can bring him to the city elders and accuse him. {21:20} They'll say, "He's stubborn, won't listen, and parties too much." {21:21} The men of the city will stone him to death; it's about cleaning up evil, and everyone will learn a lesson. {21:22} Also, if someone commits a serious crime deserving death and is hanged on a tree, {21:23} bury them the same day because a hanged person is cursed by God, and you don't want to defile the land God gave you.

{22:1} If you see your bro's ox or sheep wandering off, don't just ignore it—bring them back to your bro. {22:2} And if your bro isn't around or you don't know them, take the animals home with you and keep them safe until your bro comes looking, then give them back. {22:3} Treat lost stuff from your bro the same way—don't pretend you didn't find it. {22:4} If you see your bro's donkey or ox stuck on the road, help them out and get them back on their feet. {22:5} Guys, don't wear girl clothes, and girls, no guy clothes—God's not into that. {22:6} If you come across a bird's nest with chicks or eggs and the mama bird is there, take the babies but let the mama bird go free. {22:8} When you build a new house, put a railing around the roof to prevent accidents. {22:9} Don't mix different seeds in your vineyard; keep it pure. {22:10} Don't plow with a mixed team of ox and donkey. {22:11} Don't wear clothes made of different fabrics mixed together. {22:12} Put fringes on your clothes to remind you of God's commands. {22:13} If a man marries a woman and then hates her, spreading lies about her not being a virgin, {22:14} her parents can prove her innocence by showing the evidence to the city elders. {22:15} The dad explains that he gave his daughter to this guy, and now he's lying about her. {22:16} The elders punish the lying husband and make him pay a fine to the girl's dad; he can't divorce her. {22:17-19} But if the accusations are true and the girl isn't a virgin, she's stoned for bringing shame. {22:20-21} If a man sleeps with a married woman, both are stoned to death. {22:22} If a betrothed virgin is found having sex in the city, both are stoned. {22:25} But if a man forces a betrothed woman in the field, only he is punished. {22:23} If a man sleeps with an unmarried virgin, he must marry her and pay her father.

{23:1} If someone gets seriously injured down there or loses their private parts, they can't be part of the crew of the LORD. {23:2} A bastard won't be part of the crew of the LORD, not even for ten generations. {23:3} Ammonites and Moabites can't join the crew of the LORD, not even for ten generations, because they didn't help out with food and water when you left Egypt. {23:4} They even hired Balaam to curse you, but God turned it around for you because He loves you. {23:6} Don't try to make friends with them or wish them well forever. {23:7} Don't hate Edomites; they're family. Don't hate Egyptians either because you were once strangers in their land. {23:8} Their kids can join the crew of the LORD after three generations. {23:9} When you're going into battle, keep away from anything shady. {23:10} If someone's unclean because of something that happened at night, they need to stay outside the camp until evening, then they can wash up and come back in. {23:13} Keep an area outside the camp where you can go do your business, and make sure to cover it up. {23:14} God is with you in camp, so keep it clean and holy. {23:15} If a slave escapes to you, don't send them back to their master; let them stay among you wherever they choose. {23:17} No prostitutes among the Israelite women, and no male prostitutes among the Israelite men. {23:18} Don't bring money earned from prostitution or the price of a dog into the house of the LORD for any offering—it's all gross to God. {23:19} Don't charge interest on loans to fellow Israelites, whether it's money, food, or anything else. {23:20} You can charge interest to foreigners, but not to your own people, so you'll be blessed in everything you do in the land you're taking over.

{24:1} If a guy marries a girl but later decides she's not his vibe anymore because of something sketchy, he can write her a breakup note, give it to her, and send her packing. {24:2} After she's out of his place, she's free to marry someone else. {24:3-4} But if that second guy also ends up hating her and dumps her with a note, or if he dies, then her first husband can't take her back after that because it's gross to the LORD. {24:5} When a guy gets married, he gets a year off from war or other work to chill with his new wife. {24:6} Don't take someone's millstones as collateral—it's like taking their life. {24:7} If anyone is caught kidnapping an Israelite and selling them, that person is done for. {24:8-9} Pay attention to leprosy and follow what the priests say about it. {24:10-13} When you lend something to your buddy, don't go into their house to get collateral. {24:14} Treat poor hired workers right, whether they're from your crew or outsiders. {24:15} Don't mess with the rights of strangers, orphans, or widows. {24:16} If you forget a sheaf in your field during harvest, leave it for those in need. {24:17} Same goes for your olive trees and vineyards—leave some for the less fortunate.

{25:1} When there's beef between dudes and they bring it to court, the judges gotta make sure they're fair, siding with the righteous and calling out the wicked. {25:2} If the guilty dude deserves a beating, the judge can order it, but it's gotta be reasonable—like, forty lashes max, otherwise it's too harsh. {25:3} Don't be cruel to the ox grinding corn; let it eat while it works. {25:4} If bros live together and one dies without kids, his widow can't just marry anyone; she's gotta marry his bro and keep the family line going. {25:5} If two guys are fighting and one's wife jumps in to save her man by, you know, grabbing the other guy's privates, that's a big no-no—chop her hand off. {25:6} No cheating with different weights in your bag or different measures at home; keep it fair with the same standards for everyone. {25:7} And don't forget what Amalek did to you on the way out of Egypt—when you were tired and vulnerable, they attacked from behind. {25:8} So, when you've finally got peace and quiet in the Promised Land, wipe out the memory of Amalek—don't let it linger.

{26:1} So, when you finally roll into the land God gave you, settled in and all, {26:2} grab the first fruits from your land, put them in a basket, and head over to the place where God's name is chillin'. {26:3} Talk to the priest there and tell 'em, "Today, I'm repping the land God promised our ancestors." {26:4} The priest will take your basket and set it down at God's altar. {26:5} Then you spill to God, "My ancestors were nomads, and we ended up in Egypt with just a few of us, but look at us now—a big nation." {26:6} Egypt wasn't cool to us, though—made us slaves and all that. {26:7-8} But we cried out to the Lord, and He heard us, saw our struggles, and got us out of there with a bang—mighty hand, signs, and wonders. {26:9} He brought us here, to this awesome land flowing with milk and honey. {26:10} And now, I've brought these first fruits to you, Lord, to show some love. {26:11} Celebrate all the good stuff God's given you, your fam, the Levites, and even the strangers. {26:12} Today, God's laid down the rules—keep 'em close to your heart and soul. {26:13} You've committed to walking in God's ways, keeping His rules, and listening to His voice. {26:14} In return, God's chosen you as His special crew, and He's got big plans to boost you up.

{27:1} Moses and the elders told everyone, "Keep all the rules I'm giving you today." {27:2} When you cross over the Jordan into the land God's giving you, set up some big stones and cover them with plaster. {27:3} Write down all these laws on the stones when you cross over, heading into that sweet land flowing with milk and honey that God promised your ancestors. {27:4} Once you're across the Jordan, set up those stones on Mount Ebal and plaster them up. {27:5} Build an altar of stones there for the Lord your God, no iron tools allowed. {27:6} Use whole stones for the altar and offer burnt offerings and peace offerings to the Lord. {27:7} Eat there and have a good time in front of the Lord your God. {27:8} Write all these laws clearly on the stones. {27:9} Moses and the Levite priests told Israel, "Listen up! Today, you become God's people." {27:10} So, make sure you obey God's voice and follow His rules and statutes. {27:11} Moses said to the people, {27:12} "These tribes will bless the people on Mount Gerizim: Simeon, Levi, Judah, Issachar, Joseph, and Benjamin. {27:13} These tribes will stand on Mount Ebal to curse: Reuben, Gad, Asher, Zebulun, Dan, and Naphtali. {27:14} The Levites will say loudly to all Israel, {27:15} 'Cursed is anyone who makes idols and hides them.' The people will say, 'Amen.' {27:16}

'Cursed is anyone who disrespects their parents.' The people will say, 'Amen.' {27:17} 'Cursed is anyone who moves their neighbor's boundary marker.' The people will say, 'Amen.' {27:18} 'Cursed is anyone who causes a blind person to wander off track.' The people will say, 'Amen.' {27:19} 'Cursed is anyone who perverts justice for strangers, orphans, and widows.' The people will say, 'Amen.' {27:20} 'Cursed is anyone who sleeps with their father's wife, exposing their father's shame.' The people will say, 'Amen.' {27:21} 'Cursed is anyone who sleeps with an animal.' The people will say, 'Amen.' {27:22} 'Cursed is anyone who sleeps with their half-sister.' The people will say, 'Amen.' {27:23} 'Cursed is anyone who sleeps with their mother-in-law.' The people will say, 'Amen.' {27:24} 'Cursed is anyone who attacks their neighbor secretly.' The people will say, 'Amen.' {27:25} 'Cursed is anyone who takes money to kill an innocent person.' The people will say, 'Amen.' {27:26} 'Cursed is anyone who doesn't stick to all the rules in this law.' The people will say, 'Amen.'

{28:1} So like, if you're all about listening to what the big guy upstairs says, following all his rules and stuff, then you're gonna be like the top dog, better than any other nation out there. {28:2} And trust, all the good vibes and blessings will be raining down on you, if you're all ears for what the big man upstairs is saying. {28:3} You'll be blessed in the city and out in the boonies too. {28:4} Your kids, your crops, your livestock, everything's gonna be blessed, like straight up thriving. {28:5} Your pantry and your stash, all blessed too. {28:6} Every move you make, from stepping out to coming back home, it's gonna be blessed. {28:7} Any haters who come at you are gonna get wrecked, like they'll come at you one way but peace out seven ways. {28:8} God's gonna hook you up with blessings in everything you put your hands on, in the land he gave you. {28:9} You'll be like this holy squad for God, as promised, if you stay on his grind. {28:10} And everyone's gonna know you're repping the Lord's name, they'll be shook. {28:11} Your pockets, your livestock, your crops, it's all gonna be overflowing with blessings in the land God promised your ancestors. {28:12} Heaven's gonna open up, rain's gonna bless your land, everything you do will prosper, and you won't need to borrow from nobody. {28:13} You'll be the head honcho, not the sidekick, only on top, never at the bottom, if you stay on God's grind, doing what he says. {28:14} And don't even think about straying from God's word, not even a step to the left or right, chasing after other gods. {28:15} But if you straight up ignore what God's saying, and don't keep his rules and regs, then brace yourself for a world of hurt, 'cause all these curses are gonna hit you like a ton of bricks. {28:16} Cursed in the city, cursed in the sticks. {28:17} Your pantry and stash? Yeah, cursed too. {28:18} Your kids, your crops, your livestock? All cursed. {28:19} From the moment you step out to when you come back home, it's all cursed. {28:20} You're gonna be hit with every curse imaginable, everything you try to do will be a fail, 'til you're wiped out, all because you turned your back on God. {28:21} Sickness, disease, it's all gonna stick to you like glue, 'til you're gone from the land you were supposed to own. {28:22} You'll be hit with every sickness under the sun, relentless until you're wiped out. {28:23} Your sky's gonna be like brass, the ground beneath you like iron. {28:24} Rain? Nah, it's gonna be like powder and dust, no relief 'til you're done for. {28:25} Your enemies? Yeah, they'll have the upper hand, chasing you down 'til you're scattered everywhere. {28:26} Your dead body? Just gonna be bird and beast buffet, no one's gonna shoo 'em away. {28:27} You'll be plagued with diseases you can't shake off, no matter what you try. {28:28} Madness, blindness, confusion of mind, you'll be stumbling around like it's midnight in broad daylight, nothing's gonna go right, and no one's gonna save you. {28:29} You'll be groping around like you're blind, never finding success, just constantly getting jacked and robbed, with no one to help. {28:30} You'll marry, but someone else will slide into your partner's DMs. You'll build a house, but you won't get to live in it. You'll plant a vineyard, but you won't even taste the grapes. {28:31} Your livestock will be slaughtered before your eyes, your ride jacked, your sheep given to your enemies, and nobody's gonna step in to help. {28:32} Your kids will be taken from you and given to others, and you'll long for them all day, but you won't be able to do a thing about it. {28:33} Your hard-earned goods will be snatched up by a nation you don't even know, and you'll just keep getting crushed and oppressed. {28:34} You'll be driven crazy by the sight of everything going wrong. {28:35} God's gonna hit you with messed-up knees and legs, sores from head to toe, no healing in sight. {28:36} God will send you and your leader to a nation you never heard of, where you'll worship other gods, idols made of wood and stone. {28:37} You'll become a laughingstock, a cautionary tale, a joke among all the nations where God sends you. {28:38} You'll plant seeds, but harvest next to nothing, 'cause locusts will devour it all. {28:39} You'll plant vineyards, but won't enjoy the wine, 'cause worms will eat up your grapes. {28:40} You'll have olive trees, but no olive oil, 'cause your olives will drop off. {28:41} You'll have kids, but won't get to enjoy them, 'cause they'll be taken away into captivity. {28:42} Your trees and crops will be eaten up by locusts. {28:43} Strangers in your midst will rise above you, and you'll sink low. {28:44} They'll be lending to you, but you won't be lending to them. They'll be on top, you'll be on the bottom. {28:45} And these curses will hunt you down, catch you, and crush you, 'cause you didn't listen to God's voice and follow his rules and regulations. {28:46} They'll be a sign and a wonder on you and your descendants forever. {28:47} 'Cause you didn't serve God with joy and gladness when you had everything, now you'll serve your enemies in hunger, thirst, and lack of everything, with an iron yoke around your neck 'til you're wiped out. {28:48} God will bring a distant nation against you, like eagles swooping down, speaking a language you don't understand. {28:49} They'll be fierce and show no mercy, devouring everything you've got 'til you're done for. {28:50} They'll besiege you in all your cities, knocking down your fortified walls, in the land God gave you. {28:51} You'll eat your own children during the siege, no pity for anyone. {28:52} Even the gentlest among you will turn savage, turning on family and loved ones, 'cause life's gonna be brutal. {28:53} So like, in the middle of all this chaos, when your enemies have you trapped and stressed out, you'll end up eating your own kids—yeah, it's gonna get that bad. {28:54} The gentlest among you will turn bitter, giving evil looks to family and loved ones, 'cause everyone's gonna be desperate and struggling. {28:55} They won't even share the flesh of their kids that they eat, 'cause they've got nothing left in the siege and distress from enemies at every gate. {28:56} Even delicate women, who wouldn't dare walk outside, will turn against their own families when they're starving and trapped. {28:57} They'll hide the fact that they're eating their own children out of sheer desperation. {28:58} If you don't stick to all the rules laid out in this book and honor God's name, brace yourself for mind-blowing plagues and sicknesses that won't quit.

{28:59} You'll face all the horrors of Egypt and then some, with diseases that won't let go. {28:60} Every sickness and plague not even mentioned here will come crashing down on you until you're wiped out. {28:61} Your numbers will dwindle, from stars in the sky to barely a handful, all because you refused to listen to God. {28:62} God once rejoiced in blessing and multiplying you, but now he'll take joy in destroying and scattering you, ripping you from the land you were meant to inherit. {28:63} You'll be scattered across the globe, forced to serve foreign gods made of wood and stone. {28:64} Among these nations, you'll find no peace, just constant anxiety, failing health, and deep sorrow. {28:65} Your life will hang in the balance, living in perpetual fear day and night, with no certainty about tomorrow. {28:66} You'll wish for night in the morning and morning at night, terrified of what you see and experience. {28:67} Eventually, God will send you back to Egypt, but this time by ship—a journey you'll never return from. {28:68} There, you'll be sold into slavery, and no one will come to your rescue.

{29:1} So, like, here's the deal—the covenant words that the LORD gave to Moses for the Israelites in Moab, in addition to the one made back in Horeb. {29:2} Moses gathered all of Israel and was like, "Y'all saw firsthand everything the LORD did in Egypt to Pharaoh and his crew, right? The miracles, the signs—epic stuff." {29:3} Despite all that, the LORD didn't open your hearts or eyes or ears to get it till now. {29:4} I've led you through the wilderness for forty years; your clothes and shoes didn't wear out 'cause I'm showing off that I'm your God. {29:6} You didn't eat bread or drink booze all this time so you'd recognize who's boss. {29:7} When we rolled up on Sihon king of Heshbon and Og king of Bashan, we took 'em down and handed their turf to Reubenites, Gadites, and half the tribe of Manasseh. {29:9} Follow this covenant and prosper in all you do. {29:10} Today, you're all standing before the LORD—leaders, elders, officers, everyone: {29:11} the kids, wives, and even the strangers in camp, from the wood-choppers to the water-fetchers. {29:12} We're here to enter into this covenant and oath with the LORD today, making us His chosen people as promised to our ancestors—Abraham, Isaac, and Jacob. {29:15} And not just with those here today, but also with those not here. {29:18} We're serious about this—no turning away to worship other gods or stirring up trouble. {29:20} If anyone tries to shrug off the curse and live like it's all good, the LORD will be ticked and let loose all the curses written in this book, erasing their name from the map. {29:22} Future generations and even outsiders will be shook when they see the land's disasters and sicknesses, a wasteland like Sodom, Gomorrah, Admah, and Zeboim—totally wrecked by the LORD. {29:25} People will be asking why all this went down, and the answer's simple: they ditched the LORD's covenant, worshiping gods they didn't even know. {29:28} So the LORD booted them out of their land in rage, casting them into another place where they still are today.

{30:1} So, like, when all this stuff—the good and the bad—happens to you and you're spread across all these nations the LORD sent you to, {30:2} if you turn back to the LORD your God and follow His rules with all your heart and soul, {30:3} then God will bring you back from wherever you've been scattered, showing compassion and gathering you up. {30:4} Even if you've been tossed to the ends of the earth, God will still find you and bring you back. {30:5} You'll inherit the land your ancestors had, and God will hook you up even more than them. {30:6} He'll change your heart and your kids' hearts so you'll love Him with everything and actually live life. {30:7} And God will put all these curses on your enemies and those who messed with you. {30:8} If you come back to God and do what He says, {30:9} He'll make you successful in everything you do—your family, your work, your land—just like He did with your ancestors. {30:10} All you gotta do is listen to God, keep His laws, and really commit to Him with all you've got. {30:11} 'Cause what I'm telling you isn't some secret mission; it's right here in front of you. {30:12} You don't have to go to the ends of the earth or beyond the sky to get it; it's right here with you. {30:14} It's right on your lips and in your heart, ready for you to do it. {30:15} Look, I'm giving you two options today: choose life and good or death and bad. {30:16} Follow God, keep His rules, and you'll thrive in the land you're heading to. {30:17} But if you turn away, worship other gods, and ignore God's rules, {30:18} you're signing up for disaster; you won't last long in the land you're about to enter. {30:19} I'm putting it out there—life or death, blessing or curse—so pick life and live on, you and your kids. {30:20} Love God, obey Him, stick with Him 'cause He's your life and your future in the land promised to your ancestors—Abraham, Isaac, and Jacob.

{31:1} So Moses gathered everyone together and dropped some truth on Israel. {31:2} He's like, "I'm 120 today and can't keep up anymore. The LORD told me I won't make it across the Jordan." {31:3} But don't trip, the LORD will handle those nations for you, and Joshua will lead the way, just like the LORD said. {31:4} God's gonna deal with them like He did with Sihon and Og—remember them? {31:5} The LORD will give them over to you so you can do what I've taught you. {31:6} Stay strong and fearless, 'cause the LORD's got your back; He won't bail on you. {31:7} Moses pulled Joshua aside and hyped him up in front of everyone, telling him to take the people to their promised land and make it theirs. {31:8} The LORD's the one leading the charge; He won't ditch you. Don't be scared or worried. {31:9} Moses wrote down the law and gave it to the Levite priests carrying the covenant ark and to all the elders of Israel. {31:10} Moses told them, "Every seven years during the year of release at the feast of tabernacles, {31:11} when everyone's gathered before the LORD at His chosen place, read this law out loud for everyone to hear. {31:12} Bring everyone—men, women, kids, even visitors—so they can learn to respect the LORD and obey His law. {31:13} It's for their kids too, so they grow up knowing and fearing the LORD in the land you're heading to." {31:14} Then the LORD told Moses, "Your time's almost up; call Joshua and meet Me at the tabernacle." So Moses and Joshua headed over. {31:15} God showed up in a cloud pillar at the tabernacle door. {31:16} He told Moses, "You're gonna rest with your ancestors soon, and these people are gonna chase after foreign gods in the land they're going to, forsaking Me and breaking our deal." {31:17} God's gonna be ticked, hiding His face as they suffer many troubles and say, 'Where's God when we need Him?' {31:18} I'll totally hide from them because of the evil they do, turning to other gods. {31:19} So, write this song and teach it to the Israelites to remind them of their disobedience. {31:20} When they're living large in the promised land, getting fat and happy, they'll turn to other gods, ticking Me off and breaking our deal. {31:21} This song will be proof against them, never forgotten by their descendants, 'cause I know what they're thinking even before they get to the promised land." {31:22} Moses wrote the song that day and taught it to the Israelites. {31:23} He gave Joshua a pep talk, saying, "Stay strong; you're leading them to their promised land, and I'll be with you." {31:24} After writing down all these laws, Moses handed the book to the Levites carrying the covenant ark. {31:25} "Put this book in the side of the covenant ark as a witness against you," Moses instructed. {31:26} "I know you've rebelled; even while I'm alive, you've gone against the LORD. How much worse will it be after I'm gone?" {31:28} Moses gathered all the elders and officers to hear his final words, calling on heaven and earth as witnesses. {31:29} "I know you'll mess up after I'm gone, turning away from the LORD's way and facing evil in the future because of your wicked deeds." {31:30} Moses dropped the mic after sharing this song with the entire congregation of Israel.

{32:1} Yo, listen up, you heavens, and hear me out, earth. {32:2} My words are gonna be like rain, my speech like dew, gentle on the plants, showering blessings on the grass. {32:3} I'm shouting out the name of the LORD; give Him the props He deserves. {32:4} He's solid like a rock, flawless in His work, always just and true. {32:5} But these people, they've messed themselves up; they're nothing like His children—a twisted and rebellious bunch. {32:6} Seriously, are you really gonna treat the LORD like this, acting all foolish? Isn't He your Father who made and established you? {32:7} Remember the old days, think about all the generations past; ask your parents or elders—they'll tell you. {32:8} When the Most High divided up the nations and set boundaries, He did it with Israel in mind. {32:9} 'Cause the LORD's got His people; Jacob is His special inheritance. {32:10} He found them in the desert, in a barren wilderness, guiding and caring for them like His favorites. {32:11} Like an eagle stirring up its nest, the LORD watched over them, teaching and protecting. {32:12} He led them alone; no other gods were with them. {32:13} He gave them the best of the land's produce, honey from rocks, oil from flinty stones. {32:14} They had the finest, but they got fat and turned away from God, forgetting the Rock who saved them. {32:15} Instead, they angered Him with foreign gods and abominations. {32:16} They made Him jealous and mad with their idols. {32:17} They worshipped demons, not God, chasing after new gods their ancestors never knew. {32:18} They forgot the Rock who gave them life. {32:19} When the LORD saw this, He was disgusted with His children's rebellion. {32:20} He decided to hide His face and see what would become of them—a faithless and disobedient generation. {32:21} They made God jealous with worthless idols, so He'll make them jealous with a foolish nation. {32:22} His anger blazed like fire, burning down to the depths of the earth, consuming everything. {32:23} He'll bring disaster upon them, shooting His arrows. {32:24} They'll suffer hunger, heat, and bitter destruction, attacked by wild beasts and poisonous snakes. {32:25} Both young and old will face destruction from outside and fear from within. {32:26} He planned to scatter them, wiping out their memory from among humanity. {32:27} But He held back, not wanting their enemies to brag, thinking they defeated them on their own. {32:28} They're a nation without sense or understanding. {32:29} If only they were wise and understood their end! {32:30} How could one enemy chase a thousand, or two put ten thousand to flight, if not for the LORD allowing it? {32:31} Our Rock is nothing like theirs; even their enemies know it. {32:32} Their vine is poisonous, like Sodom's grapes, bitter and deadly. {32:33} Their wine is like dragon venom, cruel and deadly. {32:34} Isn't all this written down, sealed up in God's treasure? {32:35} Vengeance belongs to God; their downfall is coming, and it won't be delayed. {32:36} The LORD will judge His people and show mercy when He sees their power is gone. {32:37} They'll cry out to their useless gods for help, but they won't save them. {32:38} These gods, who feasted on sacrifices and drink offerings, won't come to their aid. {32:39} See, I alone am God; there's no one beside Me. I control life and death, healing and harm—no one can escape My hand. {32:40} I raise My hand to heaven and declare: I live forever. {32:41} If I sharpen My sword for judgment, I'll repay My enemies and punish those who hate Me. {32:42} My arrows will be drenched in blood, My sword will devour flesh—payback for all the enemies' wrongs. {32:43} Rejoice, nations, with His people, for He'll avenge His servants' blood and show mercy to His land and people. {32:44} So Moses and Hoshea spoke this song to the people, wrapping it up. {32:45} Moses finished sharing these words with all Israel. {32:46} He told them, "Pay attention to these words I've shared today; teach them to your kids and make sure to follow this law. {32:47} It's not just some empty talk—it's your life, and it's what will keep you going in the land you're heading to across the Jordan." {32:48} The LORD spoke to Moses that day, saying, {32:49} "Head up to Mount Nebo in Moab, overlooking Jericho, and take a look at the land of Canaan I'm giving to Israel." {32:50} "You'll die on that mountain, like Aaron died on Mount Hor and was buried." {32:51} "You messed up at Meribah-Kadesh, not honoring Me among the Israelites." {32:52} "You'll see the land from afar, but you won't step foot

{33:1} So, here's Moses, the man of God, giving Israel a dope blessing before he kicks the bucket. {33:2} He's like, "Yo, the LORD came down from Sinai, showing up from Seir to Paran, rolling with thousands of saints; and from His right hand, He dropped a fiery law for them." {33:3} The LORD loves His people; all His saints are in His hands, chilling at His feet, soaking in His wisdom. {33:4} Moses passed down the law to us, the inheritance of Jacob's crew. {33:5} He was like the king of Jeshurun when all the heads of the tribes of Israel came together. {33:6} For Reuben, he's like, "Let Reuben live and thrive; may his crew never be small." {33:7} Then for Judah, he's asking the LORD to listen up and hook Judah up against his enemies. {33:8} And for Levi, Moses is like, "Keep those Thummim and Urim with your holy ones, tested at Massah and Meribah." {33:9} Levi's crew obeyed God's word and covenant. {33:10} They're the ones teaching Jacob the rules and offering sacrifices. {33:11} Moses blesses Levi's substance and asks God to defeat anyone who rises against them. {33:12} Then he's got love for Benjamin, saying they'll dwell safely, covered by the LORD. {33:13} And for Joseph, he's praising their land, blessed with heavenly gifts and abundant resources. {33:14} The best fruits from the sun and moon, treasures from ancient mountains—all blessings for Joseph. {33:15} Joseph's got it all, including the goodwill from the One in the burning bush. {33:16} Moses wants all those blessings on Joseph's head, the one set apart from his brothers. {33:17} Joseph's glory is like a powerful bull, pushing people to the ends of the earth, with Ephraim and Manasseh numbering in the thousands. {33:18} Zebulun gets a shoutout to rejoice in their journeys, and Issachar in their tents. {33:19} They're calling the people to the mountain, offering righteous sacrifices, enjoying the riches of the seas and hidden treasures. {33:20} Then for Gad, Moses blesses their strength, dwelling like a lion, tearing into enemies. {33:21} Gad gets the first share, executing justice with Israel's leaders. {33:22} Dan's compared to a lion's cub, ready to leap from Bashan. {33:23} Naphtali's satisfied with favor and the LORD's blessing, possessing the west and south. {33:24} Asher's blessed with many children, loved by his brothers, and enjoying abundance of oil. {33:25} Their shoes are like iron and brass, matching their strength each day. {33:26} There's no one like the God of Jeshurun, riding on the heavens to help His people. {33:27} The eternal God is their refuge, supporting them always, destroying their enemies. {33:28} Israel will live in safety, with abundant harvests and dew from the heavens. {33:29} Moses wraps up, saying Israel is blessed and saved by the LORD, shielded and victorious over enemies.

{34:1} So Moses hiked up from the plains of Moab to Mount Nebo, to the top of Pisgah overlooking Jericho. The LORD showed him all the land from Gilead to Dan, {34:2} including Naphtali, Ephraim, Manasseh, Judah, all the way to the Mediterranean Sea, {34:3} and the southern region, the Jericho valley, the city of palm trees, down to Zoar. {34:4} The LORD told him, "This is the land I promised to Abraham, Isaac, and Jacob, saying I'll give it to your descendants. You're seeing it with your own eyes, but you won't cross over there." {34:5} Moses, the LORD's servant, died in Moab, just like the LORD said. {34:6} They buried him in a valley in Moab near Beth-peor, but no one knows where his grave is to this day. {34:7} Moses was 120 years old when he died, still sharp-eyed and strong. {34:8} The Israelites mourned Moses in the plains of Moab for thirty days, then the mourning period was over. {34:9} Joshua, son of Nun, was filled with wisdom because Moses laid hands on him. The Israelites listened to Joshua and followed the LORD's commands through him. {34:10} No prophet in Israel has matched Moses, whom the LORD spoke to face to face, {34:11} performing all the signs and wonders in Egypt before Pharaoh, his servants, and the entire nation, {34:12} with his mighty hand and awesome deeds witnessed by all Israel.

Joshua

✦✦✦

{1:1-2} Yo, so after Moses, the LORD's main guy, passed on, the LORD hit up Joshua, Moses' right-hand man, and was like, "Moses is gone, bro. Now it's your turn. Lead the crew across the Jordan to the land I promised the Israelites. {1:3} Wherever you step, it's yours, just like I told Moses. {1:4} From the wilderness to Lebanon, all the way to the Euphrates River and the land of the Hittites, west to the Great Sea—that's your turf. {1:5} Ain't nobody gonna mess with you. I got your back like I did with Moses; I won't bail on you. {1:6} So be bold and brave. You're gonna divide up this land for the people as their inheritance, just like I swore to their ancestors. {1:7} Stay strong and courageous, and stick to the law Moses laid down. Don't stray from it, and you'll succeed wherever you go. {1:8} Keep the law on your lips, meditate on it day and night, and then you'll make it big and have mad success. {1:9} I'm telling you, be strong and brave. Don't be scared or shook. The LORD your God is rolling with you everywhere you go. {1:10-11} Joshua then told the officers, "Get the people ready. In three days, we're crossing the Jordan to take the land the LORD's giving us." {1:12-15} And he said to the Reubenites, Gadites, and half the tribe of Manasseh, "Remember what Moses said? You can leave your families and livestock here while we cross over armed, ready to fight alongside our brethren until they also get their land. Then you can head back east." {1:16} The people replied to Joshua, "We got you. Whatever you say, we'll do. Wherever you send us, we'll go." {1:17} We followed Moses, and we'll follow you. Just make sure the LORD your God is with you like he was with Moses. {1:18} Anybody who disrespects your orders and refuses to listen to you will be dealt with—stay strong and brave, man.

{2:1} So Joshua sent two guys from Shittim to scope out Jericho on the DL. They ended up at a harlot named Rahab's place and crashed there. {2:2} Word got to the king of Jericho that Israelite dudes were snooping around, and he was shook. {2:3} The king sent for Rahab, demanding she hand over the spies who came to scope out the land. {2:4} But Rahab hid the guys and lied, saying they'd left before the gates closed. She sent the king's men on a wild chase after them. {2:6} Meanwhile, she had hidden the spies on her roof under some flax stalks. {2:7} The king's men chased after the spies toward the Jordan River but shut the city gates once they were gone. {2:8} Before the spies slept, Rahab came up to the roof. {2:9} She spilled to them how terrified her people were of Israel, knowing God had given them the land. {2:10} They'd heard about the Red Sea parting and how Israel wiped out kings Sihon and Og. {2:11} Rahab confessed their hearts melted in fear because they knew Israel's God ruled in heaven and earth. {2:12-13} She asked the spies to spare her family as a thank-you for her help. {2:14} The spies agreed, promising safety to her and her kin when they took over the land. {2:15} Rahab helped them escape by lowering them down the wall with a cord. {2:16} She told them to hide in the mountains for three days until the coast was clear. {2:17} They made a deal that she'd hang a scarlet thread from her window to identify her house. {2:18} The spies hid until it was safe, then told Joshua how scared the people of Jericho were of Israel.

{3:1} So Joshua and the crew left Shittim early in the morning and camped by the Jordan River before crossing. {3:2} Three days later, the officers gave the people instructions. {3:3} They said, "When you see the ark of the covenant and the Levite priests carrying it, follow them." {3:4} "Keep a distance of about two thousand cubits from the ark; don't get too close so you know where to go, especially since you've never been this way before." {3:5} Joshua told everyone, "Get ready; tomorrow the LORD will do some amazing stuff." {3:6} Then Joshua told the priests to carry the ark and lead the way across the river, and they did. {3:7} The LORD assured Joshua that he would be respected by all Israel, just like Moses, to show that God was with him. {3:8} Joshua instructed the priests carrying the ark to stand still in the river once they reached the edge of the water. {3:9} Joshua then gathered the Israelites and reminded them of the LORD's words. {3:10} He told them, "This is how you'll know the living God is with you, ready to kick out the Canaanites, Hittites, Hivites, Perizzites, Girgashites, Amorites, and Jebusites." {3:11} "Watch as the ark of the covenant of the Lord passes into the Jordan ahead of you." {3:12} "Now pick twelve guys, one from each tribe." {3:13} "When the priests carrying the ark step into the river, the water will pile up, allowing everyone to cross." {3:14} As they started moving toward the Jordan, the priests carrying the ark stepped into the water, and it piled up, letting the people cross over near Jericho. {3:17} The priests stood in the middle of the river on dry ground, and all the Israelites crossed over safely until everyone made it across the Jordan.

{4:1} After everyone crossed, the LORD told Joshua to select twelve men to take stones from the Jordan where the priests stood and leave them where they camped that night. {4:2} Joshua chose twelve men, one from each tribe, as the LORD instructed. {4:3} He told them to carry the stones on their shoulders, one stone for each tribe of Israel. {4:4} "These stones will be a reminder for future generations," Joshua explained, "so when your kids ask what they mean, tell them how the waters of the Jordan parted when the ark passed by, and these stones are a lasting memory." {4:5} The Israelites did as Joshua commanded, taking twelve stones from the Jordan and setting them up at their campsite. {4:6} That day, everyone saw how great Joshua was, and they respected him like they respected Moses throughout his life.

{5:1} When all the Amorite and Canaanite kings heard that the LORD dried up the Jordan for the Israelites to pass through, they freaked out and lost all hope. {5:2} Then the LORD told Joshua to get sharp knives and circumcise the Israelites again. {5:3} So Joshua made the knives and circumcised them at a place called the Hill of Foreskins. {5:4} The reason? All the men who left Egypt and were of fighting age died in the wilderness because they didn't obey the LORD. {5:5} So Joshua circumcised those born during the wilderness journey who hadn't been circumcised. {5:6-7} They wandered for forty years until all the rebellious ones died, and their kids, whom Joshua circumcised, had never been circumcised along the way. {5:8} After the circumcision, they stayed in camp until they healed. {5:9} The LORD told Joshua that he had removed the shame of Egypt from them, and they named the place Gilgal. {5:10} The Israelites camped in Gilgal and celebrated Passover on the fourteenth day of the month, eating food from the land the next day. {5:11-12} The manna stopped once they had food from Canaan. {5:13} While Joshua was near Jericho, he saw a man with a drawn sword. {5:14} The man identified himself as the captain of the LORD's army, and Joshua worshipped him. {5:15} The captain told Joshua to remove his shoes because he was standing on holy ground.

{6:1} Jericho was tightly shut because of the Israelites. {6:2} The LORD told Joshua that he had delivered Jericho, including the king and warriors, into his hands. {6:3} Joshua was instructed to march around the city with all his soldiers for six days. {6:4} On the seventh day, they were to march around the city seven times with priests blowing trumpets. {6:5} When they heard a long blast, they were to shout, and the city walls would fall flat. {6:6} Joshua instructed the priests to carry the ark and blow the trumpets while the armed men followed. Joshua ordered the people not to shout until he gave the signal on the seventh day. {6:7} When they shouted, the walls fell, and the Israelites captured the city.

{7:1} The Israelites messed up big time when Achan, from the tribe of Judah, took forbidden stuff, making God angry at them. {7:2} Joshua sent men to check out Ai near Beth-aven. {7:3} They suggested sending only a few thousand to attack Ai, but they got wrecked by Ai's forces. {7:4-5} About three thousand Israelites fled from Ai, and Ai killed thirty-six of them. {7:6} Joshua and the elders freaked out, mourning before the LORD. {7:7} Joshua was like, "God, why did you bring us here just to get owned by the Amorites? I wish we'd stayed on the other side of the Jordan!" {7:8-9} He was worried that the Israelites were turning their backs on their enemies. {7:10} The LORD told Joshua to stop lying on the ground. {7:11} God said Israel sinned by taking forbidden stuff and breaking their covenant. {7:12-15} The Israelites couldn't win battles because of this curse, and God wouldn't be with them unless they got rid of the cursed items. {7:16} Joshua divided the tribes, and Judah was chosen. {7:17} Joshua confronted Achan, who confessed to taking the forbidden items. {7:18} They found the items in Achan's tent. {7:19} Israel stoned Achan and burned everything he owned.

{8:1} God was like, "Chill, Joshua. Take your crew and head back to Ai. I'm giving you the king, the city, and everything." {8:2} Treat Ai like Jericho—take the loot, but leave the rest. Plan an ambush behind the city. {8:3} Joshua picked thirty thousand warriors for the job. {8:4} They set up the ambush close to Ai while Joshua and his crew approached the city. {8:5-6} When Ai came out to fight, Joshua acted like he was losing and retreated. {8:7} Once Ai was distracted, the ambush crew took over. {8:8} Burn the city as commanded. {8:9} The ambush crew hid between Bethel and Ai while Joshua stayed with the main group. {8:10-13} Early the next day, Joshua led the attack on Ai. {8:14-18} Ai fell for the trick and went after Joshua, leaving the city unguarded. {8:18} God told Joshua to stretch out his spear toward Ai. {8:19} The ambush crew attacked, took Ai, and set it on fire. {8:20-24} Ai's people were trapped, unable to escape. {8:25-26} Israel killed twelve thousand Ai inhabitants. {8:26} Joshua didn't stop until Ai was wiped out. {8:27} They took the loot and cattle. {8:28} Joshua burned Ai and left it in ruins. {8:29} The king of Ai was hung on a tree. {8:30} Joshua built an altar to God. {8:31} They followed Moses' law, blessing the people.

{9:1} So, when all the kings this side of the Jordan—up in the hills, valleys, and along the coast near Lebanon—heard about it, they banded together to take on Joshua and Israel. {9:2} The folks in Gibeon heard what Joshua did to Jericho and Ai and pulled a sneaky move. {9:3} They dressed up like travelers, looking worn out with old stuff. They rolled up to Joshua at camp and were like, "We're from far away, let's make a deal." {9:4} They buttered him up, talking about how they heard about God's rep from Egypt and the battles with the Amorite kings. {9:5} Joshua fell for it and made peace, swearing not to harm them. {9:6} Three days later, they found out the Gibeonites were neighbors. {9:7} The leaders were like, "We made an oath, can't touch 'em." {9:8} So, they made them do grunt work—wood chopping and water hauling—for the Israelites. {9:9} Joshua was ticked off, asking why they lied about being far away. {9:10} From then on, they were the wood-choppers and water-fetchers for Israel and the Lord's altar.

{10:1} So, when Adoni-zedek, the king of Jerusalem, heard how Joshua took down Ai and wiped it out, just like Jericho, and how Gibeon made peace with Israel and joined them, {10:2} he got scared because Gibeon was a big city, royal-level, way stronger than Ai, packed with tough dudes. {10:3} Adoni-zedek messaged other kings—Hoham of Hebron, Piram of Jarmuth, Japhia of Lachish, Debir of Eglon—saying, {10:4} "Help me take down Gibeon; they're cool with Joshua and Israel." {10:5} So, these five Amorite kings—Jerusalem, Hebron, Jarmuth, Lachish, Eglon—teamed up, camped at Gibeon, and attacked. {10:6} Gibeon sent a SOS to Joshua at Gilgal, like, "Don't ghost us; come quick and save us from these mountain Amorites." {10:7} Joshua and his warriors got moving from Gilgal. {10:8} Then the LORD told Joshua, "Don't sweat it; I've handed them over to you; they won't stand a chance." {10:9} Joshua rolled out of Gilgal all night and caught them off guard. {10:10-11} The LORD wrecked them at Gibeon, chased them to Beth-horon, Azekah, and Makkedah, and even threw hailstones at them. {10:12-13} Joshua then prayed for the sun and moon to pause until they finished off their enemies. {10:14} The LORD really had Israel's back in that epic battle. {10:15} Afterward, Joshua and Israel went back to Gilgal, victorious. {10:16} The five kings hid in a cave at Makkedah. {10:17-18} Joshua found out and had big stones rolled in front of the cave. {10:19-21} He told his crew to chase the enemies, not letting them retreat to their cities. {10:22-24} Joshua called out the kings and made his warriors step on their necks. {10:25} Joshua encouraged them, saying, "Stay strong; the LORD will handle our enemies." {10:26-27} Later, Joshua took down the kings, hanged them, and tossed them into the cave, sealing it with stones. {10:28} Joshua took Makkedah, destroyed everyone, just like Jericho's king. {10:29} Basically, Joshua wiped out all the kings and their lands as commanded by the LORD.

{11:1} When Jabin, king of Hazor, heard what was up, he hit up Jobab, king of Madon, and a bunch of other kings, {11:2} from the north in the mountains, all the way down to Chinneroth, and across to Dor in the west. {11:3} They gathered up Canaanites, Amorites, Hittites, Perizzites, Jebusites, and Hivites to go against Israel. {11:4} So, they all met up at the waters of Merom to take on Israel. {11:6} But the LORD told Joshua, "Chill; by this time tomorrow, they'll be wiped out. You'll mess up their horses and burn their chariots." {11:7} Joshua and his crew surprised them at the waters of Merom and attacked. {11:8} The LORD handed them over to Israel, who chased them all the way to Zidon and Mizrephoth-maim, smacking them down until none were left. {11:9} Joshua did what the LORD said—messed up their horses and burned their chariots. {11:10} Then Joshua took out Hazor and its king. {11:11} They wiped out everyone and burned Hazor. {11:12} Joshua took all the cities and kings, just like Moses commanded. {11:14} They took all the spoils, but everyone else got smacked down with the sword. {11:15} Joshua followed everything Moses and the LORD commanded. {11:16} He took all the land, the hills, the south country, Goshen, the valley, and more. {11:17} From mount Halak to Baal-gad, he took out all the kings. {11:18} Joshua kept at it for a long time. {11:19} No city made peace except Gibeon. {11:20} The LORD made their hearts hard so they'd fight Israel and get wiped out. {11:21} Joshua wiped out the Anakims from the mountains. {11:22} None were left except in Gaza, Gath, and Ashdod. {11:23} Joshua took the whole land as the LORD said and divided it among the tribes. Then the land had peace.

{12:1} Yo, check it. These are the kings that Israel took down on the other side of the Jordan, towards the sunrise, from the river Arnon up to Mount Hermon, including the eastern plain. {12:2} Sihon, the Amorite king of Heshbon, ruled from Aroer on the Arnon River, all the way to the Jabbok River, bordering Ammon. {12:3} His territory stretched from the Sea of Galilee to the Dead Sea, including Beth-jeshimoth and Ashdoth-pisgah in the south. {12:4} Then there's Og, the Bashan king, one of those giant dudes, who lived in Ashtaroth and Edrei, ruling over Mount Hermon, Salcah, and all of Bashan. {12:5} Moses and the Israelites took them down and handed the land to Reuben, Gad, and half of Manasseh. {12:7} Then there's the kings on the west side of the Jordan, from Baal-gad to Mount Halak, that Joshua gave to the tribes of Israel, each according to their share. {12:8} In the mountains, valleys, plains, springs, wilderness, and the southern region, they defeated the Hittites, Amorites, Canaanites, Perizzites, Hivites, and Jebusites. {12:9} There's the king of Jericho, Ai, Jerusalem, Hebron, Jarmuth, Lachish, Eglon, Gezer, Debir, Geder, Hormah, Arad, Libnah, Adullam, Makkedah, Bethel, Tappuah, Hepher, Aphek, Lasharon, Madon, Hazor, Shimron-meron, and Achshaph. {12:10} Also Taanach, Megiddo, Kedesh, Jokneam of Carmel, Dor, Gilgal, and Tirzah—making it thirty-one kings in total.

{13:1} Yo, Joshua was gettin' up there in age, and the LORD was like, "You're old, man, but there's still a ton of land left to take over." {13:2} Here's the scoop on what's left: all the Philistine territory, including Geshur, stretching from Sihor near Egypt up to Ekron, with five Philistine city crews: Gazathites, Ashdothites, Eshkalonites, Gittites, and Ekronites, plus the Avites. {13:4} Down south, it's all about Canaanite land and Mearah near Sidon, all the way to Aphek on the Amorite border. {13:5} That's the deal with the Giblites and Lebanon, from Baal-gad under Mount Hermon to the entrance of Hamath. {13:6} I'm kickin' out all the hill folks in Lebanon down to Misrephoth-maim, includin' the Sidonians. You just gotta divvy it up by lottery among the Israelites, like I told ya. {13:7} So get on with it and divide this land for inheritance among the nine tribes and half of Manasseh. {13:8} Reuben and Gad already got their share from Moses east of the Jordan, just like Moses, the LORD's right-hand man, laid it out. {13:9} From Aroer on the Arnon River, and Medeba plain up to Dibon—yeah, that's the spot. {13:10} Also, all of Sihon's cities in Heshbon, up to the Ammonite border. {13:11} That includes Gilead, Geshurite and Maachathite territories, and all of Mount Hermon and Bashan up to Salcah. {13:12} Og's kingdom in Bashan got wrecked by Moses—dude was one of the last giants. {13:13} But the Israelites never got rid of the Geshurites and Maachathites; they're still chillin' with 'em today. {13:14} Oh, and remember, the Levites don't get any land; they're all about those fire sacrifices for the LORD, just like He said.

{14:1} So, these are the spots the Israelites snagged in Canaan, divvied up by Eleazar the priest, Joshua (son of Nun), and the tribal big shots. {14:2} They drew straws for their turf, just like the LORD told Moses, for the nine tribes and the half-tribe. {14:3} Moses already divvied up land for two and a half tribes east of the Jordan, but the Levites got no land chunk. {14:4} Joseph's kids—Manasseh and Ephraim—counted as two tribes, so the Levites got zip except for some cities to chill in with space for their animals and stuff. {14:5} The Israelites followed the LORD's orders and split up the land. {14:6} Then the crew from Judah rolled up to Joshua in Gilgal, and Caleb, son of Jephunneh, the Kenezite, was like, "Yo, remember what the LORD told Moses about me and you back in Kadesh-barnea?" {14:7} I was forty when Moses sent me to check out the land, and I gave him the real scoop. {14:8} But my crewmates scared everyone, not me—I stayed true to the LORD. {14:9} Moses promised me back then that wherever I trod would be mine and my descendants' forever, because I stayed loyal to the LORD. {14:10} And here I am, still kicking at eighty-five, just like the LORD said, even after all those wilderness years. {14:11} I'm still as strong as back then, ready for battle. {14:12} So, gimme that mountain the LORD talked about. {14:13} Joshua blessed Caleb and gave him Hebron. {14:14} Hebron became Caleb's spot 'cause he stayed true to the LORD. {14:15} Hebron used to be called Kirjath-arba, named after a big shot from the Anakims. And then, peace reigned—no more war.

{15:1} So, the tribe of Judah scored this turf in Canaan, stretching all the way down to Edom's border, the Zin wilderness in the south. {15:2} Their southern edge ran from the shore of the Dead Sea, looking towards the south. {15:3} It then extended to Maalehacrabbim, passed through Zin, ascended to Kadesh-barnea, then headed to Hezron, Adar, and circled around to Karkaa. {15:4} From there, it stretched towards Azmon and reached the Egyptian border, ending at the sea—this is their southern border. {15:5} To the east, it was the Dead Sea, all the way to the end of the Jordan River. In the north, it started from the sea's bay at the Jordan's northern tip. {15:6} Heading up to Beth-hogla, passing north of Beth-arabah, then up to the stone of Bohan, Reuben's son. {15:7} From there, it moved towards Debir from the Achor Valley, northward to Gilgal before Adummim, south of the river. {15:8} Continuing up the Hinnom Valley's south side towards the Jebusites, which is Jerusalem, then up to the mountain west of Hinnom's valley, ending at the valley's north edge. {15:9} It ran from the hilltop to Nephtoah's water fountain, then to the cities of Mount Ephron, and on to Baalah, also known as Kirjath-jearim. {15:10} It looped from Baalah west to Mount Seir, along Mount Jearim, Chesalon on the north side, down to Beth-shemesh and Timnah. {15:11} It continued north towards Ekron, then to Shicron, Mount Baalah, and Jabneel, ending at the sea. {15:12} The western border reached the Mediterranean Sea. This is the Judah tribe's border according to their families. {15:13} Caleb, son of Jephunneh, got a share among the Judah tribe, including the city of Hebron, promised by the LORD to Joshua. {15:14} Caleb ousted the three Anakim sons—Sheshai, Ahiman, and Talmai—from Hebron. {15:15} Then he tackled the folks in Debir, previously called Kirjath-sepher. {15:16} Caleb threw down a challenge: whoever takes Kirjath-sepher gets his daughter Achsah as a wife. {15:17} Othniel, Caleb's brother Kenaz's son, took the challenge and married Achsah. {15:18} When she arrived, she asked Caleb for a favor, dismounting her donkey, and Caleb said, "What do you want?" {15:19} She asked for a blessing since he'd given her a dry land—she wanted springs too. So Caleb gave her upper and lower springs. {15:20} This is the Judah tribe's inheritance based on their families.

{16:1} So, Joseph's crew landed their spot from Jordan by Jericho, all the way to the water of Jericho on the east, heading into the wilderness that climbs up from Jericho to Mount Bethel. {16:2} It runs from Bethel to Luz, then moves along to the borders of Archi to Ataroth. {16:3} Going westward to Japhleti's coast, down to Beth-horon the lower, and towards Gezer, ending at the sea. {16:4} That's how Joseph's descendants, Manasseh and Ephraim, claimed their turf. {16:5} Ephraim's border stretched from Ataroth-addar to Upper Beth-horon on the east. {16:6} It extends towards the sea to Michmethah on the north side, then loops eastward to Taanath-shiloh, passing Janohah. {16:7} Heading down from Janohah to Ataroth, Naarath, and reaching Jericho, ending at the Jordan. {16:8} The border stretches westward from Tappuah to the Kanah River, ending at the sea. This is Ephraim's tribe's inheritance by their families. {16:9} Ephraim's cities were within Manasseh's inheritance, including all the cities with their villages. {16:10} They didn't kick out the Canaanites in Gezer; instead, they live among the Ephraimites to this day, paying tribute.

{17:1} Now for Manasseh, the firstborn of Joseph, specifically for Machir, the father of Gilead—being a warrior, he snagged Gilead and Bashan. {17:2} There's also a lot for the other children of Manasseh by their families—Abiezer, Helek, Asriel, Shechem, Hepher, and Shemida. {17:3} Zelophehad, Hepher's son, Gilead's descendant, had no sons, only daughters: Mahlah, Noah, Hoglah, Milcah, and Tirzah. {17:4} They approached Eleazar the priest, Joshua, and the leaders, saying, "The LORD told Moses to give us an inheritance among our family members." So, they received an inheritance alongside their father's relatives. {17:5} Manasseh got ten portions, excluding Gilead and Bashan across the Jordan. {17:6} Since Manasseh's daughters inherited alongside his sons, the rest of Manasseh's sons received the land of Gilead. {17:7} Manasseh's territory stretched from Asher to Michmethah, in front of Shechem, with the border extending towards the inhabitants of En-tappuah. {17:8} Manasseh controlled Tappuah, but Tappuah's border belonged to Ephraim's children. {17:9} The border descended to the Kanah River, south of the river. These Ephraimite cities are among the Manassehite cities, with Manasseh's border to the north of the river, ending at the sea. {17:10} Southward belongs to Ephraim, northward to Manasseh, with the sea as the border, meeting Asher in the north and Issachar in the east. {17:11} Manasseh had Beth-shean, Ibleam, Dor, Endor, Taanach, and Megiddo within Issachar and Asher—three regions. {17:12} Yet, they couldn't displace the city inhabitants; the Canaanites stayed. {17:13} As Israel grew stronger, they made the Canaanites pay tribute but didn't fully expel them. {17:14} The Josephites said to Joshua, "Why only one lot and portion for us when we're a big crew, and the LORD's been good to us?" {17:15} Joshua told them, "If you're so numerous, head to the forested area, clear it out in the land of the Perizzites and giants, if Ephraim's hill isn't enough for you." {17:16} The Josephites said, "The hill isn't cutting it for us, and the Canaanites in the valley have iron chariots, in Beth-shean, and Jezreel's valley." {17:17} Joshua said to the house of Joseph, Ephraim and Manasseh, "You're a large crew with great power; you won't just get one lot." {17:18} "The mountain will be yours; it's wooded, so clear it out. You'll drive out the Canaanites, even with their iron chariots and strength."

{18:1} So, the whole squad of Israelites gathered at Shiloh and pitched the tabernacle there. They had already conquered the land. {18:2} There were still seven tribes of Israel who hadn't gotten their land yet. {18:3} Joshua was like, "Why are you dragging your feet to take over the land the LORD gave you?" {18:4} "Pick three guys from each tribe, and I'll send them out to survey the land, then they'll come back to me." {18:5} "We'll split it into seven parts: Judah stays in the south, and Joseph's crew holds it down in the north." {18:6} "You guys map out the land into seven parts and bring me the details so we can cast lots before the LORD." {18:7} "But the Levites don't get land; they're set apart for the LORD's service. Gad, Reuben, and half of Manasseh already got their land east of the Jordan." {18:8} The men went out as instructed by Joshua to survey the land and came back to him at Shiloh. {18:9} They described the land in seven parts in a book and presented it to Joshua at Shiloh. {18:10} Joshua cast lots for them at Shiloh before the LORD and divided the land among the Israelites according to their divisions. {18:11} The tribe of Benjamin got their lot, and their land was between Judah and Joseph's tribes. {18:12} Their northern border stretched from the Jordan up to Jericho, then through the mountains westward to the wilderness of Beth-aven. {18:13} From there, it went toward Luz (Bethel) and descended to Ataroth-adar near the southern hill of Beth-horon. {18:14} The border continued southward to Kirjath-baal (Kirjath-jearim), a Judahite city, marking the western boundary. {18:15} The southern border extended from Kirjath-jearim to the Nephtoah well. {18:16} It descended to the valley of Hinnom, then to En-rogel, and onward to En-shemesh, Geliloth, and Adummim. {18:17-19} Turning north, it passed En-shemesh to the stone of Bohan, and continued toward Arabah, going down to the north bay of the Dead Sea near the Jordan's south end, marking the southern coast. {18:20} Jordan formed the eastern boundary. This was Benjamin's inheritance, encompassing their cities and villages according to their families. {18:21} The cities of Benjamin included Jericho, Beth-hoglah, Keziz Valley, Beth-arabah, Zemaraim, Bethel, Avim, Parah, Ophrah, Chephar-haammonai, Ophni, Gaba, Gibeon, Ramah, Beeroth, Mizpeh, Chephirah, Mozah, Rekem, Irpeel, Taralah, Zelah, Eleph, Jebusi (Jerusalem), Gibeath, and Kirjath—a total of fourteen cities with their villages. This was the inheritance of Benjamin's families.

{19:1-8} Next up, Simeon's crew got their piece of the pie within Judah's territory. They scored Beer-sheba, Sheba, Moladah, Hazar-shual, Balah, Azem, Eltolad, Bethul, Hormah, Ziklag, Beth-marcaboth, Hazar-susah, Beth-lebaoth, and Sharuhen—thirteen cities with their 'hoods. Plus, Ain, Remmon, Ether, and Ashan—four more cities with their 'hoods. All the towns around these cities up to Baalath-beer and Ramath down south fell to Simeon's tribe. {19:9} They hooked up with Judah for land 'cause Judah had too much. {19:10-16} Then Zebulun stepped up with the third lot, and their turf stretched to Sarid, up to the sea, Maralah, Dabbasheth, along the border of Chisloth-tabor, Daberath, Japhia, Gittah-hepher, Ittah-kazin, Remmon-methoar, Neah, Hannathon, and Jiphthah-el valley—twelve cities and their 'hoods. {19:17-23} Issachar got the fourth lot, stretching toward Jezreel, Chesulloth, Shunem, Haphraim, Shihon, Anaharath, Rabbith, Kishion, Abez, Remeth, En-gannim, En-haddah, and Beth-pazzez up to Tabor, Shahazimah, Beth-shemesh, and their border at the Jordan—sixteen cities and their 'hoods. {19:24-31} Asher's tribe drew the fifth lot, including Helkath, Hali, Beten, Achshaph, Alammelech, Amad, Misheal, Carmel, Shihor-libnath, turning east to Beth-dagon, Zebulun, Jiphthah-el valley, Beth-emek, Neiel, Cabul, Hebron, Rehob, Hammon, Kanah, and reaching great Zidon, Ramah, Tyre, and Hosah up to Achzib—twenty-two cities with their 'hoods. {19:32-39} Naphtali snagged the sixth lot, with their border from Heleph to Zaanannim, Adami, Nekeb, Jabneel, Lakum, Aznoth-tabor, Hukkok, Zebulun, Asher, Judah on the Jordan eastward. Their fortified cities included Ziddim, Zer, Hammath, Rakkath, Chinnereth, Adamah, Ramah, Hazor, Kedesh, Edrei, En-hazor, Iron, Migdal-el, Horem, Beth-anath, and Beth-shemesh—nineteen cities with their 'hoods. {19:40-48} Finally, Dan rolled with the seventh lot, bagging Zorah, Eshtaol, Ir-shemesh, Shaalabbin, Ajalon, Jethlah, Elon, Thimnathah, Ekron, Eltekeh, Gibbethon, Baalath, Jehud, Bene-berak, Gath-rimmon, Me-jarkon, Rakkon, and then grabbing Leshem after a showdown—forty-six cities with their 'hoods. {19:49-50} Once they divvied up the land, the Israelites threw Joshua a bone, giving him Timnath-serah in Ephraim's hills as the LORD had said, and Joshua built up the city and settled there. {19:51} These were the tribal territories divided up by Eleazar, Joshua, and the tribe heads at Shiloh, wrapping up the land distribution.

{20:1} Yo, the LORD spoke to Joshua, telling him to set up cities of refuge as He instructed through Moses. {20:3} These spots were for anyone who accidentally took a life—like, they didn't mean it—and needed to escape the avenger of blood. {20:4} If someone fled to one of these cities and spilled what happened to the city elders, they'd take them in, offering a safe place to crash. {20:5} If the avenger showed up, they wouldn't hand over the killer because it was an accident and not premeditated. {20:6} The killer stayed there until their case went to court, or until the high priest died; then they could go back home. {20:7} They set up Kedesh in Galilee, Shechem in Ephraim, and Kirjath-arba (Hebron) in Judah for this purpose. {20:8} Across the Jordan by Jericho, they had Bezer, Ramoth, and Golan—each from different tribes. {20:9} These cities were for all the Israelites and even strangers among them, giving shelter to anyone who unintentionally caused a death, keeping them safe until they faced trial.

{21:1} The Levite leaders approached Eleazar, Joshua, and other tribe heads at Shiloh, saying Moses had ordered cities for them to live in, along with pasture for their animals. {21:3} The Israelites followed through, giving Levites cities and land as the LORD commanded. {21:2} The Kohathites, Levite descendants of Aaron, got cities from Judah, Simeon, and Benjamin. {21:3} Other Kohathites received cities from Ephraim, Dan, and half of Manasseh—thirteen cities total. {21:4} Gershonites got cities from Issachar, Asher, Naphtali, and half of Manasseh—thirteen cities. {21:5} Merari's descendants got cities from Reuben, Gad, and Zebulun—twelve cities. {21:6} Levites received cities from Judah and Simeon, with specific mention of thirteen cities for Aaron's descendants. {21:7} Remaining Kohathites got cities from Ephraim, including Shechem, Gezer, Kibzaim, and Beth-horon—four cities. {21:8} Dan's cities included Eltekeh, Gibbethon, Aijalon, and Gath-rimmon—four cities. {21:9} Half of Manasseh contributed Tanach and Gath-rimmon—two cities. {21:10} Gershonites received Golan (in Bashan) and Beesh-terah—two cities. {21:11} Issachar provided Kishon, Dabareh, Jarmuth, and En-gannim—four cities. {21:12} Naphtali pitched in Kedesh (Galilee), Hammoth-dor, and Kartan—three cities. {21:13} Zebulun gave Jokneam and Kartah—two cities. {21:14} Reuben added Bezer, Jahazah, Kedemoth, and Mephaath—four cities. {21:15} Gad contributed Ramoth (Gilead), Mahanaim, Heshbon, and Jazer—four cities. {21:16} The LORD fulfilled His promise, giving Israel the land He swore to their ancestors. {21:17} They had peace and defeated all their enemies, experiencing every good thing the LORD promised.

{22:1} So Joshua hit up the Reubenites, Gadites, and half of Manasseh, {22:2} and he was like, "Y'all rocked it, doing everything Moses and I told you to do. {22:3} You stuck with your crew and followed God's rules all this time. {22:4} Now that your homies got that promised rest, head back to your hood and chill in the land Moses gave you on the other side of the Jordan. {22:5} But make sure you stay on top of God's commands and laws, loving Him, walking in His ways, keeping His rules, sticking with Him, and serving Him with all your heart and soul." {22:6} Then Joshua blessed them and sent them off, and they bounced back to their tents. {22:7} Moses hooked up one half of Manasseh in Bashan, and Joshua took care of the other half on this side of the Jordan. When Joshua sent them home, he blessed them, {22:8} and told them to return with mad loot—tons of livestock, silver, gold, brass, iron, and fresh gear. Split the spoils with your crew. {22:9} So the Reubenites, Gadites, and half of Manasseh bounced from Shiloh in Canaan back to Gilead, to their own land, just like the LORD told Moses. {22:10} When they hit the Jordan in Canaan, the Reubenites, Gadites, and half of Manasseh built a huge altar by the river. {22:11} When the Israelites heard, they were like, "Yo, Reuben, Gad, and Manasseh built an altar near Canaan's border at the Jordan crossing." {22:12} Israel got triggered and gathered at Shiloh, ready to wage war against them. {22:13} They sent Phinehas, Eleazar's son, to the Gilead crew—Reuben, Gad, and Manasseh. {22:14} He rolled up with ten big shots, one from each tribe, leading thousands of Israelites. {22:15} They approached Reuben, Gad, and Manasseh in Gilead, asking, {22:16} "What's up with this rebellion? Building an altar today to ditch God? {22:17} Peor's scandal wasn't enough? Even after that plague, you wanna peace out from following the LORD? {22:18} If your land's tainted, come chill in the LORD's land with us, where His tabernacle is. Don't rebel against God or us by building an altar next to His." {22:19} "Remember Achan? His screw-up hurt all of us. {22:20} If you're not rebelling, and this altar's legit, let God handle it. {22:21} The Reubenites, Gadites, and Manassehites were like, "The LORD knows. {22:22} If we're in the wrong, don't save us now. {22:23} We built this altar to honor the LORD, not for sacrifices. {22:24} It's to keep the story alive for future generations. {22:25} The LORD split us from you with the Jordan; our kids might forget Him because of that. {22:26} This altar's a witness, not for offerings, but to show we're with the LORD." {22:27} "We'd never rebel against the LORD, ditching Him today. {22:28} So when our kids ask about it, we'll say, 'Look at the LORD's altar our ancestors made.'" {22:29} "No way we'd rebel, building altars for sacrifices next to the LORD's altar." {22:30} When Phinehas and the big shots heard this, they were cool with it. {22:31} Phinehas was like, "We see God's with us since you didn't mess with Him. {22:32} They headed back to Canaan, spreading the word to the Israelites. {22:33} The Israelites were relieved and decided not to wage war or wreck Reuben and Gad's land. {22:34} Reuben and Gad named the altar "Witness," to show the LORD's the real deal.

{23:1} So, like, after a hot minute of the LORD giving Israel a breather from all their haters, Joshua got old and was feeling it in his bones. {23:2} He called all Israel together—elders, heads, judges, officers—and was like, "I'm getting up there in age, y'all. {23:3} And you've seen how the LORD your God wrecked all these nations because of us; He's the real MVP who fought for us. {23:4} Check it out, I've divided up what's left of these nations among your tribes, from the Jordan to the big sea out west. {23:5} The LORD your God will kick them out and clear the way for you to take their land, just like He promised. {23:6} So, stay strong and keep on following everything in Moses' law—no sidetracks allowed. {23:7} Don't mix with these leftover nations or even say their god's names or swear by them or serve them or bow down to them. {23:8} Stick tight to the LORD your God, just like you've been doing. {23:9} The LORD has pushed out big, tough nations in front of you; nobody could stand up against you. {23:10} One of you can chase a thousand enemies because the LORD your God fights for you, just like He promised. {23:11} So, make sure you love the LORD your God. {23:12} If you mess up and start cozying up to these leftover nations, marrying them, and hanging out with them, {23:13} you better believe the LORD your God won't clear them out anymore—they'll mess you up and cause trouble until you're gone from this awesome land He gave you. {23:14} Today's the day I'm checking out like everyone else, and you know deep down that every good thing the LORD promised you has come true; not one thing has fallen through. {23:15} But just like the good stuff came to you, the LORD will bring on all the bad stuff if you mess up, until you're kicked out of this sweet land He gave you. {23:16} If you break the covenant with the LORD your God—going off to serve other gods and bowing down to them—then get ready for the LORD's anger to light up against you, and you'll be outta here quick from this great land He hooked you up with.

{24:1} So Joshua gathered all the tribes of Israel to Shechem and called for the elders, heads, judges, and officers, and they showed up before God. {24:2} Then Joshua was like, "Listen up, everyone! The LORD God of Israel, way back when, your ancestors were on the other side of the river, including Terah, Abraham's dad, and Nahor. They were into other gods. {24:3} But I grabbed your guy Abraham from over there, took him all around Canaan, made his family grow, and gave him Isaac. {24:4} Then Isaac got Jacob and Esau. Esau got Mount Seir, but Jacob and his crew went down to Egypt. {24:5} I sent Moses and Aaron, and we gave Egypt a hard time, remember? Then I got you out. {24:6} Brought your ancestors out of Egypt, got to the sea, and the Egyptians chased you with chariots. {24:7} When you cried out, the LORD caused darkness between you and the Egyptians, then drowned them in the sea—yeah, you saw that! Then you spent a long time in the wilderness. {24:8} I got you into Amorite territory east of the Jordan; you fought them and I handed them over to you. {24:9} Then Balak of Moab tried to start something, sent for Balaam to curse you, but I shut that down and blessed you instead, saving you. {24:10} You crossed the Jordan, came to Jericho, and took on the Amorites, Perizzites, Canaanites, Hittites, Girgashites, Hivites, and Jebusites—I gave them to you. {24:12} Sent hornets ahead to chase out the Amorite kings before you—no sword or bow needed. {24:13} I gave you a land you didn't work for, cities you didn't build, vineyards and olive groves you didn't plant—now you live in them. {24:14} So, fear the LORD, serve Him faithfully, ditch the gods your ancestors worshipped, and serve the LORD. {24:15} If you're not into serving the LORD, choose today who you want to serve—gods your ancestors worshipped or the Amorite gods. As for me and my fam, we're all in for the LORD." {24:16} The people were like, "No way we're ditching the LORD for other gods! {24:17} The LORD brought us and our ancestors out of Egypt, did miracles, and protected us everywhere we went among different people. {24:18} He cleared out all the people before us, including the Amorites—so, yeah, we're serving the LORD; He's our God." {24:19} Joshua was like, "You can't just serve the LORD casually; He's holy and won't ignore your mess-ups and sins. {24:20} If you bail on the LORD and worship other gods, He'll turn against you and bring trouble after all the good He did for you." {24:21} The people insisted, "Nope, we're sticking with the LORD." {24:22} So Joshua was like, "You're witnesses; you chose the LORD to serve." They agreed, "We're witnesses." {24:23} Then Joshua told them, "Get rid of any foreign gods among you and commit to the LORD, the God of Israel." {24:24} The people were like, "We're all about serving the LORD and obeying Him." {24:25} Joshua made a covenant with them, set rules, and made it official in Shechem. {24:26} He wrote all this in God's law book, set up a big stone under an oak tree by the LORD's sanctuary. {24:27} Joshua said, "This stone's a witness—it heard all the LORD said to us, so don't deny your God." {24:28} After that, Joshua let everyone head back to their land. {24:29-30} Later on, Joshua died at 110, buried in his part of the land in Timnath-serah, Mount Ephraim, north of Gaash. {24:31} Israel stayed faithful to the LORD as long as Joshua and the elders who outlived him were around, seeing all the LORD's amazing deeds for them.

Judges

✝✝✝

{1:1} So like, after Joshua died, the Israelites were like, "Yo, who's gonna take on the Canaanites first?" {1:2} And God was like, "Judah's got this; I'm handing over the land to them." {1:3} Judah was all, "Simeon, come roll with me to fight these Canaanites, and I'll back you up later." So Simeon joined in. {1:4} Judah went up, and they wrecked the Canaanites and Perizzites in Bezek, taking out ten thousand of them. {1:5} They found Adonibezek in Bezek, fought him, and chopped off his thumbs and big toes. {1:6} Adoni-bezek tried to bounce, but they caught him, and he confessed how he had done the same to other kings. They brought him to Jerusalem, where he croaked. {1:8} Judah also took on Jerusalem, slashing and burning it down. {1:9} Later, Judah went down to battle the Canaanites in the mountains, south, and valley. {1:10} They hit up Hebron (Kirjath-arba back in the day) and wiped out Sheshai, Ahiman, and Talmai. {1:11} Then they took on Debir (previously known as Kirjath-sepher). {1:12} Caleb was like, "Whoever takes Kirjath-sepher gets my daughter Achsah." Othniel, Caleb's bro, did it and scored Achsah. {1:13} Achsah got Caleb to hook her up with a field, and he blessed her with springs too. {1:16} The Kenites rolled with Judah into the Judah wilderness. {1:17} Judah and Simeon teamed up and destroyed Zephath, renaming it Hormah. {1:18} Judah also took Gaza, Askelon, and Ekron. {1:19} God had Judah's back, helping them drive out mountain dwellers, but they couldn't boot out valley folks 'cause of their iron chariots. {1:20} They gave Hebron to Caleb, who kicked out the three Anak sons. {1:21} Benjamin didn't kick out the Jebusites from Jerusalem, so they're still chilling there. {1:22} The house of Joseph hit up Bethel, and God was on their side. {1:23} They scoped Bethel (formerly Luz). {1:24} They asked a dude from the city to show them the way in, and then they wrecked the place but let him and his fam go. {1:26} The dude moved to the Hittite land, built a city, and named it Luz. {1:27} Manasseh didn't clear out Beth-shean, Taanach, Dor, Ibleam, or Megiddo; Canaanites stayed. {1:28} When Israel got strong, they made the Canaanites pay tribute instead of fully booting them. {1:29} Ephraim left the Canaanites in Gezer, coexisting. {1:30} Zebulun also let Canaanites hang in Kitron and Nahalol, making them pay up. {1:31} Asher didn't kick out Accho, Zidon, Ahlab, Achzib, Helbah, Aphik, or Rehob; they lived among Canaanites. {1:33} Naphtali didn't clear out Beth-shemesh or Beth-anath but made them pay up.

{2:1} Yo, an angel rolled up from Gilgal to Bochim and dropped some truth: "I brought you out of Egypt and into this land, just like I promised your ancestors. I swore I'd never break our deal." {2:2} "Don't make alliances with the locals, smash their altars," but y'all didn't listen. What's the deal? {2:3} So I said, "Fine, I won't kick them out for you. They'll be a pain in your side, and their gods will trip you up." {2:4} When the angel dropped this, the people were like, "Oh no!" and started bawling. {2:5} They named the place Bochim (which means "weepers") and offered sacrifices to the LORD. {2:6} After Joshua peaced out, each Israelite went to claim their own turf. {2:7} They stayed true to the LORD during Joshua's time and while the elders who lived through it were around, seeing all the cool stuff God did. {2:8} Joshua, the LORD's servant, passed at 110. {2:9} They buried him up in Ephraim's mountains. {2:10} That whole generation passed, and a new one popped up, clueless about God and what went down in Israel's past. {2:11} The new generation messed up, serving Baal. {2:12} They ditched the LORD who freed them from Egypt and got into worshiping other gods from the neighbors, ticking off the LORD. {2:13} They totally bailed on the LORD and got into worshiping Baal and Ashtaroth. {2:14} God got mad and let spoilers and enemies trash them, selling them out. {2:15} No matter where they went, things went sour, just like God said. {2:16} But the LORD raised up judges to save them from their enemies. {2:17} They still didn't listen to the judges, though, and chased after other gods, ditching the path their ancestors followed, ignoring God's commands. {2:18} When God raised up judges, things got better; the LORD was with them as long as the judge lived, saving them from enemies. {2:19} But when the judge died, they got worse, diving deeper into idol worship and stubborn ways. {2:20} God got even hotter, saying, "Y'all broke our deal, didn't listen to me." {2:21} "So now, I'm not gonna boot out any more nations left by Joshua." {2:22} "I'll let them stick around to test if Israel will stay on the LORD's path like their ancestors did." {2:23} So God chilled on driving out those nations, not rushing it or handing them to Joshua.

{3:1} So like, these were the nations God left to test Israel, especially those who didn't experience the Canaan wars. {3:2} The idea was to teach the new generation about war since they had no clue. {3:3} It included five Philistine lords, Canaanites, Sidonians, and Hivites from Lebanon's mountains, from Baal-hermon to Hamath's border. {3:4} They were there to test if Israel would follow God's commandments, like Moses taught. {3:5} Israel lived among Canaanites, Hittites, Amorites, Perizzites, Hivites, and Jebusites. {3:6} They married their daughters, gave their daughters to their sons, and worshiped their gods. {3:7} Israel messed up big time, forgot about the LORD, and got into worshiping Baal and idols. {3:8} So God got mad and let Chushanrishathaim, king of Mesopotamia, rule over them. {3:9} When Israel cried out to the LORD, God raised up Othniel, Caleb's bro, to save them from Chushanrishathaim. {3:10} The LORD's spirit was with Othniel, who defeated Chushanrishathaim, and Israel had peace for 40 years. {3:11} Othniel died, and Israel messed up again, so the LORD let Eglon, king of Moab, mess with them. {3:13} Eglon joined forces with Ammon and Amalek, attacked Israel, and took the city of palm trees. {3:14} Israel served Eglon for 18 years. {3:15} When Israel cried to the LORD, God raised up Ehud, a lefty Benjamite, to deliver them from Moab. {3:16} Ehud made a long dagger and hid it on his thigh. {3:17} He stabbed Eglon in the belly, and the dagger got stuck in his fat. {3:18} Eglon's servants thought he was relieving himself, but he was dead. {3:19} Ehud slipped away and rallied Israel. {3:20} They defeated Moab, killing about 10,000 men, and had peace for 80 years. {3:21} After Ehud, Shamgar killed 600 Philistines with an ox goad and delivered Israel.

{4:1} So, like, after Ehud died, Israel went back to doing evil in God's eyes. {4:2} Then God let them get wrecked by Jabin, the king of Canaan, who had this general named Sisera living in Harosheth of the Gentiles. {4:3} Israel cried out because Sisera had 900 iron chariots and kept them oppressed for 20 years. {4:4} Now Deborah, a prophetess and Lapidoth's wife, was judging Israel at the time. {4:5} She hung out under a palm tree called Deborah between Ramah and Bethel, where Israelites came to her for judgments. {4:6} Deborah sent for Barak, son of Abinoam from Kedesh-naphtali, telling him that God commanded him to gather 10,000 men from Naphtali and Zebulun and head towards Mount Tabor. {4:7} She promised to lure Sisera and his army to the Kishon River where Barak would defeat them. {4:8-9} Barak was hesitant unless Deborah went with him, so she agreed, warning that the credit for the victory would go to a woman, not him. {4:10} Barak got his men from Zebulun and Naphtali, and they headed to Kedesh with Deborah. {4:11} Meanwhile, Heber the Kenite had moved away and pitched his tent near Kedesh. {4:12-13} Sisera found out about Barak and gathered his iron chariots and troops to the Kishon River. {4:14} Deborah told Barak it was go-time, and God was on their side. {4:15} The LORD messed up Sisera's army, and he bailed from his chariot, running for his life. {4:16} Barak chased the rest of Sisera's army until they were wiped out. {4:17-20} Sisera fled to Heber's tent, seeking refuge, not knowing Jael was waiting for him. {4:21} Jael, Heber's wife, tricked Sisera into sleeping, then drove a tent peg through his temples, killing him. {4:22} When Barak arrived, Jael showed him Sisera dead in her tent. {4:23} That day, God subdued Jabin, the king of Canaan, before Israel. {4:24} Israel prospered and defeated Jabin until he was no more.

{5:1} So, Deborah and Barak dropped a sick track that day, like, praising the LORD for avenging Israel. {5:2} They were all hyped 'cause the people willingly stepped up. {5:3} Listen up, kings and princes, I'm gonna sing praises to the LORD God of Israel. {5:4} When God rolled out from Seir and marched from Edom, the earth shook, and even the heavens were crying with rain. {5:5} The mountains melted before the LORD, even Sinai itself, before the God of Israel. {5:6} Back in Shamgar and Jael's time, the highways were deserted, and everyone was taking back routes. {5:7} Villages were abandoned until I, Deborah, stepped up as a leader in Israel. {5:8} They started worshiping new gods, and suddenly, there was war everywhere. Did anyone even have a shield or spear among forty thousand in Israel? {5:9} I'm all about those governors of Israel who stepped up willingly. Bless the LORD. {5:10} Speak up, you riding on white donkeys, you sitting in judgment, and you just out and about. {5:11} Those who escaped the enemy attacks, chilling by the watering holes, they'll talk about the righteous acts of the LORD, especially how He looked out for His people in the villages of Israel. {5:12} Deborah woke up and dropped some bars, and Barak led the captives, son of Abinoam. {5:13} The LORD gave him dominion over the nobles and made me boss over the mighty. {5:14} Ephraim held it down against Amalek, and Benjamin was all about it too. Governors came from Machir, and Zebulun had skilled writers. {5:15} Even Issachar's princes were with Deborah and Barak, getting into the action. {5:16} Reuben, what were you doing with the sheep? Your thoughts should've been on bigger things. {5:17} Gilead stayed across the Jordan, and why was Dan chilling in ships? Asher was coasting, staying in his harbors. {5:18} Zebulun and Naphtali risked it all in the high places of the field. {5:19} The kings fought at Taanach by Megiddo, but they left with no spoils. {5:20} The stars fought from the sky against Sisera. {5:21} The Kishon River swept them away. That's some strength, yo. {5:22} The horsehoofs got wrecked by the mighty prancing. {5:23} The angel of the LORD cursed Meroz hard because they didn't help the LORD against the enemy. {5:24} Jael, Heber's wife, is praised above all women for her bravery in the tent. {5:25} Sisera asked for water; she hooked him up with milk and butter. {5:26} Then she went full DIY with a tent peg and hammer, straight through Sisera's head. {5:27} He bowed down at her feet and didn't get up again. {5:28} Sisera's mom was worried, waiting for him to come home. {5:29} Her ladies reassured her, but nope, Sisera wasn't coming back. {5:30} They were busy dividing the spoils, with even some fancy stuff for Sisera's crew. {5:31} Let all Your enemies perish, LORD, and let those who love You shine like the sun in their strength. And then the land chilled for forty years.

{6:1} So, the Israelites were back on their nonsense, and the LORD let Midian rule over them for seven years. {6:2} Midian was all over them, so the Israelites were hiding out in mountain dens, caves, and strongholds to escape. {6:3} Whenever Israel planted crops, Midian, along with the Amalekites and the eastern tribes, would swoop in and wreck everything, leaving nothing for Israel—not even livestock. {6:4} They camped out, destroyed crops all the way to Gaza, and left Israel with nothing to survive on. {6:5} They brought their cattle and tents, swarming like grasshoppers with too many camels to count, and just wrecked the land. {6:6} Israel was broke because of Midian, so they cried out to the LORD for help. {6:7} When the Israelites cried out to the LORD about Midian, {6:8} the LORD sent a prophet to remind them how He brought them out of Egypt, saved them from oppression, and gave them the land of their enemies. {6:9} The LORD said, "I'm the one who rescued you, but you've been ignoring my commands." {6:11} Then an angel of the LORD showed up under an oak tree in Ophrah, where Joash lived. Gideon, Joash's son, was hiding out, threshing wheat by the winepress to keep it from the Midianites. {6:12} The angel told Gideon, "You're a brave one, and the LORD is with you." {6:13} Gideon was like, "Um, if the LORD is with us, why are we in this mess? Where are all the miracles we heard about?" {6:14} The LORD looked at Gideon and said, "Go, and you'll save Israel from Midian. I'm sending you." {6:15} Gideon was unsure, saying, "How can I save Israel? My family is poor, and I'm the least important." {6:16} But the LORD assured him, "I'll be with you, and you'll defeat the Midianites like it's no big deal." {6:17-18} Gideon asked for a sign, and the angel agreed to wait for his offering. {6:19-20} Gideon prepared a meal, and the angel instructed him to put it on a rock. {6:21} The angel touched the offering with his staff, and fire consumed it. Then the angel vanished. {6:22} Gideon freaked out, realizing he'd seen an angel face-to-face. {6:23} The LORD assured

Gideon he wouldn't die. {6:24} So, Gideon built an altar and named it Jehovah-shalom. {6:25-27} That night, the LORD told Gideon to tear down his father's altar to Baal and build one for the LORD. {6:28-31} When the city woke up and saw the altar destroyed, they wanted Gideon dead. {6:32} They started calling him Jerubbaal because he messed with Baal's altar. {6:33} The Midianites, Amalekites, and eastern tribes gathered in Jezreel Valley. {6:34-35} The Spirit of the LORD came upon Gideon, and he blew a trumpet to gather his men. {6:36-37} Gideon asked the LORD for a sign, using a fleece of wool. {6:38} The next morning, the fleece was soaked with dew. {6:39} Gideon asked for another sign, and that night, the fleece was dry while the ground was wet.

{7:1} So, Gideon and his crew got up early and camped near the well of Harod. The Midianites were chilling to the north, by the hill of Moreh, in the valley. {7:2} The LORD told Gideon, "You've got too many people with you. If I let y'all win, Israel might think they did it all themselves." {7:3} So Gideon told the scared ones to head home from Mount Gilead. Twenty-two thousand bounced, leaving ten thousand. {7:4} The LORD said, "Still too many. Take them to the water, and I'll weed them out. Those who drink like dogs, set them aside; those who kneel down, keep them." {7:5-6} Three hundred lapped water with their hands, while the rest knelt to drink. {7:7} The LORD said, "I'll use the three hundred who lapped to save you from Midian. Let the others bounce." {7:8} Gideon sent the rest home and kept the three hundred. The Midianite camp was down in the valley. {7:9} That night, the LORD said, "Get ready to attack; I've delivered them to you." {7:10} If Gideon was nervous, he could take his servant Phurah with him. {7:11-14} Gideon went down to the enemy camp and overheard a dream and its meaning, confirming that God would give them victory. {7:15} Gideon worshipped and returned to his crew, saying, "Let's go; the LORD has given us victory." {7:16} He split the three hundred into three groups with trumpets and lit lamps in pitchers. {7:17-20} He instructed them to follow his lead. When they blew their trumpets, they shouted, "The sword of the LORD and of Gideon!" {7:21} The enemy panicked, and chaos ensued. {7:22} The three hundred blew trumpets, and the LORD caused confusion among the enemy. {7:23} Israelites from various tribes joined the pursuit. {7:24} Gideon called for backup from Ephraim, who captured key locations. {7:25} They caught and killed two Midianite leaders, Oreb and Zeeb, bringing their heads to Gideon.

{8:1} So, the guys from Ephraim were all up in Gideon's face, asking why he didn't call them to join the fight against the Midianites. They were really giving him a hard time. {8:2} Gideon clapped back, saying, "What did I do wrong compared to you guys? Isn't what you got from the Midianites better than what we did?" {8:3} Gideon smoothed things over by pointing out that God handed over Midian's princes to them. {8:4} Gideon and his three hundred men crossed the Jordan, tired but still chasing after them. {8:5-6} He asked the people of Succoth for food for his weary crew, but they refused, questioning whether Gideon would actually defeat Zebah and Zalmunna. {8:7-9} Gideon warned them that when he returned victorious, he'd make them pay. {8:10} Zebah and Zalmunna were holed up in Karkor with their remaining forces after losing 120,000 soldiers. {8:11-13} Gideon took on the remaining troops, securing victory. {8:14} Gideon captured a young man from Succoth who described their leaders. {8:15} Gideon confronted the men of Succoth, showing them Zebah and Zalmunna, calling them out for not supporting him earlier. {8:16} Gideon punished the men of Succoth with thorns and briers. {8:17-21} He also took down the tower of Penuel and killed its people. {8:22-26} The Israelites asked Gideon to rule over them, but he refused, saying only the LORD would rule them. {8:27} Gideon made an ephod from the spoils, which led Israel astray. {8:28} Midian was defeated, and the land enjoyed peace for forty years during Gideon's time.

{9:1} So, Abimelech, Jerubbaal's son, hit up his fam in Shechem, chatting with them and all the relatives on his mom's side, like, "Yo, what's the deal? Would you rather have me, one guy, rule over you or all seventy of Jerubbaal's sons? Remember, I'm your blood." {9:2} His mom's peeps spread the word in Shechem, and everyone was vibing with Abimelech because, you know, family ties and all that. {9:3-4} They even tossed him some cash from the temple of Baal-berith, which Abimelech used to hire some shady characters to roll with him. {9:5} Then he rolled up to his dad's crib and offed all his bros, except Jotham who dipped out. {9:6} Shechem and Millo's crew then crowned Abimelech king at Shechem. {9:7-9} Jotham, though, wasn't having it. He climbed up Mount Gerizim and dropped some truth bombs on Shechem. {9:10-14} He went full parable mode, talking about trees wanting a king and all that jazz. {9:15-20} Basically, he said, "You wanted a thorn bush as king? Well, don't be surprised when it stings you back." {9:21} After dropping truth bombs, Jotham bailed to Beer to avoid Abimelech. {9:22} Three years later, trouble brewed between Abimelech and Shechem. {9:23} God stirred up drama between them. {9:24-26} This was payback for Abimelech offing Jerubbaal's seventy sons. {9:27-28} Shechem started throwing shade at Abimelech, and Gaal stepped up to challenge him. {9:29} Gaal wished he could kick Abimelech out and straight up told him to bring it on. {9:30} The next day, Abimelech went on the offensive. {9:31} He ambushed Shechem and took them down. {9:32} Abimelech and his crew attacked the tower of Shechem, burning it down with everyone inside. {9:33} Abimelech tried to burn the tower's door, but a woman dropped a millstone on his head, cracking his skull. {9:34} He asked his homie to kill him so nobody would say a woman took him out, and he went out like that. {9:35} This was payback for Abimelech offing his brothers. {9:36} Shechem got what was coming to them, just like Jotham said.

{10:1} So, after Abimelech, this dude Tola, from Issachar, stepped up to bat for Israel. He lived in Shamir up in Ephraim and judged Israel for twenty-three years before kicking the bucket and getting buried there. {10:3} Then came Jair, a Gileadite, who ruled for twenty-two years. {10:4} He had thirty sons riding around on thirty donkeys, each with their own city in Gilead named Havoth-jair. {10:5} Jair died and got laid to rest in Camon. {10:6} But the Israelites, as usual, messed up big time, worshipping all sorts of gods—Baalim, Ashtaroth, the Syrian, Sidonian, Moabite, Ammonite, and Philistine gods—totally ditching the LORD. {10:7} God got super mad and let the Philistines and Ammonites mess with Israel for eighteen years, especially hitting those on the east side of the

Jordan in Gilead. {10:9} The Ammonites even crossed the Jordan to pick fights with Judah, Benjamin, and Ephraim, causing serious distress. {10:10} Finally, Israel cried out to the LORD, admitting they'd messed up, forsaking Him for other gods. {10:11} God was like, "Um, hello? Didn't I rescue you from Egypt, the Amorites, Ammonites, and Philistines before? {10:12} Even the Zidonians, Amalekites, and Maonites were a problem until you asked for help." {10:13} But since they kept ditching Him for other gods, God was over it. {10:14} He basically said, "Go cry to your new gods when you're in trouble." {10:15} So, Israel was like, "Okay, we messed up. Do whatever, but please save us." {10:16} They tossed out their idols and focused on the LORD, which actually got to Him. {10:17} The Ammonites set up camp in Gilead, and Israel gathered in Mizpeh. {10:18} The leaders in Gilead were like, "Who's gonna lead the charge against Ammon? They'll be our top dog."

{11:1-2} So, there's this dude Jephthah from Gilead, a real tough guy, but get this—he's the son of a harlot. Gilead was his dad, and he had other legit sons with his wife who totally kicked Jephthah out, dissing him because his mom wasn't part of the fam. {11:3} Jephthah bounced to Tob and gathered a crew of rowdy dudes to hang with him. {11:4} Later on, the Ammonites start beefing with Israel. {11:5-6} The elders of Gilead then fetch Jephthah from Tob, asking him to lead the charge against Ammon. {11:7} Jephthah's like, "Hold up, weren't you the ones who kicked me out? Why come to me now that you're in trouble?" {11:8} The elders beg him to be their head and fight Ammon. {11:9-10} Jephthah's like, "Fine, but only if the LORD helps us win." {11:11} They make a deal, and Jephthah makes it official before the LORD in Mizpeh. {11:12} Jephthah sends messages to the Ammonite king, asking why they're starting trouble in his land. {11:13-14} The king claims Israel took his land after leaving Egypt, demanding it back peacefully. {11:15-18} Jephthah sets the record straight, saying Israel never touched Moab or Ammon's land. {11:19-20} He explains how Israel asked nicely to pass through Moab and Edom's land, but they got shut down and had to take the long way. {11:21-27} God helped Israel defeat Sihon, king of the Amorites, giving them their land. {11:28} The Ammonite king ignores Jephthah's messages. {11:29} Then the Spirit of the LORD hits Jephthah, and he gears up to fight the Ammonites. {11:30-31} Jephthah makes a vow to the LORD—if he wins, the first thing to greet him at home will be dedicated to God. {11:32-33} God comes through, and Jephthah defeats the Ammonites, wrecking them from Aroer to Minnith. {11:34} When Jephthah returns home, his daughter comes out to celebrate, but she's his only child. {11:35} He's devastated because of his vow to God. {11:36} His daughter accepts her fate, agreeing to what Jephthah vowed to the LORD. {11:37-39} She asks for two months to mourn her fate with her friends. {11:40} Each year, the Israelite girls mourn her fate for four days.

{12:1} So, the Ephraimites got all fired up and confronted Jephthah, asking why he didn't invite them to fight the Ammonites and threatening to burn down his house. {12:2} Jephthah clapped back, explaining they didn't show up when he needed them against the Ammonites. {12:3} He took matters into his own hands and fought the Ammonites, and God helped him win. {12:4} Then Jephthah rallied the Gileadites and clashed with Ephraim because they dissed the Gileadites as fugitives. {12:5} The Gileadites controlled the Jordan River crossings and checked if anyone claiming to be Ephraimite could say "Shibboleth" right. If they messed it up like "Sibboleth," they got smoked—42,000 Ephraimites bit the dust. {12:7} Jephthah ruled Israel for six years before he passed away and was buried in Gilead. {12:8} Next up was Ibzan from Bethlehem, leading Israel for seven years, having 30 sons and daughters who were well-traveled. {12:10} Ibzan kicked the bucket and was buried in Bethlehem. {12:11-12} Then came Elon from Zebulun, judging Israel for a decade before he died and was buried in Aijalon. {12:13} After him, Abdon from Pirathon took charge, having a huge family crew and ruling Israel for eight years before he passed away and was buried in Ephraim.

{13:1} So, the Israelites messed up again in God's eyes, and God let the Philistines rule over them for forty years. {13:2} There was this dude named Manoah from the Danites, and his wife couldn't have kids. {13:3} Then an angel appeared to her, saying she'd have a son who'd be a Nazarite from birth, no booze or unclean food for him, and he'd start delivering Israel from the Philistines. {13:6} The woman told her husband, describing this intense angel, and they wanted more guidance on raising the kid. {13:9} God listened, and the angel showed up again to the woman. {13:10} She rushed to tell her husband, and they found the angel. {13:12} Manoah wanted to know how to raise their future son. {13:16} The angel declined their food but accepted a sacrifice to the LORD. {13:17} Manoah asked the angel's name, but it was kept secret. {13:19} They sacrificed to God, and the angel did something miraculous. {13:20} As the offering burned, the angel ascended in the flame. {13:21} After that, the angel didn't show up again, and Manoah realized it was truly an angel of the LORD. {13:22} Manoah feared they'd die for seeing God, but his wife reassured him. {13:24} The woman gave birth to a son named Samson, and he grew up blessed by the LORD. {13:25} The Spirit of the LORD began to move him in the camp of Dan.

{14:1} So Samson rolled into Timnath and spotted a Philistine girl he liked. {14:2} He spilled the tea to his parents, like, "I found a girl, get her for me as a wife." {14:3} His parents were shook, asking why he wanted a Philistine when there were plenty of options from their own crew. Samson was like, "Nah, she's the one for me." {14:4} Little did they know, it was all part of God's plan to mess with the Philistines 'cause they were running the show in Israel. {14:5} As Samson was chilling in the vineyards, a lion jumped him, but with divine strength, he crushed it like it was nothing. {14:7} Then he went to chat with the girl. {14:8} Later, he checked back on the lion's carcass and found honey inside. {14:10} He threw a party with the girl, and thirty guys showed up as part of the crew. {14:12} Samson dropped a riddle, offering a bet: thirty outfits if they solved it or vice versa. {14:14} The riddle was deep—food from a lion and sweetness from strength. They couldn't crack it in three days. {14:15} On the seventh day, they pressured the girl to squeeze Samson for the answer or else they'd burn her place down. {14:16} The girl was upset Samson didn't trust her with the riddle. {14:17} She cried for days until Samson spilled the beans, and she spilled them to her people. {14:18} The guys figured out the riddle, and Samson got heated, saying they wouldn't have solved it if not for his girl telling them. {14:19} Fired up by the Spirit of the LORD, Samson went to Ashkelon, took down thirty dudes, and paid up with outfits. Then he bounced back home. {14:20} Turns out, Samson's wife got hitched to one of the guys from the party.

{15:1} So, like, after a bit during wheat harvest, Samson swung by to see his wife, thinking they'd chill together. But her dad was like, "Nah, I thought you hated her, so I hooked her up with your bro. Isn't her sis hotter? Take her instead." {15:3} Samson was like, "Okay, I'll get back at the Philistines without feeling bad about it." {15:4} He rounded up 300 foxes, tied them up in pairs with firebrands between them, and set them loose in the Philistines' fields, burning up their crops, vineyards, and olives. {15:6} When the Philistines found out, they torched Samson's wife and her dad in retaliation. {15:7} Samson vowed revenge, and he sure delivered, causing a major stir and then chilling at the top of the rock Etam. {15:9} The Philistines set up camp in Judah, spreading out in Lehi. {15:10} The dudes from Judah were like, "Why you coming at us?" The Philistines were after Samson, payback for what he did. {15:11} Three thousand guys from Judah went to Samson, asking why he brought this on them. {15:12} They were ready to hand him over, but Samson was like, "Promise not to take me out yourselves." {15:14} As they took him to Lehi, the Spirit of the LORD kicked in, and Samson broke free from his bindings. {15:15-17} He grabbed a jawbone and took down a thousand Philistines. {15:18} After that, he was super thirsty and prayed to God for help. {15:19} God came through, making water gush from the jawbone's hollow place, reviving Samson. {15:20} Samson ruled over Israel during the Philistine rule for twenty years.

{16:1} So Samson rolls into Gaza and meets this girl, and they hook up. {16:2} The locals find out Samson's there and plan to ambush him at the city gate at dawn. {16:3} But Samson's too slick—he waits till midnight, then rips the city gate off its hinges and hauls it up a hill near Hebron. {16:4} Later on, he falls for a girl named Delilah in the valley of Sorek. {16:5} The Philistine leaders bribe Delilah to find out Samson's weakness so they can take him down. {16:6-7} Delilah keeps pressing Samson to spill his secret, and he messes with her, saying if he's tied with certain ropes or cords, he'll be weak. {16:8-9} Delilah tries it, but Samson breaks free. {16:10-12} She's frustrated but keeps asking, and Samson jokes about getting tied up again. {16:13-18} Samson finally spills the beans: his strength comes from his uncut hair because he's been dedicated to God since birth. {16:19} Delilah shaves his head while he's sleeping, and Samson loses his strength. {16:20} When the Philistines attack, Samson doesn't realize he's powerless without God's spirit. {16:21} They capture him, blind him, and make him grind grain in prison. {16:22} Over time, Samson's hair starts growing back. {16:23-24} The Philistine leaders celebrate their victory over Samson. {16:25-27} At a big party, they bring Samson out to entertain them. {16:28-29} Samson prays to God for strength one last time. {16:30} He pushes down the pillars of the building, killing everyone inside, including himself. {16:31} Samson's family retrieves his body and buries him, and he's remembered for leading Israel for twenty years.

{17:1} So there's this dude from mount Ephraim named Micah. {17:2} He tells his mom, "Remember that 1100 shekels of silver you lost? Well, I took it." His mom's cool with it, blesses him, and decides to dedicate the silver to the LORD to make idols. {17:4} Micah gives the silver to a craftsman who makes graven and molten images for him. {17:5} Micah sets up a shrine with all these idols, including an ephod, and even appoints one of his sons as a priest. {17:6} Back then, Israel had no king, so everyone just did whatever seemed right to them. {17:7} Then there's this young Levite from Bethlehemjudah, part of the family of Judah, chilling there. {17:8} He leaves Bethlehemjudah and heads to mount Ephraim, finding Micah's place along the way. {17:9} Micah asks him where he's from, and he says he's a Levite from Bethlehemjudah, looking for somewhere to stay. {17:10} Micah offers him room and board, plus some cash and clothes, to be his priest. {17:11} The Levite's down with it and stays with Micah like one of his own. {17:12} Micah ordains the Levite as his priest, and he hangs out in Micah's house. {17:13} Micah's stoked, thinking having a Levite as his priest means good things from the LORD.

{18:1} So back when there wasn't any king in Israel, the tribe of Dan was on a mission to find themselves a place to settle because they hadn't gotten their piece of land among the other tribes. {18:2} The Danites sent five tough dudes from Zorah and Eshtaol to scout the land, and they ended up crashing at Micah's place in mount Ephraim. {18:3} When they recognized the voice of the young Levite at Micah's house, they asked him what he was doing there. {18:4} The Levite explained that Micah hired him to be his priest. {18:5} They told the Levite to ask God if their journey would be successful. {18:6} The priest gave them the go-ahead, saying their way was blessed by the LORD. {18:7} So the five scouts went to Laish and found the people living peacefully, like the Zidonians, without any authority oppressing them. {18:8} After checking it out, they returned to Zorah and Eshtaol and told their fellow Danites the good news. {18:9} The Danites decided to go up against Laish because they liked what they saw, and they encouraged each other not to be lazy about taking the land. {18:10} They were sure they'd find a rich and spacious place because God had promised it to them. {18:11} Six hundred armed Danites set out from Zorah and Eshtaol. {18:12} They camped near Kirjath-jearim in Judah, which they called Mahaneh-dan. {18:13} Then they moved on to mount Ephraim and arrived at Micah's house. {18:14} The five scouts revealed to the Danites that Micah had idols in his house, and they urged their tribe to consider their next move. {18:15} They then went to Micah's house, where they greeted the Levite. {18:16} The six hundred armed Danites stood guard at the gate. {18:17} The scouts entered, took the idols, and the Levite stood by with the armed men. {18:18} They took Micah's idols and asked the Levite what he was doing. {18:19} They persuaded him to come with them and be a priest for the entire tribe of Dan, promising a better deal than serving just one household. {18:20} The Levite was happy with this and joined them along with the idols. {18:21} So they left, taking their families and possessions with them. {18:22} When they were far from Micah's house, the neighbors caught up to them. {18:23} They confronted Micah, asking why he brought a whole army. {18:24} Micah realized they took his idols and priest and complained. {18:25} The Danites warned him to stay quiet or face serious consequences. {18:26} Seeing they were too strong, Micah went back home. {18:27} The Danites attacked Laish, a quiet and secure city, killing the people and burning it down. {18:28} Since Laish was isolated, there was no one to save them. {18:29} They renamed the city Dan after their ancestor Dan. {18:30} The Danites set up Micah's idols, and a descendant of Manasseh served as their priest until the land was captured. {18:31} They continued to use Micah's idols while the house of God was in Shiloh.

{19:1} So back in those days when there wasn't any king in Israel, there was this Levite dude chilling on the side of mount Ephraim. He hooked up with a girl from Bethlehemjudah as his side piece. {19:2} But then his girl started playing him, went back to her dad's crib in Bethlehemjudah, and stayed there for four months. {19:3} Her man decided to go after her, to try and talk things out and bring her back. He took his servant and a couple of donkeys, and she brought him to her dad's house. When her dad saw him, he was all hyped to meet him. {19:4} The girl's dad convinced him to stick around, so he stayed there for three days, eating, drinking, and crashing at their place. {19:5} On the fourth day, when he wanted to leave, the dad was like, "Have a bite of bread first, then you can bounce." {19:6} They ate together, and the dad was like, "Chill, stay the night, have a good time." {19:7} When the dude tried to leave again, the dad insisted he stay, so he spent another night there. {19:8} On the fifth day, he finally got up early to leave, but the dad convinced him to chill a bit longer. They hung out until afternoon, eating again. {19:9} When the man and his girl were ready to leave, her dad was like, "Come on, stay the night. The day's almost over. Stay here, have a good time, and leave early tomorrow." {19:10} But the man wasn't down to stay, so he left and passed by Jebus (Jerusalem) with his two donkeys and his girl. {19:11} By the time they got near Jebus, it was getting late, and the servant suggested they crash in the city of the Jebusites. {19:12} But the man said, "Nah, we're not staying in a city of strangers. Let's head to Gibeah." {19:13} They decided to find a place to crash in Gibeah or Ramah. {19:14} As they went by Gibeah, which belongs to Benjamin, the sun was going down. {19:15} They decided to stay in Gibeah, but no one offered them a place to crash. {19:16} Then an old man from mount Ephraim, who was staying in Gibeah where the people were Benjamites, came back from work in the evening. {19:17} He spotted the travelers in the city street and asked where they were going and where they came from. {19:18} The man explained they were traveling from Bethlehemjudah to mount Ephraim and were heading to the house of the LORD, but no one would take them in. {19:19} The old man offered them straw, provender, bread, wine, and a place to stay. {19:20} He welcomed them into his house, and they ate and drank. {19:21} While they were chilling, some wicked dudes from the city surrounded the house, demanding to see the traveler. {19:22} The old man refused and tried to reason with them. {19:23} He even offered his daughter and the man's concubine to them instead, but they weren't having it. {19:24} So the man reluctantly gave them his concubine, and they mistreated her all night. {19:25} In the morning, they let her go, and she collapsed at the door. {19:26} When the man saw her at dawn, he told her to get up, but she didn't respond. So he put her on a donkey and headed home. {19:29} When he got home, he cut her body into twelve pieces and sent them throughout Israel. {19:30} This shocked everyone who saw it, saying such a thing had never happened since the days of Egypt.

{20:1} So, like, all the kids of Israel gathered together, from Dan to Beer-sheba, including Gilead, to meet up with the LORD in Mizpeh. {20:2} The big shots from all the tribes showed up, with 400,000 soldiers ready to throw down. {20:3} When the tribe of Benjamin heard about this gathering at Mizpeh, the other Israelites were like, "Tell us what went down." {20:4} The Levite, whose woman got killed, explained, "I rolled into Gibeah with my girl to crash." {20:5} But then the guys from Gibeah attacked us, trying to kill me, and they forced themselves on my girl, and she died. {20:6} So I cut her up and sent pieces all over Israel because of their messed-up behavior. {20:7} "You're all Israelites," he said, "give me some advice here." {20:8} Everyone agreed not to go home until they sorted out Gibeah. {20:9} They decided to attack Gibeah by drawing lots. {20:10} They sent troops to gather supplies and take revenge on Gibeah. {20:11} The whole crew of Israelites assembled against Gibeah like a united force. {20:12} They sent messengers to Benjamin, demanding, "Hand over the evildoers from Gibeah so we can execute them and cleanse Israel." But the Benjaminites refused. {20:14} Instead, they rallied to defend Gibeah and fight against the rest of Israel. {20:15} The Benjaminites mobilized 26,000 swordsmen from their cities, plus 700 elite fighters from Gibeah. {20:16} Among them were 700 skilled left-handed warriors who could sling stones with deadly accuracy. {20:17} The rest of Israel, excluding Benjamin, had 400,000 sword-wielding men, all ready for battle. {20:18} Israel consulted God at the house of God, asking who should attack Benjamin first. {20:19} Israel set up camp near Gibeah and prepared to fight. {20:20} They faced off against Benjamin, getting ready for a showdown. {20:21} The Benjaminites came out of Gibeah and killed 22,000 Israelite soldiers that day. {20:22} Israel regrouped and prepared for battle the next day. {20:23} They wept before the LORD and sought counsel on whether to attack again. {20:24} Israel approached Benjamin again for battle. {20:25} Benjamin came out of Gibeah and killed 18,000 more Israelite soldiers. {20:26} Israel and the people went to the house of God, weeping and fasting. {20:27} They consulted the LORD through Phinehas, son of Eleazar, asking whether to continue the battle against Benjamin. {20:28} The LORD instructed them to go, promising victory the next day. {20:29} Israel set up an ambush around Gibeah. {20:30} On the third day, Israel faced Benjamin again at Gibeah. {20:31} Benjamin lured them away from Gibeah and attacked, killing about 30 Israelites. {20:32} Benjamin thought they were winning, but Israel pretended to retreat, drawing them out of the city. {20:33} Israel set up a trap at Baal-tamar, and the ambush from Gibeah attacked. {20:34} 10,000 chosen men from Israel fought hard against Gibeah. {20:35} The LORD gave Israel victory; they killed 25,100 Benjaminites. {20:36} Benjamin realized they were losing ground. {20:37} The ambush rushed Gibeah, destroying the city. {20:38} They signaled with smoke to coordinate their attack. {20:39} Benjamin chased after Israel, thinking they were winning again. {20:40} But when they saw the city in flames, they knew they were in trouble. {20:41} Benjamin was shocked to see disaster strike. {20:42} Israel pursued and defeated Benjamin near Gibeah. {20:43} They surrounded Benjamin, chased them down, and defeated them. {20:44} 18,000 Benjaminites were killed, including valiant warriors. {20:45} The survivors fled to the rock of Rimmon, where Israel pursued and killed 5,000. {20:46} The total casualties that day for Benjamin were 25,000 valiant men. {20:47} 600 men escaped to the rock of Rimmon and stayed there for four months. {20:48} Israel wiped out the Benjaminites, destroying their cities and all within reach.

{21:1} So, like, the dudes from Israel swore at Mizpeh, saying they wouldn't let any of their daughters marry a Benjaminite. {21:2} Then everyone hit up the house of God and stayed there till evening, crying their hearts out. {21:3} They were like, "Yo, LORD God of Israel, why'd this happen? One tribe's missing now." {21:4} Next day, they got up early, built an altar, and offered sacrifices. {21:5} They were like, "Who didn't show up at Mizpeh? They're toast." {21:6} Israel felt bad for Benjamin 'cause they were basically wiped out. {21:7} "How do we find wives for the Benjaminites if we swore not to give them our daughters?" {21:8} They were like, "Did anyone miss the Mizpeh gathering?" Turns out, no one from Jabesh-gilead came. {21:9} So they sent 12,000 tough dudes to Jabesh-gilead to take out everyone there, including women and kids. {21:10} They were instructed to wipe out all the men and women who had slept with men. {21:12} They found 400 virgin girls in Jabesh-gilead and brought them to Shiloh. {21:13} They sent peeps to the Benjaminites in Rimmon to negotiate. {21:14} The Benjaminites got wives from the saved Jabesh-gilead girls, but they still needed more. {21:15} Israel felt bad 'cause they messed up Benjamin's tribe. {21:16} The elders were like, "How do we find wives for the remaining Benjaminites since there are no women left in Benjamin?" {21:17} They wanted to keep Benjamin from getting wiped out. {21:18} But they couldn't give them their daughters due to the oath against it. {21:19} They were like, "There's a festival in Shiloh where girls dance; go there and snag wives." {21:20} So they told the Benjaminites to hide in the vineyards and grab Shiloh's dancing daughters. {21:21} If anyone complained, they'd smooth it over and say it was necessary. {21:23} The Benjaminites did it, got wives, and went back to their cities. {21:24} After that, everyone went back to their tribes and homes.

Ruth

+++

[1:1] So, back in the day when the judges were in charge, there was a serious famine in the land. This guy from Bethlehem named Elimelech, along with his wife Naomi and their two sons, decided to bounce to Moab to find food. [1:2] Elimelech's wife was Naomi, and their sons were Mahlon and Chilion. They were from Bethlehem and settled in Moab. [1:3] Sadly, Elimelech died, leaving Naomi with her two sons. [1:4] The sons married Moabite women named Orpah and Ruth, and they lived in Moab for about ten years. [1:5] Tragically, both Mahlon and Chilion died, leaving Naomi without her sons or her husband. [1:6] Naomi heard that things had gotten better in Judah, so she decided to head back with her daughters-in-law. [1:7] They set out for Judah together, but along the way, Naomi told them to go back to their families in Moab. [1:8] She blessed them and wished them well. [1:9] Naomi hoped they would find new husbands and be at peace. They cried and kissed goodbye. [1:10] Orpah and Ruth wanted to go with Naomi, but she encouraged them to stay in Moab. [1:11] She explained that she had no more sons to offer them. [1:12] Naomi urged them to go back to their families. [1:13] She didn't want them waiting around for sons that might never come. [1:14] Orpah left, but Ruth stayed with Naomi. [1:15] Naomi insisted that Ruth go back like Orpah did. [1:16] But Ruth was determined to stay with Naomi and adopt her people and her God. [1:17] She promised to stay with Naomi until death separated them. [1:18] When Naomi saw that Ruth was unwavering, she stopped trying to convince her to leave. [1:19] So, the two of them made it to Bethlehem, causing a stir in the city. [1:20] People were shocked to see Naomi back and asked if it was really her. [1:21] Naomi said to call her "Mara" (meaning bitter) instead of Naomi because of all her hardships. [1:22] Naomi and Ruth returned to Bethlehem at the start of the barley harvest.

[2:1] Naomi's husband had a wealthy relative named Boaz. [2:2] Ruth, the Moabite, asked Naomi if she could go glean in the fields to find favor with someone. Naomi said, "Sure, go for it, girl." [2:3] So Ruth went and started gleaning in Boaz's field, who happened to be related to Naomi's family. [2:4] Boaz greeted his workers, saying, "May the Lord be with you!" They replied, "And bless you too!" [2:5] Boaz asked his servant about Ruth, and the servant explained that she came with Naomi from Moab and had been working hard since morning. [2:6] Ruth asked to gather leftovers after the reapers, and she had been there pretty much all day, taking a break only briefly. [2:8] Boaz told Ruth to stay close to his crew and not go to other fields, and he made sure the guys knew not to bother her. He also let her drink from their water vessels when she got thirsty. [2:10] Ruth was amazed and asked Boaz why he was so kind to her, a stranger. [2:11] Boaz said he'd heard about her devotion to Naomi and how she left her homeland to come to a place she didn't know before. [2:12] He blessed her for trusting in the Lord, the God of Israel. [2:13] Ruth thanked Boaz for being comforting and friendly, even though she wasn't one of his usual crew. [2:14] Boaz invited Ruth to eat with them at mealtime and even offered her bread and vinegar. She sat with the workers, and Boaz personally served her roasted grain. [2:15] Boaz instructed his guys to let Ruth glean among the sheaves and even intentionally drop extra grain for her. [2:17] Ruth gleaned until evening and ended up with a whole lot of barley. [2:18] Ruth brought her haul back to Naomi, who was impressed. Naomi shared some of her own food with Ruth after Ruth had eaten her fill. [2:19] Naomi asked Ruth where she had gleaned, and Ruth told her it was Boaz's field. [2:20] Naomi praised Boaz for being so kind to both the living and the dead, acknowledging his kinship to their family. [2:21] Ruth mentioned that Boaz told her to stick around until the end of the harvest. [2:22] Naomi encouraged Ruth to stay close to Boaz's maidens and not wander into other fields. [2:23] So Ruth kept gleaning with Boaz's crew until the end of both barley and wheat harvests, staying with her mother-in-law Naomi.

[3:1] Naomi, her mother-in-law, was like, "Hey girl, shouldn't we find you a good situation?" [3:2] She's all like, "Boaz is fam, and he's chillin' at the threshing floor tonight." [3:3] Naomi tells Ruth to freshen up, put on her best outfit, and head down to the floor without making it obvious who she is until Boaz is done eating and drinking. [3:4] Naomi gives Ruth the scoop: when Boaz lies down, mark where he is and go lay down next to him. He'll let you know what's up. [3:5] Ruth's like, "I'm down for whatever you say." [3:6] So Ruth heads over, does everything Naomi said. [3:7] After Boaz eats and drinks and feels good, he crashes at the end of the grain pile, and Ruth sneaks over, uncovers his feet, and lays down. [3:8] At midnight, Boaz wakes up startled and sees Ruth at his feet. [3:9] He's like, "Who are you?" Ruth's like, "I'm Ruth, your servant. Spread your cover over me since you're a close relative." [3:10] Boaz blesses her, saying she's shown kindness by not chasing after younger guys, rich or poor. [3:11] Boaz tells Ruth not to worry; he's got her back because everyone knows she's a good woman. [3:12] Boaz admits he's a relative, but there's someone closer than him. [3:13] Boaz tells Ruth to chill until morning to see how things go with the other dude. [3:14] Ruth stays by his feet until morning, and Boaz tells her to keep it on the DL that she was there. [3:15] Boaz gives Ruth six measures of barley, and she heads back to the city. [3:16] When Ruth gets back to Naomi, she spills the tea on everything that went down. [3:17] Ruth shows Naomi the barley Boaz gave her and tells her about the plan. [3:18] Naomi's like, "Sit tight, girl. Boaz won't rest until this is sorted."

[4:1] So Boaz heads to the city gate and sits down, waiting for the other relative. [4:2] He gets ten elders to join them. [4:3] Boaz tells the other relative that Naomi's selling Elimelech's land. [4:4] He's like, "I thought I'd let you know first. If you want it, buy it. If not, tell me." The other guy's like, "I'll buy it." [4:5] Boaz drops the bomb: if he buys the land, he also has to marry Ruth to carry on her dead husband's name. {4:6} The other guy backs out because it messes with his own inheritance, so Boaz takes over. {4:7} They seal the deal like they used to in Israel—by exchanging a shoe. {4:8} Boaz buys the land and Ruth. {4:9} He announces to everyone that he's bought back Elimelech's land and married Ruth to carry on her husband's name. {4:10} Everyone's on board, blessing Boaz and Ruth. {4:11} They hope Ruth is like Rachel and Leah and wish Boaz success in Bethlehem. {4:12} They pray for Boaz to have a great family, like the one that came from Tamar and Judah. {4:13} Boaz and Ruth get married, and soon enough, Ruth has a baby boy. {4:14} The women bless Naomi, saying she's not left without family. {4:15} They predict the baby will bring joy and care for Naomi in her old age. {4:16} Naomi becomes the baby's caretaker, and the neighbors name the baby Obed, who becomes the grandfather of David.

1 Samuel

✦✦✦

{1:1} So, there's this dude named Elkanah from Ramathaimzophim, repping mount Ephraim. His fam line goes back to Jeroham, Elihu, Tohu, and Zuph. He's an Ephrathite. {1:2} Elkanah has two wives: Hannah and Peninnah. Peninnah has kids, but Hannah can't have any. {1:3} Every year, Elkanah goes to Shiloh to worship and sacrifice to the LORD of hosts. Eli's sons, Hophni and Phinehas, are priests there. {1:4} When Elkanah sacrifices, he gives portions to Peninnah and her kids, but gives Hannah a bigger share 'cause he loves her, even though the LORD closed her womb. {1:5} Peninnah keeps taunting Hannah about not having kids, making her upset because of her infertility. {1:6} This goes on every year, and every time they go to the house of the LORD, Peninnah gets under Hannah's skin, making her cry and not eat. {1:7} Elkanah tries to comfort Hannah, asking why she's sad and not eating, and if he isn't better to her than ten sons. {1:8} After eating at Shiloh, Hannah goes to pray bitterly to the LORD, crying her heart out. {1:9} She vows to dedicate her child to the LORD if He gives her a son, promising he'll serve God his whole life without cutting his hair. {1:10} While praying, Eli notices her, thinking she's drunk because she's only moving her lips. {1:11} Eli confronts her, thinking she's wasted, but she explains she's deeply troubled and pouring out her soul to the LORD. {1:12} Eli blesses her, hoping the LORD grants her request. {1:13} Hannah goes back, eats, and cheers up. {1:14-19} The next morning, they worship and return home. Elkanah knows Hannah, and the LORD remembers her. {1:20} Hannah conceives and names her son Samuel, meaning "asked of the LORD." {1:21} Elkanah and his fam offer sacrifices to the LORD yearly, honoring their vow. {1:22} Hannah stays home until Samuel is weaned, then plans to bring him to the LORD and leave him there forever. {1:23} Elkanah supports her decision, encouraging her to do what she thinks is right, and trusting in the LORD's plan.

{2:1} Hannah prayed and was like, "I'm so happy in the LORD! My enemies can't touch me because I'm rejoicing in His salvation." {2:2} There's no one as holy as the LORD; He's our rock, our God. {2:3} Don't talk big and proud; the LORD knows all and judges actions. {2:4} Powerful warriors fall, and the weak find strength. {2:5} The full become hungry, while the hungry are satisfied. Even the barren have children, while those with many kids grow weak. {2:6} The LORD brings life and death; He raises people up and brings them down. {2:7} He makes people poor and rich, humble and exalted. {2:8} He lifts the poor from the dust to sit among princes and inherit glory, for the earth is His. {2:9} His saints are protected, and the wicked will be silenced. {2:10} The LORD will crush His enemies and strengthen His anointed. {2:11} Meanwhile, Elkanah heads back home, and Samuel serves the LORD under Eli the priest. {2:12} Now Eli's sons were wicked and didn't know the LORD. {2:13} When people offered sacrifices, the priests' servants would come and take whatever they wanted for themselves, even before the fat was burnt. {2:14} They even demanded raw meat instead of cooked, and threatened force if denied. {2:15} The young men's sin was great, and people hated offering sacrifices to the LORD because of them. {2:18} But Samuel served the LORD, a child wearing a linen ephod. {2:19} His mother made him a little coat each year when they went to offer sacrifices. {2:20} Eli blessed Elkanah and his wife, asking the LORD to bless them with more children. {2:21} Hannah was blessed with more children, and Samuel grew up serving the LORD. {2:22} Eli was old and heard about his sons' misconduct with women at the tabernacle entrance. {2:23} He scolded them for dishonoring the LORD and causing people to sin. {2:24} Despite warnings, they ignored their father and faced consequences because the LORD intended to punish them. {2:25} Samuel continued to grow in favor with the LORD and people. {2:27} A man of God came to Eli, reminding him of God's past favor on his family in Egypt. {2:28} God chose Eli's family as priests and gave them offerings from Israel. {2:29} But Eli's sons dishonored God by taking the best offerings for themselves. {2:30} The LORD decided to reject Eli's family, honoring those who honor Him and despising those who reject Him.

{3:1} So Samuel was serving the LORD under Eli, and back then, hearing from the LORD was rare; there weren't many visions. {3:2} One night, Eli's eyesight was failing, and he couldn't see well. {3:3} Before the lamp of God went out in the temple where the ark was, Samuel was lying down. {3:4} Then the LORD called Samuel, and Samuel was like, "Here I am." {3:5} He ran to Eli, thinking Eli had called him, but Eli was like, "Nah, go back to bed." So Samuel did. {3:6} The LORD called Samuel again, and Samuel went to Eli, but Eli hadn't called him. {3:7} Samuel didn't know the LORD yet, and the word of the LORD wasn't revealed to him. {3:8} The LORD called Samuel again, and Eli realized it was the LORD calling Samuel. {3:9} Eli told Samuel, "If He calls you again, say, 'Speak, LORD; your servant is listening.'" So Samuel did as Eli said. {3:10} The LORD called Samuel again, and Samuel was ready to listen. {3:11} The LORD told Samuel about a big thing He was going to do in Israel that would shock everyone. {3:12} He'd make sure Eli's family faced judgment for their sins. {3:13} Eli knew this was because his sons were wicked and he didn't stop them. {3:14} So, the LORD swore that Eli's family would never be forgiven through sacrifices or offerings. {3:15} Samuel waited until morning and opened the doors of the LORD's house, but he was afraid to tell Eli what he saw. {3:16} Eli asked Samuel what the LORD said, swearing him to tell the truth. {3:17-18} Samuel shared everything with Eli; he didn't hold back. Eli accepted it, saying, "Let the LORD do what He thinks is best." {3:19} Samuel grew up, and the LORD was with him, confirming everything he said. {3:20} All Israel knew Samuel was a true prophet of the LORD, from Dan to Beer-sheba.

{4:1} Samuel's words reached all Israel, and they faced the Philistines in battle at Eben-ezer, with the Philistines at Aphek. {4:2} The Philistines fought and defeated Israel, killing about four thousand men. {4:3} When Israel wondered why they lost, they decided to bring the ark of the covenant from Shiloh, hoping it would save them. {4:4} They brought the ark, with Eli's sons Hophni and Phinehas, to the battlefield. {4:5} When the ark arrived, Israel cheered loudly, shaking the ground. {4:6} The Philistines heard and got scared, realizing the LORD was with Israel. {4:7} They feared, saying, "God's with them now; we're in trouble." {4:8} They remembered how God had punished Egypt with plagues in the wilderness. {4:9} The Philistines encouraged each other to fight like men and not become Israel's slaves. {4:10} They fought again, and this time, Israel was badly beaten; thirty thousand soldiers fell. {4:11} The ark was captured, and Eli's sons Hophni and Phinehas died. {4:12} A Benjaminite soldier rushed to Shiloh, mourning the losses. {4:13} When he arrived, he found Eli worried about the ark. {4:14} Eli asked about the commotion, and the soldier told him what happened. {4:15} Eli, old and blind, listened to the soldier's report. {4:16-18} The soldier explained the defeat and deaths, and when he mentioned the ark, Eli fell and died, bringing judgment on his family after forty years of leading Israel. {4:19} Phinehas' wife, about to give birth, heard the news and went into labor, naming her son "I-chabod" to mark the loss of God's glory from Israel.

{5:1} The Philistines snagged the ark of God and hauled it from Eben-ezer to Ashdod. {5:2} When they got it, they plopped it down in Dagon's crib. {5:3} The next morning, they found Dagon face-planted in front of the LORD's ark. They stood him back up, but the next day, Dagon was down again with his head and hands chopped off, leaving just a stump. {5:5} So, nobody steps on Dagon's threshold in Ashdod anymore. {5:6} The LORD wasn't playing; He messed up Ashdod with tumors. {5:7} The Ashdodites were like, "We can't keep this ark; it's too much for us and Dagon." {5:8} They gathered the Philistine lords and decided to send the ark to Gath. {5:9} But Gath got hit hard too, so they shipped it to Ekron. {5:10} The Ekronites panicked, thinking the ark would wipe them out. {5:11} They sent the ark back to its place, worried they'd all be done for.

{6:1} The ark stayed in Philistine territory for seven months. {6:2} They consulted priests and diviners on what to do with it. {6:3} They were told not to send it back empty-handed but to give a trespass offering. {6:4} They crafted golden tumors and mice as a peace offering to the God of Israel. {6:5-6} They were like, "Maybe He'll chill out if we give Him props." {6:7} They made a new cart and used unyoked cows to carry the ark back to Israel. {6:8} They placed the ark on the cart with the gold offerings and sent it off. {6:9} If it headed to Beth-shemesh, they figured it was God's doing; otherwise, it was chance. {6:10-12} The men did as instructed, and the cows led the way straight to Beth-shemesh, no detours. {6:13} The people of Beth-shemesh rejoiced at seeing the ark. {6:14} They offered sacrifices to the LORD. {6:15} But when they peeked into the ark, God struck down seventy men from Beth-shemesh. {6:16} The survivors were like, "Who can handle this powerful LORD?" {6:17} They sent for Kirjath-jearim to come and take the ark.

{7:1} The crew from Kirjath-jearim rolled up and brought the LORD's ark to Abinadab's pad on the hill, putting Eleazar his son in charge of it. {7:2} It stayed there in Kirjath-jearim for a grip, like twenty years, and all of Israel was feeling down, missing the LORD. {7:3} Samuel dropped wisdom to Israel, saying, "If you wanna get right with the LORD, ditch those other gods and idols, get your hearts in line, and serve Him alone; then He'll save you from the Philistines." {7:4} So Israel dumped Baal and Ashtaroth and got on board with the LORD. {7:5} Samuel was like, "Everybody meet up at Mizpeh, and I'll pray for you." {7:6} They gathered there, poured out water before the LORD, fasted, and confessed their sins. Samuel held it down, judging Israel at Mizpeh. {7:7} When the Philistines heard Israel was mobbing up at Mizpeh, their bigwigs rolled in ready to fight. {7:8} Israel was shook and asked Samuel to keep praying for them. {7:9} Samuel offered a lamb as a burnt offering and cried out to the LORD for Israel, and God came through. {7:10} While Samuel was doing his thing, the Philistines came to battle, but the LORD brought thunder and messed them up, so Israel got the W. {7:11} Israel chased down the Philistines and wrecked them. {7:12} Samuel set up a stone called Eben-ezer, saying, "The LORD helped us this far." {7:13} The Philistines were tamed and stopped messing with Israel; God had their back as long as Samuel was around. {7:14} Israel got back all the cities the Philistines took, from Ekron to Gath, and there was peace with the Amorites. {7:15} Samuel kept judging Israel his whole life, going around Bethel, Gilgal, Mizpeh, and back to Ramah, where he set up an altar to the LORD.

{8:1} Samuel got old and appointed his sons as judges over Israel. {8:2} His firstborn was Joel, and his second was Abiah; they judged in Beer-sheba. {8:3} But they didn't follow Samuel's ways; they were all about the money, taking bribes, and perverting justice. {8:4} The elders of Israel weren't having it; they came to Samuel in Ramah. {8:5} They told Samuel, "You're old, and your sons are off track; give us a king like everyone else." {8:6} Samuel wasn't feeling it; he prayed to the LORD. {8:7} The LORD told Samuel, "Listen to the people; they're rejecting Me, not you." {8:8} The LORD reminded Samuel how Israel always strayed, serving other gods. {8:9} The LORD told Samuel to go along with it but to warn them about what having a king would mean. {8:10} Samuel told the people everything the LORD said about having a king. {8:11} He said, "Here's what your king will do: take your sons for his army, make them run before his chariots, and put them to work in his fields and war machines." {8:12} "He'll take your daughters as cooks and bakers, and your best land, vineyards, and olive groves for himself." {8:13} "He'll take a tenth of your crops and give it to his officials and servants." {8:14} "He'll take your fields, vineyards, and olive groves and give them to his buddies." {8:15-17} "He'll take a tenth of your flocks, and you'll become his servants." {8:18} "And when you cry out because of your king, the LORD won't answer." {8:19-20} But the people insisted on having a king, wanting to be like everyone else, with a leader to fight their battles. {8:21} Samuel relayed all this to the LORD. {8:22} The LORD told Samuel to grant their request. Samuel then sent everyone home to await their new king.

{9:1} So, there was this dude from Benjamin named Kish, his dad was Abiel, son of Zeror, son of Bechorath, son of Aphiah—a Benjamite, and he was a real powerhouse. {9:2} Kish's son, Saul, was a total catch—good-looking, top-tier among the Israelites, towering over everyone from the shoulders up. {9:3} One day, Kish's donkeys went MIA. Kish told Saul, "Take a servant and go find 'em." {9:4} They searched Mount Ephraim, Shalisha, Shalim, even Benjamin, but nada. {9:5} When they hit Zuph, Saul's like, "Let's bail before Dad freaks." {9:6} The servant's like, "Yo, there's a legit prophet in this town—everything he says goes down. Let's hit him up for directions." {9:7} Saul's worried they got no gift for the prophet, no bread left. He's like, "What do we offer?" {9:8} The servant's got a bit of silver to spare, so they're set to pay the prophet for guidance. {9:9} Back then, folks called prophets "seers." {9:10} Saul's down, they roll to the prophet's city. {9:11} As they arrive, they see girls fetching water and ask about the seer. {9:12} The girls point them to Samuel, who's heading for the high place for a sacrifice. {9:13} They hustle into town just in time to catch Samuel before the feast. {9:14} Samuel meets them, ready for the sacrifice. {9:15} Meanwhile, the Lord told Samuel a day prior about Saul's arrival. {9:16} God's like, "Tomorrow, I'll send you a dude from Benjamin. Anoint him to lead my peeps against the Philistines—they're crying out to me." {9:17} When Samuel spots Saul, God's like, "That's the guy I was talking about. He's gonna reign over my people." {9:18} Saul finds Samuel and asks where the seer lives. {9:19} Samuel's like, "That's me. Come eat with me, and tomorrow I'll spill your secrets." {9:20} Samuel's like, "Forget the donkeys. Israel's eyeing you and your fam." {9:21} Saul's all modest, saying he's from the smallest tribe, the tiniest fam. {9:22} Samuel treats Saul like VIP, seating him with the top guests. {9:23} Samuel tells the cook to serve Saul the special portion. {9:24} Saul chows down on the feast. {9:25} Afterward, Samuel chats with Saul on the rooftop. {9:26} Next morning, Samuel's ready to send Saul off. {9:27} As they head out, Samuel pulls Saul aside for a private word from God.

{10:1} So Samuel grabs some oil, pours it on Saul's head, gives him a kiss, and says, "The Lord's chosen you to lead His crew." {10:2} After you bounce today, check by Rachel's grave near Benjamin in Zelzah. Two dudes will tell you they found the donkeys and your dad's worried sick about you. {10:3} Keep moving to the plain of Tabor—three guys heading to Bethel will greet you with food and wine. {10:4} They'll hook you up with bread. {10:5} Then head to the hill of God, where the Philistine garrison is. You'll run into prophets jamming with instruments; the Spirit of the Lord will hit you, and you'll start prophesying. {10:6} You'll be a changed person, filled with the Spirit. {10:7} When these signs happen, do what needs to be done—God's got your back. {10:8} Then head to Gilgal; I'll join you soon for sacrifices. Chill there for seven days till I arrive and tell you what's up. {10:9} As Saul turns away, God changes his heart, and all the signs Samuel mentioned happen. {10:10} When Saul reaches the hill, he meets prophets, and the Spirit hits him, and he joins in prophesying. {10:11} People who knew Saul are shocked he's prophesying, and they're like, "Is Saul one of the prophets?" {10:12} They start joking, "Is Saul joining the prophets now?" {10:13} After prophesying, Saul heads to the high place. {10:14} Saul's uncle asks where they went; Saul says they were looking for donkeys but ended up at Samuel's. {10:15} His uncle wants the scoop from Samuel. {10:16} Saul tells him they found the donkeys but keeps quiet about the kingdom stuff Samuel talked about. {10:17} Samuel calls the people to Mizpeh. {10:18} He reminds Israel how God saved them from Egypt and all oppressors. {10:19} But now they want a king, rejecting God who saved them from trouble. {10:20} Samuel lines up the tribes; Benjamin's picked. {10:21} Then within Benjamin, Saul's family gets chosen, but Saul's missing. {10:22} They ask God if Saul's coming, and God's like, "Yeah, he's hiding among the baggage." {10:23} They fetch Saul, and he stands tall among the people. {10:24} Samuel's like, "See the dude God chose—there's no one like him." {10:25} Everyone cheers for the king. {10:26} Saul heads home to Gibeah with a crew of supporters. {10:27} But some haters doubt Saul's ability to save them and offer no gifts.

{11:1} Meanwhile, Nahash the Ammonite threatens Jabesh-gilead. {11:2} He demands their right eyes for peace, shaming Israel. {11:3} The elders of Jabesh ask for a week to find help. {11:4} Messengers tell Saul, and the people cry. {11:5} Saul's like, "Why's everyone crying?" {11:6} The Spirit hits Saul, and he's furious. {11:7} Saul sends a brutal message to rally Israel against Nahash. {11:8} At Bezek, Israel gathers—300,000 from Israel, 30,000 from Judah. {11:9} They promise Jabesh help by tomorrow. {11:10} Jabesh agrees to surrender to Saul's terms. {11:11} Saul divides his troops, ambushes the Ammonites, scattering them. {11:12} People demand punishment for those who doubted Saul. {11:13} Saul shows mercy, knowing God brought salvation that day. {11:14} Samuel calls for a kingdom renewal in Gilgal. {11:15} Israel rejoices as Saul is crowned king before the Lord.

{12:1} So Samuel tells all Israel, "Yo, I heard you loud and clear. Made a king happen for y'all." {12:2} "Check it, your king's out there. I'm old and gray now, been with you since I was a kid." {12:3} "Seriously, if I've done wrong, call me out. Whose stuff did I take? Who did I cheat? Who'd I hurt? Tell me, and I'll fix it." {12:4} They're like, "Nah, you're good. Never messed with us." {12:5} Samuel's like, "God and I are witnesses—you got nothing on me." {12:6} Samuel reminds them how God worked through Moses and Aaron, bringing their ancestors out of Egypt. {12:7} "Remember all the good things God's done for you." {12:8} "God saved your ancestors from Egypt and settled them here." {12:9} "But when they forgot God, trouble came—Philistines, Moabites, Canaanites—everyone was against them." {12:10} "They cried to God, admitted their sins, and God sent deliverers like Gideon, Jephthah, and me." {12:11} "Then Nahash threatened, and you demanded a king instead of sticking with God as your leader." {12:12} "So here's your king, chosen by you, but God's still the true king." {12:13} "If you and the king fear God, follow His commands, you'll be good. But if you rebel, watch out." {12:14} "Stay true to God, and He'll keep blessing you." {12:15} "But if you mess up, you and your king will suffer." {12:16} Samuel tells them to witness God's power. {12:17} He's like, "It's harvest time; I'll ask God for thunder and rain to show you how wrong it was to demand a king." {12:18} Samuel prays, and God sends thunder and rain, scaring everyone. {12:19} People beg Samuel not to let them die for asking for a king on top of their sins. {12:20} Samuel's like, "Chill. Yeah, you messed up, but don't stop following God with all your heart." {12:21} "Don't chase useless things that can't help or save you—they're pointless." {12:22} "God won't abandon you; He chose you as His people." {12:23} "I'll keep praying for you and teaching you the right way." {12:24} "Fear God, serve Him truly, and remember all He's done for you." {12:25} "But if you keep doing wrong, you and your king will face consequences."

{13:1} Saul's been king for a year, then two, when he gathers an army. {13:2} He picks 3,000 soldiers—2,000 with him, 1,000 with Jonathan. {13:3} Jonathan strikes a Philistine garrison, and Saul spreads the news. {13:4} Israel's ready to fight. {13:5} Philistines assemble a huge army against Israel. {13:6} Israel's scared and hiding. {13:7} Some cross the Jordan to Gad and Gilead, but Saul's in Gilgal with trembling followers. {13:8} He waits seven days for Samuel but panics when Samuel's late. {13:9} Saul offers sacrifices without waiting for Samuel. {13:10} As soon as he finishes, Samuel shows up, and Saul greets him. {13:11} Samuel's like, "What did you do?" Saul's like, "People were freaking out, and you weren't here, so I did the sacrifice myself." {13:12} Samuel's disappointed; Saul didn't obey God's command. {13:13} Samuel tells Saul his kingdom won't last—God wants someone after His own heart to lead. {13:14-15} Samuel leaves for Gibeah, and Saul's left with 600 men. {13:16} Philistines camp in Michmash, and Saul's troops stay in Gibeah. {13:17} Philistine raiders split into three groups.

{14:1} So one day, Jonathan, Saul's son, tells his armor-bearer, "Yo, let's hit up the Philistine garrison across the way, but don't tell my dad." {14:2} Saul's chilling under a pomegranate tree while 600 dudes are with him. {14:3} Ahiah, the priest, is there too, wearing his ephod, but the people don't know Jonathan's gone. {14:4} The path to the Philistines has sharp rocks named Bozez and Seneh on either side. {14:5} One faces north toward Michmash, the other south toward Gibeah. {14:6} Jonathan's like, "Let's take on these uncircumcised guys; maybe the Lord will help us, no matter how many of us there are." {14:7} His armor-bearer's all in, saying, "Go for it; I've got your back." {14:8} So they reveal themselves to the garrison. {14:9} If they say, "Wait for us," they'll chill. {14:10} But if they say, "Come up," they'll attack 'cause God's given them to Jonathan. {14:11} They show themselves, and the Philistines are like, "Look, the Hebrews are coming out of hiding!" {14:12} Jonathan and his armor-bearer go up, and they start whooping Philistines 'cause God's with them. {14:13} Jonathan climbs up and takes out Philistines, followed by his armor-bearer. {14:14} In a half-acre of land, they kill about twenty dudes. {14:15} Everyone's freaking out—the garrison, raiders, even the ground shakes. {14:16} Saul's watchmen see the Philistines scattering in fear. {14:17} Saul's like, "Who's missing?" Turns out, Jonathan and his armor-bearer are gone. {14:18} Saul's like, "Bring the ark of God." {14:19} While Saul's talking to the priest, the Philistine camp gets loud. {14:20} Saul and his crew rush to battle, and chaos breaks out—everyone fighting each other. {14:21} Hebrews who sided with the Philistines now join Saul and Jonathan's crew. {14:22} Even Israelites hiding in Ephraim join the battle after hearing the Philistines flee. {14:23} God saves Israel that day, and they chase the Philistines to Beth-aven. {14:24} Israel's soldiers are hungry 'cause Saul cursed anyone who ate until evening. {14:25} They find honey on the ground but don't eat it 'cause of the oath. {14:26} Jonathan tastes honey, and his eyes light up. {14:27} Someone tells him about Saul's oath, but Jonathan's like, "I didn't hear it," and eats the honey. {14:28} People are faint from hunger. {14:29} Jonathan's like, "My dad's making things worse; look how the honey helped me." {14:30} He thinks they could've done more damage if they ate from the spoils. {14:31} They keep smiting Philistines from Michmash to Aijalon. {14:32} Everyone goes for the spoil—sheep, oxen, and they eat with the blood. {14:33} Saul finds out and says they sinned by eating with blood. {14:34} He has them sacrifice properly. {14:35} Saul builds an altar to the Lord, his first one. {14:36} Saul plans to attack the Philistines all night. {14:37} He asks God for advice, but God doesn't answer. {14:38} Saul gathers the chiefs to figure out the sin. {14:39} Saul swears even if Jonathan's guilty, he'll die. {14:40} He divides Israel into two sides—himself and Jonathan against the rest. {14:41} They cast lots, and Saul and Jonathan are chosen. {14:42} Saul wants to cast lots between him and Jonathan. {14:43} Jonathan admits to eating honey and expects to die. {14:44} Saul agrees Jonathan deserves death. {14:45} People protest; Jonathan's saved 'cause he helped Israel. {14:46} Saul stops pursuing the Philistines. {14:47} He reigns over Israel, fighting enemies everywhere. {14:48} He smites the Amalekites, freeing Israel from plunderers. {14:49} Saul's sons are Jonathan, Ishui, and Melchi-shua, with daughters Merab and Michal. {14:50} Saul's wife is Ahinoam, and Abner is his captain.

{15:1} So Samuel tells Saul, "God picked you to be king over Israel, so listen up to what He's saying." {15:2} God remembers what Amalek did to Israel after they left Egypt. {15:3} He tells Saul to wreck Amalek—wipe out everything, no mercy, men, women, babies, animals, all of it. {15:4} Saul gathers 200,000 foot soldiers and 10,000 Judahites. {15:5} He rolls up to an Amalekite city and waits in the valley. {15:6} Saul tells the Kenites, "Bounce, don't get caught up with the Amalekites 'cause you were cool to Israel." The Kenites dip. {15:7} Saul smashes Amalek from Havilah to Shur by Egypt. {15:8} He takes Amalek's king Agag alive but kills everyone else. {15:9} Saul and his crew spare Agag and the best sheep and stuff, going against God's orders. {15:10} Then God's like, "Samuel, Saul messed up." {15:11} Samuel's bummed and prays all night. {15:12} Early next morning, Samuel finds out Saul's at Carmel, then Gilgal. {15:13} Samuel confronts Saul, who's like, "I did everything God said." {15:14} Samuel's like, "Then why do I hear sheep and cows?" {15:15} Saul blames the people for keeping the good stuff to sacrifice to God, saying they destroyed the rest. {15:16} Samuel's like, "Hold up, let me tell you what God said." {15:17} He reminds Saul how God raised him up, then commanded him to destroy the Amalekites. {15:18} Samuel asks why Saul disobeyed, jumping on the spoils. {15:19} Saul blames the people again, saying they kept stuff to sacrifice in Gilgal. {15:20} Saul insists he followed God's orders, bringing Agag and only keeping stuff for sacrifices. {15:21} Samuel's like, "Does God prefer sacrifices over obedience?" {15:22} He says obeying is better than offering sacrifices. {15:23} Rebellion's like witchcraft to God; stubbornness is idolatry. Saul's rejection of God's word means he's no longer king. {15:24} Saul admits he messed up, fearing the people and disobeying God. {15:25} He asks Samuel to forgive him and worship with him. {15:26} Samuel's like, "Nah, God rejected you." {15:27} Samuel leaves, and Saul grabs his robe, tearing it. {15:28} Samuel declares God took the kingdom from Saul, giving it to someone better. {15:29} God's not human; He won't change His mind. {15:30} Saul's like, "Honor me in front of everyone; let's worship

God." {15:31} Samuel agrees, and they worship. {15:32} Samuel tells them to bring Agag. {15:33} Samuel kills Agag in Gilgal, saying his violence will be repaid. {15:34} Samuel heads home, and Saul returns to Gibeah. {15:35} Samuel never sees Saul again; he mourns, and God regrets making Saul king.

{16:1} God tells Samuel, "Stop mourning for Saul; I've ditched him as king over Israel. Grab your oil and head to Jesse the Bethlehemite's place. I've picked one of his sons to be king." {16:2} Samuel's like, "How can I do that? Saul will kill me if he finds out." God's like, "Take a cow with you and say you're sacrificing to the LORD." {16:3} Samuel calls Jesse for the sacrifice and says, "I'll show you who to anoint." {16:4} Samuel goes to Bethlehem, and the town elders freak out, asking if he's coming in peace. {16:5} Samuel's like, "All good, here for a sacrifice; everyone get ready." He sanctifies Jesse and his sons for the sacrifice. {16:6} When they arrive, Samuel sees Eliab and thinks, "He's gotta be the one God picked." {16:7} But God's like, "Nah, I don't pick based on looks; I see the heart." {16:8} Jesse brings Abinadab, but God hasn't chosen him either. {16:9} Then Shammah comes, but nope, not him either. {16:10} Samuel's like, "None of these are the one." {16:11} Samuel asks Jesse if there are more sons, and Jesse's like, "Just the youngest, David, who's out with the sheep." Samuel's like, "Go get him; we're not sitting down until he's here." {16:12} David comes in—ruddy, good-looking—and God's like, "Anoint him; he's the one." {16:13} Samuel anoints David, and the Spirit of the LORD is with him from then on. Samuel heads back to Ramah. {16:14} The LORD's Spirit leaves Saul, and he's troubled by an evil spirit. {16:15} Saul's servants suggest finding a skilled harp player to calm him when the evil spirit hits. {16:16} Saul agrees, so they find David, Jesse's son, skilled at playing the harp and a brave dude. {16:17} Saul's like, "Bring him to me." {16:18} One servant knows David and recommends him, saying God's with him. {16:19} Saul sends for David. {16:20} Jesse sends David with gifts to Saul. {16:21} David impresses Saul, becomes his armor-bearer, and Saul asks Jesse to let David stay. {16:22} When the evil spirit hits Saul, David plays the harp to soothe him, and the spirit leaves.

{17:1} So the Philistines gathered their crew for battle, chilling at Shochoh near Judah, setting up camp between Shochoh and Azekah in Ephes-dammim. {17:2} Saul and the Israelite squad also showed up, posted up by the valley of Elah, ready to face off with the Philistines. {17:3} The Philistines were up on one mountain, Israel on another, with a valley in between. {17:4} Then out comes the Philistine MVP, Goliath from Gath, standing like six cubits and a span tall. {17:5} Dude's decked out: brass helmet, iron coat of mail weighing 5,000 shekels, brass leg armor, and a heavy spear. {17:6} He's got a shield-bearer rolling with him too. {17:7} Goliath starts trash-talking Israel, challenging them to send out a warrior to face him. {17:8} He's like, "Why y'all even here? I'm Philistine; y'all just work for Saul. Send me one of your guys to fight!" {17:9} Goliath proposes a deal: if Israel's dude wins, Philistines will serve Israel; if Goliath wins, Israel will serve Philistines. {17:10} Goliath keeps taunting, daring Israel to send someone to face him. {17:11} Saul and the Israelites hear this and are terrified. {17:12} Now David, Jesse's youngest son from Bethlehem, was back home tending sheep while his three older bros, Eliab, Abinadab, and Shammah, fought with Saul. {17:13} Jesse sends David with food for his bros and their captain. {17:14} While his bros are with Saul, David's back home with the sheep. {17:15} Goliath shows up every day for 40 days, flexing on Israel. {17:17} Jesse sends David with food to check on his bros. {17:18} David heads to the battlefield and talks to his bros. {17:19} Meanwhile, Israel and Philistines are facing off in the valley of Elah. {17:20} Early one morning, David leaves the sheep with a keeper, heads to the battle line, and asks about the fight. {17:21} Israel and Philistines are geared up for battle. {17:22} David leaves his stuff with a keeper and goes to greet his bros. {17:23} Goliath steps up, talking the same trash, and David hears it. {17:24} Israel sees Goliath and panics. {17:25} They're all talking about how the king will hook up the guy who takes down Goliath. {17:26} David's like, "What's the reward for beating this dude? He's dissing God's army!" {17:27} People tell David about the reward for defeating Goliath. {17:28} Eliab, David's bro, gets ticked off at David for being there, assuming he's just nosy. {17:29} David's like, "What did I do wrong? Isn't there a reason I'm here?" {17:30} David asks others the same question, getting the same answer. {17:31} Saul hears about David's questions and sends for him. {17:32} David tells Saul he's ready to fight Goliath. {17:33} Saul doubts David, saying he's too young to take on Goliath. {17:34} David explains how he fought off lions and bears while shepherding. {17:35} David insists he can handle Goliath, just like the wild animals. {17:36} David trusts God will help him defeat Goliath. {17:37} Saul agrees, sending David off with a blessing. {17:38} Saul tries to suit up David with armor, but it's too much for him. {17:39} David sticks with what he knows—his staff, sling, and stones. {17:40} He grabs five smooth stones and heads out to face Goliath. {17:41} Goliath approaches, with his shield-bearer in tow. {17:42} Goliath looks down on David, seeing him as just a kid. {17:43} Goliath taunts David, calling him names. {17:44} Goliath threatens to feed David's flesh to the birds and beasts. {17:45} David tells Goliath he's coming in the name of God, ready to take him down. {17:46} David predicts victory, knowing God's got his back. {17:47} David declares the battle belongs to God. {17:48} David charges at Goliath. {17:49} He slings a stone, hitting Goliath in the forehead, knocking him out. {17:50} David finishes Goliath off with his own sword. {17:51} The Philistines flee when they see Goliath is down. {17:52} Israel pursues, chasing the Philistines back to their territory. {17:53} Israel celebrates their victory. {17:54} David takes Goliath's head to Jerusalem and keeps his armor. {17:55} Saul notices David's bravery and asks about his family. {17:56} Abner brings David to Saul, holding Goliath's head. {17:58} Saul learns that David is Jesse's son from Bethlehem.

{18:1} After David finished talking with Saul, Jonathan felt a deep connection with him and loved him like a brother. {18:2} Saul decided to keep David around and wouldn't let him go back home. {18:3} Jonathan and David made a pact because Jonathan cherished him so much. {18:4} Jonathan even gave David his royal robe, clothes, sword, bow, and belt. {18:5} David was on a winning streak, impressing Saul and the people, and Saul put him in charge of the army. {18:6} When David returned after defeating Goliath, the women celebrated him with singing and dancing. {18:7} They sang, "Saul has slain thousands, but David tens of thousands." {18:8}

Saul got super jealous and upset about this, thinking David might try to take over the kingdom. {18:9} Saul started keeping a close eye on David from then on. {18:10} The next day, Saul was overcome by an evil spirit, and David played music to calm him down like before, but this time Saul had a spear in hand. {18:11} Saul tried to pin David to the wall with the spear, but David dodged it twice. {18:12} Saul feared David because God was with him and had left Saul. {18:13} So Saul made David a captain over a thousand soldiers, and David gained favor with the people. {18:14} David continued to act wisely, and God was with him. {18:15} Saul grew even more afraid of David as he saw how wise David was. {18:16} Everyone in Israel and Judah loved David because he led them well. {18:17} Saul offered David his older daughter Merab in marriage, hoping David would fight the Philistines. {18:18} But David was humble, questioning why he deserved to marry into the royal family. {18:19} However, Merab was given to someone else. {18:20} Saul's other daughter Michal loved David, which pleased Saul. {18:21} Saul decided to use Michal as a trap for David by offering her to him in marriage. {18:22} Saul's servants persuaded David to accept Michal as his wife. {18:23} David questioned if it was a big deal to marry into the royal family since he was just a poor man. {18:24} Saul's servants reported David's response to Saul. {18:25} Saul told his servants to ask David for 100 Philistine foreskins as a dowry, hoping David would be killed in battle. {18:26} David agreed to this challenge and went out, killed 200 Philistines, and brought back their foreskins to Saul. {18:27} Saul gave Michal to David as his wife. {18:28} Saul realized that God was with David, and Michal loved him. {18:29} Saul became even more afraid of David and kept seeing him as an enemy. {18:30} David continued to outsmart everyone, gaining more respect and fame than anyone else around Saul.

{19:1} So Saul tells Jonathan and all his crew to take out David. {19:2} But Jonathan, being a real one, warns David and says, "Yo, my dad's out to get you. Lay low till morning, hide out, and I'll scope out the situation." {19:3} Jonathan talks David up to Saul, reminding him how David's been loyal and saved Israel from Goliath. {19:4} He's like, "Why you wanna ice David for no reason?" {19:5-6} Saul actually listens and swears David won't be killed. {19:7} Jonathan brings David back to Saul's crib like it's all good. {19:8} But war breaks out again, and David wrecks the Philistines, making them bounce. {19:9} Saul's chilling at home with a javelin, and David plays music to calm him, but Saul tries to spear him against the wall. {19:10} David dips out, and Saul keeps plotting to off him, even using his own daughter Michal to warn him. {19:11-12} Michal helps David escape through a window, then pulls a switcheroo with a dummy in the bed. {19:13-14} When Saul's goons show up, she's like, "Nah, he's sick." {19:15-17} Saul's not buying it, and Michal throws some shade back at him. {19:18-19} David hauls it to Samuel in Ramah and spills all about Saul's vendetta. {19:20-21} Saul sends more goons after David, but they get caught up prophesying with Samuel. {19:22} Saul rolls up to Ramah asking about Samuel and David, and people are like, "They're at Naioth." {19:23} So Saul shows up there too, gets hit with the spirit, and starts prophesying naked. The rumor mill starts buzzing about Saul joining the prophets.

{20:1} So David jets from Naioth in Ramah and spills to Jonathan, like, "Bro, what's my deal? Why's your dad after me?" {20:2} Jonathan's like, "No way, you're good. My dad tells me everything, big or small." {20:3} David's like, "Your dad knows I'm chill with you, but he's keeping it hush for some reason. Trust me, I'm this close to getting whacked." {20:4} Jonathan's ride-or-die, offering to help with whatever David needs. {20:5} David's got a plan for the new moon feast and asks to lay low for three days. {20:6} He tells Jonathan to cover for him, saying he's off to Bethlehem for a family thing. {20:7} They'll gauge Saul's reaction to know if he's really out to get David. {20:8} David's grateful to Jonathan and says, "If I messed up, just take me out yourself." {20:9} Jonathan's like, "No way, I'd warn you if my dad had it out for you." {20:10} David's curious how Jonathan will let him know what's up with Saul. {20:11} Jonathan's like, "Let's go to the field and hash this out." {20:12} They make a pact, calling on the Lord to be their witness. {20:14} Jonathan asks David to always show kindness to his family, even after David's enemies are gone. {20:16} They seal the deal, swearing that David's enemies will answer to God. {20:17} Jonathan's all in, swearing his loyalty to David. {20:18} He warns David he'll be missed at the feast. {20:19} After three days, David's supposed to check in at the stone Ezel. {20:20} Jonathan's got a signal with arrows to let David know if it's safe. {20:22} Depending on the arrows, David will know whether to stay or bounce. {20:23} They pray the Lord watches over their pact forever. {20:24} David goes undercover in the field while the feast kicks off. {20:25} Saul notices David's seat empty by the wall and gets suspicious. {20:27} Saul's like, "Why's Jesse's son not here?" {20:28} Jonathan covers, saying David asked to go to Bethlehem for a family thing. {20:30} Saul loses it, accusing Jonathan of siding with David against him. {20:31} He demands they bring David to him to be killed. {20:32} Jonathan's shocked and asks why David deserves death. {20:33} Saul tries to spear Jonathan, showing his true intentions. {20:34} Jonathan's outraged and skips the feast out of grief for David. {20:35} The next morning, Jonathan and David meet up in the field. {20:36} Jonathan sets up a signal with arrows and sends his lad to check it. {20:37} The arrow lands beyond the lad, signaling danger to David. {20:38} Jonathan signals the lad to hurry back, confirming the plan. {20:39} Only Jonathan and David know what's up. {20:40} Jonathan sends the lad back to town with the gear. {20:41} David shows up, they embrace, and they cry it out. {20:42} Jonathan sends David off with peace, bound by their oath to the Lord. They part ways, and Jonathan heads back to town.

{21:1} So David rolls up to Nob to see Ahimelech the priest, who's totally shook when he sees David alone and asks why he's flying solo. {21:2} David pulls a cover story, saying the king sent him on a secret mission and even kept his crew in the dark about it. {21:3} Then David asks for some bread, but all the priest has is consecrated bread, which is normally off-limits unless the guys have been keeping it clean. {21:4-6} The priest checks, and since David's crew has been pure, he hands over the holy bread. {21:7} But guess what? Saul's top herdsman, Doeg the Edomite, was chilling there, eavesdropping. {21:8} David's like, "Got any weapons here?" He's in a rush and didn't bring his gear. {21:9} The priest offers up Goliath's sword, neatly wrapped behind the ephod. David's all in for that, saying it's one-of-a-kind. {21:10} Then David takes off, scared of Saul, and heads to Achish, the king of Gath. {21:11} Achish's crew recognizes

David as the hero from the songs and dances. {21:12-13} David's freaking out and pretends to be insane, drooling and scratching at doors. {21:14} Achish is like, "Why bring this crazy dude to me?" {21:15} He kicks David out, not wanting madmen in his house.

{22:1} David then bounces to the cave of Adullam, where his fam and peeps in trouble join him, and he becomes their leader, gathering about four hundred dudes. {22:3} David heads to Mizpeh of Moab and asks the king to keep his parents safe while he figures out what God has in store. {22:4} The king takes them in while David's on the move. {22:5} The prophet Gad tells David to leave the hold and head to Judah. {22:6-8} When Saul hears about David, he's in Gibeah, looking serious with his spear and servants around him. {22:9} Doeg spills the beans to Saul about David's visit to Nob and the priest giving him bread and Goliath's sword. {22:10-15} Saul calls in Ahimelech and his crew, accusing them of conspiring against him with David. {22:16} Saul condemns Ahimelech and his house to death. {22:17} Saul orders his footmen to kill the priests, but they refuse. {22:18-21} Then Saul commands Doeg to do the dirty work, and he wipes out eighty-five priests, along with the city of Nob. Abiathar escapes and joins David, informing him of the massacre. {22:22} David feels responsible, knowing Doeg would snitch to Saul. {22:23} He assures Abiathar that he's safe with him, as they're both targets of Saul's rage.

{23:1} So David hears that the Philistines are messing with Keilah, raiding their stuff. {23:2} David checks in with God, like, "Should I go bust up these Philistines?" God's like, "Yeah, go for it, save Keilah." {23:3} But David's crew is sketched out, thinking, "We're scared here in Judah; how much worse in Keilah against the Philistine armies?" {23:4} David checks with God again, and God's like, "Go down to Keilah; I'll hand the Philistines over to you." {23:5} So David and his squad roll up, wreck the Philistines, snatch their cattle, and save Keilah. {23:6} Meanwhile, Abiathar shows up with an ephod to join David in Keilah. {23:7} Saul hears David's in Keilah and thinks, "God's given him to me; he's trapped in a town with gates and bars." {23:8} Saul calls the troops to besiege David and his crew at Keilah. {23:9} David catches on that Saul's up to no good and asks Abiathar to bring the ephod. {23:10} David's like, "God, I heard Saul's coming to wreck Keilah 'cause of me." {23:11} He asks God if the men of Keilah will give him up to Saul, and God says they will. {23:12} So David and his crew, about six hundred strong, dip out of Keilah. {23:13} Saul finds out David's gone and decides not to pursue. {23:14} David hangs in the wilderness, bunkered down, while Saul hunts him down daily. {23:15} David spots Saul on the prowl in the wilderness of Ziph. {23:16} Jonathan, Saul's son, visits David in the woods and boosts his spirits. {23:17} Jonathan's like, "Don't worry; my dad won't find you. You'll be king, and I'll have your back." {23:18} They make a pact before God, and David chills in the woods while Jonathan heads home. {23:19} But then the Ziphites rat out David to Saul, saying he's hiding in their area. {23:20} They urge Saul to come and nab David. {23:21} Saul's all grateful and sends them off to scope out David's hideout. {23:22} Saul wants the scoop on David's whereabouts, convinced he's being sly. {23:23} Saul wants them to confirm and pinpoint David's hiding spots, promising to search him out in Judah. {23:24} They head to Ziph, but David's in Maon. {23:25} Saul and his men pursue David, but David slips away. {23:26} They're like playing cat and mouse in the mountains; David's on one side, Saul's on the other, and David's scrambling to escape Saul's grasp. {23:27} Then a messenger interrupts Saul, saying, "The Philistines are back; you gotta go." {23:28} So Saul ditches the chase for David and turns toward the Philistines, calling the place Sela-hammahlekoth. {23:29} David heads to strongholds in En-gedi.

{24:1} Saul hears David's in En-gedi and mobilizes three thousand troops to hunt him down in the rocky goat lands. {24:2} Saul finds a cave to take a bathroom break, not knowing David and his crew are hiding there. {24:3} David's men are like, "This is it! God said he'd deliver Saul into your hands." So David sneaks up and cuts off a piece of Saul's robe. {24:5} David feels bad afterward. {24:6} He's like, "I can't harm God's anointed." {24:7} David stops his crew from attacking Saul. {24:8} Later, David calls out to Saul, showing him he could've killed him but chose not to.

{25:1} So Samuel kicks it, and all the Israelites gather to mourn and bury him in Ramah. David bounces to the wilderness of Paran. {25:2} In Maon, there's this big shot named Nabal, with tons of livestock, shearing sheep in Carmel. {25:3} Nabal's wife is Abigail—smart and fine—but Nabal himself is a jerk, from Caleb's family. {25:4} David hears Nabal's shearing, so he sends dudes to Carmel. {25:5} He tells them to greet Nabal and ask for some supplies. {25:6} They're like, "Peace to you, your fam, and all you got." {25:7} David's crew had protected Nabal's shepherds in Carmel, and nothing went missing. {25:8} They ask for a favor 'cause it's a good day, requesting provisions for David's crew. {25:9} The young men deliver the message and chill. {25:10} Nabal's like, "Who's David? Just another runaway servant these days." {25:11} He refuses to share his food with David's crew. {25:12} David's men report back, and David's like, "Strap up, boys." {25:13} They get ready, and about four hundred men follow David, while two hundred stay behind. {25:14} One of the young men tells Abigail what went down with David's request. {25:15} He praises David's crew for their protection. {25:16} Abigail realizes trouble's brewing and decides to act. {25:17} She loads up provisions and heads out without telling Nabal. {25:18} Abigail hurries to intercept David. {25:19} Meanwhile, David and his crew approach. {25:20} Abigail meets David on the way. {25:21} David's like, "I've been good to Nabal, and he's ungrateful." {25:22} He vows to settle the score unless Abigail intervened. {25:23} Abigail pleads with David, acknowledging Nabal's folly. {25:24} She humbles herself before David, asking for mercy. {25:25} Abigail explains Nabal's ignorance and offers gifts to David's men. {25:26} She thanks God for preventing bloodshed and evil. {25:27} Abigail presents her blessing to David and his men. {25:28} She asks for forgiveness on Nabal's behalf. {25:29} Abigail trusts that God will protect David from his enemies. {25:30} She predicts David's rise and rulership over Israel. {25:31} Abigail requests that David remember her kindness. {25:32} David praises God for sending Abigail. {25:33} He thanks her for preventing bloodshed. {25:34} David vows to spare Nabal's household because of Abigail's intervention. {25:35} He accepts her gifts and bids her peace. {25:36} Abigail returns to find Nabal partying hard. {25:37} When she tells him what happened, Nabal's heart fails him. {25:38} About ten days later, God strikes Nabal dead. {25:39} David praises God for dealing with Nabal and takes Abigail as his wife. {25:40} David's men come to Abigail, proposing marriage on David's behalf. {25:41} Abigail humbly accepts. {25:42} She joins David, becoming his wife. {25:43} David also marries Ahinoam of Jezreel. {25:44} Meanwhile, Saul marries off Michal to someone else.

{26:1} So the Ziphites slide up to Saul in Gibeah, like, "Isn't David hiding in the hill of Hachilah near Jeshimon?" {26:2} Saul's like, "Bet," and rolls down to the wilderness of Ziph with three thousand chosen Israelites to hunt David. {26:3} Saul sets up camp in Hachilah, but David's chilling in the wilderness, peeping Saul's moves. {26:4} David sends out spies who confirm Saul's arrival for real. {26:5} David checks out Saul's spot, sees him knocked out with Abner and his crew nearby. {26:6} David's like, "Who's down to roll with me and sneak up on Saul?" Abishai's like, "I'm in." {26:7} So David and Abishai creep up on Saul while he's sleeping with his spear stuck in the ground. {26:8} Abishai's ready to end Saul right there, but David's like, "Nah, can't touch the Lord's anointed." {26:9} David's like, "The Lord will handle Saul in His time." {26:10} He takes Saul's spear and water jug, and they bounce without waking anyone up 'cause the Lord put them all to sleep. {26:13} David stands far off and shouts to Abner, calling him out for failing to protect the king. {26:14} David's like, "You're supposed to be a top warrior—why'd you let this happen?" {26:15} He shows Abner Saul's stuff and calls them out for their failure. {26:17} Saul recognizes David's voice and chats with him. {26:18} David's like, "Why chase me? What did I do?" {26:19} He's like, "If God's mad at me, cool, but if it's just people, they're cursed for driving me away from God's land." {26:20} David's like, "I'm not a threat, just a flea. You're chasing me like hunting a partridge in the mountains." {26:21} Saul's like, "My bad, David. Come back—I won't mess with you again." {26:22} David points out Saul's spear and asks someone to grab it. {26:23} David's like, "God will judge us both." {26:24} Saul's like, "You're blessed, David. You'll do great things." {26:25} David peaces out, and Saul heads back home.

{27:1} So David's like, "I'm gonna get wrecked by Saul eventually. It's best for me to dip to Philistine turf quick, and Saul will give up on chasing me in Israel. That's how I'll slip out of his grip." {27:2} David bounces with his crew of six hundred to Achish, the king of Gath. {27:3} They set up shop with Achish in Gath, David and his squad, with their families, including his wives Ahinoam and Abigail. {27:4} Word gets to Saul that David's chilling in Gath, and he stops hunting for him. {27:5} David asks Achish for a spot in a smaller town, not in the royal city. {27:6} Achish hooks him up with Ziklag, which still belongs to Judah's kings today. {27:7} David kicks it in Philistine territory for a year and four months. {27:8} David and his crew raid the Geshurites, Gezrites, and Amalekites, old residents of the land from Shur to Egypt. {27:9} They wipe out everyone and take the livestock, gear, and bring it all back to Achish. {27:10} Achish asks where they've been raiding, and David lies about hitting up areas of Judah and Jerahmeelites. {27:11} David makes sure no survivors can tell Gath what he's been up to. {27:12} Achish thinks David's so hated in Israel that he'll serve him forever.

{28:1} The Philistines gear up for war against Israel, and Achish tells David he's joining the fight. {28:2} David's like, "You'll see what I can do." {28:3} Meanwhile, Samuel's dead, and Saul's banned all sorcery and wizards from Israel. {28:4} The Philistines camp in Shunem, and Saul gathers Israel at Gilboa, scared out of his mind. {28:6} Saul tries to ask the Lord for guidance, but gets nothing—no dreams, prophets, nothing. {28:7} Saul's like, "Find me a medium so I can talk to the dead." {28:8} He disguises himself and heads to a medium in Endor with two guys. {28:9} The medium's hesitant, knowing Saul's ban on sorcery, but Saul promises no harm. {28:11} Saul orders her not to spare anyone, so word doesn't get out about David's actions. {28:12} The medium thinks David's so hated that he's serving the Philistines forever. {28:15} Samuel's like, "Why'd you disturb my peace?" Saul's like, "I'm desperate, the Philistines are after me, and God's ghosting me." {28:16} Samuel's like, "God's done with you—He's given your kingdom to David." {28:18} Saul lost his kingdom for not following God's orders against Amalek. {28:19} Samuel predicts Saul and his sons will die in battle the next day. {28:20} Saul's terrified and weak, having not eaten all day. {28:21} The medium sees Saul's stressed and offers him food. {28:22} She begs him to eat before he leaves. {28:23} After refusing, Saul caves to his servants and the medium, and they eat. {28:24} The medium even prepares a feast, and they eat before heading out that night.

{29:1} So, all the Philistine armies are chilling at Aphek, while the Israelites set up camp by a fountain in Jezreel. {29:2} The Philistine big shots roll through in groups, but David and his crew hang back with Achish. {29:3} The Philistine leaders are like, "Why are these Hebrews here?" Achish vouches for David, saying he's been solid and hasn't caused any trouble. {29:4} The Philistine leaders get heated, telling Achish to send David back so he doesn't turn on them in battle. {29:5} They're like, "Isn't this David, the guy they sang about, saying Saul killed thousands but David got tens of thousands?" {29:6} Achish calls David over and tells him he's been cool, but the other Philistine leaders aren't feeling it. {29:7} So, Achish tells David to peace out quietly to avoid ticking off the other Philistine bosses. {29:8} David's like, "What's the deal? I've been loyal to you. Why can't I fight for my king against his enemies?" {29:9} Achish admits David's legit in his eyes, but he can't go against the other Philistine leaders. {29:10} Achish tells David to bounce early in the morning with his crew. {29:11} So, David and his squad head back to Philistine territory, while the Philistines head to Jezreel.

{30:1} When David and his crew get back to Ziklag after three days, they find out the Amalekites raided and burned the place, taking everyone captive. {30:2} They didn't kill anyone but took everyone and left. {30:3} David and his men reach the city and see it's burned, and their families are gone. {30:4} Everyone starts crying their hearts out until they can't cry anymore. {30:5} David's wives, Ahinoam and Abigail, are also taken captive. {30:6} David's crew blames him and talks about stoning him, but David finds strength in the Lord. {30:7} David asks the priest Abiathar to bring the ephod. {30:8} He asks God if he should pursue the Amalekites, and God tells him to go and recover everything. {30:9} So, David and six hundred men set out, leaving two hundred behind who were too tired to go further. {30:10} David and four hundred men pursue the Amalekites, while the others stay at the brook Besor. {30:11-13} They find an Egyptian in the field, give him food and water, and learn he's a servant of the Amalekites who abandoned him when he got sick. {30:14} The Egyptian tells them about the Amalekite raid. {30:15} He agrees to guide them if David spares his life. {30:16} They catch up and find the Amalekites celebrating their plunder. {30:17} David attacks from twilight till evening the next day, leaving only four hundred men who escape on camels. {30:18} David recovers everything, including his wives. {30:19} They don't miss a single thing; David recovers it all. {30:20} David takes all the livestock and declares it his spoil. {30:21} When they return to the brook Besor, David's men don't want to share with the tired ones, but David insists everyone gets an equal share. {30:22} David establishes this as a rule for Israel from that day forward. {30:23} David sends part of the spoils to the elders of Judah and other towns as gifts.

{31:1} So, the Philistines started a fight with Israel, and the Israelite dudes bounced, getting wrecked on Mount Gilboa. {31:2} The Philistines went hard after Saul and his sons; they killed Jonathan, Abinadab, and Melchi-shua, Saul's boys. {31:3} Saul was getting wrecked in the battle, hit by archers and seriously wounded. {31:4} Saul told his armorbearer, "Draw your sword and finish me off before these uncircumcised guys come and humiliate me." But the armorbearer chickened out because he was scared. So, Saul took a sword and offed himself. {31:5} When the armorbearer saw Saul was dead, he offed himself too. {31:6} Saul, his sons, the armorbearer, and all his crew died that same day. {31:7} When the Israelite dudes on the other side of the valley and across the Jordan saw Israel was running, and Saul and his sons were dead, they bailed on their cities, and the Philistines moved in. {31:8} The next day, when the Philistines came to loot the bodies, they found Saul and his sons on Mount Gilboa. {31:9} They chopped off Saul's head, stripped his armor, and spread the news in Philistine territory and among their people. {31:10} They displayed his armor in the temple of Ashtaroth and hung his body on the wall of Beth-shan. {31:11} When the peeps in Jabesh-gilead heard what the Philistines did to Saul, {31:12} all the tough guys pulled an all-nighter, snatched Saul and his sons' bodies from the wall of Beth-shan, and brought them to Jabesh, burning them there. {31:13} They buried their bones under a tree in Jabesh and fasted for seven days.

2 Samuel

✦✦✦

{1:1} So, after Saul kicked it, David came back from wrecking the Amalekites and chilled in Ziklag for a couple of days. {1:2} Then on the third day, this dude shows up, looking all messed up with torn clothes and dirt on his head. When he got to David, he bowed down. {1:3} David asked him where he came from, and he said he escaped from the camp of Israel. {1:4} David wanted to know what went down, and the guy spilled that the Israelites bailed from the battle, and lots of them got killed, including Saul and Jonathan. {1:5} David was skeptical and asked how he knew Saul and Jonathan were dead. {1:6} The guy said he stumbled upon Saul on Mount Gilboa, where Saul asked him to finish him off because he was in pain and knew he was done for. {1:7} Saul saw the guy and called out to him. {1:8} The guy told Saul he was an Amalekite. {1:9} Saul asked him to kill him, so the guy did it and snagged Saul's crown and bracelet to bring to David. {1:10} When David heard this, he tore his clothes, and all his men did the same. They mourned and fasted until evening for Saul, Jonathan, and the fallen Israelites. {1:13} David asked the guy where he was from, and he said he was an Amalekite. {1:14} David questioned him about killing the LORD's anointed king. {1:15} Then David had one of his dudes take the guy out. {1:16} David told him his blood was on his own head for admitting to killing Saul. {1:17} David then lamented Saul and Jonathan's deaths. {1:18} He wanted the story of their courage taught to the children of Judah. {1:19} He mourned the loss of Israel's beauty and strength. {1:20} David didn't want this news spreading to Gath or Askelon to avoid Philistine celebrations. {1:21} He cursed the mountains of Gilboa for abandoning Saul, the anointed one. {1:22} Jonathan and Saul were powerful and united in life and death. {1:23} They were as fast as eagles and strong as lions. {1:24} David called on the daughters of Israel to weep for Saul's splendor. {1:25} He lamented the fallen heroes, especially Jonathan. {1:26} David expressed deep sorrow for losing Jonathan, whose love was extraordinary. {1:27} He mourned the loss of mighty warriors and their weapons.

{2:1} So, after that, David hit up the LORD and asked, "Should I roll into any of the cities in Judah?" And the LORD was like, "Yeah, go for it." David was like, "Cool, which one?" And the LORD was like, "Hebron." {2:2} So David headed there with his two wives, Ahinoam and Abigail. {2:3} He brought his crew and fam with him, and they set up shop in Hebron. {2:4} The men of Judah rolled up and anointed David as king over Judah. They also let him know it was the men of Jabesh-gilead who buried Saul. {2:5} David sent a shoutout to the men of Jabesh-gilead, thanking them for burying Saul and showing kindness. {2:6} He blessed them back and promised to return the favor for their kindness. {2:7} David encouraged them to stay strong and brave because Saul was gone, and the house of Judah was backing David as king. {2:8} Meanwhile, Abner, Saul's top general, took Saul's son Ish-bosheth and set him up as king over a bunch of regions in Israel. {2:9-10} Ish-bosheth was forty years old when he became king and reigned for two years. But Judah was all about David. {2:11} David reigned over Judah from Hebron for seven and a half years. {2:12-13} Abner and Ish-bosheth's crew went out to Gibeon, and Joab and David's crew met up with them. {2:14} Abner suggested a showdown between their young bucks. {2:15-17} They went at it, and the battle got intense. {2:18} Joab had two brothers with him, Abishai and Asahel, who was as quick as a deer. {2:19} Asahel chased after Abner, not slowing down for anything. {2:20-22} Abner warned Asahel to back off, but he refused. {2:23} So Abner took him out, and everyone paused at the spot where Asahel fell. {2:24-26} Joab and Abishai kept after Abner until sunset. {2:27} Abner urged Joab to chill out and stop the fighting. {2:28} Joab called it off, and the fighting ceased. {2:29} Abner and his crew hightailed it through the night and crossed Jordan, heading to Mahanaim. {2:30} Joab regrouped and found out that nineteen of David's men were missing, including Asahel. {2:31} David's crew took down three hundred and sixty dudes from Benjamin and Abner's crew. {2:32} They buried Asahel in Bethlehem, and Joab and his crew made it back to Hebron by daybreak.

{3:1} So, there was this long-standing beef between Saul's crew and David's crew, but David kept leveling up while Saul's squad kept losing ground. {3:2} While David was posted up in Hebron, he had some kids with his wives: Amnon, Chileab, Absalom, Adonijah, Shephatiah, and Ithream. {3:3} During this ongoing war, Abner was boosting Saul's crew. {3:4} Now, Saul had a concubine named Rizpah, and Ish-bosheth called out Abner for hooking up with her. {3:5} Abner got heated and basically said, "Am I a nobody? I've been holding it down for Saul's fam, and you're gonna question me over this?" {3:6-11} He swore to transfer the kingdom from Saul's house to David's. {3:12} Abner reached out to David, proposing a partnership and offering to bring all Israel over to David's side. {3:13} David was down, but he had one condition: Abner had to bring Michal, Saul's daughter, back to him first. {3:14-15} David sent a message to Ish-bosheth, demanding Michal back. {3:16} When Michal's husband followed her, Abner sent him back. {3:17-19} Abner rallied support for David among the elders and Benjamin. {3:20} Abner and his crew came to Hebron, and David threw them a feast. {3:21} Abner offered to gather all of Israel to make a league with David so he could reign over everything he wanted. {3:22} But when Joab returned with spoils, Abner was gone, sent off in peace by David. {3:23} When Abner returned, Joab killed him in revenge for their brother Asahel's death. {3:24} David disavowed any responsibility for Abner's death, putting the blame on Joab.

{4:1} When Saul's son heard that Abner was dead in Hebron, he was shook, and all the Israelites were freaked out. {4:2-3} Saul's son had two top dudes, Baanah and Rechab, who were leaders of crews from Benjamin. {4:4} Jonathan's son, Mephibosheth, was only five when he became lame after his nurse dropped him while fleeing news of Saul and Jonathan's deaths. {4:5} Rechab and Baanah, sons of

Rimmon from Beeroth, rolled up to Ish-bosheth's house around noon. {4:6} They acted like they were there to pick up wheat but then straight up stabbed him and bounced, leaving his crib. {4:7} They found him chilling in bed, took him out, beheaded him, and ghosted into the night. {4:8} They brought Ish-bosheth's head to David in Hebron, claiming they avenged David by offing Saul's enemy. {4:9} David wasn't having it, though, and called them out for killing an innocent person. {4:10} He didn't give rewards to people who brought bad news, so why should he reward them for this? {4:11} David was done with their excuses and took them out. {4:12} He made an example of them, chopping off their hands and feet and hanging them up. But Ish-bosheth's head was buried respectfully in Abner's tomb in Hebron.

{5:1} All the Israelite tribes rolled up to David in Hebron, like, "Yo, we're fam." {5:2} They remembered how David was the real deal under Saul, leading Israel, and the LORD was all about David being in charge. {5:3} So all the elders of Israel came to Hebron, and David made a pact with them before the LORD, getting anointed king over Israel. {5:4} David was thirty when he started ruling, and he held it down for forty years. {5:5} He kicked it in Hebron over Judah for seven and a half years, then held it down in Jerusalem for thirty-three years over Israel and Judah. {5:6} David and his crew headed to Jerusalem, dealing with the Jebusites who were like, "You can't come in here unless you clear out the disabled." {5:7} But David took Zion, making it the city of David. {5:8} He was all about rewarding whoever could climb up to the gutter and take out the Jebusites. {5:9} David set up shop in the fort, naming it the city of David, and he expanded it big time. {5:10} David leveled up, and the LORD God had his back. {5:11} Hiram, king of Tyre, hooked David up with materials to build a house. {5:12} David knew the LORD established him as king for Israel's sake. {5:13} David collected more concubines and wives in Jerusalem, and they had more kids. {5:14} These are the names of his kids born in Jerusalem. {5:17} When the Philistines heard David was king, they came for him, so David played it smart and went into hiding. {5:18} The Philistines camped in the valley of Rephaim. {5:19} David asked the LORD if he should take on the Philistines, and God said, "Go for it." {5:20} David went to Baal-perazim, wrecked the Philistines, and was like, "LORD's got my back." {5:21} They left their idols, and David and his crew burned them. {5:22} The Philistines came back, and David asked the LORD what to do. {5:23} God said to circle around and attack them by the mulberry trees. {5:24} When David heard a sound in the trees, he knew it was time to move, and the LORD backed him up, wrecking the Philistines. {5:25} David took care of business from Geba to Gazer, just like God said.

{6:1} So David rounded up a crew of thirty thousand chosen Israelites. {6:2} They rolled out from Baale of Judah to bring back the ark of God, the one named after the LORD of hosts chilling between the cherubim. {6:3} They threw the ark on a new cart from Abinadab's house in Gibeah, with Uzzah and Ahio driving the cart. {6:4} Everyone was hyped, playing instruments before the LORD—harps, psalteries, timbrels, cornets, and cymbals. {6:6-7} When they hit Nachon's threshing floor, Uzzah reached for the ark, and the LORD got ticked, smiting him for the error, and Uzzah bit it right there. {6:8} David was bummed 'cause of what went down, naming the spot Perez-uzzah. {6:9} David was shook, wondering how to bring the ark to him. {6:10-11} So David ditched the ark at Obed-edom the Gittite's place. {6:12-13} When David heard Obed-edom's crib was blessed 'cause of the ark, he brought it to the city of David with mad joy. {6:14} David was vibing, dancing like crazy before the LORD in a linen ephod. {6:15} They brought the ark to David's city with shouts and trumpets. {6:16} Michal, Saul's daughter, saw David getting down and dissed him in her heart. {6:17-19} They set the ark in a tabernacle David pitched, offering sacrifices to the LORD. {6:20} Michal mocked David for how he acted, but David was like, "I was vibing for the LORD, not you." {6:21} Michal had no kids 'til she passed away.

{7:1} David finally caught a breather from all his enemies, chillin' in his crib. {7:2} He was vibing with Nathan the prophet, like, "Check it, my place is decked out in cedar, but the ark of God's just tucked away in curtains." {7:3} Nathan was like, "Bro, go for it. The LORD's got your back." {7:4-5} That night, though, the LORD hit Nathan up, saying, "Tell David, should he really build me a house to crash in?" {7:6-7} I've been rockin' tents and tabernacles since we left Egypt, never asked for a cedar crib. {7:8-9} So tell David, I picked him from sheep duty to rule Israel. {7:10-11} I'll set up a spot for my peeps, no more wanderin' or getting wrecked by wicked haters. {7:12} When David's time's up, his seed will keep the throne and build my house. {7:13} He'll make a name for me, and his kingdom's locked in for good. {7:14-15} If he slips up, I'll correct him, but my love won't bail like with Saul. {7:16} Your dynasty's set, your throne's forever. {7:17} Nathan delivered the message, straight up. {7:18-20} David was like, "Who am I, God? You've brought me this far?" {7:21} All these blessings, it's wild. {7:22} You're unmatched, LORD. {7:23} No nation's like Israel, redeemed by you, doing great things. {7:24} You've claimed Israel as yours forever. {7:25} Keep your word, LORD, make it happen. {7:26} You promised a house, now I'm here praying.

{8:1} After that, David straight up wrecked the Philistines and got Methegammah outta their grip. {8:2} He also took on Moab, measuring them out with lines—some got wrecked, some got spared, and now Moabites were paying up. {8:3} David then took on Hadadezer of Zobah when he tried to push back to the Euphrates River. {8:4} From Hadadezer, David nabbed a bunch of chariots and soldiers, keeping some horses but messing up most of the chariot crews. {8:5} When the Syrians tried to help Hadadezer, David handled them too, knocking out twenty-two thousand. {8:6} David set up shop in Damascus with garrisons, making the Syrians give him tribute. {8:7} He even snagged gold shields off Hadadezer's crew and brought them back to Jerusalem. {8:8} From Betah and Berothai, David brought back loads of brass. {8:9-12} When Toi of Hamath heard about David's wins, he sent his son Joram to give props with silver, gold, and brass. {8:13} David made a name for himself after smacking down the Syrians, taking out eighteen thousand in the valley of salt. {8:14} He stationed troops in Edom, and the Edomites became his peeps. {8:15} David ruled over all

Israel, dealing out justice. {8:16} Joab ran the show with the army, Jehoshaphat kept records, {8:17} Zadok and Ahimelech were priests, and Seraiah was the scribe. {8:18} Benaiah looked after the Cherethites and Pelethites, and David's sons were top dogs.

{9:1} David was like, "Yo, is there anyone left from Saul's fam? I wanna show 'em love 'cause of Jonathan." {9:2} There was this dude Ziba from Saul's house, so David's like, "Are you Ziba?" And Ziba's like, "Yeah, I'm your servant." {9:3} David's all, "Is there anyone left from Saul's house I can bless for God's sake?" Ziba's like, "Jonathan's got a son, but he's lame, chillin' in Lo-debar at Machir's place." {9:4} So David's like, "Where's he at?" Ziba tells him, "He's at Machir's in Lo-debar." {9:5} David sends for him and brings him back. {9:6} When Mephibosheth shows up, he bows down to David, who's like, "Mephibosheth!" And Mephibosheth's like, "I'm your servant!" {9:7} David tells him not to worry and promises to hook him up 'cause of Jonathan, giving him back Saul's land and a permanent seat at his table. {9:8} Mephibosheth's amazed and humbled, saying, "Why me, a nobody?" {9:9} David then tells Ziba to take care of everything that belonged to Saul's house, with Mephibosheth always eating at David's table. {9:10} Ziba and his crew work the land for Mephibosheth while he enjoys meals with David. {9:11} Ziba's down with it, and Mephibosheth gets treated like one of David's sons. {9:12} Mephibosheth even has a son named Micha, and everyone in Ziba's house serves Mephibosheth. {9:13} Mephibosheth stays in Jerusalem, eating with the king, but he's still lame in both feet.

{10:1} Later, the king of Ammon dies, and his son Hanun takes over. {10:2} David's like, "I wanna show kindness to Hanun for his dad's sake." So David sends his servants to console Hanun. {10:3} But the Ammonite leaders suspect David's up to something and mistreat his messengers. {10:4} Hanun shaves off half their beards and cuts their clothes, embarrassing them. {10:5} When David hears, he tells the guys to chill in Jericho until their beards grow back. {10:6} The Ammonites realize they messed up and hire a big army from Syria to fight against David. {10:7} David sends Joab and his warriors to handle business. {10:8} The battle's set at the city gate, with the Syrians facing Israel. {10:9} Joab gets ready, putting the best soldiers against the Syrians while his brother Abishai takes on the Ammonites. {10:10} They're like, "Let's do this for our people and our God." {10:11} Joab's ready to back up Abishai if needed, and vice versa. {10:12} They're all pumped up for the fight, trusting God to do what's right. {10:13} Joab and his crew crush the Syrians, who run away. {10:14} The Ammonites see the Syrians bail and retreat into the city, and Joab heads back to Jerusalem victorious. {10:15} The Syrians regroup, and Hadarezer sends more troops to face David. {10:16} They meet at Helam, and Shobach leads the Syrian army. {10:17} David gathers Israel and heads to Helam to face the Syrians. {10:18} Israel beats the Syrians, taking out seven hundred chariots and forty thousand horsemen. {10:19} After seeing this, all the kings serving Hadarezer make peace with Israel, and the Syrians stop helping the Ammonites out of fear.

{11:1} So, when it was war season and kings were out battling, David sent Joab and his crew to fight against the Ammonites and siege Rabbah, but David stayed back in Jerusalem. {11:2} One evening, David got up from bed and went on his rooftop, where he saw a fine-looking woman bathing—turns out, it was Bath-sheba, daughter of Eliam and wife of Uriah the Hittite. {11:3} David asked about her and found out who she was. {11:4} He then sent messengers, took her, and slept with her after she'd purified herself. Later, she returned home and ended up pregnant. {11:5} She let David know she was expecting. {11:6} David, realizing the situation, sent for Uriah the Hittite through Joab. {11:7} When Uriah arrived, David asked about Joab, the troops, and the battle progress. {11:8} David told Uriah to go home, wash up, and relax, even sending him a nice meal. {11:9} But Uriah stayed by the palace door with the other servants, not going home. {11:10} When David found out, he asked Uriah why he hadn't gone home. {11:11} Uriah explained that while Israel was out in tents and Joab was in the field, he couldn't just go home to his wife. {11:12} David then told Uriah to stick around longer, and he even got him drunk, hoping he'd go home—but Uriah still didn't. {11:13} The next morning, David wrote a letter to Joab, asking him to place Uriah in a dangerous battle spot and pull back so Uriah would be killed. {11:14} Joab followed orders and put Uriah where he knew the toughest fighters were. {11:15} Uriah died in the battle, and Joab sent a messenger to inform David of what went down. {11:16} The messenger delivered the news, and David heard the report. {11:17} After Uriah's wife mourned him, David brought her into his house, married her, and she had his child. However, God was not pleased with what David did.

{12:1} So, God sent Nathan to David with a story about two dudes in the same town—one rich, one poor. {12:2-3} The rich guy had tons of animals, but the poor guy had only one little lamb that was practically family to him. {12:4} When a traveler came to the rich guy, instead of using his own livestock, he took the poor guy's beloved lamb and served it to his guest. {12:5-6} David was furious and swore the guy should pay back four times what he took and showed no pity. {12:7-8} Then Nathan hit him with it: "You're that guy." God blessed David, rescued him from Saul, and gave him everything—his master's house, wives, and even more if he wanted. {12:9} But why did David do evil by killing Uriah and taking his wife? {12:10} Now the sword will never leave your family because of this. {12:11} God will stir up trouble within your own house, and your wives will be taken by your neighbor while everyone watches. {12:12} You did it secretly, but it's going down in front of everyone. {12:13} David owned up: "I messed up big time." Nathan said, "God forgives you; you won't die." {12:14} But because of this, your enemies will mock God, and the child born to you will die. {12:15} After Nathan left, the child Bath-sheba bore David fell seriously ill. {12:16-17} David prayed and fasted, lying on the ground. {12:18-19} His servants were afraid to tell him the child died, knowing how upset he'd be. {12:20} When David realized, he cleaned up and went to worship. {12:21} Later, David comforted Bath-sheba, and they had another son named Solomon, whom God loved. {12:22} Joab conquered Rabbah, and David gathered the people to take the city.

{13:1} So, like, after a while, Absalom, David's son, had a sister named Tamar, and Amnon, another son of David, was totally into her. {13:2} Amnon got so obsessed with Tamar that he pretended to be sick because he wanted to be with her. {13:3} Now, Amnon had this slick friend named Jonadab, who was like, super sneaky. {13:4} Jonadab asked Amnon why he was looking so down, and Amnon spilled that he was in love with Tamar, Absalom's sister. {13:5} So Jonadab came up with this plan for Amnon to fake being sick and ask David to send Tamar to take care of him. {13:6} Amnon followed the plan, and when David visited, Amnon asked for Tamar to come make him food in front of him. {13:7} David sent Tamar to Amnon's place to cook for him. {13:8} Tamar went there and made food, but Amnon refused to eat. {13:9-10} Then Amnon sent everyone away and asked Tamar to bring the food to him in his room. {13:11} When Tamar brought the food, Amnon grabbed her and told her to sleep with him. {13:12-13} Tamar refused, telling him it was wrong, but he didn't listen and forced himself on her. {13:14} Afterward, Amnon hated her and sent her away. {13:15} Tamar was devastated and put ashes on her head, tore her colorful clothes, and cried. {13:16} Absalom found out and comforted Tamar, but he secretly hated Amnon for what he did. {13:17} When David heard what happened, he was furious. {13:18} Two years later, Absalom planned revenge during a party, telling his servants to kill Amnon when he was drunk. {13:19} The news reached David that Absalom had killed all his sons, but it was just Amnon. {13:20} David mourned and wept. {13:21} Absalom fled to Geshur, and David longed for him, missing Amnon but grieving for Absalom.

{14:1} So Joab, David's dude, noticed that the king was softening towards Absalom. {14:2} Joab sent to Tekoah for a wise woman and asked her to pretend she was mourning, dressed in mourning clothes and not using any oil, to appeal to the king. {14:3} Joab coached her on what to say. {14:4} When the woman approached the king, she bowed down and pleaded for help. {14:5} The king asked what was wrong, and she made up a story about being a widow with two sons, one of whom killed the other, and now her family wanted to kill the surviving son, leaving her with nothing. {14:8} The king told her to go home, and he would sort it out. {14:10} The woman begged the king to protect her son. {14:11} She reminded him to remember God's law and not let revenge destroy her family. {14:18} The king asked her who was behind this, and she confessed that Joab was involved. {14:21} David agreed to bring Absalom back. {14:22} Joab thanked the king and went to fetch Absalom from Geshur. {14:24} David allowed Absalom to return home but refused to see him. {14:25} Absalom was known for his exceptional beauty throughout Israel. {14:27} Absalom had three sons and one daughter named Tamar. {14:28} Absalom lived in Jerusalem for two years without seeing the king. {14:30} When Absalom couldn't get Joab's attention, he set Joab's barley field on fire to get his attention. {14:33} Eventually, Joab brought Absalom to the king, and David kissed him.

{15:1} After this, Absalom got all decked out with chariots, horses, and fifty hype men to roll with him. {15:2} He'd wake up early and post up by the city gate, intercepting anyone with beef needing the king's judgment. {15:3} Absalom would gas them up, saying their case was solid but the king was slacking on hearing them out. {15:4} He'd talk big, saying he wished he could judge everyone and serve up justice. {15:5} Whenever someone showed respect, he'd pull them in for a kiss. {15:6} Absalom played this game with everyone in Israel coming to see the king, and he started winning them over. {15:7} Forty years later, Absalom asked David to let him dip to Hebron to fulfill a vow to the Lord. {15:8} He claimed he made this vow back when he was in Geshur in Syria, promising to serve the Lord if he got back to Jerusalem. {15:9} David gave him the green light. So Absalom dipped to Hebron. {15:10} But Absalom sent out spies throughout Israel to spread the word that he was king in Hebron. {15:11} Two hundred men from Jerusalem joined him, clueless about the plan. {15:12} Absalom got David's counselor Ahithophel on his side, and the conspiracy grew strong. {15:13} A messenger told David that Israel was all about Absalom. {15:14} David told his crew in Jerusalem they needed to bounce to avoid Absalom catching them off guard and wrecking the city. {15:15} His crew was down for whatever David decided. {15:16} So David dipped with his fam, leaving ten concubines behind to hold it down. {15:17} They left the city and camped far off. {15:18} His squad rolled with him, including six hundred warriors from Gath. {15:19} David told Ittai the Gittite to peace out and stay safe since he was new to the crew. {15:20} Ittai swore loyalty to David, willing to roll wherever he went. {15:21} David let Ittai join them. {15:22} They all crossed the brook Kidron and kept moving towards the wilderness. {15:23} Everyone was crying, and they kept moving. {15:24} Zadok and the Levites brought the ark of the covenant but set it down before David left the city. {15:25} David told Zadok to take the ark back and prayed for God's favor to return. {15:26} He left his fate to God. {15:27} David told Zadok to go back to the city with his sons. {15:28} David waited in the wilderness for news from Zadok. {15:29} Zadok and Abiathar stayed in Jerusalem. {15:30} David climbed Mount Olivet, crying and with his head covered. {15:31} He found out Ahithophel was with Absalom's crew and prayed for his advice to flop. {15:32} Hushai met David and offered to help. {15:33} David said he'd be a burden if Hushai came along. {15:34} Instead, he told Hushai to go back and pretend to be loyal to Absalom to counter Ahithophel's counsel. {15:35} David told Hushai to share intel with Zadok and Abiathar. {15:36} They had their sons, Ahimaaz and Jonathan, ready to send messages. {15:37} Hushai rolled into the city, and Absalom came into Jerusalem.

{16:1} So David was chilling, walking down the hill, when Ziba, Mephibosheth's servant, rolled up with a couple of donkeys loaded with bread, raisins, summer fruits, and a bottle of wine. {16:2} David was like, "What's the deal with all this?" Ziba said it was for the crew to eat and drink on their journey. {16:3} David asked where Mephibosheth was at, and Ziba said he stayed back in Jerusalem, thinking Israel would restore his family's kingdom. {16:4} David was like, "Cool, everything Mephibosheth had is yours now." Ziba was all about that grace from the king. {16:5} As David hit up Bahurim, Shimei, a Saul fam member, came out cursing and throwing rocks at him and his crew. {16:6} He was dissing David hard, blaming him for Saul's blood and saying God gave the kingdom to Absalom. {16:7} Abishai was ready to take him out, but David was like, "Nah, let him do his thing; maybe God wants this." {16:8-15} David accepted it as his fate. {16:9} Absalom and his crew pulled up to Jerusalem, and Ahithophel was with them. {16:16} When Hushai approached Absalom, he played it smooth, saying, "Long live the king!" {16:17} Absalom was like, "You call this loyalty, not riding with your boy?" {16:18} Hushai was like, "Nah, I'm riding with whoever the Lord and the people choose." {16:19} He played it off, saying he'd serve Absalom just like he served his dad. {16:20} Absalom asked Ahithophel for advice on what to do next. {16:21} Ahithophel told him to publicly go in on David's concubines, which would show he's really against his dad. {16:22} So they set Absalom up on the roof and did their thing in front of everyone. {16:23} Ahithophel's advice was like gold, whether for David or Absalom.

{17:1} So Ahithophel was like, "Yo Absalom, let me pick out 12,000 soldiers and go after David tonight. {17:2-3} We'll catch him off guard, make him scared, and scatter his crew. I'll take out the king, and everyone else will come back to you. {17:4} Absalom and the elders were feeling this plan. {17:5} Absalom then called Hushai over for a second opinion. {17:6} Absalom asked Hushai if they should go with Ahithophel's plan. {17:7} Hushai was like, "Nah, Ahithophel's advice isn't it right now." {17:8} He explained how David and his boys are tough and won't chill with just anyone. {17:9} David could be hiding in a pit or somewhere sneaky. {17:10} He said even the bravest dudes would freak out because they know David's crew is no joke. {17:11} Hushai suggested gathering all of Israel to Absalom and leading the battle himself. {17:12} They'd catch David off guard and wipe them all out. {17:13} If David hides in a city, they'd wreck it until nothing's left. {17:14} Absalom and the crew were vibing with Hushai's advice more than Ahithophel's, and it turned out God wanted to mess up Ahithophel's plan to punish Absalom. {17:15} Hushai spilled the beans to Zadok and Abiathar about what went down with Absalom and the elders. {17:16} Hushai sent word to David to move ASAP and not chill in the plains, or else they'd all get wrecked. {17:17-18} Jonathan and Ahimaaz stayed low-key, but a girl tipped them off, and they told David. {17:19-20} The woman hid them in a well, and Absalom's crew couldn't find them. {17:21} Later, they told David to move quickly because of Ahithophel's plan against him. {17:22} So David and his crew crossed the Jordan without losing anyone. {17:23} Ahithophel saw his plan failed, so he went home, got his stuff in order, and ended it. {17:24} David reached Mahanaim, and Absalom crossed the Jordan with the Israelites. {17:25} Absalom put Amasa in charge instead of Joab. {17:26} They set up camp in Gilead. {17:27} David got to Mahanaim, and people from Rabbah, Lodebar, and Rogelim hooked him up with food and supplies because they knew they were hungry, tired, and thirsty in the wilderness.

{18:1} So David counted up his crew and put leaders in charge of thousands and hundreds. {18:2} He sent a third of the crew with Joab, another third with Abishai (Joab's bro), and the rest with Ittai the Gittite. David was like, "I'm rolling with y'all too." {18:3} But the crew was like, "Nah, you're too valuable. Stay back and help us out from the city." {18:4} David was cool with whatever they thought was best. He stood by the gate, and everyone headed out by the hundreds and thousands. {18:5} David told Joab and Abishai to go easy on Absalom for his sake. Everyone heard the king's orders about dealing with Absalom gently. {18:6} So they clashed with Israel in the woods of Ephraim. {18:7-8} Israel got wrecked by David's crew, and a ton of dudes got taken out that day—like 20,000. {18:9} Absalom ended up caught in a tree, and a guy saw it and told Joab. {18:10-11} Joab was like, "Why didn't you finish him off? I would've paid you." {18:12-13} The guy was like, "No way I'm touching the king's son after what David said." {18:14} Joab didn't waste time—he took care of Absalom himself. {18:15} Then Joab's crew finished the job. {18:16} Joab called off the pursuit after blowing the trumpet. {18:17} They threw Absalom in a pit and piled stones on him, and Israel split. {18:18} Absalom had set up a monument for himself while he was alive, calling it Absalom's Place. {18:19}-20 Ahimaaz wanted to bring the king news, but Joab said not today because of Absalom. {18:21} Joab sent Cushi to tell David what happened. {18:22} Ahimaaz insisted on running too. {18:23} The lookout recognized Ahimaaz's run. {18:24} Ahimaaz told David everything was good, but he didn't know Absalom's fate. {18:25} Cushi delivered the news to David, and David was devastated, mourning Absalom's death.

{19:1} Joab heard that the king was bawling over Absalom. {19:2} The whole vibe of victory turned into a downer because everyone knew how torn up the king was about his son. {19:3} The people snuck back into the city that day, feeling embarrassed like when you bail during a battle. {19:4} David covered his face and cried out, "Oh my son Absalom, my son, my son!" {19:5} Joab came to the king and called him out, saying he was dissing all the peeps who saved his life and his fam from Absalom's rebellion. {19:6} Joab accused David of loving his enemies and hating his friends, basically saying David would've been happier if they all died instead of Absalom. {19:7} Joab was like, "Get up and reassure your crew. If you don't, they're outta here, and that's gonna be worse for you than anything that's happened before." {19:8} So David got up and sat in the gate, and word spread that the king was there. Everyone came before him because Israel had scattered. {19:9} The tribes of Israel started arguing, saying the king saved them from enemies and now he's bounced because of Absalom. {19:10} They were like, "Absalom's dead, so why aren't we talking about bringing the king back?" {19:11} David sent word to the priests and elders of Judah, asking why they were the slowest to bring him back when everyone else was down. {19:12} He reminded them they were family and questioned why they were dragging their feet. {19:13} David told them to appoint Amasa as captain in place of Joab. {19:14} The men of Judah were swayed and sent word for the king to return with all his peeps. {19:15} So the king came back and went to Jordan, and the people of Judah came to meet him. {19:16} Shimei and a bunch of Benjamin dudes rushed to meet David. {19:17} A thousand men of Benjamin and Ziba with his sons and servants went over Jordan with the king. {19:18} They used a ferry boat to carry the king's crew over and do whatever the king wanted. {19:19} Shimei begged for forgiveness from David for dissing him when he left Jerusalem. {19:20} He owned up to his mistakes and was the first to welcome David back. {19:21} Abishai wanted Shimei dead for dissing the LORD's anointed, but David was like, "Nah, let it go." {19:22} David shut down the sons of Zeruiah, knowing he was king over Israel. {19:23} David spared Shimei's life and made a promise to him. {19:24} Mephibosheth came to meet the king looking rough since David left. {19:25} David asked why he didn't come along, and

Mephibosheth explained he was deceived by his servant. {19:26-27} He defended himself against slander and praised David as an angel. {19:28} Mephibosheth acknowledged he was as good as dead before David's kindness. {19:29} David decided Ziba and Mephibosheth should split the land. {19:30} Mephibosheth was cool with whatever because the king was back in peace.

{20:1} There was this sketchy dude named Sheba, a troublemaker from Benjamin, who blew a trumpet and declared, "We're done with David! We're out, Israel, back to our own tents." {20:2} So everyone from Israel split from David and followed Sheba, but the men of Judah stuck with their king from Jordan to Jerusalem. {20:3} David returned to Jerusalem and took those ten concubines he had left behind, keeping them under guard but not going in with them. They lived like widows until they died. {20:4} David told Amasa to gather the men of Judah within three days and meet him. {20:5} But Amasa took longer than he was supposed to. {20:6} David told Abishai, "Sheba's trouble. Get your crew and go after him before he fortifies himself and escapes." {20:7} Joab's men, along with the Cherethites and Pelethites, and all the mighty men, went out of Jerusalem after Sheba. {20:8} When they reached Gibeon, Amasa was ahead of them. Joab's sword fell out as he walked with Amasa. {20:9} Joab asked Amasa how he was doing and then struck him in the stomach, causing his bowels to spill out, and Amasa died. Joab and Abishai continued after Sheba. {20:11} Joab's supporters followed him. {20:12} Amasa's body lay in the middle of the road, so they moved him to the field and covered him with a cloth. {20:13} After that, everyone continued to pursue Sheba. {20:14} Sheba traveled through all the tribes of Israel to Abel and Beth-maachah, and they gathered to confront him. {20:15} They besieged him in Abel of Beth-maachah, building a ramp against the city wall to bring it down. {20:16} A wise woman from the city called out to Joab. {20:17-18} When he approached, she asked if he was Joab and then spoke to him. {20:19} She explained she was a peaceful and loyal citizen, questioning why Joab wanted to destroy a city and the inheritance of the LORD. {20:20} Joab denied wanting destruction, only seeking Sheba. {20:21} The woman promised to deliver Sheba's head over the wall to Joab. {20:22} Sheba's head was thrown to Joab, and he blew a trumpet, signaling the end of the conflict. Joab returned to Jerusalem to David. {20:23-24} Joab was in charge of Israel's army, Benaiah over the Cherethites and Pelethites, Adoram over tribute, Jehoshaphat was the recorder, {20:25} Sheva the scribe, and Zadok and Abiathar were the priests. {20:26} Ira the Jairite was also a chief ruler under David.

{21:1} So there was this long famine during David's time, like three years straight. David was all like, "Yo, Lord, what's the deal?" And God was like, "It's because of Saul and his messed up crew. They offed the Gibeonites." {21:2} David called up the Gibeonites, who weren't even Israelites but leftover Amorites. Saul had it out for them, all fired up for Israel and Judah. {21:3} David asked the Gibeonites, "How can I make this right and get your blessing on our land?" {21:4} The Gibeonites were like, "We don't want money or any Israelite blood spilled. Just hand over seven of Saul's sons." David was like, "Consider it done." {21:5} The Gibeonites said, "Give us seven of Saul's sons who wronged us, and we'll hang them up for the Lord at Gibeah of Saul." David agreed, saying, "I got you." {21:7} David spared Mephibosheth, Jonathan's son, because of his oath to Jonathan. {21:8} But he handed over two sons of Rizpah, Saul's concubine, and five sons of Michal to the Gibeonites, who hanged them. {21:10} Rizpah spread sackcloth on a rock from harvest until the rain came, guarding the bodies from birds and beasts. {21:11} When David heard what Rizpah did, he took action. {21:12} David retrieved Saul and Jonathan's bones from Jabeshgilead and buried them in Benjamin. {21:15} Later, the Philistines came back for more, and David and his crew fought them. {21:16} Ishbi-benob, a giant's descendant, tried to take out David, but Abishai saved him. {21:17} After that, the men told David to stay out of battle, preserving Israel's light. {21:18} In another battle, Sibbechai killed Saph, another giant's son. {21:19} Elhanan from Bethlehem took down Goliath's brother in Gob. {21:20-21} There was also a showdown in Gath with another giant, with six fingers and toes on each side, taken out by Jonathan, David's nephew. {21:22} David and his squad handled these giants like pros.

{22:1} So David was vibing after God delivered him from all his haters, including Saul. {22:2} He was like, "God's my rock, fortress, and savior, yo. Trusting in him all the way." {22:3} God's his shield, salvation, and safe place, rescuing him from violence. {22:4} David was all about praising God, knowing he'd be saved from his enemies. {22:5} When death was closing in and wicked folks were scaring him, {22:6} it was like hell was all around him, death traps everywhere. {22:7} But in his despair, David called out to God, and God heard him from up in heaven. {22:8} The earth shook and heaven's foundations moved, 'cause God was mad. {22:9} Smoke came from God's nose, fire from his mouth, burning everything up. {22:10} God came down from the heavens, darkness under his feet. {22:11} Riding on a cherub, soaring on the wings of the wind. {22:12} Surrounded by darkness, dark waters, and thick clouds. {22:13} Bright flames came from him. {22:14} God thundered from heaven, speaking with power. {22:15} He shot arrows, scattered enemies, and brought lightning. {22:16} Even the sea's depths were exposed, the world's foundations revealed, all at God's rebuke. {22:17} God reached down, rescued David from deep waters. {22:18} He saved him from strong enemies and haters who were too much for him. {22:19} Enemies tried to strike in his worst moments, but God had his back. {22:20} God brought him to a wide-open place, delighted in him, and rewarded him. {22:21} God rewarded him for his righteousness and clean hands. {22:22} David stuck to God's ways, never strayed. {22:23} Always followed God's judgments and statutes. {22:24} He kept himself clean and upright before God. {22:25} So God rewarded him according to his righteousness. {22:26} God shows mercy to the merciful, is upright with the upright. {22:27} He's pure to the pure but not cool with the crooked. {22:28} God saves the afflicted but keeps an eye on the proud. {22:29} God's David's light, guiding him out of darkness. {22:30} With God, David did some crazy feats, running through armies and jumping over walls. {22:31} God's way is perfect, and his word is tried and true, protecting those who trust in him. {22:32} 'Cause who's God if not the LORD? And who's a solid rock if not our God? {22:33} God's David's strength and power, making his path perfect. {22:34} He made David's feet nimble like a deer's and placed him on high places. {22:35} God trained David for battle, breaking steel bows with his arms.

{22:36} He gave David the shield of salvation, making him great with his kindness. {22:37} God made his steps steady so he wouldn't slip. {22:38} David chased and destroyed his enemies, not turning back till they were done. {22:39} He wiped them out so they couldn't rise again. {22:40} God armed David for battle, subduing those who rose against him. {22:41} David crushed his enemies, no one could save them but God. {22:42} David pounded them like dust, stomped them like street dirt, scattered them everywhere. {22:44} God saved David from his people's strife, making him head over nations he didn't even know. {22:45} Strangers bowed to David, obedient when they heard of him. {22:46} Enemies hid and trembled in fear. {22:47} David's hype was all about God, his rock and savior. {22:48} God avenges David, bringing down his enemies. {22:49} God lifted David up and saved him from violence. {22:50} So David's all about giving thanks to God everywhere, singing praises to his name. {22:51} God's the real deal, saving his anointed, David and his descendants forever.

{23:1} So, like, these are the final words of David. David, Jesse's kid, was like, "Yo, listen up. I'm the one God lifted up, the chosen dude of Jacob's God, and the sick songwriter of Israel." {23:2} He was all, "The Spirit of the LORD spoke through me, and his words were on my tongue." {23:3} It's like, "The God of Israel, the Rock, told me: Whoever's in charge has to be just, ruling in respect of God." {23:4} And he's gonna be as fresh as a morning with no clouds, like when the sun's rising, or when grass sprouts after a rain. {23:5} Even though my family's not perfect with God, he made this everlasting deal with me, solid and legit. It's all about my salvation and what I really want, even if it's not what I expected. {23:6} But those worthless dudes, they're like thorns you can't grab, you gotta deal with them with iron and spears, burning them up on the spot. {23:7} They're no joke, man. {23:8} Check out these mighty men David had: Adino the Eznite, he took on 800 dudes with a spear and crushed them all at once. {23:9} Then there's Eleazar, son of Dodo, who fought the Philistines when everyone else chickened out. {23:10} He fought until his arms were jelly, but God gave him a sick victory that day. {23:11} Shammah held down a field of lentils against a whole Philistine gang. {23:12} He stood his ground, wrecked them, and scored another big win for God. {23:13} Three of the top dogs came to David during harvest time, while the Philistines camped in the valley. {23:14} David was chilling in a stronghold, while the Philistine crew was posted up in Bethlehem. {23:15} He was like, "Man, I wish I could get a drink from that Bethlehem well by the gate." {23:16} So three of his homies busted through enemy lines, got water from the Bethlehem well, and brought it back, but David poured it out as an offering to God. {23:17} He was like, "Nah, I can't drink this. It's like the blood of my boys who risked it all." {23:18} Abishai, Joab's bro, was one of the top three, took on 300 dudes and came out on top. {23:19} Super honorable, but not quite in the top three ranks. {23:20} Then there's Benaiah, son of Jehoiada, a real tough guy from Kabzeel. {23:21} He took out two Moabite warriors and a lion in the snow with just a stick. {23:22} That's the kind of stuff Benaiah pulled off, earning him mad respect. {23:23} He was even more honorable than the thirty, but still not top three. David put him in charge of his personal guard. {23:24} Asahel, Joab's bro, was one of the thirty, along with Elhanan, Shammah, Elika, Helez, Ira, Abiezer, Mebunnai, Zalmon, Maharai, and so on. {23:39} Thirty-seven badasses in total.

{24:1} So, like, God got mad at Israel again and made David think, "Hey, let's count everyone in Israel and Judah." {24:2} The king told Joab, the head honcho of the army, "Go and count all the people from Dan to Beersheba so I know how many we've got." {24:3} Joab was like, "May God increase the people a hundredfold, but why are you into this?" {24:4} But David insisted, so Joab and his crew went out to tally up the Israelites. {24:5} They traveled around, pitching camp here and there, counting folks from all over. {24:6} They hit up Gilead, Tahtim-hodshi, Dan-jaan, and Zidon, {24:7} then swung down through the Hivite and Canaanite cities, and down south to Judah and Beer-sheba. {24:8} After nine months and twenty days, they finally made it back to Jerusalem. {24:9} Joab reported the count to David: 800,000 valiant swordsmen in Israel and 500,000 in Judah. {24:10} David felt guilty after counting the people and said to God, "I messed up big time. Please forgive me for being so foolish." {24:11} The next morning, God's word came to the prophet Gad, David's seer. {24:12} Gad told David, "Here are three options; pick one and I'll make it happen." {24:13} David chose for God to decide, saying, "I'd rather rely on God's mercy than man's punishment." {24:15} So God sent a plague, and 70,000 people died from Dan to Beer-sheba. {24:16} When the angel was about to destroy Jerusalem, God stopped him and spared the people. {24:17} David confessed his sin to God, asking for the punishment to fall on him and his family instead of the innocent people. {24:18} Gad told David to build an altar to God on Araunah's threshing floor. {24:19} David obeyed and went to Araunah's place. {24:20} Araunah greeted David respectfully. {24:21} David explained he needed the site to build an altar and stop the plague. {24:22} Araunah offered everything needed for the sacrifice. {24:23} Araunah generously gave it all to David, praying for God's acceptance. {24:24} But David insisted on paying for it, saying he wouldn't offer sacrifices that cost him nothing. {24:25} So David bought the threshing floor and offered sacrifices to God, and the plague stopped.

1 Kings

✦✦✦

{1:1} So King David was hella old and couldn't stay warm even with blankets. {1:2} His crew was like, "We need to find a young hottie to keep the king warm." {1:3} They searched all over Israel and found this babe named Abishag from Shunem and brought her to the king. {1:4} She was super cute and took care of the king, but they didn't hook up. {1:5} Meanwhile, Adonijah, son of Haggith, started flexing, saying, "I'm gonna be king," and got chariots, horsemen, and fifty dudes to roll with him. {1:6} His dad never checked him, asking, "Why are you doing this?" Plus, he was good-looking and born after Absalom. {1:7} He teamed up with Joab and Abiathar the priest, and they backed Adonijah. {1:8} But Zadok the priest, Benaiah, Nathan the prophet, Shimei, Rei, and David's mighty men weren't with Adonijah. {1:9} Adonijah sacrificed sheep, oxen, and fat cattle by the stone of Zoheleth near En-rogel and invited all his brothers, the king's sons, and the royal crew. {1:10} But he didn't invite Nathan, Benaiah, the mighty men, or his bro Solomon. {1:11} Nathan told Bath-sheba, Solomon's mom, "Haven't you heard? Adonijah's claiming the throne, and David doesn't know. {1:12} Let me give you some advice to save your life and Solomon's. {1:13} Go to King David and remind him he promised you that Solomon would be king. Ask why Adonijah is reigning. {1:14} While you're talking, I'll come in and back you up." {1:15} So Bath-sheba went to the king, who was super old, with Abishag attending him. {1:16} She bowed and the king asked what she wanted. {1:17} She said, "My lord, you swore by God that Solomon would reign after you. {1:18} But now Adonijah is king and you don't even know it. {1:19} He's sacrificed a ton of animals and invited all your sons, Abiathar, and Joab, but not Solomon. {1:20} Everyone's waiting for you to declare who will be king after you. {1:21} If you don't, Solomon and I will be treated as criminals when you're gone." {1:22} While she was still talking, Nathan the prophet came in. {1:23} They told the king Nathan was there, and he bowed before the king. {1:24} Nathan asked, "My lord, did you say Adonijah will reign after you? {1:25} He's sacrificed animals and is partying with all the king's sons, the army captains, and Abiathar. They're all shouting, 'Long live King Adonijah!' {1:26} But he didn't invite me, Zadok, Benaiah, or Solomon. {1:27} Did you approve this without informing your servants who should be king after you?" {1:28} King David said, "Call Bath-sheba." She came and stood before him. {1:29} The king swore by God, who saved him from trouble, {1:30} "Just as I swore to you, Solomon will be king after me and sit on my throne. I'll make it happen today." {1:31} Bath-sheba bowed with her face to the ground and said, "May my lord King David live forever." {1:32} King David said, "Call Zadok, Nathan, and Benaiah." They came before him. {1:33} The king told them, "Take my servants and put Solomon on my mule. Take him to Gihon. {1:34} Let Zadok and Nathan anoint him as king over Israel and blow the trumpet, shouting, 'Long live King Solomon!' {1:35} Then escort him back so he can sit on my throne. He'll be king in my place. I've appointed him ruler over Israel and Judah." {1:36} Benaiah said, "Amen! May the Lord confirm it. {1:37} Just as God has been with you, may He be with Solomon and make his throne greater than yours." {1:38} So Zadok, Nathan, Benaiah, the Cherethites, and Pelethites made Solomon ride on King David's mule to Gihon. {1:39} Zadok took the horn of oil from the tabernacle and anointed Solomon. They blew the trumpet and everyone shouted, "Long live King Solomon!" {1:40} The crowd followed, playing pipes and celebrating so loudly that the ground shook. {1:41} Adonijah and his guests heard the commotion as they finished eating. Joab heard the trumpet and asked, "What's going on in the city?" {1:42} While he was speaking, Jonathan, son of Abiathar the priest, arrived. Adonijah said, "Come in, you must have good news." {1:43} But Jonathan replied, "No, King David has made Solomon king. {1:44} The king sent Zadok, Nathan, Benaiah, and the Cherethites and Pelethites with him. They put him on the king's mule, {1:45} anointed him at Gihon, and now he's reigning. The city's celebrating, and that's the noise you heard. {1:46} Solomon is sitting on the throne. {1:47} The king's servants came to congratulate King David, saying, 'May God make Solomon's name greater than yours and his throne even greater.' The king bowed in worship on his bed {1:48} and praised God for letting him see his successor on the throne." {1:49} Adonijah's guests were terrified and scattered. {1:50} Adonijah feared Solomon and grabbed the horns of the altar for protection. {1:51} Solomon was told, "Adonijah fears you and is holding onto the altar, asking you to swear not to kill him." {1:52} Solomon said, "If he proves himself worthy, he'll be fine. But if he's found guilty, he'll die." {1:53} Solomon had him brought down from the altar. Adonijah bowed to Solomon, and Solomon told him, "Go home."

{2:1} As David was about to kick the bucket, he told Solomon, {2:2} "Yo, I'm about to peace out, so be strong and act like a man; {2:3} Follow God's rules, live right, keep his commandments, and you'll succeed in whatever you do. {2:4} God promised me that if my kids stick to his ways, there'll always be one of us on Israel's throne. {2:5} Also, you know what Joab did to me and to those two commanders, Abner and Amasa—straight-up killed them in peacetime. {2:6} So use your smarts and don't let him die peacefully. {2:7} But be chill with the sons of Barzillai; they helped me when I was on the run from Absalom. {2:8} And remember Shimei, who cursed me out but I promised I wouldn't kill him. {2:9} You're wise, you know what to do—don't let him die in peace either." {2:10} David passed away and was buried in the City of David. {2:11} He ruled over Israel for forty years: seven in Hebron and thirty-three in Jerusalem. {2:12} Solomon took over the throne, and his kingdom was solid. {2:13} Then Adonijah, son of Haggith, came to Bathsheba, Solomon's mom, and she asked, "You coming in peace?" He replied, "Yeah, peace." {2:14} He added, "I have something to say." She said, "Go ahead." {2:15} He said, "You know I was supposed to be king, but it turned out to be my brother's because God wanted it that way. {2:16} I have one request, don't say no." She said, "Go on." {2:17} He asked her to talk to Solomon about letting him marry Abishag. {2:18} Bathsheba said, "Okay, I'll talk to him." {2:19} Bathsheba went to Solomon and he got up, bowed, and had a throne set for her.

She sat at his right hand. {2:20} She said, "I have a small request, don't say no." Solomon replied, "Ask away, mom, I won't refuse." {2:21} She asked for Abishag to be given to Adonijah as a wife. {2:22} Solomon answered, "Why are you asking for Abishag for Adonijah? Might as well ask for the kingdom for him too, since he's my older brother." {2:23} Then Solomon swore by the Lord, "If Adonijah hasn't sealed his fate with this, God do so to me and more. {2:24} As the Lord lives, who put me on my father's throne and established my house, Adonijah will die today." {2:25} So Solomon sent Benaiah to strike Adonijah down, and he died. {2:26} Solomon told Abiathar the priest, "Go to your estate in Anathoth. You deserve to die, but I won't kill you now because you carried the Ark and shared my father's struggles." {2:27} So Solomon removed Abiathar from being a priest, fulfilling the Lord's word about Eli's house in Shiloh. {2:28} When Joab heard the news (since he had supported Adonijah but not Absalom), he ran to the Lord's tabernacle and grabbed the altar horns. {2:29} Solomon heard about it and sent Benaiah to strike him down. {2:30} Benaiah told Joab to come out, but Joab said he'd die there. Benaiah reported this back to the king. {2:31} Solomon said, "Do what he said. Strike him down and bury him to remove the guilt Joab brought on me and my father. {2:32} The Lord will return his blood on his own head for killing two better men than himself, Abner and Amasa, without my father's knowledge. {2:33} Their blood will be on Joab and his descendants forever, but David's house and throne will have peace from the Lord forever." {2:34} So Benaiah killed Joab, and he was buried at his house in the wilderness. {2:35} Solomon put Benaiah over the army and Zadok as the new priest in place of Abiathar. {2:36} Solomon called for Shimei and told him to build a house in Jerusalem and stay there. {2:37} If he crossed the Kidron Valley, he'd be doomed. {2:38} Shimei agreed and lived in Jerusalem for a long time. {2:39} After three years, two of Shimei's servants ran off to King Achish in Gath. Shimei went to get them back. {2:40} He brought them back, but Solomon found out. {2:41} Solomon called Shimei out, reminding him of the oath he broke by leaving Jerusalem. {2:42} Solomon said, "Didn't I make you swear by the Lord that you'd die if you left? And you said it was good. {2:43} Why didn't you keep your promise?" {2:44} Solomon told him, "You know all the evil you did to my father, so the Lord will bring it back on your head. {2:45} But Solomon will be blessed, and David's throne will be secure forever." {2:46} Then Solomon commanded Benaiah to strike down Shimei, and he died, firmly establishing Solomon's kingdom.

{3:1} Solomon made a deal with Pharaoh, the king of Egypt, and married his daughter. He brought her to the City of David while he was finishing building his palace, the temple of the Lord, and the wall around Jerusalem. {3:2} But people were still sacrificing at high places since there wasn't a temple for the Lord's name yet. {3:3} Solomon loved the Lord and followed his dad David's rules, but he also sacrificed and burned incense at high places. {3:4} The king went to Gibeon to offer sacrifices because that was the main high place; Solomon offered a thousand burnt offerings there. {3:5} At Gibeon, the Lord appeared to Solomon in a dream at night, and God said, "Ask for whatever you want me to give you." {3:6} Solomon replied, "You showed great kindness to my dad David because he was faithful and righteous. You continued this kindness by giving him a son to sit on his throne today. {3:7} Now, Lord my God, you've made me king in place of my dad, but I'm just a kid and don't know how to rule. {3:8} I'm among your chosen people, a huge crowd that can't be counted. {3:9} Give me a discerning heart to govern your people and distinguish between right and wrong. Who can govern such a great people?" {3:10} The Lord was pleased that Solomon asked for this. {3:11} God said, "Because you asked for discernment to govern justly, not for a long life or riches or the death of your enemies, {3:12} I'll give you a wise and discerning heart, unlike anyone before or after you. {3:13} I'll also give you what you didn't ask for—riches and honor—so you'll be the greatest king in your lifetime. {3:14} If you walk in my ways and obey my statutes and commands like your dad David, I'll give you a long life." {3:15} Solomon woke up and realized it was a dream. He returned to Jerusalem, stood before the Ark of the Covenant, offered burnt offerings and peace offerings, and threw a feast for all his servants. {3:16} Two women, both prostitutes, came to the king and stood before him. {3:17} One said, "My lord, this woman and I live in the same house, and I gave birth while she was there. {3:18} Three days after my child was born, she also had a baby. We were alone; no one else was in the house. {3:19} One night, her baby died because she accidentally smothered it. {3:20} So she switched our babies while I was asleep, putting her dead child beside me and taking mine. {3:21} When I woke up to nurse my baby, I found it dead, but in the morning, I realized it wasn't my child." {3:22} The other woman said, "No, the living one is my son; the dead one is yours." They argued before the king. {3:23} The king said, "One says, 'This is my son, the living one, and yours is the dead one,' while the other says, 'No, yours is the dead one, and mine is the living one.'" {3:24} The king ordered, "Bring me a sword." They brought it to him. {3:25} He then said, "Cut the living child in two and give half to each woman." {3:26} The real mother, moved by love for her son, said, "Please, my lord, give her the living baby; don't kill him!" But the other woman said, "Neither of us will have him. Cut him in two!" {3:27} The king declared, "Give the living baby to the first woman. Don't kill him; she is his mother." {3:28} All Israel heard about the king's wise ruling and held him in awe because they saw God's wisdom in him to administer justice.

{4:1} So, King Solomon was the main dude over all of Israel. {4:2} Here are his squad members: Azariah, son of Zadok the priest, {4:3} Elihoreph and Ahiah, sons of Shisha, the scribes; Jehoshaphat, son of Ahilud, the recorder. {4:4} Benaiah, son of Jehoiada, was the head of the army; Zadok and Abiathar were the priests. {4:5} Azariah, son of Nathan, was in charge of the officers, and Zabud, son of Nathan, was the top official and the king's BFF. {4:6} Ahishar managed the palace, and Adoniram, son of Abda, was in charge of forced labor. {4:7} Solomon had twelve officers over all Israel who provided food for the king and his household, each one handling the supplies for one month a year. {4:8} Here are their names: The son of Hur in the hill country of Ephraim, {4:9} the son of Dekar in Makaz, Shaalbim, Beth-shemesh, and Elon-beth-hanan, {4:10} the son of Hesed in Arubboth, including Sochoh and all the land of Hepher, {4:11} the son of Abinadab in Naphoth-dor (he was married to Solomon's daughter Taphath), {4:12} Baana, son of Ahilud, in Taanach, Megiddo, and all Beth-shean, from Zarethan below Jezreel, from Beth-shean to Abel-meholah and beyond Jokmeam, {4:13} the son of Geber in Ramoth-gilead, including the towns of Jair, son of Manasseh, in Gilead, and the region of Argob in Bashan with sixty large walled cities and bronze bars, {4:14} Ahinadab, son of Iddo, in Mahanaim, {4:15} Ahimaaz in Naphtali (he married Solomon's daughter Basemath), {4:16} Baana, son of Hushai, in Asher and Aloth, {4:17} Jehoshaphat, son of Paruah, in Issachar, {4:18} Shimei, son of Elah, in Benjamin, {4:19} and Geber, son of Uri, in Gilead, the country of Sihon, king of the Amorites, and Og, king of Bashan. He was the only officer in that region. {4:20} Judah and Israel were as many as the sand on the seashore, eating, drinking, and having a good time. {4:21} Solomon ruled over all the kingdoms from the Euphrates River to the land of the Philistines and to the border of Egypt. They brought gifts and served Solomon all his life. {4:22} Solomon's daily provisions were thirty cors of fine flour and sixty cors of meal, {4:23} ten fattened cattle, twenty pasture-fed cattle, a hundred sheep and goats, as well as deer, gazelles, roebucks, and fattened poultry. {4:24} He ruled over all the region west of the Euphrates from Tiphsah to Gaza and had peace on all sides. {4:25} Judah and Israel lived safely, each man under his own vine and fig tree, from Dan to Beersheba, all the days of Solomon. {4:26} Solomon had forty thousand stalls for his chariot horses and twelve thousand horsemen. {4:27} The district governors provided supplies for King Solomon and all who came to his table, each one in his month. They made sure nothing was lacking. {4:28} They also brought barley and straw for the chariot horses and other horses to the proper places, each according to his duty. {4:29} God gave Solomon super wisdom and insight, and a mind as vast as the sand on the seashore. {4:30} Solomon's wisdom was greater than all the wisdom of the people of the East and all the wisdom of Egypt. {4:31} He was wiser than anyone else, wiser than Ethan the Ezrahite, Heman, Calcol, and Darda, sons of Mahol. His fame spread to all the surrounding nations. {4:32} He spoke three thousand proverbs, and his songs numbered a thousand and five. {4:33} He talked about plant life, from the cedar in Lebanon to the hyssop that grows out of walls. He also spoke about animals, birds, reptiles, and fish. {4:34} People from all nations came to listen to Solomon's wisdom, sent by all the kings of the world who had heard of his wisdom.

{5:1} Hiram, the king of Tyre, sent his crew to Solomon because he heard Solomon got crowned in his dad's place; Hiram was always tight with David. {5:2} Solomon hit up Hiram, saying, {5:3} "You know my dad David couldn't build a temple for the LORD because of all the beef around him, until the LORD handled his enemies. {5:4} But now, the LORD my God has given me peace on all sides, no enemies or bad vibes. {5:5} So, I'm planning to build a temple for the LORD, as He promised my dad, saying that his son would build it. {5:6} Can you command your people to cut cedar trees from Lebanon for me? My crew will work with yours, and I'll pay your workers whatever you say, because no one cuts timber like the Sidonians." {5:7} When Hiram heard Solomon's message, he was super hyped and said, "Blessed be the LORD today for giving David such a wise son to rule this great nation." {5:8} Hiram replied to Solomon, "I got your message and I'll get you all the cedar and fir timber you need. {5:9} My servants will bring them down from Lebanon to the sea, float them to the place you choose, and then you can pick them up. You just need to hook me up with food for my household." {5:10} So, Hiram gave Solomon all the cedar and fir trees he wanted. {5:11} Solomon gave Hiram twenty thousand measures of wheat for his household and twenty measures of pure oil every year. {5:12} The LORD gave Solomon wisdom as promised, and there was peace between Hiram and Solomon; they made a pact. {5:13} King Solomon drafted a labor force from all Israel; the total was thirty thousand men. {5:14} He sent them to Lebanon in shifts of ten thousand a month, spending one month in Lebanon and two months at home, with Adoniram in charge of the labor force. {5:15} Solomon had seventy thousand carriers and eighty thousand stonecutters in the hills, {5:16} plus thirty-three hundred foremen supervising the workers. {5:17} The king ordered them to quarry large, expensive stones to lay the foundation of the temple. {5:18} Solomon's builders, Hiram's builders, and the Gebalites cut and prepared the timber and stone to build the temple.

{6:1} So, like, 480 years after the Israelites bounced from Egypt, in the fourth year of Solomon's reign over Israel, in the month of Zif (the second month), he started building the LORD's crib. {6:2} The house Solomon built for the LORD was 60 cubits long, 20 cubits wide, and 30 cubits high. {6:3} The porch in front of the temple was 20 cubits long (matching the house's width) and 10 cubits wide. {6:4} He made windows with narrow frames for the house. {6:5} Against the walls of the house, Solomon built side rooms all around, both the temple and the innermost sanctuary (the oracle): he made chambers all around. {6:6} The lowest side room was 5 cubits wide, the middle was 6 cubits wide, and the third was 7 cubits wide. He made narrow ledges around the outside of the house so the beams wouldn't be attached to the walls. {6:7} The house was built with stones prepared at the quarry, so no hammer, axe, or iron tool was heard during construction. {6:8} The entrance to the middle floor was on the south side of the house, with stairs leading up to the middle floor and from there to the third floor. {6:9} Solomon finished building the house, covering it with beams and planks of cedar. {6:10} He built side rooms all around the house, 5 cubits high, attached to the house with cedar timbers. {6:11} The word of the LORD came to Solomon, saying, {6:12} "About this house you're building: if you follow my decrees, carry out my regulations, and keep all my commands, I'll keep the promise I made to David your father. {6:13} I'll live among the Israelites and won't abandon my people Israel." {6:14} So Solomon finished building the house. {6:15} He lined the interior walls with cedar boards, from the floor to the ceiling, and covered the floor with planks of juniper. {6:16} He partitioned off 20 cubits at the rear of the house with cedar boards, from floor to ceiling, to make an inner sanctuary, the Most Holy Place. {6:17} The main hall in front of this inner sanctuary was 40 cubits long. {6:18} The cedar inside the house was carved with gourds and open flowers; everything was cedar, no stone was visible. {6:19} He prepared the inner sanctuary to house the ark of the covenant of the LORD. {6:20} The inner sanctuary was 20 cubits long, 20 cubits wide, and 20 cubits high, overlaid with pure gold, and he also covered the cedar altar with gold. {6:21} Solomon overlaid the interior of the house with pure gold and placed gold chains across the front of the inner sanctuary, which was also overlaid with gold. {6:22} He covered the entire interior with gold and also the altar in the inner sanctuary. {6:23} In the inner sanctuary, he made two cherubim out of olive wood, each 10 cubits high. {6:24} Each wing of the cherubim was 5 cubits, so the wingspan of each cherub was 10 cubits. {6:25} Both cherubim were the same size and shape, each 10 cubits high. {6:26} The height of each cherub was 10 cubits. {6:27} He placed the cherubim inside the innermost room, with their wings spread out so that one wing touched one wall and the other wing touched the other wall, and their wings touched each other in the middle of the room. {6:28} He overlaid the cherubim with gold. {6:29} He decorated the walls of the house all around with carved figures of cherubim, palm trees, and open flowers, both inside and out. {6:30} He overlaid the floor of the house with gold, inside and out. {6:31} For the entrance to the inner sanctuary, he made doors out of olive wood, with five-sided doorposts. {6:32} The two doors were also made of olive wood, and he carved cherubim, palm trees, and open flowers on them, overlaying the carvings with gold. {6:33} Similarly, he made doorposts of olive wood for the entrance to the main hall, which were four-sided. {6:34} The two doors were of juniper wood; each door had two folding panels. {6:35} He carved cherubim, palm trees, and open flowers on them and overlaid the carvings with gold. {6:36} He built the inner courtyard with three rows of dressed stone and a row of cedar beams. {6:37} The foundation of the LORD's house was laid in the fourth year, in the month of Zif, {6:38} and in the eleventh year, in the month of Bul (the eighth month), the house was completed in all its details and according to its specifications. Solomon took seven years to build it.

{7:1} So, Solomon was working on his own crib for 13 years, and he finished the whole thing. {7:2} He also built the House of the Forest of Lebanon; it was 100 cubits long, 50 cubits wide, and 30 cubits high, with four rows of cedar pillars and cedar beams on the pillars. {7:3} It was covered with cedar above the beams that rested on 45 pillars, 15 in a row. {7:4} There were windows in three rows, with light facing light in three tiers. {7:5} All the doors and doorposts were square, with windows; and light faced light in three tiers. {7:6} He made a porch of pillars; it was 50 cubits long and 30 cubits wide. The porch was in front, with pillars and a thick beam in front of them. {7:7} He made a porch for his throne where he might judge, called the Porch of Judgment, covered with cedar from floor to ceiling. {7:8} His house where he lived had another courtyard within the porch, built similarly. Solomon also made a house for Pharaoh's daughter, whom he had married, similar to this porch. {7:9} All these were made of expensive stones, cut to size, sawed with saws inside and out, from the foundation to the coping, and outside toward the great courtyard. {7:10} The foundation was made of costly stones, large stones of 10 cubits and stones of 8 cubits. {7:11} Above were costly stones, cut to size, and cedar. {7:12} The great courtyard all around had three rows of cut stone and a row of cedar beams, for both the inner court of the house of the LORD and the porch of the house. {7:13} King Solomon sent for and brought Hiram from Tyre. {7:14} He was the son of a widow from the tribe of Naphtali, and his father was a man of Tyre, a skilled worker in bronze. He was filled with wisdom, understanding, and skill to work with bronze. He came to King Solomon and did all his work. {7:15} He cast two pillars of bronze, each 18 cubits high, and a line of 12 cubits measured the circumference of each. {7:16} He made two capitals of cast bronze to set on the tops of the pillars; each capital was 5 cubits high. {7:17} There were nets of checker work and wreaths of chain work for the capitals on top of the pillars; seven for one capital and seven for the other. {7:18} He made the pillars and two rows around the one network to cover the capitals on top with pomegranates, and did the same for the other capital. {7:19} The capitals on top of the pillars in the porch were of lily work, four cubits high. {7:20} The capitals on the two pillars also had pomegranates above, near the bowl-shaped part next to the network, with 200 pomegranates in rows all around the other capital. {7:21} He set up the pillars at the porch of the temple; he set up the right pillar and named it Jachin, and set up the left pillar and named it Boaz. {7:22} The tops of the pillars were decorated with lily work. So, the work of the pillars was finished. {7:23} He made a cast metal sea, 10 cubits from rim to rim, circular in shape, 5 cubits high, and 30 cubits in circumference. {7:24} Below the rim, gourds encircled it, 10 to a cubit, all around the sea. The gourds were cast in two rows when it was cast. {7:25} The sea stood on 12 oxen, three facing north, three facing west, three facing south, and three facing east; the sea was set on top of them, with their hindquarters inward. {7:26} It was a handbreadth thick, and its rim was like the rim of a cup, like a lily blossom. It held 2,000 baths. {7:27} He made ten bronze stands; each was 4 cubits long, 4 cubits wide, and 3 cubits high. {7:28} The stands were made this way: they had side panels, and the panels were between the frames. {7:29} On the panels between the frames were lions, oxen, and cherubim, and on the frames above and below the lions and oxen were wreaths of beveled work. {7:30} Each stand had four bronze wheels with bronze axles, and at the four corners were supports for a basin; the supports were cast with wreaths at each side. {7:31} The top of the stand had a circular opening half a cubit deep, with its opening a cubit and a half. It had carvings on its panels, which were square, not round. {7:32} The four wheels were underneath the panels, and the axles of the wheels were attached to the stand. Each wheel was a cubit and a half in diameter. {7:33} The wheels were made like chariot wheels; their axles, rims, spokes, and hubs were all cast metal. {7:34} There were four supports at the four corners of each stand; the supports were part of the stand itself. {7:35} On top of the stand, there was a circular band half a cubit high. The top and sides of the stand were made of one piece. {7:36} He engraved cherubim, lions, and palm trees on the surfaces of the supports and on the panels, in every available space, with wreaths all around. {7:37} This is how he made the ten stands. All of them were cast in the same molds, with the same size and shape. {7:38} He made ten bronze basins, each holding 40 baths, and each basin was 4 cubits across, one basin for each of the ten stands. {7:39} He placed five stands on the south side of the temple and five on the north side. He placed the sea on the south side, at the southeast corner of the temple. {7:40} Hiram also made the basins, shovels, and sprinkling bowls. So Hiram finished all the work he did for King Solomon on the temple of the LORD: {7:41} the two pillars, the two bowl-shaped capitals on top of the pillars, the two sets of network decorating the two bowl-shaped capitals on top of the pillars, {7:42} the 400 pomegranates for the two sets of network (200 pomegranates for each set of network, covering the bowl-shaped capitals on top of the pillars), {7:43} the ten stands with their ten basins, {7:44} the Sea and the twelve bulls under it, {7:45} the pots, shovels, and sprinkling bowls. All these objects that Hiram made for King Solomon for the temple of the LORD were of burnished bronze. {7:46} The king had them cast in clay molds in the plain of the Jordan between Sukkoth and Zarethan. {7:47} Solomon left all these things unweighed because there were so many; the weight of the bronze was not determined. {7:48} Solomon also made all the furnishings for the temple of the LORD: the golden altar, the golden table on which was the bread of the Presence, {7:49} the lampstands of pure gold (five on the right and five on the left, in front of the inner sanctuary), the gold flowers, lamps, and tongs, {7:50} the pure gold basins, wick trimmers, sprinkling bowls, dishes, and censers, and the gold sockets for the doors of the innermost room (the Most Holy Place) and for the doors of the main hall of the temple. {7:51} When all the work King Solomon did for the temple of the LORD was finished, he brought in the things his father David had dedicated—the silver, gold, and furnishings—and placed them in the treasuries of the LORD's temple.

{8:1} So, Solomon hit up all the OGs of Israel, the tribe leaders, and the heads of all the fams, and they pulled up to Jerusalem to bring the Ark of the Covenant from the City of David, aka Zion. {8:2} All the homies in Israel showed up for the feast in the seventh month, called Ethanim. {8:3} The elders rolled in, and the priests scooped up the Ark. {8:4} They brought the Ark of the LORD, the tabernacle, and all the holy stuff from the tabernacle, with the priests and Levites on duty. {8:5} Solomon and the whole squad sacrificed so many sheep and oxen, it was impossible to count. {8:6} The priests placed the Ark in the inner sanctuary, the Most Holy Place, under the wings of the cherubim. {8:7} The cherubim spread their wings over the Ark, covering it and its poles. {8:8} They pulled the poles out so their ends were visible from the Holy Place but not from outside, and they're still there to this day. {8:9} The Ark only had the stone tablets that Moses put there at Horeb, where the LORD made a covenant with Israel after they dipped from Egypt. {8:10} When the priests left the Holy Place, a cloud filled the house of the LORD, {8:11} and the priests couldn't even stand to minister 'cause the glory of the LORD filled the house. {8:12} Solomon said, "The LORD said He would chill in thick darkness. {8:13} I built a dope house for you to live in forever." {8:14} The king turned around and blessed the whole squad of Israel, who were all standing, {8:15} and he said, "Blessed be the LORD, the God of Israel, who talked to my dad David and made it happen, saying, {8:16} 'Since I brought Israel out of Egypt, I didn't choose a city from any tribe to build a house for my name, but I chose David to rule my people.' {8:17} My dad David wanted to build a house for the name of the LORD, the God of Israel. {8:18} But the LORD told my dad, 'You did well to want to build a house for my name, {8:19} but you're not gonna build it; your son will.' {8:20} The LORD made it happen, and now I'm king in my dad's place, sitting on the throne of Israel, just like the LORD promised, and I've built the house for the name of the LORD. {8:21} I put a spot there for the Ark, where the covenant of the LORD is, which He made with our ancestors when He brought them out of Egypt. {8:22} Solomon stood before the altar of the LORD in front of the whole squad of Israel and spread out his hands toward heaven: {8:23} and said, "LORD God of Israel, there's no God like you, in heaven above or on earth below, keeping your promises and mercy with your servants who walk before you with all their heart. {8:24} You've kept your word to my dad David; you spoke and made it happen today. {8:25} So now, LORD God of Israel, keep your promise to my dad David, saying there'll always be a man to sit on Israel's throne if they follow your way like he did. {8:26} And now, God of Israel, let your word come true, the one you spoke to my dad David. {8:27} But seriously, will God really live on earth? Even the highest heavens can't contain you, let alone this house I built. {8:28} But still, respect the prayer and plea of your servant, LORD my God, listening to the cry and prayer that your servant prays today: {8:29} That your eyes may be open toward this house day and night, the place where you said your name would be, hearing the prayer your servant prays toward this place. {8:30} Hear the plea of your servant and your people Israel when they pray toward this place; hear from heaven, your dwelling place, and forgive. {8:31} If someone sins against their neighbor and has to take an oath, and they come swear it at your altar in this house, {8:32} then hear from heaven and judge between your servants, condemning the guilty and acquitting the innocent. {8:33} When your people Israel get wrecked by an enemy because they sinned against you, and they turn back to you, confess your name, pray, and plead with you in this house, {8:34} then hear from heaven and forgive their sin and bring them back to the land you gave their ancestors. {8:35} When the sky is closed and there's no rain because they sinned against you, if they pray toward this place, confess your name, and turn from their sin when you afflict them, {8:36} then hear from heaven and forgive the sin of your servants and your people Israel, teaching them the right way to live, and send rain on the land you gave your people as an inheritance. {8:37} If there's famine, pestilence, blight, mildew, locusts, or caterpillars; if enemies besiege them in their land; whatever plague or sickness there is; {8:38} whatever prayer or plea is made by anyone or by all your people Israel, knowing the afflictions of their own hearts, and spreading out their hands toward this house, {8:39} then hear from heaven, your dwelling place, and forgive, act, and give to each according to their ways, since you know their hearts (for only you know every human heart), {8:40} so they may fear you all the time they live in the land you gave our ancestors. {8:41} As for the foreigner who isn't from your people Israel but comes from a far country for your name's sake {8:42} (for they'll hear of your great name and mighty hand and outstretched arm), when they come and pray toward this house, {8:43} hear from heaven, your dwelling place, and do whatever the foreigner asks, so all peoples of the earth may know your name and fear you, like your people Israel, and know that this house I built is called by your name. {8:44} When your people go out to battle against their enemy, wherever you send them, and they pray to the LORD toward the city you've chosen and the house I've built for your name, {8:45} then hear from heaven their prayer and plea and uphold their cause. {8:46} If they sin against you (for there's no one who doesn't sin), and you get angry with them and hand them over to the enemy, and they get taken captive to enemy land, far or near; {8:47} if they have a change of heart in the land where they're captive, repent, and plead with you, saying, 'We have sinned, done wrong, and acted wickedly'; {8:48} and if they turn back to you with all their heart and soul in the land of their enemies who took them captive, and pray to you toward their land, the city you chose, and the house I've built for your name, {8:49} then hear their prayer and plea from heaven, your dwelling place, and uphold their cause, {8:50} and forgive your people who sinned against you and all their offenses, and cause their captors to show them mercy; {8:51} for they are your people and your inheritance, whom you brought out of Egypt, from the iron furnace. {8:52} May your eyes be open to your servant's plea and to your people Israel's plea, listening to them whenever they call to you. {8:53} For you separated them from all the peoples of the earth to be your inheritance, as you declared through your servant Moses when you brought our ancestors out of Egypt, O Lord GOD." {8:54} When Solomon finished praying all this prayer and plea to the LORD, he stood up from before the altar of the LORD, where he had been kneeling with his hands spread out to heaven. {8:55} He stood and blessed the whole assembly of Israel in a loud voice, saying, {8:56} "Blessed be the LORD, who has given rest to his people Israel, according to all he promised; not one word has failed of all his good promise, which he spoke through his servant Moses. {8:57} May the LORD our God be with us as he was with our ancestors; may he never leave us nor forsake us. {8:58} May he turn our hearts to him, to walk in all his ways and keep his commands, decrees, and regulations, as he commanded our ancestors. {8:59} And may these words of mine, which I have prayed before the LORD, be near to the LORD our God day and night, that he may uphold the cause of his servant and the cause of his people Israel according to each day's need, {8:60} so that all the peoples of the earth may know that the LORD is God and there is no other. {8:61} And may your hearts be fully committed to the LORD our God, to live by his decrees and obey his commands, as at this time." {8:62} Then the king and all Israel with him offered sacrifices before the LORD. {8:63} Solomon offered a sacrifice of fellowship offerings to the LORD: twenty -two thousand cattle and a hundred and twenty thousand sheep and goats. So the king and all the Israelites dedicated the temple of the LORD. {8:64} On that same day, the king consecrated the middle part of the courtyard in front of the temple of the LORD, and there he offered burnt offerings, grain offerings, and the fat of the fellowship offerings, because the bronze altar before the LORD was too small to hold all these offerings. {8:65} So Solomon observed the festival at that time, and all Israel with him—a vast assembly, people from Lebo Hamath to the Wadi of Egypt. They celebrated it before the LORD our God for seven days and seven days more, fourteen days in all. {8:66} On the eighth day, he sent the people away. They blessed the king and went home, joyful and glad in heart for all the good things the LORD had done for his servant David and his people Israel.

{9:1} After Solomon finished building the house of the LORD, his own crib, and everything he wanted to do, {9:2} the LORD showed up to Solomon again, like before at Gibeon. {9:3} The LORD told him, "I heard your prayer and supplication, and I've made this house holy, where I put my name forever; my eyes and heart will always be here. {9:4} If you walk before me like your dad David, with integrity and doing everything I commanded, keeping my rules and judgments, {9:5} then I'll keep your kingdom's throne in Israel forever, just like I promised David—there'll always be someone on Israel's throne. {9:6} But if you or your kids start slippin' and don't keep my commands and go worship other gods, {9:7} I'll kick Israel out of the land I gave them, ditch this house I made holy for my name, and Israel will become a joke and insult among all people. {9:8} Passersby at this high house will be shocked and hiss, asking why the LORD did this to the land and house. {9:9} They'll answer, 'They left the LORD their God who brought their ancestors out of Egypt, got into other gods, and worshipped them—that's why the LORD brought all this trouble.' {9:10} Twenty years later, after Solomon built the two houses—the LORD's house and his own place, {9:11} King Hiram of Tyre wasn't feelin' the twenty cities Solomon gave him in Galilee, {9:12} so Hiram checked out the cities Solomon gave him, but they were trash to him. {9:13} Hiram was like, 'What are these cities, bro?' and he still calls them the Land of Cabul today. {9:14} Hiram sent the king six hundred and sixty talents of gold. {9:15} This was why King Solomon raised a levy: to build the house of the LORD, his own place, and Millo, the wall of Jerusalem, Hazor, Megiddo, and Gezer. {9:16} Pharaoh of Egypt had taken Gezer, burned it, killed the Canaanites there, and gave it as a wedding gift to Solomon's wife, Pharaoh's daughter. {9:17} Solomon rebuilt Gezer, Beth-horon lower, {9:18} Baalath, and Tadmor in the wilderness, {9:19} all the storage cities, chariot cities, horsemen cities, and everything Solomon wanted to build in Jerusalem, Lebanon, and his whole kingdom. {9:20} Solomon put the leftover Amorites, Hittites, Perizzites, Hivites, and Jebusites to work as slaves. {9:21} The Israelites couldn't fully wipe them out, so Solomon made them pay tribute as forced labor. {9:22} But he didn't enslave any Israelites; they were soldiers, servants, princes, captains, chariot officers, and cavalry. {9:23} These were the top dogs over Solomon's workforce—five hundred and fifty in charge of the workers. {9:24} Pharaoh's daughter moved to her house in the City of David that Solomon built for her, and then he built up Millo. {9:25} Solomon sacrificed three times a year at the altar he built for the LORD, burning incense at the altar in front of the LORD. He finished the house. {9:26} Solomon also had a fleet of ships at Ezion-Geber, by Eloth on the Red Sea in Edom. {9:27} Hiram sent his sea-savvy sailors with Solomon's crew. {9:28} They sailed to Ophir, got four hundred and twenty talents of gold, and brought it back to King Solomon.

{10:1} So, like, when the queen of Sheba heard about how lit Solomon's rep was because of the LORD's name, she came to test him with tough questions. {10:2} She rolled up to Jerusalem with a massive crew, camels loaded with spices, tons of gold, and precious stones, and when she met Solomon, they had a heart-to-heart about everything on her mind. {10:3} Solomon spilled all the tea—didn't keep anything from her. {10:4} When the queen of Sheba saw Solomon's wisdom and the crib he built, {10:5} his lavish meals, his servants' swag, their fresh threads, his cupbearers, and how he climbed up to the house of the LORD, she was blown away. {10:6} She told him, "Everything I heard back home about your moves and wisdom was true." {10:7} "I wasn't sure until I came and saw it with my own eyes—what I heard doesn't even scratch the surface. Your wisdom and success are way beyond the hype." {10:8} "Your crew is blessed to be around you, hearing your wisdom all day." {10:9} "Praise the LORD your God who put you on Israel's throne because He loves Israel forever, making you king to serve justice." {10:10} She hooked Solomon up with 120 talents of gold, loads of spices, and precious stones—never seen such a spice stash like what she gave him. {10:11} Also, Hiram's navy brought back mad almug trees and precious stones from Ophir. {10:12} Solomon used the almug trees to make pillars for the house of the LORD and his own crib, plus harps and lyres for the singers—no trees like those before or since. {10:13} Solomon granted the queen of Sheba everything she asked for, besides what he already gave her out of his royal generosity. Then she bounced back to her country with her squad. {10:14} In one year, Solomon got 666 talents of gold. {10:15} Plus, he cashed in from merchants, spice traders, and all the Arab kings and governors. {10:16} Solomon made 200 gold shields, each weighing 600 shekels of gold. {10:17} He also crafted 300 golden shields, each weighing three pounds of gold, and put them in the House of the Forest of Lebanon. {10:18} Solomon made a sick ivory throne, overlaying it with top-tier gold. {10:19} The throne had six steps, and the back was round, with arms on each side of the seat and two lions beside them. {10:20} Twelve lions stood on the steps, like none ever made in any kingdom. {10:21} All of Solomon's drinking vessels were gold, and all the House of the Forest of Lebanon's vessels were pure gold—no silver, not a big deal in Solomon's time. {10:22} Solomon had a fleet of Tarshish ships with Hiram's navy. Every three years, they brought gold, silver, ivory, apes, and peacocks. {10:23} Solomon surpassed all earth's kings in wealth and wisdom. {10:24} Everyone on earth wanted to hear Solomon's wisdom, which God put in his heart. {10:25} They brought him gifts—silver and gold items, clothes, armor, spices, horses, and mules—every year. {10:26} Solomon collected chariots and horsemen, amassing 1400 chariots and 12,000 horsemen stationed in cities and with him in Jerusalem. {10:27} Silver was as common as rocks in Jerusalem, and he had cedar trees aplenty, like sycamores in the valley, abundant. {10:28} Solomon imported horses from Egypt, paying top dollar to his merchants for linen yarn. {10:29} A chariot from Egypt went for 600 shekels of silver, a horse for 150, supplied for all the Hittite and Syrian kings through Solomon's dealers.

{11:1} So, like, King Solomon was really into a lot of foreign women, including Pharaoh's daughter, Moabites, Ammonites, Edomites, Sidonians, and Hittites—totally not the nations Israel was supposed to be mixing with, as the LORD had said. {11:2} God warned Israel not to get involved with these other peeps, saying they'd lead them away from Him. But Solomon was all heart-eyes for them. {11:3} He ended up with 700 wives, who were princesses, and 300 side chicks, and they totally turned his heart away from God. {11:4} When Solomon got old, his wives got him hooked on other gods, and his heart wasn't fully with the LORD like his dad David's. {11:5} Solomon started worshiping Ashtoreth, the Sidonian goddess, and Milcom, the Ammonite god—major betrayal. {11:6} He did a lot of bad stuff in God's sight and didn't stay loyal like David. {11:7} Solomon even built altars for Chemosh, the Moabite god, and Molech, the Ammonite god, just to please his foreign wives who were all about that incense and sacrifices. {11:8} All because of his foreign wives, Solomon went all-in on their gods. {11:9} God was super mad 'cause Solomon's heart was turned away, even though God had appeared to him twice! {11:10} God specifically told him not to follow other gods, but Solomon didn't listen. {11:11} So, God said to Solomon, "Since you've messed up big time and didn't keep our deal, I'm taking the kingdom from you and giving it to one of your servants. {11:12} I'll wait until after you're gone out of respect for your dad David, but your son will lose most of it." {11:13} "I won't take it all, though—keeping one tribe for David's sake and for the sake of Jerusalem, the city I chose." {11:14} Then God stirred up enemies against Solomon, like Hadad the Edomite, who fled to Egypt as a kid and later caused trouble for Solomon. {11:15} Hadad was mad 'cause David messed up his people in Edom, so he caused issues for Israel during Solomon's rule.

{12:1} So, Rehoboam rolled up to Shechem because all of Israel was there to crown him king. {12:2} Jeroboam, who had been hiding out in Egypt, heard about it and came back. {12:3} They sent for him, and Jeroboam and all Israel came to Rehoboam, saying, {12:4} "Your dad made life rough for us. Can you lighten up and we'll be cool with you?" {12:5} Rehoboam told them to come back in three days for an answer. {12:6} He asked the old heads who served Solomon for advice on what to say. {12:7} They said, "If you serve the people today and speak kindly, they'll be loyal forever." {12:8} But Rehoboam ditched their advice and asked his bros for input. {12:9} They said, "Tell them, 'My little finger is thicker than my dad's waist. {12:10} He whipped you, but I'll whip you with scorpions.'" {12:11} When Jeroboam and the people returned, Rehoboam told them he'd be even tougher than his dad. {12:12} When Israel saw this, they said, "We have no part in David's kingdom! Let's go back to our own homes." {12:17} The people of Judah stuck with Rehoboam, but Israel rebelled. {12:18} Rehoboam sent Adoram, who collected taxes, and Israel stoned him to death. Rehoboam fled back to Jerusalem. {12:19} Israel rebelled against the house of David from then on. {12:20} When Jeroboam returned, Israel made him king, except for Judah. {12:21} Rehoboam gathered troops to fight Israel and reclaim the kingdom. {12:22} But God told Shemaiah to tell them not to fight. {12:23} So they listened to God and went home. {12:25} Jeroboam fortified Shechem and Penuel. {12:26} He worried Israel would turn back to Rehoboam if they went to Jerusalem to worship, so he set up golden calves in Bethel and Dan, saying they were their gods who brought them out of Egypt. {12:31} He set up his own priests and altars, making his own feast days.

{13:1} Yo, check it, this dude straight outta Judah, on a word from the LORD, shows up in Bethel, where Jeroboam's burning incense. {13:2} He starts preaching against the altar, saying, "Yo altar, listen up! The LORD says a kid named Josiah from David's fam is gonna wreck this place, offering up these sketchy priests and even burning human bones on you." {13:3} Then he pulls a miracle, making the altar split and ashes pour out, just like the LORD said. {13:4} When Jeroboam hears this, he tries to grab him, but his hand dries up and he can't pull it back. {13:5} The altar splits and ashes spill out, just like the man of God said. {13:6} Jeroboam asks him to pray for his hand to heal, and it does. {13:7} Then Jeroboam's like, "Come chill at my place and I'll hook you up." {13:8} But the man of God's like, "Nah, not even for half your house. The LORD told me not to eat or drink here." {13:9} The LORD commanded me not to eat or drink here or return the same way I came." {13:10} So he leaves a different way. {13:11} Now, there's this old prophet in Bethel, and his sons spill the tea about what the man of God did. {13:12} The old prophet's like, "Which way did he go?" {13:13} He tells his sons to saddle up the donkey, and he goes after him. {13:14} He finds him under an oak and asks if he's the man of God from Judah. {13:15} Then he's like, "Come kick it at my place and have some grub." {13:16} But the man of God's like, "No can do, gotta follow the LORD's orders and not eat or drink here." {13:17} The LORD said no food, no drink, and don't come back the same way." {13:18} The old prophet's like, "I'm a prophet too, and an angel told me to bring you back to my crib to eat and drink." But he was lying. {13:19} So the man of God goes with him, eats and drinks. {13:20} While they're eating, the LORD's word comes to the prophet who brought him back. {13:21} The prophet tells the man of God from Judah that because he disobeyed the LORD, his body won't even get buried with his fam. {13:22} He ate and drank where he wasn't supposed to, so he won't rest with his ancestors. {13:23} After eating and drinking, he saddles up the donkey for the prophet he brought back. {13:24} On his way, a lion kills him, leaving his body in the road with the donkey and the lion standing there. {13:25} People see it and spread the word in the city where the old prophet lives. {13:26} When the old prophet hears, he's like, "That's the man of God who disobeyed the LORD." {13:27} He tells his sons to saddle the donkey again. {13:28} They find the body, the donkey, and the lion, and the lion hasn't eaten the body or hurt the donkey. {13:29} The prophet buries the man of God and mourns him. {13:30} He puts him in his own grave, and they mourn, saying, "Oh no, my brother!" {13:31} Then he tells his sons to bury him next to the man of God. {13:32} The LORD's word against the altar in Bethel and other high places will come true. {13:33} After this, Jeroboam keeps doing evil, appointing unqualified priests to high places. {13:34} This leads to sin for Jeroboam's house, setting them up for destruction.

{14:1} So, like, Abijah, Jeroboam's son, got sick. {14:2} Jeroboam tells his wife, "Yo, disguise yourself and head to Shiloh to find Ahijah the prophet. He's the one who told me I'd be king." {14:3} He sends her with some bread, cracknels, and honey, and tells her Ahijah will know what's up with the kid. {14:4} Jeroboam's wife does as he says, heads to Shiloh, and finds Ahijah's house, but Ahijah's too old to see. {14:5} The LORD tells Ahijah, "Jeroboam's wife is coming about her son, who's sick. When she shows up, pretend she's someone else." {14:6} As soon as Ahijah hears her, he's like, "Come in, Jeroboam's wife! Why the disguise? I've got heavy news for you." {14:7} Ahijah tells her to let Jeroboam know the LORD's not happy because even though he was exalted as king, he hasn't been faithful like David. {14:8} The LORD took the kingdom from David's house and gave it to Jeroboam, but he's been making other gods and idols, totally ticking off the LORD. {14:9} So, the LORD's gonna bring disaster on Jeroboam's house, wiping out every male descendant and leaving it like dung until it's gone. {14:10} Dogs will eat those who die in the city, and birds will eat those who die in the fields, just like the LORD said. {14:11} Jeroboam's wife is told to head back, and when she gets home, the child will die. {14:12} This is because he's the only one in Jeroboam's house who's decent before the LORD. {14:13} Israel will mourn and bury him, the only one in Jeroboam's family to get a proper burial, because of his good heart toward the LORD. {14:14} Also, the LORD will raise up a new king over Israel who will wipe out Jeroboam's house that very day. {14:15} The LORD will punish Israel like shaking a reed in water, uprooting them from this good land because they've been setting up groves and making the LORD angry. {14:16} Israel will suffer because of Jeroboam's sins, leading them into sin. {14:17} Jeroboam's wife heads back to Tirzah, and as soon as she reaches the doorstep, the child dies. {14:18} They bury him, and all Israel mourns according to what the LORD said through Ahijah. {14:19} You can read more about Jeroboam's deeds and reign in the history books of Israel's kings. {14:20} Jeroboam ruled for twenty-two years and then kicked it. His son Nadab took over. {14:21} Rehoboam, Solomon's son, starts ruling in Judah. He was forty-one when he began and reigned for seventeen years in Jerusalem, the LORD's chosen city. His mom's name was Naamah, an Ammonite. {14:22} But Judah was messed up, doing things that made the LORD mad, like setting up high places, idols, and groves all over. {14:23} They even had male prostitutes in the land, doing all the disgusting stuff the LORD had kicked out other nations for. {14:24} Shady stuff was going down. {14:25} In Rehoboam's fifth year, Shishak, Egypt's king, attacks Jerusalem. {14:26} He loots the treasures from the LORD's house and Rehoboam's palace, taking everything, even the gold shields Solomon made. {14:27} Rehoboam replaces them with bronze shields and hands them over to the palace guard. {14:28} When the king goes to the LORD's house, the guard brings out and returns the shields to their chamber. {14:29} If you wanna know more about Rehoboam's story, check out the chronicles of Judah's kings. {14:30} Rehoboam and Jeroboam kept beefing all their lives. {14:31} Rehoboam dies and gets buried in David's city. His mom was Naamah the Ammonite. His son Abijam takes over.

{15:1} So, like, in the eighteenth year of King Jeroboam, Abijam started ruling over Judah. {15:2} He was in charge for three years in Jerusalem. His mom's name was Maachah, daughter of Abishalom. {15:3} Abijam followed all the sinful ways of his dad, Jeroboam, and wasn't fully committed to the LORD like David. {15:4} But the LORD, for David's sake, let Abijam be a light in Jerusalem and establish his son after him to keep the city strong. {15:5} David did what was right, except for Uriah's incident. {15:6} The beef between Rehoboam and Jeroboam kept going. {15:7} You can find more about Abijam's deeds in Judah's kings' chronicles. The war between Abijam and Jeroboam kept going. {15:8} Abijam passed away and was buried in the city of David. His son Asa took over. {15:9} In the twentieth year of Jeroboam, Asa became king of Judah. {15:10} He ruled for forty-one years in Jerusalem. His mom's name was Maachah, daughter of Abishalom. {15:11} Asa did right by the LORD, like his dad David. {15:12} He cleaned up the land, getting rid of the wrong stuff his ancestors made. {15:13} He even stripped his mom Maachah of her queen status for making an idol. {15:14} Asa's heart was loyal to the LORD, even though some high places stayed. {15:15} He brought dedication gifts to the LORD's house—silver, gold, and vessels. {15:16} Asa was at war with Baasha, the king of Israel, throughout his reign. {15:17} Baasha of Israel built Ramah to block off Judah from coming and going. {15:18} Asa took the remaining treasures from the LORD's house and his palace and sent them to Benhadad of Syria to break Baasha's alliance. {15:19} Asa's like, "Let's make a deal, dude." Benhadad agrees and sends his forces to hit Israel's cities. {15:20} Baasha hears this and stops building Ramah, staying in Tirzah. {15:22} Asa announces throughout Judah that everyone's gotta help tear down Baasha's fortifications, using the materials to rebuild Geba and Mizpah. {15:23} More about Asa's deeds and cities are in Judah's kings' records. He got sick in his old age. {15:24} Asa passed away and was buried with his fathers in David's city. His son Jehoshaphat took over. {15:25} Nadab, Jeroboam's son, began ruling over Israel in Asa's second year, reigning for two years. {15:26} He messed up like his dad, making Israel sin. {15:27} Baasha of Issachar's house conspired against Nadab and killed him at Gibbethon during a siege. {15:28} Baasha took over in Asa's third year and wiped out Jeroboam's entire family, just as the LORD had foretold through Ahijah. {15:29} It was all because of Jeroboam's sins that angered the LORD. {15:31} The rest of Nadab's story is in Israel's kings' chronicles. {15:32} Asa and Baasha kept at it, fighting throughout their lives. {15:33} Baasha began his reign over all Israel in Tirzah, ruling for twenty-four years. {15:34} But he kept doing evil, following Jeroboam's sinful ways that led Israel astray.

{16:1} Then the LORD spoke to Jehu, Hanani's son, about Baasha, like, saying, {16:2} "Dude, I raised you up from nothing and made you a ruler over my people Israel. But you've been following Jeroboam's bad vibes, leading my people to sin and ticking me off with their sins." {16:3} "Now I'm gonna wipe out Baasha's descendants and his whole house, making your house just like Jeroboam's." {16:4} "Dogs will chow down on those who die in the city, and birds will feast on those who die in the fields." {16:5} You can read more about Baasha's life in Israel's kings' chronicles. {16:6} Baasha died and was buried in Tirzah, and then his son Elah took over. {16:7} The prophet Jehu, Hanani's son, also spoke the word of the LORD against Baasha and his house for all the evil he did, provoking the LORD to anger like Jeroboam and also for killing him. {16:8} Elah, Baasha's son, began ruling over Israel in Tirzah in Asa's twenty-sixth year, ruling for two years. {16:9} One of his chariot captains, Zimri, plotted against him while he was getting wasted at Arza's place in Tirzah. {16:10} Zimri rolled in, killed Elah in Asa's twenty-seventh year, and took over. {16:11} Zimri wasted no time and wiped out Baasha's entire family as soon as he took the throne—no survivors. {16:12} This fulfilled the LORD's prophecy against Baasha through Jehu the prophet. {16:13} It was all because of Baasha and Elah's sins, leading Israel astray with their idolatry. {16:14} You can read more about Elah's deeds and life in Israel's kings' chronicles. {16:15} Zimri's reign lasted only seven days in Tirzah in Asa's twenty-seventh year. The people were busy besieging Gibbethon, a Philistine town. {16:16} When they heard Zimri had offed the king, they rallied behind Omri, the army captain, making him king right then and there at the camp. {16:17} Omri and all Israel marched from Gibbethon and besieged Tirzah. {16:18} When Zimri saw the city was lost, he went into the palace and set it on fire, dying in the flames because of his sins, provoking the LORD like Jeroboam did. {16:19} More about Zimri's acts and betrayal are in Israel's kings' chronicles. {16:21} Israel split into two camps: some backed Tibni, Ginath's son, as king, while others supported Omri. {16:22} Omri's crew won out, Tibni bit the dust, and Omri reigned. {16:23} Omri started his rule over Israel in Asa's thirty-first year, reigning for twelve years, six in Tirzah. {16:24} He bought the hill of Samaria from Shemer for two talents of silver, built a city there, and named it Samaria after Shemer, the hill's owner. {16:25} But Omri was a real letdown to the LORD, worse than all before him. {16:26} He followed Jeroboam's lead, leading Israel into sin and provoking the LORD with their idolatry. {16:27} More about Omri's deeds and power are in Israel's kings' chronicles. {16:28} Omri died and was buried in Samaria, and his son Ahab took over. {16:29} Ahab, Omri's son, started ruling over Israel in Asa's thirty-eighth year, reigning in Samaria for twenty-two years. {16:30} Ahab was the worst yet, ticking off the LORD more than anyone before him. {16:31-32} And as if that wasn't bad enough, he married Jezebel, Ethbaal's daughter, king of the Sidonians, and started serving Baal, building an altar and shrine for Baal in Samaria. {16:33} Ahab outdid all the previous kings of Israel in provoking the LORD.

{17:1} So, Elijah the Tishbite, from Gilead, straight up told Ahab, "As the LORD God of Israel lives, I swear there won't be any dew or rain for years, except when I say so." {17:2} Then the LORD hit him up, saying, "Yo, head east and chill by the brook Cherith near the Jordan River." {17:3} "You'll drink from the brook, and I've told some ravens to bring you food there." {17:4} So Elijah did just that, posted up by the brook, and the ravens hooked him up with bread and meat every morning and evening; and he drank from the brook. {17:7} After a while, though, the brook dried up because of the drought. {17:8} Then the LORD hit Elijah up again, saying, "Get up and go to Zarephath in Sidon; I've told a widow there to take care of you." {17:10} So he went to Zarephath and saw a widow gathering sticks. {17:11} He called out to her, "Can you bring me some water to drink?" {17:11} As she went, he asked for bread too. {17:12} She was like, "I swear, I only have a bit of flour and oil left to make one last meal for me and my son before we die." {17:13} But Elijah reassured her, "Don't stress, just make me a small cake first; then you can make some for yourself and your son." {17:14} "The flour won't run out and the oil won't run dry until it rains again." {17:15} She did as he said, and they ate for days without running out of food. {17:16} The flour and oil never ran out, just like the LORD said through Elijah. {17:17} Later, the widow's son got seriously sick to the point of death. {17:18} She was upset and thought Elijah was there to remind her of her sins and take her son away. {17:19} Elijah took the boy to an upstairs room, laid him on his bed, and cried out to the LORD, "Have you brought this tragedy on the widow I'm staying with by taking her son?" {17:21} Elijah stretched out over the boy three times, crying out to the LORD, "Please, bring this boy's soul back." {17:22} The LORD heard Elijah's prayer, and the boy came back to life. {17:23} Elijah brought the boy downstairs and gave him to his mom, saying, "Look, your son is alive." {17:24} The woman was convinced then that Elijah was a man of God, and that the LORD's word through him was true.

{18:1} So, after a bunch of days, the LORD hit up Elijah in the third year, saying, "Go show yourself to Ahab; I'll make it rain again." {18:2} Elijah rolled up to Ahab, and there was a serious famine in Samaria. {18:3} Ahab called Obadiah, his house manager, who was a big-time God-fearing dude. {18:4} When Jezebel was offing the LORD's prophets, Obadiah hid a hundred in caves, feeding them. {18:5} Ahab told Obadiah, "Go check all the water sources; maybe we can find grass to save the animals." {18:6} They split up; Ahab went one way, Obadiah another. {18:7} As Obadiah was heading out, bam! Elijah showed up. Obadiah recognized him, fell down, and was like, "Are you my guy Elijah?" {18:8} Elijah was like, "Yup, go tell your boss Ahab, Elijah's in the house." {18:9} Obadiah was worried, "Why you tryna get me killed by Ahab? I've been loyal to God since forever!" {18:10} "I swear, Ahab's been looking for you everywhere, making everyone swear you're not around." {18:11} "Now you want me to tell him you're here? He'll kill me when you disappear!" {18:12-16} Elijah reassured him, "I'm showing myself to Ahab today, no disappearing act." {18:16} Obadiah found Ahab and spilled the beans; Ahab went to meet Elijah. {18:17} When Ahab saw Elijah, he was like, "Are you the troublemaker of Israel?" {18:18} Elijah was quick to set the record straight, "I'm not the problem; you and your fam are for ditching God's commands and following Baal." {18:19} "Gather all Israel and the Baal prophets to Mount Carmel." {18:20} Ahab rounded up everyone to Mount Carmel. {18:21} Elijah called out to the people, "How long are you gonna be indecisive? If the LORD is God, follow Him; if it's Baal, go for it." {18:22} "I'm the only prophet of the LORD left, but there are 450 Baal prophets here." {18:23-38} "Let's each set up a bull sacrifice, and whichever God answers with fire is the real deal." {18:39} When the LORD sent fire that consumed the sacrifice, wood, stones, and water, everyone was convinced. {18:40} Elijah took down the Baal prophets at the brook Kishon. {18:41} Elijah told Ahab, "Get ready, rain's coming." {18:42} Ahab ate and drank while Elijah went up to Carmel's peak, praying for rain. {18:43} He sent his servant to check the sea; after seven tries, a small cloud appeared. {18:44} Elijah told Ahab to get moving before the rain blocked him. {18:45} And sure enough, heavy rain fell as Ahab headed to Jezreel. {18:46} The LORD powered up Elijah, who outran Ahab to Jezreel's entrance.

{19:1} So, Ahab spilled the tea to Jezebel about all that Elijah had done, including taking out all the prophets. {19:2} Jezebel sent a message to Elijah, swearing she'd make him pay with his life by tomorrow. {19:3} When he heard that, he bolted and headed to Beer-sheba in Judah, leaving his servant behind. {19:4} Elijah kept going into the wilderness, sat under a tree, and straight-up asked to die, feeling like he wasn't any better than his ancestors. {19:5} While he crashed out under the tree, an angel woke him up and told him to eat. {19:6} Elijah found a cake and water by his head, so he ate and drank and crashed out again. {19:7} The angel came back, woke him up, and told him to eat again because he had a long trip ahead. {19:8} Elijah ate, drank, and then powered through with that meal for forty days and nights until he reached Mount Horeb. {19:9} He got to a cave and stayed there. The LORD hit him up and asked, "What are you doing here, Elijah?" {19:10} Elijah explained he'd been super loyal to the LORD, but Israel had ditched the covenant, torn down altars, and killed prophets, leaving him as the last one hunted down. {19:11} The LORD told him to stand on the mount, and then wild stuff happened—wind, earthquake, fire—but the LORD wasn't in any of it. {19:12} After all that, there was a quiet voice. {19:13} When Elijah heard it, he covered his face and went to the cave entrance. The voice asked again, "What are you doing here, Elijah?" {19:14} Elijah gave the same rundown about being the last loyal prophet. {19:15-16} The LORD told him to go back, anoint Hazael as king over Syria, anoint Jehu as king over Israel, and anoint Elisha as prophet to take over. {19:17-18} The LORD mentioned the surviving ones, and there were actually seven thousand who hadn't bowed to Baal. {19:19} So Elijah went and found Elisha plowing with twelve oxen, tossed his mantle over him, and dipped. {19:20} Elisha asked to say bye to his fam, but Elijah was like, "Do you, I didn't do anything to you." {19:21} Elisha roasted his oxen for the people, said peace out to his old life, and followed Elijah.

{20:1} So, Ben-hadad, the king of Syria, gathered all his crew—thirty-two kings, along with horses and chariots—and rolled up to Samaria to start some drama. {20:2} He sent messengers to Ahab, claiming all the gold, silver, and even the best-looking wives and kids as his own. {20:3} Ahab was like, "Sure, whatever you say, boss." {20:4} When the messengers came back demanding even more, Ahab was like, "Hold up, this dude's trippin'." {20:6} Ben-hadad was planning to send his crew to raid Ahab's crib the next day. {20:7} Ahab called the elders and was like, "This dude is shady, trying to take my family and riches." {20:8} Everyone agreed with Ahab—don't let Ben-hadad have his way. {20:10} Ben-hadad got all cocky, swearing that Samaria would be covered in dust by his troops. {20:11} Ahab responded, basically saying, "Don't count your chickens before they hatch." {20:12} When Ben-hadad heard this, he called to gear up and set up against the city. {20:13} Then a prophet showed up to Ahab, saying the LORD would hand over the enemy army that day. {20:14} Ahab was like, "Who's gonna make this happen?" {20:15} The prophet said it would be done by young leaders from the provinces. Ahab was put in charge of the battle. {20:16-19} They went out at noon while Ben-hadad was getting wasted with his kings. {20:20-27} The Israelites attacked, and the Syrians ran off while Ahab wrecked their horses and chariots. The prophet told Ahab to prepare for another round next year. {20:28} The Syrians thought Israel's God only worked in the hills, but they were about to learn a lesson. {20:29} The battle lasted seven days, and on the seventh, the Israelites wrecked the Syrians, killing a hundred thousand foot soldiers. {20:30} The survivors fled into the city, and a wall fell on twenty-seven thousand of them. Ben-hadad ended up hiding. {20:31} Ben-hadad's crew suggested they surrender to Ahab, hoping for mercy. {20:32} They came to Ahab with ropes around their heads, asking to spare Ben-hadad. Ahab called Ben-hadad "bro" and brought him in. {20:35} Then a prophet told another guy to hit him, but he refused. {20:36} The prophet said he'd be eaten by a lion for disobeying. {20:37} He asked someone else, who did hit him but also wounded him. {20:38} The prophet disguised himself with ashes and waited for Ahab. {20:39} He told Ahab a story about losing a prisoner and being held responsible. {20:40-41} Ahab basically said, "Your fault, your problem." {20:42} The prophet revealed himself and told Ahab he'd pay for letting someone escape destruction. {20:43} Ahab went home bummed out.

{21:1} So, there's this guy Naboth from Jezreel who had a sweet vineyard next to King Ahab's palace. {21:2-3} Ahab asked Naboth to hand over his vineyard, offering to trade it for a garden or pay up in cash, but Naboth refused, saying it's his family inheritance. {21:4} Ahab was so bummed about this that he sulked in bed and refused to eat. {21:5-6} Jezebel came in like, "Why you so down? Eat something!" {21:7-8} Jezebel basically told Ahab to man up and enjoy life, promising she'd take care of Naboth's vineyard for him. {21:9-14} She sent letters to the city elders to falsely accuse Naboth of blasphemy and get him stoned. {21:15-18} When Jezebel heard Naboth was dead, she told Ahab to go claim the vineyard. {21:19} Then Elijah shows up, telling Ahab he's in deep trouble for killing Naboth and taking the vineyard. {21:20-21} Ahab's like, "Oh great, my enemy found me," and Elijah calls him out for his evil deeds. {21:22} Elijah warns Ahab that his whole family line will face consequences for his sins. {21:23} Jezebel's fate is sealed too—she'll be eaten by dogs in Jezreel. {21:24} Ahab was the worst, influenced by his wife Jezebel to worship idols and do evil stuff. {21:25} When Ahab hears Elijah's words, he's all remorseful, wearing sackcloth and fasting. {21:26} Because Ahab humbled himself, God decided not to bring disaster in his lifetime but would punish his descendants instead.

{22:1} So, Syria and Israel chilled without any war for like three years straight. {22:2} Then in the third year, Jehoshaphat, the king of Judah, rolls up to hang with the king of Israel. {22:3} The king of Israel's like, "Yo, Ramoth in Gilead should totally be ours, but we're sleeping on it while Syria's king still holds it. {22:4} Wanna roll with me to battle for Ramoth-gilead?" Jehoshaphat's like, "Yeah, bro, I'm down. Your crew is my crew, your horses are my horses." {22:5} Jehoshaphat's all about consulting the Lord first. {22:6} So, the king of Israel gathers like four hundred prophets and asks them, "Should we go to battle at Ramoth-gilead?" And they're all like, "Yeah, dude, the Lord's got your back." {22:7} Jehoshaphat's not convinced and asks, "Isn't there another prophet of the Lord around here?" {22:8} The king of Israel's like, "Well, there's Micaiah, but I hate him because he never says anything good about me, always brings bad news." Jehoshaphat's like, "Come on, don't diss him." {22:9} So, they call for Micaiah. {22:10} The kings are chilling, looking all regal, and all the prophets are hyping them up. {22:11} Zedekiah's there making a show with iron horns, claiming the Lord will help defeat Syria. {22:12} All the prophets are chanting the same thing—go conquer Ramoth-gilead, you'll succeed. {22:13} The messenger tells Micaiah to get with the program and say something positive. {22:14} But Micaiah's like, "I'll only speak what the Lord tells me." {22:15} When Micaiah faces the kings, he tells them to go ahead and battle, they'll win because the Lord's on their side. {22:16} The king's not buying it and asks Micaiah to speak the truth from the Lord. {22:17} Micaiah shares a vision of scattered sheep without a shepherd, and the Lord says they should all go home in peace. {22:18} The king of Israel complains to Jehoshaphat, "See, I told you he's always negative." {22:19} Micaiah reveals a vision of the Lord and heavenly hosts discussing how to bring Ahab down. {22:20} A spirit offers to deceive Ahab's prophets, and the Lord approves the plan. {22:21} The spirit heads out to deceive. {22:22} The Lord allows this lying spirit to influence the prophets. {22:23} Micaiah explains how the Lord permitted lies to be spoken through the prophets. {22:24} Zedekiah gets mad and hits Micaiah, questioning how the Lord's spirit left him. {22:25} Micaiah warns Zedekiah about hiding from the consequences. {22:26} The king orders Micaiah's imprisonment. {22:27} Micaiah predicts that if the king returns safely, then the Lord didn't speak through him. {22:28} Micaiah warns the people to pay attention. {22:29} Despite all this drama, the kings go to battle. {22:30} The king of Israel disguises himself while Jehoshaphat rocks his royal robes. {22:31} The king of Syria orders his captains to focus on capturing the king of Israel. {22:32} Mistaken identity leads to chaos until Jehoshaphat calls out. {22:33} Realizing their mistake, the Syrians stop pursuing Jehoshaphat. {22:34} A random arrow hits the king of Israel, who's wounded and wants out of the battle. {22:35} The king dies, and the battle ends. {22:36} The troops disperse as the sun sets. {22:37} They bring the king's body to Samaria for burial. {22:38} His chariot's washed where dogs lick his blood, as prophesied. {22:39} You can read more about Ahab's wild life in the history books. {22:40} Ahab dies, and his son Ahaziah takes over. {22:41} Meanwhile, Jehoshaphat rules over Judah, and he's all about that peace with Israel. {22:42} Jehoshaphat was thirty-five when he started ruling and reigned for twenty-five years in Jerusalem. {22:43} He was a good king but didn't remove the high places of worship. {22:44} Jehoshaphat and Israel were cool with each other. {22:45} You can read more about Jehoshaphat's reign in the history books. {22:46} He cleaned up the remnants of idol worship left from his dad's time. {22:47} Edom didn't have its own king, just a deputy. {22:48} Jehoshaphat tried to send ships for gold but faced some setbacks. {22:49} Ahaziah wants to tag along on a voyage, but Jehoshaphat's not having it. {22:50} Jehoshaphat passes away, and his son Jehoram takes over. {22:51} Ahaziah starts ruling Israel and keeps up the idol-worshipping family tradition.

2 Kings

+++

{1:1} So, Moab decided to rebel against Israel after Ahab kicked it. {1:2} Ahaziah, the king of Israel, took a tumble through a lattice in his crib in Samaria and got sick. He sent messengers to ask Baal-zebub, the god of Ekron, if he'd recover from his illness. {1:3} But the angel of the Lord told Elijah, "Get up, go meet the king's messengers, and tell them, 'Isn't it because Israel doesn't have a God that you're running to Baal-zebub?'" {1:4} Elijah relayed God's message that Ahaziah wouldn't recover but would die in bed. Then Elijah bounced. {1:5} When the messengers returned without going to Ekron, Elijah was like, "Why'd you come back?" {1:6} They explained, "Some dude met us and told us to go back to the king with the same message from the Lord." {1:7} Ahaziah asked what this man looked like, and they described Elijah. {1:8} The king then sent a captain with fifty soldiers to get Elijah, who was chilling on a hilltop. The captain told Elijah the king wanted him to come down. {1:10} Elijah was like, "If I'm a man of God, let fire come down from heaven and toast you and your fifty soldiers." And it happened—fire consumed them. {1:11-12} The king sent another captain with fifty, but the same thing happened again. {1:13} Finally, a third captain came humbly, fell before Elijah, and begged for mercy for himself and his men. {1:14-15} The angel of the Lord told Elijah to go with this captain, and not to fear him. Elijah then went with him to the king. {1:16} Elijah repeated the Lord's message to Ahaziah, that seeking answers from Baal-zebub showed a lack of faith in God, and he would die in bed. {1:17} Ahaziah died as Elijah prophesied, and Jehoram took over in his place. {1:18} You can read more about Ahaziah's reign in the history books of Israel's kings.

{2:1} So, one day the Lord was about to snatch Elijah up to heaven in a whirlwind, and Elijah was rolling with Elisha from Gilgal. {2:2} Elijah told Elisha, "Stay here; I gotta go to Bethel 'cause the Lord sent me." Elisha was like, "I'm ride or die, man. I ain't leaving you." So they headed to Bethel. {2:3} The prophet crew in Bethel came to Elisha like, "You know Elijah's gonna be taken away today, right?" Elisha was like, "Yeah, I know. Chill out." {2:4} Then Elijah told Elisha, "Stay here in Jericho; I gotta go there 'cause the Lord sent me." Elisha's response was, "I'm sticking with you, bro." So off they went to Jericho. {2:5} The prophet squad in Jericho approached Elisha with the same news, and he was like, "Yeah, I got it. Calm down." {2:6} Elijah told Elisha again to stay put in Jordan, but Elisha was all in. They went together. {2:7} Fifty of the prophet crew watched from afar as they stood by the Jordan. {2:8} Elijah took his mantle, smacked the water, and bam! They walked over on dry ground. {2:9} After crossing, Elijah asked Elisha what he wanted before he left. Elisha said, "I want a double portion of your spirit." {2:10} Elijah was like, "That's a tough one. But if you see me taken up, you got it; if not, too bad." {2:11} As they talked, a fiery chariot and horses appeared, splitting them apart, and Elijah went up to heaven in a whirlwind. {2:12} Elisha cried out, "My father, my father! The chariot of Israel and its horsemen!" Then he took Elijah's mantle. {2:13-14} He picked up Elijah's mantle, went back to the Jordan, and smacked the water, asking, "Where's the Lord God of Elijah?" The water parted, and Elisha crossed over. {2:15} The prophet crew in Jericho saw Elisha and recognized Elijah's spirit resting on him. They bowed before him. {2:16-18} They asked Elisha to send men to find Elijah, fearing the Lord had taken him and left him somewhere. Elisha said no at first but eventually agreed. They searched for three days but found nothing. {2:19} People of the city told Elisha the water was bad and the land barren. {2:20-21} Elisha asked for a new jar with salt, went to the spring, threw in the salt, and declared healing. {2:22-23} The water was healed, just like Elisha said. They went to Bethel, and kids mocked Elisha for being bald. {2:24} Elisha cursed them, and two bears came out and mauled forty-two kids. {2:25} Afterward, Elisha went to Mount Carmel and back to Samaria.

{3:1} Jehoram, Ahab's son, started ruling Israel during Jehoshaphat's reign in Judah. He wasn't as bad as his parents 'cause he got rid of Baal's idols but stuck with Jeroboam's sins. {3:2} King Mesha of Moab paid tribute to Israel with tons of lambs and wool, but when Ahab died, Moab rebelled. {3:3} Jehoram gathered all Israel for battle against Moab, even asking Jehoshaphat and the Edomite king to join. {3:4} They freaked out when they ran out of water, thinking the Lord set them up to lose to Moab. {3:5} Jehoshaphat wanted a prophet, and they found Elisha. {3:6} Elisha wasn't feeling the Israelite king but helped out 'cause of Jehoshaphat. Elisha needed music to get in the zone before prophesying. {3:7} He said to dig ditches, and miraculously, water filled them without rain. {3:28 The Moabites, thinking the water was blood, got ready to attack, but the Israelites ambushed them. {3:9} Moab got wrecked, cities destroyed, trees cut down, and wells blocked. {3:10} Moab's king even sacrificed his son, causing outrage against Israel, and they bounced back home.

{4:1} There was this woman whose husband, a prophet dude, died, and she was stressing 'cause she owed debts. The creditor was about to take her two sons as slaves. {4:2} She went to Elisha like, "Help me out! All I got is this pot of oil." {4:3} Elisha told her to gather as many empty jars as she could from neighbors. {4:4-6} She poured the oil into the jars, and miraculously, it kept flowing until every jar was full. {4:7} Elisha told her to sell the oil, pay off the debt, and use the rest to live with her kids. {4:8} Elisha used to pass through Shunem, and this lady there was always hospitable, so he stopped by often for meals. {4:9} She told her husband they should build a room for Elisha with all the essentials, and he agreed. {4:10} Elisha stayed in that room whenever he passed by. {4:11} One day, he asked his servant to call the lady, and he promised her a son. {4:11} She ended up having a son just as Elisha predicted. {4:12} Years later, the boy got sick while working with his dad and died in his mother's lap. {4:14} She laid him on Elisha's bed and headed out. {4:15} She asked her husband for a donkey to see Elisha. {4:16} She went to Elisha at Mount Carmel. {4:17} Elisha's servant greeted her, and she said everything was cool. {4:18} Elisha knew something was up with her. {4:19} Elisha returned and revived the child. {4:37} She picked up her son and left. {4:20} Elisha went back to Gilgal, where there was a famine. {4:21} The prophets cooked a meal but accidentally used poisonous gourds. {4:22} Elisha fixed the meal by adding meal to it. {4:23} Someone brought Elisha bread and grain, and Elisha fed a hundred men with it.

{5:1} So there's this dude Naaman, big shot in Syria's army, but he's got leprosy. {5:2} The Syrians captured a little Israelite girl who served Naaman's wife. {5:3} The girl suggested Naaman go see the prophet in Samaria to cure his leprosy. {5:4-5} Naaman hears this and gets the king of Syria to send him with a ton of gifts to the king of Israel, thinking he'll heal him. {5:6-7} The king of Israel freaks out, thinking it's a setup. {5:8-9} Elisha hears about this and tells the king to send Naaman to him. {5:10} Elisha tells Naaman to dip in the Jordan seven times to be cured. {5:11-13} Naaman's mad because Elisha didn't do some dramatic healing ritual. {5:14} Finally, Naaman dips in the Jordan as instructed and is healed. {5:15-16} Naaman wants to give Elisha gifts, but Elisha refuses. {5:17-19} Naaman asks for dirt to worship the LORD in Syria. {5:20} Gehazi, Elisha's servant, sees Naaman's gifts and decides to chase after him. {5:21} Gehazi lies to Elisha about where he's been, and Elisha curses him with Naaman's leprosy.

{6:1-2} So, the prophet's crew tells Elisha, "Yo, our crib's too small. Let's hit up Jordan, grab some wood, and build a bigger spot." Elisha's like, "Go for it." {6:3} They ask him to roll with them, and he's down. {6:4-5} At the river, one dude's axe head falls in, and he freaks out because it's borrowed. {6:6-7} Elisha throws a stick in, and the iron floats. He's like, "Grab it." {6:8} Meanwhile, the king of Syria's plotting against Israel, but Elisha warns the king of Israel every time. {6:9-13} The king of Syria tries to capture Elisha, but Elisha's in Dothan. {6:14-15} So Syria sends troops to surround the city. {6:16} Elisha's servant panics, but Elisha's like, "Chill, there's more with us than them." {6:17} Elisha prays, and the servant sees angels all around. {6:18} Elisha prays again, and the Syrian soldiers go blind. {6:19-20} Elisha leads them to Samaria, and then back to Syria. {6:21-23} The king of Israel wants to attack, but Elisha's like, "Nah, feed 'em and send 'em home." {6:24} Later, Syria besieges Samaria, causing a famine. {6:25} Things get desperate; people are eating anything they can find. {6:26} The king hears a woman's plea for help. {6:27} The king blames Elisha for the famine and wants him dead. But Elisha's calm, knowing it's all in God's hands.

{7:1} Elisha drops some divine truth, saying, "Listen up, tomorrow at this time, you'll snag a deal: fine flour and barley, dirt cheap, right at Samaria's gate." {7:2} Some big shot, tight with the king, throws shade at Elisha, like, "Come on, even if God opened the sky, could this really happen?" Elisha's like, "You'll see it but won't get a taste." {7:3} Meanwhile, four lepers are chilling by the gate, thinking, "Why just sit here and rot?" {7:4} They weigh their options: stay here and starve or roll up on the Syrian camp. {7:5} So they head over at twilight and find the camp deserted—no Syrians in sight. {7:6} Turns out, God made the Syrians hear a phantom army, so they bounced, thinking they were surrounded. {7:7} The Syrians ditched everything and bolted for their lives. {7:8} The lepers stumble upon an empty tent, feast, stash some loot, and repeat. {7:9} Then they're like, "Yo, we can't keep this to ourselves. Let's tell the king." {7:10-11} They spill the beans to the gatekeeper, who alerts the palace. {7:12-13} The king assumes it's a trap, but a servant suggests sending scouts. {7:14-15} They investigate and find the Syrians' abandoned trail of stuff. {7:16} The people rush in and plunder the Syrian tents, and sure enough, food prices drop just like Elisha predicted. {7:17} The king puts the doubting lord in charge of the gate, and the people trample him to death—fulfilling Elisha's prophecy.

{8:1} So Elisha was like, "Hey, lady! Remember when I brought your kid back to life? Well, guess what? God's sending a famine for seven years. Pack up your fam and find somewhere else to chill until it's over." {8:2} The lady was like, "Cool, Elisha," and did what he said. She took her crew and bounced to Philistine land for seven years. {8:3} After seven years, she came back and went straight to the king to reclaim her house and land. {8:4} Meanwhile, the king was chatting with Gehazi, Elisha's servant, wanting to hear all about the dope miracles Elisha did. {8:5} As Gehazi was spilling the tea about how Elisha raised a dead body, the woman burst in, asking the king to sort out her property situation. Gehazi was like, "Yo, king, that's the woman and her son Elisha brought back to life." {8:6} The king was like, "Alright, let's fix this." He appointed an official to restore everything she lost, including all the crops from the day she left until now. {8:7} Meanwhile, Elisha rolled up in Damascus and found out King Ben-hadad of Syria was sick. {8:8} Ben-hadad told Hazael to bring Elisha a fat gift and ask if he'd recover from his illness. {8:9} So Hazael showed up with a bunch of stuff, asking Elisha if the king would get better. {8:10} Elisha was like, "Tell him he'll recover, but I know he's gonna die." {8:11} Elisha got emotional, and Hazael was like, "What's up, man? Why you crying?" {8:12} Elisha was like, "I know you're gonna mess things up big time for Israel—burning their forts, killing their dudes, and doing horrible things to their women and kids." {8:13} Hazael was shook, like, "Me? Do all that? Nah, I'm just a servant." {8:14} Elisha then dropped the bomb that Hazael was gonna be the king of Syria. {8:15} Later, Hazael went back to Ben-hadad, who asked what Elisha said. Hazael lied and said Elisha told him the king would recover. {8:16} Next thing you know, Hazael suffocated Ben-hadad, and boom, Hazael became the new king. {8:17} Meanwhile, in Israel, Jehoram took over as king at 32 years old, ruling for eight years. {8:18} He was a copycat of Ahab's crew, even marrying Ahab's daughter and doing evil in God's sight. {8:19} But God spared Judah because of His promise to David. {8:20} During Jehoram's rule, Edom rebelled and got their own king. {8:21} Jehoram went to battle against Edom and won, but they kept rebelling. {8:22} Edom and Libnah stayed rebellious till then. {8:23} You can read more about Jehoram's antics in the history books. {8:24} When Jehoram died, he was buried with his ancestors, and his son Ahaziah took over. {8:25} Ahaziah started his reign in the twelfth year of Joram's rule in Israel. {8:26}

He was only 22 and ruled for just one year, walking in the wicked ways of Ahab's fam since his mom was Ahab's daughter. {8:27} Ahaziah also went to battle with Joram against Syria but ended up getting hurt. {8:28} Joram went back to Jezreel to heal, and Ahaziah went to check on him because he was sick.

{9:1} So Elisha, the prophet, hit up one of his homies from the prophet crew and was like, "Yo, get ready and grab this oil, then head to Ramoth-gilead. {9:2} When you get there, find this dude Jehu, son of Jehoshaphat, and pull him aside in private. {9:3} Then pour that oil on his head and be like, "God's saying you're the new king of Israel." After that, bounce out quick, no chillin'. {9:4} The prophet homie went to Ramoth-gilead like Elisha told him. {9:5} When he got there, he found the army captains chilling. He was like, "Got something to tell you, Captain." {9:6} Jehu was like, "To me?" The homie was like, "Yeah, to you, Captain." Then he took Jehu inside, poured oil on him, and said, "God says you're the new king of Israel." {9:7} And God's got a to-do list for you—wipe out Ahab's whole fam to avenge His servants' blood, especially Jezebel's. {9:8} The whole Ahab crew's gonna be gone. God's gonna take out anyone from Ahab's line, including dudes peeing on walls and the leftovers in Israel. {9:9} Ahab's house is gonna be history, just like Jeroboam and Baasha's. {9:10} Oh, and Jezebel's gonna get eaten by dogs in Jezreel, and no one's gonna bury her. Then the prophet's homie bolted. {9:11} Jehu came out to his crew, and they were like, "Everything cool?" They were confused about the prophet homie. Jehu was like, "You know this guy and what he said." {9:12} They were skeptical, but the prophet homie spilled the same story he told Jehu. {9:13} They wasted no time and set up a hype announcement, blowing trumpets and declaring Jehu as king. {9:14} Jehu was plotting against Joram, who was hanging in Ramoth-gilead dealing with his injuries from fighting Hazael of Syria. {9:15} Joram went back to Jezreel to heal, and Jehu was like, "No one's leaving this city to snitch to Jezreel." {9:16} Jehu rode hard to Jezreel. Joram was there, and Ahaziah from Judah was visiting. {9:17} A lookout saw Jehu's crew coming and told Joram to send a horseman to check if it's peace. {9:18} The horseman met Jehu, asking about peace, and Jehu was like, "What's peace got to do with this? Follow me." The lookout saw this but didn't return. {9:19} They sent another horseman, same deal. The lookout saw them joining Jehu's group, noticing how crazy Jehu was driving. {9:20} Joram got ready to roll out with his chariot, meeting Jehu in Naboth's field. {9:21} Joram was like, "Peace, Jehu?" Jehu was like, "Peace? Nah, not while Jezebel's been wildin' with her witchcraft." {9:22} Joram panicked and tried to dip, yelling to Ahaziah about the betrayal. {9:23} But Jehu took a shot and hit Joram, who slumped in his chariot. {9:24} Jehu told his crew to toss Joram's body where Naboth got done dirty by Ahab. {9:25} Jehu was like, "Remember Naboth? The Lord's still not cool with Ahab's fam." {9:26} Jehu chased after Ahaziah, who got smoked near Ibleam. Ahaziah fled to Megiddo and died there. {9:28} They took Ahaziah's body to Jerusalem and buried him with his ancestors. {9:29} Ahaziah started his rule in Judah during Joram's eleventh year in Israel. {9:30} When Jehu hit Jezreel, Jezebel caught wind and dolled herself up to face him. {9:31} Jehu was like, "You remember Zimri? No peace for traitors." {9:32} He looked up and called out for support, and a few eunuchs showed up. {9:33} Jehu ordered them to chuck Jezebel out the window. Her blood splattered everywhere, and they trampled her. {9:34} Jehu chilled, had a meal, and was like, "Go bury this cursed queen." {9:35} They went to bury her but found only parts of her body because the dogs had taken care of the rest. {9:36} God's word through Elijah came true. {9:37} Jezebel's body was left like trash in Jezreel, like the prophecy said.

{10:1} Ahab had, like, 70 sons in Samaria. So Jehu sent letters to Samaria, to the rulers of Jezreel, the elders, and those taking care of Ahab's kids, saying, {10:2} "When this letter hits you, and you're chillin' with your master's sons, with chariots, horses, and a fortified city, pick the best son, put him on the throne, and defend your master's house." {10:3} But they were scared, like, "Two kings couldn't handle him. How can we?" {10:5} The house manager, city mayor, elders, and caretakers hit up Jehu, saying, "We got you, we're down to follow your lead. We won't make anyone king. Just tell us what's good." {10:6} So Jehu sent another letter, like, "If you're really with me, grab the heads of your master's sons and meet me in Jezreel by tomorrow." {10:7} When they got the letter, they took the king's sons, killed all 70, put their heads in baskets, and sent them to Jezreel. {10:8} A messenger told Jehu they brought the heads. Jehu was like, "Stack 'em in two piles at the gate till morning." {10:9} Next morning, Jehu stood before everyone and was like, "You all cool. I took down my master, but who took down all these?" {10:10} He basically said God's word about Ahab's house came true. {10:11} Jehu wiped out the rest of Ahab's crew in Jezreel, including his big shots, relatives, and priests, leaving no one. {10:12} Then Jehu bounced to Samaria. On the way, he met some of Ahaziah's bros. {10:14} He was like, "Grab 'em." They took 42 and killed them at the pit. {10:15} After that, Jehu met Jehonadab and was like, "You cool like me?" Jehonadab was down, so they rolled together. {10:16} Jehu was like, "Check out my loyalty to God." So they cruised in his chariot. {10:17} In Samaria, Jehu wiped out the rest of Ahab's crew, just like God said through Elijah. {10:18} Jehu gathered everyone and was like, "Ahab kinda worshipped Baal, but I'm gonna really serve him." {10:19} He told them to summon all of Baal's prophets, servants, and priests—no one missing. He had a big sacrifice for Baal planned, but he was plotting to destroy Baal's worshippers. {10:20} Jehu announced a huge Baal assembly, and all the Baal worshippers came. The house of Baal was packed. {10:21} Jehu made sure only Baal worshippers were there. {10:22} He got Baal worshippers' outfits ready. {10:23} Jehu and Jehonadab went into Baal's house and made sure only Baal worshippers were there. {10:24} While they were offering sacrifices, Jehu stationed 80 men outside, making sure none escaped. {10:25} After the sacrifice, Jehu ordered them to go in and kill everyone. They wiped them out and trashed the house. {10:26} They brought out Baal's idols, burned them, and destroyed the house. {10:27} Baal's image and house were wrecked and turned into a toilet. {10:28} Jehu wiped out Baal worship from Israel. {10:29} Even though Jehu was good against Ahab's crew, he kept worshipping golden calves in Bethel and Dan, causing Israel to sin. {10:30} God praised Jehu for taking out Ahab's crew, promising his descendants would rule Israel for four generations. {10:31} But Jehu didn't fully follow God's law and kept up Jeroboam's sins. {10:32} During Jehu's reign, the Lord started punishing Israel, with Hazael attacking from all sides. {10:35} Jehu passed away and was buried in Samaria. His son Jehoahaz took over. {10:36} Jehu ruled over Israel for 28 years in Samaria.

{11:1} When Athaliah, Ahaziah's mom, saw her son was dead, she went on a rampage and wiped out all the royal offspring. {11:2} But Jehosheba, King Joram's daughter and Ahaziah's sister, took Joash (Ahaziah's son), and they hid him from Athaliah. They stashed him and his nurse in a room in the house of the LORD for six years while Athaliah ruled the land. {11:4} In the seventh year, Jehoiada sent for the commanders, captains, and guards, brought them to the house of the LORD, and made a pact with them. He showed them Joash. {11:5} He told them, "Here's the plan: One third of you guards will watch over the king's house on the Sabbath. {11:6} Another third will be at the Sur Gate, and the remaining third will be at the gate behind the guard. {11:7} Two-thirds of you who go out on the Sabbath will guard the LORD's house around the king. {11:8} Everyone will have their weapons ready. Anyone who breaches the security will be taken down. Stick with the king wherever he goes." {11:9} The commanders followed Jehoiada's orders, taking their shifts on the Sabbath and reporting to him. {11:10} Jehoiada gave them David's spears and shields from the temple of the LORD. {11:11} The guards surrounded the king with weapons, from the temple's right corner to the left, by the altar and temple. {11:12} They brought out Joash, crowned him king, gave him the royal scrolls, anointed him, and everyone cheered, "Long live the king!" {11:13} When Athaliah heard the commotion, she stormed into the LORD's temple. {11:14} She saw the king standing by a pillar with the princes and trumpeters, and the people rejoicing and blowing trumpets. Athaliah tore her clothes and yelled, "Treason, Treason!" {11:15} Jehoiada ordered the guards to take her outside the temple grounds and kill anyone who followed her, but not in the temple. {11:16} They grabbed her by the way horses enter the king's house and killed her there. {11:17} Jehoiada made a covenant between the LORD, the king, and the people, declaring they would be the LORD's people. {11:18} The people tore down the house of Baal, smashed his altars and images, and killed Baal's priest Mattan. Officers were put in charge of the LORD's temple. {11:19} They escorted Joash from the house of the LORD to the king's house through the guard gate, and he took his seat on the throne. {11:20} The people celebrated, and the city was peaceful after they killed Athaliah near the king's house. {11:21} Joash was seven years old when he became king.

{12:1} When Jehoash took the throne in his seventh year, he ruled in Jerusalem for forty years. His mom, Zibiah from Beer-sheba, was the queen. {12:2} Jehoash followed God's ways as long as Jehoiada the priest guided him. {12:3} But the people still worshipped at the high places, offering sacrifices and burning incense there. {12:4} Jehoash told the priests, "Use all the money brought to the house of the LORD, including the dedicated offerings, to repair any damage to the temple." {12:6} But by the twenty-third year of Jehoash's reign, the repairs were still not done. {12:7} Jehoash confronted Jehoiada and the priests, asking why they hadn't fixed the temple. He ordered them to stop taking money for themselves and focus on the repairs. {12:9} Jehoiada made a chest for donations, placed it near the altar's entrance, and the doorkeepers collected all the money brought into the temple. {12:10} When they saw how much money was collected, the king's secretary and the high priest put it in bags and counted it. {12:11} They paid the workers who repaired the temple with this money, buying materials and hiring carpenters and stonemasons. {12:12-16} They used the funds to repair the temple and buy necessary supplies. {12:17} Hazael, the king of Syria, attacked Gath and then set his sights on Jerusalem. {12:18} Jehoash sent the treasures of the temple and his own possessions, including gold, to Hazael to appease him, and Hazael withdrew from Jerusalem. {12:19} The rest of Jehoash's deeds are recorded in the chronicles of the kings of Judah. {12:20} Eventually, Jehoash was assassinated by his servants in the house of Millo, and Amaziah, his son, became king after him.

{13:1} When Joash had been ruling Judah for twenty-three years, Jehoahaz, Jehu's son, took over in Samaria, ruling for seventeen years. {13:2} He wasn't good in God's eyes; instead, he kept on with Jeroboam's sinful ways that led Israel astray. {13:3} This made God angry, so he let Hazael, king of Syria, and his son Ben-hadad dominate Israel for a long time. {13:4} Jehoahaz pleaded with God because the Syrian king was crushing Israel. {13:5} God answered by sending a savior to free Israel from Syrian oppression, letting them live peacefully in their tents again. {13:6} But even after this, Israel didn't stop following Jeroboam's sinful path, and the Asherah pole in Samaria stayed put. {13:7} Jehoahaz was left with only fifty horsemen, ten chariots, and ten thousand foot soldiers because the Syrian king had wiped out the rest like threshing dust. {13:8} The rest of Jehoahaz's deeds and strength are recorded in Israel's king chronicles. {13:9} When Jehoahaz died, he was buried in Samaria, and his son Joash took over. {13:10} Thirty-seven years into Joash's rule in Judah, Jehoash, Jehoahaz's son, became king in Samaria for sixteen years. {13:11} Like his dad, he did evil in God's eyes, sticking to Jeroboam's sinful ways. {13:12} More about Joash's actions, including his battles against Judah's King Amaziah, is recorded in Israel's king chronicles. {13:13} Joash died and was buried in Samaria, and his son Jeroboam took his throne. {13:14} Elisha fell ill and eventually died, and King Joash of Israel mourned his death, calling him the "chariot and horsemen of Israel." {13:15} Elisha instructed Joash to take a bow and arrows. {13:16} He placed his hand on the bow, and Elisha put his hands over Joash's. {13:17} Elisha told Joash to shoot an arrow towards Syria's east, symbolizing victory over the Syrians in Aphek. {13:18} Then Elisha instructed Joash to strike the ground with arrows. Joash struck three times and stopped. {13:19} Elisha was upset because Joash didn't strike more; if he had, Syria would have been defeated completely. {13:20} After Elisha's death, Moabite raiders invaded the land. {13:21} During a burial, when a man's body touched Elisha's bones, he came back to life and stood up. {13:22} Hazael of Syria oppressed Israel for Jehoahaz's entire reign. {13:23} Despite this, God showed compassion due to his covenant with Abraham, Isaac, and Jacob, sparing Israel and not casting them away. {13:24} Hazael died, and his son Ben-hadad took over. {13:25} Jehoash, Jehoahaz's son, reclaimed cities from Ben-hadad in battle, defeating him three times and restoring Israel's lost territories.

{14:1} When Joash's son Jehoahaz had been king of Israel for two years, Amaziah, Joash's son, took over as king of Judah. {14:2} He was twenty-five when he started ruling and reigned twenty-nine years in Jerusalem. His mom's name was Jehoaddan from Jerusalem. {14:3} Amaziah did right in God's eyes, but not as well as his ancestor David; he followed the ways of his dad Joash. {14:4} However, he didn't remove the high places, and people kept sacrificing and burning incense there. {14:5} Once he had a solid grip on the kingdom, he had his father's assassins put to death. {14:6} But he spared the children of the murderers, following Moses' law that says not to punish children for their parents' sins. {14:7} Amaziah defeated Edom, killing ten thousand in the Valley of Salt and capturing Selah, renaming it Joktheel. {14:8} Amaziah sent messengers to Jehoash, Jehoahaz's son, king of Israel, challenging him to face off. {14:9} Jehoash of Israel responded with a parable, basically saying not to pick a fight that could end badly. {14:10} He warned Amaziah not to get cocky over defeating Edom and advised him to stay home to avoid disaster for Judah. {14:11} But Amaziah didn't listen, so Jehoash of Israel marched up to Beth-shemesh, and they faced off. {14:12} Judah lost to Israel and fled to their homes. {14:13} Jehoash captured Amaziah at Beth-shemesh, then went to Jerusalem and tore down part of its wall. {14:14} He looted the house of the LORD and the king's treasury, taking hostages, then returned to Samaria. {14:15} More about Jehoash's deeds and battles against Amaziah are in Israel's king chronicles. {14:16} Jehoash died and was buried in Samaria, and his son Jeroboam took over. {14:17} Amaziah lived fifteen years after Jehoash's death. {14:18} More about Amaziah's actions are in Judah's king chronicles. {14:19} Eventually, there was a conspiracy against Amaziah in Jerusalem, and he fled to Lachish, where he was killed. {14:20} They brought him back to Jerusalem for burial. {14:21} Judah then made Amaziah's sixteen-year-old son Azariah king in his place. {14:22} Azariah rebuilt Elath and restored it to Judah after his father's death. {14:23} In Amaziah's fifteenth year as king, Jeroboam, Joash's son, took over in Samaria and ruled for forty-one years. {14:24} He did evil in God's eyes, continuing Jeroboam's sins that led Israel astray. {14:25} Jeroboam restored Israel's borders as God had foretold through the prophet Jonah. {14:26} God saw how bitter Israel's affliction was, with no one left to help them. {14:27} God didn't want to wipe out Israel's name but saved them through Jeroboam. {14:28} More about Jeroboam's deeds, wars, and conquests are in Israel's king chronicles. {14:29} Jeroboam died, and his son Zachariah took over as king of Israel.

{15:1} When Jeroboam had been king of Israel for 27 years, Azariah, Amaziah's son, took over as king of Judah. {15:2} He was only sixteen when he started ruling and reigned for 52 years in Jerusalem. His mom's name was Jecholiah from Jerusalem. {15:3} Azariah did right by God, following his father Amaziah's example, {15:4} but he didn't get rid of the high places where people kept sacrificing and burning incense. {15:5} God struck Azariah with leprosy until he died, and during that time, his son Jotham ruled the land. {15:6} More about Azariah's deeds are in Judah's king chronicles. {15:7} Azariah passed away, and Jotham took over as king. {15:8} In Azariah's 38th year as king of Judah, Zachariah, Jeroboam's son, began ruling over Israel in Samaria for six months. {15:9} He did evil in God's sight, just like his ancestors, continuing Jeroboam's sinful ways. {15:10} Shallum, son of Jabesh, conspired against Zachariah, killed him, and took over as king. {15:11} More about Zachariah's reign is in Israel's king chronicles. {15:12} This fulfilled the Lord's word to Jehu that his descendants would rule Israel for four generations. {15:13} Shallum took over in the 39th year of Uzziah, king of Judah, reigning for a month in Samaria. {15:14} Menahem then came from Tirzah, killed Shallum, and became king. {15:15} More about Shallum's actions and conspiracy is in Israel's king chronicles. {15:16} Menahem attacked Tiphsah and its surroundings from Tirzah because they refused to open their gates to him. He even ripped open pregnant women. {15:17} Menahem began ruling over Israel in the 39th year of Azariah, king of Judah, reigning for ten years in Samaria. {15:18} He continued in the sinful ways of Jeroboam throughout his reign. {15:19} Assyria's King Pul invaded, and Menahem paid him a thousand talents of silver to confirm his hold on the kingdom. {15:20} Menahem taxed all of Israel's wealthy men to raise the money for Assyria's king. {15:21} More about Menahem's deeds are in Israel's king chronicles. {15:22} Menahem died, and his son Pekahiah took over. {15:23} In Azariah's 50th year as king of Judah, Pekahiah, Menahem's son, began ruling over Israel in Samaria for two years. {15:24} He followed in the sinful ways of Jeroboam and didn't change. {15:25} Pekah, son of Remaliah, conspired against Pekahiah, killed him in Samaria, and took the throne. {15:26} More about Pekahiah's reign is in Israel's king chronicles. {15:27} Pekah began ruling over Israel in the 52nd year of Azariah, king of Judah, reigning for twenty years in Samaria. {15:28} He continued in Jeroboam's sinful ways throughout his reign. {15:29} During Pekah's reign, Assyria's Tiglath-pileser captured parts of Israel and deported the people. {15:30} Hoshea then conspired against Pekah, killing him and taking his place in the 20th year of Jotham, Uzziah's son. {15:31} More about Pekah's deeds are in Israel's king chronicles. {15:32} In Pekah's second year as king of Israel, Jotham, Uzziah's son, began ruling over Judah. {15:33} He was 25 when he started ruling and reigned sixteen years in Jerusalem. His mom's name was Jerusha, daughter of Zadok. {15:34} Jotham did right by God, following his father Uzziah's example. {15:35} However, he didn't remove the high places where people sacrificed and burned incense, although he did build up the higher gate of the house of the Lord. {15:36} More about Jotham's deeds are in Judah's king chronicles. {15:37} During Jotham's reign, the Lord sent Rezin, king of Syria, and Pekah against Judah. {15:38} Jotham died and was buried with his fathers, and his son Ahaz took over as king.

{16:1} When Pekah had been ruling Israel for 17 years, Ahaz, Jotham's son, took over as king of Judah. {16:2} Ahaz was just twenty when he started ruling and reigned for sixteen years in Jerusalem. He didn't do right in God's sight like his ancestor David. {16:3} Instead, he followed the ways of the kings of Israel, even sacrificing his own son in the fire, mimicking the heathen practices that God had condemned. {16:4} Ahaz sacrificed and burned incense on high places, hills, and under every green tree. {16:5} Rezin, the king of Syria, and Pekah, son of Remaliah, king of Israel, attacked Jerusalem, but couldn't defeat Ahaz. {16:6} During this time, Rezin regained control of Elath for Syria and kicked out the Jews, settling Syrians there. {16:7} So Ahaz sent a plea to Tiglath-pileser, king of Assyria, asking for help against Syria and Israel. {16:8} Ahaz gathered silver and gold from the temple and his palace to send as a gift to the Assyrian king. {16:9} Tiglath-pileser agreed and attacked Damascus, capturing the people and killing Rezin. {16:10} Ahaz went to Damascus to meet Tiglath-pileser and copied an altar design he saw there, sending it to Urijah the priest to build in Jerusalem. {16:11} Urijah built the altar as instructed before Ahaz's return. {16:12} When Ahaz returned, he offered sacrifices on the new altar. {16:13} He burnt offerings, meat offerings, drink offerings, and sprinkled blood on the altar. {16:14} Ahaz then moved the bronze altar from the temple to make room for his new altar. {16:15} He ordered Urijah to use the new altar for all offerings, including those from the people. {16:16} Urijah obeyed Ahaz's commands. {16:17} Ahaz also made changes to the temple, removing the bases' borders, the laver, and the sea, placing the latter on a stone pavement. {16:18} He altered the temple's design to please the king of Assyria. {16:19} More about Ahaz's actions are recorded in Judah's king chronicles. {16:20} Ahaz passed away and was buried in the city of David, and his son Hezekiah became king.

{17:1} So like, in the twelfth year of Ahaz's rule in Judah, this dude Hoshea, Elah's son, took over Samaria for nine years, ruling over Israel. {17:2} But, man, he wasn't cool in God's eyes, you know? He did evil stuff, although not as bad as the kings before him. {17:3} Then Shalmaneser, the Assyrian king, rolls up against him. Hoshea's like, "Okay, okay," and starts serving Shalmaneser, giving him gifts. {17:4} But then Assyria's king finds out Hoshea was scheming, 'cause he reached out to So, the king of Egypt, without sending gifts to Assyria like before. So, Assyria locks him up in prison. {17:5} Then Assyria's king sweeps through the land, sieging Samaria for three years. {17:6} Finally, in Hoshea's ninth year, Assyria's king takes Samaria, deporting Israel to Assyria, scattering them across Halah, Habor by the river of Gozan, and the cities of the Medes. {17:7} 'Cause, you see, Israelites were sinning hard against God, who saved them from Egypt, straight up fearing other gods. {17:8} They were copying the heathen ways the Lord had booted out before them and the kings of Israel. {17:9} They were pulling sneaky moves against the Lord, setting up high places and idols in every city, doing stuff that really ticked off the Lord. {17:10} They set up idols and sacred poles on every hill and under every tree. {17:11} They were burning incense everywhere, just like the heathen before them, making God seriously mad. {17:12} They straight-up worshipped idols, which God specifically said not to do. {17:13} But the Lord kept warning Israel and Judah through prophets and seers to turn away from evil and obey His laws, but they weren't having it. {17:14} They were stubborn, just like their ancestors who didn't trust in the Lord. {17:15} They rejected God's statutes, covenant, and testimonies, chasing after worthless idols and becoming empty themselves, following the ways of the nations around them despite God's warnings. {17:16} They ditched all of God's commandments, making golden calves, setting up sacred poles, and worshipping the stars and Baal. {17:17} They even sacrificed their own children, practiced divination and sorcery, and sold themselves to evil, provoking the Lord to anger. {17:18} So, naturally, the Lord was ticked off and removed Israel from His sight, leaving only Judah behind. {17:19} But even Judah wasn't following God's commandments; they were copying Israel's sinful ways. {17:20} The Lord straight-up rejected all of Israel and handed them over to spoilers, kicking them out of His sight. {17:21} He split Israel from David's house, making Jeroboam king, who led Israel away from the Lord into serious sin. {17:22} The Israelites kept doing Jeroboam's sins, refusing to stop. {17:23} So the Lord removed Israel from His sight, just like He warned through His prophets. And that's how Israel got hauled off to Assyria, never to return. {17:24} Assyria's king imported folks from Babylon, Cuthah, Ava, Hamath, and Sepharvaim to replace the Israelites in Samaria, and these new folks settled there. {17:25} At first, these new peeps didn't fear the Lord, so He sent lions to munch on them. {17:26} They freaked out and asked the Assyrian king to send them a priest to teach them about the God of the land. {17:27} So Assyria sends one of the deported priests to teach them the ropes. {17:28} This priest settles in Bethel, teaching them how to worship the Lord. {17:29} But these nations still made their own gods and put them in the high places that the Samaritans made. {17:30} Each nation made its own gods, like the Babylonians making Succoth-benoth and the folks from Cuth making Nergal. {17:31} Everyone was making their own gods and doing their own thing. {17:32} They feared the Lord but also set up their own priests in the high places to make sacrifices. {17:33} They kinda served the Lord but also worshipped their own gods, just like the nations they were brought from. {17:34} They're still doing this today, not fearing the Lord or obeying His laws, ordinances, or commandments. {17:35} The Lord made a covenant with them, telling them not to fear other gods or worship them or sacrifice to them. {17:36} They should only worship and sacrifice to the Lord, who saved them from Egypt with great power. {17:37} They should always obey God's statutes, ordinances, laws, and commandments, never fearing other gods. {17:38} They must never forget the covenant with the Lord or fear other gods. {17:39} Instead, they should fear the Lord, who will deliver them from all their enemies. {17:40} But, alas, they didn't listen and kept doing their own thing. {17:41} So these nations still fear the Lord but also worship their idols, just like their fathers did.

{18:1} So, like, in the third year of Hoshea, Elah's son, being king of Israel, Hezekiah, Ahaz's son, took over Judah's throne. {18:2} He was twenty-five when he started ruling and reigned for twenty-nine years in Jerusalem. His mom's name was Abi, Zachariah's daughter. {18:3} Now, this dude Hezekiah was legit in God's eyes, doing all the right things just like his ancestor David. {18:4} He got rid of all those high places, smashed idols, cut down groves, and even destroyed that bronze serpent Moses made because folks were burning incense to it. He called it "Nehushtan." {18:5} He totally trusted in the Lord God of Israel, and no king of Judah before or after him was as cool as Hezekiah. {18:6} He was all about sticking with the Lord, never straying, and keeping all those commandments Moses got from God. {18:7} And you know what? The Lord had his back, blessing everything Hezekiah did. He even rebelled against the Assyrian king and refused to serve him. {18:8} Hezekiah took down the Philistines, rolling all the way to Gaza, from watchtower to fortified city. {18:9} In Hezekiah's fourth year, which was Hoshea's seventh, the Assyrian king Shalmaneser showed up at Samaria and besieged it. {18:10} After three years, they took Samaria in Hezekiah's sixth year, which was Hoshea's ninth. {18:11} Assyria's king deported Israel to Assyria, scattering them across Halah, Habor by the river of Gozan, and the cities of the Medes because they ignored God's voice, broke His covenant, and dissed Moses' commands. {18:13} Then, in Hezekiah's fourteenth year, Sennacherib, the Assyrian king, attacked all of Judah's fortified cities and took them. {18:14} Hezekiah tried to make peace, sending a message to the Assyrian king in Lachish, saying he messed up and would pay up. The Assyrian king demanded 300 talents of silver and 30 talents of gold. {18:15} Hezekiah coughed up all the silver from the Lord's house and his own palace. {18:16} He even stripped gold from the temple doors and pillars and handed it over to Assyria's king. {18:17} Then Assyria sent Tartan, Rabsaris, and Rabshakeh from Lachish to Hezekiah with a huge army against Jerusalem. They arrived and stood by the conduit of the upper pool near the highway. {18:18} When they called for the king, out came Eliakim, Hilkiah's son, in charge of the household, along with Shebna the scribe and Joah the recorder. {18:19} Rabshakeh told them to relay to Hezekiah that the Assyrian king was asking what Hezekiah was thinking, trusting in Egypt for help against Assyria. {18:20} He mocked Hezekiah's confidence in Egypt, comparing it to leaning on a fragile reed that breaks and hurts you, dissing Egypt's reliability. {18:21-22} He suggested that trusting in the Lord wasn't smart either, pointing out that Hezekiah had trashed the Lord's high places and altars. {18:23} Rabshakeh offered horses if Judah could even use them. {18:24} He questioned Hezekiah's reliance on Egypt for chariots and horsemen, claiming Assyria was sent by the Lord to destroy Judah. {18:25} Eliakim, Shebna, and Joah asked Rabshakeh to speak in Syrian so the people wouldn't understand, but Rabshakeh loudly proclaimed the king of Assyria's words in Hebrew, mocking Hezekiah's reliance on God to save Jerusalem.

{19:1} So, when King Hezekiah heard the news, he freaked out, tearing his clothes, putting on sackcloth, and heading straight to the house of the LORD. {19:2} He sent Eliakim, the head of his crew, Shebna the scribe, and the elder priests, all rocking sackcloth, to Isaiah the prophet, Amoz's son. {19:3} They were like, "Hezekiah says it's a total disaster today—like, trouble, insults, and blasphemy. We're stuck, unable to handle this." {19:4} Hezekiah hoped that the LORD would hear the insults from Rabshakeh, the Assyrian king's dude, who dissed the living God, and maybe God would step in for the few of us left. {19:5} So, Hezekiah's crew met up with Isaiah. {19:6} Isaiah was like, "Tell your boss not to sweat the insults from Assyria's crew. {19:7} I'm sending a vibe their way, and they'll bail out, hearing some rumor, and head back home. Assyria's king is gonna meet his end there." {19:8} Rabshakeh bounced back and found Assyria's king chilling near Libnah after leaving Lachish. {19:9} When he heard that Tirhakah, Ethiopia's king, was coming to fight him, he sent more messages to Hezekiah, basically saying, "Don't trust your God to save you from Assyria's king." {19:10} He's like, "You've seen what Assyria's done to other lands—total destruction. You really think you'll be spared?" {19:11} He's doubting big time. {19:12} Look at all those nations Assyria's wiped out, just like Gozan, Haran, Rezeph, and the people of Eden in Thelasar. {19:13} Where are Hamath's king, Arpad's king, Sepharvaim's king, Hena, and Ivah? {19:14} Hezekiah got the letter from the messengers, read it, then went to the LORD's house and spread it out before Him. {19:15} Hezekiah prayed, "LORD God of Israel, who's between the cherubim, You're the God, the real deal, who made heaven and earth." {19:16} "LORD, listen up, look around, and check out what Sennacherib said, dissing You." {19:17} He's like, "Sure, Assyria's kings have wrecked nations and their gods—just man-made stuff, wood and stone, so of course, they're gone." {19:18} "Save us from Assyria, so everyone knows You're the only real God." {19:20} Isaiah messaged Hezekiah, "God heard your prayer against Assyria's king, Sennacherib." {19:21} God's like, "Zion's daughter thinks you're a joke, Assyria. Jerusalem's daughter's laughing at you." {19:22} "Who're you dissing and challenging? You're picking a fight with the Holy One of Israel." {19:23} "You bragged about your chariots and invasion plans, but I'm not impressed." {19:24} "You've done a lot, but I'm the one who made it happen, turning your fancy places into ruins." {19:25} "I've known all along, and now I'm showing my power by defending these cities." {19:26} "So yeah, Assyria's peeps are weak, scared, and easily trampled, like grass on the roof." {19:27} "I see you, your actions, your anger against Me." {19:28} "Because you're mad at Me, I'll lead you back where you came from." {19:29} "Here's a sign: this year, eat what grows on its own, next year too. Then sow and reap as normal." {19:30} "The remaining Judah folks will thrive, taking root and bearing fruit." {19:31} "A remnant will come from Jerusalem and Mount Zion, all because of my zeal." {19:32} "Assyria's king won't set foot in this city or shoot an arrow at it. He won't even get close." {19:33} "He'll retreat the same way he came, not touching this city, says the LORD." {19:34} "I'm protecting this city for My sake and because of my servant David." {19:35} That night, the angel of the LORD wiped out 185,000 Assyrians. {19:36} Sennacherib left, went back to Nineveh, and while worshipping his god Nisroch, his sons killed him and fled to Armenia. Esar-haddon, his son, took over as king.

{20:1} So, Hezekiah was seriously sick, like almost to death. Then Isaiah, the prophet, rolled up and told him straight from the LORD, "Get your house in order 'cause you're gonna kick it; you won't make it." {20:2} Hezekiah turned away, faced the wall, and hit up the LORD with a prayer, saying, {20:3} "LORD, remember how I've been real with You, doing good stuff in Your eyes." Hezekiah was bawling hard. {20:4} Before Isaiah even left the courtyard, the LORD hit him up, saying, {20:5} "Go back to Hezekiah, leader of my crew, and tell him the LORD, the God of your dad David, heard his prayer and saw his tears. He's gonna heal you. On the third day, you'll be back at the house of the LORD." {20:6} "Plus, I'm throwing in another fifteen years for you, saving you and this city from Assyria's king. This is for Me and my dude David." {20:7} Isaiah said, "Take some figs." They put it on the boil, and Hezekiah got better. {20:8} Hezekiah asked Isaiah, "How will I know for sure the LORD will heal me and I'll be at the house of the LORD in three days?" {20:9} Isaiah said, "You want the shadow to go forward ten degrees or back ten degrees?" {20:10} Hezekiah said, "Going down ten degrees is easy. Make it go back ten degrees." {20:11} Isaiah called out to the LORD, and the shadow went back ten degrees on Ahaz's sundial. {20:12} Meanwhile, Berodach-baladan from Babylon sent Hezekiah letters and gifts after hearing he was sick. {20:13} Hezekiah showed off everything in his crib, from silver and gold to spices and armor—nothing was off-limits. {20:14} Isaiah came back, asking Hezekiah, "What did these guys say, and where they from?" Hezekiah said, "They're from far-off Babylon." {20:15} Isaiah asked, "What did they see in your house?" Hezekiah said, "They peeped everything. I showed them all my stuff." {20:16} Isaiah dropped some truth, saying, {20:17} "Everything in your crib, including what your ancestors saved, will end up in Babylon. The LORD said so—nothing's staying." {20:18} "Even your future sons will get taken away, serving as eunuchs in Babylon's king's palace." {20:19} Hezekiah was like, "Cool with me. If there's peace and truth while I'm around, that's all that matters." {20:20} "And the other stuff Hezekiah did, his power moves like making a pool and bringing water to the city—are they not in the king's chronicles?" {20:21} Hezekiah passed away and Manasseh, his son, took over.

{21:1} So Manasseh was only twelve when he started ruling, and he held it down for fifty-five years in Jerusalem. His mom's name was Hephzi-bah. {21:2} But here's the kicker—he went all evil, just like the nations the LORD kicked out before Israel. {21:3} Manasseh rebuilt all those high places his dad Hezekiah tore down. He set up altars for Baal, made groves like Ahab did, and started worshipping the whole celestial crew. {21:4} He even built altars in the LORD's house, the place where the LORD said His name would be. {21:5} Altars for every heavenly host were in the house of the LORD's two courts. {21:6} And get this—he made his own kid pass through fire, practiced divination, cast spells, consulted spirits, and magicians. He was all about angering the LORD with wickedness. {21:7} Manasseh even put a carved image of the grove in the LORD's house, the place the LORD said to David and Solomon, "This is where I'm repping forever." {21:8} The LORD promised not to move Israel's feet from their land if they stuck to His commands and Moses' law. {21:9} But they blew it, and Manasseh led them to out-evil the nations the LORD already booted. {21:10} Then the LORD's prophets came through, saying, {21:11} "Manasseh's evil deeds top even the Amorites'. He made Judah sin with idols." {21:12} So the LORD dropped a bomb—huge evil on Jerusalem and Judah that'll have everyone's ears ringing. {21:13} He'd wipe Jerusalem clean like a dish, flipping it upside down. {21:14} The LORD would ditch the remnant of His inheritance, handing them over to enemies as prey. {21:15} All because they'd been doing evil and ticking off the LORD since their Egypt days. {21:16} Manasseh spilled so much innocent blood that it flooded Jerusalem, on top of leading Judah into wickedness. {21:17} You can read all about Manasseh's deeds and sins in the kings' chronicles of Judah. {21:18} Manasseh bit the dust and got buried in his own backyard, while Amon, his son, took over. {21:19} Amon was twenty-two when he started ruling, holding it down for just two years in Jerusalem. His mom was Meshullemeth. {21:20} But Amon followed in his dad's footsteps, doing evil like Manasseh. {21:21} He was all about the idols his dad worshipped and walked in his evil ways. {21:22} Amon ditched the LORD God of his ancestors and didn't walk in the LORD's ways. {21:23} His servants had enough and offed him in his crib. {21:24} The people then took care of those who conspired against Amon and made Josiah, his son, king. {21:25} You can find more about Amon's deeds in the kings' chronicles of Judah. {21:26} Amon was laid to rest in his tomb, and Josiah took over the throne.

{22:1} So Josiah was only eight when he started running things, and he held it down for thirty-one years in Jerusalem. His mom's name was Jedidah, daughter of Adaiah from Boscath. {22:2} And check it—he did right by the LORD, following in David his dad's footsteps, not swerving left or right. {22:3} By the time Josiah hit eighteen, he sent Shaphan, son of Azaliah, the scribe, to the house of the LORD, saying, {22:4} "Go see Hilkiah the high priest, tally up the silver collected at the door by the people. {22:5} Then hand it to the workers overseeing the LORD's house to fix it up, {22:6} hire carpenters, builders, and masons, and buy timber and hewn stone to patch things up." {22:7} They didn't even need to count the money 'cause they were honest about it. {22:8} Hilkiah the high priest tells Shaphan, "Yo, found the book of the law in the LORD's house." Hilkiah hands it to Shaphan, who reads it. {22:9} Shaphan comes back to the king, "We got the money and gave it to the workers fixing the LORD's house." {22:10} Shaphan shows the king the book Hilkiah gave him, and he reads it before the king. {22:11} When the king hears the words of the law, he tears his clothes. {22:12} The king tells Hilkiah, Ahikam, Achbor, Shaphan, and Asahiah, "Go ask the LORD for me, for the people, and for Judah, about the words of this book we found. The LORD's wrath is big 'cause our ancestors didn't listen to what's written about us." {22:13-14} So they go to Huldah the prophetess, wife of Shallum, keeper of the wardrobe, in Jerusalem, and chat with her. {22:15-16} She tells them, "Tell the man who sent you that the LORD's bringing evil on this place, just like what's written in the book Josiah read. {22:17} 'Cause they ditched me and worshipped other gods, my anger's fired up and won't chill. {22:18-19} But tell the king of Judah, 'Cause you humbled yourself and felt for this place's fate, I heard you. {22:20} "I'll let you go in peace before things get worse." They told the king what Huldah said.

{23:1} So the king hit up all the elders of Judah and Jerusalem to gather. {23:2} Then he rolled up to the house of the LORD with all the people—men, women, priests, prophets, and everyone—and read the book of the covenant to them. {23:3} Standing by a pillar, the king made a vow to the LORD, promising to walk in His ways, keep His commandments, and obey His statutes with all their heart and soul. The people stood with him on that. {23:4} Then the king ordered Hilkiah the high priest, the priests of the second order, and the doorkeepers to haul out all the vessels made for Baal, the grove, and the host of heaven from the temple. They burned them outside Jerusalem in the Kidron fields and took the ashes to Bethel. {23:5} He kicked out the idolatrous priests appointed by the kings of Judah to burn incense in the high places and around Jerusalem—those who burned incense to Baal, the sun, moon, planets, and heavenly hosts. {23:6} The king dragged the grove from the house of the LORD outside Jerusalem to the Kidron brook, burned it, crushed it to powder, and scattered the dust over graves. {23:7} He demolished the houses of the male cult prostitutes near the house of the LORD, where women made hangings for the grove. {23:8} Gathering all the priests from the cities of Judah, he defiled the high places from Geba to Beersheba and tore down the high places at the city gates. {23:9} Although the high place priests didn't come to Jerusalem, they ate unleavened bread with their fellow priests. {23:10} Josiah desecrated Topheth in the Valley of Hinnom to stop anyone sacrificing their children to Molech. {23:11} He got rid of the horses dedicated to the sun near the LORD's house, burned the chariots of the sun with fire. {23:12} Josiah tore down the altars on Ahaz's roof and in the house of the LORD's court, tossing the dust into the Kidron brook. {23:13} He defiled the high places to the right of the Mount of Corruption, built by Solomon for Ashtoreth, Chemosh, and Milcom—abominations to the Zidonians, Moabites, and Ammonites. {23:14} Breaking the idols and cutting down the groves, he filled the places with human bones. {23:15} He destroyed the altar at Bethel and the high place Jeroboam built to make Israel sin, burning and pulverizing it along with the grove. {23:16} Josiah saw tombs on the mountain and had the bones taken out, burned them on the altar, defiling it as the LORD's prophet foretold. {23:17} When Josiah saw a tomb, they told him it belonged to the man of God who denounced his altar in Bethel. {23:18} Josiah left the bones undisturbed, as commanded. {23:19} He obliterated the high places in Samaria built by the kings of Israel that angered the LORD, doing as he did in Bethel. {23:20} Josiah executed the high place priests on their altars, burning human bones, then returned to Jerusalem. {23:21} He told everyone to keep the Passover to the LORD as written in the covenant book. {23:22} No Passover like this had been held since the days of the judges or the kings of Israel and Judah. {23:23} This Passover went down in Josiah's eighteenth year of reign. {23:24} Josiah got rid of all the sorcerers, wizards, idols, and abominations in Judah and Jerusalem to honor the law of Moses. {23:25} No king before or after Josiah turned to the LORD with all their heart, soul, and might, following the law of Moses. {23:26} But the LORD didn't back down from His anger toward Judah for all of Manasseh's provocation. {23:27} The LORD planned to reject Judah like He did Israel, casting off Jerusalem and His chosen house. {23:28} More of Josiah's deeds are written in Judah's kings' chronicles. {23:29} During his reign, Pharaoh Nechoh of Egypt fought Assyria at the Euphrates River. Josiah opposed him and died at Megiddo. {23:30} They brought Josiah's body back to Jerusalem, and the people made his son Jehoahaz king. {23:31} Jehoahaz was twenty-three and reigned three months in Jerusalem. His mom was Hamutal, daughter of Jeremiah of Libnah. {23:32} Like his ancestors, Jehoahaz did evil in the LORD's sight. {23:33} Pharaoh Nechoh imprisoned him at Riblah in Hamath and imposed a tribute on Judah. {23:34} Nechoh made Josiah's son Eliakim king, renaming him Jehoiakim, and took Jehoahaz to Egypt, where he died. {23:35} Jehoiakim paid silver and gold to Pharaoh, taxing the people as Pharaoh demanded. {23:36} Jehoiakim was twenty-five and reigned eleven years in Jerusalem. His mom was Zebudah, daughter of Pedaiah of Rumah. {23:37} Jehoiakim followed his ancestors' evil ways in the LORD's eyes.

{24:1} So Nebuchadnezzar, the king of Babylon, showed up during Jehoiakim's reign and Jehoiakim became his puppet for three years before rebelling. {24:2} The LORD sent bands of Chaldeans, Syrians, Moabites, and Ammonites against Judah to wreck it, just like the prophets said. {24:3} This was all happening because of Judah's sins, especially those of Manasseh. {24:4} Judah was full of innocent blood, which the LORD wouldn't let slide. {24:5} The rest of Jehoiakim's story is in the kings of Judah's chronicles. {24:6} Jehoiakim died, and his son Jehoiachin took over. {24:7} The king of Egypt didn't come back out of his land because Babylon took everything from the river of Egypt to the Euphrates. {24:8} Jehoiachin was only eighteen when he started ruling and lasted three months in Jerusalem. His mom was Nehushta. {24:9} He followed his dad's evil ways. {24:10} That's when Nebuchadnezzar's crew showed up, and Jerusalem got surrounded. {24:11} Nebuchadnezzar himself rolled in and laid siege to the city. {24:12} Jehoiachin surrendered to Nebuchadnezzar in his eighth year. {24:13} They hauled off all the treasures from the LORD's house, including Solomon's gold stuff, just like the LORD said. {24:14} They took everyone from Jerusalem—princes, warriors, craftsmen, leaving only the poorest. {24:15} Jehoiachin, his mom, wives, officers, and top folks all got carted off to Babylon. {24:16} Seven thousand strong guys, plus a thousand craftsmen and smiths, got taken as captives to Babylon. {24:17} Nebuchadnezzar put Zedekiah, Jehoiachin's uncle, on the throne and renamed him. {24:18} Zedekiah was twenty-one when he started ruling and lasted eleven years in Jerusalem. His mom was Hamutal. {24:19} He did the same evil as Jehoiakim. {24:20} Because of the LORD's anger, Jerusalem and Judah got kicked out, thanks to Zedekiah rebelling against Babylon's king.

{25:1} So in the ninth year of his rule, on the tenth day of the tenth month, Nebuchadnezzar, the king of Babylon, showed up with his crew and set up camp against Jerusalem, building forts all around it. {25:2} They kept Jerusalem under siege until Zedekiah's eleventh year. {25:3} By the fourth month, on the ninth day, the city was hit hard with famine, and there was no food left. {25:4} The city walls were breached, and the soldiers slipped out at night through the gate by the king's garden, while the Chaldeans surrounded the city. Zedekiah tried to escape toward the plain. {25:5} But the Chaldean army caught up to him in the plains of Jericho, and his entire army scattered. {25:6} They captured Zedekiah and brought him to Nebuchadnezzar at Riblah, where they judged him. {25:7} They killed Zedekiah's sons before his eyes, gouged out his eyes, put him in bronze chains, and took him to Babylon. {25:8} Then, in the nineteenth year of Nebuchadnezzar's reign, on the seventh day of the fifth month, Nebuzaradan, the captain of the guard, who served the king of Babylon, arrived in Jerusalem. {25:9} He burned down the LORD's house, the king's palace, and all the important houses in Jerusalem. {25:10} The Chaldean army, with Nebuzaradan, tore down the city walls. {25:11} Nebuzaradan took the rest of the people in the city, along with those who had surrendered to the king of Babylon, and carried them away. {25:12} Only the poorest people were left behind to work the vineyards and fields. {25:13} The Chaldeans broke apart the bronze pillars, bases, and the bronze sea from the LORD's house, and took the bronze to Babylon. {25:14} They also took away all the bronze and gold utensils used for worship. {25:15} They took the gold and silver firepans, bowls, and other items from the LORD's house. {25:16} They even took the two bronze pillars, the bronze sea, and the stands that Solomon had made for the LORD's house. {25:17} One pillar was eighteen cubits tall, with a three-cubit-high bronze capital and bronze pomegranates around it. The second pillar was similar. {25:18} The captain of the guard took the chief priest Seraiah, the second priest Zephaniah, and three doorkeepers. {25:19} He also took an officer overseeing the soldiers, five men who were with the king, the chief scribe of the army who mustered the people, and sixty other men. {25:20} Nebuzaradan brought them to the king of Babylon at Riblah, where the king executed them. Thus, Judah was taken from their land. {25:22} The people left in Judah were put under Gedaliah, the son of Ahikam, as ruler by Nebuchadnezzar. {25:23} When the army captains and their men heard that Nebuchadnezzar had made Gedaliah governor, they came to Mizpah— including Ishmael, Johanan, Seraiah, and Jaazaniah, with their men. {25:24} Gedaliah promised them safety, urging them to serve Babylon's king and dwell in the land. {25:25} But in the seventh month, Ishmael, of royal blood, and ten men attacked Gedaliah, killing him and the Jews and Chaldeans with him at Mizpah. {25:26} The people, fearing the Chaldeans, fled to Egypt, from the least to the greatest, including army captains. {25:27} In the thirty-seventh year of Jehoiachin's captivity, in the twelfth month, on the twenty-seventh day, Evil-merodach, the king of Babylon, released Jehoiachin from prison. {25:28} He treated him kindly, setting him above other kings in Babylon. {25:29} Jehoiachin's prison clothes were replaced, and he ate at the king's table for life. {25:30} He received a daily allowance from the king for the rest of his days.

1 Chronicles

+++

{1:1} So there's Adam, Sheth, Enosh, {1:2} Kenan, Mahalaleel, and Jered, {1:3} Then Henoch, Methuselah, and Lamech, {1:4} After them, Noah, Shem, Ham, and Japheth. {1:5} Japheth's crew included Gomer, Magog, Madai, Javan, Tubal, Meshech, and Tiras. {1:6} Gomer's sons were Ashchenaz, Riphath, and Togarmah. {1:7} Javan's crew: Elishah, Tarshish, Kittim, and Dodanim. {1:8} Ham had Cush, Mizraim, Put, and Canaan. {1:9} Cush had Seba, Havilah, Sabta, Raamah, and Sabtecha. Raamah had Sheba and Dedan. {1:10} Cush's son Nimrod was a big deal. {1:11-12} Mizraim's crew included Ludim, Anamim, Lehabim, Naphtuhim, Pathrusim, Casluhim (they're the Philistines), and Caphthorim. {1:13-16} Canaan had Zidon, Heth, Jebusites, Amorites, Girgashites, Hivites, Arkites, Sinites, Arvadites, Zemarites, and Hamathites. {1:17-18} Shem's crew: Elam, Asshur, Arphaxad, Lud, Aram, Uz, Hul, Gether, and Meshech. {1:18} Arphaxad had Shelah, who had Eber. {1:19-23} Eber had Peleg and Joktan—earth divided in Peleg's day, and Joktan's crew was Almodad, Sheleph, Hazarmaveth, Jerah, Hadoram, Uzal, Diklah, Ebal, Abimael, Sheba, Ophir, Havilah, and Jobab. {1:24-27} Shem's line: Arphaxad, Shelah, Eber, Peleg, Reu, Serug, Nahor, Terah, and then Abram, also known as Abraham. {1:28} Abraham's sons were Isaac and Ishmael. {1:29-31} Ishmael's kids: Nebaioth, Kedar, Adbeel, Mibsam, Mishma, Dumah, Massa, Hadad, Tema, Jetur, Naphish, and Kedemah. {1:32} Abraham's concubine Keturah had Zimran, Jokshan, Medan, Midian, Ishbak, and Shuah, and Jokshan's sons were Sheba and Dedan. {1:33} Midian's crew: Ephah, Epher, Henoch, Abida, and Eldaah. {1:34} The kings of Edom before any king in Israel were Bela, Jobab, Husham, Hadad, Samlah, Shaul, Baal-hanan, and Hadad (again), with various dukes in Edom: Timnah, Aliah, Jetheth, Aholibamah, Elah, Pinon, Kenaz, Teman, Mibzar, Magdiel, and Iram.

{2:1} So, like, these are the sons of Israel: Reuben, Simeon, Levi, Judah, Issachar, Zebulun, {2:2} Dan, Joseph (yeah, that Joseph!), and Benjamin, Naphtali, Gad, and Asher. {2:3} Judah's sons were Er, Onan, and Shelah—three born to him from Shua the Canaanite woman. Er was not cool with the Lord, so the Lord took him out. {2:4} Tamar, his daughter-in-law, gave birth to Pharez and Zerah for Judah. So, all of Judah's sons were five. {2:5} Pharez's sons were Hezron and Hamul. {2:6} Zerah's sons were Zimri, Ethan, Heman, Calcol, and Dara—five in total. {2:7} Carmi's sons included Achar, who brought trouble to Israel by doing something cursed. {2:8} Ethan's son was Azariah. {2:9} Hezron's sons were Jerahmeel, Ram, and Chelubai. {2:10} Ram had Amminadab, who had Nahshon, a prince of Judah. {2:11} Nahshon had Salma, who had Boaz, {2:12} Boaz had Obed, who had Jesse. {2:13} Jesse's sons were Eliab (the firstborn), Abinadab, Shimma, Nethaneel, Raddai, {2:14} Ozem, and David (yep, the David!). {2:16} David's sisters were Zeruiah and Abigail, and Zeruiah had Abishai, Joab, and Asahel—three dudes. {2:17} Abigail had Amasa, and Amasa's dad was Jether the Ishmaelite. {2:18} Caleb, son of Hezron, had kids with Azubah and Jerioth. Their sons were Jesher, Shobab, and Ardon. {2:19} After Azubah passed, Caleb married Ephrath, who gave birth to Hur. {2:20} Hur had Uri, who had Bezaleel. {2:21} Hezron also married Machir's daughter, Gilead's dad, when he was sixty and had Segub. {2:22} Segub had Jair, who ruled twenty-three cities in Gilead. {2:23} Jair took Geshur and Aram's towns with Kenath, sixty cities in all—part of Machir's family. {2:24} After Hezron passed, Abiah (Hezron's wife) had Ashur, father of Tekoa. {2:25} Jerahmeel's firstborn, Ram, had Bunah, Oren, Ozem, and Ahijah. {2:26} Ram had another wife, Atarah, who was Onam's mom. {2:27} Ram's firstborn, Maaz, had Jamin and Eker. {2:28} Onam had Shammai and Jada. Shammai's sons were Nadab and Abishur. {2:29} Abishur's wife was Abihail, and they had Ahban and Molid. {2:30} Nadab's sons were Seled and Appaim, but Seled died childless. {2:31} Appaim's son was Ishi, and Ishi's son was Sheshan, whose daughter was Ahlai. {2:32} Shammai's brother Jada had Jether and Jonathan, but Jether died childless. {2:33} Jonathan's sons were Peleth and Zaza. They were all Jerahmeel's descendants. {2:34} Sheshan had no sons, only daughters, and his Egyptian servant, Jarha, married one of his daughters and had Attai. {2:36} Attai had Nathan, who had Zabad, {2:37} Zabad had Ephlal, who had Obed, {2:38} Obed had Jehu, who had Azariah, {2:39} Azariah had Helez, who had Eleasah, {2:40} Eleasah had Sisamai, who had Shallum, {2:41} Shallum had Jekamiah, who had Elishama. {2:42} Caleb's brother Jerahmeel had Mesha, father of Ziph, and Mareshah, father of Hebron. {2:43} Hebron's sons were Korah, Tappuah, Rekem, and Shema. {2:44} Shema had Raham, father of Jorkoam, and Rekem had Shammai. {2:45} Shammai's son was Maon, who was the father of Beth-zur. {2:46} Caleb's concubine Ephah had Haran, Moza, and Gazez, and Har.

{3:1} So, like, these were David's kids born in Hebron: Amnon (from Ahinoam the Jezreelitess), Daniel (from Abigail the Carmelitess), {3:2} Absalom (Maachah's son, Talmai king of Geshur's daughter), Adonijah (Haggith's son), {3:3} Shephatiah (Abital's son), and Ithream (Eglah's son)—all six were born in Hebron. David ruled Hebron for seven years and six months, then thirty-three years in Jerusalem. {3:5} In Jerusalem, he had Shimea, Shobab, Nathan, and Solomon (from Bath-shua Ammiel's daughter). {3:6} Ibhar, Elishama, Eliphelet, Nogah, Nepheg, Japhia, Elishama, Eliada, and Eliphelet—nine in total. {3:9} These were David's sons, not counting his concubines' sons or Tamar. {3:10} Solomon's son was Rehoboam, then Abia, Asa, Jehoshaphat, {3:11} Joram, Ahaziah, Joash, Amaziah, Azariah, Jotham, {3:13} Ahaz, Hezekiah, Manasseh, Amon, and Josiah. {3:15} Josiah's sons were Johanan, Jehoiakim, Zedekiah, and Shallum. {3:16} Jehoiakim's sons were Jeconiah and Zedekiah. {3:17} Jeconiah's sons were Assir and Salathiel. {3:18} Pedaiah had Malchiram, Pedaiah, Shenazar, Jecamiah, Hoshama, and Nedabiah. {3:19} Pedaiah's sons were Zerubbabel and Shimei. Zerubbabel had Meshullam, Hananiah, and Shelomith. {3:20} Hananiah had Pelatiah and Jesaiah; Rephaiah had Arnan, Obadiah, and

Shechaniah. {3:22} Shechaniah had Shemaiah, and Shemaiah's sons were Hattush, Igeal, Bariah, Neariah, and Shaphat—six in total. {3:23} Neariah had Elioenai, Hezekiah, and Azrikam—three. {3:24} Elioenai had Hodaiah, Eliashib, Pelaiah, Akkub, Johanan, Dalaiah, and Anani—seven in total.

{4:1} So, like, Judah's sons were Pharez, Hezron, Carmi, Hur, and Shobal. {4:2} Reaiah, Shobal's son, had Jahath, who had Ahumai and Lahad—these were the Zorathites. {4:3} Also, Etam's father had Jezreel, Ishma, Idbash, and their sister Hazelelponi. {4:4} Penuel was Gedor's father, and Ezer was Hushah's dad—both were Hur's sons, Ephratah's firstborn and Bethlehem's father. {4:5} Ashur from Tekoa had two wives, Helah and Naarah. {4:6} Naarah had Ahuzam, Hepher, Temeni, and Haahashtari. {4:7} Helah's sons were Zereth, Jezoar, Ethnan. {4:8} Coz's sons were Anub, Zobebah, and Aharhel's son, Harum's family. {4:9} Jabez was super honorable, and his mom named him Jabez because she had him with much sorrow. {4:10} Jabez prayed to God, asking for blessings, protection, and to keep him from evil—and God granted his request. {4:11} Chelub's brother Shuah had Mehir, who was Eshton's dad. {4:12} Eshton had Beth-rapha, Paseah, and Tehinnah, Irnahash's father. {4:13} Kenaz had Othniel and Seraiah; Othniel had Hathath. {4:14} Meonothai had Ophrah; Seraiah had Joab, the valley of Charashim's founder—they were craftsmen. {4:15} Caleb's son Jephunneh had Iru, Elah, Naam, and Kenaz. {4:16} Jehaleleel's sons were Ziph, Ziphah, Tiria, Asareel. {4:17} Ezra had Jether, Mered, Epher, Jalon, Miriam, Shammai, Ishbah, Eshtemoa's father. {4:18} Jehudijah, Mered's wife, had Jered, Heber, Jekuthiel—Bithiah, Pharaoh's daughter, whom Mered married. {4:19} Hodiah, Naham's sister, had Keilah the Garmite and Eshtemoa the Maachathite. {4:20} Shimon had Amnon, Rinnah, Ben-hanan, Tilon; Ishi had Zoheth, Ben-zoheth. {4:21} Shelah, Judah's son, had Er (Lecah's father), Laadah (Mareshah's father), Ashbea's linen workers' families. {4:22} Jokim, Chozeba's men, Joash, Saraph, Moab's rulers, Jashubi-lehem—ancient facts. {4:23} These were potters, plant and hedge dwellers working for the king. {4:24} Simeon's sons were Nemuel, Jamin, Jarib, Zerah, Shaul; {4:25} Shallum, Mibsam, Mishma, Hamuel, Zacchur, Shimei. {4:27} Shimei had sixteen sons and six daughters; but not all family multiplied like Judah's children. {4:28-31} They lived in Beer-sheba, Moladah, Hazar-shual, Bilhah, Ezem, Tolad, Bethuel, Hormah, Ziklag, Bethmarcaboth, Hazar-susim, Beth- birei, Shaaraim—until David's reign. {4:32} Their villages were Etam, Ain, Rimmon, Tochen, Ashan—five cities; {4:33} and all the surrounding villages unto Baal. {4:34-35} Meshobab, Jamlech, Joshah, Joel, Jehu, Seraiah, Asiel's son. {4:36} Elioenai, Jaakobah, Jeshohaiah, Asaiah, Adiel, Jesimiel, Benaiah, Ziza, Allon's son, Jedaiah's son, Shimri's son, Shemaiah's son—princes in their families.

{5:1} So, like, Reuben was the firstborn of Israel, but he messed up by sleeping with his dad's wife, so his birthright got passed to Joseph's sons. {5:2} Judah ended up becoming the top dog among his brothers and produced a ruler, but the birthright belonged to Joseph. {5:3} Reuben's sons were Hanoch, Pallu, Hezron, and Carmi. {5:4-6} Joel's lineage was Shemaiah, Gog, Shimei, Micah, Reaia, Baal, and Beerah, who got carried off by Tilgath-pilneser, the Assyrian king. {5:7} Jeiel and Zechariah were prominent among Reuben's brethren. {5:8} Bela, son of Azaz and Joel's descendant, lived in Aroer up to Nebo and Baal-meon. {5:9} He expanded eastward toward the Euphrates River because their cattle flourished in Gilead. {5:10} During Saul's time, they fought the Hagarites and settled throughout the east of Gilead. {5:11} Gad's children lived in Bashan up to Salchah. {5:12} Joel was their leader, followed by Shapham, Jaanai, and Shaphat in Bashan. {5:13-17} Other Gadites were Michael, Meshullam, Sheba, Jorai, Jachan, Zia, and Heber—seven in total. {5:18} The combined warriors of Reuben, Gad, and half of Manasseh numbered 44,760 skilled in battle. {5:19-20} They defeated the Hagarites—Jetur, Nephish, and Nodab—with God's help. {5:21-22} They seized 50,000 camels, 250,000 sheep, 2,000 donkeys, and 100,000 men. {5:23} The half tribe of Manasseh flourished from Bashan to Mount Hermon. {5:24} Epher, Ishi, Eliel, Azriel, Jeremiah, Hodaviah, and Jahdiel were their brave and renowned leaders. {5:25} Sadly, they later turned away from God and worshiped local gods, leading to their downfall and Assyrian captivity.

{6:1} So, like, Levi's fam consisted of Gershon, Kohath, and Merari. {6:2} Kohath's crew was Amram, Izhar, Hebron, and Uzziel. {6:3} Amram's squad was Aaron, Moses, and Miriam. Aaron's posse included Nadab, Abihu, Eleazar, and Ithamar. {6:4-10} Eleazar had Phinehas, who had Abishua, who had Bukki, who had Uzzi, who had Zerahiah, who had Meraioth, who had Amariah, who had Ahitub, who had Zadok, who had Ahimaaz, who had Azariah, who had Johanan, who had Azariah, the one who did priest stuff in Solomon's temple in Jerusalem. {6:11-15} Azariah had Amariah, who had Ahitub, who had Zadok, who had Shallum, who had Hilkiah, who had Azariah, who had Seraiah, who had Jehozadak, who got taken captive when Nebuchadnezzar wrecked Judah and Jerusalem. {6:16} Levi had Gershom, Kohath, and Merari. {6:17} Gershom had Libni and Shimei. {6:18} Kohath had Amram, Izhar, Hebron, and Uzziel. {6:19} Merari had Mahli and Mushi. These were the Levite families. {6:20-21} Gershom's fam included Libni, Jahath, Zimmah, Joah, Iddo, Zerah, and Jeaterai. {6:22-24} Kohath's line had Amminadab, Korah, Assir, Elkanah, Ebiasaph, Assir (again), Tahath, Uriel, Uzziah, and Shaul. {6:25} Elkanah had Amasai and Ahimoth. {6:26-27} Elkanah's sons were Zophai, Nahath, Eliab, and Jeroham. {6:28} Samuel's sons were Vashni and Abiah. {6:29-30} Merari's crew included Mahli, Libni, Shimei, Uzza, Shimea, Haggiah, and Asaiah. {6:31} These peeps were in charge of the temple tunes after the ark chilled. {6:32} They sang at the tabernacle until Solomon built the temple in Jerusalem, then they stuck to their gig order. {6:33-38} These were the ones who served, even with their kids. Among the Kohathites, Heman was a singer, son of Joel, son of Shemuel, son of Elkanah, son of Jeroham, son of Eliel, son of Toah, son of Zuph, son of Elkanah (again), son of Mahath, son of Amasai, son of Elkanah (again), son of Joel (again), son of Azariah, son of Zephaniah, son of Tahath, son of Assir, son of Ebiasaph, son of Korah, son of Izhar, son of Kohath, son of Levi, son of Israel. {6:39-43} Heman's bro was Asaph, son of Berachiah, son of Shimea, son of Michael, son of Baaseiah, son of Malchiah, son of Ethni, son of Zerah, son of Adaiah, son of Ethan, son of Zimmah, son of Shimei, son of Jahath, son of Gershom, son of Levi. {6:44-47} Merari's fam was on the left: Ethan, son of Kishi, son of Abdi, son of Malluch, son of Hashabiah, son of Amaziah, son of Hilkiah, son of Amzi, son of Bani, son of Shamer, son of Mahli, son of Mushi, son of Merari, son of Levi. {6:48} Their Levite bros handled all kinds of temple service. {6:49} But Aaron and his sons handled the altar, incense, and holy stuff, following Moses' commands. {6:50-53} Aaron's sons were Eleazar, Phinehas, Abishua, Bukki, Uzzi, Zerahiah, Meraioth, Amariah, Ahitub, Zadok, and Ahimaaz. {6:54-56} Aaron's fam got land and cities in Judah, including Hebron and Caleb's fields. {6:57-59} Judah's cities went to Aaron's sons: Hebron, Libnah, Jattir, Eshtemoa, Hilen, Debir, Ashan, and Beth-shemesh. {6:60} From Benjamin, they got Geba, Alemeth, and Anathoth. Thirteen cities in all. {6:61} Kohath's sons in Manasseh got ten cities. {6:62} Gershom's sons got thirteen cities from Issachar, Asher, Naphtali, and Manasseh in Bashan. {6:63} Merari's sons got twelve cities from Reuben, Gad, and Zebulun. {6:64} Israel gave these cities with their lands to the Levites. {6:65} They got cities from Judah, Simeon, and Benjamin. {6:66} Kohath's leftover families got cities from Ephraim. {6:67-70} They got cities of refuge like Shechem, Gezer, Jokmeam, Beth-horon, Aijalon, and Gath-rimmon. {6:71} Gershom's sons got Golan and Ashtaroth in Manasseh. {6:72-75} From Issachar, they got Kedesh and Daberath, and from Naphtali, they got Ramoth and Anem. {6:76} Naphtali gave them Kedesh, Hammon, and Kirjathaim. {6:77} Zebulun gave Rimmon and Tabor. {6:78} Reuben gave Bezer, Jahzah, Kedemoth, and Mephaath. {6:79} Gad gave Ramoth, Mahanaim, Heshbon, and Jazer.

{7:1} So, like, Issachar's crew included Tola, Puah, Jashub, and Shimrom, making four in total. {7:2} Tola's sons were Uzzi, Rephaiah, Jeriel, Jahmai, Jibsam, and Shemuel, who were the heads of their fam, known for being brave and strong dudes. In David's time, they had a whopping 22,600 warriors. {7:3} Uzzi had Izrahiah, who had Michael, Obadiah, Joel, and Ishiah, totaling five, all big shots. {7:4} These dudes, organized by their fams and generations, formed a fighting force of 36,000 because they had lots of wives and kids. {7:5} The rest of Issachar's fams were also tough, adding up to 87,000 mighty warriors. {7:6} Moving on to Benjamin, we've got Bela, Becher, and Jediael, making three. {7:7} Bela's crew included Ezbon, Uzzi, Uzziel, Jerimoth, and Iri, totaling five, all tough leaders with a headcount of 22,034. {7:8} Becher's sons were Zemira, Joash, Eliezer, Elioenai, Omri, Jerimoth, Abiah, and Anathoth, all of them sons of Becher. {7:9} Their tally was 20,200 mighty men. {7:10} Jediael's sons included Bilhan, who had Jeush, Benjamin, Ehud, Chenaanah, Zethan, Tharshish, and Ahishahar, totaling 17,200 warriors. {7:13} Naphtali's crew was Jahziel, Guni, Jezer, and Shallum, sons of Bilhah. {7:14} Manasseh had Ashriel and Machir (by his concubine), the dad of Gilead. {7:15} Machir married Huppim and Shuppim's sister Maachah, who had Zelophehad. {7:16} Maachah gave birth to Peresh and Sheresh, and they had Ulam and Rakem. {7:17} Ulam's son was Bedan, part of Gilead's fam. {7:20} Ephraim's fam tree goes from Shuthelah down to Tahath. {7:18} Non's son was Jehoshuah.

{8:1} So, like, Benjamin had Bela as his firstborn, then Ashbel, Aharah, Nohah, and Rapha following. {8:2} Bela's sons were Addar, Gera, Abihud, Abishua, Naaman, Ahoah, Gera again, Shephuphan, and Huram. {8:3} Ehud's crew, the heads of Geba, moved to Manahath, including Naaman, Ahiah, Gera, who had Uzza and Ahihud. {8:4} Shaharaim had kids in Moab, after sending them away; Hushim and Baara were his wives. {8:5-11} With Hodesh, his wife, he had Jobab, Zibia, Mesha, and Malcham, along with Jeuz, Shachia, and Mirma. Hushim had Abitub and Elpaal. {8:12} Elpaal's sons were Eber, Misham, Shamed, who built Ono and Lod. {8:13} Beriah and Shema were heads in Aijalon, driving out Gath's folks. {8:14} More sons followed, including Ahio, Shashak, Jeremoth, Zebadiah, Arad, Ader, Michael, Ispah, Joha, and others. {8:15} These leaders dwelled in Jerusalem. {8:16} The father of Gibeon, Maachah's husband, lived in Gibeon with his sons, including Abdon, Zur, Kish, Baal, Nadab, Gedor, Ahio, and Zacher. {8:17} Ner begat Kish, and Kish begat Saul, who had Jonathan, Malchi-shua, Abinadab, and Esh-baal. {8:18} Jonathan's son was Merib-baal, and Merib-baal had Micah. {8:19} Micah's sons were Pithon, Melech, Tarea, and Ahaz. {8:20} Ahaz had Jehoadah, Alemeth, Azmaveth, Zimri, and Moza. {8:21} Azel had six sons: Azrikam, Bocheru, Ishmael, Sheariah, Obadiah, and Hanan. {8:39} Eshek's sons were Ulam, Jehush, and Eliphelet. {8:22} Ulam's sons were mighty warriors and skilled archers, totaling 150 descendants.

{9:1} Yo, so everyone in Israel was counted by family lines and documented in the kings' records of Israel and Judah, who got exiled to Babylon for their wrongdoing. {9:2} The first peeps who settled back in their spots were Israelites, priests, Levites, and Nethinims. {9:3} In Jerusalem, there were folks from Judah, Benjamin, Ephraim, and Manasseh. {9:4} Uthai, descendant of Pharez from Judah, was there. {9:5} Shilonites like Asaiah and his crew were also around. {9:6} Zerah's descendants included Jeuel and six hundred and ninety others. {9:7} Among Benjamin's crew were Sallu, Ibneiah, Elah, and Meshullam. {9:8-9} Plus, their homies totaled nine hundred and fifty-six. All these dudes were big shots in their families. {9:10} Among the priests were Jedaiah, Jehoiarib, and Jachin. {9:11-12} Azariah was a high-up priest, and so were Adaiah and Maasiai. {9:13} The Levites numbered a thousand seven hundred and sixty, all skilled for God's work. {9:14-18} Shemaiah, Bakbakkar, Heresh, and Mattaniah were Levites too. {9:19} Shallum and his Korahite fam looked after the tabernacle gates. {9:20} Phinehas once ruled over them, and the Lord was with him. {9:21} Two hundred and twelve peeps were gatekeepers as David and Samuel set them up. {9:22} Gatekeepers covered the house from all sides. {9:23} They camped around God's house and opened it every morning. {9:24} Some handled the holy items daily. {9:25} Others managed the sanctuary's offerings. {9:26} Mattithiah was in charge of the pans. {9:33} The singers were also busy round the clock. {9:27} These Levite leaders lived in Jerusalem. {9:28} In Gibeon, Jehiel's crew stayed, including Abdon, Zur, Kish, Baal, and more. {9:29} Saul's line included Jonathan, Malchi-shua, Abinadab, and Esh-baal.

{10:1} Yo, the Philistines were up against Israel, and the Israelite dudes bounced from them, getting wrecked on Mount Gilboa. {10:2} The Philistines kept chasing Saul and his sons, taking down Jonathan, Abinadab, and Malchi-shua. {10:3} Saul got hit bad by archers in the battle. {10:4} Saul asked his armorbearer to end him, but the dude was scared. So Saul offed himself with a sword. {10:5} When the armorbearer saw Saul was gone, he did the same. {10:6} Saul, his three sons, and his whole fam were wiped out. {10:7} Israelite dudes in the valley saw this and bailed, leaving their cities to the Philistines. {10:8} Next day, the Philistines looted the dead and found

Saul and his sons on Mount Gilboa. {10:9} They took Saul's head and armor, spreading the news in Philistia. {10:10} They put Saul's gear in their temple, even his head in Dagon's temple. {10:11-12} When Jabesh-gilead heard, they sent dudes to get Saul and his sons' bodies, burying them under an oak and fasting seven days. {10:13} Saul's death was because he dissed the Lord's word and asked a spirit medium instead of God. {10:14} That's why God handed the kingdom to David.

{11:1} So, all of Israel pulled up to David at Hebron, saying, "Yo, we're fam." {11:2} They were like, "Even when Saul was king, you were the one leading us out and bringing us back. God told you, 'You're gonna be the shepherd of my people Israel, and you'll be the ruler over them.'" {11:3} So all the elders of Israel came to King David at Hebron, and he made a pact with them there before God. They anointed David as king over Israel, just like the Lord said through Samuel. {11:4} David and all of Israel then headed to Jerusalem, aka Jebus, where the Jebusites lived. {11:5} The Jebusites were like, "You ain't getting in here," but David still took the fortress of Zion, now the City of David. {11:6} David announced, "Whoever takes out the Jebusites first will be the chief and captain." Joab, son of Zeruiah, stepped up first and became chief. {11:7} David lived in the fortress, so they called it the City of David. {11:8} He built up the city all around, from Millo to the surrounding areas, and Joab fixed up the rest. {11:9} David kept getting stronger because the Lord of hosts was with him. {11:10} Here are the names of David's top warriors who had his back in his kingdom, along with all Israel, to make him king, just as the Lord had said. {11:11} The top warrior was Jashobeam, a Hachmonite, who took down 300 enemies with his spear in one go. {11:12} Next was Eleazar, son of Dodo the Ahohite, one of the top three warriors. {11:13} He was with David at Pas-dammim when the Philistines gathered for battle in a field of barley, and the people ran from the Philistines. {11:14} They stood their ground in the middle of the field, defended it, and defeated the Philistines, with God giving them a great victory. {11:15} Three of the thirty chief warriors went down to the rock to David at the cave of Adullam, while the Philistine army camped in the Valley of Rephaim. {11:16} David was in the stronghold, and the Philistine garrison was in Bethlehem. {11:17} David wished for some water from the well near the gate of Bethlehem. {11:18} The three warriors broke through the Philistine lines, drew water from the well at Bethlehem, and brought it to David. But he refused to drink it and poured it out as an offering to the Lord. {11:19} He said, "God forbid I drink this! It's like drinking the blood of these men who risked their lives." So, he didn't drink it. These were the mighty acts of the three warriors. {11:20} Abishai, Joab's brother, was chief of another three warriors. He took out 300 enemies with his spear and was as famous as the top three. {11:21} He was more honored than the other two of this group and became their commander, though he didn't reach the level of the first three. {11:22} Benaiah, son of Jehoiada, a valiant man from Kabzeel, did many great deeds. He killed two Moabite warriors who were like lions, and on a snowy day, he went down into a pit and killed a lion. {11:23} He also killed an Egyptian giant who was five cubits tall. The Egyptian had a spear like a weaver's beam, but Benaiah attacked him with a staff, snatched the spear from the Egyptian's hand, and killed him with it. {11:24} Benaiah did these things and was as famous as the top three warriors. {11:25} He was more honored than the thirty but didn't reach the level of the first three. David put him in charge of his bodyguard. {11:26} The other valiant warriors were Asahel, Joab's brother, Elhanan, son of Dodo from Bethlehem, {11:27} Shammoth the Harorite, Helez the Pelonite, {11:28} Ira, son of Ikkesh from Tekoa, Abi-ezer from Anathoth, {11:29} Sibbecai the Hushathite, Ilai the Ahohite, {11:30} Maharai from Netophah, Heled, son of Baanah from Netophah, {11:31} Ithai, son of Ribai from Gibeah in Benjamin, Benaiah the Pirathonite, {11:32} Hurai from the ravines of Gaash, Abiel the Arbathite, {11:33} Azmaveth the Baharumite, Eliahba the Shaalbonite, {11:34} The sons of Hashem the Gizonite, Jonathan, son of Shage the Hararite, {11:35} Ahiam, son of Sacar the Hararite, Eliphal, son of Ur, {11:36} Hepher the Mecherathite, Ahijah the Pelonite, {11:37} Hezro the Carmelite, Naarai, son of Ezbai, {11:38} Joel, brother of Nathan, Mibhar, son of Hagri, {11:39} Zelek the Ammonite, Naharai the Berothite, armor-bearer of Joab, son of Zeruiah, {11:40} Ira the Ithrite, Gareb the Ithrite, {11:41} Uriah the Hittite, Zabad, son of Ahlai, {11:42} Adina, son of Shiza the Reubenite, a leader of the Reubenites, and thirty with him, {11:43} Hanan, son of Maacah, Joshaphat the Mithnite, {11:44} Uzzia the Ashterathite, Shama and Jehiel, sons of Hothan the Aroerite, {11:45} Jediael, son of Shimri, and Joha his brother the Tizite, {11:46} Eliel the Mahavite, Jeribai, and Joshaviah, sons of Elnaam, and Ithmah the Moabite, {11:47} Eliel, Obed, and Jaasiel the Mezobaite.

{12:1} So, here's the squad that rolled up to David in Ziklag while he was hiding out from Saul, son of Kish. These were the elite fighters, real war heroes. {12:2} They were armed with bows and could throw stones and shoot arrows with both hands. They were from Saul's tribe, Benjamin. {12:3} The leader was Ahiezer, then Joash, sons of Shemaah the Gibeathite; also Jeziel, Pelet, sons of Azmaveth; Berachah, and Jehu the Antothite, {12:4} Ismaiah the Gibeonite, a top warrior among the thirty and their leader; Jeremiah, Jahaziel, Johanan, and Josabad the Gederathite, {12:5} Eluzai, Jerimoth, Bealiah, Shemariah, Shephatiah the Haruphite, {12:6} Elkanah, Jesiah, Azareel, Joezer, Jashobeam, the Korhites, {12:7} and Joelah, Zebadiah, sons of Jeroham from Gedor. {12:8} From the Gadites, some hardcore fighters joined David in the wilderness. These dudes could handle shields and bucklers, had faces like lions, and were as fast as deer on the mountains. {12:9} Ezer was the leader, Obadiah the second, Eliab the third, {12:10} Mishmannah the fourth, Jeremiah the fifth, {12:11} Attai the sixth, Eliel the seventh, {12:12} Johanan the eighth, Elzabad the ninth, {12:13} Jeremiah the tenth, Machbanai the eleventh. {12:14} These Gadites were the captains of the army; the least of them could take on a hundred, and the best could handle a thousand. {12:15} These guys crossed the Jordan in the first month when it was overflowing its banks, and they made everyone in the valleys run away, both to the east and west. {12:16} Then some from Benjamin and Judah came to David's stronghold. {12:17} David went out to meet them and said, "If you're here to help me, we're good. But if you're here to betray me to my enemies, even though I haven't wronged anyone, let God judge and punish you." {12:18} Then the Spirit came upon Amasai, the leader of the captains, and he said, "We're with you, David, son of Jesse. Peace to you and your helpers, because your God helps you." So David welcomed them and made them leaders of his troops. {12:19} Some from Manasseh also joined David when he was with the Philistines against Saul, but they didn't end up helping because the Philistine leaders sent David away, fearing he'd turn against them and join Saul. {12:20} When David went to Ziklag, more from Manasseh joined him: Adnah, Jozabad, Jediael, Michael, Jozabad, Elihu, and Zilthai, leaders of thousands in Manasseh. {12:21} They helped David against the raiding bands because they were all valiant warriors and commanders in the army. {12:22} Day by day, more warriors came to David until he had a massive army, like the army of God. {12:23} Here's the count of the armed troops who came to David at Hebron to transfer Saul's kingdom to him, as the Lord had said. {12:24} From Judah, there were 6,800 armed with shields and spears, ready for battle. {12:25} From Simeon, 7,100 brave warriors for the fight. {12:26} From Levi, 4,600. {12:27} Jehoiada, leader of the Aaronites, came with 3,700 men. {12:28} Zadok, a young and valiant warrior, brought 22 leaders from his family. {12:29} From Benjamin, Saul's tribe, 3,000 men, most of whom had been loyal to Saul's house until then. {12:30} From Ephraim, 20,800 brave warriors, renowned in their families. {12:31} From the half-tribe of Manasseh, 18,000 designated by name to come and make David king. {12:32} From Issachar, 200 leaders who understood the times and knew what Israel should do; all their relatives were under their command. {12:33} From Zebulun, 50,000 seasoned warriors who could keep rank; they were not divided in heart. {12:34} From Naphtali, 1,000 officers and 37,000 men with shields and spears. {12:35} From Dan, 28,600 experienced warriors. {12:36} From Asher, 40,000 who went to war, ready for battle. {12:37} From the east side of the Jordan, from Reuben, Gad, and the half-tribe of Manasseh, 120,000 armed with all kinds of weapons. {12:38} All these warriors, skilled in battle formation, came to Hebron with a single purpose: to make David king over all Israel. Everyone else in Israel was also united in making David king. {12:39} They spent three days there with David, eating and drinking, because their relatives had provided for them. {12:40} Even those from nearby Issachar, Zebulun, and Naphtali brought food on donkeys, camels, mules, and oxen—loads of provisions like flour, fig cakes, raisins, wine, oil, oxen, and sheep. There was plenty of joy in Israel.

{13:1} So, David talked it over with the leaders of thousands and hundreds, basically every head honcho. {13:2} David then told the whole squad of Israel, "If you all think it's cool and it's God's will, let's reach out to our bros all over Israel, including the priests and Levites in their towns and outskirts, to gather everyone here. {13:3} Let's bring the ark of our God back to us, since we didn't seek it during Saul's days." {13:4} Everyone was down for it because it felt right to all the people. {13:5} So David gathered all of Israel, from Shihor in Egypt to the entrance of Hamath, to bring the ark of God from Kirjath-jearim. {13:6} David and all Israel went to Baalah, aka Kirjath-jearim in Judah, to bring up the ark of the LORD, who dwells between the cherubim, whose name is called on it. {13:7} They put the ark of God on a new cart from the house of Abinadab, driven by Uzza and Ahio. {13:8} David and all Israel were jamming out before God with all their might, with songs, harps, lyres, tambourines, cymbals, and trumpets. {13:9} When they got to Chidon's threshing floor, Uzza reached out to steady the ark because the oxen stumbled. {13:10} God got angry at Uzza and struck him down for touching the ark, so he died right there before God. {13:11} David was upset because God had struck Uzza, so that place is called Perez-uzza to this day. {13:12} David got scared of God that day and wondered, "How can I ever bring the ark of God to me?" {13:13} So David didn't bring the ark to the City of David but instead took it to the house of Obed-edom the Gittite. {13:14} The ark of God stayed with Obed-edom's family for three months, and God blessed his whole household and everything he had.

{14:1} Meanwhile, Hiram, the king of Tyre, sent messengers to David with cedar wood, masons, and carpenters to build him a palace. {14:2} David realized that God had confirmed him as king over Israel, lifting up his kingdom for the sake of His people, Israel. {14:3} David took more wives in Jerusalem and had more sons and daughters. {14:4} Here are the names of his kids born in Jerusalem: Shammua, Shobab, Nathan, and Solomon, {14:5} Ibhar, Elishua, Elpelet, {14:6} Nogah, Nepheg, Japhia, {14:7} Elishama, Beeliada, and Eliphelet. {14:8} When the Philistines heard that David was anointed king over all Israel, they all came to hunt him down. David heard about it and went out to face them. {14:9} The Philistines had spread out in the valley of Rephaim. {14:10} David asked God, "Should I go up against the Philistines? Will you deliver them into my hand?" God answered, "Go up, and I will deliver them into your hand." {14:11} So they went up to Baal-perazim, and David defeated them there. David said, "God has burst through my enemies by my hand like a flood," so they called the place Baal-perazim. {14:12} The Philistines abandoned their idols there, and David ordered them to be burned. {14:13} The Philistines came back and spread out in the valley again. {14:14} David asked God again, and God said, "Don't go straight up; circle around and attack them in front of the mulberry trees. {14:15} When you hear the sound of marching in the tops of the mulberry trees, move out to battle because God has gone ahead of you to strike the Philistine army." {14:16} David did as God commanded, and they struck down the Philistines from Gibeon to Gezer. {14:17} David's fame spread everywhere, and the LORD made all the nations fear him.

{15:1} David built himself some cribs in the City of David and made a spot for the ark of God, pitching a tent for it. {15:2} Then David said, "Only the Levites can carry the ark of God because the LORD picked them to do it and serve Him forever." {15:3} David gathered everyone in Israel to Jerusalem to bring up the ark of the LORD to the place he had set up. {15:4} He got together the descendants of Aaron and the Levites: {15:5} From the sons of Kohath: Uriel the chief and 120 of his bros; {15:6} From the sons of Merari: Asaiah the chief and 220 of his bros; {15:7} From the sons of Gershom: Joel the chief and 130 of his bros; {15:8} From the sons of Elizaphan: Shemaiah the chief and 200 of his bros; {15:9} From the sons of Hebron: Eliel the chief and 80 of his bros; {15:10} From the sons of Uzziel: Amminadab the chief and 112 of his bros. {15:11} David called for Zadok and Abiathar the priests and the Levites Uriel, Asaiah, Joel, Shemaiah, Eliel, and Amminadab. {15:12} He told them, "You are the leaders of the Levites. Purify yourselves, you and your bros, so you can bring up the ark of the LORD God of Israel to the spot I prepared for it. {15:13} Because last time we didn't do it right, the LORD our God struck us down for not seeking Him properly." {15:14} So the priests and Levites purified themselves to bring up the ark of the LORD God of Israel. {15:15} The Levites carried the ark of God on their shoulders with poles, just like Moses commanded according to God's word. {15:16} David told the chief Levites to appoint their bros as singers with musical instruments—harps, lyres, and cymbals—to make a joyful sound. {15:17} So the Levites chose Heman son of Joel; his bros Asaph son of Berechiah; and from the sons of Merari, their bro Ethan son of Kushaiah; {15:18} and with them their second-degree bros Zechariah, Ben, Jaaziel, Shemiramoth, Jehiel, Unni, Eliab, Benaiah, Maaseiah, Mattithiah, Elipheleh, Mikneiah, Obed-edom, and Jeiel, the gatekeepers. {15:19} The singers Heman, Asaph, and Ethan were appointed to play the brass cymbals; {15:20} Zechariah, Aziel, Shemiramoth, Jehiel, Unni, Eliab, Maaseiah, and Benaiah played psalteries on Alamoth; {15:21} Mattithiah, Elipheleh, Mikneiah, Obed-edom, Jeiel, and Azaziah played harps on the Sheminith to excel. {15:22} Chenaniah, the chief of the Levites, was in charge of the singing because he was skilled at it. {15:23} Berechiah and Elkanah were doorkeepers for the ark. {15:24} Shebaniah, Jehoshaphat, Nethaneel, Amasai, Zechariah, Benaiah, and Eliezer, the priests, blew the trumpets before the ark of God, and Obed-edom and Jehiah were doorkeepers for the ark. {15:25} So David, the elders of Israel, and the captains over thousands went to bring up the ark of the covenant of the LORD from the house of Obed-edom with joy. {15:26} When God helped the Levites carrying the ark of the covenant of the LORD, they sacrificed seven bulls and seven rams. {15:27} David was dressed in a robe of fine linen, as were all the Levites carrying the ark, the singers, and Chenaniah, the song leader. David also wore a linen ephod. {15:28} So all Israel brought up the ark of the covenant of the LORD with shouts, the sound of cornet, trumpets, cymbals, making noise with psalteries and harps. {15:29} As the ark of the covenant of the LORD came into the City of David, Michal, Saul's daughter, looked out the window and saw King David dancing and celebrating, and she despised him in her heart.

{16:1} They brought the ark of God and set it up in the tent that David had prepped for it. Then they offered burnt sacrifices and peace offerings to God. {16:2} When David finished offering the sacrifices, he blessed everyone in the name of the LORD. {16:3} He hooked everyone up with a loaf of bread, a piece of meat, and a flagon of wine, both the dudes and the ladies. {16:4} David assigned some of the Levites to serve in front of the ark of the LORD, to record, and to thank and praise the LORD God of Israel: {16:5} Asaph was the leader, with Zechariah, Jeiel, Shemiramoth, Jehiel, Mattithiah, Eliab, Benaiah, and Obed-edom as his squad; Jeiel played psalteries and harps, and Asaph rocked the cymbals; {16:6} Benaiah and Jahaziel the priests were on trumpets continually before the ark. {16:7} That day, David gave Asaph and his crew a psalm to thank the LORD. {16:8} "Give thanks to the LORD, call on His name, and tell everyone about His awesome deeds. {16:9} Sing to Him, sing psalms, and talk about all His wonderful works. {16:10} Glory in His holy name; let those who seek the LORD rejoice. {16:11} Seek the LORD and His strength, always seek His presence. {16:12} Remember the amazing things He has done, His wonders, and the judgments He has spoken; {16:13} You descendants of Israel, His servant, children of Jacob, His chosen ones. {16:14} He is the LORD our God; His judgments are everywhere on earth. {16:15} Always remember His covenant, the word He commanded to a thousand generations; {16:16} The covenant He made with Abraham, and His oath to Isaac; {16:17} He confirmed it to Jacob as a decree, to Israel as an everlasting covenant, {16:18} Saying, 'I'll give you the land of Canaan, your inheritance.' {16:19} When you were few in number, few indeed, and strangers in it, {16:20} And you wandered from nation to nation, from one kingdom to another, {16:21} He allowed no one to wrong them; He rebuked kings for their sake, {16:22} Saying, 'Don't touch My anointed ones, do My prophets no harm.' {16:23} Sing to the LORD, all the earth; proclaim His salvation day by day. {16:24} Declare His glory among the nations, His marvelous works among all people. {16:25} For the LORD is great and highly praised; He is to be feared above all gods. {16:26} For all the gods of the peoples are idols, but the LORD made the heavens. {16:27} Splendor and majesty are before Him; strength and joy are in His place. {16:28} Give to the LORD, families of the peoples, give to the LORD glory and strength. {16:29} Give to the LORD the glory due His name; bring an offering and come before Him. Worship the LORD in the splendor of His holiness. {16:30} Tremble before Him, all the earth; the world is firmly established, it cannot be shaken. {16:31} Let the heavens be glad and the earth rejoice; let them say among the nations, 'The LORD reigns!' {16:32} Let the sea and all that fills it resound; let the fields and everything in them exult. {16:33} Then the trees of the forest will sing for joy before the LORD, for He is coming to judge the earth. {16:34} Give thanks to the LORD, for He is good; His faithful love endures forever. {16:35} And say, 'Save us, God of our salvation; gather and rescue us from the nations, so that we may give thanks to Your holy name and rejoice in Your praise.' {16:36} Blessed be the LORD God of Israel from everlasting to everlasting." And all the people said, "Amen," and praised the LORD. {16:37} David left Asaph and his crew there before the ark to minister regularly according to each day's requirements. {16:38} He left Obed-edom and his 68 bros to be gatekeepers; Obed-edom son of Jeduthun and Hosah were in charge. {16:39} Zadok the priest and the other priests were stationed at the tabernacle of the LORD at the high place in Gibeon. {16:40} They were to offer burnt offerings regularly, morning and evening, on the altar of burnt offerings according to the Law of the LORD, which He commanded Israel. {16:41} With them were Heman and Jeduthun and the rest chosen to give thanks to the LORD, because His love endures forever. {16:42} Heman and Jeduthun were responsible for the music, with trumpets and cymbals and the other instruments for sacred song. The sons of Jeduthun were gatekeepers. {16:43} Then all the people went home, and David returned home to bless his household.

{17:1} So David was chilling in his crib, and he said to Nathan the prophet, "Yo, I'm living in this dope cedar house, but the ark of the covenant is just under some curtains." {17:2} Nathan replied, "Go for it, dude! God's got your back." {17:3} But that night, God hit up Nathan with a message, {17:4} "Tell David, 'This is what the LORD says: You're not the one to build me a house to live in. {17:5} I've never lived in a house, ever since I brought Israel out of Egypt. I've moved from tent to tent, from one tabernacle to another. {17:6} Did I ever ask any of the judges I appointed to lead Israel, 'Why haven't you built me a cedar house?' {17:7} So tell my servant David, 'This is what the LORD of hosts says: I took you from the pasture, from following sheep, to be the leader of my people Israel. {17:8} I've been with you wherever you went and have defeated all your enemies before you. Now I'll make your name as famous as the greatest names on earth. {17:9} And I'll provide a place for my people Israel and plant them so they can have their own home and not be disturbed again. Wicked people won't oppress them anymore, like they did at the beginning, {17:10} and since the time I appointed judges over my people Israel. I'll also subdue all your enemies. Moreover, I declare that the LORD will build a house for you. {17:11} When your time comes to join your ancestors, I'll raise up one of your offspring to succeed you, one of your own sons, and I'll establish his kingdom. {17:12} He will build a house for me, and I'll establish his throne forever. {17:13} I will be his father, and he will be my son. I'll never withdraw my love from him, as I withdrew it from the one who preceded you. {17:14} I'll settle him in my house and my kingdom forever, and his throne will be established forever.'" {17:15} Nathan relayed all these words and the entire vision to David. {17:16} Then King David went in and sat before the LORD, saying, "Who am I, LORD God, and what is my family, that you have brought me this far? {17:17} And as if this were not enough in your sight, O God, you have spoken about the future of my house. You've treated me like a high-ranking person, LORD God. {17:18} What more can David say to you for honoring your servant? You know your servant, {17:19} LORD. For the sake of your servant and according to your will, you have done this great thing and made all these great promises known. {17:20} There is no one like you, LORD, and there is no God but you, as we have heard with our own ears. {17:21} And who is like your people Israel—the one nation on earth whose God went out to redeem a people for himself and to make a name for himself, and to perform great and awesome wonders by driving out nations before your people, whom you redeemed from Egypt? {17:22} You made your people Israel your very own forever, and you, LORD, have become their God. {17:23} And now, LORD, let the promise you have made concerning your servant and his house be established forever. Do as you promised, {17:24} so that your name will be great forever. Then people will say, 'The LORD Almighty, the God over Israel, is Israel's God!' And the house of your servant David will be established before you. {17:25} You, my God, have revealed to your servant that you will build a house for him. So your servant has found courage to pray before you. {17:26} You, LORD, are God! You have promised these good things to your servant. {17:27} Now, please bless the house of your servant, so that it may continue forever in your sight; for you, LORD, have blessed it, and it will be blessed forever."

{18:1} So after all this, David totally owned the Philistines, conquered them, and took over Gath and its towns from their control. {18:2} He also defeated Moab, and the Moabites became his servants, bringing him gifts. {18:3} David then went on to smash Hadarezer, king of Zobah, all the way to Hamath, establishing his rule by the Euphrates River. {18:4} David captured 1,000 chariots, 7,000 horsemen, and 20,000 foot soldiers from Hadarezer. He disabled all the chariot horses, keeping only 100 chariots. {18:5} When the Syrians of Damascus tried to help Hadarezer, David wiped out 22,000 of them. {18:6} David then placed garrisons in Damascus, and the Syrians became his servants, also bringing gifts. The LORD protected David wherever he went. {18:7} David took the gold shields from Hadarezer's officers and brought them to Jerusalem. {18:8} From Tibhath and Chun, Hadarezer's cities, David took a lot of bronze, which Solomon later used to make the bronze sea, pillars, and vessels. {18:9} When Tou, king of Hamath, heard about David's victories over Hadarezer, {18:10} he sent his son Hadoram to King David to ask how he was and to congratulate him for defeating Hadarezer, who had been at war with Tou. Hadoram brought all kinds of gold, silver, and bronze items. {18:11} King David dedicated these treasures to the LORD, along with the silver and gold he had taken from other nations like Edom, Moab, the Ammonites, the Philistines, and Amalek. {18:12} Abishai, son of Zeruiah, also killed 18,000 Edomites in the Valley of Salt. {18:13} David put garrisons in Edom, and all the Edomites became his servants. The LORD protected David wherever he went. {18:14} So David ruled over all Israel, bringing justice and fairness to all his people. {18:15} Joab, son of Zeruiah, was the commander of the army; Jehoshaphat, son of Ahilud, was the recorder. {18:16} Zadok, son of Ahitub, and Abimelech, son of Abiathar, were priests; Shavsha was the scribe; {18:17} Benaiah, son of Jehoiada, was over the Cherethites and Pelethites; and David's sons were chief officials at the king's side.

{19:1} So, after all this, Nahash, king of the Ammonites, died, and his son took over. {19:2} David was like, "I'll show kindness to Hanun, son of Nahash, 'cause his dad was good to me." So he sent messengers to comfort him about his dad. David's crew rolled up in Ammon to comfort Hanun. {19:3} But the Ammonite leaders were like, "Yo, you really think David's honoring your dad by sending these guys? Nah, they're here to spy and overthrow the land!" {19:4} So Hanun shaved David's crew, cut their clothes at the butt, and sent them packing. {19:5} Some people told David how his men got treated, and he sent for them, telling them to chill at Jericho until their beards grew back before returning. {19:6} Realizing they made themselves hated by David, Hanun and the Ammonites hired a thousand talents of silver for chariots and horsemen from Mesopotamia, Syria-Maachah, and Zobah. {19:7} They got 32,000 chariots and the king of Maachah with his troops, who camped before Medeba. The Ammonites also gathered from their cities to battle. {19:8} When David heard this, he sent Joab and all the mighty warriors. {19:9} The Ammonites set up battle at the city gate, with the kings by themselves in the field. {19:10} Joab saw the battle was on both fronts, so he picked Israel's best to fight the Syrians. {19:11} The rest he put under his bro Abishai's command to face the Ammonites. {19:12} Joab said, "If the Syrians are too tough for me, you help. If the Ammonites are too tough for you, I'll help you. {19:13} Be brave and fight hard for our people and cities of God. Let the LORD do what He thinks is good." {19:14} Joab and his troops advanced against the Syrians, and they fled. {19:15} Seeing the Syrians flee, the Ammonites also fled from Abishai and went into the city. Then Joab went back to Jerusalem. {19:16} When the Syrians saw they lost to Israel, they called reinforcements from beyond the river, with Shophach, the captain of Hadarezer's army, leading them. {19:17} David heard about it, gathered all Israel, crossed the Jordan, and faced them. They set up battle, and the Syrians fought him. {19:18} But the Syrians ran from Israel. David killed 7,000 chariot fighters, 40,000 foot soldiers, and Shophach, their captain. {19:19} Seeing they were beaten, Hadarezer's servants made peace with David and served him. The Syrians didn't help the Ammonites anymore.

{20:1} The next year, when kings go to war, Joab led the army, destroyed the Ammonite country, and besieged Rabbah. David stayed in Jerusalem, and Joab captured Rabbah and destroyed it. {20:2} David took the king's crown, which weighed a talent of gold and had precious stones, and put it on his head. He also took a lot of loot from the city. {20:3} He brought out the people there and cut them with saws, iron harrows, and axes. He did this to all Ammonite cities, then David and all the people returned to Jerusalem. {20:4} Later, there was another war with the Philistines at Gezer. Sibbechai the Hushathite killed Sippai, a descendant of the giants, subduing them. {20:5} Another battle with the Philistines happened, where Elhanan, son of Jair, killed Lahmi, Goliath's brother, whose spear was like a weaver's beam. {20:6} Again, there was war at Gath, where there was a huge dude with 24 fingers and toes, six on each hand and foot, another giant's son. {20:7} When he defied Israel, Jonathan, son of Shimea, David's brother, killed him. {20:8} These were descendants of the giant in Gath, and they were defeated by David and his crew.

{21:1} So, Satan was like, "Let's mess with Israel," and made David count them. {21:2} David told Joab and the leaders, "Go count everyone from Beersheba to Dan, and bring me the numbers." {21:3} Joab was like, "Why? The LORD can make us way more than we are. Aren't they all your servants? Why do this and bring trouble on Israel?" {21:4} But David insisted, so Joab went and counted everyone in Israel and came back to Jerusalem. {21:5} Joab reported to David: Israel had a million and a hundred thousand sword-wielding men, and Judah had four hundred seventy thousand. {21:6} But he didn't count Levi and Benjamin because he thought the king's order was wrong. {21:7} God was mad about this and struck Israel. {21:8} David said to God, "I messed up big time by doing this. Please forgive me, I acted foolishly." {21:9} The LORD told Gad, David's seer, {21:10} "Go tell David, 'The LORD says: I'm giving you three choices; pick one for me to do to you.'" {21:11} Gad told David, {21:12} "Three years of famine, three months of running from your enemies, or three days of the LORD's sword—pestilence in the land with the angel of the LORD wrecking Israel. Think it over and let me know." {21:13} David told Gad, "I'm in deep trouble. Let me fall into the LORD's hands, 'cause His mercy is great. But don't let me fall into human hands." {21:14} So, the LORD sent a plague on Israel, and 70,000 people died. {21:15} God sent an angel to destroy Jerusalem, but as he was doing it, the LORD felt bad and told the angel, "That's enough, stop now." The angel was by Ornan the Jebusite's threshing floor. {21:16} David saw the angel of the LORD with a drawn sword over Jerusalem and he and the elders, in sackcloth, fell on their faces. {21:17} David said, "Wasn't it me who ordered the count? I sinned and did evil. But these people, what did they do? Let your hand be against me and my family, not them." {21:18} Then the angel told Gad to tell David to set up an altar to the LORD at Ornan's threshing floor. {21:19} David followed Gad's instructions from the LORD. {21:20} Ornan saw the angel and his sons hid. He was threshing wheat. {21:21} When David came, Ornan saw him, bowed down with his face to the ground. {21:22} David asked Ornan to sell him the threshing floor to build an altar to stop the plague. {21:23} Ornan said, "Take it, my king! And I'll give you oxen for burnt offerings, threshing tools for wood, and wheat for the grain offering. I give it all." {21:24} But David said, "No, I'll pay full price. I won't offer to the LORD something that cost me nothing." {21:25} So David paid Ornan 600 shekels of gold for the place. {21:26} David built an altar there, offered burnt and peace offerings, and called on the LORD. God answered with fire from heaven on the altar. {21:27} The LORD told the angel to put his sword away. {21:28} When David saw that the LORD answered him at Ornan's threshing floor, he sacrificed there. {21:29} The LORD's tabernacle made by Moses and the altar were at that time in the high place at Gibeon. {21:30} But David couldn't go there to seek God because he was scared of the angel's sword.

{22:1} Then David was like, "This is the spot for the LORD God's house and the altar for Israel's burnt offerings." {22:2} He ordered all the foreigners in Israel to gather and got masons to carve stones for God's house. {22:3} David stocked up on tons of iron for the gate nails and joints, and so much brass it couldn't be weighed. {22:4} He also got a massive amount of cedar wood, brought by the Zidonians and Tyrians. {22:5} David said, "My son Solomon is young and inexperienced, and the LORD's house must be super awesome and famous everywhere. So, I'll get everything ready before I die." And David prepared a lot. {22:6} Then he called Solomon and told him to build a house for the LORD God of Israel. {22:7} David told Solomon, "Son, I wanted to build a house for the LORD my God, {22:8} but God said, 'You have shed too much blood and waged big wars; you can't build my house. {22:9} You'll have a son named Solomon who will bring peace and rest to Israel. {22:10} He will build my house, he'll be my son, and I'll be his father. I'll make his kingdom's throne strong forever.' {22:11} So, my son, may the LORD be with you and help you build His house as He said. {22:12} May the LORD give you wisdom and understanding to lead Israel and keep His laws. {22:13} You'll succeed if you follow the rules and judgments the LORD gave Moses. Be strong and brave; don't be afraid or discouraged. {22:14} I've worked hard to prepare 100,000 talents of gold, a million talents of silver, and so much brass and iron it's uncountable. Plus, I've got timber and stone ready, and you can add more. {22:15} You've got plenty of workers: stone and timber cutters, and skilled craftsmen for every kind of work. {22:16} There's no limit to the gold, silver, brass, and iron. So get to work, and may the LORD be with you." {22:17} David also told all the princes of Israel to help Solomon, {22:18} saying, "The LORD your God is with you and has given you peace on every side. He handed the land's inhabitants to me, and it's under the LORD and His people. {22:19} So, focus your hearts and souls on seeking the LORD your God. Get up and build the sanctuary for the LORD God, to bring in the ark of the covenant and the holy vessels of God, into the house built for the LORD's name."

{23:1} When David got old and felt like he'd seen it all, he made Solomon his son the king over Israel. {23:2} He got all the big shots of Israel, along with the priests and the Levites, together. {23:3} Now, the Levites were counted from age thirty and up, and there were a total of 38,000 of them. {23:4} Out of those, 24,000 were assigned to work on the house of the LORD, 6,000 were officers and judges, {23:5} 4,000 were gatekeepers, and another 4,000 praised the LORD with musical instruments that David had made for praising. {23:6} David split them into groups according to Levi's sons: Gershon, Kohath, and Merari. {23:7} Laadan and Shimei were part of the

Gershonites. {23:8} Laadan's sons were Jehiel, Zetham, and Joel, three in all. {23:9} Shimei's sons were Shelomith, Haziel, and Haran, also three. These were the Gershonite fathers. {23:10} Shimei's sons were Jahath, Zina, Jeush, and Beriah, four in total. {23:11} Jahath was the main guy, followed by Zizah; Jeush and Beriah didn't have many kids, so they were counted together under their father's house. {23:12} Kohath had Amram, Izhar, Hebron, and Uzziel, four sons. {23:13} Amram's sons were Aaron and Moses. Aaron and his sons were set apart forever to do holy stuff like burning incense to the LORD, serving Him, and blessing in His name. {23:14} Moses, the man of God, had sons from the Levites. {23:15} Moses's sons were Gershom and Eliezer. {23:16} Gershom's main dude was Shebuel, {23:17} while Eliezer's main guy was Rehabiah. Eliezer didn't have any other sons, but Rehabiah had a bunch. {23:18} Izhar's main guy was Shelomith, {23:19} Hebron had Jeriah, Amariah, Jahaziel, and Jekameam. {23:20} Uzziel had Micah and Jesiah. {23:21} Merari had Mahli and Mushi. Mahli's sons were Eleazar and Kish. {23:22} Eleazar had no sons, only daughters, who were taken by their cousins, Kish's sons. {23:23} Mushi's sons were Mahli, Eder, and Jeremoth, three in all. {23:24} These were Levi's sons, sorted by their fathers' houses. They were the main guys in their families, counted by names and roles, starting from age twenty, responsible for working in the house of the LORD. {23:25} David said, "The LORD God of Israel has given His people rest so they can stay in Jerusalem forever. {23:26} The Levites won't have to carry the tabernacle or its stuff anymore. {23:27} David's last words made the Levites' starting age for service twenty and up. {23:28} They were assigned to assist Aaron's sons in the house of the LORD, in the courts, chambers, and in purifying holy things, along with other tasks. {23:29} They handled the showbread, fine flour for offerings, unleavened cakes, pan-baked and fried stuff, and all sorts of measurements. {23:30} They stood every morning to thank and praise the LORD, and did the same in the evening. {23:31} They offered burnt sacrifices to the LORD on Sabbaths, new moons, and set feasts, according to His commands, always before the LORD. {23:32} They were in charge of the tabernacle, the holy place, and helping Aaron's sons in the house of the LORD.

{24:1} So, like, these are the divisions of Aaron's sons. The dudes were Nadab, Abihu, Eleazar, and Ithamar. {24:2} But Nadab and Abihu bit the dust before their dad and didn't have kids, so Eleazar and Ithamar took over the priest gig. {24:3} David sorted them out, giving Zadok (Eleazar's son) and Ahimelech (Ithamar's son) their roles and tasks. {24:4} Turns out there were more big shots from Eleazar's side than Ithamar's side, so that's how they split it. Eleazar's crew had sixteen main dudes from their father's house, while Ithamar's side had eight. {24:5} They drew lots to decide who did what, and it turned out that Eleazar's sons and Ithamar's sons got roles as governors in the sanctuary and the house of God. {24:6} Shemaiah, the son of Nethaneel, wrote it all down for the king, the princes, Zadok the priest, Ahimelech (Abiathar's son), and the big bosses of the priests and Levites. Each household got picked for Eleazar and Ithamar. {24:7} First up was Jehoiarib, then Jedaiah, Harim, Seorim, Malchijah, Mijamin, Hakkoz, Abijah, Jeshua, Shecaniah, Eliashib, Jakim, Huppah, Jeshebeab, Bilgah, Immer, Hezir, Aphses, Pethahiah, Jehezekel, Jachin, Gamul, Delaiah, and Maaziah. {24:8} These were the rotations for their service in the house of the LORD, just like how the LORD God of Israel told Aaron. {24:9} The other sons of Levi were like: Amram's son was Shubael, who had Jehdeiah. {24:10} Rehabiah's son Isshiah was the first, {24:11} and Izhar's son was Shelomoth, who had Jahath. {24:12} Hebron's sons were Jeriah, Amariah, Jahaziel, and Jekameam. {24:13} Uzziel's son was Michah, and Michah's son was Shamir. {24:14} Michah's brother Isshiah had Zechariah. {24:15} Merari had Mahli and Mushi, and Jaaziah's sons were Beno, Shoham, Zaccur, and Ibri. {24:16} Mahli had a son named Eleazar, who didn't have any kids. {24:17} Kish's son was Jerahmeel. {24:18} Mushi's sons were Mahli, Eder, and Jerimoth. Those were the sons of the Levites from their father's houses. {24:19} They also cast lots before David the king, Zadok, Ahimelech, and the big bosses of the priests and Levites, the main dudes over the younger ones.

{25:1} So, like, David and his squad put the sons of Asaph, Heman, and Jeduthun in charge of jamming out with harps, psalteries, and cymbals. The total crew working it out was: {25:2} Of Asaph's sons: Zaccur, Joseph, Nethaniah, and Asarelah, all under Asaph's guidance, spitting lyrics as per the king's order. {25:3} Jeduthun's squad: Gedaliah, Zeri, Jeshaiah, Hashabiah, and Mattithiah, six in all, rocking out under their dad's lead with harps to thank and praise the LORD. {25:4} Heman's crew: Bukkiah, Mattaniah, Uzziel, Shebuel, Jerimoth, Hananiah, Hanani, Eliathah, Giddalti, Romamti-ezer, Joshbekashah, Mallothi, Hothir, and Mahazioth. {25:5} These dudes were Heman's band, dropping spiritual beats and getting divine wisdom, with Heman getting blessed with fourteen sons and three daughters from God. {25:6} All these dudes followed their dad's lead in singing for the LORD, rocking cymbals, psalteries, and harps, doing their thing for the house of God as ordered by the king to Asaph, Jeduthun, and Heman. {25:7} So, all in all, including their well-trained bros in the art of LORD's jams, there were two hundred eighty-eight in the crew. {25:8} They rolled dice, no matter if they were big shots or newbies, everyone got a shot. {25:9} First roll went to Asaph's Joseph, second to Gedaliah, along with his twelve brothers and sons. {25:10} Then it was Zaccur's turn, also with his twelve brothers and sons. {25:11} Izri got the fourth roll, again with his twelve brothers and sons. {25:12} Next was Nethaniah, same deal with his twelve brothers and sons. {25:13} Bukkiah got the sixth roll, with his twelve brothers and sons. {25:14} Jesharelah got the seventh roll, same setup with his twelve brothers and sons. {25:15} Jeshaiah got the eighth roll, yup, with his twelve brothers and sons. {25:16} Mattaniah got the ninth roll, you guessed it, with his twelve brothers and sons. {25:17} Shimei got the tenth roll, same setup with his twelve brothers and sons. {25:18} Azareel got the eleventh roll, you know the drill, with his twelve brothers and sons. {25:19} Hashabiah got the twelfth roll, ditto with his twelve brothers and sons. {25:20} Shubael got the thirteenth roll, same deal with his twelve brothers and sons. {25:21} Mattithiah got the fourteenth roll, with his twelve brothers and sons. {25:22} Jeremoth got the fifteenth roll, you get it, with his twelve brothers and sons. {25:23} Hananiah got the sixteenth roll, same setup with his twelve brothers and sons. {25:24} Joshbekashah got the seventeenth roll, with his twelve brothers and sons. {25:25} Hanani got the eighteenth roll, you know, with his twelve brothers and sons. {25:26} Mallothi got the nineteenth roll, with his twelve brothers and sons. {25:27} Eliathah got the twentieth roll, same deal with his twelve brothers and sons. {25:28} Hothir got the twenty-first roll, with his twelve brothers and sons. {25:29} Giddalti got the twenty-second roll, ditto with his twelve brothers and sons. {25:30} Mahazioth got the twenty-third roll, same setup with his twelve brothers and sons. {25:31} And Romamti-ezer got the twenty-fourth roll, yup, with his twelve brothers and sons.

{26:1} So, like, about the security team: Meshelemiah, Kore's kid from the Asaph crew, held it down. {26:2} His sons were Zechariah, Jediael, Zebadiah, Jathniel, Elam, Jehohanan, and Elioenai. {26:3} Obed-edom's sons, the bouncers, were Shemaiah, Jehozabad, Joah, Sacar, Nethaneel, Ammiel, Issachar, and Peulthai, blessed by God. {26:4} Shemaiah's sons, the muscle, were Othni, Rephael, Obed, Elzabad, and their tough cousins, Elihu and Semachiah. {26:5} The Obed-edom crew, including sons and cousins, were sixty-two strong, all skilled for the job. {26:6} Meshelemiah's crew, eighteen strong, were also ready to throw down. {26:7} Hosah, from Merari's fam, had Simri as head honcho, even though he wasn't firstborn, his dad put him in charge, along with Hilkiah, Tebaliah, and Zechariah, thirteen in total. {26:8} The porters, sixty-two from Obed-edom's crew, and eighteen from Meshelemiah's squad, were ready for their shifts in the LORD's crib. {26:9} They rolled dice, small or big, to decide their shifts at each gate, {26:10} Shelemiah got the east gate, Zechariah's wise son got the north gate, {26:15} Obed-edom got the south gate, {26:16} and Shuppim and Hosah handled the west gate, with Shallecheth gate on the side, set up for security. {26:17} Six Levites guarded the east, four a day north and south, and two Levites took care of Asuppim gate. {26:18} Four Levites were stationed at Parbar, and two at the causeway. {26:19} These were the gate assignments for the Korahites and Merarites. {26:20} Ahijah managed the house of God's treasures and dedicated items. {26:21} Laadan's crew, Jehieli, managed the treasures. {26:24} Shebuel, Moses' grandson, managed the treasures, while his brother Rehabiah and others took care of David's dedications. {26:27} Spoils from battles were dedicated to maintain the LORD's crib. {26:29} Chenaniah and his sons handled Israel's external affairs as officers and judges. {26:30} Hashabiah and his tough Hebronite crew, seventeen hundred strong, handled business west of the Jordan, serving the LORD and the king. {26:31} Among them was Jerijah, a standout leader, and forty years later, they found mighty warriors at Jazer of Gilead. {26:32} Two thousand seven hundred strong men were made chiefs by King David over the Reubenites, Gadites, and half tribe of Manasseh, handling all matters of God and the king.

{27:1} So, like, the Israelites were all organized, with chief dads, thousand captains, hundred captains, and officers serving the king. Each month, a course of them, totaling twenty-four thousand, did their thing, rotating in and out. {27:2} Jashobeam led the first month's crew, also twenty-four thousand strong. {27:3} Perez's kid was head honcho for the first month. {27:4} Dodai, an Ahohite, handled the second month, with his crew of twenty-four thousand. {27:5} Benaiah, a top priest, commanded the third month, also with twenty-four thousand. {27:6} Benaiah, one of the mighty thirty, had his son Ammizabad in his crew. {27:7} Asahel and Zebadiah ruled the fourth month, with their twenty-four thousand. {27:8} Shamhuth handled the fifth month, with his crew of twenty-four thousand. {27:9} Ira the Tekoite was in charge of the sixth month, with his twenty-four thousand. {27:10} Helez from Ephraim led the seventh month, with his twenty-four thousand. {27:11} Sibbecai from Zarhites was up for the eighth month, with his twenty-four thousand. {27:12} Abiezer from Benjamin took the ninth month, also with twenty-four thousand. {27:13} Maharai, another Zarhite, led the tenth month, with his twenty-four thousand. {27:14} Benaiah from Ephraim was the boss for the eleventh month, with his twenty-four thousand. {27:15} Heldai from Othniel wrapped it up for the twelfth month, still with twenty-four thousand. {27:16} Each tribe had its ruler: Eliezer for Reuben, Shephatiah for Simeon, Hashabiah for Levites, and Zadok for Aaronites, among others. {27:23} David didn't count those under twenty, as God promised to increase Israel's numbers like the stars. {27:24} Joab started counting but stopped due to divine wrath, and it wasn't recorded in David's chronicles. {27:25} Azmaveth managed the king's treasures, and Jehonathan handled the storehouses. {27:26} Ezri supervised the field workers, {27:27} Shimei took care of the vineyards, Zabdi handled the wine cellars, {27:28} Baal-hanan managed the olive and sycomore trees, while Joash looked after the oil cellars. {27:29} Shitrai oversaw the herds in Sharon, and Shaphat managed those in the valleys. {27:30} Obil took care of the camels, and Jehdeiah handled the donkeys. {27:31} Jaziz was in charge of the flocks. All of them managed King David's riches. {27:32} Jonathan, David's uncle, was a wise advisor, while Jehiel was with the king's sons. {27:33} Ahithophel was the king's counselor, and Hushai was his buddy. {27:34} After Ahithophel, Jehoiada and Abiathar took charge, and Joab led the king's army.

{28:1} So David gathered all the big shots of Israel, tribe leaders, company captains, stewards, officers, mighty dudes, and all the brave souls to Jerusalem. {28:2} Then David, standing tall, was like, "Listen up, fam! I wanted to build a chill crib for God's stuff, but He said nah, 'cause I've been too much of a warrior. {28:3} But God's cool with Solomon doing it. He chose me to rule, picked Judah as the main tribe, and singled out Solomon to be king. {28:4} Solomon's the chosen one to reign on God's throne. {28:5} God promised Solomon a long-lasting kingdom if he sticks to the divine rules. {28:6} So, Solomon, my dude, you're up to build God's pad and courts. He's like a son to God now. {28:7} If Solomon keeps it real and obeys God, his reign's set for eternity. {28:8} So, peeps, keep God's commands to hold onto this dope land forever and pass it down to your kids. {28:9} And you, Solomon, gotta know God, serve Him with all you got. He knows your vibes, so seek Him. If you dip, though, God won't play, yo. {28:10} God chose you to build His crib, so stay strong and get it done. {28:11} David hooked Solomon up with blueprints for everything: porches, cribs, treasure spots, chill rooms, and even the mercy seat spot. {28:12} He got all the deets by the spirit: layouts, chambers, treasures, and all that jazz. {28:13} Covers everything: priest shifts, Levite gigs, and all the house chores. {28:14} Gave gold and silver for all the tools, including candlesticks and tables. {28:15} Gold for candlesticks and silver for the tables, weighed out to fit. {28:16} More gold for the shewbread tables and silver for the others. {28:17} Also gold for fleshhooks, bowls, cups, and basins, and silver for silver basins. {28:18} Even gold for the incense altar and the cherub chariot guarding the ark. {28:19} God laid it all out for David to write down, every detail of the blueprint. {28:20} David told Solomon to stay strong, 'cause God's got his back until the job's done. {28:21} Priests, Levites, and skilled workers are down to help, and everyone's ready to follow Solomon's lead.

{29:1} So David, the OG king, was like, "Listen up, y'all! Solomon, my boy, is God's chosen one, but he's still young and green, and this task is massive. This palace ain't for us, it's for the big man upstairs." {29:2} "I've gone all out, prepped gold, silver, brass, iron, wood, onyx stones, bling stones, and all sorts of gems, plus heaps of marble." {29:3} "Because I love God's house so much, I've dropped my own stash of gold and silver for the cause." {29:4} "Check this out: 3000 talents of gold from Ophir and 7000 talents of refined silver to bling out the walls." {29:5} "And everyone who's down to contribute to God's crib today?" {29:6} "Well, the big shots, tribe leaders, and work crew bosses all stepped up and donated like bosses." {29:7} "They dropped 5000 talents of gold, 10,000 drams, 10,000 talents of silver, 18,000 talents of brass, and a whopping 100,000 talents of iron." {29:8} "The folks with precious stones also chipped in for the Lord's treasure." {29:9} "People were hyped to give, doing it with pure hearts, and David was stoked." {29:10} "So David gives a shoutout to the big man upstairs in front of everyone, praising Him forever." {29:11} "God, you're the bomb! You've got all the power and glory, ruling over everything." {29:12} "Riches and honor? That's all You, God. You're the boss, making everything awesome." {29:13} "Thanks for everything, God. You're the real MVP." {29:14} "Who am I, really? Everything we got is from You anyway." {29:15} "We're just passing through, our days are like a Snapchat story, here and gone." {29:16} "God, all this stuff we're using to build Your house? It's all from You." {29:17} "You know my heart, God, and I'm stoked to give. Seeing everyone else chip in is rad." {29:18} "God of our ancestors, keep this vibe going, and keep everyone's hearts in the right place." {29:19} "And hook up Solomon with the skills to do the job right, following all Your rules and building this palace." {29:20} "Now it's time for the whole crew to give props to the Lord. Everyone bows down, worshiping God and the king." {29:21} "They throw down sacrifices, offering up a thousand bullocks, rams, and lambs, with drink offerings, for all Israel." {29:22} "Then they throw a lit party, celebrating Solomon as the new king and Zadok as the priest." {29:23} "Solomon takes the throne, and things start looking up; all Israel is on board." {29:24} "Even David's crew and all the mighty men are backing Solomon." {29:25} "God blesses Solomon big time, making him the flyest king Israel's ever seen." {29:26} "That's how David, son of Jesse, ruled over Israel." {29:27} "He was king for 40 years, seven in Hebron and 33 in Jerusalem." {29:28} "He dies a legend, old and rich, and Solomon takes over." {29:29} "All David's deeds, from start to finish, are written in the books of Samuel, Nathan, and Gad." {29:30} "It covers his whole reign, his ups and downs, and everything that went down in Israel and beyond."

2 Chronicles

✦✦✦

{1:1} So Solomon, David's kid, leveled up big time in his kingdom, and God was totally backing him, making him a big deal. {1:2} Then Solomon hit up all of Israel, the squad leaders, judges, and every big shot in the country. {1:3} They all rolled to the high spot in Gibeon, where Moses set up shop for God back in the day. {1:4} David had brought the Ark there, setting it up in a tent in Jerusalem, and Solomon and the crew were all about it. {1:5} Solomon rolled up to the brass altar, in front of God's tent, and dropped a thousand burnt offerings on it. {1:6} That night, God pops up to Solomon and says, "Ask me anything." {1:7} Solomon's like, "God, you hooked up my dad, and now it's my turn. Make good on your promises to him. You made me king over this huge nation." {1:8} "So, how about you bless me with some wisdom and knowledge? I gotta lead this massive crew, so I need the smarts to do it right." {1:9} God's like, "Yo, since you're asking for wisdom and not just chasing riches and fame, I got you. You'll be the wisest dude ever, and I'll throw in riches and honor too, no one's gonna top that." {1:10} Then Solomon rolls back to Jerusalem and takes charge of Israel. {1:11} He's building up his army, scoring 1400 chariots and 12,000 horsemen. {1:12} He's stacking up silver and gold in Jerusalem like it's nothing, and importing cedar like it grows on trees. {1:13} Plus, he's importing horses from Egypt and linen yarn for his crew. {1:14} He's even hooking up other kings with chariots and horses, making deals left and right.

{2:1} Solomon's thinking, "It's time to build a crib for God and a palace for myself." {2:2} He's got 70,000 workers on load-bearing duty, 80,000 cutting stone, and 3600 supervising the crew. {2:3} Then he hits up King Huram of Tyre, saying, "You helped out my dad, now do the same for me." {2:4} "I'm building a house for God, for all the worship and offerings, forever." {2:5} "This house is gonna be huge, 'cause our God is the real deal." {2:6} "But honestly, no house can contain God, I'm just building it to offer sacrifices." {2:7} "So, hook me up with a skilled craftsman in gold, silver, bronze, iron, and all that, like my dad had." {2:8} "And send over some cedar and other trees from Lebanon, 'cause your guys know how to work it." {2:9} "We need tons of timber for this epic house I'm building." {2:10} "And I'll pay your crew with 20,000 measures of wheat, barley, wine, and oil." {2:11} King Huram hits back, "God's loving you, man, that's why you're king." {2:12} He's like, "Bless God for giving David a son like you, ready to build a house for God." {2:13} "I'm sending over a top-notch craftsman to help out." {2:14} This dude's got skills in everything, just like your crew back home. {2:15} "Send over the supplies, and we'll bring the wood from Lebanon straight to you." {2:16} "We got this." {2:17} Solomon counts up all the foreigners in Israel, just like his dad did, and it's a hefty 153,600. {2:18} He puts 70,000 to work carrying stuff, 80,000 to cut stone, and 3600 to keep everyone in check.

{3:1} So Solomon starts building God's crib in Jerusalem on Mount Moriah, where God appeared to his dad David, on Ornan the Jebusite's spot. {3:2} He kicks off on the second day of the second month, four years into his reign. {3:3} Solomon gets the lowdown on building God's house: it's 60 cubits long and 20 cubits wide. {3:4} The porch matches the house, 20 cubits long and 120 high, decked out in pure gold. {3:5} Inside, he's got cedar walls gilded with gold, palm trees, and chains. {3:6} Blinging out the house with precious stones and gold from Parvaim. {3:7} Everything gets the gold treatment: beams, posts, walls, and even the doors, with cherubims engraved on the walls. {3:8} The most holy part matches the house's dimensions, all overlaid with fine gold weighing 600 talents. {3:9} Nails are gold too, and he even gold-plated the upper chambers. {3:10} In the holy house, he crafts two gold-covered cherubims. {3:11} Each cherub's wings are 20 cubits long, reaching across the house. {3:12} The wings touch each other and the walls, with faces toward each other. {3:13} These cherubims are 20 cubits wide, standing on their feet, faces inward. {3:14} Solomon makes a swanky veil with blue, purple, crimson, and cherubim patterns. {3:15} Then he sets up two 35-cubit pillars outside the house, each with a 5-cubit topper. {3:16} Chains hang from the tops with 100 pomegranates. {3:17} He names one pillar Jachin and the other Boaz.

{4:1} Plus, he crafts a 20-cubit brass altar, 20 cubits wide and 10 cubits tall. {4:2} There's a massive molten sea, 10 cubits wide and 5 cubits high, with oxen decorations and 3000 baths capacity. {4:3} Twelve oxen hold it up, facing each direction. {4:4} It's got a handbreadth thickness, with lily flower designs. {4:5} He's got ten washbasins for offerings, plus the priests' sea for washing. {4:6} Ten gold candlesticks and ten tables fill the temple, along with 100 golden basins. {4:7} He sets up the priestly court with brass doors. {4:8} The sea's on the east side, and Huram crafts pots, shovels, and basins. {4:9} Huram finishes off the job, making two pillars with decorations and pomegranates. {4:10} Plus, bases, lavers, and a sea with 12 oxen under it. {4:11} All the brass gear's cast in the Jordan plain. {4:12} Solomon goes all out, making loads of brass gear. {4:13} He covers the whole temple in gold, from altars to tables. {4:14} Gold lamps, flowers, and snuffers are part of the package. {4:15} Everything's made of pure gold, even the doors.

{5:1} So, like, Solomon wraps up all the work for God's crib, bringing in all the stuff his dad David dedicated—silver, gold, instruments—and stashing them in God's treasure trove. {5:2} Then he gets the elders and tribe leaders together to haul the Ark of the Covenant to Jerusalem from Zion. {5:3} Everyone shows up for the big feast in the seventh month. {5:4} The elders roll in, and the Levites carry the ark. {5:5} They bring in the ark, the tabernacle, and all the holy gear, with priests and Levites handling the heavy lifting. {5:6} Solomon and the whole gang sacrifice so many sheep and oxen you couldn't count 'em all. {5:7} The priests slide the ark into its spot under the cherubim's wings in the holy place. {5:8} Those cherubim spread their wings over the ark, covering it and its poles. {5:9} They pull out the poles so you can see them from the holy place but not from outside. And they're still there to this day. {5:10} Inside the ark are just the two tablets Moses dropped in there at Horeb, back when God made a deal with Israel in Egypt. {5:11} When the priests bail from the holy place—'cause they're all sanctified and not sticking to a schedule—and the singers, with their cymbals, harps, and hundred and twenty trumpets, all get going. {5:12-13} They all get in sync, making one massive sound, praising God and shouting about His mercy, and bam, the crib's filled with a cloud—the glory of God's all up in there. {5:14} The priests can't even stand up to do their thing 'cause of the cloud, that's how filled up with God's glory the crib is.

{6:1} So, like, Solomon's like, "Yo, God's all about that thick darkness vibe." {6:2} "But hey, I've hooked You up with a dope house, a forever spot to chill." {6:3} Then the king turns to the whole squad of Israel and blesses them, and everyone's standing there soaking it in. {6:4} He's like, "Props to the big man upstairs, who's made good on everything He told my dad David." {6:5} "Ever since we bounced from Egypt, God's been clear: Jerusalem's His jam, and David's His main man." {6:6} "David was all about building God a crib, but God was like, 'Nah, but your kid can hook it up.'" {6:7} David was all about that house for God's name, but God was like, "Cool idea, but not your job, David." {6:8} "But check it, God's kept His word. Here I am, sitting on the throne, and this house is all about God's name." {6:9} "And boom, here's the Ark, with God's covenant inside, chilling like a boss." {6:12} Then he's standing by the altar, in front of everyone, throwing his hands up. {6:13} He's set up this brass platform, five cubits long, five wide, and three high, right in the court. He hops up on it, gets on his knees, and throws his hands up to the sky, {6:14} saying, "God of Israel, You're the real MVP, no one else comes close, always keeping Your promises and showing love to Your peeps who stay loyal." {6:15} "You kept it real with David my dad, just like You said, and here we are today." {6:16} "So, God of Israel, stick to Your word for David, and make sure his descendants stay on point with Your law, just like he did." {6:17} "And let what You promised David come true." {6:18} "But for real, can God actually chill with us on Earth? Like, even the heavens can't contain Him, let alone this crib I built." {6:19} "So, God, listen up to my prayer and my peeps' prayers, hear us out and forgive us when we mess up." {6:20} "Keep Your eyes on this crib day and night, where You said You'd put Your name, and listen up when we pray toward this place." {6:21} "Listen up to us and our prayers, whether we're here or calling out to You from wherever. Listen up from heaven, and when You do, forgive us." {6:22} "If someone messes with their neighbor and has to swear an oath at Your altar here, {6:23} then hear from heaven and make things right, punishing the bad and backing up the good." {6:24} "And if we get wrecked by our enemies 'cause we messed up, but then we're like, 'Our bad, God, please forgive us' and pray toward this crib," {6:25} "then hear from heaven, forgive our screw-ups, and bring us back to the land You promised us and our ancestors." {6:26} "And if things get rough, like no rain and stuff, 'cause we screwed up, but then we pray toward this place and own up to our mistakes," {6:27} "then hear from heaven, forgive us, and teach us the right way to live, and bring rain to the land You gave us." {6:28} "If there's famine, disease, or enemies on our doorstep, and we pray here, pouring out our hearts," {6:29} "then listen from heaven, Your place, and forgive us, treating us each as we deserve, 'cause You know what's up with everyone's hearts." {6:31} "So we'll stay in line with Your ways as long as we're living in the land You promised our ancestors." {6:32} "And if someone not from Israel shows up, all hyped about Your name and what You can do, and prays here," {6:33} "then hear from heaven, Your spot, and do whatever they're asking, so everyone on Earth knows Your name, just like Your peeps do, and knows this crib is all about You." {6:34} "And if we head out to battle and pray toward this city You picked and this crib I built for You," {6:35} "then listen up from heaven, hear our prayers, and have our backs." {6:36} "If we mess up (and let's be real, everyone does), and You get mad and let our enemies smack us around and drag us off," {6:37} "but then we wise up wherever we end up, and pray and say, 'Sorry, we messed up,'" {6:38} "and we're all in, praying toward home, this city, and this crib for You," {6:39} "then listen from heaven, Your spot, to our prayers and forgive us, 'cause we're Your people who slipped up." {6:40} "So, God, keep Your eyes and ears peeled for the prayers here

{7:1} So, when Solomon finished his prayer, bam! Fire comes down from heaven, torching those sacrifices, and the whole place gets lit up with the Lord's glory. {7:2} The priests couldn't even roll into the crib 'cause it was overflowing with God's glory. {7:3} And when the Israelites peeped that fire show and the Lord's glory, they dropped to the ground, worshipping and praising the Lord, shouting, "He's all good, and His mercy lasts forever." {7:4} Then King Solomon and the crew offered up sacrifices to the Lord. {7:5} Solomon went all out, sacrificing 22,000 oxen and 120,000 sheep, fully dedicating the house of God. {7:6} The priests were doing their thing, the Levites were jamming on the Lord's instruments, and everyone was vibing to David's tunes, praising the Lord 'cause His mercy lasts forever. The priests blasted the trumpets, and all Israel stood in awe. {7:7} Solomon consecrated the court in front of the Lord's house for sacrifices since the bronze altar he made couldn't handle all the offerings. {7:8} Then they threw down for a week-long party, with all of Israel, from Hamath to the River of Egypt, turning up. {7:9} On the eighth day, they kept it solemn, dedicating the altar for another week and partying for seven days straight. {7:10} When they wrapped it up on the 23rd day of the seventh month, everyone went back home stoked, feeling the love from the Lord to David, Solomon, and all of Israel. {7:11} So, Solomon wrapped up the Lord's house and his own house, crushing everything he set out to do. {7:12} Then, the Lord rolls up on Solomon at night and tells him, "Yo, I heard your prayer, and I'm picking this place as my crib for sacrifices." {7:13-14} "If I shut up the heavens or send disasters, but my peeps humble themselves, pray, seek my face, and turn from their bad vibes, I'll listen up, forgive, and heal their land." {7:15} "From now on, I'm tuning in to prayers from this spot. {7:16} I've picked and blessed this house so my name's always here, and I'll keep my eyes and heart locked in." {7:17-18} "If you stay on track like your pops David, keeping my commands and laws, I'll keep your throne solid, just like I promised David." {7:19-20} "But if you bail on my rules, chase other gods, and diss me, I'll yank you out of this land I gave you, ditch this house I blessed, and make it a joke among nations." {7:21} "This house will be a shocker to everyone, making them wonder why the Lord wrecked this land and house." {7:22} "And they'll learn it's 'cause they ditched the Lord who brought them out of Egypt, chasing other gods instead."

{8:1} After twenty years of grinding, building both the Lord's crib and his own pad, Solomon was flexing hard. {8:2} He took the cities that Huram hooked him up with and made them poppin', letting the Israelites move in. {8:3} Then he rolled up to Hamathzobah and straight up dominated. {8:4} Built up Tadmor in the desert and stocked up on store cities in Hamath. {8:5} And he beefed up Beth-horon, both upper and lower, fortifying them with walls, gates, and bars. {8:6} Solomon was building all over the place, from Jerusalem to Lebanon, flexing his dominion. {8:7-8} As for the leftover Hittites, Amorites, Perizzites, Hivites, and Jebusites, not part of the Israel squad, Solomon made them cough up cash as tribute. {8:9} He didn't make Israelites slaves for his projects, but he had them as warriors, top-ranking officers, and cavalry commanders. {8:10} These were the big shots in King Solomon's crew, 250 bosses running the show. {8:11} Solomon moved Pharaoh's daughter out of David's crib to her own spot 'cause he wanted to keep it holy where the Lord's ark had been. {8:12-13} Then he dropped burnt offerings on the Lord's altar every day, sticking to Moses' command on Sabbaths, New Moons, and big feasts three times a year. {8:14-15} He organized the priests and Levites just like his dad David ordered, and the gatekeepers kept watch, all as David, the man of God, commanded. {8:16} Solomon's hustle was real, from laying the foundation of the Lord's crib to finishing it up, making it tight. {8:17} Then he hit up Ezion-geber and Eloth by the Red Sea in Edom. {8:18} Huram hooked him up with ships and sea-savvy sailors, cruising to Ophir and hauling back 450 talents of gold for King Solomon.

{9:1} When the queen of Sheba heard about Solomon's rep, she came through with hard questions, rolling deep with camels loaded with spices, gold, and precious stones. {9:2} Solomon schooled her on everything, holding back nothing. {9:3} When she saw Solomon's wisdom and his baller house, she was blown away. {9:4} Checking out his crib, his servants, their gear, his crew, and even the stairs leading to the Lord's house, she was shook. {9:5} She told Solomon she heard the hype, but seeing it for herself, she was mind-blown, saying he's even greater than the rumors. {9:7} She praised Solomon's crew for getting to be around his wisdom all the time. {9:8} She shouted out to the Lord, thanking Him for putting Solomon on the throne, using him to bring justice and righteousness to Israel. {9:9} She hooked Solomon up fat with gold, spices, and precious stones, nothing like it had ever been seen before. {9:10} Huram's crew and Solomon's crew brought back more gold and precious stuff from Ophir, even some sweet trees. {9:11} Solomon hooked up the Queen with everything she wanted, plus more than she brought. Then she bounced back to her hood with her crew. {9:13} In one year alone, Solomon racked up 666 talents of gold, not counting what traders brought in. {9:22} Solomon's stacks and smarts had him on top of the game, outclassing every king on the block. {9:23} Every king wanted to hang with Solomon, soaking up his wisdom that God blessed him with. {9:24} They all came through with gifts, silver, gold, clothes, armor, spices, horses, and mules, showing love every year. {9:25} Solomon had 4,000 stalls for horses and chariots and 12,000 horsemen, posted up in chariot cities and chilling in Jerusalem. {9:26} He reigned over all the kings from the river to the Philistine land and Egypt. {9:27} Silver was as common as rocks in Jerusalem, and cedar trees were as plenty as sycamores in the lowlands. {9:28-29} They brought Solomon horses from Egypt and everywhere else. {9:30} Solomon's whole story, from start to finish, is all written up in Nathan the prophet's book, Ahijah the Shilonite's prophecy, and Iddo the seer's visions against Jeroboam. {9:31} Solomon ruled in Jerusalem over all of Israel for 40 years before he passed, joining his ancestors, and Rehoboam took over.

{10:1} Rehoboam pulled up in Shechem, and all of Israel showed up to crown him king. {10:2} When Jeroboam, who bounced to Egypt to dodge Solomon's vibe, heard about it, he jetted back. {10:3} They hit him up, so Jeroboam and the crew rolled up to Rehoboam, saying, {10:4} "Your old man had us working hard. Ease up a bit, and we got your back." {10:5} Rehoboam told them to chill for three days. Then they bounced. {10:6} Rehoboam hit up Solomon's OGs for advice, asking how to respond. {10:7} They were like, "If you're cool and speak good vibes, they'll ride with you forever." {10:8} But Rehoboam ghosted the OGs and hit up his crew instead. {10:9} He was like, "What should I tell them?" {10:10} His day-one squad said, "Tell them you'll be tougher than your dad. He whipped them; you'll scorch them." {10:11-14} So Jeroboam and the crew came back, and Rehoboam said what his crew advised, doubling down on the hardship. {10:15} The king didn't listen to the people because it was part of God's plan, fulfilling what He told Ahijah to say to Jeroboam. {10:16} When Israel saw Rehoboam wasn't budging, they bounced, saying, "We're done with David's fam. Everyone back to their own turf." So Israel dipped. {10:17} But the Israelites in Judah stayed put under Rehoboam's rule. {10:18} Rehoboam sent out his tax dude, but the Israelites stoned him to death. Rehoboam dipped quick back to Jerusalem. {10:19} Israel rebelled against David's line up until now.

{11:1} Rehoboam got back to Jerusalem and rallied 180,000 warriors from Judah and Benjamin to fight Israel and bring them back under his rule. {11:2-4} But God told Shemaiah, "Tell Rehoboam and the Judah and Benjamin crew not to fight their brothers. Peace out." So they backed off. {11:5} Rehoboam kicked it in Jerusalem, building up defense cities in Judah. {11:6-10} He hooked up Bethlehem, Etam, and Tekoa, among others. {11:11-12} He beefed up the forts, stocked them with supplies, and had Judah and Benjamin backing him up. {11:13} Priests and Levites from all over Israel rolled to Rehoboam's side. {11:14} They left their old spots and came to Judah and Jerusalem because Jeroboam shut them out. {11:15} He set up priests for high places, demons, and the idols he made. {11:16} People from all over Israel came to Jerusalem to worship the Lord. {11:17} They held it down for Judah and made Rehoboam strong for three years, sticking to David and Solomon's path. {11:18-20} Rehoboam married Mahalath and Abihail, having a bunch of kids. {11:21} He was all about Maachah, Absalom's daughter, even though he had 18 wives and 60 side pieces, racking up 28 sons and 60 daughters. {11:22} He made Abijah, Maachah's son, the top dog, thinking he'd be king. {11:23} Rehoboam spread out his kids all over Judah and Benjamin, setting them up with food and gear. And he kept chasing after more wives.

{12:1} After Rehoboam got his kingdom on lock and felt himself, he ditched God's rules, dragging all Israel down with him. {12:2} In year five of Rehoboam's reign, Shishak, the Egyptian king, rolled up to Jerusalem because they dissed the Lord. {12:3} He came with 1,200 chariots, 60,000 horsemen, and a bunch of peeps from Egypt, Libya, Sudan, and more. {12:4} Shishak took Judah's fortified cities and hit up Jerusalem. {12:5} Then Prophet Shemaiah showed up, calling out Rehoboam and Judah's leaders, saying they'd turned their backs on God, so now Shishak's got them. {12:6} Hearing this, Judah's leaders and Rehoboam humbled themselves, admitting God's righteousness. {12:7} God peeped their humbleness and told Shemaiah He wouldn't let Shishak wreck Jerusalem, but they'd still be Shishak's minions to learn a lesson. {12:8-9} Shishak raided Jerusalem, taking all the goodies from the Lord's house and the king's palace, including Solomon's gold shields. {12:10} Rehoboam swapped out the gold shields for brass ones, handing them over to his palace guards. {12:11} Every time the king hit up the Lord's house, the guards took the shields, storing them away. {12:12} When Rehoboam humbled himself, God chilled out, not wiping him out entirely, and Judah prospered. {12:13} Rehoboam's rule in Jerusalem was tight. He was 41 when he started, ruling 17 years. His mom was Naamah, an Ammonite. {12:14} But he messed up, not getting his heart right with God. {12:15} You can peep Rehoboam's whole story in Shemaiah and Iddo's records. And he stayed beefing with Jeroboam. {12:16} Rehoboam passed away, and his son Abijah took over.

{13:1-2} Abijah started ruling Judah when he was 18, holding it down for three years. His mom, Michaiah, was from Gibeah. And he kept battling Jeroboam. {13:3} Abijah brought 400,000 soldiers to the showdown, while Jeroboam rocked up with 800,000 fierce fighters. {13:4-5} Abijah set up shop on Mount Zemaraim, throwing shade at Jeroboam and Israel, reminding them God gave the kingdom to David and his descendants forever. {13:6-7} He called out Jeroboam for rebelling against his boss, Solomon's son, and gathering shady peeps against Rehoboam. {13:8} Abijah called out Jeroboam's crew for trying to mess with God's kingdom, rolling with golden calves like they're gods. {13:9} They ditched the Lord's priests and made their own, offering sacrifices to nothing. {13:10} But Abijah was repping the Lord, sticking with the Aaronic priests and Levites, handling God's business. {13:11} They kept the daily sacrifices, incense, showbread, and golden lampstand in check, unlike Jeroboam's crew who turned their backs on God. {13:12} With God on their side and priests blasting trumpets, Abijah told Israel not to mess with the Lord, but they didn't listen. {13:13} Jeroboam pulled a sneaky move, ambushing Judah from behind, trapping them in a battle sandwich. {13:14} When Judah saw they were surrounded, they prayed, and the priests blasted their trumpets. {13:15-16} Judah let out a battle cry, and God wrecked Jeroboam and Israel in front of Abijah's crew. {13:16} Israel bounced, and God handed them over to Judah. {13:17} Abijah's crew went to town, slaying 500,000 of Israel's top warriors. {13:18-19} Judah took the win, relying on the Lord, and snagged some cities from Jeroboam, like Bethel, Jeshanah, and Ephrain. {13:20} Jeroboam never recovered and bit the dust. {13:21} Abijah flexed, marrying 14 wives and having 22 sons and 16 daughters. {13:22} You can peep more about Abijah's life in the prophet Iddo's records.

{14:1} After Abijah kicked it with his ancestors and got buried in David's city, his son Asa took over. Things chilled for ten years. {14:2-4} Asa did what God liked, tearing down altars to other gods, smashing idols, and making sure Judah followed God's law. {14:5} He even trashed all the high places and idols in Judah, keeping the kingdom peaceful. {14:6} Asa beefed up Judah's defenses, enjoying peace because God gave it to him. {14:7} So Asa was like, "Let's fortify these cities while the land's peaceful because God's got our backs." And they built and prospered. {14:8} Asa's army was stacked: 300,000 soldiers from Judah and 280,000 from Benjamin, all tough warriors. {14:9} Then Zerah the Ethiopian rolled up with a million-man army and 300 chariots, setting up camp in Mareshah. {14:10} But Asa wasn't having it. He faced off with Zerah in the valley of Zephathah and called on God for backup. {14:11} God wrecked the Ethiopians, and they fled. Asa's crew chased them to Gerar, smashing them up and snagging tons of loot. {14:12} They raided all the nearby cities too, spreading fear with all the loot they snagged, and then headed back to Jerusalem.

{15:1} God's spirit hit Azariah, Oded's son, and he met Asa, dropping some truth on him and Judah. {15:2} Azariah was like, "God's with you as long as you're with Him, but if you ditch Him, He'll ditch you." {15:3} Israel had been lacking God, priests, and laws for a while, but when they turned to God in their trouble, He showed up. {15:5} Those were rough times, with no peace for anyone, and God was bringing down some serious trouble. {15:7} So stay strong and don't slack, because your hard work's gonna pay off. {15:8} Asa heard this and took action, tossing out all the idols in Judah and Benjamin and fixing up the Lord's altar. {15:9} He called everyone, including foreigners from Ephraim, Manasseh, and Simeon, to Jerusalem for a big meeting in the third month of Asa's reign. {15:11} They offered 700 oxen and 7,000 sheep to God as part of a deal to seek Him with all their hearts. {15:13} And they made a vow that anyone who didn't seek God would get the boot, no matter who they were. {15:14} They shouted and blasted trumpets, swearing their loyalty to God. {15:15} Judah was stoked about it, swearing to seek God with all their hearts, and God hooked them up with peace. {15:16} Asa even kicked his mom Maachah out for making idols, destroying her idol and burning it at Kidron Brook. {15:17} But he didn't get rid of all the high places in Israel, although his heart stayed true to God his whole life. {15:18} Asa brought all the stuff his dad dedicated to God's house, plus his own silver, gold, and vessels. {15:19} And there wasn't any war until Asa's 35th year of ruling.

{16:1} So in Asa's 36th year of ruling, Baasha, the king of Israel, rolled up on Judah and set up a blockade at Ramah to keep Asa boxed in. {16:2} Asa pulled out some cash from the treasury and hit up Ben-hadad, the king of Syria, asking him to break his alliance with Baasha and help him out. {16:4} Ben-hadad was down, so he sent his army captains to wreck some of Israel's cities like Ijon, Dan, and

Abelmaim, plus all the store cities of Naphtali. {16:5} When Baasha caught wind of this, he stopped building at Ramah and backed off. {16:6} Asa then swooped in, grabbed the materials Baasha was using, and used them to beef up Geba and Mizpah. {16:7} But then Hanani, the prophet, called Asa out, saying he blew it by trusting the king of Syria instead of God. {16:9} Hanani told him he acted stupidly and that he'd have wars from now on. {16:10} Asa got mad and chucked Hanani in the slammer, and he started cracking down on the people too. {16:12} Asa's life story's all in the history books of Judah and Israel. {16:13} In Asa's 39th year of ruling, he got super sick in his feet, but instead of praying to God, he hit up the doctors. {16:14} Asa kicked the bucket in his 41st year of ruling and got buried in a fancy tomb he made himself in David's city, with a big funeral and all.

{17:1} Jehoshaphat, Asa's son, took over, flexing on Israel with some military moves. {17:2} He beefed up defenses in all of Judah's cities and even in Ephraim, where Asa had taken over before. {17:3} God had Jehoshaphat's back because he followed David's footsteps and didn't mess with Baal. {17:5} Because of that, God hooked Jehoshaphat up, with Judah bringing him gifts, making him rich and famous. {17:6} Jehoshaphat was all about God, taking down the high places and groves in Judah. {17:7} In his third year of ruling, he sent teachers throughout Judah to spread the word, backed up by Levites and priests. {17:9} They taught the people all about God's law, hitting up every city in Judah. {17:10} Everyone around Judah got scared of God, so they didn't mess with Jehoshaphat. {17:11} Even the Philistines started bringing him gifts, and the Arabians hooked him up with a ton of livestock. {17:12} Jehoshaphat got even richer, building castles and store cities in Judah. {17:14} Here's the military stats: Judah had Adnah leading 300,000 soldiers, Jehohanan with 280,000, and Amasiah with 200,000. {17:17} Benjamin brought Eliada with 200,000 soldiers armed with bows and shields, and Jehozabad with 180,000 ready for battle. {17:19} These dudes served the king, alongside others stationed in fortified cities all over Judah.

{18:1} So Jehoshaphat was living large, chilling with Ahab, getting that cash and respect. {18:2} After a while, he rolls down to Ahab's spot in Samaria. Ahab throws him a fat party with sheep and oxen and talks him into joining a mission to Ramoth-gilead. {18:3} Ahab's like, "You down to roll?" and Jehoshaphat's like, "Yeah, bro, me and my crew got your back in this war." {18:4} But Jehoshaphat's got doubts, so he's like, "Hold up, let's ask God first." {18:5} Ahab rounds up 400 prophets and asks if they should go to battle, and they're all like, "Yeah, go for it, God's got your back." {18:6} But Jehoshaphat's not convinced and asks if there's another prophet they can check with. {18:7} Ahab's like, "There's one guy, Micaiah, but I hate him because he always brings bad news." {18:8} So Ahab sends for Micaiah, and they're all sitting there in their royal gear while the prophets hype them up. {18:10} One of the prophets, Zedekiah, even gets some iron horns and says, "God says you'll gore Syria with these." {18:11} All the prophets are backing Ahab, saying, "Go to Ramoth-gilead and win, God's got your back." {18:12} So they send for Micaiah, telling him to get with the program and say something good. {18:13} But Micaiah's like, "I'm only saying what God tells me, period." {18:14} When he faces the king, he's like, "Sure, go and win," but the king knows he's being sarcastic. {18:15} The king's like, "Seriously, tell me the truth." {18:16} So Micaiah says he saw Israel scattered like sheep with no shepherd, and God said they should go home in peace. {18:17} Ahab's like, "See, I told you he never says anything good." {18:18} Micaiah's like, "Well, here's what I really saw, God's chilling on his throne with all his angels." {18:19} God's asking who's gonna take out Ahab, and some spirits step up with ideas. {18:20} One spirit offers to be a lying spirit in the prophets' mouths, and God's like, "Yeah, go for it." {18:22} So now God's put lies in the prophets' mouths to mess with Ahab. {18:23} Zedekiah gets mad and slaps Micaiah, asking how he got a different message. {18:24} Micaiah's like, "You'll see when you're hiding." {18:25} Ahab's done with him, sending him off to jail until he comes back victorious. {18:26} Micaiah's like, "If you come back in one piece, I ain't speaking for God." {18:28} So Ahab and Jehoshaphat head to Ramoth-gilead. {18:29} Ahab's like, "I'm gonna disguise myself, you stay royal." So Ahab goes incognito and they head to battle. {18:30} The Syrian king tells his chariot commanders to only focus on Ahab. {18:31} But when they see Jehoshaphat, they think he's Ahab and start attacking, until Jehoshaphat cries out and God saves him. {18:33} A random dude shoots Ahab with an arrow, and he's like, "Get me outta here, I'm hit!" {18:34} Ahab stays propped up in his chariot until he dies at sunset, and the battle rages on.

{19:1} So Jehoshaphat, the king of Judah, heads back home to Jerusalem all chill and peaceful. {19:2} Then Jehu, son of Hanani the seer, rolls up and drops some truth bombs on him, like, "Bruh, why you gotta back up the ungodly and be cool with those who hate God? That's just asking for trouble from the man upstairs." {19:3} But hey, Jehu acknowledges that Jehoshaphat's got some good stuff going on, like clearing out those groves and getting his heart set on seeking God. {19:4} Jehoshaphat sets up shop in Jerusalem and starts preaching, bringing people from all over back to worshipping the Lord. {19:5} He's like, "Let's get some judges in every city, and make sure they're not just doing it for show, but because they're all about God." {19:6} He tells the judges, "You're not just judging for people, but for the big guy upstairs who's got your back." {19:7} Jehoshaphat's all about that fear of the Lord, making sure everyone's on the straight and narrow, no favoritism or shady deals allowed. {19:8} Back in Jerusalem, Jehoshaphat's setting up a legit team of Levites, priests, and elders to handle all the legal stuff, making sure they're handling disputes according to God's law. {19:9} He's like, "You gotta do this in reverence for the Lord, with honesty and sincerity." {19:10} He's telling them, "If your bros come to you with beef, make sure you sort it out according to God's rules, so nobody ends up with divine wrath on their doorstep." {19:11} Jehoshaphat's got Amariah the head priest and Zebadiah in charge of king's business, and he's like, "Stay strong and do what's right, and God's got your back."

{20:1} So, like, after all that drama, the Moabites, Ammonites, and some other crew rolled up on Jehoshaphat for a showdown. {20:2} And Jehoshaphat gets word that a huge army's coming from across the sea, all the way from Hazazon-tamar (that's En-gedi, btw).

{20:3} Dude starts freaking out, but then he's like, "Okay, gotta hit up the big guy upstairs," and declares a fast throughout Judah. {20:4} Everyone's like, "Let's get together and ask the Lord for help!" So they come from all over Judah to seek God. {20:5} Jehoshaphat's standing in the house of the Lord, talking to the people, when he's like, "God, you're the boss of heaven and earth, right? Ain't nobody gonna mess with you!" {20:6} He's reminding everyone how God hooked them up with this land and a place to worship. {20:7} Jehoshaphat's like, "Remember how God kicked out the old residents for us? Now these dudes wanna take it back!" {20:8} He's like, "We're here, God, crying out to you. Save us from this mess!" {20:9} Jehoshaphat's like, "If things get bad, we're coming to you, God, right here in this house. And we know you'll help us out." {20:10} He's like, "These Moabites and Ammonites? You stopped us from messing with them back in Egypt, and now they're coming for us! What's up with that?" {20:11} He's calling out their betrayal, like, "We didn't mess with them, and now they're trying to kick us out of our own land!" {20:12} Jehoshaphat's straight-up honest, like, "We can't handle this on our own, God. We're counting on you." {20:13} So everyone's standing there, Jehoshaphat, the whole crew, even the kids, waiting for God to come through. {20:14} Then this dude Jahaziel gets filled with the Spirit and starts talking to everyone, saying, "Listen up! Don't be scared of this huge army. God's got this!" {20:15} He's like, "Tomorrow, go out and face them. They'll be at the cliff of Ziz. But you won't even need to fight. Just watch what God's gonna do." {20:16} He's telling them where to find the enemy and how God's gonna handle it. {20:17} Jahaziel's like, "Chill out, Judah and Jerusalem. God's got your back. Tomorrow, head out, and God will be with you." {20:18} So Jehoshaphat bows down, everyone's worshiping God, and it's a whole vibe. {20:19} Then the Levites start hyping up the crowd, praising God with loud voices. {20:20} Next morning, they're up and ready, and Jehoshaphat's like, "Trust in God, y'all! He's got this." {20:21} So they start marching, praising God for his mercy. {20:22} And when they start singing and praising, God throws the enemy into confusion, and they start fighting each other. {20:23} The Ammonites and Moabites turn on the people of Mount Seir, wiping each other out. {20:24} When Judah gets to the lookout, all they see is dead bodies—enemy down! {20:25} They hit the jackpot with loot, so much they can't even carry it all. {20:26} After blessing God, they head back to the valley of Berachah, where they had their victory party. {20:27} They head back to Jerusalem, Jehoshaphat leading the way, everyone partying because God gave them the win. {20:28} They get to the house of the Lord with music blasting. {20:29} And word spreads about how God fought for Israel, and everyone's freaking out. {20:30} Jehoshaphat's kingdom enjoys some peace and quiet, all thanks to God. {20:31} Jehoshaphat was 35 when he became king and ruled for 25 years in Jerusalem. His mom's name was Azubah, daughter of Shilhi. {20:32} He's walking the same path as his dad Asa, doing what's right by God. {20:33} But those high places for idol worship? Yeah, they're still around, 'cause people haven't fully turned to God yet. {20:34} All the rest of Jehoshaphat's story is in the books of Jehu the son of Hanani, mentioned in the kings of Israel. {20:35} After all that success, Jehoshaphat teams up with Ahaziah, who's not exactly a saint. {20:36} They're trying to build ships for trade, but it doesn't end well. {20:37} Some prophet calls out Jehoshaphat for hooking up with Ahaziah, and their ships end up wrecked. Tough luck.

{21:1} So, like, Jehoshaphat kicks the bucket and gets buried in the city of David. Then his son Jehoram takes over. {21:2} Jehoshaphat had a bunch of brothers: Azariah, Jehiel, Zechariah, Azariah (again), Michael, and Shephatiah. These were all his sons. {21:3} Jehoshaphat hooked them up with some sick gifts and fortified cities in Judah, but he passed the kingdom to Jehoram 'cause he was the oldest. {21:4} When Jehoram takes over, he's like, "I gotta secure my position," and straight-up murders all his brothers and some other princes. {21:5} Jehoram's 32 when he starts ruling and lasts eight years in Jerusalem. {21:6} He's totally following in the messed-up footsteps of the kings of Israel, even marrying Ahab's daughter. And yeah, he's evil in God's eyes. {21:7} But God's like, "Nah, I won't wipe out the house of David 'cause of my promise to David." {21:8} During Jehoram's time, the Edomites break free and make their own king. {21:9} Jehoram's like, "Nuh-uh, not on my watch," and beats them in battle. But they keep rebelling. Same with Libnah, 'cause Jehoram ditched God. {21:10} He sets up idol worship spots in Judah and gets the people doing all sorts of shady stuff. {21:11} Then Elijah the prophet sends him a letter, straight-up calling him out for his wickedness. {21:12} Elijah's like, "You're not walking in your dad Jehoshaphat's or grandpa Asa's footsteps. You're acting just like the evil kings of Israel, leading Judah and Jerusalem into sin." {21:13} He's like, "You're messing up big time, killing your own brothers who were better than you!" {21:14} Elijah's like, "God's gonna smack your people, your family, and your stuff with a major plague." {21:15} "And you? You're gonna get seriously sick, your bowels falling out day by day." {21:16} God stirs up trouble with the Philistines, Arabians, and Ethiopians, and they wreck Judah. {21:17} They straight-up raid Jehoram's palace, taking everything, including his family, except for his youngest son Jehoahaz. {21:18} But God's not done. He hits Jehoram with an incurable disease in his bowels. {21:19} After two years of agony, his bowels literally fall out, and he dies a miserable death. And nobody even bothers with a proper funeral for him. {21:20} Jehoram was 32 when he started ruling, lasted eight years, and died without anyone missing him. They bury him in the city of David, but not with the other kings.

{22:1} The people of Jerusalem make Jehoram's youngest son Ahaziah king 'cause the Arabians killed off all the older ones. So Ahaziah takes over. {22:2} Ahaziah's 42 when he becomes king and only lasts a year. His mom's name is Athaliah, daughter of Omri. {22:3} He's just as messed up as the kings of Israel 'cause his mom's his advisor in all things evil. {22:4} He does so much evil that even after his dad dies, he keeps being wicked with his mom's help. {22:5} He takes her advice and teams up with Joram, king of Israel, to fight Hazael, king of Syria. But it goes south, and Joram gets wrecked. {22:6} Joram gets hurt and heads to Jezreel to recover, and Ahaziah goes to visit him. {22:7} But that's a bad move 'cause Jehu's on a mission from God to wipe out Ahab's house, and Ahaziah gets caught in the crossfire. {22:8} Jehu finds Ahaziah's relatives and kills them, 'cause they're all connected to Ahab's house. {22:9} They hunt down Ahaziah, find him hiding in Samaria, and bring him to Jehu, who takes him out. They bury him, saying, "He's Jehoshaphat's son who actually followed God." And with that, Ahaziah's family loses their grip on the kingdom. {22:10} When Athaliah sees her son's dead, she goes on a killing spree, wiping out all the royal heirs of Judah. {22:11} But one brave woman, Jehoshabeath, hides Ahaziah's son Joash and saves him from the massacre. {22:12} Joash stays hidden in the house of God for six years while Athaliah rules the land.

{23:1} So, like, in the seventh year, Jehoiada gets all pumped up and forms a crew with some top dudes: Azariah, Ishmael, Azariah (again), Maaseiah, and Elishaphat. {23:2} They roll around Judah, rounding up all the Levites from every city and the big shots from Israel, and they all meet up in Jerusalem. {23:3} Then they all make a pact with the king at God's house, and he's like, "Yo, the king's son is gonna rule, just like the LORD said about David's sons." {23:4} Here's the plan: One-third of you, including priests and Levites, guard the doors on the Sabbath. {23:5} Another third chill at the king's crib, and the last third guard the foundation gate. Everyone else hangs out in the LORD's house courtyard. {23:6} But only priests and Levites can go inside 'cause they're holy. Everyone else keeps watch for the LORD. {23:7} The Levites gotta surround the king, armed and ready. Anyone else who tries to crash gets the axe. Stick with the king when he comes and goes. {23:8} So everyone follows Jehoiada's orders, taking shifts on the Sabbath, just like he said. {23:9} Jehoiada hooks up the crew with spears, shields, and armor from King David's stash in God's house. {23:10} Then they line up, armed to the teeth, from one side of the temple to the other, by the altar and the king, ready to protect. {23:11} They bring out the king's son, crown him, give him the scrolls, and make him king. Jehoiada and his sons anoint him and shout, "Long live the king!" {23:12} When Athaliah hears the party going down, she crashes it, accusing everyone of treason. {23:13} But when she sees the king all decked out and everyone cheering, she loses it, yelling "Treason!" {23:14} Jehoiada kicks her out and tells the guards to kill anyone who follows her. But he's like, "Don't off her in God's house." {23:15} So they drag her out to the horse gate by the king's house and take her out there. {23:16} Jehoiada seals the deal between the people and the king to be all about the LORD. {23:17} Then they wreck the house of Baal, smashing his altars and idols, and take out Baal's priest Mattan. {23:18} Jehoiada organizes the temple stuff just like King David wanted, with priests and Levites offering sacrifices and singing praises as written in Moses's law. {23:19} They post guards at the temple gates to keep out anything impure. {23:20} They roll out with the king from God's house through the high gate into his crib and set him on the throne. {23:21} Everyone's stoked, and the city's chill again after they take out Athaliah.

{24:1} So Joash starts running the show when he's only seven, and he's in charge for a whopping forty years in Jerusalem. His mom's name is Zibiah from Beer-sheba. {24:2} While Jehoiada the priest is calling the shots, Joash does everything right in God's eyes. {24:3} Jehoiada even gets himself two wives and starts a family. {24:4} Later on, Joash decides it's time to fix up God's house. {24:5} He tells the priests and Levites to hit up all the cities in Judah and gather money from Israel every year to fix up the temple. But the Levites drag their feet. {24:6} Joash calls out Jehoiada like, "Dude, why aren't the Levites following Moses's command to bring in donations for the tabernacle?" {24:7} He's mad 'cause Athaliah's sons trashed God's house and gave all the dedicated stuff to Baal. {24:8} So they make a donation chest and put it outside the temple gate. {24:9} They announce throughout Judah and Jerusalem to bring in the donations as Moses commanded in the wilderness. {24:10} Everybody's stoked and throws their cash in until they've filled the chest. {24:11} When they bring it to the king's office and see all the money, the king's scribe and the high priest's officer haul it off, empty it, and bring it back for more donations. They do this every day, collecting loads of cash. {24:12} Joash and Jehoiada use the money to hire workers to fix up the temple, hiring masons, carpenters, and metalworkers. {24:13} The workers do their thing, and the temple is restored to its former glory. {24:14} They use the leftover money to make fancy vessels for the temple and keep offering burnt sacrifices to God as long as Jehoiada's around. {24:15} But Jehoiada gets old and passes away at the ripe old age of a hundred and thirty. {24:16} They bury him with the kings in the city of David because he did right by God and his house. {24:17} After Jehoiada's gone, the princes of Judah start whispering in Joash's ear, and he listens to them. {24:18} They ditch God's house and start worshipping groves and idols, which ticks off God, bringing His wrath on Judah and Jerusalem. {24:19} God sends prophets to bring them back to Him, but they don't listen. {24:20} Then the Spirit of God comes upon Zechariah, Jehoiada's son, and he calls out the people for disobeying God's commandments, warning them they won't prosper if they keep ditching God. {24:21} But they turn on Zechariah and stone him to death in the temple courtyard at the king's command. {24:22} Joash forgets all the good Jehoiada did for him and orders Zechariah's death. When Joash dies, he's like, "God, you deal with it." {24:23} Toward the end of the year, the Syrian army comes against Joash, killing all the princes and sending the spoils to the king of Damascus. {24:24} The Syrians may have had a small army, but God gave them victory because Joash and his peeps turned their backs on God. So Joash gets what's coming to him. {24:25} When the Syrians leave, Joash is left with some serious diseases, and his own servants take him out for the blood of Zechariah's sons, killing him in his bed. They bury him in the city of David, but not with the other kings. {24:26} The ones who took him out were Zabad, a son of Shimeath the Ammonitess, and Jehozabad, a son of Shimrith the Moabitess. {24:27} If you wanna know more about Joash's reign and what went down, check out the kings' book. His son Amaziah takes over after him.

{25:1} So Amaziah takes the throne when he's twenty-five, ruling for twenty-nine years in Jerusalem. His mom's Jehoaddan from Jerusalem. {25:2} He tries to do right by God, but his heart's not totally in it. {25:3} Once he's settled in, he deals with the servants who offed his dad. {25:4} But he's chill about it, following the law of Moses that says each person's responsible for their own sins, not their fam's. {25:5} Then he gets Judah organized, appointing captains and numbering his troops. He's got 300,000 top-notch soldiers ready for battle. {25:6} He even hires 100,000 tough guys from Israel, dropping some serious coin for them. {25:7} But a God-fearing dude shows up, warning him not to bring the Israelite army 'cause God's not vibing with them. {25:8} He's like, "If you go, be ready to lose 'cause God's got the power to help or smack you down." {25:9} Amaziah's worried about the cash he dropped on the Israelites, but the guy's like, "God can hook you up with way more than that." {25:10} So Amaziah sends the Israelite crew home, ticking them off big time. {25:11} He gears up and heads out to battle, laying the smackdown on the Edomites, taking out 10,000. {25:12} Then he's like,

"Yo, let's toss 10,000 off a cliff," and they do it. Brutal. {25:13} But the soldiers he sent home go on a rampage, wrecking cities in Judah and snagging some loot. {25:14} After kicking Edom's butt, Amaziah brings home their gods and starts worshiping them, which ticks off God big time. {25:15} So God sends a prophet to call him out, asking why he's worshiping gods who couldn't even save their own people. {25:16} Amaziah's like, "Who are you to speak to me like that?" and the prophet's like, "You're toast 'cause you didn't listen to me." {25:17} Amaziah tries to make peace with Joash, king of Israel, but Joash ain't having it, hitting him with a sick burn about thistles and cedars. {25:18} Basically telling him to chill 'cause he ain't all that. {25:19} But Amaziah's pride won't let him back down, and God lets him fall hard 'cause he started worshiping Edom's gods. {25:20} So Joash rolls up and smacks Judah down, sending Amaziah packing. {25:21} They face off at Beth-shemesh, and Judah gets wrecked. {25:22} Joash drags Amaziah back to Jerusalem, busts up the walls, and loots the place. {25:23} He even nabs all the gold, silver, and temple goodies, taking hostages back to Samaria. {25:24} Amaziah's son Uzziah takes over when he dies. {25:25} Amaziah lives for fifteen years after Joash kicks the bucket. {25:26} You can read all about Amaziah's ups and downs in the history books. {25:27} Once Amaziah ditches God, a conspiracy goes down in Jerusalem, and he hightails it to Lachish. They track him down and take him out. {25:28} They parade his body on horses and bury him with his ancestors.

{26:1} Then the people of Judah crown Uzziah king at sixteen, taking over from his pops, Amaziah. {26:2} He fixes up Eloth, bringing it back under Judah's wing. {26:3} Uzziah rules for fifty-two years, starting when he's sixteen. His mom's Jecoliah from Jerusalem. {26:4} He's a solid king, following in Amaziah's footsteps. {26:5} He's all about God while Zechariah's around, and God blesses him with success. {26:6} He takes on the Philistines, wrecking their walls and building up Judah's cities. {26:7} God's got his back, helping him against the Philistines and the Arabians. {26:8} The Ammonites even start paying tribute to him 'cause he's that legit. {26:9} He beefs up Jerusalem's defenses, building towers and digging wells. {26:10} He's all about that farming life, with cattle and vineyards everywhere. {26:11} He's got a massive army, well-trained and ready for action. {26:12} Leading them are 2,600 top dogs. {26:13} And they've got a whopping 307,500 troops ready to throw down. {26:14} Uzziah hooks them up with top-notch gear, shields, spears, helmets, the works. {26:15} He even invents some crazy weapons for Jerusalem's towers. Uzziah's name is spreading far and wide 'cause he's straight-up balling. {26:16} But when he's riding high, he gets cocky and decides to burn incense in the temple, something only priests are supposed to do. {26:17} Azariah and eighty other priests call him out, but he ain't having it. {26:18} They tell him to bail, but he loses it and tries to burn incense anyway. Then BAM, leprosy hits him right in the face. {26:19} The priests see it and kick him out of there quick. {26:20} He's a leper till he dies, living in isolation. His son Jotham takes over ruling. {26:21} Isaiah the prophet writes up all the stuff Uzziah did, good and bad. {26:22} He kicks the bucket and gets buried with his ancestors.

{27:1} So Jotham takes the throne at twenty-five, ruling for sixteen years in Jerusalem. His mom's Jerushah, daughter of Zadok. {27:2} He's pretty solid, keeping it real with God like his dad Uzziah, but he's not about that temple life. And the people? Yeah, they're still shady. {27:3} He's all about construction, beefing up the high gate of the temple and stacking up the walls of Ophel. {27:4} Plus, he's building cities in the Judah mountains and throwing up castles and towers in the forests. {27:5} He throws down with the Ammonite king and comes out on top. And check it, the Ammonites cough up mad cash and grain as tribute. They keep it coming for three years straight. {27:6} Jotham's flexing hard 'cause he's staying true to God. {27:7} You wanna know more? Check out the history books for all the deets on Jotham's reign and battles. {27:8} He's twenty-five when he starts ruling and goes strong for sixteen years in Jerusalem. {27:9} When Jotham bites the dust, they lay him to rest in David's city, and his son Ahaz takes over.

{28:1} Ahaz steps up at twenty, ruling for sixteen years in Jerusalem. But he's no David, that's for sure. {28:2} He's all about copying the kings of Israel, even getting into making idols for Baal. {28:3} This dude's burning incense to pagan gods, even sacrificing his own kids in the fire. Sick, right? {28:4} He's all over the place with his worship, setting up altars everywhere, even under trees. {28:5} God's had enough and lets Syria take him down, hauling off a bunch of Judah's people to Damascus. And Israel? They lay a smackdown on him too. {28:6} Pekah, Remaliah's son, wipes out 120,000 Judah warriors in one day 'cause they've ditched God. {28:7} Some Ephraim warrior takes out the king's son and a bunch of others. {28:8} Israel carts off 200,000 captives, plus loads of loot, back to Samaria. {28:9} But then this prophet named Oded steps in, calling them out for their rage against Judah and telling them to release the captives. {28:10} Some Ephraim big shots agree, realizing they've already screwed up big time. {28:11} They set the captives free and take care of them, making sure they're good to go back home. {28:16} Ahaz is so desperate, he hits up the Assyrian kings for help. {28:17} 'Cause, you know, the Edomites are causing trouble again, raiding Judah and snatching up captives. {28:18} And the Philistines? They're taking over Judah's cities in the lowlands and the south, making themselves at home. {28:19} God's punishing Judah 'cause of Ahaz's screw-ups, leaving them exposed and vulnerable. {28:20} So Tilgath-pilneser rolls up, causing Ahaz grief but not actually helping him. {28:21} Ahaz starts robbing God's house and his own palace to buy Assyria's help, but it's a bust. {28:22} Ahaz keeps dissing God even when things get tough. Total jerk move. {28:23} He starts worshiping the gods of Damascus, thinking they'll save him. Spoiler alert: they don't. They wreck him and Israel. {28:24} Ahaz goes all out, trashing God's house, setting up altars all over Jerusalem. {28:25} Everywhere you look in Judah, there's high places for burning incense to other gods, just ticking off God even more. {28:26} Check out the history books for all the stuff Ahaz did, from start to finish. {28:27} Ahaz kicks the bucket and gets buried in Jerusalem, but they don't put him in the kings' tombs. His son Hezekiah takes over.

{29:1} Hezekiah takes over at twenty-five, ruling for twenty-nine years in Jerusalem. His mom's Abijah, daughter of Zechariah. {29:2} Dude's legit, following God like his OG, David. {29:3} First year on the job, first month, he's like, "Let's open up this temple, yo." {29:4}

He calls in the priests and Levites, like, "Time to clean house, fam." {29:5} He's all, "Levites, get yourselves together, clean up this holy spot." {29:6} Our ancestors messed up big time, dissing God and turning their backs on him. {29:7} They straight-up neglected the temple, shutting doors, blowing out lamps, not even burning incense or making offerings to God. {29:8} God's wrath hit Judah and Jerusalem hard, leaving them messed up. {29:9} Our peeps got wrecked, families torn apart, all 'cause of this. {29:10} Hezekiah's like, "Let's make things right with God and dodge his wrath." {29:11} He tells his sons, "Don't slack off. God chose you to serve him, so step up." {29:12} Levites start rolling in, ready to clean house, each group doing their thing. {29:13} They all get together, getting themselves right, following the king's orders and God's word to purify the temple. {29:16} Priests get busy cleaning up the temple, hauling out all the junk into the courtyard. {29:17} They start cleaning on the first of the month and finish up on the sixteenth, eight days of hard work. {29:18} They hit up Hezekiah like, "Temple's squeaky clean, altar's ready to roll, and check it, we found all the stuff Ahaz trashed." {29:20} Hezekiah's up at the crack of dawn, rallying the city big shots, heading to the temple. {29:21} They bring a bunch of animals for sacrifices, covering all the bases for the kingdom and the sanctuary. {29:22} Priests get to work, spilling blood on the altar like it's nobody's business. {29:23} Then they bring out the goats for the sin offering, laying hands on them before the kill. {29:24} Priests do their thing, making things right with God for all Israel. {29:25} Levites bust out the instruments, just like David and the prophets ordered. {29:26} Music's pumping, priests got their trumpets going. {29:27} Hezekiah's like, "Time for the burnt offering," and the worship starts blasting. {29:28} Whole congregation's in on it, singing, playing, until the offering's done. {29:29} When it's all over, everyone bows down and worships. {29:30} Hezekiah's all, "You're in with God now, so bring your sacrifices and thanks to the temple." {29:31} People start bringing in sacrifices and thank offerings, just overflowing with gratitude. {29:32} They bring in tons of animals for burnt offerings, like, seventy bullocks, a hundred rams, and two hundred lambs. {29:33} Plus, they're dropping six hundred oxen and three thousand sheep as consecrated offerings. {29:34} But there aren't enough priests to handle it all, so the Levites step up, keeping things in check. {29:35} Burnt offerings are lit, with fat from peace offerings and drink offerings for each one. Temple's running smooth. {29:36} Hezekiah's stoked, the people are pumped, 'cause God got them sorted, and it happened fast.

{30:1} Hezekiah hits up everyone in Israel and Judah, even sending texts to Ephraim and Manasseh, saying, "Yo, come to the temple in Jerusalem and let's celebrate Passover for the Lord." {30:2} He's all, "We missed the Passover deadline, but let's do it in the second month." {30:3} 'Cause the priests and the people weren't ready yet, you know? {30:4} Everybody's down with the plan, for real. {30:5} So they spread the word all over, from Beer-sheba to Dan, like, "Passover party in Jerusalem, let's go!" {30:6} Messengers hit the road with the king's letters, saying, "Come back to God, y'all, and he'll have your back." {30:7} He's like, "Don't be like your ancestors who messed up big time." {30:8} "Chill out, be cool with God, and worship him. That's how you avoid getting wrecked by his wrath." {30:9} He's like, "If you get back to God, your peeps in captivity might catch a break and come back home." {30:10} Messengers go out, but some people just laugh it off, thinking it's a joke. {30:11} But some folks from Asher, Manasseh, and Zebulun are like, "Okay, let's do this," and head to Jerusalem. {30:12} In Judah, God's got everyone on the same page, following the king's orders and God's word. {30:13} So a huge crowd shows up in Jerusalem for the Feast of Unleavened Bread in the second month, like, packed house. {30:14} They clean up the temple, tossing out all the altars and stuff into the Kidron Valley. {30:15} Then they do Passover on the fourteenth day of the second month. Priests and Levites get serious, bringing in the burnt offerings to the temple. {30:16} They stick to the rules, just like Moses laid out. Priests do the blood sprinkling, Levites handle the rest. {30:17} 'Cause some people weren't ready, Levites step in to help with the Passover sacrifices. {30:18} Lots of folks, even from Ephraim, Manasseh, Issachar, and Zebulun, weren't fully clean but still chow down on Passover. Hezekiah's like, "God, forgive them," and God's cool with it, healing the people. {30:19} He's like, "If you're sincere about seeking God, even if you're not perfectly clean, God's got you." {30:20} And God listens to Hezekiah, and everyone's happy. {30:21} People party for seven days straight in Jerusalem, priests and Levites singing and jamming out to God. {30:22} Hezekiah's chatting with the Levites, giving props to those who teach about God. They feast for a week, offering peace offerings and confessing to God. {30:23} Everyone's like, "Let's keep the party going!" and they celebrate for another seven days, pumped up. {30:24} Hezekiah hooks up the congregation with a ton of animals for sacrifices, and the princes chip in too. Lots of priests get themselves ready for duty. {30:25} Everyone in Judah, along with priests, Levites, and even visitors from Israel, are stoked. {30:26} Jerusalem's lit with joy, like it hasn't been since Solomon's time. {30:27} Priests bless the people, their prayers reaching up to God's place in heaven.

{31:1} When it's all done, Israelites head back home, smashing idols, cutting down groves, and wrecking altars all over Judah and Benjamin, even in Ephraim and Manasseh, wiping out every trace of idolatry. Then everyone heads back to their cities. {31:2} Hezekiah sets up the priests and Levites for their duties, making sure they handle sacrifices, give thanks, and praise God at the temple gates. {31:3} He even sorts out offerings for mornings, evenings, Sabbaths, new moons, and festivals, all according to God's law. {31:4} He tells the Jerusalem peeps to give the priests and Levites their share, keeping them focused on God's law. {31:5} Soon as the word goes out, Israelites start bringing in the first fruits, tithes, and holy offerings, overflowing with abundance. {31:6} Even folks from Judah cities chip in with their tithes, stacking them up. {31:7} They start piling up the offerings in the third month, finishing up by the seventh month. {31:8} Hezekiah and the princes check out the piles and bless God and his people. {31:9} Hezekiah's like, "What's up with all this?" and talks to the priests and Levites about the heaps. {31:10} Chief priest Azariah's like, "Since people started bringing in offerings, we've got more than enough to eat and plenty left over. God's been good to us." {31:11} So Hezekiah tells them to make storage rooms at the temple, and they do, faithfully bringing in offerings, tithes, and dedicated stuff. {31:12} Cononiah and Shimei oversee everything, with Jehiel, Azaziah, Nahath, Asahel, Jerimoth, Jozabad, Eliel, Ismachiah, and Benaiah helping out, all under Hezekiah and Azariah's command. {31:13} Kore's in charge of the freewill offerings, making sure they're distributed right. {31:14} Eden,

Miniamin, Jeshua, Shemaiah, Amariah, and Shecaniah handle priestly duties, giving to their fellow priests according to their schedule, no matter if they're big or small. {31:15} They even take care of the little ones, wives, sons, and daughters, making sure everyone's on board with staying holy. {31:16} Priests and Levites from three years old and up get their daily portion for temple service, according to their duties and schedules. {31:17} Priests trace their ancestry, Levites start at twenty, all sticking to their duties as laid out by their ancestors. {31:18} Everyone, from the littlest to the oldest, their wives and kids, is part of the plan to stay holy. {31:19} Aaron's descendants, priests in the outskirts, make sure everyone gets their share, following the rules for priests and Levites. {31:20} Hezekiah's all about doing good, right, and true stuff in God's eyes. {31:21} Every project he takes on for God's house, the law, and God's commands, he's all in, and it works out.

{32:1} So, after all that went down and everything got set up, Sennacherib, the Assyrian king, rolled in, ready to take over Judah, eyeing those fortified cities like they were his new digs. {32:2} When Hezekiah peeped Sennacherib's arrival and his plan to throw down with Jerusalem, he huddled up with his crew to cut off the water supply from outside the city, and they came through. {32:3} They rounded up a bunch of folks to block up all the fountains and the stream running through the land, asking, "Why should the Assyrians roll up and find an easy water source?" {32:4} Hezekiah also beefed up the defenses, fixing the busted wall, building it higher, adding another layer outside, and sprucing up the city defenses. {32:5} He even rallied the people, pumping them up in the city gate, giving them a pep talk, like, "Stay strong, y'all! Don't trip about Sennacherib or his squad. We got more backup than they do." {32:6} He was all about that positive vibe, telling the people not to stress, because while Sennacherib's packing human muscle, they got the LORD God on their side to handle business. And the people were all about what Hezekiah was preaching, totally chilling. {32:9} But then Sennacherib, the big boss of Assyria, sent his henchmen to Jerusalem, while he himself was busy laying siege to Lachish with his full force, sending a message to Hezekiah and all the folks in Jerusalem, like, "Yo, what's your plan here, trusting that the LORD will bail you out of my grip?" {32:10} He straight-up called out Hezekiah, saying he was leading them to a famine and thirst-induced death, claiming Hezekiah was promising divine rescue from the Assyrian king's hand. {32:11} Sennacherib tried to throw shade, saying Hezekiah tore down all the other altars, telling everyone to worship at one, burning incense there. {32:12} He bragged about how none of the gods of other lands could save them from his conquests, throwing major doubt on the power of Judah's God. {32:13} He even mocked Hezekiah, saying no god had ever stood a chance against Assyria, so why should Judah's God be any different? {32:16} His goons kept dissing the LORD and Hezekiah, writing letters railing against the God of Israel, spreading doubt and fear among the people on the city walls. {32:17} They straight-up dissed the God of Jerusalem, treating Him like just another human-made deity. {32:20} That's when Hezekiah and the prophet Isaiah hit up heaven with prayers and cries for help. {32:21} And the LORD sent an angel to wipe out all the Assyrian big shots, sending Sennacherib back home in disgrace. And when he got back, his own fam took him out in his own temple. {32:22} So, the LORD saved Hezekiah and the Jerusalem crew from Sennacherib and his squad, keeping them safe from all sides. {32:23} People started showing mad love, bringing gifts to the LORD in Jerusalem and Hezekiah, making him a legend among the nations. {32:24} But then Hezekiah got super sick, prayed hard, and got a sign from the LORD. {32:25} But Hezekiah let it go to his head, getting all prideful, which brought down the LORD's wrath on him and Judah. {32:26} But Hezekiah and the Jerusalem crew eventually humbled themselves, so the LORD held off on the wrath during Hezekiah's time. {32:27} Hezekiah was rolling in cash and respect, stacking up treasures and setting up storerooms for all kinds of riches. {32:28} He even made sure there was plenty of food, wine, and livestock, with all the facilities to keep them cozy. {32:29} He hooked up cities and livestock for days, blessed with mad wealth from God. {32:30} Hezekiah even redirected the Gihon stream, making things smooth in the city of David, and everything he touched turned to gold. {32:31} But when Babylon's big shots came knocking, asking about the miracles, God let Hezekiah deal with them solo, to see what was really in his heart. {32:32} You can find more about Hezekiah's hustle and his goodness in Isaiah's vision and the kings' chronicles of Judah and Israel. {32:33} When Hezekiah passed, they gave him a proper send-off, burying him in the royal tombs, and everyone in Judah and Jerusalem showed him love even in death. Then his son Manasseh took over.

{33:1} So, Manasseh was like, twelve years old when he started ruling, and he was in charge for, like, fifty-five years in Jerusalem. {33:2} But he was totally not cool in the LORD's eyes, you know, doing all the messed up stuff that the heathens, who got kicked out by the LORD before, used to do. {33:3} He rebuilt those high places that his dad Hezekiah tore down, set up altars for Baal, made groves, worshipped all the stars and stuff, totally not vibing with the LORD's deal. {33:4} Oh, and he even put altars in the LORD's house, even though the LORD was like, "This is where my name's staying forever, yo." {33:5} And he set up altars for all the stars in the LORD's house courtyards, like, seriously? {33:6} He even made his kids go through fire rituals in the valley of Hinnom, did all sorts of witchy stuff, majorly ticking off the LORD. {33:7} Then, he put up a carved idol in the LORD's house, even though God was all about David and Solomon, saying, "This is the place where I'm gonna stay forever." {33:8} God was like, "I won't kick Israel out of their land anymore if they just follow my rules through Moses." {33:9} But Manasseh led Judah and Jerusalem down a bad path, worse than the heathens the LORD already wiped out. {33:10} The LORD tried talking sense to Manasseh and his crew, but they were like, "Nah, we're good." {33:11} So, the LORD let the Assyrian army captains snatch up Manasseh, dragging him off to Babylon like a thorn bush. {33:12} When he hit rock bottom, Manasseh reached out to the LORD, humbled himself big time, prayed hard. {33:13} And the LORD listened, showed him mercy, and brought him back to Jerusalem, making him king again. That's when Manasseh finally got it, realizing the LORD was the real deal. {33:14} After all that drama, Manasseh got busy building a serious wall around the city of David, beefing up defenses, posting guards everywhere. {33:15} He kicked out all those foreign gods and idols from the LORD's house and Jerusalem, tossing them out of the city for good. {33:16} Then, he fixed up the LORD's altar, started making sacrifices, and told Judah to get their act together and serve the LORD, God of Israel. {33:17} But even though people still sacrificed in the high places, at least they were only doing it for the LORD. {33:18} The rest of Manasseh's story, his prayers to God, and the prophecies he got from the seers, all written down in the kings of Israel's book. {33:19} His prayers, how God listened, all his screw-ups, where he built those high places and idols before he got humble, all there in the seers' writings. {33:20} Manasseh kicked the bucket, joining his ancestors in the grave, buried right at his place. Then his son Amon took over. {33:21} Amon was like, twenty-two when he started ruling, only lasted two years in Jerusalem. {33:22} But, just like his dad, he was on the wrong side of the LORD, sacrificing to all those carved idols Manasseh set up. {33:23} He didn't even try to humble himself before the LORD, unlike his old man Manasseh, just kept on doing more messed up stuff. {33:24} And then, his own crew turned against him, taking him out in his own house. {33:25} But the people weren't having it, they went after those who plotted against King Amon, making his son Josiah the new king.

{34:1} So, Josiah was, like, eight years old when he started running the show, and he held it down in Jerusalem for, like, thirty-one years. {34:2} He was all about doing what's right in the LORD's eyes, walking the same path as his ancestor David, never swerving off course. {34:3} By the time he hit his eighth year in power, even though he was still a young gun, he started seeking the God of his old man David. And by the twelfth year, he was on a mission, cleaning house in Judah and Jerusalem, tearing down those high places, groves, and all those graven and molten images. {34:4} He straight-up wrecked the altars of Baal right in front of everyone, chopped down those high-flying idols, smashed the groves and images, turning them to dust and scattering it over the graves of those who worshipped them. {34:5} He even burned up the bones of the priests on their own altars, purging Judah and Jerusalem of all that mess. {34:6} He didn't stop there either, taking his clean-up crew to cities all over, from Manasseh to Ephraim to Simeon and beyond, getting rid of every last trace of idolatry. {34:7} Once he was done smashing idols and tearing down altars, he bounced back to Jerusalem, mission accomplished. {34:8} By the time he hit his eighteenth year on the throne, with the land and the temple all cleaned up, he sent out his squad to fix up the house of the LORD. {34:9} When they hit up Hilkiah the high priest, they handed over the cash collected from all over, from Manasseh and Ephraim to the leftovers of Israel, Judah, and Benjamin. And then they bounced back to Jerusalem. {34:10} They handed the loot over to the workers in charge of the temple, making sure they had what they needed to fix up the place. {34:11} They even hooked up the builders with funds to cop some fresh stone and timber, to patch up the houses the kings of Judah had trashed. {34:12} The crew put in work, staying true to the task, with Jahath and Obadiah, the Levites, overseeing the project, and Zechariah and Meshullam, from the Kohathites, getting things moving. And they had some Levites who were musical wizards too. {34:13} They handled everything from carrying heavy loads to overseeing all kinds of work, with Levite scribes, officers, and bouncers in the mix. {34:14} Then, when they brought out the loot from the temple, Hilkiah stumbled upon a copy of the law of the LORD given by Moses. {34:15} He hit up Shaphan the scribe, like, "Yo, check it, I found the law of the LORD in the house of the LORD." And Hilkiah passed the book to Shaphan. {34:16} Shaphan took the book to Josiah, giving him the lowdown, saying, "Everything you wanted us to do, consider it done." {34:17} He let Josiah know they sorted out the cash from the temple and passed it on to the overseers and the workers. {34:18} Then Shaphan filled Josiah in, telling him Hilkiah hooked him up with the book, and he read it out loud for the king. {34:19} When Josiah heard what was written in the law, he was shook, tearing his clothes in response. {34:20} Josiah ordered Hilkiah, Ahikam, Abdon, Shaphan, and Asaiah to hit up the LORD and get the scoop on what was up with the book they found. {34:21} He was like, "Find out what's going on for me and the rest of Judah and Israel. The LORD's seriously ticked off because our ancestors didn't keep His word." {34:22} So they all rolled up to Huldah the prophetess, the wife of Shallum, the son of Tikvath, who was in charge of the wardrobe. And they were like, "Fill us in." {34:23} Huldah told them straight from the LORD, "Go back and tell the king this: I'm bringing down some serious heat on this place, all the curses written in that book you found. {34:25} Because they ditched me and started burning incense to other gods, ticked me off with all their handmade junk, I'm unleashing my fury on this place, and it won't be stopped." {34:26} But for Josiah, the king who reached out, here's the deal: "Because you got soft and showed humility when you heard my words against this place and its people, tearing your clothes and crying out to me, I heard you loud and clear." {34:28} "You'll peace out and be laid to rest in peace, never seeing the crapstorm I'm bringing on this place and its people." And they gave the king the rundown. {34:29} Josiah rounded up all the elders of Judah and Jerusalem. {34:30} Then he hit up the temple with all the people, big and small, priests and Levites, and read them the riot act straight from the book they found in the house of the LORD. {34:31} He stood his ground, making a solid commitment before the LORD to follow His commandments and keep the covenant written in that book with all his heart and soul. {34:32} He got everyone in Jerusalem and Benjamin to swear to it, and the people of Jerusalem kept it real with the covenant of their God, the God of their ancestors. {34:33} Josiah went all out, clearing out every last abomination from all the lands belonging to Israel, making everyone present in Israel serve the LORD their God. And they stayed true to the LORD, the God of their ancestors, for as long as Josiah lived.

{35:1} So, Josiah threw a lit passover party for the LORD in Jerusalem, and they slaughtered the passover lambs on the fourteenth day of the first month. {35:2} He put the priests on duty and hyped them up for their service in the house of the LORD. {35:3} Then he told the Levites, who were all about teaching Israel and dedicated to the LORD, "Yo, put that holy ark in the house Solomon built; don't stress about carrying it around. Serve the LORD your God and His people Israel." {35:4} "Get yourselves organized by your family clans, following the plan laid out by David and Solomon." {35:5} "Stand ready in the holy place according to your family divisions, alongside your Levite brethren." {35:6} "Then get ready for the passover, cleanse yourselves, and prep your brothers to follow the LORD's word through Moses." {35:7} Josiah hooked the people up with lambs and goats for the passover offerings, thirty thousand lambs and three thousand bulls, all from his own stash. {35:8} His crew of bosses willingly gave more, including Hilkiah, Zechariah, and Jehiel, who tossed in twenty-six hundred small cattle and three hundred oxen for the passover offerings. {35:9} Conaniah,

Shemaiah, Nethaneel, Hashabiah, Jeiel, and Jozabad, the top Levites, chipped in with five thousand small cattle and five hundred oxen for the Levites' passover offerings. {35:10} They got everything ready as ordered by the king, with the priests in their positions and the Levites in their courses. {35:11} They slaughtered the passover lambs, the priests sprinkled the blood, and the Levites skinned the animals. {35:12} They sorted out the burnt offerings, distributing them according to family divisions to offer to the LORD, following Moses's instructions. And they did the same with the oxen. {35:13} They roasted the passover lambs as required, while boiling up the holy offerings to be distributed quickly among the people. {35:14} After that, they prepped for themselves and the priests because the priests, the sons of Aaron, were busy offering burnt offerings and fat until nightfall. So the Levites took care of themselves and the priests. {35:15} The singers, sons of Asaph, followed David's orders, alongside Asaph, Heman, and Jeduthun the king's seer, while the porters held it down at every gate, staying on duty. The Levites had their backs, getting things ready for them. {35:16} Everything went down on the same day, with the passover celebrated and burnt offerings made on the LORD's altar, just like King Josiah commanded. {35:17} All the Israelites who were there kept the passover and the feast of unleavened bread for seven days. {35:18} This passover was off the charts, unlike any other in Israel since the time of Samuel the prophet. None of the kings of Israel threw a passover bash like Josiah did, along with the priests, Levites, and everyone from Judah, Israel, and Jerusalem who showed up. {35:19} This epic passover went down in the eighteenth year of Josiah's reign. {35:20} After all that, when Josiah had the temple sorted, along comes Necho, king of Egypt, to throw down with Charchemish by the Euphrates. {35:21} Josiah tries to reason with him, sending ambassadors like, "Bro, I ain't got beef with you. God told me to hustle, so don't mess with God, who's got my back, or He'll wreck you." {35:22} But Josiah ain't backing down, disguising himself to throw down with Necho, ignoring God's warning delivered by Necho. They clash in the valley of Megiddo. {35:23} Josiah catches an arrow from the archers and tells his crew, "Get me outta here; I'm hurt bad." {35:24} They switch him to another chariot and haul him back to Jerusalem, where he kicks the bucket and gets buried in his family's tomb. All of Judah and Jerusalem mourn for Josiah. {35:25} Jeremiah joins in the lament, with all the singers and wailers making sure Josiah's legacy lives on, writing it all down in their mournful tunes. {35:26} The rest of Josiah's epic deeds, his goodness, it's all written in the LORD's law. {35:27} Everything he did, from start to finish, it's all there in the books of the kings of Israel and Judah.

{36:1} So, the squad in Jerusalem were like, "Yo, let's crown Jehoahaz, Josiah's son, as king." {36:2} Jehoahaz was only twenty-three when he took the throne and only lasted three months before Egypt shut him down, making him pay up a hundred talents of silver and a talent of gold. {36:3} Then Egypt's king was like, "Nah, Eliakim, Jehoahaz's bro, you're up next," and changed his name to Jehoiakim. Jehoahaz got shipped off to Egypt. {36:5} Jehoiakim, twenty-five at the start, ruled for eleven years, but he was straight-up evil in God's eyes. {36:6} Nebuchadnezzar from Babylon rolled in, chained up Jehoiakim, and dragged him off to Babylon, even snatching up some holy gear from the LORD's house. {36:9} Then Jehoiachin, just eight years old, took over, but he was also on the wrong side of God's vibe, lasting only three months and ten days before Nebuchadnezzar swooped in, took him to Babylon, and installed Zedekiah as king. {36:11} Zedekiah, twenty-one when he started, ruled for eleven years, but he wasn't feeling Jeremiah's messages from the LORD. {36:14} Everyone, from the top priests to the regular folks, went off the rails, polluting the LORD's house in Jerusalem with all kinds of messed-up stuff. {36:16} God kept sending messages, but they straight-up dissed His messengers and ignored His prophets until God's wrath boiled over, and there was no going back. {36:17} So Nebuchadnezzar rolled in, wrecking the young, the old, and everyone in between, no mercy. {36:18} He looted the LORD's house and the royal treasury, hauling everything back to Babylon. {36:19} Then they torched God's house, smashed up Jerusalem's walls, and burned down all the fancy buildings, destroying all the precious stuff. {36:20} Those who survived got hauled off to Babylon as slaves, serving Nebuchadnezzar and his crew until Persia took over. {36:21} All of this went down just like Jeremiah said, until the land had its rest for seventy years, in line with God's word. {36:22} Then Cyrus, king of Persia, came on the scene, stirred up by God to make a big announcement, saying God gave him all the kingdoms and told him to rebuild His house in Jerusalem. {36:23} So, Cyrus put it out there for anyone who wanted to join the building crew to head to Jerusalem with God's blessing.

Ezra

✛✛✛

{1:1} So, like, in Cyrus's first year as Persia's king, God nudged Cyrus to make a big announcement across his whole kingdom, even writing it down, saying, {1:2} "Yo, Cyrus here! God, the big guy up in the sky, hooked me up with all the kingdoms on Earth. He's like, 'Build me a crib in Jerusalem, yo!' That's in Judah, by the way." {1:3} Cyrus was all, "Anyone down to help out? If you're with God, go for it, head to Jerusalem, and get building for the LORD, who's all about Israel, chillin' in Jerusalem." {1:4} And anyone left behind should pitch in with cash, gold, goods, animals, and extra offerings for God's crib in Jerusalem. {1:5} So, the leaders of Judah and Benjamin, plus the priests and Levites, and anyone else feeling the vibe from God, were ready to roll and build the LORD's house in Jerusalem. {1:6} Everyone around them chipped in with silver, gold, goods, animals, and all kinds of fancy stuff, not holding back. {1:7} Even Cyrus himself busted out the goods from the LORD's house that Nebuchadnezzar swiped and stashed in his own spot. {1:8} Cyrus handed them over to Sheshbazzar, the Judah prince, with Mithredath keeping count. {1:9} Here's the score: thirty gold plates, a thousand silver plates, twenty-nine knives, {1:10} thirty gold bowls, four hundred and ten silver bowls, and a thousand other fancy items. {1:11} In total, there were five thousand four hundred golden and silver items that Sheshbazzar brought back with the crew from Babylon to Jerusalem.

{2:1} So, like, all these folks who bounced back from being locked up in Babylon, thanks to Nebuchadnezzar, they returned to their hood in Jerusalem and Judah, each to their own turf; {2:2} Rollin' with Zerubbabel were Jeshua, Nehemiah, Seraiah, Reelaiah, Mordecai, Bilshan, Mizpar, Bigvai, Rehum, and Baanah. Total headcount of the Israelite homies: {2:3} The Parosh crew was two thousand one hundred seventy-two. {2:4} Shephatiah's squad was three hundred seventy-two. {2:5} Arah's clique was seven hundred seventy-five. {2:6} Pahath-moab, reppin' Jeshua and Joab, rolled deep with two thousand eight hundred twelve. {2:7} Elam's posse was a cool one thousand two hundred fifty-four. {2:8} Zattu's squad was nine hundred forty-five. {2:9} Zaccai's crew was seven hundred sixty. {2:10} Bani's squad was six hundred forty-two. {2:11} Bebai's crew was six hundred twenty-three. {2:12} Azgad's crew was a solid one thousand two hundred twenty-two. {2:13} Adonikam's squad was six hundred sixty-six. {2:14} Bigvai's squad was two thousand fifty-six. {2:15} Adin's clique was four hundred fifty-four. {2:16} Ater of Hezekiah's squad was ninety-eight. {2:17} Bezai's crew was three hundred twenty-three. {2:18} Jorah's clique was a hundred twelve. {2:19} Hashum's squad was two hundred twenty-three. {2:20} Gibbar's crew was ninety-five. {2:21} Bethlehem's posse was a hundred twenty-three. {2:22} Netophah's crew was fifty-six. {2:23} Anathoth's squad was a hundred twenty-eight. {2:24} Azmaveth's clique was forty-two. {2:25} Kirjath-arim, Chephirah, and Beeroth's squad was seven hundred forty-three. {2:26} Ramah and Gaba's crew was six hundred twenty-one. {2:27} Michmas's squad was a hundred twenty-two. {2:28} Bethel and Ai's posse was two hundred twenty-three. {2:29} Nebo's crew was fifty-two. {2:30} Magbish's squad was a hundred fifty-six. {2:31} The other Elam's crew was a cool one thousand two hundred fifty-four. {2:32} Harim's squad was three hundred twenty. {2:33} Lod, Hadid, and Ono's posse was seven hundred twenty-five. {2:34} Jericho's crew was three hundred forty-five. {2:35} Senaah's squad was three thousand six hundred thirty. {2:36} The priests from Jedaiah's crew, representing Jeshua's fam, were nine hundred seventy-three. {2:37} Immer's clique was a thousand fifty-two. {2:38} Pashur's squad was a thousand two hundred forty-seven. {2:39} Harim's squad was a thousand seventeen. {2:40} The Levites from Jeshua and Kadmiel's crew, from Hodaviah's fam, were seventy-four. {2:41} Asaph's squad of singers was a hundred twenty-eight. {2:42} The porters, from Shallum, Ater, Talmon, Akkub, Hatita, and Shobai's crew, were a hundred thirty-nine. {2:43} The Nethinims, from Ziha, Hasupha, Tabbaoth, Keros, Siaha, Padon, Lebanah, Hagabah, Akkub, Hagab, Shalmai, and Hanan's crew, were four hundred fifty-three. {2:44} Giddel, Gahar, and Reaiah's crew was forty-nine. {2:45} Rezin, Nekoda, and Gazzam's crew was forty-seven. {2:46} Uzza, Paseah, and Besai's squad was fifty-eight. {2:47} Asnah, Mehunim, and Nephusim's crew was a hundred sixty-three. {2:48} Bakbuk, Hakupha, and Harhur's squad was a hundred eighty-one. {2:49} Bazluth, Mehida, and Harsha's crew was forty-eight. {2:50} Barkos, Sisera, and Thamah's posse was a hundred fifty-seven. {2:51} Neziah and Hatipha's squad was fifty-two. {2:52} Solomon's servants' crew, including Sotai, Sophereth, Peruda, Jaalah, Darkon, and Giddel's squad, was hundred ninety-two. {2:53} The total headcount of peeps coming back from Tel-melah, Tel-harsa, Cherub, Addan, and Immer was six hundred fifty-two. {2:54} Habaiah, Koz, and Barzillai's crew was sixty-eight. {2:55} Sotai, Sophereth, and Peruda's squad was hundred twenty-three. {2:56} Jaalah, Darkon, and Giddel's crew was forty-eight. {2:57} Shephatiah, Hattil, and Pochereth of Zebaim's squad was a hundred twenty-three. {2:58} In total, including the Nethinims and Solomon's servants' kids, there were three hundred ninety-two. {2:59} And those who couldn't trace their lineage from Tel-melah, Tel-harsa, Cherub, Addan, and Immer numbered six hundred fifty-two. {2:60} Habaiah, Koz, and Barzillai's crew, who married into Barzillai the Gileadite's family, tried to get legit but couldn't prove their lineage, so they got booted from the priesthood as tainted. {2:61} They were told by the head honcho not to chow down on the holy grub until a priest with the Urim and Thummim stepped up. {2:62} So the whole crowd, including servants and maids, totaled forty-two thousand three hundred sixty; along with two hundred singers and musicians, and a solid crew of horses, mules, camels, and donkeys. {2:63} The big shot fathers, when they hit up the LORD's crib in Jerusalem, threw down some serious cash to set up shop for God: sixty-one thousand drams of gold, five thousand pounds of silver, and a hundred priestly threads. {2:64} So the priests, Levites, regular folks, singers, porters, and Neth

{3:1} So, like, when the chill vibes of the seventh month hit and the Israelite fam were posted up in their cities, they all linked up in Jerusalem like one big crew. {3:2} Jeshua, son of Jozadak, and his priest squad, along with Zerubbabel, son of Shealtiel, and his crew, built up the altar of the God of Israel, you know, to drop some sick burnt offerings as written in Moses' law. {3:3} They set the altar up on its base, 'cause they were low-key shook by the locals, and started offering up burnt offerings to the LORD, morning and night. {3:4} They even threw down for the Feast of Tabernacles, following the script, and offered up the daily burnt offerings, you know, sticking to the usual routine. {3:5} Then they hit up the continuous burnt offerings, including for the new moons and all the other lit feasts of the LORD, plus anyone who wanted to chip in with a freewill offering. {3:6} They started dropping those burnt offerings to the LORD from the first day of the seventh month, even though they hadn't laid down the foundation for the LORD's crib yet. {3:7} They were throwing cash at the masons and carpenters, hooking them up with food, drink, and oil, shipping in those cedar trees from Lebanon to Joppa, just like Cyrus, the king of Persia, had hooked them up. {3:8} Then, in the second year of their setup in God's crib in Jerusalem, in the second month, Zerubbabel, Jeshua, the leftover priests and Levites, and all the other ex-captives who rolled into Jerusalem, recruited Levites aged twenty and up to get the house of the LORD moving. {3:9} Jeshua and his sons, Kadmiel and his sons, and the sons of Judah all teamed up to get the work crew going in God's crib, joined by the sons of Henadad and their Levite crew. {3:10} When the builders laid down the temple's foundation, they had the priests decked out in their gear with trumpets, and the Levites, sons of Asaph, with cymbals, jamming out to praise the LORD, following David's playbook. {3:11} They belted out tunes together, giving props and thanks to the LORD, 'cause He's dope and His love for Israel is forever. And the whole squad shouted loud when they praised the LORD, 'cause they finally laid down the foundation for the LORD's crib. {3:12} But a bunch of old-timers, priests, Levites, and OG dads who had seen the first temple, straight-up cried when they saw the new foundation, while others were hyped as heck, shouting for joy. {3:13} It was so loud, you couldn't even tell if the noise was cheers or tears; it echoed far and wide, fam.

{4:1} But when the haters from Judah and Benjamin caught wind that the ex-captives were building a temple for the LORD God of Israel, {4:2} they rolled up to Zerubbabel and the OG dads, talking about joining forces, claiming they worshipped the same God since the days of Esarhaddon, king of Assyria, who brought them up here. {4:3} Zerubbabel, Jeshua, and the other OG dads of Israel straight-up shut them down, saying they had no business building a house for their God. They were gonna handle it themselves, just like King Cyrus ordered. {4:4} But the locals weren't having it; they straight-up messed with the heads of the people of Judah, making their building project a real pain. {4:5} They even hired haters to sabotage them, pulling this shady move from Cyrus' reign all the way to Darius, king of Persia. {4:6} And when Ahasuerus was on the throne, right at the start of his reign, they snitched on the peeps of Judah and Jerusalem. {4:7} Artaxerxes was on the throne when Bishlam, Mithredath, Tabeel, and their crew wrote to him in Persian, but with a Syriac twist, spitting some venom about Judah and Jerusalem. {4:8} Rehum, the bigwig, and Shimshai, the secretary, penned a letter dissing Jerusalem to Artaxerxes like this: {4:9} Rehum, Shimshai, and their crew, including the Dinaites, Apharsathchites, Tarpelites, Apharsites, Archevites, Babylonians, Susanchites, Dehavites, and Elamites, sent a letter to Artaxerxes, laying it down. {4:10} They included all the other nations Asnapper brought over and planted in Samaria and beyond the river at that time. {4:11} Here's the gist of the letter they sent to Artaxerxes: "Your loyal peeps here wanna chat, bro. {4:12} FYI, those Jews you sent back here are straight-up rebelling, building up this sketchy city, Jerusalem, and fixing up the walls and stuff. {4:13} Just saying, if they finish this city and walls, they ain't gonna pay taxes, tolls, or customs, and you'll be outta pocket, king. {4:14} So, since we're on the palace payroll and can't stand seeing you disrespected, we're giving you the heads-up. {4:15} Check the records; you'll see Jerusalem's been nothing but trouble for kings and provinces, stirring up trouble since way back. That's why it got wrecked, yo. {4:16} Just so you know, if they rebuild this city and walls, you're gonna lose out big time." {4:17} Artaxerxes hit them back with a message for Rehum, Shimshai, and the crew in Samaria and beyond: "Chill vibes, bros, and at such a time. {4:18} I read your letter loud and clear. {4:19} I've checked it out, and turns out Jerusalem's been causing trouble for a hot minute, rebelling against kings and starting drama. {4:20} There've been some real kings over Jerusalem who had control over the whole region, making everyone pay up. {4:21} So, tell your crew to lay off and stop building the city until I say otherwise. {4:22} Don't mess this up; it's not good for the king's rep." {4:23} When Rehum, Shimshai, and their crew read Artaxerxes' letter, they sped off to Jerusalem, forcing the Jews to stop working by any means necessary. {4:24} And just like that, the work on God's crib in Jerusalem came to a halt. It stayed that way until the second year of Darius, king of Persia's reign.

{5:1} So, like, Haggai and Zechariah, the prophets, slid into the DMs of the Jews in Judah and Jerusalem, speaking on behalf of the God of Israel, ya know. {5:2} Then Zerubbabel, son of Shealtiel, and Jeshua, son of Jozadak, got to work building up God's crib in Jerusalem, with the prophets backing them up. {5:3} While they were at it, Tatnai, the governor on this side of the river, and his crew, rolled up with questions, asking who gave them permission to build and fortify this place. {5:4} So, we hit them back, asking for the names of the dudes leading this project. {5:5} But God had the elders of the Jews' backs, and Tatnai couldn't shut them down until it got kicked up to Darius. That's when they shot back a letter about the whole situation. {5:6} Here's the scoop on the letter Tatnai and his squad sent to King Darius: {5:7} They started it off with the usual greetings, keeping it chill. {5:8} They told the king they scoped out the scene in Judea, where they're putting together this massive house for the big God, with solid stones and timber flying up. {5:9} They even hit up the elders with the same questions about who gave them the green light for this project. {5:10} They made sure to get their names too, so they could pass them along to the king. {5:11} The elders hit them back, saying they're just doing what the God of heaven and earth told them to do, rebuilding the house that a big-shot king of Israel put up way back when. {5:12} But then, our ancestors ticked off the big guy upstairs, so He let Nebuchadnezzar, the king of Babylon, wreck the place and drag everyone off to

Babylon. {5:13} But in Cyrus the king of Babylon's first year, he was like, "Let's rebuild this temple!" {5:14} And Cyrus hooked them up with all the gold and silver stuff Nebuchadnezzar swiped from God's house in Jerusalem, bringing it back and handing it to this dude named Sheshbazzar, who he made governor. {5:15} Cyrus told Sheshbazzar to take the goods and rebuild the temple in Jerusalem. {5:16} So, Sheshbazzar got to it, laying down the foundation for God's house in Jerusalem, and they've been at it ever since, but still ain't finished. {5:17} So, if the king's feeling generous, he can check the records in Babylon and see if Cyrus really gave the green light to build God's house in Jerusalem, then let us know what's up.

{6:1} So, like, King Darius dropped a decree, and they went searching in the archives over in Babylon where they stash all their loot. {6:2} They found this scroll in Achmetha, in some fancy palace in the Medes province, and it was like, "Yo, in the first year of Cyrus, he was all about rebuilding God's crib in Jerusalem, you feel? Make it sturdy, like 60 cubits high and wide, with three rows of big stones and fresh timber." {6:3-4} And Cyrus was like, "And let's hook them up with the cash from my palace to fund it." Plus, he wanted all the gold and silver stuff Nebuchadnezzar swiped from God's temple in Jerusalem to get sent back there. {6:6-7} Then Darius was like, "Hey, Tatnai and crew, back off and let the Jews do their thing. Don't mess with the construction of God's house." {6:8-9} And he told them to cough up whatever the Jews needed from the royal stash, no delays. They were supposed to keep the sacrifices and prayers flowing smoothly. {6:10} Anyone trying to mess with this decree would have their house wrecked and be left hanging on their own timber. Darius was serious about protecting God's house. {6:12} So, Tatnai and his crew got on it real quick, following Darius's orders. {6:14} With Haggai and Zechariah hyping them up, the Jewish elders got to work, finishing the job just as God, Cyrus, Darius, and Artaxerxes commanded. {6:15} They wrapped it all up on the third day of Adar in Darius's sixth year on the throne. {6:16} Then the Israelites, priests, Levites, and the rest of the crew celebrated the dedication of God's house, throwing down with a hundred bulls, two hundred rams, and four hundred lambs. They even sacrificed twelve goats for a sin offering, one for each tribe of Israel. {6:18} They organized the priests and Levites for duty, just like Moses said in his book. {6:19} The folks who came back from captivity even kept the Passover on the fourteenth day of the first month, all pure and legit. {6:20} Priests and Levites got cleaned up together, then they slaughtered the Passover for everyone, including themselves and their priest homies. {6:21-22} The Israelites who returned from exile, along with those who had kept themselves separate from the pagan filth in the land, had a feast for seven days, celebrating big time. The Lord had them feeling joyful, and even got the king of Assyria to have their back and help out with God's house. It was lit.

{7:1} So, like, after all that went down, when Artaxerxes was running the show in Persia, Ezra, son of Seraiah, Azariah's kid, and Hilkiah's grandchild, you know, that whole crew, was doing his thing. {7:2} Ezra was on point with the law of Moses, God's gift to Israel, and Artaxerxes was totally down to grant whatever Ezra asked for, thanks to God's favor. {7:3} So Ezra bounces from Babylon with some of the Israelites, priests, Levites, singers, gatekeepers, and the Nethinims, heading for Jerusalem in Artaxerxes's seventh year. {7:8-9} He rolls into Jerusalem in the fifth month of that year, leaving Babylon on the first day of the first month and getting there on the first day of the fifth month, all because God's got his back. {7:10} Ezra was all about seeking and teaching God's law in Israel, straight up. {7:11-13} And Artaxerxes hooks him up with a letter, giving him and any Israelites, priests, or Levites who want to go to Jerusalem the green light. {7:14-16} He's like, "Take all the silver, gold, and whatever else you need for God's house in Jerusalem. Do whatever seems right with the rest, and make sure all the temple stuff is on point." {7:17-20} He's even like, "Use this cash to buy all the animals and offerings you need for sacrifices, and whatever's left, do what God wants with it." {7:21} And he tells the treasury folks to hook Ezra up pronto whenever he asks for stuff, no questions asked. {7:22-23} Artaxerxes is serious about making sure God's house is taken care of, 'cause he doesn't want any trouble with God. {7:24} Plus, he's like, "Hands off the temple crew. No tolls, tributes, or taxes on them." {7:25-26} Ezra's supposed to set up judges and teach the people God's laws, and anyone not down with God's law and the king's law is in for some serious consequences. {7:27-28} Ezra's thanking God for putting it in Artaxerxes's heart to make the temple fly, and he's grateful for the king's favor, feeling pumped because God's got his back, gathering up Israel's top dogs to roll with him.

{8:1} So, like, these are the main dudes and their family tree who rolled with me from Babylon when Artaxerxes was calling the shots. {8:2} We had Phinehas's boy Gershom, Ithamar's kid Daniel, and David's descendant Hattush, you know? {8:3} Shechaniah's offspring Zechariah led a crew of one-fifty dudes. {8:4} Elihoenai, son of Zerahiah, repped for the Pahath-moab fam with two hundred guys. {8:5} Jahaziel's son had a posse of three hundred from Shechaniah's line. {8:6} Ebed, son of Jonathan, rolled deep with fifty dudes from Adin. {8:7} Jeshaiah, son of Athaliah, had a squad of seventy from Elam. {8:8} Zebadiah, son of Michael, held it down with eighty from Shephatiah's crew. {8:9} Joab's son Obadiah brought two hundred and eighteen guys. {8:10} Josiphiah's kid had a squad of a hundred and sixty. {8:11} Bebai's son Zechariah had twenty-eight in his crew. {8:12} Johanan, Hakkatan's son, led a hundred and ten guys from Azgad's fam. {8:13} Adonikam's boys Eliphelet, Jeiel, and Shemaiah had sixty dudes. {8:14} Uthai and Zabbud from Bigvai's fam rolled with seventy guys. {8:15} We chilled by the Ahava River in tents for three days, scoping out the peeps and realizing there were no Levites among us. {8:16-17} So, I hit up some chiefs and smart dudes and sent them to Iddo, the boss in Casiphia, asking for Levite helpers for God's house. {8:18-20} By God's grace, we got a Levite dude named Sherebiah and his crew, eighteen in total, plus twenty from Merari's fam. {8:21} I called for a fast by the Ahava River, seeking guidance from God for us and our fam. {8:22} I didn't wanna ask the king for soldiers 'cause we told him God's got our back, so we prayed for God's help. {8:23} We fasted, prayed, and God came through for us. {8:24-29} Then, I picked twelve priests and Levites and weighed out the offerings, silver, and gold for God's house, making sure they were kept holy. {8:30} The priests and Levites took everything and brought it to Jerusalem. {8:31-32} We left Ahava on the twelfth day of the first month and got to Jerusalem safe and sound, chilling for three days. {8:33-34} On the fourth day, we weighed everything at the temple with Meremoth and some Levites. {8:35} The returnees from captivity offered sacrifices to God: twelve bullocks, ninety-six rams, seventy-seven lambs, and twelve goats for sin. {8:36} We delivered the king's orders to his officials, and they helped out the people and the temple.

{9:1} So, like, when all this went down, the leaders came up to me, saying, "Yo, Israelites, priests, and Levites are mingling with the locals, adopting their messed up ways—Canaanites, Hittites, Perizzites, Jebusites, Ammonites, Moabites, Egyptians, Amorites. {9:2} They're even marrying their daughters and sons! The holy crew's mixing it up big time, and the leaders are the main culprits here." {9:3} When I heard this, I was shook. Ripped my clothes, pulled out hair from my head and beard, and just sat there, stunned. {9:4} All who feared God's words gathered around, and I stayed shocked until the evening sacrifice. {9:5} Then, at the evening sacrifice, I got up from my shock, ripped my clothes again, and got on my knees, praying to the Lord. {9:6} I was like, "God, I'm embarrassed to even look at you, man. Our sins are sky high, and we're drowning in trespasses." {9:7} "Since our ancestors' time, we've been messing up big time. Kings, priests—all of us—have been handed over to foreign rulers, facing swords, captivity, and shame." {9:8} "But hey, God showed us some mercy, leaving us a remnant, a little hope, to set up the temple and give us a fighting chance." {9:9} "Even though we were slaves, God didn't ditch us. He showed us mercy in the eyes of the Persian kings, helping us rebuild our home and put up walls." {9:10} "Now, God, what can we even say? We ditched your commands." {9:11} "You warned us about the filthy ways of this land, but we didn't listen." {9:12} "So, we gotta stop marrying into these messed up families, seeking their peace and prosperity. We gotta stay strong and enjoy the land you gave us." {9:13} "Despite all our mess-ups, you didn't punish us as much as we deserved. You still gave us a way out." {9:14} "But if we keep messing up and getting tangled up with these abominations, you'll be mad, and there'll be nothing left of us." {9:15} "God of Israel, you're righteous. We're still here, but we're guilty as charged. We can't even stand before you because of all this."

{10:1} So, like, after Ezra poured out his heart in prayer and confessed, straight-up crying and throwing himself down before the house of God, a massive crowd gathered—men, women, and kids—everyone was bawling their eyes out. {10:2} Then Shechaniah, son of Jehiel, one of Elam's crew, spoke up, saying, "Bro, we totally messed up with our marriages to the locals. But hey, there's hope if we get our act together." {10:3} "Let's make a pact with God to ditch these wives and their kids, just like our leaders and those who respect God's rules suggest. Let's do this by the book." {10:4} "You're the man for this job, Ezra. We've got your back. Be brave and handle it." {10:5} So Ezra got everyone—the priests, the Levites, all of Israel—to swear they'd follow through. And they swore, no backing down. {10:6} After that, Ezra bounced from the house of God and crashed at Johanan's crib. He didn't eat or drink because he was grieving over everyone's screw-ups. {10:7} They spread the word throughout Judah and Jerusalem, calling all the exiles to come to Jerusalem ASAP. {10:8} Anyone who didn't show up within three days, following the advice of the leaders and elders, would lose all their stuff and get kicked out of the community. {10:9} Within three days, everyone from Judah and Benjamin rolled into Jerusalem. It was the ninth month, the twentieth day, and they were all chilling in front of the house of God, trembling from the cold and the heavy rain. {10:10} Ezra stepped up and laid it out, "Y'all messed up, marrying these locals and adding to Israel's mess." {10:11} "Now own up to God, do what's right, cut ties with these foreigners." {10:12} The whole crowd shouted back, "You're right, Ezra, we're on it." {10:13} But they were like, "Bro, there's so many of us, it's pouring rain, and this ain't a quick fix. We've all messed up big time." {10:14} "Let's get our leaders to stand up and schedule meetings. Every dude with a foreign wife needs to show up, along with the city elders and judges, until God's anger cools off." {10:15} Only a few dudes were on the job, like Jonathan and Jahaziah, with Meshullam and Shabbethai helping out. {10:16} The exiles got with the program. Ezra and the heads of the families, with everyone's names on the list, got together on the first day of the tenth month to sort this mess out. {10:17} They wrapped things up with all the dudes who had foreign wives by the first day of the first month. {10:18} Turns out, even some of the priest's sons had married foreigners—Jeshua's crew: Maaseiah, Eliezer, Jarib, Gedaliah. {10:19} They pledged to ditch their wives and offered a ram for their screw-up. {10:20} More dudes were guilty, like Hanani and Zebadiah from Immer's family. {10:21} Also, Harim's sons: Maaseiah, Elijah, Shemaiah, Jehiel, Uzziah. {10:22} Pashur's sons: Elioenai, Maaseiah, Ishmael, Nethanel, Jozabad, Elasah. {10:23} Plus, Levites: Jozabad, Shimei, Kelaiah, Kelita, Pethahiah, Judah, Eliezer. {10:24} Singers like Eliashib, and porters Shallum, Telem, Uri. {10:25} Also, dudes from Israel: Parosh's sons—Ramiah, Jeziah, Malchiah, Miamin, Eleazar, Malchijah, Benaiah. {10:26} Elam's sons—Mattaniah, Zechariah, Jehiel, Abdi, Jeremoth, Eliah. {10:27} Zattu's sons—Elioenai, Eliashib, Mattaniah, Jeremoth, Zabad, Aziza. {10:28} Bebai's sons—Jehohanan, Hananiah, Zabbai, Athlai. {10:29} Bani's sons—Meshullam, Malluch, Adaiah, Jashub, Sheal, Ramoth. {10:30} Pahath-moab's sons—Adna, Chelal, Benaiah, Maaseiah, Mattaniah, Bezalel, Binnui, Manasseh. {10:31} Harim's sons—Eliezer, Ishijah, Malchiah, Shemaiah, Shimeon, Benjamin, Malluch, Shemariah. {10:32} Hashum's sons—Mattenai, Mattathah, Zabad, Eliphelet, Jeremai, Manasseh, Shimei. {10:33} Bani's sons—Maadai, Amram, Uel, Benaiah, Bedeiah, Chelluh. {10:34} More dudes were guilty—Maadai, Amram, Uel. {10:35} Benaiah, Bedeiah, Chelluh. {10:36} Vaniah, Meremoth, Eliashib. {10:37} Mattaniah, Mattenai, Jaasau. {10:38} Bani, Binnui, Shimei. {10:39} Shelemiah, Nathan, Adaiah. {10:40} Machnadebai, Shashai, Sharai. {10:41} Azareel, Shelemiah, Shemariah. {10:42} Shallum, Amariah, Joseph. {10:43} Nebo's sons—Jeiel, Mattithiah, Zabad, Zebina, Jadau, Joel, Benaiah. {10:44} All these dudes married foreign wives, and some even had kids with them.

Nehemiah

✦✦✦

{1:1} So, like, Nehemiah, son of Hachaliah, starts spitting some truths. It was in Chisleu, the twentieth year, when I was chilling in Shushan's palace. {1:2} Then Hanani, one of my bros, rolls up with some Judah homies. I'm like, "What's the scoop on the Jews who made it out and what's the deal with Jerusalem?" {1:3} And they're like, "Dude, those left from the captivity are struggling big time. Jerusalem's wall is wrecked, and the gates are toast." {1:4} I'm hit hard when I hear this, so I break down, weep for days, fast, and pray to the big man upstairs. {1:5} "God of heaven, you're awesome and merciful to those who dig you. Listen up, please." {1:6} "Hear my prayer, day and night, for Israel. We messed up big time, me and my fam." {1:7} "We blew it, didn't keep your rules from Moses." {1:8} "Remember what you told Moses? Mess up, get scattered. But if we come back to you, even if we're scattered to the ends of the earth, you'll bring us back." {1:9} "We're your crew, your people, redeemed by your power." {1:10} "God, listen to our prayers and make things right, especially today. Show me some love, I'm just the king's cupbearer."

{2:1} Fast forward to Nisan, twentieth year of King Artaxerxes, and wine's flowing. I serve the king wine, but I've never been sad in front of him before. {2:2} The king's like, "Why the long face? You ain't sick." I freak out a bit. {2:3} "Long live the king! But I can't be happy when my hometown's wrecked, and my ancestors' tombs are trashed." {2:4} So, I pray to God on the low. {2:5} I'm like, "King, if you're cool with it and I'm still your fave, send me to Judah to rebuild." {2:6} The king and queen are like, "Sure, how long you gone be?" We set a date. {2:7} I'm like, "Hook me up with some letters to the governors and the forest keeper for supplies." The king's down, thanks to God's blessing. {2:9} I hit up the governors with the king's letters, with army captains and horsemen in tow. {2:10} When Sanballat and Tobiah hear about it, they're not happy. Someone caring about Israel's welfare? Nope, they ain't having it. {2:11} So, I make it to Jerusalem and lay low for three days. {2:12} One night, I sneak out with a few dudes. I don't spill the beans about my plans, just me and my trusty steed. {2:13} I scope out the damaged walls and burnt gates by the valley gate and the dung gate. {2:14} Then I try the fountain gate and the king's pool, but my horse can't get through. {2:15} I check out the wall by the brook, then sneak back in through the valley gate. {2:16} The leaders don't know what's up; I haven't spilled the tea to anyone yet. {2:17} I gather the crew and say, "Look at the mess we're in. Let's rebuild the wall so we're not a laughingstock." {2:18} I share how God's got my back and the king's down with the plan. They're all in for the rebuild. {2:19} But when Sanballat, Tobiah, and Geshem hear, they mock us, asking if we're rebelling against the king. {2:20} I clap back, "God's got us, so we're building. But you? You got no part in this."

{3:1} So, Eliashib the high priest and his crew of priests kicked things off by fixing up the sheep gate, making it all holy and setting up the doors. They kept at it until they reached the tower of Meah and the tower of Hananeel. {3:2} Then it was the guys from Jericho's turn, and Zaccur, son of Imri, was right there with them. {3:3} The sons of Hassenaah took charge of the fish gate, sorting out the beams, doors, locks, and bars. {3:4} Meremoth, son of Urijah, and Meshullam, son of Berechiah, along with Zadok, son of Baana, pitched in next. {3:5} But the Tekoites got lazy, their leaders didn't even bother to help. {3:6} Jehoiada and Meshullam took on the old gate, fixing it up good. {3:7} Melatiah, Jadon, and their crew from Gibeon and Mizpah went all the way to the governor's throne. {3:8} Uzziel, the goldsmith, and Hananiah, the apothecary's son, fortified Jerusalem's broad wall. {3:9} Rephaiah, ruler of half of Jerusalem, and Jedaiah, over by his own house, got to work too. {3:10} Hattush and Malchijah stepped up next, followed by Hashub and Malchiah. {3:11} Malchijah and Hashub took care of their piece and the tower of the furnaces. {3:12} Shallum, ruler of half of Jerusalem, and his daughters didn't hold back either. {3:13} Hanun and the Zanoah crew fixed the valley gate up to the dung gate. {3:14} Malchiah made sure the dung gate was back in action, representing part of Beth-haccerem. {3:15} Shallun spruced up the gate of the fountain, all the way to the king's garden and down to the city of David's stairs. {3:16} Nehemiah took on a chunk near Beth-zur and the sepulchers of David, even the pool and the house of the mighty. {3:17} The Levites, Rehum and Hashabiah, held it down too. {3:18} Bavai, Benjamin, and Azariah made sure Keilah was covered. {3:19} Ezer and Baruch handled their spots, then Meremoth came in for another piece. {3:20} Then came the priests and the plain dudes, making sure their houses were good to go. {3:21} Benjamin, Hashub, and Azariah did their part too. {3:22} Then the priests from the plain stepped in. {3:23} Benjamin, Hashub, and Azariah held it down by their houses. {3:24} Binnui got his hands dirty, making sure Azariah's house was sorted. {3:25} Palal, Pedaiah, and the crew took care of business by the king's high house and the prison court. {3:26} The Nethinims set up shop in Ophel, all the way to the water gate and beyond. {3:27} The Tekoites made sure the great tower and Ophel's wall were solid. {3:28} The priests made sure their houses were good from above the horse gate. {3:29} Zadok and Shemaiah were on it too, by their own houses and the east gate. {3:30} Hananiah and Hanun's son, along with Meshullam, got busy too. {3:31} Malchiah, the goldsmith's son, and the merchants sorted out the gate Miphkad. {3:32} Between the corner and the sheep gate, the goldsmiths and merchants made sure everything was tight.

{4:1} When Sanballat heard we were building the wall, he got seriously mad and started dissing the Jews hard. {4:2} He even talked smack in front of his buddies and the Samarian army, like, "What do these weak Jews think they're doing? Can they even finish it? Can they bring back these rocks from the trash?" {4:3} Tobiah, that Ammonite dude, was there too, saying, "Even if a fox climbed up, it would break their wall down!" {4:4} We prayed to God, asking Him to see how they were disrespecting us, and we asked Him to deal with them. {4:5} We didn't want their sins to be forgotten, 'cause they really ticked God off with their insults. {4:6} But we kept building anyway, joining the wall up to half its height 'cause we were determined. {4:7} When Sanballat, Tobiah, and their crew heard the walls were up and the holes were getting fixed, they flipped out and planned to attack Jerusalem and stop the work. {4:8} But we stayed prayed up and posted a watch day and night. {4:9} Judah was like, "We're worn out and there's so much trash, we can't keep building!" {4:10} Meanwhile, our haters were planning a sneak attack to stop the work. {4:11} Our neighbors kept warning us that enemies were lurking around, ready to ambush us. {4:12} So, I organized the people, putting guards on the low and high points of the wall, armed with swords, spears, and bows. {4:13} I encouraged everyone not to be scared and to remember the Lord, then we got back to work. {4:14} When our enemies heard we were ready, and God shut down their plans, we went back to work without fear. {4:15} From then on, half of us worked while the other half stood guard with weapons, and the leaders had our backs. {4:16} Those building the wall had swords strapped to their sides, ready to defend, and the trumpet guy stayed close. {4:17} Everyone worked with one hand and held a weapon with the other. {4:18} And I told the leaders and the people, "The work's huge, and we're spread out, but if you hear the trumpet, come to our defense 'cause God's got our backs." {4:19} So we worked hard, with half of us holding spears from sunrise to sunset. {4:20} I also told everyone to stay in Jerusalem at night, ready to guard while others worked during the day. {4:21} None of us took off our clothes, except to wash them, 'cause we knew we had to stay alert.

{5:1} There was this huge outcry from the people and their spouses against their fellow Jews. {5:2} Some were like, "Yo, we got mad kids to feed, so we're taking out loans to buy food and survive." {5:3} Others were saying, "We had to mortgage our lands and houses just to buy food 'cause there's a famine." {5:4} And then there were those who were forced to borrow money to pay the king's taxes, putting their lands and vineyards up as collateral. {5:5} We're all in the same boat, man, our kids are suffering, and some of them are even being sold into slavery because we're so broke. {5:6} When I heard all this, I was livid. {5:7} So I called out the nobles and rulers for charging interest on loans to their own people. I gathered everyone for a serious talk. {5:8} I reminded them how we'd bought back our Jewish brothers who were sold to foreigners, and now they wanna sell them off again? I shut them down real quick. {5:9} I told them straight up that what they were doing wasn't cool, and they should fear God instead of letting our enemies disrespect us. {5:10} Me and my crew could've easily charged them interest too, but I was like, nah, let's drop this whole usury thing. {5:11} I demanded they give back the lands, vineyards, olive groves, houses, and even the interest and crops they'd taken from their own people. And they agreed. {5:12} I even made them swear to it in front of the priests. {5:13} Then I shook out my pockets, symbolizing how God should shake out anyone who doesn't keep their promise. And everyone said "Amen" and praised the Lord. And they actually followed through with it. {5:14} Since I became governor, I didn't take any perks that the previous governors did. {5:15} Those guys were milking the people, but I didn't 'cause I respected God too much. {5:16} I was all in on building the wall, and I didn't even buy any land. All my peeps were focused on the work. {5:17} I even had a hundred and fifty Jews and officials eating at my table, not to mention all the foreigners around us. {5:18} They hooked me up with one ox, six prime sheep, and poultry every day, plus a stash of wine every ten days. But I never took any of the governor's food because the people were already struggling. {5:19} Yo, God, remember all the good stuff I did for these people, okay?

{6:1} When our enemies heard the wall was finished and there were no holes, they got shook. {6:2} Sanballat and Geshem tried to set up a meeting to mess with me, but I wasn't having it. {6:3} I was like, "Sorry, I'm busy building stuff. I can't just dip out whenever." {6:4} They kept trying to set up meetings, but I kept shutting them down. {6:5} Then Sanballat straight up sent me a letter accusing me of planning to rebel and become king. {6:6} He even said I'd hired prophets to spread the word in Jerusalem. Total lies. {6:7} But Sanballat was persistent, trying to scare me into meeting him to talk strategy. {6:8} I hit him back, telling him none of his accusations were true, and he was just making stuff up. {6:9} They were all trying to scare us, saying we'd get too weak to finish the work. So I prayed for strength. {6:10} Then some dude, Shemaiah, tried to get me to hide in the temple, but I was like, "Nah, I'm not running scared." {6:11} Turns out, he was paid off by Tobiah and Sanballat to spook me. {6:12} They were hoping I'd mess up and give them more reasons to talk trash about me. {6:13} But I saw through their scheme and stayed true. {6:14} God, don't forget what Tobiah, Sanballat, and that prophetess Noadiah did to me. They were shady as heck. {6:15} So, yeah, we finished the wall in just fifty-two days. {6:16} When our haters saw the wall was done, they felt small and knew God was on our side. {6:17} The nobles in Judah were chatting with Tobiah, and his letters were reaching them. {6:18} Some Judah peeps were even sworn to him, and his son was married into one of the big families. {6:19} They were spreading lies about me and telling Tobiah everything I said. And Tobiah kept sending me threatening letters.

{7:1} So, like, once the wall was done and I got the doors up and the bouncers, singers, and Levites were all sorted, {7:2} I put my bro Hanani and this dude Hananiah in charge of Jerusalem 'cause they were solid and respected God big time. {7:3} I told them, "Keep those gates shut until the sun's blazing, and when you're there, make sure to lock up tight and set up watches all around the city, each person guarding their own hood." {7:4} Now, the city was massive, but there weren't that many people living there, and a lot of houses still needed to be built. {7:5} But then, my dude God put it in my head to organize everyone by their family tree. So, I dug up this old genealogy record of those who first came back from Babylon, and here's what I found: {7:6} These were the OGs who came back from exile under Nebuchadnezzar: Zerubbabel, Jeshua, Nehemiah, Azariah, Raamiah, Nahamani, Mordecai, Bilshan, Mispereth, Bigvai, Nehum, and Baanah. And here's the headcount: {7:8} Parosh had 2,172 peeps, {7:9} Shephatiah had 372, {7:10} Arah had 652, {7:11} Pahath-moab and Jeshua and Joab had 2,818, {7:12} Elam had 1,254, {7:13} Zattu had 845, {7:14} Zaccai had 760, {7:15} Binnui had 648, {7:16} Bebai had 628, {7:17} Azgad had 2,322, {7:18} Adonikam had 667, {7:19} Bigvai had 2,067, {7:20} Adin had 655, {7:21} Ater had 98,

{7:22} Hashum had 328, {7:23} Bezai had 324, {7:24} Hariph had 112, {7:25} Gibeon had 95, {7:26} Bethlehem and Netophah had 188, {7:27} Anathoth had 128, {7:28} Bethazmaveth had 42, {7:29} Kirjath-jearim, Chephirah, and Beeroth had 743, {7:30} Ramah and Gaba had 621, {7:31} Michmas had 122, {7:32} Bethel and Ai had 123, {7:33} The other Nebo had 52, {7:34} The other Elam had 1,254, {7:35} Harim had 320, {7:36} Jericho had 345, {7:37} Lod, Hadid, and Ono had 721, {7:38} Senaah had 3,930, {7:39} The priests: Jedaiah's descendants, from Jeshua's house, had 973, {7:40} Immer had 1,052, {7:41} Pashur had 1,247, {7:42} Harim had 1,017, {7:43} The Levites: Jeshua, Kadmiel, and Hodevah's descendants had 74, {7:44} The singers: Asaph's descendants had 148, {7:45} The porters: Shallum, Ater, Talmon, Akkub, Hatita, and Shobai's descendants had 138, {7:46-60} The Nethinims: Ziha, Hashupha, Tabbaoth, Keros, Sia, Padon, Lebana, Hagaba, and Shalmai's descendants had 392, {7:61} Some folks from Telmelah, Telharesha, Cherub, Addon, and Immer came too, but they couldn't trace their ancestry to Israel. {7:62} Delaiah, Tobiah, and Nekoda's descendants were 642. {7:63} The priests: Habaiah, Koz, and Barzillai's descendants, who married one of Barzillai the Gileadite's daughters, had 1,247. {7:64} Some dudes tried to prove their lineage but failed, so they got kicked out of the priesthood. {7:65} The governor told them not to eat the holy stuff until a priest with Urim and Thummim showed up. {7:66} Altogether, there were 42,360 peeps, plus 7,337 servants, and 245 singers. {7:67} They had 736 horses, 245 mules, 435 camels, and 6,720 donkeys. {7:68} Some of the big shots pitched in: the governor donated a thousand gold coins, fifty bowls, and 530 priestly garments. {7:71} And other leaders threw in 20,000 gold coins and 2,200 pounds of silver. {7:72} Plus, the rest of the people chipped in 20,000 gold coins, 2,000 pounds of silver, and 67 priestly garments. {7:73} So, priests, Levites, porters, singers, some people, Nethinims, and all of Israel went back to their cities. And when the seventh month rolled around, the Israelites were chilling in their cities.

{8:1} So, like, everyone gathered at the spot in front of the water gate and asked Ezra, the scribe, to bring out the book of the law of Moses that the LORD told Israel to follow. {8:2} And Ezra the priest brought the law before the whole crowd, men and women, everyone who could understand, on the first day of the seventh month. {8:3} He read from morning till noon in front of the water gate, and everyone listened intently to the book of the law. {8:4} Ezra stood up on this wooden platform they made for him, and by his side were Mattithiah, Shema, Anaiah, Urijah, Hilkiah, and Maaseiah on one side, and Pedaiah, Mishael, Malchiah, Hashum, Hashbadana, Zechariah, and Meshullam on the other. {8:5} When Ezra opened the book, everyone stood up because he was up higher than everyone else, and they all stayed standing. {8:6} Then Ezra blessed the LORD, the great God, and the people shouted "Amen, Amen!" while lifting their hands and bowing down to worship with their faces to the ground. {8:7} Jeshua, Bani, Sherebiah, Jamin, Akkub, Shabbethai, Hodijah, Maaseiah, Kelita, Azariah, Jozabad, Hanan, Pelaiah, and the Levites helped people understand the law, and everyone stayed in their spots. {8:8} They read the law of God clearly and explained it, making sure everyone got it. {8:9} Then Nehemiah, Ezra, and the Levites teaching the people said, "Today is holy to the LORD your God, so don't cry or be sad." But the people were crying when they heard the words of the law. {8:10} Nehemiah told them, "Go and have a feast, eat good food, drink sweet stuff, and share with those who don't have anything prepared. Today's a special day to the Lord, so don't be sad; the joy of the LORD is your strength." {8:11} The Levites told everyone to chill out because it was a holy day, so no need to be bummed out. {8:12} After hearing the words, everyone went to eat, drink, share food, and have a big party because they understood what they were taught. {8:13} The next day, the big shots, priests, and Levites gathered to understand the law better. {8:14} They found out from the law that the Israelites were supposed to live in booths during the seventh month festival. {8:15} So, they spread the word to everyone in every city, saying, "Go grab olive branches, pine branches, myrtle branches, palm branches, and thick tree branches to build booths," just like it was written. {8:16} People went and made booths on their roofs, in their courtyards, at the house of God, in the street of the water gate, and at the gate of Ephraim. {8:17} Everyone who came back from exile made booths and sat in them, and there was a lot of joy because Israel hadn't celebrated like this since the days of Jeshua, son of Nun. {8:18} Every day, from the first to the last, they read from the book of the law of God. They celebrated the feast for seven days, and on the eighth day, they had a big gathering, just like it's supposed to be.

{9:1} On the twenty-fourth day of this month, the Israelites came together, fasting, wearing sackcloth, and dusting themselves with earth. {9:2} The descendants of Israel separated themselves from all outsiders, confessed their sins, and the sins of their ancestors. {9:3} They stayed in their spots, reading from the law of the LORD their God for a quarter of the day, then spent another quarter confessing and worshiping the LORD their God. {9:4} On the stairs, the Levites—Jeshua, Bani, Kadmiel, Shebaniah, Bunni, Sherebiah, Bani, Chenani—cried out loud to the LORD their God. {9:5} Then the Levites, Jeshua, Kadmiel, Bani, Hashabniah, Sherebiah, Hodijah, Shebaniah, Pethahiah, said, "Praise the LORD your God forever! Blessed be your glorious name, exalted above all blessings and praise." {9:6} "You, LORD, you alone, made heaven and earth and everything in it, the seas and all that's in them, and you sustain them all. Even the heavenly beings worship you." {9:7} "You are the LORD God who chose Abram, brought him out of Ur of the Chaldees, and renamed him Abraham." {9:8} "You found his heart faithful and made a covenant with him to give the land to his descendants. You've kept your word because you're righteous." {9:9} "You saw our ancestors' suffering in Egypt, heard their cries by the Red Sea," {9:10} "performed signs and wonders against Pharaoh and his people, showing that you're in charge." {9:11} "You split the sea, letting them walk through on dry land, and tossed their pursuers into the depths like a stone into mighty waters." {9:12} "You guided them with a cloudy pillar by day and a pillar of fire by night to light their way." {9:13} "You came down on Mount Sinai, spoke to them from heaven, gave them right judgments, true laws, good statutes, and commandments." {9:14} "You made known to them your holy Sabbath, gave them laws and statutes through Moses." {9:15} "You gave them bread from heaven when they were hungry, water from a rock when they were thirsty, and promised them the land you swore to give them." {9:16} "But they and our ancestors acted arrogantly, ignored your commandments," {9:17} "and refused to obey, forgetting your wonders. Instead, they rebelled, appointed a leader to take them back to slavery. But you, God, are forgiving, gracious, merciful, slow to anger, and abounding in steadfast love; you didn't abandon them." {9:18} "Even when they made a molten calf and said, 'This is your god who brought you out of Egypt,' you didn't forsake them." {9:19} "Despite their rebellion, you didn't abandon them in the wilderness; the pillar of cloud and fire stayed with them, guiding their way." {9:20} "You gave them your good spirit to instruct them, didn't withhold manna from their mouths, and provided water for their thirst." {9:21} "You sustained them for forty years in the wilderness, providing for all their needs; their clothes didn't wear out, and their feet didn't swell." {9:22} "You gave them kingdoms and nations, handing over the lands of Sihon, Heshbon, and Og king of Bashan." {9:23} "You multiplied their descendants like the stars in the sky and brought them into the land promised to their ancestors." {9:24} "So, they went in, possessed the land, and you subdued its inhabitants before them, giving them kings and peoples' hands to do as they pleased." {9:25} "They captured fortified cities, a fertile land, full of houses filled with goods, wells, vineyards, olive groves, and fruit trees. They ate, were satisfied, and reveled in your great goodness." {9:26} "Yet they disobeyed, rebelled against you, disregarded your law, killed your prophets who warned them, and committed great provocations." {9:27} "You delivered them into the hands of their enemies who oppressed them. When they cried out to you in their distress, you heard them from heaven and, in your abundant mercy, sent them deliverers who saved them from their enemies' hands." {9:28} "But after they had rest, they did evil before you again. So, you handed them over to their enemies' power. Yet, when they cried out to you again, you heard from heaven, delivering them many times because of your mercy." {9:29} "You warned them to return to your law, but they acted arrogantly, didn't listen to your commandments, and sinned against your judgments. Still, you're patient, warned them through your Spirit in your prophets, but they wouldn't listen, so you gave them into the hands of other peoples." {9:30} "For many years, you were patient with them, warning them through your Spirit and prophets, but they refused to listen, so you handed them over to other nations." {9:31} "Yet, for your great mercies' sake, you didn't utterly destroy them or forsake them, for you're a gracious and merciful God." {9:32} "Now, our God, the great, mighty, and awesome God who keeps his covenant and mercy, don't overlook the trouble that has come upon us, our kings, princes, priests, prophets, ancestors, and all your people, from Assyrian kings to this day." {9:33} "You're just in all that has happened to us; we've done wrong." {9:34} "Our kings, princes, priests, and ancestors haven't kept your law, haven't listened to your commandments and testimonies against them." {9:35} "They haven't served you in your kingdom, despite your goodness, in the large, fertile land you gave them; they didn't turn away from their evil deeds." {9:36} "Today, we're servants in the land you gave our ancestors to enjoy its fruits and goodness, yet we're slaves in it." {9:37} "The land yields abundantly for the kings you've set over us because of our sins. They have dominion over our bodies and livestock, doing as they please, and we're in great distress." {9:38} "So, we're making a firm covenant, writing it down, and our leaders, Levites, and priests are sealing it."

{10:1} So, like, Nehemiah, the big boss, son of Hachaliah, and Zidkijah, sealed the deal. {10:2} Then there's Seraiah, Azariah, Jeremiah, {10:3} Pashur, Amariah, Malchijah, {10:4} Hattush, Shebaniah, Malluch, {10:5} Harim, Meremoth, Obadiah, {10:6} Daniel, Ginnethon, Baruch, {10:7} Meshullam, Abijah, Mijamin, {10:8} Maaziah, Bilgai, Shemaiah—these were the priests. {10:9} Then the Levites: Jeshua son of Azaniah, Binnui of the Henadad crew, Kadmiel; {10:10} And their crew: Shebaniah, Hodijah, Kelita, Pelaiah, Hanan, {10:11} Micha, Rehob, Hashabiah, {10:12} Zaccur, Sherebiah, Shebaniah, {10:13} Hodijah, Bani, Beninu. {10:14} The head honchos: Parosh, Pahath-moab, Elam, Zatthu, Bani, {10:15} Bunni, Azgad, Bebai, {10:16} Adonijah, Bigvai, Adin, {10:17} Ater, Hizkijah, Azzur, {10:18} Hodijah, Hashum, Bezai, {10:19} Hariph, Anathoth, Nebai, {10:20} Magpiash, Meshullam, Hezir, {10:21} Meshezabeel, Zadok, Jaddua, {10:22} Pelatiah, Hanan, Anaiah, {10:23} Hoshea, Hananiah, Hashub, {10:24} Hallohesh, Pileha, Shobek, {10:25} Rehum, Hashabnah, Maaseiah, {10:26} Plus Ahijah, Hanan, Anan, {10:27} Malluch, Harim, Baanah. {10:28} And all the rest of the crew—the priests, Levites, doorkeepers, singers, Nethinims, and anyone else who separated themselves from foreign influences to follow God's law—along with their families, everyone who knew and understood what was up; {10:29} They were tight with their crew, the VIPs, and took a solemn oath to stick to God's law given by Moses, and to obey all the LORD's commands, judgments, and statutes; {10:30} They swore they wouldn't let their kids marry outsiders or take spouses from other tribes. {10:31} They pledged not to buy anything from the locals on the Sabbath or holy days, and to let the land rest every seventh year, canceling all debts. {10:32} They committed to fund the temple's service, contributing a third of a shekel per person annually for God's crib; {10:33} Covering everything from showbread to sacrifices, from weekly offerings to festivals and sin offerings to atone for Israel. {10:34} They drew lots to decide who'd bring wood offerings to the temple, following the ancestral schedule, burning it all on the LORD's altar, just like the law says; {10:35} They promised to bring the first fruits of their crops and trees every year to the house of the LORD; {10:36} They'd also offer up their firstborn sons and livestock, as the law dictates, to the priests who serve in God's house; {10:37} They'd give the first fruits of their dough, offerings, wine, oil, and fruit to the priests in the temple chambers, and the Levites would get a cut in every city; {10:38} When the Levites collected tithes, the priests would be there to supervise, making sure a tenth of the tithe went to the temple treasury; {10:39} Because both Israelites and Levites were responsible for bringing grain, wine, and oil offerings to the temple chambers where the sacred vessels, priests, doorkeepers, and singers were, and they were all committed to not abandoning God's house.

{11:1} So, like, the big shots of the people moved to Jerusalem, and the rest drew straws: one out of ten got to live in the holy city, and the other nine parts got spread out in other cities. {11:2} Everyone cheered on the dudes who volunteered to live in Jerusalem. {11:3} Now, these were the main players who lived in Jerusalem, but in Judah's cities, everyone stuck to their own turf: Israelites, priests, Levites, temple servants, and Solomon's peeps. {11:4} In Jerusalem, some Judeans and Benjaminites set up camp. Among the Judeans were Athaiah, descended from Perez; {11:5} And Maaseiah, from a long line, with 468 brave dudes from Perez's crew. {11:6} Among the Benjaminites were Sallu, Gabbai, and Sallai, totaling 928. {11:9} Joel and Judah kept things in check in the city. {11:10} Among the priests were Jedaiah and Jachin. {11:11} Seraiah ran the show at God's house. {11:12} 822 of their relatives pitched in, including Adaiah.

{11:13} 242 dads led the way, with Amashai. {11:14} Plus, there were 128 mighty dudes led by Zabdiel. {11:15} The Levites included Shemaiah, Shabbethai, and Jozabad. {11:16} They handled the temple's day-to-day stuff. {11:17} Mattaniah led prayers, Bakbukiah and Abda backed him up. {11:18} In the holy city, there were 284 Levites. {11:19} The gatekeepers Akkub, Talmon, and co. numbered 172. {11:20} The rest of Israel's priests and Levites lived in Judah's cities, each on their own turf. {11:21} The temple servants lived in Ophel, with Ziha and Gispa in charge. {11:22} Uzzi oversaw the Levites in Jerusalem, with Asaph's descendants leading the choir. {11:23} The king made sure the singers got their daily share. {11:24} Pethahiah, representing Judah's clan, handled people's issues with the king. {11:25} Judeans settled in various villages, like Kirjath-arba and Dibon. {11:26} They spread out to places like Jeshua and Moladah. {11:27} Even as far as Hazar-shual and Beer-sheba. {11:28} From Ziklag to Zanoah, they covered a lot of ground. {11:29} Their territory reached from Beer-sheba to Hinnom Valley. {11:30} Meanwhile, Benjaminites lived in Michmash, Anathoth, and more. {11:31} Geba, Anathoth, and other spots housed Benjamin's crew. {11:32} They claimed spots like Anathoth and Nob. {11:33} And had places like Ramah and Gittaim. {11:34} Even Lod and Ono were on their turf. {11:35} Craftspeople settled in the valley. {11:36} Levites were spread throughout Judah and Benjamin.

{12:1} So, like, here are the priests and Levites who rolled with Zerubbabel and Jeshua: Seraiah, Jeremiah, Ezra, Amariah, Malluch, Hattush, Shechaniah, Rehum, Meremoth, Iddo, Ginnetho, Abijah, Miamin, Maadiah, Bilgah, Shemaiah, Joiarib, Jedaiah, Sallu, Amok, Hilkiah, Jedaiah, the main squad in Jeshua's time. {12:8} Plus the Levites: Jeshua, Binnui, Kadmiel, Sherebiah, Judah, and Mattaniah, who handled the gratitude vibe with their crew. {12:9} Bakbukiah and Unni and their squad held down the watch. {12:10} Jeshua's line: Joiakim, then Eliashib, then Joiada, {12:11} And Joiada's kid Jonathan, who became Jaddua. {12:12} In Joiakim's time, the priestly VIPs were: Meraiah from Seraiah's crew, Hananiah from Jeremiah, Meshullam from Ezra, Jehohanan from Amariah, Jonathan from Melicu, Joseph from Shebaniah, Adna from Harim, Helkai from Meraioth, Zechariah from Iddo, Meshullam from Ginnethon, Zichri from Abijah, Piltai from Miniamin, Moadiah's crew, Shammua from Bilgah, Jehonathan from Shemaiah, Mattenai from Joiarib, Uzzi from Jedaiah, Kallai from Sallai, Eber from Amok, Hashabiah from Hilkiah, Nethaneel from Jedaiah. {12:22} The Levites in Eliashib, Joiada, Johanan, and Jaddua's time were top-tier, along with the priests, up to Darius the Persian's era. {12:23} Levi's top dogs were listed in the records up to Johanan, Eliashib's kid. {12:24} Leading Levites were Hashabiah, Sherebiah, and Jeshua, alongside their squad, keeping the Davidic vibe alive. {12:25} Mattaniah, Bakbukiah, Obadiah, Meshullam, Talmon, and Akkub held it down at the gates. {12:26} This was during Joiakim, Jeshua's son, and Nehemiah's time as governor, and Ezra the priest, the scribe. {12:27} At the wall dedication, they brought in Levites from everywhere to celebrate with mad joy, singing, cymbals, and harps. {12:28} Singers came from all around, even the farthest villages, 'cause Nehemiah hooked them up with cribs. {12:30} Priests and Levites purified themselves, the people, the gates, and the wall. {12:31} I led the Judah bosses on the wall, with two crews giving thanks, one on each side, even past the dung gate. {12:32} After them were Hoshaiah, half the Judah bosses, Azariah, Ezra, Meshullam, Judah, Benjamin, Shemaiah, Jeremiah. {12:35} Some priest's sons rocked trumpets: Zechariah, Jonathan's kid, Shemaiah's grandson, Mattaniah's great-grandson, Michaiah's great-great-grandson, Zaccur's great-great-great-grandson, Asaph's descendant. {12:36} With Shemaiah, Azarael, Milalai, Gilalai, Maai, Nethaneel, Judah, Hanani, vibing on David's instruments, and Ezra on deck. {12:37} At the fountain gate, they took the stairs up from David's city, past the water gate. {12:38} The other crew of thanks-givers rolled opposite, and I tagged along, half the people on the wall, past the tower of the furnaces to the broad wall. {12:39} Then from above Ephraim's gate to the sheep gate, stopping at the prison gate. {12:40} So the two crews of thanks-givers were in the house of God, along with me and half the bosses. {12:41} Priests Eliakim, Maaseiah, Miniamin, Michaiah, Elioenai, Zechariah, Hananiah rocked trumpets. {12:42} Maaseiah, Shemaiah, Eleazar, Uzzi, Jehohanan, Malchijah, Elam, Ezer sang, with Jezrahiah leading. {12:43} Big sacrifices and big vibes went down that day; everyone was lit 'cause God had them vibing hard, even the fam heard it from afar. {12:44} Some were assigned to manage the treasures, offerings, firstfruits, and tithes, bringing in what was due for the priests and Levites, making Judah happy for their peeps. {12:45} Singers and porters stayed on duty, keeping things pure, following David and Solomon's commands. {12:46} Back in David and Asaph's time, they were the OGs of praise and thanks to God. {12:47} During Zerubbabel and Nehemiah's days, all Israel took care of the singers and porters, making sure they were good, and they kept things holy for the Levites, who kept it holy for Aaron's kids.

{13:1} So, like, they were reading from the book of Moses to the people, and they found this rule that the Ammonites and Moabites couldn't join the crew of God ever, {13:2} 'cause they didn't hook up the Israelites with food and water when they needed it, but instead hired Balaam to curse them. But our God flipped that curse into a blessing. {13:3} When they heard this law, they kicked out all the mixed-up people from Israel. {13:4} Before this, Eliashib, the priest, was tight with Tobiah, {13:5} and he even gave him a swanky room in the house of God where they used to stash offerings, incense, and all the stuff for the Levites, singers, and porters, as well as the priests' offerings. {13:6} I wasn't around at that time 'cause I was outta town, but in the 32nd year of Artaxerxes king of Babylon, I came back to Jerusalem. {13:7} When I got there, I heard about Eliashib's shady deal with Tobiah, so I kicked Tobiah's stuff outta that room in God's house. {13:8} It really bugged me, so I cleared out the room and had it cleaned up. Then I put back all the stuff for God's house, like the offerings and incense. {13:10} I noticed that the Levites weren't getting what they were supposed to 'cause they'd all bailed to work their own fields. {13:11} I called out the rulers on this and was like, "Why are we neglecting God's house?" So I got them sorted and back in their place. {13:12} Then all of Judah brought in their tithes of grain, wine, and oil to the treasuries. {13:13} I put Shelemiah the priest, Zadok the scribe, and Pedaiah the Levite in charge of the treasuries, and Hanan, Mattaniah's descendant, was next to them. 'Cause they were reliable and responsible for distributing to their fellow Levites. {13:14} God, don't forget the good stuff I did for your house and its duties. {13:15} I saw some folks in Judah working on the Sabbath, bringing in loads of stuff to Jerusalem, even selling stuff on the Sabbath. {13:16} There were even Tyrians selling fish and stuff in Jerusalem on the Sabbath. {13:17} So I called out the Judah big shots on this, asking them why they were disrespecting the Sabbath. {13:18} I reminded them how our ancestors messed up, and that disrespecting the Sabbath would just bring more trouble on Israel. {13:19} So, when it started getting dark on the Sabbath, I ordered the gates to be shut tight until after the Sabbath, and I posted my own peeps there to make sure no one brought in loads on the Sabbath. {13:20} The merchants and sellers had to stay outside Jerusalem overnight a couple times 'cause of this. {13:21} I warned them not to camp around the wall anymore, threatening to lay hands on them if they did. After that, they stopped showing up on the Sabbath. {13:22} I told the Levites to clean up and keep watch at the gates to keep the Sabbath holy. God, remember this and go easy on me, yeah? {13:23} Also, I saw some Jews marrying folks from Ashdod, Ammon, and Moab. {13:24} Their kids were even speaking a mix of languages, not just Jewish, but whatever their parents spoke. {13:25} I chewed them out, cursed them, even got physical with some, and made them swear not to marry off their kids to foreigners. {13:26} Didn't Solomon mess up by marrying foreign women? Even though God loved him and made him king over Israel, those foreign women led him astray. {13:27} So should we listen to you and do this huge wrong by marrying foreigners? {13:28} One of Joiada's descendants was even married to Sanballat the Horonite's daughter, so I kicked him out too. {13:29} God, remember how they defiled the priesthood and the covenant and clean-up I did. {13:30} I kicked out all the foreigners and put the priests and Levites back in charge of their duties. {13:31} And I made sure there were enough offerings for the priests and Levites. God, remember the good stuff I did, yeah?

Esther

✦✦✦

{1:1} So, like, this happened when Ahasuerus was king, ruling from India to Ethiopia, over like, 127 provinces. {1:2} In those days, King Ahasuerus was chilling on his throne in Shushan the palace. {1:3} In the third year of his reign, he threw a massive feast for all his VIPs: the big shots from Persia and Media, plus the nobles and princes from all over. {1:4} He flexed his wealth and power for a solid 180 days, showing off his kingdom's riches and his own majesty. {1:5} After that, he threw another bash for everyone in Shushan, from the high rollers to the regular folks, lasting seven days in the palace garden courtyard. {1:6} The place was decked out with white, green, and blue hangings, held up by fine linen cords and purple rings on marble pillars. The beds were gold and silver, on a floor of red, blue, white, and black marble. {1:7} They were sipping royal wine from all sorts of gold cups, each one different, and there was plenty to go around, fitting the king's status. {1:8} And get this, the drinking was totally chill, no one was forced to do anything. The king made sure everyone could do whatever they wanted. {1:9} Queen Vashti threw her own party for the ladies in the royal palace. {1:10-11} On the last day, when the king was feeling pretty lit, he ordered his crew to bring Queen Vashti to show off her beauty wearing the royal crown. 'Cause she was a sight to see, you know? {1:12} But Queen Vashti straight-up refused to come when the king's guys called her, and that really ticked the king off, he was heated. {1:13} So he turned to his advisors, who were all about knowing the deal with laws and stuff. {1:14-16} Memucan stepped up, along with the other top dogs, and they were like, "Vashti didn't just disrespect the king, she dissed all the princes and people in every province!" {1:17-18} They were worried that if word got out, all the women would start thinking they could disrespect their husbands too, and that's not a vibe they wanted. {1:19} So, they suggested the king make it law that Vashti could never come before him again and give her royal status to someone better. {1:20} When this decree went out across the kingdom, all the wives were supposed to respect their husbands, no matter who they were. {1:21} The king and his crew were into the idea, so they went ahead with Memucan's plan. {1:22} They sent out letters to every province in every language, declaring that every man should be in charge at home, and that's how it went down.

{2:1} So, like, once King Ahasuerus had cooled off from being mad, he started thinking about Vashti and what went down with her. {2:2} Then his crew of servants suggested, "Hey, let's find some hot young babes for the king." {2:3} They set up this whole search party across the kingdom to find the hottest chicks and bring them to Shushan Palace, under the watch of this guy named Hege. {2:4} The plan was to pick the girl who pleased the king the most to be the new queen instead of Vashti. The king was totally on board with that. {2:5} Oh, and in Shushan, there was this dude named Mordecai, a Jewish guy who got taken away from Jerusalem. {2:6} He raised his cousin Esther, who was a total babe, after her parents died. {2:7} So when the king's order went out and all these girls were rounded up, Esther got pulled into the mix too. {2:8-9} She totally caught the king's eye and got special treatment from Hegai, along with her crew of maidens. They even got the VIP spot in the women's house. {2:10} Esther kept her background on the down-low, just like Mordecai told her to. {2:11} Meanwhile, Mordecai was posted up outside, checking in on Esther and keeping tabs on her. {2:12} So, like, every girl had to go through this twelve-month beauty regimen, with six months of myrrh and six months of sweet perfumes and stuff. {2:13} When it was her turn to meet the king, Esther could ask for anything to take with her from the women's house to the king's crib. {2:14} She'd chill with the king for one night and then head back to the second women's house. If the king was feeling her vibe, she'd get called back again. {2:15} When Esther's turn came, she kept it simple and just took what Hegai suggested. And everybody thought she was a total queen. {2:16} So Esther got upgraded to the main event, moving into the king's palace in the tenth month of the seventh year of his reign. {2:17} The king was totally smitten with Esther and gave her mad respect, even more than all the other girls. He even crowned her queen instead of Vashti. {2:18} Then the king threw this epic party, celebrating Esther's new status, and he hooked up the provinces with some gifts, you know, keeping the vibes right. {2:19} After the whole queen selection ordeal, Mordecai started hanging out at the king's gate. {2:20} Esther still kept her family background hush-hush, just like Mordecai told her. She was all about following his lead. {2:21} While Mordecai was posted up, two of the king's homies, Bigthan and Teresh, got mad at the king and wanted to take him out. {2:22} Mordecai found out and looped Esther in, and she let the king know what was up, giving props to Mordecai. {2:23} The plot got exposed, and both Bigthan and Teresh got hung up on a tree. It all got recorded in the king's history books.

{3:1} So, after all that drama, King Ahasuerus decided to boost this guy Haman, promoting him above all the other big shots. {3:2} And all the king's crew at the gate had to bow down and show respect to Haman because the king said so. But Mordecai wasn't about to bow down to him. {3:3} The other servants were like, "Why you gotta disobey the king, Mordecai?" {3:4} They kept pressuring him, trying to see if he'd change his mind, 'cause they knew he was Jewish. {3:5} Haman got seriously ticked off when he saw Mordecai still wasn't showing him respect. {3:6} He wasn't just mad at Mordecai; he wanted to take out all the Jews in the kingdom because of him. {3:7} So they cast lots to pick a date to wipe out the Jews, from the first month to the twelfth month, a whole year. {3:8} Haman went to the king and was like, "Yo, there's this group of people in your kingdom who don't follow your rules. You gotta let me take care of them." {3:9} Haman offered to pay big bucks to make it happen. {3:10} The king was like, "Cool, you got it," and gave Haman his signet ring as a sign of approval. {3:11} He basically gave Haman free rein to do whatever he wanted with the Jews. {3:12} So they wrote up these official letters, sealed with the king's ring, and sent them out to all the provinces, saying it was cool to wipe out the Jews. {3:13} These letters went out, saying it was open season on Jews of all ages, to be wiped out in one day. {3:14} The decree was posted up everywhere, getting everybody ready for the big day. {3:15} While all this was going down, the king and Haman were just chilling and sipping drinks, but the city of Shushan was freaking out.

{4:1} When Mordecai saw what was up, he was totally devastated. He ripped his clothes, threw on some sackcloth and ashes, and hit the streets, crying his heart out. {4:2} He even went to the king's gate, but you can't roll up there looking like that. {4:3} All over the kingdom, Jews were mourning hard, fasting, and shedding tears, rocking the sackcloth and ashes vibe. {4:4} Esther's crew heard about Mordecai's scene and told her. She was shook and tried to send him some fresh threads, but he wasn't having it. {4:5} Esther got her boy Hatach, one of the king's chamberlains, to find out what was going on with Mordecai. {4:6} So Hatach hit the streets to find Mordecai at the king's gate. {4:7} Mordecai filled him in on everything, including Haman's shady deal to pay off the king's treasury to take out the Jews. {4:8} He even gave Hatach a copy of the official decree to show Esther, telling her to step up to the king and plead for her people. {4:9} Hatach ran back and spilled all the tea to Esther. {4:10} Esther hit up Hatach again, telling him to relay a message to Mordecai. {4:11} She broke it down, reminding everyone that if you roll into the king's court uninvited, you're risking your life unless the king's feeling generous. But she hadn't been summoned in over a month. {4:12} Hatach filled Mordecai in on Esther's words. {4:13} Mordecai hit her back, saying, "You can't think you'll be safe just because you're the queen. Maybe you got here for a reason, to save your people." {4:14} Esther shot back, telling Mordecai to gather all the Jews in Shushan and fast for three days, including her and her girls. Then she'd hit up the king, breaking the rules, and if she goes down, she goes down. {4:17} Mordecai bounced and followed Esther's orders to the letter.

{5:1} So on the third day, Esther suited up in her royal gear and posted up in the king's inner court, right across from his crib. {5:2} When the king peeped Esther chilling there, she caught his eye, and he extended the golden sceptre to her. Esther came through and touched it. {5:3} The king was like, "What's good, Queen Esther? What do you want? I'll hook you up, even half the kingdom." {5:4} Esther played it smooth, inviting the king and Haman to a banquet she had set up for them that day. {5:5} The king was down and told Haman to hurry up and get ready for the feast. {5:6} At the wine-filled banquet, the king was all ears for Esther's request. {5:7} Esther laid it down, saying, "Here's what I need." {5:8} She asked if she'd won the king's favor, could they do what she asked? She invited them both to another banquet the next day. {5:9} Haman was stoked after the banquet until he saw Mordecai posted up at the king's gate, not showing him any love. {5:10} He tried to play it cool, but as soon as he got home, he called up his squad and his wife Zeresh. {5:11} Haman bragged about his riches, his fam, and how he was big time with the king, even getting an exclusive invite from Esther. {5:12} But none of that mattered as long as Mordecai was chilling at the king's gate. {5:13} Zeresh and the crew were like, "Build a fifty-cubit-high gallows, and tomorrow, ask the king to hang Mordecai on it. Then come party it up at Esther's banquet." Haman was all in and got the gallows built.

{6:1} So, like, the king couldn't catch any Z's that night, so he was like, "Bring me the history book," and they read it to him. {6:2} Turns out, Mordecai had snitched on those two chamberlains trying to take out the king. {6:3} The king was like, "What did we do to honor Mordecai for this?" His crew was like, "Umm, nothing, bro." {6:4} Then the king was like, "Who's outside?" Guess who? Haman, ready to ask for Mordecai's head. {6:5} They were like, "Yo, Haman's waiting." So the king was like, "Bring him in." {6:6} Haman strolled in, thinking he was about to get a VIP treatment. {6:7} The king was like, "What should we do for someone I wanna show off?" Haman thought, "Obviously, me." {6:8} Haman suggested giving this person the king's fly outfit, his whip, and his crown, and parading him through town. {6:9} The king was like, "Cool, do that for Mordecai, the dude posted at my gate. Don't miss a thing." {6:10} So Haman had to eat humble pie, decked out Mordecai, and gave him the royal treatment, announcing him as the king's fave. {6:11} Mordecai went back to his gate chill spot, while Haman booked it home, totally bummed out, hiding his face in shame. {6:12} He spilled his guts to his wife and friends about what went down. They were like, "If Mordecai's a Jew, you're doomed, bro." {6:14} While they were still talking smack, the king's crew showed up, rushing Haman to Esther's shindig.

{7:1} So the king and Haman rolled up to Esther's party. {7:2} The next day, at the wine-fueled bash, the king was like, "Esther, what's your deal? I'll hook you up, even half the kingdom." {7:3} Esther was like, "If you really dig me, King, spare my life and save my people." {7:4} She spilled the tea about how they were all set to be wiped out. {7:5} The king was like, "Who's the jerk trying to pull this off?" {7:6} Esther pointed straight at Haman. Dude was sweating buckets in front of the king and queen. {7:7} The king bounced from the party, mad as heck, while Haman tried to plead for his life with Esther, knowing he was toast with the king. {7:8} When the king came back, he saw Haman lying on Esther's bed and flipped. He was like, "Is this guy really gonna try something with the queen right in front of me?" They covered Haman's face. {7:9} Then one of the king's guys was like, "Yo, Haman built a fifty-cubit-high gallows for Mordecai." The king was like, "Hang him on that." {7:10} So they hung Haman on the gallows meant for Mordecai. That cooled the king down real quick.

{8:1} So, like, on that day King Ahasuerus was all, "Yo, Esther, you can have Haman's pad, since he's outta here." Mordecai also stepped up to the king 'cause Esther spilled the beans about him. {8:2} The king was like, "Here, Mordecai, take Haman's bling," and Esther put Mordecai in charge of Haman's crib. {8:3} Esther wasn't done yet. She went back to the king, crying and all, begging him to cancel Haman's evil plan against the Jews. {8:4} The king was like, "Esther, what's up?" and he offered her his golden scepter. {8:5} Esther was like, "If you're cool with it and I'm still your fave, let's undo Haman's hateful letters trying to wipe out the Jews." {8:6} She couldn't handle seeing her people suffer like that. {8:7} The king was all, "Esther, I hooked you up with Haman's place, and he's toast on his own gallows for messing with the Jews." {8:8} He told them to write whatever they wanted for the Jews, sealed with his ring, 'cause once it's signed, it's locked in. {8:9} So, they got all the scribes together in the third month and wrote up the deal according to Mordecai's orders, for all the provinces from India to Ethiopia, in every language. {8:10} They sent out letters on horses, mules, camels, and dromedaries, granting the Jews the right to defend themselves on the thirteenth day of the twelfth month. {8:11} The Jews were given the green light to gather and defend themselves against anyone who tried to harm them, and take whatever loot they could. {8:12} This was going down in every province on the same day. {8:13} The decree went out everywhere, and the Jews were ready to fight back. {8:14} The king's orders were spread fast by the postal service. And the decree went out from Shushan the palace. {8:15} Mordecai left the king's presence looking fly in royal blue and white, rocking a big gold crown, and draped in fancy linen and purple threads. Shushan was lit, celebrating Mordecai's new status. {8:16} The Jews were vibing with light, joy, and honor. {8:17} Everywhere the king's orders reached, the Jews threw parties, and even some locals converted to Judaism out of respect.

{9:1} So, like, in the twelfth month, which is Adar, on the thirteenth day, when the king's orders were about to go down, the day when the enemies of the Jews thought they'd get the upper hand (but it totally flipped, and the Jews were in charge), {9:2} the jews in every city across King Ahasuerus' turf got together to shut down anyone trying to mess with them. Nobody could even step to them 'cause everyone was scared stiff. {9:3} All the big shots in the provinces, the deputies, and even the king's officers were backing the Jews 'cause they were terrified of Mordecai. {9:4} Mordecai was straight up famous in the king's crib, and word about him spread everywhere. He just kept getting more legendary. {9:5} The Jews straight-up wrecked their enemies with swords, bringing the pain, and doing whatever they wanted to those who hated them. {9:6} In Shushan, they took out five hundred dudes. {9:7} They got Parshandatha, Dalphon, Aspatha, {9:8} Poratha, Adalia, Aridatha, {9:9} Parmashta, Arisai, Aridai, and Vajezatha, the ten sons of Haman, and smoked 'em, but they didn't even touch the loot. {9:10} The body count in Shushan was reported to the king. {9:12} The king was like, "Yo, Esther, they took out five hundred dudes in Shushan, including Haman's ten sons. What's the deal everywhere else?" He was all ears for Esther's request. {9:13} Esther was like, "If it's cool with you, let the Jews in Shushan keep going tomorrow like they did today, and hang Haman's sons on the gallows." {9:14} The king was down, and the decree went out from Shushan, and Haman's sons got hung. {9:15} In Shushan, the Jews kept it going on the fourteenth, taking out three hundred more, but still no looting. {9:16} Meanwhile, Jews in other provinces were defending themselves and chilling from their enemies, taking out seventy-five thousand foes, but they kept it clean, no loot grabbing. {9:17} They kicked back on the thirteenth and fourteenth, making it a feast and celebration. {9:18} The Shushan crew did the same on the thirteenth, fourteenth, and fifteenth, keeping the party going. {9:19} Even the Jews in the villages celebrated on the fourteenth, sharing food and sending gifts. {9:20} Mordecai sent letters to all the Jews in the king's provinces, near and far, {9:21} telling them to celebrate the fourteenth and fifteenth of Adar every year, commemorating the days when they went from sadness to joy, mourning to partying, and sharing with the needy. {9:22} The Jews were all in, making sure these days were locked in every year, for all generations, families, provinces, and cities, so Purim would never be forgotten. {9:23} They committed to keeping these days as Mordecai wrote to them. {9:24} This was all because Haman, the Agagite, tried to wipe out the Jews, but his plan backfired, and he ended up on the gallows, along with his sons. {9:25} When Esther went before the king, he made sure Haman's evil plot against the Jews came back on him and his sons. {9:26} That's why they call these days Purim, after the lot Haman cast. And everyone was all about it, spreading the word and keeping the tradition alive. {9:27} Esther and Mordecai backed up these plans with their authority, making sure everyone stuck to the script, and no one forgot the fasting and crying. {9:28} They wanted Purim to be remembered and celebrated everywhere, for all time. {9:29} Queen Esther and Mordecai made it official with another letter. {9:30} They sent it out to all the Jews in the hundred twenty-seven provinces of Ahasuerus' kingdom, spreading peace and truth. {9:31} They made sure everyone knew the deal about Purim, just as Mordecai and Esther laid it out, including the fasting and crying. {9:32} Esther's decree made Purim official, written in the records.

{10:1} King Ahasuerus taxed the land and the islands. {10:2} All his epic deeds and how he boosted Mordecai's rep are all written down in the king's records. {10:3} Mordecai was next in line to King Ahasuerus, super respected among the Jews, always looking out for his people's welfare and spreading peace among his peeps.

Job

+++

{1:1} So, like, there was this dude named Job in Uz, and he was totally legit—like, perfect and always doing the right thing. He was all about fearing God and avoiding anything shady. {1:2} He had seven sons and three daughters, which was pretty rad. {1:3} His bank account was stacked with seven thousand sheep, three thousand camels, five hundred oxen, five hundred donkeys, and a massive crew of servants. He was basically the top dog in the east. {1:4} His kids would throw these huge parties at each other's places, and Job would be all, "Nah, gotta make sure my fam's in check," and he'd hook them up with burnt offerings, just in case they messed up and dissed God. He was always on that grind. {1:6} One day, when the heavenly crew was checking in with God, Satan rolled up too. {1:7} God was like, "What's up, Satan? Where you been?" And Satan's all, "Just cruising the Earth, you know, doing my thing." {1:8} Then God's like, "Yo, peep Job—he's the real deal, no one else like him, always staying true to Me." {1:9} But Satan's like, "Come on, God, Job only praises You 'cause You're always looking out for him. Take away his stuff, and watch him flip." {1:10} God's like, "Fine, Satan, do your thing, but don't mess with Job himself." So Satan bounced. {1:13-19} While Job's kids were partying it up, disaster strikes. First, some raiders jack all his livestock and off his servants. Then, a freak lightning storm roasts his sheep and more of his crew. After that, a gang of raiders roll in and take off with his camels and kill more of his servants. And if that wasn't enough, a gnarly windstorm wipes out the house where his kids are partying, and they all bite it. {1:20} Job's reaction? He's crushed, but he keeps it real with God, falls to the ground, and worships, saying, "I came into this world with nothing, and I'll leave with nothing. God gives, God takes away—praise God no matter what." {1:21} Through all this, Job keeps his head on straight and doesn't blame God for any of it.

{2:1} Round two: the heavenly crew reports for duty again, and Satan's back too. {2:2} This time, Satan messes with Job's health, hitting him with nasty boils from head to toe. {2:3} Job's wife is like, "Curse God and die, man," but Job's like, "Nah, you're talking crazy. We take the good with the bad from God—no hating." Job's still keeping it real, no matter what. {2:4} Job's crew hears about his troubles and come to be there for him. {2:5} When they spot Job from afar, they're so bummed they start crying, tearing their clothes, and throwing dust in the air. {2:6} They just sit with Job in silence for a whole week, 'cause they can see how much he's hurting.

{3:1} So, like, Job just couldn't hold it in anymore and straight-up cursed the day he was born. {3:2} He was like, "Yo, check it," {3:3} "Let that day be totally dark, like, don't even let God look at it. {3:4} Bring on the darkness, death, and clouds—make it spooky AF. {3:5} That night? Let it be super lonely, with no happy sounds. {3:6} And forget counting it as a regular day of the year, or even a month. {3:7} Let people who are into cursing curse it. {3:8} Let it be the worst for those who know how to summon evil spirits. {3:9} May the twilight stars go dark, and may it never see the dawn. {3:10} Because it didn't keep me locked up in my mom's womb to spare me this suffering. {3:11} Why didn't I just kick the bucket at birth? {3:12} Why did I even get knees to crawl with or breasts to feed from? {3:13} I could've been chilling in the grave, partying with kings and big shots. {3:14} Or hanging with rich dudes who built themselves fancy tombs. {3:15} Or I could've been like a stillborn, never seeing the light of day. {3:16} There, the wicked stop causing trouble, and the exhausted find peace. {3:17-19} Prisoners and rulers are equal; slaves are free from their masters. {3:20} Why should life be given to those in agony, and why should those with bitter souls keep on living? {3:21} They crave death more than hidden treasures. {3:22} They're stoked when they find a grave. {3:23} Why give light to someone whose path is hidden and who God has trapped? {3:24} I'm not even hungry before I groan, and my cries come pouring out like water. {3:25} My worst fears have come true, and what I dreaded has happened. {3:26} I never had peace or safety, even when things were calm, trouble was lurking.

{4:1} Then Eliphaz the Temanite chimes in, saying, {4:2} "Yo, if we try to talk to you, you gonna get mad? But we gotta speak up, man." {4:3} "You've helped so many people when they were down and out." {4:4} "You've been like a rock for those stumbling, helping them stand firm." {4:5} "But now it's you who's struggling, and you're losing it. {4:6} Wasn't your faith, confidence, and integrity your thing?" {4:7} "Think about it—innocent people don't get wiped out. So what's up?" {4:8} "I've seen it myself: people who do evil reap what they sow. {4:9} God's wrath wipes them out, and His breath blows them away. {4:10} Even fierce lions lose their teeth and their cubs scatter." {4:11} "The mighty lion loses his prey, and his offspring go hungry." {4:12} "One time, I had this trippy dream and got this heavy message." {4:13} "In the dead of night, when everyone's asleep, fear hit me hard, making my bones rattle." {4:14-15} "I felt a presence, and every hair on my body stood on end." {4:16} "It just stood there, but I couldn't make out what it was. There was just silence until I heard a voice, like," {4:17} "Can humans be more righteous than God? Can a person be purer than their maker?'" {4:18} "God doesn't even trust His angels; He finds fault in even them." {4:19} "So why would He trust us, made from dust, easily crushed?" {4:20} "We're destroyed from dawn to dusk, ignored by everyone." {4:21} "Doesn't their wisdom die with them?"

{5:1} So, like, if you're looking for answers, who you gonna call? And which influencer saint are you gonna hit up? {5:2} 'Cause getting all worked up just messes you up, and jealousy just wrecks you. {5:3} I've seen fools rising up, but then BAM, their whole setup gets cursed. {5:4} Their kids ain't safe, and they get crushed in the courts with no one to save them. {5:5} Hungry folks snatch up their crops, thieves clean them out, and they're left with nothing. {5:6} Bad stuff doesn't just happen out of nowhere; trouble's just part of life. {5:7} Man, life's like born into trouble, you know, like sparks flying up. {5:8} But yo, I'm gonna turn to God and lay it all out, 'cause He does some crazy stuff nobody can even figure out. {5:9} He's the one who makes it rain and waters the fields, lifting up the lowly and giving hope to the downtrodden. {5:10} He messes with the plans of the schemers, so they can't pull off their shady moves. {5:11} Those who think they're so smart get caught up in their own mess, and the stubborn get tripped up. {5:12} But God looks out for the poor, keeping them safe from harm. {5:13} So yeah, those who have it rough but still listen to God, they're blessed. {5:18} 'Cause even when He hits hard, He's also the one who heals. {5:14} He'll get you through six kinds of trouble, and in the seventh, you'll still be standing. {5:15} Even in famines and wars, He's got your back. {5:16} You won't have to worry about haters talking smack or destruction when it rolls through. {5:17} You'll laugh at disaster and famine, not even sweating the wild beasts. {5:18} Even the rocks and animals will be chill with you. {5:19} Your home will be peaceful, and you won't mess up. {5:20} Your descendants will be as numerous as blades of grass, and you'll live a long life, like a mature crop.

{6:1} But then Job's like, "Yo, can't you see how heavy my suffering is?" {6:2} "It's heavier than all the sand on the beach; my words get swallowed up." {6:3} "The Almighty's arrows are stabbing me; His terrors are attacking me." {6:4} "Does a donkey bray when it's got food, or an ox moo when it's munching?" {6:5} "Can you eat food without seasoning, or an egg without salt?" {6:6-7} "The stuff I can't even stand to touch is like my daily meals now." {6:8} "Man, I wish God would just end it all; I'm over this." {6:9-10} "At least then I'd have some peace, even if it meant going out in pain. I haven't kept quiet about God's truth." {6:11-12} "What's my strength good for, or why should I even bother living?" {6:13} "I've got nothing left; wisdom's left me hanging." {6:14} "Friends should be supportive when you're down, but they've ditched me and lost their respect for God." {6:15} "My friends are like dried-up streams, gone when the going gets tough." {6:16} "They're like ice that melts when it's warm, disappearing when things get hot." {6:17-18} "Their paths twist and turn, leading nowhere and ending in nothing." {6:19-20} "They hoped for something, but got nothing; they showed up and were embarrassed." {6:21-22} "Now you're acting all shook; you see how messed up I am and freak out." {6:23} "Did I ask for your help? Did I say, 'Hey, give me stuff'?" {6:24} "Teach me, and I'll shut up; show me where I messed up." {6:25} "Good advice hits hard, but what are you trying to prove with all this arguing?" {6:26} "You think you can correct someone who's desperate? It's like trying to catch the wind." {6:27} "You've been harsh to the fatherless and dug pits for your friends." {6:28} "So chill and look at me; it's obvious if I'm lying." {6:29} "Don't be unjust; my righteousness is on the line here." {6:30} "Am I saying messed-up stuff? Can't I tell right from wrong?"

{7:1} Ain't life just like a gig shift? You clock in, grind it out, and then you're outta there. {7:2} I'm just here, waiting for this shift to end like a servant craving shade or a worker waiting for payday. {7:3} But instead, I'm stuck with endless nights and days of nothingness. {7:4} I lay down, hoping to wake up and it'll all be over, but it's just tossing and turning till dawn. {7:5} My body's falling apart, covered in sores and dirt, skin all messed up. {7:6} My days fly by faster than a TikTok vid, and I'm left with no hope. {7:7} Life's just a breath, and I can't see any good coming my way. {7:8} People used to see me, but now it's like I'm invisible. {7:9} It's like disappearing into thin air, gone and forgotten. {7:10} Once you're in the ground, that's it, no coming back. {7:11} So, I'm gonna vent, let it all out, because I'm done pretending everything's fine. {7:12} Like, why are you watching me so closely, like I'm some kind of sea monster? {7:13} I try to sleep, but you hit me with nightmares, making me dread waking up. {7:14-15} It's like my soul would rather die than keep living like this. {7:16} Living forever? Nah, I'm good. Let me peace out; life's just a big fat zero. {7:17} Like, why even bother with us humans? What's the point of caring about us? {7:18} Can't you just leave me alone for a sec? Let me catch my breath. {7:19} Yeah, I messed up, but why are you punishing me like this? {7:20} Why won't you forgive me and let me move on? 'Cause soon enough, I'll be sleeping in the dirt, and you won't even notice.

{8:1} Then this dude Bildad pipes up, asking Job how long he's gonna keep ranting. {8:2} He's like, "Seriously, your words are like a hurricane. When's it gonna stop?" {8:3} "Does God play favorites? Is He unfair?" {8:4} "If your kids messed up, that's on them, not God." {8:5} "You gotta turn back to God, man, and pray for forgiveness." {8:6} "If you were innocent, God would totally hook you up." {8:7} "Even if you started small, you'd end up huge, rolling in success." {8:8} "Check out history, man, learn from the past." {8:9} "We're just here for a sec, clueless about life." {8:10} "Listen to the wise; they'll drop some real knowledge." {8:11} "Can plants grow without water? No way." {8:12} "They wither up quick if they're not looked after." {8:13} "That's what happens to those who forget about God." {8:14} "Their hopes get crushed like a flimsy spider web." {8:15} "They'll lean on their houses, but they won't stand; they'll grip them tight, but they won't last." {8:16} "They might look fresh now, but they'll be uprooted soon." {8:17} "Their roots will wrap around rocks, clinging to nothing." {8:18} "Once they're gone, it'll be like they were never there." {8:19} "Their joy will vanish, and others will rise in their place." {8:20} "God doesn't mess with the righteous; He leaves the wicked to their own demise." {8:21} "But if you turn back to Him, you'll be laughing again, rejoicing." {8:22} "Those who hate you will be ashamed, and the homes of the wicked will crumble."

{9:1} So, Job's like, "I get it, but how can anyone be square with God?" {9:2} Trying to argue with Him? You won't even get a word in; He's too slick for that. {9:3} God's got mad power, man. He's flipping mountains like it's nothing. {9:4} He's shaking the earth like a snow globe, making the stars hit snooze. {9:5} And you can't even question Him; He's on a whole other level. {9:6} God's playing 4D chess while we're stuck in checkers. {9:7} He's running the whole show, from sunrise to sunset. {9:8} Painting the sky like it's His canvas, surfing the waves like it's a breeze. {9:9} Making constellations and chilling in the south. {9:10} His moves are so next level, we can't even keep up. {9:11} He's passing by, and I don't even notice. {9:12} Who can stop Him when He decides to do something? {9:13} You think you're all that, but you're nothing compared to Him. {9:14} Even if I was squeaky clean, I wouldn't dare to argue with Him. {9:15} I'd rather plead for mercy than try to prove myself innocent. {9:16} Like, if I called out to Him, would He even listen? {9:17} He's hitting me with storms and pain for no reason. {9:18} Can't even catch my breath; it's all bitterness and pain. {9:19} If I try to defend myself, I just end up condemning myself. {9:20} Even if I claim to be flawless, it just proves I'm delusional. {9:21} Even if I was perfect, I wouldn't even recognize myself. {9:22} He's taking out the good and the bad; it's like a messed-up game to Him. {9:23} If disaster strikes, He's laughing while innocent folks suffer. {9:24} It's like the wicked are running the show, hiding behind their masks. {9:25} My days are like a race car; zooming by, not a moment of peace. {9:26} Gone in a flash, like ships in the night or an eagle swooping down. {9:27} I try to forget my troubles, but I know I won't get off easy. {9:28} I'm drowning in sorrow, and I know I won't be let off the hook. {9:29} If I'm a sinner, why bother trying? {9:30} Even if I scrub myself clean, I'll still end up in the mud. {9:31} No matter what, I'll end up in the dirt, rejected and filthy. {9:32} I can't argue with Him; there's no mediator between us. {9:33} If only He'd back off and stop scaring me, then maybe I could speak up without fear. {9:34} But that's just wishful thinking. {9:35} It's just not happening.

{10:1} I'm so over life; I'm just gonna let it all out, speaking from the depths of my soul. {10:2} God, please, tell me what I did wrong. {10:3} Is it fun for You to crush me and side with the wicked? {10:4} Do You see like we do? {10:5} Do You live like us? {10:6} Are You keeping tabs on my sins? {10:7} You know I'm not evil, but You're still handing out punishment. {10:8} You made me, but now You're breaking me? {10:9} I'm just clay in Your hands; are You gonna crush me back into dust? {10:10} Did You pour me out like milk and turn me into cheese? {10:11} You dressed me up in skin and bones, but now You're tearing me apart. {10:12} You gave me life, but now You're destroying me. {10:13} You know all this stuff, God; it's all on You. {10:14} If I mess up, You're watching, and You won't let me off easy. {10:15} If I'm bad, I'm screwed, but even if I'm good, I won't catch a break. {10:16} I'm drowning in confusion; it's like I'm in a crazy game, and You're pulling all the strings. {10:17} You're piling on the evidence against me, getting angrier by the minute. {10:18} Why'd You even bother bringing me into this messed-up world? {10:19} I wish I was never born, just a blip from the womb to the grave. {10:20} My days are numbered; just let me catch a break before I'm gone forever. {10:21} Before I'm swallowed up by darkness and death's shadow. {10:22} A land of pure darkness, where chaos reigns, and light is swallowed whole.

{11:1} So Zophar, the Naamathite, pops up and goes, {11:2} "You really think a bunch of words gonna cut it? Can a chatterbox like you be righteous?" {11:3} "Your lies gonna shut everyone up? When you're being shady, ain't nobody gonna call you out?" {11:4} "You claim your teachings are pure, that you're squeaky clean." {11:5} "But wouldn't it be sweet if God spoke up, laid out some wisdom and showed you up?" {11:6} "Know this, God ain't even given you the full wrath you deserve." {11:7} "Can you even comprehend God? Can you figure out the Almighty?" {11:8} "It's like trying to reach heaven; what can you do? Deeper than hell; what can you grasp?" {11:9} "Bigger than earth, wider than the sea." {11:10} "If God decides to act, who can stop him?" {11:11} "He sees through the fakers, spots the wickedness, you think he won't check you?" {11:12} "You may think you're wise, but you're just a clueless fool." {11:13} "If you straighten up and reach out to him; if you ditch the sin and clean up your act." {11:14} "Then you can hold your head high without shame, be solid, and fearless." {11:15} "You'll forget your misery, it'll be like water under the bridge." {11:16} "Your future gonna shine brighter than noon; you'll glow like the morning." {11:17} "You'll be secure, hopeful, chilling in safety." {11:18} "You'll rest without fear, folks will come to you." {11:19} "But the wicked gonna fail, their hope gonna fade."

{12:1} And Job claps back, saying, {12:2} "Oh, you guys are the wise ones, huh? Wisdom gonna die with you." {12:3} "But I'm no slouch, I know stuff too, who doesn't know this?" {12:4} "I'm mocked by my neighbors, even when I call on God, I get laughed at." {12:5} "The unstable are despised by the comfortable." {12:6} "The wicked thrive, God showers them with blessings." {12:7} "Ask the animals, they'll teach you; ask the birds, they'll tell you." {12:8} "Even the earth has lessons; fish got stories to share." {12:9} "Everyone knows it's God's handiwork." {12:10} "He holds the soul of every living thing, the breath of all mankind." {12:11} "Words are tested by the ear, food by the mouth." {12:12} "Old folks got wisdom, age brings understanding." {12:13} "He's got wisdom, strength, counsel, and understanding." {12:14} "He breaks down, you can't rebuild; he shuts up, there's no opening." {12:15} "He withholds water, it dries up; he releases it, floods come." {12:16} "With him is strength and wisdom, he deceives and reveals." {12:17} "He leads counselors astray, makes judges fools." {12:18} "He strips kings of power, wraps their waist with defeat." {12:19} "He humiliates princes, topples the mighty." {12:20} "He silences the wise, confuses the old." {12:21} "He puts down princes, weakens the strong." {12:22} "He uncovers mysteries, brings light to darkness." {12:23} "He builds up nations, then tears them down; he enlarges them, then shrinks them again." {12:24} "He confounds the leaders, makes them wander in confusion." {12:25} "They stumble in darkness, like drunkards."

{13:1} Yo, I've peeped all that, heard it loud and clear. {13:2} Whatever you know, I know too, I'm no less than you. {13:3} I'm itching to chat with the Big Guy, wanna hash it out with God. {13:4} But y'all are straight up lying, playing at being helpful but ain't worth a dime. {13:5} If you'd just zip it, that'd be the smart move. {13:6} Listen up to what I gotta say, pay attention to my words. {13:7} You really gonna talk smack for God? Be deceitful on his behalf? {13:8} You gonna butter him up? Argue for God? {13:9} Think it's cool for him to grill you? Or you gonna clown him like one bro mocks another? {13:10} He'll call you out if you're two-faced. {13:11} Ain't his awesomeness gonna freak you out? His dread gonna hit you hard? {13:12} Your memories are like ash, your bodies just clay. {13:13} Shut it, let me speak my piece, let whatever come, come. {13:14} Why am I risking it all? Even if I'm wiped out, I'll still trust him, but I'll stick to my ways. {13:15} He's got my back, a faker won't stand before him. {13:16} Listen closely to what I'm saying, hear me out. {13:17} Look, I got my case in order; I know I'm in the right. {13:18} Who's gonna argue with me? If I keep quiet, I'm as good as dead. {13:19} Just don't do two things to me; then I won't hide from you. {13:20} Ease off, don't scare me with your dread. {13:21} Call me, I'll answer; or let me speak, and you reply. {13:22} How many wrongs and sins do I have? Show me my mess-ups. {13:23} Why you hiding your face, treating me like an enemy? {13:24} You gonna crush a withered leaf? Chase after dry straw? {13:25} You're hitting me with harsh words, making me pay for my young mistakes. {13:26} You got my feet in cuffs, watching every step, leaving your mark. {13:28} And I'm wasting away like rotten fruit, like a moth-eaten shirt.

{14:1} A person's life is short and full of drama. {14:2} They pop up like a flower, then bam, they're gone, just a fleeting shadow. {14:3} Why even bother judging someone like that? {14:4} Can't make something clean out of something dirty. {14:5} You got their days numbered, set their limits; they can't go beyond. {14:6} Just let them rest, they'll finish their time like a hired hand. {14:7} There's hope for a chopped-down tree, it might grow back, sprout new branches. {14:8} Even if its roots get old and its stump dies, with a bit of water, it'll bud again. {14:9} But a person dies and fades away, where do they go? {14:10} Like water drying up from a sea, they lie down and don't rise till the heavens are gone. {14:11} I wish you'd stash me in the grave, keep me hidden till your anger's past, set a time for me, and remember me. {14:12} If a person dies, will they live again? I'll wait all my days till things change. {14:13} You call, I'll answer; you'll long for the work of your hands. {14:14} You're keeping tabs on me now, aren't you? {14:15} My wrongs are all locked up, my sins sewn tight. {14:16} Mountains crumble, rocks move, and water erodes stones. {14:17} You wash away the stuff that grows on earth's dust and crush the hope of people. {14:18} You're always on top, they pass away; you change their looks and send them off. {14:19} Their kids rise to honor, they don't even know; they're brought low, but they don't even notice. {14:20} But they're in pain, their soul's hurting within.

{15:1} So Eliphaz, the Temanite, jumps in and goes, {15:2} "Think a smart dude should talk nonsense and fill up on hot air?" {15:3} "Should he waste time with useless chatter? Or spit out speeches that do no good?" {15:4} "You've thrown fear out the window, ignore prayer before God." {15:5} "Your mouth spills out your sin, you choose to be sneaky." {15:6} "Your own words condemn you, not me; your lips rat you out." {15:7} "You think you're the first dude ever? Or were you around before the hills?" {15:8} "You heard God's secrets? Keep wisdom all to yourself?" {15:9} "What do you know that we don't? What's your special insight?" {15:10} "We got old dudes with us, way older than your pops." {15:11} "You think you got some exclusive connection with God?" {15:12} "Why you acting all high and mighty? What's with the shady looks?" {15:13} "You turning against God with your words?" {15:14} "What's a person, that they can be clean? Born of a woman, that they can be righteous?" {15:15} "They don't even trust their own holy ones; even the heavens ain't clean to them." {15:16} "Man's more messed up than you think, guzzling sin like water." {15:17} "I'll lay it out for you, listen up; wise words passed down from generations." {15:18} "Earth was given to them alone, no outsider stepping in." {15:19} "Wicked folks suffer all their days, never knowing how long they got." {15:20} "They hear doom approaching even in their good times." {15:21} "They don't think they'll ever escape darkness, they're hunted by the sword." {15:22} "They're desperate for food, knowing darkness is just around the corner." {15:23} "Trouble and pain haunt them, like a warrior ready for battle." {15:24} "They're against God, trying to stand up to the Almighty." {15:25} "They go at him head-on, relying on their fatness and strength." {15:26} "They live in deserted places, in empty houses ready to crumble." {15:27} "They won't get rich, their wealth won't last, and they won't see the light of day." {15:28} "They won't escape darkness; their life will wither away like dry branches." {15:29} "Their deception leads to nothing, their end is emptiness." {15:30} "Their time will come, their hopes will fade away." {15:31} "They'll fall before their time, their future won't be bright." {15:32} "They'll lose everything, like a vine shedding unripe grapes." {15:33} "The congregation of hypocrites will be deserted, fire will consume their dishonest dwellings." {15:34} "They scheme evil, give birth to emptiness, and their belly churns out deceit."

{16:1} Then Job claps back, saying, {16:2} "Heard enough of this; you're all terrible comforters." {16:3} "When will the pointless words stop? What makes you think you can answer?" {16:4} "I could talk like you if I were in your shoes, I could dish out words against you." {16:5} "But I'd rather comfort you with my words, ease your pain with what I say." {16:6} "But nothing I say makes me feel better; holding back doesn't help either." {16:7} "Now I'm worn out; you've destroyed my friends." {16:8} "You've marked me with wrinkles, my frailty shows on my face." {16:9} "He attacks me in his anger, hating me; his eyes sharpen against me." {16:10} "They open their mouths wide against me; they slap me on the cheek with insults; they gang up on me." {16:11} "God's handed me over to the godless, into the hands of the wicked." {16:12} "I was at peace, but he shattered me; he grabbed me by the neck, shook me to pieces, and made me a target." {16:13} "His archers surround me; he tears through my insides, pouring out my guts on the ground." {16:14} "He keeps hitting me, one blow after another; he charges at me like a giant." {16:15} "I've put on sackcloth, rubbed my face in the dust." {16:16} "My face is swollen from crying, my eyelids are like the shadow of death." {16:17} "But I'm innocent; my prayer is pure." {16:18} "Earth, don't cover up my blood; let my cry be heard." {16:19} "My witness is in heaven, my advocate is on high." {16:20} "My friends mock me; I pour out my tears to God." {16:21} "I wish someone could argue my case with God, like a friend pleading for a neighbor!" {16:22} "Soon I'll go to a place where I can't come back from."

{17:1} So, like, my breath stinks, my days are like over, and the graves are practically calling my name. {17:2} Ain't I surrounded by haters? Can't catch a break with their mocking. {17:3} Just end it already, give me some assurance; who's gonna back me up here? {17:4} 'Cause you've blocked their understanding; you won't give 'em a chance. {17:5} If you butter up your friends, even your kids will turn away. {17:6} People talk trash about me, like I'm some joke. {17:7} I'm so bummed out, my eyes are practically useless, and my body feels like a shadow. {17:8} Good guys are gonna be shocked at this, and the innocent will stand up to the fakes. {17:9} The righteous will keep doing their thing, getting stronger and stronger. {17:10} But seriously, where are the wise ones among you? I can't find a single one. {17:11} My days are done, my plans are wrecked, even my thoughts are messed up. {17:12} It's like I'm living in darkness all the time; the light barely lasts. {17:13} If I wait around, I'm practically living in the grave already. {17:14} I'm like talking to death, calling it my family. {17:15} But where's my hope now? Who's gonna see it? {17:16} We're all headed to the grave, resting in the dirt together.

{18:1} Then this guy Bildad, he's like, "When are you gonna stop with the talk? Listen up, then we'll speak." {18:3} "Why you treating us like animals, thinking we're trash?" {18:4} "Your anger's tearing you apart; think the whole earth's gonna shake for you?" {18:5} "Nah, wicked folks' lights are gonna go out, their fire's gonna die." {18:6} "Darkness will fill their homes, their candles will flicker out." {18:7} "Their strength will fail them, their own plans will backfire." {18:8} "They're gonna fall into their own traps, get caught up in their own schemes." {18:9} "Trouble's gonna trip them up, they're gonna get wrecked by their own plans." {18:10} "They'll walk right into traps, stumbling into their own downfall." {18:11} "Fear's gonna chase 'em down, make 'em run." {18:12} "They'll starve, and destruction's gonna be right there with 'em." {18:13} "Their skin's gonna waste away, death's gonna take 'em." {18:14} "They'll lose all confidence, be terrified outta their minds." {18:15} "Their homes will be wrecked, brimstone scattered all over." {18:16} "Their roots will dry up, their branches cut off." {18:17} "Nobody's gonna remember 'em, they'll fade into nothing." {18:18} "From light to darkness, they're gonna get chased outta here." {18:19} "No kids, no family left behind; they'll be forgotten." {18:20} "People in the future are gonna be shocked at how messed up their lives were." {18:21} "Yeah, that's what happens to the wicked who don't know squat about God."

{19:1} So, like, Job's like, "Seriously, guys?" {19:2} "How long you gonna keep on dissing me and tearing me down with your words?" {19:3} "You've roasted me like ten times already, and you're not even embarrassed by how distant you've become?" {19:4} "Even if I messed up, that's on me, not you." {19:5} "If you're trying to make yourselves look good by putting me down, just know it's God who's put me in this mess." {19:6} "I've been crying out for justice, but it's like my voice isn't even heard." {19:7} "He's blocked every path I try to take and surrounded me with darkness." {19:8} "To top it off, he's stripped me of everything I had, taken away all my dignity." {19:9} "I'm completely destroyed, with no hope left, like a tree with its roots ripped out." {19:10} "And now, he's turned his anger against me, treating me like an enemy." {19:11} "It's like his armies are coming after me, setting up camp all around my home." {19:12} "My friends and family have all abandoned me, treating me like a stranger." {19:13} "Even my closest relatives act like they don't know me anymore." {19:14} "My buddies have ditched me, and even my childhood friends have forgotten me." {19:15} "My own household treats me like a stranger; I'm an outsider in my own home." {19:16} "I call out to my servants, but they don't even bother to respond." {19:17} "Even my wife acts like she doesn't know me, despite all I've done for our family." {19:18} "Even the kids make fun of me; I stand up, and they talk smack." {19:19} "All my close friends despise me now; the ones I loved have turned against me." {19:20} "I'm skin and bones, barely hanging on." {19:21} "Have some compassion, guys; God's hand is heavy on me." {19:22} "Why are you treating me like you're God, not satisfied until I'm completely destroyed?" {19:23} "I wish my words could be written down and remembered forever." {19:24} "Like, engraved in stone for all to see." {19:25} "I know my redeemer's out there, gonna come through for me in the end." {19:26} "Even if my body's destroyed, I'll still see God with my own eyes." {19:27} "I'll see him for myself, no one else; even if I'm at my lowest." {19:28} "You should be asking yourselves why you're going after me; the real issue lies with me." {19:29} "Better watch out for what's coming; wrath's gonna bring down the hammer, and you'll know there's a reckoning."

{20:1} Then Zophar's like, "Okay, listen up, I gotta say something real quick." {20:2} "I've been holding back, but I gotta speak my mind." {20:3} "I've heard your insults, and I gotta respond with some truth." {20:4} "Haven't you realized by now that the wicked don't last long? Their happiness is just a flash in the pan." {20:5} "Even if they seem to have it all, they'll disappear in no time." {20:6} "They'll be forgotten, like they never even existed." {20:7} "People will be like, 'Where'd they go?'" {20:8} "Their dreams will vanish, like they were never real." {20:9} "Nobody will see them again, their place will be empty." {20:10} "Their kids will have to give back what they took from the poor, making things right." {20:11} "Their past mistakes will come back to haunt them, sticking with them till the end." {20:12} "Even if they enjoy their evil deeds for a while, it'll turn sour in the end." {20:13} "They'll try to hang onto their wickedness, but it'll destroy them from the inside." {20:14} "Their wealth won't last; God'll make sure it's all taken away." {20:15} "They'll taste the venom of their own deeds, and it'll be their downfall." {20:16} "They'll suffer the consequences of their actions; there's no escaping it." {20:17} "They won't enjoy the good things in life; their days of luxury are over." {20:18} "They'll have to give back what they stole, and they won't enjoy it." {20:19} "Their guilty conscience will keep them from finding peace; they won't enjoy what they have." {20:20} "There'll be nothing left for them to enjoy; their wealth and possessions will vanish." {20:21} "They won't be able to find peace or satisfaction; their wealth won't save them." {20:22} "When they're about to indulge, God'll bring down his fury on them, ruining their feast." {20:23} "They'll try to escape, but they won't get away from God's judgment." {20:24} "They'll flee from danger, but it'll catch up to them; they won't escape." {20:25} "Disaster will strike them, and they won't know what hit them." {20:26} "They'll be consumed by darkness, with no one to save them." {20:27} "Their sins will be exposed for all to see; the earth will rise up against them." {20:28} "Their wealth will disappear, and everything they have will be gone in a flash." {20:29} "That's the fate of the wicked, decreed by God."

{21:1} Job's like, "Hold up, let me drop some truth on you." {21:2} "Listen up, and let this be your reality check." {21:3} "Let me speak my piece; after that, you can keep clowning on me." {21:4} "Look, if I'm complaining, it's not about humans; and even if it were, wouldn't I have a reason to be upset?" {21:5} "Pay attention and be amazed; just shut up and listen." {21:6} "Even thinking about this stuff freaks me out, sends shivers down my spine." {21:7} "So why do bad guys get to live it up, get old, and be all powerful?" {21:8} "They've got their families with them, watching their success." {21:9} "Their houses are secure, and they don't worry about God punishing them." {21:10} "Their animals have no trouble reproducing, and their kids are carefree." {21:11} "They've got their little ones running around, having a blast." {21:12} "They're partying it up with music and celebration." {21:13} "They live it up, then BAM, they're in the grave."

{21:14} "They're like, 'God, leave us alone; we're not interested in your rules.'" {21:15} "Who needs God? What's in it for us if we pray?" {21:16} "Their happiness isn't in their hands; I want nothing to do with their wicked ways." {21:17} "But how often do bad guys get what's coming to them? God dishes out suffering when he's ticked off." {21:18} "They're like dry grass blown away by the wind, easily swept away." {21:19} "God keeps track of their wrongdoing, and eventually, they'll face the consequences." {21:20} "They'll see their own destruction and face the wrath of the Almighty." {21:21} "What's the point of enjoying life after you're gone?" {21:22} "Can anyone teach God a lesson? He's the ultimate judge." {21:23} "Some people die peacefully, while others suffer till the end." {21:24} "Some live in luxury, while others can't even enjoy a meal." {21:25} "In the end, they all end up in the dirt, covered in worms." {21:26} "I know what you're thinking, and you're dead wrong about me." {21:27} "You're asking where the wicked live? You ever talk to people passing by?" {21:28} "The wicked are doomed to destruction, facing God's wrath." {21:29} "Who's gonna confront them about their wickedness? Who's gonna make them pay for what they've done?" {21:30} "They're headed for the grave, and that's where they'll stay." {21:31} "Even the ground they lie in will seem sweet; everyone who comes after will follow in their footsteps." {21:32} "So, how can you comfort me with lies? Your answers are all empty."

{22:1} Then Eliphaz is like, "Can we really benefit God? Does he gain anything from our wisdom?" {22:2} "Is God impressed by your righteousness? Does it matter to him if you're perfect?" {22:3} "Will he punish you out of fear? Will he argue with you in court?" {22:4} "Your wickedness is pretty clear; your sins are countless." {22:5} "You've cheated your brother, stripped the needy, and denied help to the hungry." {22:6} "While you were living it up, the poor suffered." {22:7} "You ignored the thirsty and left the hungry with nothing." {22:8} "But the powerful prospered, and the honorable lived in luxury." {22:9} "You've left widows destitute and broken the arms of orphans." {22:10} "Now you're surrounded by trouble and fear." {22:11} "Darkness surrounds you, and disaster strikes without warning." {22:12} "God's up there in the sky, way above us; can you even comprehend how high?" {22:13} "You question if God knows what's going on; can he see through the clouds?" {22:14} "Thick clouds block his view, and he moves in mysterious ways." {22:15} "Have you ever thought about the path of the wicked?" {22:16} "They're washed away by floods, their foundations destroyed." {22:17} "They say to God, 'Get lost! What can you do for us?'" {22:18} "Yet he still blesses them, but I want nothing to do with their evil plans." {22:19} "The righteous see this and rejoice, while the innocent laugh at their downfall." {22:20} "Our wealth may be gone, but the fire consumes the remnants of the wicked." {22:21} "Get to know God, and find peace; that's where true happiness lies." {22:22} "Listen to his teachings and keep them close to your heart." {22:23} "Turn back to God, and rid your life of sin." {22:24} "Then you'll be as rich as gold, with God as your protector." {22:25} "You'll find joy in God, and you'll be able to look him in the eye." {22:26} "You'll pray, and he'll answer; you'll keep your promises to him." {22:27} "You'll decree something, and it'll happen; light will guide your way." {22:28} "When others fall, you'll lift them up; the humble will find salvation." {22:29} "God will rescue the innocent, and your hands will be clean in his sight." {22:30} "The pure of heart will be saved, and justice will prevail."

{23:1} Job's like, "Here we go again." {23:2} "Today's complaint? It's rough, man. Worse than my groans." {23:3} "I wish I knew where to find God; I'd march right up to him." {23:4} "I'd plead my case and lay out my arguments." {23:5} "I'd want to hear what he has to say to me, understand his response." {23:6} "But nah, he wouldn't come at me with all his power; he'd give me strength." {23:7} "Then we could have a real talk, and maybe I'd finally get some relief from my judge." {23:8} "But no matter which way I go, I can't find him; he's playing hide and seek." {23:9} "I look around, but I can't see him anywhere." {23:10} "But hey, he knows where I'm at; when he's done testing me, I'll come out shining like gold." {23:11} "I've stuck to his path and never turned away." {23:12} "I've followed his commands, treasured his words more than food." {23:13} "But hey, he does what he wants; who can change his mind?" {23:14} "He's got plans for me, and he's got plenty more where that came from." {23:15} "But his presence? It freaks me out; just thinking about it makes me tremble." {23:16} "God's messing with my heart, and the Almighty's got me all shook up." {23:17} "I haven't been left in the dark, but God hasn't shown me the light either."

{24:1} "Why don't those who claim to know God see what's going on?" {24:2} "Some people mess with the rules, stealing flocks and animals." {24:3} "They're heartless, taking advantage of orphans and widows." {24:4} "They push the poor around, forcing them into hiding." {24:5} "They're like wild animals scavenging for food, up at the crack of dawn to steal." {24:6} "They harvest crops they didn't plant and reap the rewards of the wicked." {24:7} "They leave people out in the cold, with nothing to keep them warm." {24:8} "They're drenched by mountain rains, seeking shelter in the rocks." {24:9} "They exploit the vulnerable, taking advantage of the poor." {24:10} "They strip people naked and steal their food." {24:11} "They live it up while others suffer." {24:12} "People cry out in pain, but God doesn't seem to notice." {24:13} "They reject the light and don't know the path to righteousness." {24:14} "They're criminals, preying on the weak and vulnerable." {24:15} "They think they can hide their sins, but they can't escape judgment." {24:16} "They do their dirty work in the dark, thinking they won't get caught." {24:17} "But their deeds are like death in the morning; everyone sees their wickedness." {24:18} "They're cursed, their lives full of misery; they don't know the path of righteousness." {24:19} "Drought and heat destroy them, just like their sins consume them." {24:20} "They'll be forgotten, consumed by worms; their wickedness will be their downfall." {24:21} "They mistreat the barren and ignore the needs of widows." {24:22} "They think they're untouchable, but their time will come." {24:23} "Even if they seem safe, God's watching their every move." {24:24} "They may seem powerful for a while, but they'll be cut down like wheat." {24:25} "And if what I'm saying isn't true, who's gonna prove me wrong?"

{25:1} So Bildad jumps in, saying, "God's all about power and respect, bringing peace up high." {25:2-3} "Who can even count his armies? Everyone gets touched by his light." {25:4} "But seriously, how can any human be right with God? We're just born into sin."

{25:5} "Even the moon ain't shining in comparison, and the stars ain't pure to him." {25:6} "We're nothing compared to God, just worms."

{26:1} Job fires back, "What good are you to someone powerless? How do you help the weak?" {26:2} "You got no wisdom to share, no real insight." {26:3} "Who's even listening to your words? Where's your understanding coming from?" {26:4} "God's got the whole universe in his hands, even the dark places." {26:5} "He's got everything under control, from the north to the sea." {26:6} "The heavens themselves shake at his power; who can even comprehend it?" {26:7} "We've only scratched the surface of what God's capable of."

{27:1} Job's not done yet, saying, "As long as I'm breathing, I won't speak lies or give in." {27:2} "I won't deny my integrity, even if it kills me." {2:3} "Let my enemies face the same fate as the wicked." {27:4} "What hope does a hypocrite have when God takes their life?" {27:5} "Will a hypocrite even call on God when trouble hits?" {27:6} "I'll teach you about God's power, won't hide a thing." {27:7} "This is what awaits the wicked and oppressors from God." {27:8} "Their children will suffer, never satisfied." {27:9} "They'll die alone, with no one to mourn them." {27:10} "They might gather wealth, but the righteous will inherit it." {27:11} "Terrors will grip them like a storm in the night." {27:12} "No escaping from God's judgment; they'll be hissed out of their place."

{28:1} So, like, there's totally places where you find silver and gold, you know? {28:2} Iron's dug up from the earth, and brass is melted down from rocks. {28:3} Water flows from the earth, man, and then just disappears. {28:4} You can find cool stuff like sapphires and gold in the earth, it's wild. {28:5} Dude's out here moving mountains and carving out rivers, finding all the good stuff. {28:6} But where do you find wisdom, man? Like, seriously, where's that place? {28:7} I dropped some knowledge, and they were just soaking it up, man. {28:8} And God's like, "Yo, fear me, that's wisdom, and stay away from evil, that's understanding."

{29:1} Job's like, "Back in the day, life was sweet, man. God was looking out for me." {29:2} People saw me and showed respect, even the elders, you know? {29:3} I was helping out the poor and the widows, spreading joy and righteousness. {29:4} I was like a superhero for the poor, dude. {29:5} After I spoke, they were just silent, soaking it all in. {29:6} I was the boss, man, leading the way and comforting those who were down.

{30:1-8} Bro, now the younger dudes are totally dissing me, man. Like, I wouldn't even let their dads hang with the dogs from my flock. They were so desperate they had to eat weeds and roots, dude. {30:9} Now they're making fun of me, using me as their punchline. {30:10} They straight-up hate me, man, not even holding back from spitting in my face. {30:11} They've just let loose, man, no boundaries anymore. {30:12-13} These young guns are getting bold, messing with me and trying to trip me up. {30:14} They hit me hard, like a flood, dude, just crashing over me. {30:15} Terrors are chasing me down, man, like I'm being pursued by a storm. {30:16-18} I'm totally drained, man, these afflictions got me. {30:19} I'm in the mud now, feeling as worthless as dust and ashes. {30:20} I'm calling out, but it's like no one's listening, man. {30:21} God's out here being harsh with me, like, seriously against me. {30:22} Bro, I was out here caring for others, and now I'm just getting hit with darkness. {30:23} I feel like I'm hanging with dragons and owls, man, like, total isolation. {30:24} My vibe's all messed up, man, my music's turned into mourning.

{31:1} I made a deal with myself, like, why even entertain thoughts about a girl, you know? {31:2} If I saw someone in need, man, I was there for them, always. {31:3} God's terror was real to me, man, like, I couldn't handle it. {31:4} I wasn't banking on gold, man, or putting my trust in riches. {31:5} I wasn't out here flexing because I had money, dude, that's not my vibe. {31:6} I wasn't getting hyped about the sun shining or the moon looking fresh. {31:7} If my homies were craving something, man, I'd make sure they got it.

{32:1} So, like, those three dudes finally stopped going back and forth with Job 'cause he thought he was all right in his own eyes. {32:2} And then this Elihu dude, son of Barachel the Buzite, got all fired up, man, against Job and his friends 'cause they were justifying themselves instead of God. {32:3} Like, just 'cause you're old doesn't mean you're always wise, you know? {32:4} So Elihu's like, "I'm stepping in, man, 'cause God's the one who's really in charge here."

{33:1} Yo, Job, listen up to what I gotta say, man, 'cause my words are coming straight from the heart. {33:2} If you got something to say, lay it out for me, bro, I'm ready to hear you out. {33:3} But, dude, if you're acting all innocent while God's calling you out, that's not cool, man. {33:4} Sometimes God's trying to get through to us, but we're just not getting it, you know? {33:5} He's like, "Look, man, sometimes I gotta let you go through tough times to set you straight." {33:6} If you're cool with God, man, he'll hook you up, make you feel fresh and young again. {33:7} So, like, God's always working things out for us, bringing us back from dark times into the light. {33:8} So, Job, just chill and listen to what I gotta say; I'm here to drop some wisdom on you.

{34:1} So Elihu was like, "Yo, listen up fam, I got some wisdom to drop." {34:2} He's like, "All you smart folks, lend me your ears, 'cause I'm dropping knowledge bombs." {34:3} He's saying, "Just like you taste food with your mouth, you gotta test out words with your ears." {34:4} Then he's like, "Let's be real and figure out what's good and what's not." {34:5} And he's calling out Job, saying, "Job's out here claiming he's all righteous, but he's saying God's unjust to him." {34:6} Job's like, "Why should I lie and say I'm in the wrong when I'm not?" {34:7} Elihu's throwing shade at Job, saying he's chugging down scorn like water. {34:8} He's like, "Job's rolling with the wrong crowd, hanging out with shady characters." {34:9} Job's even saying it's useless to be tight with God. {34:10} Elihu's dropping truth bombs, saying God ain't about that wicked life. {34:11} He's saying, "God's fair, and everyone gets what they deserve." {34:12} Basically, God ain't messing with injustice. {34:13} Elihu's asking who put Job in charge of the world. {34:14} He's saying if God wanted to, he could wipe us all out. {34:15} We're all gonna die and turn to dust eventually. {34:16} Elihu's like, "If you're smart, you'll listen to me." {34:17} He's questioning if it's cool for someone who's against what's right to be in charge. {34:18} Like, is it okay to call out a king as wicked or a prince as ungodly? {34:19} Elihu's saying God doesn't play favorites, rich or poor, we're all made by him. {34:20} He's saying people can bite it in an instant, and the powerful will fall without anyone laying a finger on them. {34:21} God sees everything we do, there's no hiding from him. {34:22} Even in the darkest places, God sees the shady stuff people do. {34:23} Elihu's saying God won't dish out more than we deserve. {34:24} He'll crush the mighty and put others in their place. {34:25} God knows what's up and he'll wreck those who deserve it. {34:26} He'll make an example out of the wicked for everyone to see. {34:27} Because they turned away from God and ignored his ways. {34:28} God hears the cries of the poor and afflicted. {34:29} When he brings peace, who can stir up trouble? And when he hides his face, who can see him? Whether it's a nation or an individual, no one can mess with God. {34:30} Elihu's saying, if hypocrites rule, it's gonna mess everyone up. {34:31} It's only right to admit when we're wrong and promise not to do it again. {34:32} Elihu's like, "Teach me if I'm messing up, I'll stop." {34:33} Whether we agree or not, God's gonna do what's fair. {34:34} He's like, "If you're smart, you'll listen to me." {34:35} Basically, Job's talking nonsense without knowing what's up. {34:36} Elihu's saying Job needs to be put to the test for backing up wicked folks. {34:37} Job's just adding rebellion to his sin, talking trash against God.

{35:1} Elihu keeps going, {35:2} asking Job if he really thinks he's more righteous than God. {35:3} He's like, "What's in it for you to be clean from sin?" {35:4} Elihu's ready to clap back at Job and his crew. {35:5} He's saying, "Look at the sky, it's way above you, man." {35:6} If you sin, what's that gonna do to God? {35:7} If you're righteous, what's God getting from you? {35:8} Your wickedness might hurt someone like you, but your goodness could help out a fellow human. {35:9} 'Cause of all the messed up stuff going on, people cry out, but no one's asking where God's at. {35:10} Nobody's recognizing God, who brings joy even in the dark times. {35:11} He's saying God teaches us more than animals and birds. {35:12} People cry out, but prideful jerks don't get an answer. {35:13} God ain't paying attention to empty words. {35:14} Even if you think you can't see him, he's all about justice. {35:15} But since people ain't seeing it, they're facing his anger without even realizing it. {35:16} That's why Job's just babbling on without knowing what he's talking about.

{36:1} Elihu's back at it again, {36:2} saying, "Just hold up a sec, I got more to say on God's behalf." {36:3} He's like, "I'm pulling wisdom from far and wide, gonna give props to my Creator." {36:4} He's swearing his words are legit, 'cause he's got mad knowledge. {36:5} Check it, God's hella mighty, not playing favorites, flexing both strength and smarts. {36:6} He's not saving the wicked, but he's looking out for the underdogs. {36:7} God's eyes are on the righteous, hooking them up, even with kings on their thrones, making them top dogs. {36:8} Even if they're in deep trouble, he'll show them their wrongs and tell them to straighten up. {36:9} He's giving them a reality check and telling them to quit their shady business. {36:10} If they listen up and serve him, they'll live the good life, but if they don't, they'll bite it. {36:11} But hypocrites just keep piling up the anger, not even crying out when they get busted. {36:12} They're gone before they even get old, living among the filth. {36:13} But God's looking out for the poor and oppressed, opening their eyes to what's up. {36:14} He would've hooked you up, Job, but you chose the path of the wicked, so now you're facing the consequences. {36:15} God's all about rescuing the downtrodden and shining a light on injustice. {36:16} He would've freed you from your troubles and set you up with the good stuff. {36:17} But you messed up, so watch out for his wrath 'cause no amount of cash can save you. {36:18} You think your riches matter to him? Nah, not even your bling can buy you out of trouble. {36:19} Don't wish for the night when people get wiped out, and don't choose evil over suffering. {36:20} God's the one with the power, teaching us all, unmatched by anyone. {36:21} Who's gonna question him? He's the boss. {36:22} Remember to give props to God, everyone can see his work. {36:23} He's way beyond us, and we can't even begin to understand his ways. {36:24} God's work is mind-blowing, and we're just seeing a glimpse of it. {36:25} He's way bigger than us, and his years are countless. {36:26} He controls even the tiniest drops of water, making it rain whenever he wants. {36:27} Rain or shine, it's all under his command. {36:28} Clouds drop rain all over the place, thanks to God. {36:29} Can anyone understand how clouds work, or the thunder that rolls through them?

{37:1} My mind's blown by all this, it's like my heart's doing backflips. {37:2} Listen up to the roar of God's voice, echoing all over the earth. {37:3} His voice reaches everywhere, and his lightning lights up the sky. {37:4} When he speaks, it's like thunder, and ain't nobody stopping him. {37:5} God's thunder is crazy, doing things we can't even wrap our heads around. {37:6} He tells the snow to fall, and controls all kinds of weather. {37:7} He shuts down everyone's plans so we can see his work. {37:8} Animals hunker down when storms come, staying in their spots. {37:9} Storms come from all directions, bringing cold and heat. {37:10} Frost comes from God's breath, freezing up the waters. {37:11} He waters the clouds, making them shine bright. {37:12} Everything obeys his orders, doing whatever he says. {37:13} He sends storms for correction, or to water the land, or just to show mercy. {37:14} So listen up, Job, and think about how awesome God's works are. {37:15} Do you know when God makes the clouds light up? {37:16} Do you understand how he balances the clouds, with all his perfect knowledge? {37:17} Ever noticed how warm your clothes are when the south wind blows? {37:18} Did you help God stretch out the sky, strong as metal? {37:19} We're clueless about what to say to him, 'cause it's too mind-blowing. {37:20} If anyone tried to talk to him, they'd get swallowed up. {37:21} People can't see the light in the clouds when the wind blows them away. {37:22} Good weather comes from the north, where God's got his majesty. {37:23} We can't figure out the Almighty, he's all about power, judgment, and justice. {37:24} People respect him 'cause he ain't impressed by anyone's smarts.

{38:1} So then, God's like, "Yo, Job, listen up!" {38:2} He's all, "Who do you think you are, spouting off all this stuff without knowing squat?" {38:3} "Man up, Job, 'cause I'm about to drop some truth bombs on you. Get ready to answer me." {38:4} "Where were you when I was laying down the foundations of the earth? Can you even comprehend?" {38:5} "Who measured it all out, huh? Who marked out the boundaries?" {38:6} "Do you know how it's all held together? Or who laid down that cornerstone?" {38:7} "And remember when the morning stars were singing and all the sons of God were cheering?" {38:8} "Or how about when I locked up the sea with doors and put clouds around it?" {38:9} "I made clouds its clothes and wrapped it in darkness like a baby." {38:10} "Then I set its boundaries and told it, 'This far you may come, but no farther; here is where your proud waves halt.'" {38:11} "Did you command the morning to come, or show the dawn its place?" {38:12} "So it could grab the earth by its edges and shake the wicked out of it?" {38:13} "The earth changes like clay under a seal; things shift around like clothes." {38:14} "The wicked are stripped of their light, and their raised arms are broken." {38:15} "Did you explore the springs of the sea or walk in the recesses of the deep?" {38:16} "Have the gates of death been shown to you? Have you seen the gates of the deepest darkness?" {38:17} "Do you know the paths to their dwellings?" {38:18} "Where does darkness reside? Where is its place?" {38:19} "Can you take it to its haunts and set it on its homeward path?" {38:20} "Do you know this because you were born then, or because the number of your days is so great?" {38:21} "Have you entered the storehouses of the snow or seen the storehouses of the hail?" {38:22} "Which I reserve for times of trouble, for days of war and battle?" {38:23} "By what way is the lightning distributed, or the east wind scattered over the earth?" {38:24} "Who cuts a channel for the torrents of rain, and a path for the thunderstorm?" {38:25} "To water a land where no one lives, an uninhabited desert," {38:26} "To satisfy a desolate wasteland and make it sprout with grass?" {38:27} "Does the rain have a father? Who fathers the drops of dew?" {38:28} "From whose womb comes the ice? Who gives birth to the frost from the heavens?" {38:29} "Who has the wisdom to count the clouds? Who can tip over the water jars of the heavens?" {38:30} "Do you hunt the prey for the lioness and satisfy the hunger of the lions?" {38:31} "Who provides food for the raven when its young cry out to God and wander about for lack of food?

{39:1} "Do you know the time when the mountain goats give birth? Or can you mark when the deer gives birth?" {39:2} "Can you count the months they are pregnant or know the time they give birth?" {39:3} "They crouch down and bring forth their young; their labor pains are over." {39:4} "Their young thrive and grow strong in the wilds; they leave and do not return." {39:5} "Who let the wild donkey go free? Who untied its ropes?" {39:6} "I gave it the wasteland as its home, the salt flats as its habitat." {39:7} "It laughs at the commotion in the town; it does not hear a driver's shout." {39:8} "It ranges the hills for its pasture and searches for any green thing." {39:9} "Will the wild ox consent to serve you? Will it stay by your manger at night?" {39:10} "Can you hold it to the furrow with a harness? Will it till the valleys behind you?" {39:11} "Will you rely on it for its great strength? Will you leave your heavy work to it?" {39:12} "Can you trust it to bring in your grain and gather it to your threshing floor?" {39:13} "The wings of the ostrich flap joyfully, though they cannot compare with the wings and feathers of the stork." {39:14} "She lays her eggs on the ground and lets them warm in the sand," {39:15} "Unmindful that a foot may crush them, that some wild animal may trample them." {39:16} "She treats her young harshly, as if they were not hers; she cares not that her labor was in vain," {39:17} "For God did not endow her with wisdom or give her a share of good sense." {39:18} "Yet when she spreads her feathers to run, she laughs at horse and rider." {39:19} "Do you give the horse its strength or clothe its neck with a flowing mane?" {39:20} "Do you make it leap like a locust, striking terror with its proud snorting?" {39:21} "It paws fiercely, rejoicing in its strength, and charges into the fray." {39:22} "It laughs at fear, afraid of nothing; it does not shy away from the sword." {39:23} "The quiver rattles against its side, along with the flashing spear and lance." {39:24} "In frenzied excitement, it eats up the ground; it cannot stand still when the trumpet sounds." {39:25} "At the blast of the trumpet, it snorts, 'Aha!' It catches the scent of battle from afar, the shout of commanders and the battle cry." {39:26} "Does the hawk take flight by your understanding and spread its wings toward the south?" {39:27} "Does the eagle soar at your command and build its nest on high?" {39:28} "It dwells on a cliff and stays there at night; a rocky crag is its stronghold." {39:29} "From there it looks for food; its eyes detect it from afar." {39:30} "Its young ones feast on blood, and where the slain are, there it is."

{40:1} So, God's like, "Yo, Job, let me drop some wisdom on you." {40:2} "Think you can challenge the Almighty? You got something to say, then say it!" {40:3} Job's like, "Okay, okay, I hear you." {40:4} "I'm, like, nothing compared to you. I'll just keep quiet." {40:5} "I spoke once, I won't say anything more. Twice, that's it, I'm done." {40:6} Then God's back, "Alright, Job, man up! Let's talk." {40:7} "You think you can question my judgment? You think you can judge me and be righteous?" {40:8} "Got an arm like mine? Can you roar like me?" {40:9} "Get yourself all decked out in majesty and glory, Job. Let's see what you got." {40:10} "Unleash your wrath on the proud and bring them down." {40:11} "Look at those who are full of themselves and humble them." {40:12} "Crush the wicked and hide them in the dirt." {40:13} "Then maybe I'll acknowledge that you can save yourself." {40:14} "Now check out Behemoth, this massive creature I made. He munches on grass like a boss." {40:15} "He's got power in his muscles and strength in his belly." {40:16} "His tail sways like a massive cedar tree, his bones are like iron bars." {40:17} "He's the king of God's creations, and he ain't afraid of nothing." {40:18} "He chills under shady trees, in reeds and swamps." {40:19} "Rivers are like drinks to him; he can gulp down the Jordan without a care." {40:20} "He's got eyes like lasers, and nothing can catch him off guard."

{41:1} "Now, can you catch Leviathan with a fishing rod? Can you tie him up with a rope?" {41:2} "Can you stick a hook in his nose or pierce his jaw with a spear?" {41:3} "Will he beg you for mercy? Will he speak to you with soft words?" {41:4} "Will he make a deal with you or become your lifelong servant?" {41:5} "Will you play with him like a pet or keep him on a leash for your girls?" {41:6} "Will your buddies throw a party with him or sell him off to merchants?" {41:7} "Can you pierce his skin with arrows or his head with harpoons?" {41:8} "Touch him once, and you'll remember the battle forever." {41:9} "Just looking at him is terrifying; who can stand up to me?"

{41:10} "No one is brave enough to mess with him; who's got the guts to stand before me?" {41:11} "Who can take from me and expect to be repaid? Everything under heaven is mine." {41:12} "I won't hide his powers or his impressive appearance." {41:13} "Who can strip off his outer coat or approach him with a bridle?" {41:14} "Who can open his jaws? His teeth are terrifying!" {41:15} "His scales are like shields, sealed up tight." {41:16} "They're so close together, not even a breath can pass between." {41:17} "They're joined together so tightly; they can't be pulled apart." {41:18} "When he sneezes, light flashes; his eyes are like the dawn." {41:19} "Fire shoots from his mouth; smoke pours from his nostrils." {41:20} "His breath sets coals on fire; flames blaze from his mouth." {41:21} "Strength resides in his neck; dismay goes before him." {41:22} "His flesh is firm and immovable; you can't budge him." {41:23} "His heart is hard as a stone; nothing can make him flinch." {41:24} "When he rises up, even the mightiest tremble; they retreat before his thrashing." {41:25} "Weapons shatter against him; spears and arrows are useless." {41:26} "Iron is nothing but straw to him, and bronze is like rotten wood." {41:27} "Arrows don't make him flee; slingstones are like bits of straw to him." {41:28} "Darts are like stubble to him; he laughs at the sound of a spear." {41:29} "Sharp objects are beneath him; he spreads sharp objects like mud." {41:30} "He churns the sea like a boiling pot; he makes the sea like a jar of ointment." {41:31} "He leaves a shining wake behind him; the sea seems white with foam." {41:32} "There's no creature on earth like him; he's fearless." {41:33} "He's king over all the proud." {41:34} "And that's Leviathan for you."

{42:1} Then Job's like, "Okay, I get it. You can do anything; no one can stop you." {42:2} "Who am I to question you? I've been talking nonsense, things way over my head." {42:3} "So, here I am, ready to listen and learn. I was just talking without knowing squat." {42:4} "I've heard about you, but now I see for myself." {42:5} "I take back everything I said; I'm sorry for doubting you." {42:6} "I'm totally humbled now, sitting here covered in dust and ashes." {42:7} So, after God talks to Job, he's like, "Yo, Eliphaz, you and your buddies messed up big time. You didn't speak the truth like Job did." {42:8} "Go offer sacrifices, and Job will pray for you. Otherwise, I might have to set you straight." {42:9} So, Eliphaz and the crew do what God says, and God accepts Job's prayer. {42:10} And then God blesses Job big time; he gets twice as much as before. {42:11} Everybody comes to support Job, and they bring him gifts and money. {42:12} Job becomes even wealthier, with tons of animals and kids. {42:13} He's got seven sons and three daughters, and they're all beautiful. {42:14} And they all live happily ever after, with Job seeing his descendants for four generations. {42:17} And Job dies, old and satisfied with life.

Psalms

{1:1} Yo, shout out to the homie who ain't vibin' with the shady crew, or chillin' with sinners, or hangin' with the haters. {1:2} Nah, this dude's all about that divine law grind, day and night, ya feel? {1:3} He's like a lit tree by the water, always fruitful and never dry, straight prosperin' in whatever he does. {1:4} But them shady folks? They're like chaff in the wind, blown away and forgotten. {1:5} They ain't gonna stand when the judgment goes down, or chill with the righteous crew. {1:6} 'Cause the Big Guy upstairs knows what's up with the righteous, but those shady types? They're gonna fade away, no doubt.

{2:1} Why the world gotta be so extra, trippin' and imagining stuff? {2:2} Leaders actin' all tough, schemin' against the Big Guy and his chosen, talkin' smack like, "Let's break free from their rules!" {2:3} But Big Guy just chillin' up there, laughin' at 'em, straight clownin'. {2:4} And when he's done laughin', he's gonna lay down some truth and shut 'em down real quick. {2:5} Don't mess with Big Guy, or he'll unleash his wrath and ruin your day, for real. {2:6} But check it, Big Guy's got his King holdin' it down on Zion, his holy turf. {2:7} Big Guy's like, "That's my Son, right there, born to rule." {2:8} Ask him for anything, and he's hookin' it up, givin' you the whole world as your playground. {2:9} He's gonna crush your enemies like it's nothin', shatter 'em like pottery. {2:10} So, yo, kings and rulers, wise up and show some respect, 'cause Big Guy's the real deal. {2:11} Serve Big Guy with some respect, and celebrate with a little fear and trembling. {2:12} Kiss up to his Son, 'cause you don't wanna tick him off even a little bit. Bless up to anyone who puts their trust in them.

{3:1} Big Guy, it's gettin' real out here, with all these haters comin' at me. {3:2} Everybody's talkin' trash, sayin', "No way Big Guy's gonna help him." {3:3} But you got my back, Big Guy, my shield and my glory, keepin' me strong. {3:4} I holler at you, and you hear me out, straight from your holy turf. {3:5} I lay down and crash, and when I wake up, it's all thanks to you, Big Guy. {3:6} Ain't scared of no mob, even if they're mobbin' on all sides. {3:7} Step up, Big Guy, save me from these haters, knock 'em down like dominoes. {3:8} Salvation's all you, Big Guy, blessin' your peeps like nobody else.

{4:1} Listen up, Big Guy, when I call out to you, the one who keeps it real when times get tough. {4:2} Yo, people, how long you gonna keep disrespectin' me, lovin' the drama and chasin' lies? {4:3} But peep this, Big Guy's got his squad, and he hears me when I call. {4:4} Keep it real, stay away from the dirt, think about your actions when you hit the hay. {4:5} Do right, trust in Big Guy, that's the move. {4:6} Some folks be askin', "Where's the good stuff at?" Big Guy, shine your light on us. {4:7} You bring more joy than cash flow and fine wine. {4:8} I'm chillin' in peace, sleepin' sound, 'cause you, Big Guy, keep me safe.

{5:1} Big Guy, listen up to what I'm sayin', peep my thoughts. {5:2} Hear me out when I call, my King, my main dude, 'cause I'm prayin' straight to you. {5:3} You'll catch me hollerin' at you in the mornin', Big Guy, my eyes on you. {5:4} You ain't about that wicked life, Big Guy, evil can't hang with you. {5:5} Fools ain't got no place with you, Big Guy, you can't stand those who do dirt. {5:6} You gonna wreck those liars, Big Guy, hate those who shed blood and talk smack. {5:7} But me? I'm all about your mercy, Big Guy, worshipin' you with respect in your holy crib. {5:8} Lead me down the right path, Big Guy, 'cause I got enemies lurkin' 'round every corner. {5:9} They talk big, but they're straight-up wicked, their words just coverin' up their foul hearts. {5:10} Crush 'em, Big Guy, let 'em fall flat on their faces 'cause they've crossed you. {5:11} But for those who trust in you, Big Guy, it's all joy and celebration, 'cause you got their back. {5:12} You gonna bless the righteous, Big Guy, surround 'em with your favor like a shield.

{6:1} Yo, God, don't be all mad at me, and don't go all crazy on me, okay? {6:2} I'm like, super weak here, God, please heal me 'cause I'm totally freaking out. {6:3} My soul is like, seriously stressed, God, how long is this gonna go on? {6:4} God, come on, save me, like, do it for your mercy's sake. {6:5} 'Cause, like, when you're dead, you can't even remember God, and in the grave, who's gonna thank you, right? {6:6} I'm, like, exhausted from crying all night, my bed's like a pool and my tears are soaking my sheets. {6:7} My eyes are wrecked from crying, I feel ancient 'cause of all my haters. {6:8} Get outta here, you jerks, God's heard me crying, okay? {6:9} God's heard my prayer, and he's gonna answer it. {6:10} All my enemies better get embarrassed and stressed out real quick.

{7:1} Yo, God, I'm putting all my trust in you, so, like, save me from all these people coming after me, okay? {7:2} Don't let them tear me apart like a lion, 'cause nobody else is gonna save me. {7:3} God, if I messed up, if I did anything wrong, {7:4} if I've hurt someone who was chill with me for no reason, yeah, I've done that, okay? {7:5} Let my enemies come at me, let them stomp me down and trash my rep. {7:6} God, get all fired up against my haters, show up and lay down some justice. {7:7} Then everyone will see you're in charge. {7:8} God's gonna judge people, and he'll judge me based on how I've kept it real. {7:9} Let the wickedness of the wicked end, but keep it real with the righteous, 'cause God knows what's up with people's hearts. {7:10} My protection comes from God, he's got my back 'cause I keep it real.

{8:1} Yo, God, your name is straight fire everywhere, you're like, totally ruling the heavens. {8:2} Even little kids know what's up 'cause you shut down haters and bullies. {8:3} When I check out the stars and stuff, I'm like, dang, God, you're so huge and we're so tiny. {8:4} Like, why do you even care about us? {8:5} But you've still given us mad respect and power. {8:6} You put everything under our feet, from animals to the whole ocean. {8:7} God, your name's seriously awesome, like, everywhere.

{9:1} Yo, I'm gonna shout you out big time, God, for all the amazing stuff you do. {9:2} I'm pumped to be on your team, God, I'm gonna sing your praises loud. {9:3} When my enemies try to mess with me, they're gonna fall flat in front of you. {9:4} 'Cause you're always on point with justice, sitting up there making things right. {9:5} You shut down the bad guys, wiping their names out forever. {9:6} Haters are gonna lose in the end, their evil plans are gonna flop. {9:7} But God's always gonna be here, ready to bring justice. {9:8} He's gonna set things straight for everyone. {9:9} God's a safe space for those who get pushed around, especially when times get tough. {9:10} People who know what's up are gonna trust in you, God, 'cause you never ditch your crew. {9:11} Sing about God, let everyone know what he's done. {9:12} When he checks out the scene, he's got our backs, he doesn't forget the little guy's cries. {9:13} Yo, God, have some mercy on me, check out my struggles with my enemies, you're the one who lifts me up from the edge of disaster. {9:14} So I can shout out your praises to everyone, celebrating your saves. {9:15} Haters are gonna fall into the traps they set for others, it's gonna backfire on them big time. {9:16} God's known for his justice, and the wicked are gonna get caught up in their own evil. {9:17} They're gonna end up in a bad place, along with anyone who forgets about God. {9:18} 'Cause the needy aren't gonna be ignored forever, and the poor aren't gonna get left hanging. {9:19} God, rise up and show everyone who's really in charge. {9:20} Scare 'em straight, God, so they remember they're just human.

{10:1} God, where you at when things get rough? {10:2} The jerks with all the power are trashing the little guys, let them get caught in their own schemes. {10:3} They brag about their evil plans and worship money, stuff that you can't stand. {10:4} They're so full of themselves, they don't even think about you. {10:5} They're always causing trouble, they don't care about your rules, and they just laugh at their enemies. {10:6} They think they're untouchable, like they'll never face any consequences. {10:7} They're all about cursing and lying, spreading hate and lies. {10:8} They lurk around, waiting to attack innocent people, targeting the poor. {10:9} They're like sneaky lions, waiting to pounce on the helpless. {10:10} They act all innocent, but it's just a front to take advantage of the weak. {10:11} They think you've forgotten about them, that you're never gonna call them out. {10:12} God, rise up and don't forget about the little guys. {10:13} Why do these jerks disrespect you? They act like you won't ever hold them accountable. {10:14} But you see everything, you'll pay them back for their evil, 'cause the poor trust in you, you're their lifeline. {10:15} Break the power of the wicked, search out their evil until there's none left. {10:16} God's gonna be in charge forever, and all those jerks are gonna be wiped out. {10:17} God, you've heard the cries of the oppressed, you're gonna get them ready, you're listening to their prayers. {10:18} So they can finally get justice, and the bullies won't be able to push them around anymore.

{11:1} Yo, I trust in the LORD: Why y'all telling me to dip like a bird to its crib? {11:2} Look, the baddies got their bows bent, arrows ready to snipe the good hearts on the low. {11:3} If the foundations get wrecked, what can the real ones do? {11:4} The LORD's chilling in his holy spot, his throne's in heaven: he sees everything, checking out everyone. {11:5} The LORD tests the real ones, but he can't stand the wicked and those who love violence. {11:6} For the wicked, he's gonna rain down traps, fire, and brimstone; that's what they're getting served. {11:7} The righteous LORD loves righteousness; his face shines on the upright.

{12:1} Help, LORD; the good ones are disappearing; the faithful are fading among the people. {12:2} They all talk trash to their neighbors, speaking fake flattery with double hearts. {12:3} The LORD's gonna shut up all those flattering lips and boastful tongues. {12:4} They say, "With our words we'll win; our lips are ours; who's the boss over us?" {12:5} Because of the oppression of the poor and the needy's cries, the LORD says, "Now I'll step in; I'll keep them safe from those who diss them." {12:6} The LORD's words are pure, like silver refined in a furnace, purified seven times. {12:7} You'll keep them safe, LORD, preserving them from this generation forever. {12:8} The wicked are everywhere when the worst people are on top.

{13:1} How long will you forget me, LORD? Forever? How long will you hide your face from me? {13:2} How long must I wrestle with my thoughts and daily sorrow in my heart? How long will my enemy win over me? {13:3} Look at me and answer, LORD my God. Light up my eyes, or I'll sleep the sleep of death; {13:4} Or my enemy will say, "I've beaten him," and my foes will celebrate when I stumble. {13:5} But I trust in your mercy; my heart rejoices in your salvation. {13:6} I'll sing to the LORD because he's been so good to me.

{14:1} The fool says in his heart, "There's no God." They're corrupt, doing vile deeds; no one does good. {14:2} The LORD looks down from heaven on all people to see if anyone understands and seeks God. {14:3} They've all turned away and become filthy; no one does good, not even one. {14:4} Do all these evil-doers have no sense? They eat up my people like bread and don't call on the LORD. {14:5} They're in great fear, for God is with the righteous. {14:6} You shame the plans of the poor, but the LORD is their refuge. {14:7} I wish salvation for Israel would come from Zion! When the LORD brings back his people, Jacob will rejoice, and Israel will be glad.

{15:1} LORD, who can chill in your tent? Who can vibe on your holy hill? {15:2} The one who lives blamelessly, does what's right, and speaks truth from the heart; {15:3} Who doesn't talk smack, doesn't do dirty to their neighbor, or throw shade; {15:4} Who despises the vile but honors those who fear the LORD; who keeps their word even when it hurts; {15:5} Who doesn't lend money for interest or take bribes against the innocent. Whoever does these things will never be shaken.

{16:1} Save me, God, 'cause I trust you. {16:2} My soul says, "LORD, you're my everything; my goodness doesn't reach you. {16:3} But it's for the saints on earth, the awesome ones I delight in. {16:4} Those chasing other gods will have more sorrows; I won't join their bloody offerings or speak their names. {16:5} The LORD is my inheritance and my cup; you got my back. {16:6} The lines have fallen for me in sweet spots; I've got a great heritage. {16:7} I bless the LORD for his advice; even at night, my heart instructs me. {16:8} I keep the LORD always before me; with him at my right hand, I won't be shaken. {16:9} My heart's happy, my glory rejoices; my body rests in hope. {16:10} You won't leave my soul in hell; you won't let your Holy One see decay. {16:11} You show me life's path; in your presence is fullness of joy; at your right hand are eternal pleasures.

{17:1} Listen, LORD, to what's right, pay attention to my cry, hear my prayer from honest lips. {17:2} Let my verdict come from you; see what's fair. {17:3} You've tested my heart, visited me at night, tried me, and found nothing; I decided my mouth won't sin. {17:4} By your words, I've avoided the paths of the destroyer. {17:5} Keep me steady on your paths, so my footsteps won't slip. {17:6} I call on you, God, 'cause you'll hear me; listen to my prayer. {17:7} Show your amazing love, you who save those who trust in you from their enemies. {17:8} Keep me as the apple of your eye, hide me under your wings. {17:9} Protect me from the wicked who oppress me, my deadly enemies surrounding me. {17:10} They're arrogant, speaking proudly with their mouths. {17:11} They've surrounded us, watching our every step, ready to pounce. {17:12} They're like lions hungry for prey, lurking in secret spots. {17:13} Arise, LORD, stop them, bring them down; save me from the wicked with your sword. {17:14} Save me from worldly men, who only have this life; their bellies are full of your treasure, they leave wealth to their kids. {17:15} But I'll see your face in righteousness; I'll be satisfied when I wake, seeing your likeness.

{18:1} I love you, LORD, my strength. {18:2} The LORD is my rock, fortress, and deliverer; my God, my strength, in whom I trust; my shield, and the horn of my salvation, my high tower. {18:3} I call on the LORD, worthy to be praised, and I'm saved from my enemies. {18:4} Death's sorrows surrounded me, floods of ungodly men scared me. {18:5} The grave's sorrows surrounded me, death's traps caught me. {18:6} In distress, I called the LORD, cried to my God; he heard me from his temple, my cry reached his ears. {18:7} Then the earth shook and quaked, the hills' foundations moved because he was angry. {18:8} Smoke rose from his nostrils, devouring fire from his mouth; coals blazed. {18:9} He parted the heavens and came down with darkness under his feet. {18:10} He rode a cherub, flying on the wings of the wind. {18:11} He made darkness his hiding place; dark waters and thick clouds surrounded him. {18:12} From his brightness, thick clouds passed with hailstones and fiery coals. {18:13} The LORD thundered from heaven, the Highest gave his voice with hailstones and fiery coals. {18:14} He sent out arrows, scattering them; he shot lightning and confused them. {18:15} The waters' channels appeared, the earth's foundations were exposed at your rebuke, LORD, at the blast of your breath. {18:16} He reached down from on high and took me, drawing me out of deep waters. {18:17} He rescued me from my powerful enemy, from those who hated me and were too strong for me. {18:18} They confronted me in my day of disaster, but the LORD was my support. {18:19} He brought me out into a spacious place; he rescued me because he delighted in me. {18:20} The LORD rewarded me for my righteousness; he repaid me for my clean hands. {18:21} I've kept the LORD's ways and haven't wickedly turned from my God. {18:22} All his laws are before me; I haven't turned away from his decrees. {18:23} I've been blameless before him and kept myself from sin. {18:24} The LORD repaid me for my righteousness, for my clean hands in his sight. {18:25} With the faithful, you show yourself faithful; with the blameless, you show yourself blameless. {18:26} With the pure, you show yourself pure; with the devious, you show yourself shrewd. {18:27} You save the humble but bring low those with haughty eyes. {18:28} You light my lamp, LORD; my God brightens my darkness. {18:29} With your help, I can advance against a troop; with my God, I can scale a wall. {18:30} God's way is perfect; the LORD's word is flawless; he shields all who take refuge in him. {18:31} For who is God besides the LORD? And who is the Rock except our God? {18:32} It's God who arms me with strength and keeps my way secure. {18:33} He makes my feet like a deer's and sets me on the heights. {18:34} He trains my hands for battle; my arms can bend a bow of bronze. {18:35} You make your saving help my shield, your right hand sustains me, your help has made me great. {18:36} You provide a broad path for my feet so my ankles don't give way. {18:37} I pursued my enemies and overtook them; I didn't turn back till they were destroyed. {18:38} I crushed them so they couldn't rise; they fell beneath my feet. {18:39} You armed me with strength for battle; you humbled my adversaries before me. {18:40} You made my enemies turn their backs in flight, and I destroyed my foes. {18:41} They cried for help, but no one saved them; to the LORD, but he didn't answer. {18:42} I beat them as fine as windblown dust; I trampled them like dirt in the streets. {18:43} You delivered me from the attacks of the people; you made me the head of nations. {18:44} People I didn't know serve me as soon as they hear me. {18:45} Foreigners cower before me; they lose heart and come trembling from their strongholds. {18:46} The LORD lives! Praise be to my Rock! Exalted be God my Savior! {18:47} He is the God who avenges me, who subdues nations under me. {18:48} He saves me from my enemies; you exalted me above my foes; from a violent man you rescued me. {18:49} Therefore I'll praise you, LORD, among the nations; I'll sing praises to your name. {18:50} He gives his king great victories; he shows unfailing love to his anointed, to David and his descendants forever.

{19:1} The heavens declare God's glory; the skies show his handiwork. {19:2} Day after day they pour forth speech; night after night they reveal knowledge. {19:3} They have no speech, they use no words; no sound is heard from them. {19:4} Yet their voice goes out into all the earth, their words to the ends of the world. In the heavens, God has pitched a tent for the sun. {19:5} It's like a bridegroom coming out of his chamber, like a champion rejoicing to run his course. {19:6} It rises at one end of the heavens and makes its circuit to the other; nothing is deprived of its warmth. {19:7} The law of the LORD is perfect, refreshing the soul; the statutes of the LORD are trustworthy, making wise the simple. {19:8} The precepts of the LORD are right, giving joy to the heart; the commands of the LORD are radiant, giving light to the eyes. {19:9} The fear of the LORD is pure, enduring forever; the decrees of the LORD are firm, and all of them are righteous. {19:10} They're more precious than gold, than much pure gold; they're sweeter than honey, than honey from the honeycomb. {19:11} By them your servant is warned; in keeping them there's great reward. {19:12} But who can discern their own errors? Forgive my hidden faults. {19:13} Keep your servant also from willful sins; may they not rule over me. Then I'll be blameless, innocent of great transgression. {19:14} May these words of my mouth and this meditation of my heart be pleasing in your sight, LORD, my Rock and my Redeemer.

{20:1} May the LORD answer you when you're in trouble; may the name of the God of Jacob protect you. {20:2} May he send you help from the sanctuary and grant you support from Zion. {20:3} May he remember all your sacrifices and accept your burnt offerings. {20:4} May he give you the desire of your heart and make all your plans succeed. {20:5} We'll shout for joy over your victory and lift up our banners in the name of our God. May the LORD grant all your requests. {20:6} Now I know that the LORD saves his anointed; he answers him from his heavenly sanctuary with the victorious power of his right hand. {20:7} Some trust in chariots and some in horses, but we trust in the name of the LORD our God. {20:8} They're brought to their knees and fall, but we rise up and stand firm. {20:9} LORD, give victory to the king! Answer us when we call.

{21:1} Yo, the king's gonna be hyped about your strength, God, and he's gonna be lit about your salvation, like, for real! {21:2} You hooked him up with everything he asked for, no holding back, straight up. {21:3} You're all about blessing him with the good stuff, even throwing a sick gold crown on his head. {21:4} He asked for a long life, and you were like, "Sure thing, forever and ever." {21:5} Your salvation's got him feeling himself, you've decked him out with honor and majesty. {21:6} You've made him the luckiest dude ever, he's smiling non-stop 'cause of your favor. {21:7} 'Cause the king's putting all his trust in you, God, and because of your mercy, he's standing firm. {21:8} Your enemies don't stand a chance, God's gonna find 'em all and take 'em down. {21:9} When God gets mad, it's like they're toast in a fiery oven, he's gonna wreck 'em with his wrath. {21:10} They won't even leave a legacy, God's wiping out their entire bloodline. {21:11} 'Cause they tried to pull some shady stuff against you, but they couldn't follow through. {21:12} So you're gonna make 'em turn tail when you bust out your arrows against 'em. {21:13} God, you're the real deal, and we're gonna sing and praise your power big time.

{22:1} My God, my God, why you gotta leave me hanging? Why you so distant when I need you? {22:2} I'm crying out to you all day long, but it's like you're not even listening, even in the dead of night. {22:3} But I know you're holy, God, you're all about soaking up the praise of your people. {22:4} Our ancestors trusted in you, and you came through for them every time. {22:5} They called out to you, and you rescued them, they put their trust in you and never got let down. {22:6} But here I am, feeling like nothing, just a joke to everyone, totally disrespected. {22:7} They're all laughing at me, making fun of me, talking trash about me. {22:8} They're saying, "If he trusts in God so much, why doesn't God come through for him?" {22:9} But you're the one who brought me into this world, you gave me hope from day one. {22:10} I've been counting on you since before I was even born, you've always been my God. {22:11} Don't bail on me now, trouble's closing in and I've got no one else to turn to. {22:12} It's like I'm surrounded by a bunch of raging bulls, they're closing in on me from all sides. {22:13} They're opening their mouths like hungry lions, ready to tear me apart. {22:14} I feel drained, like all my strength's gone, my heart's melting like wax inside me. {22:15} I'm dried up and parched, my tongue's sticking to the roof of my mouth, and I'm sinking into the ground. {22:16} 'Cause these dogs are closing in on me, a gang of wicked people's got me trapped, they're nailing me to the ground. {22:17} I can count all my bones, they're staring at me like vultures waiting to swoop in. {22:18} They're divvying up my clothes, casting lots for my stuff. {22:19} But don't leave me hanging, God, you're my strength, hurry up and help me out. {22:20} Save me from the sword, rescue me from these savage dogs. {22:21} Pull me out of the lion's den, 'cause you've heard my cries for help from way back. {22:22} I'll shout out your name to all my peeps, I'll sing your praises in front of everyone. {22:23} All you God-fearing folks, give him props, all you descendants of Jacob, give him glory, and show him respect, all you descendants of Israel. {22:24} 'Cause God hasn't ignored my suffering, he hasn't turned away from me when I needed him, he heard my cries for help. {22:25} I'll sing your praises loud and clear in front of everyone, I'll keep my promises to you in front of all those who respect you. {22:26} The humble will eat and be satisfied, they'll praise the LORD, and their hearts will live forever. {22:27} Everyone everywhere will remember and turn to the LORD, and all the nations will bow down before him. {22:28} 'Cause the LORD's in charge, he's the ruler of all nations. {22:29} Everyone on earth will worship him, even those who end up in the dust, 'cause no one can save themselves. {22:30} Future generations will serve him, and they'll be known as the LORD's people. {22:31} They'll come and tell everyone about the amazing things he's done.

{23:1} The LORD's like my personal hype man, I won't need anything else. {23:2} He's got me chilling in the best spots, leading me to the calmest waters. {23:3} He's got my back, guiding me along the right paths for his own rep. {23:4} Even if I'm walking through the scariest places, I won't be scared 'cause he's right there with me, comforting me with his strength and support. {23:5} He's setting up a feast for me right in front of my enemies, blessing me like crazy, overflowing my cup. {23:6} Goodness and mercy are gonna stick with me all my days, and I'm gonna kick it in God's house forever.

{24:1} The whole world belongs to the LORD and everyone living in it. {24:2} He's the one who set it all up, building it on top of the seas and the rivers. {24:3} Who gets to hang out with the LORD? Who gets to stand in his holy spot? {24:4} Only those with clean hands and pure hearts, who aren't into faking it or lying. {24:5} They'll get blessings from the LORD, and he'll hook 'em up with salvation. {24:6} This is the kind of people who really get God, who really go after him, Jacob's crew. {24:7} Open up, you ancient gates, let the King of glory in! {24:8} Who's this King of glory? The LORD, he's strong and fierce, he's the LORD, the undefeated warrior. {24:9} Open up, you ancient gates, let the King of glory in! {24:10} Who 's this King of glory? The LORD of angel armies, he's the King of glory!

{25:1} God, I'm lifting up everything I've got to you. {25:2} I'm all in, God, don't let me get embarrassed, don't let my enemies win. {25:3} Make sure those who trust in you don't end up ashamed, but let those who betray you get what's coming to 'em. {25:4} Teach me your ways, God, show me where to go. {25:5} Lead me down the right path, teach me what's real, 'cause you're the one who saves me, and I'm banking on you all day long. {25:6} Remember, LORD, all your love and kindness, 'cause you've been showing it since way back. {25:7} Don't hold my past against me, God, forgive me 'cause you're good. {25:8} You're the best, God, that's why you teach sinners how to do it right. {25:9} You show the humble what's up, leading them in your ways. {25:10} Your love and truth are for everyone who keeps your covenant and follows your rules. {25:11} God, forgive my huge mistakes, 'cause they're stacking up. {25:12} Anyone who respects the LORD gets the inside scoop, he shows 'em what's up. {25:13} They'll have it easy, chilling like they own the place, and their kids will inherit everything. {25:14} The LORD shares his secrets with those who respect him, he lets 'em in on his plans. {25:15} I've got my eyes on you, LORD, 'cause you're gonna pull me out of this mess. {25:16} Turn to me, show me some love 'cause I'm feeling alone and beat down. {25:17} My problems are huge, so get me out of this mess. {25:18} Look at how much I'm hurting, how much I'm suffering, and forgive all the wrong stuff I've done. {25:19} Check out my enemies, they're everywhere and they hate me like crazy. {25:20} Protect me, save me, don't let me down 'cause I'm trusting in you. {25:21} Keep me honest and true, 'cause I'm counting on you. {25:22} Save your people, God, from all their problems.

{26:1} Check me out, LORD; I've been straight-up real and I trust you, so I won't slip. {26:2} Test me, LORD, and check my heart and mind. {26:3} Your kindness is always in front of me, and I've lived in your truth. {26:4} I don't hang with fake people, and I avoid hypocrites. {26:5} I can't stand evildoers and won't chill with the wicked. {26:6} I'll keep my hands clean and stay around your altar, LORD, {26:7} to shout thanks and talk about your amazing works. {26:8} LORD, I love your house, the place where your glory stays. {26:9} Don't count me with sinners or my life with murderers, {26:10} whose hands are full of mischief and bribes. {26:11} But I'll keep it real; save me and be kind to me. {26:12} I'm standing strong; in the gatherings, I'll praise the LORD.

{27:1} The LORD is my light and savior; who should I fear? The LORD is my strength; who's gonna scare me? {27:2} When the wicked came at me, they stumbled and fell. {27:3} Even if an army surrounds me, my heart won't fear; if war breaks out, I'll stay confident. {27:4} One thing I want from the LORD: to live in his house all my life, to see his beauty and seek him in his temple. {27:5} In tough times, he'll hide me in his shelter and set me high on a rock. {27:6} Now my head is higher than my enemies around me, and I'll offer joyful sacrifices and sing praises to the LORD. {27:7} Listen, LORD, when I cry out; be kind and answer me. {27:8} You said, "Seek my face," and my heart says, "I'll seek your face, LORD." {27:9} Don't hide from me or turn away in anger; you've been my help. Don't leave or abandon me, God of my salvation. {27:10} Even if my parents abandon me, the LORD will take me in. {27:11} Teach me your way, LORD, and lead me on a smooth path because of my enemies. {27:12} Don't hand me over to my enemies; false witnesses are attacking me, people who breathe out violence. {27:13} I would've lost hope if I didn't believe I'd see the LORD's goodness in the land of the living. {27:14} Wait for the LORD; be strong and take heart, and wait for the LORD

{28:1} I cry to you, LORD, my rock; don't be silent, or I'll be like those who go down to the pit. {28:2} Hear my pleas when I cry out, lifting my hands toward your holy place. {28:3} Don't drag me away with the wicked, who speak peace to their neighbors but have evil in their hearts. {28:4} Give them what they deserve for their actions, their wicked deeds; repay them according to what they've done. {28:5} Because they ignore the LORD's works and his actions, he'll tear them down and not rebuild them. {28:6} Praise the LORD, for he has heard my cries for mercy. {28:7} The LORD is my strength and shield; my heart trusts him, and he helps me. My heart leaps for joy, and I'll thank him with my song. {28:8} The LORD is the strength of his people, a fortress of salvation for his anointed one. {28:9} Save your people and bless your inheritance; shepherd them and carry them forever.

{29:1} Give the LORD glory and strength, you mighty ones. {29:2} Give the LORD the glory due his name; worship him in the beauty of holiness. {29:3} The LORD's voice is over the waters; the God of glory thunders, the LORD over many waters. {29:4} The LORD's voice is powerful and majestic. {29:5} The LORD's voice breaks the cedars; he shatters the cedars of Lebanon. {29:6} He makes Lebanon skip like a calf and Sirion like a young wild ox. {29:7} The LORD's voice strikes with flashes of lightning. {29:8} The LORD's voice shakes the desert; he shakes the wilderness of Kadesh. {29:9} The LORD's voice twists the oaks and strips the forests bare. In his temple, everyone cries, "Glory!" {29:10} The LORD sits enthroned over the flood; the LORD is king forever. {29:11} The LORD gives strength to his people; the LORD blesses them with peace.

{30:1} I'll exalt you, LORD, for you lifted me up and didn't let my enemies rejoice over me. {30:2} LORD my God, I cried to you for help, and you healed me. {30:3} LORD, you brought me up from the grave and kept me alive so I wouldn't go down to the pit. {30:4}

Sing to the LORD, you saints, and praise his holy name. {30:5} His anger lasts only a moment, but his favor lasts a lifetime; weeping may stay for the night, but joy comes in the morning. {30:6} When I felt secure, I said, "I won't ever be shaken." {30:7} LORD, when you favored me, you made my mountain stand firm; but when you hid your face, I was dismayed. {30:8} I called to you, LORD; I begged for mercy. {30:9} What gain is there in my destruction, in me going down to the pit? Will the dust praise you? Will it proclaim your faithfulness? {30:10} Hear, LORD, and be merciful to me; LORD, be my help. {30:11} You turned my wailing into dancing; you removed my sackcloth and clothed me with joy, {30:12} so my heart can sing your praises and not be silent. LORD my God, I'll praise you forever.

{31:1} Yo, God, I'm trusting you all the way, so don't let me down, keep me from getting embarrassed. Come through for me 'cause you're righteous. {31:2} Listen up, God, hook me up quick, be my solid rock, my fortress where I can chill and feel safe. {31:3} You're my ride-or-die, God, lead me for your own rep's sake. {31:4} Rescue me from the traps these haters set, 'cause you're my strength. {31:5} I'm putting my life in your hands, God, you've saved me, you're the real deal. {31:6} I can't stand fake people and their lies, but I'm all about trusting in you, God. {31:7} I'm gonna party hard in your mercy 'cause you've peeped my struggles and known my pain. {31:8} You didn't let my enemies win, you gave me room to breathe. {31:9} Show me some love, God, I'm struggling here, feeling drained and down. {31:10} My life's been a rollercoaster of grief and pain, my strength's fading 'cause of my mistakes. {31:11} I've been dissed by my enemies, especially by my neighbors, and even my friends are scared to chill with me. {31:12} I'm like a ghost, forgotten and broken, like a wrecked car on the side of the road. {31:13} Haters been talking smack and plotting against me, trying to take me out. {31:14} But I put all my trust in you, God, you're my ride-or-die. {31:15} My fate's in your hands, God, save me from these haters and the drama they bring. {31:16} Shine your light on me, God, save me 'cause you're all about mercy. {31:17} Don't let me down, God, 'cause I've called out to you. Let the haters get what's coming to them, let 'em fade away into nothing. {31:18} Shut down the liars and their trash talk against the real ones. {31:19} Your goodness is off the charts for those who respect you, showing off for those who trust in you. {31:20} Keep us safe in your chill zone away from all the drama and gossip. {31:21} Praise the LORD, 'cause he's come through for me big time, even in tough times. {31:22} Sometimes I felt like you were ignoring me, but you still heard me out when I cried to you. {31:23} All you peeps who love God, show him some love, 'cause he's got your back and he's gonna deal with the fakers. {31:24} Stay strong, keep the faith, and God will give you the strength you need.

{32:1} If you've been forgiven, you're blessed, man, 'cause your sins are covered. {32:2} Blessed is the one who's not carrying that guilt around, who's keeping it real. {32:3} When I kept quiet about my mess, it was eating me up inside. {32:4} Day and night, I felt the weight of it all, like I was dried up and thirsty. Pause and think about that. {32:5} But when I owned up to my mistakes and came clean with you, God, you forgave me. Pause and think about that. {32:6} That's why every real one turns to you when they're in trouble, 'cause even in the worst storms, you keep 'em safe. {32:7} You're like a safe space for me, God, keeping me out of trouble and surrounding me with your jams of deliverance. Pause and think about that. {32:8} I'm gonna teach you, show you the way to go, keeping my eye on you the whole time. {32:9} Don't be dumb like a horse or a mule, not getting it, needing a bit and bridle to stay on track. {32:10} Wicked people are gonna have it rough, but those who trust in God, they're gonna be swimming in mercy. {32:11} So, happy vibes in the LORD, all you righteous peeps, shout it out, all you with pure hearts.

{33:1} Get hyped, you righteous ones, 'cause praising the LORD is the way to go. {33:2} Jam out to the LORD with your tunes, sing to him with your strings and beats. {33:3} Drop a fresh track for him, play it skillfully, crank up the volume. {33:4} 'Cause the LORD's word is solid, and everything he does is legit. {33:5} He's all about fairness and justice, and the earth's full of his goodness. {33:6} He spoke, and boom, the heavens were made, and everything in 'em came from his breath. {33:7} He scooped up the sea like it was nothing, storing it up like treasure. {33:8} Everybody should respect the LORD, stand in awe of him, 'cause when he speaks, it happens. {33:9} He's got his eye on those who respect him, those who trust in his mercy. {33:10} He's got their back, saving them from death and keeping 'em alive when things get rough. {33:11} We're banking on the LORD, 'cause he's our help and our shield. {33:12} Our hearts are gonna be pumped 'cause we trust in him, knowing he's got our backs. {33:13} So, LORD, show us your love, 'cause we're hoping in you. {33:14} Give us your mercy, LORD, like we're counting on you to do. {33:15} Pause and think about how I'm always singing your praises and talking about how legit you are. {33:16} Let's get it, LORD, stand up for what's right, rescue my soul from those lions. {33:17} I'll be giving you props in front of everyone, praising you like crazy. {33:18} Don't let my haters get the last laugh, don't let 'em win. {33:19} They don't want peace, they're all about stirring up trouble for the chill peeps. {33:20} They're talking smack, thinking they've got it all figured out, but you've seen it all, LORD, don't stay silent. {33:21} So, step up, LORD, judge my case, you're my God and my Lord. {33:22} Bring on the verdict, LORD, and don't let my enemies celebrate over me. {33:23} Don't let 'em say, "We got him!" Let 'em know you got my back. {33:24} Let 'em be ashamed and embarrassed, those who enjoy seeing me suffer. {33:25} Let my tongue never stop praising you, LORD, all day, every day. Pause and think about that.

{34:1} I'm giving the LORD props all day, every day, his praise is always on my lips. {34:2} My soul's all about boasting in the LORD, and when the humble peeps hear about it, they'll be stoked. {34:3} Come on, let's make a big deal about the LORD, let's lift his name up together. {34:4} I reached out to the LORD, and he came through for me, taking away all my fears. {34:5} Those who look to him are gonna shine, their faces won't be covered in shame. {34:6} I was struggling, but the LORD heard me out and saved me from all my problems. {34:7} The LORD's angels got my back, surrounding me and keeping me safe. {34:8} Check it out, taste and see that the LORD's legit, blessed is the one who trusts in him. {34:9} So, respect the LORD, all you who belong to him, 'cause if you do, you won't be left wanting. {34:10} Even strong lions go hungry, but those who look to the LORD won't miss out on anything good. {34:11} Listen up, kids, I'm gonna teach you how to respect the LORD. {34:12} Want a good life with plenty of days? Keep your tongue in check and stay away from evil. {34:13} Turn away from evil, do good, and go after peace like it's your job. {34:14} The LORD's got his eye on the righteous, and he listens to their prayers. {34:15} But he's not feeling the evil ones, he's cutting them off from the earth. {34:16} When the righteous cry out, the LORD hears them and saves them from all their troubles. {34:17} The LORD's close to those with a broken heart, saving those who are crushed in spirit. {34:18} Yeah, the righteous go through some tough times, but the LORD's there to rescue them every time. {34:19} He's keeping all their bones intact, not a single one gets broken. {34:20} Evil's gonna take out the wicked, and those who hate the righteous will end up empty-handed. {34:21} But the LORD's redeeming the souls of his peeps, and none of those who trust in him will end up empty-handed.

{35:1} Step up, LORD, and fight for me against my enemies, take up your shield and defend me. {35:2} Grab your weapons, LORD, and stand up for me, tell my soul, "I got you." {35:3} Let my enemies be embarrassed and put to shame, those who want to see me fail. {35:4} Let them be blown away like chaff in the wind, let your angels chase them down. {35:5} Let their path be dark and slippery, let your angels give 'em a hard time. {35:6} They set traps for me for no reason, digging pits to trip me up. {35:7} Let them fall into their own traps and be destroyed by their own schemes. {35:8} And I'll be partying in the LORD's victory, celebrating his salvation. {35:9} All my bones are gonna shout, "LORD, you're the real MVP, saving the weak from the strong, the poor and needy from those who would exploit them." {35:10} Haters tried to throw shade on me, accusing me of stuff I didn't do. {35:11} They paid me back with evil for the good I did for them. {35:12} But when they were in trouble, I was there for them, mourning and fasting for them. {35:13} I treated them like family, but they celebrated when I was down and out, even when I didn't know it. {35:14} They talked trash about me, mocked me at their parties, gnashing their teeth in hatred. {35:15} LORD, how long you gonna watch this? Save my soul from their attacks, my precious life from these lions. {35:16} I'm gonna thank you in front of everyone, praising you in the big crowd. {35:17} Don't let my enemies celebrate over me for no reason, and don't let them wink at each other in secret hate. {35:18} They're not about peace, they're all about stirring up trouble for the chill folks. {35:19} They're talking smack, saying, "We got him!" but you've seen it all, LORD, don't stay silent. {35:20} So, stand up, LORD, and fight for me, you're my God and my Lord. {35:21} Bring on the verdict, LORD, and don't let my enemies celebrate over me. {35:22} Don't let them say, "We got him!" Let 'em know you got my back. {35:23} So, get up and take action, LORD, stand up for me, my God and my Lord. {35:24} Judge me, LORD my God, according to your righteousness, and don't let them celebrate over me. {35:25} Don't let them say, "We got him!" Don't let them rejoice in my downfall. {35:26} Let them be embarrassed and ashamed, those who enjoy seeing me suffer. {35:27} But let those who support my cause shout for joy and be glad, saying, "The LORD is great, he's all about his servant's success." {35:28} And I'll be singing about your righteousness and praising you all day long. Pause and think about that.}

{36:1} The wicked's sin whispers in my heart, "There's no fear of God in their eyes." {36:2} They hype themselves up until their badness is exposed. {36:3} Their words are lies and deceit; they've ditched wisdom and doing good. {36:4} They plot mischief in bed, setting themselves on a sketchy path and not rejecting evil. {36:5} Your mercy, LORD, reaches the skies, and your faithfulness touches the clouds. {36:6} Your righteousness is like huge mountains; your judgments are deep like the ocean. LORD, you save both people and animals. {36:7} Your lovingkindness is epic, God! So, humans trust in the shade of your wings. {36:8} They're fully satisfied with your house's richness and drink from your river of delights. {36:9} With you is the fountain of life; in your light, we see light. {36:10} Keep your lovingkindness going for those who know you, and your righteousness for the upright-hearted. {36:11} Don't let pride stomp on me, and don't let the wicked push me around. {36:12} The workers of evil have fallen; they're knocked down and can't get up.

{37:1} Don't trip over evildoers or be jealous of those who do wrong. {37:2} They'll be cut down like grass and wither like green plants. {37:3} Trust in the LORD and do good; you'll live in the land and be safe. {37:4} Take joy in the LORD, and he'll give you your heart's desires. {37:5} Commit your path to the LORD, trust him, and he'll make it happen. {37:6} He'll make your righteousness shine like the dawn, and your justice like the noonday sun. {37:7} Chill in the LORD and wait for him; don't stress over those who succeed in their wicked plans. {37:8} Stop being angry and drop the rage; don't stress, it only leads to evil. {37:9} Evildoers will be cut off, but those who hope in the LORD will inherit the land. {37:10} In a bit, the wicked will be no more; you'll look for them and they'll be gone. {37:11} But the meek will inherit the land and enjoy great peace. {37:12} The wicked plot against the righteous and gnash their teeth at them. {37:13} But the Lord laughs at the wicked, for he knows their day is coming. {37:14} The wicked draw swords and bend bows to bring down the poor and needy and to kill those who live upright lives. {37:15} But their swords will pierce their own hearts, and their bows will be broken. {37:16} Better the little the righteous have than the wealth of many wicked. {37:17} For the power of the wicked will be broken, but the LORD supports the righteous. {37:18} The LORD knows the days of the blameless, and their inheritance will last forever. {37:19} They won't be ashamed in times of trouble; in days of famine, they'll have plenty. {37:20} But the wicked will perish; the LORD's enemies will be like the beauty of the fields, they will vanish—vanish like smoke. {37:21} The wicked borrow and do not repay, but the righteous give generously. {37:22} Those the LORD blesses will inherit the land, but those he curses will be cut off. {37:23} The LORD makes firm the steps of the one who delights in him. {37:24} Though they stumble, they will not fall, for the LORD upholds them with his hand. {37:25} I was young and now I'm old, yet I have never seen the righteous forsaken or their children begging bread. {37:26} They are always generous and lend freely; their children will be a blessing. {37:27} Turn from evil and do good; then you will dwell in the land forever. {37:28} For the LORD loves the just and will not forsake his faithful ones. Wrongdoers will be completely destroyed; the offspring of the wicked will perish. {37:29} The righteous will inherit the land and dwell in it forever. {37:30} The mouths of the righteous utter wisdom, and their tongues speak what is just. {37:31} The law of their God is in their hearts; their feet do not slip. {37:32} The wicked lie in wait for the righteous, intent on putting them to death. {37:33} But the LORD will not leave them in the power of the wicked or let them be condemned when brought to trial. {37:34} Hope in the LORD and keep his way. He will exalt you to inherit the land; when the wicked are destroyed, you will see it. {37:35} I have seen a wicked and ruthless man flourishing like a luxuriant native tree, {37:36} but he soon passed away and was no more; though I looked for him, he could not be found. {37:37} Consider the blameless, observe the upright; a future awaits those who seek peace. {37:38} But all sinners will be destroyed; there will be no future for the wicked. {37:39} The salvation of the righteous comes from the LORD; he is their stronghold in time of trouble. {37:40} The LORD helps them and delivers them; he delivers them from the wicked and saves them, because they take refuge in him.

{38:1} LORD, don't rebuke me in your anger or discipline me in your wrath. {38:2} Your arrows have pierced me, and your hand has come down on me. {38:3} Because of your wrath there is no health in my body; there is no soundness in my bones because of my sin. {38:4} My guilt has overwhelmed me like a burden too heavy to bear. {38:5} My wounds fester and are loathsome because of my sinful folly. {38:6} I am bowed down and brought very low; all day long I go about mourning. {38:7} My back is filled with searing pain; there is no health in my body. {38:8} I am feeble and utterly crushed; I groan in anguish of heart. {38:9} All my longings lie open before you, Lord; my sighing is not hidden from you. {38:10} My heart pounds, my strength fails me; even the light has gone from my eyes. {38:11} My friends and companions avoid me because of my wounds; my neighbors stay far away. {38:12} Those who want to kill me set their traps, those who would harm me talk of my ruin; all day long they scheme and lie. {38:13} I am like the deaf, who cannot hear, like the mute, who cannot speak; {38:14} I have become like one who does not hear, whose mouth can offer no reply. {38:15} LORD, I wait for you; you will answer, Lord my God. {38:16} For I said, "Do not let them gloat or exalt themselves over me when my feet slip." {38:17} For I am about to fall, and my pain is ever with me. {38:18} I confess my iniquity; I am troubled by my sin. {38:19} Many have become my enemies without cause; those who hate me without reason are numerous. {38:20} Those who repay my good with evil lodge accusations against me, though I seek only to do what is good. {38:21} LORD, do not forsake me; do not be far from me, my God. {38:22} Come quickly to help me, my Lord and my Savior.

{39:1} I said, "I will watch my ways and keep my tongue from sin; I will put a muzzle on my mouth while in the presence of the wicked." {39:2} So I remained utterly silent, not even saying anything good. But my anguish increased; {39:3} my heart grew hot within me. While I meditated, the fire burned; then I spoke with my tongue: {39:4} "Show me, LORD, my life's end and the number of my days; let me know how fleeting my life is. {39:5} You have made my days a mere handbreadth; the span of my years is as nothing before you. Everyone is but a breath, even those who seem secure. Selah. {39:6} Surely everyone goes around like a mere phantom; in vain they rush about, heaping up wealth without knowing whose it will finally be. {39:7} But now, Lord, what do I look for? My hope is in you. {39:8} Save me from all my transgressions; do not make me the scorn of fools. {39:9} I was silent; I would not open my mouth, for you are the one who has done this. {39:10} Remove your scourge from me; I am overcome by the blow of your hand. {39:11} When you rebuke and discipline anyone for their sin, you consume their wealth like a moth—surely everyone is but a breath. Selah. {39:12} Hear my prayer, LORD, listen to my cry for help; do not be deaf to my weeping. I dwell with you as a foreigner, a stranger, as all my ancestors were. {39:13} Look away from me, that I may enjoy life again before I depart and am no more."

{40:1} I waited patiently for the LORD; he turned to me and heard my cry. {40:2} He lifted me out of the slimy pit, out of the mud and mire; he set my feet on a rock and gave me a firm place to stand. {40:3} He put a new song in my mouth, a hymn of praise to our God. Many will see and fear the LORD and put their trust in him. {40:4} Blessed is the one who trusts in the LORD, who does not look to the proud, to those who turn aside to false gods. {40:5} Many, LORD my God, are the wonders you have done, the things you planned for us. None can compare with you; were I to speak and tell of your deeds, they would be too many to declare. {40:6} Sacrifice and offering you did not desire—but my ears you have opened—burnt offerings and sin offerings you did not require. {40:7} Then I said, "Here I am, I have come—it is written about me in the scroll. {40:8} I desire to do your will, my God; your law is within my heart." {40:9} I proclaim your saving acts in the great assembly; I do not seal my lips, LORD, as you know. {40:10} I do not hide your righteousness in my heart; I speak of your faithfulness and your saving help. I do not conceal your love and your faithfulness from the great assembly. {40:11} Do not withhold your mercy from me, LORD; may your love and faithfulness always protect me. {40:12} For troubles without number surround me; my sins have overtaken me, and I cannot see. They are more than the hairs of my head, and my heart fails within me. {40:13} Be pleased to save me, LORD; come quickly, LORD, to help me. {40:14} May all who want to take my life be put to shame and confusion; may all who desire my ruin be turned back in disgrace. {40:15} May those who say to me, "Aha! Aha!" be appalled at their own shame. {40:16} But may all who seek you rejoice and be glad in you; may those who long for your saving help always say, "The LORD is great!" {40:17} But as for me, I am poor and needy; may the Lord think of me. You are my help and my deliverer; you are my God, do not delay.

{41:1} Blessed is the one who looks out for the poor; the LORD's got their back in tough times. {41:2} The LORD will keep them safe and alive, and they'll be blessed on earth; He won't let their enemies win. {41:3} The LORD will help them when they're sick, making them feel better. {41:4} I said, "LORD, have mercy on me; heal my soul, for I've sinned against you." {41:5} My enemies talk trash about me, saying, "When will he die and be forgotten?" {41:6} Even when they visit me, they speak nonsense and gather bad thoughts, then spread them around. {41:7} All who hate me whisper together, plotting against me. {41:8} They say, "A wicked disease clings to him;

now that he's down, he won't get up." {41:9} Even my close friend, whom I trusted and shared bread with, has turned against me. {41:10} But you, LORD, be merciful and lift me up so I can repay them. {41:11} I know you're on my side because my enemy doesn't triumph over me. {41:12} You uphold me in my integrity and set me before you forever. {41:13} Blessed be the LORD God of Israel from everlasting to everlasting. Amen and Amen.

{42:1} Just like a deer thirsts for water, my soul thirsts for you, God. {42:2} My soul craves God, the living God; when can I come and be with Him? {42:3} My tears have been my food day and night, while people constantly ask, "Where is your God?" {42:4} I remember these things and pour out my soul because I used to go with the crowd to the house of God with joy and praise. {42:5} Why are you down, my soul? Why so disturbed? Hope in God, for I will praise Him for His help. {42:6} My soul is downcast, so I remember you from the land of Jordan, the heights of Hermon, from Mount Mizar. {42:7} Deep calls to deep in the roar of your waterfalls; all your waves and breakers have swept over me. {42:8} By day the LORD directs His love, at night His song is with me—a prayer to the God of my life. {42:9} I say to God my Rock, "Why have you forgotten me? Why must I go about mourning, oppressed by the enemy?" {42:10} My enemies taunt me, saying daily, "Where is your God?" {42:11} Why are you downcast, my soul? Why so disturbed within me? Hope in God, for I will yet praise Him, my Savior and my God.

{43:1} Vindicate me, God, and defend my cause against an ungodly nation; rescue me from deceitful and unjust people. {43:2} You are God my strength, so why have you rejected me? Why must I go about mourning, oppressed by the enemy? {43:3} Send out your light and truth; let them lead me to your holy mountain, to your dwelling place. {43:4} Then I will go to the altar of God, my joy and delight; I will praise you with the harp, God, my God. {43:5} Why are you downcast, my soul? Why so disturbed within me? Hope in God, for I will yet praise Him, my Savior and my God.

{44:1} We've heard it with our own ears, God; our ancestors told us what you did in their days, long ago. {44:2} You drove out the nations with your hand and planted our ancestors; you crushed the peoples and made our ancestors flourish. {44:3} They didn't win the land by their own sword, nor did their own arm save them; it was your right hand, your arm, and the light of your face, for you loved them. {44:4} You are my King and my God, who decrees victories for Jacob. {44:5} Through you, we push back our enemies; through your name, we trample foes. {44:6} I don't trust in my bow; my sword doesn't bring me victory. {44:7} But you give us victory over our enemies and put our adversaries to shame. {44:8} In God, we make our boast all day long, and we will praise your name forever. Selah. {44:9} But now, you have rejected and humbled us; you no longer go out with our armies. {44:10} You made us retreat before the enemy, and our adversaries have plundered us. {44:11} You gave us up to be devoured like sheep and scattered us among the nations. {44:12} You sold your people for a pittance, gaining nothing from their sale. {44:13} You have made us a reproach to our neighbors, the scorn and derision of those around us. {44:14} You have made us a byword among the nations; the people shake their heads at us. {44:15} I live in disgrace all day long, and my face is covered with shame. {44:16} At the taunts of those who reproach and revile me, because of the enemy, who is bent on revenge. {44:17} All this happened to us, though we had not forgotten you or been false to your covenant. {44:18} Our hearts had not turned back; our feet had not strayed from your path. {44:19} But you crushed us and made us a haunt for jackals; you covered us over with deep darkness. {44:20} If we had forgotten the name of our God or spread out our hands to a foreign god, {44:21} would not God have discovered it, since he knows the secrets of the heart? {44:22} Yet for your sake, we face death all day long; we are considered as sheep to be slaughtered. {44:23} Awake, Lord! Why do you sleep? Rouse yourself! Do not reject us forever. {44:24} Why do you hide your face and forget our misery and oppression? {44:25} We are brought down to the dust; our bodies cling to the ground. {44:26} Rise up and help us; redeem us because of your unfailing love.

{45:1} My heart is stirred by a noble theme as I recite my verses for the king; my tongue is the pen of a skillful writer. {45:2} You are the most excellent of men, and your lips have been anointed with grace since God has blessed you forever. {45:3} Gird your sword on your side, you mighty one; clothe yourself with splendor and majesty. {45:4} In your majesty ride forth victoriously in the cause of truth, humility, and justice; let your right hand achieve awesome deeds. {45:5} Let your sharp arrows pierce the hearts of the king's enemies; let the nations fall beneath your feet. {45:6} Your throne, O God, will last forever and ever; a scepter of justice will be the scepter of your kingdom. {45:7} You love righteousness and hate wickedness; therefore God, your God, has set you above your companions by anointing you with the oil of joy. {45:8} All your robes are fragrant with myrrh and aloes and cassia; from palaces adorned with ivory, the music of the strings makes you glad. {45:9} Daughters of kings are among your honored women; at your right hand is the royal bride in gold of Ophir. {45:10} Listen, daughter, and pay careful attention: Forget your people and your father's house. {45:11} Let the king be enthralled by your beauty; honor him, for he is your lord. {45:12} The city of Tyre will come with a gift; people of wealth will seek your favor. {45:13} All glorious is the princess within her chamber; her gown is interwoven with gold. {45:14} In embroidered garments, she is led to the king; her virgin companions follow her—those brought to be with her. {45:15} Led in with joy and gladness, they enter the palace of the king. {45:16} Your sons will take the place of your fathers; you will make them princes throughout the land. {45:17} I will perpetuate your memory through all generations; therefore, the nations will praise you forever and ever.

{46:1} God's like our ultimate safe space and strength, always there to help us out when things get rough. {46:2} So, like, we're not gonna trip, even if everything around us goes cray cray, like if the whole earth starts shaking and mountains are thrown into the ocean. {46:3} Even if the seas get all wild and the mountains start shaking, we're still gonna keep it cool. Pause and let that sink in.

{46:4} There's this dope river flowing through God's city, making everyone chill and happy, especially in the holy spot where the Most High kicks it. {46:5} God's right there in the middle of it all, making sure nothing messes with his city. He's got her back, showing up early to help out. {46:6} The haters may freak out, and kingdoms might crumble, but when God speaks, the whole earth listens. {46:7} The LORD's rolling with us, and the God of Jacob's got our backs. Pause and let that sink in. {46:8} Check it out, peep the crazy stuff God's done on the earth, leaving it all wrecked. {46:9} He shuts down wars all over the place, breaking bows, and burning chariots like it's NBD. {46:10} So, just chill and recognize that God's in charge. He's gonna get props from everyone, everywhere. {46:11} The LORD of hosts is on our side, and the God of Jacob's our safe space. Pause and let that sink in.

{47:1} Yo, clap your hands and shout out to God with some major hype. {47:2} 'Cause the Most High God is legit scary, ruling over the whole earth like a boss. {47:3} He's got other peeps under our feet, giving us the upper hand. {47:4} He's chosen our spot for us, showing mad love to Jacob. Pause and let that sink in. {47:5} God's showing up with a shout, and the LORD's bringing the noise like a trumpet blast. {47:6} Let's drop some sick beats for God, singing praises to our King like it's our jam. {47:7} 'Cause God's the king of the whole earth, so let's sing some praises with some serious understanding. {47:8} He's ruling over all the peeps, chilling on his holy throne. {47:9} Everyone's coming together, showing love to the God of Abraham, 'cause the whole earth belongs to God, and he's getting mad props.

{48:1} The LORD is off the charts, and we gotta give him mad love in the city where he's chilling, up on his holy mountain. {48:2} Mount Zion's got the best views, bringing joy to the whole earth. It's the spot of the great King. {48:3} God's known for being a safe space in her palaces. {48:4} When the kings rolled through, they couldn't believe what they saw and bounced out real quick. {48:5} They saw it for themselves and were blown away, bouncing out in a hurry. {48:6} Fear gripped them hard, like labor pains on a mom-to-be. {48:7} God wrecked the ships of Tarshish with an east wind. {48:8} We heard about it, and now we've seen it in the city of the LORD of hosts, the city of our God. He's gonna keep it going forever. Pause and let that sink in. {48:9} We've thought about your loving kindness, God, kicking it in your temple. {48:10} Your name goes worldwide, God, bringing justice to the ends of the earth. Your right hand is all about doing what's right. {48:11} Let Mount Zion throw a party, and let the daughters of Judah get hyped about your judgments. {48:12} Take a stroll around Zion, check out her towers. {48:13} Look closely at her defenses, peep her palaces, and pass it all down to the next generation. {48:14} 'Cause this God is our God forever and ever. He's gonna guide us, even through death.

{49:1} Listen up, everyone, from the highest to the lowest, rich and poor alike. {49:2} My mouth's gonna drop some wisdom, and my thoughts are gonna be all about understanding. {49:3} I'm gonna be all ears for some deep stories, sharing them with some sick beats on the harp. {49:4} So, why should I stress when bad times roll in, when my enemies are circling around me? {49:5} They trust in their wealth and brag about how loaded they are, {49:6} But none of that cash can save them or pay off God. {49:7} 'Cause paying off God is way too expensive, and it's not gonna last forever. {49:8} They think they're gonna live forever and avoid death and decay, {49:9} But they see wise folks and fools alike kick the bucket, leaving all their loot behind. {49:10} Even though they thought their wealth would last forever, they're gonna end up in the same place as the animals. {49:11} That's just plain dumb. But hey, their kids think they're onto something. Pause and let that sink in. {49:12} They're gonna end up in the grave like sheep, while the righteous have the upper hand in the morning. Their beauty's gonna fade away in the grave, far from their fancy houses. {49:13} But God's gonna save my soul from the power of the grave; he's gonna take me in. Pause and let that sink in. {49:14} Don't stress when someone gets rich or when their mansion gets even bigger. {49:15} 'Cause when they kick the bucket, they're not taking anything with them. Their glory's not following them to the grave. {49:16} Even though they praised themselves while they were alive, everyone's gonna forget about them when they're gone. {49:17} They're gonna join their ancestors in the grave, never to see the light again. {49:18} So, even though they were living the high life, not getting it, they're gonna end up like the animals.

{50:1} The Almighty God, the LORD, is speaking up, calling out to the whole earth from sunrise to sunset. {50:2} Out of Zion, the most beautiful spot, God's shining bright. {50:3} Our God's coming, and he's not holding back. Fire's gonna blaze in front of him, with a storm raging all around. {50:4} He's calling out to the heavens and the earth, ready to judge his people. {50:5} Gather all the holy ones to him, those who've made a deal with him through sacrifice. {50:6} The heavens are gonna declare his righteousness, 'cause God's the judge himself. Pause and let that sink in. {50:7} Listen up, my people, 'cause I've got something to say. Israel, I'm laying it all out for you: I'm God, your God. {50:8} I'm not gonna get on your case about your sacrifices or burnt offerings, 'cause they've been on point. {50:9} I don't need any bulls from your house or goats from your pens, {50:10} 'Cause every animal out there is mine, from the forests to the hills. {50:11} I know every bird in the mountains and every wild beast out there. They're all mine. {50:12} If I was hungry, I wouldn't even tell you. 'Cause the whole world is mine, and everything in it. {50:13} Do you think I'm gonna chow down on bull meat or drink goat blood? {50:14} Nah, what I want is some thanksgiving and for you to keep your promises to me, the Most High. {50:15} And when trouble comes knocking, call on me. I'll rescue you, and then you can shout out my praises. {50:16} But for the wicked, God's got some questions. What gives you the right to talk about my rules or make deals with me? {50:17} You hate being told what to do and toss my words aside. {50:18} When you see a thief, you're cool with it, and you're down with cheaters. {50:19} Your mouth's all about evil, and your tongue spins lies. {50:20} You sit around talking trash about your own family, even your own brother. {50:21} You've done all this, and I've stayed quiet. But don't think I'm like you. I'm gonna call you out and set things straight. {50:22} So, listen up, all you forgetful peeps. Don't make me tear you apart with no one to save you. {50:23} Anyone who offers praise is giving me props, and anyone who gets their act together, I'll show them some real salvation.

{51:1} Yo, God, I'm begging you, show me some love like you always do; wipe out all my screw-ups 'cause you're all about that mercy. {51:2} Scrub me clean from all the bad stuff I've done, and get rid of my sin completely. {51:3} 'Cause I know I messed up, and my guilt's always on my mind. {51:4} I get it, God, I messed up big time, and it's all on you. You're totally justified in calling me out on it. {51:5} I've been a hot mess since day one, even before I was born, I was already in trouble. {51:6} You're all about truth in the heart, so teach me wisdom deep down inside. {51:7} Make me squeaky clean, God, wash away all my dirt till I'm whiter than snow. {51:8} Fill me up with joy and happiness, so even my broken bones can celebrate. {51:9} Don't look at my sins, just wipe them out completely. {51:10} Give me a fresh start, God, make my heart clean and give me a new attitude. {51:11} Don't push me away, God; don't take your Spirit away from me. {51:12} Bring back the joy of being saved, and keep me going with a free spirit. {51:13} Then I'll teach other screw-ups your ways, and they'll turn to you. {51:14} Save me from feeling guilty, God, my savior; then I'll sing about how awesome you are. {51:15} Open my mouth, Lord, so I can shout out your praises. {51:16} 'Cause you're not into sacrifices; if you were, I'd totally do it. You're all about a broken heart and spirit, God; that's what you're into. {51:17} God, you're not gonna turn away someone who's really sorry and humble. {51:18} Do some awesome stuff in Zion, God; build up the walls of Jerusalem. {51:19} Then you'll be into our sacrifices—our burnt offerings will be on point.

{52:1} Yo, why you bragging about being bad, you big shot? God's goodness is always around. {52:2} Your tongue's all about causing trouble, like a sharp razor, cutting people down with lies. {52:3} You love being bad more than being good; lying comes more naturally to you than speaking the truth. Pause and let that sink in. {52:4} You're all about spreading gossip and lies, you sneaky talker. {52:5} God's gonna wipe you out for good, yank you out of your comfort zone, and kick you out of the land of the living. Pause and let that sink in. {52:6} The righteous will see it all go down, and they'll laugh at you. {52:7} Look at this dude, not trusting in God but in his riches, getting strong in his wickedness. {52:8} But me, I'm chillin' like a green olive tree in God's crib, trusting in his mercy forever. {52:9} I'll keep praising you forever 'cause you've got it going on, and I'll keep waiting on your name 'cause it's legit awesome.

{53:1} This fool's saying there's no God; they're all messed up and doing messed up stuff, not one of them's doing anything good. {53:2} God's checking out the scene from heaven, looking for anyone who gets it, anyone who's looking for him. {53:3} But they're all turning their backs on him, going off the rails and getting filthy; there's not a single one doing anything good. {53:4} Don't these bad dudes get it? They're munching on God's people like they're snacks but not even bothering to call out to God. {53:5} They're freaking out for no reason, 'cause God's smashing their plans to pieces, putting them to shame 'cause he can't stand them. {53:6} Can't wait for God to come and save us from all this mess! When he brings his people back, Jacob's gonna party, and Israel's gonna be stoked.

{54:1} God, save me by your name and show me what's up with your power. {54:2} Listen up, God, hear my prayers; pay attention to what I'm saying. {54:3} 'Cause these strangers are coming after me, and haters are trying to mess me up; they're not thinking about you, God. Pause and let that sink in. {54:4} But God's got my back; he's there for everyone who's got my back. {54:5} He's gonna pay back all the evil my enemies do to me; cut them down with the truth. {54:6} I'll bring my offerings to you freely; I'll praise your name, LORD, 'cause it's awesome. {54:7} 'Cause you've saved me from all kinds of trouble, and I've seen you take care of my enemies.

{55:1} Yo, God, listen to my prayers; don't ignore what I'm asking. {55:2} Pay attention to me, hear me out; I'm freaking out and making some noise. {55:3} 'Cause my enemies are talking trash, and wicked people are coming after me; they're not thinking about you, and they hate me. {55:4} I'm hurting real bad inside, and I'm scared to death. {55:5} I'm shaking with fear, and I feel like I'm drowning in horror. {55:6} I wish I could just fly away like a bird and find some peace. {55:7} I'd go far away and hide out in the wilderness. Pause and let that sink in. {55:8} I'd get away from this storm and find some peace and quiet. {55:9} God, break up their plans and shut them down; I've seen nothing but violence and trouble in this city. {55:10} They're up to no good day and night, causing trouble and spreading sadness. {55:11} Wickedness is everywhere, and you can't even walk down the street without seeing lies and deceit. {55:12} It's not some enemy I could deal with; it's someone I trusted, my friend and companion. {55:13} We were tight, sharing everything, even going to church together. {55:14} Let them get what's coming to them; let them go straight to hell, 'cause there's nothing but wickedness where they are. {55:15} But me, I'm gonna call on God, and he's gonna save me. {55:16} Morning, noon, and night, I'm gonna pray and shout out to God, and he's gonna hear me. {55:17} He's saved me from all kinds of battles 'cause he's always got my back. {55:18} God's gonna hear and mess them up, even though they've been doing the same old thing forever. Pause and let that sink in. {55:19} They've turned against their friends and broken their promises. {55:20} Their words might sound sweet, but they've got war in their hearts; they talk smooth, but they're ready to stab you in the back. {55:21} Give all your worries to God, and he'll hold you up; he won't let anything mess with the good people. {55:22} But you, God, you'll bring them down into the dirt of destruction; wicked and deceitful people won't last long, but I'm sticking with you.

{56:1} Yo God, have mercy on me, cuz these people tryna eat me alive; they fightin' me every single day. {56:2} My enemies be on my case daily, there's so many of 'em, God most High. {56:3} When I'm scared, I put my trust in You. {56:4} I'll praise Your word in God; I've put my trust in You, and I ain't scared of what people can do to me. {56:5} They twist my words every day; all they think about is doing me dirty. {56:6} They squad up, hide, track my moves, and plot against me. {56:7} Will they get away with their evil? Nah, God, take 'em down in Your anger. {56:8} You see my struggles; keep my tears in Your bottle, ain't they in Your book? {56:9} When I cry out to You, my enemies will retreat; this I know, for God is with me. {56:10} I'll praise God's word; in the LORD I'll praise His word. {56:11}

In God, I've put my trust; I ain't scared of what people can do to me. {56:12} Your promises are on me, God; I'll give You my praises. {56:13} You saved my soul from death; won't You keep my feet from stumbling, so I can walk before You in the light of the living?

{57:1} Have mercy on me, God, have mercy on me, cuz my soul trusts in You; I'll chill in the shadow of Your wings till these troubles pass. {57:2} I'll cry out to God Most High, to the One who gets things done for me. {57:3} He'll send help from heaven and save me from those who wanna devour me. Selah. God will send His mercy and truth. {57:4} My soul's chillin' with lions, lying among fiery dudes, whose teeth are spears and arrows, and their tongues are sharp swords. {57:5} Be exalted, God, above the heavens; let Your glory be over all the earth. {57:6} They set traps for me; my soul's bowed down; they dug a pit in front of me, but they fell into it themselves. Selah. {57:7} My heart's fixed, God, my heart's fixed; I'll sing and give praise. {57:8} Wake up, my glory; wake up, psaltery and harp; I'll wake up early. {57:9} I'll praise You, Lord, among the people; I'll sing to You among the nations. {57:10} Your mercy is great to the heavens, and Your truth to the clouds. {57:11} Be exalted, God, above the heavens; let Your glory be over all the earth.

{58:1} Do y'all really speak righteousness, congregation? Do y'all judge uprightly, sons of men? {58:2} Nah, y'all work wickedness in your hearts and weigh out violence on the earth. {58:3} The wicked are wild from birth; they go astray speaking lies as soon as they're born. {58:4} Their poison is like a serpent's poison; they're like a deaf snake that won't listen to the charmer. {58:5} They don't hear the voice of charmers, no matter how good the charm. {58:6} Break their teeth in their mouths, God; break out the big teeth of the young lions, LORD. {58:7} Let them vanish like water running away; when they shoot their arrows, let them be like they're broken. {58:8} Let them disappear like a snail melting away, like a stillborn child who never sees the sun. {58:9} Before your pots can feel the thorns, God will sweep them away, both alive and in His wrath. {58:10} The righteous will be happy when they see vengeance; they'll wash their feet in the blood of the wicked. {58:11} People will say, "Yeah, there's a reward for the righteous; surely there's a God who judges on earth."

{59:1} Save me from my enemies, my God; protect me from those who rise up against me. {59:2} Save me from evildoers; rescue me from bloodthirsty people. {59:3} Look, they lie in wait for me; the mighty gather against me, not for my sin or my wrongdoing, LORD. {59:4} They run and prepare themselves without my fault; wake up to help me and see. {59:5} You, LORD God of hosts, the God of Israel, wake up to visit all the nations; don't show any mercy to wicked traitors. Selah. {59:6} They come back at evening, making noise like dogs, and go around the city. {59:7} Look, they belch out with their mouths; swords are in their lips, for who hears, they say? {59:8} But You, LORD, laugh at them; You hold all the nations in derision. {59:9} I'll wait for You, His strength; for God is my defense. {59:10} The God of my mercy will meet me; God will let me see my desire on my enemies. {59:11} Don't kill them, or my people might forget; scatter them by Your power and bring them down, Lord our shield. {59:12} For the sin of their mouth and the words of their lips, let them be taken in their pride; for the curses and lies they utter. {59:13} Consume them in Your wrath, consume them till they're no more, and let them know that God rules in Jacob to the ends of the earth. Selah. {59:14} At evening let them return, making noise like dogs, and go around the city. {59:15} Let them wander up and down for food, and grumble if they aren't satisfied. {59:16} But I'll sing of Your power; I'll sing aloud of Your mercy in the morning, for You've been my defense and refuge in the day of my trouble. {59:17} To You, my strength, I'll sing praises; for God is my defense, the God of my mercy.

{60:1} God, You've cast us off, scattered us, and been displeased; turn back to us again. {60:2} You made the earth tremble and broke it; heal its cracks, for it shakes. {60:3} You've shown Your people hard things; made us drink the wine of confusion. {60:4} You've given a banner to those who fear You, to be displayed because of the truth. Selah. {60:5} That Your beloved may be delivered; save with Your right hand and hear me. {60:6} God has spoken in His holiness; I will rejoice, I'll divide Shechem and measure out the Valley of Succoth. {60:7} Gilead is mine, and Manasseh is mine; Ephraim is the strength of my head; Judah is my lawgiver. {60:8} Moab is my washbasin; over Edom I'll throw my shoe; Philistia, shout in triumph because of me. {60:9} Who will bring me into the strong city? Who will lead me to Edom? {60:10} Won't You, God, who cast us off? Won't You, God, who didn't go out with our armies? {60:11} Give us help from trouble, for human help is useless. {60:12} Through God we'll do valiantly; for He will trample down our enemies.

{61:1} Yo, God, listen up; check out my prayer. {61:2} When life's got me feeling overwhelmed, I'm reaching out to you from wherever I am, asking you to guide me to a higher place. {61:3} You've always been my shelter, my safe spot from all the haters. {61:4} I'm gonna stick with you forever, hanging out in your crib and trusting in your protection. Pause and think about that. {61:5} You've heard my promises, God, and you've given me the same blessings you give to those who respect you. {61:6} You're gonna keep the king going strong, making his reign last for generations. {61:7} He'll be chilling with you forever, so hook him up with some mercy and truth to keep him going strong. {61:8} And I'll keep singing your praises forever so I can keep my promises to you every day.

{62:1} My soul's just waiting on God; he's the one who's gonna save me. {62:2} He's my rock and my salvation, my defense; nothing's gonna shake me. {62:3} How long are you gonna keep plotting against people, trying to take them down? You're gonna get wrecked, just like a falling wall or a wobbly fence. {62:4} All you care about is tearing people down from their greatness, loving to lie and deceive. Pause and think about that. {62:5} I'm putting all my hope in God 'cause I know he's got my back. {62:6} He's my rock and my salvation, my defense; nothing's gonna shake me. {62:7} God's where it's at for me—my salvation, my glory, my strength, my safe spot. {62:8} Trust in him all the time; pour your heart out to him, 'cause God's our safe spot. Pause and think about that. {62:9} People, no matter how low or high they are, they're just worthless compared to God. {62:10} Don't put your trust in oppressing others or getting rich; if your wealth grows, don't let it go to your head. {62:11} God's got all the power; that's what I've heard, and I'm sticking with it. {62:12} And God, you're all about mercy; you give everyone what they deserve.

{63:1} God, you're my God; I'm up early seeking you out. My soul's thirsty for you, craving you in this dry and thirsty place where there's no water. {63:2} I wanna see your power and glory, just like I've seen it in your house. {63:3} 'Cause your love is better than life itself; I can't help but praise you. {63:4} I'm gonna bless you as long as I live, lifting my hands up in your name. {63:5} You satisfy my soul like nothing else can; my mouth's gonna praise you with joyful lips. {63:6} Even when I'm lying in bed, I'm thinking about you; even in the middle of the night, I'm meditating on you. {63:7} 'Cause you've always been my help, and I find joy in the shadow of your wings. {63:8} My soul's sticking close to you; your right hand's got me covered. {63:9} But those who try to destroy me will end up in the grave. {63:10} They're gonna fall by the sword, becoming food for scavengers. {63:11} But the king's gonna find joy in God; anyone who swears by him is gonna shine, but liars will be silenced.

{64:1} God, hear me out when I pray; keep me safe from my enemies' threats. {64:2} Hide me from their evil schemes, from the rebellion of those who do wrong. {64:3} They sharpen their tongues like swords and aim their bitter words like arrows. {64:4} They plot in secret against the innocent, shooting at them suddenly and without fear. {64:5} They encourage each other to do evil, planning their traps in secret, thinking no one will catch them. {64:6} But God's gonna hit them with his own arrows, suddenly bringing them down. {64:7} Their own words are gonna come back to bite them, and everyone who sees it will run away scared. {64:8} People are gonna see what God does and be amazed at his work. {64:9} The righteous are gonna be happy in the LORD and trust in him, and all those with honest hearts will shine.

{65:1} Praise is waiting for you, God, in Zion; we're gonna keep our promises to you. {65:2} You're the God who listens to prayers; everyone's gonna come to you. {65:3} Our sins might be overwhelming, but you're gonna wipe them away. {65:4} Blessed is the person you choose to be close to you, living in your house; they're gonna be happy with all the good stuff in your temple. {65:5} You answer us with awesome deeds, God of our salvation; you're the hope of everyone, even those at the ends of the earth and beyond the sea. {65:6} You're the one who sets the mountains in place with your strength, all powerful. {65:7} You calm the raging seas and the noisy waves, and you calm the shouting of the nations. {65:8} Everyone's in awe of your amazing power; you make the morning and evening sing for joy. {65:9} You take care of the earth, watering it and enriching it with rivers full of water; you provide grain for us when we need it. {65:10} You water the fields and make them fertile; you soften them with showers and bless their crops. {65:11} You crown the year with your goodness, and your paths overflow with abundance. {65:12} The wilderness pastures are covered with flocks, and the hills are full of joy on every side. {65:13} The fields are covered with sheep, and the valleys are full of wheat; everyone's shouting for joy and singing praises.

{66:1} Yo, everyone, make some noise for God! {66:2} Sing and hype up His name, make His praise epic. {66:3} Tell God, "Your works are awesome! Your power makes enemies bow down." {66:4} Everyone on Earth will worship You and sing Your name. Selah. {66:5} Come check out God's works: He's awesome in what He does for people. {66:6} He turned the sea into dry land; we walked through the water on foot. Let's celebrate Him there. {66:7} He rules forever with power; He sees all nations. Don't let rebels get too cocky. Selah. {66:8} Bless our God, everyone, make His praise heard loud and clear: {66:9} He keeps our soul alive and keeps us steady. {66:10} You tested us, God; You refined us like silver. {66:11} You trapped us and put heavy loads on us. {66:12} People walked over our heads; we went through fire and water, but You brought us to a good place. {66:13} I'll go to Your house with burnt offerings; I'll keep my promises to You, {66:14} That my lips promised, that I spoke when I was in trouble. {66:15} I'll offer You fat animals, with the smell of rams; I'll offer bulls and goats. Selah. {66:16} Come listen, all who respect God, and I'll tell you what He did for me. {66:17} I called out to Him, praising Him with my voice. {66:18} If I held sin in my heart, the Lord wouldn't listen: {66:19} But God really listened and heard my prayer. {66:20} Blessed be God, who didn't ignore my prayer or His mercy.

{67:1} God, be kind to us and bless us; shine Your face on us. Selah. {67:2} So that Your way is known on Earth, Your saving power among all nations. {67:3} Let the people praise You, God; let everyone praise You. {67:4} Let nations be happy and sing for joy: because You judge fairly and guide nations on Earth. Selah. {67:5} Let the people praise You, God; let everyone praise You. {67:6} Then the Earth will give its harvest, and God, our own God, will bless us. {67:7} God will bless us, and everyone on Earth will respect Him.

{68:1} Let God rise up, let His enemies scatter: let those who hate Him run away. {68:2} Like smoke blown away, drive them away: like wax melting before fire, let the wicked perish before God. {68:3} But let the good people be happy; let them celebrate before God, super happy. {68:4} Sing to God, praise His name: lift up the one who rides on the clouds by His name JAH, and celebrate before Him. {68:5} A dad to orphans and a judge for widows is God in His holy home. {68:6} God sets the lonely in families; He frees prisoners, but rebels live in a dry land. {68:7} God, when You led Your people out, when You marched through the desert; Selah: {68:8} The Earth shook, the sky dropped rain at God's presence, even Sinai shook at God's presence, the God of Israel. {68:9} You, God, sent a lot of rain, refreshing Your tired inheritance. {68:10} Your people settled there; You, God, provided for the poor out of Your goodness. {68:11} The Lord gave the command: many people announced it. {68:12} Kings and armies ran away: and the women at home shared the loot. {68:13} Even if you sleep among the sheep pens, you'll have wings of a dove covered with silver, and feathers with yellow gold. {68:14} When the Almighty scattered kings, it was like snow falling on Salmon. {68:15} The mountain of God is like the mountain of Bashan;

a high mountain like the mountain of Bashan. {68:16} Why do you look with envy, high mountains? This is the mountain God chose to live in; the Lord will stay there forever. {68:17} God's chariots are twenty thousand, even thousands of angels: the Lord is among them, as in Sinai, in the holy place. {68:18} You went up on high, took captives; you received gifts for people, even for rebels, so the Lord God might live there. {68:19} Praise the Lord, who daily loads us with benefits, the God of our salvation. Selah. {68:20} Our God is a God who saves; the escape from death belongs to the Lord God. {68:21} But God will crush the heads of His enemies, the hairy scalp of those who keep on sinning. {68:22} The Lord said, "I will bring them back from Bashan, I will bring them back from the depths of the sea: {68:23} So your feet may be covered in your enemies' blood, and the tongues of your dogs too." {68:24} They saw Your procession, God; the procession of my God, my King, into the holy place. {68:25} The singers led the way, the musicians followed; among them were young women playing tambourines. {68:26} Praise God in the big gathering, praise the Lord from the fountain of Israel. {68:27} There is little Benjamin, leading them, the princes of Judah and their group, the princes of Zebulun and Naphtali. {68:28} God has ordered your strength: show Your power, God, You who have acted for us. {68:29} Because of Your temple at Jerusalem, kings will bring You gifts. {68:30} Rebuke the beast among the reeds, the herd of bulls with the calves of the nations, till they bow down with silver pieces: scatter the nations who delight in war. {68:31} Envoys will come from Egypt; Ethiopia will quickly reach out to God. {68:32} Sing to God, kingdoms of the Earth; sing praises to the Lord; Selah: {68:33} To Him who rides on the ancient skies; He speaks with a mighty voice. {68:34} Credit God with strength; His majesty is over Israel, and His power is in the skies. {68:35} God, You are awesome in Your holy places: the God of Israel gives strength and power to His people. Praise be to God.

{69:1} Save me, God; for the waters are up to my neck. {69:2} I sink in deep mud, where there's no place to stand: I've come into deep waters, and the floods overwhelm me. {69:3} I'm tired of crying: my throat is dry: my eyes fail while I wait for my God. {69:4} Those who hate me without a reason outnumber the hairs on my head: my powerful enemies try to destroy me wrongfully: I had to return what I didn't steal. {69:5} God, You know my foolishness; my sins aren't hidden from You. {69:6} Don't let those who wait for You, Lord God of hosts, be ashamed because of me: don't let those who seek You be disgraced because of me, God of Israel. {69:7} Because for Your sake I have endured scorn; shame has covered my face. {69:8} I've become a stranger to my siblings, and an outsider to my mother's children. {69:9} My passion for Your house consumes me; the insults of those who insult You have fallen on me. {69:10} When I cried and fasted, they mocked me for it. {69:11} I wore sackcloth as my clothing; I became a joke to them. {69:12} Those who sit at the gate gossip about me; I became the song of drunkards. {69:13} But I pray to You, Lord, at a favorable time: God, in Your great love, hear me in Your truth of salvation. {69:14} Deliver me from the mud, and don't let me sink: rescue me from those who hate me, and from deep waters. {69:15} Don't let the floodwaters engulf me, or the depths swallow me up, or the pit close its mouth over me. {69:16} Answer me, Lord, for Your loving kindness is good: turn to me in Your great compassion. {69:17} Don't hide Your face from Your servant; I'm in trouble: answer me quickly. {69:18} Come near and rescue me: redeem me because of my enemies. {69:19} You know how I am insulted, shamed, and disgraced: all my enemies are before You. {69:20} Insults have broken my heart; I'm in despair: I looked for sympathy, but there was none; for comforters, but found none. {69:21} They put gall in my food and gave me vinegar for my thirst. {69:22} Let their feast become a trap, and their celebrations a snare. {69:23} Let their eyes be darkened so they can't see; make their bodies shake continually. {69:24} Pour out Your anger on them, let Your fierce anger overtake them. {69:25} Let their homes {69:26} Yo, they be straight up hatin' on the dude you smacked down, talkin' smack 'bout the ones you wrecked. {69:27} Like, pile up their sins, God, and don't even let 'em near your goodness. {69:28} Cancel their names from the cool list, don't even let 'em hang with the righteous. {69:29} But yo, I'm feelin' low and sad, so like, save me, God, and lift me up high. {69:30} I'm gonna shout out to God with a sick track, and give him props with some mad thanks. {69:31} That's gonna vibe with the Lord better than a beefy bull with horns and hooves. {69:32} The chill peeps gonna see that and be stoked, and if you're seekin' God, your heart's gonna come alive. {69:33} 'Cause God's all about helpin' out the strugglers, he ain't about ditchin' his peeps. {69:34} Let everything in the sky and on the earth give him props, even the oceans and all the creatures. {69:35} 'Cause God's gonna save Zion, and build up the towns of Judah, so his crew can chill there and own it. {69:36} His loyal homies gonna inherit that spot, and all those who dig his vibe gonna kick it there.

{70:1} Yo, God, hurry up and rescue me, come through ASAP, Lord. {70:2} Make those haters who wanna see me wiped out feel dumb and embarrassed, turn 'em around and mess 'em up. {70:3} Let 'em get what's comin' to 'em for talkin' trash, those jerks who think they're all that. {70:4} But everyone who's got your back, God, let 'em be pumped and stoked, and anyone who's down with your salvation, keep 'em shoutin', "God's the bomb!" {70:5} But me, I'm feelin' broke and desperate, so come on, God, I need your help, you're my only hope; don't ghost me, Lord.

{71:1} Yo, Lord, I'm putting all my trust in you; don't let me get confused. {71:2} Save me with your righteousness, and help me out; listen up, and rescue me. {71:3} Be my solid hangout spot, where I can always chill; you've given the green light to save me 'cause you're my rock and my fortress. {71:4} My God, get me out of the clutches of the wicked, the unrighteous and cruel ones. {71:5} 'Cause you're my hope, Lord GOD; I've been trusting in you since I was a kid. {71:6} You've had my back since day one, even before I was born; you're the one who brought me into this world, so my shoutouts are always gonna be about you. {71:7} I may seem strange to a lot of people, but you're my solid hideout. {71:8} Let me be all about praising you and giving you props all day long. {71:9} Don't ditch me when I'm old and grey; don't bail on me when I'm losing my strength. {71:10} My enemies are talking smack about me, plotting against my soul. {71:11} They're saying, "God's abandoned him; let's mess him up 'cause there's no one to save him." {71:12} God, don't keep your distance; come through quick and help me out. {71:13} Let those who mess with me get wrecked and shut down; let them be covered in shame and disgrace, those who want to see me hurt. {71:14} But I'm gonna keep on hoping, and I'll keep praising you even more. {71:15} I'll keep talking about your righteousness and your salvation all day long; 'cause honestly, I can't even count how many times you've come through for me. {71:16} I'm gonna roll with the strength of the Lord GOD; I'll be all about your righteousness, and yours only. {71:17} God, you've been schooling me since I was young; and I've been shouting out your amazing deeds ever since. {71:18} Even now, when I'm old and grey, God, don't leave me hanging; let me show off your strength to this generation and to all who come after. {71:19} Your righteousness is off the charts, God; you've done some incredible things. Seriously, who's even close to being like you? {71:20} You've put me through some tough times, but you're gonna bring me back to life again; you're gonna lift me up from the lowest of lows. {71:21} You're gonna make me even greater and comfort me all around. {71:22} I'm gonna praise you with music, with the psaltery and the harp, O my God, the Holy One of Israel. {71:23} My lips are gonna be jumping for joy when I sing to you; and my soul, which you've saved, is gonna be feeling it. {71:24} My tongue's gonna be all about your righteousness all day long; 'cause those who want to see me hurt are gonna be left speechless, embarrassed and ashamed.

{72:1} God, give the king your judgments, and your righteousness to the king's son. {72:2} He's gonna rule your people with fairness, and the poor with justice. {72:3} The mountains are gonna bring peace to the people, and even the little hills, through fairness. {72:4} He's gonna stand up for the poor, rescue the needy children, and crush the oppressor. {72:5} People are gonna respect him as long as the sun and moon are in the sky, for generations to come. {72:6} He's gonna come down like rain on freshly cut grass, like showers watering the earth. {72:7} Righteousness is gonna flourish during his rule, and there's gonna be plenty of peace as long as the moon is shining. {72:8} He's gonna have authority from sea to sea, from the river to the ends of the earth. {72:9} People in the wilderness are gonna bow down to him; even his enemies are gonna bite the dust. {72:10} Kings from all over are gonna bring him gifts; rulers from distant lands are gonna pay their respects. {72:11} All kings are gonna bow down to him; all nations are gonna serve him. {72:12} 'Cause he's gonna rescue the needy when they cry out; he'll help out the poor and those who have no one else. {72:13} He's gonna show mercy to the poor and needy, and save their souls from trouble. {72:14} He's gonna save them from lies and violence; their lives are gonna be precious in his sight. {72:15} He's gonna live a long life, and people are gonna give him gifts of gold from Sheba; they're gonna pray for him all the time, and he'll be praised every day. {72:16} There's gonna be plenty of crops, even on the tops of mountains; the harvest will shake like Lebanon, and the cities will flourish like grass. {72:17} His name's gonna last forever; it'll shine as long as the sun, and people from all over the world are gonna call him blessed. {72:18} Blessed be the LORD God, the God of Israel, the one who does amazing things. {72:19} And blessed be his glorious name forever; let the whole earth be filled with his glory. Amen, and Amen. {72:20} That's the end of David's prayers, son of Jesse.

{73:1} God's been good to Israel, especially to those with clean hearts. {73:2} But me? I almost lost my way; I nearly slipped up. {73:3} 'Cause I got jealous watching fools live it up, seeing the wicked succeed. {73:4} They don't suffer like other folks; they're not plagued like everyone else. {73:5} Their pride is like a chain around them; violence is their trademark. {73:6} They're fat with success, with more than they could ever want. {73:7} They're corrupt and talk trash about oppressing others; they're all high and mighty. {73:8} They even mouth off against heaven itself, and their tongues strut across the earth. {73:9} They act like God doesn't even know what's going on; they think the Most High isn't paying attention. {73:10} That's why people turn to them and lap up everything they say. {73:11} And they ask, "How can God know what's happening? Is the Most High even paying attention?" {73:12} Look at these godless people, living it up in the world and getting richer. {73:13} And here I am, trying to keep my heart pure and my hands clean, but it feels like it's all for nothing. {73:14} 'Cause I'm constantly hit with trouble and disciplined every morning. {73:15} If I start talking like this, I'll betray your children, God. {73:16} Trying to figure this out just messed with my head until... {73:17} I entered your sanctuary, God, and then I understood what happens to the wicked in the end. {73:18} You set them up for disaster, pushing them towards destruction. {73:19} They're brought to ruin in an instant; they're completely terrified. {73:20} It's like waking up from a bad dream; when you're done with them, Lord, you'll despise their memory. {73:21} That's when my heart felt the pain, and I was kicked in the gut. {73:22} I was so stupid and clueless, acting like an animal in front of you. {73:23} But even then, you were with me; you held me by my right hand. {73:24} You guide me with your advice, and afterward, you'll honor me. {73:25} Who else do I have in heaven but you? And here on earth, there's nothing I desire more than you. {73:26} My body and my heart might give out, but God, you're the strength of my heart and my forever portion. {73:27} Those who are far from you will perish; you destroy all who are unfaithful to you. {73:28} But for me, getting close to God is the best thing ever; I've put my trust in the Lord GOD, so I'm gonna tell everyone about your amazing works.

{74:1} God, why have you abandoned us forever? Why are you so angry with the sheep of your pasture? {74:2} Remember your people, the ones you've chosen long ago, the tribe you've redeemed as your own. Don't forget about Mount Zion, where you live. {74:3} Look at all the destruction the enemy has caused in the sanctuary; they're trashing the place where your name is honored. {74:4} Your enemies are causing chaos in your meeting places; they're setting up their flags as signs of victory. {74:5} They're famous for smashing everything in sight, like lumberjacks taking down trees. {74:6} But now they're wrecking all the artwork with axes and hammers. {74:7} They've set fire to your sanctuary, defiling the place where your name resides, reducing it to rubble. {74:8} They said to themselves, "Let's wipe them out altogether!" They burned down all the places of worship throughout the land. {74:9} We're not seeing any miraculous signs; there are no prophets left, and no one knows how long this is gonna last. {74:10} God, how long are our enemies gonna mock us? Will they blaspheme your name forever? {74:11} Why are you holding back, God? Pull your hand out and take action! {74:12} You've always been our King, working salvation in the world. {74:13} You split the sea with your power, crushing the heads of sea monsters. {74:14} You crushed the heads of Leviathan and fed him to the creatures of the wilderness. {74:15} You split open springs and streams; you dried up mighty rivers. {74:16} The day belongs to you, and so does the night; you set the boundaries of the earth and made summer and winter. {74:17} Don't forget how your enemies insult you, LORD, how foolish people mock your name. {74:18} Don't let your dove be captured by the flock of vultures; don't forget about your poor and oppressed people forever. {74:19} Remember your covenant with us, because the dark corners of the earth are filled with violence. {74:20} Don't let the oppressed return home empty-handed; let the poor and needy praise your name. {74:21} Rise up, God, and defend yourself; remember how fools insult you all day long. {74:22} Don't ignore the voices of your enemies; their shouting gets louder every day. {74:23} Don't ignore the haters' voices, God; their noise keeps getting louder by the minute.

{75:1} Yo, God, we're giving you major thanks; your name's all up in our mouths 'cause your amazing deeds speak for themselves. {75:2} When I'm in charge, I'm gonna judge everyone fair and square. {75:3} The whole earth and everyone in it is hanging on by a thread, and I'm the one holding it all together. Selah. {75:4} I'm telling the fools to wise up and warning the wicked not to get cocky: {75:5} Don't be showing off and talking smack with your stubborn attitude. {75:6} 'Cause getting ahead doesn't come from any direction you expect; it's all in God's hands. {75:7} He's the real judge; he takes down one and puts up another. {75:8} God's got this cup, and it's filled with some serious red stuff, a mix that'll knock you out; he's gonna make the wicked drink it all the way to the bottom. {75:9} But me? I'm gonna keep on declaring and praising the God of Jacob forever. {75:10} I'm gonna shut down all the wicked haters, but the righteous ones? They're gonna rise up even higher.

{76:1} In Judah, God's got street cred, his name's top-notch in Israel. {76:2} His crib's in Zion, and his pad's in Jerusalem. {76:3} That's where he shuts down the enemy's weapons, breaks their bows, shields, and swords. Selah. {76:4} Yo, he's way more lit than any mountain out there. {76:5} The tough guys get wrecked, they're knocked out cold; ain't nobody can even lift a finger. {76:6} When God gets on their case, even their rides get KO'd, chariots and horses straight knocked out. {76:7} God's the one you don't wanna mess with, who can stand up to him when he's ticked off? {76:8} When God speaks up from heaven, even the earth shuts up and listens, {76:9} 'Cause when God steps in to lay down the law, he's all about savin' the humble on earth. Selah. {76:10} Even the anger of people ends up praising you, and whatever's left of their fury, you shut it down. {76:11} So, like, give props to the Lord, and everyone around him should come bearing gifts to the one you gotta show respect to. {76:12} He shuts down the pride of princes, he's got kings shakin' in their boots.

{77:1} I'm straight up callin' out to God, shoutin' out to him, and he's listenin'. {77:2} When I'm strugglin', I'm lookin' for the Lord; I'm cryin' out all night, can't find no peace. {77:3} Thinkin' 'bout God's got me feelin' troubled, complainin' 'bout my situation, feelin' overwhelmed. Selah. {77:4} I can't even sleep 'cause I'm so stressed out; I'm so messed up, I can't even speak. {77:5} I'm thinkin' 'bout the old days, rememberin' ancient times. {77:6} I'm replayin' my jams from back in the day, thinkin' hard, searchin' deep. {77:7} Wonderin', is God gonna ditch us for good? Is he ever gonna show us some love again? {77:8} Has he forgotten how to be kind? Has he given up on keepin' his promises? Selah. {77:9} Is God done bein' merciful? Is he so mad he's shuttin' us out? Selah. {77:10} But then I remember, this is just me trippin'; I remember the awesome stuff God's done. {77:11} I'm thinkin' 'bout all the things the Lord's done, rememberin' all his amazing deeds. {77:12} I'm gonna mull over everything God's done, and talk about all the cool stuff he's pulled off. {77:13} God's always doin' his thing in his holy place; there ain't nobody as awesome as our God. {77:14} God's the one who does crazy stuff, showin' off his power to all the people. {77:15} He saved his peeps with his mighty arm, the descendants of Jacob and Joseph. Selah. {77:16} Even the waters saw God and freaked out; the depths were shook. {77:17} The clouds poured down rain, the skies boomed with thunder; God's arrows were flyin' all over. {77:18} His voice echoed through the heavens, lightnin' up the world; the earth was shakin' and quakin'. {77:19} God's path is through the sea, his tracks through mighty waters, but nobody knows where he's headed. {77:20} He led his people like a boss, hand in hand with Moses and Aaron.

{78:1} Listen up, fam, pay attention to what I'm sayin'; open your ears to my words. {78:2} I'm gonna drop some truth bombs, spill some ancient secrets: {78:3} Stuff we heard from our folks, things they told us about way back. {78:4} We ain't keepin' this stuff to ourselves; we're passin' it on to the next generation, tellin' 'em 'bout the awesome stuff the Lord's done, his power, his miracles. {78:5} 'Cause God set things up in Jacob, laid down the law in Israel, told our ancestors to pass it all on to their kids. {78:6} So the next generation would know about it, and the kids after them, so they could tell their kids too, {78:7} Yo, peeps gotta trust in God, not forgettin' all the dope stuff He's done and keepin' His rules, ya know? {78:8} Don't be like them old heads, actin' all stubborn and rebellious, not stayin' loyal to God and keepin' it real with Him. {78:9} Even them Ephraim homies, strapped up with bows, punked out when it was time to throw down. {78:10} They straight-up broke the deal with God, refused to follow His laws. {78:11} Forgot all the crazy miracles God flexed on 'em, like back in Egypt and Zoan. {78:12} Dude was droppin' miracles left and right, splitin' seas and stuff. {78:13} Led 'em with clouds in the day, and lit 'em up with fire at night. {78:14} Even cracked rocks in the desert to quench their thirst. {78:15} Straight-up brought streams from rocks, like, rivers flowin' in the desert, man. {78:16} But they kept on dissin' God, tickin' Him off in the desert. {78:17} Always testin' God, askin' for munchies to satisfy their cravings. {78:18} They even talked smack, doubtin' if God could hook 'em up with grub in the desert. {78:19} But check it, God was straight-up mad, fire burnin' against Jacob, His anger lit against Israel. {78:20} 'Cause they didn't trust in God or His salvation, even though He brought clouds and opened up the heavens. {78:21} Dropped manna like it was rain, and hooked 'em up with that heavenly bread. {78:22} They chowed down on angel food, their bellies full, but while the food was still in their mouths... {78:23} God's rage came down on 'em, takin' out their finest, smitin' Israel's top dogs. {78:24} But even after all that, they kept on sinning, doubtin' God's miracles. {78:25} So God let 'em wander in emptiness, their years filled with trouble. {78:26} They only came crawlin' back to God when things got tough, seekin' Him early in the morn. {78:27} Rememberin' that God was their rock, the high God their redeemer. {78:28} But even then, they was talkin' smack with their mouths, lyin' to God with their tongues. {78:29} Their hearts weren't right with Him, and they weren't loyal to His covenant. {78:30} But God, bein' full of compassion, forgave their mess-ups, didn't let His anger burn 'em up. {78:31} 'Cause He knew they were just flesh, here today, gone tomorrow. {78:32} But they kept on pushin' His buttons in the desert, provokin' Him left and right. {78:33} God did some crazy stuff back then, turnin' rivers to blood and wreckin' Egypt with plagues. {78:34} But they straight-up forgot all that, didn't even remember when He saved 'em from their enemies. {78:35} God's like, "I chose you, but you still actin' shady." {78:36} They just kept frontin' with their words, lyin' to God's face. {78:37} Their hearts weren't true, and they couldn't keep it real with His covenant. {78:38} But God, bein' merciful, forgave their wrongs, held back His full wrath time and time again. {78:39} 'Cause He knew they were just flesh, here today, gone tomorrow. {78:40} But they kept on pushin' His buttons in the desert, causin' trouble left and right. {78:41} Doubtin' God, tryna box in the Holy One of Israel. {78:42} Forgot all the miracles He did in Egypt, the wonders in Zoan. {78:43} Turnin' rivers to blood, and wreckin' Egypt with plagues. {78:44} Smackin' 'em with all sorts of pests, from flies to frogs. {78:45} Messin' with their crops, lettin' bugs and locusts wreck 'em. {78:46} Destroyin' their vines and trees with hail and frost. {78:47} Even takin' out their livestock with hail and lightning bolts. {78:48} God was straight-up furious, unleashing His wrath and trouble on 'em. {78:49} Sendin' angels of destruction, takin' lives with pestilence. {78:50} No mercy, just death, 'cause they pushed Him too far. {78:51} Even smacked Egypt's firstborn, the pride of Ham's tents. {78:52} But God led His own people out like sheep, protectin' 'em in the wilderness. {78:53} Keepin' 'em safe, while the sea swallowed up their enemies. {78:54} Guidin' 'em to His holy mountain, the place He bought with His own hand. {78:55} Kickin' out the heathen, dividin' up the land for His chosen ones. {78:56} But they kept testin' God, not keepin' His rules. {78:57} Actin' shady, just like their ancestors, turnin' away like a broken bow. {78:58} Makin' God mad with their idols and high places. {78:59} God was ticked, straight-up disgusted with Israel. {78:60} So He bounced from Shiloh, the tent He set up among His peeps. {78:61} Lettin' the enemy run wild, takin' His glory and strength. {78:62} Even lettin' His people get wrecked by the sword, showin' His wrath to His own inheritance. {78:63} Fires blazed, takin' out their youth, no weddings for the maidens. {78:64} Priests got smoked, widows left with no one to mourn 'em. {78:65} But then God woke up, like a beast outta slumber, roar of a champ after a good drink. {78:66} Smackin' His enemies from behind, makin' 'em perpetual losers. {78:67} Even dissed Joseph's crib, skippin' Ephraim, choosin' Judah's tribe. {78:68} Buildin' His temple like a boss, firm like the earth He set up forever. {78:69} He chose David, the shepherd boy, took him from the fields to lead Israel. {78:70} Guided 'em with integrity and skill, like a boss. {78:70} So God picked David, pulled him from his boring sheep gig, {78:71} Swapped lambs for leading Israel and Jacob, His peeps. {78:72} He kept 'em fed, heart full of integrity, hands skillful in guidance.

{79:1} Yo, God, these haters be messin' with your turf, {79:2} Treatin' your holy crib like trash, Jerusalem's a wreck. {79:3} Blood spillin' like water, bodies left for the birds and beasts. {79:4} We're a joke to our neighbors, laughed at and mocked. {79:5} How long you gonna stay mad, Lord? Your jealousy burnin' like fire. {79:6} Pour out your rage on those clueless heathens, and kingdoms who don't know you. {79:7} They're tearin' up Jacob's hood, leavin' it in ruins. {79:8} Forget our past sins, God, show us some love quick 'cause we're down in the dumps. {79:9} Save us, God of our salvation, for your rep's sake, wipe our sins clean. {79:10} Why should the haters ask, "Where's their God?" Show 'em, Lord, make 'em pay for spillin' our blood. {79:11} Hear the cries of the captives, save those marked for death with your mighty power. {79:12} Give our neighbors seven times the shame they gave you, Lord. {79:13} We'll keep reppin' you forever, givin' you props for all generations.

{80:1} Listen up, Shepherd of Israel, leading Joseph like a boss, {80:2} Get your game on before Ephraim, Benjamin, and Manasseh, come save us. {80:3} Turn us around, God, shine your face on us, then we'll be safe. {80:4} How long you gonna stay mad at our prayers, Lord of hosts? {80:5} We're chowin' down on tears, drinkin' 'em up like waterfalls. {80:6} We're a joke to our neighbors, enemies laughin' it up. {80:7} Turn us around, God of hosts, shine your face on us, then we'll be safe. {80:8} You brought a vine outta Egypt, kicked out the haters, and planted it. {80:9} You made room for it, let it take root, now it's takin' over. {80:10} Covered the hills with its shade, its branches like giant trees. {80:11} Reachin' out to the sea, branches stretchin' to the river. {80:12} But why'd you let it get wrecked, its fences torn down? {80:13} Boars and wild beasts tearin' it up, devourin' the fields. {80:14} Come back, God of hosts, check out your vineyard from heaven, {80:15} The one you planted with your right hand, the branch you made strong. {80:16} It's burned up, cut down, destroyed by your anger. {80:17} Lay your hand on the man at your right hand, the son of man you made strong. {80:18} We won't turn away from you, revitalize us, and we'll call on your name. {80:19} Turn us around, Lord God of hosts, shine your face on us, then we'll be safe.

{81:1} Sing it loud for God, our strength! Make some joyful noise for the OG, the God of Jacob. {81:2} Grab a jam, bring in the drums, the sweet vibes of the harp, and the guitar. {81:3} Blast that trumpet on the new moon, at the appointed time, on our lit feast day. {81:4} 'Cause this was the deal for Israel, a law laid down by the God of Jacob. {81:5} He set it up back in Joseph's day, as a proof, when he dipped out of Egypt and I was clueless about the language. {81:6} I took off his heavy load, his hands were freed from the grind. {81:7} You called out when things got rough, and I came through; I answered you with some thunder, tested you at the waters of Meribah. Selah. {81:8} Listen up, my people, I got something to say: Israel, if you pay attention, {81:9} There won't be any strange gods among you; you won't bow down to any weird idols. {81:10} I'm the LORD your God, the one who brought you out of Egypt; open wide, and I'll hook you up. {81:11} But you didn't listen to me, my people rejected me. {81:12} So I let them do their thing, follow their own plans. {81:13} Man, if only they had listened to me, walked in my ways! {81:14} I would've wrecked their enemies, turned my hand against their haters. {81:15} Those who hate the LORD would've been kissing up to him; they'd be around forever. {81:16} He would've been feeding them the best, honey straight from the rock, keeping them satisfied.

{82:1} God's chilling with the powerful squad; he's sorting stuff out among the big shots. {82:2} How long are you gonna be unfair, taking the side of the bad guys? Selah. {82:3} Stand up for the poor and parentless; give the afflicted and needy a fair shake. {82:4} Rescue the poor and needy; get them out of the clutches of the bad guys. {82:5} They're clueless, won't understand a thing; they're walking in the dark, messing up everything. {82:6} I said, "You're like gods, all of you are children of the Most High." {82:7} But you're gonna kick the bucket like everyone else, fall like any other leader. {82:8} Rise up, God, sort out this earth; 'cause it's all yours anyway.

{83:1} Yo, God, don't stay quiet; speak up and don't hold back. {83:2} Check it, your enemies are making a ruckus; those who hate you are getting bold. {83:3} They're plotting against your people, scheming against your hidden ones. {83:4} They're saying, "Let's wipe 'em out as a nation, so nobody remembers Israel." {83:5} They're all in on this, working together against you: {83:6} Edom, Ishmaelites, Moab, Hagarenes; {83:7} Gebal, Ammon, Amalek; the Philistines and the folks from Tyre; {83:8} Even Assyria's in on it, helping out the descendants of Lot. Selah. {83:9} Treat them like you did the Midianites, like Sisera and Jabin at Kison's brook: {83:10} They're history, like what happened at Endor, turned to crap for the earth. {83:11} Make their big shots like Oreb, Zeeb, all their princes like Zebah and Zalmunna: {83:12} They wanted to snatch up God's houses as their own. {83:13} My God, make them spin like wheels; scatter them like chaff in the wind. {83:14} Burn them up like fire burns wood, like flames torch mountains; {83:15} Chase them down with your storm, scare them with your tempest. {83:16} Slap them with shame, so they'll seek out your name, LORD. {83:17} Let them be embarrassed and messed up forever; let them be put to shame and destroyed. {83:18} So everyone knows that you, whose name is JEHOVAH, are the top dog over everything.

{84:1} Man, your digs are dope, LORD of hosts! {84:2} My soul's itching for your crib, yeah, I'm dying to chill in your courts; my heart and flesh are begging for the living God. {84:3} Even the birds found a spot to crash, where they can build their nests, at your altars, LORD of hosts, my King, my God. {84:4} Those who kick it in your crib are blessed; they're always shouting your praises. Selah. {84:5} Blessed are those who find their strength in you; their hearts are all about your ways. {84:6} They turn barren places into oases; the rain fills up the pools. {84:7} They're getting stronger and stronger; each one shows up in Zion, ready to vibe with God. {84:8} LORD God of hosts, listen up to my prayer; pay attention, God of Jacob. Selah. {84:9} Look at us, God, our shield, check out your chosen one's face. {84:10} A day in your crib beats a thousand anywhere else; I'd rather be a doorman in your house than chill in the wicked's tents. {84:11} 'Cause you, LORD God, you're like a sun and shield, you hand out grace and glory; you don't hold back anything good from those who walk the straight and narrow. {84:12} LORD of hosts, blessed are those who trust in you.

{85:1} LORD, you've been real good to your land; you brought Jacob back from captivity. {85:2} You've forgiven your people's mess-ups, covered all their sins. Selah. {85:3} You dropped the anger, put a lid on the rage. {85:4} Turn us around, God of our salvation; chill out on the anger toward us. {85:5} Are you gonna stay mad at us forever? Keep your anger going for all time? {85:6} Nah, bring us back to life again, so your people can party it up. {85:7} Show us some love, LORD, and give us your salvation. {85:8} I'm all ears for what God the LORD has to say; he's bringing peace to his peeps and his saints, but they better not go back to their dumb ways. {85:9} Those who fear him are gonna get hooked up real soon; glory's gonna set up shop in our land. {85:10} Mercy and truth are teaming up; righteousness and peace are tight. {85:11} Truth's popping up from the ground; righteousness is peeking down from the sky. {85:12} Yeah, the LORD's bringing the good stuff, and our land's gonna be popping with blessings. {85:13} Righteousness is leading the way, setting us on the right path.

{86:1} Hey God, listen up and hear me out 'cause I'm struggling and need help. {86:2} Keep my soul safe; I'm tryin' to stay holy. My God, save your servant who trusts you. {86:3} Show me some mercy, Lord; I'm cryin' out to you every day. {86:4} Make your servant's soul happy 'cause I'm liftin' it up to you, Lord. {86:5} You're so good, Lord, ready to forgive and full of mercy for everyone who calls on you. {86:6} Listen to my prayer, Lord, and pay attention to my requests. {86:7} When I'm in trouble, I'll call on you, 'cause I know you'll answer. {86:8} There's no god like you, Lord, and no works like yours. {86:9} All nations you made will come and worship before you, Lord, and glorify your name. {86:10} You do awesome things, 'cause you're the only true God. {86:11} Teach me your ways, Lord, so I can walk in your truth; unite my heart to respect your name. {86:12} I'll praise you, Lord my God, with all my heart and glorify your name forever. {86:13} Your mercy's great toward me; you saved my soul from the lowest hell. {86:14} God, proud people are against me, violent mobs want my soul; they don't acknowledge you. {86:15} But you, Lord, are full of compassion, gracious, patient, and overflowing with mercy and truth. {86:16} Turn to me and show me mercy; give your strength to your servant, save your handmaid's son. {86:17} Show me a sign of your goodness, so my haters will see and be ashamed 'cause you helped and comforted me.

{87:1} God's foundation is on the holy mountains. {87:2} The Lord loves the gates of Zion more than all the dwellings of Jacob. {87:3} Awesome things are said about you, city of God. Selah. {87:4} I'll mention Rahab and Babylon to those who know me: look, Philistia, Tyre, and Ethiopia; this person was born there. {87:5} And of Zion, it'll be said, "This one and that one were born in her"; the Highest himself established her. {87:6} The Lord will count, when he writes up the people, that this person was born there. Selah. {87:7} The singers and players on instruments are there: all my springs are in you.

{88:1} Lord, God of my salvation, I've cried day and night before you. {88:2} Let my prayer come before you; listen to my cry. {88:3} My soul's full of troubles, my life is close to the grave. {88:4} I'm counted with those who go down to the pit, like a person with no strength. {88:5} Free among the dead, like the slain lying in the grave, whom you don't remember, cut off from your hand. {88:6} You've put me in the lowest pit, in darkness and the depths. {88:7} Your wrath is heavy on me, you've afflicted me with all your waves. Selah. {88:8} You've distanced my friends from me, made me disgusting to them; I'm trapped and can't escape. {88:9} My eye mourns because of my affliction; Lord, I call daily on you, reaching out my hands to you. {88:10} Will you show wonders to the dead? Will the dead rise and praise you? Selah. {88:11} Will your lovingkindness be declared in the grave, your faithfulness in destruction? {88:12} Will your wonders be known in the dark, and your righteousness in the land of forgetfulness? {88:13} But I've cried out to you, Lord; in the morning, my prayer comes before you. {88:14} Lord, why do you reject my soul? Why do you hide your face from me? {88:15} I'm afflicted and ready to die since my youth; I suffer your terrors, I'm distracted. {88:16} Your fierce wrath overwhelms me, your terrors have cut me off. {88:17} They surround me daily like water, they completely engulf me. {88:18} You've taken my loved ones and friends away from me, made me a stranger to them.

{89:1} I'll sing of the Lord's mercies forever; with my mouth, I'll make your faithfulness known to all generations. {89:2} I've said, Mercy will last forever; your faithfulness is established in the heavens. {89:3} I've made a covenant with my chosen one, I've sworn to David my servant: {89:4} I'll establish your seed forever and build up your throne for all generations. Selah. {89:5} The heavens will praise your wonders, Lord, your faithfulness in the assembly of the saints. {89:6} Who in the sky can compare to the Lord? Who among the mighty can be like the Lord? {89:7} God is greatly feared in the assembly of the saints and held in reverence by all around him. {89:8} Lord God of hosts, who's mighty like you, Lord? Your faithfulness surrounds you. {89:9} You rule the raging sea; when the waves rise, you still them. {89:10} You crushed Rahab like one of the slain; you've scattered your enemies with your strong arm. {89:11} The heavens and the earth are yours; you founded the world and everything in it. {89:12} You created the north and the south; Tabor and Hermon rejoice in your name. {89:13} Your arm is mighty, your hand strong, your right hand high. {89:14} Righteousness and justice are the foundation of your throne; mercy and truth go before you. {89:15} Blessed are the people who know the joyful sound; they walk, Lord, in the light of your presence. {89:16} They rejoice in your name all day and are exalted in your righteousness. {89:17} You're the glory of their strength; by your favor, our horn is exalted. {89:18} The Lord is our defense; the Holy One of Israel is our king. {89:19} You spoke in a vision to your holy one, saying, I've given help to one who's mighty; I've exalted a chosen one from the people. {89:20} I found David my servant; I've anointed him with my holy oil. {89:21} My hand will support him, my arm will strengthen him. {89:22} The enemy won't outsmart him, the wicked won't oppress him. {89:23} I'll crush his foes before him and strike down those who hate him. {89:24} My faithfulness and mercy will be with him; in my name, his horn will be exalted. {89:25} I'll set his hand over the sea, his right hand over the rivers. {89:26} He'll call to me, "You're my Father, my God, and the rock of my salvation." {89:27} I'll make him my firstborn, the highest of the kings of the earth. {89:28} My mercy will stay with him forever, my covenant will stand firm with him. {89:29} I'll make his seed endure forever, his throne like the days of heaven. {89:30} If his children forsake my law and don't walk in my judgments, {89:31} If they break my statutes and don't keep my commandments, {89:32} Then I'll punish their sin with the rod, their iniquity with stripes. {89:33} But I won't take away my lovingkindness from him, nor let my faithfulness fail. {89:34} I won't break my covenant or change what I've said. {89:35} Once I've sworn by my holiness, I won't lie to David. {89:36} His seed will endure forever, his throne like the sun before me. {89:37} It'll be established forever like the moon, a faithful witness in the sky. Selah. {89:38} But you've rejected and been angry with your anointed. {89:39} You've renounced the covenant with your servant, defiled his crown by throwing it to the ground. {89:40} You've broken down all his walls, brought his strongholds to ruin. {89:41} Everyone who passes by plunders him; he's a reproach to his neighbors. {89:42} You've exalted the right hand of his enemies, made all his foes rejoice. {89:43} You've turned the edge of his sword and haven't supported him in battle. {89:44} You've ended his splendor, cast his throne to the ground. {89:45} You've shortened his youth, covered him with shame. Selah. {89:46} How long, Lord? Will you hide yourself forever? Will your wrath burn like fire? {89:47} Remember how brief my time is; why did you create all humans for nothing? {89:48} What man can live and not see death? Can he save his soul from the grave? Selah. {89:49} Lord, where's your former lovingkindness, which you swore to David in your truth? {89:50} Yo, God, remember the shade thrown at your squad; I'm holding onto all the hate from these big shots; {89:51} They've been dragging your name, Lord; they're trash-talking your chosen one. {89:52} Bless up, Lord, forever and always. Amen and Amen.

{90:1} God, you've been our safe space through all the generations. {90:2} Before the mountains or the earth were a thing, from forever ago to forever, you're God. {90:3} You turn humans back to dust, saying, "Go back to where you came from, folks." {90:4} A thousand years to you are like yesterday, gone in a blink, like a night shift. {90:5} You sweep them away like a flood; they crash like they're asleep; in the morning, they're like grass that sprouts up. {90:6} It blooms in the morning and then by evening, it's cut down and wilts. {90:7} We're wiped out by your anger; your rage is stressing us out. {90:8} You've got our sins in plain sight, our secret fails in your spotlight. {90:9} Our days are ending in your wrath; we live out our years like a story told. {90:10} We get seventy years, eighty if we're strong, but those years are full of struggle; they're soon over, and we bounce. {90:11} Who knows how hardcore your anger is? Your wrath matches the fear you deserve. {90:12} Teach us to count our days right, so we can get a wise heart. {90:13} Come back, Lord! How long will it be? Have some mercy on your servants. {90:14} Hit us up early with your love, so we can celebrate and be glad all our days. {90:15} Make us happy for as long as you've made us suffer, for the years we've seen bad times. {90:16} Show your deeds to your servants, and your glory to their kids. {90:17} Let the Lord's beauty be on us; establish the work of our hands for us; yeah, establish the work of our hands.

{91:1} Chill in the secret spot of the Most High, you'll be safe under the Almighty's shade. {91:2} I'm telling you, the LORD's my safe space, my fortress; my ride-or-die, I trust in him. {91:3} He'll totally save you from traps and nasty diseases. {91:4} He'll cover you like a cozy blanket, and you can trust him like you trust your bestie; his truth's gonna protect you. {91:5} You won't sweat the night terrors or dodging arrows during the day. {91:6} Not scared of darkness diseases or high noon destruction. {91:7} Even if a thousand go down beside you, or ten thousand at your right hand, you're good. {91:8} You'll just watch as the bad guys get what's coming to them. {91:9} 'Cause you made the LORD your home base, the Most High's where you kick it. {91:10} Nothing bad's gonna happen to you, no plagues crashing at your place. {91:11} 'Cause he's got his crew of angels looking out for you, keeping you safe wherever you go. {91:12} They'll even catch you if you trip, so you won't stub your toe on a rock. {91:13} You'll stomp on lions and snakes, trample those beasts underfoot. {91:14} 'Cause you're all about him, he's got your back; he's gonna lift you up 'cause you know his name. {91:15} When you call out, he'll be there; he's got your back when things get tough, gonna rescue you and give you props. {91:16} You'll have a long, epic life, and he'll show you his salvation.

{92:1} It's dope to thank the LORD and jam out to his name, Most High. {92:2} Spreading the word about your kindness in the morning, and your faithfulness every night, {92:3} With some sick tunes on a ten-string guitar, and the harp bringing those good vibes. {92:4} 'Cause you, LORD, make me happy with what you do; I'll celebrate the awesome stuff you make. {92:5} LORD, your works are amazing, and your thoughts are deep, like, seriously deep. {92:6} Only a dummy wouldn't get it; fools just don't understand. {92:7} When bad people pop up like weeds, and all those troublemakers start strutting their stuff, it's just 'cause they're doomed. {92:8} But you, LORD, you're forever at the top. {92:9} 'Cause your enemies, LORD, they're gonna bite it; all the troublemakers are gonna scatter. {92:10} But you'll hook me up, make my status rise like a unicorn's horn; I'll be dripping with fresh blessings. {92:11} I'll see my enemies get what's coming to them, hear all about their downfall. {92:12} The good guys are gonna thrive like palm trees, grow tall like cedars in Lebanon. {92:13} Those who stick with the LORD's crew are gonna flourish in his hangouts. {92:14} They'll stay fruitful even in their golden years, staying healthy and thriving. {92:15} Showing everyone that the LORD is straight up righteous; he's my rock, and there's no shady business with him.

{93:1} The LORD's running the show, dressed to impress; he's got the whole world in check. {93:2} His throne's been set up forever; he's been around since forever. {93:3} The floods might get loud, but the LORD's even louder; he's stronger than the wildest waves. {93:4} LORD, you're way more powerful than the roar of the ocean. {93:5} Your rules are rock solid; your house is all about holiness, LORD, now and forever.

{94:1} LORD God, you're the boss of payback; show yourself, God of payback, let's see what you got. {94:2} Step up, you judge of the earth; give the proud what they deserve. {94:3} LORD, how long are the bad guys gonna party? How long are they gonna win? {94:4} How long are they gonna talk trash and brag about being jerks? {94:5} They're messing with your people, LORD, hurting the ones you care about. {94:6} They're killing the helpless, taking out widows and orphans. {94:7} And they have the nerve to say, "God doesn't see; the God of Jacob doesn't pay attention." {94:8} Seriously, wake up, you clueless people; when are you gonna wise up, you fools? {94:9} God made ears, you think he can't hear? He made eyes, you think he can't see? {94:10} He's the one who trains the nations, you think he won't correct them? He's the one who teaches us stuff; you think he doesn't know? {94:11} The LORD knows what's going on in people's heads; he knows it's all empty. {94:12} Happy is the one you teach, LORD, and train in your law, {94:13} 'Cause you give them a break from tough times until you take out the trash. {94:14} The LORD won't ditch his people; he won't bail on his crew. {94:15} Fairness is coming back strong; those with honest hearts will follow it. {94:16} Who's gonna stand up to the bad guys for me? Who's gonna take on the jerks for me? {94:17} If the LORD hadn't had my back, I would've been toast by now. {94:18} When I felt like I was slipping, your kindness, LORD, caught me. {94:19} In the middle of all my crazy thoughts, your comfort was everything to me. {94:20} You think a throne built on evil is gonna hang with you? A throne that makes evil laws? {94:21} They're ganging up on good people, condemning innocent lives. {94:22} But the LORD's my bodyguard; he's my safe space. {94:23} He's gonna make them pay for their evil, cut them off for good; the LORD our God's gonna take them out.

{95:1} Let's bust out some tunes for the LORD; let's get loud and thank the rock who saves us. {95:2} Let's bring our gratitude, make some noise with our jams. {95:3} 'Cause the LORD's a big deal, way bigger than any other gods. {95:4} He's got the whole world in his hands, even the big mountains. {95:5} The sea's his, he made it; his hands crafted the dry land. {95:6} So let's come correct and worship him; let's bow down and show some respect to the LORD who made us. {95:7} 'Cause he's our God, and we're his squad; we're his crew, and he's always got our back. If you hear him calling you today, {95:8} Don't brush it off like they did in the past, when they tested him and saw what he could do. {95:9} They pushed him for forty years, and he was done with their drama, saying, "These people just don't get it; they don't know how to follow me." {95:10} In his anger, he swore they wouldn't find rest in his place.

{96:1} Sing a new track to the Lord: sing to the Lord, all the earth. {96:2} Sing to the Lord, bless his name; spread the news of his salvation daily. {96:3} Tell his glory among the nations, his wonders among all people. {96:4} For the Lord is awesome and totally deserves our praise; he's to be feared above all gods. {96:5} All the other nations' gods are just idols, but the Lord made the heavens. {96:6} Honor and majesty are in front of him; strength and beauty are in his sanctuary. {96:7} Give to the Lord, families of the people, give to the Lord glory and strength. {96:8} Give to the Lord the glory due to his name; bring an offering and roll up into his courts. {96:9} Worship the Lord in the beauty of holiness; tremble before him, all the earth. {96:10} Say among the nations, "The Lord rules!"

The world is set and unmovable; he judges the people fairly. {96:11} Let the heavens be hyped, and let the earth be glad; let the sea roar and all that's in it. {96:12} Let the field be stoked and all in it; then all the trees of the forest will sing for joy {96:13} Before the Lord, because he's coming to judge the earth; he'll judge the world with righteousness and the people with his truth.

{97:1} The Lord rules; let the earth celebrate; let all the islands be glad. {97:2} Clouds and darkness surround him; righteousness and justice are his throne's foundation. {97:3} Fire goes before him and burns up his enemies all around. {97:4} His lightning lights up the world; the earth sees and trembles. {97:5} The hills melt like wax at the Lord's presence, at the presence of the Lord of all the earth. {97:6} The heavens announce his righteousness, and all the people see his glory. {97:7} All who worship images and boast in idols are embarrassed; worship him, all gods. {97:8} Zion heard and was happy; the daughters of Judah rejoiced because of your judgments, Lord. {97:9} For you, Lord, are the highest over all the earth; you are lifted far above all gods. {97:10} You who love the Lord, hate evil; he protects the lives of his faithful; he saves them from the wicked. {97:11} Light is spread for the righteous, and joy for the upright in heart. {97:12} Rejoice in the Lord, you righteous ones; and give thanks to his holy name.

{98:1} Sing a new song to the Lord because he's done awesome things; his right hand and his holy arm have won him the victory. {98:2} The Lord has shown his salvation; he's revealed his righteousness to the nations. {98:3} He's remembered his love and faithfulness to Israel; all the earth's ends have seen our God's salvation. {98:4} Make a joyful noise to the Lord, all the earth; break out in praise and sing for joy. {98:5} Sing to the Lord with the harp; with the harp and melodious song. {98:6} With trumpets and the blast of the ram's horn, make a joyful noise before the Lord, the King. {98:7} Let the sea and all it contains roar, the world and those who live in it. {98:8} Let the rivers clap their hands; let the hills sing for joy together {98:9} Before the Lord, because he's coming to judge the earth; he'll judge the world with righteousness and the people with fairness.

{99:1} The Lord rules; let the people shake; he sits between the cherubim; let the earth move. {99:2} The Lord is great in Zion; he's above all the people. {99:3} Let them praise your great and awesome name; it's holy. {99:4} The King loves justice; you establish fairness, you do what's right in Jacob. {99:5} Lift up the Lord our God, and worship at his footstool; he's holy. {99:6} Moses and Aaron were among his priests, and Samuel among those who call on his name; they called on the Lord, and he answered them. {99:7} He spoke to them in the cloudy pillar; they kept his laws and the statutes he gave them. {99:8} You answered them, Lord our God; you were a forgiving God to them, but you punished their misdeeds. {99:9} Lift up the Lord our God, and worship at his holy hill; for the Lord our God is holy.

{100:1} Make a joyful noise to the Lord, all you lands. {100:2} Serve the Lord with gladness; come before him with joyful songs. {100:3} Know that the Lord is God; he made us, and we belong to him; we are his people, the sheep of his pasture. {100:4} Enter his gates with thanksgiving and his courts with praise; give thanks to him and praise his name. {100:5} For the Lord is good; his mercy lasts forever; his faithfulness continues through all generations.

{101:1} Yo, I'm gonna drop some bars about mercy and justice; yo, LORD, I'm singing to you. {101:2} Gonna be smart about how I roll, keep it real in my crib, keeping it 💯. {101:3} No shady stuff on my screen; I'm ghosting anyone who's shady AF. {101:4} If you're fake, you're out; I don't hang with no shady crew. {101:5} If you're talking smack behind backs, I'm cutting you off; no room for arrogant vibes. {101:6} My squad's gonna be the real deal; only rolling with those who keep it 💯. {101:7} Liars and cheats ain't welcome here; I'm keeping it real, no fakes allowed. {101:8} I'm cleaning house early, kicking out all the phonies; making sure this place stays legit.

{102:1} Yo, LORD, hear me out; answer me quick when I'm in a jam. {102:2} Don't ghost me when I'm struggling; listen up and reply ASAP. {102:3} My days are dragging like endless drama, bones feeling burnt out. {102:4} My heart's heavy, feeling drained; forgetting to even eat. {102:5} Groaning so much, my skin's sticking to my bones. {102:6} Feeling like a lonely bird in the wilderness, like an outcast in the desert. {102:7} Watching from the sidelines, feeling isolated. {102:8} Haters throwing shade all day, got beef with me non-stop. {102:9} I've been eating sadness for breakfast, drinking tears for hydration. {102:10} Feeling the heat of your anger and wrath; you lift me up, then bring me down. {102:11} Days slipping away like shadows, wilting like grass. {102:12} But you, LORD, you're forever; your legacy goes on and on. {102:13} You'll rise up, show mercy to Zion; it's time to bless her. {102:14} Your peeps love her walls, cherish her dust. {102:15} Nations will respect your name, kings will bow to your glory. {102:16} When you rebuild Zion, you'll shine in all your glory. {102:17} You'll hear the cries of the helpless, not ignoring their prayers. {102:18} This story's gonna be told for generations; people yet to be born will praise you. {102:19} You're watching from your holy place in the sky, seeing everything. {102:20} Hearing the cries of the prisoners, freeing those on death row. {102:21} Making your name known in Zion, your praise echoing in Jerusalem. {102:22} When everyone gathers to worship you, you'll be there. {102:23} You weakened me on my journey, shortened my days. {102:24} I begged you, "Don't take me now; your legacy lasts forever." {102:25} You laid the earth's foundation long ago; the heavens are your masterpiece. {102:26} They'll fade away, but you'll endure; changing them like clothes, but you remain the same. {102:27} You're forever; your years never end. {102:28} Your servants' children will thrive, their legacy secure before you.

{103:1} Shout out to the LORD; calling on his name, spreading the word about his deeds. {103:2} Singing his praises, dropping some sick rhymes about his wonders. {103:3} Glorifying his holy name, making those who seek him hype. {103:4} Searching for the LORD and his strength, always seeking his presence. {103:5} Remembering all the awesome things he's done; his mercy and love. {103:6} Yo, descendants of Abraham, Jacob's crew, listen up. {103:7} The LORD's our God, laying down justice everywhere. {103:8} He's always remembering his promises, passed down for generations. {103:9} He's cool, not always throwing shade; his mercy's endless. {103:10} He doesn't hold our mistakes against us; his love is sky-high for those who respect him. {103:11} His mercy's as high as the sky, reaching those who honor him. {103:12} As far as east is from west, he's wiped out our sins. {103:13} He's like a chill dad, showing love to those who respect him. {103:14} He knows we're just human; he knows we're made of dust. {103:15} Our lives are like grass, flourishing briefly like flowers. {103:16} But his love lasts forever, even to our grandkids. {103:17} For those who keep his promises and remember his commands. {103:18} He's got his throne up in the sky, ruling over everything. {103:19} Shout out to the LORD, you mighty angels, obeying his commands. {103:20} Bless the LORD, all you heavenly hosts, doing his bidding. {103:21} Bless the LORD, all his creations, everywhere he rules. {103:22} Yo, soul, shout out to the LORD; praise him with all you've got.

{104:1} Big shout out to the LORD, yo, he's lit; decked out in honor and power. {104:2} Wrapped up in light like it's his fashion statement; stretching out the sky like it's his VIP lounge. {104:3} Laying down his crib in the deep waters; cruising on clouds like it's his ride. {104:4} His angels are like supernatural DJs; his crew bringing the heat. {104:5} He laid down the earth's foundation, making sure it stays put. {104:6} Covered it up with oceans like a cozy blanket; waters towering over the mountains. {104:7} When he speaks, nature listens; his thunder makes everything bounce. {104:8} Rivers flowing down the mountains, carving their paths. {104:9} He set boundaries for the waters; they know their place. {104:10} Springs gushing in the valleys, watering the hills. {104:11} Giving drinks to all the animals; even the wild donkeys get their fill. {104:12} Birds making homes in the trees, singing their hearts out. {104:13} Watering the hills, satisfying the earth with its bounty. {104:14} Growing grass for the cattle, herbs for us to enjoy. {104:15} Wine to make us happy, oil to make us shine, bread to keep us strong. {104:16} The LORD's trees are always fresh, like those cedars in Lebanon. {104:17} Home to birds; even the storks chill there. {104:18} High hills are playgrounds for wild goats; rocks are hangouts for hyraxes. {104:19} The moon marks the seasons; the sun knows when to clock out. {104:20} Darkness falls, and the nocturnal creatures come out to play. {104:21} Lions roaring for their dinner, looking up to heaven for their meal ticket. {104:22} Sun rises, they retreat to their dens; humans head out to grind till dusk. {104:23} Yo, LORD, your work is insane; in wisdom, you made it all. {104:24} Earth's loaded with your riches; you're the ultimate flex. {104:25} The ocean's vast, teeming with life; creatures big and small. {104:26} Ships sailing, Leviathan's playing in the waves. {104:27} All creatures waiting on you for their grub; when you give, they're all set. {104:28} You open your hand, they're satisfied; you hide your face, they freak out. {104:29} Take away their breath, they're gone; back to dust they go. {104:30} You send out your spirit, they're created; you renew the face of the earth. {104:31} LORD, your glory lasts forever; you're stoked about your creations. {104:32} You look at the earth, it shakes; you touch the mountains, they smoke. {104:33} I'll sing to the LORD as long as I live; praising my God while I've got breath. {104:34} Thinking about him's sweet; glad to be in his crew. {104:35} Let the sinners vanish from the earth; let the wicked be no more. Big shout out to the LORD; praise the LORD, yo!

{105:1} Yo, props to the LORD; call out his name, spread the word about his epic deeds. {105:2} Singing to him, dropping beats about his amazing works. {105:3} Celebrating his holy name; all who seek him, get hyped. {105:4} Chasing after the LORD and his power; always looking for his face. {105:5} Remembering all the dope stuff he's done; his wonders and righteous verdicts. {105:6} Hey, descendants of Abraham, Jacob's posse, listen up. {105:7} The LORD's our God; his verdicts reach every corner of the earth. {105:8} He never forgets his promises, passed down for ages. {105:9} The deal he made with Abraham, the oath he swore to Isaac. {105:10} Keeping the same deal with Jacob, making it law for Israel forever. {105:11} Promising them the land of Canaan, their inheritance. {105:12} When they were just a handful; few and far between in a foreign land. {105:13} Moving from place to place, from nation to nation. {105:14} No one messed with them; kings got called out for them. {105:15} "Don't mess with my chosen ones," he warned, "and don't diss my prophets." {105:16} He even brought a famine on their turf, cutting off their food supply. {105:17} Sent Joseph ahead as a slave; sold him off for some coins. {105:18} Shackled him in chains, imprisoned him unfairly. {105:19} But his word proved true; the LORD's plan tested him. {105:20} Pharaoh sent for him, released him from prison, set him free. {105:21} Made him ruler of his palace, manager of his possessions. {105:22} To control his princes as he pleased, teach his elders wisdom. {105:23} Israel ended up in Egypt; Jacob stayed in the land of Ham. {105:24} And they multiplied like crazy, stronger than their haters. {105:25} Turned their enemies' hearts against them, made them plot against his people. {105:26} Sent Moses his servant, and Aaron his chosen one. {105:27} They showed off his signs and wonders in Egypt. {105:28} Sent darkness, but no one rebelled; they obeyed his word. {105:29} Turned their water into blood, killed their fish. {105:30} Frogs everywhere, even in their king's palace. {105:31} Sent swarms of flies and gnats, all over their land. {105:32} Hail instead of rain, fiery lightning in their land. {105:33} Destroyed their vines and fig trees, shattered their trees. {105:34} Sent locusts, devouring everything in sight, too many to count. {105:35} Ate up all the plants, stripped the land bare. {105:36} Killed all the firstborn, the pride of their strength. {105:37} But he led his people out with silver and gold; not a weakling among them. {105:38} Egypt rejoiced when they left; fear of them fell on their enemies. {105:39} Covered them with a cloud by day; gave them fire to light their way at night. {105:40} They asked for meat, he sent them quail; satisfied them with heavenly bread. {105:41} Split a rock, water gushed out; flowed like a river in the desert. {105:42} He remembered his sacred promise, made to Abraham his servant. {105:43} He brought out his people with joy, his chosen ones with singing. {105:44} Gave them the lands of their enemies; they took over the labor of others. {105:45} So they could keep his laws and obey his instructions. Big shout out to the LORD!

{106:1} Yo, shout out to the LORD! Give props to the LORD, 'cause he's awesome: his vibes last forever. {106:2} Who can even describe the LORD's epic deeds? Who can show off all his praise? {106:3} Blessed are those who keep it real with judgment, and always do what's right. {106:4} Remember me, LORD, with the love you got for your squad: visit me with your salvation; {106:5} So I can see the good of your chosen ones, rejoice in the happiness of your nation, and flex with your inheritance. {106:6} We messed up like our ancestors, we committed wrongs, we acted wickedly. {106:7} Our ancestors didn't get your wonders in Egypt; they forgot your many mercies; they provoked you at the sea, even at the Red Sea. {106:8} But you saved them for your name's sake, to show off your mighty power. {106:9} You rebuked the Red Sea and it dried up: you led them through the depths like it was the wilderness. {106:10} And you saved them from the haters, and redeemed them from the enemy's hand. {106:11} The waters covered their enemies: not one was left. {106:12} Then they believed your words; they sang your praise. {106:13} But they quickly forgot your works; they didn't wait for your counsel: {106:14} They craved like crazy in the wilderness, and tested God in the desert. {106:15} So you gave them what they asked for, but sent emptiness into their soul. {106:16} They envied Moses in the camp, and Aaron, the holy one of the LORD. {106:17} The earth opened and swallowed Dathan, and covered the company of Abiram. {106:18} A fire blazed among their company; the flames burnt up the wicked. {106:19} They made a calf in Horeb, and worshipped a molten image. {106:20} They traded their glory for an image of an ox that eats grass. {106:21} They forgot God their savior, who did great things in Egypt; {106:22} Amazing works in the land of Ham, and awesome things by the Red Sea. {106:23} So he said he'd destroy them, if Moses, his chosen one, hadn't stood in the breach, to turn away his anger, so he wouldn't destroy them. {106:24} They despised the promised land, they didn't believe his word: {106:25} They whined in their tents, and didn't listen to the LORD's voice. {106:26} So he raised his hand against them, to overthrow them in the wilderness: {106:27} To overthrow their descendants among the nations, and scatter them across lands. {106:28} They joined themselves to Baal-peor, and ate sacrifices offered to the dead. {106:29} They made him mad with their inventions, and a plague broke out among them. {106:30} Then Phinehas stood up and intervened: and the plague was stopped. {106:31} And it was counted to him as righteousness through all generations forever. {106:32} They angered him at the waters of Meribah, so things went badly for Moses because of them: {106:33} They provoked his spirit, so he spoke rashly with his lips. {106:34} They didn't destroy the nations the LORD had told them to: {106:35} Instead, they mixed with the nations and learned their ways. {106:36} They served their idols: which became a trap for them. {106:37} They sacrificed their sons and daughters to demons, {106:38} And shed innocent blood, the blood of their sons and daughters, whom they sacrificed to Canaan's idols: and the land was stained with blood. {106:39} They were defiled by their own deeds, and played the harlot with their own inventions. {106:40} So the LORD's anger burned against his people, and he hated his own inheritance. {106:41} He handed them over to the nations; and those who hated them ruled over them. {106:42} Their enemies oppressed them, and they were subdued under their power. {106:43} Many times he delivered them; but they rebelled with their plans, and were humbled for their sin. {106:44} Yet he saw their distress, when he heard their cry: {106:45} And he remembered his covenant with them, and relented because of his great mercy. {106:46} He made them pitied by all who took them captive. {106:47} Save us, LORD our God, and gather us from the nations, to give thanks to your holy name, and to triumph in your praise. {106:48} Blessed be the LORD God of Israel from everlasting to everlasting: and let everyone say, Amen. Praise the LORD.

{107:1} Give thanks to the LORD, for he is good: his mercy lasts forever. {107:2} Let the redeemed of the LORD say this, those he redeemed from the enemy's hand; {107:3} And gathered them from the lands, from the east, west, north, and south. {107:4} They wandered in the wilderness, finding no city to live in. {107:5} Hungry and thirsty, their souls fainted within them. {107:6} Then they cried out to the LORD in their trouble, and he delivered them from their distress. {107:7} He led them by a straight way to a city where they could settle. {107:8} Oh, that people would praise the LORD for his goodness, and for his wonderful works to humanity! {107:9} For he satisfies the thirsty and fills the hungry with good things. {107:10} Some sat in darkness and in the shadow of death, bound in affliction and chains; {107:11} Because they rebelled against God's words and despised the counsel of the Most High. {107:12} So he humbled their hearts with labor; they stumbled, and there was no one to help. {107:13} Then they cried to the LORD in their trouble, and he saved them from their distress. {107:14} He brought them out of darkness and the shadow of death, and broke their chains. {107:15} Oh, that people would praise the LORD for his goodness, and for his wonderful works to humanity! {107:16} For he breaks down gates of bronze and cuts through bars of iron. {107:17} Some became fools through their rebellion and suffered for their sins. {107:18} They loathed all food and came near the gates of death. {107:19} Then they cried to the LORD in their trouble, and he saved them from their distress. {107:20} He sent out his word and healed them; he rescued them from the grave. {107:21} Oh, that people would praise the LORD for his goodness, and for his wonderful works to humanity! {107:22} Let them sacrifice thank offerings and tell of his works with songs of joy. {107:23} Those who go down to the sea in ships, who do business on the mighty waters; {107:24} They saw the works of the LORD, his wonderful deeds in the deep. {107:25} For he spoke and stirred up a tempest that lifted high the waves. {107:26} They mounted up to the heavens and went down to the depths; in their peril, their courage melted away. {107:27} They reeled and staggered like drunkards; they were at their wits' end. {107:28} Then they cried out to the LORD in their trouble, and he brought them out of their distress. {107:29} He stilled the storm to a whisper; the waves of the sea were hushed. {107:30} They were glad when it grew calm, and he guided them to their desired haven. {107:31} Oh, that people would praise the LORD for his goodness, and for his wonderful works to humanity! {107:32} Let them exalt him in the assembly of the people and praise him in the council of the elders. {107:33} He turned rivers into a desert, flowing springs into thirsty ground; {107:34} And fruitful land into a salt waste, because of the wickedness of those who lived there. {107:35} He turned the desert into pools of water and the parched ground into flowing springs; {107:36} There he brought the hungry to live, and they founded a city where they could settle. {107:37} They sowed fields and planted vineyards that yielded a fruitful harvest; {107:38} He blessed them, and their numbers greatly increased, and he did not let their herds diminish. {107:39} Then their numbers decreased, and they were humbled by oppression, calamity, and sorrow. {107:40} He pours contempt on nobles and made them wander in a trackless waste. {107:41} But he lifted the needy out of their affliction and increased their families like flocks. {107:42} The upright see and rejoice, but all the wicked shut their mouths. {107:43} Let the wise heed these things and consider the LORD's great love.

{108:1} My heart is steadfast, O God; I will sing and make music with all my soul. {108:2} Wake up, psaltery and harp: I'm waking up early. {108:3} I'm gonna praise you, LORD, among the people; I'm singing praises to you among the nations. {108:4} Your mercy is epic above the heavens, and your truth reaches to the clouds. {108:5} Be exalted, God, above the heavens; let your glory be over all the earth. {108:6} Save your beloved; help with your right hand, and answer me. {108:7} God spoke in his holiness; I'm hyped, I'll split up Shechem and measure out the valley of Succoth. {108:8} Gilead is mine; Manasseh is mine; Ephraim is the strength of my head; Judah is my lawgiver. {108:9} Moab is my washbasin; over Edom, I'll toss my shoe; I'll flex over Philistia. {108:10} Who will bring me to the strong city? Who will lead me to Edom? {108:11} Won't you, God, who cast us off? And won't you, God, go out with our armies? {108:12} Help us from trouble; human help is pointless. {108:13} Through God, we'll do bravely; he's the one who'll stomp our enemies.

{109:1} Don't stay silent, God of my praise; {109:2} Wicked and deceitful mouths are open against me; they've spoken against me with lies. {109:3} They surrounded me with hate words and fought me for no reason. {109:4} For my love, they're my enemies, but I'm all about prayer. {109:5} They repaid me evil for good and hatred for my love. {109:6} Set a wicked person over him; let Satan stand at his right hand. {109:7} When he's judged, let him be condemned; let his prayer be a sin. {109:8} Let his days be few; let someone else take his position. {109:9} Let his kids be fatherless and his wife a widow. {109:10} Let his kids wander and beg; let them seek their bread from desolate places. {109:11} Let the creditor seize all he has; let strangers take his work. {109:12} Let no one show him mercy; let no one be kind to his fatherless kids. {109:13} Let his family line be cut off; in the next generation, let their name be erased. {109:14} Let his ancestors' sins be remembered by the LORD; don't let his mom's sin be erased. {109:15} Let these sins always be before the LORD; let him cut off their memory from the earth. {109:16} Because he didn't remember to show mercy, but persecuted the poor and needy, even to kill the brokenhearted. {109:17} As he loved cursing, let it come to him; as he didn't delight in blessing, let it be far from him. {109:18} He wore cursing like a garment; let it seep into him like water, like oil into his bones. {109:19} Let it be like the clothes covering him and the belt he always wears. {109:20} Let this be the LORD's reward to my enemies and to those who speak evil against me. {109:21} But do this for me, O GOD the Lord, for your name's sake; because your mercy is good, deliver me. {109:22} I'm poor and needy, and my heart is wounded inside me. {109:23} I'm fading like the evening shadow; I'm shaken off like a locust. {109:24} My knees are weak from fasting, and my body is thin. {109:25} I'm a joke to them; they look at me and shake their heads. {109:26} Help me, LORD my God; save me according to your mercy, {109:27} So they'll know that this is your hand; you, LORD, have done it. {109:28} Let them curse, but you bless; when they attack, let them be ashamed, but let your servant rejoice. {109:29} Let my enemies be clothed with shame; let them cover themselves with their own disgrace like a robe. {109:30} I'll greatly praise the LORD with my mouth; I'll praise him in a crowd. {109:31} He stands at the right hand of the needy to save them from those who condemn their souls.

{110:1} The LORD said to my Lord, "Sit at my right hand until I make your enemies your footstool." {110:2} The LORD will send out your mighty scepter from Zion; rule among your enemies. {110:3} Your people will offer themselves freely on the day of your power, in holy splendor; your youth will come to you like dew from the morning's womb. {110:4} The LORD has sworn and will not change his mind, "You are a priest forever after the order of Melchizedek." {110:5} The Lord is at your right hand; he will crush kings on the day of his wrath. {110:6} He will judge among the nations, heaping up the dead and crushing the rulers of many lands. {110:7} He will drink from a brook along the way; therefore he will lift up his head.

{111:1} Yo, big shout out to the LORD! I'm gonna give props to the LORD with all my heart, kicking it with the squad of the righteous and in the congregation. {111:2} Check it, the LORD's works are straight fire, sought after by everyone who's into that stuff. {111:3} His work is mad respectable and dope; his righteousness lasts forever. {111:4} He's made sure his epic works are remembered; the LORD is all about grace and compassion. {111:5} He hooks up those who respect him with grub; always keeping his covenant in mind. {111:6} He's shown his crew the power of his works, hooking them up with the goods from the nations. {111:7} His hands are all about truth and justice; his commands are legit. {111:8} They're solid forever and ever, done with straight-up truth and integrity. {111:9} He sent redemption to his people; he's got his covenant locked down forever. Holy and reverend is his name. {111:10} Respect for the LORD is where wisdom starts; those who follow his commands are legit. His praise lasts forever.

{112:1} Big ups to the LORD! Blessed is the one who respects the LORD and loves his commands. {112:2} His crew's gonna be boss on the earth; the next generation of the righteous is gonna be blessed. {112:3} Wealth and riches are gonna be in his crib, and his righteousness is gonna last forever. {112:4} When darkness hits, the righteous are gonna shine bright; they're all about grace, compassion, and doing what's right. {112:5} A good person shows love and helps out; they handle their business with wisdom. {112:6} They're gonna stand firm forever; the righteous are gonna be remembered forever. {112:7} They're not gonna stress about bad news; they trust in the LORD with all their heart. {112:8} Their heart is steady; they're not scared, even when they see their enemies fall. {112:9} They're all about sharing and helping the needy; their righteousness lasts forever. They're gonna be honored big time. {112:10} The wicked are gonna see it and be shook; they're gonna be raging with envy and fade away. The desires of the wicked are gonna be history.

{113:1} Praise the LORD! All you servants of the LORD, give mad props to the name of the LORD. {113:2} Blessed be the name of the LORD now and forever. {113:3} From sunrise to sunset, the LORD's name is gonna be praised. {113:4} The LORD is way up there, above all nations, his glory reaching beyond the heavens. {113:5} Who's even close to the LORD our God, kicking it up high? {113:6}

He takes time to check out what's up in heaven and on earth. {113:7} He raises up the poor from the dirt, lifting the needy from the lowest places. {113:8} So they can hang with the big shots, even the big shots of his crew. {113:9} He hooks up the barren woman, making her a happy mom. Praise the LORD.

{114:1} When Israel bounced out of Egypt, Jacob's crew from a land with a strange language; {114:2} Judah was where it was at for him, and Israel was his turf. {114:3} The sea peeped it and split; the Jordan River got pushed back. {114:4} The mountains were jumping like they hit the dance floor, and the little hills were bouncing like they were feeling the vibe. {114:5} What was up with you, sea, making a run for it? What about you, Jordan, backing up? {114:6} You mountains, what's with the dance moves? You little hills, catching that vibe? {114:7} Shake in your boots, earth, in the presence of the Lord, in the presence of the God of Jacob; {114:8} Who turned the rock into a water fountain, and the flint into a flowing stream.

{115:1} Not about us, LORD, not about us, but all about your name getting the glory, for your mercy and your truth's sake. {115:2} Why would the other nations ask, "Where's their God now?" {115:3} But our God's up in the heavens, doing whatever he pleases. {115:4} Their idols are just silver and gold, man-made junk. {115:5} They got mouths but can't talk, eyes but can't see, {115:6} Ears but can't hear, noses but can't smell, {115:7} Hands but can't touch, feet but can't walk, and they don't say squat. {115:8} Those who make them are just as useless; everyone who trusts in them is a joke. {115:9} Israel, put your trust in the LORD; he's got your back. {115:10} House of Aaron, trust in the LORD; he's got your back. {115:11} All you who respect the LORD, trust in the LORD; he's got your back. {115:12} The LORD hasn't forgotten about us; he's gonna bless us, bless Israel's house, bless Aaron's house. {115:13} He's gonna bless all who respect the LORD, from the smallest to the greatest. {115:14} The LORD's gonna hook you up more and more, you and your crew. {115:15} You're blessed by the LORD who made heaven and earth. {115:16} The heavens belong to the LORD, but he gave the earth to us humans. {115:17} Dead folks don't praise the LORD, neither do those who go down to the grave. {115:18} But we're gonna praise the LORD from now on, forever. Praise the LORD.

{116:1} Yo, I'm all about the LORD because he heard me out when I was pleading. {116:2} Since he listened up, I'm gonna keep hitting him up as long as I'm alive. {116:3} I was deep in the struggles of death, feeling the heat of hell; trouble and sorrow were my jam. {116:4} So I called out to the LORD; "Yo, LORD, save my soul," I begged. {116:5} The LORD's all about grace and righteousness; our God's got that mercy vibe. {116:6} He's got the backs of the simple folk; when I was down, he lifted me up. {116:7} Now I'm chilling; the LORD's been mad generous to me. {116:8} He saved my butt from death, dried up my tears, and kept me from falling. {116:9} I'm gonna keep it real with the LORD as long as I'm alive. {116:10} I stayed faithful even when life got real tough; {116:11} In my rush, I said, "Everybody's a liar." {116:12} So, what can I give back to the LORD for all he's done for me? {116:13} I'll take that cup of salvation and keep calling on the LORD. {116:14} I'll keep my promises to the LORD in front of everyone. {116:15} The LORD values the death of his peeps. {116:16} LORD, I'm totally your servant, the son of your servant-girl; you set me free. {116:17} I'm gonna thank you big time, offer up my sacrifices, and keep calling on your name. {116:18} I'll keep my promises to the LORD in front of everyone, in the LORD's house, in Jerusalem. Praise the LORD.

{117:1} Everybody, worldwide, give props to the LORD; all you people, show him love. {117:2} His mercy game is strong, and the LORD's truth lasts forever. Praise the LORD.

{118:1} Big ups to the LORD; he's all good because his mercy lasts forever. {118:2} Israel, let's give a shout; his mercy lasts forever. {118:3} House of Aaron, join in; his mercy lasts forever. {118:4} All you who respect the LORD, join the chorus; his mercy lasts forever. {118:5} When I was in a tight spot, I called on the LORD, and he hooked me up big time. {118:6} With the LORD on my side, I ain't afraid; what can humans do to me? {118:7} The LORD's got my back with those who help me out; so I'm gonna see victory over my haters. {118:8} Trusting the LORD is way better than relying on people. {118:9} Trusting the LORD is way better than relying on leaders. {118:10} All the nations tried to mess with me, but I shut them down in the name of the LORD. {118:11} They came at me from all sides, but I shut them down in the name of the LORD. {118:12} They swarmed me like bees, but they got shut down like thorns in a fire, all in the name of the LORD. {118:13} You tried to knock me down hard, but the LORD had my back. {118:14} The LORD's my strength and my jam; he's the one who saved me. {118:15} The righteous parties up big time; the LORD's right hand gets it done. {118:16} The LORD's right hand is lifted high; it's all about victory. {118:17} I ain't going down; I'm gonna live and tell everyone about the LORD's works. {118:18} The LORD put me through some tough times, but he didn't let me go down for the count. {118:19} Open up the gates of righteousness for me; I'm coming in to praise the LORD. {118:20} These are the LORD's gates, where only the righteous get in. {118:21} I'm gonna give you props; you listened to me and became my savior. {118:22} The stone that the builders rejected is now the cornerstone. {118:23} This is all the LORD's doing; it's amazing in our eyes. {118:24} This day, made by the LORD, is gonna be lit; we're gonna rejoice and be stoked. {118:25} Save us now, LORD; send us prosperity, please. {118:26} Blessed is the one who comes in the name of the LORD; we bless you from the LORD's house. {118:27} God is the LORD who gave us light; tie up the sacrifice with cords to the altar's horns. {118:28} You're my God, and I'm gonna praise you; you're my God, and I'm gonna lift you up. {118:29} Big shout out to the LORD; he's all good because his mercy lasts forever.

{119:1} Yo, big shoutout to those who stay true to the path, walking in the LORD's law. {119:2} Props to those who keep his teachings and are all about seeking him with everything they got. {119:3} They ain't out here doing wrong; they stay on that righteous grind.

{119:4} You straight up told us to stick to your rules like glue. {119:5} Man, I wish I could stay on track with your laws all the time! {119:6} If I can do that, I won't ever feel ashamed 'cause I'll be respecting all your commands. {119:7} Once I learn your righteous ways, I'll praise you with all my heart. {119:8} I'm sticking to your rules, LORD; please don't ditch me. BETH. {119:9} How's a young person gonna keep their act clean? By living according to your word. {119:10} I've been searching for you with everything I got; don't let me stray from your commands. {119:11} I keep your word close to my heart so I don't mess up. {119:12} Yo, LORD, big ups to you; teach me your rules. {119:13} I'm out here spreading the word from your mouth. {119:14} Your teachings are my jam, worth more to me than stacks of cash. {119:15} I'll think about your rules and respect your ways. {119:16} Your statutes bring me joy; I won't forget your word. GIMEL. {119:17} Be good to me, LORD, so I can keep on living and sticking to your word. {119:18} Open my eyes to see the amazing stuff in your law. {119:19} I feel like a stranger sometimes; don't hide your commands from me. {119:20} I'm always craving your judgments; they're my lifeline. {119:21} You put those arrogant fools in their place, the ones who stray from your commands. {119:22} Keep me away from shame and disrespect; I've been keeping your teachings close. {119:23} Even when big shots talk trash about me, I'm all about meditating on your rules. {119:24} Your teachings are my joy and my guidance. DALETH. {119:25} I feel stuck in the dirt sometimes; give me life according to your word. {119:26} I've laid out my struggles before you, and you listened; teach me your rules. {119:27} Help me understand your precepts so I can talk about your amazing works. {119:28} Sometimes I feel crushed; give me strength according to your word. {119:29} Keep me away from lies; give me your law with grace. {119:30} I've chosen the path of truth; your judgments guide me. {119:31} I'm sticking to your testimonies; don't let me down, LORD. {119:32} I'll run the race of your commands once you expand my heart. HE. {119:33} Teach me your statutes, LORD, and I'll follow them till the end. {119:34} Give me wisdom, and I'll keep your law with all my heart. {119:35} Guide me on the path of your commands; that's where I find joy. {119:36} Keep my heart away from greed; I'm all about your testimonies. {119:37} Turn my eyes from useless stuff; keep me on your path. {119:38} Make sure your word sticks with me; I'm all about respecting you. {119:39} Keep me safe from shame; your judgments are legit. {119:40} I'm all about your rules; give me life according to your righteousness. VAU. {119:41} Send your mercy my way, LORD, along with your salvation, just like you said you would. {119:42} Then I'll have something to say to those who diss me 'cause I trust in your word. {119:43} Don't let me stop speaking the truth; I'm all about hoping in your judgments. {119:44} Your law is my jam, now and forever. {119:45} I'll walk freely 'cause I'm all about your precepts. {119:46} I'll talk about your testimonies even in front of kings without shame. {119:47} Your commands are my joy 'cause I love 'em. {119:48} I'm all about your commands; I'll lift 'em up and think about 'em all day long. ZAIN. {119:49} Don't forget your promise to me, LORD; it's what keeps me going. {119:50} Your word is my comfort in tough times; it's what keeps me going. {119:51} Even when haters mock me, I stick to your law. {119:52} I remember your judgments from way back; they comfort me. {119:53} It freaks me out when I see wicked folks ignoring your law. {119:54} Your statutes are my jams, even when I'm far from home. {119:55} I remember your name at night and keep your law. {119:56} I've stayed true to your precepts. CHETH. {119:57} You're my main deal, LORD; I'm all about keeping your word. {119:58} I've been begging for your favor with everything I got; be cool with me just like you promised. {119:59} I've been reflecting on my actions and turning toward your testimonies. {119:60} I'm quick to follow your commands; no time for delay. {119:61} Even when jerks try to mess with me, I won't forget your law. {119:62} I'll wake up at midnight to thank you for your righteous judgments. {119:63} I hang out with those who respect you and keep your precepts. {119:64} Your mercy fills the earth; teach me your statutes. TETH. {119:65} You've been good to me, LORD, just like you said you would. {119:66} Give me wisdom and understanding 'cause I believe in your commands. {119:67} Before I got put through the wringer, I was all over the place, but now I'm sticking to your word. {119:68} You're good and you do good things; teach me your statutes. {119:69} Those proud haters spread lies about me, but I'm sticking to your precepts with everything I got. {119:70} Their hearts are thick with evil, but I'm all about your law. {119:71} It was good for me to go through hard times 'cause now I know your statutes. {119:72} Your word means more to me than a ton of gold and silver. {119:73} Your hands made me and shaped me: give me understanding so I can learn your rules. {119:74} Those who respect you will be hyped when they see me, because I've hoped in your word. {119:75} I know, LORD, that your judgments are legit, and you've faithfully put me through trials. {119:76} Please let your kindness comfort me, as you promised your servant. {119:77} Let your tender mercies come to me, so I can live, because your law is my joy. {119:78} Let the proud be ashamed, for they've wronged me for no reason, but I'll focus on your rules. {119:79} Let those who fear you turn to me, those who know your testimonies. {119:80} Let my heart be solid in your statutes, so I won't be ashamed. {119:81} My soul is drained waiting for your salvation, but I hope in your word. {119:82} My eyes fail looking for your word, saying, "When will you comfort me?" {119:83} I'm like a dried-up wineskin in the smoke, but I don't forget your rules. {119:83} Yo, I feel like I'm out here getting smoked like a bottle in the haze, but I ain't forgetting your rules. {119:84} How long till you handle those haters coming at me, LORD? When you gonna serve up justice? {119:85} These arrogant jerks are setting traps for me, ain't even following your rules. {119:86} Your commands are solid, but they're coming at me sideways; help me out here. {119:87} They nearly wiped me out, but I didn't ditch your precepts. {119:88} Bring me back to life with your kindness, and I'll stick to what you say. LAMED. {119:89} Your word's set in stone up there in heaven, LORD. {119:90} Your faithfulness lasts through all generations; you built the earth, and it's staying put. {119:91} Everything's still running according to your rules; everything's doing what you say. {119:92} If it wasn't for your law being my jam, I'd be done for in all this trouble. {119:93} I'll never forget your rules; they're what keeps me going. {119:94} I'm yours, so save me; I've been all about your rules. {119:95} The bad ones are waiting to take me out, but I'm staying focused on your testimonies. {119:96} I've seen the end of everything, but your commandments cover everything. MEM. {119:97} Man, I'm all about your law! It's what I'm thinking about all day. {119:98} Your rules make me smarter than my enemies 'cause they're always on my mind. {119:99} I know more than my teachers 'cause I'm all about your testimonies. {119:100} I've got more sense than the old heads 'cause I'm sticking to your rules. {119:101} I'm steering clear of all the bad stuff so I can stick to your word. {119:102} I haven't strayed from your judgments 'cause you taught me right. {119:103} Your words taste so good, even better than honey in my mouth! {119:104}

Your rules give me understanding, so I can't stand anything false. NUN. {119:105} Your word lights up my path like a lamp and guides me. {119:106} I promised to stick to your righteous judgments, and I'm gonna keep that promise. {119:107} I'm going through a lot, so give me life like you promised in your word. {119:108} LORD, accept what I'm saying and teach me your judgments. {119:109} I'm always on the edge, but I'm not forgetting your law. {119:110} The bad ones are trying to trip me up, but I'm staying on your path. {119:111} Your testimonies are my inheritance forever; they make my heart happy. {119:112} I'm all in, ready to keep your rules till the end. SAMECH. {119:113} I hate useless thoughts, but I'm all about your law. {119:114} You're my safe place and my shield; I'm putting my trust in your word. {119:115} Get away from me, you troublemakers; I'm sticking to what my God says. {119:116} Keep me going according to your word, so I don't lose hope. {119:117} Hold me up, and I'll be safe; I'll always respect your rules. {119:118} You've stomped out those who don't follow your rules 'cause they're all about deceit. {119:119} You've gotten rid of all the bad ones; that's why I love your testimonies. {119:120} I'm trembling with fear before you, afraid of what you'll do. AIN. {119:121} I've been fair and just; don't let my oppressors get the best of me. {119:122} Stand up for me, make sure those arrogant ones don't crush me. {119:123} I'm desperate for your salvation and your righteous word. {119:124} Treat me with mercy and teach me your rules. {119:125} I'm your servant; give me insight so I can understand your testimonies. {119:126} It's time for you to step in, LORD; they've trashed your law. {119:127} That's why I love your commands more than gold, even more than the finest gold. {119:128} I think your rules are spot on; that's why I hate every false way. PE. {119:129} Your testimonies are amazing, so I'm sticking to 'em. {119:130} Your words shed light and give understanding to the clueless. {119:131} I'm thirsty for your commands, panting for 'em like someone who's been running. {119:132} Look at me and be kind, just like you are to those who love your name. {119:133} Guide my steps by your word; don't let sin control me. {119:134} Save me from getting crushed by people, and I'll keep your rules. {119:135} Shine your face on me and teach me your rules. {119:136} I'm crying rivers of tears 'cause people aren't following your law. TZADDE. {119:137} You're righteous, LORD, and your judgments are fair. {119:138} Your rules are straight-up righteous and totally reliable. {119:139} I'm burning with passion 'cause my enemies are ignoring your words. {119:140} Your word is pure; that's why I love it. {119:141} I might be small and overlooked, but I'm not forgetting your rules. {119:142} Your righteousness lasts forever, and your law is the truth. {119:143} Even though I'm in trouble and pain, your commands are what I enjoy. {119:144} Your testimonies are righteous forever; give me understanding, and I'll live. KOPH. {119:145} I'm crying out to you with everything I got; hear me, LORD; I'll stick to your rules. {119:146} I'm crying out to you; save me, and I'll keep your testimonies. {119:147} I'm up before dawn, crying out to you; I'm putting my hope in your word. {119:148} I'm up all night, thinking about your word. {119:149} Listen to me and treat me with kindness, LORD, just like you do with those who love you. {119:150} The troublemakers are getting closer, but they're far from your law. {119:151} You're close by, LORD, and all your rules are true. {119:152} I've known for a long time that your testimonies are solid forever. RESH. {119:153} Look at my troubles and save me; I won't forget your law. {119:154} Stand up for me and save me; give me life like you promised. {119:155} The bad ones are far from being saved 'cause they don't care about your rules. {119:156} Your mercy is huge, LORD; give me life according to your judgments. {119:157} I've got plenty of enemies, but I'm not forgetting your testimonies. {119:158} Seeing people break your word hurts me; they're not keeping it. {119:159} Look at how much I love your rules; treat me with kindness, LORD. {119:160} Your word has always been true, and your judgments are solid forever. SCHIN. {119:161} Kings are coming after me for no reason, but I'm respecting your word. {119:162} I'm celebrating every time I hear your word, like finding a huge treasure. {119:163} I hate lies, but I'm all about your law. {119:164} I'm praising you seven times a day 'cause your judgments are fair. {119:165} Those who love your law have real peace; nothing can make them stumble. {119:166} I'm counting on your salvation and sticking to your commands. {119:167} I'm holding onto your testimonies tight 'cause I love 'em so much. {119:168} I'm keeping your rules and testimonies 'cause you see everything I do. TAU. {119:169} Hear me out, LORD; give me insight according to your word. {119:170} Listen to my plea; save me according to your word. {119:171} I'll be singing your praises once you teach me your rules. {119:172} I'll be talking about your word 'cause all your commandments are right. {119:173} Help me out here 'cause I'm all about your rules. {119:174} I'm longing for your salvation, LORD, and I'm loving your law. {119:175} Let me live, and I'll praise you; your judgments will guide me. {119:176} I've gone off track like a lost sheep; come find me 'cause I'm not forgetting your commands.

{120:1} When I was stressed, I called out to God, and He heard me. {120:2} Save me, Lord, from fake people and liars. {120:3} What will you get, lying tongue? What's your fate? {120:4} Sharp arrows and burning coals. {120:5} Ugh, living in Mesech and camping in Kedar is rough. {120:6} I've been stuck with people who hate peace for too long. {120:7} I'm all about peace, but when I speak, they're all about war.

{121:1} I'm looking up to the hills for help. {121:2} My help comes from the Lord, who made heaven and earth. {121:3} He won't let you trip; the one watching over you won't fall asleep. {121:4} Look, the one watching over Israel never sleeps or slumbers. {121:5} The Lord is your protector; He's your shade at your right hand. {121:6} The sun won't burn you by day, nor the moon by night. {121:7} The Lord will keep you safe from all evil; He will guard your soul. {121:8} The Lord will guard your coming and going, now and forever.

{122:1} I was hyped when they said, "Let's go to the Lord's house." {122:2} Our feet will stand within your gates, Jerusalem. {122:3} Jerusalem is built like a city that's all connected. {122:4} That's where the tribes go up, the tribes of the Lord, to give thanks to His name. {122:5} Thrones of judgment are there, the thrones of David's house. {122:6} Pray for Jerusalem's peace; may those who love you be secure. {122:7} Peace be within your walls and security within your towers. {122:8} For the sake of my family and friends, I will say, "Peace be with you." {122:9} For the sake of the house of the Lord our God, I will seek your good.

{123:1} I lift my eyes to you, the one who lives in heaven. {123:2} Look, just like servants look to their master's hand, and a maiden to her mistress's hand, our eyes look to the Lord our God until He shows us mercy. {123:3} Have mercy on us, Lord, have mercy, because we've had more than enough contempt. {123:4} Our soul has had more than enough of the mockery from those who are at ease and the contempt from the proud.

{124:1} If the Lord hadn't been on our side, let Israel now say, {124:2} If the Lord hadn't been on our side when people attacked us, {124:3} They would have swallowed us alive when their anger flared against us. {124:4} The waters would have overwhelmed us; the torrent would have swept over our soul. {124:5} The raging waters would have swept over our soul. {124:6} Blessed be the Lord, who didn't let us be torn apart by their teeth. {124:7} Our soul has escaped like a bird from a trap; the trap is broken, and we have escaped. {124:8} Our help is in the name of the Lord, who made heaven and earth.

{125:1} Those who trust in the Lord are like Mount Zion, which can't be moved but stands forever. {125:2} Just like the mountains surround Jerusalem, the Lord surrounds His people now and forever. {125:3} The wicked's power won't rest on the land given to the righteous, so the righteous won't use their hands to do wrong. {125:4} Do good, Lord, to those who are good, to those who are upright in heart. {125:5} But those who turn to crooked ways, the Lord will lead away with the evildoers. Peace be upon Israel.

{126:1} When the LORD brought back the crew from Zion's lockdown, we were like, "Is this real life?" {126:2} Our mouths were straight-up laughing, and we were belting out tunes; even the other nations were like, "Dang, the LORD hooked them up big time!" {126:3} The LORD's been coming through for us big time, and we're stoked about it. {126:4} Yo, LORD, flip our situation like the dry season flips the streams down south. {126:5} Those who've been crying their eyes out while planting seeds will straight-up party when the harvest comes in. {126:6} Anyone who's been grinding and shedding tears, carrying precious seeds, best believe they're gonna come back with shouts of joy, hauling in their crops.

{127:1} If the LORD ain't building the house, then all that construction work's for nothing; if the LORD ain't keeping watch over the city, the night shift's pointless. {127:2} Working overtime, burning the midnight oil, stressing over stuff—yeah, that's a waste of time. The LORD's got his favorites catching some Z's. {127:3} Kids are a blessing from the LORD, a reward for your hard work. {127:4} Like arrows in the hands of a skilled archer, so are kids born in your prime. {127:5} Blessed is the parent with a full quiver; their kids won't back down, even at the city gates.

{128:1} Big ups to anyone who respects the LORD and walks the walk. {128:2} You'll enjoy the fruits of your labor, living your best life. {128:3} Your partner's gonna be like a lush vine by your crib, and your kids? They'll be like fresh olive branches around your dinner table. {128:4} That's how you know someone's blessed, when they're all about the LORD. {128:5} The LORD's gonna bless you from Zion; you'll see nothing but good vibes in Jerusalem all your days. {128:6} And yeah, you'll live to see your grandkids, with peace reigning over Israel.

{129:1} Man, since I was young, Israel's been catching all kinds of grief. {129:2} They've been messing with me since I was a kid, but they couldn't take me down. {129:3} They've been tearing up my back like plowers in a field, making long furrows. {129:4} But the LORD's on point; he's cut the cords of the wicked. {129:5} Let those haters who can't stand Zion get shut down and turned away. {129:6} Let them dry up like grass on the roof before it even grows. {129:7} Ain't nobody gathering that grass to make hay, and nobody's binding it up into sheaves. {129:8} And when they pass by, ain't nobody blessing them in the name of the LORD.

{130:1} I've been crying out to you from the bottom of the barrel, LORD. {130:2} Lord, hear me out; listen up to my prayers. {130:3} If you start keeping track of all the wrongs, Lord, who's gonna stand? {130:4} But you're all about forgiveness, so people show you respect. {130:5} I'm waiting for the LORD, my soul's hanging on to his promises. {130:6} I'm waiting for the LORD more eagerly than people waiting for the sunrise. {130:7} Israel, put your hope in the LORD; he's all about mercy and redemption. {130:8} And he's gonna redeem Israel from all their mess-ups.

{131:1} Yo, Lord, my heart's not arrogant, and my eyes aren't prideful; I don't get involved in stuff that's too big or complex for me. {131:2} I've calmed down and chilled, like a kid weaned from his mom; my soul is like a weaned child. {131:3} Israel, put your hope in the Lord now and forever.

{132:1} Lord, remember David and all he went through: {132:2} How he promised the Lord and made a vow to the Mighty One of Jacob; {132:3} "I won't enter my house or go to bed, {132:4} I won't let my eyes sleep or my eyelids rest, {132:5} Until I find a place for the Lord, a dwelling for the Mighty One of Jacob." {132:6} We heard about it in Ephrathah; we found it in the fields of Jaar. {132:7} Let's go to His dwelling place; let's worship at His footstool. {132:8} Arise, Lord, and go to Your resting place, You and the ark of Your strength. {132:9} May Your priests be clothed with righteousness, and Your saints shout for joy. {132:10} For the sake of Your servant David, don't reject Your anointed one. {132:11} The Lord swore an oath to David, a sure promise He won't revoke: "One of your descendants I will place on your throne. {132:12} If your children keep My covenant and the statutes I teach them, their children will sit on your throne forever." {132:13} For the Lord has chosen Zion, He has desired it for His dwelling: {132:14} "This is My resting place forever; here I will dwell, for I have desired it. {132:15} I will bless her with abundant provisions; her poor I will satisfy with food. {132:16} I will clothe her priests with salvation, and her saints will shout for joy. {132:17} There I will make a horn grow for David and set up a lamp for My anointed one. {132:18} I will clothe his enemies with shame, but his crown will shine."

{133:1} Check it out, how good and pleasant it is when siblings live together in unity! {133:2} It's like precious oil poured on the head, running down on the beard, Aaron's beard, down to the collar of his robes. {133:3} It's like the dew of Hermon falling on Mount Zion. For there the Lord commands His blessing, life forevermore.

{134:1} Yo, bless the Lord, all you servants of the Lord who stand by night in the house of the Lord. {134:2} Lift up your hands in the sanctuary and bless the Lord. {134:3} May the Lord, Maker of heaven and earth, bless you from Zion.

{135:1} Praise the Lord. Praise the name of the Lord; praise Him, you servants of the Lord. {135:2} You who stand in the house of the Lord, in the courts of the house of our God, {135:3} Praise the Lord, for the Lord is good; sing praises to His name, for that is pleasant. {135:4} For the Lord has chosen Jacob for Himself, Israel for His treasured possession. {135:5} I know that the Lord is great, that our Lord is greater than all gods. {135:6} The Lord does whatever pleases Him, in the heavens and on the earth, in the seas and all their depths. {135:7} He makes clouds rise from the ends of the earth; He sends lightning with the rain and brings out the wind from His storehouses. {135:8} He struck down the firstborn of Egypt, both man and beast. {135:9} He sent signs and wonders into the midst of Egypt, against Pharaoh and all his servants. {135:10} He struck down many nations and killed mighty kings— {135:11} Sihon, king of the Amorites, Og, king of Bashan, and all the kings of Canaan— {135:12} And He gave their land as an inheritance, an inheritance to His people Israel. {135:13} Your name, Lord, endures forever, Your renown, Lord, through all generations. {135:14} For the Lord will vindicate His people and have compassion on His servants. {135:15} The idols of the nations are silver and gold, made by human hands. {135:16} They have mouths, but cannot speak, eyes, but cannot see. {135:17} They have ears, but cannot hear, nor is there breath in their mouths. {135:18} Those who make them will be like them, and so will all who trust in them. {135:19} Praise the Lord, house of Israel; praise the Lord, house of Aaron; {135:20} Praise the Lord, house of Levi; you who fear Him, praise the Lord. {135:21} Praise be to the Lord from Zion, to Him who dwells in Jerusalem. Praise the Lord.

{136:1} Yo, shoutout to the LORD, 'cause he's legit good, and his love never runs out. {136:2} Big ups to the God of all gods, 'cause his love's on repeat, no cap. {136:3} Same vibe for the Lord of all lords, 'cause his love's everlasting, you feel? {136:4} He's the one pulling off those sick miracles, and yeah, his love's forever. {136:5} Shoutout to the big man who whipped up the heavens with mad wisdom, 'cause his love's eternal. {136:6} And he's the one who laid out the earth like a boss over the waters, and yeah, his love's always there. {136:7} Plus, he's the dude who made those lit lights in the sky, and yeah, his love's never-ending. {136:8} The sun holds it down in the day, 'cause his love's on repeat. {136:9} And when night falls, the moon and stars come through, 'cause his love's forever. {136:10} Remember when he put Egypt on blast with that firstborn move? Yeah, his love's eternal. {136:11} And when he busted Israel outta there? You guessed it, his love never quits. {136:12} With pure strength and a flexed-out arm, he did his thing, 'cause his love's timeless. {136:13} Splitting the Red Sea like it's no biggie? That's him, and his love's always on. {136:14} Leading Israel through like a boss? Yeah, his love's forever. {136:15} And Pharaoh? Yeah, he got wrecked in the Red Sea, 'cause his love's always there. {136:16} Leading his crew through the desert? You know it, 'cause his love's eternal. {136:17} Taking out those big shot kings? Yeah, his love's forever. {136:18} And those famous kings? Yeah, he dealt with them too, 'cause his love's never-ending. {136:19} Sihon, king of the Amorites? Yeah, his love's eternal. {136:20} Same goes for Og, king of Bashan. You know the deal, 'cause his love's always on. {136:21} And he hooked Israel up with their own spot, 'cause his love's timeless. {136:22} Making it legit for Israel? You bet, 'cause his love's forever. {136:23} He never forgets about us, even when we're down and out, 'cause his love's never-ending. {136:24} And he's always got our back against our enemies, 'cause his love's eternal. {136:25} Making sure everyone's fed? That's him, and his love's forever. {136:26} Big shoutout to the God up in heaven, 'cause his love never quits.

{137:1} Yo, by the rivers of Babylon, that's where we posted up and shed some tears, thinking about Zion. {137:2} We straight-up hung our instruments on the willow trees, feeling some type of way. {137:3} 'Cause those who took us captive wanted us to sing, but we weren't feeling it. Singing the LORD's songs in a foreign place? Nah, fam. {137:4} How are we supposed to vibe with Jerusalem on our minds? {137:5} Swear, if I forget about Jerusalem, may I forget how to do anything right. {137:6} If Jerusalem ain't my top joy, then may I forget how to even speak. {137:7} Remember when Edom talked smack about Jerusalem? Yeah, keep that in mind, LORD. {137:8} Babylon, you're gonna get yours, trust. Whoever pays you back for what you did to us, they'll be living their best life. {137:9} Yeah, payback's gonna hit hard, especially for what you did to our kids.{137:8} Yo, daughter of Babylon, you're doomed! Props to anyone who pays you back for what you did to us. {137:9} And whoever takes your kids and smashes them against rocks, that's some heavy payback.

{138:1} I'm gonna big up the LORD with all my heart, even in front of other gods, I'm gonna sing his praises. {138:2} I'm gonna show respect to his holy temple and shout out his name for his love and truth, 'cause his word is top-tier. {138:3} When I was down and out, he came through and gave me strength. {138:4} All the big shots on earth gonna give the LORD props when they hear what he's about. {138:5} They're gonna vibe with the LORD's ways 'cause his glory is off the charts. {138:6} Even though the LORD's up there, he's still got love for us regular folks, but he keeps the proud at a distance. {138:7} When I'm in a tight spot, he's gonna revive me, protect me from my haters, and come through with that right-hand save. {138:8} The LORD's gonna see through whatever I'm dealing with, 'cause his love's eternal. He better not abandon what he's started.

{139:1} LORD, you know me inside out. {139:2} You know when I'm chilling and when I'm on the move, you understand my thoughts from a mile away. {139:3} You know my whole deal, inside and out. {139:4} Every word I'm gonna say, you're already on it, LORD. {139:5} You've got me surrounded, front and back, you've got your hand on me. {139:6} Your knowledge is way beyond me; I can't even wrap my head around it. {139:7} Where can I go where you're not there? Where can I hide from you? {139:8} If I go to the highest heights or the deepest depths, you're still there, LORD. {139:9} Even if I catch the sunrise and jet to the farthest seas, you're right there with me. {139:10} Your hand's gonna guide me, your grip's gonna keep me. {139:11} Even in the darkest times, you're gonna light up my life. {139:12} Darkness can't hide me from you; night's just as bright as day for you. {139:13} You made me from the ground up; you put me together in my mom's womb. {139:14} I'm gonna give you props 'cause you made me awesome; your work is mind-blowing, and I know it. {139:15} You didn't miss a beat when you made me; every detail was perfect. {139:16} You saw me before I even came together; you had every part of me mapped out. {139:17} Your thoughts about me are priceless, LORD; there's too many to count. {139:18} If I tried to tally them up, they'd be more than all the sand on the beach. And when I wake up, you're still with me. {139:19} You're gonna take out the bad guys, LORD; so get them away from me, those bloodthirsty jerks. {139:20} They talk trash about you, LORD, and use your name like it's nothing. {139:21} Don't I hate those who hate you, LORD? Don't I get worked up over those who disrespect you? {139:22} I straight-up can't stand those guys; they're my enemies. {139:23} Check me out, God, and know where I'm coming from; put me to the test and see what's up with my thoughts. {139:24} Check if there's any shady business in me and guide me on the right path, forever.

{140:1} Save me from the bad dudes, LORD; keep me safe from the violent ones. {140:2} They're always scheming and getting ready for war. {140:3} Their tongues are as sharp as knives, and they've got poison in their words. Selah. {140:4} Keep me safe from those wicked hands; don't let them mess up my life. {140:5} They're setting traps for me, trying to trip me up. Selah. {140:6} But I'm telling you, LORD, you're my God; listen to my prayers. {140:7} You're the one who's got my back in the middle of the battle, LORD. {140:8} Don't let the bad guys get what they want; don't let their evil plans succeed. Selah. {140:9} Let their own words come back to bite them, those who try to trap me. {140:10} Let them get burned up and thrown in the fire, never to rise again. {140:11} Don't let those who talk smack about you get anywhere; let their evil ways come back to haunt them. {140:12} I know you're gonna stand up for the oppressed and the poor, LORD. {140:13} The righteous are gonna praise your name, and the upright are gonna hang with you.

{141:1} Yo, LORD, I'm hitting you up real quick; listen to my voice when I call out to you. {141:2} Let my prayers come at you like burning incense, and when I lift my hands, it's like the evening sacrifice. {141:3} Put a guard on my mouth, LORD; keep me from saying dumb stuff. {141:4} Don't let me be tempted to do anything shady or hang out with sketchy people doing evil stuff, and keep me away from their fancy treats. {141:5} If good people gotta check me, I'm cool with it; if they gotta call me out, it's like they're pouring oil on my head. Even when they're going through tough times, I'm gonna keep praying for them. {141:6} When the big shots get taken down, they'll hear my words 'cause they're sweet. {141:7} We're like scattered bones at death's door, like wood being chopped on the ground. {141:8} But I'm keeping my eyes on you, GOD the Lord; I trust in you, don't leave me hanging. {141:9} Keep me safe from the traps they're setting and from the evil plans of those doing wrong. {141:10} Let the bad guys fall into their own traps while I make my getaway.

{142:1} I'm calling out to the LORD loud and clear; I'm telling him all my troubles. {142:2} I'm laying it all out in front of him, pouring out my heart. {142:3} When I'm feeling overwhelmed, you know where I'm at, LORD. They've set traps for me in secret. {142:4} I look around, and there's no one on my side; no one cares about me. {142:5} But I'm saying to you, LORD, you're my safe place, my only hope in this world. {142:6} Listen up quick 'cause I'm in deep trouble; save me from those who are after me 'cause they're stronger than I am. {142:7} Get me out of this mess so I can praise your name; good people will come around me 'cause you're gonna hook me up big time.

{143:1} Listen to my prayer, LORD, and answer me faithfully and righteously. {143:2} Don't judge me too harshly; no one's perfect in your eyes. {143:3} My enemies are coming after me hard; they've knocked me down and left me in the dark, feeling dead inside. {143:4} I'm overwhelmed with sadness; my heart feels empty. {143:5} But I'm thinking about all the times you came through in the past; I'm meditating on your amazing deeds and the work of your hands. {143:6} I'm reaching out to you; my soul is thirsty for you like a dry, thirsty land. Selah. {143:7} Listen to me quick, LORD; I'm running on empty here. Don't turn your face away from me, or I'll end up in the pit like everyone else. {143:8} Let me hear about your loving kindness in the morning 'cause I'm trusting in you. Show me which way to go 'cause I'm lifting my soul up to you. {143:9} Save me from my enemies; I'm running to you to hide me. {143:10} Teach me to do what you want; you're my God, and your spirit is good. Lead me on the right path. {143:11} Give me life again, LORD, for the sake of your reputation. Get me out of trouble 'cause you're righteous. {143:12} Take care of my enemies in your kindness, and get rid of all those who are causing me grief 'cause I'm your servant.

{144:1} Shout out to the LORD, my strength, who trains me to fight and defend myself. {144:2} You're my rock, my fortress, my safe place, my deliverer, my shield, and the one I trust to keep my people in line. {144:3} LORD, what's up with humans that you pay attention to us? We're like a breath, here one moment and gone the next. {144:4} We're like a shadow that disappears; our days are fleeting. {144:5} Come down, LORD, and shake things up; touch the mountains, and make 'em smoke. {144:6} Throw lightning bolts and scatter my enemies; shoot your arrows and take 'em out. {144:7} Reach down from above; save me from deep waters and the grip of those foreign to you. {144:8} Their mouths are full of lies, and their right hands are raised in deceit. {144:9} I'm gonna bust out a fresh tune for you, God; I'll play it on my ten-stringed instrument. {144:10} You're the one who gives victory to kings; you saved David from the deadly sword. {144:11} Save me from the grip of strangers, whose mouths are full of lies, and their right hands are raised in deceit. {144:12} Let our kids grow up strong and healthy, like trees in their prime; let our daughters be beautiful like the inside of a palace. {144:13} Let our storehouses be full, providing all kinds of goods; let our flocks multiply by the thousands and tens of thousands in our fields. {144:14} Let our oxen be strong for plowing, with no gaps in the fences, no crime in the streets. {144:15} Happy are the people in a situation like ours; yeah, happy are the people whose God is the LORD.

{145:1} I'm gonna big up you, God, my king; I'm gonna bless your name forever and ever. {145:2} Every single day, I'll give you props, and I'll keep on praising your name forever and ever. {145:3} You're the greatest, LORD, no one can top you, and your greatness is beyond understanding. {145:4} One generation's gonna tell the next about all the cool stuff you've done and how powerful you are. {145:5} I'm gonna talk about how awesome and mighty you are, and about all the cool stuff you do. {145:6} People are gonna talk about your powerful deeds, and I'll tell everyone how amazing you are. {145:7} They're gonna share stories of your goodness and sing about your righteousness. {145:8} You're so chill and compassionate, slow to get mad, and super merciful. {145:9} You're good to everyone, and your love covers all your creations. {145:10} Everything you make is gonna praise you, LORD, and your loyal followers will bless you. {145:11} They're gonna talk about your kingdom's glory and brag about your power. {145:12} They'll let everyone know about your mighty deeds and your glorious kingdom. {145:13} Your kingdom's gonna last forever, and your rule's gonna last for all generations. {145:14} You hold up everyone who's fallen and lift up everyone who's bowed down. {145:15} Everyone's eyes are on you; you give them what they need at the right time. {145:16} You open your hand and satisfy the desires of every living thing. {145:17} You're always right in what you do, and everything you make is pure. {145:18} You're close to everyone who calls on you, everyone who calls on you honestly. {145:19} You're gonna do what people want when they respect you; you'll hear them when they cry out, and you'll save them. {145:20} You take care of everyone who loves you, but you're gonna take out all the wicked ones. {145:21} My mouth's gonna sing your praises, LORD, and let everyone praise your holy name forever and ever.

{146:1} Yo, praise the Lord. My soul, praise the Lord. {146:2} As long as I live, I'll praise the Lord; I'll sing to my God as long as I'm breathing. {146:3} Don't trust in influential people, they can't help. {146:4} When they die, they return to dust, and their plans vanish. {146:5} Happy is the one who gets help from the God of Jacob and hopes in the Lord. {146:6} He made the heaven, earth, sea, and everything in them; He keeps it real forever. {146:7} He serves justice for the oppressed and feeds the hungry. The Lord frees the prisoners. {146:8} The Lord opens the eyes of the blind; He lifts up those who are bent down. The Lord loves the righteous. {146:9} The Lord watches over foreigners, supports orphans and widows, but He messes up the plans of the wicked. {146:10} The Lord will reign forever, your God, Zion, for all generations. Praise the Lord.

{147:1} Praise the Lord! It's lit to sing praises to our God; it's fun and proper. {147:2} The Lord builds up Jerusalem and gathers Israel's outcasts. {147:3} He heals the broken-hearted and bandages their wounds. {147:4} He counts the stars and calls them by name. {147:5} Great is our Lord, and mighty in power; His wisdom is infinite. {147:6} The Lord lifts up the humble; He throws the wicked to the ground. {147:7} Sing to the Lord with thanks; make music to our God on the harp. {147:8} He covers the sky with clouds, provides rain for the earth, and makes grass grow on the hills. {147:9} He gives food to the animals and to the young ravens when they call. {147:10} He doesn't delight in the strength of the horse or the legs of a man. {147:11} The Lord takes pleasure in those who fear Him, who hope in His love. {147:12} Praise the Lord, Jerusalem; praise your God, Zion. {147:13} He strengthens your gates and blesses your people within you. {147:14} He brings peace to your borders and fills you with the finest wheat. {147:15} He sends His command to the earth; His word runs swiftly. {147:16} He spreads snow like wool and scatters frost like ashes. {147:17} He hurls down His hail like pebbles; who can withstand His icy blast? {147:18} He sends His word and melts them; He stirs up His breeze, and the waters flow. {147:19} He reveals His word to Jacob, His laws, and decrees to Israel. {147:20} He has not done this for any other nation; they do not know His laws. Praise the Lord.

{148:1} Praise the Lord! Praise the Lord from the heavens; praise Him in the heights above. {148:2} Praise Him, all His angels; praise Him, all His heavenly hosts. {148:3} Praise Him, sun and moon; praise Him, all you shining stars. {148:4} Praise Him, you highest heavens and you waters above the skies. {148:5} Let them praise the name of the Lord, for He commanded, and they were created. {148:6} He established them forever and ever; He issued a decree that will never pass away. {148:7} Praise the Lord from the earth, you great sea creatures and all ocean depths, {148:8} Lightning and hail, snow and clouds, stormy winds that do His bidding, {148:9} You mountains and all hills, fruit trees and all cedars, {148:10} Wild animals and all cattle, small creatures and flying birds, {148:11} Kings of the earth and all nations, you princes and all rulers on earth, {148:12} Young men and women, old men, and children. {148:13} Let them praise the name of the Lord, for His name alone is exalted; His splendor is above the earth and the heavens. {148:14} He has raised up a horn for His people, the praise of all His faithful servants, of Israel, the people close to His heart. Praise the Lord.

{149:1} Praise the Lord! Sing to the Lord a new song, His praise in the assembly of His faithful people. {149:2} Let Israel rejoice in their Maker; let the people of Zion be glad in their King. {149:3} Let them praise His name with dancing and make music to Him with timbrel and harp. {149:4} For the Lord takes delight in His people; He crowns the humble with victory. {149:5} Let His faithful people rejoice in this honor and sing for joy on their beds. {149:6} May the praise of God be in their mouths and a double-edged sword in their hands, {149:7} To inflict vengeance on the nations and punishment on the peoples, {149:8} To bind their kings with fetters, their nobles with shackles of iron, {149:9} To carry out the sentence written against them—this is the glory of all His faithful people. Praise the Lord.

{150:1} Praise the Lord! Praise God in His sanctuary; praise Him in His mighty heavens. {150:2} Praise Him for His acts of power; praise Him for His surpassing greatness. {150:3} Praise Him with the sounding of the trumpet; praise Him with the harp and lyre. {150:4} Praise Him with timbrel and dancing; praise Him with the strings and pipe. {150:5} Praise Him with the clash of cymbals; praise Him with resounding cymbals. {150:6} Let everything that has breath praise the Lord. Praise the Lord.

Proverbs

✦✦✦

{1:1} Yo, listen up! These are the wise words of Solomon, son of David, king of Israel. {1:2} They're all about gaining wisdom, understanding, and insight. {1:3} You gotta be open to learning and getting wisdom, knowing what's right and fair. {1:4} It's all about making the simple wise and giving young folks knowledge and good judgment. {1:5} Smart people listen and learn more, and those who understand gain wise advice. {1:6} It's about understanding sayings, deciphering wise words, and figuring out tricky riddles. {1:7} The start of wisdom? It's respecting the Lord, but fools just laugh at wisdom and good advice. {1:8} My dude, listen to your dad's teachings, and don't ignore your mom's rules. {1:9} They're like a cool necklace and a stylish headband, making you look good. {1:10} But if shady folks try to lure you into trouble, don't fall for it. {1:11} If they're planning to do something sketchy, steer clear. {1:12} They think they can get away with anything, but nah, they're just digging their own graves. {1:13} They're all about easy money and quick wins, but it's just trouble waiting to happen. {1:14} They might offer to share, but don't join them; you don't wanna go down their path. {1:15} My dude, don't follow their lead; stay away from their ways. {1:16} They're all about trouble, rushing into evil like it's a race. {1:17} But it's all gonna backfire, just like a trap set in plain sight. {1:18} They're plotting against themselves, setting traps for their own lives. {1:19} That's just how it goes for greedy people; they end up destroying themselves. {1:20} Wisdom's out there, calling out to everyone, shouting wisdom in the streets. {1:21} She's out in the open, speaking her mind, calling out in the city. {1:22} But how long will you keep being naive? Why do you enjoy being foolish? Why hate knowledge? {1:23} Listen to wisdom's warnings; she's offering you a chance to learn and grow. {1:24} But if you keep ignoring her, don't be surprised when she starts laughing at your troubles. {1:25} You turned your back on her advice, so when disaster strikes, she won't be there for you. {1:26} You'll be left alone to face your fears and suffer the consequences of your choices. {1:27} When trouble hits like a storm, and you're left in ruins, she won't be there to help. {1:28} You'll call for her, but she won't answer; you'll look for her, but she'll be nowhere to be found. {1:29} Because you rejected knowledge and refused to respect the Lord. {1:30} You didn't want wise advice; you laughed at all the warnings. {1:31} So you'll get what you deserve; your own actions will come back to haunt you. {1:32} Ignoring wisdom will lead to your downfall, and following foolishness will be your destruction. {1:33} But those who listen to wisdom will live in safety and be free from fear.

{2:1} My dude, if you really listen to what I'm saying and treasure my advice, {2:2} Pay attention to wisdom and focus on understanding; {2:3} If you crave knowledge and shout out for insight, {2:4} If you search for wisdom like it's treasure buried deep, {2:5} Then you'll understand what it means to respect the Lord and discover the knowledge of God. {2:6} Because wisdom comes from the Lord; knowledge and understanding flow from Him. {2:7} He stores up wisdom for those who do right; He's a shield for those who walk with integrity. {2:8} He guards the paths of justice and protects those who are faithful to Him. {2:9} Then you'll understand what's right, just, and fair, and you'll find every good path. {2:10} When wisdom fills your heart and knowledge brings you joy, {2:11} Discretion will watch over you, and understanding will protect you. {2:12} It'll keep you away from evil and those who speak twisted things. {2:13} They leave the straight path to walk in dark ways, {2:14} Finding joy in doing wrong and delighting in the evil they plan. {2:15} Their ways are crooked, and they're always twisting the truth. {2:16} But wisdom will protect you from the smooth talk of a tempting woman, from the flattery of a stranger. {2:17} She's abandoned her husband and forgotten her marriage vows. {2:18} Her house leads to death and her paths to the grave. {2:19} No one who goes to her comes back; they'll never return to the paths of life. {2:20} But if you follow the ways of good people and stay on the paths of the righteous, {2:21} You'll live in the land and remain there forever. {2:22} But the wicked will be removed from the land, and the treacherous will be uprooted.

{3:1} Yo, son, don't forget my rules; keep 'em close to your heart. {3:2} They'll hook you up with a long, peaceful life. {3:3} Don't ditch kindness and truth; wear 'em like bling, etch 'em in your heart. {3:4} You'll score major points with God and people. {3:5} Trust big time in the LORD, not just in what you think. {3:6} Let him guide your every move, and you'll stay on track. {3:7} Don't think you're all that; respect God and stay away from trouble. {3:8} It's like health for your body and strength for your bones. {3:9} Share your blessings with God and others, starting with the first chunk of what you earn. {3:10} Then watch your bank account blow up with blessings. {3:11} Don't hate it when God corrects you; he's just showing love like a dad to his favorite kid. {3:12} Happy is the dude who's wise and understands stuff. {3:13} Wisdom is better than cash or gold; it's more precious than rubies. {3:14} It's got a long, rich life in one hand and wealth and honor in the other. {3:15} Wisdom's ways are smooth, and its paths lead to peace. {3:16} Grab onto wisdom like it's a lifeline; everyone who holds onto it is happy. {3:17} God used wisdom to set up the world, and understanding to make the heavens. {3:18} He busted open the depths of the sea and made the clouds pour down rain. {3:19} Keep wisdom and good sense in your sights; they'll keep you alive and looking fresh. {3:20} Then you can walk your path without tripping up. {3:21} You'll sleep like a baby, without a care in the world. {3:22} Don't stress about what could go wrong; trust God, and he'll keep you safe. {3:23} Don't hold back good when you can do it, and don't put off helping your neighbor when you can. {3:24} Don't plot evil against your neighbor, especially when they're chill with you. {3:25} Don't pick fights for no reason, especially when they haven't done anything to you. {3:26} Don't be jelly of bullies; don't copy their moves. {3:27} God's not down with jerks, but he's tight with the righteous. {3:28} The wicked are cursed, but the righteous get blessed. {3:29} Wisdom leads to glory, but fools get nothing but shame.

{4:1} Listen up, kids, your old man's dropping some knowledge. {4:2} I'm giving you the good stuff; don't forget it. {4:3} I used to be young too, my mom's favorite. {4:4} She taught me the ropes; now I'm passing them on to you. {4:5} Get wisdom and understanding; don't let them out of your sight. {4:6} Hold onto them like your life depends on it; love 'em, and they'll love you back. {4:7} Wisdom is key; grab onto it with everything you've got. {4:8} Show wisdom some love, and it'll boost you up big time. {4:9} It's like wearing a crown of glory on your head. {4:10} Listen to what I'm saying, and you'll live a long time. {4:11} I've been showing you the smart way to go; stick with it. {4:12} Your steps won't be shaky, and you won't trip up. {4:13} Grab onto teaching and don't let go; it's your lifeline. {4:14} Don't walk down the wrong path or hang with the wrong crowd. {4:15} Stay far away from trouble; don't even think about getting involved. {4:16} They're always up to no good, and they can't sleep until they've caused chaos. {4:17} But doing good leads to a bright future, shining brighter every day. {4:18} The path of the wicked is dark and full of pitfalls. {4:19} Listen up, son; pay attention to my words. {4:20} Keep 'em in your sight, and etch 'em into your heart. {4:21} They'll give you life and keep you healthy. {4:22} Guard your heart above all else; it's where life starts. {4:23} Keep your mouth in check, and stay away from lies. {4:24} Look straight ahead; don't get distracted. {4:25} Think about where you're going, and stick to the path. {4:26} Don't stray to the right or the left; stay away from evil.

{5:1} Hey, listen up, my dude! Pay attention to my wisdom, and tune in to my understanding. {5:2} That way, you'll know how to act smart and keep your lips sealed with knowledge. {5:3} 'Cause let me tell you, when a smooth-talking lady comes around, it's like honey dripping from her lips and oil sliding down. {5:4} But watch out, 'cause in the end, she's bitter as wormwood and cuts like a double-edged sword. {5:5} Her path leads straight to death, and her steps head right for the grave. {5:6} You won't even see it coming 'cause her ways are twisted, and you won't know where you're going. {5:7} So, listen up, kids, and don't stray from my advice. {5:8} Stay far away from her, don't even go near her house. {5:9} 'Cause if you do, you'll lose your honor to someone else, and your best years will be wasted. {5:10} Strangers will end up with your wealth, and you'll work for someone else's benefit. {5:11} And in the end, you'll regret it when you're old and worn out, wondering why you didn't listen to instruction and hated being corrected. {5:12} You'll realize you were almost caught up in all kinds of trouble, right in front of everyone. {5:13} So, drink from your own well and stay faithful to your own wife. {5:14} Let your love be shared only with her, not with some random stranger. {5:15} Enjoy your life with the woman you married when you were young, {5:16} Let her be your source of joy, and always be captivated by her love. {5:17} Why risk it all for some other woman? Why embrace a stranger when you have all you need at home? {5:18} Remember, the Lord sees everything you do; He knows all your actions. {5:19} The wicked will get caught in their own traps and be held by the ropes of their own sins. {5:20} They'll die without instruction, lost in their own foolishness.

{6:1} My dude, if you make a promise for a friend or shake hands with a stranger, {6:2} You're setting a trap for yourself with your own words; you'll be caught by what you say. {6:3} So, do something about it now, my dude, and get yourself out of that situation before it's too late; go, apologize, and make things right. {6:4} Don't even think about sleeping; don't close your eyes for a second. {6:5} Free yourself like a deer escaping from a hunter or a bird flying from a trap. {6:6} Lazybones, learn a lesson from the ants and wise up. {6:7} They don't have a boss, but they work hard all summer and gather food at harvest. {6:8} How long will you keep sleeping? When will you wake up and get to work? {6:9} Just a little more sleep, a little more slumber, and a little more folding of the hands to rest— {6:10-11} And poverty will hit you like a thief, and need will come upon you like an armed bandit. {6:12} Watch out for those troublemakers, the ones with twisted mouths. {6:13} They wink, they shuffle their feet, they point with their fingers; {6:14} They're always plotting evil and stirring up trouble. {6:15} Their downfall will come suddenly, and there'll be no way to escape. {6:16} The Lord hates these six things, and the seventh disgusts Him even more: {6:17} Pride, lying tongues, hands that kill innocent people, {6:18} Hearts that plan wicked things, feet that race to do wrong, {6:19} False witnesses who tell lies, and those who stir up trouble among friends. {6:20} My dude, never forget your dad's teachings, and always stick to your mom's advice. {6:21} Keep them close to your heart, and wear them around your neck like a necklace. {6:22} Let them guide you wherever you go, protect you while you sleep, and talk to you when you wake up. {6:23} Because they're like a light showing you the right way to live; they'll keep you away from bad women and their smooth talk. {6:24} Don't even think about lusting after her beauty or letting her seduce you with her eyes. {6:25} 'Cause chasing after a loose woman will only lead to ruin; she'll hunt you down like a precious prize. {6:26} Can you hold fire against your chest without burning your clothes? {6:27} Can you walk on hot coals without burning your feet? {6:28} It's the same with sleeping with another man's wife; you won't go unpunished. {6:29} People don't mind a thief who steals because he's hungry, {6:30-31} But if he's caught, he has to pay back seven times what he stole and give up everything he owns. {6:32} But whoever commits adultery is just plain stupid; he's destroying himself. {6:33} He'll get hurt and dishonored, and his shame will never go away. {6:34} Jealousy makes people furious, and they won't stop until they get revenge. {6:35} They won't accept anything you offer, no matter how much you try to make up for it with gifts.

{7:1} Yo, dude, hold onto my advice like it's your phone charger; keep my rules close by. {7:2} Stick to my rules, and you'll live; treat my teachings like they're lit. {7:3} Wear 'em like bling, etch 'em into your heart. {7:4} Call wisdom your sis and understanding your fam; they'll keep you away from shady people with smooth talk. {7:5} I peeped out my window and saw this clueless guy strollin' down the street, headin' straight for trouble. {7:6} He meets this chick who's all dolled up, playin' him like a pro. {7:7} She's loud and out there, never home, always lurkin' around. {7:8} She lures him into her crib, playin' him like a fiddle. {7:9} Late at night, when it's dark and sketchy, she pounces. {7:10} She's dressed to impress, slick and sly. {7:11} She reels him in with her sweet talk, and he falls for it. {7:12} He follows her like a sheep to the slaughter, clueless as can be. {7:13} Before he knows it, he's trapped, clueless as a bird in a snare.

{7:14} She's all like, "I got sacrifices and stuff; let's party." {7:15} She's smooth talkin', actin' like she's been lookin' for him all night. {7:16} She's got her bed all decked out, like a VIP suite. {7:17} Her crib smells like a fancy spa. {7:18} She's all about that Netflix and chill till dawn. {7:19} She's playin' him, sayin' her man's away on a trip. {7:20} He's got cash and won't be back till payday. {7:21} She sweet talks him into her trap, flatterin' him till he's hooked. {7:22} He falls for it like a fish swallowin' a hook. {7:23} Before he knows it, he's in too deep, clueless till the end. {7:24} Listen up, kids, don't fall for her game; stay on track. {7:25} Don't let your heart lead you astray; don't get caught in her web. {7:26} She's taken down plenty before, even strong dudes have fallen for her tricks. {7:27} Her crib's like a one-way ticket to disaster, leadin' straight to death.

{8:1} Wisdom's callin' out; understanding's got somethin' to say. {8:2} She's on the block, droppin' wisdom bombs. {8:3} She's shoutin' from the rooftops, at the city gates, and by the doors. {8:4} Listen up, fellas, I'm talkin' to all y'all. {8:5} Don't be dumb; get wise, and open your heart. {8:6} I'm droppin' truth bombs; my words are on point. {8:7} I spit straight facts; lies make me sick. {8:8} My words are all about doin' what's right; there's no shady business here. {8:9} They're easy to understand for those who get it, straight talk for those who know what's up. {8:10} Take my advice over cash any day; wisdom's worth more than gold. {8:11} Wisdom's better than any bling; nothin' compares to it. {8:12} I hang out with good sense and find out cool stuff. {8:13} Hatin' evil is the way to go; pride, arrogance, and lies? Not my thing. {8:14} I'm all about good advice and solid wisdom; I'm the real deal. {8:15} I'm the reason kings rule and judges do justice. {8:16} I'm the secret weapon behind rulers and leaders. {8:17} I dig those who dig me, and those who look for me find me. {8:18} I bring wealth and honor; my blessings last forever. {8:19} My wisdom's better than any cash; my profit beats the best silver. {8:20} I lead the way to what's right and fair; I'm all about justice. {8:21} I hook up those who love me with the good stuff; I fill their pockets with blessings. {8:22} The LORD had me from day one, before anything else existed. {8:23} I've been around since forever, before the world even began. {8:24} I was there before the oceans, before the springs started flowin'. {8:25} Before the mountains rose up, I was there, checkin' out the scene. {8:26} Before God made the earth, the fields, even the dust, I was chillin'. {8:27} I was there when God set up the skies, when he marked out the horizon. {8:28} I saw him set up the clouds and strengthen the deep waters. {8:29} I watched him put the sea in its place, makin' sure it stayed put. {8:30} I was right there with him, checkin' out the world he made. {8:31} I was pumped about the earth, hangin' out with the human crew. {8:32} So listen up, kids; those who follow my lead are blessed. {8:33} Pay attention, get smart, and don't ignore me. {8:34} Blessed is the one who listens to me, waitin' for me like it's their job. {8:35} Whoever finds me finds life and gets God's love. {8:36} But those who diss me only hurt themselves; hatin' on me is like diggin' their own grave.

{9:1} Yo, wisdom built her crib, laid down seven solid pillars like a boss. {9:2} She cooked up a feast, busted out the wine, and set the table with style. {9:3} Sent out her squad, hollering from the rooftops, calling out to anyone clueless or lacking wisdom. {9:4} She's like, "Yo, you simple? Slide in here. Need some smarts? I gotchu." {9:5} "Come vibe with me, feast on my bread, sip on my wine. Let's get enlightened." {9:6} "Dump the fools, come roll with wisdom and live large with understanding." {9:7} "You try to school a hater, you'll catch flak. Call out a bad dude, you'll catch heat." {9:8} "Don't waste time schooling a hater; they'll just hate you more. But wise up a homie, and they'll be down for you." {9:9} "Give knowledge to the wise, they'll level up. Teach a righteous dude, and they'll soak up more game." {9:10} "Start with fearing the big G, that's where wisdom begins. Get to know what's holy, that's true understanding." {9:11} "Stick with me, and you'll live longer, live better." {9:12} "You wise? You're wise for yourself. You play the fool? You're on your own with that mess." {9:13} "But check it, a dumb chick is loud, clueless, and clueless some more." {9:14} "She's posted up at her door, trying to snag whoever's passing by, thinking stolen snacks are sweet and secret grub's a vibe." {9:15} "But she's clueless; her crib's a danger zone, her guests are in for a one-way trip to the underworld."

{10:1} "Okay, fam, listen up. Solomon's dropping some truth bombs. A wise kid makes their pops proud, but a fool brings their momma down." {10:2} "Wicked wealth? Worthless. Righteousness? Saves your butt from death." {10:3} "Big G won't let good folks starve, but He'll toss the wicked's riches in the trash." {10:4} "Lazy hustlers end up broke, but the grind never fails to stack that paper." {10:5} "Hustle in the summer, that's smart. Slacking in the harvest? That's just embarrassing." {10:6} "Good folks get blessed; troublemakers get their mouths shut." {10:7} "Good people are remembered well, but wicked names? Straight-up trash." {10:8} "Wise folks take orders, but blabbermouths trip up." {10:9} "Walk the straight and narrow, you're solid. Stray off course, you'll get called out." {10:10} "Winking leads to trouble. Babbling fools? They trip over their words." {10:11} "A righteous mouth spreads life, but wicked words cover up evil deeds." {10:12} "Hate stirs up drama; love keeps it real and covers mistakes." {10:13} "Smart folks drop wisdom; fools get smacked with a reality check." {10:14} "Wisdom stash knowledge, but fools talk themselves into trouble." {10:15} "Rich folks think they're untouchable, but poverty's the real danger zone for the poor." {10:16} "Hustle brings life to the righteous; wickedness leads to more sin." {10:17} "Stick to the path of instruction, or you'll be lost without a map." {10:18} "Hiding hate with lies? Spreading rumors? Straight-up foolishness." {10:19} "Too many words? You're gonna slip up. Keep quiet? That's wise." {10:20} "A righteous tongue is like gold; a wicked heart's worthless." {10:21} "Good words feed the soul; fools starve for wisdom." {10:22} "Big G's blessings make you rich, and there's no downside." {10:23} "Fools think messing around is fun, but the wise stay woke." {10:24} "Wickedness? It's coming back to bite you. Righteous folks? They get what they hope for." {10:25} "Wickedness fades away like a storm, but the righteous? They're steady like a rock." {10:26} "Lazy folks? They're like vinegar to your teeth or smoke in your eyes; just irritating." {10:27} "Respecting Big G adds years to your life, but wickedness? It's a shortcut to an early exit." {10:28} "Good folks? They're all about hope and joy. Wicked folks? Their hopes? They're toast." {10:29} "Walking in Big G's ways gives you strength, but straying off? That's a one-way ticket to disaster." {10:30} "Righteous folks? They're planted firm; wicked ones? They're getting evicted." {10:31} "Wise mouths know what's up, but wicked tongues? They're getting cut off." {10:32} "Good words from good people? That's what's up. Wicked talk? Just twisted nonsense."

{11:1} When you use fake vibes, it's like a major no-no for the big guy upstairs, but when you're legit, it's like his favorite thing ever. {11:2} If you're all about yourself, you're bound to feel some major embarrassment, but if you're humble, that's where the real wisdom's at. {11:3} Keep it real, and you'll stay on track, but if you're all about the shady stuff, you're just setting yourself up for a major fail. {11:4} Money won't save you when things get real, but being righteous? That's your ticket out of trouble. {11:5} Doing what's right guides your path, but if you're shady, you're just digging your own grave. {11:6} Keep it legit, and you'll stay outta trouble, but if you're all about breaking the rules, you're gonna get busted. {11:7} When a shady dude bites the dust, all his big plans go down with him, but when a good person checks out, hope still lives on. {11:8} Good people make it out of tough spots, but the shady ones? They're just trading places with 'em. {11:9} Talking trash about your neighbor? Not cool. But being wise? That's how you dodge drama. {11:10} When good stuff happens to good people, everyone's celebrating, but when the bad guys get what's coming to 'em, it's like party time. {11:11} Good folks lift up a city, but the shady ones? They're tearing it down with their mouths. {11:12} If you're clueless, you'll diss your neighbor, but if you're smart, you'll keep quiet. {11:13} Gossiping spills secrets, but having a loyal vibe? That's how you keep stuff on the DL. {11:14} Without good advice, you're heading for disaster, but with a solid crew to back you up, you're golden. {11:15} Co-signing for a stranger? Bad move. But hating that kinda deal? That's smart. {11:16} A chill chick keeps her honor, and strong people keep their cash. {11:17} Doing good vibes? It's like a boost for your soul, but being cruel? That's just hurting yourself. {11:18} Shady moves? They'll trip you up, but doing what's right? That's where you score big. {11:19} Living right? That's your lifeline, but chasing evil? It's a dead end. {11:20} Shady hearts? They're a major turnoff for the big guy, but walking the straight and narrow? He's all about it. {11:21} The wicked might team up, but they're still gonna get what's coming to 'em, while the righteous? They're coming out on top. {11:22} A cool chick who's got no chill? Yeah, she's like a diamond in a pig's snout. {11:23} Good vibes only? That's what the righteous are all about, but the wicked? They're just asking for trouble. {11:24} Some peeps spread the love and keep on winning, but if you're stingy, you're headed for broke. {11:25} Being generous? It's like leveling up, and those who water others? They're getting hydrated too. {11:26} Hoarding stuff? Yeah, the people aren't gonna be happy with you, but selling it off? That's where the blessings flow. {11:27} Seek out the good stuff, and you'll find some major perks, but if you're all about causing trouble? Brace yourself. {11:28} Trusting in your riches? Not gonna end well, but being righteous? That's where you'll flourish. {11:29} Messing up your own home life? Yeah, that's gonna blow up in your face, but having some smarts? That's where the real power's at. {11:30} Doing good? It's like planting a tree of life, and leading others to good vibes? That's some next-level wisdom. {11:31} The good guys? They're gonna get what's coming to 'em, and the wicked? They won't be getting off easy either.

{12:1} If you're into learning, you're all about leveling up, but if you can't handle criticism? Yeah, you're not the brightest bulb. {12:2} Being on the good side? That's where you'll find favor, but if you're all about shady deals, you're gonna get called out. {12:3} Trying to build something on shady vibes? Yeah, that's not gonna last, but being righteous? You're standing on solid ground. {12:4} A chill partner? They're like a crown on your head, but someone who's all about drama? They're like poison to your bones. {12:5} Good peeps? They're thinking straight, but the shady ones? They're all about the sneaky stuff. {12:6} Shady talk? It's all about causing trouble, but speaking up for what's right? That's how you dodge disaster. {12:7} Shady folks? They're gonna crash and burn, but the righteous ones? They're standing strong. {12:8} If you're wise, you're gonna get props, but if you're all about stirring up drama, you're gonna get dissed. {12:9} Being humble and having a crew? It's better than acting like you're all that and being broke. {12:10} Treating animals right? That's what a good person does, but being cruel? Yeah, that's just plain heartless. {12:11} Working hard? That's how you put food on the table, but chasing after empty dreams? That's just dumb. {12:12} Shady folks? They're all about causing trouble, but being rooted in what's right? That's where the real fruit's at. {12:13} Watch what you say; it could land you in hot water, but being on the up and up? That's how you dodge disaster. {12:14} Spreading good vibes? That's how you fill up your tank, and putting in the work? You're gonna see some major payback. {12:15} Thinking you're right all the time? Yeah, that's a major red flag, but listening to advice? Now that's smart. {12:16} When a fool gets mad, everyone knows about it, but a wise person? They're all about keeping it chill. {12:17} Speaking truth? That's all about doing what's right, but lying? Yeah, that's just shady. {12:18} Some words? They're like a dagger to the heart, but words of wisdom? They're healing. {12:19} Truth? It's gonna stand the test of time, but lies? They're just gonna crumble eventually. {12:20} Cooking up evil plans? Yeah, that's just plain shady, but making peace? That's where the good vibes are at. {12:21} Good people? They're not gonna get blindsided by evil, but the wicked? They're in for a world of hurt. {12:22} Lying? Yeah, that's a major no-no for the big guy, but being real? That's where it's at. {12:23} Smart folks? They know when to keep quiet, but fools? They're all about shouting out their nonsense. {12:24} Putting in the work? That's how you take charge, but being lazy? Yeah, that's gonna cost you. {12:25} Feeling down? A kind word can turn it all around, but spreading negativity? That's just gonna bring everyone down. {12:26} The righteous? They're in a league of their own, but following the wicked? That's just leading to trouble. {12:27} If you're lazy, you're not gonna eat, but if you're diligent, you're gonna see some major rewards. {12:28} Walking the righteous path? It's all about life, but going down the wrong road? Yeah, that's a dead end.

{13:1} So, peep this, a smart kid listens up when dad drops knowledge, but a hater? Nah, they can't handle the truth. {13:2} Speak good vibes, eat good vibes; but if you're all about breaking the rules, you're just inviting trouble. {13:3} Keep your mouth shut, keep your life chill; but if you're all about running your mouth, you're asking for trouble. {13:4} Lazy souls want it all but end up with nada; but those who hustle? They're living large. {13:5} Real ones hate lies; but fakes? They're straight-up embarrassing. {13:6} Doing right keeps you on track, but being shady? Yeah, that's just asking for a fall. {13:7} Some flex like they're loaded but are actually broke; others keep it humble but got stacks. {13:8} Rich folks think they're untouchable; but the poor? They're too busy to even care. {13:9} Good vibes shine bright; but haters? Yeah, their light's about to go out. {13:10} Drama only comes from pride; but if you're smart, you're all about that wisdom. {13:11} Quick cash never lasts; but if you're grinding? You're stacking up for real. {13:12} Delayed dreams hurt the heart, but when they finally come true? That's the good stuff. {13:13} Diss the truth, and you're setting yourself up for a fall; but those who respect the rules? They're in for some real rewards. {13:14} Wise laws keep you living large and dodging trouble; but those who ignore them? Yeah, they're just asking for trouble. {13:15} Having smarts earns you respect, but if you're all about breaking the rules? Life's gonna be tough. {13:16} Smart moves come from knowing what's up, but fools? They just lay all their cards on the table. {13:17} Shady messengers? They're heading straight for trouble; but if you're loyal and true? You're bringing that good vibe health. {13:18} Ignore good advice, and you'll end up broke and ashamed; but if you're all about learning and growing? Yeah, you're in for some real respect. {13:19} Achieving your dreams? Sweet satisfaction; but if you're stuck in your evil ways? Yeah, that's just messed up. {13:20} Roll with the wise, and you'll level up; but if you're hanging with fools? Yeah, you're setting yourself up for a fall. {13:21} Trouble's always chasing down the rule breakers, but if you're all about doing right? Yeah, good things are coming your way. {13:22} Good folks leave behind a legacy for generations to come; but all that shady wealth? Yeah, it's just waiting to be passed on to the righteous. {13:23} Some folks got plenty, just 'cause they know how to hustle; but others? Yeah, they're clueless and end up losing everything. {13:24} Spare the discipline, and you're not doing your kid any favors; but if you love 'em, you'll set 'em straight early on. {13:25} Good folks eat 'til they're satisfied, but the wicked? Yeah, they're always left wanting more.

{14:1} Smart ladies? They're building their empire; but fools? Yeah, they're tearing it all down with their own hands. {14:2} Keep it real, fear the Big G; but if you're all about doing things your way? Yeah, you're disrespecting the man upstairs. {14:3} Foolish mouths? Just asking for trouble; but wise words? They'll keep you out of trouble. {14:4} No hustle, no gain; but if you're putting in the work? Yeah, you're gonna see some real results. {14:5} Real talk? A trustworthy witness won't lie; but a liar? Yeah, they'll spin a web of lies. {14:6} Haters act like they're searching for wisdom, but they ain't finding nothing; but those who get it? Yeah, it's like second nature to 'em. {14:7} Dip out when you're around a fool who's all talk and no action; 'cause real knowledge? Yeah, it's not coming from them. {14:8} Smart folks know their way around, but fools? Yeah, they're always scheming. {14:9} Fools laugh off sin, but those who do right? They're winning respect. {14:10} Your own struggles? Yeah, only you know how much they sting; but outsiders? They just don't get it. {14:11} Wicked houses? Yeah, they're crumbling down; but righteous homes? They're thriving. {14:12} Thinking you're on the right path might feel good, but if it leads to destruction? Yeah, you're in for a rude awakening. {14:13} Even when you're laughing, there might be pain deep down; 'cause that joy? Yeah, it's not always gonna last. {14:14} Slipping back into old ways? Yeah, that's just gonna fill you with regret; but staying true to yourself? Yeah, that's where real satisfaction lies. {14:15} Naive folks believe everything they hear, but the wise? They're always checking their steps. {14:16} Smart folks steer clear of trouble, but fools? They're charging in, full steam ahead. {14:17} Quick tempers? Yeah, they lead to dumb decisions; but those with wicked plans? Yeah, they're straight-up hated. {14:18} Simpletons? Yeah, they just keep on making the same mistakes; but those with smarts? Yeah, they're crowned with wisdom. {14:19} Evil bows down to good; but those who do wrong? Yeah, they're shut out from the righteous. {14:20} Poor folks? Yeah, even their neighbors ain't feeling 'em; but the rich? Yeah, they got friends coming out the woodwork. {14:21} Diss your neighbor? Yeah, that's a sin; but showing mercy to the poor? Yeah, that's where the real happiness is at. {14:22} Those who plot evil? Yeah, they're way off track; but those who show kindness and honesty? Yeah, they're the real winners. {14:23} Hard work always pays off; but if you're all talk and no action? Yeah, you're just gonna end up broke. {14:24} Wise folks? Yeah, they're stacking up that wealth; but fools? Yeah, they're just throwing their money away. {14:25} A true friend will always have your back; but a fake one? Yeah, they're just full of lies. {14:26} Fear of the Big G? Yeah, that's where you find real confidence; and for their kids? Yeah, they got a safe place to land. {14:24} Yo, for smart peeps, their riches are like the ultimate flex; but for fools? Yeah, their stupidity just screams out loud. {14:25} Real ones save lives with their truth bombs, but those who lie? Yeah, they're just spreading toxic vibes. {14:26} Being all about respecting the Big G? Yeah, that's where the real confidence comes from; and for their kids? Yeah, they got a safe space to vibe. {14:27} Big G's respect is like a fountain of life, keeping you away from all the sketchy stuff that leads to trouble. {14:28} Having a big crew? Yeah, it's a sign of respect for the king; but if you're rolling solo? Yeah, it's a one-way ticket to losing everything. {14:29} Keeping your cool? Yeah, that's a sign of real smarts; but if you're quick to blow up? Yeah, you're just inviting chaos. {14:30} Having a healthy mindset? Yeah, it's like the key to living your best life; but being jealous? Yeah, it eats away at you from the inside. {14:31} Messing with the poor? Yeah, it's like dissing the Big G himself; but showing them love and respect? Yeah, that's where the real blessings come in. {14:32} Wicked folks? Yeah, they're gonna get what's coming to them eventually; but the righteous? Yeah, they're holding out hope even in the face of death. {14:33} Wisdom? Yeah, it's deep in the hearts of those who really get it; but for fools? Yeah, they're just out here exposing themselves. {14:34} Doing what's right? Yeah, it's what lifts a nation up; but living foul? Yeah, it's a stain on everyone. {14:35} The king's all about showing love to smart servants; but if you're bringing shame? Yeah, you better watch out for his wrath.

{15:1} Speaking calmly can totally defuse a heated situation, but throwing shade just amps up the anger. {15:2} Smart peeps know how to drop knowledge bombs, but fools? They're all about spewing nonsense. {15:3} The big guy upstairs sees everything, both the good and the bad. {15:4} Keeping it real with your words? It's like a breath of fresh air, but being all twisted up inside? That's just gonna mess you up. {15:5} Ignoring your old man's advice? Not smart. But listening up when you're called out? Now that's wise. {15:6} Good vibes in a righteous home? That's where the treasure's at, but shady business? It's just asking for trouble. {15:7} Wise words spread knowledge, but fools? They're all about ignorance. {15:8} The wicked's offerings? Yeah, they make the big guy sick, but when the upright pray? That's what he's all about. {15:9} The wicked's path? It's a no-go zone for the big guy, but those chasing after what's right? He's all over that. {15:10} Getting called out for your mistakes? It stings, but turning away from correction? That's a one-way ticket to trouble. {15:11} The big guy's got his eye on everything, even our inner thoughts. {15:12} Scoffers? They're not into being called out, and they're definitely not hanging with the wise crowd. {15:13} A happy heart? It shows on your face, but carrying around sorrow? It's a real spirit breaker. {15:14} Smart folks are hungry for knowledge, but fools? They're just feeding on nonsense. {15:15} Life's rough for the down-and-out, but those with a positive vibe? It's like a never-ending party. {15:16} A little with respect for the big guy? Way better than being loaded and dealing with constant drama. {15:17} Sharing a humble meal with love beats out a fancy spread with hate any day. {15:18} Getting all worked up? It's a recipe for drama, but staying chill? That's how you keep the peace. {15:19} Lazy paths? They're like walking through thorns, but doing what's right? It's a smooth ride. {15:20} Making your pops proud? That's what a wise kid does, but dissing your mom? Not cool. {15:21} Foolishness might seem fun to clueless peeps, but those who've got their act together? They're walking tall. {15:22} Going it alone? Yeah, you're setting yourself up for failure, but listening to advice? That's how you get things done. {15:23} Saying the right thing at the right time? It's a real mood lifter. {15:24} Walking the righteous path? It's like rising above the mess below. {15:25} The big guy takes down the prideful, but he's all about supporting those who've lost everything. {15:26} Wicked thoughts? They're a major turnoff for the big guy, but pure words? Yeah, he's loving that. {15:27} Greedy for cash? You're just causing trouble for your own fam, but turning down bribes? That's where real living's at. {15:28} Righteous peeps think before they speak, but the wicked? They're just spewing out evil. {15:29} The big guy's not vibing with the wicked crowd, but he's all ears for the prayers of the righteous. {15:30} Good news? It's like a party for your soul, and a positive vibe? It's good for your bones. {15:31} Listening up when life calls you out? That's how you hang with the smart crew. {15:32} Ignoring advice? Yeah, you're not doing your soul any favors, but taking criticism? That's how you grow. {15:33} Revering the big guy? That's where wisdom starts, and showing some humility? Yeah, that's how you get honored.

{16:1} Whatever plans you're cooking up and whatever you say? It's all coming from the big guy upstairs. {16:2} Thinking you're all clean? Yeah, that's just your own opinion, but the big guy? He sees right through it. {16:3} Trusting the big guy with your plans? That's how you stay on track. {16:4} Even the wicked? Yeah, they're playing a role in the big guy's plan. {16:5} Proud vibes? They're a major turnoff for the big guy, and teaming up with other proud peeps? Yeah, that's not gonna end well. {16:6} Mercy and truth? They're like a cleanse for wrongdoing, and fearing the big guy? That's how you steer clear of trouble. {16:7} Living in a way that pleases the big guy? It's like making peace with your enemies. {16:8} A little bit with righteousness? It's way better than rolling in cash without doing what's right. {16:9} You might think you're in control, but the big guy's the one calling the shots. {16:10} Kings speaking truth? It's like they're channeling divine wisdom, and sticking to what's right? Yeah, that's how you rule. {16:11} Fairness? It's all part of the big guy's plan, and making sure everything's on the level? Yeah, that's his work. {16:12} Kings doing shady stuff? Yeah, that's a major no-go, 'cause their throne? It's built on righteousness. {16:13} Kings dig truth-tellers, and those speaking straight up? Yeah, they're all about that. {16:14} Pissing off a king? It's like signing your own death warrant, but being wise? That's how you calm things down. {16:15} Basking in the king's favor? It's like life itself, and being on his good side? It's like rain in a drought. {16:16} Getting wisdom? Way better than scoring gold, and understanding? Yeah, that's worth more than silver. {16:17} Walking the straight and narrow? It's how you avoid disaster, and staying true to your path? It's how you save your soul. {16:18} Pride? It's a one-way ticket to destruction, but humility? That's how you rise above. {16:19} Being humble? Yeah, that's where it's at, and sharing the spoils with the proud? Not a good look. {16:20} Handling stuff with wisdom? It's how you find success, and trusting in the big guy? It's like winning the happiness lottery. {16:21} Smart folks? They're known for their wisdom, and speaking with kindness? Yeah, that's how you boost your brainpower. {16:22} Having understanding? It's like a fountain of life, but listening to fools? That's just asking for trouble. {16:23} Wise hearts? They teach wise things, and their words? They're like medicine for your soul. {16:24} Saying the right thing? It's like honey for the soul, sweet and good for your bones. {16:25} Thinking you're on the right track? Yeah, that might lead to disaster. {16:26} Working hard? Yeah, that's how you eat, but being greedy? It's like an endless hunger. {16:27} Digging up evil? Yeah, it's like playing with fire, and spreading rumors? That's how you break up friendships. {16:28} Stirring up trouble? Yeah, that's a specialty of the troublemakers, but the righteous? They're all about spreading goodness. {16:29} Leading others down a bad path? Yeah, that's not cool, but standing firm against it? That's real strength. {16:30} Plotting evil? It's like brewing trouble, and letting those words fly? Yeah, that's just asking for trouble. {16:31} Being old and wise? It's like wearing a crown, but only if you've walked the righteous path. {16:32} Keeping your cool? Yeah, that's way better than being a tough guy, and mastering yourself? That's true strength. {16:33} Life might seem random, but the big guy's the one pulling the strings.

{17:1} Yo, it's better to chill with a dry snack in peace than to be stuck in a drama-filled mansion. {17:2} Check it, a smart worker ends up with more respect than a screw-up kid, and they even get a piece of the pie. {17:3} You know how silver and gold get purified? Well, the Big G tests hearts, no joke. {17:4} Those shady types love listening to lies, and liars? They're all ears for gossip. {17:5} Dissin' the poor is like dissin' the Big G himself, and anyone celebrating someone's downfall? Yeah, they're in for some payback. {17:6} Grandkids make old folks proud, and a dad's pride is his kids. {17:7} Talking smart ain't a look for fools, and leaders? They shouldn't be caught lyin'. {17:8} Gifts are like flexin' jewels to those who get 'em; wherever they go, they bring good vibes. {17:9} Covering up mistakes shows love, but spreading gossip? Yeah, that's how you lose friends. {17:10} Smart folks take criticism to heart, but fools? Yeah, they never learn, no matter how hard you hit 'em. {17:11} Rebels only bring trouble on themselves, so they better watch out for what's coming. {17:12} You'd rather meet an angry bear than deal with a fool and their foolishness. {17:13} Returnin' evil for good? Yeah, that's just asking for trouble to move in. {17:14} Stirring up fights? Yeah, it's like opening the floodgates; better to squash it before it blows up. {17:15} Defending the wicked and dissin' the just? Yeah, that's a one-way ticket to being hated by the Big G. {17:16} Why a fool thinks they can buy wisdom when they ain't even got the heart for it? Beats me. {17:17} Friends got your back through thick and thin, and brothers? Yeah, they're there when things get rough. {17:18} Making deals without understanding? Yeah, that's just setting yourself up for trouble. {17:19} Loving drama? Yeah, you're inviting destruction; and if you're all about making a scene? Yeah, you're heading for trouble. {17:20} Negative vibes? Yeah, they never lead to anything good; and if you're all about causing trouble with your words? Yeah, you're just asking for it. {17:21} Having a fool for a kid? Yeah, that's a one-way ticket to disappointment; and a dad stuck with a fool? Yeah, that's just sad. {17:22} Keeping it light and happy? Yeah, it's like medicine for the soul; but feeling down? Yeah, it's like drying up from the inside out. {17:23} Using bribes to twist justice? Yeah, that's shady business; and those who got real smarts? Yeah, they see through the nonsense. {17:24} Smart ones? Yeah, they're focused on what matters; but fools? Yeah, they're always chasing after the next shiny thing. {17:25} Being stuck with a foolish kid? Yeah, it's like a never-ending headache for parents; and seeing good folks get punished? Yeah, that's just messed up. {17:26} Punishing the innocent? Yeah, it's just not right; and treating leaders unfairly? Yeah, that's not gonna fly. {17:27} Wise ones know when to keep quiet, and those with real understanding? Yeah, they're all about that positive energy. {17:28} Even a fool can seem wise if they keep their mouth shut; and someone who knows when to stay quiet? Yeah, they're seen as smart.

{18:1} When you're hungry for knowledge, you're gonna go after it; and fools? Yeah, they're too caught up in themselves to care about learning. {18:2} A fool ain't interested in understanding; they just wanna talk about themselves all day. {18:3} When troublemakers show up, drama's not far behind, and with shame comes disgrace. {18:4} Wise words run deep, and real wisdom flows like a never-ending stream. {18:5} Showing favoritism to the wicked? Yeah, that's just not cool, especially if it means trampling on the righteous. {18:6} Fools are always starting fights with their big mouths; and their words? Yeah, they're just asking for trouble. {18:7} A fool's words? Yeah, they're like a one-way ticket to disaster; and their lies? Yeah, they're like traps for their own souls. {18:8} Gossip? Yeah, it's like a dagger to the heart, cutting deep; and those who spread it? Yeah, they're stirring up trouble. {18:9} Lazy folks? Yeah, they're just as bad as those who waste everything away. {18:10} Trusting in the Big G? Yeah, it's like finding shelter in a storm; and thinking your riches make you invincible? Yeah, it's just pride talking. {18:11} Feeling untouchable 'cause you're rich? Yeah, that's just fooling yourself; and thinking you're better than everyone else? Yeah, that's just arrogance. {18:12} Pride comes before a fall, and humility comes before honor. {18:13} Shooting off your mouth before you know what's up? Yeah, that's just plain dumb; and it's only gonna lead to embarrassment. {18:14} A strong spirit can handle anything life throws its way, but a crushed spirit? Yeah, that's hard to bear. {18:15} Smart ones are always learning, and those who listen? Yeah, they're on a quest for knowledge. {18:16} Being generous opens doors, and it gets you in front of some important people. {18:17} Thinking you're in the right? Yeah, you better be ready for someone to call you out; 'cause your neighbors? Yeah, they see everything. {18:18} Settling disputes with chance? Yeah, sometimes it's the best way to end the drama; and when the mighty step aside? Yeah, it's like clearing the path for peace. {18:19} Making up with a offended sibling? Yeah, it's harder than breaking into a fortress; and family fights? Yeah, they're like prison bars. {18:20} Speaking wise words? Yeah, it's like filling up on good food; and when you're always chatting? Yeah, you're just never satisfied. {18:21} Words can bring life or death, and those who love talking? Yeah, they're gonna eat the fruit of their words. {18:22} Finding a good partner? Yeah, it's like winning the jackpot; and getting in good with the Big G? Yeah, it's like getting a stamp of approval. {18:23} Rich folks? Yeah, they're not always the friendliest; and the poor? Yeah, they're just trying

{19:1} It's way better to be broke but honest than to be all shady and dumb. {19:2} Ignorance? Not a good look, and rushing into stuff? Yeah, that's just asking for trouble. {19:3} Being foolish just messes up your life, and blaming the big guy for your mess? Not cool. {19:4} Having money attracts friends, but being poor? Yeah, it's lonely out here. {19:5} Lying? You're gonna get caught, and there's no getting away from it. {19:6} People sucking up to the rich and powerful? It's like a popularity contest, but true friendship? That's where it's at. {19:7} Poor folks? They're like outcasts, even from their own family, and no matter how much they beg, nobody's sticking around. {19:8} Getting wise? That's how you look out for yourself, and understanding? It's the key to success. {19:9} Liars? Yeah, they're gonna get what's coming to them, and those spreading falsehoods? They're headed for trouble. {19:10} Fools finding joy? Not a good vibe, and servants bossing around their superiors? Yeah, that's not the way things work. {19:11} Holding back your temper? That's real maturity, and forgiving someone's mistakes? That's true strength. {19:12} Tick off the king? It's like messing with a lion, but getting in his good books? It's like getting blessed with morning dew. {19:13} A foolish kid? Yeah, that's a headache for his old man, and a nagging wife? She's like a leaky faucet. {19:14} Inheriting wealth? It's a family thing, but finding a smart partner? That's a gift from above. {19:15} Being lazy? It's like falling into a deep sleep, and loafing around? Yeah, that's just asking to go hungry. {19:16} Following the rules? It's how you protect yourself, but ignoring them? Yeah, that's a one-way ticket to disaster. {19:17} Helping out the poor? It's like lending a hand to the big guy himself, and he's gonna pay you back big time. {19:18} Discipline your kid while there's still hope, and don't hold back, even if he's crying. {19:19} Hot-headed folks? Yeah, they're gonna get burned, and even if you rescue them once, you'll just have to do it again. {19:20} Listen to advice and learn, so you'll be wise down the road. {19:21} People have all sorts of plans, but only the big guy's plan sticks. {19:22} Wanting to do good? Yeah, that's what counts, and being poor? Way better than being a liar. {19:23} Revering the big guy? It leads to a good life, and those who do? They won't get hit with disaster. {19:24} Lazy folks? They won't even lift a finger to feed themselves. {19:25} Teach a troublemaker a lesson, and others will think twice, but give advice to someone smart? Yeah, they'll get it. {19:26} Disrespecting your parents? Yeah, that's shameful, and pushing them away? It's a disgrace. {19:27} Son, don't listen to bad advice that leads you away from knowledge. {19:28} Wicked people mock justice, and the mouths of the evil are full of wrongdoing. {19:29} Scorners? They're in for a rude awakening, and fools? Yeah, they're gonna get what's coming to them.

{20:1} Booze might seem fun, but it's trouble waiting to happen, and falling for it? Yeah, that's not smart. {20:2} Tick off the king? It's like stirring up a lion, and messing with him? You're just hurting yourself. {20:3} Peace? It's a good look, but fools? They're all about drama. {20:4} Lazy folks? They won't even work in the cold, but come harvest time, they'll be begging with empty hands. {20:5} People hide their true thoughts, but those who understand? Yeah, they'll figure it out. {20:6} Everyone brags about themselves, but finding someone truly reliable? That's rare. {20:7} Doing right? It's a good vibe, and your kids? Yeah, they'll thank you for it. {20:8} A king who brings justice? Yeah, he's clearing out all the bad vibes, just with a glance. {20:9} Who can claim they're pure? Yeah, that's a tough sell, and trying to fool the big guy? Not gonna happen. {20:10} Cheating in business? It's a major turnoff for the big guy, and using rigged scales? Yeah, that's not cool. {20:11} Even kids? Yeah, they're judged by their actions, whether they're pure or not. {20:12} Hearing and seeing? Yeah, that's all thanks to the big guy. {20:13} Loving sleep? It'll lead you to poverty, but staying awake? Yeah, that's how you stay fed. {20:14} Bargaining? It's all talk, but once the deal's done? Yeah, that's when the boasting starts. {20:15} Money and jewels? They're cool, but speaking wisdom? That's priceless. {20:16} Putting up collateral for a stranger? Yeah, that's risky business, and trusting a stranger? Not smart. {20:17} Lies might taste sweet at first, but in the end? Yeah, you'll be spitting out gravel. {20:18} Planning? It's best done with advice, and going to war? It's a serious decision. {20:19} Gossipers? They spill secrets, so don't get mixed up with them. {20:20} Curse your parents? Yeah, that's like snuffing out your own light. {20:21} Quick money? It might seem good at first, but in the end? Yeah, it won't bring blessings. {20:22} Don't seek revenge; let the big guy handle it, and he'll come through for you. {20:23} Rigged scales? Yeah, the big guy's not vibing with that, and lying? Not cool. {20:24} People's steps? Yeah, they're guided by the big guy, but understanding your own path? That's a tough one. {20:25} Fooling around with sacred stuff? Yeah, it's a trap, and making promises you can't keep? Not smart. {20:26} A wise ruler? Yeah, he's taking down the bad guys, and turning the tables on them. {20:27} People's spirits? Yeah, they're like flashlights for the big guy, searching out all their secrets. {20:28} Mercy and truth? They're what keeps a ruler going, and his throne? It's built on mercy. {20:29} Young folks? Yeah, they've got energy for days, and old folks? They're like living history books. {20:30} Sometimes pain cleans out the bad vibes, and getting disciplined? It's like a reset button for your soul.

{21:1} So, like, the king's vibe is totally controlled by the Big G, kinda like how rivers flow wherever they wanna go. {21:2} Everyone thinks they're doing what's right, but the Big G knows what's really up in our hearts. {21:3} Big G vibes more with justice and fairness than fancy rituals and sacrifices. {21:4} Acting all high and mighty, yeah, that's a big no-no; it's straight-up sin. {21:5} People who hustle hard are all about that success, but those who rush into stuff end up with nada. {21:6} Lying to get rich? Yeah, that's just a one-way ticket to disaster town. {21:7} Doing shady stuff? Yeah, it's gonna come back to bite you hard. {21:8} The way some folks roll is sketchy AF, but the pure-hearted? Yeah, they're all about doing right. {21:9} Better to chill on the roof than deal with a drama queen in a big house. {21:10} Wicked souls? Yeah, they're all about that evil life; they ain't got love for anyone. {21:11} When haters get what's coming to them, it's a wake-up call for the clueless; and when the wise learn something new, they level up. {21:12} The righteous peep the scene and know what's up with the wicked's crib; but the Big G? Yeah, He's gonna shut them down eventually. {21:13} Ignoring the cries of the needy? Yeah, that's just asking for trouble. {21:14} A sneaky bribe can calm even the angriest soul, and a well-timed reward can squash any beef. {21:15} Doing what's right brings joy to the soul, but for the shady? Yeah, it's gonna end in ruin. {21:16} Straying from wisdom? Yeah, that's a one-way ticket to a dead-end life. {21:17} Those all about the good stuff? Yeah, they're the real winners in life. {21:18} Wicked souls? Yeah, they're just a disaster waiting to happen. {21:19} Better to kick it in the wild than deal with a toxic vibe at home. {21:20} Wise folks? Yeah, they're sitting on treasure, but fools? Yeah, they blow through it like it's nothing. {21:21} Doing what's right and showing love? Yeah, that's where the real blessings are at. {21:22} Smart moves can take down even the toughest obstacles. {21:23} Keeping quiet can save you from a world of trouble. {21:24} Being all proud and arrogant? Yeah, that's a one-way ticket to nowhere. {21:25} Lazy vibes? Yeah, they're gonna lead to your downfall; you gotta hustle if you wanna make it. {21:26} Always wanting more but never giving back? Yeah, that's not a good look; but the righteous? Yeah, they're all about sharing the love. {21:27} Even the Big G ain't feeling the gifts from shady peeps; imagine what He thinks about their twisted motives. {21:28} Liars? Yeah, they're gonna get what's coming to them; but those who listen? Yeah, they're gonna keep it real. {21:29} Wicked souls? Yeah, they're all about that hard exterior, but the upright? Yeah, they know where they're headed. {21:30} Ain't no way to outsmart the Big G; He's always one step ahead. {21:31} Preparing for battle is cool and all, but real safety? Yeah, that's in the Big G's hands.

{22:1} A solid rep? Yeah, it's way better than stacking cash or chasing clout. {22:2} Rich or poor, we're all made by the Big G. {22:3} Being smart means seeing trouble coming and dodging it; but the clueless? Yeah, they just walk right into it. {22:4} Humility and respect for the Big G? Yeah, that's where the real wealth, honor, and life are at. {22:5} Sketchy situations are everywhere, but those who stay true to themselves? Yeah, they're gonna stay clear of the drama. {22:6} Teaching kids the right way? Yeah, that's gonna pay off big time down the road. {22:7} Rich folks calling the shots, and borrowers? Yeah, they're just slaves to debt. {22:8} Planting seeds of evil? Yeah, you're gonna harvest trouble; and anger? Yeah, it's only gonna lead to more problems. {22:9} Being generous brings blessings; sharing your bread with the needy? Yeah, that's where it's at. {22:10} Kick out the haters, and peace will follow; ain't nobody got time for drama. {22:11} Those with pure hearts? Yeah, they're gonna win over even the kings with their words. {22:12} The Big G? Yeah, He's keeping tabs on everything and shutting down the lies. {22:13} Lazy souls making excuses? Yeah, they're just asking for trouble. {22:14} Falling for temptation? Yeah, it's like falling into a deep hole; and those hated by the Big G? Yeah, they're gonna fall hard. {22:15} Foolishness might start in the heart, but a little tough love can straighten things out real quick. {22:16} Exploiting the poor for personal gain? Yeah, it's gonna backfire big time. {22:17} Listen up to the wise words and let them sink in deep. {22:18}

Holding onto wisdom? Yeah, it's like having the perfect comeback ready at all times. {22:19} Trusting in the Big G? Yeah, that's where real security lies. {22:20} I've dropped some real wisdom on you today; it's up to you to take it to heart. {22:21} Knowing the truth? Yeah, that's gonna give you the answers when you need 'em. {22:22} Don't mess with the poor or the afflicted; the Big G's got their back, and He's not gonna let anyone mess with them. {22:23} Angry friends? Yeah, they're bad news; don't get caught up in their drama. {22:24} Making shady deals? Yeah, that's just asking for trouble. {22:25} Don't sign up for other people's messes, or you'll end up in one yourself. {22:26} If you can't pay up, don't get involved in debt; it's just gonna lead to more problems. {22:27} Why put yourself in a tight spot if you can't handle it? {22:28} Don't mess with what's been established for generations. {22:29} See someone grinding hard? Yeah, they're gonna rise to the top; they ain't messing with the small fry.

{23:1} So, when you're dining with a VIP, scope out the scene before you dig in. {23:2} And seriously, if you're all about stuffing your face, you better check yourself before you wreck yourself. {23:3} Don't be drooling over his fancy food; it's all a front. {23:4} Don't bust your butt trying to get rich; sometimes you gotta let go of your own plans. {23:5} Think you can rely on wealth? Nah, it's as fleeting as a bird in flight. {23:6} Don't cozy up to someone with bad vibes or eyeing their fancy spread; they're not sincere. {23:7} They might act all hospitable, but they're not really with you. {23:8} That gourmet bite you took? Yeah, you might end up regretting it and losing your sweet talk. {23:9} Don't waste wisdom on fools; they'll just brush you off. {23:10} Don't mess with property lines or mess with orphans' fields; they've got a big protector. {23:11} Pay attention to lessons and soak up knowledge. {23:12} Don't hold back on discipline for your kid; a little tough love won't kill them. {23:13} Discipline them when needed; it'll save their soul from disaster. {23:14} Don't hold back on discipline; it could save them from a world of hurt. {23:15} If you're smart, it makes me happy too. {23:16} When you talk sense, it's like music to my ears. {23:17} Don't be jealous of troublemakers; stick to fearing the big guy all day long. {23:18} Trust me, the troublemakers will get what's coming to them; your hopes won't be dashed. {23:19} Listen up, be smart, and stay on the right path. {23:20} Don't hang out with heavy drinkers or party animals; they're headed for ruin. {23:21} Drinking and overeating? Yeah, they'll lead you to poverty and rags. {23:22} Respect your folks, especially when they're older. {23:23} Invest in truth and don't sell out for anything; wisdom, advice, and understanding are priceless. {23:24} Proud parents love a righteous kid; having a wise child brings joy. {23:25} Your folks will be over the moon when they see you doing well. {23:26} Follow my lead, kid, and pay attention to how I do things. {23:27} Getting involved with the wrong crowd? It's like diving into a pit; steer clear. {23:28} They're always scheming and dragging others into trouble. {23:29} Who ends up miserable? Yeah, those who party too hard and pick fights for no reason. {23:30} Hang around at bars too long, and you'll end up with more trouble than you bargained for. {23:31} Don't let the sight of booze tempt you; it's trouble waiting to happen. {23:32} Trust me, it'll bite back like a venomous snake. {23:33} Booze will cloud your judgment and make you say dumb stuff. {23:34} You'll feel lost and helpless, just like a ship lost at sea or someone stuck on a mast. {23:35} They'll mess you up without you even realizing it, and then you'll be craving it all over again.

{24:1} Don't envy bad company or wish you were with them; they're all about causing trouble. {24:2} They're always plotting mischief and stirring up trouble. {24:3} Building a solid life takes wisdom and understanding; that's how you set yourself up for success. {24:4} Fill your life with valuable knowledge, and you'll be rolling in riches. {24:5} Smart people are strong, and knowledge gives you power. {24:6} Plan your moves wisely, and safety comes in having a bunch of good advisors. {24:7} Fools don't have a clue; they're too clueless to speak up. {24:8} Those scheming for evil? Yeah, they're asking for trouble. {24:9} Foolish thoughts lead to trouble, and scoffers are just plain annoying. {24:10} If you can't handle tough times, you're not as strong as you think. {24:11} Don't turn a blind eye to those in danger or ignore those facing death; you can't play dumb and act like you didn't know. {24:12} God knows what's in your heart and watches over your soul; he'll judge everyone based on their actions. {24:13} Sweet like honey, wisdom is good for you and satisfies your soul. {24:14} When you find wisdom, it's like hitting the jackpot; you won't be disappointed. {24:15} Don't mess with good folks' homes or mess with where they rest; they'll bounce back even stronger. {24:16} Good people stumble, but they get back up; troublemakers just keep falling into trouble. {24:17} Don't celebrate when your enemies fall or get all excited when they stumble; it's not a good look. {24:18} God sees everything, and if you're gloating over someone's misfortune, he might turn his anger away from them. {24:19} Don't stress over evil people or be jealous of the wicked; they won't get away with it forever. {24:20} Bad people won't get a happy ending; their light will be snuffed out. {24:21} Respect the big guy and those in authority; don't mess with those who are always causing chaos. {24:22} Their downfall will come suddenly; who knows what disaster awaits them? {24:23} It's not cool to play favorites or show bias in judgment. {24:24} Calling evil good? Yeah, people won't stand for that; they'll hate you for it. {24:25} But those who speak truth? They'll be respected and receive blessings. {24:26} People appreciate honesty, and those who give the right answers are well-loved. {24:27} Get your work done first, then worry about building your dream house. {24:28} Don't lie about your neighbor, and don't deceive with your words. {24:29} Don't stoop to their level and seek revenge; let karma handle it. {24:30} I walked past a lazy person's field, and it was a mess; it was overgrown and falling apart. {24:31} It was a wake-up call for me; I learned something just by looking at it. {24:32} A little laziness leads to poverty and want, just like a traveler who never stops.

{25:1} Yo, these are some more of Solomon's lit proverbs that the crew of Hezekiah, the king of Judah, put down. {25:2} God keeping secrets is dope, but kings? Yeah, they're all about uncovering the truth. {25:3} The sky's high, the earth's deep, and kings? Yeah, you can't read their minds. {25:4} Purify that silver, and you'll get some top-notch bling. {25:5} Keep the wicked away from the king, and his reign's gonna be righteous. {25:6} Don't try to flex in front of the king or big shots; it's better to be invited up than put down in front of everyone. {25:7} Don't rush into arguments; you'll end up embarrassed when your neighbor schools you. {25:8} Handle issues directly with your neighbor; don't spill secrets to others, or you'll regret it. {25:9} You spill secrets, you're gonna get burned; keep it real with your neighbor. {25:10} A well-timed word is like gold on silver; it's all about that finesse. {25:11} Wise advice on listening ears? Yeah, that's like rocking gold earrings. {25:12} A reliable messenger in tough times? Yeah, they're like a cold drink on a hot day, refreshing the soul. {25:13} Flexing with fake gifts? Yeah, that's like clouds teasing rain; it's all show and no substance. {25:14} Patience can persuade even the toughest critics; soft words can break down walls. {25:15} Enjoy honey, but don't overdo it, or you'll end up puking it out; moderation is key. {25:16} Don't overstay your welcome at your neighbor's place; give them some space, or they'll start to resent you. {25:17} Spreading lies? Yeah, that's like swinging a maul and shooting arrows; it's gonna cause serious damage. {25:18} Trusting the untrustworthy? Yeah, that's like having a broken tooth or a dislocated foot; it's gonna hurt. {25:19} Singing to a heavy heart? Yeah, that's like taking someone's coat in the cold or pouring vinegar on baking soda; it's just gonna make things worse. {25:20} Being kind to your enemy? Yeah, that's like putting coals on their head; it'll mess with their mind, and Big G will notice. {25:21} Just like the north wind clears the sky, a stern look shuts down gossip. {25:22} Better to chill alone than deal with drama from a loudmouth or a big house. {25:23} Good news when you're thirsty for it? Yeah, that's like cold water on a hot day; it's refreshing AF. {25:24} Seeing a good person fall because of some fool? Yeah, it's like seeing a clean spring turn murky. {25:25} Too much honey? Yeah, it's not good for you; chasing fame? Yeah, it's overrated. {25:26} Losing control? Yeah, it's like having no defenses; you're wide open to anything.

{26:1} Giving honor to a fool? Yeah, that's like snow in the summer or rain during harvest; it just doesn't make sense. {26:2} A baseless curse? Yeah, it's like a bird flying around for no reason; it's not gonna stick. {26:3} Fools need discipline like horses need whips and asses need bridles. {26:4} Sometimes, it's best not to argue with a fool, or you'll end up looking like one. {26:5} But sometimes, you gotta put fools in their place, or they'll never learn. {26:6} Sending a fool to deliver a message? Yeah, it's like cutting off your own feet; you're just asking for trouble. {26:7} Fools don't make sense; their words are like a lame person's legs, all messed up. {26:8} Giving honor to a fool? Yeah, it's like loading up a slingshot with a rock; it's pointless. {26:9} Letting a fool run his mouth? Yeah, it's like letting a drunk play with a thorn; it's gonna end badly. {26:10} Big G sees it all, and He'll deal with fools and troublemakers in His own time. {26:11} Fools going back to their foolish ways? Yeah, it's like a dog eating its own vomit; it's just nasty. {26:12} Thinking you're all that? Yeah, there's more hope for a fool than for someone like you. {26:13} Lazy excuses? Yeah, it's like saying there's a lion in the street; it's just avoiding responsibility. {26:14} Lazy folks on their beds? Yeah, they're like doors on their hinges, just swinging back and forth. {26:15} Too lazy to even feed themselves? Yeah, that's just sad; they can't even bring their hand to their mouth. {26:16} Lazy people think they're smarter than everyone else; it's like they've got seven brains, but they can't even think straight. {26:17} Getting involved in other people's drama? Yeah, it's like grabbing a dog by the ears; you're just asking to get bit. {26:18} Starting trouble? Yeah, it's like throwing fire, arrows, and death around; it's gonna end in disaster. {26:19} Tricking your neighbor and then saying it was all a joke? Yeah, that's just messed up. {26:20} Stirring up drama? Yeah, it's like adding wood to a fire; it just keeps things burning. {26:21} Spreading gossip? Yeah, it's like adding fuel to the fire; it's gonna make things worse. {26:22} Spreading rumors? Yeah, it's like stabbing someone in the gut; it's gonna hurt deep. {26:23} Smooth talk with evil intentions? Yeah, it's like covering a broken pot with silver paint; it's still broken inside. {26:24} Hating someone but pretending to be cool? Yeah, it's like hiding a knife behind your back; it's gonna come out eventually. {26:25} Smooth talk might sound good, but don't fall for it; there's all kinds of messed up stuff going on behind the scenes. {26:26} Hiding hate with lies? Yeah, it's gonna come out eventually, and everyone will see how shady you really are. {26:27} Digging a pit for others? Yeah, you're gonna fall in yourself; rolling a stone? Yeah, it's gonna roll back on you. {26:28} Lying tongues might seem friendly, but they're just setting you up for a fall.

{27:1} Don't flex about tomorrow; you never know what's gonna go down. {27:2} Let others hype you up, not your own mouth; let strangers give you props, not yourself. {27:3} A stone's heavy, sand's weighty, but a fool's rage? Heavier than both combined. {27:4} Wrath's brutal, anger's off the charts, but envy? That's a whole different beast. {27:5} Tough love beats hidden affection any day. {27:6} A friend's honest criticism stings, but an enemy's sweet talk? Deceptive AF. {27:7} When you're stuffed, even honey tastes gross; but when you're starving, anything's delicious. {27:8} Like a bird leaving its nest, wandering from your place ain't wise. {27:9} Just like perfume cheers you up, a good friend's advice hits the spot. {27:10} Stick close to your friends and your dad's pals; they're better backup than distant family in a crisis. {27:11} Be smart, kid, and make me proud; I need good comebacks for the haters. {27:12} Smart folks see trouble coming and bail; fools? They walk right into it and get smacked. {27:13} Don't cosign for strangers or get mixed up with sketchy folks. {27:14} Loud praise in the morning? That's a curse, not a blessing. {27:15} Like a dripping faucet on a rainy day, a nagging woman is the worst. {27:16} Sharpen your buddies like iron sharpens iron; make each other better. {27:17} Take care of what's yours, and you'll reap the rewards; serve your boss well, and you'll get props. {27:18} Just like you see your reflection in water, people see who you really are. {27:19} Hell and destruction are insatiable, just like human desires. {27:20} Like refining silver and gold, life tests you and brings out your true character. {27:21} No matter how hard you try, you can't fix a fool; their stupidity is here to stay. {27:22} Stay on top of your business and know your stuff; ignorance won't cut it. {27:23} Take care of your assets and know your investments. {27:24} Riches come and go, but does royalty last forever? {27:25} Grass and hay sprout up, and mountains produce herbs; that's just how it is. {27:26} Your animals provide for you, and you provide for your household. {27:27} Don't let your eyes off those in need; caring for others brings blessings.

{28:1} Wicked folks run scared for no reason; the righteous? They're as fearless as lions. {28:2} When a nation screws up, leaders multiply; but with smart folks in charge, things stay stable. {28:3} A broke dude oppressing other broke folks? That's like a storm wiping out food crops. {28:4} Those who ditch the rules praise troublemakers, but the law-abiders? They call them out. {28:5} Evil minds can't grasp fairness, but those who seek the big guy? They get it. {28:6} Better to be broke but honest than rich but shady. {28:7} Obeying the rules? That's a smart move; hanging with troublemakers? That's just embarrassing for your folks. {28:8} Hoarding wealth through shady means? Eventually, it'll end up in the hands of someone who actually cares. {28:9} Ignore the rules, and even your prayers won't get through. {28:10} Leading good people down a bad path? You'll fall into your own trap; but the righteous? They get the good stuff. {28:11} Rich dudes might think they're smart, but it's the poor ones who see through their BS. {28:12} When good people win, everyone celebrates; but when jerks rise to power, decent folks hide. {28:13} Covering up your mistakes won't get you anywhere; own up to them, and you might get some mercy. {28:14} Those who stay humble? They're onto something; but those who think they're all that? They're headed for trouble. {28:15} Like a savage beast ruling over the poor, a wicked leader causes chaos. {28:16} A clueless ruler's just a bully, but one who hates greed? That's a leader worth keeping around. {28:17} Shedding innocent blood? You're running straight into disaster; no one's gonna stop you. {28:18} Walk the straight and narrow, and you'll be safe; but veer off course, and you'll crash and burn. {28:19} Tend to your own business, and you'll have plenty; chase after nonsense, and you'll end up broke. {28:20} Stay loyal, and blessings will come your way; rush into riches, and you'll be guilty as sin. {28:21} Playing favorites? Not cool; some people will sell out for a scrap of bread. {28:22} Greed leads to disaster, but some people just can't see it coming. {28:23} Offering tough love later is better than sugarcoating things now. {28:24} Stealing from your parents and pretending it's NBD? You're just as bad as a criminal. {28:25} A prideful heart stirs up trouble, but trusting in the big guy? That's where it's at. {28:26} Trusting your gut alone? That's just dumb; walk with wisdom, and you'll stay safe. {28:27} Helping out the needy? You won't go lacking; turning a blind eye? You're asking for trouble. {28:28} When the bad guys rise, people scatter; but when they fall, the good guys step up.

{29:1} Bro, if you keep ignoring advice and acting all stubborn, you're gonna crash and burn without a chance to fix it. {29:2} When good people are running the show, everyone's vibing; but when it's the shady ones in charge, it's just one big downer. {29:3} Choosing wisdom? Yeah, that's gonna make your old man proud; but hanging with the wrong crowd? That's just gonna drain your wallet. {29:4} A king who's all about fairness keeps the kingdom steady, but one who's into bribes? Yeah, he's gonna mess it all up. {29:5} Watch out for those who butter up their neighbors; they're setting them up for a fall. {29:6} Bad dudes? Yeah, they're just setting traps for themselves, but the righteous? They're chilling and celebrating. {29:7} Good peeps look out for the poor, but the wicked? Yeah, they couldn't care less. {29:8} Haters gonna bring trouble to the city, but smart ones? Yeah, they're all about keeping the peace. {29:9} Arguing with a fool? Yeah, it's pointless; whether they're raging or laughing, you're not gonna get anywhere. {29:10} The wicked hate those who stand for what's right, but the righteous? Yeah, they're all about saving lives. {29:11} Fools blabber everything, but the wise? Yeah, they know when to keep it on the down-low. {29:12} If a leader buys into lies, his whole crew's gonna be shady. {29:13} Poor or deceitful, they're all the same in Big G's eyes. {29:14} A king who's just with the poor? Yeah, his throne's gonna last, like, forever. {29:15} Discipline and correction? Yeah, they bring wisdom, but letting a kid run wild? Yeah, it's just gonna embarrass his mom. {29:16} More bad dudes mean more trouble, but the righteous? Yeah, they'll see them fall. {29:17} Teaching your kid right from wrong? Yeah, that's gonna give you peace; it's all about raising them up right. {29:18} Without a vision, people lose their way, but sticking to the rules? Yeah, that's where the real happiness is. {29:19} You can talk to a servant all day, but it's actions that count; words won't change a thing. {29:20} Someone who can't control their words? Yeah, they're worse than a fool; at least there's hope for them. {29:21} Treating your servant right from day one? Yeah, they'll be like family in the end. {29:22} Angry people stir up drama, and furious ones? Yeah, they're just full of trouble. {29:23} Being all proud? Yeah, that's gonna bring you down, but staying humble? Yeah, that's where true honor lies. {29:24} Hanging with thieves? Yeah, you're hating on yourself; you'll hear cursing and say nothing. {29:25} Fear of others traps you, but trusting in Big G? Yeah, that's where true safety is. {29:26} Everyone's trying to please the boss, but in the end, it's Big G who decides. {29:27} Good people can't stand the sight of evil, and the wicked? Yeah, they can't stand those who do what's right.

{30:1} Check it, these are the words of Agur, son of Jakeh, the real talk he spit to Ithiel and Ucal. {30:2} I'm telling you, I'm more clueless than anyone; I ain't got all the answers. {30:3} I haven't got wisdom from school or the holy stuff. {30:4} Who can do all that crazy stuff? Yeah, who's got the answers? Big G, that's who. {30:5} Every word Big G speaks is pure gold; trust Him, and you're covered. {30:6} Don't mess with His words, or you'll get called out for lying. {30:7} Bro, I've got two requests for you; don't ignore me before I'm out: {30:8} Keep me away from lies and empty dreams; I just need enough to get by. {30:9} I don't want to be rich and forget Big G, or poor and steal, dragging His name through the mud. {30:10} Don't go snitching on a servant; they'll curse you out, and you'll be the one in trouble. {30:11} Some folks disrespect their parents and bring bad vibes; {30:12} Others think they're all clean but are still dirty on the inside. {30:13} Some folks are all about themselves, thinking they're top-notch. {30:14} Their words are sharp as knives, cutting down the poor and needy. {30:15} Greed is insatiable

{31:1} Lemuel, the king, got some real wisdom from his mom. {31:2} She was like, "What's up, my son? What's up, my baby boy? What's up, my promise kid?" {31:3} Lemuel, stay away from those who drain your energy, man, and don't get tangled up in stuff that messes kings up. {31:4} Kings ain't supposed to be chugging wine or princes hitting the hard stuff; it messes with their heads. {31:5} They start sipping, forget the rules, and start messing with justice for the underdogs. {31:6} But for those down on their luck, pour them a drink; for those feeling low, give them some wine. {31:7} Let them drown their sorrows and forget their troubles. {31:8} Speak up for those who can't speak, defend the rights of the destitute. {31:9} Use your voice to judge fairly and fight for the poor and needy. {31:10} Where can you find a solid chick? She's worth more than any jewels, man. {31:11} Her man trusts her completely; he's got no reason to worry about anything. {31:12} She's got his back all the time, never causing trouble. {31:13} She's all about that DIY life, spinning wool and weaving flax. {31:14} She's like a merchant ship, bringing in food from all over. {31:15} Up before dawn, making sure everyone's fed, including her staff. {31:16} She's business savvy, investing in land and planting vineyards. {31:17} She's strong and capable, always ready for whatever comes her way. {31:18} She knows her stuff is good, and she's up working late into the night. {31:19} She's hands-on, working the spindle and the distaff. {31:20} She's generous to the poor, always reaching out to help the needy. {31:21} She's not afraid of a little cold; her whole family's dressed to impress. {31:22} She's stylish, rocking tapestry and silk, decked out in purple. {31:23} Her man's got respect in the community, sitting with the elders at the gates. {31:24} She's a businesswoman, making and selling linen and belts. {31:25} Strength and dignity are her trademarks, and she's smiling at the future. {31:26} She's wise and kind, speaking with grace and wisdom. {31:27} She runs her household like a boss and doesn't waste time lounging around. {31:28} Her kids and her man shower her with praise and blessings. {31:29} Plenty of ladies do good, but she's in a league of her own. {31:30} Charm and beauty fade, but a woman who respects Big G, now that's something worth praising. {31:31} Let her works speak for themselves; she deserves all the props she gets.

Ecclesiastes

✚✚✚

{1:1} So, like, here's what the Preacher, son of David, had to say, king in Jerusalem and all that jazz. {1:2} Like, everything's pointless, says the Preacher, like seriously, it's all just pointless. {1:3} What's the point of busting your butt when nothing really matters? {1:4} Generations come and go, but the earth's here forever. {1:5} The sun rises and sets, doing its thing like clockwork. {1:6} The wind blows here, there, and everywhere, just going around in circles. {1:7} Rivers flow into the sea, but it never fills up; they just go right back where they came from. {1:8} Everything's a grind, man; you can't ever get enough of what you see or hear. {1:9} What's happened before is gonna happen again, and there's nothing new under the sun. {1:10} Like, has anything ever really been brand new? Nah, it's all been done before. {1:11} Nobody remembers what happened before, and nobody's gonna remember what happens after. {1:12} So, like, I was king over in Jerusalem, doing my thing. {1:13} I was all about seeking wisdom and figuring out life's mysteries, but let me tell you, it's tough being human. {1:14} I've seen it all, and guess what? It's all just a big letdown. {1:15} You can't straighten out what's crooked, and you can't count what's missing. {1:16} I thought I had it all figured out, you know, but even with all my wisdom, life's still a drag. {1:17} I dove headfirst into wisdom, madness, and stupidity, and let me tell you, it's all a headache. {1:18} The more you know, the more you realize how messed up everything is.

{2:1} So, I figured, why not have some fun and enjoy life? But even that's just empty. {2:2} Laughter's overrated, man, and so is having a good time. {2:3} I tried drowning myself in wine while still keeping it real with wisdom, you know? {2:4} I built big houses, planted vineyards, you name it, I did it. {2:5} Gardens, orchards, trees, you get the picture. {2:6} Pools, servants, you name it, I had it. {2:7} Silver, gold, all that jazz, it was mine. {2:8} Singers, musicians, the whole shebang, I had 'em all. {2:9} I was the man, topping everyone who came before me. {2:10} I didn't hold back on anything; I went all in on enjoying life, but guess what? It was all for nothing. {2:11} I looked at everything I'd done, and it was all just a waste of time. {2:12} So, I checked out wisdom, stupidity, and everything in between, but what's the point? {2:13} Wisdom's better than being dumb, obviously, but even that's not gonna save you. {2:14} Smart folks see where they're going; fools stumble around in the dark. {2:15} So, I'm no better off than a fool, and why did I even bother being smart? It's all empty. {2:16} Nobody's gonna remember the wise guy any more than the idiot; we all end up forgotten in the end. {2:17} So, life sucks, man; working your butt off is just depressing, because it's all pointless. {2:18} Yeah, I hate everything I've worked for, knowing some other dude's gonna inherit it all. {2:19} Who knows if he'll be smart or just a total moron? Either way, he's getting everything I slaved for. {2:20} So, I just gave up on everything I worked so hard for. {2:21} Some dude might work his butt off, being all smart and fair, but in the end, some lazy bum's gonna get it all. What a joke. {2:22} So, what's the point of all this hard work and heartache? {2:23} Life's just one big pain, man; you never get a break. It's all empty. {2:24} So, like, the best thing you can do is just chill, enjoy life, and thank God for whatever good comes your way. {2:25} Like, who can enjoy life more than I did, right? {2:26} God gives good people wisdom, joy, all that good stuff, but the bad guys? They just keep working themselves to death for nothing. It's all just pointless and depressing.

{3:1} Everything's got its time, you know? There's a time to be born and a time to die, a time to plant and a time to uproot, {3:2} a time to kill and a time to heal, a time to tear down and a time to build, {3:3} a time to cry and a time to laugh, a time to mourn and a time to dance, {3:4} a time to chuck rocks and a time to gather them, a time to hug and a time to back off, {3:5} a time to win and a time to lose, a time to keep and a time to toss, {3:6} a time to rip and a time to patch, a time to shut up and a time to speak up, {3:7} a time to love and a time to hate, a time for war and a time for peace. {3:8} What's the point of all the hard work anyway? {3:9} I've seen people grind away at stuff, but what's the payoff? {3:10} God's made everything beautiful in its time; we just can't wrap our heads around the big picture. {3:11} I get it now; life's about enjoying yourself and doing good while you're at it. {3:12} Just eat, drink, and enjoy the fruits of your labor; it's all a gift from Big G. {3:13} Whatever God does, it's here to stay; you can't add or subtract from it. He does it to keep us in check. {3:14} What's happened before is happening now, and what's coming has already been. God's all about history repeating itself. {3:15} I've seen the good and the bad in this world, the injustice and the righteousness, and I know there's a time for everything. {3:16} I've thought it over; God's gonna judge everyone, the good and the bad, 'cause everything's got its time. {3:17} I've thought about the human condition, how God lets us see our true nature, that we're no better than animals. {3:18} What happens to us happens to animals too; we're all in the same boat. Life's pretty meaningless when you think about it. {3:19} We all end up in the same place, dust to dust, no matter who we are. {3:20} Who knows if our spirits go up while animals' spirits go down to the ground? {3:21} So, I figure the best thing to do is enjoy what you've got while you're here; that's all you're gonna get. {3:22} Then I went back to thinking about all the oppression in the world, how the oppressed cry out with no one to comfort them, and the oppressors just keep on going.

{4:1} I saw how messed up things are and wished those who've passed on were better off than those still alive. {4:2} Yep, better to be dead than to see all the messed-up stuff happening now. {4:3} Better still is someone who hasn't even been born yet, who hasn't seen all the junk going down. {4:4} I thought about how people envy each other's success, but even that's just a load of stress and emptiness. {4:5} The lazy dude just sits around, wasting away. {4:6} It's better to have a little and be chill than to have a lot and be stressed out. {4:7} Then I saw more nonsense happening; this one guy's working his butt off, but for what? {4:8} He's got no family, no friends, just piles of cash, and he's asking himself, "What's the point?" That's just sad. {4:9} Two heads are better than one; they can help each other out. {4:10} 'Cause when one falls, the other can pick them up. But pity the lonely soul who's got no one to lend a hand. {4:11} Two are stronger than one, and three are even stronger; unity's where it's at. {4:12} Better to be poor and smart than an old, clueless king who won't listen to anyone. {4:13} 'Cause even if you come out of prison to rule, you might end up broke again. {4:14} I've seen it all; from kings to commoners, no one's got it easy. {4:15} People come and go, but no one's gonna remember them. It's all just pointless and annoying.

{5:1} Yo, when you roll up to God's crib, listen up more than you talk, okay? Don't be dropping dumb sacrifices; that's just whack. They don't even realize they're messing up. {5:2} Don't be mouthing off or rushing to say stuff before God; He's up in the heavens, and you're down here, so keep it chill and keep your words short. {5:3} Dreams come from being busy, and fools yap on and on. {5:4} If you make a promise to God, don't slack off on it; He ain't down with fools who break their promises. Stick to your word. {5:5} It's better not to promise at all than to promise and then bail. {5:6} Don't let your mouth get you in trouble, especially in front of the angel; don't be making excuses, or God might get mad and wreck your stuff. {5:7} Dreaming too much and talking too much? Total waste of time. Just fear God and keep it real. {5:8} If you peep some shady stuff going down, don't trip; the big boss upstairs sees it all, and He's above even the highest big shots down here. {5:9} Everybody gets a piece of the pie from the earth, even the king gets his hands dirty in the field. {5:10} Loving cash won't satisfy you; wanting more won't do it either. It's all just empty, trust. {5:11} When you're stacking cash, there are just more mouths to feed, and in the end, what's the point? Just looking at your stuff with your eyes? Lame. {5:12} A hard-working dude sleeps soundly, even if he's living simple, but the rich dude can't even catch a break. {5:13} I've seen some messed-up stuff, like hoarding riches to your own hurt. {5:14} Riches can vanish in a heartbeat, leaving you with nothing to show for it, not even for your kid. {5:15} You come into this world with nothing, and you leave with nothing; all that hard work, and what's it worth? {5:16} It's all pointless, man; you work your butt off for nothing, just chasing after the wind. {5:17} You're stuck in darkness all your days, with nothing but sadness and sickness. {5:18} But hey, here's the real deal: eat, drink, enjoy what you've got, 'cause that's your slice of the pie, courtesy of God. {5:19} If God blesses you with cash and goodies, enjoy it, man; it's a gift straight from above. {5:20} You won't even remember half your life because God fills your heart with joy.

{6:1} Here's some messed-up stuff I've seen: it's common for dudes to get blessed by God with everything they want, but they can't even enjoy it; some random stranger ends up enjoying their stuff. How messed up is that? {6:2} If a dude's got everything, but he can't even enjoy it, that's just sad, man; it's like a sickness. {6:3} Even if a dude has a ton of kids and lives forever, if he's not happy and doesn't even get a decent burial, it's better he wasn't born. {6:4} He comes in with nothing and leaves in darkness, forgotten by all. {6:5} At least he didn't have to deal with life's BS. {6:6} Even if he lived forever, it wouldn't make a difference; we all end up in the same place. {6:7} You work your butt off just to eat, but you're never satisfied. {6:8} What's the difference between a wise dude and a fool, or a poor dude who knows how to play the game? {6:9} Seeing something cool is better than always wanting something else; that's just empty and frustrating. {6:10} Everything's already been done, man; it's just the same old story. {6:11} With all this pointless stuff going on, what's the point, right? {6:12} Like, who knows what's good for us in this life? We're just chasing shadows, man; who knows what's gonna happen after we're gone?

{7:1} Having a solid rep is better than having the fanciest cologne, and kicking the bucket beats popping into this world. {7:2} Going to a funeral's better than hitting up a party; it makes you think about life. {7:3} Sadness is better than laughter; it makes you grow. {7:4} Wise peeps hang at funerals, while fools party it up. {7:5} It's better to get wisdom from smart folks than to vibe with fools. {7:6} Foolish laughter's like crackling thorns under a pot; it's all just empty noise. {7:7} Being oppressed can drive a wise person nuts, and getting bribed can mess you up. {7:8} The end of something's better than the beginning, and being patient's better than being full of yourself. {7:9} Don't rush to get angry; that's dumb. {7:10} Don't go saying the old days were better; that's not wise. {7:11} Wisdom's good, especially when you've got cash, but wisdom's what really gives life. {7:12} Wisdom and money can protect you, but wisdom's the real deal. {7:13} Think about God's work; some things you can't straighten out. {7:14} Enjoy the good times, but remember, bad times come too; it's all part of life. {7:15} Seen it all during my time on this Earth: sometimes good folks suffer while bad ones thrive. {7:16} Don't be too righteous or too wise; it's not worth destroying yourself over. {7:17} Don't be too wicked or foolish either; why cut your life short? {7:18} It's good to find balance; that's where fearing God comes in. {7:19} Wisdom's better than a whole squad of strong folks. {7:20} No one's perfect; everyone messes up sometimes. {7:21} Don't pay too much attention to what others say; you might hear your own servants cursing you. {7:22} Sometimes you know deep down you've cursed others too. {7:23} I've tried to be wise, but it's tough. {7:24} Some things are just too deep to figure out. {7:25} I've searched for wisdom and knowledge, even explored foolishness and madness. {7:26} Women can be more dangerous than death itself, trapping hearts and minds. {7:27} I've tried to figure it all out, but there's always more to learn. {7:28} I've found one decent guy out of a thousand, but not one woman among them stands out. {7:29} Here's what I know: God made people good, but they've come up with all kinds of messed-up stuff.

{8:1} Who's as wise as that one dude who can break things down? Wisdom lights up your face and changes your vibe. {8:2} Stick to obeying the king's orders, swearing by God's name. {8:3} Don't rush out of the king's sight or get caught up in evil; he's in charge, and he does what he wants. {8:4} The king's word holds power; who's gonna question him? {8:5} Obeying the king keeps you safe, and wise folks know the right time for everything. {8:6} 'Cause there's a time and place for everything, and that's why life's so tough. {8:7} No one knows what's coming next; who can predict the future? {8:8} No one can control when they die; it's like being in a war with no way out. {8:9} Seen it all, and sometimes those in charge make things worse for everyone. {8:10} I've seen wicked folks buried like saints, and soon everyone forgets about their evil deeds. {8:11} When evil goes unpunished, people think they can get away with anything. {8:12} Even if a sinner lives a long life doing wrong, it's better for those who fear God. {8:13} But for the wicked, life's like a shadow, fading away without fearing God. {8:14} Life's unfair sometimes; good folks suffer like the bad ones, and vice versa. {8:15} So, might as well enjoy life while you can; eating, drinking, and having fun's the best we can do with the time we've got. {8:16} When I tried to understand everything happening in the world, it kept me up at night. {8:17} I realized I can't fully understand God's work; even the wisest person can't figure it all out.

{9:1} So, like, I've been thinking hard about this, and here's the deal: whether you're righteous, wise, or just doing your thing, it's all in God's hands. Nobody can predict love or hate based on what's going down. {9:2} Everything's the same for everyone: good stuff happens to both the good and the bad, the clean and the dirty, the religious and the not-so-religious. It's like, what goes around comes around, you know? {9:3} It's messed up, man; we're all in the same boat, and deep down, people are just full of evil. Life's crazy, and then we die. {9:4} But hey, as long as you're alive, there's hope, right? Being alive, even if you're not the top dog, beats being dead. {9:5} At least the living know they're gonna kick the bucket someday, but once you're dead, it's lights out, and nobody remembers you. {9:6} All that love, hate, and envy? It's all gone once you're six feet under, man. You don't get a piece of the action anymore. {9:7} So just go enjoy life, eat good food, drink up, and party on, 'cause God's cool with it now. {9:8} Keep yourself looking fresh, smelling good, and live it up with your bae while you still can. That's what life's about, you feel? {9:9} So live it up with your girl, make the most of every moment, 'cause that's all you got in this crazy world. {9:10} Whatever you do, do it with all your heart, 'cause once you're in the ground, there's no more chances to do anything. {9:11} I've seen it, man; life ain't fair. Being the fastest, the strongest, or the smartest don't mean squat. Sometimes it's just luck of the draw. {9:12} You never know when your time's up, just like fish getting caught in a net or birds snagged in a trap. {9:13} I've seen some real wisdom out there, man, and it's impressive. {9:14} There was this one time in a small town, a wise dude saved everyone, but no one even remembered him afterward. {9:15} So yeah, wisdom beats strength any day, but people don't always see it that way. {9:16} Wise words are heard in silence, not in the chaos of fools ruling the roost. {9:17} Wisdom's better than weapons of war, but one idiot can mess up a whole lot of good.

{10:1} Even a little bit of stupidity can ruin a wise dude's rep, just like dead flies stinking up perfume. {10:2} A wise dude's got it together, but a fool's a hot mess. {10:3} When a fool tries to act smart, everyone knows he's faking it. {10:4} If the boss starts tripping, don't bail; sometimes keeping your cool can smooth things over big time. {10:5} I've seen some messed-up stuff go down because of bad leadership. {10:6} Fools get all the glory, while the rich end up on the bottom. {10:7} I've seen nobodies riding high, while the big shots walk around like they're nobody. {10:8} If you dig a hole, you might fall into it; break a fence, and you might get bit. {10:9} Playing with rocks or chopping wood? Watch out, or you'll get hurt. {10:10} If your tools aren't sharp, you'll just end up working harder, but wisdom can save the day. {10:11} Even without magic, snakes still bite; and someone who talks too much is no better. {10:12} Wise words are smooth, but fools just trip over their own tongues. {10:13} Foolish talk starts dumb and ends up causing trouble. {10:14} Fools love to hear themselves talk, but who knows what's coming next? {10:15} Foolish people wear themselves out because they don't know where they're going. {10:16} It's a disaster when a kid's in charge, and everyone's partying in the morning. {10:17} But it's all good when the boss knows what's up and parties at the right time, for the right reasons. {10:18} Laziness brings everything crashing down, and doing nothing just makes it worse. {10:19} Parties are for laughs, and booze brings the fun, but money solves all problems. {10:20} Don't diss the king, not even in your head, and don't trash-talk the rich in private; you never know who's listening.

{11:1} Throw your bread out on the water; it'll come back to you later. {11:2} Share your stuff with a bunch of people; you never know when bad stuff's gonna happen. {11:3} When it rains, it pours; and when a tree falls, it stays where it falls. {11:4} If you wait for perfect conditions, you'll never get anything done. {11:5} Just like you don't know how stuff grows inside a mom, you can't figure out everything God's up to. {11:6} Plant your seeds in the morning and don't hold back; who knows which ones will thrive? {11:7} Light's nice, and so is seeing the sun. {11:8} But even if you live a long time, don't forget there are dark days too; life's just full of ups and downs. {11:9} Enjoy your youth, but remember, God's gonna judge you for everything. {11:10} So, chill out, let go of the bad stuff, 'cause being young is fleeting.

{12:1} Remember God while you're young, before things get tough. {12:2} Before life gets dark and gloomy, while you still got energy. {12:3} When your body starts to fail you, and you can't do what you used to. {12:4} When you can't do the things you love anymore, and life starts feeling empty. {12:5} When you're scared of everything, and life just feels heavy. {12:6} Before you kick the bucket, and your body turns to dust. {12:7} Your body goes back to the earth, and your spirit goes back to God. {12:8} Everything's meaningless, says the wise preacher. {12:9} He tried to teach people wisdom and put a bunch of proverbs in order. {12:10} He tried to use good words and tell the truth. {12:11} Wise words are like a kick in the butt, coming from one shepherd. {12:12} So, listen up, my dude, too much reading will wear you out. {12:13} Here's the deal: Fear God and do what He says, 'cause that's what life's all about. {12:14} God's gonna judge everything you do, even the secret stuff.

Song of Songs

✛✛✛

{1:1} So, here's the ultimate love jam from Solomon. {1:2} Let him lay one on me, 'cause his love's better than a fine wine. {1:3} Your scent is like top-tier perfume, no wonder all the girls are into you. {1:4} Lead me, and we'll run together; the king's taken me to his place, and we're gonna be living it up, remembering our love more than any party. {1:5} Yeah, I'm not the fairest, but I'm rocking it, just like those cool tents and curtains. {1:6} Don't judge me for my tan; the sun's been rough on me. My family wasn't too keen on me, making me do all the hard work, but hey, I've got my own thing going. {1:7} Tell me, babe, where you chillin' with your crew at noon? I don't wanna be left wandering around alone. {1:8} If you're lost, just follow the crowd and hang with the shepherds. {1:9} I'm comparing you to Pharaoh's chariot crew, babe. You're top-notch. {1:10} Your bling is on point, babe, those jewels and gold chains. {1:11} We're decking you out in gold and silver. {1:12} When the king's chilling, my scent fills the room. {1:13} My love's like a bundle of myrrh, staying close to my heart all night. {1:14} My babe's like a sweet-smelling flower in the En-gedi vineyards. {1:15} You're beautiful, babe, those eyes are captivating. {1:16} You're a total stunner, babe, and our love nest is lit. {1:17} Our place is top-notch, cedar beams and fir rafters.

{2:1} I'm the bomb, the best flower around. {2:2} Like a lily among thorns, that's how amazing my love is. {2:3} My babe's like an apple tree among the regular trees, standing out. Chilling with him is sweet, and his love is like honey. {2:4} He's taken me to the party spot, and love's his vibe. {2:5} Keep me close with wine and apples; I'm lovesick. {2:6} His arms around me, cozy and snug. {2:7} Ladies, don't mess with my love vibes, let us do our thing. {2:8} Babe's on his way, leaping over mountains, skipping over hills. {2:9} He's like a deer, peeking through the window at me. {2:10} He's calling me to join him, saying winter's over, time to chill. {2:11} Flowers blooming, birds singing, and love's in the air. {2:12} It's time to get moving, babe, the world's waking up. {2:13} The figs are out, the vines are smelling good. Babe, it's time to roll. {2:14} Hey, my love, show yourself, I wanna see you and hear your voice; it's music to my ears. {2:15} Let's deal with those pesky foxes wrecking our vines, babe, before they ruin everything. {2:16} You're mine, and I'm yours, babe, chilling among the lilies. {2:17} Until dawn breaks and shadows disappear, return to me like a deer on the mountains of Bether.

{3:1} So, like, last night I was lying in bed, searching for my soulmate, but couldn't find them anywhere. {3:2} I'm gonna get up now and hit the streets, hoping to find my soulmate. But no luck yet. {3:3} I asked the city guards if they've seen my soulmate, but they didn't know. {3:4} Eventually, I found my soulmate and held on tight, not letting go until I brought them home. {3:5} Hey, girls of Jerusalem, don't go waking up love until it's ready. {3:6} Who's this coming out of the wilderness, smelling all fancy with perfumes and stuff? {3:7} Check out Solomon's bed, surrounded by his tough crew. {3:8} They're all armed, ready for anything that comes their way. {3:9} Solomon's got a sweet ride made from Lebanese wood. {3:10} It's decked out with silver, gold, and all sorts of fancy stuff, fit for the girls of Jerusalem. {3:11} Girls of Zion, check out King Solomon on his big day, looking sharp with his crown.

{4:1} Wow, you're beautiful, babe, with those lovely eyes and your hair. {4:2} Your teeth are perfect, and your lips are like scarlet. {4:3} Your neck is like a tower, and your breasts are like twin roes. {4:4} Your beauty blows my mind. {4:5} Your breasts are like twin roes among the lilies. {4:6} Until dawn, I'll be chilling on the mountain, soaking in the scenery. {4:7} Babe, you're flawless. {4:8} Come with me from Lebanon, babe, from the mountains and the wild places. {4:9} You've stolen my heart, babe, with just one look. {4:10} Your love is better than wine, and you smell amazing. {4:11} Your lips are like honey, and your clothes smell divine. {4:12} You're like a secret garden, babe, full of beauty. {4:13} Your plants are like an orchard, with all sorts of goodies. {4:14} Sweet scents and spices, a fountain of gardens. {4:15} Your garden is like paradise, flowing with life. {4:16} Come on, wind, blow through my garden, let those sweet smells spread. Let my beloved come and enjoy the fruits of my garden.

{5:1} So, I'm chilling in my garden, right? Just vibing with my crew. Got my myrrh, spice, honeycomb, honey, wine, and milk on lock. Come through, friends, let's party and drink up, my beloveds. {5:2} I'm half asleep, but my heart's wide awake, 'cause I hear my boo knocking. He's like, "Open up, babe, it's me, your love, your dove, your everything. My head's dripping with dew, and my hair's soaked in the night's mist." {5:3} I'm like, "Hold up, I just took off my coat. Why should I put it back on? I washed my feet, why should I get 'em dirty again?" {5:4} Then he reaches in through the door, and I'm all like, "Whoa, my heart skipped a beat." {5:5} I rush to open the door, but he's already gone, and I'm left hanging. I'm searching for him, but he's ghosted me. {5:6} I get attacked by these city guards, they beat me up, snatched my veil. {5:7} I'm begging you, girls of Jerusalem, if you find my guy, let him know I'm lovesick. {5:8} They're like, "Girl, why you trippin' over this guy? What's so special about him?" {5:9} I'm like, "My boo's one in a million, he's the real deal." {5:10} My guy's got that mixed-race vibe, white and ruddy, and he's the best among ten thousand. {5:11} His head's pure gold, hair all wild like a raven. {5:12} His eyes are like doves by the river, washed with milk, looking fresh. {5:13} He's got that golden touch, belly shining like ivory with sapphire inlays. Legs like marble pillars on gold bases, face like Lebanon, majestic as the cedars. {5:14} He's got the sweetest lips, babe, and he's just perfect in every way. He's my boo and my BFF, girls of Jerusalem.

{6:1} "Hey babe, where'd your guy go? We wanna help you find him." {6:2} My guy's just chilling in his garden, picking flowers and enjoying the scenery. {6:3} It's all good, babe, we're in this together, chilling among the lilies. {6:4} Girl, you're stunning, like Tirzah, beautiful as Jerusalem, and fierce as an army with banners. {6:5} Stop staring at me, babe, you're too much to handle. Your hair's like a flock of goats in Gilead. {6:6} Your teeth are perfect, like sheep coming from a wash, every one with a twin, none missing. {6:7} Your temples are like pomegranate slices hidden in your hair. {6:8} There's queens and concubines galore, but my babe's the only one for me, the queen bee. {6:9} She's unique, one in a million. Everyone's singing her praises, queens, concubines, you name it. {6:10} Who's that shining like the morning, bright as the moon, clear as the sun, and fierce as an army with banners? {6:11} I was just checking out the garden, seeing the fruits and vines, and bam, suddenly I'm feeling invincible. {6:12} Come back, babe, we wanna see you again. What's so special about you? You're like an army marching in perfect formation.

{7:1} Your kicks are on point, princess! Your whole vibe is lit, like crafted by a master. {7:2} Your style's like a party, always ready to turn up. {7:3} Your vibe is so twin roes, girl. {7:4} Your look is like top-tier, from head to toe. {7:5} Your whole vibe's like royalty, babe. {7:6} You're just too good to be true, babe, seriously. {7:7} Your whole vibe's like a palm tree, and your curves are like grape clusters. {7:8} I'm gonna climb that palm tree, grab those grapes. Your scent's like apples, girl. {7:9} Your kisses are sweet like wine, girl, making even the sleepers talk. {7:10} I'm all about my boo, and he's all about me. {7:11} Let's bounce, babe, let's hit the town. {7:12} Let's check out the vineyards, see what's popping. That's where I'll show you some love. {7:13} I got all sorts of treats for you, babe.

{8:1} Wish you were like my bro, so I could kiss you without anyone tripping. {8:2} I'd show you around, introduce you to my fam, and we'd have some bomb drinks. {8:3} Hold me close, babe, and let's vibe together. {8:4} Hey, girls of Jerusalem, don't mess with my love until he's ready. {8:5} Who's that strolling in, arm in arm with her boo? I know where you came from, babe, and I'm here for it. {8:6} Keep me close to your heart, babe, like a permanent vibe. Love's no joke, it's serious stuff. {8:7} Love's unstoppable, no matter what. {8:8} We got a little sis, but she's not quite there yet. What should we do for her? {8:9} If she's solid, we'll hook her up. If she's not quite there, we'll help her out. {8:10} I'm solid, babe, and my curves are like towers. That's how I caught his eye. {8:11} Solomon had this lit vineyard, and he rented it out for a pretty penny. {8:12} My vineyard's on point, Solomon, but you can have your cut. {8:13} You're chilling in the gardens, and your crew's listening. Let me hear you too. {8:14} Hurry up, babe, and come vibe with me in the mountains.

Isaiah

✦✦✦

{1:1} So, peep this vision Isaiah had, right? He's talking about Judah and Jerusalem back in the day when Uzziah, Jotham, Ahaz, and Hezekiah were ruling. {1:2} Yo, heaven and earth, listen up! The LORD's dropping truth bombs here: "I raised you all like my own kids, and what do you do? You rebel against me." {1:3} Even animals know their owner, but Israel? Nah, they clueless. My people ain't even thinking straight. {1:4} Israel, you messed up nation, full of sin and corruption. You've turned your back on the LORD, ticked off the Holy One of Israel, and stepped backward into trouble. {1:5} Why keep getting smacked down? You just gonna rebel even harder? Your whole deal is messed up, from head to toe. {1:6} Ain't nothing right with you, just wounds, bruises, and festering sores left untreated. Your country's wrecked, cities burnt to the ground, land snatched up by strangers right before your eyes. {1:7} Zion's like a shack in a vineyard, a shack in a cucumber patch, a city under siege. {1:8-9} If the LORD hadn't left us a tiny remnant, we'd be toast like Sodom and Gomorrah. {1:10} Listen up, rulers of Sodom, and pay attention, people of Gomorrah. {1:11} What's the point of all your sacrifices? God's sick of 'em. He's drowning in burnt offerings, but he ain't feeling it. {1:12} When you come to worship, who asked for all this? Treading his courts like you own the place? {1:13} Your worship's a joke to him, your rituals make him sick. New moons, Sabbaths, assemblies - it's all garbage. {1:14} Even your feasts make God gag. He's tired of putting up with your nonsense. {1:15} You raise your hands, but God's turning away. You pray, but he ain't listening. Your hands are stained with blood. {1:16} Get yourselves cleaned up, ditch the evil you're doing. Stop being jerks and learn to do good. Help out the oppressed, stand up for the fatherless, speak up for the widows. {1:17-19} Let's talk, says the LORD. Even if your sins are scarlet, he'll make 'em white as snow. Even if they're red like crimson, he'll make 'em wooly white. {1:20} If you're down to play ball, you'll enjoy the good life. But if you keep being stubborn and rebellious, you're gonna get wrecked by the sword. The LORD said it, so it's going down. {1:21} How'd the faithful city turn into a prostitute? Once it was all about justice and righteousness, now it's full of killers. {1:22} Your purity's gone, your wine watered down. {1:23} Your leaders are corrupt, hanging with thieves, loving bribes, chasing after rewards. They don't care about the orphans, and widows can't even get a hearing. {1:24} So the LORD's like, "Alright, time to deal with my enemies, time to get some payback." {1:25} He's gonna clean house, get rid of the junk, purify you like silver, get rid of all the trash. {1:26} Then he'll bring back righteous leaders, wise counselors. Then you'll be called the city of righteousness, the faithful city. {1:27} Zion's gonna be saved by justice, and her people by righteousness. {1:28} But the rebellious and sinful? They're gonna get wiped out together. Those who ditched the LORD are gonna get swallowed up. {1:29-30} You'll be ashamed of your idol groves and gardens. You'll wither like a dying oak, like a garden without water. {1:31} The mighty will be tinder, their work a spark. Both will blaze up, and no one will put it out.

{2:1} Now, here's what Isaiah saw about Judah and Jerusalem. {2:2} In the future, the LORD's house will be the top spot, higher than any hill. Everyone's gonna be flocking there. {2:3} People will be like, "Yo, let's hit up the LORD's house, learn some righteous ways, and walk in his paths. The law's gonna come from Zion, and the word of the LORD from Jerusalem." {2:4} He's gonna be the judge, sorting out the nations, making peace. They'll turn their weapons into tools for farming and gardening. No more war, just chill vibes. {2:5} Yo, house of Jacob, let's walk in the LORD's light. {2:6} But y'all turned your backs on God's people, filling up with all kinds of foreign ideas, acting like the Philistines. You're into wealth, fortune-telling, and hanging with strangers. {2:7} Your land's stacked with cash, treasure galore, horses, and chariots. {2:8} But you're all about idols, worshipping stuff you made with your own hands. {2:9} Bowing down to idols, big or small? That ain't gonna fly. So, don't expect any mercy. {2:10} Duck and cover, hide from the LORD's wrath and his majestic glory. {2:11} Pride's gonna get knocked down, arrogance brought low, and only the LORD's gonna shine. {2:12} The day of reckoning's coming for the proud and lofty, and they'll be humbled. {2:13} The tall trees and high mountains will get leveled, along with all the fancy towers and walls. {2:14} No more showing off. {2:15} People are gonna hide in caves, terrified of the LORD's power when he shakes the earth. {2:16} They'll toss their fancy idols into rat holes and bat caves. {2:17} So, quit trusting in humans, 'cause they're just a breath in the wind. Who cares about them?

{3:1} Yo, peep this: the big man upstairs, the one in charge, is stripping Jerusalem and Judah of everything they rely on—food, water, even their leaders and experts. {3:2} Gone are the tough guys, the warriors, the judges, the prophets, the wise ones, and the old heads. {3:3} Say goodbye to the army captains, the respected folks, the advisors, the skilled workers, and the smooth talkers. {3:4} Instead, they're gonna have kids running the show, and babies making the calls. {3:5} It's gonna be chaos—people oppressing each other left and right, disrespecting their elders, and dishonoring the respectable. {3:6} You'll have folks begging others to lead just because they've got clothes on their back, not because they're fit for it. {3:7} But even those asked won't want the job because they've got nothing to offer. {3:8} Why's all this happening? 'Cause they're going against the big guy upstairs, and that never ends well. {3:9} Their faces show it all—they're as guilty as sin, no hiding it. They're in for a rough ride with all the bad they've brought upon themselves. {3:10} Good news for the righteous, though—they'll reap what they sow. {3:11} But for the wicked, it's gonna be rough—they're gonna get what they deserve. {3:12} My people are getting trampled by kids and ruled by women. Those leading them are leading them astray, messing up their paths. {3:13} But the big guy's stepping in to set things straight, to judge the people. {3:14} He's gonna call out the elders and leaders for exploiting the poor, for hoarding what isn't rightfully theirs. {3:15} Why do you beat down my people and grind the faces of the poor? Asks the big guy upstairs. {3:16} And as for you, Zion's ladies, with your haughty attitude, strutting around, making eyes at everyone, clinking your jewelry—watch out. {3:17} The big guy's gonna humble you, expose your secrets, and bring you down a notch. {3:18} He's gonna strip away all your fancy jewelry and accessories, leaving you exposed. {3:19} No more bling, no more fancy clothes, just plain and simple. {3:20} You're gonna lose all your flashy gear and be left with nothing but the basics. {3:21} No more rings, no more nose rings, just stripped down to nothing. {3:22} All your fancy outfits, your designer gear, your accessories—gone. {3:23} The mirrors, the fine linens, the fancy hats—all of it's out. {3:24} And instead of smelling sweet, there's gonna be stench; instead of belts, there'll be rips; instead of nice hair, baldness; instead of beauty, ashes. {3:25} Your men will fall in battle, your warriors defeated. {3:26} Your gates will mourn, your city left deserted.

{4:1} And then there'll be seven women chasing after one guy, begging to be associated with him just to save face. {4:2} But on that day, things are gonna look up for those who survived. {4:3} The ones left in Zion and Jerusalem will be called holy, each one written in the book of life. {4:4} Once the big guy upstairs cleans up the mess and purges the city, things will start looking up. {4:5} He's gonna set up a defense around Zion, a cloud by day and a fire by night, protecting it all. {4:6} There'll be shelter from the heat and storms, a safe haven for all.

{5:1} Alright, check it, I'm about to drop a verse about my main squeeze and his vineyard. So, my guy's got this sick vineyard on a super lush hill, right? {5:2} He goes all out, fences it, clears out the rocks, plants the best vines, throws up a tower, even sets up a winepress. Dude's expecting top-notch grapes, but what does he get? Straight-up wild ones. {5:3} Yo, peeps of Jerusalem and Judah, I need y'all to judge something between me and my vineyard. {5:4} Like, what else could my guy have done for his vineyard? He did everything, but instead of good grapes, it's all wild and unruly. {5:5} So, here's the deal: I'm tearing down the fences, letting it get trashed, breaking down the walls, and letting it get trampled. {5:6} It's gonna be a wasteland, no pruning, no digging, just weeds and thorns. Plus, I'm putting the clouds on notice, no rain for this place. {5:7} 'Cause this vineyard is Israel, God's chosen crew, but instead of justice, there's oppression, and instead of righteousness, it's all crying and chaos. {5:8} And woe to those who keep gobbling up land, joining house to house till there's no space left, trying to be all alone in the world. {5:9} God's saying, "I see it all, and soon, these fancy houses will be empty and abandoned." {5:10} Even if you have ten acres, you'll barely get a bath's worth of grapes, and your harvest will be pitifully small. {5:11} And woe to those who start drinking at the crack of dawn and keep going till the night's lit with wine. {5:12} They're all about the parties, the music, the wine, but they couldn't care less about God's work or what he's up to. {5:13} So, my peeps end up in captivity 'cause they're clueless, and even the big shots are starving, thirsty for some real knowledge. {5:14} And hell's opening wide, swallowing up all their glory, riches, and pride. {5:15} The lowly get brought down, the mighty humbled, and the proud? Yeah, they're getting a reality check. {5:16} But God's gonna come out on top with his righteous judgments, and he'll be praised for his holiness. {5:17} Then the lambs will graze in peace, and strangers will feast on the abandoned lands of the fat cats. {5:18} Woe to those who haul around sin like it's some kind of fancy accessory, dragging it behind them like a cart. {5:19} They're all like, "Come on, God, do something so we can see it, let's see what this Holy One's got." {5:20} But woe to those who twist good and evil, light and dark, sweet and bitter, like it's some kind of messed-up game. {5:21} And woe to those who think they're so smart, so clever in their own eyes. {5:22} Woe to the heavy drinkers, the party animals, who twist justice for a price and deny the innocent their rights. {5:23-24} Their end? It's gonna be like stubble in a fire, chaff in the wind, 'cause they've trashed God's law and disrespected his word. {5:25} So, God's ticked off at his people, and he's laying down the law, shaking things up big time. But even after all that, he's still reaching out, his hand still stretched out in mercy. {5:26} He's gonna raise a flag to the nations, calling them in from afar with a whistle, and they're gonna come rushing in. {5:27} They'll be unstoppable, no breaks, no sleep, no loose belts or busted shoe laces. {5:28} Their weapons sharp, their bows ready, horses hooves like flint, wheels spinning like a whirlwind. {5:29} They'll roar like lions, seizing their prey and carrying it off with no one to stop them. {5:30} And when they hit, it'll be like the sea roaring, darkness and despair everywhere, even the light swallowed up by the darkness.

{6:1} So, when King Uzziah died, I had this vision of the Lord chilling on his throne, high and mighty, filling up the whole temple. {6:2-3} And these seraphim dudes were there, with six wings each, covering their faces and feet, and flying around, shouting, "Holy, holy, holy is the LORD of hosts! His glory fills the whole earth!" {6:4} The place was shaking, smoke everywhere from the shout. {6:5} And I'm just like, "Dang, I'm screwed! I'm surrounded by foul-mouthed people, and now I'm seeing the King, the LORD of hosts, in the flesh." {6:6} Then one of the seraphim flew over with a hot coal, grabbed with tongs from the altar, and touched my lips with it. "Your sins are wiped clean," he said. {6:7-8} And then I heard the Lord asking, "Who can I send? Who's up for the task?" And I was like, "Right here, send me!" {6:9} And God's like, "Go tell these people to listen up but not understand, to look but not get it. Make 'em fat and deaf, blind to the truth, so they won't repent and be healed." {6:10-11} And I'm like, "How long, God?" And he's like, "Till the cities lie in ruins, the houses empty, and the land deserted." {6:12} Until there's almost no one left. {6:13} But even then, a remnant will survive and bounce back, like trees shedding their leaves but still standing strong, because the holy seed will keep this going.

{7:1} So, back in the day when Ahaz, Jotham's kid, was ruling Judah, Rezin from Syria and Pekah, Remaliah's son, from Israel thought they'd take a shot at Jerusalem in a war but couldn't pull it off. {7:2} Word got to King David's fam that Syria and Ephraim were teaming up, and it freaked them out—like trees swaying in a strong wind. {7:3} Then the Big Guy upstairs tells Isaiah, "Yo, go meet Ahaz with your son Shearjashub by the waterway in the fuller's field." {7:4} And Isaiah's supposed to tell Ahaz, "Chill, bro. Don't stress over those two firebrands, Rezin and Remaliah's kid, and their anger." {7:5} 'Cause they're plotting against Judah, saying, "Let's roll up and mess with them, and pop a king in there, maybe Tabeal's boy." {7:6} But the Big Guy's like, "Nah, that ain't happening." {7:7} "Syria's boss is Rezin, and Ephraim's gonna fall apart within 65 years, not even a nation anymore." {7:8-9} "Ephraim's boss is Samaria, and Remaliah's kid's calling the shots there. If you don't believe it, you won't see it happen." {7:10-11} Later, the Big Guy talks to Ahaz again, saying, "Ask for a sign, anything, from the depths to the skies." {7:12} But Ahaz is like, "Nah, I won't ask, won't test the Big Guy." {7:13} Then the Big Guy's like, "Seriously? You're buggin'. You're tiring out people, but now you're trying to tire out God too?" {7:14-15} So, the Big Guy himself drops a bomb: "Check it, a virgin's gonna have a son named Immanuel. He'll live it up on butter and honey, learning good from bad." {7:16} "By the time he knows right from wrong, the land you dread will be deserted by its kings." {7:17} "The Big Guy's bringing trouble on you and your crew, from Assyria, the same day Ephraim split from Judah, led by the Assyrian king." {7:18-21} "On that day, Egypt's flies and Assyria's bees will swarm and sting everywhere." {7:22} "There'll be milk aplenty, and everyone left will be living the butter and honey life." {7:23} "But where there used to be vineyards worth a fortune, there'll be nothing but thorns and thistles." {7:24} "People will resort to bows and arrows because the land's overrun with thorns." {7:25} "But the hills that were once tilled will be open grazing, free from thorns, perfect for cattle and sheep."

{8:1} Later on, the Big Guy tells me, "Grab a big scroll and write 'Maher-shalal-hash-baz' on it." {8:2} "Before that kid can even talk, Damascus and Samaria's riches will be plundered by the Assyrian king." {8:3} "These people are turning away from me, looking to Rezin and Remaliah's kid for help." {8:4} "The Assyrian king's gonna roll through Judah, like floodwaters, up to the neck." {8:5} "But don't stress, God's with us, so any plans against us will flop." {8:6} "I'm telling you, don't get caught up in what these folks are saying, don't be scared like them." {8:7} "Fear the Big Guy, not them." {8:8} "Some will stumble, fall, and get trapped because of him." {8:15} "So, keep spreading the word, and my followers will hold onto it tight." {8:9} "Me and the kids God gave me are gonna be like a sign in Israel, thanks to the Big Guy living on Mount Zion."

{9:1} So, like, even though things were rough before, it's not gonna be as bad as when Zebulun and Naphtali got hit up, and then Galilee got it worse. {9:2} The ones stuck in the dark are finally seeing some serious light, especially those chilling in the shadow of death. Light's shining bright on them now. {9:3} You've beefed up the nation, but the vibe's not getting any happier. They're kinda celebrating, but it's more like the joy of a harvest or splitting up the loot. {9:4} You've totally smashed the oppressors' grip, just like in the good old days of Midian's defeat. {9:5} 'Cause, like, battles usually have all this noise and blood, but this time it's all about fire and destruction. {9:6} 'Cause guess what? A kid's been born, a son's been given, and he's gonna be in charge of everything. And check out his names: Wonder, Counselor, Mighty God, Eternal Dad, Prince of Peace. {9:7} His rule and peace? They're never gonna end, sitting on David's throne, making sure everything's fair and square from now till forever. And God's totally gonna make it happen. {9:8} God's dropping some knowledge on Jacob, and Israel's feeling it. {9:9} Even Ephraim and Samaria, who are pretty full of themselves, are gonna get a wake-up call. {9:10} They're talking big, like, "Yeah, things fell apart, but we'll build back stronger." But God's got other plans. {9:11} He's gonna sic Rezin's enemies on him, teaming up to bring him down. {9:12} Syrians in front, Philistines in the back, they're gonna chow down on Israel with no mercy. And God's still not done being mad. {9:13} 'Cause even after all that, the people aren't turning back to God or seeking him out. {9:14} So, God's gonna chop off both the leaders and the followers, the high and the low, all in one go. {9:15} The honored ones, they're gonna fall just like the prophets spreading lies. {9:16} 'Cause the leaders are leading everyone astray, and the ones following them are gonna get wrecked. {9:17} And God's not even gonna spare the young or the vulnerable 'cause everyone's being fake and wicked, talking nonsense. And God's still mad about it. {9:18} 'Cause wickedness is like a fire, burning up everything in its path, from thorns and briers to the deepest forests, leaving nothing but smoke behind. {9:19} All because God's ticked off, the land's gonna be dark and the people fuel for the fire. No one's gonna spare their own brother. {9:20} People are gonna be desperate, starving on one side, eating their own flesh on the other. {9:21} Manasseh and Ephraim, they're gonna turn on each other, teaming up against Judah. And guess what? God's still not done being mad.

{10:1} Woe to those making unjust laws, writing up oppression like it's some kind of prescription. {10:2} They're totally messing with justice, robbing the poor, and preying on the vulnerable. {10:3} But when the day of reckoning comes, when everything falls apart, where are they gonna turn for help? What'll happen to all their boasting? {10:4} 'Cause without God, they're gonna end up under the oppressor's thumb, crushed with the rest of the losers. And God's still not done being mad. {10:5} Assyria, you're just a tool in God's angry hand, a weapon for his wrath. {10:6} He's sending you against a hypocritical nation, giving you the green light to plunder and trample them like dirt on the streets. {10:7} But that's not what you're thinking, right? Your plan's not to destroy nations left and right. {10:8} But you're acting like your leaders are all kings. {10:9} Seriously, who do you think you are? Calno, Carchemish, Hamath, Arpad, Samaria, Damascus? {10:10} You're not better than those other kingdoms with their idols. {10:11} And just like you wrecked Samaria, you think you're gonna do the same to Jerusalem? {10:12} But when God's done with Jerusalem, when he's wrapped up his work on Mount Zion, he's gonna punish you, Assyria, for your arrogance. {10:13} You're saying, "I did all this by myself, with my own strength and wisdom." You're acting like you're some kind of superpower, robbing nations and crushing them like bugs. {10:14} But just like a bird builds its nest, you've gathered up all this wealth, but God's gonna bring you down. {10:15} Can an axe brag about the one who swings it? Can a saw show off against the one who handles it? You're just tools in God's hand, nothing more. {10:16} So, God's gonna slim down the fat cats, strip away their glory, and light a fire that'll consume all the thorns and briers in one go. {10:17} The light of Israel will be like a fire, burning up all the thorns and briers in one day. {10:18} It'll devour everything, from the grand forests to the lush fields, leaving nothing but ashes behind. {10:19} Only a few trees will be left standing in the once-thick forest, easy enough for a kid to count. {10:20} And when that day comes, the surviving remnant of Israel and Jacob won't be relying on the ones who hurt them but on the LORD, the Holy One of Israel, for real. {10:21} They're gonna return to the mighty God, no more looking to human strength. {10:22} 'Cause even though Israel's as numerous as the sand, only a small remnant will return, 'cause God's decree of destruction is gonna overflow with righteousness. {10:23} The Lord GOD of hosts is gonna carry out this decree, fully and decisively, throughout the land. {10:24-25} So, God's saying to his people in Zion, "Don't sweat Assyria. Yeah, they're gonna smack you around, but it won't last long, and my anger will fade with their destruction." {10:26} And just like God did at Oreb's rock and in the Red Sea, he's gonna stir things up against Assyria. {10:27} And when that day comes, Assyria's oppression will be lifted from your shoulders, and their yoke will be destroyed because of God's anointing. {10:28} Assyria's rolling through all these towns, setting up camp, but God's saying, "Not for long."

{11:1} So, there's gonna be this dude, a descendant of Jesse, and he's gonna be like a new shoot growing from Jesse's family tree. {11:2} The Big Guy's spirit is gonna be all over him—wisdom, understanding, counsel, strength, knowledge, and respect for the Big Guy. {11:3} He'll be super sharp in respecting the Big Guy and won't judge by what he sees or hears. {11:4} He'll be all about fairness, especially for the poor and the humble. He's gonna shut down the wicked just by speaking and breathing. {11:5} Righteousness will be his belt, and faithfulness his waistband. {11:6} It's gonna be wild—wolves chilling with lambs, leopards kicking it with goats, and even little kids leading them around. {11:7} Cows and bears will graze together, and lions will be munching on straw like oxen. {11:8} Babies will be playing near snake holes, and toddlers will be chilling by vipers' nests. {11:9} No harm or destruction will go down in the Big Guy's holy turf 'cause the whole world will be filled with his knowledge, like the seas are filled with water. {11:10} There's gonna be this new branch from Jesse's family tree, and everyone, including non-Jews, will be drawn to him. It's gonna be lit. {11:11} And the Big Guy's gonna step in again, a second time, to bring back his peeps who got scattered all over—Assyria, Egypt, Pathros, Cush, Elam, Shinar, Hamath, and even the islands. {11:12} He'll set up a sign for the nations, gather up the outcasts of Israel, and bring back Judah's scattered crew from all corners of the earth. {11:13-14} Ephraim's jealousy of Judah and Judah's rivalry with Ephraim will be history. They'll team up against their enemies, Philistines to the west, Edomites, Moabites, and Ammonites. {11:15} The Big Guy's gonna shut down the Red Sea and smack the Nile with his powerful hand, splitting it into seven streams so folks can walk through on dry land. {11:16} There's gonna be a highway for the leftover peeps from Assyria, just like when they rolled out of Egypt.

{12:1} And when that day comes, you're gonna be like, "Yo Big Guy, thanks for calming down and comforting me." {12:2} You'll be shouting, "God's got my back! I trust him, no fear, 'cause he's my strength and my jam, my salvation!" {12:3} So get hyped, 'cause you're gonna be drawing water from the wells of salvation with pure joy. {12:4} You'll be giving mad props to the Big Guy, spreading the word about how awesome he is, and telling everyone how high his name is lifted. {12:5} Sing loud and proud to the Big Guy 'cause he's done some amazing stuff, and everyone's gonna know about it. {12:6} So, all you Zion residents, shout it out 'cause the Holy One of Israel is in your midst, and he's legit.

{13:1} So Isaiah's got the scoop on Babylon, here's what's up. {13:2} Hoist up a flag on the tallest peak, yell out loud so everyone hears, and give 'em a wave to head to the fancy folks' place. {13:3} I've called up my elite crew, my anger squad who dig my vibe. {13:4} It's gonna be loud in the hills, like a massive party, all the nations showing up for the showdown. God's rallying the troops for battle. {13:5} They're rolling in from far away, from the ends of the sky, it's God himself with his wrathful gear to wreck the whole place. {13:6} Brace yourselves, 'cause the big day of God's wrath is coming, and it's gonna be a total wipeout. {13:7} Everyone's gonna be freaking out, hearts melting, hands trembling. {13:8} Fear's gonna grip 'em, pain's gonna hit 'em hard, like labor pains. They'll be stunned, staring at each other with faces flushed with fear. {13:9} The day of God's wrath is gonna be brutal, wiping out the sinners, leaving the land desolate. {13:10} Even the stars and constellations won't shine, the sun'll be dark, and the moon won't give its light. {13:11} God's gonna punish the world for its evil, take down the arrogant and haughty, putting the wicked in their place. {13:12} People are gonna be more valuable than gold from Ophir. {13:13} God's gonna shake up the heavens, and the earth's gonna quake in his anger. {13:14} It'll be chaos, everyone scrambling back to their own people and lands. {13:15} Anyone caught's gonna get skewered, and anyone joined with 'em's gonna fall by the sword. {13:16} Even their kids won't be spared, houses plundered, wives violated, it's gonna be brutal. {13:17} God's gonna stir up the Medes, who won't care about gold or silver, slashing through young and old alike, no mercy for kids. {13:18} Babylon, once so glorious, gonna be like Sodom and Gomorrah, a wasteland. {13:19} Forever deserted, no one living there, just wild animals and eerie creatures. {13:20} Arabs won't camp there, shepherds won't rest their flocks there. {13:21} It's gonna be a haunt for desert creatures, with owls and satyrs taking over. {13:22} The time's coming soon, and it won't be delayed.

{14:1} But hey, there's hope for Jacob and Israel. Strangers gonna join 'em, sticking with the house of Jacob. {14:2} People'll bring 'em back, they'll own servants and maids from the land God gave 'em. {14:3} One day, God's gonna give 'em rest from their troubles and fears, from all the hard times they've been through. {14:4} They'll mock the king of Babylon, saying, "Look who's fallen now, the mighty city's done for." {14:5} God's crushed the wicked rulers. {14:6} The tyrant who ruled with an iron fist is now on the run, with no one to stop his downfall. {14:7} The whole earth's at peace, bursting into songs of joy. {14:8} Even the trees are celebrating, glad that the threat's gone. {14:9} Hell's fired up, welcoming the king of Babylon, along with all the other big shots. {14:10} They'll mock him, saying, "You're just like us now, weak and helpless." {14:11} His grandeur's turned to rot, his music silenced by worms. {14:12} He who thought he could rival God, brought down to the dust. {14:13} You wanted to be like God, now you're headed to the depths of hell. {14:14} But you're gonna fall, not rise like you thought. {14:15} People'll stare at you in disbelief, wondering how you, who shook kingdoms, ended up like this. {14:16} You, who turned the world into a wasteland, who kept prisoners locked away, now lying in disgrace. {14:17} All the kings, once powerful, now resting in their tombs. {14:18} But you, cast out like trash, no proper burial for you. {14:19} Your descendants won't be honored, wiped out like you were. {14:20} God's gonna punish 'em for their sins, making sure they never rise again. {14:21} Their children'll pay for their parents' sins, never ruling or building cities. {14:22} God's wiping out Babylon, not even leaving a name behind. {14:23} Turning it into a wasteland, fit only for animals and ponds. {14:24} God's made up his mind, and nothing's gonna change his plans. {14:25} He's gonna crush the Assyrians in his land, trample 'em in his mountains, freeing his people from their grip. {14:26} His plans aren't just for one nation but for the whole earth. {14:27} Who can stop God's plans? No one. {14:28} In the year that King Ahaz died, this message came: {14:29} Don't celebrate, all you Philistines, just because the rod that struck you is broken. From that serpent's root will come an adder, and its offspring will be a fiery flying serpent. {14:30} The poorest of the poor will find food, and the needy will lie down in safety. But I will destroy your root with famine, and it will kill your remnant. {14:31} Wail, O gate! Cry out, O city! All of you, Philistia, are melted away in fear. For a cloud of smoke is coming from the north, and there will be no stragglers in its ranks. {14:32} What answer shall be given to the envoys of that nation? The LORD has established Zion, and in her, the afflicted of his people will find refuge.

{15:1} Yo, here's the lowdown on Moab. In one night, Ar of Moab got wrecked, silenced for good; same thing happened to Kir of Moab. {15:2} Everyone's headed to Bajith and Dibon, hitting up the high spots to cry. Moab's crying over Nebo and Medeba; they're all shaving their heads and cutting off beards. {15:3} They're rocking sackcloth in the streets, crying on rooftops and everywhere, shedding mad tears. {15:4} Heshbon and Elealeh are wailing, and you can hear it all the way to Jahaz. Moab's soldiers are losing it; life's just too heavy for them. {15:5} My heart breaks for Moab; their refugees are fleeing to Zoar, like a young cow. They're climbing up Luhith, weeping all the way; crying destruction on the road to Horonaim. {15:6} The waters of Nimrim are dried up; the grass is gone, no green in sight. {15:7} So they're hauling all their stuff to the Brook of the Willows. {15:8} Moab's cries are echoing everywhere, from Eglaim to Beerelim. {15:9} Dimon's waters are bloody; more trouble is coming, like lions for Moab's survivors.

{16:1} Send a lamb to the ruler from Sela to the desert, to the mountain of Zion's daughter. {16:2} The Moabite girls at the Arnon fords will be like scared birds kicked out of their nest. {16:3} Get some advice, do what's right; be a shadow at noon, hide the outcasts, don't snitch on the wanderers. {16:4} Let my outcasts stay with you, Moab; be a safe spot for them from the oppressor. The tyrant's done, the destruction's over, oppressors are gone. {16:5} Mercy will set up the throne; someone will sit on it in David's tent, ruling with truth, justice, and quick righteousness. {16:6} We've heard all about Moab's pride and arrogance, but his boasts are just lies. {16:7} So Moab will wail for Moab, everyone will wail; they'll mourn for the foundations of Kir-hareseth, definitely hit hard. {16:8} The fields of Heshbon and the vines of Sibmah are suffering; foreign rulers trashed their best plants, reaching Jazer and wandering through the desert. Their branches stretched out over the sea. {16:9} So I'll cry for the vines of Sibmah like Jazer does; I'll drench you with my tears, Heshbon and Elealeh. The shouting for your summer fruits and harvest is gone. {16:10} Joy and gladness are gone from the fields; no singing or shouting in the vineyards, no wine pressing. I've ended the shouts of joy. {16:11} My heart sounds like a harp for Moab, my insides for Kir-haresh. {16:12} When Moab gets tired of the high places and heads to their sanctuary to pray, it won't work out. {16:13} This is what the LORD has said about Moab for a while. {16:14} But now the LORD says, within three years, like a hired worker's time, Moab's glory will be trashed, with all their big numbers, and the leftovers will be tiny and weak.

{17:1} So, peeps, check it out—Damascus is straight-up wrecked, like, completely trashed. {17:2} Aroer's cities? Deserted. They're just spots for sheep to chill without anyone bothering them. {17:3} Ephraim's stronghold? Gone. Same with Damascus's rule. They're gonna be as faded as Israel's former glory, says the Big Guy. {17:4} And Jacob's once grand rep? It's gonna fade, his muscles turning to mush. {17:5} It's gonna be like when you're gathering crops, but there's hardly anything left, just a few grapes hanging on, a couple on each branch. {17:6} But there'll still be a little something left, like when you shake an olive tree and a few olives drop. The Big Guy's calling it. {17:7} When stuff gets rough, people are gonna start looking up, turning to the Holy One of Israel. {17:8} They're gonna ditch their handmade altars and groves, realizing they ain't worth squat. {17:9} Strong cities? Yeah, they're gonna be like abandoned branches, left behind 'cause of Israel. Total ghost towns. {17:10} And why's all this happening? 'Cause y'all forgot about God, your rock. So now, instead of planting good stuff, you're gonna be stuck with garbage. {17:11} You'll put in the work, but when it's time to harvest, it's gonna be a disaster. {17:12} Oh, and here's a warning for the loud nations—those who roar like the sea: The Big Guy's gonna shut you down, scatter you like chaff before the wind. {17:13} You'll come crashing like waves, but God's gonna put you in your place, making you run away like dust in the wind. {17:14} And when all's said and done, trouble's gonna hit hard, but by morning, it'll be gone. That's what happens to those who mess with us.

{18:1} Oh, and another woe to those shady lands beyond Ethiopia's rivers, sending out messengers in boats to distant nations. {18:2} They're telling them, "Yo, go tell those folks who've been through it all that we're coming." {18:3} Everybody's gonna see when God raises the flag and blows the horn. {18:4} 'Cause God's chilling, watching over everything, like the sun on a clear day or dew in the morning. {18:5} Before the harvest, when everything's ripe, he's gonna prune it all, chopping off the dead branches. {18:6} And what's left? It's gonna be bird food and wild animal hangouts. {18:7} But in the end, all those scattered and beaten-down folks are gonna bring their tribute to the LORD of hosts, to the place where his name shines brightest, Mount Zion.

{19:1} Yo, here's the lowdown on Egypt. The LORD is rolling in on a swift cloud, and Egypt's idols are gonna freak out, their hearts melting. {19:2} I'll turn the Egyptians against each other, bro against bro, neighbor against neighbor, city against city, kingdom against kingdom. {19:3} Egypt's spirit will fail, their plans destroyed. They'll seek idols, charmers, mediums, and wizards for help. {19:4} I'll hand the Egyptians over to a harsh ruler; a fierce king will control them, says the LORD of hosts. {19:5} The sea waters will dry up, the river wasted. {19:6} They'll redirect the rivers, and the defensive streams will dry up, reeds and rushes will wither. {19:7} The plants by the brooks, everything sown there, will wither and disappear. {19:8} The fishers will mourn, all who cast hooks into the brooks will lament, and those who spread nets on the waters will languish. {19:9} Those who work in fine flax and weave networks will be confused. {19:10} The workers in sluices and fish ponds will be shattered. {19:11} The princes of Zoan are fools, Pharaoh's wise counselors are brutish. How can you say to Pharaoh, "I'm the son of the wise, son of ancient kings"? {19:12} Where are your wise men now? Let them tell you what the LORD of hosts has planned for Egypt. {19:13} The princes of Zoan are fools, the princes of Noph are deceived; they've led Egypt astray, the backbone of its tribes. {19:14} The LORD has mixed a spirit of confusion in Egypt; they've made Egypt err in all its works, like a drunk staggering in his vomit. {19:15} Egypt won't have any work for head or tail, palm branch or reed. {19:16} On that day, Egypt will be like women, trembling in fear because of the LORD's hand, which He shakes over it. {19:17} The land of Judah will terrify Egypt; everyone who mentions it will be afraid because of what the LORD of hosts has planned against it. {19:18} On that day, five cities in Egypt will speak the language of Canaan and swear allegiance to the LORD of hosts; one will be called the City of Destruction. {19:19} On that day, there will be an altar to the LORD in the middle of Egypt and a pillar to the LORD at its border. {19:20} It will be a sign and witness to the LORD of hosts in Egypt. When they cry to the LORD because of oppressors, He'll send them a savior and defender to rescue them. {19:21} The LORD will be known to Egypt, and the Egyptians will know the LORD, offering sacrifices and offerings; they'll make vows to the LORD and keep them. {19:22} The LORD will strike Egypt, striking and healing it. They'll return to the LORD, and He'll respond to their pleas and heal them. {19:23} On that day, there'll be a highway from Egypt to Assyria. Assyrians will go to Egypt, and Egyptians to Assyria, and they'll worship together. {19:24} On that day, Israel will be the third along with Egypt and Assyria, a blessing in the midst of the earth. {19:25} The LORD of hosts will bless them, saying, "Blessed be Egypt my people, Assyria my handiwork, and Israel my inheritance."

{20:1} In the year Tartan came to Ashdod, sent by Sargon, king of Assyria, and captured it, {20:2} the LORD spoke through Isaiah son of Amoz, saying, "Take off your sackcloth and sandals." He did so, walking naked and barefoot. {20:3} The LORD said, "Just as my servant Isaiah has walked naked and barefoot for three years as a sign against Egypt and Ethiopia, {20:4} so will the king of Assyria lead away Egyptian prisoners and Ethiopian captives, young and old, naked and barefoot, with buttocks bared, shaming Egypt. {20:5} They'll be dismayed and ashamed of Ethiopia their hope and Egypt their glory. {20:6} The inhabitants of this coastland will say, 'Look, this is what happened to those we hoped for, who fled to for help against the king of Assyria! How will we escape?'"

{21:1} Yo, here's the scoop on the desert by the sea—it's like a wild storm coming from the desert, a real scary place. {21:2} I had this intense vision where backstabbers were doing their thing, and the spoilers were spoiling. Elam and Media, they're up to no good. But I've shut down all their drama. {21:3} Man, I'm feeling it deep in my gut, like labor pains hitting hard. I'm shook just thinking about it. {21:4} My heart's racing, and I'm freaking out. What used to bring me joy now just scares me. {21:5} It's time to get ready, keep watch, eat, drink, and gear up, leaders. {21:6} God told me to set up a lookout, someone to keep an eye out and report back. {21:7} So, this lookout sees some crazy stuff, like chariots and all, and he's freaking out. {21:8} He's like, "There's a lion out there!" I'm telling you, this guy's been on the lookout nonstop. {21:9} And then he spots another group of dudes, and he's like, "Babylon's toast, man! Their idols are smashed to bits!" {21:10} It's like my job to share what God's telling me. {21:11} Now, listen up—here's what's going down in Dumah. They're calling out from Seir, asking what's up with the night. {21:12} The lookout's like, "Morning's coming, but then it's back to darkness. If you wanna know more, ask away." {21:13} And check this—Arabia's got issues too. They're gonna be camping out in the woods. {21:14} But Tema's stepping up, offering water and bread to those in need. {21:15} They're running from swords and bows, just trying to survive the war. {21:16} God's saying within a year, Kedar's gonna lose its shine. {21:17} And Kedar's mighty warriors? Yeah, they're gonna be few and far between. God's calling the shots.

{22:1} Here's the deal with the valley of vision—why are you all hanging out on rooftops? {22:2} You used to be so lively, but now it's like a ghost town. {22:3} Your leaders have split, and anyone left is getting captured. {22:4} I'm done comforting you. It's a day of trouble, with God tearing down walls and people crying out. {22:5} Elam's ready for battle, and Kir's bringing out the shields. {22:6} Get ready for chariots filling your valleys and horsemen posted at the gates. {22:7} The armor's off, and everyone's checking out the defenses. {22:8} And then, Judah's secrets are exposed, and everyone's eyeing up their defenses. {22:9} You've seen the city's weak spots, gathered water from the lower pool, and even tore down houses to reinforce the walls. {22:10} You're prepping for battle, but you're not looking to God, the one who made it all. {22:11} So, God's calling for mourning and sadness instead of partying. {22:12} But some are like, "Let's eat, drink, and be merry, 'cause tomorrow we might die." {22:13-14} But God's saying this mess ain't gonna be cleared up until y'all straighten out. {22:15} God's telling me to go talk to this Shebna dude, and ask why he's building a fancy tomb. {22:16} He's gonna be in for a rude awakening 'cause God's gonna boot him out big time. {22:17} He's gonna get tossed around like a ball and end up in a far-off land. {22:18} He's losing his power, and his fancy stuff's will become a disgrace. {22:19} His days of glory are over.

{23:1} The drama about Tyre: Cry, ships of Tarshish, 'cause Tyre's wrecked, no houses left, no entryways; they found out from the land of Chittim. {23:2} Chill, islanders; merchants from Zidon, who sail over the sea, filled you up. {23:3} The seed of Sihor, the river's harvest, is her income; she's the marketplace for nations. {23:4} Be ashamed, Zidon: the sea, the mighty sea, says, "I don't labor or give birth, don't raise young men or bring up virgins." {23:5} Egypt's news will make them freak out like Tyre's news did. {23:6} Head over to Tarshish; cry, islanders. {23:7} Is this your happy city, ancient since forever? Her feet will take her far to live as a stranger. {23:8} Who planned this against Tyre, the crowning city, whose merchants are princes, whose traders are honored? {23:9} The LORD of hosts planned it to humble all pride, to bring all honored ones into contempt. {23:10} Flow through your land like a river, daughter of Tarshish; your strength is gone. {23:11} He stretched his hand over the sea, shook kingdoms; the LORD ordered the destruction of the merchant city, its strongholds wrecked. {23:12} He said, "No more joy for you, oppressed virgin, daughter of Zidon: go to Chittim, but you won't find rest there." {23:13} Look at the land of the Chaldeans; they weren't even a thing until Assyria set it up for desert dwellers: they built towers and palaces and then wrecked it. {23:14} Cry, ships of Tarshish; your stronghold is destroyed. {23:15} And it'll be that Tyre will be forgotten for seventy years, like the lifespan of a king: after seventy years, Tyre will be like a forgotten harlot. {23:16} Take a harp, walk the city, forgotten harlot; play sweet music, sing lots of songs, so you'll be remembered. {23:17} After seventy years, the LORD will check in on Tyre, and she'll go back to her old ways, hooking up with all the kingdoms of the world. {23:18} But her profits and wages will be set apart for the LORD: they won't be saved or stored up; they'll go to those who live in the LORD's presence, to eat well and wear durable clothes.

{24:1} Check it out, the LORD's gonna empty the earth, wreck it, turn it upside down, and scatter everyone. {24:2} It'll be the same for everyone: people and priests, servants and masters, maids and mistresses, buyers and sellers, lenders and borrowers, creditors and debtors. {24:3} The land will be totally emptied and plundered, 'cause the LORD said so. {24:4} The earth mourns and fades away, the world withers and fades, the proud people of the earth waste away. {24:5} The earth is defiled by its people; they've broken the laws, changed the rules, and violated the eternal covenant. {24:6} That's why a curse devours the earth, and its people are punished; the inhabitants are burned up, and few are left. {24:7} The new wine mourns, the vine withers, all the happy-hearted sigh. {24:8} The fun of tambourines is over, the noise of partying ends, the joy of the harp stops. {24:9} They won't drink wine with songs; strong drink will be bitter to those who drink it. {24:10} The city of chaos is shattered; every house is shut up so no one can enter. {24:11} There's a crying for wine in the streets; all joy is darkened, and the land's happiness is gone. {24:12} The city is left in ruins, and the gate is destroyed. {24:13} It'll be like this in the land among the people, like the shaking of an olive tree, like the gleaning of grapes after the harvest is over. {24:14} They'll lift up their voices, they'll sing for the LORD's majesty, they'll shout from the west. {24:15} So, honor the LORD in the east, the name of the LORD God of Israel in the islands of the sea. {24:16} From the ends of the earth, we hear songs: "Glory to the Righteous One." But I said, "I'm wasting away, woe to me! The treacherous betray, and they betray treacherously." {24:17} Terror, pit, and snare await you, earth's inhabitants. {24:18} Whoever flees the sound of terror will fall into a pit, and whoever climbs out of the pit will be caught in a snare; the floodgates of heaven are open, and the earth's foundations shake. {24:19} The earth is broken, split apart, violently shaken. {24:20} The earth staggers like a drunk, sways like a hut; its rebellion weighs it down, and it falls, never to rise again. {24:21} On that day, the LORD will punish the powers in the heavens above and the kings on the earth below. {24:22} They'll be herded together like prisoners in a dungeon; they'll be shut up in prison and punished after many days. {24:23} The moon will be disgraced, the sun ashamed; the LORD will reign on Mount Zion and in Jerusalem, with great glory before its elders.

{25:1} Yo, God, you're the real MVP! I'm gonna lift you up and give you props for all the amazing stuff you've done. Your plans from way back are solid, straight-up truthful. {25:2} You turned cities into ruins, left fortresses deserted. Those fancy palaces? They're history, never gonna be rebuilt. {25:3} So now, even the toughest folks are giving you props. Scary nations are shaking in their boots because of you. {25:4} You've always had our backs, especially when we're down and out. You're our shelter in the storm, our shade from the heat, protecting us when things get crazy. {25:5} You'll silence the noise of our enemies, cooling things down like a cloud on a scorching day. The bullies will be brought low. {25:6} And here's the deal—God's throwing a massive party on this mountain. It's gonna be a feast with the best food and drinks, straight-up gourmet. {25:7} He's gonna wipe away all the messed-up stuff covering people's eyes, unveiling the truth to everyone. {25:8} Death's getting wrecked, and God's wiping away tears. He's lifting the shame off his people, no more putting up with their nonsense. God's said it, so it's going down. {25:9} People will be shouting, "This is our God! We've been waiting for him, and he's come through big time. We're pumped about his salvation!" {25:10} And here, on this mountain, God's gonna show his power, stomping on Moab like trampled straw. {25:11} He'll put an end to their pride and take away their loot. {25:12} Those high walls they trusted in? Yeah, God's gonna bring 'em crashing down, laying 'em flat in the dust.

{26:1} When that day comes, we'll be singing in Judah, bragging about our strong city and how God's our ultimate defense. {26:2} Open up the gates, let in the righteous crew who stick to the truth. {26:3} God keeps those chill vibes going for anyone who's got their mind set on him, 'cause they trust him big time. {26:4} So, keep putting your trust in God—he's got the power to last forever. {26:5} He takes down the big shots, levels the playing field, and brings the proud to their knees. {26:6} It's the little guys who come out on top in the end. {26:7} The righteous path is straight up, and God knows what's good. {26:8} We've been waiting for God to show up and do his thing, longing for his name to be remembered. {26:9} We've been reaching out to God, even when things were rough, hoping everyone would learn what's right when God steps in. {26:10} But even if the wicked catch a break, they still won't learn. They'll keep doing wrong, ignoring God's greatness. {26:11} When God shows up with his power, they'll see it, and they'll be sorry they ever doubted. {26:12} God's got peace lined up for us 'cause he's the one who's been making things happen all along. {26:13} We've had other rulers, but we're sticking with you, God. You're the only one worth mentioning. {26:14} Those other rulers are history, never coming back. You took 'em out and wiped their memory clean. {26:15} You've built us up as a nation, spreading us out across the globe. {26:16} When we were in trouble, we came running to you, pouring out our hearts when things got tough. {26:17} We've been through some real pain, just like a woman in labor, crying out in agony. {26:18} We've been through it all, but we haven't seen any change. The world's still messed up. {26:19} But here's the kicker—your people aren't staying down. We'll rise up from the dust, shouting for joy 'cause your blessings are like the morning dew, bringing new life to the earth. {26:20} So, let's all hunker down for a bit, hiding out until the storm blows over. {26:21} 'Cause when God comes out to set things straight, he's gonna hold everyone accountable. The earth's gonna reveal all its secrets, and there won't be any more hiding from the truth.

{27:1} So, like, when that epic day rolls around, the big dude upstairs with his massive sword is gonna wreck Leviathan, that sneaky snake, and also take out that dragon chilling in the sea. {27:2} And on that day, we're gonna sing about this sick vineyard of red wine. {27:3} The Lord's like, "I got this, fam. I'll keep it hydrated 24/7, ain't no one gonna mess with it." {27:4} He's all chill, not into fury, but if anyone tries to mess with him, he'll just plow through them and burn 'em up. {27:5} Or if someone's down to vibe with his strength, they can totally make peace with him. {27:6} And he's gonna make Jacob's crew thrive, like Israel's gonna be poppin' with fruit all over the place. {27:7} Did he smack Jacob around like Jacob smacked others? Nah, it's more like he's debating with them, holding back his power when things get rough. {27:8} It's like, when Jacob starts getting its act together, the Lord's like, "Cool, I'll ease up." {27:9} This is how Jacob's gonna get rid of its bad vibes and sins—by ditching all the old altars and stuff. {27:10} But even the fortified cities are gonna be ghost towns, overrun by nature and forgotten. {27:11} When things start falling apart, they're gonna be like, "Oh snap, we should've listened!" {27:12} Then the Lord's gonna gather up Israel, one by one, from all over the place. {27:13} And he's gonna blow that big trumpet, calling everyone back to Jerusalem to worship him.

{28:1} Yo, Ephraim's got a wake-up call—no more partying for them. {28:2} 'Cause the Lord's got this powerful force that's gonna wreck shop, like a mega storm. {28:3} Prideful Ephraim's gonna get trampled, and all that flashy stuff they had is gonna fade away. {28:4} Their glory's gonna disappear like a flower in your hand—you blink, and it's gone. {28:5} But for the true believers, the Lord's gonna be their crown of glory, giving them strength and wisdom. {28:6} And for those fighting the good fight, he's gonna have their backs. {28:7} But some folks, they've totally lost it with all the drinking—they're so wasted, they can't even see straight. {28:8} It's like everywhere you look, there's puke and filth, no place is clean. {28:9} So who's gonna learn from the Lord? Those who've moved on from baby stuff. {28:10} It's all about learning bit by bit, like piece by piece, until it starts making sense. {28:11} 'Cause when the Lord tries to talk to people, they're like, "Huh? Speak up, we don't get it." {28:12} He's saying, "Chill out, find some peace with me," but they're not having it. {28:13} So instead of getting it all at once, they keep stumbling and falling back. {28:14} Listen up, you arrogant rulers in Jerusalem, 'cause you're in for a reality check. {28:15} You think you've got it all figured out, making deals with death and thinking you're safe? Nah, that ain't gonna fly. {28:16} The Lord's laying down the real deal in Zion—a solid foundation you can trust. {28:17} He's bringing justice and righteousness, washing away all the lies and hiding places. {28:18} Your shady deals with death and hell? Yeah, they're getting canceled, and when the storms hit, you'll be wiped out. {28:19} It's gonna be relentless, day and night, until you can't even keep up with the chaos. {28:20} You think you're covered, but you're gonna find out real quick that it's not gonna be enough. {28:21} The Lord's gonna shake things up, doing his thing in ways you never expected. {28:22} So don't be acting all tough, 'cause the Lord's got a plan, and it's gonna happen, no doubt. {28:23} Pay attention, listen up to what the Lord's saying. {28:24} Think about it—does a farmer plow all day just to mess around? {28:25} Once the field's ready, they start planting all sorts of stuff in there. {28:26} 'Cause the Lord's the one teaching them, showing them how to do it right. {28:27} They don't use the same methods for everything—each crop gets its own treatment. {28:28} They know when to stop, when to let things be. {28:29} It's all part of the Lord's plan, and it's pretty amazing how it all works out.

{29:1} Yo, peeps, check it—Ariel, where David chilled? Every year, they're all about them sacrifices, yo. {29:2} But I'm 'bout to wreck Ariel, bringin' down mad heaviness and sorrow. It's gonna be straight-up Ariel-town up in here, fam. {29:3} I'll be camping 'round ya, layin' siege with my crew, raisin' forts like it's Fortnite. {29:4} And you? You'll be brought down, speakin' from the ground, voice low like some ghost whisperin' from the dust. {29:5} All them strangers crowdin' around? They'll be like tiny dust specks, and the haters? Just blowin' away like chaff, yo. {29:6} God's droppin' thunder, earthquakes, and all sorts of chaos. It's gonna be lit with fire, fam. {29:7} All them nations comin' at Ariel? They'll be like a faded dream when you wake up starvin'. {29:8} They'll dream of feasting, but wake up hungry; dream of quenchin' their thirst, but wake up parched. {29:9} They'll be actin' drunk, but not from sippin' on wine, staggerin' 'round like they're wasted but not from the strong stuff. {29:10} 'Cause God's gonna knock 'em out with a spiritual knockout punch, closin' their eyes and shuttin' down their prophets and rulers. {29:11} They'll be clueless, like tryna read a sealed book, passin' it to someone smart who's like, "Nah, can't do it." {29:12} Then they'll pass it to some clueless dude who's like, "Nah, not me." {29:13} God's callin' 'em out, yo! They talk the talk, but their hearts are miles away, just goin' through the motions they learned from others. {29:14} But God's droppin' some serious truth bombs on 'em, blowin' the minds of their so-called wise ones and hidin' the understanding of their so-called smart ones. {29:15} They're playin' hide and seek with God, tryna keep their shady deals in the dark, actin' like nobody's watchin'. {29:16} But they got it twisted, thinkin' they can pull a fast one on the Creator. Like, can a clay pot say to the potter, "You didn't make me"? Can a piece of art diss its artist? {29:17} Just wait a bit longer, and the barren land will be poppin' off like a wild party. It's gonna be wild!

{30:1} Yo, big bummer for those rebellious kids, says the LORD, who seek advice everywhere but from me, and rely on their own ways, not on my spirit, just piling up sin upon sin. {30:2} They're all about heading to Egypt for help, not even asking me; they're all about Pharaoh's strength, trusting in Egypt's shade! {30:3} But guess what? Relying on Pharaoh will only bring you shame, and trusting in Egypt will only leave you confused. {30:4} 'Cause Pharaoh's peeps were chilling in Zoan, and his ambassadors were hitting up Hanes. {30:5} But they were all embarrassed, relying on a nation that can't help or do squat for them, just a big disappointment and a shame. {30:6} Oh, and here's another thing: a message about the beasts of the south, heading into a land of trouble and pain, carrying their loot on donkeys and camels to a place that won't even benefit them. {30:7} 'Cause Egypt's help? Useless and empty. That's why I've been saying, their strength is in just chilling. {30:8} So, I'm like, write this down, make it clear, so it sticks for ages: these people are rebellious and refuse to listen to the LORD's law. {30:9} They're like, "Hey, prophets, don't give us real talk; just tell us what we wanna hear, even if it's lies." {30:10} They're like, "Stop talking about God; we don't wanna hear about Him." {30:11} But this is what the Holy One of Israel says: because you ignore my word and trust in oppression and deceit, {30:12} your sin will be like a wall about to collapse, suddenly giving way. {30:13-14} It'll be shattered like a potter's vessel, smashed beyond recognition, with nothing left to scoop fire or water from. {30:15} But if you return to me and chill, you'll be saved; find peace and strength in that, but you ain't into it. {30:16} Nah, you're all, "Nah, we'll ride horses and be swift," but guess what? Your pursuers will be even swifter. {30:17} A thousand will flee at the shout of one; five will make you run, till you're left like a flag on a mountain, or a sign on a hill. {30:18} But yo, the LORD is patient, hoping to show you grace, waiting to be exalted and show mercy, 'cause He's all about judgment. Blessed are those who wait for Him. {30:19} Soon peeps will live in Zion and Jerusalem, crying no more, 'cause God will be super gracious, hearing your cries and answering. {30:20} Even if things get tough, and you face adversity and affliction, your teachers won't be MIA anymore; you'll see them. {30:21} And you'll hear a voice behind you saying, "This is the way, walk in it," whenever you turn left or right. {30:22} You'll be tossing out those silver and gold idols like used tampons, saying, "Get outta here!" {30:23} Then God will bless your crops and make everything fat and plentiful; your livestock will feast in large pastures. {30:24-25} Even on the high mountains and hills, there'll be rivers and streams on the day when the towers fall. {30:26} And on that day, the moon will shine as bright as the sun, and the sun will be seven times brighter, healing His people's wounds. {30:27} Yo, the LORD's coming from far away, burning with anger, heavy burdened; His words are like fire, and His breath is like a flood, sifting the nations with a sieve of vanity, leading them astray. {30:28} But yo, there'll be singing, like at a holy festival; joy, like when you're heading to the mountain of the LORD, to the mighty One of Israel. {30:29-30} And the LORD will make His voice heard, showing His strength and anger, with fire, storms, and hailstones. {30:31} 'Cause it's the LORD's voice that will strike down the Assyrians, who once struck with a rod. {30:32} And wherever the LORD's staff lands, there will be music and battle against His enemies. {30:33} For Tophet has long been ready, prepared for the king; it's deep and wide, a place of fire and wood, kindled by the LORD's breath, like a stream of sulfur.

{31:1} Woe to those who go to Egypt for help, relying on horses, and trusting in chariots 'cause they got many, and in horsemen 'cause they're super strong; but they don't look to the Holy One of Israel or seek the LORD! {31:2} Yet He's wise too and will bring disaster and won't take back His words: He'll rise against the house of evildoers and against the help of those who do wrong. {31:3} Now, Egyptians are just humans, not God; their horses are flesh, not spirit. When the LORD stretches out His hand, both the helper and the helped will fall, and they'll all fail together. {31:4} The LORD told me, just like a lion growling over its prey, and even if a bunch of shepherds show up, he won't be scared by their shouting or humbled by their noise: that's how the LORD of hosts will come down to fight for Mount Zion and its hill. {31:5} Like birds flying, the LORD of hosts will defend Jerusalem; He'll protect it, deliver it, and save it. {31:6} Turn back to Him whom Israel's children have deeply rebelled against. {31:7} In that day, everyone will toss away their silver and gold idols that they made, which are just sinful. {31:8} The Assyrian will fall by a sword, but not a man's; a sword not wielded by humans will devour him. He'll run from the sword, and his young men will be put to shame. {31:9} He'll retreat to his stronghold out of fear, and his princes will panic at the signal, says the LORD, whose fire is in Zion and furnace is in Jerusalem.

{32:1} Check it out, a king will rule righteously, and princes will rule justly. {32:2} Each one will be like a shelter from the wind, a refuge from the storm, like rivers of water in a dry place, like the shadow of a big rock in a weary land. {32:3} The eyes of those who see won't be dim, and the ears of those who hear will listen. {32:4} The rash will understand knowledge, and the stammerers will speak clearly. {32:5} No more will the vile person be called noble, nor the scoundrel be considered generous. {32:6} The vile person speaks villainy, his heart plans wickedness, to practice hypocrisy, to spread lies about the LORD, leaving the hungry empty and withholding water from the thirsty. {32:7} The scoundrel's methods are evil; he devises wicked schemes to ruin the poor with lies, even when the needy speak the truth. {32:8} But the noble plan noble things, and by noble things they stand. {32:9} Listen up, you complacent women; hear my voice, you careless daughters; listen to what I'm saying. {32:10} In a bit, you carefree women will be troubled; the grape harvest will fail, and the gathering won't come. {32:11} Tremble, you complacent women; be troubled, you careless ones; strip off your clothes and put on sackcloth. {32:12} They will mourn for the fields, for the fruitful vines. {32:13} The land of my people will grow thorns and briers, yes, all the houses of joy in the joyous city; {32:14} The palaces will be abandoned, the busy city deserted; the forts and watchtowers will become dens forever, a joy for wild donkeys, a pasture for flocks; {32:15} Until the spirit is poured on us from above, and the wilderness becomes a fruitful field, and the fruitful field is considered a forest. {32:16} Then justice will dwell in the wilderness, and righteousness will live in the fruitful field. {32:17} The work of righteousness will be peace; and the effect of righteousness will be quietness and confidence forever. {32:18} My people will live in peaceful homes, in secure dwellings, and in undisturbed places of rest. {32:19} Even when hail flattens the forest and the city is leveled completely. {32:20} Blessed are you who sow beside all waters, who let the ox and the donkey roam freely.

{33:1} Yo, listen up, if you're out there spoiling others but ain't getting any payback, or playing dirty when no one's playing dirty with you, watch out 'cause when you stop your shady business, it's gonna come back to bite you. {33:2} Oh Lord, be cool with us; we've been waiting on you. Be our strength every morning, and our savior when things get rough. {33:3} When chaos breaks out, people scatter, and when you step up, nations get shook. {33:4} And all that loot you've been hoarding? It's gonna get snatched up like caterpillars on a rampage. {33:5} The Lord's on top, bringing justice and righteousness to Zion. {33:6} Wisdom and knowledge will keep us steady, and the fear of the Lord is where it's at. {33:7} But their tough guys will be crying for help, and the peacekeepers will be in tears. {33:8} The roads are deserted, travelers have stopped, 'cause covenants are broken, cities are ignored, and no one cares. {33:9} The earth is mourning, Lebanon's cut down, and all the fruitful places are wasted. {33:10} But now the Lord's gonna rise up and make his move. {33:11} You'll end up with nothing but straw and stubble, and your own actions will consume you like fire. {33:12} People will be burnt up like lime, and thorns will be turned to ashes in the fire. {33:13} So, peeps near and far, check out what the Lord's been up to, and recognize his power. {33:14} Sinners in Zion are scared stiff, and hypocrites are freaking out. Who can handle the fire? {33:15} Only those who walk the straight and narrow, who reject oppression and bribery, and turn away from evil. {33:16} They'll be living it up, safe and sound, with all they need. {33:17} They'll see the king in all his glory and the far-off lands. {33:18} But for the wicked, it's gonna be terrifying. {33:19} They'll face a people they can't understand, speaking a language they can't comprehend. {33:20} But for those in Zion, it's gonna be chill—Jerusalem's gonna be a peaceful spot, never to be disturbed. {33:21} With the Lord as our judge, lawgiver, and king, we're gonna be saved. {33:22} But for the enemies, their plans will fall apart, and even the weak will get a piece of the spoils. {33:23} No one will be sick, and everyone's sins will be forgiven.

{34:1} Hey, everyone, listen up—earth, world, and everything in it. {34:2} The Lord's mad at all the nations, and his fury's on their armies. He's gonna wipe 'em out. {34:3} Their dead will be left out to rot, and their blood will stain the mountains. {34:4} Even the heavens are gonna be shaken up, and all their host will fall like leaves. {34:5} The Lord's sword is gonna come down hard, bringing judgment to all. {34:6} Blood will flow, and there'll be sacrifices aplenty. {34:7} It's gonna be a bloodbath, with even the unicorns joining in. {34:8} 'Cause it's payback time, the Lord's year of vengeance for Zion. {34:9} The land will turn to pitch, and the sky will rain brimstone. {34:10} The fires won't stop, and the smoke will rise forever, turning the land to waste. {34:11} But it won't be inhabited by humans, just wild beasts and desolation. {34:12} Leaders will be nowhere to be found, and the nobles will be gone. {34:13} Thorns and brambles will take over, with dragons ruling the roost. {34:14} It's gonna be a wild scene, with all sorts of creatures making themselves at home. {34:15} Vultures will gather, nesting in the shadows, and it's gonna be a real party. {34:16} So read up on what the Lord's got planned, 'cause it's all going down as he said. {34:17} He's divvying it all up, and it's gonna be ours forever, from generation to generation.

{35:1} Yo, check it out, the wilderness and lonely spots are gonna be lit, the desert's gonna be popping like a rose garden. {35:2} It's gonna bloom like crazy, with mad joy and singing, getting all that glory from Lebanon, Carmel, and Sharon; they're gonna see the glory of the LORD and our awesome God. {35:3} So, yo, help out those with weak hands and shaky knees. {35:4} Tell those with scared hearts to chill, not to stress, 'cause God's coming with vengeance and salvation. {35:5} Then the blind will see, the deaf will hear, {35:6} the lame will jump like deer, and the mute will sing, 'cause water's gonna flow in the desert, streams in the wilderness. {35:7} Even dry ground will be like a pool, thirsty land will become springs; even where dragons used to chill, grass will grow. {35:8} And there'll be a sick highway called the Way of Holiness; only the clean can roll on it, and even clueless wanderers won't get lost. {35:9} No lions or wild beasts, just the redeemed strolling around. {35:10} And those saved by the LORD will come back to Zion, singing and full of everlasting joy, leaving behind all the sadness and sighs.

{36:1} So, in the fourteenth year of King Hezekiah, Sennacherib, the king of Assyria, rolled up on all the fortified cities of Judah and took 'em. {36:2} Then the king of Assyria sent Rabshakeh with a huge army to Jerusalem, and he posted up by the conduit of the upper pool in the highway of the fuller's field. {36:3} So, Eliakim, Hilkiah's son, Shebna the scribe, and Joah, Asaph's son, the recorder, stepped up. {36:4} And Rabshakeh was like, "Tell Hezekiah, what's up with trusting in Egypt? 'Cause, like, Pharaoh's just a broken reed, man. {36:5} And if you're thinking you got some sick war strategy, tell me, who you trustin' that makes you rebel against me?" {36:6} He's all, "So, you think you can lean on Egypt? Nah, man, it's gonna backfire, just like when a reed pierces your hand. That's Pharaoh for ya." {36:7} He's like, "And if you're thinking, 'Oh, we trust in the LORD,' well, didn't Hezekiah tear down His altars and high places? He even told y'all to worship at this altar here." {36:8} Then he's all, "So, make a deal with my king, and I'll hook you up with two thousand horses if you can even find enough riders. {36:9} How you gonna stand against even the least of my master's servants? You're putting your trust in Egypt for chariots and horses?" {36:10} He's like, "Did I come up against this land without the LORD telling me to destroy it? God straight-up said, 'Go and wreck this place.'" {36:11} Then Eliakim, Shebna, and Joah were like, "Yo, speak to us in Aramaic, we get that. Don't talk in Hebrew where everyone can hear." {36:12} But Rabshakeh's like, "Did my king send me to you or to the dudes on the wall? They're the ones who are gonna eat their own crap and drink their own pee with you." {36:13} So, Rabshakeh stood up and yelled in Hebrew, saying, "Listen up, peeps! Here's what the great king of Assyria says." {36:14} He's like, "Don't let Hezekiah fool you; he can't save you." {36:15} He's like, "Don't trust Hezekiah or the LORD when he says this city won't be handed over to the king of Assyria." {36:16} "Don't listen to Hezekiah; just make a deal with me and come out. I'll let you eat from your own vine and fig tree and drink from your own well. {36:17} Until I take you to a land just like yours, with food and wine, bread and vineyards." {36:18} "Don't let Hezekiah trick you into thinking the LORD will save you. Have any of the gods of other nations saved them from the king of Assyria?" {36:19} "Where are the gods of Hamath and Arphad? Where are the gods of Sepharvaim? Did they save Samaria from me?" {36:20} "So, who among all the gods out there has saved their people from me? Why would the LORD save

Jerusalem from me?" {36:21} But they kept quiet, not saying a word, 'cause the king said not to respond. {36:22} So, Eliakim, Shebna, and Joah went back to Hezekiah, tore their clothes, and told him everything Rabshakeh said.

{37:1} So, like, when King Hezekiah heard that stuff, he totally freaked out, tore his clothes, put on some sackcloth, and went to the temple. {37:2} Then he sent his crew to Isaiah, like Eliakim, Shebna, and some priest elders, all decked out in sackcloth, with a message from Hezekiah. {37:3} He was like, "Dude, today is straight-up messed. We're in deep trouble, getting dissed big time. It's like trying to give birth but having zero strength." {37:4} "Maybe the big man upstairs will hear about how Rabshakeh, the Assyrian king's henchman, is dissing the living God. So, Isaiah, can you throw up some prayers for the ones left standing?" {37:5} So, Hezekiah's squad rolled up to Isaiah's place. {37:6} Isaiah was like, "Tell your boss not to stress about those haters. God's got this. The Assyrian king's crew can talk smack, but they'll get theirs soon." {37:7} "I'm gonna send some chaos their way. Rabshakeh will hear some rumors and bounce back to his own turf. Then, he's gonna eat steel in his own backyard." {37:8} So, Rabshakeh peaced out and found out the Assyrian king was busy elsewhere. {37:9} When he heard that Tirhakah, the Ethiopian king, was rolling in for a fight, Rabshakeh sent a message to Hezekiah. {37:10} He was like, "Don't let your God fool you, Hezekiah. He's saying Jerusalem won't fall to the Assyrians, but look at all the other lands they wrecked." {37:11} "You've seen what we did to other places. Think you'll escape?" {37:12} "What happened to the gods of the places we trashed? Gone, just like that. Your turn's coming, buddy." {37:13} "Where are those other kings now? Gone with the wind, my dude." {37:14} So, Hezekiah got the message, headed to the temple, and laid it all out before God. {37:15} Then he hit up God with a prayer session.

{38:1} So, like, Hezekiah was seriously sick, like, about to kick the bucket. Then Isaiah, the prophet, rolled up to him and dropped a bombshell from the Big Man upstairs, saying, "Get your affairs in order, dude, 'cause you're outta here." {38:2-3} Hezekiah was like, "Hold up, God, hear me out," and started pouring his heart out in prayer, bawling his eyes out. {38:4-5} Then God hit Isaiah up with a message, like, "Tell Hezekiah I heard his cries and saw his tears. Tell him I'm adding 15 more years to his life and throwing in some city-saving bonus points." {38:6-8} "Oh, and check this out, I'm gonna flip time back on the sundial by ten notches to prove I mean business." {38:9} So, Hezekiah jotted down his thoughts when he was on his deathbed and then made a full recovery. {38:10} He was like, "Thought I was done for, ready to meet the Grim Reaper at death's door, but looks like I've been saved from the brink." {38:11} "I thought I'd never see the light of day again, never kick it with the living, but here I am, back in the game." {38:12} "My days felt numbered, like a tent packed up, my life hanging by a thread, but now I'm feeling the recovery vibes." {38:13} "I thought I'd be torn apart, bones shattered like a lion's prey, but now it's a whole new day." {38:14} "I was chirping like a bird in sorrow, mourning like a dove, eyes strained looking up, feeling oppressed, hoping for a break." {38:15} "What can I say? God spoke, and now here I am, living softly, still feeling the bitterness but grateful for the second chance." {38:16} "God's the real MVP, bringing me back from the brink, giving life to my spirit." {38:17} "I was drowning in bitterness, but God showed me love, pulling me out of the pit, tossing my sins out of sight." {38:18-19} "The dead can't sing your praises, can't celebrate you, but the living sure can. I'm here to spread the word, from one generation to the next." {38:20-21} "God was ready to save me, so now we're jamming out in the house of the Lord, singing songs with stringed instruments for the rest of our days." {38:21} Isaiah was like, "Yo, grab some figs, slap 'em on the boil, and watch Hezekiah bounce back." {38:22} Hezekiah was like, "What's the sign that I'm good to hit up the house of the Lord again?"

{39:1} So, like, at that time Merodach-baladan, the son of Baladan, king of Babylon, slid some letters and a gift to Hezekiah 'cause he heard he'd been sick and bounced back. {39:2} Hezekiah was stoked and flexed his crib, showing off all his dope stuff—silver, gold, spices, precious ointments, armor, and everything in his stash. He didn't hold back, showing them everything he had. {39:3} Then Isaiah the prophet rolled up to Hezekiah, like, "What's the deal with these dudes? Where they from?" And Hezekiah was like, "They're from way out in Babylon, man." {39:4} So Isaiah's all, "What'd they peep in your crib?" And Hezekiah's like, "Everything, man. Showed 'em all my stash, no secrets." {39:5} Then Isaiah drops the bomb, "Listen up, Hezekiah, here's what the LORD's saying." {39:6} "The day's coming when everything in your crib, and all your ancestors' loot, is gonna get hauled off to Babylon. LORD said it, so it's happening." {39:7} "And they're gonna snatch up your sons too, make 'em eunuchs in the king of Babylon's palace." {39:8} Hezekiah's like, "Cool with me, Isaiah. Peace and truth in my time."

{40:1} Yo, peeps, cheer up! God's saying it's all good for His crew. {40:2} Speak kindly to Jerusalem, let her know the war's over, her sins are forgiven. She got double grace for all her mess-ups. {40:3} Listen up to the voice in the wild, making a path for the LORD, straight through the desert. {40:4} Valleys gonna rise up, mountains and hills gonna lay low, all the twisted paths gonna be straightened, rough places smoothed out. {40:5} And everyone's gonna see the glory of the LORD together, 'cause what He says, goes. {40:6} Dude's like, "What should I say?" All flesh is temporary, like grass, flowers—they fade 'cause the LORD's breath blows on 'em. People? Just grass, man. {40:7} Grass withers, flowers fade, 'cause the LORD's breath blows on 'em. People? Just grass, man. {40:8} Grass withers, flowers fade, but God's Word? It's solid, forever. {40:9} Yo, Zion, spread the good news, climb up high and shout it out to Jerusalem—don't hold back! Say to Judah's cities, "Check out your God!" {40:10} The Lord GOD's coming in strong, His arm's taking charge. He's got rewards and work lined up. {40:11} He's gonna care for His peeps like a shepherd, gathering 'em up, carrying the lambs, leading gently those with young. {40:12} Who measured the waters in the palm of his hand, marked out the heavens with his handspan, measured out the dust of the earth, weighed the mountains and hills? {40:13} Who's His advisor? Who taught Him? {40:14} Who's His counselor? Who schooled Him in justice and knowledge, showed Him the path of understanding? {40:15} Nations are like a drop in the bucket, dust on a scale. Islands? They're nothing to Him. {40:16} Lebanon's not enough for a fire, its beasts not enough for a burnt offering. {40:17} All nations are nothing to Him, less than nothing, just vanity. {40:18} So, who you gonna compare to God? What you gonna liken to Him? {40:19} People make idols, gold-plating 'em, casting silver chains. {40:20} Some poor sap picks a tree that won't rot, hires a craftsman to carve an idol that won't budge. {40:21} Don't you know? Haven't you heard? Wasn't it told to you from the start? Haven't you understood since the earth was founded? {40:22} Dude sits on the earth's circle, peeps below look like grasshoppers. He stretches out the heavens like a curtain, sets them up like a tent. {40:23} He makes rulers worthless, judges nothing. {40:24} They won't take root, won't grow. Dude's gonna blow on 'em, they'll wither away, get swept up like stubble. {40:25} So, who you gonna compare to me? Who's my equal? asks the Holy One. {40:26} Look up high, see who made all this, calls 'em out by name—'cause of His power, not one's missing. {40:27} Why you saying, "My way's hidden from the LORD, my cause is ignored by my God"? {40:28} Don't you know? Haven't you heard? The everlasting God, the LORD, Creator of the earth's ends, never gets tired, never gets weary. His understanding's beyond searching. {40:29} He gives power to the tired, increases the strength of the weak. {40:30} Even young dudes get tired and drop, {40:31} but those who wait on the LORD get their strength renewed. They soar like eagles, run without getting tired, walk without fainting.

{41:1} Yo, islands, hush up and let the people get their act together, then let's talk it out and judge together. {41:2} Who's the one who raised up that righteous dude from the east, called him up, gave him nations to rule over? He made 'em dust for his sword and stubble for his bow. {41:3} He chased 'em down and came out on top, even in places he hadn't been before. {41:4} Who's been making things happen since way back? Me, the LORD, the OG, from the beginning to the end, that's who. {41:5} When the islands saw it, they freaked out, and the ends of the earth got scared and came close. {41:6} They all helped each other out, saying, "Stay strong, bro." {41:7} So the carpenter cheered on the goldsmith, and the dude who smoothed out metal encouraged the guy who hammered on the anvil, saying, "It's ready to be soldered," and they nailed it down so it wouldn't budge. {41:8} But you, Israel, you're my servant, Jacob, my chosen one, Abraham's descendant, my buddy. {41:9} I plucked you from the ends of the earth, called you from the top dogs, and told you, "You're my servant, I chose you, and I'm not letting you go." {41:10} Don't sweat it, 'cause I'm with you. Don't freak out, 'cause I'm your God. I'll make you strong, help you out, and support you with my righteous hand. {41:11} Check it, anyone who's been ticked off at you will be embarrassed and humiliated—they'll be worthless. Those who've gone up against you will vanish into thin air. {41:12} You'll look for 'em but won't find 'em, even those who fought against you will be worthless, like they never existed. {41:13} 'Cause I, the LORD your God, will hold your hand, saying, "Don't be afraid, I got your back." {41:14} Don't trip, Jacob, even you, Israelites, 'cause I got you, says the LORD, your redeemer, the Holy One of Israel. {41:15} I'll make you into a new, sharp tool for threshing, so you can crush mountains and turn hills to dust. {41:16} You'll scatter 'em with the wind and whirlwind, and you'll rejoice in the LORD, celebrating the Holy One of Israel. {41:17} When the poor and needy are looking for water and can't find any, when they're desperate, I, the God of Israel, will hear them and won't abandon them. {41:18} I'll make rivers flow in high places and springs in valleys. I'll turn the wilderness into a pool and dry land into springs. {41:19} I'll plant cedar, acacia, myrtle, and olive trees in the wilderness, and fir, pine, and box trees in the desert, so everyone can see, know, understand, and recognize that the LORD did this, and the Holy One of Israel created it. {41:20} Bring it on, says the LORD, make your case, says the King of Jacob. {41:21} Let 'em show us what'll happen, tell us about past events, so we can understand and know what's coming. {41:22} Predict the future, if you can, so we can know if you're really gods. Do something good or bad to impress us and make us pay attention together. {41:23-24} But you're worthless, and your work's worthless too. Anyone who chooses you is disgusting. {41:25} I brought someone from the north, and he's coming. From the east, he'll call on my name and crush princes like mortar and clay. {41:26} Who predicted this from the start, so we could say he's righteous? Nope, no one. No one heard your words, and no one's saying anything. {41:27} The first one will say to Zion, "Look, they're here," and I'll send someone to Jerusalem with good news. {41:28} But I looked around, and there was no one, not even a counselor who could answer a word when I asked. {41:29} They're all useless, their works are worth nothing, their idols are worthless, just wind and confusion.

{42:1} Look at my servant, the one I support, my chosen one who makes me happy. I've put my spirit on him; he'll bring justice to the nations. {42:2} He won't shout or make a scene in the streets. {42:3} He won't break a bruised reed or snuff out a smoldering wick; he'll bring justice faithfully. {42:4} He won't give up or be discouraged until he establishes justice on earth, and the islands wait for his law. {42:5} So says God the LORD, the one who made the heavens, stretched them out, spread out the earth and all that comes from it, the one who gives breath to the people on it and spirit to those who walk on it. {42:6} I, the LORD, called you in righteousness, will hold your hand, keep you, and make you a covenant for the people, a light for the Gentiles. {42:7} He'll open blind eyes, free prisoners, and release those sitting in darkness from prison. {42:8} I am the LORD; that's my name, and I won't give my glory to another or my praise to idols. {42:9} Past events have happened, and I'm declaring new things. Before they happen, I'm telling you about them. {42:10} Sing a new song to the LORD, praise him from the ends of the earth, you who sail the sea and everything in it, you islands and their inhabitants. {42:11} Let the wilderness and its towns raise their voices, the settlements where Kedar lives; let the people of Sela sing, let them shout from the mountaintops. {42:12} Let them give glory to the LORD and declare his praise on the islands. {42:13} The LORD will go out like a mighty man, stirring up jealousy like a warrior. He'll cry out, roar, and prevail against his enemies. {42:14} I've been quiet for a long time, holding back, but now I'll cry out like a woman in labor; I'll destroy and devour all at once. {42:15} I'll make mountains and hills desolate, dry up all their vegetation, turn rivers into islands, and dry up the pools. {42:16} So, like, I'll totally guide the blind down paths they never even knew existed, lighting up the darkness for them and straightening out all the messed-up stuff. I'm not gonna bail on them, you know? {42:17} Those who trust in idols, thinking they're like, divine and all, are gonna be majorly embarrassed and turned away. {42:18} Yo, listen up, you deaf ones, and open your eyes, you blind ones, so you can actually see. {42:19} Who's more blind than my servant, or deafer than the messenger I sent? Who's more blind than someone who's supposed to know better, or more blind than the LORD's servant? {42:20} They see a lot of stuff, but they don't really get it; they hear a bunch, but they're not really listening. {42:21} The LORD's totally stoked about doing what's right; he's gonna make the law super important and respectable. {42:22} But dang, my people are getting totally ripped off and jacked up; they're trapped and hidden away, no one's rescuing them or even saying, "Hey, let's fix this." {42:23} Who's paying attention to this? Who's actually listening and thinking about what's gonna happen next? {42:24} Who let Jacob get looted and Israel get robbed? Wasn't it the LORD, the one we dissed by not following his rules? They wouldn't walk the walk or obey his laws, so he got super mad and went all out on them, but they didn't even realize it or care.

{43:1} Yo, peeps, listen up, 'cause the LORD who made you, Jacob, and formed you, Israel, is speaking. Don't trip, 'cause I got your back—I redeemed you, called you by name, you're mine. {43:2} When you go through tough times, I'll be there, keeping you from getting swamped, even when it feels like you're walking through fire, you won't get burned. {43:3} 'Cause I'm the LORD your God, the Holy One of Israel, your Savior. I traded Egypt, Ethiopia, and Seba for you. {43:4} You're precious to me, honored, loved. I'll swap people for you, give up nations for your life. {43:5} So, chill out, 'cause I'm with you. I'll bring your descendants from everywhere, gather 'em up from all over. {43:6} I'll tell the north, "Let 'em go," and the south, "Don't hold 'em back." Bring my sons from far away, my daughters from the ends of the earth. {43:7} Everyone called by my name, I made 'em for my glory, formed 'em, created 'em. {43:8} Bring out the blind who can see and the deaf who can hear. {43:9} Let all the nations gather and people assemble. Who among them can declare this, show us what happened in the past? Let 'em bring their witnesses to justify themselves or hear the truth. {43:10} You're my witnesses, says the LORD, my chosen servant, so you know and believe me, understand that I'm the real deal. Before me, no God was formed, and there won't be one after me. {43:11} I, only I, am the LORD, and there's no other savior beside me. {43:12} I declared, saved, and showed, even when there was no other god among you. So you're my witnesses that I'm God. {43:13} Even before the day began, I am He, and no one can snatch you from my hand. I'll do what I want, who's gonna stop me? {43:14} So says the LORD, your redeemer, the Holy One of Israel: For your sake, I sent to Babylon and brought down all their big shots, the Chaldeans, whose shouts echo from their ships. {43:15} I am the LORD, your Holy One, Israel's creator, your King. {43:16} So says the LORD, who makes a way in the sea, a path in mighty waters. {43:17} He brings out chariots, horses, armies, and power, but they'll lie down, never to rise again, extinguished, like snuffed-out wicks. {43:18} Forget about the past, don't dwell on old stuff. {43:19} 'Cause I'm about to do something new, it's already springing up, don't you see it? I'll make a way in the wilderness, rivers in the desert. {43:20} Even the wild animals will honor me, dragons and owls, 'cause I'm providing water in the wilderness, rivers in the desert, quenching the thirst of my chosen people. {43:21} I formed this people for myself, they'll shout my praise. {43:22} But you haven't called on me, Jacob, you've been ignoring me, Israel. {43:23} You haven't brought me your offerings, honored me with sacrifices. I didn't make you serve me with offerings or wear you out with incense. {43:24} You haven't bought me sweet cane with money, or filled me with the fat of your sacrifices. You've made me serve with your sins, wearied me with your iniquities. {43:25} But I, even I, am the one who blots out your transgressions for my own sake, won't remember your sins. {43:26} Remind me of what I've done, let's argue it out, declare your case so you can be justified. {43:27} Your first father sinned, and your leaders have rebelled against me. {43:28} So I've profaned the leaders of the sanctuary, given Jacob over to destruction, Israel to scorn.

{44:1} But now, listen up, Jacob my servant, Israel, whom I've chosen. {44:2} So says the LORD, who made you, formed you from the womb, who'll help you—don't be afraid, Jacob, my servant, Jesurun, whom I've chosen. {44:3} 'Cause I'll pour water on the thirsty, floods on dry ground. I'll pour out my Spirit on your descendants, my blessing on your offspring. {44:4} They'll sprout up among the grass, like willows by streams. {44:5} One will say, "I belong to the LORD," another will use Jacob's name, and another will sign up to the LORD, calling themselves Israel. {44:6} So says the LORD, the King of Israel, and his redeemer, the LORD of hosts: I'm the first, the last, and there's no God beside me. {44:7-8} Who else can declare and order things like I do, since I appointed the ancient people? Let them declare what's coming. Don't be afraid, don't forget, I've told you from the beginning. You're my witnesses. Is there any God beside me? Nope, I don't know any. {44:9} All those who make idols are worthless, their precious things won't profit them. They're their own witnesses, blind and ignorant, they'll be ashamed. {44:10} Who made a god, molded an idol that's good for nothing? {44:11} Their creators will be ashamed, they're just ordinary people. Let them gather together, they'll be afraid, ashamed together. {44:12} The blacksmith works in the coals, hammers out the idol with his strong arms, hungry and weak. {44:13} The carpenter measures it out, marks it with a line, shapes it with planes, and marks it with a compass, making it look like a man, a beautiful idol that'll stay in the house. {44:14} He cuts down cedars, chooses cypresses and oaks from the forest, plants an ash tree, and the rain nourishes it. {44:15} Then it becomes fuel for a person to burn, to keep warm, bake bread, even make a god and worship it, a carved image to bow down to. {44:16} He burns part for fire, cooks food, and says, "Ah, I'm warm, I've seen the fire." {44:17} The rest he makes into a god, a carved image, and falls down to worship it, pray to it, saying, "Save me, you're my god." {44:18} They don't know or understand, their eyes are shut, hearts closed. {44:19} No one stops to think, no

{45:1} Yo, check it, the LORD's speaking straight to Cyrus, sayin', "I got your back, bro. I'm gonna make nations bow before you, openin' gates like it's nothin'. And I'll hook you up with mad treasures, so you know it's me, the real deal, the God of Israel." {45:2} I'll pave the way for you, smooth out all the bumps, breakin' down any barriers in your path. {45:3} And those hidden riches? Yeah, I'm handin' 'em over, so you see who's really runnin' the show. {45:4} I'm doin' this for my people, Jacob and Israel, even though you might not realize it yet. {45:5} I'm the LORD, ain't no one else. I got your back even if you don't know it. {45:6} Everyone gonna know who's callin' the shots, from sunrise to sunset. I'm the only game in town. {45:7} I'm the one makin' everything happen, bringin' peace and even stirrin' up trouble when I need to. {45:8} Heaven's droppin' some righteousness, earth's poppin' with salvation, all 'cause I said so. {45:9} Don't be messin' with your Maker, you're just clay in the potter's hands. {45:10} Don't diss your pops or your mom, 'cause I'm the one who brought you into this world. {45:11} I'm the Holy One of Israel, I know what's up. {45:12} I made everything, stretched out the heavens, got all the stars in line. {45:13} I got your back, Cyrus, you're gonna rebuild my city and let my people go, no strings attached. {45:14} Even Egypt, Ethiopia, and the Sabeans gonna bow down to you, knowin' that the real power's with you. {45:15} I might be low-key sometimes, but I'm still your God, savin' the day. {45:16} Anybody makin' idols gonna be embarrassed real quick. {45:17} But Israel, you're safe with me, forever. {45:18} I made everything for a reason, so don't doubt it. {45:19} I ain't keepin' secrets, I'm all about truth and righteousness. {45:20} Listen up, all you survivors out there, stop worshipin' useless idols. {45:21} Who else but me can predict the future? I'm the only one who's got your back. {45:22} Look to me for salvation, I'm the real deal. {45:23} Every knee's gonna bow, every tongue's gonna swear loyalty to me, you can count on it. {45:24} Those who trust in me gonna find strength and righteousness. {45:25} Israel's seed gonna be justified and glorify me.

{46:1} Idols like Bel and Nebo? They're worthless, can't even carry themselves. {46:2} They're all captured, useless in the end. {46:3} Listen up, Israel, I've been with you since day one. {46:4} I got you covered from cradle to grave, 'cause I made you, and I'm gonna see you through. {46:5} Who you gonna compare me to? No one can match up. {46:6} People wastin' their cash on idols, thinkin' they'll save 'em. {46:7} Carrying idols around like they mean somethin', but they're just dead weight. {46:8} Remember this, wise up, you rebellious folks. {46:9} I'm the OG God, ain't nobody like me, and I call the shots from start to finish. {46:10} I see it all, from beginning to end, and what I say goes, no question. {46:11} I'll bring in whoever I need to get the job done, you can bet on it. {46:12} Pay attention, you stubborn ones, righteousness is comin' close. {46:13} My salvation's on the way, and it ain't takin' forever. And I'm settin' up shop in Zion for all to see, 'cause that's where my glory's at.

{47:1} Alright, listen up Babylon, you ain't gonna be called soft and delicate no more. Time to get down and dirty, grindin' away like there's no tomorrow. {47:2} Your secrets ain't stayin' hidden, your shame's gonna be out in the open. I'm comin' for vengeance, and I ain't playin' nice. {47:3} The LORD, our redeemer, he's about to show you who's boss. {47:4} So sit down, shut up, Babylon, your reign's over. {47:5} You thought you were untouchable, but you're about to get a reality check. {47:6} You messed with my people, showed 'em no mercy, and now it's payback time. {47:7} You thought you'd reign forever, but you ain't think about the consequences. {47:8} Livin' it up, thinkin' you're untouchable, but it's all gonna come crashing down on you. {47:9} Your wickedness ain't gonna save you, your sorcery's gonna backfire big time. {47:10} Trustin' in your evil ways, thinkin' nobody's watchin'? Think again. {47:11} Disaster's comin' for you, and you ain't gonna see it comin'. {47:12} Keep relyin' on your tricks, your magic ain't gonna save you. {47:13} All your advisors ain't gonna do squat when the heat comes. {47:14} Your merchants ain't gonna be able to bail you out, they'll desert you when things get rough. {47:15} You're goin' down, Babylon, ain't nobody gonna save you.

{48:1} Yo, listen up, Jacob and Israel, you claim to follow the LORD but you ain't doin' it right. {48:2} You claim to be all about Jerusalem, but you ain't livin' up to it. {48:3} I've been tellin' you what's up from the jump, and it's all goin' down just like I said. {48:4} You're stubborn as heck, but I've been warnin' you since day one. {48:5} I ain't lettin' you give credit to your idols for my work. {48:6} I've been droppin' truth bombs on you, but you ain't payin' attention. {48:7} You think you know it all, but you don't know squat. {48:8} You've been ignorin' me since day one, but I know how you really are. {48:9} I'm holdin' back my anger for now, but don't push it. {48:10} I've been testin' you, puttin' you through the fire. {48:11} I ain't doin' this for you, I'm doin' it for me, so my name stays clean. {48:12} Listen up, Jacob and Israel, I'm the first and the last, the one who laid the earth's foundation and stretched out the heavens. {48:13} Gather 'round and listen up, who else can predict the future like me? The LORD's got Babylon's number. {48:14} I called the shots, and Babylon's gonna get what's comin' to 'em. {48:15} It's all goin' down just like I said, Babylon's gonna get a beatdown. {48:16} Come closer, listen up, I ain't been keepin' secrets. {48:17} I'm your redeemer, your guide, listen to me and you'll prosper. {48:18} If only you'd listened to me from the start, you'd be livin' in peace and prosperity. {48:19} Your descendants would be numerous and prosperous, never forgotten. {48:20} Get outta Babylon, run from the Chaldeans, shout it from the rooftops, the LORD's savin' Jacob. {48:21} He kept you hydrated in the desert, even made water flow from a rock. {48:22} But there ain't no peace for the wicked, says the LORD.

{49:1} Yo, listen up, all you folks out there, even if you're miles away. The big man upstairs has been calling the shots since before I was even born, he's been talking about me since my mom was carrying me. {49:2} He's given me this slick tongue, sharp as a sword, and kept me hidden away until it was time to do my thing. {49:3} He's telling me, "You're my main dude, Israel, the one I'm gonna shine through." {49:4} I was like, "Man, I've been putting in work, but it feels like I'm spinning my wheels." But hey, my boss upstairs knows what's up. {49:5} So now, the big guy who made me from the start has a plan: even if Israel's still scattered, I'm gonna shine like a boss in his eyes, and he's gonna be my backup. {49:6} And get this, it's not just about Israel anymore; I'm going global, bringing light to everyone, not just the hometown crowd. {49:7} The big man upstairs, the one who saves Israel and is totally holy, is backing me up. Even if people diss me, kings are gonna take notice and show some respect because of the big guy who's got my back. {49:8} The big man's telling me, "When the time's right, I've got your back. I'll make sure you're legit and set you up as the real deal." {49:9} I'll be telling prisoners to break free and those in the dark to show themselves. They'll find their way, no more hunger or thirst, and no scorching sun, 'cause the big guy's got their back, leading them to water. {49:10} He's even gonna make the mountains into highways, and everyone's gonna come running, from all over the place. {49:11} So, shout out to the heavens, earth, and mountains; the big man's giving his people some TLC and showing mercy to those who've had a rough time. {49:12} But some are feeling abandoned, thinking the big guy forgot about them. {49:13} But hey, even if a mom forgets her kid, the big man won't forget about us. He's got us marked, always on his mind. {49:14} Your kids will come running back to you, even the ones who caused trouble before. {49:15} So get ready, 'cause even the nations are gonna pitch in and help out, carrying your kids in their arms and on their shoulders. {49:16} Even kings will step up as babysitters and queens as wet nurses, bowing down to you, 'cause they know who's in charge. {49:17} So don't worry about the bullies and those who messed you up; they'll be the ones scrambling to get out of your way. {49:18} Look around, everyone's coming to you, swearing loyalty like it's a fashion trend, decking you out like a bride. {49:19} Your once-desolate land will be bursting at the seams with people, and those who thought they got the best of you will be long gone. {49:20} Your kids will be like, "This place is too cramped, make room!" {49:21} You'll be wondering where all these kids came from, feeling abandoned and alone, but don't worry, the big guy's got a plan. {49:22} He's gonna rally the nations and show everyone what's up, bringing your kids back home in style. {49:23} So, chill out, those who trust in the big man; he won't let you down. {49:24} Can the tough guys keep what they've taken, or will those they've captured be set free? {49:25} But hey, the big guy says even the toughest captors will lose their grip, and those who've been oppressed will be set free. {49:26} And those who messed with you? Yeah, they're gonna get what's coming to them, big time.

{50:1} So, the big guy's like, "Where's the paperwork for your mom's divorce? Who's claiming you owe them?" But hey, it's not because of some debt; you've messed yourselves up with your own mistakes. {50:2} So, when the big guy calls, why's everyone ghosting? He's still got the power to save, to make the oceans dry up with just a word. {50:3} He can even cover the sky in darkness and make sackcloth out of the clouds. {50:4} He's given me the gift of gab, so I know how to drop wisdom when it's needed; he's always there, teaching me what's up. {50:5} I'm all ears when he's talking, not rebellious or running away. {50:6} I've taken hits and kept on going, not hiding my face in shame or backing down. {50:7} 'Cause the big guy's got my back; I won't be embarrassed. I'm standing strong, not backing down. {50:8} Who's gonna step up and challenge me? Let's face off, but trust me, you won't win. {50:9} The big guy's got my back; who's gonna stand against me? They'll all fade away like old clothes, eaten up by moths. {50:10} So, if you're feeling lost in the dark with no light, trust in the big guy's name and lean on him. {50:11} But for those who try to make it on their own, relying on their own light, they'll end up in a world of hurt.

{51:1} Yo, listen up all you righteousness seekers, pay attention! Check out where you come from, remember your roots. {51:2} Think about Abraham and Sarah, they're the OGs. I blessed them, and I'm gonna bless you too. {51:3} Zion, get ready for some comfort, I'm gonna turn your wastelands into paradise. {51:4} My law's coming, it's gonna shine a light for everyone. {51:5} My righteousness is right around the corner, salvation's on the move, and I'm gonna bring justice. {51:6} Look up, the heavens are gonna disappear like smoke, but my salvation's gonna last forever. {51:7} If you know what's right, don't be scared of what people say. {51:8} Those who oppose you? They're gonna fade away like moth-eaten clothes, but my righteousness? It's here to stay. {51:9} Time to wake up, arm of the LORD, remember who's in charge here. {51:10} Remember how I parted the sea? Yeah, that was me. {51:11} Those who trust in me? They're coming back to Zion singing, joy replacing sorrow. {51:12} I'm the one comforting you, so why you sweatin' what mere mortals can do? {51:13} Forgettin' who made you? Remember who stretched out the heavens and laid the earth's foundation. {51:14} I'm the one who's got your back, so stand tall, Jerusalem. {51:15} You've been through some tough times, but I'm takin' that cup of suffering outta your hands, passin' it on to those who oppressed you.

{52:1} Wake up, Zion, put on your best threads, 'cause only the pure are comin' in. {52:2} Dust yourself off, Jerusalem, shake off those chains. {52:3} You sold yourselves for nothin', but I'm buyin' you back, no cash required. {52:4} My people went through hell, but it wasn't their fault. {52:5} They've been howlin' under oppression, and my name's been dragged through the mud. {52:6} But they'll know who I am, and they'll know it's me speaking. {52:7} How awesome are the messengers bringin' good news, proclaimin' peace and salvation. {52:8} Your watchmen are gonna sing in unison when I bring Zion back. {52:9} Let the ruins of Jerusalem rejoice, 'cause I've comforted my people and redeemed Jerusalem. {52:10} Everyone's gonna see the salvation I bring, no one's gonna miss it. {52:11} Get outta there, leave the unclean behind, be pure as you carry the LORD's vessels. {52:12} No need to rush, I'm leading the way, and I've got your back. {52:13} Check it, my servant's gonna be smart, he's gonna be top dog. {52:14} He'll shock a lot of people, lookin' worse than anyone ever did. {52:15} He'll change the game for many nations, leavin' kings speechless.

{53:1} Yo, who's actually buying into what we're saying? And who's really seeing the big man's power? {53:2} He's gonna come up like a little plant in a dry spot, not looking all fancy or anything. {53:3} People are straight up dissing him, treating him like garbage. We're acting like we don't even know him. {53:4} But get this, he's taking on all our pain and suffering, even though we thought he was getting what he deserved. {53:5} Turns out, he's taking hits for our screw-ups, getting beat down for our mistakes. His suffering brings us peace, and his scars are our healing. {53:6} We've all gone off on our own, doing our own thing, and the big man's laying it all on him. {53:7} He's getting slammed and not saying a word, taking it like a lamb to the slaughter. {53:8} They dragged him off and did him dirty, but who's even talking about his side of the story? He got cut off before he could even tell it, all because of our screw-ups. {53:9} He ended up buried with the bad guys, but he did nothing wrong, not a single lie came out of his mouth. {53:10} But it's all good, 'cause the big man's cool with it. He's gonna see the light at the end of the tunnel, living on and doing the big man's work.

{53:11} He'll see the results of all he's been through and be satisfied, 'cause he's gonna set things straight for a lot of people. {53:12} So, he'll get a piece of the action with the big shots, sharing the spoils 'cause he gave everything, even his life, for us screw-ups.

{54:1} Hey, you who've been feeling empty and like you've got nothing to show, start singing! Even if you've never had kids, you're gonna have more than those who've been married forever, says the big man upstairs. {54:2} Make room, spread out your living space, and don't hold back. Your influence is gonna spread far and wide, bringing life to places that were once dead. {54:3} Don't worry about running out of room; your descendants are gonna take over new territory, making even the deserted cities thrive. {54:4} Don't sweat it; you won't be embarrassed or ashamed anymore. You'll forget all about the tough times and the loneliness, 'cause your Maker's got your back. {54:5} Your connection with the big man is like a marriage; he's got your back no matter what. He's the ultimate power in the universe. {54:6} You may have felt abandoned and alone, but the big man's picking you up and dusting you off. {54:7} He may have stepped back for a bit, but he's coming back with open arms and loads of mercy. {54:8} He might have seemed ticked off for a moment, but he's all about showing you love that lasts forever, says the big man who saves you. {54:9} Just like he promised never to flood the earth again like in Noah's time, he's promising never to give up on you or scold you again. {54:10} Even if the earth falls apart and the hills crumble, his love for you will never fade, and his promise of peace will never be broken, says the big man who's all about showing mercy. {54:11} So, you who've been through the storm and back, feeling like nobody's got your back, check this out: I'm gonna decorate your life with the finest materials, making you shine like precious jewels. {54:12} Your life's gonna be like a work of art, with beauty everywhere you look. {54:13} Your kids are gonna be straight-up wise, and they're gonna know peace like nobody's business. {54:14} You'll be established in righteousness, far from oppression and fear. {54:15} Anyone who tries to mess with you is gonna fall flat on their face. {54:16} I'm the one who made the people who make weapons, and I'm the one who controls how they're used. {54:17} No weapon formed against you will succeed, and anyone who tries to take you down will get shut down. This is what I promise to all my faithful servants, says the big man upstairs.

{55:1} Yo, anyone feelin' thirsty? Come chill by the water, even if your pockets are empty. You can grab some grub, sip on some wine and milk, all on the house. {55:2} Why waste your cash on stuff that won't fill you up? Listen up and chow down on the good stuff, let your soul feast on that richness. {55:3} Tune in and come vibe with me, your soul's gonna be livin' large. I'll hook you up with a rock-solid deal, like David-style mercy that lasts forever. {55:4} David's been repping my squad hard, leading the way for the people. {55:5} Watch out, 'cause nations you never knew about are gonna be all up in your DMs, thanks to the LORD reppin' hard. {55:6} Better hit up the LORD while he's around, give him a shout while he's still close by. {55:7} Time for the wicked to ditch their ways and the shady ones to drop their schemes. Come back to the LORD, he's all about that mercy and forgiveness. {55:8} My thoughts ain't like yours, says the LORD. My ways? Way above yours. {55:9} Rain and snow do their thing, makin' the earth lush and fruitful. {55:10} My word? It's gonna go out and get stuff done, no coming back empty-handed. {55:11} Get ready to bounce with joy, peace leadin' the way. Even the mountains and trees are gonna be hyped. {55:12} No more thorns or briars, just good vibes all around, all to give props to the LORD.

{56:1} Listen up, keep it real and do what's right. My salvation's comin' in hot, and my righteousness? 'Bout to be lit. {56:2} Props to anyone who stays true, keeps the Sabbath holy, and keeps their hands clean from evil. {56:3} Don't let outsiders front like they're not part of the fam, or eunuchs think they're left out. {56:4} If they're down with the Sabbath and down with me, they're gonna get VIP treatment in my crib. {56:5} Even better than sons and daughters, they're gonna get a name that lasts forever. {56:6} Outsiders who come to rep the LORD, keep the Sabbath legit, and roll with my crew? They're gonna get the royal treatment too. {56:7} They'll be kickin' it on my holy mountain, vibin' in my house of prayer. I'm accepting all offerings and sacrifices, 'cause my house is for everyone. {56:8} The LORD's bringin' in the outcasts of Israel, and he's not stoppin' there. {56:9} Hey, all you wild animals, come feast. {56:10} But these watchmen? Straight up clueless. Dumb dogs who can't even bark, too busy snoozin'. {56:11} Always hungry, always greedy, never satisfied. Shepherds who can't even understand their own flock, just lookin' out for themselves. {56:12} They're like, "Let's party, get wasted!" Always livin' for today, never thinkin' 'bout tomorrow.

{57:1} So, like, righteous people are dying, and nobody even cares. The kind-hearted are taken away, but nobody stops to think that maybe it's because they're being spared from the messed-up future. {57:2} They're just chilling in peace, catching some Z's, each one walking their path of goodness. {57:3} But yo, you sons of sorcery, offspring of cheaters and players, what's your deal? {57:4} Who are you mocking? Who are you sticking your tongues out at? You're just a bunch of liars, getting all hyped up over idols and sacrificing kids in the valleys and under rocks. {57:5} You're all about those idols, even sacrificing to them by the stream. Like, seriously, is that supposed to make me happy? {57:6} Setting up shop on high mountains, making sacrifices left and right. {57:7} You even got cozy with other gods, making secret pacts and loving every minute of it. {57:8} You've got all these secret spots for worship, but you forgot about me. You're out there chasing after others, enlarging your territory, and loving every minute of it. {57:9} You're out here rubbing elbows with kings, wearing expensive perfume, and sending messengers all over the place, stooping down low for what? {57:10} You're exhausted from running around, but you won't admit defeat. You found some thrill in your life, so you're not willing to change your ways. {57:11} Who are you scared of? Who are you trying to impress with your lies? You forgot all about me, but I've been quiet for too long, and you're not even scared of me anymore. {57:12} I'll lay out your righteousness and your deeds, but guess what? They ain't gonna save you. {57:13} Cry out all you want, gather your little groups, but it's all gonna blow away like dust. Those who trust in me, though, they're gonna inherit the land and take over my holy mountain. {57:14} They'll be saying, "Clear the way, make it easy for my people." {57:15} 'Cause I'm the big boss, chilling in my eternal crib, hanging out with the humble and the brokenhearted, giving them life. {57:16} I'm not gonna be angry forever 'cause that would just be too much for y'all. {57:17} I was mad 'cause you were all about chasing after what you wanted, but now I'm gonna heal you up. {57:18} I'll guide you and bring comfort to you and all your crew who've been crying. {57:19} I'm all about spreading peace and healing, whether you're near or far. {57:20} But for the wicked, it's like they're constantly tossed around in a storm, stirring up dirt and filth. {57:21} They won't find peace, says my big man upstairs.

{58:1} So, like, shout it out, don't hold back, let everyone know where they're messing up, especially the house of Jacob. {58:2} They act all religious, seeking me out every day, acting like they're all about doing what's right and sticking to the rules. {58:3} But then they're all, "Why doesn't God notice us when we fast and pray?" But guess what? You're fasting for all the wrong reasons, just to start fights and act tough. {58:4} Is that what fasting's about? Trying to show off and pick fights? Nah, that's not gonna cut it, especially not today. {58:5} This is what real fasting looks like: standing up against injustice, freeing the oppressed, and breaking every chain of oppression. {58:6} It's about sharing what you have with those in need, giving shelter to the homeless, clothing the naked, and not turning away from your own family. {58:7} Then your light will shine like the morning, your healing will come quickly, and your righteousness will lead the way. {58:8} When you call out, I'll be there; when you cry, I'll answer. But first, you gotta let go of oppression and stop pointing fingers and talking trash. {58:9} If you help out the hungry and care for the afflicted, then your light will shine even in the darkest times, and your darkness will be as bright as noonday. {58:10} I'll guide you through every struggle, satisfy your soul in the dry seasons, and make you thrive like a well-watered garden. {58:11} Your people will rebuild what's been torn down, restore what's been broken, and be known as the ones who fix things up. {58:12} If you treat the Sabbath with respect and honor it as a day of rest and worship, focusing on me and not on your own desires or words, {58:13} then you'll find joy in me, and I'll lift you up to great heights and bless you with the inheritance of your ancestors, 'cause I said so.

{59:1} Check it, the LORD's got mad power, ain't nothin' holding him back from savin'; his ears ain't deaf to your cries. {59:2} But yo, it's your sins that got you ghosted by God, he ain't even lookin' your way 'cause you're so messed up. {59:3} Your hands are covered in blood, fingers full of wickedness, and your lips? Spittin' lies left and right. {59:4} Ain't nobody speakin' up for justice or truth, they're all about that fake life, schemin' and causing chaos. {59:5} They're hatching snake eggs and spinning webs of deceit; mess with their stuff and you're done for. {59:6} But their webs ain't gonna cover 'em up; their evil deeds are out in the open for everyone to see. {59:7} They're all about that wicked life, running towards evil and shedding innocent blood. {59:8} They don't know the first thing about peace, always walking down crooked paths, and there's no chill in sight. {59:9} We're lost in the dark, waiting for a light that never comes; it's like we're blind, stumbling around even in broad daylight. {59:10} We're growling like bears, mourning like doves, looking for justice and salvation, but it's nowhere to be found. {59:11} Our sins are stacked up against us, and there's no escaping the consequences; truth's been trampled, and there's no fairness in sight. {59:12} It's like justice took a U-turn, and truth got kicked to the curb; ain't nobody standing up for what's right. {59:13} We're straight-up lying and rebelling against the LORD, talking smack and stirring up trouble from the heart. {59:14} Justice is a joke, and truth got lost in the streets; even doing good gets you targeted. {59:15} The LORD sees it all and ain't pleased; there's no one stepping up to make things right. {59:16} He looks around, sees no one's got it together, so he rolls up his sleeves and brings salvation himself; righteousness is his armor, and he's ready to throw down. {59:17} He's suiting up with righteousness and salvation, ready to bring the smackdown on his enemies; even the far-off islands gonna feel it. {59:18} People gonna learn to fear the LORD from all corners of the earth; when trouble comes knockin', the LORD's spirit gonna raise the standard. {59:19} The Redeemer's coming to Zion, and those who turn from their wicked ways gonna get blessed, says the LORD. {59:20} As for me, this is my deal with them, says the LORD: my spirit and my words ain't ever leaving their mouths, from now on, forever.

{60:1} Rise and shine, 'cause your time's come, and the LORD's glory's shining on you. {60:2} Darkness might be creeping in, but the LORD's light's gonna outshine it all. {60:3} The nations gonna flock to your light, and kings gonna be drawn to your brightness. {60:4} Look around, everyone's heading your way; your peeps coming from afar, daughters in tow. {60:5} You gonna be overflowing with blessings, 'cause everyone's bringing their A-game to you. {60:6} Gifts pouring in from every direction, camels and dromedaries loaded with gold and incense, all singing the LORD's praises. {60:7} Even the nomads bringing their flocks to honor you, offerings piling up on the altar, and I'm about to bless the house big time. {60:8} Who are these speeding in like clouds, like doves to their nest? {60:9} Even the far-off islands waiting for their cue, ships loaded with riches for the LORD, 'cause he's shown you mad love. {60:10} Outsiders gonna rebuild your walls, and their kings gonna serve you; I might've laid the smackdown on you before, but now it's all about the love. {60:11} Your gates staying open 24/7, no breaks, so everyone can bring their riches to you, and kings can come pay their respects. {60:12} Any nation that tries to front gonna get wrecked; those fools gonna end up in ruins. {60:13} The best of the best coming your way, making your sanctuary shine; I'm about to make my presence known in a big way. {60:14} Your former enemies gonna be bowing down at your feet, calling you the city of the LORD, the pride of Israel. {60:15} You might've been rejected and hated before, but now you're gonna be the envy of the world, bringing joy for generations. {60:16} You'll be sucking up the wealth of the nations, knowing that I, the LORD, am your Savior and Redeemer, the boss of Israel. {60:17} I'm upgrading your bling game big time, swapping out brass for gold, iron for silver, wood for bronze; your leaders gonna be all about peace, and your rulers gonna be all about fairness. {60:18} Ain't gonna be no violence or destruction in your hood anymore; your walls gonna be called Salvation, your gates Praise. {60:19} Forget the sun and moon, 'cause the LORD himself gonna be your everlasting light, and your God your glory. {60:20} No more sunsets or moonsets, 'cause the LORD's light gonna be shining on you all day, every day, and your days of mourning are over. {60:21} Your crew gonna be all righteous, owning the land forever; they're gonna be my handiwork, showing off my skills. {60:22} Even the smallest crew gonna blow up big time; I, the LORD, gonna make it happen, right on schedule.

{61:1} Yo, the Spirit of the Lord GOD is all up in me, 'cause He chose me to spread good vibes to the humble, sent me to mend broken hearts, set captives free, and unlock the cells for those stuck. {61:2} I'm here to declare it's all good in the hood with the Lord, and to bring the day of payback from our big guy upstairs; to comfort all the sad homies. {61:3} I'm all about giving those who are down and out a glow-up, turning their sorrows into joy, and swapping out their gloom for some hype, so they can shine like stars for the Lord. {61:4} They'll rebuild what's been trashed, fix up the old ruins, and spruce up the rundown cities, making 'em brand new. {61:5} Even outsiders will pitch in, tending to your flocks and working your fields. {61:6} But you, you're gonna be the Lord's VIPs, known as His top crew, living large off the blessings of the nations. {61:7} You'll get double the blessings for your past shame, and while they're celebrating, you'll be rolling in joy forever. {61:8} 'Cause the Lord's all about justice and hates when people steal and act all fake for religious stuff. He's gonna set things straight and make a forever deal with you. {61:9} Your kids will be famous among the nations, and everyone will know you're blessed by the Lord. {61:10} I'm gonna party hard for the Lord 'cause He's decked me out in salvation gear and righteousness threads, like a bride and groom all dressed up. {61:11} Just like the earth brings forth its plants and gardens bloom, the Lord's gonna make righteousness and praise shine for everyone to see.

{62:1} I won't keep quiet for Zion's sake or rest for Jerusalem's sake until their righteousness shines bright and their salvation blazes like a torch. {62:2} Everyone will see Zion's goodness, and all the kings will recognize their glory. They'll get a fresh name from the Lord's mouth. {62:3} Zion's gonna be like a crown jewel in the Lord's hands, a royal crown in the hands of their God. {62:4} No more feeling abandoned or land left empty; they'll be called "My Delight Is in Her" and "Married Land" 'cause the Lord's into them, and their land will be booming. {62:5} Like a happy groom with his bride, that's how God's gonna rejoice over Zion. {62:6} I've stationed guards on your walls, Jerusalem, who won't ever keep quiet, day or night. You who talk about the Lord, don't stop shouting praises until Jerusalem's the talk of the town. {62:7} Keep at it, don't let up until Jerusalem's a shining star on the world stage. {62:8} The Lord's made a serious promise: no more letting your enemies feast on your crops or drink your wine. {62:9} Instead, those who've worked the fields will chow down and give props to the Lord; those who've harvested will throw back some drinks in the holy courts. {62:10} So get ready, open up those gates, clear the way for the people, smooth out the roads, and hoist up a flag for all to see. {62:11} The Lord's shouting from one end of the earth to the other, saying to Zion's daughter, "Your Savior's on His way, bringing His reward with Him, ready to get to work." {62:12} They'll call you "Holy People," "Redeemed by the Lord," and you, Jerusalem, you'll be known as "Sought After," "A City Not Forsaken."

{63:1} Yo, who's rolling in from Edom, decked out in fresh gear from Bozrah, looking all majestic and flexing their strength? It's me, speaking the truth and packing some serious saving power. {63:2} But why you all red in your outfit, like you've been stomping grapes in a vineyard? {63:3} I've been handling business solo, squashing my enemies in anger and leaving their blood all over my fit. {63:4} It's payback time, and my squad's getting redeemed, no doubt. {63:5} I looked around for backup, but it was crickets, so I had to handle it myself, fueled by my own fury. {63:6} I'm gonna crush my enemies and leave them wasted, bringing their strength to the ground. {63:7} Let's talk about the Lord's kindness and how He's blessed us, showing mad love to Israel and hooking them up big time. {63:8} He's always been about his people, never swerving, always holding it down as their Savior. {63:9} In their struggles, He's felt it too, sending His angel to save them, carrying them through the tough times. {63:10} But they messed up big time, ticking off the Holy Spirit, turning God against them. {63:11} But then He remembered the good old days with Moses, asking where the one who led them out of Egypt was at. {63:12} The one who split the sea and made a name for Himself, leading them through like a boss. {63:13} He guided them through the deep, like a skilled rider through the wilderness, keeping them from falling. {63:14} Just like a beast rests in the valley, the Lord's Spirit gave them peace and led them, making His name shine. {63:15} Yo, check it from up above, from your holy crib; where's your passion and strength, your love and mercy? Are they on lockdown? {63:16} You're still our main man, even if Abraham doesn't know us, and Israel acts clueless. You've always been our Father, our Redeemer; your name's been solid forever. {63:17} Lord, why'd you let us stray, hardening our hearts against you? Come back for your crew's sake, for your tribe's inheritance. {63:18} Your holy peeps barely had a grip on the land, and now our enemies are trampling your sanctuary. {63:19} We're yours, but you let them run the show; they ain't even repping your name.

{64:1} We wish you'd bust open the sky and come down, make the mountains shake at your presence. {64:2} Like when fire melts stuff down, make it known to your haters, so the nations straight up quake. {64:3} You've pulled off some crazy stuff we never saw coming, making mountains tremble at your arrival. {64:4} From way back, nobody's seen or heard of anyone like you, doing what you do for those who wait for you. {64:5} You hook up those who keep it real and stay true to you, but we've messed up big time, and we're counting on you to save us. {64:6} We're all messed up and our good deeds are like trash; we're fading fast, blown away by our sins. {64:7} Nobody's even calling out to you, getting fired up to grab hold of you; you turned your back on us and let us get wrecked by our sins. {64:8} But listen up, Lord, you're our Father; we're the clay, and you're the potter; we're all your handiwork. {64:9} Don't stay mad forever, Lord, don't keep bringing up our sins; just look, we're all your people. {64:10} Your holy cities are deserted, Zion's a ghost town, Jerusalem's in ruins. {64:11} Our holy crib, where our ancestors praised you, is burnt to the ground, and all our good stuff is wrecked. {64:12} Are you gonna sit back and watch this go down, Lord? Are you gonna stay silent while we suffer?

{65:1} Yo, I'm out here for those who ain't even checkin' for me, and I'm showing up for those who ain't even searchin'; I'm like, "Here I am, here I am," to a crew who ain't even reppin' my name. {65:2} I'm reaching out all day to a bunch of rebels who be walking down messed up paths, doing their own thing. {65:3} They keep getting on my nerves, sacrificing in shady places, burning incense to idols; they chill in graveyards, eating forbidden grub—total disrespect. {65:4} They act all high and mighty, like, "Stay back, I'm too holy for you," but they just stink up the place with their arrogance. {65:5} But check it, I ain't staying silent; I'm gonna pay 'em back for all the junk they've pulled, straight up. {65:6-7} Your sins, and the sins of your ancestors, are gonna catch up with you, burning incense on mountains and dissing me left and right; y'all gonna get what's coming to you. {65:8} So listen up, I ain't gonna wipe everyone out 'cause of a few bad apples; there's still some good ones in the mix. {65:9} I'm gonna raise up a remnant from Jacob and Judah, my chosen crew gonna inherit the land and make it theirs. {65:10} And places like Sharon gonna be chill spots for my peeps, a place where they can kick back and vibe with me. {65:11} But you, you're straight-up ditching me, forgetting about my holy mountain, setting tables for false gods and offering drinks to idols. {65:12} So I'm marking you for destruction, you're all gonna get wrecked 'cause you ignored my calls, turned away from my words, and did your own messed-up thing. {65:13} But peep this, my servants gonna eat and drink, rejoice and celebrate, while you gonna be left starving and thirsty, ashamed and crying. {65:14} My crew gonna be singing with joy, while you gonna be crying in despair, howling in frustration. {65:15} You gonna be a curse to my chosen ones, 'cause I'm taking you out and giving my servants a new name. {65:16} Those who bless themselves on earth gonna do it in the name of the true God; those who swear oaths gonna swear by the God of truth, 'cause the past troubles gonna be forgotten, wiped clean from my sight. {65:17} New heavens and a new earth coming your way; the old stuff ain't even gonna be remembered. {65:18} But y'all gonna be hyped for what I'm bringing, especially Jerusalem—gonna be a party town, and her people gonna be lit. {65:19} I'm gonna be vibing with Jerusalem, partying with my people; no more crying, only good vibes. {65:20} No more babies dying young or old folks missing out; everyone gonna live long, happy lives, and even if you're a sinner, you'll be cursed. {65:21} They gonna build houses and live in 'em, plant vineyards and enjoy the fruit, no more getting kicked out or watching others enjoy what you planted. {65:22} 'Cause my people gonna enjoy the fruits of their labor for as long as they live, no more working for nothing, 'cause they're blessed by the LORD. {65:23} They gonna be a blessed generation, their kids gonna thrive alongside 'em, and everything they do gonna prosper. {65:24} Before they even ask, I'm gonna answer; while they're still talking, I'm gonna listen. {65:25} Wolves and lambs gonna chill together, lions gonna munch on straw like cows; ain't gonna be no hurtin' or destroyin' on my holy mountain, says the LORD.

{66:1} So listen up, the heavens are my throne, and the earth is my footstool; where you gonna build a house for me? Where's my chill spot? {66:2} Everything out here is made by me, says the LORD, but I'm checkin' out the ones who are humble and respect my word. {66:3} Offering sacrifices ain't gonna cut it if your heart ain't right; you're choosing your own way and getting off on doing what's wrong. {66:4} So I'm gonna let you have your way, and your worst fears gonna come true, 'cause you ignored my calls and did what I hate. {66:5} Listen up, all you who respect the LORD's word; your haters who dissed you for my sake gonna be put to shame, but I'm coming through for you. {66:6} I'm bringing judgment to my enemies, loud and clear, from the city and the temple, it 's all coming down. {66:7} Jerusalem gonna pop out a baby before she even feels the labor pains; she gonna have kids without the struggle. {66:8} Who's ever seen anything like this? Nations popping up out of nowhere, just like that? When Zion goes into labor, she's gonna birth her children quick. {66:9} You think I'd start something and not finish it? Think I'd bring life and not bring it to term? That's not how I roll, says your God. {66:10} So get hype with Jerusalem, all you who love her; rejoice with her, all you who mourned for her. {66:11} You gonna get blessed, satisfied with all the good stuff she brings; you gonna drink deep from her glory and be filled with joy. {66:12} 'Cause I'm bringing peace to Jerusalem like a flowing river, and the glory of the nations gonna pour in; you gonna be carried on her hip and dandled on her knees. {66:13} I'm gonna comfort you like a loving mother, and you gonna find your peace in Jerusalem. {66:14} When you see all this go down, your heart gonna be full of joy, your bones gonna be strong; and my servants gonna know my blessing, while my enemies gonna feel my wrath. {66:15} Get ready, 'cause the LORD's coming with fire and chariots, ready to unleash his anger and rebuke with flames. {66:16} With fire and sword, the LORD gonna judge everyone, and there's gonna be a lot of casualties. {66:17} Those who think they're holier-than-thou, eating all kinds of forbidden stuff in their gardens, gonna get taken out, says the LORD. {66:18} I know what y'all been up to, and I'm bringing all nations to witness my glory. {66:19} I'm sending survivors to tell the nations about me, to places like Tarshish, Pul, and Lud, places that ain't heard of me yet; they gonna declare my glory among the nations. {66:20} They gonna bring your brothers and sisters as an offering to the LORD from all nations, riding in on horses, chariots, and all sorts of fancy rides, to my holy mountain Jerusalem, just like the Israelites bring their offerings in clean vessels to the LORD's house. {66:21} And I'm gonna choose some of them to be priests and Levites, says the LORD. {66:22} Just like the new heavens and earth I'm making gonna last forever, so will your descendants and your name remain before me, says the LORD. {66:23} Every month, every week, all flesh gonna come worship before me, says the LORD. {66:24} And they gonna see the bodies of those who rebelled against me, their worms ain't gonna die, and their fire ain't gonna be put out; they gonna be a sight to behold, a warning to all.

Jeremiah

✦✦✦

{1:1} Yo, these are the words of Jeremiah, son of Hilkiah, one of the priests from Anathoth in Benjamin's hood. {1:2} The LORD's word hit him during the days of Josiah, son of Amon, king of Judah, in year thirteen of his reign. {1:3} The word also came during Jehoiakim's rule, son of Josiah, until the eleventh year of Zedekiah, son of Josiah, up to when Jerusalem got captured in month five. {1:4} The LORD then spoke to me, saying, {1:5} "Before I even formed you in the womb, I knew you; before you popped out, I set you apart and made you a prophet to the nations." {1:6} I said, "Ah, Lord GOD, I can't speak; I'm just a kid." {1:7} But the LORD replied, "Don't say you're just a kid; you'll go where I send you and say what I tell you." {1:8} "Don't be scared of them, 'cause I'm with you to save you," says the LORD. {1:9} Then the LORD touched my mouth and said, "Look, I've put my words in your mouth. {1:10} Today, I appoint you over nations and kingdoms to uproot, tear down, destroy, overthrow, build, and plant." {1:11} The LORD asked me, "Jeremiah, what do you see?" I said, "I see a rod of an almond tree." {1:12} The LORD said, "Good eye! I'm watching to make sure my word comes true." {1:13} The LORD spoke to me again, "What do you see?" I said, "I see a boiling pot, tilting from the north." {1:14} The LORD said, "Trouble's coming from the north on all the land's inhabitants. {1:15} I'm calling all northern kingdoms; they'll set their thrones at Jerusalem's gates and attack all Judah's cities." {1:16} I'll pass judgment on them for their wickedness, abandoning me, burning incense to other gods, and worshipping their own creations. {1:17} So get ready, stand up, and tell them everything I command you. Don't freak out, or I'll make you look foolish in front of them. {1:18} Today, I've made you a fortified city, an iron pillar, and bronze walls against the whole land, kings, officials, priests, and people of Judah. {1:19} They'll fight you but won't win, 'cause I'm with you to save you," says the LORD.

{2:1} The LORD's word came to me again, saying, {2:2} "Go shout this to Jerusalem: The LORD says, 'I remember your youthful devotion, your bridal love, when you followed me in the wilderness, a barren land.' {2:3} Israel was holy to the LORD, the first fruits of his harvest; anyone who ate it faced disaster," says the LORD. {2:4} Listen up, house of Jacob and all Israel's families: {2:5} The LORD says, "What did your ancestors find wrong with me to stray far, chasing worthless idols and becoming worthless themselves? {2:6} They didn't ask, 'Where's the LORD who brought us out of Egypt, led us through the deserts, pits, drought, and death's shadow, where no one lives?' {2:7} I brought you to a fertile land to enjoy its fruit and goodness, but you defiled my land and made my heritage disgusting. {2:8} The priests didn't ask, 'Where's the LORD?' Those who handle the law didn't know me, leaders rebelled against me, prophets prophesied by Baal, chasing useless stuff. {2:9} So I still bring charges against you," says the LORD, "and against your grandkids too. {2:10} Cross to the coasts of Kittim and look; send to Kedar, observe closely, see if anything like this has happened. {2:11} Has a nation changed its gods, which aren't gods? But my people swapped their glory for useless idols. {2:12} Be shocked, heavens, be horrified and desolate," says the LORD. {2:13} "My people have done two evils: they've ditched me, the living water source, and dug broken cisterns that can't hold water. {2:14} Is Israel a servant, a slave by birth? Why is he plundered? {2:15} Young lions roared at him, growling, laying waste his land; his cities are burned, uninhabited. {2:16} The men of Memphis and Tahpanhes have shaved your head. {2:17} Haven't you brought this on yourself by abandoning the LORD your God when he led you on the way? {2:18} Why now go to Egypt for the Nile's waters or Assyria for the Euphrates? {2:19} Your wickedness will punish you, your backsliding will rebuke you. Realize and see how evil and bitter it is to forsake the LORD your God and have no awe of me," says the Lord GOD Almighty. {2:20} "Long ago I broke your yoke, tore off your chains, but you said, 'I won't serve!' Indeed, on every high hill and under every green tree you sprawled out, playing the harlot. {2:21} I planted you like a choice vine, all pure seed. How did you turn into a corrupt, wild vine? {2:22} Even if you wash with soap and use lots of cleansing powder, your guilt is still before me," declares the Lord GOD. {2:23} "How can you say, 'I'm not defiled; I haven't followed the Baals'? Look at your behavior in the valley; know what you've done—you're a swift she-camel running here and there, {2:24} a wild donkey accustomed to the desert, sniffing the wind in her craving—in her heat, who can restrain her? Any males seeking her won't tire themselves; they'll find her during mating season. {2:25} Don't run until your feet are bare and your throat is dry. But you said, 'It's no use! I love foreign gods, and I must go after them.' {2:26} As a thief is disgraced when caught, so the people of Israel are disgraced—they, their kings, officials, priests, and prophets. {2:27} They say to wood, 'You are my father,' and to stone, 'You gave me birth.' They've turned their backs to me and not their faces. Yet when they're in trouble, they say, 'Come and save us!' {2:28} Where then are the gods you've made for yourselves? Let them come if they can save you when you're in trouble! For you have as many gods as you have towns, Judah. {2:29} Why do you bring charges against me? You all have rebelled against me," declares the LORD. {2:30} "In vain I've punished your children; they didn't respond to correction. Your sword has devoured your prophets like a ravenous lion. {2:31} You people of this generation, consider the word of the LORD: Have I been a desert to Israel or a land of great darkness? Why do my people say, 'We are free to roam; we won't come to you anymore'? {2:32} Does a young woman forget her jewelry, a bride her wedding ornaments? Yet my people have forgotten me, days without number. {2:33} How skilled you are at pursuing love! Even the worst of women can learn from your ways. {2:34} On your clothes is found the lifeblood of the innocent poor, though you didn't catch them breaking in. Yet in spite of all this, {2:35} you say, 'I'm innocent; he's not angry with me.' But I will pass judgment on you because you say, 'I haven't sinned.' {2:36} Why do you go about so much, changing your ways? You'll be disappointed by Egypt as you were by Assyria. {2:37} You'll also leave that place with your hands on your head, for the LORD has rejected those you trust; you won't prosper by them.

{3:1} So like, imagine this: if a dude dumps his girl, and she goes and hooks up with someone else, can he just take her back like nothing happened? That's like majorly messed up, right? But check it, you've been playing around with all these other guys, but the LORD's like, "Come back to me, I'm still down for you." {3:2} Look around, you've been getting busy in all the wrong places, like some desert rendezvous or something, messing up the whole vibe of the land with your shenanigans. {3:3} And because of all that, the blessings ain't even flowing anymore; you got a stubborn attitude, refusing to feel any shame. {3:4} But for real, ain't it time you started calling out to me like, "Yo, Dad, you've been there since day one, help me out"? {3:5} Is the LORD gonna stay mad forever? Nah, but you've been talking and acting foul for way too long. {3:6} Then the LORD was like, "Look at what Israel's been up to, climbing every mountain and chilling under every tree, acting all shady." {3:7} And I'm there telling Israel, "Come back to me," but she ain't listening. Even Judah peeped that and didn't learn from it. {3:8} I had to put Israel on blast for all the messed-up stuff she was doing, even gave her a breakup notice, but Judah just ignored the warning and joined in on the mess. {3:9} Israel's been so loose with her ways that she's defiled the whole land, getting it on with idols and statues. {3:10} And even with all that, Judah's only half-heartedly trying to come back to me, acting all fake, says the LORD. {3:11} So the LORD's like, "Israel might have some excuses, but Judah's got none." {3:12} But yo, there's still hope for Israel; the LORD's like, "Come back, I ain't gonna hold a grudge forever; I'm merciful like that." {3:13} Just admit you messed up, confess your sins to the LORD, stop chasing after every foreign thing, and start listening to me, says the LORD. {3:14} Yo, backsliding crew, listen up, the LORD's married to you; I'll pick a few of you from each hood and bring you back to Zion. {3:15} And I'm hooking you up with some real spiritual leaders who gonna feed you wisdom and understanding. {3:16} And when you start thriving in the land, ain't nobody gonna talk about the old religious relics anymore; it's gonna be a whole new vibe. {3:17} Jerusalem gonna be known as the LORD's spot, and all the nations gonna gather there in his name; ain't nobody gonna be following their wicked desires anymore. {3:18} In those days, Judah and Israel gonna be tight, rolling out from the north to the land their ancestors got blessed with. {3:19} But yo, I was like, "How can I even treat you like my kids and bless you with a dope land, when you keep turning away from me?" {3:20} It's like when a wife straight ghosts her husband; that's how you've been treating me, Israel, says the LORD. {3:21} You can hear the cries of Israel all over, begging for forgiveness, realizing they've forgotten their God. {3:22} So they're coming back, saying, "We're ready to turn things around, LORD, you're our God." {3:23} But seriously, looking to the hills for salvation? Nah, real salvation comes from the LORD our God, that's the deal with Israel. {3:24} It's like our shame has swallowed up everything good, from our youth till now, 'cause we've been disobeying the LORD. {3:25} Israel, if you come back to me and clean up your act, you won't have to bounce.

{4:1} So like, Israel, if you wanna make things right, come back to me; ditch all the messed-up stuff you've been doing, and we can work things out. {4:2} And swear by the LORD, for real, in truth and righteousness; then everyone's gonna be shouting out blessings in his name. {4:3} The LORD's telling the folks in Judah and Jerusalem, "Yo, you gotta prepare your hearts, stop sowing seeds among thorns." {4:4} Circumcise your hearts, Judah, and get rid of all that messed-up stuff, 'cause if you don't, my anger's gonna blaze outta control. {4:5} Spread the word in Judah, let everyone know in Jerusalem; sound the alarm, gather the crew, let's huddle up and head to the safe spots. {4:6} Raise the flag for Zion and don't hesitate; 'cause I'm bringing trouble from the north, a major beatdown. {4:7} The enemy's coming like a lion, tearing up the place, making it desolate; your cities gonna be ghost towns. {4:8} So put on your mourning clothes, start crying and wailing, 'cause the LORD's anger ain't letting up. {4:9} It's gonna be a day of reckoning, even the king's heart gonna fail, and the priests and prophets gonna be shook. {4:10} I was like, "Man, LORD, you got these people all fooled, saying there's peace when the sword's ready to strike." {4:11} When disaster hits, it's gonna be like a dry wind blowing in from the wilderness, not refreshing, just destructive. {4:12} It's like a storm coming straight at us, and I'm gonna lay down the verdict. {4:13} The enemy gonna roll in like dark clouds, chariots moving like a whirlwind, faster than eagles; we're in deep trouble. {4:14} Jerusalem, clean up your act if you wanna be saved; how long you gonna let your messed-up thoughts linger? {4:15} Trouble's coming from all directions, from Dan in the north to mount Ephraim. {4:16} Spread the word to everyone, especially Jerusalem; enemies coming from far off, ready to take us down. {4:17} They're surrounding us like guards in a field 'cause we've rebelled against the LORD. {4:18} You brought this on yourselves with your messed-up ways, and now you gotta deal with the consequences. {4:19} I'm hurting deep down, like my guts are twisted up; my soul can't find peace 'cause I hear the war drums beating. {4:20} It's chaos everywhere, the whole land's in ruins; everything's gone in the blink of an eye. {4:21} How long we gotta endure this misery? 'Cause my people been acting dumb, clueless about who I am; they're all about doing evil, but when it comes to doing good, they're clueless. {4:22} I looked around, and it's like everything's messed up, no order, no light in the heavens. {4:23} The earth's trembling, hills shaking; it's like humanity's vanished, birds flown away. {4:24} I'm seeing a once fertile land turned into a wasteland, cities in ruins 'cause of the LORD's fierce anger. {4:25} The LORD said it's gonna be desolate, but he won't totally wipe us out. {4:26} The earth's gonna mourn, skies gonna be dark 'cause the LORD's spoken it, decided it, and ain't backing down. {4:27} The whole city's gonna run scared at the sound of approaching enemies; they'll hide in the woods, climb rocks, but no one's gonna be left. {4:28} And when everything's stripped away, what's left? Even if you try to look good on the outside, your lovers gonna diss you, hunt you down. {4:29} It's like the cries of a woman in labor, the anguish of giving birth; that's how Zion feels, her soul weary from all the bloodshed.

{5:1} Yo, run around the streets of Jerusalem and check out if you can find anyone who does what's right and seeks the truth; if you do, I'll pardon it. {5:2} Even though they say, "The LORD lives," they're totally lying. {5:3} LORD, don't your eyes see the truth? You've punished them, but they didn't care; you consumed them, but they refused to take the hint: they've made their faces harder than rock and won't come back. {5:4} So I was like, these folks are clueless and poor; they don't know the LORD's way or his judgment. {5:5} I'll go talk to the big shots; they know the LORD's way and his judgment: but they've broken all the rules and ditched their responsibilities. {5:6} That's why a lion from the forest will kill them, and a wolf in the evenings will attack them, and a leopard will stalk their cities: anyone who goes out will get torn to bits because their wrongdoings are so many, and their betrayals are increasing. {5:7} How can I forgive you for this? Your kids have ditched me and sworn by fake gods: when I fed them well, they cheated and hung out at the harlots' houses. {5:8} They're like well-fed horses in the morning, each one neighing after his neighbor's wife. {5:9} Shouldn't I punish for these things? says the LORD: shouldn't my soul take revenge on a nation like this? {5:10} Go up on her walls and wreck them; but don't destroy completely: take away her defenses because they don't belong to the LORD. {5:11} The house of Israel and the house of Judah have been super shady against me, says the LORD. {5:12} They've lied about the LORD and said, "It's not him; no disaster will come upon us; we won't see sword or famine." {5:13} The prophets are full of hot air, and the word isn't in them: so they'll get what they deserve. {5:14} So here's what the LORD God of hosts says, "Because you said this, I'll make my words in your mouth fire, and these people wood, and it'll burn them up." {5:15} Listen, I'm bringing a nation from far away against you, Israel, says the LORD: it's a mighty and ancient nation, a nation whose language you don't know and can't understand. {5:16} Their quiver is like an open grave; they're all mighty warriors. {5:17} They'll eat up your harvest and your bread, which your kids should eat: they'll eat up your flocks and herds; they'll eat up your vines and fig trees: they'll destroy your fortified cities that you trust in with the sword. {5:18} But even in those days, says the LORD, I won't completely destroy you. {5:19} And when you ask, "Why is the LORD our God doing all this to us?" you'll answer them, "Because you ditched me and served other gods in your land, so now you'll serve strangers in a land that isn't yours." {5:20} Announce this to the house of Jacob, and spread the word in Judah, saying, {5:21} Listen up, you foolish people without understanding; you have eyes but don't see; you have ears but don't hear. {5:22} Don't you fear me? says the LORD: won't you tremble at my presence, the one who set the sand as the boundary for the sea, by a perpetual decree, so it can't pass it: even though the waves toss, they can't prevail; though they roar, they can't pass over it? {5:23} But these people have stubborn and rebellious hearts; they've turned away and left. {5:24} They don't even say in their hearts, "Let's fear the LORD our God, who gives rain in its season: the early and the late rain; he keeps for us the appointed weeks of the harvest." {5:25} Your sins have turned these things away, and your wrongdoings have kept good things from you. {5:26} Among my people are wicked people; they lie in wait like someone setting traps; they set traps and catch people. {5:27} Like a cage full of birds, so are their houses full of deceit: that's why they've become rich and powerful. {5:28} They've grown fat and sleek; they surpass the deeds of the wicked: they don't judge the cause of the fatherless, so they prosper; and they don't defend the rights of the needy. {5:29} Shouldn't I punish for these things? says the LORD: shouldn't my soul take revenge on a nation like this? {5:30} A shocking and horrible thing has happened in the land; {5:31} The prophets prophesy lies, and the priests rule by their own authority; and my people love it that way: but what will you do in the end?

{6:1} Hey, kids of Benjamin, gather to flee out of Jerusalem, blow the trumpet in Tekoa, and light a signal fire in Beth-haccerem: because disaster is coming from the north, great destruction. {6:2} I've compared the daughter of Zion to a beautiful and delicate woman. {6:3} The shepherds with their flocks will come to her; they'll pitch their tents all around her; each one will feed in his place. {6:4} Get ready for war against her; let's attack at noon. Woe to us! The day is ending, and the shadows of the evening are stretching out. {6:5} Let's go at night and destroy her palaces. {6:6} This is what the LORD of hosts says: Cut down trees and build a siege ramp against Jerusalem: this city must be punished; it's full of oppression. {6:7} Just as a well keeps its water fresh, so she keeps her wickedness fresh: violence and destruction are heard in her; sickness and wounds are constantly before me. {6:8} Be warned, Jerusalem, or I'll turn away from you; I'll make your land desolate, uninhabited. {6:9} This is what the LORD of hosts says: They'll glean the remnant of Israel like a vine; turn back your hand as a grape gatherer among the branches. {6:10} Who can I speak to and warn so they'll hear? Their ears are closed, and they can't listen: the word of the LORD is offensive to them; they have no delight in it. {6:11} I'm full of the LORD's fury; I'm tired of holding it in: I'll pour it out on the children in the street, and on the young men gathered together: even the husband and wife will be taken, the elderly and those advanced in years. {6:12} Their houses will be turned over to others, along with their fields and wives: because I'll stretch out my hand against the inhabitants of the land, says the LORD. {6:13} From the least to the greatest, everyone is greedy for gain; from prophet to priest, everyone deals falsely. {6:14} They treat my people's wounds superficially, saying, "Peace, peace," when there is no peace. {6:15} Were they ashamed when they committed these abominations? No, they weren't at all ashamed; they didn't even blush: so they'll fall among the fallen; when I punish them, they'll be brought down, says the LORD. {6:16} This is what the LORD says: Stand at the crossroads and look; ask for the ancient paths, where the good way is, and walk in it, and you'll find rest for your souls. But they said, "We won't walk in it." {6:17} I appointed watchmen over you, saying, "Listen to the sound of the trumpet." But they said, "We won't listen." {6:18} Therefore hear, you nations, and know, O congregation, what's happening among them. {6:19} Hear, O earth: I'll bring disaster on these people, the fruit of their schemes, because they haven't listened to my words, and they've rejected my law. {6:20} Why do you bring me incense from Sheba, and sweet cane from a far country? Your burnt offerings aren't acceptable, nor are your sacrifices pleasing to me. {6:21} So this is what the LORD says: I'll put obstacles before these people; parents and children together will stumble over them; neighbors and friends will perish. {6:22} This is what the LORD says: Look, a people is coming from the north, a great nation is being stirred up from the farthest parts of the earth. {6:23} They hold bows and spears; they're cruel and show no mercy; their voices roar like the sea, and they ride on horses, ready for battle against you, daughter of Zion. {6:24} We've heard the report of them; our hands hang limp: anguish has gripped us, pain like a woman in labor. {6:25} Don't go out into the field, don't walk on the road; for the enemy has a sword, and terror is on every side. {6:26} O my people, put on sackcloth and roll in ashes: mourn as if for an only son, a bitter lamentation:

because the destroyer will suddenly come upon us. {6:27} I've made you a tester of metals among my people, so you may know and test their ways. {6:28} They're all stubborn rebels, spreading slander; they're bronze and iron; they're all corrupt. {6:29} The bellows blow fiercely to burn away the lead with fire; but the refining is in vain because the wicked are not removed. {6:30} People will call them rejected silver because the LORD has rejected them.

{7:1} So like, the LORD hit up Jeremiah with a message, you know? He was like, "Jeremiah, head to the entrance of my crib and drop some truth bombs on these Judah peeps coming to worship me." {7:2} Then the LORD was all, "Listen up, Judah crew! If you wanna keep living large in this hood, you gotta clean up your act." {7:3} He was like, "Quit with the fake vibes and shady dealings, and I'll let you chill here." {7:4} "Stop frontin' like just 'cause you're in my temple, everything's cool. I see through that." {7:5} "If you wanna stay, step up your game, show some love to your neighbors, and stop messing with innocent peeps." {7:6} "Don't be shady to strangers, orphans, and widows, and don't spill innocent blood. And ditch those other gods; they're just trouble." {7:7} "Then I'll hook you up in this spot, just like I promised your ancestors, forever and ever." {7:8} "But yo, don't be believing those lies, 'cause they ain't worth squat." {7:9} "You out here stealing, killing, cheating, and worshipping fake gods like Baal, then rolling up in my house acting all innocent? Nah, not cool." {7:10} "You really think you can pull off that fake vibe, acting all innocent in my crib after doing all that shady stuff?" {7:11} "Nah, this place ain't a hideout for crooks. I see everything, and it ain't pretty." {7:12} "Remember what went down in Shiloh? Yeah, that's what happens when you mess with me." {7:13} "I've been hitting you up early, trying to set you straight, but you ain't even listening." {7:14} "So I'm gonna treat this place like Shiloh, and your promises like trash." {7:15} "I'll boot you outta here, just like I did with your fam from Ephraim." {7:16} "Don't even bother praying for these fools; they ain't gonna listen to you, and I ain't gonna listen to them." {7:17} "You see what's going down in Judah? It's straight-up messed up." {7:18} "They out here baking cakes for the queen of heaven, trying to get me heated." {7:19} "But who they really getting mad at? Themselves." {7:20} "So guess what? My anger's gonna blow up this place, and ain't nothing gonna stop it." {7:21} "Yo, forget about your burnt offerings and sacrifices; I never asked for that in the first place." {7:22} "I just wanted you to obey me and walk in my ways, but you straight-up ignored that." {7:23} "You never listened, always doing your own thing, and now you're worse off than before." {7:24} "I sent prophets to you, but you brushed 'em off and went your own way." {7:25} "So go ahead, tell 'em what's up, but they ain't gonna listen. Call out to 'em, but they ain't gonna answer." {7:26} "This nation ain't about listening to me or taking correction; truth's gone MIA." {7:27} "Jerusalem, cut off your hair and start mourning 'cause you've been straight-up rejected." {7:28} "This nation ain't got no time for the LORD's truth; they've been playing themselves." {7:29} "Judah's done some evil stuff, polluting my house with their abominations." {7:30} "They out here sacrificing their kids in the valley of Hinnom, straight-up disobeying me." {7:31} "So, it's gonna be a new name for that place, and it ain't gonna be pretty." {7:32} "Dead bodies gonna pile up in Tophet, and there won't be enough space to bury 'em all." {7:33} "They gonna be food for the birds and beasts, and ain't nobody gonna scare 'em away." {7:34} "And I'm shutting down the party in Judah and Jerusalem; ain't gonna be no more celebrations 'cause the land gonna be a wasteland."

{8:1} "Oh, and don't forget about digging up the bones of Judah's kings, princes, priests, prophets, and all the Jerusalem peeps; they gonna be left out in the open, no proper burial for 'em." {8:2} "Their idols gonna be exposed for what they are, useless and forgotten." {8:3} "People gonna choose death over life 'cause they'd rather keep doing their evil thing." {8:4} "So, why you gonna fall and not get back up? Why you turning away and not coming back?" {8:5} "Jerusalem, why you always falling back into your old ways? You cling to lies and refuse to change." {8:6} "I've been listening, but you ain't been speaking right. Nobody's owning up to their wickedness; they just keep on doing their thing." {8:7} "Even birds know when it's time to migrate, but my people can't figure out what's right." {8:8} "You think you're so smart, with the law of the LORD in your hands? Nah, you're just fooling yourselves." {8:9} "Wise ones feeling ashamed 'cause they rejected the word of the LORD; ain't no wisdom in that." {8:10} "So, I'm handing over your wives and fields to others 'cause y'all greedy and deceitful, from the prophets to the priests." {8:11} "They out here trying to patch things up with empty words, talking about peace when there ain't none." {8:12} "They ain't even ashamed of their abominations, can't even blush. So they gonna fall like everyone else when judgment comes." {8:13} "I'm gonna wipe out their crops, their land gonna be barren 'cause they've been straight-up disobedient." {8:14} "Why you just sitting there? Get moving, find some shelter, 'cause trouble's on its way!" {8:15} "You were hoping for peace and healing, but all you got was trouble." {8:16} "You can hear the enemy's horses coming from miles away; they're here to wreck everything." {8:17} "I'm sending serpents among you, and they ain't gonna be tamed; they gonna bite you, and there ain't nothing you can do about it." {8:18} "When I try to comfort myself, I feel nothing but despair." {8:19} "Listen to the cries of my people, far from home, asking where I am. But they've brought this on themselves with their idols and foolishness." {8:20} "Harvest's done, summer's over, and you're still stuck in trouble." {8:21} "I'm hurting for my people, feeling black and blue." {8:22} "Isn't there any hope left? Where are the healers? Why aren't my people getting better?"

{9:1} Oh man, if my head was like a water faucet and my eyes were like a fountain, I'd cry non-stop for my fallen people! {9:2} I wish I could find a chill spot in the wild to escape from my folks, 'cause they're all cheaters and shady AF. {9:3} They use their tongues like bows shooting lies; they don't stand up for the truth; they just keep doing bad stuff and don't even know me, says the LORD. {9:4} Be careful of your neighbor, don't trust even your bro, 'cause everyone is trying to one-up each other and spreading rumors. {9:5} They all trick their neighbors and never tell the truth; they train their tongues to lie and work hard to do wrong. {9:6} You're living in a world of lies; they refuse to know me because of their deceit, says the LORD. {9:7} So, the LORD of hosts says, "I'm gonna melt and test them; what else can I do for my people?" {9:8} Their tongue is like a deadly arrow; they talk nice to their neighbor but are planning to stab them in the back. {9:9} Shouldn't I deal with this? says the LORD; shouldn't I get revenge on a nation like this? {9:10} I'll cry for the mountains and the deserted fields because they're burnt up, no one can walk through, and even the animals are gone. {9:11} I'll turn Jerusalem into ruins and make Judah's cities empty. {9:12} Who's smart enough to get this? Who has heard from the LORD and can explain why the land is destroyed and empty like a desert? {9:13} The LORD says, "Because they ditched my law and didn't listen to me or walk in my ways, {9:14} but followed their own hearts and worshipped Baal like their ancestors taught them," {9:15} so the LORD of hosts, the God of Israel, says, "I'm gonna feed them bitter stuff and give them poisoned water. {9:16} I'll scatter them among nations they and their ancestors never knew, and I'll send a sword after them until they're wiped out." {9:17} The LORD of hosts says, "Think about it and call the mourning women to come; get the skillful ones to wail for us, {9:18} and let them hurry and cry so our eyes overflow with tears." {9:19} A voice of crying is heard from Zion, "We're ruined! We're so ashamed because we've left our land and our homes are destroyed." {9:20} Listen to the LORD's word, you women; let your ears take in what he's saying. Teach your daughters how to wail and your neighbors how to mourn, {9:21} 'cause death has climbed in through our windows and entered our palaces, cutting off the kids in the streets and the young men in the squares. {9:22} Say, "The LORD says, 'The dead bodies of men will lie like dung in the fields and like grain left behind by the reaper, with no one to gather them.'" {9:23} The LORD says, "Don't let the wise boast in their wisdom, the strong boast in their strength, or the rich boast in their riches. {9:24} But if you're gonna brag, brag that you understand and know me, that I am the LORD who practices kindness, justice, and righteousness on the earth, for I delight in these things," says the LORD. {9:25} "Look, the days are coming," says the LORD, "when I'll punish all who are circumcised only in the flesh— {9:26} Egypt, Judah, Edom, Ammon, Moab, and all who live in the desert, for all these nations are uncircumcised, and Israel is uncircumcised in heart."

{10:1} Listen to the word the LORD speaks to you, house of Israel. {10:2} The LORD says, "Don't follow the ways of the nations or be terrified by signs in the heavens, even though the nations are terrified by them. {10:3} The customs of the peoples are worthless; they cut a tree out of the forest, a craftsman shapes it with his axe. {10:4} They decorate it with silver and gold and fasten it with hammer and nails so it won't topple. {10:5} They're like scarecrows in a cucumber field; they can't speak; they have to be carried because they can't walk. Don't be afraid of them; they can't do harm nor can they do any good." {10:6} There's no one like you, LORD; you are great, and your name is mighty in power. {10:7} Who should not fear you, King of the nations? This is your due. Among all the wise leaders of the nations and in all their kingdoms, there's no one like you. {10:8} They are all senseless and foolish; they are taught by worthless wooden idols. {10:9} Hammered silver is brought from Tarshish and gold from Uphaz; what the craftsman and goldsmith have made is then dressed in blue and purple—all made by skilled workers. {10:10} But the LORD is the true God; he is the living God, the eternal King. When he is angry, the earth trembles; the nations cannot endure his wrath. {10:11} Tell them this: "These gods, who did not make the heavens and the earth, will perish from the earth and from under the heavens." {10:12} But God made the earth by his power; he founded the world by his wisdom and stretched out the heavens by his understanding. {10:13} When he speaks, the waters in the heavens roar, and he makes clouds rise from the ends of the earth. He sends lightning with the rain and brings out the wind from his storehouses. {10:14} Everyone is senseless and without knowledge; every goldsmith is shamed by his idols. The images he makes are a fraud; they have no breath in them. {10:15} They are worthless, the objects of mockery; when their judgment comes, they will perish. {10:16} He who is the Portion of Jacob is not like these, for he is the Maker of all things, including Israel, the people of his inheritance—the LORD Almighty is his name. {10:17} Gather up your belongings to leave the land, you who live under siege. {10:18} For this is what the LORD says: "At this time I will hurl out those who live in this land; I will bring distress on them so that they may be captured." {10:19} Woe to me because of my injury! My wound is incurable! Yet I said to myself, "This is my sickness, and I must endure it." {10:20} My tent is destroyed; all its ropes are snapped. My children are gone from me and are no more; no one is left now to pitch my tent or to set up my shelter. {10:21} The shepherds are senseless and do not inquire of the LORD; so they do not prosper, and all their flock is scattered. {10:22} Listen! The report is coming—a great commotion from the land of the north! It will make the towns of Judah desolate, a haunt of jackals. {10:23} LORD, I know that people's lives are not their own; it is not for them to direct their steps. {10:24} Discipline me, LORD, but only in due measure—not in your anger, or you will reduce me to nothing. {10:25} Pour out your wrath on the nations that do not acknowledge you, on the peoples who do not call on your name. For they have devoured Jacob; they have devoured him completely and destroyed his homeland.

{11:1} Yo, Jeremiah got hit up by the LORD again, and this time it was like, "Listen up, Judah crew, and all you peeps in Jerusalem." {11:2} "You gotta hear this covenant deal and spread the word." {11:3} "Anyone who ain't down with this covenant deal is straight-up cursed." {11:4} "Back when I brought your ancestors outta Egypt, I laid down the rules: obey me, and we cool." {11:5} "I promised your ancestors a dope land, flowing with milk and honey, and here you are." {11:6} "Spread the word in every hood, and make sure they know the deal." {11:7} "I've been trying to set you straight since Egypt days, but you just ain't listening." {11:8} "Y'all straight-up ignored me and did your own thing, so now you gotta face the consequences." {11:9} "There's a whole conspiracy going down in Judah and Jerusalem, and y'all ain't even woke to it." {11:10} "You're back to your old wicked ways, ignoring my words and chasing after other gods." {11:11} "So here's the deal: I'm bringing the pain, and when you cry out to me, I ain't gonna hear it." {11:12} "You gonna be out there praying to your fake gods, but they ain't gonna save you when trouble hits." {11:13} "You got so many altars to false gods in Judah and Jerusalem, it's like every street's got one." {11:14} "Don't even bother praying for these people; I ain't listening when they cry out for help." {11:15} "What's my beloved doing in my house, acting all scandalous with others and disrespecting what's holy?" {11:16} "I called you a green olive tree with good fruit, but now I'm burning it down 'cause you messed up." {11:17} "Judah and Jerusalem gonna face the consequences for their wickedness and their idol worship." {11:18} "I've seen what's going down, and I know what they're up to." {11:19} "They're plotting against me, trying to cut down the tree and erase my name." {11:20} "But I trust in you, LORD, to bring justice, 'cause I've laid it all out for you." {11:21} "Those fools from Anathoth trying to shut me up, but they gonna get what's coming to them." {11:22} "I'm gonna bring punishment on them, wiping out their young and starving their families." {11:23} "There ain't gonna be no survivors in Anathoth; they're gonna feel my wrath."

{12:1} "LORD, you're righteous, but I gotta ask: why do the wicked thrive while the righteous suffer?" {12:2} "They're flourishing while they're speaking your name, but their hearts are far from you." {12:3} "But you know me, LORD; you've seen my heart. Bring judgment on them like sheep for the slaughter." {12:4} "How long we gotta watch the land suffer 'cause of the wicked? Even the animals are feeling it, thinking you won't see their end." {12:5} "If I'm struggling with the small stuff, how can I handle the big stuff? If peace ain't even safe, what chance do we have in chaos?" {12:6} "Even my own fam's turning against me, calling out to the masses to betray me. Can't trust 'em, even if they're sweet-talkin'." {12:7} "I'm done with my heritage; I've handed it over to my enemies." {12:8} "My heritage's like a lion roaring against me; I can't stand it anymore." {12:9} "My heritage's like a bird with everyone against it, surrounded by beasts ready to devour." {12:10} "Too many leaders have trashed my land, turned it into a wasteland." {12:11} "It's empty, mourning for me, but nobody's paying attention." {12:12} "The enemy's taken over, spreading through the land; the LORD's sword's gonna bring destruction everywhere." {12:13} "They planted wheat but got thorns; worked hard but got nothing; they're gonna regret it 'cause the LORD's furious." {12:14} "LORD's gonna deal with all the evil neighbors messing with Israel's inheritance, kicking 'em out and bringing Judah back." {12:15} "After kicking them out, I'll show compassion and bring them back to their land." {12:16} "If they learn from Israel's ways and swear by the LORD's name, they'll be part of my people." {12:17} "But if they don't obey, I'm wiping 'em out, plain and simple."

{13:1} So the LORD was like, "Yo, Jeremiah, grab a lit linen belt and wear it. Don't wash it." {13:2} So I copped the belt and rocked it as the LORD told me to. {13:3} Then the LORD hit me up again, saying, {13:4} "Take that belt you got and head to the Euphrates. Stash it in a crack in the rocks." {13:5} So I went, hid it by the Euphrates, just as the LORD said. {13:6} After a while, the LORD was like, "Get up, go back to the Euphrates, and grab that belt I told you to hide." {13:7} So I went back, dug it up, and the belt was trashed, totally useless. {13:8} Then the LORD told me, {13:9} "That's how I'm gonna wreck the pride of Judah and Jerusalem. {13:10} These evil people who ignore my words and follow their own vibes and other gods are gonna end up like that useless belt. {13:11} Just like a belt clings to a dude's waist, I wanted Israel and Judah to cling to me, so they could be my people and bring me praise and glory, but they wouldn't listen. {13:12} So, tell them this: The LORD, God of Israel, says, 'Every bottle will be filled with wine.' And they'll be like, 'Duh, we know that.' {13:13} Then you say, 'The LORD says He's gonna fill everyone in this land – kings, priests, prophets, and all Jerusalem – with drunkenness. {13:14} He'll smash them together, fathers and sons, with no mercy, no pity, total destruction.' {13:15} Listen up, don't be proud, the LORD has spoken. {13:16} Give glory to the LORD before it gets dark, and you trip and fall. If you ignore Him, He'll turn your light into the shadow of death, deep darkness. {13:17} If you don't listen, I'll cry in secret because of your pride, my tears will flow because the LORD's people are taken captive. {13:18} Tell the king and queen to humble themselves and sit down, because their crowns are coming off. {13:19} The southern cities will be shut down, no one will open them; Judah will be taken captive, all of it. {13:20} Look up and see those coming from the north. Where's your beautiful flock now? {13:21} What will you say when He punishes you? You trained them to be rulers over you; won't your pains be like a woman in labor? {13:22} If you wonder why this is happening, it's because of your huge sins, your skirts are pulled up, your heels exposed. {13:23} Can an Ethiopian change his skin, or a leopard his spots? Neither can you do good when you're used to doing evil. {13:24} So I'll scatter them like chaff blown by the desert wind. {13:25} This is your lot, the portion I have decreed, because you've forgotten me and trusted in lies. {13:26} So I'll pull up your skirts over your face, and your shame will be seen. {13:27} I've seen your adulteries and lustful neighings, your shameless whoring. Woe to you, Jerusalem! When will you ever be clean?

{14:1} The word of the LORD came to Jeremiah about the drought: {14:2} Judah mourns, its cities languish, they lie in the dirt, and the cry of Jerusalem goes up. {14:3} Nobles send their servants for water; they find no water and return with empty jars, ashamed and dismayed, their heads covered. {14:4} The ground is cracked because there's no rain; the farmers are ashamed, covering their heads. {14:5} Even the deer abandons her newborn in the field because there's no grass. {14:6} Wild donkeys stand on barren heights, panting like jackals, their eyes failing for lack of food. {14:7} LORD, our sins testify against us, but for your name's sake, do something; our backsliding is many, we've sinned against you. {14:8} O Hope of Israel, Savior in times of trouble, why are you like a stranger in the land, like a traveler staying only a night? {14:9} Why are you like a man taken by surprise, like a warrior powerless to save? Yet you are among us, LORD, and we are called by your name; do not forsake us! {14:10} This is what the LORD says about this people: They love to wander; they do not restrain their feet. So the LORD does not accept them; He will remember their wickedness and punish them for their sins. {14:11} The LORD said to me, "Do not pray for the well-being of this people. {14:12} Even if they fast, I will not listen to their cry; though they offer burnt offerings and grain offerings, I will not accept them. Instead, I will destroy them with the sword, famine, and plague." {14:13} But I said, "Alas, Sovereign LORD! The prophets keep telling them, 'You will not see the sword or suffer famine. Indeed, I will give you lasting peace in this place.'" {14:14} Then the LORD said to me, "The prophets are prophesying lies in my name. I have not sent them or appointed them or spoken to them. They are prophesying to you false visions, divinations, idolatries, and the delusions of their own minds. {14:15} Therefore, this is what the LORD says about the prophets who are prophesying in my name: I did not send them, yet they are saying, 'No sword or famine will touch this land.' Those same prophets will perish by sword and famine. {14:16} And the people they are prophesying to will be thrown into the streets of Jerusalem because of the famine and sword. There will be no one to bury them, their wives, their sons, or their daughters. I will pour out on them the calamity they deserve. {14:17} "Speak this word to them: 'Let my eyes overflow with tears night and day without ceasing; for the Virgin

Daughter, my people, has suffered a grievous wound, a crushing blow. {14:18} If I go into the country, I see those slain by the sword; if I go into the city, I see the ravages of famine. Both prophet and priest go about their business in the land they know not.'" {14:19} Have you rejected Judah completely? Do you despise Zion? Why have you afflicted us so that we cannot be healed? We hoped for peace, but no good has come, for a time of healing, but there is only terror. {14:20} We acknowledge our wickedness, LORD, and the guilt of our ancestors; we have indeed sinned against you. {14:21} For the sake of your name, do not despise us; do not dishonor your glorious throne. Remember your covenant with us and do not break it. {14:22} Do any of the worthless idols of the nations bring rain? Do the skies themselves send down showers? No, it is you, LORD our God. Our hope is in you, for you do all this.

{15:1} So, the LORD was like, "Even if Moses and Samuel were here, I'm done with these people. Get 'em outta my sight." {15:2} "And when they're like, 'Where we gonna go?' Tell 'em, 'You're marked for death, the sword, famine, or captivity.'" {15:3} "I'm sending four kinds of punishment: swords, savage dogs, birds of prey, and wild beasts." {15:4} "They're gonna get scattered everywhere 'cause of Manasseh's evil in Jerusalem." {15:5} "Nobody's gonna show pity or ask how they're doing." {15:6} "They ditched me, so now it's payback time; I'm tired of forgiving." {15:7} "I'll make 'em suffer, strip 'em of kids, and destroy 'em 'cause they won't change." {15:8} "Widows everywhere, and a spoiler attacking at noon; chaos and terror." {15:9} "Even those who had it all are gonna suffer; there's no escape from their enemies." {15:10} "Man, I'm cursed! Even though I didn't do anything wrong, everyone's hating on me." {15:11} "But don't worry, there's hope for you; even in the tough times, the enemy will treat you well." {15:12} "Can iron break iron? No way. But your wealth and treasures will be taken away for your sins." {15:13} "You'll be dragged to a land you don't know 'cause my anger's burning hot." {15:14} "No more talk about the Exodus; it's gonna be about my bringing them back from everywhere they've been scattered." {15:15} "I'll protect you from the wicked and the terrible."

{16:1} "The LORD said some heavy stuff to me." {16:2} "Don't even think about getting married or having kids here." {16:3} "All those born here will suffer; they'll die horribly and won't even get a proper burial." {16:4} "Don't bother mourning for them; my peace is gone from this place." {16:5} "Both the big shots and the nobodies will die here, and nobody's gonna mourn." {16:6} "No mourning, no shaving heads, no cutting yourselves for the dead." {16:7} "No mourning rituals, no comforting the bereaved." {16:8} "Stay away from parties and feasts." {16:9} "No more joy, gladness, weddings, or celebrations." {16:10} "When they ask why all this evil, tell 'em it's 'cause their ancestors ditched me for other gods." {16:11} "They're worse than their ancestors, all following their own evil desires." {16:12} "So I'm kicking them out into a land where they'll serve other gods day and night, without my favor." {16:13} "But if they come back to me and separate the precious from the worthless, they'll be my voice." {16:14} "They'll fight against you, but they won't win 'cause I'm with you." {16:15} "I'll deliver you from the wicked and the terrible." {16:16} "I'll send people to gather them and others to hunt them down, from every corner." {16:17} "I see everything they do; they can't hide from me or their sins." {16:18} "I'll double their punishment for defiling my land with their detestable acts." {16:19} "People will realize their ancestors believed in lies and worthless things." {16:20} "Making gods that aren't even real? Seriously?" {16:21} "I'll make sure they know my power and who I am, once and for all."

{17:1} Yo, the sin of Judah's like engraved with an iron pen, point sharp as a diamond, right on their hearts and altars. {17:2} Their kids remember the altars and groves by the green trees on high hills. {17:3} My mountain in the field, I'll give your treasures and high places for sin across your borders to the spoil. {17:4} You, yourself, will lose the heritage I gave you and serve your enemies in a land you don't know, cuz you made me super angry, and it'll burn forever. {17:5} The LORD says, "Cursed is the one who trusts in humans and turns away from the LORD. {17:6} They'll be like a bush in the desert, not seeing good times, living in parched places, salty and uninhabited. {17:7} Blessed is the one who trusts in the LORD, whose hope is the LORD. {17:8} They'll be like a tree planted by water, spreading roots by the river, not fearing heat, always green, not worried in drought, and never failing to bear fruit. {17:9} The heart is deceitful and super wicked, who can understand it? {17:10} I, the LORD, search the heart and test the mind, giving everyone according to their ways and the fruit of their deeds. {17:11} Like a partridge sitting on eggs it didn't lay, the one who gets rich unjustly will lose it all in mid-life and end up a fool. {17:12} A glorious high throne is our sanctuary from the start. {17:13} O LORD, hope of Israel, everyone who forsakes you will be ashamed, their names written in the dust because they left the LORD, the fountain of living waters. {17:14} Heal me, LORD, and I'll be healed; save me, and I'll be saved, for you are my praise. {17:15} They say to me, "Where's the word of the LORD? Let it come now!" {17:16} I haven't hurried away from being your shepherd, nor desired the disaster day. You know what I said was right before you. {17:17} Don't be a terror to me; you're my hope in the day of evil. {17:18} Let my persecutors be ashamed, but not me; let them be dismayed, not me. Bring the day of disaster on them, double destruction. {17:19} The LORD told me, "Go stand in the gate where the kings of Judah come in and out, and in all Jerusalem's gates. {17:20} Tell them to hear the word of the LORD, kings of Judah, all Judah, and Jerusalem's inhabitants entering these gates. {17:21} The LORD says, "Don't carry a load on the Sabbath or bring it through Jerusalem's gates. {17:22} Don't carry loads out of your houses on the Sabbath or do any work. Keep the Sabbath holy, as I commanded your ancestors. {17:23} They didn't listen, stiffened their necks, didn't hear or accept instruction. {17:24} If you listen to me, says the LORD, and don't bring loads through the city gates on the Sabbath but keep it holy, not doing any work, {17:25} Then kings and princes on David's throne, riding chariots and horses, along with the people of Judah and Jerusalem's inhabitants, will enter these gates, and this city will last forever. {17:26} People will come from Judah's cities, around Jerusalem, Benjamin's land, the plain, the mountains, and the south, bringing burnt offerings, sacrifices, grain offerings, incense, and thank offerings to the LORD's house. {17:27} But if you don't listen and keep the Sabbath holy, and carry loads through Jerusalem's gates on the Sabbath, I'll start a fire in its gates that'll burn down Jerusalem's palaces, unquenchable.

{18:1} The word from the LORD to Jeremiah: {18:2} Get up and go to the potter's house; I'll let you hear my words there. {18:3} I went to the potter's house and saw him working on his wheel. {18:4} The pot he was shaping from clay got messed up, so he reshaped it as he saw fit. {18:5} The LORD's word came to me: {18:6} House of Israel, can't I do with you like this potter? You're clay in my hands, O Israel. {18:7} If I announce that a nation or kingdom is to be uprooted, torn down, and destroyed, {18:8} But if that nation I warned turns from its evil, I'll relent and not bring the disaster I planned. {18:9} If I announce that a nation or kingdom is to be built up and planted, {18:10} But if it does evil in my sight and disobeys me, I'll reconsider the good I intended. {18:11} So, tell Judah and Jerusalem: The LORD says, "I'm preparing disaster against you. Turn from your evil ways and improve your actions." {18:12} But they'll say, "It's hopeless! We'll follow our own plans and act on our own evil intentions." {18:13} Therefore, the LORD says: Ask among the nations, who has heard such things? Israel's done a horrible thing. {18:14} Does snow vanish from Lebanon's rocks or cool mountain streams dry up? {18:15} Yet my people have forgotten me, burning incense to worthless idols, causing them to stumble off the ancient paths onto muddy trails. {18:16} Their land will be desolate, a perpetual hissing; everyone passing by will be astonished and shake their heads. {18:17} Like an east wind, I'll scatter them before their enemies. I'll show them my back, not my face, in their day of disaster. {18:18} They said, "Let's plot against Jeremiah; the law won't be lost from the priests, nor counsel from the wise, nor words from the prophets. Let's attack him with our words and ignore his messages." {18:19} Listen to me, LORD! Hear my enemies' accusations. {18:20} Should good be repaid with evil? They dug a pit to take my life. Remember how I stood before you to speak good for them, to turn your wrath away. {18:21} So, hand their children over to famine; pour out their blood by the sword. Let their wives be childless and widows, their men slain by disease and battle. {18:22} Let cries be heard from their homes when raiders suddenly attack them. They dug a pit to catch me and hid snares for my feet. {18:23} But you, LORD, know all their plots to kill me. Don't forgive their sins or blot out their offenses. Let them be overthrown before you; deal with them in your anger.

{19:1} So, God was like, "Yo, go grab a potter's clay jar and gather some elders and priests." {19:2} "Then head to the valley of Hinnom and drop some truth bombs there." {19:3} "Tell the kings of Judah and the peeps in Jerusalem, I'm bringing some serious bad vibes to this place; it's gonna be shocking." {19:4} "They've ditched me, offered sacrifices to other gods, and spilled innocent blood." {19:5} "They're even sacrificing their kids to Baal, something I never asked for or even thought about." {19:6} "So, the day's coming when this place will be known as the Valley of Slaughter, not Tophet." {19:7} "Their plans will fail, enemies will take 'em out, and their bodies will be bird and beast buffet." {19:8} "This city will be a ghost town, a laughingstock; people will be shocked by its disasters." {19:9} "They'll even resort to cannibalism during the siege." {19:10} "Break the jar in front of everyone, symbolizing how this city and its people will be shattered." {19:11} "Just like a broken pot, they'll be beyond repair, buried in Tophet till there's no space left." {19:12} "Jerusalem will be as defiled as Tophet, all because they worshipped other gods on their rooftops." {19:13} "Jeremiah went and preached this, then stood in the temple court." {19:14} "He warned of the city's impending doom because they refused to listen." {19:15} "Meanwhile, Pashur, the priest, got wind of Jeremiah's prophecies and put him in stocks." {19:16} "Next day, Pashur let him out, and Jeremiah dropped some truth bombs on him too." {19:17} "God's like, 'Your name ain't Pashur anymore; it's Terror on Every Side.'" {19:18} "You and your crew are gonna be captured, killed, and buried in Babylon." {19:19} "Everything in the city, its wealth, labor, and treasures, will be plundered and taken to Babylon." {19:20} "Even you, Pashur, and your fam, are gonna end up in Babylon, where you'll die for spreading lies."

{20:1} "Jeremiah's feeling betrayed by God, tired of being mocked and hated." {20:2} "He's fed up, but God's words burn inside him, and he can't keep silent." {20:3} "Despite the threats and mockery, God's on his side, and his enemies will stumble and fail." {20:4} "He's praying for vengeance on them, trusting in God's justice." {20:5} "He sings praises to God for rescuing him from evil dudes." {20:6} "He curses the day he was born, wishing he'd never seen the light of day." {20:7} "He even curses the dude who told his dad he had a son, wishing he'd never been born." {20:8} "Why bother living a life full of pain and shame?"

{21:1} So, Jeremiah got a message from the LORD when King Zedekiah sent Pashur son of Melchiah and Zephaniah son of Maaseiah the priest to him, saying, {21:2} "Yo, Jeremiah, can you ask the LORD for help? Nebuchadnezzar, king of Babylon, is waging war on us. Maybe the LORD will do something awesome for us like He did before, and make Nebuchadnezzar back off." {21:3} Jeremiah told them, "Here's what you need to say to Zedekiah: {21:4} The LORD God of Israel says, 'I'm going to turn your weapons against you. The ones you're using to fight the king of Babylon and the Chaldeans who are besieging you outside the walls, I'm bringing them right into the heart of the city. {21:5} I'll be fighting against you myself with an outstretched hand and a powerful arm, in anger, fury, and great wrath. {21:6} I'm going to strike the people in this city, both humans and animals; they'll die from a terrible plague. {21:7} After that, says the LORD, I'm going to hand over King Zedekiah of Judah, his officials, and the people who survive the plague, the sword, and the famine to Nebuchadnezzar, king of Babylon, and to their enemies who want to kill them. Nebuchadnezzar will slaughter them without mercy or pity.' {21:8} And to this people, you need to say, 'The LORD says, "Look, I'm giving you a choice between the way of life and the way of death. {21:9} If you stay in this city, you'll die by the sword, famine, or plague. But if you go out and surrender to the Chaldeans who are besieging you, you'll live, and your life will be spared. {21:10} I have decided to bring disaster on this city and not good, says the LORD. It will be handed over to the king of Babylon, and he will burn it down."' {21:11} And concerning the royal family of Judah, tell them, 'Hear the word of the LORD; {21:12} O house of David, the LORD says, "Administer justice every morning and rescue those who have been robbed from their oppressor, or my anger will blaze out like fire, and it will burn uncontrollably because of your evil deeds. {21:13} Look, I'm against you, you who live in the valley, on the rocky plateau, says the

LORD. You who say, 'Who can come against us? Who can enter our homes?' {21:14} I will punish you according to what you've done, says the LORD. I will start a fire in your forests that will consume everything around it.'"

{22:1} The LORD says, 'Go down to the palace of the king of Judah and tell him this: {22:2} Hear the word of the LORD, O king of Judah, who sits on David's throne, you, your officials, and your people who enter these gates. {22:3} This is what the LORD says: "Do what is just and right. Rescue the oppressed from their oppressor. Don't exploit or do violence to the foreigner, the fatherless, or the widow, and don't shed innocent blood in this place. {22:4} If you really do this, then kings who sit on David's throne will come through the gates of this palace, riding in chariots and on horses, with their officials and their people. {22:5} But if you don't obey these words, I swear by myself, says the LORD, that this palace will become a ruin."' {22:6} For this is what the LORD says concerning the house of the king of Judah: 'You are like Gilead to me, like the summit of Lebanon, but I will surely make you like a wilderness, like towns not inhabited. {22:7} I will send destroyers against you, each with his weapons, and they will cut down your fine cedar beams and throw them into the fire. {22:8} Many nations will pass by this city and ask one another, "Why has the LORD done such a thing to this great city?" {22:9} And the answer will be, "Because they have forsaken the covenant of the LORD their God and have worshipped and served other gods."' {22:10} Don't weep for the dead king or mourn his loss; rather, weep bitterly for the one who is exiled, because he will never return or see his native land again. {22:11} For this is what the LORD says about Shallum (Jehoahaz) son of Josiah, who succeeded his father as king of Judah but has gone from this place: 'He will never return. {22:12} He will die in the place where they have led him captive; he will not see this land again.' {22:13} Woe to him who builds his palace by unrighteousness, his upper rooms by injustice, making his own people work for nothing, not paying them for their labor. {22:14} He says, 'I will build myself a great palace with spacious upper rooms.' So he makes large windows in it, panels it with cedar, and decorates it in red. {22:15} Does it make you a king to have more and more cedar? Did not your father have food and drink? He did what was right and just, so all went well with him. {22:16} He defended the cause of the poor and needy, and so all went well. Is that not what it means to know me? declares the LORD. {22:17} But your eyes and your heart are set only on dishonest gain, on shedding innocent blood and on oppression and extortion.' {22:18} Therefore this is what the LORD says about Jehoiakim son of Josiah king of Judah: 'They will not mourn for him: "Alas, my brother! Alas, my sister!" They will not mourn for him: "Alas, my master! Alas, his splendor!" {22:19} He will have the burial of a donkey—dragged away and thrown outside the gates of Jerusalem.' {22:20} Go up to Lebanon and cry out, let your voice be heard in Bashan, cry out from Abarim, for all your allies are crushed. {22:21} I warned you when you felt secure, but you said, 'I will not listen!' This has been your way since your youth; you have not obeyed me. {22:22} The wind will drive all your shepherds away, and your allies will go into exile. Then you will be ashamed and disgraced because of all your wickedness. {22:23} You who live in 'Lebanon,' who are nestled in cedar buildings, how you will groan when pangs come upon you, pain like that of a woman in labor! {22:24} 'As surely as I live,' declares the LORD, 'even if you, Jehoiachin son of Jehoiakim king of Judah, were a signet ring on my right hand, I would still pull you off. {22:25} I will deliver you into the hands of those who want to kill you, those you fear—Nebuchadnezzar king of Babylon and the Babylonians. {22:26} I will hurl you and the mother who gave you birth into another country, where neither of you was born, and there you both will die. {22:27} You will never come back to the land you long to return to.' {22:28} Is this man Jehoiachin a despised, broken pot, an object no one wants? Why will he and his children be hurled out, cast into a land they do not know? {22:29} O land, land, land, hear the word of the LORD! {22:30} This is what the LORD says: 'Record this man as if childless, a man who will not prosper in his lifetime, for none of his offspring will prosper, none will sit on the throne of David or rule anymore in Judah.'

{23:1} God's like, "Listen up, fam, I'm talking to you." {23:2} "You pastors out there who should be taking care of my peeps, you've messed up big time." {23:3} "But don't trip, I'm gonna gather the leftovers from all over and bring them back home." {23:4} "I'll appoint some good shepherds to look after them, so they won't be stressing anymore." {23:5} "Check it, a righteous king from David's line is coming, and he's gonna rule with justice." {23:6} "Under his rule, Judah will be safe, and Israel will chill." {23:7} "The day's coming when nobody will talk about Egypt; instead, they'll talk about the north country and how I brought my people back." {23:8} "They'll settle down in their own land, no more wandering." {23:9} "My heart's hurting because of these fake prophets; they're messing everything up." {23:10} "The land's full of cheaters, and because of all the lies, it's a mess." {23:11} "Even the religious leaders are messed up; they're doing dirt in my own house." {23:12} "They're heading for disaster, slipping and falling in the dark." {23:13} "The prophets in Samaria are fools, leading my people astray." {23:14} "And the ones in Jerusalem are just as bad, cheating, lying, and supporting the bad guys." {23:15} "So, I'm gonna give them a taste of their own medicine, some bitter stuff to swallow." {23:16} "Don't listen to these fake prophets; they're just talking nonsense." {23:17} "They're telling everyone peace and safety, even to those doing whatever they want." {23:18} "But who's really heard from me and understood my message?" {23:19} "Get ready for some serious trouble, especially for the wicked." {23:20} "My anger won't cool down until I've done what I said; you'll see it happen." {23:21} "I didn't send these prophets, but they're out here running their mouths." {23:22} "If they actually listened to me, they'd help my people turn away from their messed-up ways." {23:23} "I'm not some distant God; I'm right here, seeing everything." {23:24} "You can't hide from me; I'm everywhere." {23:25} "I've heard these prophets talking nonsense, claiming they had visions and dreams." {23:26} "How long are they gonna keep lying to themselves and everyone else?" {23:27} "They're trying to make people forget about me and follow their own dreams, just like they did with Baal." {23:28} "If a prophet has a dream, let him speak it, but if he has my word, let him speak it faithfully." {23:29} "My word's like a fire and a hammer; it's gonna break through anything." {23:30} "I'm against these prophets who steal my words and claim them as their own." {23:31} "I'm against those who speak lies in my name." {23:32} "I'm against those who spread false dreams and lead my people astray." {23:33} "If anyone asks what's up with the Lord, tell them nothing; I've left them." {23:34} "And if anyone keeps talking about the Lord's burden, they're gonna get what's coming to them." {23:35} "Just ask, 'What's the Lord saying?' and 'What's he doing?'" {23:36} "Stop talking about the Lord's burden; everyone's gonna carry their own load because you've twisted my words." {23:37} "Ask the prophets, 'What's the Lord saying?' and 'What's he doing?'" {23:38} "Since you keep saying 'the Lord's burden,' even though I told you not to, I'm gonna forget about you and your city." {23:39} "You're gonna face everlasting shame and disgrace."

{24:1} "God gave me a vision of two baskets of figs, one good and one rotten, after Nebuchadnezzar took some peeps from Judah to Babylon." {24:2} "The good figs represent those I'll bring back to their land; the bad figs represent Zedekiah and his crew, who'll face trouble." {24:3} "The good will be blessed, and the bad will face the consequences." {24:4} "That's the deal from the Lord, straight up."

{25:1} So, in the fourth year of Jehoiakim, son of Josiah, king of Judah, and the first year of Nebuchadnezzar, king of Babylon, a word came to Jeremiah about all the people of Judah; {25:2} Jeremiah the prophet spoke to all the people of Judah and the peeps in Jerusalem, saying, {25:3} "From the thirteenth year of Josiah, son of Amon, king of Judah, until today, for twenty-three years, the word of the LORD has come to me, and I've been speaking to y'all, but you haven't listened. {25:4} The LORD sent all His prophets to you, but you ignored them and didn't even bother to listen. {25:5} They said, 'Yo, turn from your evil ways and actions, and you can live in the land the LORD gave you and your ancestors forever. {25:6} Don't chase other gods to serve and worship them, making me mad with the works of your hands; then I won't harm you.' {25:7} But you didn't listen to me, says the LORD, and made me angry with your actions to your own detriment. {25:8} So, because you didn't listen to my words," says the LORD of hosts, {25:9} "I'm bringing all the families from the north, including Nebuchadnezzar, king of Babylon, my servant, to destroy this land and its people, and all the surrounding nations, making them an astonishment, a hissing, and a perpetual desolation. {25:10} I'll take away their joy, happiness, the voices of bride and groom, the sound of grinding mills, and the light of lamps. {25:11} This whole land will be desolate and shocking, and these nations will serve the king of Babylon for seventy years. {25:12} When the seventy years are up, I'll punish the king of Babylon and that nation for their iniquity," says the LORD, "and make the land of the Chaldeans desolate forever. {25:13} I'll bring upon that land all my words I've pronounced against it, everything written in this book that Jeremiah has prophesied against all the nations. {25:14} Many nations and great kings will make slaves of them too, and I'll repay them according to their deeds and the works of their hands." {25:15} This is what the LORD, God of Israel, told me: "Take this cup of my fury from my hand and make all the nations I send you to drink it. {25:16} They'll drink it, stagger, and go crazy because of the sword I'm sending among them." {25:17} So, I took the cup from the LORD's hand and made all the nations drink it, the ones the LORD sent me to: {25:18} Jerusalem and the cities of Judah, their kings and officials, making them a desolation, an astonishment, a hissing, and a curse, like today; {25:19} Pharaoh, king of Egypt, his servants, his officials, and all his people; {25:20} all the mixed people, all the kings of the land of Uz, all the kings of the land of the Philistines (Ashkelon, Gaza, Ekron, and the leftover people of Ashdod); {25:21} Edom, Moab, and the Ammonites; {25:22} all the kings of Tyre, all the kings of Sidon, and the kings of the coastlands across the sea; {25:23} Dedan, Tema, Buz, and all those who cut the corners of their hair; {25:24} all the kings of Arabia, and all the kings of the mixed people living in the desert; {25:25} all the kings of Zimri, all the kings of Elam, and all the kings of Media; {25:26} all the kings of the north, far and near, one after another, and all the kingdoms on the face of the earth. And the king of Sheshach will drink after them. {25:27} So, tell them this: This is what the LORD of hosts, the God of Israel, says: "Drink, get drunk, vomit, fall, and don't get up because of the sword I'm sending among you." {25:28} If they refuse to take the cup from your hand to drink, tell them this is what the LORD of hosts says: "You will certainly drink. {25:29} I'm starting to bring disaster on the city called by my name, and you expect to go unpunished? You won't be unpunished because I'm bringing a sword against all the inhabitants of the earth," declares the LORD of hosts. {25:30} So, prophesy all these words against them and say: "The LORD will roar from on high, and from His holy dwelling, He will shout loudly. He will roar against His land and shout like those who tread the grapes, against all who live on the earth. {25:31} The noise will resound to the ends of the earth, for the LORD has a case against the nations. He will judge all humanity and put the wicked to the sword," declares the LORD. {25:32} This is what the LORD of hosts says: "Look! Disaster is spreading from nation to nation; a mighty storm is rising from the ends of the earth." {25:33} On that day, those slain by the LORD will be everywhere—from one end of the earth to the other. They won't be mourned, gathered, or buried, but will be like dung lying on the ground. {25:34} Wail, you shepherds, and cry out; roll in the dust, you leaders of the flock. The days of your slaughter have come, and you will fall and be shattered like fine pottery. {25:35} The shepherds will have nowhere to flee, the leaders of the flock no place to escape. {25:36} Listen to the cries of the shepherds, the wailing of the leaders of the flock, for the LORD is destroying their pasture. {25:37} The peaceful meadows will be laid waste because of the LORD's fierce anger. {25:38} He has left His den like a lion, for their land is a desolate wasteland because of the oppressor's sword and because of the LORD's fierce anger.

{26:1} Early in the reign of Jehoiakim, son of Josiah, king of Judah, this word came from the LORD: {26:2} "This is what the LORD says: Stand in the courtyard of the LORD's house and speak to all the people of the towns of Judah who come to worship in the LORD's house. Tell them everything I command you; don't leave out a word. {26:3} Maybe they'll listen, and each will turn from their evil ways. Then I'll relent and not bring the disaster I was planning because of their evil deeds. {26:4} Say to them: This is what the LORD says: If you do not listen to me and follow my law, which I've set before you, {26:5} and if you don't listen to the words of my servants the prophets, whom I've sent to you again and again (though you haven't listened), {26:6} then I'll make this house like Shiloh and this city a curse among all the nations of the earth." {26:7} The priests, the prophets, and all the people heard Jeremiah speak these words in the house of the LORD. {26:8} But as soon as Jeremiah finished telling all the people everything the LORD had commanded him to say, the priests, the prophets, and all the people seized him and said, "You must die! {26:9} Why do you prophesy in the LORD's name that this house will be like Shiloh and this city desolate and uninhabited?" And all the people crowded around Jeremiah in the house of the LORD. {26:10} When the officials of Judah heard about these things, they went up from the king's palace to the house of the LORD and took their places at the entrance of the New Gate of the LORD's house.{26:11} So, like, the priests and prophets were all up in the princes' and people's faces, saying, "Yo, this dude's gotta go! He's been dissing the city, and y'all heard it yourselves." {26:12} Then Jeremiah was like, "Listen up, y'all. The big man upstairs sent me to drop truth bombs on this city and its peeps. {26:13} So, like, if you wanna avoid the drama, start acting right and listen to what the big guy says. He might change his mind about wrecking you." {26:14-15} "As for me, do whatever, but just know if you off me, innocent blood's on your hands, and this city's cursed. The big guy sent me to spit facts, yo." {26:16} Then the princes and everyone else were like, "Hold up, hold up. This dude ain't gotta die. He's just spitting truths in the name of our God." {26:17-19} And then some elders piped up, saying, "Yo, remember Micah back in the day? He warned about this stuff too, and he didn't get whacked for it. Maybe offing this dude ain't the move." {26:20} And there was this other dude, Urijah, speaking the same language as Jeremiah about this city and land, and when King Jehoiakim heard it, he tried to ice Urijah, but the dude ran to Egypt. {26:21} So, Jehoiakim sent a squad to Egypt, grabbed Urijah, brought him back, and whacked him. But Jeremiah had some backup, Ahikam, so they couldn't touch him.

{27:1} So, like, when Jehoiakim was ruling in Judah, the Lord hit up Jeremiah with this message: {27:2} "Jeremiah, bro, make some bonds and yokes, and rock them on your neck." {27:3} "Then send them to all these kings: Edom, Moab, Ammonites, Tyrus, Zidon, through the messengers coming to Zedekiah in Judah." {27:4} "Tell 'em this is from the Lord: I made everything, and I've given it to Nebuchadnezzar, even the animals." {27:5} "All nations gotta serve him and his descendants until his time's up, then others will take over." {27:6} "Anyone who won't serve him will face the sword, famine, and disease until they're gone." {27:7} "So don't listen to those prophets telling you not to serve Babylon; they're lying and leading you astray." {27:8} "The nations that submit to Babylon will stay in their land and live, but those who resist will be punished." {27:9} "Ignore those prophets, diviners, and dreamers saying you won't serve Babylon; they're lying to you." {27:10} "They're just trying to get you kicked out and destroyed." {27:11} "But those who serve Babylon will chill in their own land and thrive." {27:12} "I told Zedekiah the same thing: serve Babylon and live." {27:13} "Why risk death by ignoring my warning?" {27:14} "So, don't believe those prophets saying you won't serve Babylon; they're straight-up lying." {27:15} "I didn't send them; they're just spreading lies in my name, leading you and themselves into trouble." {27:16} "I even told the priests and the people the same thing: don't listen to those prophets saying the temple stuff will come back soon from Babylon; it's all lies." {27:17} "Serve Babylon, and you'll survive; why let the city get wrecked?" {27:18} "And if those prophets claim they're legit, let them pray I don't let Babylon take any more stuff from the temple or the king's palace." {27:19} "But the vessels Nebuchadnezzar didn't take when he exiled Jeconiah and the nobles will eventually end up in Babylon." {27:20} "That's the deal; they'll stay there until I bring them back." {27:21} "Everything left in the temple and the king's palace will also go to Babylon, but one day, I'll bring them back." {27:22} "So, don't stress; it's all part of the plan."

{28:1} "Then, in Zedekiah's fourth year, Hananiah, this prophet from Gibeon, rolls up with some wild claims." {28:2} "He's like, 'Yo, the Lord said I broke Babylon's yoke.'" {28:3} "He's saying in two years, all the temple stuff Nebuchadnezzar took will be back, along with the captives." {28:4} "But Jeremiah's like, 'Sure, okay, if that's what the Lord's really saying.'" {28:5} "Then Jeremiah drops truth in front of everyone, saying prophets before him predicted wars and disasters, not peace like Hananiah's saying." {28:6} "But Jeremiah's like, 'Word, if that's what the Lord's saying, let it happen.'" {28:7} "But then he hits Hananiah with the real talk, saying he's speaking lies." {28:8} "Those true prophets predicted wars and disasters, not peace." {28:9} "So, if Hananiah's prophecy comes true, then we'll know he's legit." {28:10} "Hananiah grabs Jeremiah's yoke and breaks it, spouting more about breaking Babylon's yoke in two years." {28:11} "Then he peaces out, leaving Jeremiah to do his thing." {28:12} "Later, the Lord hits up Jeremiah, telling him to tell Hananiah he didn't break wooden yokes, but he's about to bring iron ones." {28:13} "All these nations will serve Babylon, as I've decreed." {28:14} "So, Jeremiah's like, 'Sorry, Hananiah, but you're wrong.'" {28:15} "You're leading the people astray with your lies, so the Lord's gonna take you out." {28:16} "And true to the word, Hananiah bites the dust that same year."

{29:1} Alright, check it, Jeremiah shot this letter from Jerusalem to the elders, priests, prophets, and all the peeps Nebuchadnezzar took to Babylon, including Jeconiah, the queen, and others, through Elasah and Gemariah, who Zedekiah sent. {29:2} This was after Jeconiah and crew bounced from Jerusalem. {29:3} So, Zedekiah sent this letter to Nebuchadnezzar, saying, "Yo, the Lord says to build houses, plant gardens, get married, and pray for Babylon, 'cause when it's good there, it's good for you." {29:4} "Don't listen to your own prophets and dreamers; they're spitting lies in the Lord's name." {29:5} "But after 70 years, I'll bring you back and do good stuff for you." {29:6} "I got good plans for you, not bad ones." {29:7} "Just pray to me, seek me, and you'll find me." {29:8} "Those prophets in Babylon ain't legit; they're just leading you astray." {29:9} "They're lying in my name; I didn't send them." {29:10} "So after 70 years, I'll hook you up, and you'll be back here." {29:11} "I got plans for you, fam, plans for peace, not disaster." {29:12} "Just call on me, and I'll listen." {29:13} "Seek me with all your heart, and you'll find me." {29:14} "I'll bring you back and gather you from everywhere you got scattered." {29:15} "But since you're saying the Lord raised up prophets in Babylon, watch out." {29:16} "The Lord's gonna deal with those kings and peeps left behind, sending them war, famine, and disease." {29:17} "They're gonna be like nasty figs, uneatable and cursed." {29:18} "Because they ignored my warnings through my prophets." {29:19} "Listen up, all you exiles; these lying prophets are gonna get what's coming to them." {29:20} "The Lord's saying to Ahab and Zedekiah, who are lying in his name, Nebuchadrezzar's gonna take care of them." {29:21} "They're gonna get roasted just like Zedekiah and Ahab." {29:22} "Because they've been doing shady stuff and lying in the Lord's name." {29:23} "Jeremiah's got a message for Shemaiah too." {29:24} "The Lord's saying, 'You're gonna get punished for your lies and leading people astray.'" {29:25} "He was calling himself a prophet and causing chaos." {29:26} "So why didn't you call him out, Zephaniah?" {29:27} "He was saying this captivity would be short, but nah, build your houses and stay put." {29:28} "And Zephaniah read Jeremiah's letter aloud." {29:29} "Then the Lord hit up Jeremiah again, saying, 'Tell the peeps in exile about Shemaiah.'" {29:30} "He's been spewing lies, and I didn't send him." {29:31} "So I'm gonna deal with him and his descendants for leading people astray."

{30:1} "Now, here's what the Lord's saying to Jeremiah." {30:2} "Write down everything I've told you in a book." {30:3} "I'm gonna bring back the exiles, Israel and Judah, to the land I gave their ancestors." {30:4} "But it ain't gonna be easy; there's gonna be fear and trembling." {30:5} "It's gonna be rough, like dudes in labor, faces pale with fear." {30:6} "It's gonna be a time of trouble, but they'll make it through." {30:7} "And when it's over, no one's gonna mess with them." {30:8} "I'm gonna break their chains and set them free." {30:9} "They'll serve me and David their king, and I'll raise him up for them." {30:10} "So don't stress, Jacob, I got you; you'll come back and chill in peace." {30:11} "Even though I'll punish other nations, I won't wipe you out completely." {30:12} "Your wounds are bad, but I'll heal them." {30:13} "There's no one else to help you, no meds to heal you." {30:14} "Your lovers have forgotten you 'cause I've punished you for your sins." {30:15} "Your suffering's deep 'cause your sins are many." {30:16} "But those who mess with you will get messed up too." {30:17} "I'll bring healing, and they'll know you're Zion, not abandoned." {30:18} "I'll rebuild your city and show mercy on your homes." {30:19} "There'll be joy and thanksgiving, and I'll increase your numbers." {30:20} "Your kids will be plentiful, and your community will be strong." {30:21} "Your leaders will come from among you, and they'll approach me with all their hearts." {30:22} "You'll be my people, and I'll be your God." {30:23} "But for the wicked, there's gonna be a storm coming." {30:24} "The Lord's anger won't stop until he's done what he planned." {30:25} "You'll see it all in the end."

{31:1} Yo, God's like, "I got the back of all the fams in Israel, and they're gonna be my squad." {31:2} He's saying, "Even those who survived the chaos got my blessing in the wild, especially my boy Jeremiah when I helped him chill." {31:3} God's been with me since forever, saying, "I've had mad love for you non-stop; that's why I've been all about showing you kindness." {31:4} He's like, "I'm gonna rebuild you, Israel, and you'll be lit again, decked out with your vibes, dancing and celebrating." {31:5} "You'll be planting vines up in the hills, and people will be snacking on the grapes like it's NBD." {31:6} "There's gonna be a day when everyone's hyped to head to Zion and kick it with the Lord." {31:7} God's like, "Time to throw down some beats for Jacob and give some shout-outs for Israel. Spread the word, give thanks, and pray for the crew." {31:8} "I'll bring them back from everywhere, even the blind, the pregnant, and those going through it. It's gonna be a big reunion." {31:9} "They'll come back with tears, but I'll guide them gently, like a loving parent." {31:10} "Listen up, world, and broadcast it far and wide: God, who scattered Israel, is gonna bring them together like a boss shepherd." {31:11} "I've rescued Jacob and got him back from those stronger than him." {31:12} "So let's party up in Zion, celebrating all the blessings I'm bringing: food, wine, and good times. They're gonna be feeling like a well-watered garden, with no more sadness." {31:13} "The party's gonna be jumping, from the young to the old, 'cause I'm turning their sorrow into joy." {31:14} "My peeps will be living large, satisfied with all the goodness I'm bringing," says the Lord. {31:15} "But, yo, there's some real talk too: crying and mourning heard all around, especially Rachel crying for her lost children, refusing to be comforted." {31:16} "But I'm telling her, 'Chill, wipe those tears, 'cause there's hope on the horizon; those kids are coming home.'" {31:17} "Believe it, there's light at the end of the tunnel. Your kids will be back home, safe and sound." {31:18} "I hear Ephraim laying it all out: 'You disciplined me, and I took it like a champ. Turn me around, and I'll get back on track; you're my God, after all.'" {31:19} "Once I got turned around, I was all in. I was like, 'Dang, I really messed up, feeling so ashamed of my past.'" {31:20} "Is Ephraim still close to my heart? You bet. I've been real torn up about him; I'm gonna show him some serious love," says the Lord. {31:21} "Set some reminders, make some bold moves. Keep your eyes on the road, Israel, and head back to your hometowns." {31:22} "Yo, rebellious daughter, how long you gonna keep messing up? God's pulling off some crazy stuff here: a girl's gonna be chasing a dude." {31:23} "This is gonna be the talk of the town when I bring my crew back from the struggle: 'God's blessing you, land of justice and holiness.'" {31:24} "Everyone's gonna be chilling in Judah, farming and raising livestock, because I've given them rest." {31:25} "I've given peace to the weary and joy to the sorrowful." {31:26} "When I woke up, it was all good vibes; my sleep was mad sweet." {31:27} "Check it, there's more good stuff coming: I'm gonna fill Israel and Judah with people and animals, like I've always said." {31:28} "Just like I've been watching to tear down, I'm gonna be watching to build up," says the Lord. {31:29} "No more blaming the past; everyone's gonna be responsible for their own actions." {31:30} "So, yeah, if you're messing up, you're gonna feel it; your mistakes are gonna bite you back." {31:31} "Here's the deal: I'm gonna make a fresh covenant with Israel and Judah, not like the old one from Egypt that they broke. This time, I'm putting my law in their hearts." {31:32} "They won't need a crash course in knowing me; from the top dogs to the newbies, they'll all be tight with me. I'm wiping the slate clean." {31:33} "Check it, I'm the one keeping the lights on in the sky, making the waves crash, and my name? It's the Lord of the Universe." {31:34} "As long as the sun and moon shine, Israel will be around. I ain't giving up on them, no matter what."

{32:1} So, like, this message popped up for Jeremiah from the big man upstairs during Zedekiah's reign, which was also when Nebuchadrezzar was doing his thing. {32:2} At that time, the Babylonian army had Jerusalem on lockdown, and Jeremiah was stuck in the king's crib's courtyard, locked up tight. {32:3} Zedekiah was all like, "Why you gotta be such a downer, Jeremiah? Always saying Babylon's gonna take over the city and stuff." {32:4} "And guess what? You won't escape, Zedekiah; you're gonna have a face-to-face chat with Nebuchadrezzar himself, and it won't be pretty." {32:5} "He's gonna haul you off to Babylon, and you'll be chilling there until further notice. And yeah, fighting against the Chaldeans ain't gonna do squat for you." {32:6} Jeremiah's like, "Got a message from the man upstairs, y'all." {32:7} "So, my cousin Hanameel rolls up in the courtyard, talking about selling his land in Anathoth. He says I got first dibs 'cause it's family and all." {32:8} "He hands me the pitch in the courtyard, just like the big man said he would, and starts pitching his land in Anathoth, repping that Benjamin life. He's all like, 'You gotta buy this land; it's in the fam, bro.'" {32:9} "So, I drop seventeen shekels of silver and seal the deal, like, 'This is legit.'" {32:10} "I make it official, sign the papers, get some witnesses, and weigh out the cash. All by the book, yo." {32:11} "Then I hand over the paperwork to Baruch, with all eyes on us in the courtyard." {32:12} "I pass it to Baruch in front of Hanameel and the crew, with all the homies watching." {32:13} "And I'm like, 'Baruch, hold onto these papers tight, man. Keep 'em safe for a long time.'" {32:14} "God's saying, 'Put those papers in a jar so they last, 'cause one day, people will be buying and selling land again in this place.'" {32:15} "God's like, 'Don't worry, houses and fields will be back on the market in this land.'" {32:16} "After handing off the paperwork to Baruch, I'm like, 'Yo, big man upstairs, you made the heavens and the earth, ain't nothing too tough for you.'" {32:17} "You're all about love and justice, dishing out what's deserved." {32:18} "You're the real deal, God Almighty, checking out everyone's moves and paying back accordingly." {32:19} "You're all about the big plans and making things happen, keeping an eye on everyone and serving up consequences." {32:20} "You've been dropping miracles since Egypt, making a name for yourself." {32:21} "You busted Israel out of Egypt with style, throwing down signs, wonders, and straight-up terror." {32:22} "And then you hooked them up with this sweet land, just like you promised their ancestors." {32:23} "But they blew it, didn't follow your rules, and now they're paying the price. It's all on them." {32:24} "Now look, the enemy's at the gates, just like you said. The city's toast, and it's playing out right before our eyes." {32:25} "You told me to buy land even though Babylon's about to take over the place." {32:26} "Then God's like, 'Jeremiah, listen up.'" {32:27} "He's like, 'I'm the big boss, the God of all humanity. Nothing's too tough for me, remember?'" {32:28} "So, God's saying, 'Babylon's gonna roll in and take this city, just like I said. And they're gonna torch it, especially the houses where people worshiped other gods.'" {32:29} "Why? 'Cause Israel and Judah have been nothing but trouble, making me mad since day one, doing all sorts of messed-up stuff." {32:30} "So, God's like, 'Jerusalem's been ticking me off for ages, from the day they built it. I'm done with it.'" {32:31} "And why? 'Cause the people of Israel and Judah, from the top dogs to the regular Joes, have been driving me nuts with their nonsense." {32:32} "They've turned their backs on me, ignored my warnings, and trashed my house with their idols." {32:33} "They've had their chance to shape up, but nope, they turned their backs on me instead." {32:34} "They've polluted my temple with their filth, setting up shrines to worship other gods." {32:35} "They're even sacrificing their kids to these false gods, something I never even told them to do. It's a total disaster." {32:36} "But here's the deal: despite all this, I'm still gonna bring back the people who've been scattered, including those from other countries." {32:37} "I'm bringing them back home, and they're gonna live in peace." {32:38} "They'll be my crew, and I'll be their God, no doubt." {32:39} "I'm gonna unify them, make 'em all fear me, for their own good and the good of their kids." {32:40} "And I'm making a forever pact with them; I won't ever ditch 'em, but I'll make sure they stay loyal to me." {32:41} "I'm stoked to do good for them, and I'm planting them in this land with all my heart and soul." {32:42} "Just like I brought down the hammer with all the bad stuff, I'm gonna come through with all the good stuff I promised." {32:43} "And yeah, people will be buying land again in this supposedly desolate place." {32:44} "Folks will be buying and selling in Benjamin, Jerusalem, Judah, the mountains, valleys, and southern lands, 'cause I'm bringing back the exiles, says the big man upstairs."

{33:1} So, like, the big man upstairs hit up Jeremiah again, while he was still chilling in the prison courtyard, saying, {33:2} "Listen up, I'm the one who made everything, formed it all, and I go by the name of the LORD. {33:3} Hit me up, and I'll clue you in on some mind-blowing stuff you ain't even heard of yet." {33:4} "Now, peep this, I've got something to say about the houses in this city and the houses of the kings of Judah that got wrecked by the enemy. {33:5} They tried to throw down with the Chaldeans, but it just ended up filling the place with dead bodies, thanks to my anger and fury over their wickedness." {33:6} "But check it, I'm gonna bring healing and cure, reveal some peace and truth, and bring back Judah and Israel from captivity, rebuilding them like they were at the start. {33:7} I'll wipe their slate clean of all the dirt they've done against me, pardon all their sins, and they'll be a name of joy and honor to all the nations." {33:8} "Everyone's gonna hear about the good I'm doing for them and be shaking in their boots over the blessings I'm dropping." {33:9} "And yo, there'll be voices of joy and gladness again, weddings, praises to the LORD, and sacrifices in His house because I'm bringing back the land's prosperity." {33:10} "And this place that everyone thought would be empty? Nah, it's gonna be bumping again, with people and animals and all that jazz." {33:11} "People will be shouting praises to the LORD because of all the good stuff happening, and I'm gonna restore the land's prosperity, just like before." {33:12} "In all the cities, shepherds will be chilling with their flocks, just living their best lives." {33:13} "And the flocks will be all over the place, in the mountains, valleys, and everywhere else, just like the good old days." {33:14} "I'm gonna make good on all the promises I made to Israel and Judah." {33:15} "And in those days, the Branch of righteousness will sprout up for David, bringing judgment and righteousness to the land." {33:16} "Judah will be saved, Jerusalem will be secure, and they'll be known as 'The LORD our righteousness.'" {33:17} "Because let me tell you, David's line will always have someone on the throne, and the Levite priests won't ever run out of folks to handle their sacrifices." {33:18} "I'm keeping my end of the deal, no worries." {33:19} "Now, peep this, if you can mess with the laws of nature, then maybe you can mess with my promises to David and the Levite priests, but that ain't happening." {33:20} "As much as you can't count the stars or measure the sand, that's how I'm gonna multiply David's descendants and the Levites serving me." {33:21} "Now, let's talk about what these people are saying, dissing on the two families I chose, acting like I've rejected them. {33:22} If I break my promise about day and night, then yeah, maybe I'll break my promise to David and the Levite priests." {33:23} "But nah, that's not happening. David's line and the Levites are sticking around, no matter what."

{34:1} "Now, here's the deal. When Nebuchadnezzar and his crew were laying siege to Jerusalem and its cities, I had something to say to Zedekiah, king of Judah." {34:2} "I told him straight up, 'Babylon's gonna wreck this place, burn it to the ground.'" {34:3} "You ain't escaping, Zedekiah, you're getting nabbed, eyeball to eyeball with the king of Babylon, and then it's off to Babylon for you." {34:4} "But don't stress, you won't die by the sword, just a peaceful death, and people will mourn you, because I said so." {34:5} "So, Jeremiah dropped this knowledge on Zedekiah while Babylon was doing its thing, hitting up Jerusalem and the remaining cities of Judah." {34:6} "After Zedekiah made this deal with the people of Jerusalem, promising freedom to all their Hebrew servants, everyone was down with it." {34:7} "But then they changed their minds, brought back their former servants, and put them back into slavery." {34:8} "So I hit up Jeremiah again, saying, 'Check this out, I made a deal with your ancestors when I brought them out of Egypt, but they didn't stick to it." {34:9} "I said after seven years, let your Hebrew servants go free, but they didn't listen. You tried to do right, but then you went and messed it all up again." {34:10} "So, since you didn't keep your end of the deal about setting your servants free, I'm declaring freedom for you, but not the good kind. You're gonna face war, disease, famine, and get scattered all over the place." {34:11} "And those who broke the covenant by cutting that calf in half, I'm serving them up to their enemies, their dead bodies as a feast for the birds and beasts." {34:12} "And Zedekiah and his crew? Yeah, they're getting handed over to their enemies, including Babylon's army, and they're gonna get wrecked." {34:13} "I'm gonna command it, and they're gonna come back and take this city, burning it down. And all the cities of Judah are gonna be ghost towns."

{35:1} So, like, God's message came to Jeremiah when Jehoiakim was ruling Judah, saying, {35:2} "Yo, go hit up the Rechabites' crib, bring 'em to the house of the Lord, and hook 'em up with some wine." {35:3} So Jeremiah rolls with Jaazaniah and the whole Rechabite crew to the temple. {35:4} He takes them to this chamber, and there's all this wine waiting for them. {35:5} Jeremiah's like, "Drink up, fam." {35:6} But they're like, "Nah, man. Our ancestor Jonadab said no to the vino, and we've been sticking to that rule for ages." {35:7} "We don't build houses, plant crops, or own land; we're all about that tent life, keeping it real as strangers in this land." {35:8} "We've been following Jonadab's orders to the letter, no wine for us or our kids, and no fancy houses either." {35:9} "Nope, no houses, vineyards, or fields for us. Just tents and obedience to Jonadab's commands." {35:10-11} "So, when Nebuchadnezzar came knocking, we bounced to Jerusalem, scared of the Babylonians and the Syrians." {35:12} Then God hits up Jeremiah again, saying, {35:13} "Tell the people of Judah and Jerusalem, 'Why you gotta be so stubborn? Listen to my words, yo.'" {35:14} "The Rechabites have been loyal to Jonadab's command not to drink wine, but y'all keep ignoring me." {35:15} "I've been sending prophets, begging y'all to turn from your wicked ways and worship only me, but nope, y'all ain't listening." {35:16} "The Rechabites are following their ancestor's commands, but y'all ain't following mine. So, here's the deal:" {35:17} "I'm bringing all the bad stuff I promised on Judah and Jerusalem 'cause y'all ain't listening to me, even though I've been calling out to you." {35:18} Jeremiah tells the Rechabites, "God's pleased with you for sticking to Jonadab's rules; you'll always have a representative before God." {35:19} "Jonadab's legacy is gonna stand forever before God."

{36:1} Now, in Jehoiakim's fourth year as king, God hits up Jeremiah again, saying, {36:2} "Grab a notebook and write down everything I've told you about Israel, Judah, and all the nations since Josiah's time." {36:3} "Maybe if the people of Judah hear all the bad stuff coming their way, they'll straighten up, and I can forgive them." {36:4} So, Jeremiah calls up Baruch and tells him to write down everything God's said. {36:5} But Jeremiah can't go to the temple himself, so he sends Baruch in his place. {36:6} Baruch's supposed to read God's words to the people in the temple and all over Judah. {36:7} Maybe they'll pray and change their ways, 'cause God's seriously ticked off at them. {36:8} Baruch follows Jeremiah's orders, reading God's words in the temple. {36:9} Then, in Jehoiakim's fifth year, they call for a fast in Jerusalem, and Baruch reads God's words to everyone. {36:10} He even reads them to the officials in the temple. {36:11} One of those officials, Michaiah, goes to the king's palace and tells the others what he heard Baruch read. {36:12} So all the big shots send Jehudi to fetch Baruch and his scroll. {36:13} They're like, "Baruch, bring that scroll over here; we wanna hear it for ourselves." {36:14} Baruch's like, "Okay, sure," and brings the scroll. {36:15} They're like, "Read it to us," so Baruch does. {36:16} And when they hear it, they freak out and decide to tell the king everything. {36:17} They ask Baruch how he wrote down all this stuff, and he's like, "Jeremiah told me, and I wrote it down." {36:18-19} They're like, "Wow, okay," and tell Baruch and Jeremiah to hide. {36:20} They head to the king's court but stash the scroll in a room, then spill all the tea to the king. {36:21} So the king sends Jehudi to grab the scroll, and Jehudi reads it to the king and all his posse. {36:22} The king's chilling by the fire when Jehudi starts reading. {36:23} He reads a few pages, then slices up the scroll and tosses it into the fire. {36:24} Nobody freaks out, not even the king or his crew. {36:25} A couple of guys try to stop the king, but he won't listen. {36:26} So the king sends some guys to nab Baruch and Jeremiah, but God hides them. {36:27-28} Then God tells Jeremiah to write it all down again, all the stuff Jehoiakim burned. {36:29} And tell Jehoiakim, "You burned the scroll 'cause it said Babylon's gonna wreck this place, but now you're really screwed." {36:30} "You won't have an heir on David's throne, and you'll be thrown out, roasting in the sun by day and freezing at night." {36:31} "You and your crew are gonna pay for your sins, and all the bad stuff I said is gonna happen to you 'cause you didn't listen." {36:32} So Jeremiah writes it all down again with Baruch's help, and they add even more stuff.

{37:1} So, like, Zedekiah takes over from Coniah 'cause Nebuchadnezzar made him king in Judah. {37:2} But neither Zedekiah, his crew, nor the peeps in Judah listen to God's words through Jeremiah. {37:3} Zedekiah sends Jehucal and Zephaniah to Jeremiah, like, "Yo, pray to God for us." {37:4} Jeremiah's out and about 'cause they haven't thrown him in jail yet. {37:5} Then when Pharaoh's army shows up, the Chaldeans bounce from Jerusalem. {37:6} Then God hits up Jeremiah, saying, {37:7} "Tell Zedekiah Pharaoh's army ain't gonna save him; they're heading back to Egypt. And those Chaldeans? They're coming back to wreck Jerusalem." {37:8} "Don't fool yourselves; the Chaldeans ain't leaving." {37:9} "Even if you beat 'em up, they'll still come back and torch the city." {37:10} So, even if you beat up the Chaldeans, they'll come back and burn the city down. {37:11} So when the Chaldeans bail 'cause of Pharaoh's army, {37:12} Jeremiah splits from Jerusalem. {37:13} But at the Benjamin Gate, Irijah accuses him of defecting to the Chaldeans. {37:14} Jeremiah's like, "Nah, that's fake news," but Irijah drags him to the princes anyway. {37:15} They're mad at Jeremiah, so they beat him up and throw him in prison. {37:16} Jeremiah's stuck in the dungeon for days, {37:17} until Zedekiah secretly brings him out and asks if God's got any messages. Jeremiah's like, "Yep, you're getting handed over to Babylon." {37:18} Jeremiah's like, "What'd I do to deserve this? And where are those prophets who said Babylon wouldn't touch us?" {37:19-20} "Listen up, Zedekiah. Don't send me back to that prison or I might kick the bucket there." {37:21} So Zedekiah moves him to a better prison spot and gives him bread until it runs out.

{38:1} Then Shephatiah, Gedaliah, Jucal, and Pashur hear Jeremiah's words: {38:2} "Stay in the city, you'll die. Surrender to the Chaldeans, you'll live." {38:3} "The city's going down to Babylon." {38:4} The princes are like, "Let's kill Jeremiah; he's demoralizing the troops." {38:5} Zedekiah's like, "Fine, do whatever." {38:6} So they chuck Jeremiah into Malchiah's dungeon with no water, just muck. {38:7} But Ebed-melech, a palace dude, hears about it and tells Zedekiah, who's chilling at the Benjamin Gate. {38:8} Ebed-melech's like, "Dude, Jeremiah's gonna starve to death down there." {38:9-10} So Zedekiah sends Ebed-melech and some guys to rescue Jeremiah before he croaks. {38:11-12} They lower some rags down to Jeremiah and tell him to put them under his armpits for cushioning. {38:13} They haul Jeremiah out of the pit, and he stays in the prison court. {38:14} Zedekiah pulls Jeremiah aside in the temple and is like, "Spill the beans, Jeremiah, I won't snitch." {38:15} Jeremiah's like, "If I tell you, will you kill me? And if I give you advice, will you listen?" {38:16} Zedekiah swears not to kill him or let others harm him. {38:17} So Jeremiah tells Zedekiah, "If you surrender to Babylon, you'll live. If not, you're toast." {38:18-19} Zedekiah's like, "But the Jews who've already gone over to the Chaldeans might make fun of me." {38:20} Jeremiah's like, "Don't worry, they won't." "Listen to God, and you'll be okay." {38:21-22} But if you refuse, God says all the women left in your palace will mock you as you sink in the muck, and your family will be captured. {38:23-24} Zedekiah's like, "Keep this on the down-low, and you won't die." {38:25} "But if the princes ask, don't hide anything from them, or they might kill you." {38:26} "Just say you asked not to go back to Jonathan's house to die." {38:27} So the princes grill Jeremiah, and he tells them everything Zedekiah said. And they leave him alone 'cause they don't suspect anything. {38:28} So Jeremiah chills in the prison court until Babylon takes over Jerusalem.

{39:1} So, like, in the ninth year of Zedekiah's rule over Judah, in the tenth month, Nebuchadnezzar, the king of Babylon, and his crew rolled up on Jerusalem, and they straight-up surrounded it. {39:2} Then, in the eleventh year of Zedekiah's reign, in the fourth month, on the ninth day, they busted through the city's defenses. {39:3} And all the big shots from Babylon, like Nergal-sharezer, Samgar-nebo, Sarsechim, Rab-saris, Nergal-sharezer, Rabmag, and the rest of the crew, they all showed up and kicked it at the main gate. {39:4} When King Zedekiah peeped them and their army, he and his soldiers bolted out of the city under the cover of darkness, sneaking out through the king's garden gate between the walls and heading out into the open plain. {39:5} But the Babylonian army was on their tail, and they caught up with Zedekiah in the Jericho plains, nabbed him, and dragged him off to Nebuchadnezzar in Riblah, where he got his judgment. {39:6} Then Nebuchadnezzar himself watched as they offed Zedekiah's sons right in front of him and took out all the nobles of Judah. {39:7} And just to rub it in, they blinded Zedekiah, put him in chains, and hauled him off to Babylon. {39:8} The Babylonians torched the king's palace, the people's houses, and knocked down the walls of Jerusalem. {39:9} Nebuzar-adan, the captain of the guard, rounded up the remaining folks in the city and those who surrendered to him and shipped them off to Babylon as captives. {39:10} But he left behind the poorest of the poor in Judah, hooking them up with vineyards and fields. {39:11-12} Now, Nebuchadnezzar gave Nebuzar-adan a special mission concerning Jeremiah, telling him, "Look after him, don't hurt him, just do whatever he says." {39:13} So Nebuzar-adan, Rab-saris, Nergal-sharezer, Rabmag, and the rest of the Babylonian bigwigs went and fetched Jeremiah out of prison and handed him over to Gedaliah, son of Ahikam, to take care of. {39:14-15} While Jeremiah was still locked up, the LORD dropped some wisdom on him, saying, "Yo, go talk to Ebed-melech the Ethiopian. I'm bringing some bad stuff down on this city, but I got your back, bro."

{40:1} After Nebuzar-adan let Jeremiah loose from Ramah, where he'd been dragged along with the other captives, {40:2} he was like, "Yeah, God's not happy with what went down here. You guys messed up, and now you're paying for it." {40:3-4} "But hey, I'm setting you free today. If you wanna come with me to Babylon, cool. If not, do your thing, man. The whole land's open to you." {40:5} Before he bounced, Nebuzar-adan told Jeremiah, "You can go chill with Gedaliah or do whatever. Here's some grub for the road." {40:6} So Jeremiah linked up with Gedaliah and posted up in Mizpah with the locals. {40:7-8} When the field captains and their crews heard that Gedaliah was in charge, they all rolled up to Mizpah, including Ishmael, Johanan, Jonathan, Seraiah, the sons of Ephai, Jezaniah, and their squads. {40:9} Gedaliah assured them, "No need to stress. Serve the Chaldeans, live good, everything's gonna be alright." {40:10} "Me? I'm kicking it here at Mizpah, but you guys, go gather up your goods and settle back into your cities." {40:11} When the Jews scattered all over heard that there was a remnant left in Judah under Gedaliah's rule, they all came back, gathering in Mizpah and stocking up on supplies. {40:12} But Johanan and the field captains pulled Gedaliah aside and warned him about Ishmael's plot to take him out, but Gedaliah brushed it off as lies.

{41:1} So, like, in the seventh month, Ishmael and his crew roll up to Gedaliah's spot in Mizpah, acting all chill and breaking bread. {41:2} But then Ishmael straight-up goes all savage on Gedaliah, the Babylon-appointed governor, and wipes him out with his posse. {41:3} He doesn't stop there; he takes out all the Jews with Gedaliah, plus the Chaldeans and even the soldiers. {41:4} And get this, nobody even knows about it until the next day. {41:5} Meanwhile, some dudes with their faces shaved and clothes ripped, all mourning and stuff, show up with offerings for the temple. {41:6} Ishmael, pretending to be all sympathetic, meets them, then turns around and massacres them too. {41:7} But he spares these ten guys who offer him treasure, tossing the rest into a pit. {41:8-9} The pit's the same one King Asa made, and Ishmael fills it up with bodies. {41:10} Then he kidnaps everyone left in Mizpah, including the king's daughters, and heads for Ammon. {41:11} But when Johanan and his squad catch wind of Ishmael's madness, {41:12} they roll up on him by the big waters in Gibeon. {41:13} When Ishmael's crew sees Johanan, they're stoked. {41:14} So all the people Ishmael nabbed bounce and join up with Johanan. {41:15} Ishmael and eight of his goons manage to escape to Ammon. {41:16} Johanan and his crew round up everyone Ishmael kidnapped, plus the survivors from Gibeon, {41:17} and they peace out to Chimham near Bethlehem, thinking Egypt's safer 'cause Ishmael offed Gedaliah.

{42:1-3} Then everyone, from the top dogs to the regular folk, comes to Jeremiah asking him to pray for them and seek God's guidance 'cause they're freaked out. {42:4} Jeremiah's like, "I got you; I'll pray and tell you whatever God says." {42:5} They're all, "May God be our witness; we'll do whatever He says." {42:6} "Whether it's good or bad, we're down to obey." {42:7} Ten days later, God hits up Jeremiah with a message. {42:8-9} So Jeremiah calls Johanan and his crew, along with everyone else, and delivers God's word. {42:10} "If you stay in this land, I'll rebuild and protect you 'cause I regret messing you up." {42:11} "Don't be scared of Babylon's king; I got your back." {42:12} "I'll show you mercy and bring you back home." {42:13} "But if you bail to Egypt and ignore God's voice," {42:14} "thinking it's all chill there, you're dead wrong." {42:15-16} "If you head to Egypt, you'll face the sword and famine, and you'll die there." {42:17} "Anyone who goes to Egypt is doomed; none will escape the disaster." {42:18} "Just like I wrecked Jerusalem, I'll bring the same fury upon you in Egypt, making you a curse and a reproach." {42:19} "Don't even think about going to Egypt; I'm warning you now." {42:20} "You pretended to be all about seeking God's will, but you never listened to me." {42:21} "I told you what God said, but you ignored Him, so now you're toast." {42:22} "You'll die by sword, famine, and disease in the place you wanted to go."

{43:1} When Jeremiah finished delivering God's message, Azariah, Johanan, and their crew of big shots accused him, saying, "Nah, you're lying. God didn't send you to tell us not to go to Egypt." {43:-2-3} They straight-up accused Jeremiah of being a puppet for Baruch, trying to sell them out to the Chaldeans. {43:4} But Johanan and his crew didn't care about what the LORD said; they dipped from Judah anyway. {43:5-6} They rounded up everyone left, including the refugees who came back, and headed to Egypt, not caring about God's warning. {43:7} So they ended up in Egypt, disobeying God's word, and landed in Tahpanhes. {43:8-9} Then the LORD hit up Jeremiah in Tahpanhes, telling him, "Grab some big stones, stash them in the clay by Pharaoh's crib, and let everyone peep them." {43:10} And he was like, "Tell them I'm gonna bring Nebuchadnezzar over, park his throne on those stones, and he'll run Egypt." {43:11} "He'll wreck Egypt, bringing death, captivity, and the sword." {43:12} "Egypt's gods? Toast. He's gonna clean house and stroll out peacefully." {43:13} "He'll even smash Beth-shemesh's idols and torch the Egyptian gods' cribs."

{44:1} Then Jeremiah got another word from the LORD about the Jews in Egypt, chilling in Migdol, Tahpanhes, Noph, and Pathros. {44:2} God was like, "Y'all saw how I wrecked Jerusalem and Judah for your wickedness, right? Now they're ghost towns." {44:3} "You messed up big time, burning incense and bowing down to random gods, even though I warned you not to." {44:4} "I sent my prophets to warn you, but you wouldn't listen, doing the stuff I hate." {44:5} "You kept doing your thing, ignoring me, and now look at Judah and Jerusalem." {44:6} "They're ruins, thanks to your rebellion." {44:7} "So why keep piling on evil by dragging your families to Egypt, making yourselves cursed and despised?" {44:8} "Burning incense to other gods in Egypt? Seriously? You're cutting yourselves off from me and becoming a joke among the nations." {44:9} "Don't forget how your ancestors and kings messed up too. You're just repeating history." {44:10} "You haven't learned a thing, ignoring my law and doing your own thing." {44:11} "So now I'm turning against you, ready to wipe out all of Judah." {44:12} "Anyone who heads to Egypt to chill will end up dead, from the least to the greatest." {44:13} "I'll punish those in Egypt like I punished Jerusalem, with sword, famine, and disease." {44:14} "None of the remnant in Egypt will escape; they'll all face the consequences." {44:15} "Even when you were burning incense to other gods, life was good, huh? But now, with me out of the picture, you're suffering." {44:16} But the people were like, "Nah, we're doing things our way. We're gonna keep worshipping the queen of heaven and pouring out drink offerings, just like we used to." {44:17} They straight-up ignored Jeremiah, sticking to their plan to worship other gods. {44:18} Jeremiah was like, "Look, when you stopped worshipping the queen of heaven, life went downhill. But go ahead, keep pretending it's all good." {44:19} "You think offering cakes and drinks to the queen of heaven without your men is gonna save you?" {44:20-21} Then Jeremiah was like, "Seriously, you think the LORD forgot how you worshipped other gods in Judah and Jerusalem? That's why everything's messed up now." {44:22} "Your wickedness pushed God too far, and now your land is a wasteland, just like today." {44:23} "Because you sinned and ignored God's law and warnings, this is happening." {44:24} Jeremiah was like, "Listen up, all of you, even the ladies. You're gonna get what's coming to you." {44:25} "You made vows to the queen of heaven, and you're gonna pay up." {44:26} "God's swearing off Egypt; his name won't even be mentioned there anymore." {44:27} "Everyone in Egypt's doomed to die by sword and famine until they're wiped out." {44:28} "Only a few will survive and return to Judah, proving whose words stand true, mine or yours." {44:29} "And as a sign, God's gonna punish you right here, showing you his words are no joke." {44:30} "Just like Zedekiah fell, Pharaoh-hophra's next, marked for doom."

{45:1} So, like, Jeremiah drops some wisdom on Baruch, basically saying, "Bro, I get you're stressed, but don't trip. God's got this." {45:2} He's like, "Look, everything you've built, God's gonna tear it down. And all those plans you had? Forget about 'em." {45:3} "Just chill, man. God's gonna spare your life wherever you go, even if everyone else is doomed."

{46:1} Then Jeremiah gets a vision about Egypt and Pharaoh's crew. {46:2} He's like, "Yo, Nebuchadnezzar's gonna wreck Egypt's army big time." {46:3-4} "Get ready for battle, folks." {46:4} "Suit up, horses! Let's go!" {46:5} "But why they turning tail and running? Fear's got 'em shook." {46:6} "Ain't nobody escaping. They're all gonna bite it up north by the Euphrates." {46:7} "Who's this flood rolling in?

It's Egypt, thinking they're gonna drown out everyone else." {46:8} "Egypt's like a tsunami, thinking it's gonna wipe out everything." {46:9} "They're calling in everyone, but it's gonna be a massacre." {46:10} "This is God's day of reckoning. The sword's gonna drink deep of their blood." {46:11} "Egypt's tryna heal, but it ain't gonna work. They're doomed." {46:12} "Everybody's heard how Egypt's fallen. They're all just stumbling over each other." {46:13} "Nebuchadnezzar's coming for Egypt, no doubt." {46:14} "Spread the word in Egypt, get ready for the slaughter." {46:15} "Why'd your warriors chicken out? 'Cause God scared 'em off." {46:16} "They're dropping like flies, and they just wanna go home." {46:17} "Pharaoh's just noise now; his time's up." {46:18} "Swear on the name of the Lord, destruction's coming." {46:19} "Egypt's gonna be empty and desolate." {46:20} "Egypt might look fine, but it's doomed from the north." {46:21} "Even their hired guns are bailing. They know it's over." {46:22} "Egypt's gonna get chopped down like a forest." {46:23} "They're gonna swarm Egypt like locusts, unstoppable." {46:24} "Egypt's gonna be humiliated, handed over to the north." {46:25} "God's gonna punish Egypt and their gods, even Pharaoh." {46:26} "They'll be handed over to Nebuchadnezzar." {46:27} "But Jacob, don't sweat it. God's got your back." {46:28} "Fear not, Jacob. God's gonna do what He promised."

{47:1} So, like, Jeremiah gets a download from the big man upstairs about the Philistines, right before Pharaoh hits up Gaza. {47:2} God's like, "Check it, a flood's coming from the north, gonna wreck everything in its path, and no one's gonna escape." {47:3} "When the enemy rolls in with their horses and chariots, parents ain't even gonna look back for their kids, they're gonna be so freaked out." {47:4} "The day of reckoning's coming for the Philistines, gonna wipe out everyone and everything, even the helpers from Tyre and Sidon." {47:5} "Gaza's gonna be wrecked, Ashkelon too. How long you gonna keep mourning, huh?" {47:6} "God's sword, it's itching for action. But how can it chill when God's given it a mission against Ashkelon and the seashore?"

{48:1} Now onto Moab, God's like, "Nebo's doomed, Kiriathaim's toast, Misgab's going down." {48:2} "Moab's days of glory are over. They're scheming against Heshbon, but it's all gonna blow up in their faces." {48:3} "Horonaim's gonna be a hot mess, total destruction." {48:4} "Moab's done for, even the little ones are gonna feel the pain." {48:5} "Tears are gonna flow non-stop, from Luhith to Horonaim, it's gonna be a disaster." {48:6} "Run for your lives, Moabites, like you're running from a wildfire." {48:7} "Moab's thinking they're all that, trusting in their riches and their gods. But they're all gonna get snatched up, even their deity Chemosh." {48:8} "No city's gonna escape the spoiler's wrath. The valleys will be wrecked, the plains destroyed, just like God said." {48:9} "Moab, you better sprout wings and fly, 'cause your cities are gonna be ghost towns." {48:10} "Cursed be anyone who tries to deceive God or holds back their sword from bloodshed." {48:11} "Moab's been living the easy life, never been through the grind. But now the party's over, wanderers are gonna wreck everything." {48:12} "Moab's gonna be ashamed of Chemosh, just like Israel was ashamed of Bethel." {48:13} "It's gonna be a rough time for Moab, folks. But they brought it on themselves." {48:14} "Thought you were tough, Moab? Think again. Your cities are wrecked, your warriors gone." {48:15} "Moab's about to face some serious pain, and it's coming fast." {48:16} "Everybody's gonna mourn for Moab, even those who knew them well." {48:17} "How did Moab, once so strong, fall so hard?" {48:18} "You used to be so proud, Dibon, but now you're gonna suffer." {48:19} "Aroer, keep watch, ask anyone who's escaped what's going down." {48:20} "Moab's finished, folks. Spread the word, Arnon, Moab's done for." {48:21} "Judgment's hitting everywhere, from Holon to Jahazah." {48:22} "From Dibon to Nebo, Moab's getting wrecked." {48:23} "From Kiriathaim to Bethgamul, from Beth-meon to Kerioth, Moab's getting trashed, near or far." {48:24-25} "Moab's power's gone, their strength broken, says God." {48:26} "Time to get Moab wasted, 'cause they thought they were better than God. Now they're gonna wallow in their own mess." {48:27} "Remember how you laughed at Israel? Well, now it's your turn to cry." {48:28} "Moabites, get out of the cities, find some rocks to hide in, like scaredy cats." {48:29} "Moab, you're so full of yourself, but you're about to eat humble pie." {48:30} "I know you're mad, Moab, but that's not gonna change anything. Your lies won't save you." {48:31} "I'm gonna mourn for Moab, cry for all of them." {48:32} "I'll cry for Sibmah like I cried for Jazer. Your crops are ruined, Moab, your harvest's gone." {48:33} "No more joy or gladness in Moab, just destruction." {48:34} "From Heshbon to Elealeh, from Zoar to Horonaim, Moab's gonna wail." {48:35} "No more sacrifices on the high places, no more incense to idols." {48:36} "My heart breaks for Moab, like a flute playing a sad tune. Your riches are gone, Moab." {48:37} "Everyone's gonna be mourning on the rooftops of Moab, in the streets, 'cause Moab's shattered, no one's gonna want them anymore." {48:38} "Moab's gonna be a laughingstock, a disgrace to everyone." {48:39} "Moab's gonna be a joke, a laughingstock to everyone around them." {48:40} "Moab's gonna try to fly away like an eagle, but there's no escaping their fate." {48:41} "Kerioth's captured, the strongholds surprised, Moab's warriors are gonna be like scaredy cats." {48:42} "Moab's gonna be wiped out, 'cause they thought they were better than God." {48:43} "Fear, traps, and snares are waiting for Moab." {48:44} "Try to run, Moab, you'll fall into a pit. Try to climb out, you'll get caught in a trap. It's Moab's year of reckoning, says God." {48:45} "Those who fled to Heshbon for safety are gonna find themselves in the middle of the fire. Chemosh's people are gonna be taken captive, sons and daughters alike." {48:46} "But one day, Moab's gonna come back from captivity, says God. That's the end of Moab's story."

{49:1} Yo, peeps, listen up 'bout the Ammonites, God's like, "Yo, ain't Israel got any heirs? Why's their king chillin' in Gad and his homies livin' in his crib? {49:2} Imma bring some war vibes to Rabbah, it's gonna be a mess, and Israel gonna be like, 'Yo, this place ours now.' {49:3} Heshbon, you gonna cry 'cause Ai got trashed, Rabbah's ladies, grab your sackcloth, it's a mourning sitch. Their king, priests, and big shots? They're gonna get nabbed. {49:4} Yo, why you flexin' in the valleys, Rabbah? You used to be on top, but now you're all, 'Who gon' mess with me?' {49:5} Well, guess what, trouble's comin' from all sides, you'll be scattered, ain't no one gonna save you. {49:6} But after all that drama, I'll bring the Ammonites back home, says the Lord. {49:7} Edom, you ain't so wise no more? Your counsel vanished, huh? {49:8} Better run and hide, Dedan crew, 'cause Esau's gonna get hit hard, it's his time for a beatdown. {49:9} Even if pickers come for your grapes, they won't leave any behind; thieves gonna clean you out. {49:10} Esau's gonna get wrecked, secrets exposed, fam scattered, and no one can hide. {49:11} Even if you're left with no parents, I got your back, kids and widows, trust me. {49:12} The Lord says, 'You thought you were safe, Edom? Nah, you gonna feel it too.' {49:13} Bozrah's gonna be a wasteland, a curse, and all its cities, straight-up ruins. {49:14} Word's out from the Lord, the nations are rallying against you, Edom, time to face the music. {49:15} You gonna be small and hated among nations, Edom, that's what's up. {49:16} Your arrogance's gonna backfire, Edom, no matter how high and mighty you feel. {49:17} Edom's gonna be a ghost town, peeps gonna be shook passing through. {49:18} Just like Sodom and Gomorrah, Edom's gonna be a no-go zone, no one living there. {49:19} Edom's gonna face off with a lion, but I'll make it peace out quick. Who's gonna step up? Ain't nobody like me, says the Lord. {49:20} So, listen up to the Lord's plan against Edom, they're gonna get wrecked, just a few left standing. {49:21} Everybody's gonna feel the tremors when Edom falls, echoes heard across the seas. {49:22} Edom might flex like an eagle, but when it's time, they'll be scared like a woman in labor. {49:23} Damascus, you're gonna freak out, bad news got you shook, can't catch a break. {49:24} Damascus gonna bolt, fear gonna grip 'em, pain like childbirth. {49:25} Once a city of joy, now deserted, what happened, Damascus? {49:26} Young bloods gonna drop in the streets, warriors gonna be wiped out, says the Lord. {49:27} Damascus' walls gonna be lit up, palaces turned to ashes. {49:28} Kedar and Hazor, you're next on Babylon's hit list, time to scram. {49:29} Babylon's coming for your tents, your flocks, your gear, and your camels, and y'all gonna be scared stiff. {49:30} Hazor, you better hide deep, Babylon's got plans for you. {49:31} Babylon's coming for that easy target, the land without defenses. {49:32} Babylon's gonna loot and scatter y'all, no escaping their wrath. {49:33} Hazor's gonna be a wasteland forever, ain't nobody gonna live there. {49:34} The Lord's got beef with Elam too, they ain't getting off easy. {49:35} Elam's gonna get wrecked, their power gonna be shattered. {49:36} Elamites gonna scatter everywhere, nowhere to run from the Lord's anger. {49:37} Elam's gonna face their enemies and the Lord's fury, swords gonna come for 'em till they're done. {49:38} The Lord's gonna set up shop in Elam, take out their rulers, says the Lord. {49:39} But one day, Elam's gonna bounce back, says the Lord.

{50:1} Yo, Babylon, you're in for it, says Jeremiah. {50:2} Nations gonna hear about your downfall, idols gonna be wrecked, no hiding the shame. {50:3} A nation's coming from the north to wreck you, Babylon, leaving nothing behind. {50:4} Israel and Judah gonna find their way back to God, seeking him with tears. {50:5} They gonna seek the Lord and never forget the deal they make. {50:6} My people lost, shepherds failed 'em, they've been wandering and forgetting their roots. {50:7} Enemies been feasting on 'em, thinking they're in the right 'cause Israel messed up with God. {50:8} Get outta Babylon, leave Chaldea, be like goats leading the flock out. {50:9} Babylon's getting hit by a squad from the north, arrows gonna fly true, no wasted shots. {50:10} Babylon's gonna get looted, the looters gonna be satisfied, says the Lord. {50:11} Babylon, you thought you were living the good life, but now you're gonna get wrecked. {50:12} Babylon's gonna be humiliated, a wasteland, a deserted desert. {50:13} Wrath's gonna leave Babylon uninhabited, people gonna be shocked at her downfall. {50:14} Babylon's enemies gonna gather against her, shouting for vengeance, bringing down her foundations. {50:15} Babylon's donezo, her deal with the devil's catching up, time for payback. {50:16} Harvesters gonna bail, fearing the enemy's sword, everyone running back to their own. {50:17} Israel's scattered like sheep, chewed up by Assyria and Babylon. {50:18} But the Lord's gonna punish Babylon just like he did Assyria. {50:19} Israel gonna come back home, chill in Carmel and Bashan, living the good life. {50:20} In those days, Israel's sins gonna be wiped clean, says the Lord. {50:21} Merathaim and Pekod, Babylon's enemies, gonna get wiped out too. {50:22} Sounds of war and destruction echoing everywhere. {50:23} Babylon, once the big shot, now crumbling, a laughingstock. {50:24} Babylon caught off guard, snared by the Lord 'cause she messed with him. {50:25} The Lord's got his weapons ready, unleashing his anger on Babylon. {50:26} Babylon's storehouses gonna be raided, nothing left standing. {50:27} Slaughter gonna hit Babylon hard, their cattle gonna be toast. {50:28} Survivors gonna flee to Zion, spreading word of the Lord's vengeance. {50:29} Archers gonna surround Babylon, no escape, payback's coming. {50:30} Babylon's youth gonna fall, warriors gonna be wiped out, says the Lord. {50:31} The Lord's against Babylon's pride, time for payback's here. {50:32} Babylon's pride gonna lead to its fall, fires gonna consume everything around it. {50:33} Israel and Judah oppressed together, but the Lord's their redeemer, gonna bring justice and trouble to Babylon. {50:34} Swords gonna hit Babylon's rulers, wise ones, liars, and all, no mercy. {50:35} Swords gonna be on everyone in Babylon, princes, wise guys, even the mixed crowds, all gonna suffer. {50:36} Babylon's mightiest gonna be terrified, horses gonna fail 'em. {50:37} Babylon's treasures gonna be robbed, waters gonna dry up, 'cause they're obsessed with idols. {50:38} Babylon's gonna be a haunt for wild beasts, deserted forever, no one living there again. {50:39} Just like Sodom and Gomorrah, Babylon's gonna be wiped out, forever deserted. {50:40} Babylon's days numbered, peeps from all over gonna rise up against it. {50:41} They're gonna be armed to the teeth, ruthless, and unstoppable, coming for Babylon. {50:42} Babylon's king gonna hear and freak out, pain gonna hit 'em hard. {50:43} Babylon's gonna face a lion's wrath, but they gonna flee, 'cause who's gonna step up against the Lord? {50:44} Who's gonna step up against the Lord? Babylon's gonna run scared, but who can stop the Lord's plans? {50:45} Listen up to the Lord's plans against Babylon, they're gonna get wrecked. {50:46} Babylon's fall gonna shake the earth, cries gonna echo among the nations.

{51:1} Yo, peep this message from the Big Guy: I'm sending a storm to wreck Babylon and anyone who's got beef with me. {51:2} Babylon's gonna get hit with a fierce wind, and her land will be laid bare when trouble comes knocking. {51:3} Archers, get ready to shoot; warriors, gear up and show no mercy. {51:4} Babylon's gonna be a war zone, with bodies littering the streets. {51:5} But don't trip, Israel and Judah ain't forgotten by their God, even though they messed up big time. {51:6} If you're smart, bounce out of Babylon now and save yourselves; God's about to lay down some serious payback. {51:7} Babylon used to be a big deal, but now she's fallen and everyone's mourning. {51:8} She's wrecked beyond repair, so grab some ointment, but it ain't gonna help much. {51:9} We tried to fix Babylon up, but she's a lost cause. Time to bail and head back home; her judgment's coming. {51:10} Let's give props to God for bringing justice; spread the word in Zion. {51:11} The Medes are hyped up and ready to take down Babylon; it's all part of God's plan for payback. {51:12} Babylon, brace yourself; the attack's coming, and God's calling the shots. {51:13} Babylon, with all your riches, your days are numbered because of your greed. {51:14} God's gonna flood Babylon with enemies, and they'll raise a battle cry against her. {51:15} God's the master of creation, from the heavens to the earth; he controls it all. {51:16} His voice shakes the heavens, unleashes storms, and stirs up the winds. {51:17} People are dumb for trusting in idols; they're worthless and breathless. {51:18} Idols are a joke, doomed to perish when judgment comes. {51:19} But Israel's different; they're God's chosen, not some man-made statues. {51:20} Israel, you're like my weapon of mass destruction; with you, I'll crush nations and kingdoms. {51:21} You'll wreck horses, chariots, men, women, young, and old. {51:22} You'll break everything in Babylon, from shepherds to farmers to rulers. {51:23} Babylon's gonna pay for all the evil she did, right in front of everyone. {51:24} God's gonna make Babylon and the Chaldeans pay for their crimes against Zion. {51:25} Babylon, you're in for it; God's against you, and you're going down hard. {51:26} You won't even get a rock for a memorial; you'll be a desolate wasteland forever. {51:27} Babylon, get ready; God's calling in the troops from every nation to take you down. {51:28} The Medes and their allies are gearing up for battle, and Babylon's days are numbered. {51:29} Babylon's trembling with fear; God's judgment's coming, turning her into a ghost town. {51:30} Babylon's soldiers are too scared to fight; they're hiding in their bunkers like scaredy-cats. {51:31} Babylon's defenses are crumbling; messengers are racing to tell the king the city's been breached. {51:32} The city's surrounded, the bridges are burning, and the enemy's closing in. {51:33} Babylon's like a threshing floor, ready to be trampled; her time's almost up. {51:34} Nebuchadnezzar thought he could devour us, but he's gonna get what's coming to him. {51:35} We'll shout Babylon's violence back at her, and her blood will be on her own hands. {51:36} God's gonna dry up Babylon's sea and make her springs run dry. {51:37} Babylon's gonna be a wasteland, a haunt for dragons, and a hissing for everyone. {51:38} Her people will roar in terror, but their defenses won't hold; they'll toil in vain and face the flames. {51:39} God'll make 'em drunk with destruction, so they'll pass out and never wake up. {51:40} They'll be led to the slaughter like lambs; their leaders will be treated like goats. {51:41} Babylon, you're finished; everyone's shocked at your downfall. {51:42} The flood's coming for Babylon; she's drowning in her own destruction. {51:43} Her cities will be desolate wastelands, abandoned by all. {51:44} God's gonna punish Babylon's gods and make 'em cough up what they swallowed. {51:45} My people, get out of Babylon and save yourselves from God's wrath. {51:46} Don't freak out over rumors; Babylon's destruction's coming, and it's gonna be loud and clear. {51:47} God's gonna judge Babylon's idols and leave her land in ruins. {51:48} Heaven and earth will celebrate Babylon's downfall as invaders pour in from the north. {51:49} Just like Babylon laid waste to Israel, she's gonna get what's coming to her from all over. {51:50} If you made it out alive, don't stick around; remember God and think about Jerusalem. {51:51} We're ashamed; strangers have invaded God's sanctuary. {51:52} Babylon's idols are gonna get what's coming to them, and the wounded will groan throughout her land. {51:53} Even if Babylon reached for the stars, God would still bring her down. {51:54} Babylon's gonna wail as destruction sweeps in from the Chaldeans. {51:55} God's plundered Babylon and silenced her mighty shouts. {51:56} Her defenders are defeated, their weapons useless; God's gonna repay them for their evil. {51:57} Babylon's leaders will be knocked out cold, sleeping forever, says the LORD of hosts. {51:58} Babylon's walls will crumble, her gates will burn, and her people will work for nothing and suffer in flames. {51:59} This is the message Jeremiah gave Seraiah when he went to Babylon with Zedekiah; Seraiah was a low-key dude. {51:60} Jeremiah wrote down all this doom for Babylon and told Seraiah to read it there. {51:61} After reading it, Seraiah was to toss the scroll into the Euphrates, symbolizing Babylon's fall. {51:62} Babylon's gonna sink and never rise again, just like God said. That's the end of Jeremiah's words against Babylon.

{52:1} So, like, Zedekiah was 21 when he started ruling, and he ruled for 11 years in Jerusalem. His mom, Hamutal, was the daughter of Jeremiah from Libnah. {52:2} But yo, he was straight-up evil, just like Jehoiakim. {52:3} The Big Guy was so ticked off that he let Jerusalem and Judah get wrecked until they got booted out of his sight, all 'cause Zedekiah tried to rebel against the king of Babylon. {52:4-5} Then in his ninth year of ruling, on the tenth day of the tenth month, Nebuchadnezzar and his crew rolled up to Jerusalem and set up camp. They had the city on lockdown until Zedekiah's eleventh year. {52:6} By the fourth month of that year, on the ninth day, the city was starving—no bread anywhere. {52:7} So the city got breached, and the soldiers dipped out, sneaking through a gate near the king's garden while the Chaldeans were busy surrounding the place. {52:8} But the Chaldean army wasn't having it; they caught up to Zedekiah in Jericho's plains, and his squad bailed on him. {52:9-11} They snagged Zedekiah and dragged him to Nebuchadnezzar in Riblah. And yo, Nebuchadnezzar made him watch as he offed Zedekiah's kids, then took out all the Judah big shots. {52:12} In the fifth month, on the tenth day of Nebuchadnezzar's nineteenth year, Nebuzaradan, the head honcho of Babylon's guard, showed up in Jerusalem. {52:13} He torched the LORD's crib, the king's pad, and every other house in the city. {52:14} Then Nebuzaradan and his crew tore down all of Jerusalem's walls. {52:15} They hauled off some of the poor folks, the leftovers in the city, and anyone who surrendered to Babylon. {52:16} But they left behind a few of the poorest peeps to work the land. {52:17} They jacked all the brass stuff from the LORD's house—pillars, bases, and that giant brass bath. {52:18} They snagged all the brass kitchenware too. {52:19} And they swiped the gold and silver utensils from the temple. {52:20-23} They even took Solomon's fancy brass stuff—two pillars, a giant bath, and twelve brass bulls. {52:24} They grabbed the head priest Seraiah, the second priest Zephaniah, and three doorkeepers. {52:25} They also took an army eunuch, seven of the king's crew, and the army's head scribe, plus 60 regular folks. {52:26} Nebuzaradan dragged them all to Nebuchadnezzar in Riblah. {52:27} And Nebuchadnezzar offed them there. So, yeah, Judah got exiled from their own turf. {52:28} In Nebuchadnezzar's seventh year, he snatched 3,023 Jews. {52:29} Then in his eighteenth year, he took 832 more from Jerusalem. {52:30} And in his twenty-third year, Nebuzaradan nabbed 745 Jews. That's a total of 4,600 people. {52:31} Then in the 37th year of Jehoiachin's exile, on the 25th day of the 12th month, Evil-merodach, the new king of Babylon, showed Jehoiachin some love. {52:32} He hooked him up with a VIP spot above the other ex-kings in Babylon. {52:33} And he traded in Jehoiachin's prison threads for some fresh gear. {52:34} Jehoiachin got fed by the king of Babylon every day until he kicked the bucket. That's how it went down, fam.

Lamentations

✛✛✛

{1:1} Yo, check it, Jerusalem used to be poppin', full of peeps, like a queen among cities. But now? She's like a widow, paying tribute to everyone. {1:2} She's straight-up bawling every night, tears streaming down her face. All her so-called friends? They turned on her, flipping the script, now they're her enemies. {1:3} Judah's been snatched up, living in exile, no chill vibes anywhere. Persecutors all up in her grill, no escape in sight. {1:4} Zion's streets are sad, no parties happening, gates deserted. Even the priests and the girls are feeling down, it's a rough time. {1:5} Her haters? They're winning, thanks to God dropping some serious punishment for all the messed-up stuff she did. Her kids? Locked up by the enemy. {1:6} Jerusalem's lost her shine, leaders running scared, no strength left. {1:7} Remembering the good times when Jerusalem was on top, now she's alone, haters mocking her. {1:8} Jerusalem messed up big time, stripped naked for all to see. Feeling down and out, looking back in regret. {1:9} Dirty secrets exposed, no one to comfort her. Yo, God, check out this mess, the enemy's flexing hard. {1:10} Enemies raiding her crib, even trespassing in her holy place. God's commandments thrown out the window. {1:11} Everybody's hungry, trading their stuff for food just to survive. God, see what's up, I'm feeling low. {1:12} Passersby, peep this, see if anyone's had it as bad as me. God's anger's fierce, got me feeling wrecked. {1:13} It's like fire in my bones, can't escape it, feeling trapped and drained. {1:14} God's got me in a chokehold, no strength left, handed over to those I can't beat. {1:15} God's crushing my crew, young ones getting crushed like grapes in a winepress. {1:16} Tears flowing non-stop, no one to comfort me, my kids suffering, enemy's winning. {1:17} Reaching out for help, but nobody's there, enemies closing in from all sides. Jerusalem's a hot mess, treated like garbage. {1:18} God's righteous, I messed up big time, feeling the pain, my young ones taken away. {1:19} Asked for help, but got betrayed, even the priests and elders couldn't handle it. {1:20} God, I'm hurting bad, inside and out, chaos everywhere. {1:21} Enemies loving my suffering, but their day's coming, gonna be just like me. {1:22} Let God see the pain, payback time for all who messed with me.

{2:1} God's wrath raining down on Zion, destroying everything, no mercy. {2:2} Crushing everything in sight, no pity, bringing it all down, wrecking the kingdom. {2:3} No mercy for Israel, God's fury burning like wildfire, consuming everything. {2:4} God's aiming his arrows, taking out everything beautiful in Zion, unleashing his fury. {2:5} God's like an enemy, swallowing up Israel's beauty, leaving nothing but mourning and sorrow. {2:6} Ripping apart the holy place, destroying everything, no more celebrations, dissing the leaders. {2:7} God's done with the altar, hating on the sanctuary, letting enemies tear down the walls. {2:8} Destroying Zion's defenses, no holding back, even the walls are crying out in pain. {2:9} Gates smashed, leaders in exile, law gone, prophets silent. {2:10} Elders sitting in dust, mourning in silence, young ones hanging their heads low. {2:11} Crying till my eyes run dry, feeling the pain in my gut, watching my people suffer. {2:12} Kids asking for food, but there's none, dying in the streets while their moms watch in despair. {2:13} God, I'm hurting bad, like the sea, who can heal me? {2:14} Prophets spewing nonsense, ignoring the real issues, no escape from captivity. {2:15} Enemies mocking Jerusalem's downfall, saying, "Wasn't this the city everyone praised?" {2:16} Enemies celebrating, saying, "We got 'em!" God's wrath fulfilled, enemies gloating. {2:17} God did what he said he'd do, no mercy, enemies celebrating, getting the last laugh. {2:18} Crying out to God day and night, can't hold back the tears, can't stop the pain. {2:19} God, see our suffering, our kids starving in the streets. {2:20} God, look at what you've done, kids starving, priests and prophets slain in your sanctuary. {2:21} Young and old lying dead in the streets, my kids slaughtered, no mercy from you. {2:22} God's unleashed terror on us, nobody escaped, the ones I raised and cared for, gone.

{3:1} Yo, I've been through some real tough times, feeling the wrath of the Big Guy's rod. {3:2} He's led me into darkness, no light in sight. {3:3} It's like he's turned against me, his hand on me all day long. {3:4} My body's all messed up, skin wrinkled, bones broken. {3:5} He's built walls around me, filled with bitterness and pain. {3:6} I'm stuck in dark places, feeling like I'm already dead. {3:7} Can't break free, weighed down by heavy chains. {3:8} Even when I cry out, he ignores my prayers. {3:9} My paths are all messed up, nothing but obstacles. {3:10} Feels like he's stalking me, waiting to attack like a bear or a lion. {3:11} He's messed up my life, left me feeling empty. {3:12} Like he's aiming arrows at me, ready to strike. {3:13} Those arrows pierce right through me, causing even more pain. {3:14} I'm a laughingstock, everyone's mocking me all day long. {3:15} He's filled me with bitterness, made me feel drunk with suffering. {3:16} Even my teeth are messed up, broken by stones, covered in ashes. {3:17} Can't find any peace, forgotten what it feels like. {3:18} Thought I was done for, but then I remembered the LORD's mercy. {3:19} I can't forget all the pain and suffering, it's burned into my memory. {3:20-21} But even in my lowest moments, I still have hope. {3:22} It's only by the LORD's mercy that we're not wiped out completely, his compassion never runs dry. {3:23} Every morning, it's like a fresh start, his faithfulness is off the charts. {3:24} The LORD's got my back, he's all I need, so I'll keep hoping in him. {3:25} He's good to those who wait for him, who seek him with all their heart. {3:26} It's cool to hope and wait quietly for the LORD's help. {3:27} Sometimes you gotta take on challenges when you're young. {3:28} Just gotta sit in silence and deal with it, carry the weight on your shoulders. {3:29} Sometimes you gotta humble yourself, look for hope even in the dust. {3:30} Take the hits without fighting back, let the insults roll off you. {3:31-32} 'Cause the LORD won't abandon us forever, even when he brings us grief, he'll show compassion, 'cause he's all about that mercy. {3:33} He's not out here trying to hurt us, he's just trying to teach us. {3:34} He's not about crushing people, turning justice upside down. {3:35} He's not about messing with people's rights in front of the Big Guy. {3:36} The LORD ain't down with unjust stuff. {3:37} Who's gonna make stuff happen if the LORD didn't say so? {3:38} Good and bad don't come from anywhere but the Most High. {3:39} So why complain when we mess up? {3:40} Let's take a look at ourselves, turn back to the LORD. {3:41} Lift up our hearts and hands to God in heaven. {3:42} We messed up big time, but you haven't forgiven us. {3:43} You've been angry, punished us, shown no mercy. {3:44} Covered yourself in clouds, ignoring our prayers. {3:45} Made us the laughingstock of the world. {3:46} Enemies everywhere, talking trash, bringing fear and destruction. {3:47} We're living in fear, trapped in a nightmare. {3:48} Tears flow like rivers, seeing the devastation. {3:49} Can't stop crying, hoping for a glimpse of you, LORD. {3:50} Waiting for you to look down from heaven. {3:51} My heart hurts seeing all the suffering. {3:52} Enemies chasing me down for no reason, like I'm some bird. {3:53} They've taken my life, thrown me in a dungeon, and dropped a stone on me. {3:54} Overwhelmed by waves, feeling cut off from everything. {3:55} Called out to you, LORD, from the depths of despair. {3:56} You heard me, don't ignore my cries. {3:57} You came close when I called, saying, "Don't be afraid." {3:58} You've stood up for me, saved my life. {3:59} You've seen the wrong they've done, so judge them. {3:60} You've seen all their schemes against me. {3:61} Their insults never stop, LORD, they're relentless. {3:62} Their lies and plots, they never quit. {3:63} They're always there, like a bad song playing on repeat. {3:64} Pay them back for what they've done, LORD. {3:65} Make them feel the pain, let your curse fall on them. {3:66} Pursue them with anger, wipe them out under your heavens.

{4:1} Yo, how did our bling lose its shine? The top-quality stuff now looking cheap, and our holy spots? Trashed in every hood. {4:2} Our once-golden boys, now treated like basic pottery, no respect for their hustle. {4:3} Even sea creatures caring for their young better than our people, acting cold-hearted like desert birds. {4:4} Babies parched and starving, mouths dry, crying out for bread but getting nada. {4:5} The rich now scraping by in the streets, once living large now hugging trash heaps. {4:6} Our punishment worse than Sodom's quick wipeout, no mercy, no escape. {4:7} Our holy ones once shining bright, now dark and wasted away, unrecognizable, skin clinging to bones. {4:8} Those killed by the sword getting off easier than those dying of hunger, wasting away without a crumb to eat. {4:9} Desperate moms cooking their own kids, the ultimate horror in our destruction. {4:10} God's fury unleashed, burning down Zion, foundations crumbling. {4:11} Kings and folks worldwide shocked that enemies breached Jerusalem's gates. {4:12} Prophets and priests guilty of bloodshed, stumbling around like blind fools, defiling themselves with gore. {4:13} People telling them to scram, too filthy to touch, kicked out, wandering among the nations. {4:14} God's anger dividing us, no more mercy, dissing the priests, ignoring the elders. {4:15} We hoped for help that never came, watching in vain, our days numbered. {4:16} Enemies stalking us, can't even walk the streets in peace, our time's up. {4:17} Persecutors faster than eagles, chasing us down everywhere. {4:18} Our beloved leader taken down, leaving us exposed, no refuge among the nations. {4:19} Shout out to Edom, celebrating our downfall, but their turn's coming, gonna be lit. {4:20} Zion's paid for her sins, no more captivity, but Edom, you're next, your sins exposed.

{5:1} God, remember our suffering, check out our shame. {5:2} Strangers taking over our land, foreigners in our homes. {5:3} Orphans and widows everywhere, abandoned and alone. {5:4} Paying for water, buying firewood, no rest from our oppressors. {5:5} Forced to work for Egyptians and Assyrians, just to eat. {5:6} Our ancestors sinned, and we're stuck dealing with the fallout. {5:7} Servants ruling over us, no one to rescue us from their grip. {5:8} Risking our lives for bread, dodging swords in the wilderness. {5:9} Skin blackened from famine, feeling the heat like an oven. {5:10} Women violated in Zion, girls in Judah's cities. {5:11} Leaders hanged, elders disrespected. {5:12} Young men grinding at the mill, kids crushed under the weight. {5:13} Elders missing from the gate, young ones silent without music. {5:14} Our joy gone, replaced by mourning. {5:15} Crown snatched from our heads, woe to us for our sins! {5:16} Our hearts faint, our eyes dim with tears. {5:17} Zion's a wasteland, foxes ruling the roost. {5:18} But you, God, stay steady forever, your throne enduring through the ages. {5:19} Why you ghosting us, God? Come back and renew us like back in the day. {5:20} You've totally ditched us, super mad at us.

Ezekiel

✦✦✦

{1:1} So, like, it was the thirtieth year, fourth month, fifth day, and I was chilling by the river Chebar with the other captives, when suddenly, the sky cracked open, and I got a peek at some divine visions. {1:2} It was like, the fifth year of king Jehoiachin's lockup, when God's word came straight to Ezekiel, son of Buzi, right there in Chaldea by the Chebar, and you could totally feel the divine vibe. {1:3} Then I saw this massive whirlwind from the north, blazing with fire and this intense amber glow, and in the middle of it all, there were these four living beings, looking all human-like but with some wild features. {1:4} Each had four faces and four wings, and their feet were like, solid, shining brass. {1:5} Their wings touched each other, and they moved straight ahead, no turning around. {1:6} And get this, they had faces of a human, a lion, an ox, and an eagle, with wings that stretched up, two covering their bodies. {1:7} They went straight ahead, following the spirit, no turning around. {1:8} These creatures glowed like fiery coals, moving among them was like lightning in a storm. {1:9} It was like they were flashing in and out, moving as fast as lightning. {1:10} Then there were these wheels by the creatures, with these crazy rings full of eyes, and wherever the creatures went, the wheels followed, lifted by the spirit within them. {1:11} It was like, when the creatures moved, the wheels moved, when they stopped, the wheels stopped, the spirit totally in sync. {1:12} And there was this crazy crystal-like firmament above them, with wings spread out, making this thunderous noise like a massive waterfall or the voice of a whole army. {1:13} When they stood still, they lowered their wings, and this voice from above spoke to them. {1:14} Above the firmament was this throne, glowing like sapphire, with this figure that looked like a dude on it, surrounded by this fiery glow. {1:15} And from his waist up, it was this fiery blaze, and from his waist down, it was this bright light, like a rainbow on a rainy day. {1:16} It was like this dude was surrounded by this rainbow-like brightness, the very image of the Lord's glory. And when I saw it, I just hit the floor, overwhelmed by it all, and heard this voice speaking to me.

{2:1} Then this voice was like, "Yo, Ezekiel, stand up, I got something to tell you." {2:2} And as soon as it spoke, this energy hit me, lifting me to my feet, so I could hear what it had to say. {2:3} The voice was all, "Ezekiel, I'm sending you to the Israelites, this stubborn bunch who've been rebelling against me, generation after generation." {2:4} "They're a bunch of stubborn brats, but I'm sending you to speak my truth to them, whether they listen or not, they gotta know a prophet's been in their midst." {2:5} And even though they're rebellious as heck, don't be scared of them, or their words, even if they come at you with all kinds of threats. {2:6} "You gotta speak my truth, whether they wanna hear it or not, even if they're as rebellious as they come." {2:7} "Don't be like them, Ezekiel, don't rebel against me like they do, just speak my words, and eat up what I give you." {2:8} And then, I looked, and there was this hand with a scroll, written inside and out with all kinds of heavy stuff, like laments, mourning, and woe.

{3:1} So, like, the dude was all, "Hey, son of man, munch on whatever you find; eat this scroll and then go chat with the peeps of Israel." {3:2} So I was like, "Sure thing," and chowed down on that scroll. {3:3} And he's all, "Dude, fill up on this scroll I'm giving you," so I did, and it tasted like honey, all sweet and stuff. {3:4} Then he's like, "Alright, go hit up the Israel crew and speak my words to 'em." {3:5} He's like, "You're not talking to some foreign folks with a different language; this is straight up Israel." {3:6} "I'm not sending you to some other peeps with a different language you can't understand; if I did, they'd actually listen to you." {3:7} "But nah, Israel won't listen; they're too stubborn and hard-hearted." {3:8} "I'm making you tough, bro, so don't sweat it when they give you attitude." {3:9} "Your forehead's harder than rock; don't be scared of 'em, even if they're a bunch of rebels." {3:10} "And listen up, take in everything I tell you, bro, and listen up real good." {3:11} "Then go tell your peeps, whether they wanna listen or not, what the Lord's gotta say." {3:12} Suddenly, I'm lifted up, hearing this crazy loud voice behind me, shouting about the glory of the Lord. {3:13} And I'm hearing these wild noises of living creatures and wheels, it's nuts. {3:14} So, I get lifted up and taken away, feeling all bitter and fired up, but knowing the Lord's got me. {3:15} Next thing I know, I'm chilling with these captives by the river, and I'm just sitting there, shocked, for like a week. {3:16-17} After a week, the Lord's word comes to me, saying, "Son of man, I'm making you a lookout for Israel, so listen up and warn 'em on my behalf." {3:18} "If you don't warn the wicked, and they die in their sin, that's on you; but if you do warn 'em and they still don't change, at least you saved yourself." {3:19} "And if a righteous dude turns bad and you don't warn him, his blood's on your hands; but if you do warn him and he stays good, you're good too." {3:20-21} "So, just let 'em know; if they hear you, cool, if not, that's on them." {3:22} "Now, go out to the open space, I gotta chat with you there." {3:23} So I'm like, "Alright," and head out, and there's the glory of the Lord, just like I saw before, and I'm on the ground again. {3:24} Then, the spirit's in me, getting me back on my feet, and telling me to lock myself up in my house. {3:25} "They're gonna tie you up, so you can't move around among 'em," he says. {3:26} "Your tongue's gonna stick to the roof of your mouth, so you can't speak; these people are too rebellious." {3:27} "But when I talk to you, I'll open your mouth, and you'll tell 'em what I say, whether they listen or not, 'cause, you know, rebellious and stuff."

{4:1} Then he's like, "Hey you, son of man, grab a tile and draw Jerusalem on it." {4:2} "Act like you're attacking it, build forts, set up camps, and all that." {4:3} "And take this iron pan, it's like a wall between you and the city; go face it and pretend to siege it." {4:4} "Lie down on your left side, to symbolize the sin of Israel, one day for each year of their wrongdoing." {4:5} "They've been sinning for 390 years, so you gotta lay there for that long." {4:6} "Then switch to your right side, representing the sin of Judah, 40 days, each one for a year." {4:7} "Focus on Jerusalem, keep your arm exposed, and prophesy against it." {4:8} "And I'll tie you up so you can't turn around until you're done with the siege." {4:9} "Grab some wheat, barley, beans, lentils, millet, and fitches, mix 'em up, and make bread, one loaf for each day you're lying down, 390 days." {4:10} "You'll eat 20 shekels of it every day, and drink water, one-sixth of a hin." {4:11-12} "Cook it over dung, 'cause that's how the Israelites are gonna eat when they're exiled." {4:13} "So, yeah, that's how they're gonna eat, even in other lands where I'll send 'em." {4:14} And I'm like, "Uh, Lord, I've never eaten gross stuff like that, never ate anything unclean." {4:15} But he's like, "I'm telling you, use cow dung instead," so I do. {4:16} "Oh, and by the way, son of man, I'm gonna mess up the food supply in Jerusalem, so they'll have to ration their bread and water, and they'll be shocked and dismayed." {4:17} "They're gonna be desperate for food and water, and they'll waste away because of their sin."

{5:1} Yo, Ezekiel, grab a sharp knife and a razor, then shave your head and beard. Next, get some scales and weigh the hair. {5:2} Burn a third of it in the city when the siege days are over, take another third and chop it with a knife, and scatter the remaining third in the wind. I'll chase them down with a sword. {5:3} Also, take a few strands and stash them in your clothes. {5:4} Then take some more and throw them into the fire, it'll spread throughout Israel like wildfire. {5:5} God's like, "Yo, this is Jerusalem, placed right in the middle of nations, but it's gone worse than all of them, rejecting my laws and statutes." {5:6} "You've messed up more than any other nation, so I'm against you, and I'll judge you in front of everyone." {5:7} "You've multiplied wickedness, disobeying my laws and imitating the nations around you." {5:8} "So, I'm gonna diminish you, and my eye won't spare you, no mercy here." {5:9} "Your punishment will be like nothing before because of your disgusting behavior." {5:10} "You'll reach such a low point that fathers will eat their sons, and sons will eat their fathers. I'll scatter the remaining people to the winds." {5:11} "Because you've defiled my sanctuary with your abominations, I won't hold back my judgment." {5:12} "One-third will die from disease, another from famine, and the last by the sword. I'll chase the rest with a sword." {5:13} "Then you'll know I mean business, and they'll know I'm the LORD when my fury is unleashed upon them." {5:14} "I'll make you a waste and a disgrace among the nations, visible for all to see." {5:15} "You'll be a reproach, a mockery to all around when I execute my anger and fury upon you. I've said it, and I'll do it." {5:16} "I'll hit you with famine and worsen it until you're desperate, breaking your food supply." {5:17} "Famine, wild animals, death—all of it's coming for you. I've spoken."

{6:1} Then the LORD was like, "Yo, Ezekiel, listen up." {6:2} "Focus on Israel's mountains and start prophesying against them." {6:3} "Tell 'em, I'm bringing a sword, destroying their high places." {6:4} "Their altars will be deserted, their idols shattered, and their dead bodies strewn before them." {6:5} "I'll lay the dead right at their idol's feet, scattering their bones everywhere." {6:6} "Their cities will be laid waste, their altars destroyed, and their idols smashed. It's all gonna be gone." {6:7} "The dead will pile up, and they'll know I'm the LORD." {6:8} "But I'll leave a few alive, scattered among the nations, just so they remember me." {6:9} "They'll realize how much they've screwed up, and they'll regret it all." {6:10} "They'll know I'm the LORD, and I wasn't joking about the punishment." {6:11} "So, smack your hand and stomp your foot, lamenting the evil of Israel's house. They'll fall by the sword, famine, and disease." {6:12} "Some will die far away, some close by, and some besieged in the city. My fury will be complete." {6:13} "Then they'll know I'm the LORD when their dead lie among their idols, all over the place." {6:14} "I'll stretch out my hand, making the land desolate, worse than the wilderness. They'll know I'm the LORD."

{7:1} So, like, the Lord hit me up again with a message, saying, {7:2} "Yo, son of man, listen up, 'cause the Lord's saying to Israel, 'It's game over, man, it's over for all corners of the land.'" {7:3} "The end's here, and I'm bringing down my anger on you, judging you for all the messed-up stuff you've been doing." {7:4} "I ain't holding back; I'm gonna hit you with everything you got coming, and you're gonna know it's me, the Lord, who's doing it." {7:5} "Seriously, it's bad news, like, really bad news; it's here, it's watching, it's happening." {7:6} "The end's here, morning's come, and it's not a good morning; it's trouble time, and there's no turning back." {7:7} "The day of reckoning's here, and it's not gonna be pretty; no one's gonna be safe from what's coming." {7:8} "I'm about to unleash my fury on you, finishing what I started, judging you for all the messed-up stuff you've done." {7:9} "No mercy, no holding back; I'm gonna give you what you deserve, and you're gonna know it's me, the Lord, doing it." {7:10} "You see the day coming? Yeah, it's here, and it's not good; pride's taken root, and it's gonna be your downfall." {7:11} "Violence is everywhere, wickedness is rampant, and there won't be anyone left, no one to mourn for them." {7:12} "It's happening, the end's near; no one's gonna be celebrating or mourning, 'cause everyone's gonna feel the wrath." {7:13} "No one's gonna get their stuff back; this vision's for real, and there's no going back to the way things were." {7:14} "They're getting ready for battle, but no one's gonna fight; my wrath's coming down on everyone." {7:15} "It's chaos everywhere, with violence, disease, and famine; no one's safe, whether they're in the city or out in the fields." {7:16} "But those who survive are gonna be like doves in the mountains, mourning for their sins." {7:17} "Everyone's gonna be weak, feeble, like water; no one's gonna have any strength left." {7:18} "People are gonna be wearing sackcloth, horrified and ashamed, with bald heads and shame on their faces." {7:19} "They're gonna throw their money in the streets, but it won't save them from the Lord's wrath; they won't find any satisfaction, no matter how much they have." {7:20} "They may have had some fancy stuff, but they turned it into idols and abominations; now it's all gonna be taken away from them." {7:21} "I'm handing it over to strangers to plunder, to the wicked to spoil; they're gonna defile it all." {7:22} "I'm turning away from them, letting them defile my sanctuary; robbers are gonna break in and desecrate it." {7:23} "The land's full of violence, the city's full of crime; it's time to bring in the worst of the worst to take over." {7:24} "I'm gonna let the heathens take over their houses, put an end to the strong and their sacred places." {7:25} "Destruction's coming, and they're gonna seek peace, but there won't be any." {7:26} "It's gonna be one disaster after another, and they'll be looking for answers from prophets, but they won't find any; the priests won't have any guidance, and the elders won't have any counsel." {7:27} "The king's gonna mourn, the prince's gonna be desolate, and the people are gonna suffer for their sins; I'm gonna judge them according to what they've done, and they're gonna know it's the Lord."

{8:1} "So, in the sixth year, in the sixth month, on the fifth day of the month, while I was chilling at home, the elders of Judah were there, and then bam, the hand of the Lord God hit me." {8:2} "And suddenly, I'm seeing this crazy vision of fire, blazing bright, from his waist down, fire; and from his waist up, this intense brightness, like amber." {8:3} "And then, he reaches out his hand, grabs me by the hair, and lifts me up between heaven and earth, showing me this vision of Jerusalem, right at the gate where they got this jealousy-inducing idol." {8:4} "And there it is, the glory of the God of Israel, just like I saw before, chilling there." {8:5} "And he's like, 'Yo, son of man, look north'; so I do, and there it is, this idol at the gate of the altar, making everyone jealous." {8:6} "He's like, 'Check this out, son of man, see what they're doing?' It's all messed up, and they're just getting started." {8:7} "And then he takes me to this hole in the wall, and I'm like, 'What's up with this?' and he's like, 'Dig into it,' so I do, and there's a door." {8:8} "He's like, 'Go on in,' so I do, and I see all this messed-up stuff they're doing." {8:9} "There's all these creepy images, abominable beasts, and idols plastered all over the walls." {8:10} "And then there's these seventy elders of Israel, with incense burning, and it's all shady, dark stuff they're up to." {8:11} "And he's like, 'Yo, son of man, peep what they're doing in secret, thinking I don't see; they think I've abandoned them.'" {8:12} "He's like, 'There's more,' so I look, and it's even worse." {8:13} "Then he takes me to the entrance of the Lord's house, and there's women weeping for some dude named Tammuz." {8:14} "He's like, 'You see this?' and I'm like, 'Yeah,' and he's like, 'It's gonna get worse.'" {8:15} "He takes me inside the temple, and there's these guys worshiping the sun, with their backs to the Lord's temple." {8:16} "And he's like, 'You see this too?' and I'm like, 'Yeah,' and he's like, 'They're messed up, filling the land with violence, and they're gonna pay for it.'" {8:17} "I'm gonna bring down my fury on them, no holding back, even if they cry out to me; they're gonna know it's the Lord."

{9:1} So, I heard this loud voice saying, "Yo, get those in charge of the city here, each with their weapon." {9:2} Then six dudes rolled up from the north, packing heat, and one of them, dressed in linen with an inkhorn, stood by the brass altar. {9:3} The glory of God moved from the cherub to the temple threshold. God told the linen guy to mark those who mourn over the city's sins. {9:4} To the others, he's like, "Go after him and start smiting. Show no mercy, just go for it." {9:5} "Slay everyone, young and old, but spare those marked. Start with the elders." {9:6} So, they went out and started killing. {9:7} God's like, "Defile the house, fill the courts with bodies." They went and did it. {9:8} While they were at it, I fell on my face and pleaded, "God, are you gonna destroy all of Israel because of Jerusalem's mess?" {9:9} He's like, "The sins of Israel and Judah are too much, the land's full of blood, and they think I don't see." {9:10} "My eye won't spare them, they'll get what they deserve." {9:11} The linen guy reported back, "Did what you said, boss."

{10:1} I looked and saw a throne-like sapphire above the cherubim. {10:2} God told the linen guy, "Go between the wheels, grab fire, and scatter it over the city." He did it. {10:3} The cherubim stood by as the linen guy went in, and the cloud filled the inner court. {10:4} The glory of God moved from the cherub to the temple threshold, filling the place with brightness. {10:5} The sound of the cherubim's wings was loud, like the voice of God. {10:6} The linen guy was told to take fire from between the wheels. He did it. {10:7} A cherub handed him the fire, and he went out. {10:8} The cherubim had the form of a human hand under their wings. {10:9} Each cherub had four wheels, one beside each, and they looked like beryl stones. {10:10} Each wheel had the same appearance, like a wheel within a wheel. {10:11} They moved without turning, following wherever the head looked. {10:12} Their whole body, backs, hands, wings, and wheels were full of eyes. {10:13} It was called a wheel. {10:14} Each cherub had four faces: a cherub, a man, a lion, and an eagle. {10:15} When the cherubim moved, the wheels moved. {10:16} When they lifted their wings, the wheels didn't turn. {10:17} They stood when the cherubim stood and lifted themselves when the cherubim did, for the spirit of the living creature was in them. {10:18} Then the glory of God left the temple threshold and stood over the cherubim. {10:19} The cherubim lifted their wings and rose from the earth, with the wheels beside them at the east gate, and the glory of God above them. {10:20} This was the creature I saw by the Chebar River, and I knew they were the cherubim. {10:21} Each had four faces and wings, and human hands under their wings. {10:22} Their faces were the same as those by the Chebar River, and they moved straight ahead.

{11:1} So, the spirit took me to the east gate of the Lord's house, and there were twenty-five dudes chillin', including Jaazaniah and Pelatiah, big shots in the city. {11:2} And the spirit's like, "Yo, son of man, check it, these are the guys stirring up trouble, giving bad advice in this city." {11:3} "They're like, 'Nah, we good, let's build houses; this city's our safe space, and we're the ones in control.'" {11:4} "So, prophesy against them, son of man, let 'em know what's up." {11:5} Then the Lord's spirit hit me up, saying, "Speak up, son, this is what the Lord says: I know what y'all are thinking, every last one of you." {11:6} "Y'all been shedding blood left and right in this city, filling the streets with corpses." {11:7} "So here's the deal: those corpses you've piled up? They're like the meat in a pot, and this city's the pot; but I'm gonna pull you out of there." {11:8} "You've been afraid of the sword? Well, get ready, 'cause it's coming for you," says the Lord. {11:9} "I'll drag you out of here, hand you over to strangers, and serve up some justice." {11:10} "You're gonna fall by the sword; I'll judge you right on the border of Israel, and you'll know it's me, the Lord." {11:11} "This city won't be your safe space anymore, and you won't be in control; I'll judge you right on the border of Israel." {11:12} "You'll know it's me, the Lord, 'cause you haven't followed my rules, instead, you've been copying the heathens around you." {11:13} Then, when I was prophesying, Pelatiah dropped dead. I hit the floor, freaking out, like, "Lord, are you gonna wipe out all of Israel?" {11:14} Then the Lord hit me up again, saying, {11:15} "Listen, son, your peeps, your whole crew, even all of Israel, they're the ones the people of Jerusalem are saying, 'Get lost, this land is ours.'" {11:16} "But here's the deal: even though I've scattered them among the nations, I'll still be there for them, like a little sanctuary wherever they go." {11:17} "I'll gather them up from all over, bring 'em back to Israel, and they'll clean up the place, getting rid of all the nasty stuff." {11:18} "They'll roll in, clean up house, and I'll give 'em new hearts and spirits, so they'll finally follow my rules and be my peeps." {11:19} "Then they'll do what's right, and they'll be my crew, and I'll be their God." {11:20} "But those who keep chasing after their nasty idols and abominations? They're gonna get what's coming to 'em, says the Lord." {11:21} "Then the cherubim did their thing, wheels spinning, and the glory of the God of Israel hovered over them." {11:22} "And the Lord's glory left the city, chilling on a mountain to the east." {11:23} "Later, the spirit took me in a vision to Chaldea, to the exiles. The vision was over." {11:24} "I told the exiles everything the Lord showed me."

{12:1} "Then the Lord hit me up, saying," {12:2} "Listen, son, you're surrounded by a bunch of rebellious peeps who don't see or hear anything; they're straight-up stubborn." {12:3} "So, son, pack up your stuff and move it around during the day in front of 'em; maybe they'll get the message, even though they're stubborn." {12:4} "Carry your stuff out during the day, like you're moving, and then at night, do the same in front of 'em, like you're going into exile." {12:5} "Dig through the wall where they can see you, and carry your stuff out that way." {12:6} "Do it all in front of 'em, carrying your stuff out at twilight, covering your face so you can't see the ground; it's a sign for Israel." {12:7} "So I did what the Lord said: moved my stuff during the day, like I was going into exile, and at night, I dug through the wall and carried it out." {12:8} "Next morning, the Lord hit me up again," {12:9} "Listen, son, haven't the rebellious peeps been asking you what you're doing?" {12:10} "Tell 'em, 'This is about the prince in Jerusalem and all the Israelites there; what I'm doing is a sign for them: they're going into exile.'" {12:11} "The prince among 'em will carry his stuff at twilight, digging through the wall to get out; he'll cover his face so he can't see the ground." {12:12} "I'll spread my net over him, and he'll be caught in my trap, dragged off to Babylon, where he'll die without ever seeing it." {12:13} "I'll scatter all those around him to the winds, and they'll be hunted down with the sword." {12:14} "They'll know I'm the Lord when I scatter 'em among the nations and spread 'em out." {12:15} "But I'll leave a few of 'em untouched, so they can tell everyone about their nasty deeds among the nations; then they'll know I'm the Lord." {12:16} "Then the word of the Lord hit me up again, saying," {12:17} "Listen, son, the people of Israel are saying, 'This vision's way off, it's for some distant future.'" {12:18} "So tell 'em, 'This ain't no distant future; what I'm saying's gonna happen soon.'" {12:19} "Their land's gonna be a wasteland, and they'll eat and drink in fear and astonishment because of all the violence." {12:20} "Their cities will be destroyed, their land laid waste; then they'll know I'm the Lord." {12:21} "Then the word of the Lord hit me up, saying," {12:22} "Listen, son, what's this saying I keep hearing in Israel: 'Time drags on, and nothing's happening'?" {12:23} "Tell 'em, 'That's gonna stop; things are gonna happen, and soon.'" {12:24} "No more fake visions or lying divinations among Israel." {12:25} "I'm the Lord; what I say is gonna happen, and it ain't gonna take long. In your lifetime, rebellious house, I'm speaking and making it happen," says the Lord. {12:26} "The word of the Lord hit me up again, saying," {12:27} "Listen, son, the people of Israel are saying, 'This vision's for way off in the future; he's talking about stuff that won't happen for ages.'" {12:28} "So tell 'em, 'No more waiting; what I've said is gonna happen, and soon,' says the Lord."

{13:1} So, God hit me up, saying, {13:2} "Yo, son of man, call out those fake prophets in Israel. Tell 'em to listen up to what God's gotta say, not just make stuff up." {13:3} God's like, "Those foolish prophets are clueless, just following their own vibe, not seeing squat!" {13:4} "Israel's prophets are like desert foxes, slick but worthless." {13:5} "They ain't patching up the gaps or building defenses for Israel when trouble hits." {13:6} "They're into all this fake stuff, claiming it's from God when it's not, giving people false hope." {13:7} "You ever seen such a joke? Claiming God said stuff He didn't?" {13:8} "So, because they're all about lies and vanity, I'm coming for 'em. God's against those fakers." {13:9} "I'm gonna deal with those prophets who peddle lies, they won't be part of my crew or get in on Israel's future. They'll know I mean business." {13:10} "They've been fooling my people, promising peace where there's none. It's like building a flimsy wall, thinking it'll hold up against a storm." {13:11} "That wall's coming down hard, hit by storms, hail, and wind. When it crumbles, they'll be like, 'Where'd that protection go?'" {13:12} "I'll tear it down myself in fury, exposing its weakness, and those fakers will get what's coming." {13:13} "That wall they've built with lies? I'm tearing it down with a storm and fury, leaving nothing behind. They'll realize I mean business." {13:14} "I'm smashing that wall they built with lies, bringing it down to the ground. They'll be toast, and they'll know it's me, God, who did it." {13:15} "Their wall? Gone. Them? Done. Those prophets in Jerusalem promising peace? None to be found, says God." {13:16} "You, son of man, call out the women prophets too, prophesying from their own hearts. They're just as guilty." {13:17} "They're making soul traps, promising life but delivering death, all for some bread and barley." {13:18} "But I'm coming for their traps, setting those souls free. They won't be able to hunt my people anymore, and they'll know it's me, God." {13:19} "They've been making the good guys sad and supporting the bad guys, promising life where there's none. But that's over now." {13:20} "I'm freeing my people from their lies, delivering them from their grip. They'll know I mean business." {13:21} "Because they've been spreading lies and false visions, I'm taking back control. They won't be able to deceive my people anymore, and they'll know it's me, God." {13:22} "Now, some Israel elders came to me, and God had a word for them." {13:23} "It's like this: when the land's acting up, I'll bring down the hammer. Famine, beasts, sword, or pestilence, nothing will be spared."

{14:1} So, some of the Israel elders rolled up to me, took a seat, and then God hit me up with a message, saying, {14:2} "Listen up, son of man, these dudes got their hearts full of idols, messing up big time. Should I even bother answering when they come asking?" {14:3} "Tell 'em straight: anyone in Israel with idols in their heart, showing off their sin for all to see, and then trying to get a word from a prophet, I'll give 'em an answer that matches their idol count." {14:4} "I'm doing this to expose Israel's heart problem, 'cause they're all distant from me, too caught up in their idols." {14:5} "So, tell Israel to wise up, ditch the idols, and turn away from all the messed-up stuff they're into." {14:6} "This goes for everyone, even strangers hanging out in Israel, if they're setting up idols in their hearts and then trying to ask about me, I'll deal with them myself." {14:7} "I'm gonna turn against anyone pulling that stunt, making 'em a cautionary tale. They'll be cut off from my crew, and they'll know who's boss." {14:8} "And if a prophet gets duped into saying stuff, it's on them. I'll deal with them too, wiping 'em out from among my people." {14:9} "They'll pay for their sin, prophets and those who listen to 'em alike, so Israel stays on track with me." {14:10-11} "This is so Israel stays on point with me, being my crew, and me being their God, says the Lord GOD." {14:12} "Then God hit me up again, saying," {14:13} "Yo, son of man, when the land's acting up, trespassing hard, I'm gonna step in. Famine, wiping out people and beasts, it's all on the table." {14:14} "Even if Noah, Daniel, and Job were around, they'd only save themselves by their righteousness, says the Lord GOD." {14:15} "If I let nasty beasts loose and they wreck the land, leaving it deserted, not even these three legends could save anyone else, just themselves." {14:16} "Even if they were around, I swear, says the Lord GOD, they'd only save themselves, leaving the land a wasteland." {14:17} "If I bring out the sword on that land, cutting off people and beasts, same deal. Even if those three were there, they'd only save themselves." {14:18} "They wouldn't save anyone else, just themselves, swears the Lord GOD." {14:19} "Or if I send a plague, pouring out my anger, wiping out people and beasts, same story. Even with Noah, Daniel, and Job, they'd only save themselves." {14:20} "They'd only save themselves through their righteousness, says the Lord GOD." {14:21} "So, if I bring all four of my heavy punishments on Jerusalem—sword, famine, beasts, and plague—cutting off people and beasts," {14:22} "There'll still be a few left, sons and daughters. You'll see 'em and understand why I had to bring down the hammer on Jerusalem. You'll get it, says the Lord GOD." {14:23} "Their ways and deeds will give you comfort, and you'll know I had good reason for everything I did, says the Lord GOD."

{15:1} So, the big man upstairs hit me up again, like, "Yo, listen up, dude." {15:2} He's all like, "Check it, son of man, what makes a vine so special compared to any ol' tree or branch?" {15:3} "Can you make anything useful out of vine wood? Nah, it just gets tossed into the fire for fuel, burns up real quick." {15:4} "Even when it's whole, it ain't good for much. So, imagine what it's like after it's been burnt up." {15:5} "That's exactly what's gonna happen to the folks in Jerusalem, straight up." {15:6} "I'm gonna be against them, they'll face one fire after another, and then they'll know I'm the real deal." {15:7} "Their land's gonna be a wasteland 'cause they've been acting all shady, says the big man." {15:8} "They've been trespassing on some serious boundaries, and now they're gonna pay the price."

{16:1} Then the big man upstairs hit me up again, dropping some serious truth bombs. {16:2} He's like, "Yo, son of man, tell Jerusalem what's up with all their messed-up stuff." {16:3} "Here's the deal, Jerusalem: you're from Canaan, your parents were Amorites and Hittites." {16:4} "And let's talk about your birth – nobody cared about you, you were left out in the open, totally neglected." {16:5} "But I came along and saw you all messed up, covered in your own blood, and I was like, 'Live!'" {16:6} "I hooked you up big time, made you grow and shine, gave you the works." {16:7} "You went from zero to hero, decked out in the finest, looking fly." {16:8} "When the time was right, I made a covenant with you, covered you up, and claimed you as mine." {16:9} "I cleaned you up, washed away all that blood, and anointed you with oil." {16:10} "I dressed you in the finest threads, hooked you up with the best gear." {16:11} "I blinged you out with jewelry, bracelets, chains – you name it, I gave it to you." {16:12} "You were dripping in gold and silver, looking like royalty, all because of me." {16:13} "Everyone was talking about you, how beautiful you were because of the way I made you look." {16:14} "But you let it all go to your head, started playing the field, hooking up with anyone who came your way." {16:15} "You took your fancy clothes and used them to decorate your high places, acting all scandalous." {16:16} "You even took the bling I gave you and made idols to worship, totally disrespecting me." {16:17} "You took my gifts and used them to cheat on me, setting up a whole scandalous scene." {16:18} "You even took the food I gave you and offered it to your idols as a sacrifice, like, what?" {16:19} "You went as far as sacrificing your own kids to these idols, like, seriously?!" {16:20} "You've been so messed up, getting involved with all sorts of shady dealings, but you don't even remember where you came from." {16:21} "You've been building these fancy places to worship all over the place, offering yourself up to anyone who passes by." {16:22} "You're acting like a straight-up cheater, forgetting about our covenant and going after other lovers." {16:23} "After all the messed-up stuff you've done, it's time for some serious consequences, no more playing around." {16:24} "You've built yourself up, but now it's all gonna come crashing down. It's judgment time." {16:25} "You've been flaunting yourself everywhere, but now you're gonna be exposed for who you really are." {16:26} "You've been messing around with all your neighbors, thinking you can get away with it, but I've had enough." {16:27} "I'm handing you over to those who hate you, and they're gonna show you no mercy." {16:28} "You've been hooking up with everyone, trying to fill that void, but you're never satisfied." {16:29} "You've been spreading your scandals far and wide, but it's all gonna catch up to you." {16:30} "You're acting like a desperate fool, doing whatever it takes to satisfy your desires." {16:31} "You've been setting up your shady businesses everywhere, but you're not even getting paid for it." {16:32} "You're like a cheating spouse, taking on all these lovers instead of sticking with me." {16:33} "Other people pay for their services, but you're the one paying them, trying to get them to come back for more." {16:34} "You're unlike any other, even in your scandalous ways. But it's all gonna catch up to you." {16:35} "So, listen up, you scandalous one, here's what's gonna go down." {16:36} "You've been exposing yourself to everyone, getting involved in all sorts of shady stuff." {16:37} "Now, I'm gonna gather up all your lovers and haters and expose you for who you really are." {16:38} "You're gonna face judgment for all your scandals and bloodshed, and it's gonna be brutal." {16:39} "Your fancy places and high places? They're all gonna come crashing down, and you'll be left stripped and exposed." {16:40} "You'll face the wrath of those you've wronged, and they won't hold back." {16:41} "Your houses will burn, and you'll be judged in front of everyone. It's game over for your scandalous ways." {16:42} "But once it's all said and done, I'll chill out, and you'll never act scandalous again." {16:43} "You've forgotten where you came from and all the messed-up stuff you've done. But it's all gonna catch up to you." {16:44} "People will talk about you and your scandals, comparing you to your shady family." {16:45} "You're just like your scandalous mama, hating on your husband and kids, and your sisters are no better." {16:46} "Your family tree's full of scandalous folks, from Samaria to Sodom, and you're the worst of them all." {16:47} "But even they didn't stoop to your level. You've outdone them all with your scandals." {16:48} "As sure as I'm alive, your sister Sodom didn't pull the stuff you've been pulling. You've taken it to a whole new level." {16:49} "Sodom's downfall was pride and neglecting the needy. But you? You're on a whole other level of messed up." {16:50} "You've been proud and scandalous, committing abominations left and right. That's why I took them out." {16:51} "Compared to you, Samaria's practically innocent. But you've made excuses for your sisters and justified your own scandals." {16:52} "You've judged others while doing worse yourself. You're gonna get what's coming to you." {16:53} "When I bring back Sodom and Samaria, your time's up. You'll be ashamed of what you've done." {16:54} "You'll be humiliated as your sisters rise again, and you'll realize what a mess you've made." {16:55} "When your sisters come back, you'll be right there with them, but it won't be pretty." {16:56} "You never mentioned Sodom when you were at your peak, but now you're the one everyone's talking about." {16:57} "Before your scandals were exposed, you were surrounded by folks who looked down on you." {16:58} "But now, your scandals are out in the open for everyone to see. You've got no one to blame but yourself." {16:59} "So, here's the deal: I'm gonna treat you just like you've treated me, breaking our covenant and acting all scandalous." {16:60} "But I'll still remember the good times we had and make a fresh start with you." {16:61} "You'll look back on all your mess and feel ashamed when I bring back your sisters and make things right." {16:62} "I'll make a new covenant with you, and you'll know that I'm the real deal." {16:63} "You'll remember all the messed-up stuff you did and be too ashamed to even speak. But I'll be cool with you, and we'll move on."

{17:1} So, like, the big man upstairs hit me up, saying, {17:2} "Listen up, dude, drop a riddle on the Israel crew; {17:3} Here's the deal: There's this massive eagle with flashy feathers, swoops down on Lebanon, snags the top branch of a cedar tree. {17:4} Cuts off the top, takes it to a city of traders. {17:5} Then he plants it in a primo spot, by some big waters, like, making it thrive. {17:6} It grows into this vine, branches reaching out, roots digging deep. {17:7} Then another eagle shows up, and this vine leans toward him, reaching out, hoping for some watering action. {17:8} Planted in prime soil, it's supposed to flourish, but will it? Nah, it's gonna get yanked out, wither up, no chance. {17:9} You feeling me? It's gonna wither, fade away, no one to save it. {17:10} Planted or not, it's gonna wither when the east wind blows, dried up in its own furrows. {17:11} Then God hits me up again, saying, {17:12} "Tell these rebellious folks what's up: The Babylonian king rolls into Jerusalem, takes the king and his crew back to Babylon. {17:13} Snatches some royal blood, makes a deal, takes some top-tier folks. {17:14} That's how he keeps things under control, not letting Jerusalem get too big for its britches. {17:15} But the king flips, tries to cozy up to Egypt, looking for help. Will it work? Nah, he'll get what's coming, break the deal, and get wrecked. {17:16} Swear to God, he's gonna die in Babylon, where he dissed the king who put him there. {17:17} Even with Egypt's backup, they ain't gonna save him in battle. {17:18} Breaking that deal was a big mistake, he ain't getting out of this. {17:19} So, God's like, "I'm gonna hit him with what he deserves, my oath and covenant, they're coming back to bite him." {17:20} I'm gonna trap him, drag him to Babylon, make him pay for crossing me. {17:21} His crew's gonna get wiped out, those left will scatter, and they'll know I called the shots. {17:22} God's saying, "I'm gonna take a cutting from that big cedar tree, plant it high up, make it thrive. {17:23} In Israel's highest peak, it's gonna grow, be huge, provide shade for birds. {17:24} Every tree's gonna see it, know I'm in charge, raising up the low ones, knocking down the high ones. {17:25} Word up, I'm doing it, says the Lord GOD."

{18:1} Then God's back at it, saying, {18:2} "What's with this saying in Israel? 'Parents eat sour grapes, kids get sour too?' {18:3} No way, not anymore, says the Lord GOD. {18:4} Everyone's got their own soul, man. If you mess up, you're gonna pay. {18:5} But if you're living right, doing your thing, you're good. {18:6} Not messing with idols, not messing with your neighbor's spouse, keeping clean. {18:7} Helping the needy, being fair, doing what's right. {18:8} Not taking advantage, not being shady, doing right by people. {18:9} Walking the walk, following the rules, staying true; that's the deal, you'll be cool, says the Lord GOD. {18:10} But if your kid's a total jerk, does the opposite, messing up left and right, {18:11} Ignoring all the good stuff, getting into shady business, doing all the wrong things. {18:12} Being greedy, doing dirty, worshipping idols, it's a mess. {18:13} Taking advantage, being greedy; he's gonna get what's coming, that's on him. {18:14} But if he sees his dad's mistakes, learns from them, does better, {18:15} Not messing with idols, not messing with neighbors' spouses, {18:16} Helping the needy, being honest, doing right, {18:17} Not getting involved in shady deals, being fair, following the rules; he's good, won't pay for his dad's mess-ups. {18:18} But if his dad was a total jerk, messing with his own people, he's gonna pay for it. {18:19} So, don't ask why, man. If the kid does right, he's good, even if his dad messed up. {18:20} Everyone's responsible for their own actions, no passing the blame. {18:21} But if the bad guy turns it around, starts living right, he's good, won't get what's coming. {18:22} Past mistakes? Forget about 'em. If he's living right, he's good, says the Lord GOD . {18:23} God's like, "I don't want the wicked to die, I want 'em to change their ways and live." {18:24} But if the good guy goes bad, starts doing wrong, he's gonna pay for it, no getting out of it. {18:25} Don't be saying God's not fair. Listen up, Israel, my way's fair, yours ain't. {18:26} If a good guy goes bad and dies for it, that's on him. {18:27} But if a bad guy changes his ways, starts living right, he's gonna live. {18:28} Because he sees his mistakes, turns it around, he's good, won't die. {18:29} So, Israel, don't be saying God's not fair. My way's fair, yours ain't. {18:30} So, I'm gonna judge you based on your actions, Israel. Turn it around, ditch the bad stuff, and you won't be ruined by it. {18:31} Get rid of your mess-ups, get a fresh start, why throw your life away, Israel? {18:32} God's like, "I don't want anyone to die for their mistakes. Turn it around, and live."

{19:1} Yo, peep this lament for the OGs of Israel, {19:2} So, like, imagine this: your mom's a total lioness, chilling with other lions, raising her cubs in the mix. {19:3} She's all nurturing and stuff, but one of her cubs grows up wild, snatching prey, straight up eating people. {19:4} Word gets out, and he gets snatched up, chained and hauled to Egypt. {19:5} Mom sees that her first cub's a lost cause, so she tries again with another. {19:6} But he ends up just like his bro, wreaking havoc, laying waste to cities. {19:7} He's out there, wrecking palaces, making the land desolate with his roar. {19:8} Eventually, the homies from all around trap him, and he's stuck in their pit. {19:9} They lock him up, haul him off to Babylon, never to be heard from again in the hills of Israel. {19:10} Now, your mom, she used to be like a thriving vine, planted by the water, fruitful and lush. {19:11} She had it all — strong rulers, towering branches, standing tall among the others. {19:12} But then fury strikes, and she's torn from her roots, cast down, dried up, her strength broken and burned. {19:13} Now she's stuck in the wilderness, dry and barren. {19:14} Her branches catch fire, devouring her fruit, leaving her with no strength to rule. This is some heavy lamenting, man.

{20:1} So, fast forward to the seventh year, fifth month, tenth day, some Israel elders roll up to chat with the LORD, chilling with me. {20:2} Then boom, the LORD drops some truth on me, saying, {20:3} "Yo, son of man, talk to these Israel elders. But let me tell you, I ain't here to play 20 questions with them." {20:4} "You gonna call them out, son of man? You gonna make 'em face the messed-up stuff their ancestors did?" {20:5} "Tell 'em this, son of man: Back in the day, when I chose Israel and flexed on them in Egypt, I laid down the law." {20:6} "I had big plans for them, leading them to a dope land flowing with milk and honey, the best spot around." {20:7} "But they straight up rebelled, chasing after idols like it was the new trend. I was like, 'I'm your God, don't forget it!'" {20:8} "But nah, they dissed me, clung to their idols, so I had to lay down some divine fury right there in Egypt." {20:9} "But I held back, didn't want my name getting dragged through the mud by the heathens watching." {20:10} "So, I haul them out of Egypt, into the wilderness, and drop some truth bombs on 'em." {20:11} "I give 'em my laws, my sabbaths, everything they need to live right. But they're like, 'Nah, we good.'" {20:12} "They straight up trash my sabbaths, chase after idols like they're going out of style. So, I'm like, 'Fine, you do you.'" {20:13} "But I'm not done yet. I got more tricks up my sleeve. I'm gonna scatter 'em, disperse 'em, let 'em taste some real hardship." {20:14} "They're gonna get some laws that ain't so sweet, judgments that'll make 'em squirm. And I'll make 'em realize I'm the LORD, no doubt." {20:15} "But even then, they ain't learning. They're still chasing idols, polluting my sabbaths. So close, yet so far." {20:16} "But I ain't giving up. I'll still bring 'em back, show 'em who's boss. They'll know I'm the LORD, no question." {20:17} "I'll make 'em pass under the rod, sift out the rebels, the ones who dissed me. They won't step foot in Israel, you hear me?" {20:18} "But to the rest of y'all, Israel, I got a message: Go ahead, worship your idols, but don't drag my name through the mud again with your trash." {20:19} "When you finally get it together and come back to me, we'll do things right. I'll accept your offerings, your firstfruits, all that good stuff." {20:20} "You'll be back in my good books, and the heathens will see that I'm the real deal." {20:21} "And when I finally bring you back to Israel, you'll look back at your past, your messed-up ways, and be like, 'Damn, we were jacked up.'" {20:22} "But I did it all for my name's sake, not 'cause you deserved it. Remember that, Israel." {20:23} "I ain't done with you yet. I'm gonna scatter you, disperse you, let you taste some real struggle." {20:24} "Because you dissed me, trashed my laws, chased after idols. So, I'm gonna let you learn the hard way." {20:25} "I'll give you laws that ain't so sweet, judgments that'll make you squirm. I'll make you realize I'm the LORD." {20:26} "So, listen up, son of man, and tell Israel this: Your ancestors dissed me big time, straight-up crossed the line." {20:27} "But I'm still gonna rule over you, with a mighty hand, pouring out my fury. You'll see, I ain't playing around." {20:28} "I'll bring you out from among the nations, gather you up, and lay down the law." {20:29} "And when you finally come to your senses and worship idols no more, you'll know I'm the real deal." {20:30} "But until then, keep offering your gifts, sacrificing your kids, polluting yourselves with idols. But don't expect me to answer when you call." {20:31} "You think you can just copy the heathens, serving wood and stone? Think again." {20:32} "I'm gonna rule over you with a mighty hand, pouring out my fury. You'll see, I'm not to be messed with."

{21:1} So, like, the big man upstairs hits me up, saying, {21:2} "Yo, dude, focus on Jerusalem and spit some truth at the holy spots, and call out Israel, like, 'God's coming for you, and it's gonna get messy. I'm gonna take out both the good and the bad.'" {21:3} "Check it, I'm gonna whip out my sword and start slicing and dicing, taking out everyone from south to north. I want everyone to know I mean business." {21:4} "Since I'm taking out both the righteous and the wicked, my sword is gonna be out and about, wrecking everyone's day." {21:5} "Once that sword's out, it's staying out. No going back." {21:6} "So, bro, start groaning and moaning in front of everyone, showing how messed up things are gonna get." {21:7} "And when people ask why you're acting all bummed, tell 'em it's because bad stuff is coming, and everyone's gonna freak out." {21:8} "God's chatting me up again, saying," {21:9} "Get ready to preach, man. Tell 'em a sword's getting sharpened and shined up, ready to do some serious damage." {21:10} "This sword ain't for partying. It's gonna wreck shop, ignoring anyone who tries to stop it." {21:11} "It's all polished up and ready to be wielded, destined for destruction." {21:12} "So, dude, start wailing and crying, 'cause this is gonna hit hard. It's gonna mess up my people, especially the big shots." {21:13} "And even though some might think this is all a joke, it's no laughing matter. Things are gonna get real." {21:14} "So, bro, keep prophesying and clapping your hands, 'cause the sword's gonna keep swinging, especially at the big shots who think they're safe in their mansions." {21:15} "I'm aiming this sword at all their defenses, making their hearts drop and their homes crumble." {21:16} "They won't know which way to turn, left or right. It's gonna be chaos." {21:17} "I'm gonna clap my hands too, calming down my anger. I said it, and I'm gonna do it." {21:18} "God's back at it, saying," {21:19} "Hey, you, pick two paths, 'cause Babylon's sword is coming. They're gonna hit both Ammon and Judah, especially Jerusalem." {21:20} "The king of Babylon's all set, using magic and superstition to decide who to attack." {21:21} "He's got his eye on Jerusalem, planning out the siege and destruction." {21:22} "But it's all gonna be a sham, a false prediction. They might swear oaths, but they're gonna get what's coming to 'em." {21:23} "So, because they're not getting away with anything, they're gonna be captured and punished." {21:24} "Because they've been so wicked, it's all coming back to bite 'em. God's not forgetting a thing." {21:25} "And you, you rotten prince of Israel, your time's up. Your reign of terror's ending." {21:26} "God's saying, 'Take off that crown, 'cause things are changing. The lowly are gonna rise, and the high and mighty are gonna fall.'" {21:27} "There's gonna be so much upheaval, but it's all leading to the rightful ruler taking charge." {21:28} "And you, keep prophesying, dude, about the Ammonites and their disgrace. Tell 'em the sword's out and ready to slice and dice, bringing judgment." {21:29} "They might be feeling smug, but it's all gonna come crashing down on 'em. Their time's up." {21:30} "Think I'm gonna let 'em off easy? Nah, they're gonna get what's coming to 'em, right where they started all this mess." {21:31} "I'm gonna unleash my wrath on 'em, handing 'em over to ruthless conquerors to wipe 'em out." {21:32} "They're gonna be fuel for the fire, forgotten and gone. 'Cause God said so."

{22:1} "Then God hits me up again, saying," {22:2} "Yo, you, gonna lay down the truth on that messed up city? Show 'em all their dirty laundry." {22:3} "Let 'em know they've been spilling blood and making idols left and right." {22:4} "They're guilty as sin, defiling themselves with their wicked ways." {22:5} "They're gonna be a laughingstock, mocked by everyone near and far." {22:6} "All the big shots have been in on it, exploiting everyone they could." {22:7} "They've shown no respect for family or outsiders, oppressing the vulnerable at every turn." {22:8} "They've trashed what's holy and treated my Sabbaths like they're nothing." {22:9} "They're spreading lies and bloodshed, partying it up in the mountains and getting down and dirty." {22:10} "They've been getting freaky with their family members, taking bribes and cheating their neighbors, forgetting all about me." {22:11} "It's a mess, and I'm fed up. I'm gonna smack 'em down for their greed and corruption." {22:12} "So, I'm gonna slap 'em silly for all the blood they've spilled and the filth they've spread." {22:13} "Think they can handle what's coming? Nah, they're gonna crumble when I'm through with 'em. 'Cause I said so." {22:14} "I'm gonna scatter 'em all over, cleaning up their mess wherever they go." {22:15} "They'll know it's me who's in charge, no doubt about it." {22:16} "God's back at it, saying," {22:17} "Israel's become worthless, like a pile of junk metals in a furnace. They're all impurities." {22:18} "So, I'm gonna gather 'em up and throw 'em in the fire, melting 'em down and leaving 'em there." {22:19} "Just like you melt down metals in a furnace, I'm gonna melt down these people in my anger and fury." {22:20} "They'll be as helpless as silver in the fire, realizing it's me, God, who's unleashing my wrath on 'em." {22:21} "Once they're in that fire, they'll know who's boss." {22:22} "Just like silver melts in the furnace, they're gonna melt under my fury. And they'll know it was me, God, who did it." {22:23} "Then God's back with more, saying," {22:24} "Hey, tell 'em they're like a barren wasteland, never getting any rain when they need it." {22:25} "Their prophets are like hungry lions, devouring anyone in their path, taking everything for themselves." {22:26} "Their priests are breaking all the rules, treating what's holy like it's nothing, blurring the lines between right and wrong." {22:27} "Their leaders are like wolves, tearing people apart for profit." {22:28} "Their prophets are all talk, spewing lies in my name when I never said a word." {22:29} "The people are just as bad, oppressing the poor and needy, taking advantage of strangers." {22:30} "I looked for someone to stand up for what's right, but there was no one. So, I'm gonna bring down my wrath on 'em, giving 'em what they deserve." {22:31} "They brought this on themselves, and now they're gonna pay the price, just like I said."

{23:1} Yo, God hit me up again, saying, {23:2} "Hey dude, there were these two girls, both from the same mom: {23:3} They were wildin' out in Egypt back in the day, losing their V-cards there. {23:4} Their names were Aholah, the older one, and Aholibah, her sis: they were mine, and they had kids. So here's the deal; Samaria is Aholah, and Jerusalem is Aholibah. {23:5} Aholah cheated on me, crushing on her Assyrian neighbors, {23:6} who were all dripped out in blue, leaders and hotshot riders. {23:7} She hooked up with these Assyrians, and got into all their idols. {23:8} She never stopped her old habits from Egypt where she had her wild times. {23:9} So, I handed her over to her Assyrian crushes. {23:10} They exposed her, took her kids, and killed her; she became infamous among women when they judged her. {23:11} When Aholibah saw this, she went even harder with her lovers and was more of a wild child than her sis. {23:12} She got obsessed with the Assyrians too, all their captains and riders. {23:13} I saw she was corrupted just like her sister. {23:14} She escalated, getting into Babylonian guys painted on the walls. {23:15} These dudes were all decked out, looking like princes. {23:16} She was instantly hooked and sent messengers to them in Babylon. {23:17} The Babylonians came over, and they defiled her, and she got tired of them. {23:18} She flaunted her actions, and I got fed up with her too. {23:19} Yet, she kept reminiscing about her wild times in Egypt. {23:20} She lusted after dudes with big assets and vigorous energy. {23:21} She remembered the lewdness of her youth in Egypt. {23:22} So, God said, "Aholibah, I'm bringing your old lovers against you. {23:23} The Babylonians, Chaldeans, and all the Assyrians with them: all those hotties. {23:24} They will come at you with chariots and shields and judge you by their standards. {23:25} I'll unleash my jealousy; they'll cut off your nose and ears, and kill your kids. {23:26} They'll strip you of your clothes and jewels. {23:27} I'll end your lewdness from Egypt, and you won't look back. {23:28} I'll deliver you to those you hate. {23:29} They'll deal with you hatefully, take your stuff, and expose your whoredoms. {23:30} I'm doing this because you went whoring after the heathen and their idols. {23:31} You followed your sister's path, so you'll drink her cup. {23:32} God says, "You'll drink deep and large from your sister's cup, be laughed at and scorned. {23:33} You'll be drunk and sorrowful, filled with desolation, like your sister Samaria. {23:34} You'll drink it, suck it dry, and break the shards, tearing yourself apart. {23:35} God says, "Since you forgot me and threw me away, bear your lewdness and whoredoms. {23:36} God said to me, "Son of man, will you judge Aholah and Aholibah? Tell them their abominations; {23:37} They committed adultery and had blood on their hands, sacrificed their kids to idols. {23:38} They defiled my sanctuary and profaned my sabbaths. {23:39} After killing their kids for idols, they came to my sanctuary the same day. {23:40} They sent for men from afar, dressed up for them, and sat on a fancy bed with my incense and oil. {23:41} They set a table and had a crowd, including desert men who put bracelets and crowns on them. {23:42} They committed more whoredoms. {23:43} I said to her, "Will they now commit whoredoms with her, and she with them?" {23:44} They went in unto her, like a harlot: so they went to Aholah and Aholibah. {23:45} Righteous men will judge them like adulteresses and murderers. {23:46} God says, "I'll bring a mob against them and let them be robbed and spoiled. {23:47} The mob will stone them and kill their kids, burning their houses. {23:48} This will stop lewdness in the land, teaching all women a lesson. {23:49} They'll repay your lewdness, and you'll know I am the Lord GOD.

{24:1} In the ninth year, tenth month, tenth day, God spoke to me, {24:2} "Son of man, mark this day: the king of Babylon is attacking Jerusalem. {24:3} Tell the rebellious house, God says, "Set on a pot, pour water into it: {24:4} Gather the pieces, the thigh and shoulder, fill it with choice bones. {24:5} Take the best of the flock, burn the bones under it, and boil it well. {24:6} God says, "Woe to the bloody city, the pot with scum! Bring it out piece by piece. {24:7} Her blood is in her midst; she put it on a rock, not the ground. {24:8} This caused fury for vengeance; her blood is on the rock. {24:9} God says, "Woe to the bloody city! I'll make the fire pile great. {24:10} Heap on wood, kindle the fire, consume the flesh, and let the bones burn. {24:11} Set the pot empty on the coals, to melt its filthiness. {24:12} Her scum won't leave; her scum will be in the fire. {24:13} In her filthiness is lewdness: I've tried to purge her, but she won't be clean. {24:14} I, the LORD, have spoken; it will happen, I won't change my mind. They'll judge you according to your ways. {24:15} God's word came to me, saying, {24:16} "Son of man, I'm taking away your wife with a stroke: don't mourn or weep. {24:17} Don't cry, bind your head, put on shoes, don't cover your lips, or eat bread from others. {24:18} I spoke to the people in the morning: in the evening my wife died; I did as commanded. {24:19} The people asked me, "What does this mean for us?" {24:20-21} I told them, God says, "I'll profane my sanctuary, the desire of your eyes, and your kids will fall by the sword. {24:22} You'll do as I did: not mourn or weep; {24:23} You'll wear your headgear and shoes, but pine away for your iniquities. {24:24} Ezekiel is a sign: you'll do as he did, and know I am the Lord GOD. {24:25} When I take from them their strength, joy, and kids, {24:26} the escapee will tell you, {24:27} and your mouth will be opened, and you'll speak. You'll be a sign to them, and they'll know I am the LORD.

{25:1} Yo, the big man upstairs hit me up again, saying, {25:2} "Bro, focus on the Ammonites and drop some truth bombs on them." {25:3} I'm like, "Listen up, Ammonites, God's got some words for you. You were all smug when my crib got trashed, and when Israel and Judah got wrecked. So now you're gonna get handed over to the dudes from the east. They'll crash at yours, eat your grub, and chill." {25:4} "Rabbah, your main spot? Yeah, it's gonna be a hangout for camels. You'll be left out cold, and that's on you." {25:5} "Because you were all cheering when Israel got messed up, now you're gonna get wrecked too." {25:6} "You were clapping and stomping all happy when Israel got messed up? Well, now it's your turn. I'm coming for you, and I'll hand you over to other nations. You're done." {25:7} "Moab and Seir were talking smack about Judah too? Well, they're getting a piece of the action. I'll open Moab up to the east guys too. No one's gonna remember you, Ammonites." {25:8} "Edom got beef with Judah? Yeah, they're getting it too. I'll lay them to waste, starting from Teman. They'll know my wrath." {25:9} "And I'll make sure Israel gives Edom a taste of their own medicine. They're gonna pay for their actions, big time." {25:10} "Philistines acting all tough? They're gonna regret it. I'll lay them to waste too, and they'll know who's boss." {25:11} "I'm bringing the heat on Tyre now. They're gonna feel the wrath of Babylon, big time."

{26:1} So, in the eleventh year, on the first of the month, God hits me up again, saying, {26:2} "Bro, Tyre's talking smack about Jerusalem, thinking they're all that. Well, they're in for a rude awakening." {26:3} "I'm coming for you, Tyre. I'll bring nations against you like waves crashing on the shore." {26:4} "Your walls and towers? Yeah, they're coming down. You'll be left like a barren rock." {26:5} "Your city's gonna be a fishing spot in the sea. That's how done you are." {26:6} "Even your countryside's gonna get wrecked. You'll know who's boss when your people start dropping." {26:7} "Nebuchadrezzar's rolling in from the north with his army. You better watch out." {26:8} "He's gonna tear down your walls, set up camp against you, and crush you." {26:9} "Your defenses won't stand a chance against him. Your city's gonna shake when he rolls in." {26:10} "His army's gonna trample your streets. Your people are gonna get wrecked, and your riches plundered." {26:11} "Your city's gonna be left in ruins. No more tunes playing, no more parties." {26:12} "Your city's gonna be a ghost town, never to be rebuilt. That's a promise from the man upstairs." {26:13} "People are gonna mourn your downfall. Your glory days are over." {26:14} "You're gonna be like a deserted rock, never to rise again. That's the word of God." {26:15} "Your downfall's gonna shake the islands. Everyone's gonna know when your time's up." {26:16} "Even the big shots of the sea will tremble at your fall. Your glory's gone, and they know it." {26:17} "They're gonna mourn your loss and wonder how such a mighty city fell." {26:18} "The islands will quake at your demise. Your end will send shockwaves." {26:19} "Your city's gonna be left deserted, drowned in the deep. You'll sink into oblivion." {26:20} "You'll join the ranks of ancient cities buried in the earth. Your glory days are gone, and you'll never be found again." {26:21} That's the word from the man upstairs.

{27:1} The word of the LORD came again unto me, saying, {27:2} Now, son of man, take up a lamentation for Tyrus; {27:3} And say unto Tyrus, "Yo, you who chill at the entry of the sea, the ultimate dealer of goods for many islands, the Lord GOD says: Tyrus, you said, 'I'm flawless.' {27:4} Your borders are in the seas, and your builders made you super pretty. {27:5} They made all your ship boards from fir trees of Senir and used cedars from Lebanon for your masts. {27:6} They made your oars from the oaks of Bashan, and your benches were of ivory from the isles of Chittim. {27:7} Your sails were of fine linen from Egypt, and your coverings were blue and purple from the isles of Elishah. {27:8} The folks from Zidon and Arvad were your sailors, and your wise men, Tyrus, were your pilots. {27:9} The elders of Gebal and their wise men were your calkers, and all the ships of the sea with their mariners were there to trade your goods. {27:10} Men from Persia, Lud, and Phut were in your army, and they hung their shields and helmets in you, showing off your splendor. {27:11} Men of Arvad and your army were on your walls all around, and the Gammadims were in your towers. They hung their shields on your walls, making your beauty perfect. {27:12} Tarshish traded with you because of your many riches; they exchanged silver, iron, tin, and lead for your goods. {27:13} Javan, Tubal, and Meshech traded people and bronze vessels in your market. {27:14} Those from the house of Togarmah traded horses, horsemen, and mules. {27:15} Men of Dedan were your merchants; many islands traded with you and brought ivory and ebony as gifts. {27:16} Syria traded with you because of your many products; they dealt with you in emeralds, purple, embroidered work, fine linen, coral, and agate. {27:17} Judah and the land of Israel traded wheat from Minnith, Pannag, honey, oil, and balm in your market. {27:18} Damascus traded with you for your many products, wine of Helbon, and white wool. {27:19} Dan and Javan going back and forth traded bright iron, cassia, and calamus in your market. {27:20} Dedan traded in precious clothes for chariots. {27:21} Arabia and all the princes of Kedar traded with you in lambs, rams, and goats.

{27:22} The merchants of Sheba and Raamah traded with you in spices, precious stones, and gold. {27:23} Haran, Canneh, Eden, the merchants of Sheba, Asshur, and Chilmad were your merchants. {27:24} They traded in all sorts of things: blue clothes, embroidered work, and chests of rich apparel bound with cords, and made of cedar among your merchandise. {27:25} The ships of Tarshish sang of you in your market, and you were replenished and made very glorious in the midst of the seas. {27:26} Your rowers brought you into great waters; the east wind has broken you in the midst of the seas. {27:27} Your riches, your fairs, your merchandise, your mariners, and your pilots, your calkers, and the occupiers of your merchandise, and all your men of war that are in you, and all your company in the midst of you, shall fall into the midst of the seas in the day of your ruin. {27:28} The suburbs shall shake at the sound of the cry of your pilots. {27:29} And all that handle the oar, the mariners, and all the pilots of the sea, shall come down from their ships; they shall stand upon the land. {27:30} And they shall make their voice heard against you and shall cry bitterly and cast dust upon their heads; they shall wallow in the ashes. {27:31} They shall make themselves bald for you and gird themselves with sackcloth, and they shall weep for you with bitterness of heart and bitter wailing. {27:32} And in their wailing, they shall take up a lamentation for you and lament over you, saying, 'What city is like Tyrus, like the destroyed in the midst of the sea?' {27:33} When your wares went out of the seas, you filled many people; you enriched the kings of the earth with your riches and your merchandise. {27:34} In the time when you shall be broken by the seas in the depths of the waters, your merchandise and all your company in the midst of you shall fall. {27:35} All the inhabitants of the isles shall be astonished at you, and their kings shall be very afraid; they shall be troubled in their faces. {27:36} The merchants among the people shall hiss at you; you shall be a terror, and never shall you be any more.

{28:1} The word of the LORD came again unto me, saying, {28:2} Son of man, say unto the prince of Tyrus, 'The Lord GOD says: Because your heart is lifted up, and you said, 'I am a God, I sit in the seat of God, in the midst of the seas;' yet you are a man, and not God, though you set your heart as the heart of God: {28:3} Behold, you are wiser than Daniel; there is no secret they can hide from you. {28:4} With your wisdom and your understanding you have gotten riches, and have gotten gold and silver into your treasures. {28:5} By your great wisdom and by your trade, you have increased your riches, and your heart is lifted up because of your riches. {28:6} Therefore the Lord GOD says: Because you have set your heart as the heart of God; {28:7} Behold, I will bring strangers upon you, the terrible of the nations, and they shall draw their swords against the beauty of your wisdom, and they shall defile your brightness. {28:8} They shall bring you down to the pit, and you shall die the deaths of those slain in the midst of the seas. {28:9} Will you still say before him that slays you, 'I am God?' but you shall be a man, and no God, in the hand of him that slays you. {28:10} You shall die the deaths of the uncircumcised by the hand of strangers, for I have spoken it, says the Lord GOD. {28:11} Moreover, the word of the LORD came unto me, saying, {28:12} Son of man, take up a lamentation upon the king of Tyrus, and say unto him, 'The Lord GOD says: You seal up the sum, full of wisdom and perfect in beauty. {28:13} You have been in Eden the garden of God; every precious stone was your covering: the sardius, topaz, and the diamond, the beryl, the onyx, and the jasper, the sapphire, the emerald, and the carbuncle, and gold. The workmanship of your tabrets and of your pipes was prepared in you in the day you were created. {28:14} You are the anointed cherub that covers, and I have set you so. You were upon the holy mountain of God; you walked up and down in the midst of the stones of fire. {28:15} You were perfect in your ways from the day you were created until iniquity was found in you. {28:16} By the multitude of your merchandise, they have filled the midst of you with violence, and you have sinned. Therefore, I will cast you as profane out of the mountain of God, and I will destroy you, O covering cherub, from the midst of the stones of fire. {28:17} Your heart was lifted up because of your beauty; you have corrupted your wisdom by reason of your brightness. I will cast you to the ground; I will lay you before kings that they may behold you. {28:18} You have defiled your sanctuaries by the multitude of your iniquities, by the iniquity of your trade. Therefore, I will bring forth a fire from the midst of you; it shall devour you, and I will bring you to ashes upon the earth in the sight of all them that behold you. {28:19} All they that know you among the people shall be astonished at you; you shall be a terror, and never shall you be any more.' {28:20} Again the word of the LORD came unto me, saying, {28:21} Son of man, set your face against Zidon, and prophesy against it, {28:22} And say, 'The Lord GOD says: Behold, I am against you, O Zidon, and I will be glorified in the midst of you. They shall know that I am the LORD when I have executed judgments in her and am sanctified in her. {28:23} For I will send pestilence into her, and blood into her streets; the wounded shall be judged in the midst of her by the sword upon her on every side, and they shall know that I am the LORD. {28:24} And there shall be no more a pricking brier unto the house of Israel, nor any grieving thorn of all that are round about them, that despised them. They shall know that I am the Lord GOD.' {28:25} Thus says the Lord GOD: When I shall have gathered the house of Israel from the people among whom they are scattered and shall be sanctified in them in the sight of the heathen, then shall they dwell in their land that I have given to my servant Jacob. {28:26} And they shall dwell safely therein, and shall build houses and plant vineyards. They shall dwell with confidence when I have executed judgments upon all those that despise them round about them. They shall know that I am the LORD their God."

{29:1} So, like, in the tenth year, on the tenth month, on the twelfth day of the month, the Big Guy upstairs hit me up, saying, {29:2} "Yo, dude, focus on Pharaoh, the ruler of Egypt, and drop some truth bombs on him and all of Egypt: {29:3} Tell him, 'God's not vibing with you, Pharaoh, you're acting all big and mighty, but guess what? I'm about to reel you in like a fish on a line.' {29:4} "I'm gonna hook you up, Pharaoh, with some serious trouble. Your rivers will be full of fish stuck to your scales, and then I'll leave you stranded in the wilderness, a buffet for wild animals. {29:5} "Egypt will know I mean business because they've been as reliable as a broken umbrella for Israel. {29:6} "When Israel leaned on Egypt, it just crumbled under pressure. {29:7} "So, here's the deal, Pharaoh, a sword's coming your way, wiping out everything, man and beast alike. {29:8} "Egypt's gonna be a ghost town, and they'll finally get that I'm the boss around here because they've been acting like they own the Nile. {29:9} "You've been talking big about your river, but I'm about to make Egypt a barren wasteland. {29:10} "I'm gonna wreck your whole scene, Egypt, from top to bottom, from Syene to Ethiopia. {29:11} "Ain't nobody gonna be walking or even crawling through there for forty years. {29:12} "Egypt's gonna be a mess, just like the other wastelands, and I'll scatter the Egyptians everywhere. {29:13} "But after forty years, I'll bring them back home, and they'll be chillin' in Pathros, but it'll be a low-key setup. {29:14} "They'll be at the bottom of the rankings, not bossing over other nations anymore. {29:15} "They won't be anyone's go-to ally anymore; Israel won't even give them a second thought. They'll know who's really in charge." {29:16} So, like, Egypt won't be Israel's safety net anymore; they'll remember their wrongs, but they'll know it's all on me, God. {29:17} Then, in the twenty-seventh year, on the first day of the first month, God hit me up again, saying, {29:18} "Dude, remember when Nebuchadnezzar went all out on Tyre, but got nothing for it? Well, I'm gonna give him Egypt as payment. {29:19} "Egypt's gonna be his jackpot, and he'll take everything, and it's all because they worked for me, says the Lord." {29:20} "And in that day, Israel's gonna start flexing again, and they'll know I'm the real deal."

{30:1} Then, God's word came to me again, saying, {30:2} "Yo, son of man, get ready to drop some bad news: {30:3} "The day of reckoning is almost here, a dark day for the nations. {30:4} "Egypt's gonna get hit hard, and Ethiopia's gonna feel the pain too, with death everywhere. {30:5} "Ethiopia, Libya, Lydia, and all the other mixed-up people, they're all gonna bite the dust, along with Egypt's supporters. {30:6} "Egypt's gonna take a major fall, from Syene to everywhere else, swords gonna be swinging. {30:7} "And they'll know it's me, God, when Egypt goes up in flames and all their buddies bail on them. {30:8} "Messengers are gonna scare the Ethiopians stiff, just like Egypt's gonna be, 'cause the end is nigh." {30:9} "And Nebuchadnezzar's gonna make Egypt tap out, with his army and all, they'll leave nothing but bodies. {30:10} "I'll dry up the rivers and hand Egypt over to strangers, making it a wasteland. I said it, and I'll do it." {30:11} "Babylon's gonna bring the pain, drawing swords on Egypt, leaving a trail of destruction. {30:12} "I'll wreck Egypt, destroy their idols, and strike fear into their hearts. They'll know I'm in charge." {30:13} "I'll bring chaos to Noph, fire to Zoan, and judgment to No. {30:14} "Sin's gonna feel my wrath, and No's gonna be torn apart, with Noph facing constant distress." {30:15} "The young guns of Aven and Pi-beseth are gonna fall, and these cities are gonna get taken over." {30:16} "Dark days are coming to Tehaphnehes, with Egypt's strength fading away, covered in clouds, and her daughters taken as captives." {30:17} "That's how I'm gonna roll in Egypt, and they'll know it's me, God." {30:18} Then, in the eleventh year, on the seventh day of the first month, God hit me up again, saying, {30:19} "I broke Pharaoh's arm, and it ain't getting fixed anytime soon. {30:20} "So, I'm against Pharaoh, breaking both his strong and already broken arms, making him drop his sword. {30:21} "Egyptians are gonna be scattered everywhere, and I'll give Babylon's king the power, but Pharaoh's gonna be groaning in pain. {30:22} "I'll make sure Babylon's king is the real deal, and Egypt's gonna know it when he brings the heat. {30:23} "Egyptians will be scattered, and they'll know I'm in charge.'"

{31:1} So, like, in the eleventh year, on the first day of the third month, the Big Guy upstairs hit me up, saying, {31:2} "Yo, bro, talk to Pharaoh, the king of Egypt, and his crew: Who do you think you're like with all your swagger? {31:3} Check it, the Assyrian was like this huge tree in Lebanon, chillin' with dope branches, casting mad shade, standin' tall and all. {31:4} Water was his homie, makin' him big, flowin' around his roots, hydrating him and his homies nearby. {31:5} So, naturally, he's towering over all the other trees, his branches flexin' hard 'cause of all that water. {31:6} Birds were crashing in his branches, and all sorts of critters were poppin' out babies underneath, and nations were vibin' in his shade. {31:7} He was straight-up beautiful, with those long branches of his, rooted by some prime water source. {31:8} Even the trees in God's garden couldn't outshine him; fir trees, chestnut trees, none could match his vibe. {31:9} I hooked him up with all those branches, and suddenly, all the other trees in Eden were jelly. {31:10} So here's the deal, because he got too big for his britches, thinking he's the top dog, I'm handin' him over to some serious dudes from other lands; they're gonna handle him for his wicked ways. {31:11} They're gonna give him what's coming to him 'cause he got too cocky. {31:12} And now, he's gonna get wrecked, his branches scattered, his boughs broken, and everyone's bailing on him. {31:13} Birds are gonna chill on his ruins, and animals will be all over his broken branches. {31:14} It's a lesson, man, so that no other tree tries to one-up themselves, thinkin' they're all that. {31:15} When he bites the dust, I'm throwin' a mourning party; I'll calm down the chaos, and even Lebanon's gonna feel the loss. {31:16} Nations are gonna freak when they hear he's gone, along with all the other top-tier trees; they'll find solace in the depths of the earth. {31:17} They're all headed to the underworld, along with those who got taken out by the sword, including his posse who used to chill in his shade among the nations. {31:18} So, who else is flexin' like you among the Eden trees? But you, Pharaoh, you're headed for the same fate, down with the uncircumcised and those slain by the sword, says the Big Guy.

{32:1} Fast forward to the twelfth year, first day of the twelfth month, and again, the Big Guy's hittin' me up, sayin', {32:2} "Bro, drop a sad rap for Pharaoh, king of Egypt. Picture him like a young lion, fierce among nations, or a massive whale causing chaos in the seas. {32:3} Here's the deal, I'm gonna cast my net over him with a whole crew, and they're gonna reel him in. {32:4} Then I'm just gonna toss him out on dry land, let the birds have a field day, and the beasts too. {32:5} His flesh is gonna be like a buffet for the mountains, fillin' up the valleys with his height. {32:6} And his blood? Yeah, that's gonna water the land, all the way to the mountains, turning the rivers into crimson streams. {32:7} When I'm done with him, the sky's gonna go dark, stars hiding, clouds blocking the sun, and the moon's gonna go MIA. {32:8} Total blackout, man, darkness everywhere, courtesy of the Big Guy. {32:9} I'll mess with people's heads big time, bringin' destruction to places they never even heard of. {32:10} Everyone's gonna be shook, kings trembling, swords trembling, people fearing for their lives when he goes down. {32:11} 'Cause guess what? Babylon's king's gonna bring the pain. {32:12} He's gonna mow down Pharaoh's crew, all those mighty warriors, strip Egypt of its swag, leaving nothing but ruins. {32:13} Even the beasts are gonna get wiped out, no more footprints trampling through. {32:14} I'll turn their waters thick like oil. {32:15} Egypt's gonna be a ghost town, stripped of its glory, and when I'm done, they'll know who's boss. {32:16} This is the rap they'll spit when they mourn

Egypt, nations' daughters crying out for the fallen land and its crew. {32:17} Now it's the twelfth year, fifteenth day of the month, and once again, the Big Guy's dropping truth bombs, saying, {32:18} "Bro, wail for Egypt's massive crew, toss 'em down with the famous nations' daughters, into the pits with the rest. {32:19} Who do you think you're prettier than? You're headed down with the uncircumcised. {32:20} They're gonna fall among the slain, delivered to the sword, so bring 'em on, round 'em up. {32:21} Even the tough guys from the underworld are gonna give him a hard time, hanging with the uncircumcised, slain by the sword. {32:22} Assyria's there too, with all its homies, graves all around, terrorizing the living. {32:23} Their graves line the pit, causing fear while they were alive. {32:24} Elam's there too, surrounded by graves, all uncircumcised, slain by the sword, heading down with their shame. {32:25} They're all lying among the slain, uncircumcised, even though they were once feared. {32:26} Meshech, Tubal, and their whole crew, same deal, uncircumcised and slain by the sword, causing terror in the living world. {32:27} But they're not chillin' with the mighty dead, heading straight to hell with their war gear. {32:28} They're just gonna be another broken crew among the uncircumcised, lying with those slain by the sword. {32:29} Edom's kings and princes, they're in the mix too, lying with the uncircumcised, down with the slain and those going to the pit. {32:30} Northern princes and all the Zidonians, they're all going down with the slain, feeling embarrassed by their once-mighty selves. {32:31} Pharaoh's gonna peep this scene, finding solace in seeing his crew all together, slain by the sword, says the Big Guy. {32:32} 'Cause I've brought terror to the living world, and he's gonna lie among the uncircumcised, just like his crew, says the Big Guy.

{33:1} So, like, the Big Guy hit me up again, saying, {33:2} "Yo, son of man, talk to your homies and tell 'em this: when I bring the sword down on a land, and the locals pick someone to be their lookout, {33:3} if he peeps the sword coming and blows the horn to warn the crew, {33:4} anyone who hears the horn but ignores it, and then gets taken out by the sword, that's on them. {33:5} They heard the horn but brushed it off; their bad if they get taken out. But anyone who takes the warning saves themselves. {33:6} But if the lookout sees the sword coming but doesn't blow the horn to warn the crew, and then someone gets taken out, it's on the lookout for not doing his job; their blood's on his hands. {33:7} So, son of man, I made you the lookout for the house of Israel. You gotta listen to what I'm saying and give 'em a heads-up from me. {33:8} When I tell a wicked person they're gonna get what's coming to 'em, if you don't warn 'em to turn their life around, they'll get what's coming, but you'll have to answer for it. {33:9} But if you do warn 'em, and they still refuse to change, they'll get what's coming, but at least you did your part. {33:10} So, yo, tell the house of Israel this: if they're drowning in their own mess, wondering how they're gonna survive, here's the deal: {33:11} As the Big Guy lives, he ain't into seeing the wicked crash and burn. He wants 'em to change their ways and live. So, turn it around, people! Why throw your lives away? {33:12} Listen up, son of man, tell your crew this: being righteous won't save you when you mess up, and being wicked won't seal your fate if you turn things around. {33:13} If I promise a righteous person they'll live, but they start acting shady, all their good deeds won't matter when they get what's coming. {33:14} But if I tell a wicked person they're done for, and they do a 180, doing what's right and paying back what they owe, they'll live. {33:15} If the wicked start making things right, giving back what they stole, living right, they'll live, no question. {33:16} Their past sins won't count against them; they're in the clear as long as they do right. {33:17} But here's the kicker: the house of Israel's complaining that I'm not fair, but they're the ones who ain't playing fair. {33:18} When a righteous person goes off the rails and starts doing wrong, they'll get what's coming. But if a wicked person turns their life around and starts doing right, they'll live. {33:19} And yet, they still say I'm not fair. Israel, I'm judging each of you by what you do. {33:20} Then, on the fifth day of the tenth month in the twelfth year of our captivity, a survivor from Jerusalem came to me, saying, "The city's toast." {33:21} Before he arrived, the Big Guy had me speechless, but as soon as the survivor showed up, my mouth was opened, and I could speak again. {33:22} Then the Big Guy hit me up, saying, {33:23} "Yo, son of man, those folks left in the wastelands of Israel are talking smack, saying, 'Abraham was just one dude, and he got the whole land. But we're a whole bunch, so this land's ours.' {33:24} Tell 'em this from me: you're eating blood, worshipping idols, and shedding blood, but you think you deserve this land? {33:25} You're relying on violence, committing abominations, and messing around with your neighbors' spouses, and you think you should inherit the land? {33:26} Tell 'em this: by my life, those left in the wastelands will fall by the sword, the ones in the open fields will become beast chow, and those hiding in forts and caves will die from disease. {33:27} I'll make the land desolate, strip it of its pride, and the mountains of Israel will be deserted, with no one passing through. {33:28} Then they'll know I'm the Big Guy, when I turn their land into a wasteland because of their messed-up ways. {33:29} And you, son of man, your people are still gossiping about you by the walls and doors, talking about how they're so into hearing what the Big Guy has to say. {33:30} They come to you like they're all about it, sitting there listening to your words, but their hearts are chasing after their desires. {33:31} You're like a dope song to them, with a sick beat and killer lyrics, but they're just vibing to your words without acting on 'em. {33:32} And when all this goes down, and trust me, it will, then they'll know a prophet was among them.

{34:1} Then the Big Guy hit me up again, saying, {34:2} "Yo, son of man, drop some truth bombs on the leaders of Israel for me. {34:3} Tell 'em they're in for a world of hurt 'cause they're only looking out for themselves, not the people they're supposed to be leading. {34:4} They're living large off the backs of their flock, not taking care of 'em like they should. {34:5} The sick and injured get no love, the lost and strays don't get found, and instead of searching for 'em, they're ruling with force and cruelty. {34:6} So the flock gets scattered, left as easy prey for all sorts of predators. {34:7} Shepherds, listen up, 'cause the Big Guy's got something to say: {34:8} "As I live, because my flock got wrecked and no one cared, I'm coming for you shepherds. I'll hold you accountable and stop you from feeding off my flock. {34:9} So, shepherds, get this: I'm against you, and I'll rescue my flock from your grip so you can't feed off 'em anymore. {34:10} Here's the deal: I'm gonna search for my lost sheep and bring 'em back from wherever they've been scattered, even in the darkest of days. {34:11} Just like a shepherd gathers their flock, I'll find my sheep and rescue 'em from all the places they've been scattered. {34:12} I'll bring 'em back from the nations, gather 'em from the lands, and bring 'em to their own turf, where they'll chill by the rivers and live it up in their homeland. {34:13} I'll lead 'em to lush pastures and high mountains, where they'll chill in comfort. {34:14} I'll make sure they're fed and rested, says the Big Guy. {34:15} I'll take care of my flock, providing everything they need, says the Big Guy. {34:16} I'll find the lost, bring back the strays, heal the injured, and strengthen the weak. But the fat and strong, I'll judge 'em harshly. {34:17} And as for you, my flock, I'll be the judge between you, sorting out the winners and losers. {34:18} You think it's cool to graze on the best pastures and then trample down the rest? To drink from clean waters and then muck 'em up with your hooves? {34:19} Meanwhile, my flock gets leftovers, drinking what you've muddied up. {34:20} So here's the deal: I'm gonna judge between the fat sheep and the skinny ones. {34:21} Because you've been shoving the weak around, butting 'em with your horns, and scattering 'em, I'll save my flock from you and judge between them. {34:22} I'll appoint one shepherd over 'em, my servant David; he'll take care of 'em like I would. {34:23} And I, the Big Guy, will be their God, with David as their leader. {34:24} I'll make a peace deal with 'em, kick out the wild beasts, and let 'em chill in safety. {34:25} They'll live securely in the wild, sleeping without fear. {34:26} The land and the areas around my hill will be blessed, with showers coming at the right time. {34:27} The trees will bear fruit, the land will flourish, and they'll know I'm the Big Guy when I break their chains and free 'em from their oppressors. {34:28} They won't be prey for other nations or food for wild beasts anymore; they'll live safely without fear. {34:29} I'll raise up a famous leader for 'em, and they won't go hungry or face shame from other nations again. {34:30} Then they'll know I'm their God, and they're my people, says the Big Guy. {34:31} And you, my flock, you're my crew, and I'm your God, says the Big Guy."

{35:1} Yo, so the Big Guy hit me up, like, "Yo, son of man, peep this: you gotta lay it down on Mount Seir, prophesy on it and let 'em know what's up. {35:2} Tell 'em, 'Check it, Mount Seir, the Big Guy's got beef with you. I'm about to wreck your whole vibe. {35:3} I'mma stretch out my hand and leave you straight desolate. {35:4} Your cities? Toast. You'll be ghost town central, and you'll know who's the real deal: me, the LORD. {35:5} 'Cause you've been holding a grudge forever and shedding Israelite blood like it's nothing when they were down and out. {35:6} So, I swear, I'm gonna make you bleed like you never bled before since you got no love for blood. {35:7} Mount Seir's gonna be a wasteland, no one coming or going. {35:8} Your mountains are gonna be littered with bodies, casualties of the sword. {35:9} You're gonna stay desolate, no cities coming back, and you'll know who's boss: me, the LORD. {35:10} 'Cause you've been running your mouth about owning Israel's turf, thinking you're all that, when the LORD was chillin' there. {35:11} So, I'mma match your anger and envy, and when I'm done, Israel's gonna see who's got their back. {35:12} And you'll realize I'm the real deal when I hear all the smack you've been talking about Israel's mountains, saying they're yours to devour. {35:13} You've been boasting against me, multiplying your words like you're some big shot. I've heard it all. {35:14} When the whole earth's partying, you'll be left alone, desolate just like you wished on Israel. {35:15} You thought it was funny when Israel was down and out, now you'll be the one feeling lonely, Mount Seir, and all your buddies, too.

{36:1} Oh, and you, son of man, drop some truth bombs on the mountains of Israel, saying, 'Listen up, mountains of Israel, the LORD's got something to say. {36:2} 'Cause the haters been talking trash, claiming even the ancient high places are theirs. {36:3} So, let 'em know, they've left you in ruins, dissed you everywhere, treating you like a joke for the other nations to laugh at. {36:4} But yo, mountains of Israel, listen up: the LORD's got your back, even in your desolation, in your forsaken cities, mocked by the rest of the world. {36:5} 'Cause I've been speaking out against the haters, against all those who dissed my land, with joy in their hearts, trying to kick Israel out. {36:6} So, prophesy about Israel, tell 'em, 'I've been furious 'cause you've been carrying the shame of the nations. {36:7} But yo, the LORD's raising his hand, and those haters around you? They'll bear their own shame. {36:8} But you, mountains of Israel, you're gonna thrive, bringing forth fruit for my people. {36:9} 'Cause I'm all about you, I'm turning things around, getting you all tilled and sown. {36:10} I'm bringing back the people of Israel, filling up the cities, rebuilding what's been wasted. {36:11} I'm multiplying everything, man and beast, making things better than before. You'll see, I'm the LORD. {36:12} Israel's gonna reclaim you as their inheritance, and you won't be snatched away from them anymore. {36:13} 'Cause you've been accused of being a land that devours people, but no more, says the LORD. {36:14} You won't be taking lives or causing nations to mourn anymore, says the LORD. {36:15} You won't bear the shame of the nations or the reproach of the people anymore, says the LORD. {36:16} And yo, the word of the LORD came to me, saying, {36:17} 'Yo, son of man, Israel messed up big time when they were living in their own land, defiling it with their wicked ways. {36:18} So, I let loose my fury on them for shedding blood and worshiping idols, polluting the land. {36:19} I scattered them among the nations, judging them for their actions. {36:20} And when they ended up among the nations, they made my name look bad by claiming they were my people, but their actions said otherwise. {36:21} But I had to look out for my rep, which Israel trashed among the nations they went to. {36:22} So, tell Israel, 'It's not for your sake I'm doing this, but for the sake of my holy name, which you've dragged through the mud among the nations. {36:23} I'm gonna make my name holy again, which you've made profane in the eyes of the nations, and they'll know I'm the LORD when I show my holiness through you. {36:24} 'Cause I'm bringing you back from among the nations, gathering you from all over and bringing you back to your own land. {36:25} Then I'mma cleanse you with some fresh water, washing away all your filthiness and idolatry. {36:26} I'm giving you a new heart and a new spirit, taking out that stony heart and giving you a heart of flesh. {36:27} I'm putting my spirit within you, making you walk in my ways, keeping my commandments and doing what's right. {36:28} You'll live in the land I gave your ancestors, and you'll be my people, and I'll be your God. {36:29} I'll save you from all your uncleanness, bringing abundance to your crops and no more famine. {36:30} Your trees will bear fruit, and your fields will flourish, and you won't be ashamed among the nations anymore. {36:31} You'll remember your past wickedness and be disgusted with yourselves for your sins and abominations. {36:32} This ain't for your sake, Israel, it's for mine, says the LORD. You should be ashamed of yourselves for your actions, O house of Israel. {36:33} So, says the LORD, when I cleanse you from your sins, I'll let you dwell in your cities, and the wastelands will be rebuilt. {36:34} The desolate land will be tilled again, seen as a blessing by all who pass by. {36:35} They'll say, 'This land, once desolate, is like paradise now,' and the ruined cities will be rebuilt and inhabited. {36:36} Then the nations around you will know that I, the LORD, rebuild what's been destroyed and plant what's been desolate. I've spoken it, and I'll make it happen. {36:37} So, says the LORD, Israel's gonna come asking for my blessing, and I'll multiply them like a flock. {36:38} Just like the holy feasts in Jerusalem, those waste cities will be filled with people, and they'll know I'm the LORD.

{37:1} So, the Big Guy's power swept me up and dropped me in this valley packed with bones, like, everywhere. {37:2} These bones? Super dry, like they've been here forever. {37:3} And the Big Guy's like, "Yo, can these bones come back to life?" And I'm like, "Yo, Big Guy, you know best." {37:4} Then he's like, "Prophesy to these bones, tell 'em to listen up." {37:5} And he's like, "Check it, I'm bringing breath back into you, you'll be alive again." {37:6} "I'll deck you out with muscles, flesh, skin, the whole deal, and then breathe life into you, so you'll know who's boss: me, the LORD." {37:7} So I'm laying down the prophecy, and there's this crazy noise, bones rattling together. {37:8} I look, and boom, they're all fleshed out, but still no breath. {37:9} Then he's like, "Prophesy to the wind, son of man, tell it to bring breath to these dead dudes." {37:10} So I do my thing, and suddenly they're breathing, standing up like an army. {37:11} And the Big Guy's like, "Yo, son of man, these bones are Israel, feeling dried up and hopeless. {37:12} Prophesy to 'em, tell 'em I'm bringing 'em back from the grave, back to Israel." {37:13} "When I do this, they'll know I'm the LORD, bringing 'em back and putting my spirit in 'em." {37:14} "I'll settle 'em in their own land, and they'll know it's me, the LORD, who's making it happen." {37:15} Then the Big Guy hits me up again, saying, {37:16} "Yo, son of man, grab a stick, write 'Judah' on it, and another one for 'Joseph' and his crew. {37:17} Stick 'em together, they're gonna be one in your hand." {37:18} "When people ask, 'What's up with the sticks?' Tell 'em I'm bringing together Israel from all over, making them one nation, living safely in their land." {37:19} "The sticks? They'll be right there, in your hand, for everyone to see." {37:20} "I'll bring Israel back from among the nations, gather 'em up, and bring 'em back to their land." {37:21} "They'll be one nation, with one king, and no more division or idol worship. {37:22} "They'll be my people, and I'll be their God, with David as their king forever." {37:23} "I'll make a covenant of peace with 'em, and my sanctuary will be with 'em forevermore." {37:24} "The nations will see that I, the LORD, sanctify Israel with my sanctuary in their midst."

{38:1} Then the Big Guy's word comes to me again, saying, {38:2} "Son of man, get ready to lay it down on Gog, the boss of Magog, and all his crew. {38:3} Tell him, 'I'm coming for you, Gog, ready to take you down.'" {38:4} "I'll hook you up, drag you out with your army, decked out in armor, ready to roll." {38:5} "Persia, Ethiopia, Libya, they'll all be there with their gear." {38:6} "Gomer and Togarmah, too, and a bunch of others." {38:7} "Get ready, gather your crew, and be on guard." {38:8} "In the future, you'll come against my restored Israel, who's been living safely." {38:9} "You'll come like a storm, covering the land with your army." {38:10} "But when you have your evil plan, I'll be ready for you." {38:11} "You'll come against unwalled villages, peaceful people, to take their stuff." {38:12} "To plunder and prey on those who've rebuilt their lives." {38:13} "And the nations will be like, 'What you doing, Gog? Trying to rob us blind?'" {38:14} "So, son of man, tell Gog, 'When Israel's chilling safely, you'll know it.'" {38:15} "Then you'll come from the north with your massive army." {38:16} "But I'll bring you against my land, so the nations will see my power through you, Gog." {38:17} "They'll remember the prophets who spoke of your coming against Israel." {38:18} "And when you come against Israel, my fury's gonna be off the charts." {38:19} "There'll be earthquakes, shaking everything up in Israel." {38:20} "Everything's gonna tremble at my presence, even the mountains." {38:21} "Swords will be turned against each other, and I'll unleash pestilence and destruction." {38:22} "Rain, hail, fire, brimstone, the works." {38:23} "Through all this, I'll show my power, and the nations will know I'm the LORD."

{39:1} Yo, so peep this, son of man, it's time to throw shade at Gog, you feel? The Lord GOD's like, "Yo, Gog, I'm coming for you, chief prince of Meshech and Tubal." {39:2} I'm gonna flip you around, leave only a sixth of your crew, then drag you from up north and drop you on the mountains of Israel. {39:3} I'm snatching your bow from your left hand and making your arrows drop from your right. {39:4} You're gonna eat dirt on those Israeli mountains along with your squad, and the scavengers and wild animals are gonna feast on you. {39:5} You're gonna faceplant in the open field 'cause I said so, says the Lord GOD. {39:6} I'm lighting up Magog and those chillin' on the islands, just so they know I'm the LORD. {39:7} I'll make my name pop in the middle of Israel, and I ain't letting anyone disrespect it anymore. The world's gonna know I'm the LORD, the real deal in Israel. {39:8} Yeah, it's happening, it's going down, says the Lord GOD; this is the day I've been talking about. {39:9} The Israelis in the cities are gonna come out, torching and burning weapons - shields, bucklers, bows, arrows, spears, you name it - they're burning that stuff for seven years. {39:10} They won't need to chop trees or take wood from the forest 'cause they're burning up the weapons they captured, taking back what was taken from them, says the Lord GOD. {39:11} On that day, Gog's gonna get his own burial ground in Israel, in the valley east of the sea, and it's gonna be named after him - Hamon-gog. {39:12} It's gonna take seven months for Israel to bury the bodies, cleansing the land. {39:13} Everyone's gonna pitch in with the burial, making it a day of honor when I show off, says the Lord GOD. {39:14} They'll appoint people to keep cleaning up after seven months, searching the land for any remains. {39:15} Whoever spots a bone will mark it with a sign until the cleanup crew buries it in Hamon-gog Valley. {39:16} They'll even name a city Hamonah. That's how they're gonna clean up the land. {39:17} Yo, son of man, listen up, says the Lord GOD; tell all the birds and beasts to come to my big feast in the mountains of Israel. {39:18} They're gonna chow down on the powerful ones, drinking the blood of the big shots - rams, lambs, goats, bulls, the best of the best. {39:19} They'll pig out until they're stuffed, drinking blood until they're wasted, all from the sacrifice I'm throwing. {39:20} That's how they'll feast at my table - horses, chariots, soldiers, the whole deal, says the Lord GOD. {39:21} I'm gonna flex on the nations, showing off the judgment I've brought and the smackdown I've laid. {39:22} That's how Israel will know I'm their

God from that day forward. {39:23} And the nations will know why Israel got jacked up - they messed up and got punished. They crossed me, so I turned away and let their enemies deal with them. {39:24} They got what they deserved for their dirtiness and sins, and I turned away from them. {39:25} But now I'm gonna bring Jacob back from exile, show mercy to all of Israel, and get protective of my holy name. {39:26} After they've taken their licks and faced their trespasses, living safely without fear, I'm gonna gather them back from their enemy's lands and make a statement among the nations. {39:27} That's when they'll know I'm the LORD who sent them off among the nations, but brought them back to their own land, leaving none behind. {39:28} And I won't ignore them anymore; I'm gonna pour out my spirit on the house of Israel, says the Lord GOD.

{40:1} So, like, in the twenty-fifth year of our exile, at the start of the year, on the tenth of the month, exactly fourteen years after the city was wrecked, the LORD reached out to me and took me there. {40:2} In some God-given vision, I found myself in Israel, chilling on a tall mountain, checking out what looked like a city framework down south. {40:3} Then this dude showed up, looking all shiny like brass, with a measuring tape and a measuring rod, standing at the gate. {40:4} He's like, "Look closely, listen up, and pay attention to everything I'm showing you; you gotta tell the Israelites what's up." {40:5} There's this outer wall around the house, and this dude's got a six-cubit-long measuring rod, measuring the building's width and height. {40:6} Then he rolls up to the east gate, measuring the thresholds and stairways, which are one reed wide. {40:7} Each little room is one reed long and wide, with five cubits between them, and the gate's threshold is one reed. {40:8} He also measures the gate's inner porch, one reed wide. {40:9} The porch itself is eight cubits, with two-cubit posts, all inside the gate. {40:10} Three little rooms are on each side of the east gate, three on this side, three on that side, all the same size, with matching posts. {40:11} The gate's entry is ten cubits wide, with the gate itself thirteen cubits long. {40:12} There's a one-cubit space on each side of the gate, and the little rooms are six cubits wide on each side. {40:13} The gate's length, including the arches, is twenty-five cubits, facing each other. {40:14} The gate's posts are sixty cubits long, extending to the gate's court. {40:15} From the gate entrance to the inner porch's front, it's fifty cubits. {40:16} There are small windows in the little rooms, with palm trees on the posts, and the arches and windows all around. {40:17} He takes me to the outer court, where there are chambers and a pavement, thirty chambers on the pavement. {40:18} The pavement near the gates is lower. {40:19} He then measures the breadth from the front of the lower gate to the outer court's front, a hundred cubits eastward and northward. {40:20} Next, he checks out the north gate of the outer court, measuring its length and width. {40:21} It's got three little rooms on each side, just like the first gate, with matching posts and arches, fifty cubits long and twenty-five cubits wide. {40:22} There are windows, arches, and palm trees just like the east gate, with seven steps leading up to it. {40:23} The inner gate faces the north and east, with a hundred cubits between gates. {40:24} He then takes me to the south gate, measuring its posts and arches just like the others. {40:25} There are windows and arches all around, fifty cubits long and twenty-five cubits wide. {40:26} Seven steps lead up to it, with palm trees on the posts. {40:27} There's a gate in the inner court toward the south, with a hundred cubits between gates. {40:28} He brings me to the inner court through the south gate, measuring its posts, arches, and windows just like the others. {40:29} It's fifty cubits long and twenty-five cubits wide, with arches facing the outer court. {40:30} There are palm trees on the posts, with eight steps leading up to it. {40:31} Then he takes me to the east gate, measuring it just like the others. {40:32} The little rooms, posts, arches, and windows are all measured, fifty cubits long and twenty-five cubits wide. {40:33} It faces the outer court, with palm trees on the posts and eight steps leading up to it. {40:34} There are chambers and entries by the gate's posts, where they washed the offerings. {40:35} There are two tables in the gate's porch on each side, for slaughtering burnt offerings, sin offerings, and trespass offerings. {40:36} On the outside, by the north gate's entry, there are two more tables, and two more on the porch by the gate. {40:37} Eight tables in total, for slaughtering sacrifices, are set up by the gate's side. {40:38} These four tables are made of hewn stone for burnt offerings, a cubit and a half long, a cubit and a half wide, and a cubit high, with hooks for flesh. {40:39} Outside the inner gate are the singers' chambers, and their view is toward the south, one at the east gate facing north. {40:40} He says, "This chamber faces south and is for the priests who manage the house. {40:41} The one facing north is for the priests who manage the altar; they're Zadok's descendants from Levi, who come near to the LORD to serve Him. {40:42} He measures the court, a hundred cubits long and wide, square-shaped, with the altar in front of the house. {40:43} Then he brings me to the porch of the house, measuring each post, five cubits on each side, with the gate three cubits wide on each side. {40:44} The porch is twenty cubits long and eleven cubits wide, with steps leading up to it and pillars by the posts on both sides.

{41:1} So, like, he took me to the temple and peeped the posts, six cubits wide on both sides, just like the tabernacle. {41:2} The door was ten cubits wide, with five cubits on each side, and it was forty cubits long and twenty cubits wide. {41:3} Then he measured the inside post, two cubits, and the door, six cubits wide and seven cubits high. {41:4} The length was twenty cubits and the width twenty cubits in front of the temple, and he's like, "Yo, this is the most holy spot." {41:5} The wall of the house was six cubits thick, and each side chamber was four cubits wide, surrounding the house on every side. {41:6} The side chambers were stacked three high, thirty in total, and they were built into the house's wall, but they didn't go through it. {41:7} There were ramps and twists going up to the side chambers, making the house wider and taller as you went up. {41:8} The foundation of the side chambers was six great cubits high. {41:9} The outer wall for the side chambers was five cubits thick, leaving space for the chambers inside. {41:10} There was twenty cubits of space between the chambers surrounding the house on every side. {41:11} The doors of the side chambers faced the open space, one to the north and one to the south, with a five-cubit space all around. {41:12} The building in front of the separate area was seventy cubits wide and had a five-cubit thick wall all around, and it was ninety cubits long. {41:13} The house, the separate area, and the building, including their walls, were all one hundred cubits long. {41:14} The width of the front of the house and the separate area to the east was also one hundred cubits. {41:15} He measured the length of the building behind the separate area, with its galleries on both sides, one hundred cubits, including the inner temple and the porches of the court. {41:16} The doorposts, narrow windows, and galleries on three levels, with wood paneling around, reaching from the ground to the windows, all around the house, were measured. {41:17} They covered the area above the door, inside and outside, and the entire wall around, inside and out, by measure. {41:18} Cherubim and palm trees were carved into the walls, with a palm tree between each cherub, and each cherub had two faces. {41:19} The faces of the cherubim were toward the palm trees, one face toward the palm tree on one side and the face of a young lion toward the palm tree on the other side, all around the house. {41:20} Cherubim and palm trees were carved from the ground up to above the door, even on the wall of the temple. {41:21} The temple posts were square, and the face of the sanctuary was like the appearance of the other. {41:22} The wooden altar was three cubits high and two cubits long, with corners, length, and walls all made of wood, and he's like, "This is the table before the LORD." {41:23} The temple and the sanctuary had two doors each, with two leaves for each door, two leaves for one door and two for the other. {41:24} Cherubim and palm trees were carved on the temple doors, just like on the walls, and thick planks were on the porch outside. {41:25} There were narrow windows and palm trees on the porch sides and on the side chambers of the house, along with thick planks. {41:26} The windows were narrow and had palm trees on both sides of the porch, and the side chambers of the house had thick planks.

{42:1} Then he took me out to the outer court, heading north, into the chamber opposite the separate area and in front of the building to the north. {42:2} The north door was one hundred cubits long and fifty cubits wide. {42:3} There were three stories of galleries opposite the twenty cubits for the inner court and opposite the pavement for the outer court, with gallery facing gallery in three stories. {42:4} There was a ten-cubit wide walkway leading to the chambers, and the doors faced north. {42:5} The upper chambers were shorter because the galleries were higher than the lower and middle chambers of the building. {42:6} They were in three stories but didn't have pillars like the courtyard pillars, so the building was narrower than the lower and middle chambers from the ground. {42:7} The wall outside the chambers, facing the outer court and in front of the chambers, was fifty cubits long. {42:8} The chambers in the outer court were fifty cubits long, and in front of the temple were one hundred cubits. {42:9} The entryway was under these chambers on the east side, leading into them from the outer court. {42:10} The chambers were built into the thickness of the court wall, facing the separate area and the building. {42:11} The entrance was like the chambers facing north, with the same measurements and doors. {42:12} The north and south chambers facing the separate area were holy chambers where the priests who approached the LORD would eat the most holy offerings, lay the most holy things, and offer the grain offering, sin offering, and guilt offering because the place was holy. {42:13} When the priests entered, they wouldn't leave the holy place and go into the outer court wearing the clothes they ministered in, because they were holy; instead, they would leave them there and put on other clothes to approach the things for the people. {42:14} When he finished measuring the inner house, he took me out to the gate facing east and measured it all around. {42:15} He measured the east side with a measuring rod, five hundred rods, all around. {42:16} He measured the north side, five hundred rods, all around. {42:17} He measured the south side, five hundred rods, all around. {42:18} He turned toward the west and measured five hundred rods with a measuring rod. {42:19} He measured all four sides, with a wall all around, five hundred rods long and five hundred rods wide, to separate the sanctuary from the common place.

{43:1} After that, he took me to the gate, the one facing east. {43:2} And, OMG, the glory of the God of Israel was coming from the east, and His voice was like a waterfall, and the earth was lit up with His glory. {43:3} It was just like the vision I had seen when I came to destroy the city; it was like the vision I saw by the river Chebar, and I fell on my face. {43:4} The glory of the LORD came into the house through the east-facing gate. {43:5} The spirit lifted me up and brought me to the inner court, and the glory of the LORD filled the house. {43:6} I heard Him speaking to me from the house, and the man was standing next to me. {43:7} He said, "Son of man, this is where my throne is, where my feet rest, where I'll live among the Israelites forever. The house of Israel will never defile my holy name again, neither they nor their kings, with their promiscuity or the dead bodies of their kings in their high places. {43:8} By setting their threshold next to mine, and their doorposts beside my doorposts, with only a wall between me and them, they defiled my holy name with their abominations. So I consumed them in my anger. {43:9} Now, let them stop their promiscuity and get rid of the dead bodies of their kings far from me, and I will live among them forever. {43:10} Son of man, show this house to the Israelites so they may be ashamed of their sins. Let them measure the pattern. {43:11} If they are ashamed of all they've done, show them the design of the house, its layout, exits, entrances, and all its forms, ordinances, and laws. Write it down in their sight so they may follow the whole design and all its regulations and do them. {43:12} This is the law of the house: on top of the mountain, its entire surrounding area will be most holy. Behold, this is the law of the house. {43:13} These are the measurements of the altar in cubits (each cubit is a cubit and a hand breadth): the base shall be a cubit, the width a cubit, and the border around its edge half a cubit. This shall be the height of the altar. {43:14} From the base on the ground to the lower ledge shall be two cubits, and the width one cubit. From the smaller ledge to the larger ledge shall be four cubits, and the width one cubit. {43:15} The altar hearth shall be four cubits high, and four horns shall project upward from the hearth. {43:16} The hearth shall be twelve cubits long and twelve cubits wide, square in its four corners. {43:17} The upper ledge shall be fourteen cubits long and fourteen wide, with a half-cubit border around it. The base shall be a cubit high all around, and its steps shall face east. {43:18} He said to me, "Son of man, this is what the Lord GOD says: These are the regulations for the altar on the day it is built, to offer burnt offerings and sprinkle blood on it. {43:19} You are to give a young bull for a sin offering to the Levitical priests of the family of Zadok, who come near to minister to me, declares the Lord GOD. {43:20} Take some of its blood and put it on the four horns of the altar, on the four corners of the ledge, and around the rim, and cleanse and purify the altar. {43:21} Take the bull for the sin offering and burn it in the designated area of the temple, outside the sanctuary. {43:22} On the second day, offer a male goat without defect for a sin offering, and the altar will be cleansed as it was cleansed with the bull. {43:23} When you have finished purifying it, offer a young bull without defect and a ram from the flock without defect. {43:24} Present them before the LORD, and the priests shall sprinkle salt on them and sacrifice them as a burnt offering to the LORD. {43:25} For seven days you are to provide a male goat daily for a sin offering. You are also to provide a young bull and a ram from the flock, both without defect. {43:26} For seven days, they are to make atonement for the altar and cleanse it; thus, they will dedicate it. {43:27} At the end of these days, from the eighth day onward, the priests are to present your burnt offerings and fellowship offerings on the altar. Then I will accept you, declares the Lord GOD."

{44:1} Then he brought me back to the outer gate of the sanctuary, the one facing east, and it was shut. {44:2} The LORD said to me, "This gate is to remain shut. It must not be opened; no one may enter through it. It is to remain shut because the LORD, the God of Israel, has entered through it. {44:3} The prince himself is the only one who may sit inside the gateway to eat in the presence of the LORD. He is to enter by way of the portico of the gateway and go out the same way." {44:4} Then the man brought me by way of the north gate to the front of the temple. I looked and saw the glory of the LORD filling the temple of the LORD, and I fell facedown. {44:5} The LORD said to me, "Son of man, look carefully, listen closely, and give attention to everything I tell you concerning all the regulations regarding the LORD's temple. Give attention to the entrance to the temple and all the exits of the sanctuary. {44:6} Say to rebellious Israel, 'This is what the Lord GOD says: Enough of your detestable practices, people of Israel! {44:7} In addition to all your other detestable practices, you brought foreigners uncircumcised in heart and flesh into my sanctuary, desecrating my temple while you offered me food, fat, and blood, and you broke my covenant. {44:8} Instead of carrying out your duty in regard to my holy things, you put others in charge of my sanctuary. {44:9} This is what the Lord GOD says: No foreigner uncircumcised in heart and flesh is to enter my sanctuary, not even the foreigners who live among the Israelites. {44:10} The Levites who went far from me when Israel went astray and who wandered from me after their idols must bear the consequences of their sin. {44:11} They may serve in my sanctuary, having charge of the gates of the temple and serving in it; they may slaughter the burnt offerings and sacrifices for the people and stand before the people and serve them. {44:12} But because they served them in the presence of their idols and made the house of Israel fall into sin, therefore I have sworn with uplifted hand that they must bear the consequences of their sin, declares the Lord GOD. {44:13} They are not to come near to serve me as priests or come near any of my holy things or my most holy offerings; they must bear the shame of their detestable practices. {44:14} Yet I will put them in charge of the duties of the temple and all the work that is to be done in it. {44:15} But the Levitical priests, who are descendants of Zadok and who faithfully carried out the duties of my sanctuary when the Israelites went astray from me, are to come near to minister before me; they are to stand before me to offer sacrifices of fat and blood, declares the Lord GOD. {44:16} They alone are to enter my sanctuary; they alone are to come near my table to minister before me and serve me as guards. {44:17} When they enter the gates of the inner court, they are to wear linen clothes; they must not wear any woolen garment while ministering at the gates of the inner court or inside the temple. {44:18} They are to wear linen turbans on their heads and linen undergarments around their waists. They must not wear anything that makes them perspire. {44:19} When they go out into the outer court where the people are, they are to take off the clothes they have been ministering in and leave them in the sacred rooms and put on other clothes, so that the people are not consecrated through contact with their garments. {44:20} They must not shave their heads or let their hair grow long, but they are to keep the hair of their heads trimmed. {44:21} No priest is to drink wine when he enters the inner court. {44:22} They must not marry widows or divorced women; they may marry only virgins of Israelite descent or widows of priests. {44:23} They are to teach my people the difference between the holy and the common and show them how to distinguish between the unclean and the clean. {44:24} In any dispute, the priests are to serve as judges and decide it according to my ordinances. They are to keep my laws and my decrees for all my appointed festivals, and they are to keep my Sabbaths holy. {44:25} A priest must not defile himself by going near a dead person, except for a father or mother, son or daughter, brother or unmarried sister . {44:26} After he is cleansed, he must wait seven days. {44:27} On the day he goes into the inner court of the sanctuary to minister in the sanctuary, he is to offer a sin offering for himself, declares the Lord GOD. {44:28} I am to be the only inheritance the priests have. You are to give them no possession in Israel; I will be their possession. {44:29} They will eat the grain offerings, the sin offerings, and the guilt offerings; and everything in Israel devoted to the LORD will belong to them. {44:30} The best of all the firstfruits and of all your special gifts will belong to the priests. You are to give them the first portion of your ground meal so that a blessing may rest on your household. {44:31} The priests must not eat anything, whether bird or animal, found dead or torn by wild animals.

{45:1} Yo, when you gotta divide up the land, like, for inheritance, you gotta give some of it to the big guy upstairs, you know, God? Yeah, make it holy and stuff. It's gotta be like, 25K long and 10K wide, and that whole area's gotta be super holy, like, all around it. {45:2} Then, there's this chunk of land, 500 by 500, and like, fifty cubits all around for the suburbs. {45:3} And you use that to measure out the 25K by 10K for the sanctuary and the super holy place. {45:4} Priests get dibs on the holy land part, you know, to do their priestly stuff. It's their pad and it's all holy. {45:5} Levites get a chunk too, you know, for their gig, like, 20 chambers worth. {45:6} And there's this city part, 5K wide and 25K long, like, right across from the holy part. It's for all of Israel. {45:7} And then, there's this bit for the big shot, the prince, on both sides of the holy part and the city part, from west to east. It's all balanced, you know? {45:8} The prince gets his slice in Israel, but no more trampling on the people, got it? The rest of the land goes to the tribes of Israel. {45:9} God's like, "Yo, princes, enough with the violence and the scamming. Start dishing out justice and fairness. Cut the people some slack, okay?" {45:10} Everything's gotta be fair and square, like, no cheating with the scales or the measurements. {45:11} Same deal with the measurements, you know? Keep it all consistent. {45:12} And there's this money system, like, 20 shekels, 25 shekels, 15 shekels, you know? {45:13} Offerings gotta be like, a sixth of this and a sixth of that, you know, wheat and barley. {45:14} And don't forget the oil, like, a tenth of it from a big batch. {45:15} Plus, there's this lamb thing, like, one out of every 200, super top-quality, for offerings and peace stuff. God's cool with it. {45:16} Everyone chips in for the prince's offerings, you know? {45:17} The prince's job is to handle all the offerings and feasts and stuff, making things right for Israel. {45:18} And then God's like, "Okay, first of the month, get a young bull, no blemishes, and clean up the sanctuary." {45:19} Throw some blood around, you know, on the house posts and the altar corners, make things right. {45:20} And every seventh day, same deal, for anyone who messes up. {45:21} Passover's like, a big deal on the fourteenth day of the first month, seven days of unleavened bread. {45:22} The prince gets a bull for a sin offering on that day. {45:23} During the feast, it's like, seven days, seven bulls, seven rams, and a goat for sin every day. {45:24} Plus, there's grain and oil, you know, for the offerings. {45:25} Then, in the seventh month, same thing for seven days, offerings and oil.

{46:1} So, the inner court gate facing east stays closed during the week, but opens on Sabbath and new moon days. {46:2} The prince comes in through the porch gate, and the priests set up his offerings while he chills by the gate. Then he leaves, but they don't close the gate till evening. {46:3} People come to worship at this gate on Sabbaths and new moons too. {46:4} The prince's Sabbath offering is like, six flawless lambs and a ram. {46:5} Plus grain for the ram and whatever grain he can afford for the lambs, and oil. {46:6} New moon's like, a young bull, six lambs, and a ram, all spotless. {46:7} Same deal with the grain and oil, you know? {46:8} Prince goes in and out through the gate porch, you know? {46:9} But during feasts, people go in one gate and out another, keeping things moving. {46:10} So, like, the prince is with the crew, you know? When they go in, he goes in; when they bounce, he bounces. {46:11} During the parties and the big events, the meat offering is like, a set amount for a bullock, a ram, and lambs based on what he can give, plus oil. {46:12} If the prince feels like making a personal offering to God, they open the east gate for him. He does his thing, like on Sabbath, and then he dips. They close the gate after he leaves. {46:13} Every day, they gotta bring a fresh lamb for a burnt offering, no defects allowed, you know? {46:14} Plus, they gotta whip up a meat offering every morning, with a portion of grain and oil, like a regular thing for God. {46:15} They gotta keep this ritual going every morning, no breaks, like, a continuous burnt offering. {46:16} God's like, if the prince gives his sons a gift, it's theirs, you know, inheritance and all. {46:17} But if he gives a gift from his inheritance to a servant, they get it until the year of freedom, then it goes back to the prince. His sons keep their inheritance though. {46:18} The prince can't mess with people's land, like, no unfair grabs to kick them out. His sons get their inheritance straight from him, so people don't lose their land. {46:19} So, he takes me through this side entrance into the priest's chambers, facing north, and there's stuff on the west sides too. {46:20} Then he's like, "This is where the priests cook up the offerings, you know, so they don't take them outside and make people holy." {46:21} Then he takes me out to the outer court and shows me these courts in each corner, all the same size. {46:22} They got buildings all around, with cooking spots underneath, like, in rows. {46:23} These are the cooking spots for the priests, you know, where they do their thing. {46:24} He tells me, "These are the spots where they cook, where the house ministers boil up the people's sacrifices."

{47:1} So, dude took me back to the house door, and bam, water's gushing out from under it, heading east. The house faces east, and the water's flowing from the right side of the house, south of the altar. {47:2} Then he led me out of the north gate and showed me this sick scene where water's flowing out on the right side. {47:3} He starts measuring eastward with his line, and after a thousand cubits, we're ankle-deep in water. {47:4} Another thousand, and it's up to our knees. Another one, and it's waist-deep. {47:5} Then we hit this river, too deep to cross, perfect for a swim. {47:6} Dude's like, "Seen enough?" Then we head back to the riverbank. {47:7} There are tons of trees on both sides of the riverbank. {47:8} He tells me the water's gonna flow east, into the desert and then into the sea, making the waters there fresh. {47:9} And wherever the river flows, there'll be tons of life and a huge variety of fish. {47:10} Fishermen are gonna line the shores, casting nets and hauling in loads of fish. {47:11} But the marshy areas will stay salty. {47:12} Along the riverbanks, there'll be trees bearing fruit all year, and their leaves won't wither. Their fruit will be for food, and their leaves for healing. {47:13} God says, "Here's how the land's gonna be divvied up among the twelve tribes, with two portions for Joseph." {47:14} Everyone's gonna get a fair share, just like I promised your ancestors. {47:15} Here's the deal on the northern border, from the Great Sea to Hethlon to Zedad. {47:16} Hamath, Berothah, Sibraim, between Damascus and Hamath, Hazar-hatticon near Hauran. {47:17} The northern border runs from the sea to Hazar-enan, Damascus, and northward to Hamath. {47:18} The eastern border runs from Hauran, Damascus, Gilead, and the Jordan River to the Dead Sea. {47:19} The southern border goes from Tamar to Kadesh to the River and the Great Sea. {47:20} And the western border is the Great Sea to Hamath. {47:21} The land will be divided among the tribes of Israel. {47:22} It'll be assigned by lot, including to foreigners living among you, who will be treated as citizens. {47:23} Foreigners will inherit land according to the tribe where they settle, says God.

{48:1} Now here's the rundown of the tribes from north to south, starting with Dan. {48:2} Then Asher, {48:3} Naphtali, {48:4} Manasseh, {48:5} Ephraim, {48:6} Reuben, {48:7} and Judah. {48:8} Judah's offering will be 25,000 reeds wide and as long as one of the other portions, with the sanctuary in the middle. {48:9} The offering to the Lord will be 25,000 by 10,000 reeds. {48:10} A portion of this will be for the priests, with 25,000 to the north and south and 10,000 to the east and west, with the sanctuary in the middle. {48:11} This will be for the Zadokite priests who remained faithful. {48:12} The portion offered to the Lord by the Levites will border the priests' land. {48:13} Next to the priests' land, the Levites will get 25,000 by 10,000 reeds. {48:14} They can't sell any of it, as it's holy to the Lord. {48:15} The remaining 5,000 reeds will be for the city, with space for living and suburbs. {48:16} The city will be square, with 4,500 reeds on each side. {48:17} There'll be 250 reeds of suburbs around the city on all sides. {48:18} The remaining 10,000 reeds will be for common use, to support the city. {48:19} This land will serve all the tribes of Israel. {48:20} The total offering will be 25,000 by 25,000 reeds, with the city in the middle. {48:21} Next to the priests' land and the city, there'll be a portion for the prince. {48:22}

Between Judah and Benjamin, this portion will belong to the prince. {48:23} From east to west, Benjamin will have a portion. {48:24} Then Simeon, {48:25} Issachar, {48:26} Zebulun, {48:27} and Gad. {48:28} And along Gad's southern border will be Tamar to Kadesh, along the River to the Great Sea. {48:29} This is how the land will be divided among the tribes, says the Lord God. {48:30} The city will have gates named after the tribes of Israel: three on the north, one each for Reuben, Judah, and Levi. {48:31} Three on the east, one each for Joseph, Benjamin, and Dan. {48:32} Three on the south, one each for Simeon, Issachar, and Zebulun. {48:33} And three on the west, one each for Gad, Asher, and Naphtali. {48:34} The city will be 18,000 reeds around, and its name will be "The Lord Is There."

Daniel

+++

{1:1} So, like, in the third year of Jehoiakim's rule over Judah, Nebuchadnezzar, the king of Babylon, rolls up to Jerusalem and starts a whole siege scene. {1:2} God's like, "Here you go, Nebby, take Jehoiakim and some stuff from my crib." So Nebby takes the loot back to Babylon, flexing it in his god's treasure house. {1:3} Then Nebby tells Ashpenaz, his eunuch head honcho, to round up some Israelite VIPs and big shots. {1:4} He's like, "Get me kids who look good, are smart AF, and can spit Chaldean game." {1:5} And Nebby sets them up with a three-year VIP meal plan, aiming to have them join his entourage at the end. {1:6} Among them are these Judah homies: Daniel, Hananiah, Mishael, and Azariah. {1:7} Nebby renames them, like, 'cause he's the boss: Daniel's now Belteshazzar, Hananiah's Shadrach, Mishael's Meshach, and Azariah's Abed-nego. {1:8} But Daniel's like, "Nah, not feeling that Babylonian grub or booze, yo." So he asks Ashpenaz for a pass. {1:9} And boom, Daniel's suddenly the eunuch crew's favorite. {1:10} Ashpenaz's sweating though, worried Nebby'll roast him if Daniel and the squad start looking raggedy. {1:11} Daniel hits up Melzar, the head eunuch on duty, and proposes a test run: ten days on a plant-based diet. {1:12} Melzar's like, "Alright, bet," and agrees to the veggie plan. {1:13} Ten days later, Daniel and crew are looking fresh, outshining all the other kids chowing down on Nebby's feast. {1:14} Melzar's sold, so he swaps their meals for plants only. {1:15} God blesses the squad with mad wisdom, and Daniel's all about decoding dreams and visions. {1:16} At the end of the trial, Nebby's boys are looking fly on veggies and water. {1:17} God hooks the four up with wisdom and knowledge, especially Daniel with his dream game. {1:18} Once the training's up, Ashpenaz presents them to Nebby. {1:19} Nebby vibes with them, especially Daniel and crew, so they get a prime spot in his crew. {1:20} Nebby quizzes them, and they outshine all the other mystics in the realm, like, by tenfold. {1:21} And Daniel's a player in Babylon until Cyrus takes over.

{2:1} Next year, Nebby's tossing and turning, stressing over dreams. {2:2} So he rings up his mystic squad: magicians, astrologers, the whole shebang. {2:3} He's like, "Decode this dream I had, or else." {2:4} They're like, "Cool, what did you dream?" {2:5} Nebby's all, "I forgot, but you better tell me or it's over for you." {2:6} But if they come through, Nebby's talking rewards and respect. {2:7} They're still stuck, so Nebby's fuming and orders a magician massacre. {2:8} Nebby's getting impatient, knowing they're stalling. {2:9} He threatens them with death for their lies and stalls. {2:10} The mystics admit no one can pull this off, not even the divine squad. {2:11} Nebby's realizing this is some next-level stuff only the gods can decode. {2:12} He's mad, so he orders a hit on all the wise folks in Babylon. {2:13} The hit's out, and Daniel and the squad are on the list. {2:14} Daniel hits up Arioch, Nebby's hitman, with some wise words. {2:15} He's like, "Why the rush, bro?" So Arioch spills the tea. {2:16} Daniel's cool, asking Nebby for time to figure it out. {2:17} He briefs the squad and asks God for help. {2:18} God's got Daniel's back, and the squad prays they don't get axed. {2:19} That night, Daniel dreams and deciphers the code, praising God. {2:20} He's all, "God's the GOAT, giving wisdom and power." {2:21} God controls everything, from kings to knowledge, no cap. {2:22} He's got the 411 on everything, from the darkest secrets to the light. {2:23} Daniel's giving thanks, knowing God's the plug for wisdom and insight. {2:24} Daniel's back on it, convincing Arioch not to off the wise folks. {2:25} Arioch takes Daniel to Nebby, saying he's got the scoop. {2:26} Nebby's like, "Can you break down my dream, Daniel?" {2:27} Daniel's like, "Not me, but the big man upstairs can." {2:28} Only God can unlock this level of intel, revealing what's up with Nebby's dreams. {2:29} It's all about Nebby's future, and only God's got the inside scoop. {2:30} Daniel's like, "This ain't about me flexing, but so you know what's really up." {2:31} Nebby's dream? A massive statue, shining bright but low-key terrifying. {2:32} It's got a gold head, silver chest, brass belly, iron legs, and mixed clay feet. {2:33} Then a stone without hands smashes the feet, crumbling the statue into dust. {2:34} The wind blows it all away, leaving nothing behind. {2:35} The stone? It becomes a massive mountain, taking over the whole scene. {2:36} Daniel's like, "Okay, Nebby, here's the lowdown." {2:37} Nebby's the top dog, with God hooking him up big time. {2:38} He's ruling over everything, top-tier status. {2:39} But after him, it's downhill, with other kingdoms coming in. {2:40} Each one's weaker, but still packing a punch. {2:41} Eventually, the kingdom splits, weak in some areas but strong in others. {2:42} People try to mix it up, but it's not working out. {2:43} Mixing iron and clay? Not a good combo. {2:44} But one day, God's setting up shop, and it's game over for all the other kingdoms. {2:45} Nebby's dream? It's a wrap, and Daniel's breaking it down for him. {2:46} Nebby's bowing down, giving Daniel props, and offering up sacrifices. {2:47} He's all, "Your God? The real deal, revealing all the secrets." {2:48} Nebby hooks Daniel up, making him a big shot, ruler of Babylon's province, and boss of the wise guys. {2:49} Daniel's like, "Yo, can my crew get in on this action?" So Nebby hooks up Shadrach, Meshach, and Abed-nego, with Daniel chilling at the king's gate.

{3:1} So, King Nebuchadnezzar made this giant golden statue, like 90 feet high and 9 feet wide, and put it up in the plain of Dura in Babylon. {3:2} He then called all the big shots - the princes, governors, captains, judges, treasurers, counselors, sheriffs, and all the regional bosses - to come to the statue's dedication. {3:3} So all these important people showed up and stood in front of the statue. {3:4} Then a herald shouted out, "Listen up, everyone from every nation and language! {3:5} When you hear the music from the cornet, flute, harp, sackbut, psaltery, dulcimer, and all other instruments, you need to bow down and worship the golden statue. {3:6} If you don't, you'll be thrown into a blazing furnace immediately." {3:7} So, as soon as everyone heard the music, they all bowed down and worshiped the golden statue. {3:8} But some Chaldeans went to snitch on the Jews. {3:9} They told King Nebuchadnezzar, "Long live the king! {3:10} You made a rule that everyone must bow down and worship the golden statue when they hear the music, {3:11} and if they don't, they'll be thrown into the blazing furnace. {3:12} Well, there are some Jews you put in charge of Babylon – Shadrach, Meshach, and Abed-nego – who aren't paying attention to you, King. They don't serve your gods or worship the statue." {3:13} This made Nebuchadnezzar super mad, so he ordered Shadrach, Meshach, and Abed-nego to be brought to him. {3:14} When they arrived, he asked them, "Is it true you don't serve my gods or worship the golden statue? {3:15} If you're ready now, when you hear the music, bow down and worship the statue. If you do, great. If not, you'll be thrown into the blazing furnace, and what god can save you from my hands?" {3:16} Shadrach, Meshach, and Abed-nego replied, "Nebuchadnezzar, we don't need to defend ourselves to you in this. {3:17} If you throw us in the furnace, the God we serve is able to save us from it, and He will rescue us from your power. {3:18} But even if He doesn't, we want you to know we won't serve your gods or worship the golden statue." {3:19} This made Nebuchadnezzar even angrier, and his face twisted with rage. He ordered the furnace to be heated seven times hotter than usual. {3:20} Then he commanded his strongest soldiers to tie up Shadrach, Meshach, and Abed-nego and throw them into the blazing furnace. {3:21} So, they tied them up fully clothed and threw them into the furnace. {3:22} Because the king's command was so urgent and the furnace so hot, the flames killed the soldiers who threw Shadrach, Meshach, and Abed-nego in. {3:23} And Shadrach, Meshach, and Abed-nego fell, bound, into the blazing furnace. {3:24} But suddenly, King Nebuchadnezzar jumped up in amazement and asked his advisers, "Didn't we tie up and throw three men into the fire?" They replied, "Yes, King." {3:25} He exclaimed, "Look! I see four men, unbound, walking around in the fire unharmed, and the fourth looks like a son of the gods." {3:26} Nebuchadnezzar then approached the furnace and shouted, "Shadrach, Meshach, and Abed-nego, servants of the Most High God, come out!" So they came out of the fire. {3:27} All the important people gathered around and saw that the fire hadn't harmed their bodies, their hair wasn't singed, their clothes weren't scorched, and they didn't even smell like smoke. {3:28} Nebuchadnezzar praised their God, saying, "Blessed be the God of Shadrach, Meshach, and Abed-nego, who sent his angel to rescue them! They trusted in Him and defied my command, willing to give up their lives rather than serve or worship any god except their own. {3:29} Therefore, I decree that anyone who says anything against the God of Shadrach, Meshach, and Abed-nego will be cut into pieces, and their houses turned into rubble, for no other god can save this way." {3:30} Then the king promoted Shadrach, Meshach, and Abed-nego in Babylon.

{4:1} King Nebuchadnezzar sent this message to people of every nation and language in the world: "Peace and prosperity to you! {4:2} I want to share the amazing signs and wonders the Most High God has done for me. {4:3} His miracles are incredible, and His kingdom is everlasting, His rule endures from generation to generation. {4:4} I, Nebuchadnezzar, was at home in my palace, content and prosperous. {4:5} But I had a dream that frightened me; the images and visions terrified me. {4:6} So I ordered all the wise men of Babylon to come and interpret the dream for me. {4:7} When the magicians, enchanters, astrologers, and diviners came, I told them the dream, but they couldn't interpret it. {4:8} Finally, Daniel (also called Belteshazzar after my god), who has the spirit of the holy gods, came before me, and I told him the dream. {4:9} I said, 'Belteshazzar, chief of the magicians, I know you have the spirit of the holy gods and that no mystery is too difficult for you. Here is my dream; interpret it for me. {4:10} These are the visions I saw while lying in bed: I looked, and there before me stood a tree in the middle of the earth. Its height was enormous. {4:11} The tree grew large and strong, and its top touched the sky; it was visible to the ends of the earth. {4:12} Its leaves were beautiful, its fruit abundant, and on it was food for all. Under it, the wild animals found shelter, and the birds lived in its branches; from it, every creature was fed. {4:13} In the visions I saw while lying in bed, I looked, and there before me was a holy messenger, coming down from heaven. {4:14} He called in a loud voice: 'Cut down the tree and trim off its branches; strip off its leaves and scatter its fruit. Let the animals flee from under it and the birds from its branches. {4:15} But let the stump and its roots, bound with iron and bronze, remain in the ground, in the grass of the field. Let him be drenched with the dew of heaven, and let him live with the animals among the plants of the earth. {4:16} Let his mind be changed from that of a man and let him be given the mind of an animal, till seven times pass by for him. {4:17} The decision is announced by messengers, the holy ones declare the verdict, so that the living may know that the Most High is sovereign over all kingdoms on earth and gives them to anyone he wishes and sets over them the lowliest of people.' {4:18} This is the dream I, King Nebuchadnezzar, had. Now, Belteshazzar, tell me what it means, for none of the wise men in my kingdom can interpret it for me. But you can, because the spirit of the holy gods is in you." {4:19} Then Daniel (also called Belteshazzar) was greatly perplexed for a time, and his thoughts terrified him. So the king said, "Belteshazzar, do not let the dream or its meaning alarm you." Belteshazzar answered, "My lord, if only the dream applied to your enemies and its meaning to your adversaries! {4:20} The tree you saw, which grew large and strong, with its top touching the sky, visible to the whole earth, {4:21} with beautiful leaves and abundant fruit, providing food for all, giving shelter to the wild animals, and having nesting places in its branches for the birds—{4:22} Your Majesty, you are that tree! You have become great and strong; your greatness has grown until it reaches the sky, and your dominion extends to distant parts of the earth. {4:23} "Your Majesty saw a holy one, a messenger, coming down from heaven and saying, 'Cut down the tree and destroy it, but leave the stump, bound with iron and bronze, in the grass of the field, while its roots remain in the ground. Let him be drenched with the dew of heaven; let him live with the wild animals, until seven times pass by for him.' {4:24} "This is the interpretation, Your Majesty, and this is the decree the Most High has issued against my lord the king: {4:25} So like, they're gonna kick you out of the human zone, and you'll be chilling with the wild animals, munching on grass like a cow, and getting soaked with dew from the sky for seven times, until you realize that the big boss upstairs is the real deal in running the show on Earth, handing out kingdoms to whoever he wants. {4:26} And remember when they said to leave the tree roots intact? Well, that means your kingdom will be waiting for you once you've figured out that the heavens are in charge. {4:27} So, hey king, listen to my advice: clean up your act, ditch the sins, and start being kind to the less fortunate. Maybe then you can stretch out your chill vibes a bit longer. {4:28} And guess what? All this stuff totally happened to King Nebuchadnezzar. {4:29} Fast forward twelve months, and he's strutting around his palace in Babylon, feeling all proud and mighty. {4:30} He's like, "Check out this epic Babylon I built with my own mad skills, all for my own glory." {4:31} But before he can finish his bragging, a voice from the heavens drops the bomb: "Yo Nebuchadnezzar, your reign's over, dude." {4:32} And just like that, he's booted from civilization, hanging out with the wildlife, chomping on grass, and waiting out those seven times until he gets the memo that the most High is the real boss. {4:33} And boom, right then and there, it all goes down as predicted: Nebuchadnezzar's living that grass-eating, dew-soaked life until he's looking more like a bird than a king. {4:34} But eventually, after some serious time out in the wild, Nebuchadnezzar has a total lightbulb moment. He looks up to the heavens, gets his smarts back, and starts praising the big guy upstairs, recognizing his everlasting power and dominion over everything. {4:35} He's like, "Yo, everybody on Earth is basically nothing compared to the Almighty, who does whatever he wants, whenever he wants. Can't mess with that." {4:36} And just like that, Nebuchadnezzar's back in business, with all his glory and honor restored, and everyone's lining up to get his advice. He's back on top, even more majestic than before. {4:37} So now Nebuchadnezzar's all about giving props to the King of heaven, whose works are all about truth and justice. And he's learned his lesson: mess with pride, and you'll get put in your place.

{5:1} So, like, Belshazzar the king throws this lit party for a thousand of his crew, popping bottles and vibing. {5:2} He's sipping on his drink when he's like, "Yo, bring out those fancy cups we snagged from Jerusalem's temple. Let's flex with them." {5:3} So they bust out these holy cups, and everyone's drinking and shouting out praises to their bougie gods of gold, silver, bronze, iron, wood, and stone. {5:4} Then out of nowhere, this freaky hand appears, writing on the wall by the candlelight. Belshazzar's shook, seeing this hand writing. {5:5} His vibe completely changes, and he's freaking out, knees knocking together and all. {5:6} He screams for his mystic crew, demanding they decode this wall graffiti. He's like, "Whoever cracks this gets the VIP treatment, gold chain, and third in command!" {5:7} But none of his wise guys can read it or explain it. Belshazzar's tripping, and his crew's jaws are dropping. {5:8} Then the queen shows up, dropping knowledge about Daniel, the OG from his dad's reign. She's like, "This dude's got divine wisdom, yo. Let him check it out." {5:9} So they bring in Daniel, and Belshazzar's like, "Aren't you that dude from Judah my dad brought here?" {5:10} He's heard about Daniel's wisdom and insight, unlike these other fake mystics. {5:11} Belshazzar's desperate, offering up those same rewards to Daniel if he can crack the code. {5:12} Daniel's like, "Hold up, keep your bling. I got you, though." {5:13} Daniel lays it down, reminding Belshazzar about his dad's rise and fall, and how he's following in the same footsteps. {5:14} He's like, "You're acting all high and mighty, dissing the real God while praising these fake gods. Not cool, bro." {5:15} Then Daniel reads the writing on the wall, dropping the bomb: "Your kingdom's over, Belshazzar. God's clocked your time." {5:16} Belshazzar's like, "Say what?!" Daniel's got the scoop: "Your kingdom's done, weighed, and split up between the Medes and Persians." {5:17} Belshazzar sticks to his word, hooking Daniel up with the promised rewards and title. {5:18} But that same night, Belshazzar's out, and Darius the Mede takes over.

{6:1} Darius decides to set up his administration, with Daniel leading the pack. {6:2} Daniel's the top dog, making sure everything's on point, so the king doesn't take an L. {6:3} But the other dudes in power are hating on Daniel, trying to find some dirt on him, but they come up empty-handed. {6:4} They're like, "We gotta find something to trip up Daniel, but he's squeaky clean." {6:5} So they plot against him using his faith as bait. {6:6} They butter up King Darius, getting him to sign this crazy decree: no one can pray to anyone except the king for a whole month. {6:7} They lay it on thick, saying it's to boost the king's rep. {6:8} Yo, king, you gotta stamp that decree and sign it, and don't be changing it up, you know, 'cause that's the law of the Medes and Persians, and that stuff doesn't get altered. {6:9} So King Darius was like, "Sure, I'll sign it." {6:10} And Daniel, he knew the deal, man. As soon as he found out the decree was signed, he went home, opened his windows toward Jerusalem, and got down on his knees three times a day to pray and thank his God, just like he always did. {6:11} And these other dudes were like, "Hey, we caught Daniel praying to his God again." {6:12} So they went to the king and were like, "Hey, remember that decree you signed? Well, Daniel's breaking it big time." {6:13} And they're all, "Daniel doesn't care about your decree, King. He's still praying three times a day." {6:14} When the king heard this, he was so bummed out, man. He really wanted to help Daniel, so he tried all day to figure something out. {6:15} But these guys were like, "Sorry, King, once you make a decree, it's set in stone." {6:16} So the king was like, "Okay, bring Daniel here." And they tossed him into the lion's den. But before they sealed it up, the king was like, "Your God will save you, Daniel." {6:17} Then they sealed it up tight so nobody could change their minds about Daniel. {6:18} The king was so stressed out, he didn't even eat or listen to music that night. {6:19} Early the next morning, he rushed to the lion's den. {6:20} When he got there, he was freaking out, calling for Daniel. "Yo, Daniel, can your God save you from these lions?" {6:21} And Daniel was like, "Hey, King, I'm still here." {6:22} "My God sent an angel to shut those lions' mouths 'cause he knows I'm innocent. I didn't do anything wrong to you either, King." {6:23} The king was relieved, man. He ordered them to pull Daniel out, and guess what? Daniel wasn't even scratched because he trusted in his God. {6:24} Then the king was like, "Okay, you guys who accused Daniel, you're going in the den." And before they even hit the bottom, the lions wrecked 'em. {6:25} King Darius sent out a message to everyone, like, "Hey, peace to you all." {6:26} "I'm making it law that everyone in my kingdom better show respect to Daniel's God 'cause he's the real deal, eternal, and his kingdom will last forever." {6:27} "He saved Daniel from the lions, man, that's some serious power." {6:28} And Daniel? Yeah, he did pretty well during Darius's reign, and even when Cyrus took over.

{7:1} So, like, in the first year of Belshazzar king of Babylon, Daniel had this wild dream, you know, visions and stuff, while he was chilling in his bed. Then he wrote it all down, you know, spilled the tea on what he saw. {7:2} Daniel starts spilling the deets, right? He's like, "Yo, I had this lit vision in the dead of night, and there were these four crazy winds battling it out over this massive sea, fam." {7:3} Then, out of nowhere, four huge beasts pop out of the sea, each one totally different from the others, like, no cap. {7:4} The first beast was like a lion with eagle's wings, but then its wings got snatched and it started standing up like a human with feelings and all.

{7:5} Next up, there's this other beast, a bear, right? It's leaning on one side, and it's chomping down on three ribs like it's lunchtime. {7:6} Then, yo, there's this leopard with four wings and four heads, getting all the power moves, like, flexing its dominion. {7:7} And just when you thought it couldn't get crazier, there's this fourth beast, straight-up terrifying, with iron teeth and ten horns. It's like something out of a nightmare, fam. {7:8} And peep this, Daniel's checking out these horns, and then this little horn pops up, like, "Hey, I'm here to steal the show with my human-like eyes and big talk." {7:9} Then Daniel's like, "Hold up, I saw thrones getting tossed around, and this OG called the Ancient of days is posted up, looking fresh in his all-white threads." {7:10} There's this whole setup, like, a million angels serving up looks, and the ultimate judge is laying down the law with the books wide open, ready for the tea. {7:11} Daniel's shook by the big talk coming from that horn, but then it gets served, like, game over, and it's thrown into the fire. {7:12} And the other beasts, they lose their power, but they're still hanging around for a bit, like they got an extended stay or something. {7:13} Then Daniel spots this dude, Son of Man, cruising in on clouds, rolling up to the Ancient of days, getting VIP treatment. {7:14} And boom! This dude gets handed the keys to the kingdom, all the nations gotta bow down to him, 'cause his rule is forever, and ain't nobody breaking that. {7:15} Daniel's vibe gets totally bummed out, like, his spirit's down in the dumps, and these visions got him all twisted up. {7:16} So he's like, "Yo, what's the deal with all this?" And this wise dude spills the tea, explaining the whole shebang. {7:17} Those four beasts? They're four kings, straight up. They're coming in hot from the earth. {7:18} But peep this, the saints of the Most High are about to snatch that kingdom and hold onto it for eternity. That's their gig, no cap. {7:19} Then Daniel's like, "Hit me with more info on that fourth beast, 'cause it's freaking me out, with its metal teeth and all." {7:20} And those ten horns? Yeah, they're kings too. But this one horn's like, "Check me out, I'm the boss," and starts throwing shade like it's nobody's business. {7:21} That horn? It's on a mission to mess with the saints, and it's winning. But then the Ancient of days shows up, and it's game over for that horn. {7:22} The saints finally get their time to shine, taking over the kingdom like it's their birthright, 'bout time, right? {7:23} And Daniel hears it straight: That fourth beast? It's gonna wreck the whole world, breaking it into pieces like it's no biggie. {7:24} And those ten horns? Yeah, they're kings too, but this new horn's got its own agenda, taking out three kings and causing chaos. {7:25} This new horn's got a mouthful, talking smack against the Most High, messing with the saints, and trying to rewrite the rules. But its days are numbered. {7:26} The endgame? That horn's gonna get what's coming to it, losing its power and getting tossed out for good. {7:27} And in the end, the saints are taking over, ruling the world like bosses, and everyone's gotta bow down. That's the way the cookie crumbles. {7:28} So yeah, that's the whole deal. Daniel's still shook, but he's keeping it low-key, processing everything in his head.

{8:1} Fast forward to year three of king Belshazzar's reign, and Daniel's back with more visions, like it's a sequel or something. {8:2} He's zoning out by the river Ulai, when suddenly, bam, another vision hits him, this time in Shushan, chilling in the palace. {8:3} Daniel's checking out this ram with two horns, one bigger than the other, just vibing by the river. {8:4} This ram's on a power trip, going west, north, and south, wrecking everything in its path, and nobody's stepping up to stop it. {8:5} Then out of nowhere, there's this goat charging in from the west, not even touching the ground, with a big horn front and center. {8:6} The goat goes full-on rage mode, smashing into the ram and taking it down, no contest. {8:7} That ram's no match, getting wrecked by the goat, and nobody's coming to its rescue. {8:8} So then this goat gets even stronger, but then its big horn gets snapped off, and four new horns pop up in its place, heading in all directions. {8:9} And from one of those horns, a little one sprouts up, growing big and causing chaos in all directions. {8:10} This little horn's got big dreams, messing with the stars, trashing the place, and taking on the big shots. {8:11} It even starts beef with the top dog, messing with the daily routine and trashing the holy place. {8:12} It's like a full-on war against the sacred, throwing truth to the curb, and making power moves left and right. {8:13} Daniel's overhearing some angels chatting, wondering how long this madness is gonna last, with the holy place getting trampled on. {8:14} And the response? Two thousand and three hundred days, then it's cleanup time for the holy place. {8:15} So, like, when I, Daniel, peeped the vision and tried to figure it out, boom, this dude shows up looking like a regular dude. {8:16} And then I hear this voice, like, from the riverbanks, calling out to Gabriel, telling him to break it down for me. {8:17} So Gabriel slides up to where I'm at, and I'm straight up scared, fall flat on my face. But he's like, "Get it together, dude, 'cause this vision's all about the end times." {8:18} As he's talking, I'm out cold, face down in the dirt, but he taps me and wakes me up. {8:19} Then he's like, "Check it, I'm about to spill the tea on what's gonna happen when the end comes." {8:20} That ram you saw? Yeah, that's Media and Persia doing their thing. {8:21} And that wild goat? That's Greece, and that big horn? That's their OG king. {8:22} But once he's out of the picture, four new kingdoms are gonna rise, but they won't have his power. {8:23} And when those kingdoms hit rock bottom with their sins, this fierce-faced king's gonna step up, straight out of a thriller movie, speaking in riddles and messing stuff up. {8:24} This dude's gonna be mighty, but it ain't gonna be his own power, wrecking stuff left and right, especially messing with the holy folks. {8:25} He's gonna be slick, making craftiness his game, boosting his ego, and even taking on the Prince of princes. But he's gonna get wrecked, no hands needed. {8:26} And that vision you heard? It's legit, so lock it up 'cause it's gonna be a hot minute before it all goes down. {8:27} So I'm out, fainting and sick for days, but then I'm back on my grind, handling the king's business, still shook by the vision, but nobody's really getting it.

{9:1} So like, in the first year of Darius, son of Ahasuerus, from the Medes crew, taking over the Chaldean scene; {9:2} I, Daniel, peeped some books and got the deets on the seventy years vibe, straight from Jeremiah's prophecy, feeling it deep in my soul. {9:3} I'm all about that prayer life, fasting, rocking the sackcloth, and dusting myself in ashes, like, seeking the Big Guy upstairs. {9:4} I hit up the Lord, confessing my sins, giving props to His greatness, and owning up to our mess-ups. {9:5} We messed up big time, doing all sorts of shady stuff, totally ghosting on Your rules, God. {9:6} And we totally blew off Your prophets too, which was major shade. {9:7} We're all about that confusion life now, thanks to our screw-ups, spreading everywhere 'cause we couldn't keep it together. {9:8} Confusion city, that's us, from the top dogs to the regular peeps, all 'cause we dropped the ball, God. {9:9} But hey, You're all about that mercy and forgiveness, even when we're off the rails. {9:10} We straight-up ignored Your rules, God, laid down by Your prophet squad. {9:11} The whole Israel squad broke Your laws, ditching Your vibe, so the curse hit us hard, just like You warned in Moses' law 'cause we messed up big time. {9:12} We got what was coming, big time, facing a world of hurt, worse than anywhere else, 'cause Jerusalem got hit like no other. {9:13} Moses called it right, we got what we deserved, but we didn't even ask for forgiveness until it was too late. {9:14} You watched it all go down, God, 'cause we didn't listen to You, but You're always on point with Your moves. {9:15} We get it, God, You did some epic stuff back in the day, but we're still here screwing up. {9:16} So, God, be chill, let go of that anger towards Jerusalem, Your holy turf, 'cause we've been blowing it big time, and now we're a laughing stock. {9:17} Listen up, God, hear my prayer and turn that frown upside down on Your empty crib, all for Your rep's sake. {9:18} My God, open Your ears and eyes to our mess, and the city reppin' Your name, 'cause we ain't asking for forgiveness based on our actions but on Your mad love. {9:19} Hear us out, forgive us, and don't sleep on this, God, 'cause Your city and Your crew are all about repping Your name. {9:20} So, while I'm spitting rhymes in prayer, owning up to my sins and the screw-ups of my crew, laying it down for Your holy spot; {9:21} Boom! Gabriel slides in like he owns the place, hitting me up around sunset. {9:22} He's like, "Yo, Daniel, I'm here to drop some wisdom on you." {9:23} From the get-go of your prayer session, I was dispatched to drop some knowledge 'cause you're a real one, Daniel, so get ready for some real talk about visions. {9:24} Check it, Daniel, seventy weeks are gonna go down for your crew and your city, wrapping up the drama, ending the sin fest, making peace for the mess, bringing in the good vibes forever, sealing up all those visions and prophecies, and crowning the ultimate holy spot. {9:25} Listen up and get it straight, from the moment the order goes out to rebuild Jerusalem till the big boss, the Messiah, shows up, it's gonna be a wild ride of seven weeks plus sixty-two weeks, with the streets and walls rebuilt in the middle of some serious chaos. {9:26} And then, after those sixty-two weeks, the Messiah's gonna get taken out, not for Himself though. Then, a new ruler's posse is gonna trash the city and sanctuary, bringing it to a watery end, with desolation and war ruling the scene till the end of days. {9:27} And for one final week, this ruler's gonna make deals left and right, but halfway through, he's shutting down the sacrifices and going full-on desolation mode with all kinds of nasty stuff, until it all goes down as planned.

{10:1} Fast-forward to the third year of Cyrus, king of Persia, and I'm getting some major insights, for real, Daniel, who's also known as Belteshazzar, and this vision is legit, but it's gonna be a minute before it all goes down. {10:2} So, in those days, I'm vibing on a three-week mourning sesh. {10:3} No tasty grub, no meat or wine, and definitely no self-care routines until those three weeks are up. {10:4} Then, on the twenty-fourth day of the first month, I'm chilling by the Hiddekel riverbank. {10:5} And then, boom, I spy this dude, decked out in some fresh linen, gold bling, and a glow-up like no other, shining brighter than lightning with eyes on fire, and his whole vibe was like polished brass. {10:6} This dude's voice? Straight-up surround sound, no joke. {10:7} So, I'm the only one catching this vision, while my crew's running for the hills 'cause they're shook. {10:8} Left solo, I'm soaking in this epic vision, but I'm on the verge of passing out 'cause it's too much to handle. {10:9} Even though I'm fading fast, I'm still tuning in to this celestial show. {10:10} Then, out of nowhere, I feel a hand lifting me up, getting me on my knees. {10:11} And this dude's like, "Yo, Daniel, you're all good, stand tall, 'cause I'm here for you." And I'm there, shaking in my boots. {10:12} But he's like, "Chill, Daniel, from day one of your quest for wisdom and your humble vibes before God, your words were heard, and I'm here for you." {10:13} But it wasn't smooth sailing, yo, 'cause the Persian big shot was throwing shade for twenty-one days, until Michael, the heavy hitter, swooped in to back me up against the Persian crew. {10:14} Now, I'm here to drop some truth bombs about what's gonna go down with your squad in the future, 'cause this vision is playing out for a hot minute. {10:15-16} So, like, after he said all that stuff to me, I was just like staring at the ground, totally speechless, you know? Then this guy, kinda looking like a regular dude, touched my lips. So, I opened my mouth and was like, "Hey man, this vision is seriously freaking me out, I feel totally drained." {10:17} I was like, "How can I even talk to you, man? I've got no strength left, I can barely breathe." {10:18} Then he came back, still looking like a regular guy, and he gave me some energy, you know, like a boost. {10:19} He was like, "Hey, dude, chill out, peace be with you. Stay strong, okay?" And after he said that, I felt pumped up, and I was like, "Okay, go ahead and talk, you've got me feeling stronger." {10:20} Then he was like, "You know why I'm here? I gotta go back and deal with this prince of Persia, and after that, here comes the prince of Greece." {10:21} But he was like, "I'll tell you what's written in the scripture of truth. And I gotta tell you, nobody's got my back on this except Michael, your prince."

{11:1} Yo, so like, in the first year of Darius the Mede, ya boy stood up to back him up and make sure he's solid. {11:2} And now, peep this, there's gonna be three more kings in Persia, but the fourth one? Yeah, he's gonna be ballin' outta control, richer than all of 'em combined. And he's gonna flex that cash to stir up trouble against Greece. {11:3} Then this boss king's gonna step up, ruling like a boss with mad power. {11:4} But then his kingdom's gonna get wrecked and split into four, not even his fam's gonna keep it, 'cause it's gonna be snatched up by someone else. {11:5} The southern king's gonna be all swole and powerful, with one of his boys even stronger, ruling over mad lands. {11:6} So, after a while, they gonna try to make peace, but it ain't gonna work out for her or him. They gonna get played, along with everyone who helped 'em. {11:7} But yo, someone from her crew gonna step up and come with an army, wrecking the northern king's fortress and taking over. {11:8} And he gonna haul off Egypt's gods, their VIPs, and all their fancy silver and gold gear. And he gonna chill longer than the northern king. {11:9} Then the southern king's gonna bounce back to his turf. {11:10} But his sons gonna stir up trouble, assembling a huge army. One of 'em's gonna roll in, cause chaos, then retreat to his stronghold. {11:11} The southern king's gonna get heated and come at him, but the northern king's gonna crush him, despite the huge army. {11:12} After that beatdown, he gonna be feeling himself, taking out tens of thousands, but it ain't gonna make him stronger. {11:13} 'Cause then the northern king gonna come back with an even bigger army, loaded with cash, after a few years. {11:14} Lots of folks gonna turn against the southern king, even some of his own people gonna try to make things happen, but they gonna fail. {11:15} So the northern king gonna roll up, take over some fortified cities, and the southern king's army ain't gonna stand a chance. {11:16} No one gonna be able to stop him, he gonna even chill in the holy land and wreck it. {11:17} He gonna set his sights on expanding his kingdom, and he gonna try to get in good with this one girl, but she gonna be like, "Nah." {11:18} After that, he gonna target some islands, but some prince gonna shut him down and turn his own schemes against him. {11:19} Then he gonna try to go back to his turf, but he gonna trip and fall, and no one gonna find him. {11:20} After that, some tax collector gonna rise up in his place, but he ain't gonna last long, no drama, no battles. {11:21} Then this shady character gonna step up, not getting the royal treatment, but sliding into power with smooth talk. {11:22} He gonna come in like a flood, overwhelming everyone, even messing with the covenant's prince. {11:23} And after making deals, he gonna come up strong with a small crew. {11:24} He gonna roll into the richest spots, doing things no one before him has done, spreading out the loot, making plans against strongholds for a while. {11:25} Then he gonna amp up his power, ready to take on the southern king with a massive army. The southern king gonna get riled up, but he gonna have plans against him. {11:26} Even his own peeps gonna turn on him, and his army gonna get wrecked, with many falling in battle. {11:27} Both these kings gonna be plotting mischief and lying to each other, but their schemes ain't gonna work out in the end, 'cause it's all set for a certain time. {11:28} Then he gonna bounce back to his turf loaded with loot, but he gonna be against the holy covenant, doing his thing, then heading back home. {11:29} At the appointed time, he gonna come back toward the south, but it ain't gonna go like before. {11:30} 'Cause ships from far away gonna mess with him, so he gonna be ticked off, turning against the holy covenant, hooking up with those who forsake it. {11:31} He gonna have his crew backing him, defiling the holy stronghold, stopping the daily sacrifices, and setting up some messed-up stuff. {11:32} Those who turn on the covenant gonna fall for his smooth talk, but those who know their God gonna stand strong, doing big things. {11:33} Some folks gonna spread knowledge to many, but they gonna face swords, flames, captivity, and looting for a while. {11:34} When they fall, they gonna get a little help, but many gonna stick with them for the wrong reasons. {11:35} Those with understanding gonna fall, getting tested and purified until the appointed time comes, 'cause it's all set. {11:36} The king gonna do whatever he wants, puffing himself up above all gods, saying crazy stuff against the God of gods, and he gonna keep winning until it's all done. {11:37} He ain't gonna care about his ancestors' God or what women want or any god, 'cause he gonna think he's above all that. {11:38} But he gonna honor some new god in his place, decking it out with gold, silver, and fancy stuff. {11:39} He gonna be all about this new god, boosting it up, letting it rule over many, and divvying up the land for profit. {11:40} When the end times come, the southern king gonna come at him, but then the northern king gonna roll in like a storm, with chariots, horses, and ships, taking over countries left and right. {11:41} He gonna even hit up the holy land, wrecking many places, but some gonna escape his grip, like Edom, Moab, and the big shots from Ammon. {11:42} He gonna reach out to other lands, and even Egypt ain't gonna escape. {11:43} He gonna snag all the gold, silver, and precious stuff from Egypt, and even the Libyans and Ethiopians gonna be under his thumb. {11:44} But then news gonna come from the east and north, freaking him out, so he gonna go all out to destroy and ruin many. {11:45} Finally, he gonna set up shop between the seas on some holy mountain, but that's when his time's up, and no one gonna save him.

{12:1} So, like, when everything goes down, Michael's gonna step up, you know, he's like the big protector for your people. And it's gonna be crazy, man, like a level of trouble that's never been seen before, and at that time, everyone whose name is in the book gets saved. {12:2} And check this out, some of those who are sleeping in the ground are gonna wake up, some to live forever, and some to face everlasting shame and contempt. {12:3} Those who are wise are gonna shine like the sky, and those who lead others to do right will shine like stars forever and ever. {12:4} But you, Daniel, gotta keep these words to yourself and seal up the book until the end times, you know? People are gonna be running all over the place, and knowledge is gonna be off the charts. {12:5} Then I looked, and there were these two others, one on each side of the riverbank. {12:6} And one of them asked the dude dressed in linen, who was standing on the water, "Hey, how long till all this crazy stuff ends?" {12:7} And the guy on the water raised both hands to heaven and swore by the eternal living dude that it's gonna be for a time, times, and half a time, and when the power of the holy people gets scattered, then it's game over. {12:8} I heard all this, but I didn't really get it, so I was like, "Yo, what's gonna happen at the end of all this?" {12:9} And he was like, "Chill, Daniel, these words are locked up tight until the end comes." {12:10} Lots of people are gonna get cleaned up and tested, but the wicked are gonna keep doing their thing, clueless as ever. But the smart ones? Oh, they'll get it. {12:11} And from the time they stop the daily sacrifices and set up that abomination that messes everything up, it's gonna be 1,290 days. {12:12} Happy is the one who waits and makes it to 1,335 days. {12:13} But you, Daniel, just do your thing until the end comes. Then you can rest, and you'll get what's coming to you.

Hosea

✦✦✦

{1:1} Yo, peep this word from the big man upstairs that came to Hosea, son of Beeri, back in the days of Uzziah, Jotham, Ahaz, and Hezekiah, kings of Judah, and during Jeroboam's reign over Israel. {1:2} So, God's like, "Hosea, go get yourself a wife who's been around the block, and have some kids with her, 'cause this land's been gettin' down and dirty, cheatin' on me left and right." {1:3} So Hosea's like, "Cool," and hooks up with Gomer, daughter of Diblaim, and she pops out a son. {1:4} Then God's like, "Name him Jezreel, 'cause pretty soon I'm gonna dish out some payback on the house of Jehu for the bloodshed in Jezreel and put an end to Israel's reign." {1:5} And when that day comes, Israel's gonna get wrecked in the valley of Jezreel. {1:6} Then Gomer gets pregnant again and has a daughter. And God's like, "Name her Lo-Ruhamah, 'cause I'm done showin' mercy to Israel; they're gonna get wiped out." {1:7} But Judah, they'll get some love from me and get saved by their God, not by war machines and battles. {1:8} After Lo-Ruhamah's weaned, Gomer has another son. {1:9} God's like, "Call him Lo-Ammi, 'cause you guys ain't my people, and I ain't your God. {1:10} But don't worry, Israel's gonna be too numerous to count, like sand on the beach, and they'll go from being nobodies to being called the sons of the living God. {1:11} Judah and Israel will come together under one leader, and it's gonna be a huge deal.

{2:1} So tell your bros they're 'Ammi,' and your sis's they're 'Ru-hamah.' {2:2} And tell your mom she ain't my wife anymore, and I ain't her husband. She needs to ditch her cheating ways and get her act together. {2:3} Otherwise, I'll strip her bare and leave her like a desert, thirsty and alone. {2:4} Her kids won't get any mercy from me; they're the products of her infidelity. {2:5} She's been chasing after her other lovers, thinking they provide for her, but she forgets I'm the one who gave her everything. {2:6} So I'm gonna block her path with thorns and walls so she can't find her way. {2:7} She'll chase after her lovers but won't catch 'em; she'll look for 'em but won't find 'em. Then she'll be like, "Guess I'll go back to my first man; things were better back then." {2:8} But she doesn't realize it was me who gave her food, wine, and money, which she wasted on Baal. {2:9} So I'll take back what I gave her, her food and wine, and leave her with nothing. {2:10} Then I'll expose her infidelity for all to see, and no one will save her from me. {2:11} I'll put an end to her parties and celebrations. {2:12} Her vineyards and fig trees, the gifts from her lovers, I'll destroy them all and turn them into a wilderness where wild animals roam. {2:13} She'll pay for her worship of Baal, decking herself out with jewelry and chasing after other gods, forgetting all about me, says the LORD. {2:14} But then, I'll win her back; I'll take her to the wilderness and speak tenderly to her. {2:15} I'll give her back her vineyards and make the valley of Achor a door of hope. She'll sing there like she did in her youth when she first left Egypt. {2:16} She'll call me 'Husband' instead of 'Master.' {2:17} I'll wipe out the names of Baal from her mouth, and she won't remember them anymore. {2:18} I'll make a covenant with the animals, and they'll live in peace. {2:19} I'll marry her forever, in righteousness and justice, with love and compassion. {2:20} I'll be faithful to her, and she'll know it's me, the LORD. {2:21} When that day comes, I'll answer her prayers, and the heavens and the earth will respond. {2:22} The earth will produce crops, and everyone will prosper. {2:23} I'll claim those who were not my people as my own, and they'll call me their God.

{3:1} So, like, the big man upstairs told me, "Yo, go show some love to this woman who's, like, cheating on her man. Just like how I show love to the Israelites, who be worshiping other gods and getting lit on wine." {3:2} So I dropped some cash on her, fifteen silver coins, and some barley, like a ton of it. {3:3} And I told her, "You gotta chill with me for a while, no messing around with other dudes. And I'll be loyal to you too." {3:4} 'Cause the Israelites gonna be without a king, no prince, no sacrifices, no idols, no fancy priest clothes, and no lucky charms for a while. {3:5} But then they gonna come back to God, looking for Him and David their king, showing some respect for God and His goodness in the future.

{4:1} Listen up, Israel crew, 'cause the big man upstairs got beef with y'all, 'cause there's no truth, mercy, or knowledge of God around here. {4:2} Y'all out here swearing, lying, killing, stealing, and hooking up left and right, causing chaos and bloodshed. {4:3} So the whole land gonna be mourning, everyone gonna be feeling down, even the animals and fish gonna suffer. {4:4} Don't bother arguing or calling each other out, 'cause y'all act like you're arguing with God Himself. {4:5} That's why you gonna fall in the day, and even the prophets gonna fall with you at night, and I'm gonna mess up your mom too. {4:6} My people messed up 'cause they don't know better, rejecting knowledge, so I'm gonna reject them as my priests. 'Cause they forgot God's law, I'm gonna forget about their kids. {4:7} They got more sinful as they grew, so I'm gonna turn their glory into shame. {4:8} They chow down on sin like it's their favorite meal, loving their wickedness. {4:9} The people and the priests all messed up the same way, so they gonna get what's coming to them. {4:10} They gonna eat, but it won't be enough, they gonna hook up, but they won't get anywhere, 'cause they stopped paying attention to the Lord. {4:11} Hookups and booze mess with your head big time. {4:12} My people out here asking their idols for advice, listening to sticks and stones, 'cause they're all caught up in cheating on God. {4:13} They sacrificing on mountaintops, burning incense wherever they please, under trees, 'cause they think it's a vibe. So, their daughters gonna be out there hooking up, and their wives gonna be cheating on them. {4:14} I ain't gonna punish their daughters or wives for hooking up 'cause they're all mixed up with other folks anyway, partying with the wrong crowd. So, anyone who can't see what's wrong gonna fall. {4:15} Even though Israel's out here hooking up, Judah better not follow suit. And don't go to Gilgal or Beth-aven making false oaths in the name of the Lord. {4:16}

Israel's sliding back like a stubborn cow, so God gonna let 'em roam free like a lamb in a big field. {4:17} Ephraim's all in with idols, so just leave 'em be. {4:18} Their drinks taste sour, they're always hooking up, and their leaders are all about getting gifts and bribes. {4:19} They're caught up in their own mess, and they gonna be embarrassed 'cause of their sacrifices.

{5:1} Yo, listen up, priests, Israel, and the royal fam, 'cause judgment's coming your way. You've been setting traps like on Mizpah and spreading nets like on Tabor. {5:2} And these rebels are deep into their violence, even though I've been calling them out. {5:3} I know what's up with Ephraim, and I see Israel's messed up too. Ephraim's all about that unfaithfulness, and Israel's totally tainted. {5:4} They ain't trying to turn back to God, they're just drowning in their own wickedness, clueless about the LORD. {5:5} Israel's pride is in their face, so they're gonna fall hard for their sins, and Ephraim's going down with them. Even Judah's gonna feel the heat. {5:6} They'll try to seek God with their flocks and herds, but they won't find Him 'cause He's turned His back on them. {5:7} They've betrayed the LORD, birthing all kinds of messed-up kids. Pretty soon, they'll be wiped out along with their possessions. {5:8} Sound the alarm in Gibeah, blow the trumpet in Ramah, and scream out in Bethaven, Benjamin's next. {5:9} Ephraim's gonna be deserted when judgment hits, and I've made it clear what's gonna happen to Israel. {5:10} The leaders of Judah are like boundary-busting thieves, so I'm gonna pour out my wrath on 'em like water. {5:11} Ephraim's getting crushed and broken in judgment 'cause they've been eagerly following the wrong orders. {5:12} So I'm gonna be like a moth to Ephraim, and rot to the house of Judah. {5:13} When Ephraim and Judah see how messed up they are, they'll try to get help from Assyria and King Jareb, but it won't work. {5:14} 'Cause I'll be like a lion to Ephraim, and a young lion to Judah. I'll tear 'em up and bail, and nobody's gonna save 'em. {5:15} I'm gonna bounce and chill until they own up to their mess and start looking for me when they're in trouble.

{6:1} So let's get real and come back to the LORD. Yeah, He's been tough on us, but He's gonna heal us up and patch us back together. {6:2} After a couple days, He'll revive us, and on the third day, He'll raise us up, and we'll be living large in His sight. {6:3} Then we'll know what's up if we stick with it and keep seeking the LORD. His presence is gonna be as refreshing as the morning and as life-giving as the rain to the earth. {6:4} Yo, Ephraim, what am I gonna do with you? And Judah, same question. Your loyalty is as flimsy as morning fog and as fleeting as dew. {6:5} That's why I've been laying it down through the prophets and dropping truth bombs with my words. And my judgments shine like the morning light. {6:6} 'Cause what I'm really after is compassion, not empty sacrifices, and I want people to know me more than offering burnt offerings. {6:7} But they've straight-up broken the covenant like a bunch of dudes. They've been shady right in front of me. {6:8} Gilead's become a den of iniquity, tainted with blood. {6:9} And the priests are acting like highway robbers, teaming up to do some messed-up stuff. {6:10} I've seen some messed-up things go down in Israel's crib. Ephraim's all about that unfaithfulness, and Israel's totally tainted. {6:11} Even you, Judah, got a grim future ahead when I turn the tide for my people.

{7:1} Yo, when I was about to help out Israel, then Ephraim's dirt got exposed, and Samaria's wickedness came to light: they straight-up lying, and thieves be raiding without a care. {7:2} And they ain't even realizing I'm peeping all their foul moves; their own actions got 'em caught up, right in front of me. {7:3} They're making the king happy with their wickedness, and the princes are loving their lies. {7:4} They're all cheating, like an oven getting hot with the baker's fire, not stopping till the dough's leavened. {7:5} On the king's big day, the princes get him wasted on wine; he's chilling with the mockers. {7:6} They're prepping their hearts like an oven, scheming all night while the baker sleeps; in the morning, it's blazing hot. {7:7} They're all fired up like an oven, devouring their judges; all their kings have fallen, and not one of them calls out to me. {7:8} Ephraim's out here mixing it up with other nations; Ephraim's like a pancake burned on one side. {7:9} Strangers are draining his strength, and he don't even know it; gray hairs popping up, but he's clueless. {7:10} And Israel's too proud to turn back to the LORD, not even after all this. {7:11} Ephraim's like a clueless bird, calling out to Egypt, heading to Assyria. {7:12} But when they go, I'm setting my trap; I'll bring 'em down like birds from the sky, just like I promised. {7:13} It's gonna be rough for them! They've run away from me; destruction's coming 'cause they crossed the line, even though I tried to save 'em, they've been lying to my face. {7:14} They ain't been praying from the heart, just crying out in their beds; they only gather for food and wine, rebelling against me. {7:15} Even though I strengthened them, they're still plotting against me. {7:16} They come back, but not to the Most High; they're like a faulty bow, and their leaders will fall by the sword for all their trash talk; that's their fate in Egypt.

{8:1} Time to sound the alarm! They're about to face the wrath of the LORD, 'cause they've broken my covenant and disobeyed my law. {8:2} Now Israel's gonna cry out, "Oh God, we know you!" {8:3} But they've turned away from what's good, so now their enemies are on their tail. {8:4} They've set up kings without my approval, made princes without my knowledge; they've crafted idols from their silver and gold, sealing their own fate. {8:5} Samaria, your golden calf's got you ditched; I'm mad as hell at you! How long till you get your act together? {8:6} 'Cause that calf you made ain't gonna cut it; it ain't no god! That calf of Samaria's getting smashed to pieces. {8:7} They've been sowing the wind, and now they're gonna reap the whirlwind; they've got nothing to show for it, and if they do, strangers will snatch it up. {8:8} Israel's doomed; they'll be scattered among the nations like a worthless vessel. {8:9} They're off to Assyria, acting like a wild donkey, going it alone; Ephraim's out there buying affection. {8:10} Yeah, they've been trying to cozy up to other nations, but I'm gathering them up now, and they're gonna feel the weight of their rulers. {8:11} 'Cause Ephraim's built all these altars for sinning, and those altars will just lead them to more sin. {8:12} I gave them my law, but they treated it like some foreign thing. {8:13} They're offering sacrifices, but I ain't buying it; now I'm gonna remember their sins and hold 'em accountable; they'll end up back in Egypt. {8:14} 'Cause Israel's forgotten their Maker, building temples left and right, and Judah's building up fortified cities, but I'll send fire to burn it all down, even their fancy palaces.

{9:1} Yo, Israel, chill with the celebrations, 'cause you've been cheating on God, chasing after rewards like thirsty folks at a party. {9:2} Your fields and vineyards ain't gonna produce squat, and your wine stash gonna run dry. {9:3} You ain't gonna be chilling in the Lord's land; instead, you'll end up back in Egypt, munching on sketchy food in Assyria. {9:4} Your offerings ain't gonna cut it with the Lord, and your sacrifices gonna be as worthless as stale bread at a funeral. {9:5} What you gonna do when it's time to get serious with God, huh? {9:6} Destruction's coming, and Egypt gonna scoop you up, while your once-fancy stuff becomes overrun with weeds. {9:7} The reckoning's here, Israel's gonna feel it; prophets sounding crazy 'cause of all the sin and hate. {9:8} The watchmen supposed to be on God's side, but now they're setting traps and spreading hate even in His house. {9:9} You've gone off the deep end, just like in the Gibeah days; God ain't forgetting your mess. {9:10} I remember when you were fresh and promising, but now you're into all sorts of shameful stuff. {9:11} Ephraim's glory gonna fade fast, from birth to the grave, and even when they have kids, they'll be left with nothing. {9:12} Even if they raise kids, I'm taking 'em away; it's gonna be rough when I'm done with 'em. {9:13} Ephraim's like a nice spot, but they're bringing up kids for destruction. {9:14} God, give 'em what they deserve, messed-up pregnancies and dry nursing. {9:15} All their mess is in Gilgal, where God's had enough of 'em; He's kicking 'em out and cutting ties with their leaders. {9:16} Ephraim's done for, their roots dried up, not even the best of their kids gonna make it. {9:17} God's done with 'em 'cause they wouldn't listen; now they're gonna wander aimlessly among other nations.

{10:1} Israel's like a dead vine, only producing for themselves, making more altars as their wealth grows. {10:2} Their hearts all over the place, about to get busted for their false worship; God gonna wreck their altars and trash their idols. {10:3} Now they're acting like they don't need a king 'cause they don't fear the Lord; what good's a king gonna do now? {10:4} They're all talk, making false promises and deals, but it's gonna bite 'em back hard. {10:5} Samaria's shaking 'cause of their idolatry, mourning the loss of their glory. {10:6} They gonna be handed over to Assyria as a gift, Ephraim getting embarrassed, and Israel regretting their choices. {10:7} Samaria's king gone like foam on water. {10:8} Their sinful places gonna be wiped out, overrun with weeds, and they gonna wish the mountains would bury 'em. {10:9} Israel's been sinning since Gibeah days; they've been warned, but they never learned. {10:10} God's gotta discipline 'em, and folks gonna come against 'em when they're stuck in their wicked ways. {10:11} Ephraim's stubborn like a heifer, but God's gonna tame 'em; Judah's gonna plow, and Jacob's gonna break new ground. {10:12} Start living right, reap mercy; time to turn to the Lord before He showers righteousness on you. {10:13} You've sowed wickedness, reaped trouble; trusted in your strength, but it's gonna fail you. {10:14} Chaos gonna break out, and their forts gonna be wrecked, just like Shalman did to Beth-arbel. {10:15} Bethel gonna bring the hammer down 'cause of all their evil; Israel's king gonna get axed in no time.

{11:1} Back when Israel was just a kid, I was all about him, even called him out of Egypt like my own son. {11:2} But they bounced when I called; straight-up started worshipping Baalim and burning incense to idols. {11:3} I even showed Ephraim some love, guided them by the hand, but they didn't even realize I was healing them. {11:4} I treated them like family, pulling them close with love, easing their burdens, and feeding them. {11:5} But nah, they ain't going back to Egypt; they'd rather have the Assyrians as their kings 'cause they refused to come back to me. {11:6} And now the sword's gonna mess up their cities and wipe out their plans, all because they're stubbornly turning away from me. {11:7} My people keep sliding back from me; even though they're called to the Most High, none of them wanna lift him up. {11:8} How can I give you up, Ephraim? How can I let you go, Israel? How can I treat you like Admah or set you up like Zeboim? My heart's a mess, torn up inside; I'm feeling all kinds of regret. {11:9} But I won't let my anger loose; I won't go back on my promise to Ephraim 'cause I'm God, not just some human; I'm the Holy One right here with you, and I ain't abandoning the city. {11:10} Eventually, they'll come back to following the LORD; he'll roar like a lion, and when he does, even the kids from the west will shake in fear. {11:11} They'll be shaking like a bird flying out of Egypt or a dove from Assyria, but I'll settle them back in their homes, says the LORD. {11:12} Ephraim's all about lying, and the house of Israel's full of deceit, but Judah's still holding it down with God, staying true to the saints.

{12:1} Ephraim's chasing after empty promises, following every new trend, just piling on lies and destruction; they're making deals with the Assyrians and shipping oil off to Egypt. {12:2} And Judah's gonna catch it too; Jacob's gonna get what's coming to him based on his actions. {12:3} He's been wrestling since he was in the womb, and by his strength, he's been going toe-to-toe with God. {12:4} Yeah, he even wrestled with an angel and won; he cried and begged for mercy, found God in Bethel, and that's where he spoke with us. {12:5} 'Cause the LORD God of hosts is his name; the LORD's the one they'll remember. {12:6} So turn back to your God; show mercy and justice, and keep on waiting for God, always. {12:7} This guy's a total scammer, got deceitful scales in his hands; he's all about oppressing others. {12:8} And Ephraim's out here boasting, "Look at me, I'm rich! I've made it big without doing anything wrong!" {12:9} But I'm still the LORD your God, been with you since Egypt, and I'll bring you back to living in tents, just like during the festivals. {12:10} I've sent prophets, had plenty of visions, used metaphors, all through the prophets' work. {12:11} But seriously, what's up with the sin in Gilead? They're just empty, sacrificing bulls in Gilgal; their altars are like piles of rocks in the fields. {12:12} Jacob ended up in Syria, and Israel worked for a wife; yeah, they herded sheep for a wife. {12:13} And it was a prophet who led Israel out of Egypt, and by a prophet, they were protected. {12:14} But Ephraim really ticked God off; now he's gonna leave the blood on their hands, and their Lord's gonna bring back the shame upon them.

{13:1} When Ephraim was big talkin', he was top dog in Israel; but when he started worshiping Baal, he got wrecked. {13:2} Now they're all about sinning, making silver idols, thinking they're smart; they even say folks should kiss these calf idols when they sacrifice. {13:3} But they're gonna fade like morning clouds, vanish like dew, blown away like chaff, and vanish like smoke. {13:4} But I'm still the Lord, been with you since Egypt, ain't no other savior besides me. {13:5} I knew you back in the wilderness, during the dry times. {13:6} You had plenty, got all proud, forgot about me. {13:7} So now I'm gonna pounce like a lion, stalk like a leopard. {13:8} I'll come at 'em like a bear robbed of her cubs, tear into 'em like a lion; they're done for. {13:9} Israel, you brought this on yourself, but I'm your only hope. {13:10} I'll be your king, who else gonna save you in all your cities? Remember those judges you wanted? {13:11} I gave you a king, but I took him away too. {13:12} Ephraim's sins are packed in tight, hidden away. {13:13} They're in for pain like a woman in labor, acting like fools. {13:14} But I'll rescue 'em from the grave, redeem 'em from death; Death and the grave gonna get it. {13:15} Even if they're thriving, the Lord's gonna dry 'em up, spoil all their treasures. {13:16} Samaria gonna be a ghost town, 'cause they rebelled; swords gonna fall, babies gonna suffer, women gonna be torn up.

{14:1} Israel, get back to the Lord, your sins got you down. {14:2} Bring some words, turn to the Lord, ask Him to forgive, we'll offer our praises. {14:3} No more relying on Assyria or idols; we won't ride horses or worship our handmade gods; the Lord's where the mercy's at. {14:4} I'll fix their mess, love 'em freely, my anger's cooled. {14:5} I'll be like dew to Israel, they'll thrive like lilies, rooted like Lebanon. {14:6} They'll spread like branches, beautiful like olive trees, smellin' fresh like Lebanon. {14:7} Those who stick with the Lord will come alive, grow like corn and vines; their scent gonna be sweet like Lebanon's wine. {14:8} Ephraim's gonna wise up, ditch those idols; I've heard and seen him, he's like a thriving fir tree, fruit comin' from me. {14:9} Who's smart enough to get this? Those who understand the Lord's ways, walkin' right; but those who mess up, they're in for a fall.

Joel

✦✦✦

{1:1} So, like, here's what went down, the message from the big man upstairs to this dude named Joel, son of Pethuel. {1:2} Yo, listen up, all you old heads, and pay attention, everyone living in this hood. Did anything like this ever happen in your time, or even back in the day with your folks? {1:3} Spread the word to your kids, and let them spread it to their crew, and keep passing it on to the next generation. {1:4} So, first, the locusts come and munch on everything, then the caterpillars swoop in, and finally, the palmerworms finish off what's left. {1:5} Wake up, you party animals, and start bawling, all you wine lovers, 'cause the supply's been cut off. {1:6} There's this savage nation rolling through my turf, mad strong and countless, with teeth like lions tearing everything up. {1:7} They wrecked my vineyard, stripped my fig trees, leaving them bare and useless; it's like a ghost town out here. {1:8} Cry like a girl who just got dumped before her wedding day. {1:9} There ain't gonna be no more offerings at the crib of the LORD; even the priests are mourning. {1:10} The fields are trashed, the land's grieving; all the crops are toast, wine's dried up, and the oil's gone stale. {1:11} Farmers, feel the shame; vineyard keepers, start howling 'cause your harvest is a bust. {1:12} Everything's dried up, from the vines to the fig trees; even the pomegranates and palms are withering away, leaving no joy for anyone. {1:13} Get ready to mourn, priests; cry out, altar crew; spend the night in sackcloth, servants of my God, 'cause the offerings ain't coming. {1:14} Time to get serious, call a fasting sesh, gather everyone, young and old, in the house of the LORD, and start begging for mercy. {1:15} It's a dark day, y'all; the LORD's day of reckoning is here, and it's gonna be brutal. {1:16} Can't you see? No more feasting or partying at God's house? It's all gone. {1:17} Crops rotting in the fields, storehouses empty, barns falling apart; there's nothing left. {1:18} Even the animals are freaking out, herds wandering aimlessly 'cause there's no food, flocks left stranded with no pasture. {1:19} LORD, we're calling out to you 'cause the wildfires have scorched the wilderness, burning up all the trees. {1:20} Even the wildlife's crying out to you; the streams are dried up, and the fires have turned the wilderness into a wasteland.

{2:1} Yo, blow the horn in Zion, sound the alarm on my holy turf; everyone better be shaking in their sneakers 'cause the LORD's day is coming, it's like, right around the corner. {2:2} It's gonna be pitch black, with thick clouds covering the sky, like the break of dawn spreading over the mountains; a huge army's rolling in, never seen anything like it, and won't ever again. {2:3} They're like a blazing inferno, leaving destruction in their wake; the land's Eden in front of them, but a desolate wasteland behind 'em, and nothing's gonna escape. {2:4} They look like horses, charging into battle, swift like horsemen on the move. {2:5} Their approach sounds like a stampede on the mountaintops, roaring like a wildfire devouring everything in its path, a fierce army ready for war. {2:6} People gonna be freaking out when they see 'em, faces turning pale with fear. {2:7} They'll run like champs, scaling walls like soldiers, marching in formation without breaking ranks. {2:8} Ain't nobody gonna mess with them; they'll walk straight ahead, even through swords, without a scratch. {2:9} They'll raid the city, scaling walls and sneaking in through windows like thieves. {2:10} The earth's gonna shake before 'em, the heavens gonna tremble; sun and moon gonna go dark, stars losing their shine. {2:11} And the LORD's voice will thunder before his army; it's gonna be a massive showdown 'cause his crew's no joke; his day is gonna be lit, but also terrifying; who's gonna be able to handle it? {2:12} So, like, right now, says the LORD, turn back to me with everything you got, with fasting, crying, and mourning; {2:13} tear up your hearts, not just your clothes, and come back to the LORD your God 'cause he's all about that grace and mercy, slow to anger, full of kindness, and willing to turn away from punishment. {2:14} Who knows? Maybe he'll change his mind, leave behind a blessing, offerings of food and drink for the LORD your God. {2:15} Blow the horn in Zion, call for a fast, gather everyone for a serious gathering. {2:16} Get everyone together, young and old, bring out the kids and even the babies; let the newlyweds leave their honeymoon suite and the bride her dressing room. {2:17} And let the priests, God's crew, start crying out for mercy, pleading between the porch and the altar, saying, "Spare your people, LORD, don't let them become a joke for the pagans to mock, questioning where their God is." {2:18} Then the LORD will get protective over his land and show some love to his people. {2:19} Yeah, the LORD's gonna come through, saying, "I'll hook you up with crops, wine, and oil, so you'll be chill, and I won't let the haters clown on you anymore among the nations. {2:20} I'll kick that northern army outta here, sending 'em to a desolate wasteland, stinking up the place with their rottenness 'cause they thought they were all that." {2:21} So, don't trip, land; start celebrating 'cause the LORD's gonna do some epic stuff. {2:22} Even you animals out there, don't be scared; the wilderness is gonna come back to life, with trees bearing fruit, vines producing grapes. {2:23} So, party on, Zion crew, rejoice in the LORD your God 'cause he's already sending rain to make it all happen, the early and late rains coming in the first month. {2:24} Fields gonna be overflowing with wheat, and the wine and oil gonna be pouring out. {2:25} And I'm gonna make up for all the years those locusts and caterpillars destroyed, the palmerworms and cankerworms, my army that wrecked your fields. {2:26} You'll have plenty to eat, be totally satisfied, and give props to the LORD your God, who's been coming through in a big way; my people ain't ever gonna be ashamed. {2:27} And you'll know that I'm right here with Israel, that I'm the LORD your God, and there's no one else; my people ain't never gonna feel ashamed. {2:28} Then, later on, I'm gonna pour out my spirit on everyone, young and old; your kids gonna have visions, and the elders gonna dream big dreams. {2:29} Even the servants, even the help, gonna get in on the action when I pour out my spirit. {2:30} And I'm gonna make things go crazy in the skies and on the earth, blood, fire, and billowing smoke. {2:31} Sun's gonna go dark, moon turning red before the LORD's epic day comes, the one that's super terrifying. {2:32} But whoever calls on the LORD's name gonna be saved; in Zion and Jerusalem, there's gonna be deliverance, just like the LORD promised, for those he chooses.

{3:1} Yo, peep this, in those days when I bring Judah and Jerusalem back from being exiled, {3:2} I'm gonna gather all the nations and bring them down to this spot called the valley of Jehoshaphat, where I'll lay down some truth for messing with my people, Israel, scattering them all over the place and splitting up my turf. {3:3} They've been treating my people like commodities, trading boys for pleasure and girls for booze, just to get their drink on. {3:4} And what's up with you, Tyre, Sidon, and all you coast dwellers? You think you can pay me back? Well, guess what? Whatever you throw my way, I'll bounce it right back at you, quick and fast. {3:5} You've been jacking my silver and gold, swiping all my precious stuff and stashing it in your temples like it's yours. {3:6} And you even went and sold off the peeps from Judah and Jerusalem to the Greeks, shipping them out far from home. {3:7} But check this, I'm gonna bring them back from where you sold them and give you a taste of your own medicine. {3:8} Then I'll flip the script and have the children of Judah selling your sons and daughters to the Sabeans, a far-off crew; the LORD's calling the shots here. {3:9} Spread the word to all the nations: it's time to gear up for war, wake up the warriors, and get ready to throw down. {3:10} Turn your farming tools into weapons, and let the weak act tough. {3:11} Round up your crews, all you non-believers, and bring 'em to the party; and bring down your toughest players, LORD. {3:12} It's gonna be a wake-up call for all the non-believers, bringing them to the valley of Jehoshaphat, where I'll lay down the law for everyone. {3:13} Time to bring in the harvest 'cause the wickedness is off the charts; the press is overflowing, and it's time to reap what they've sown. {3:14} The valley's gonna be packed with people making choices 'cause the LORD's day is right around the corner. {3:15} Sun and moon gonna go dark, stars dimming their shine. {3:16} The LORD's gonna roar out of Zion, making his voice heard from Jerusalem; the whole world's gonna shake, but the LORD's gonna be the rock for his people, Israel. {3:17} Then everyone's gonna know that I'm the LORD, chilling in Zion, my holy turf; Jerusalem's gonna be pure, with no outsiders passing through. {3:18} And when that day comes, the mountains gonna be flowing with new wine, hills pouring out milk, all the rivers of Judah flowing with water, and a fountain popping up from the house of the LORD, watering the valley of Shittim. {3:19} Egypt gonna be a ghost town, and Edom a barren wasteland, paying the price for messing with the children of Judah, shedding innocent blood in their land. {3:20} But Judah and Jerusalem gonna stand strong forever, from one generation to the next. {3:21} 'Cause I'll cleanse their blood, the blood I haven't cleansed yet; 'cause the LORD's posted up in Zion.

Amos

✦✦✦

{1:1} So, peep this, it's Amos, chilling with the herds in Tekoa, dropping some truth bombs about Israel back in the days of Uzziah king of Judah and Jeroboam son of Joash king of Israel, two years before the big earthquake. {1:2} He's like, "The LORD's gonna roar from Zion, and his voice is gonna echo from Jerusalem; even the shepherds' hangouts gonna feel it, and Carmel's gonna dry up." {1:3} The big man upstairs says, "For three strikes against Damascus, and make it four, I ain't turning a blind eye; they've been wrecking Gilead with iron threshers." {1:4} But then, he's like, "I'm gonna bring the heat to Hazael's crib and toast Ben-hadad's palaces." {1:5} "Damascus's days are numbered, and the people of Syria gonna end up in Kir." {1:6} Next up, Gaza's on blast for jacking the whole population and handing them over to Edom. {1:7} "Gonna set Gaza's walls on fire, and Ashdod and Ashkelon gonna get wiped out." {1:8} "Ekron's gonna feel my wrath too; the Philistines ain't gonna be left standing." {1:9} Then, Tyre's getting called out for handing the whole crew over to Edom and forgetting about the homie covenant. {1:10} "Tyrus's walls gonna be toast too, just you wait." {1:11} Edom's turn next for coming at his brother with no mercy, keeping that rage on simmer forever. {1:12} "Teman's gonna get lit up, and Bozrah's palaces are gonna be history." {1:13} Ammon's up next, getting flamed for some heinous acts in Gilead. {1:14} "Rabbah's walls gonna catch fire too, and it's gonna be chaos in battle, with a storm to top it off." {1:15} "Their king and his crew gonna end up in chains," says the LORD.

{2:1} Now Moab's turn for some divine smackdown, burning the king of Edom's bones to lime. {2:2} "Moab's palaces in Kirioth gonna be toast, and it's gonna be a loud, fiery end." {2:3} "Judges and princes of Moab, you're outta here," says the LORD. {2:4} Judah's getting called out too for dissing the LORD's laws, going astray like their ancestors. {2:5} "Jerusalem's palaces gonna be BBQ central," says the big man upstairs. {2:6} And Israel? Oh, they're in trouble for selling out the righteous for cash and exploiting the poor for kicks. {2:7} "They're even messing with the meek and disrespecting my name," says the LORD. {2:8} "They're lounging around on stolen goods, getting drunk in the house of their gods." {2:9} "I wiped out the Amorites, tall as cedars and strong as oaks, from top to bottom," says the LORD. {2:10} "I even dragged you out of Egypt, led you through the wilderness for forty years, just to give you the Amorites' land." {2:11} "And what do I get? You turn your prophets into party animals and tell them to shut up," says the LORD. {2:12-13} "You're weighing me down like a cart full of sheaves," says the LORD. {2:14} "The fast and the furious gonna crash, the strong gonna lose their muscle, and the mighty ain't gonna save themselves," says the LORD. {2:15} "Nobody's gonna have the skills to handle a bow, run like the wind, or ride like a pro," says the LORD. {2:16} "Even the bravest gonna run for cover, stripped down to nothing," says the LORD.

{3:1} Listen up, fam, the LORD's dropping some truth bombs on you, Israelites, and the whole crew I brought outta Egypt. {3:2} He's like, "Outta all the families on the block, I've only been vibing with you, so when you mess up, expect consequences." {3:3} Can two roll together unless they're on the same page? {3:4} Will a lion roar in the woods without a snack? Will a young lion growl if it hasn't caught anything? {3:5} Can a bird get caught in a trap if there's no bait? Can someone spring a trap if there's nothing in it? {3:6} If a trumpet blares in the city, and people ain't shook, and if bad stuff goes down and the LORD ain't in the mix? Nah. {3:7} The Lord GOD don't do anything without giving his prophets a heads-up. {3:8} When the lion roars, you bet people gonna be scared; when the Lord GOD speaks, who can help but spill the tea? {3:9} Spread the word in Ashdod and Egypt's high-rises, and tell 'em to head to the hills of Samaria and check out the chaos and suffering. {3:10} 'Cause these peeps don't know how to do right, says the LORD; they're all about violence and robbery in their fancy digs. {3:11} So the LORD's like, "Enemies gonna swarm your turf, strip you of your strength, and ransack your mansions." {3:12} Just like a shepherd rescues scraps from a lion's mouth, that's how a few Israelites in Samaria will be saved, hanging on by a thread. {3:13} Listen up, House of Jacob, says the Lord GOD, the OG of heaven's armies. {3:14} When I come to settle the score with Israel, I ain't sparing Bethel's altars; they're getting wrecked, and their horns are hitting the ground. {3:15} Summer homes gonna get wrecked with the winter pads; ivory towers gonna crumble, and the swanky cribs gonna be history, says the LORD.

{4:1} Yo, you rich folks in Samaria, listen up; you're oppressing the poor, crushing the needy, and living it up. {4:2} The Lord GOD swears by his name; your days of luxury gonna come crashing down, and you and your fam gonna be dragged out like fish on hooks. {4:3} You'll be fleeing through the breaches in your walls, like cows stampeding out of a pen, and the LORD's gonna bring you down. {4:4} He's like, "Keep sinning at Bethel, keep piling up transgressions at Gilgal, keep bringing your sacrifices, and tithes, like it's all good." {4:5} "Go ahead, bring your leavened thanksgiving sacrifices and flex your free offerings, Israelites; it's all good in your book," says the Lord GOD. {4:6} "I've even given you empty stomachs and bread shortages in your fancy cities, but you still ain't turning back to me," says the LORD. {4:7} "I held back the rain when there were still three months left till harvest; I made it rain on one town but not another, leaving some thirsty and others flooded, but you still ain't turning back to me," says the LORD. {4:8} "People from two or three towns gonna flock to one just to get a drink, but they'll still be thirsty; but you still ain't turning back to me," says the LORD. {4:9} "I've hit you with blight and mildew, even when your gardens and vineyards were booming, but you still ain't turning back to me," says the LORD. {4:10} "I've sent plagues like in Egypt, killed your youth with the sword, taken away your horses, and made your camps reek, but you still ain't turning back to me," says the LORD. {4:11} "I've wiped some of you out like Sodom and Gomorrah survivors plucked from the flames, but you still ain't turning back to me," says the LORD. {4:12} "So get ready to face me, Israel, 'cause I'm coming for you," says the LORD. {4:13} "I'm the one who made the mountains and the wind, who knows your thoughts, and brings the dawn, and walks the highest places on earth; The LORD, The God of hosts, that's my name."

{5:1} Yo, peep this rant I got against you, Israel fam. {5:2} Israel's like a fallen queen, donezo and deserted on her own turf, with no one to help her up. {5:3} Listen up, 'cause the big man upstairs says this: even if a whole city goes out to battle, only a fraction gonna make it back, and that's straight-up facts for Israel. {5:4} But here's the deal, straight from the big guy: if you wanna keep breathing, start searching for me. {5:5} But don't bother with Bethel, Gilgal, or Beer-sheba; they're all gonna get wrecked. {5:6} Seek the LORD or you'll get burned, especially if you're chilling in Joseph's hood, 'cause there won't be anyone to put out the fire in Bethel. {5:7} Y'all who twist justice and ditch righteousness, you better watch out 'cause the big man's coming for you. {5:8} Seek the one who made the stars and can flip day into night, 'cause that's the LORD's name. {5:9} He's the one who hooks up the weak against the strong, so don't mess with him. {5:10} But you guys hate anyone who speaks the truth and treats the poor like dirt. {5:11} You live large off the backs of the poor, stacking up your fancy houses and vineyards, but you ain't gonna enjoy any of it. {5:12} The big guy knows all about your shady deals and dirty tricks, how you oppress the righteous and take bribes, turning justice upside down. {5:13} So when things get rough, the wise keep quiet 'cause it's a messed-up time. {5:14} Start doing good instead of evil if you wanna survive, and maybe the LORD, the God of armies, will have your back. {5:15} Hate evil, love good, and bring fairness back to your courts; maybe then the LORD will show some love to the leftovers of Joseph. {5:16} But here's the scoop from the big guy, there's gonna be crying in every street and mourning on every road. {5:17} Everywhere you look, there'll be sadness 'cause the LORD's passing through. {5:18} You fools who can't wait for the LORD's day, thinking it's gonna be all sunshine and rainbows, better think again; it's gonna be pitch black, no light in sight. {5:19} It's gonna be like running from a lion and bumping into a bear, or hiding indoors and getting bit by a snake. {5:20} Yeah, the day of the LORD gonna be darker than a black hole, no light at all. {5:21} I ain't feeling your festivals or smelling your sacrifices; I'm done with your religious gatherings. {5:22} Even if you bring me all your offerings, I'm not interested; your fancy livestock can stay put. {5:23} Stop with the music; I ain't listening to your songs anymore. {5:24} Instead, let justice flow like a river, and righteousness like a never-ending stream. {5:25} Remember those forty years in the wilderness? Yeah, you offered sacrifices, but you also worshiped other gods. {5:26} You carried around idols like Moloch and Chiun, stars you made for yourselves. {5:27} So now you're gonna be hauled off into exile beyond Damascus, says the LORD, God of armies.

{6:1} You guys chilling in Zion and Samaria, thinking you're top dogs, better listen up; trouble's coming your way. {6:2} Take a trip to Calneh, then hit up Hamath and Gath of the Philistines; see if they're better off than you. {6:3} You're ignoring the warning signs and cozying up to corruption. {6:4} You're living it up in luxury, feasting on the best, and partying like there's no tomorrow. {6:5} You're all about the music and the good times, just like David. {6:6} You're guzzling wine and slathering on expensive oils, but you don't give a damn about the suffering of Joseph. {6:7} So now you're gonna be the first ones taken captive, and your fancy feasts gonna be history. {6:8} The LORD's swearing on his own name that he's sick of your pride, and he's gonna wreck your cities and everything in 'em. {6:9} Even if there's just ten of you left in a house, you're all gonna die. {6:10} When the grim reaper comes for you, your relatives ain't even gonna give you a proper burial; they'll just tell you to shut up and deal with it, 'cause mentioning the LORD's name ain't gonna help. {6:11} 'Cause when the LORD commands it, he's gonna tear down the mansions and the shacks alike. {6:12} Trying to farm on a rock? Plowing with oxen on solid ground? That's as dumb as turning justice into poison and righteousness into bitterness. {6:13} You're all pumped up about nothing, thinking you're invincible 'cause of your own strength. {6:14} But guess what? The LORD's gonna bring a nation against you, Israel, and they're gonna mess you up from Hemath to the wilderness river.

{7:1} So, peep this, fam, the big man upstairs showed me something wild: he whipped up a swarm of grasshoppers right when the crops were coming in after the king's harvest. {7:2} When those bugs finished chomping down on everything, I was like, "Yo, God, please forgive us! How's Jacob gonna bounce back? Dude's tiny." {7:3} And guess what? The big man changed his mind about wrecking us. He was like, "Nah, not gonna happen." {7:4} Then he showed me something else: the big man called down fire to wreck stuff, and it totally messed up the deep waters. {7:5} So I'm like, "God, chill! How's Jacob gonna survive? He's small-time." {7:6} And God's like, "Yeah, gonna give you a pass on this one too." {7:7} Then he shows me this scene: the Lord's standing on a wall with a plumbline, ready to measure up his people. {7:8} And the LORD tells me, "Yo, Amos, what do you see?" I'm like, "A plumbline, obviously." Then the Lord says, "Check it, I'm about to drop the hammer on my peeps in Israel. Not gonna give 'em a break this time. {7:9} The high places gonna be wrecked, the holy sites trashed, and I'm coming after Jeroboam's crew with a vengeance. {7:10} So this priest from Bethel named Amaziah hits up King Jeroboam like, "Yo, this Amos dude's stirring up trouble, man. The land can't handle his truth bombs." {7:11} 'Cause Amos is out here preaching, "Jeroboam's gonna bite it, and Israel's gonna get kicked out of their own turf." {7:12} Then Amaziah's like, "Yo, Amos, peace out! Go preach somewhere else, like in Judah, and leave us alone." {7:13} "And don't you dare come back to Bethel," he adds, "that's the king's turf." {7:14} But Amos claps back, "I ain't no fancy prophet, just a regular dude who used to herd sheep and pick fruit. {7:15} But then the LORD called me up and was like, 'Go tell Israel what's up.'" {7:16} "So listen up," Amos tells Amaziah, "I ain't gonna hold back on Israel or Isaac's crew." {7:17} "And here's the deal from the big man upstairs: your wife's gonna be hooking, your kids gonna get sliced up, your land's gonna get divided, and you gonna die in enemy territory. And Israel? Yeah, they're getting booted out too.

{8:1} Then the big man upstairs shows me a basket of summer fruit. {8:2} He's like, "Amos, what do you see?" And I'm like, "A basket of summer fruit, duh." Then God's like, "That's it, game over for my people Israel. Not cutting 'em any slack this time." {8:3} "And those temple songs gonna turn into wails," says the LORD. "Dead bodies everywhere, with nobody making a sound." {8:4} "Listen up, you greedy swindlers," God says, "you're sucking the life out of the poor, making their lives miserable. {8:5} You're just waiting for religious holidays to be over so you can make a quick buck. {8:6} Buying up the poor for peanuts and selling off the scraps. {8:7} And I swear by Jacob's greatness, I ain't forgetting any of this. {8:8} The land gonna shake with terror, and everyone's gonna mourn. It's gonna be like a flood, washing everything away like Egypt's flood. {8:9} "And get this," God says, "I'm gonna make the sun set at noon and darken the earth in broad daylight. {8:10} Turning your parties into funerals and your songs into sob fests. Sackcloth and bald heads everywhere, mourning like you lost your only child." {8:11} "And here's the kicker," says the LORD, "I'm gonna send a famine, not of food or water, but of my words. {8:12} People gonna be searching high and low, from sea to sea, trying to find a word from the LORD, but coming up empty. {8:13} And on that day, even the young and the beautiful gonna be fainting from thirst. {8:14} Those fools who swear by Samaria's sins and worship false gods gonna fall and never get back up again.

{9:1} So, check it, I peeped the LORD chilling on the altar, and he's like, "Yo, smack the doorframe so hard the whole place shakes. Slice 'em all in the head, and even if they try to run, they ain't escaping." {9:2} He's straight-up saying, "Even if they dig to hell or climb to heaven, I'm dragging them back down. And if they try to hide on Carmel or at the bottom of the sea, I'll find 'em and send serpents after 'em." {9:3} "Even if they get captured by their enemies," he adds, "I'll command the sword to finish 'em off. I'm watching, and it ain't for good." {9:4} Then he drops this bomb, saying he's the one who can make the land melt just by touching it, and everyone's gonna be mourning. The flood's coming, and ain't nobody gonna escape, just like Egypt's flood. {9:5} He's the dude who's got his game strong in heaven and on earth, commanding the seas to pour out onto the earth. That's the LORD for you. {9:6} And then he's like, "Yo, Israel, don't act like you're special. I brought you outta Egypt, but I've helped out other folks too, like the Philistines and Syrians." {9:7} "But don't get it twisted," he warns, "I'm watching that sinful kingdom, and it's gonna get wrecked. But I'll leave a piece of Jacob standing." {9:8} "I'm gonna scatter Israel among nations like grain in a sieve," he says, "but not one little bit is gonna slip through." {9:9} And he ain't playing when he says, "All the sinners in my crew gonna get taken out by the sword, thinking they're untouchable." {9:10} Then he's dropping some hope, talking about raising up David's fallen tabernacle and fixing it up like the old days. {9:11} He's planning to let them have Edom and the heathen, giving them a piece of the action. {9:12} And he's like, "Get ready for some crazy times, where planting and harvesting happen at the same time, and wine flows like rivers from the mountains." {9:13} "I'm bringing back my people from captivity," he declares. "They'll rebuild cities, plant vineyards, and live it up. They'll never be uprooted again from the land I gave 'em." That's the word from the LORD.

Obadiah

✦✦✦

{1:1} So, peep this vision from Obadiah. The LORD's dropping some truth bombs about Edom, like there's a rumor going around from the big man upstairs, and he's sending out a message to all the nations: "Let's team up and take down Edom." {1:2} He's like, "Yo, I've made you small among the nations, and everybody's straight-up hating on you." {1:3} "Your pride's messing you up," he tells them, "thinking you're untouchable up there in your rock fortress, acting like nobody can bring you down." {1:4} "But I'll drag you down from your high horse," says the LORD, "even if you're chilling among the stars." {1:5} "If thieves came for you, they'd clean you out," he warns, "and if grape pickers showed up, they wouldn't leave a single grape." {1:6} "Your secrets ain't safe," he says, "I'm uncovering all your shady stuff." {1:7} "Your buddies are turning on you," he adds, "the ones who were all cozy with you are stabbing you in the back." {1:8} "I'm wiping out the wise guys from Edom," he declares, "and understanding's going out the window." {1:9} "Even your tough guys will be shook," he warns, "so I can wipe out everyone in Edom." {1:10} "Because you messed with your brother Jacob," he says, "you're gonna be shamed and cut off forever." {1:11} "When bad stuff went down for Jacob," he reminds them, "you were right there cheering it on like you were one of the crew." {1:12} "You should've kept your distance," he scolds, "and not gloated over Judah's troubles or talked big when they were in distress." {1:13} "You had no business barging in," he tells them, "when my people were suffering, or snatching their stuff when they were down." {1:14} "You shouldn't have been blocking their escape routes," he says, "or handing over survivors to their enemies when they were in trouble." {1:15} "The reckoning's coming," he warns, "whatever you did to others is coming right back at you." {1:16} "You partied on my holy mountain?" he questions, "Well, now all the nations are gonna party too, and it's gonna be like they never existed." {1:17} "But on Mount Zion," he promises, "there's gonna be salvation and purity, and Jacob's crew gonna get their land back." {1:18} "Jacob's gonna blaze like fire," he predicts, "Joseph's gonna be a flame, and Esau's gonna be left as ash." {1:19} "The south's gonna take over Esau's land," he says, "and the plains gonna belong to the Philistines. Ephraim and Samaria will grab Gilead, and Benjamin's gonna snag some too." {1:20} "Israel's gonna reclaim what's theirs," he assures, "even up to Zarephath. And Jerusalem's exiles in Sepharad? They'll snag the southern cities." {1:21} "Saviors gonna rise up on Mount Zion," he declares, "and it's gonna be the LORD's kingdom."

Jonah

✦✦✦

{1:1} So, Jonah gets a DM from the big man upstairs, saying, "Yo, Jonah, get up and head to Nineveh, that mega city, and call them out on their messed-up ways, 'cause I've had enough." {1:2-3} But Jonah's like, "Nah, I'm outta here," and books it to Tarshish, trying to ghost the LORD. He hits up Joppa and hops on a ship bound for Tarshish, trying to dip from the LORD's presence. {1:4} But the LORD sends a crazy storm over the sea, and the ship's getting wrecked. {1:5} The sailors freak out, praying to their gods and tossing their stuff overboard to lighten the load. Meanwhile, Jonah's passed out below deck. {1:6} The captain's like, "Wake up, dude! Pray to your God so maybe we won't die!" {1:7} They're all like, "Let's cast lots to see who brought this bad juju." Guess whose number comes up? Jonah's. {1:8} They're like, "Spill it, man! What's your deal? Where you from and what's your job?" {1:9} Jonah's like, "I'm Hebrew, and I worship the LORD, the God of heaven, who made everything." {1:10} The sailors are freaking out, knowing Jonah's running from the LORD. {1:11} They're desperate for the storm to stop, so Jonah's like, "Toss me overboard, and the sea will chill. It's because of me this storm's going down." {1:12} They try to row to shore but no dice; the storm's too wild. {1:13} They're like, "Sorry, LORD, don't blame us for this guy's life," and toss Jonah overboard. Suddenly, the sea calms down. {1:14} The sailors are shook and start worshipping the LORD, making promises and all. {1:15} And then, out of nowhere, a giant fish swallows Jonah whole, and he's stuck in there for three days and nights.

{2:1} Jonah's trapped in the fish's belly, so he starts praying to the LORD. {2:2} He's like, "LORD, I was drowning, but you heard me out. I was in the pits of despair, and you came through." {2:3} "You tossed me into the deep, and I was surrounded by waves and floods. But somehow, you pulled me out." {2:4} "Even when I felt abandoned, I knew I could count on you, LORD." {2:5} "I was drowning, completely submerged, with seaweed wrapped around my head." {2:6} "I felt like I was at rock bottom, but you rescued me, God." {2:7} "When I was at my lowest, I remembered you, LORD, and my prayers reached you." {2:8} "People who chase after fake stuff are missing out on your mercy." {2:9} "But I'm gonna keep my promise and give thanks to you, LORD. Salvation comes from you." {2:10} Then the LORD tells the fish to spit Jonah out onto dry land.

{3:1} So, the LORD hits up Jonah again, like, "Yo, Jonah, round two. Head to Nineveh, that huge city, and preach the message I gave you." {3:2-3} Jonah's like, "Fine, fine," and heads to Nineveh, following the LORD's orders. Nineveh was massive, like, three days to walk across. {3:4} Jonah strolls into the city, takes a day's walk, and starts yelling, "In forty days, Nineveh's going down!" {3:5} The people of Nineveh freak out and believe God. They declare a fast, put on sackcloth, from the big shots to the nobodies. {3:6} Even the king hears about it, strips off his royal robes, puts on sackcloth, and chills in ashes. {3:7} He sends out this decree: no one, not even animals, can eat or drink. Everyone's gotta rock sackcloth and beg God for mercy, turning away from their messed-up ways. {3:8} God sees what they're doing, how they're changing their ways, and decides not to wreck them like He said.

{4:1} But Jonah's ticked off big time and throws a fit. {4:2} He's like, "Seriously, God? I knew this would happen! That's why I ran away to Tarshish. 'Cause I knew you're all about forgiveness and compassion." {4:3} "Just kill me now, LORD. I'd rather die than deal with this." {4:4} God's like, "Really, Jonah? You mad about a plant?" {4:5} So Jonah storms out of the city, sets up camp, and waits to see what happens. {4:6} God's like, "I got you," and makes this huge plant grow to shade Jonah. Jonah's thrilled. {4:7} But the next day, God sends a worm to kill the plant, and Jonah's back in the sun, dying. {4:8} He's like, "Death seems better than this," all dramatic. {4:9} God's like, "Still mad about the plant, Jonah?" Jonah's like, "Yeah, I'd rather die over a plant." {4:10} Then God's like, "You cared about that plant, but what about Nineveh? There are over a hundred and twenty thousand people there who don't know right from wrong, not to mention the animals!"

Micah

✜✜✜

{1:1} So, like, the LORD dropped some knowledge on Micah, the Morasthite, back when Jotham, Ahaz, and Hezekiah were running things in Judah. Micah's vibe was all about Samaria and Jerusalem. {1:2} He's like, "Yo, everyone, listen up! Earth, pay attention, and let the Lord GOD be your witness, straight from His holy temple." {1:3} Micah's dropping truth bombs, saying the LORD's stepping out of His crib, about to stomp all over the high places. {1:4} Mountains melting, valleys splitting like wax in a fire, and rivers rushing downhill – that's the scene when the LORD shows up. {1:5} Why's all this happening? Because Jacob and the house of Israel messed up big time. Samaria's at fault, and so is Jerusalem. {1:6} Samaria's getting wrecked, turned into rubble, and its idols smashed to bits. {1:7} Micah's on about burning idols and the consequences of shady deals. {1:8} He's getting dramatic, wailing and howling, going bare and baring his soul, making a scene like some mythical creature. {1:9} The wound's too deep to heal, hitting Judah and even reaching Jerusalem's doorstep. {1:10} Micah's like, "Don't spread the word, don't shed tears in Gath. Save your sorrow for your own hood." {1:11} Some towns are in for it, stripped of dignity, left to face the music alone. {1:12} Maroth's hopeful but gets hit with bad news from the LORD. {1:13} Lachish, you're not off the hook; you kick-started the sin train for Zion. {1:14} More bad news for Moresheth-gath, and Achzib's kings are living a lie. {1:15} But there's hope for Mareshah, with an heir on the way to bring back the glory. {1:16} Bald up, shave your heads in mourning, 'cause your kids are getting taken away captive.

{2:1} Micah's laying down some harsh truths, calling out those scheming evil in bed and seizing land and houses by force. {2:2} They're greedy, oppressing folks left and right. {2:3} Micah's warning them, saying the LORD's got something lined up, and they won't be able to escape. {2:4} It's gonna be a sad song when they lose everything, and their land's divided up. {2:5} They'll have no say in the LORD's congregation. {2:6} Some haters tell the prophets to shut up, but they won't silence the truth. {2:7} Micah's like, "Yo, house of Jacob, is the LORD's spirit running low? Nah, His words do good for those who keep it real." {2:8} But lately, Israel's acting shady, robbing folks on the street like they're at war. {2:9} They're kicking women and kids out of their homes, stripping away God's glory. {2:10} Micah's telling them to bounce, 'cause their spot's tainted and heading for destruction. {2:11} False prophets talking about partying instead of truth are just leading the people astray. {2:12} But Micah's got hope, talking about gathering up the remnant of Israel like a shepherd rounding up the flock. {2:13} The leader's stepping up, breaking through the gates, and the LORD's leading the charge.

{3:1} Alright, listen up, Jacob's big shots and Israel's high rollers, ain't it your job to know what's right? {3:2} But nah, y'all hate what's good and love what's messed up. Y'all strip people down to their bones, tearing 'em apart like meat for a pot. {3:3} You're out here feasting on my people, breaking 'em down like they're food for the pot, smashing their bones like they're cooking up a stew. {3:4} And when you finally cry out to the LORD, He ain't gonna hear you, 'cause you've been straight-up wicked. {3:5} The LORD's got some words for those prophets who lead His people astray, talking peace with their mouths while they're ready to fight anyone who ain't feeding them. {3:6} So darkness is gonna be your vibe, with no visions and no divine insight. The sun's gonna set on you prophets, and it's gonna be dark days ahead. {3:7} Then those fortune tellers and diviners gonna be ashamed, with no answers from God to save 'em. {3:8} But me, I'm powered up by the LORD, ready to call out Jacob and Israel for their mess. {3:9} So listen up, Jacob's big shots and Israel's high rollers, you hate what's fair and twist everything right. {3:10} Y'all building up Zion with blood and Jerusalem with wickedness. {3:11} Your leaders are corrupt, your priests are only in it for the cash, and your prophets just want a payday. But y'all still gonna act like the LORD's on your side? Nah, punishment's coming your way. {3:12} Zion's gonna get plowed like a field, and Jerusalem's gonna be left in ruins. It's gonna be a wild scene.

{4:1} But in the future, the LORD's house is gonna be the main spot, rising above everything else. People gonna flock to it from all over. {4:2} Nations gonna come, saying, "Let's check out the LORD's place and learn His ways." The law's gonna come from Zion, and the word of the LORD from Jerusalem. {4:3} He's gonna bring judgment on nations near and far, turning weapons into tools for farming. War's gonna be a thing of the past. {4:4} Everyone gonna chill under their own vine and fig tree, with no fear in sight, 'cause the LORD's spoken. {4:5} People gonna rep their own gods, but we're sticking with the LORD forever. {4:6} The LORD's gonna gather up those who've been scattered and afflicted, making 'em strong again. {4:7} He's gonna make the weak into a remnant and the distant ones into a strong nation. The LORD's gonna rule over 'em from Mount Zion forever. {4:8} And you, tower of the flock, stronghold of Jerusalem, your power's coming back, along with your kingdom. {4:9} So why you crying out? Ain't there a king in charge? Your advisors may be gone, but it's just labor pains before something new's born. {4:10} It's gonna be rough, like giving birth, 'cause you're heading out of the city to Babylon. But that's where the LORD's gonna save you from your enemies. {4:11} And now all these nations wanna mess with you, looking to defile you. {4:12} But they don't know what the LORD's planning. He's gonna gather 'em up like sheaves on the threshing floor. {4:13} So get ready to rise up, daughter of Zion, 'cause you're gonna be tough as iron, smashing through your enemies. And everything they've gained? Yeah, it's gonna belong to the LORD, ruler of the whole earth!

{5:1} Okay, listen up, squad! We're under siege, and they're gonna smack the judge of Israel right in the face. {5:2} But yo, Bethlehem Ephratah, even though you're small compared to the rest, out of you will come the big boss ruler of Israel, straight from ancient times. {5:3} He's gonna let them have it until the time comes for the birth of the baby mama; then his peeps will come back to the children of Israel. {5:4} And when he steps up, he's gonna be powered by the LORD, representing big time, all the way to the ends of the earth. {5:5} This dude's gonna bring peace, even when the Assyrians roll in, we'll rally against them with seven shepherds and eight top dogs. {5:6} We're gonna wreck Assyria and Nimrod's land, saving ourselves from the Assyrians when they come our way. {5:7} And the remaining crew of Jacob will spread out, blessing folks like dew and rain, no waiting around for anyone. {5:8} Jacob's leftovers among the nations will be fierce, like a lion among other animals, tearing stuff up with no one to stop them. {5:9} They'll lay the smackdown on their enemies, cutting them off for good. {5:10} When that day comes, I'm wiping out your horses and chariots, toppling your cities and strongholds. {5:11} Say goodbye to your witchcraft and soothsayers, your idols and statues – all gone. {5:12} Your groves will be uprooted, your cities destroyed. {5:13} And I'll unleash my fury on the nations like they've never seen before.

{6:1} Now, listen up! The LORD's calling you out to stand up for what's right, to let the hills hear your voice. {6:2} Mountains, get ready to hear the LORD's beef with His people; He's got some issues with Israel, and He's gonna hash it out. {6:3} My people, what have I done to you? How have I worn you out? Tell me. {6:4} Remember how I brought you out of Egypt, how I sent Moses, Aaron, and Miriam ahead of you. {6:5} Remember Balak and Balaam, and how they tried to curse you but failed? That's how righteous the LORD is. {6:6} So, how do I approach the LORD, show respect to the Most High? Burnt offerings? Year-old calves? {6:7} Is He impressed by a bunch of rams or gallons of oil? Should I offer up my firstborn for my sins? Nah, man. {6:8} The LORD's already laid it out for you – do what's right, show mercy, and walk humbly with God. {6:9} The LORD's calling out to the city, and the wise will listen up. {6:10} Are there still crooked treasures in the homes of the wicked? {6:11} Are they still cheating with false measures and deceitful scales? {6:12} 'Cause the rich are full of violence, the people are lying left and right. {6:13} So, brace yourselves – I'm gonna make you sick and desolate because of your sins. {6:14} You'll eat but never be satisfied, you'll reach out but never grab hold; what you do manage to grab, I'll hand over to the sword. {6:15} You'll sow, but never reap; tread olives, but never anoint yourselves; and though there's sweet wine, you won't drink any. {6:16} You're following the same messed up ways as Omri and Ahab's crew, so get ready for some serious consequences.

{7:1} Dang, I'm feeling low! Like when you're hoping for a bunch of summer fruit, but there's barely anything left to snack on. My soul's craving that first ripe fruit, but it's nowhere to be found. {7:2} The good dudes are gone, man! Ain't nobody upright anymore. They're all out here scheming, hunting down their own brothers like it's some kind of game. {7:3} They're getting all evil with both hands, you feel me? The big shots, the judges, they're all about that reward, and they're not hiding it either. It's like they're wrapping up their wickedness as a gift or something. {7:4} Even the so-called "best" among them is like a prickly bush, and the ones who seem upright are sharper than a thorn hedge. Their day of reckoning is coming, and they're gonna be freaking out big time. {7:5} Don't trust anyone, man. Keep your guard up, even with your closest homies. {7:6} 'Cause it's a messed-up world where sons disrespect their fathers, daughters turn against their mothers, and even family members become enemies. {7:7} But me? I'm looking to the man upstairs. I'll wait it out for my God, 'cause I know He's got my back. {7:8} Don't get too happy when I'm down, haters. 'Cause when I fall, I'm bouncing back, and even in my darkest moments, the man upstairs is my guiding light. {7:9} I'll take whatever punishment I've got coming 'cause I messed up, but I know my God's gonna come through for me. He's gonna bring me out into the light, and I'll see His justice. {7:10} And when my enemies see it go down, they're gonna be ashamed, especially the ones who dared to ask, "Where's your God now?" They'll be trampled down like dirt in the streets. {7:11} When it's time to rebuild, the haters won't have a say anymore. {7:12} And when that day comes, my God's gonna come through for me, from every direction, even from Assyria and all those fortified cities. {7:13} But let's be real, the land's gonna be a mess because of the junk people are pulling. {7:14} Take care of your people, God, the ones you've chosen. They're out here solo, like sheep in the woods. Let them chill in the lush pastures like in the good old days. {7:15} Show us some crazy stuff, like you did back in the Egypt days. {7:16} The nations are gonna see all this and be shook. They'll be speechless, trembling in fear of our God. {7:17} They'll be crawling in the dirt like snakes, scared out of their minds because of the power of our God. {7:18} Seriously, who's like our God? He forgives our mess-ups, doesn't hold onto grudges forever, 'cause showing mercy is His thing. {7:19} He's gonna give us another chance, have pity on us, and wipe out all our screw-ups. He's tossing our sins into the deepest part of the ocean. {7:20} That's a promise He made to our ancestors way back when, and He's gonna stick to it, showing love to Jacob and keeping His word to Abraham.

Nahum

✦✦✦

{1:1} So, there's this heavy news about Nineveh, straight from Nahum the Elkoshite's vision book. {1:2} God's got major FOMO, and he's all about revenge; he's gonna take out his anger on his enemies big time. {1:3} God's not quick to rage, but when he does, watch out! He's got the power to shake things up, even control the weather. {1:4} He can calm the seas and dry up rivers like it's nothing, leaving places like Bashan, Carmel, and Lebanon feeling parched. {1:5} Mountains tremble, hills melt, and the whole earth gets scorched in his presence. {1:6} Nobody can stand up to his anger; it's like a wildfire, tearing everything down in its path. {1:7} But for those who trust in him, God's a safe haven in tough times; he's got their backs. {1:8} But for the wicked, it's gonna be like a flood wiping them out, with darkness hot on their heels. {1:9} Don't even try to mess with God; he'll wipe you out completely, and there won't be a second chance. {1:10} Those who act wickedly, thinking they're tough, are gonna get burned up like dry stubble. {1:11} There are some evil schemers out there, but they're gonna get what's coming to them. {1:12} Even if they seem quiet and harmless, they'll get taken down when God comes through. {1:13} God's gonna set people free from oppression and break their chains for good. {1:14} Nineveh's gonna get wrecked so bad, they won't even be remembered. {1:15} But for Judah, there's good news on the horizon; keep the faith and celebrate, 'cause the wicked are gonna be history.

{2:1} The one bringing destruction is on the move, so brace yourself and get ready for battle. {2:2} God's turned his back on Jacob and Israel 'cause they've been totally emptied out and left in ruins. {2:3} The warriors are decked out in red, with flaming chariots causing chaos everywhere. {2:4} Chariots are gonna be racing through the streets like lightning bolts, creating chaos everywhere. {2:5} The enemies will stumble, rushing to defend themselves, but they won't stand a chance. {2:6} Gates will be opened, and palaces will crumble. {2:7} The city's gonna be overrun, with everyone fleeing in fear. {2:8} Nineveh might seem strong, but they're gonna run when things get tough. {2:9} Take whatever riches you can, 'cause Nineveh's gonna be left empty and desolate. {2:10} The city's gonna be a total wreck, and everyone's gonna be freaking out. {2:11} Once a place of power, now it's just a ghost town. {2:12} God's against Nineveh, and he's gonna tear down everything they've built. {2:13} The enemy's gonna get burned, and their messengers won't be heard from again.

{3:1} Woe to Nineveh, the city soaked in lies and robbery; the looters won't quit. {3:2} There'll be the sound of whips, rattling wheels, and horses galloping; chaos everywhere. {3:3} The soldiers will be armed to the teeth, and there'll be bodies everywhere. {3:4} It's payback time for Nineveh's wickedness, and they're gonna be exposed for all to see. {3:5} God's gonna shame them and make them a laughingstock. {3:6} They'll be covered in filth and disgrace. {3:7} Anyone who looks at them will run away in horror. {3:8} Nineveh might've been a big deal once, but now they're doomed. {3:9} Their allies won't be able to save them; they'll be taken captive. {3:10} They'll be drunk with fear and confusion. {3:11} Their defenses will crumble like fig trees in a storm. {3:12} People will scatter, and there'll be no one to gather them up. {3:13} There's no healing for Nineveh's wounds; their destruction is permanent. {3:14} They'll face fire and swords, total devastation. {3:15} They'll be overrun like locusts, leaving nothing behind. {3:16} Their leaders will disappear like bugs, fleeing when things get tough. {3:17} The rulers will be useless, and the people will scatter. {3:18} There's no escaping the consequences of their wickedness.

Habakkuk

+++

{1:1} Yo, so peep this heavy revelation from Habakkuk the prophet. {1:2} Dude's straight-up asking God, "How long you gonna ignore my cries for help, especially when I'm seeing all this violence and you're not doing squat to stop it?" {1:3} He's like, "Why you gotta show me all this messed-up stuff, God? It's like violence and chaos everywhere I look, and nobody's doing anything about it." {1:4} And it's wild 'cause the law's just sitting there gathering dust, and justice? Forget about it! The bad guys are all over the righteous ones, and the courts? They're just spitting out wrong judgments left and right. {1:5} And yo, check this out, God's like, "Watch closely, 'cause I'm 'bout to do something so crazy, you won't even believe it when you hear about it." {1:6} He's bringing in the Chaldeans, this hardcore nation, to straight-up take over land that ain't even theirs. {1:7} These Chaldeans? They're no joke, man. They're fierce and terrifying, and they don't need anyone to tell them how to do their thing. {1:8} Their horses are faster than leopards, and their horsemen? They're coming from all over, swooping in like eagles ready to chow down. {1:9} They're all about violence, sucking it up like a strong east wind, and they're gonna gather up captives like they're scooping sand. {1:10} They're gonna mock kings, laugh at princes, and straight-up trash every fortress they come across. {1:11} But then they're gonna get cocky and start thinking it's all because of their own strength. {1:12} And Habakkuk's like, "God, you're eternal, man! We ain't gonna be wiped out by these punks. You're using them to dish out some tough love, but you've got this." {1:13} He's saying, "God, you're too pure to even look at evil, so why are you chilling while these treacherous dudes go after the righteous?" {1:14} Like, are we just gonna be like fish in a net, with no one to protect us? {1:15} These Chaldeans? They're treating their weapons like gods, worshiping their strength and success. {1:16} They're all about their weapons, thinking that's where their power and prosperity come from. {1:17} They're gonna keep on slaughtering nations without a care in the world.

{2:1} So, Habakkuk's like, "I'm gonna wait and see what God's gotta say about all this. I'll be watching and waiting for his response." {2:2} And then God's like, "Write this down plain and simple so everybody can get it, and they better run with it once they do." {2:3} He's saying, "This vision might take a minute, but it's gonna happen, so just chill and wait for it." {2:4} And then God drops some truth: "If you're full of yourself, you ain't gonna make it. But if you're righteous, you're gonna live by faith." {2:5} And then he calls out those who party too hard and get all proud and greedy, never satisfied and always wanting more, even if it means stepping on others. {2:6} He's like, "Everyone's gonna clown on this guy, saying, 'Woe to the one who's all about that greed and luxury! How long you gonna keep it up?'" {2:7} He's saying, "You're gonna get blindsided real quick, and your enemies are gonna take everything you got." {2:8} 'Cause you know what? You've been messing with too many nations, shedding blood left and right. {2:9} Woe to the dude who's all about building his empire, thinking he's invincible! {2:10} You're bringing shame on your own house, man, taking out whole nations and messing with your own soul. {2:11} Even the very stones and beams are gonna cry out against you for all the evil you've done. {2:12} Woe to the guy who's building his fortune on bloodshed and wickedness! {2:13} God's like, "You think you're making progress, but you're just spinning your wheels, man. It's all gonna be for nothing." {2:14} 'Cause one day, the whole earth's gonna know about God's glory, covering it like the ocean covers the sea. {2:15} Woe to the one who's getting others wasted just to take advantage of them! {2:16} Your glory's gonna be turned to shame, and God's gonna make you pay for your wickedness. {2:17} 'Cause all the violence you've unleashed is gonna come crashing down on you, like the terror of Lebanon, making everyone afraid. {2:18} Seriously, what's the point of idols? They're just dumb statues that can't do anything. {2:19} Woe to the fool who thinks a lifeless statue can teach or save them! {2:20} But God? He's up in his temple, and everyone better quiet down and show some respect.

{3:1} Habakkuk's dropping a prayer, straight fire, on Shigionoth. {3:2} He's saying, "God, I've heard what you're about, and it's intense. But show up again, man! Show us what you're made of and remember to bring the mercy." {3:3} He's describing God's grand entrance, like he's rolling in from Teman and Mount Paran, all majestic and covered in glory. {3:4} His brightness is like the sun, and he's got power just oozing from him. {3:5} Pestilence and burning coals? That's just God's entourage. {3:6} He's measuring up the earth, scattering nations, and shaking mountains like they're nothing. {3:7} He's seeing Cushan and Midian trembling before him. {3:8} Was God mad at the rivers or something? Nah, he's just rolling in on his chariots of salvation. {3:9} He's got his bow ready, keeping his word, and splitting the earth with rivers. {3:10} Mountains are shaking, waters are overflowing, and the deep's shouting for joy. {3:11} Even the sun and moon are standing still at God's command, stunned by his power. {3:12} He's marching through lands, threshing nations, and showing up with a whole army. {3:13} He's coming to save his people, smashing heads and exposing wickedness to the core. {3:14} He's taking down villages and scattering enemies like a whirlwind. {3:15} He's walking through the sea like it's no big deal. {3:16} Habakkuk's like, "Yo, when I heard all this, I was shaking in my boots. But I know that when trouble comes, I can find rest in God." {3:17} Even if everything goes wrong, even if there's no food or livestock, he's still gonna rejoice in God. {3:18} 'Cause God's his strength, giving him the skills to navigate life's highs and lows. {3:19} The LORD God's got his back, making him as nimble as a deer, ready to conquer any challenge. And yo, pass me them stringed instruments 'cause I gotta jam out to this.

Zephaniah

✦✦✦

{1:1} Yo, listen up, this is the word from the man Zephaniah, son of Cushi, grandson of Gedaliah, great-grandson of Amariah, and great-great-grandson of Hizkiah, back in the days of Josiah, son of Amon, king of Judah. {1:2} God's straight-up saying, "I'm gonna wipe everything off the map, no joke." {1:3} Humans, animals, birds, fish, you name it, it's all getting wiped out. And anyone hanging with the wicked? They're getting cut off too. {1:4} God's throwing down on Judah and Jerusalem, taking out all traces of Baal worship and those shady priests. {1:5} He's after the ones worshipping the stars, swearing by both God and some other deity named Malcham. {1:6} And those who turned away from God or never even bothered to seek him? They're in for it too. {1:7} So everyone better hush up and show some respect, 'cause judgment day's coming, and God's got a big sacrifice planned. {1:8} When that day hits, the high and mighty are gonna get theirs, along with anyone rocking weird outfits. {1:9} God's taking down the ones living large on violence and deception, no exceptions. {1:10} And when that day rolls in, it's gonna be chaos and mayhem, with cries echoing from every corner. {1:11} Maktesh, you're gonna feel it hard 'cause all your big shots are getting wiped out, along with anyone swimming in silver. {1:12} God's gonna light up Jerusalem with a search party, taking out the ones chilling in their comfort zones, thinking God won't do a thing. {1:13} Their stuff? It's gonna be up for grabs, their houses left deserted, their dreams of prosperity turning to dust. {1:14} The big showdown's coming, and it's gonna hit hard, with the tough guys shedding tears left and right. {1:15} It's gonna be a day of reckoning, total chaos and darkness, with no escape from God's wrath. {1:16} The cities will be under siege, the towers crumbling, and the alarm bells ringing loud and clear. {1:17} People will be stumbling around like they're blind, paying for their sins with their lives. {1:18} Money won't save them from God's fury; he's gonna burn it all down, clearing the land in record time.

{2:1} So, everyone better come together, especially you nation that's been getting the cold shoulder. {2:2} Get your act together before it's too late, before God's anger blows up in your face. {2:3} If you're humble and seeking God's way, maybe you'll catch a break when the storm hits. {2:4} Gaza's gonna be a ghost town, and Ashkelon? Total wasteland. {2:5} Oh, and you Philistines? God's got a bone to pick with you too, wiping you out completely. {2:6} Your coastal towns? They'll be for shepherds and their flocks, nothing more. {2:7} But hey, there's hope for the remnant of Judah; they'll find shelter and freedom in God's presence. {2:8} Moab and Ammon, you've been talking trash about God's people? Big mistake. {2:9} God's gonna turn you into a barren wasteland, a cautionary tale for the ages. {2:10} You brought this on yourselves with your pride and arrogance against God's people. {2:11} God's gonna show you who's boss, making the whole world bow down to him. {2:12} Even Ethiopia's gonna feel God's wrath. {2:13} Assyria, you're next on God's hit list, with Nineveh becoming a ghost town. {2:14} Flocks will roam where cities once stood, with birds nesting in the ruins, singing songs of desolation. {2:15} That once-proud city will become a wasteland, a place for wild animals, a symbol of shame for all who pass by.

{3:1} Shame on you, you corrupt city, oppressing everyone in sight. {3:2} You ignored God's warnings, refused to change your ways, and kept your distance from him. {3:3} Your leaders are like hungry lions, your judges like wolves waiting to pounce. Your prophets? They're full of hot air, and your priests? They've trashed the sacred spaces. {3:4} But God's still there, doing what's right every single day, while the wicked just keep on sinning without shame. {3:5} God's brought down nations, turned their cities to rubble, but you still haven't learned your lesson. {3:6} God gave you a chance to shape up, but you just kept on corrupting everything you touched. {3:7} So now, you better wait on God, 'cause when he finally moves, it's gonna be game over for everyone. {3:8} God's gonna round up the nations, bring them all together, and pour out his wrath on them, burning up the whole earth. {3:9} But for those who turn back to God, he's gonna give them a fresh start, with a new language and a renewed purpose. {3:10} Even the farthest corners of the earth will come back to God, offering their worship and praise. {3:11} And on that day, you won't be ashamed of your past, 'cause God's taking out the ones who strutted around in pride, humbling them before his holy mountain. {3:12} God's gonna leave behind a humble and faithful remnant, trusting in him alone. {3:13} They'll be people of integrity, speaking the truth without deceit, living in peace without fear. {3:14} So let's sing and shout, 'cause God's taken away our punishment and defeated our enemies. {3:15} With God in our midst, there's no more fear, no more darkness, only joy and peace. {3:16} So don't be afraid, Jerusalem, and don't give up, Zion. {3:17} God's power is with us, saving us, rejoicing over us with love and singing. {3:18} He's gathering up all who've suffered and been shamed, giving them a reason to celebrate. {3:19} So get ready for a turnaround, 'cause God's gonna rescue the oppressed and bring them honor and praise everywhere they go. {3:20} And when that day comes, when God brings us back from exile, he'll make us known and praised throughout the world, showing everyone his power and love.

Haggai

✦✦✦

{1:1} So, like, in the second year of Darius the king, on the first day of the sixth month, Haggai the prophet dropped some truth bombs to Zerubbabel, the Judah governor, and Joshua, the high priest, saying, {1:2} "Yo, the big man upstairs says this crew keeps saying it ain't time to rebuild his crib. {1:3} But then Haggai came in hot with more words from the big man, saying, {1:4} "Seriously, you're chilling in your fancy houses while God's house is a dump? {1:5} So, like, the big man says, 'Check yourselves.' {1:6} You're hustling hard but getting squat, eating and drinking but still hungry and thirsty, dressing up but staying cold, and earning wages only to watch them disappear like they're going into a bag with holes. {1:7} The big man's like, 'Seriously, think about your ways, guys.' {1:8} He's saying, 'Get off your butts, gather some wood, and build my house, and I'll be stoked, and I'll get some glory out of it,' says the big man. {1:9} You're expecting big things, but it's all coming up short, and when you bring it home, it's like the big man just blows it away. Why? 'Cause his house is a wreck, and you're all about your own cribs. {1:10} So now, the sky's holding back the dew, and the earth's holding back the crops. {1:11} And the big man's calling for a drought, hitting everything from the crops to the livestock to the daily grind. {1:12} Then Zerubbabel, Joshua, and the crew got real and started working on God's house, fearing the big man. {1:13} And Haggai, speaking for the big man, was like, 'I got your back,' says the big man. {1:14} And the big man pumped up Zerubbabel, Joshua, and the rest of the crew, and they got busy building the house of the big man. {1:15} This all went down on the twenty-fourth day of the sixth month, second year of Darius.

{2:1} Fast forward to the seventh month, twenty-first day, Haggai's back with another message from the big man, saying, {2:2} "Time to talk to Zerubbabel, Joshua, and the rest of the squad, asking, {2:3} 'Who's still around from back in the day when this house was lit? And how does it look now? Like trash, right?' {2:4} But the big man's like, 'Stay strong, Zerubbabel, Joshua, and crew, and get to work, 'cause I got your back,' says the big man. {2:5} 'Remember the deal we made back in Egypt? My spirit's still with you, so don't trip.' {2:6} 'Cause soon, I'm gonna shake up everything, the heavens, the earth, the sea, and the dry land. {2:7} All the nations are gonna feel it, and everyone's gonna want a piece of this house, and I'm gonna fill it with glory,' says the big man. {2:8} 'Oh, and by the way, I own all the silver and gold,' says the big man. {2:9} 'The new house's gonna be even more lit than the old one, and it's gonna be all about peace,' says the big man. {2:10} Fast forward again to the twenty-fourth day of the ninth month, second year of Darius, Haggai's back with more from the big man, saying, {2:11} "Yo, ask the priests about the law, like if touching holy stuff makes other stuff holy." {2:12} So, like, if someone's unclean touches stuff, does it make it unclean? And the priests are like, "Yeah, duh." {2:13} And Haggai's like, "Exactly! That's how the big man sees you guys and your work, all unclean." {2:14} And now, let's think back to before we even laid a stone in God's house. {2:15} From then till now, things have been rough, with harvests cut in half and work going to waste. {2:16} I've hit you with everything from blight to hail, but you still haven't turned back to me, says the big man. {2:17} So, like, from the day we laid the foundation of God's house, let's think about it, okay? {2:18} Are your crops still in the barn? Are your vines, fig trees, and olive trees still bare? From today, I'm gonna start blessing you. {2:19} And then, on the twenty-fourth day of the month, the big man's back with more for Zerubbabel, saying, {2:20} "I'm gonna shake things up, overthrow kingdoms, and bring down chariots and horses. {2:21} But Zerubbabel, my dude, I'm gonna make you a boss signet ring, 'cause I've chosen you," says the big man.

Zechariah

✦✦✦

{1:1} So, like, in the second year of Darius, in the eighth month, Zechariah got a message from the big man upstairs, saying, {1:2} "Yo, the big man's been seriously ticked off with your ancestors." {1:3} So tell them, 'The big man's saying, 'Turn to me, and I'll turn to you,' says the big man. {1:4} Don't be like your ancestors who ignored the prophets' warnings to turn from their wicked ways," but they didn't listen, says the big man. {1:5} "Where are those ancestors now? Do the prophets live forever?" {1:6} "My words and laws given through the prophets did get through to your ancestors, and they admitted that they got what they deserved," says the big man. {1:7} On the twenty-fourth day of the eleventh month, in the second year of Darius, another message came to Zechariah, saying, {1:8} "I had this wild vision of a dude riding a red horse among some myrtle trees in a valley, with red, speckled, and white horses behind him." {1:9} "So I asked, 'What's up with these?' And the angel told me, 'I'll clue you in.'" {1:10} "The dude among the myrtle trees said they're the big man's squad sent to check out the whole earth." {1:11} "They reported back, 'Everything's chill everywhere; it's all quiet.'" {1:12} "But then the angel was like, 'Yo, big man, how long are you gonna stay mad at Jerusalem and Judah? It's been seventy years already!'" {1:13} "And the big man responded with good and comforting words." {1:14} "So the angel was like, 'Spread the word: the big man's super protective of Jerusalem and Zion.'" {1:15} "He's mega ticked at the nations who messed with you when he was only a little upset." {1:16} "But now he's back in Jerusalem, ready to show mercy and rebuild his house," says the big man. {1:17} "Keep spreading the word: my cities will prosper, Zion will be comforted, and Jerusalem will be chosen again." {1:18} "Then I saw four horns, and I asked, 'What are those?' And the angel was like, 'Those horns scattered Judah, Israel, and Jerusalem.'" {1:19} "Then he showed me four carpenters, and I was like, 'What are they for?' And he said, 'They're here to scare off the horns that scattered Judah.'"

{2:1} "Now onto chapter two, I looked up again and saw a dude with a measuring line, and I was like, 'Where you going?' And he was like, 'I'm measuring Jerusalem to see how big it is.'" {2:2} "Then another angel went to meet him, telling him to spread the word that Jerusalem will be packed with people and animals, no walls needed, and the big man will be her fiery protection and glory." {2:3} "So, like, get out of Babylon, Zion, and free yourselves," says the big man. {2:4} "After all the suffering, the big man's sending me to the nations who messed with you; messing with you is like poking the big man in the eye." {2:5} "And when I shake my hand at them, they'll become slaves, and you'll know the big man sent me." {2:6} "So sing and celebrate, daughter of Zion, 'cause I'm coming to live among you," says the big man. {2:7} "And many nations will join the big man's crew, and they'll know the big man sent me to you." {2:8} "And the big man will claim Judah as his own in the holy land and pick Jerusalem again." {2:9} "Everyone better hush before the big man; he's rising up from his holy pad."

{3:1} So, like, there's Joshua the high priest, chilling with the angel of the big man upstairs, and Satan's lurking at his right, ready to throw shade. {3:2} Then the big man's like, "Nah, Satan, I rebuke you, man! Jerusalem's my pick, and Joshua here's like a fire survivor, saved from the flames." {3:3} Joshua's decked out in rags, but the big man's like, "Get those dirty threads off him and slap on some fresh gear. I'm wiping his slate clean and giving him a whole new wardrobe." {3:4-5} Then I'm like, "Yo, put a cool hat on him too," and they hook him up, and the angel's just chilling there. {3:6-7} And the angel's like, "Listen up, Joshua, if you walk the talk and keep my rules, you'll run the show in my crib and stroll among these angels." {3:8} "Hey, Joshua, and your crew, you guys are gonna blow minds. I'm bringing out my secret weapon, the BRANCH." {3:9} "Check out this stone I'm setting before Joshua, engraved with seven eyes. I'm wiping out the land's sin in a day." {3:10} "When that day comes, everyone will be living their best life, chilling under their vines and fig trees, no drama."

{4:1} Then the angel's back, jolting me awake like I just got pulled from a deep sleep. {4:2} He's like, "What do you see?" and I'm like, "A gold lampstand with seven lamps on it and two olive trees on either side." {4:3} And he's dropping wisdom, saying, "This is the big man's plan for Zerubbabel: not by power or strength, but by his spirit." {4:4} "Mountains, you think you're big? Not in Zerubbabel's way; he'll level you and bring out the cornerstone with shouts of 'Grace, grace!'" {4:5} "Zerubbabel's got this; he started the project, and he'll finish it. That's how you'll know the big man sent me." {4:6} "Don't sleep on small beginnings; Zerubbabel's got the vision, and those seven lamps are the big man's eyes, scanning the whole deal." {4:7} So I'm like, "What's with the olive trees?" {4:8} And he's like, "Those trees are the oil source, flowing through the golden pipes, bringing the juice." {4:9} "Those two are the big man's MVPs, holding it down for him worldwide."

{5:1} So, like, I turn around and check out the scene, and there's this freaky flying scroll, you know? {5:2} And the dude's like, "What's up? What do you see?" And I'm like, "Uh, there's this scroll, it's like twenty cubits long and ten cubits wide." {5:3} Then he's like, "That's the curse, man. It's going out to nail all the thieves and oath-breakers. No one's getting away with it." {5:4} "I'm sending it out," says the big man, "and it's crashing into the houses of thieves and those who lie in my name. It's wrecking everything in there, timber and stones alike." {5:5} Then the angel's like, "Hey, check this out," and I'm like, "What now?" {5:6} And he's like, "It's an ephah, representing all the shady stuff going on." {5:7-8} "Look, there's a lead weight on it, symbolizing wickedness," and he drops it in. {5:9}

Then I see two women with wings, like storks, lifting the ephah up, way high. {5:10} So I'm like, "Where are they taking it?" {5:11} And he's like, "They're setting up shop in Shinar, laying down roots there."

{6:1} And then I glance around again, and I see four chariots rolling out from between two brass mountains. {6:2-3} First one's got red horses, second one's black, third one's white, and the fourth one's got some mixed-color horses. {6:4} So I'm like, "What's the deal with these rides?" {6:5} And he's like, "Those are the heavenly spirits, doing their thing under the big man's orders." {6:6-7} "The black ones head north, then the white ones follow, and the mixed ones head south." {6:8-9} And he's like, "The ones heading north have settled the big man's spirit up there." {6:10} Then the big man's like, "Go get some peeps from Babylon, and go visit Josiah's house." {6:11} "Bring some bling and crown Joshua the high priest." {6:12} "Tell him he's the BRANCH, and he's gonna build the temple for the big man." {6:13} "He's not just building it; he's bringing the glory and ruling on his throne as a priest too, bringing peace." {6:14} "The crowns are for Helem, Tobijah, Jedaiah, and Hen, as a reminder in the big man's temple." {6:15} "Those from far away will come and help build the temple, and then you'll know it's the big man who sent me, but only if you listen up and obey his voice."

{7:1} So, like, in the fourth year of King Darius, the big man upstairs drops some knowledge on Zechariah on the fourth day of the ninth month, you feel me? {7:2-3} They sent some dudes to the house of God to pray and chat with the priests and prophets, asking, "Should we keep up this mourning routine in the fifth month, like we've been doing for years?" {7:4} Then the big man's like, "Tell everyone this," {7:5-6} "When you were fasting and mourning in the fifth and seventh months all those seventy years, were you really doing it for me, or just for yourselves?" {7:7} "Didn't you ignore the warnings of the past prophets when Jerusalem was doing well, thinking you were untouchable?" {7:8} More divine talk to Zechariah: "Here's the deal," {7:9-10} "You gotta do right by each other, show some compassion, and stop messing with the vulnerable." {7:11} But nah, they were stubborn and closed off, refusing to listen to reason. {7:12-13} They hardened their hearts, ignoring the law and the old prophets' words, which totally ticked off the big man. {7:14} So, the big man scattered them everywhere, leaving the land empty and desolate after them.

{8:1-2} The big man's like, "I'm super protective of Zion, you know? I'm back in Jerusalem's corner big time." {8:3} "Jerusalem's gonna be all about truth, and my mountain's gonna be super holy." {8:4} "Old folks will chill in the streets with their canes, and the city will be buzzing with kids playing." {8:5} "It might seem unreal to the few left, but it's all good in my eyes," says the big man. {8:6} "I'm gonna save my people from all directions, bring them back to Jerusalem, and they'll be my crew, living righteously." {8:7} "Stay strong, those of you who've been listening to the prophets since we laid down the temple's foundation." "The future's looking bright; prosperity's on the horizon." {8:8} "You've been a curse, but I'll turn it around; don't sweat it, just stay strong." {8:9} "Keep it real with your neighbors, bring peace and truth to your community; don't even think about stirring up trouble." {8:10} "Forget fasting; it's all about joy and celebration now. Love truth and peace." {8:11} "People from all over will be hyped to pray and seek the big man, even the strong nations will join in." {8:12} "In those days, ten people from different places will grab onto a Jew's coat, wanting in on that divine connection."

{9:1} Yo, peep this word from the big man in the land of Hadrach, with Damascus chilling. When everyone's eyes, even the tribes of Israel, are on the big man. {9:2} Hamath's in the mix too, along with Tyre and Sidon, thinking they're all smart. {9:3-4} But check it, Tyre's all about stacking cash, but the big man's gonna kick her to the curb and wreck her in the sea, burning her up. {9:5} Ashkelon and Gaza are gonna freak out, and Ekron's gonna be embarrassed because their king's gonna bite it, and Ashkelon's gonna be a ghost town. {9:6-7} Some random dude's gonna take over Ashdod, and the Philistines' arrogance is getting chopped down. {9:8} The big man's gonna protect his turf from invaders, and no oppressors are getting through anymore, 'cause he's watching. {9:9} So, Zion and Jerusalem, get hyped! Your king's rolling in, humble and bringing salvation on a donkey. {9:10} No more war machines for Ephraim and Jerusalem; peace talks for everyone! {9:11-12} The big man's sealing the deal with his covenant, setting prisoners free. {9:13-14} Judah's gonna be flexing with bows, and Ephraim's sons are gonna lay the smackdown on Greece. {9:15} The big man's gonna defend his crew, they're gonna wreck enemies with sling stones, party hard, and be filled up like bowls on the altar. {9:16} They'll be the big man's favorite people, shining like jewels in his land. {9:17} The big man's goodness and beauty are off the charts, and there's gonna be plenty of food and drink to go around.

{10:1} So, hit up the big man for some rain when it's dry, 'cause he's gonna hook it up with showers, blessing the fields. {10:2} Those idols and diviners ain't saying squat; they're just spinning lies and giving false hope. {10:3} The big man's ticked at the bad leaders, but he's showing love to Judah, making them warriors. {10:4-5} They're gonna come out swinging, ready to stomp on their enemies, 'cause the big man's got their backs. {10:6} Judah and Joseph are gonna get swole again, 'cause the big man's feeling merciful; they'll be back in the game like they never left. {10:7-8} Ephraim's gonna be feeling pumped, and their kids are gonna be partying, all because of the big man. {10:9-10} He's gonna scatter them among the nations, but they'll remember him, and come back stronger. {10:11} The big man's gonna dry up rivers and crush the pride of Assyria and Egypt. {10:12} He's gonna empower them to walk tall in his name, you feel?

{11:1} Yo, Lebanon, open up your doors 'cause there's gonna be some fire burning up your cedars. {11:2} Fir trees, start howling 'cause the mighty cedar has fallen, and the big shots are getting wrecked. Oaks of Bashan, get ready to cry 'cause your forest party's over. {11:3} Shepherds, you're gonna hear some wailing 'cause your glory days are done. Young lions, start roaring 'cause Jordan's pride is toast. {11:4} The big man upstairs says, "Feed the flock of the slaughter." {11:5} These greedy owners are killing them off and not feeling guilty, even thanking the big man for making them rich. And their own shepherds don't give a darn. {11:6} The big man's done feeling sorry for them; he's handing them over to their neighbors and kings to wreck the place. {11:7} But hey, you poor ones, I got your back. I took two sticks, Beauty and Bands, and looked after the flock. {11:8} I ditched three lousy shepherds in one month 'cause they made me sick, and I made them sick too. {11:9} So I said, "No more feeding for you." Let the ones who die, die, and those who need to go, go. The rest can feast on each other. {11:10} Then I snapped my staff, Beauty, to break the deal I made with everyone. {11:11} And just like that, the deal was off, and the poor folks who trusted me knew it was the real deal. {11:12} I asked them to pay up, and they tossed me thirty pieces of silver. {11:13} The big man said, "Throw it to the potter, that's what they valued me at." So I chucked the silver to the potter in the big man's house. {11:14} Then I snapped my other stick, Bands, to break the bond between Judah and Israel. {11:15} The big man said, "Get ready for a foolish shepherd." {11:16} 'Cause I'm bringing in a shepherd who won't give a hoot about the lost, won't care for the young, won't heal the hurt, or feed the hungry. He's just gonna feast on the fat ones and tear them apart. {11:17} Woe to that sorry excuse for a shepherd who ditches the flock! His arm's gonna be useless, and his eye's gonna be blind as a bat.

{12:1} Listen up, Israel, 'cause here's what the big man's saying, the one who made the heavens and the earth and crafted our spirits. {12:2} Get this, Jerusalem's gonna be a real nerve-racker for everyone around, especially when they're attacking Judah and Jerusalem. {12:3} Jerusalem's gonna be a heavy stone for everyone; trying to mess with it will end up breaking them, even if the whole world gangs up on it. {12:4} When that day comes, I'm gonna freak out every horse and rider, and I'll be watching Judah's back, blinding every horse. {12:5} The leaders of Judah will be feeling pumped, knowing Jerusalem's got their back, all thanks to the big man. {12:6} They're gonna blaze through their enemies like a wildfire, burning them up on every side, and Jerusalem will be back where it belongs. {12:7} The big man's gonna save Judah first, so the house of David and Jerusalem don't get all high and mighty over them. {12:8} When that day comes, even the weakest among them will be as strong as David, and the house of David will be as mighty as the big man's angels. {12:9} And when that day comes, I'm gonna take down every nation that tries to mess with Jerusalem. {12:10} I'll pour out grace and mercy on the house of David and Jerusalem, and they'll see me, the one they pierced, and they'll mourn for me like they've lost their own child, grieving bitterly. {12:11} There'll be mourning in Jerusalem like the mourning at Hadadrimmon in the valley of Megiddo. {12:12-13} Every family will mourn separately, with the house of David and Nathan, Levi and Shimei, each on their own. {12:14} Every family will mourn separately, with their wives apart.

{13:1} When that day rolls around, there's gonna be a clean-up fountain open to the house of David and the folks in Jerusalem, for washing away sins and getting rid of the grime. {13:2} And let me tell ya, when that day hits, I'm wiping out all the idol names from the land; no one will even remember them anymore. Plus, I'm kicking out the phony prophets and those nasty spirits from the neighborhood. {13:3} And get this, if anyone tries to keep on prophesying lies, even their own parents are gonna call them out and shut them down. They won't even let them live when they start spewing falsehoods in the name of the big man upstairs. {13:4} So when that day comes, those prophets are gonna be embarrassed about every vision they cooked up; they won't even bother wearing those rough garments to deceive anymore. {13:5} They'll be like, "Nah, I'm not a prophet, just a regular dude. I learned how to herd cattle since I was a kid." {13:6} And someone's gonna ask, "Hey, what happened to your hands?" And they'll be like, "Oh, just some wounds I got hanging out with my pals." {13:7} Time to wake up, sword, and get ready to take down my shepherd buddy, says the big man. Strike down the shepherd, and the sheep are gonna scatter, and I'll be dealing with the little ones myself. {13:8} And let me tell ya, in every corner of the land, two-thirds are gonna get wiped out and bite the dust, but the other third is gonna make it through. {13:9} I'll put that third through the fire, refining them like silver and testing them like gold. They'll call on my name, and I'll answer; they'll be my people, and they'll call me their God.

{14:1} Look out, 'cause the big man's day is coming, and your loot's gonna be divided right in front of you. {14:2} 'Cause I'm rallying all the nations against Jerusalem for a showdown; they'll take the city, loot the houses, and mistreat the women. Half the city will end up in captivity, but the rest won't be wiped out. {14:3} Then the big man's gonna step in and throw down with those nations, just like in the old battles. {14:4} He'll plant his feet on the Mount of Olives, splitting it down the middle towards the east and west, making a massive valley. Half the mountain will shift north, and half south. {14:5} When that goes down, you better bolt to the mountain valley 'cause it's gonna stretch all the way to Azal. You'll flee like you did during King Uzziah's earthquake days, and the big man and his crew will show up. {14:6} And on that day, it won't be bright or dark; it'll be a unique day known only to the big man, not day or night, but it'll light up when evening rolls in. {14:7} Living waters will flow from Jerusalem, heading towards both seas, running year-round, even in summer and winter. {14:8} The big man's gonna rule the whole earth, and there'll only be one king in charge, and everyone will know his name. {14:9} The land's gonna flatten out from Geba to Rimmon south of Jerusalem, and it'll be raised up and settled, from Benjamin's gate to the first gate, the corner gate, and all the way to the king's winepresses. {14:10-11} People will live there without fear of destruction; Jerusalem will be a safe place to call home. {14:12} But anyone who tries to mess with Jerusalem will face a terrible fate; their flesh will rot while they're still standing, their eyes will rot in their sockets, and their tongues will rot in their mouths. {14:13} And when that day comes, there'll be chaos from the big man among them; they'll turn against each other, neighbor against neighbor. {14:14} And Judah's gonna throw down in Jerusalem, snagging all the wealth from the surrounding nations in abundance. {14:15} And the animals in those tents will be hit with the same plague as their owners. {14:16} And every surviving nation that came against Jerusalem will have to show up every year to worship the big man, the LORD of hosts, and celebrate the feast of tabernacles. {14:17} And if any families refuse to show up in Jerusalem to worship the big man, no rain for them. {14:18} And if Egypt doesn't show up, they'll get hit with the same plague the big man will dish out to those who skip the feast of tabernacles. {14:19} That's gonna be Egypt's punishment and the punishment for all the nations who skip out on the feast. {14:20} On that day, even the horse bells will ring out "Holiness unto the LORD," and the pots in the LORD's house will be as sacred as the bowls at the altar. {14:21} Every pot in Jerusalem and Judah will be sacred to the big man, and anyone who sacrifices will come and cook in them. And on that day, there won't be a single Canaanite in the big man's house.

Malachi

✚✚✚

{1:1} So, like, this is the message from the big man, Malachi, to Israel. {1:2} He's all like, "Yo, I've totally loved you guys." And they're all, "Um, how exactly?" And he's like, "Dude, remember how I favored Jacob over Esau, his bro?" {1:3} "Yeah, I totally dissed Esau, left his mountains a wreck, and let wild animals take over his turf." {1:4} "And check this out, Edom's like, 'We'll bounce back,' but I'm all, 'Nah, I'll wreck your rebuild plans.' They'll be known as the bad guys forever." {1:5} "And you'll see, and you'll be like, 'Wow, the big man's reputation is lit all the way from Israel's borders.'" {1:6} "So, you know, a son respects his dad, and a servant fears his boss, right? But you priests diss me and act clueless." {1:7} "You're offering up junk on my altar, then acting like it's no biggie. My table's sacred, and you're treating it like trash." {1:8} "Seriously, if you offer trash to your governor, would he be cool with it? Nope, didn't think so." {1:9} "So, like, ask God to cut you some slack, 'cause you're the reason things are messed up. But will he even listen? Doubt it." {1:10} "You're not even bothered to shut the temple doors for free. I'm so over you; I won't accept your offerings." {1:11} "But hey, my name's gonna be huge among the Gentiles, and they'll be offering incense and legit sacrifices everywhere, showing me respect." {1:12} "But you've totally trashed my rep by dissing my table and the food on it. You're calling my offerings garbage, which is totally disrespectful." {1:13} "You're like, 'Ugh, this is so boring,' and you're bringing lame offerings. Seriously? You think I'm gonna accept that?" {1:14} "Anyone who tries to scam me by vowing to give me something worthless is in for a rude awakening. I'm a boss, and my name's feared by all."

{2:1} "Listen up, priests, this is for you. {2:2} If you don't start showing respect and giving props to my name, I'm gonna curse you and your blessings. Actually, I already have, 'cause you're not taking this seriously." {2:3} "I'm gonna mess up your future and smear dung all over your faces, even at your fancy feasts, and you'll be hauled away with it." {2:4} "But remember, I made a covenant with Levi, and he respected me and brought peace. {2:5} He spoke truth and walked with integrity, turning people away from sin." {2:6} "Priests should be wise and teach the law, but you've gone off track and led many astray, ruining Levi's legacy." {2:7} "So, yeah, you've become a joke, 'cause you haven't followed my ways and played favorites with the law." {2:8} "That's why I've made you a laughingstock; you've ignored my ways and shown favoritism in the law." {2:9} "We all have the same dad, and one God created us all, so why are you betraying each other and breaking our ancestors' covenant?" {2:10} "Judah's messed up big time, marrying foreign gods and disrespecting what I hold sacred." {2:11} "Anyone who does this, big shot or small fry, is getting cut off from Jacob's crew, even if they offer sacrifices to me." {2:12} "You're crying and wailing, but I'm not listening 'cause you're treating your wives like dirt. She's your partner and part of our deal." {2:13} "You're all fake crying at the altar, but it means nothing to me; I won't accept your offerings." {2:14} "You're asking why things are going wrong? Because you've betrayed your spouses, dissed my covenant, and think doing evil is cool." {2:15} "You're praising the arrogant and letting evil thrive, even testing my patience." {2:16} "But those who respect me talk it out and look out for each other. I've got their backs, like a dad with his loyal kid." {2:17} "You've worn me out with your nonsense, acting like evil's cool and questioning my sense of justice."

{3:1} "I'm sending my messenger to pave the way, and the big boss you're waiting for will show up unexpectedly. The messenger of our covenant will arrive, and you'll be stoked." {3:2} "But who's gonna handle his arrival? He's coming in hot, like a refiner's fire, and he's all about purifying and cleaning house." {3:3} "He'll purify the priests like silver and gold, so they can offer righteous sacrifices." {3:4} "Then Judah and Jerusalem's offerings will finally be pleasing to me, like back in the good old days." {3:5} "But I'm also gonna judge the sorcerers, adulterers, liars, and those who exploit the vulnerable. They better watch out." {3:6} "I'm the same big boss, never changing. That's why you guys are still around, despite your antics." {3:7} "But you've been ditching my rules since forever. Come back to me, and I'll come back to you. But you're like, 'How exactly?'" {3:8} "Seriously, are you guys robbing me? 'Cause it sure seems like it. You're holding out on your tithes and offerings." {3:9} "You're cursed for holding back; the whole nation's holding out on me." {3:10} "Bring all your tithes to the storehouse, so there's enough for everyone. Try it, and see if I don't open the floodgates of blessings." {3:11} "I'll protect your crops from pests, so you'll have a bumper harvest, and everyone will call you blessed." {3:12} "You've talked tough to me, but you're like, 'What did we say?' You've said serving me is pointless, and you're wondering why you should bother." {3:13} "You're like, 'Why bother serving God? What do we get out of it?' You've been walking around like you're all that, tempting fate." {3:14} "But the ones who respect me, they're talking about it and looking out for each other. I've got their backs, and they're on my VIP list." {3:15} "Soon, it'll be clear who's on the right side and who's not, who's serving me and who's not." {3:16}" Those who respect me talk and look out for each other. I've got their backs, like a dad with his loyal kid." {3:17} "They're mine, and I'll spare them when I act. I'll treat them like a proud dad treats his kid." {3:18} "Then you'll see who's righteous and who's wicked, who's serving God and who's not."

{4:1} "Check it, a day's coming that'll be lit, burning up the proud and wicked like stubble. It'll leave 'em with nothing, says the big boss." {4:2} "But for those who respect my name, the Sun of righteousness will rise with healing in his wings. They'll bounce back, growing strong like calves." {4:3} "They'll crush the wicked under their feet like ashes, when I make my move," says the big boss. {4:4} "Don't forget the law of Moses, which I gave to all Israel, with its rules and judgments." {4:5} "I'm sending Elijah before the big, scary day. He'll bring families together, or else I'll have to drop a major curse on the earth."

THE NEW
TESTAMENT

Contents

✦✦✦

Matthew...1

Mark...12

Luke...19

John...31

Acts...42

Romans...55

1 Corinthians...62

2 Corinthians...68

Galatians..72

Ephesians...75

Philippians...78

Colossians..80

1 Thessalonians..82

2 Thessalonians..84

1 Timothy...85

2 Timothy...87

Titus...89

Philemon..90

Hebrews...91

James..96

1 Peter..98

2 Peter..100

1 John...101

2 John...103

3 John...104

Jude..105

Revelation...106

Matthew

✦✦✦

{1:1} So this is the fam tree of Jesus Christ, son of David, son of Abraham. {1:2} Abraham had Isaac; Isaac had Jacob; Jacob had Judas and his crew; {1:3} Judas had Phares and Zara with Thamar; Phares had Esrom; Esrom had Aram; {1:4} Aram had Aminadab; Aminadab had Naasson; Naasson had Salmon; {1:5} Salmon had Booz with Rachab; Booz had Obed with Ruth; Obed had Jesse; {1:6} Jesse had David the king; David had Solomon with Urias' ex; {1:7} Solomon had Roboam; Roboam had Abia; Abia had Asa; {1:8} Asa had Josaphat; Josaphat had Joram; Joram had Ozias; {1:9} Ozias had Joatham; Joatham had Achaz; Achaz had Ezekias; {1:10} Ezekias had Manasses; Manasses had Amon; Amon had Josias; {1:11} Josias had Jechonias and the gang when they were exiled to Babylon; {1:12} Jechonias had Salathiel post-Babylon; Salathiel had Zorobabel; {1:13} Zorobabel had Abiud; Abiud had Eliakim; Eliakim had Azor; {1:14} Azor had Sadoc; Sadoc had Achim; Achim had Eliud; {1:15} Eliud had Eleazar; Eleazar had Matthan; Matthan had Jacob; {1:16} Jacob had Joseph, Mary's hubby, and they had Jesus, aka Christ. {1:17} So from Abe to David, that's 14 generations; from David to Babylonian exile, another 14; and from Babylon to Christ, yep, 14 more. {1:18} Now let's talk about Jesus' birth: Mary was with Joseph but preggo by the Holy Ghost before they got busy. {1:19} Joseph, being cool and all, didn't want to shame Mary, so he planned to break it off quietly. {1:20} But then an angel showed up in his dream, like, "Joe, don't stress; take Mary as wifey 'cause that baby's divine." {1:21} She's gonna have a son named Jesus, here to save folks from their sins. {1:22-23} This was all to fulfill what the prophet said about a virgin having a son named Emmanuel (meaning God with us). {1:24} So Joseph woke up and did what the angel said, marrying Mary. {1:25} They kept it chill until after Jesus was born, and that's when they named him Jesus.

{2:1} When Jesus was born in Bethlehem, Judea, during Herod's reign, some wise dudes from the east rolled up to Jerusalem, {2:2} asking, "Yo, where's the newborn King of the Jews at? We saw his star back east and came to pay respects." {2:3} When Herod heard this, he and all of Jerusalem were shook. {2:4} Herod then gathered up all the big-shot priests and scholars and asked them where the Christ was supposed to be born. {2:5} They were like, "Bethlehem, for real. The prophet said so." {2:6} "Bethlehem, you ain't no small fry among Judea's towns. A ruler's coming out of you, leading Israel." {2:7} So Herod secretly got the lowdown from the wise men on when the star appeared. {2:8} Then he sent them off to Bethlehem, saying, "Go find the kid. Let me know so I can worship him too." {2:9} The wise men bounced, and boom, the star they saw led them right to where the child was. {2:10} Seeing the star, they were stoked beyond belief. {2:11} When they got to the house, they saw the child with Mary, and they bowed down and worshipped him, opening up their treasures—gold, frankincense, and myrrh. {2:12} Then they got a heads-up in a dream not to go back to Herod, so they split a different way. {2:13} After they left, an angel hit up Joseph in a dream, saying, "Get up, take the kid and Mary, and jet to Egypt. Herod's gunning for the kid." {2:14} Joseph woke up, took the fam in the dead of night, and skedaddled to Egypt. {2:15} They chilled there until Herod kicked the bucket, fulfilling what the prophet said about calling his son out of Egypt. {2:16} When Herod realized the wise men played him, he went berserk, sending out a hit on all the toddlers in Bethlehem and nearby, under two years old, based on the wise men's deets. {2:17} Cue Jeremiah's prophecy coming true about the crying and mourning in Rama for the lost children. {2:18-20} When Herod finally bit the dust, an angel appeared to Joseph in Egypt, saying, "Go back to Israel; those after the kid are gone." {2:21} Joseph took the kid and Mary and returned to Israel. {2:22} But hearing that Archelaus was ruling in Judea in Herod's place, Joseph got nervous and, after another divine dream, steered towards Galilee instead. {2:23} They settled in Nazareth, fulfilling the prophets' words about him being a Nazarene.

{3:1} Back in the day, John the Baptist showed up, preaching in the wilds of Judea, {3:2} telling everyone to repent because the kingdom of heaven was about to go down. {3:3} This dude was the one Isaiah talked about, yelling in the desert to get ready for the Lord and straighten out his path. {3:4} John was rocking camel-hair threads with a leather belt, snacking on locusts and wild honey. {3:5} People from Jerusalem, Judea, and all over the Jordan region came out to him, {3:6} getting baptized in the Jordan River and owning up to their wrongs. {3:7} But when John peeped the Pharisees and Sadducees rolling up to his baptism, he called them out, saying, "You snakey bunch, who told you to dodge what's coming?" {3:8} "Show you've really changed your ways by your actions." {3:9} "Don't just rely on being Abraham's descendants; God can make kids of Abraham from these rocks." {3:10} "The axe is ready to chop down any tree that doesn't produce good fruit, burning it up." {3:11} "I baptize with water, but the next guy after me? He's way bigger than I am—I'm not even worthy to carry his kicks." {3:12} "He'll clean house, separating the good from the useless and burning up the worthless." {3:13} Then Jesus rolled up from Galilee to get baptized by John in the Jordan. {3:14} John tried to stop him, saying, "I need your baptism, not the other way around." {3:15} But Jesus was like, "Nah, we gotta do this to do things right." So John went along with it. {3:16} After Jesus got baptized, he came out of the water, and boom, the heavens opened up, and the Spirit of God came down like a dove and landed on him. {3:17} Then a voice from heaven was like, "This is my awesome Son, and I'm totally pleased with him."

{4:1} So Jesus, led by the Spirit, headed out into the wilderness to face off with the devil. {4:2} After fasting for forty days and nights, he was starving. {4:3} That's when the tempter showed up, saying, "If you're really the Son of God, turn these stones into bread." {4:4} Jesus shut him down, quoting Scripture, "We don't just live on bread, but on every word from God." {4:5} Next, the devil took him to the holy city and perched him on the temple's highest point, {4:6} daring him to jump, saying angels would catch him. {4:7} Jesus hit back with more Scripture, "Don't test God like that." {4:8} Then the devil took him to a mountain peak, showing him all the kingdoms and their glory, {4:9} offering it all if Jesus bowed down to worship him. {4:10} Jesus was like, "Get lost, Satan. Only God deserves worship." {4:11} The devil bounced, and angels came to chill with Jesus. {4:12} When Jesus heard John got locked up, he split for Galilee. {4:13} He left Nazareth and set up shop in Capernaum by the sea, near Zebulun and Naphtali's borders, {4:14-16} fulfilling what Isaiah said about Galilee and its people seeing a great light. {4:17} From then on, Jesus preached, "Repent, 'cause the kingdom's right here." {4:18} As Jesus strolled by the Sea of Galilee, he spotted Simon (Peter) and Andrew casting nets, 'cause they were fishermen. {4:19} He told them, "Follow me; I'll make you fish for people." {4:20} They ditched their nets and tagged along. {4:21} Further down, he saw James and John in a boat with their dad, fixing nets, and called them too. {4:22} They bailed on the boat and their dad to follow Jesus. {4:23} Jesus traveled all over Galilee, teaching, preaching the kingdom, and healing folks with all kinds of issues. {4:24} His rep spread through Syria; sick folks from everywhere came for healing—diseases, torments, possession, you name it. {4:25} Huge crowds trailed him from Galilee, Decapolis, Jerusalem, Judea, and beyond the Jordan.

{5:1} Jesus sees this huge crowd, heads up to a mountain, sits down, and his crew gathers around him. {5:2} Then he starts dropping wisdom, like, "Blessed are those who are humble in spirit, 'cause they'll inherit heaven." {5:3} "And blessed are those who mourn, 'cause they'll find comfort." {5:4} "Oh, and blessed are the meek 'cause they're taking over the earth." {5:5} "And if you're hungry for righteousness, you'll be satisfied." {5:6} "Show some mercy, and you'll get mercy back." {5:7} "Keep your heart pure, and you'll see God." {5:8} "Peacemakers? Yeah, they're like God's kids." {5:9} "And if you catch heat for doing right, heaven's yours." {5:10-12} "So, if people start dissing you, or worse, just because you're with me, keep your head up. Your reward's gonna be huge up there, just like how they dissed the prophets before you." {5:13} "You guys are the spice of the earth. But if you lose your flavor, you're useless, just tossed aside." {5:14} "You're the light in this world. A city on a hill can't be hidden." {5:15-16} "You don't light a lamp and then hide it under a basket. Let your light shine so everyone sees the good you do and gives props to your heavenly Father." {5:17} "Oh, and don't think I'm here to trash the rules. I'm here to fulfill 'em." {5:18} "In fact, not even the smallest part of the rules is gonna disappear until everything's on point." {5:19} "If anyone tries to break these rules and teaches others to do the same, they won't rank high in heaven. But those who do and teach them, they're the real MVPs up there." {5:20} "Seriously though, your righteousness has gotta top those religious big shots, or you won't even make it into heaven." {5:21} "You've heard the old rule about not murdering? Well, getting heated without a cause puts you in the hot seat too." {5:22} "Calling someone names? That's like getting sent to court. Calling someone a fool? That's fire, literally." {5:23-24} "So, if you're about to give an offering but remember someone's got beef with you, squash that first, then drop your gift." {5:25-26} "And if you're in a disagreement, settle it quickly before it blows up in court, and you end up in the slammer." {5:27} "Now, about cheating in relationships? Yeah, even lusting after someone's a problem." {5:28} "If something's causing you to mess up, get rid of it, 'cause losing an eye or a hand's better than the whole body ending up in deep trouble." {5:29} "And about divorce? Except for certain reasons, splitting up and getting hitched again leads to trouble." {5:30} "And don't be making all these promises. Just keep it simple with a yes or no. Anything more's just shady." {5:31} "You've heard about 'eye for an eye'? Forget that. Don't fight back against evil. If someone slaps you, offer the other cheek. If they sue you for your shirt, give 'em your coat too. If they make you go a mile, go two. And if someone needs something, don't be stingy." {5:32} "Oh, and love your enemies, bless those who diss you, do good to haters, and pray for the ones treating you like trash." {5:33} "That's how you roll like children of your heavenly Father, who doesn't play favorites with the sunshine or the rain." {5:34} "Loving those who love you? Everyone does that. Greetin' just your buddies? Even tax collectors do that. So step up, be as perfect as your heavenly Father."

{6:1} Yo, don't be flexing your good deeds in front of everyone just to get props. That's not how you score heavenly rewards, fam. {6:2} When you give to those in need, don't be like those fake peeps who announce it with trumpets. They just want that spotlight. Trust, they already got their reward. {6:3} Keep it lowkey when you help out—let your left hand not know what your right hand's up to. {6:4} Do good in secret, and your heavenly Father, who sees what's up behind the scenes, will give you props out in the open. {6:5} And when you pray, don't be like those show-offs who love praying in public to get noticed. They're all about that attention. For real, they got what they wanted already. {6:6} Nah, when you pray, do it in private—get in your zone, shut the door, and talk to your heavenly Father like it's just you two. He'll give you that shout-out where everyone can see. {6:7} Don't go repeating empty words like those outsiders who think more talk means better results. {6:8} Nah, don't play yourself like that—your Father already knows what you need before you even ask. {6:9-10} When you pray, keep it real like this: "Heavenly Father, you're top-tier. Let your kingdom come, and your will go down here just like it's up there. {6:11} Give us what we need today. {6:12} Forgive us our wrongs like we forgive others. {6:13} Keep us away from trouble and bad vibes. Yours is the kingdom, the power, and the glory, forever. Amen." {6:14-15} And remember, if you forgive others, your heavenly Father's got your back too. But if you're holding grudges, don't expect any forgiveness. {6:16} Now, about fasting—don't be gloomy like those fakers trying to look all spiritual. They're just trying to get noticed. Trust, they got what they wanted. {6:17-18} When you fast, keep it low-profile—freshen up, look good, and keep it between you and your Father who's got your back. {6:19} Don't be stacking up earthly treasures that can fade away or get swiped. {6:20} Invest in heavenly treasures that last—no rust or thieves up there. {6:21} Where your heart's at, that's where your focus should be. {6:22} Your eyes are the window to your soul. Keep it clear and focused, and your whole being will be lit. {6:23} But if your vision's messed up, everything's gonna be dark. If your inner light is dark, it's a major vibe killer. {6:24} You can't be loyal to two bosses—it's either God or money. Pick one. {6:25} So don't stress about food, drinks, or outfits. Life's more than just that, right? {6:26} Check out the birds—they don't work, but they're fed by your heavenly Father. And you're way more valuable than them. {6:27} Can worrying add an inch to your height? Nah, fam. {6:28-29} So why stress about clothes? Look at the flowers—they don't grind, but they're styled better than King Solomon. {6:30} If God takes care of nature like that, won't he look after you, even if you're low-key doubting? {6:31} So don't trip about what to eat, drink, or wear. That's what the outsiders stress about. {6:32} Your heavenly Father knows what's up—you're covered. {6:33} First, focus on God's kingdom and doing right. Everything else? Sorted. {6:34} Live for today—tomorrow's got its own worries. You got this.

{7:1} Yo, don't be quick to judge others if you don't wanna get judged back. {7:2} How you dish it out is how it's coming right back atcha. {7:3} Why you trippin' over a speck in your bro's eye when you got a whole plank in yours? {7:4} How you gonna offer to clear their eye when yours is all messed up? {7:5} Sort yourself out first, then you can help your bro out. {7:6} Don't waste what's sacred on those who don't respect it, or share your valuable stuff with those who'll just trash it. {7:7} Ask for what you need, go look for it, knock on doors—doors will open up for you. {7:8} Everyone who asks receives, everyone who seeks finds, and whoever knocks, it's gonna be opened up for them. {7:9} You wouldn't give your kid a rock if they asked for bread, right? {7:10} Or a snake if they wanted fish? {7:11} If you, imperfect as you are, know how to give good things to your kids, imagine how much more your heavenly Father's got your back when you ask him? {7:12} Treat others like you wanna be treated—it's the golden rule, straight from the law and the prophets. {7:13} Go through the narrow gate, not the wide one that leads to destruction. Most peeps are on that wide path, but it ain't where you wanna be. {7:14} The real deal's the narrow road that leads to life, but only a few find it. {7:15} Watch out for fake prophets rocking sheep's clothing but are really savage wolves inside. {7:16} You'll know 'em by their actions. Good trees give good fruit, bad trees give bad fruit. {7:17} A good tree can't produce bad fruit, and a bad tree can't produce good fruit. {7:18-19} Trees that don't produce good fruit? They're getting chopped down and tossed in the fire. {7:20} You'll recognize 'em by what they produce. {7:21} Not everyone shouting "Lord, Lord" gets into heaven—only those doing the will of the heavenly Father. {7:22} Some peeps will be like, "But we did all this cool stuff in your name!" {7:23} Jesus will straight up say, "I never knew you—get lost, you lawbreakers." {7:24} So if you hear my words and actually do 'em, you're like a smart person building on solid ground. {7:25} Storms may come, but your house won't budge 'cause it's on a rock. {7:26} But if you hear my words and ignore 'em, you're like a fool building on sand. {7:27} When the storms hit, that house is gone—talk about a major collapse. {7:28} After Jesus dropped these truths, people were shook 'cause he wasn't preachin' like the usual crew—he had that authority.

{8:1} After Jesus came down from the mountain, a big crowd was all up following him. {8:2} Then a leper came up to him, bowed down, and was like, "Yo, Lord, if you're down for it, you can totally heal me." {8:3} Jesus reached out and touched him, saying, "I'm down—be clean." And bam, right then and there, the leprosy was gone. {8:4} Jesus told him, "Keep it on the low, but go show yourself to the priest and offer what Moses said, just to prove what's up." {8:5} When Jesus rolled into Capernaum, a centurion came up, asking for help. {8:6} He was like, "Lord, my servant's at home, all messed up with palsy." {8:7} Jesus said, "I'll come and sort him out." {8:8} But the centurion was humble, saying, "Nah, I'm not worthy for you to come—just say the word, and my servant will be healed." {8:9} He knew about authority, 'cause when he says something, it happens. {8:10} Jesus was impressed, saying, "I haven't seen faith like this, not even in Israel." {8:11} He even dropped a bomb, saying peeps from all over will be chilling with the OGs—Abraham, Isaac, and Jacob—in heaven. {8:12} But those who think they're in but aren't? They're out, in the dark, crying and grinding their teeth. {8:13} Jesus told the centurion to bounce, and just like he believed, his servant got healed right then. {8:14} Jesus hit up Peter's house and saw his mother-in-law laid up with a fever. {8:15} He reached out, touched her hand, and the fever was gone. She got up and started taking care of 'em. {8:16} Later that evening, they brought a bunch of possessed and sick peeps to Jesus, and he straight-up cast out the evil spirits with his words and healed 'em all. {8:17} This fulfilled what the prophet Isaiah said about taking on our sickness and pain. {8:18} When Jesus saw the huge crowd, he was like, "Let's dip to the other side." {8:19} Then a scribe was like, "I'm down to follow you wherever." {8:20} Jesus was real, saying, "Foxes got dens, birds got nests, but I ain't got a crib." {8:21} Another disciple was like, "Can I bury my dad first?" {8:22} Jesus dropped wisdom, "Follow me, and let the dead deal with their own." {8:23} They all hopped on a ship with Jesus. {8:24} Then a wild storm hit, and the ship was getting slammed by waves while Jesus was knocked out. {8:25} They woke him up, panicking, like, "Lord, save us—we're gonna drown!" {8:26} Jesus was like, "Why y'all scared? Y'all got weak faith." Then he stood up, told the storm to chill, and it went dead calm. {8:27} They were shook, saying, "Who is this dude? Even the wind and sea listen to him!" {8:28} When they reached the other side, they ran into two dudes possessed by demons, straight out of the tombs and fierce. {8:29} The demons were like, "What do you want with us, Jesus, Son of God? You here to mess us up before our time?" {8:30} Nearby, there was a herd of pigs. {8:31} The demons begged to go into the pigs, and Jesus was like, "Go for it." {8:32} They bounced into the pigs, which went crazy and stampeded into the sea, drowning. {8:33} The pig farmers ran off, telling everyone what went down with the possessed dudes. {8:34} The whole city was shook and wanted Jesus to bounce from their hood.

{9:1} So Jesus hopped on a boat, crossed over, and rolled into his own city. {9:2} Check it—some dudes brought a guy with palsy lying on a bed. Jesus saw their faith and was like, "Dude, cheer up—your sins are forgiven." {9:3} But then some scribes in their heads were like, "This dude's dissing." {9:4} Jesus read their minds and was like, "Why you thinking evil stuff?" {9:5} He dropped a question, "What's easier: saying 'Your sins are forgiven' or 'Get up and walk'?" {9:6} To show he's legit, Jesus told the guy, "Get up, grab your bed, and head home." {9:7} The guy got up and bounced home. {9:8} The crowd was shook and praised God for giving such power to people. {9:9} Later, Jesus saw a dude named Matthew at the customs spot and was like, "Come follow me." Matthew got up and followed. {9:10} While Jesus was chilling at a house eating, a bunch of tax collectors and sinners showed up and ate with him and his crew. {9:11} The Pharisees were salty, asking the disciples, "Why's your teacher eating with sinners?" {9:12} Jesus heard and dropped truth, "Healthy peeps don't need a doc—sick ones do." {9:13} He schooled them, "Learn what 'I desire mercy, not sacrifice' means. I'm here for the sinners, not the righteous." {9:14} John's disciples came up asking why they and the Pharisees fast but Jesus' crew doesn't. {9:15} Jesus was like, "Can you mourn at a wedding while the party's on? But when the party's over, then you fast." {9:16} You can't patch old clothes with new fabric, or the tear gets worse. {9:17} You don't put new wine in old bottles—new goes with new, and both stay fresh. {9:18} While Jesus talked, a ruler came up, saying his daughter was dead but would live if Jesus touched her. {9:19} Jesus and his crew followed. {9:20} On the way, a woman with a twelve-year issue of blood touched Jesus' cloak, thinking she'd be healed. {9:21-22} Jesus turned and said, "Cheer up—your faith made you well." She was healed instantly. {9:23} They got to the ruler's house, and people were making noise. {9:24-25} Jesus said, "She's not dead—just sleeping." They laughed, but Jesus took her hand, and she got up. {9:26} Word spread fast about this. {9:27} As Jesus left, two blind dudes followed, yelling, "Son of David, have mercy!" {9:28} Inside, Jesus asked if they believed he could heal them. They said, "Yes, Lord." {9:29} Jesus touched their eyes, saying, "Your faith did it." {9:30} Their eyes opened, and Jesus told them to keep it on the down-low. {9:31} But they spread the news everywhere. {9:32} Later, they brought a mute demon-possessed guy to Jesus. {9:33} After casting out the demon, everyone was amazed. {9:34} The Pharisees accused Jesus of using demonic power. {9:35} Jesus traveled, teaching, preaching, and healing all kinds of sickness and disease among the people. {9:36} Seeing the crowds, Jesus felt compassion—they were lost, like sheep without a shepherd. {9:37} He told his crew, "The harvest is huge, but the workers are few. {9:38} Pray to send more workers into the harvest."

{10:1} Jesus gathered up his crew of twelve and hooked them up with powers against evil spirits, to kick them out and heal all kinds of sickness and disease. {10:2} So here's the squad: Simon (aka Peter) and his bro Andrew, James (son of Zebedee) and his bro John, {10:3} Philip, Bartholomew, Thomas, Matthew (the ex-tax collector), James (son of Alphaeus), Lebbaeus (also called Thaddaeus), {10:4} Simon the Canaanite, and Judas Iscariot, who later turned on Jesus. {10:5} Jesus sent them out with a mission: skip the Gentile and Samaritan spots, and head straight for lost Israelites. {10:6} Preach the kingdom of heaven, heal the sick, cleanse lepers, raise the dead, and boot out demons. {10:7} Don't carry cash—give freely as you've received. {10:8} No gold, silver, or brass in your wallets, no extra gear or clothes; the work is its own reward. {10:9} When you hit a town, find out who's legit and crash with them. {10:10} Be chill when you greet a house—if they're cool, leave your blessing; if not, take it back. {10:11-15} If they diss you, shake their dust off and bounce; it'll be worse for them than Sodom and Gomorrah on judgment day. {10:16} Jesus warned them: you're like sheep in a wolf pack, so be smart and harmless. {10:17} Watch out for haters—they'll drag you before councils and beat you up in synagogues. {10:18} You'll face governors and kings for my sake, as a witness to them and the Gentiles. {10:19} Don't stress about what to say when they haul you in; the Spirit will speak through you. {10:20} It's not you talking—it's the Spirit of your Father. {10:21} Families will turn on each other, but stay strong; endure till the end for salvation. {10:22} People will hate you because of me, but keep going—those who hold out will be saved. {10:23} If they chase you in one city, bounce to another; you won't finish hitting up all of Israel before I come back. {10:24} You're not above me; a disciple's like the master, a servant like the boss. {10:25} If they called me Beelzebub, expect them to diss you too. {10:26} Don't fear them—everything hidden will come out eventually. {10:27} Speak what I tell you in the light, preach it on the rooftops. {10:28} Fear the One who can destroy body and soul in hell, not those who can only kill the body. {10:29} Sparrows are cheap, but God knows when even one falls. {10:30} He's got your back down to the hairs on your head. {10:31} You're more valuable than many sparrows. {10:32} Confess me before people, and I'll confess you to my Father. {10:33} Deny me, and I'll deny you. {10:34} I'm not here to bring peace but a sword, to divide even families. {10:35} Love for me should surpass love for family. {10:36} Your enemies might be in your own household. {10:37} If you don't pick up your cross and follow me, you're not worthy of me. {10:38} Lose your life for my sake, and you'll find it. {10:39} If you welcome my messengers, you welcome me and the One who sent me. {10:40} Hospitality to my followers won't go unrewarded.

{11:1} After Jesus finished briefing his squad of twelve, he bounced to their cities to teach and preach. {11:2-3} Meanwhile, John the Baptist, locked up in prison, heard about Jesus' moves and sent two of his crew to ask, "Yo, are you the one we've been waiting for, or should we keep our eyes peeled for someone else?" {11:4-5} Jesus didn't trip; he just told them, "Go back and tell John what you've seen and heard: the blind see, the lame walk, lepers get cleansed, the deaf hear, the dead come back to life, and good news gets shared with the poor. {11:6} Blessed is anyone who doesn't get shook by me." {11:7} As John's crew left, Jesus turned to the crowd and said, "What were you expecting when you went out to see John in the wild? A pushover swayed by whatever's blowing? {11:8} Nah, John's no softie dressed in fancy threads like palace VIPs. {11:9} You were looking for a prophet? Well, John's way more than that. {11:10} He's the messenger written about, clearing the path for the big boss. {11:11} Seriously, out of everyone born, John the Baptist stands tall, but even the least in heaven's kingdom has a higher rank. {11:12} Since John's time, folks have been pushing into the kingdom of heaven, grabbing it like it's theirs. {11:13} All the prophets and the law paved the way up to John. {11:14} If you can get it, John's the Elijah everyone's been waiting for. {11:15} Listen up if you've got ears!" {11:16-17} Then Jesus dropped this truth bomb: "This generation is like kids in the market, calling the shots but never happy with the music. {11:18} John came doing his thing, fasting and all, and they call him possessed. {11:19} But when I show up, eating and chilling, they call me a glutton and a party animal, buddy-buddy with tax collectors and sinners. {11:20} Man, some cities where I've done crazy miracles still haven't turned around; {11:21} it's gonna be rough for them on judgment day. {11:22} Tyre and Sidon would've changed their ways if they saw what went down, but you, Chorazin and Bethsaida, you're in for it. {11:23} Capernaum, high and mighty, you're headed down unless you change your tune. {11:24} Sodom would've made it if they had what you've seen!" {11:25-26} Jesus took a moment and said, "Shoutout to you, Father, the boss of heaven and earth, for keeping things hidden from the smart and revealing them to the simple. {11:27} Everything's in my hands from the Father, and only I really know him—and whoever I decide to spill the beans to. {11:28} So, if you're tired of the grind and feeling weighed down, come chill with me—I'll give you a break. {11:29} Take my lead; I'm laid-back and humble, and you'll find peace. {11:30} My vibe is easy, and my load won't weigh you down.

{12:1} So Jesus, chilling on the Sabbath, strolled through a field with his crew, who were starving and started munching on some corn. {12:2} The Pharisees, always on watch, were like, "Yo, your crew is breaking Sabbath rules!" {12:3-4} Jesus clapped back, "Haven't you read what David did when he was hungry? He ate the showbread, which was only for priests." {12:5} "And y'all know the priests work on the Sabbath in the temple, right?" {12:6} Jesus dropped a bomb, saying he's greater than the temple. {12:7} "If you knew what 'I desire mercy, not sacrifice' meant, you wouldn't be dissing the innocent." {12:8} "And FYI, the Son of Man calls the shots on the Sabbath." {12:9} Jesus bounced to the synagogue, and there they found a dude with a withered hand. {12:10} The Pharisees were itching to trap him, asking if healing on the Sabbath was cool. {12:11-12} Jesus clapped back again, "If your sheep fell into a pit on the Sabbath, wouldn't you save it? How much more valuable is a person than a sheep?" {12:13} Then he told the man, "Stretch out your hand," and it was healed instantly. {12:14} The Pharisees, salty as ever, plotted against Jesus. {12:15} But Jesus knew and dipped out, with a crowd trailing him for more miracles. {12:16} He told them to keep it low-key. {12:17} This all went down to fulfill what Isaiah said about the servant who shows mercy and justice to the Gentiles. {12:18} Jesus healed a demon-possessed, blind, and mute dude, blowing everyone's minds. {12:19} But the Pharisees accused him of devil magic. {12:20} Jesus called them out, saying a kingdom divided against itself won't last. {12:21} "If I'm casting out demons by God's Spirit, then God's kingdom is here." {12:22} Jesus laid down the law, forgiving sins and blasphemies but warning about the unforgivable sin against the Holy Spirit. {12:23} "A good tree produces good fruit, and a rotten tree, rotten fruit. Your words show what's in your heart." {12:24} "You'll answer for every idle word on judgment day."

{13:1} So Jesus bounced from the crib and posted up by the beach. {13:2} Mad people pulled up, so he hopped in a boat and started dropping knowledge while everyone chilled on the shore. {13:3} He dropped some real talk in stories, like this farmer who went to plant. {13:4} Some seeds fell on the path and got snatched up by birds. {13:5} Others landed on rocky spots and sprouted fast but got fried by the sun with no roots to hold on. {13:6-7} Then there were seeds among thorns, but the weeds choked 'em out. {13:8} But some seeds hit good ground and blew up with fruit—some a hundredfold, some sixty, some thirty. {13:9} If you get it, you get it. {13:10} The crew was like, "Why you using stories, bro?" {13:11} Jesus said, "You're blessed to get it; others ain't ready for these truths." {13:12} "If you already know, you'll get more; if not, you'll lose what you got." {13:13} "They're blind and deaf to this, just like the prophet Isaiah said." {13:14} "You guys are lucky; you're tuned in." {13:15} "Listen up about this farmer." {13:16} "Some hear the kingdom word but don't get it, and the devil snatches it away." {13:17} "Others get hyped but don't last when things get tough." {13:18} "Some get distracted by life and money, and the word fizzles out." {13:19} "But those who get it and grow good roots bear fruit big-time." {13:20} Jesus drops another story: a dude planted good seeds, but an enemy threw in weeds while everyone slept. {13:21} "An enemy messed things up," the farmer said. {13:22} They wanted to pull the weeds, but the farmer said wait till harvest to sort it out. {13:23} Let the wheat grow till then. {13:24} Another story: the kingdom's like a mustard seed, tiny but grows huge. {13:25} It's like leaven hidden in dough, making it all rise. {13:26} Jesus spoke only in stories to fulfill the prophecy. {13:27} He breaks it down for the crew: the Son of Man sows good seeds, the field's the world, the good seeds are kingdom peeps, and the weeds are evil ones. {13:28} At the end, the weeds get burned. {13:29} Righteous ones will shine, but you gotta get it to get it. {13:30} Again, the kingdom's like finding treasure in a field, selling all for that gem. {13:31} It's like a merchant chasing the best pearls and going all in for one. {13:32} And it's like a net pulling all sorts, sorting good from bad at the end. {13:33} The bad get tossed, and it's not pretty. {13:34} Jesus asks if they get it; they're like, "For sure." {13:35} Teachers of the kingdom drop new and old knowledge. {13:36} Jesus wraps it up and dips out. {13:37} Back home, he drops wisdom and works, blowing minds. {13:38} People were shook, like, "Isn't this the carpenter's kid?" {13:39} They weren't feeling it, but Jesus drops truth: prophets are slept on at home.

{14:1} Herod the ruler dude heard about Jesus blowing up, {14:2} and was like telling his crew, "Yo, this has gotta be John the Baptist back from the dead, that's why he's pulling off these sick miracles." {14:3} 'Cause Herod had grabbed John and locked him up for dissing Herodias, his brother Philip's wifey. {14:4} John told him straight up, "You can't be with her, bro." {14:5} Herod wanted to off him, but he chickened out 'cause people thought John was a prophet. {14:6} Anyway, at Herod's bash, Herodias's daughter danced and Herod was into it. {14:7} So he swears to give her whatever she asks for. {14:8} Her mom coached her to ask for John's head on a platter. {14:9} Herod was bummed but he had to keep his word, so he ordered John's execution. {14:10} They chopped off John's head and served it up to the girl who took it to her mom. {14:11-12} John's crew buried him and filled in Jesus. {14:13} Jesus bounces to a quiet place when he hears, and peeps followed him on foot. {14:14} He sees a huge crowd and feels for them, so he heals their sick. {14:15} Evening rolls in, and the disciples are like, "We're in the middle of nowhere, send these peeps home to grab grub." {14:16} Jesus is like, "Nah, they can chill here. Give 'em something to eat." {14:17} They're like, "All we got is five loaves and two fish." {14:18} Jesus is like, "Bring 'em here." {14:19} He tells everyone to sit, takes the food, blesses it, breaks it, and gives it out. {14:20} Everyone eats and is stuffed; they collect twelve baskets of leftovers. {14:21} There were about five thousand men there, plus women and kids. {14:22} Jesus sends the crew ahead in a boat while he sends the crowd away. {14:23} Then he chills on a mountain praying solo till evening. {14:24} Meanwhile, the boat's in rough seas 'cause of the wind. {14:25} Around dawn, Jesus walks out to them on the water. {14:26-27} The disciples freak, thinking it's a ghost, but Jesus tells 'em to chill, it's him. {14:28} Peter's like, "If it's really you, let me walk on water too." {14:29-30} Jesus is like, "Sure." Peter starts but panics and sinks, crying for help. {14:31} Jesus saves him, but calls him out for doubting. {14:32-33} The wind stops when they get back in the boat, and the crew worships Jesus, saying he's really the Son of God. {14:34} They hit up Gennesaret, {14:35} and the locals bring all their sick peeps, asking just to touch Jesus' clothes, and they're all cured.

{15:1} So, like, these scribes and Pharisees from Jerusalem roll up to Jesus, saying, {15:2} "Yo, why don't your squad follow the old traditions and wash their hands before eating?" {15:3} Jesus is like, "Why you gotta break God's commandments with your traditions?" {15:4} He's like, "God said, 'Respect your parents,' but you guys twist it." {15:5} "You say if someone gives to their parents, it's all good, even if they diss 'em." {15:6} "Y'all just cancel God's rules with your traditions." {15:7} He calls them out as hypocrites, quoting Isaiah, {15:8} about how they talk the talk but their hearts ain't in it. {15:9} They worship for nothing, teaching human rules as God's. {15:10} Then Jesus tells the crowd, "Listen up and get this straight:" {15:11} "It's not what goes in your mouth that messes you up, it's what comes out." {15:12} His squad's like, "Yo, the Pharisees are ticked off after hearing this." {15:13} Jesus is like, "Anything not planted by my Father gets pulled out." {15:14} "Leave 'em be, they're blind guides leading blind folks, and they'll both end up in trouble." {15:15} Peter's like, "Explain this parable, bro." {15:16} Jesus is like, "You still don't get it?" {15:17} "Food goes in, gets digested, and flushed out. It's words that come from the heart that mess you up." {15:18} "Evil stuff like thoughts, murders, cheating, stealing, lies, and insults, that's what's messed up." {15:19-20} "Eating without washing your hands doesn't mess you up." {15:21} Jesus peaces out to Tyre and Sidon. {15:22} Then this Canaanite woman shows up, begging Jesus to help her daughter tormented by a demon. {15:23} He ignores her, and his crew's like, "Send her away, she's bugging us." {15:24} But Jesus is like, "I'm here for the lost sheep of Israel." {15:25-26} She begs again, and he's like, "It's not cool to give kids' food to dogs." {15:27} She's like, "True, but even dogs get crumbs from the table." {15:28} Jesus is impressed by her faith and heals her daughter. {15:29} Jesus splits and heads near the Sea of Galilee, chilling on a mountain. {15:30} Huge crowds show up, bringing the disabled, and Jesus heals them all. {15:31} People are blown away seeing the mute speak, the crippled walk, and the blind see, praising God. {15:32} Jesus tells his crew, "I feel for these folks; they've been with us three days and got nothing to eat. I won't send them off starving." {15:33} His crew's like, "How are we gonna feed them all in the middle of nowhere?" {15:34} Jesus asks, "What do you got?" They're like, "Seven loaves and a few fish." {15:35} He tells everyone to sit, {15:36} takes the food, thanks God, breaks it, and gives it to his crew, who pass it out to the crowd. {15:37} Everyone eats and is full, and they collect seven baskets of leftovers. {15:38} About four thousand men ate, not counting women and kids. {15:39} Jesus sends the crowd away, hops on a boat, and heads to Magdala's shores.

{16:1} The Pharisees and Sadducees roll up to Jesus, wanting him to drop a heavenly sign. {16:2-3} Jesus is like, "You can predict the weather by looking at the sky, but can't read the signs of the times? Hypocrites." {16:4} He's like, "This messed-up generation just wants a show; no signs except Jonah's coming." Then he bounces. {16:5} His crew forgets bread when they get to the other side. {16:6-7} Jesus is like, "Watch out for the Pharisees' and Sadducees' influence." {16:8} Jesus sees them stressing about bread and calls them out for their lack of faith. {16:9-10} He's like, "Remember the five loaves for five thousand, and the leftovers? Or the seven loaves for four thousand?" {16:11-12} He's like, "I ain't talking about bread; watch out for the Pharisees' and Sadducees' teachings." {16:13} Jesus hits Caesarea Philippi and asks his squad who people think he is. {16:14} They're like, "Some say John the Baptist, Elijah, Jeremiah, or a prophet." {16:15} Jesus asks, "But who do you say I am?" {16:16} Peter's like, "You're the Christ, Son of the living God." {16:17} Jesus gives props to Peter, saying it's a divine revelation. {16:18} He's like, "You're Peter, and on this rock, I'll build my church; hell can't touch it." {16:19} He gives Peter the keys to heaven, letting him bind and loose stuff on earth and heaven. {16:20} Then he tells them to keep it on the down-low that he's the Christ. {16:21} Jesus starts explaining he's gotta head to Jerusalem, suffer, and get killed, but rise on the third day. {16:22} Peter's like, "Nah, Lord, that ain't happening to you." {16:23} Jesus calls him out, saying, "Get behind me, Satan! You're not about God's plan." {16:24} Jesus tells his crew, "If you wanna roll with me, deny yourself, carry your cross, and follow." {16:25} "If you try to save your life, you'll lose it; lose it for my sake, and you'll find it." {16:26} "What's it worth to gain the world but lose your soul? Or trade it away?" {16:27} "The Son of Man's coming in his glory with angels, rewarding everyone as they deserve." {16:28} He's like, "Some here won't die till they see me coming in my kingdom."

{17:1} After about a week, Jesus takes Peter, James, and John up a big mountain alone. {17:2} There, Jesus starts glowing like crazy, face shining like the sun, and his clothes pure white. {17:3} Suddenly, Moses and Elijah show up, chatting with Jesus. {17:4} Peter's like, "Yo, let's chill here! We'll set up three tents—for you, Moses, and Elijah." {17:5} While he's talking, a bright cloud covers them, and a voice booms out, "This is my Son, and I'm proud of him; listen to him." {17:6} The disciples freak out, falling face-first, scared. {17:7} Jesus calms them, saying, "Get up, no need to be scared." {17:8} When they look up, it's just Jesus. {17:9} As they head down, Jesus tells them to keep quiet about what they saw until he rises from the dead. {17:10} Later, the disciples ask, "Why do the scribes say Elijah has to come first?" {17:11} Jesus explains, "Elijah will come and fix things first." {17:12} "But, yo, Elijah already came, and they didn't recognize him, treating him however they wanted. It'll be the same for the Son of Man." {17:13} The disciples realize he's talking about John the Baptist. {17:14-15} When they get back to the crowd, a man kneels before Jesus, asking for mercy for his son who's a mess—falling into fire and water due to being a lunatic. {17:16} The dad brought him to the disciples, but they couldn't help. {17:17-18} Jesus is like, "Seriously, how long do I gotta put up with this messed-up lack of faith?" He heals the boy. {17:19} Later, the disciples ask Jesus privately why they couldn't heal the boy. {17:20} Jesus tells them, "It's your lack of faith. Even a tiny bit of faith can move mountains." {17:21} "But some problems need prayer and fasting to fix." {17:22-23} While they're in Galilee, Jesus tells them he'll be betrayed and killed by men, but rise again on the third day, leaving them feeling crushed. {17:24} When they reach Capernaum, tax collectors ask Peter if Jesus pays tribute. {17:25} Peter says yes. Inside, Jesus asks Peter, "Who do kings tax—their own kids or strangers?" {17:26} Peter says, "Strangers." Jesus says, "Then we're exempt. But to avoid problems, go fish, and the first catch will have a coin for us to pay."

{18:1} The disciples roll up to Jesus like, "Who's gonna be the top dog in heaven, huh?" {18:2-3} Jesus grabs a kid, plops them in the middle, and says, "Listen up—unless you change and become like kids, forget about heaven." {18:4} "If you can humble yourself like this kid, that's how you become the big shot in heaven." {18:5} "And if you welcome a kid in my name, it's like you're welcoming me." {18:6} "But if you mess with these little believers, you'd be better off with a millstone around your neck and a dive into the deep sea." {18:7} Jesus drops truth bombs about offenses: they'll happen, but woe to the one causing them! {18:8} "If your hand or foot leads you to sin, chop 'em off; better to enter life maimed than be thrown into eternal fire." {18:9} "Same goes for your eye—if it causes you to sin, pluck it out; better one-eyed in heaven than two-eyed in hell." {18:10-11} "Don't mess with these little ones; their angels are always with my Father." {18:12-13} "Imagine a shepherd with a hundred sheep; if one strays, he leaves the rest to find it and celebrates big time when he does." {18:14} "God doesn't want any of these little ones to be lost." {18:15} "If your bro wrongs you, talk it out; if he listens, you've won him over." {18:16} "If not, bring a couple buddies to confirm things." {18:17} "If he still won't listen, tell the whole crew; if he ignores them, treat him like an outsider." {18:18} "Whatever you decide on earth is decided in heaven." {18:19} "If two of you agree on something, God's on board." {18:20} "Whenever two or three gather in my name, I'm there too." {18:21} Peter's like, "How many times should I forgive my bro—seven times?" {18:22} Jesus schools him, "Nah, seventy times seven." {18:23} Then Jesus lays down a story about forgiveness, comparing it to a king settling accounts with his servants. {18:24} The king shows mercy, forgiving a huge debt, but that servant turns around and bullies another servant over a much smaller debt. {18:25} The king finds out and calls out the first servant, furious that he didn't show the same mercy. {18:26} "That's how my heavenly Father will treat you if you don't forgive others from your heart."

{19:1} After Jesus wrapped up his talk, he bounced from Galilee and headed over to Judaea by the Jordan. {19:2} Big crowds were trailing him, and he was healing folks left and right. {19:3} Then the Pharisees came up, trying to trip him up, asking, "Can a guy divorce his wife for any reason?" {19:4} Jesus replied, "Haven't you read? God made them male and female from the start." {19:5-6} "A man leaves his parents and sticks with his wife; they become one flesh—what God joins, no one should split." {19:7} They push back, "Why did Moses say we could divorce?" {19:8} Jesus explains, "Moses allowed it because you're hard-headed, but that wasn't the plan from the get-go." {19:9} "If a guy divorces his wife for anything other than cheating and marries someone else, that's adultery; same if someone marries a divorced person." {19:10} The disciples hear this and are like, "Well, maybe it's better not to get hitched at all." {19:11} Jesus tells them, "Not everyone can handle this—only those it's meant for." {19:12} "Some are eunuchs from birth, others because of people, and some choose it for heaven's sake. If you get it, you get it." {19:13} Then people bring kids for Jesus to bless, but the disciples try to stop them. {19:14-15} Jesus says, "Let the kids come; heaven's all about them." {19:16} Later, a dude asks, "What good deed gets me eternal life?" {19:17} Jesus questions, "Why call me good? Only God's truly good. To get eternal life, keep the commandments." {19:18-19} The man's like, "Which ones?" Jesus lists 'em: no murder, adultery, stealing, lying, honor your parents, and love your neighbor as yourself. {19:20} The guy's like, "I've nailed those since forever—what's next?" {19:21} Jesus says, "Sell your stuff, give to the poor, and follow me for treasure in heaven." {19:22} The guy's bummed 'cause he's loaded. {19:23} Jesus tells his crew, "Rich folks will struggle to enter heaven." {19:24} "It's easier for a camel to squeeze through a needle's eye than for a rich person to get into God's kingdom." {19:25} The disciples are shook, like, "Who can be saved then?" {19:26} Jesus says, "For humans, it's impossible, but God can pull off anything." {19:27} Peter's like, "Yo, we've ditched everything for you; what's in it for us?" {19:28-29} Jesus tells them, "You'll rule with me in the new era; those who've given up stuff for my sake will gain big time." {19:30} "The first will be last, and the last will be first."

{20:1} There was this homeowner who went out early in the morning to hire workers for his vineyard. {20:2} He agreed to pay them a penny for the day's work and sent them off. {20:3} Around the third hour, he saw more folks hanging out idle in the marketplace. {20:4} He told them to join in and promised a fair wage. {20:5} He did the same at the sixth and ninth hours. {20:6} Then, at the eleventh hour, he found more people just standing around and asked why they hadn't been hired all day. {20:7} They said no one had hired them, so he sent them to work, promising they'd be paid what was right. {20:8} When evening came, he had his manager pay the workers, starting from the last hired to the first. {20:9} Those hired last, at the eleventh hour, got a penny each. {20:10} The first workers thought they'd get more, but they also received a penny each. {20:11-12} They complained to the homeowner, saying it wasn't fair since they worked longer in the heat. {20:13-15} The homeowner responded, "I didn't cheat you; you agreed to work for a penny. Take what's yours and go. I can do what I want with my money, right?" {20:16} "The last will be first, and the first will be last—lots are called, but few are chosen." {20:17} Jesus headed to Jerusalem with the twelve disciples and dropped some truth on them. {20:18-19} He told them he'd be betrayed to the religious leaders, condemned to death, and handed over to be mocked, beaten, and crucified—but he'd rise again on the third day. {20:20-21} Then Zebedee's mom brought her sons to Jesus, asking if they could have top spots in his kingdom. {20:22} Jesus asked if they could handle what he was about to face, and they said they could. {20:23-24} Jesus told them they'd experience his trials but deciding who sits next to him isn't his call—it's for those chosen by his Father. {20:25} When the other disciples heard, they got mad at Zebedee's sons. {20:26} Jesus explained that his followers shouldn't act like rulers do; instead, they should serve others. {20:27-29} "I'm not here to be served but to serve and give my life for many." {20:30} As they left

Jericho, a huge crowd followed Jesus. {20:30} Two blind men on the roadside cried out for mercy, calling Jesus the Son of David. {20:31} Jesus stopped and asked what they wanted. {20:32} They asked to see again, and Jesus healed them on the spot, and they started following him.

{21:1} When they got close to Jerusalem, they came to Bethphage on the Mount of Olives, and Jesus sent two of his crew ahead. {21:2} He told them to head into the nearby village and they'd find a donkey and a colt tied up; he wanted them brought to him. {21:3} If anyone asks what they're doing, they should say, "The Lord needs them," and they'll be sent without a fuss. {21:4-5} This was to fulfill a prophecy that said, "Tell the people of Zion, your King is coming, humble, riding on a donkey, and a colt, the foal of a donkey." {21:6} The disciples did exactly as Jesus said, {21:7} and brought the donkey and colt to him, placing their clothes on them, and Jesus sat on the donkey. {21:8} A huge crowd spread their clothes on the road, while others cut branches and spread them out. {21:9} The people walking ahead and behind shouted, "Hosanna to the Son of David! Blessed is he who comes in the name of the Lord! Hosanna in the highest!" {21:10} When Jesus entered Jerusalem, the whole city was buzzing, asking, "Who is this?" {21:11} The crowd answered, "This is Jesus, the prophet from Nazareth in Galilee." {21:12} Jesus then went into the temple and kicked out those buying and selling, flipping the tables of the money changers and sellers of doves, {21:13} and said, "This place should be a house of prayer, but you've turned it into a den of thieves." {21:14} The blind and lame came to him in the temple, and he healed them. {21:15} When the religious leaders saw all this and heard children praising Jesus in the temple, they were upset, {21:16} and asked Jesus if he heard what they were saying. Jesus replied, "Of course; haven't you read, 'Out of the mouths of babes and infants, you have perfected praise'?" {21:17} After that, Jesus left for Bethany and stayed there for the night. {21:18} The next morning, as he returned to the city, he felt hungry. {21:19} He saw a fig tree by the road but found no fruit, only leaves, so he said, "May you never bear fruit again!" And right away, the fig tree withered. {21:20} The disciples were amazed at how quickly it withered. {21:21} Jesus told them, "If you have faith and don't doubt, not only can you do what happened to the fig tree, but you can also say to this mountain, 'Be lifted up and thrown into the sea,' and it will happen. {21:22} Whatever you ask for in prayer, believing, you will receive." {21:23} When Jesus entered the temple, the chief priests and elders approached him while he was teaching, asking, "By what authority are you doing these things, and who gave you this authority?" {21:24} Jesus replied, "I'll ask you one question, and if you answer, I'll tell you by what authority I do these things. {21:25} Where did John's baptism come from—heaven or from humans?" They discussed it among themselves, {21:26} saying, "If we say 'from heaven,' he'll ask why we didn't believe John. But if we say 'from humans,' we fear the crowd because they believe John was a prophet." {21:27} So they told Jesus, "We don't know." Jesus said, "Then I won't tell you by what authority I do these things." {21:28-29} "What do you think? A man had two sons. He told the first one to work in the vineyard, and he refused but later changed his mind and went. {21:30} Then he told the second son to go, and he said he would but didn't. {21:31} Which of the two did what the father wanted?" They said the first one. Jesus said, "The tax collectors and prostitutes will enter the kingdom of God ahead of you. {21:32} John came to show you the right way, but you didn't believe him, while the tax collectors and prostitutes did. Even after seeing this, you didn't change your minds and believe him." {21:33} Then Jesus told them another story: "There was a landowner who planted a vineyard, put a wall around it, dug a winepress, and built a watchtower. {21:34} When it was time for the harvest, he sent his servants to the tenants to collect his fruit. {21:35} The tenants beat one servant, killed another, and stoned a third. {21:36} The landowner sent more servants, and the tenants treated them the same way. {21:37} Finally, he sent his son, thinking they would respect him. {21:38} But the tenants said, 'This is the heir. Let's kill him and take his inheritance.' {21:39} So they threw him out of the vineyard and killed him. {21:40-41} Now, when the landowner returns, what will he do to those tenants?" They said he would bring those wicked men to a miserable end and give the vineyard to other tenants who will give him the fruits at the right time. {21:42} Jesus said, "Haven't you read in the Scriptures: 'The stone that the builders rejected has become the cornerstone; this is from the Lord, and it is wonderful in our eyes'? {21:43} Therefore, I tell you, the kingdom of God will be taken away from you and given to a people who will produce its fruit. {21:44} Anyone who falls on this stone will be broken to pieces; anyone on whom it falls will be crushed." {21:45} When the chief priests and Pharisees heard his stories, they knew he was talking about them. {21:46} But because they were afraid of the crowd, they didn't arrest him—they thought he was a prophet.

{22:1} Jesus dropped another parable on them, saying, {22:2} "The kingdom of heaven is like this king who threw a wedding bash for his son. {22:3} He sent out invites, but the guests blew him off. {22:4} So, he sent out more invites, saying, 'Dinner's ready—come through!' {22:5} But they brushed it off and went back to their own stuff—farming, business, you name it. {22:6} Some even mistreated and killed his messengers. {22:7} The king got mad and sent his crew to take care of those murderers and burn their city down. {22:8-9} Then he told his servants, 'The party's still on, but those first guests ain't worthy—hit up the streets and invite anyone you find.' {22:10} So the servants hit the streets and brought in everyone, good and bad, and the party was lit. {22:11} But when the king showed up, he peeped a dude without the right gear for the party. {22:12} The king was like, 'Homie, how'd you get in here without the right fit?' The guy was speechless. {22:13} So the king told his crew, 'Tie him up and toss him out where there's darkness and crying.' {22:14} "For many are invited, but only a few get chosen." {22:15} Later on, the Pharisees tried to trap Jesus with some questions. {22:16} They sent their crew with the Herodians, saying, 'Yo, you're real and teach God's way without playing favorites. {22:17} So, tell us, should we pay taxes to Caesar or what?' {22:18} Jesus knew what was up and called them out, "Why you trying to test me, fakes?" {22:19} Then he asked for a coin and pointed out Caesar's face on it. {22:20-21} They were shook and bounced after Jesus told them, 'Give Caesar his stuff and give God what's God's.' {22:22-23} The same day, the Sadducees tried to trip Jesus up about the afterlife, {22:24} asking about a law where a guy's brother marries his widow if he dies childless—this happened with seven brothers. {22:25} In the resurrection, who's she gonna be married to out of all seven?" {22:26} Jesus schooled them, "Y'all don't know what's up—no marriage in the afterlife; it's angel vibes up there." {22:27} Then he hit them with scripture, "God's not about the dead, but the living." {22:28} The Pharisees heard how Jesus shut down the Sadducees and got together. {22:29} One of them, a lawyer, asked Jesus, "Yo, what's the top commandment in the law?" {22:30} Jesus laid it down, "Love God with everything you got, and love your neighbor like you love yourself." {22:31} "That's the whole deal right there, folks—the law and the prophets hang on these two." {22:32} While they were all there, Jesus hit them with a question, {22:33} "What's your take on the Messiah? Who's his pops?" They said, "David's son." {22:44} Jesus dropped wisdom, "How does David call him Lord then?" {22:34} No one had a comeback, and they stopped trying to test Jesus with questions after that.

{23:1} Jesus was speaking to the crowd and his crew, saying, {23:2} "Check it—those scribes and Pharisees act like they're in charge, but don't follow their lead. {23:3} They pile on rules but won't lift a finger to help. {23:4} They love showing off, wearing fancy gear and grabbing the best seats. {23:5} They're all about appearances, not the real deal. {23:6} Always after the VIP treatment and titles. {23:7-8} Don't let them call the shots—Christ's the real boss, and we're all on the same level. {23:9} Don't go calling anyone 'father' on earth—only one Father in heaven. {23:10-11} The greatest among you? Yeah, they're the ones serving others. {23:12-13} But those scribes and Pharisees? Hypocrites! Blocking heaven for others while doing nothing themselves. {23:14} They prey on widows and show off with long prayers—big trouble awaits them. {23:15} Making converts but leading them astray. {23:16} They focus on trivial oaths while missing the big picture. {23:17} Blind guides, straining at gnats but swallowing camels. {23:18} Ignoring justice, mercy, and faith while obsessing over minor tithes. {23:19} Cleaning the outside but full of greed inside. {23:20} Like fancy tombs—pretty outside but rotten inside. {23:21} Serpents and vipers—can't escape their fate. {23:22} God sends messengers, but they'll mistreat and kill them. {23:23} They'll be held accountable for all the righteous blood spilled. {23:24} It's on this generation. {23:25} Jerusalem, Jerusalem—rejecting prophets sent to gather them. {23:26} Your house is a ghost town. {23:27} You won't see me again until you welcome me with open arms.

{24:1} So Jesus bailed from the temple, and his crew rolled up to him to check out the temple's setup. {24:2} Jesus was like, "Y'all peeping this? I'm telling you, not one stone is staying stacked; it's all gonna get wrecked." {24:3} Later, on the Mount of Olives, the disciples slid up to Jesus on the low, asking, "When's this gonna go down? And how we gonna know you're pulling up and it's endgame?" {24:4} Jesus dropped knowledge, "Stay woke, don't let nobody play you." {24:5} "Fakes gonna pop up in my name, claiming 'I'm the Messiah,' trying to trick everyone." {24:6} "You'll hear about wars and rumors, but chill, this is just the start—endgame ain't here yet." {24:7} "Nations gonna go at it, kingdoms clashing, plus famines, diseases, earthquakes—global chaos vibe." {24:8} "All this is just the beginning of the madness." {24:9} "Soon they'll be hunting you down, hating on you, just 'cause you rep me." {24:10} "Betrayals, beefs, and hate spreading like wildfire." {24:11} "Fake prophets gonna rise up, playing everyone." {24:12} "With sin going wild, love's gonna take an L." {24:13} "But stay true till the end, that's your ticket." {24:14} "First, gospel gotta hit up the whole world—then it's a wrap." {24:15} "When you peep the ultimate disrespect in the holy spot, like Daniel called out—y'all better split." {24:16} "Run for the hills if you're in Judea." {24:17} "On the roof? Stay up there; don't even grab your gear." {24:18} "Out in the fields? Forget grabbing your jacket." {24:19} "Tough times for moms and moms-to-be." {24:20} "Pray your escape ain't in winter or on the Sabbath." {24:21} "Things gonna get real ugly, like never before." {24:22} "If these days don't get cut short, nobody's making it out alive—luckily, the faithful get a break." {24:23} "Don't believe the hype if they say 'Christ is here or there.'" {24:24} "Fakes coming with signs and wonders, trying to fool even the real ones." {24:25} "I'm giving you the heads up." {24:26} "If they say 'He's chilling in the desert or locked up in a room,' don't buy it." {24:27} "My return? It's gonna be quick and bright, like lightning." {24:28} "Where the drama is, that's where the buzzards gather." {24:29} "Right after the chaos, the sky's going dark, stars dropping—total celestial meltdown." {24:30} "Then, you'll see my sign in the sky, and everyone's gonna feel it when I pull up in the clouds, flexing hard." {24:31} "Angels with a loud trumpet call—snatching up my crew from all over." {24:32} "Here's a tip: peep the fig tree; when it starts popping, summer's close—same vibe with these signs." {24:33} "When all this goes down, you know it's game time, right at the doorstep." {24:34} "For real, this generation won't pass till it's all done." {24:35} "Sky and earth can fade, but my words? Eternal." {24:36} "Nobody knows the day or hour, not even angels—only the big man upstairs." {24:37} "Like Noah's days, life was normal till the flood wiped everyone—my return's gonna be like that." {24:38} "People eating, marrying, doing life—then, bam, I'm here." {24:39} "Just like back then, caught off guard till it's too late." {24:40} "Two chilling in the field—one out, one left." {24:41} "Two on the grind—one out, one left." {24:42} "Stay woke, you don't know when I'm showing up." {24:43} "If the homeowner knew the drill, they'd be ready, not caught slipping." {24:44} "So, be ready 'cause I'm sliding in when you least expect." {24:45} "Who's the real MVP? The loyal, wise servant on duty when I pop back." {24:46} "Blessed is that servant—holding it down till I'm back." {24:47} "Trust, I'm giving him the keys to the kingdom." {24:48} "But if that shady servant thinks I'm taking too long—starts messing with the crew, partying it up—" {24:49} "I'm showing up when he ain't ready, dropping the hammer." {24:50} "No slack for the fake—just weeping and grinding teeth."

{25:1} Imagine the kingdom of heaven like this: ten girls, all waiting to link up with the bridegroom, rolled out with their lamps. {25:2} Half were on point, the other half? Not so much. {25:3} The slackers forgot to pack extra oil, while the savvy ones came prepared. {25:4} When the bridegroom took his time, they all passed out. {25:6} Then at midnight, the shout went out: "He's here! Roll out to meet him!" {25:7} So, they all freshened up their lamps. {25:8} The unprepared ones begged the others for oil since theirs ran dry. {25:9} But the wise ones said, "Nah, gotta hit up the store yourselves." {25:10} While they were out shopping, the bridegroom showed up, and the ready ones dipped into the party while the door slammed shut on the others. {25:11} Later, the slackers showed up, banging on the door, "Let us in!" {25:12} But the bridegroom was like, "Sorry, don't know you." {25:13} Moral of the story: stay woke 'cause you never know when the Son of Man's pulling up. {25:14} Another vibe: a dude traveling abroad, entrusted his crew with his stash. {25:15} Gave five to one, two to another, and one to the last, based on their skills. {25:16} The five-talent dude doubled his hustle, turning five into ten. {25:17} Likewise, the two-talent dude flipped his to four. {25:18} But the one-talent guy hid his in the ground. {25:19} After a minute, the boss returned to settle up. {25:20} The five-talent guy flexed, "Doubled up your cash, boss." {25:21} Boss was like, "Solid work, I'll boost your rank; join the celebration." {25:22} The two-talent guy did the same, earning props. {25:23} Boss was like, "Well done, join the party." {25:24} But the one-talent dude made excuses, calling his boss harsh. {25:25} Gave back what he had, unchanged. {25:26} Boss wasn't having it, calling him lazy and shady. {25:27} Said he should've invested, then he'd have something to show. {25:28} So, boss took his talent and gave it to the top earner. {25:29} 'Cause those who hustle get more, but those who slack lose everything. {25:30} Then he banished the slacker to the dark, where there's crying and grinding teeth. {25:31} Now, when the Son of Man returns in glory with his crew, taking his throne, {25:32} he'll gather all nations, sorting them like a shepherd with sheep and goats. {25:33} The sheep get VIP treatment, but the goats? Left out. {25:34} The King tells the good ones, "Come through, inherit the kingdom, you've been real since day one." {25:35} 'Cause they fed him, gave him drink, welcomed him, clothed him, visited him when he was down. {25:36} To the others, it's "Peace out, into eternal fire prepared for the haters." {25:37} 'Cause they ignored his needs when he was hungry, thirsty, homeless, sick, or locked up. {25:38} He's like, "You slept on me, so you slept on yourself." {25:39} The haters get sent off to forever punishment, but the real ones? Living that eternal life.

{26:1} So, when Jesus finished dropping knowledge, he told his crew, {26:2} "Y'all know in two days it's Passover, and I'm about to get betrayed and crucified." {26:3} So the big shots—chief priests, scribes, and elders—gathered at Caiaphas's place, {26:4} plotting how to sneakily nab Jesus and off him. {26:5} But they were like, "Not during the festival, or people will riot." {26:6} Meanwhile, Jesus was chilling at Simon the leper's pad in Bethany, {26:7} when this woman rolls up with a pricey jar of ointment and pours it on his head while they're eating. {26:8} His crew was shook, like, "Why the waste?" {26:9} They thought that cash could've helped the poor. {26:10} Jesus was like, "Chill, she did a good thing for me." {26:11} "You'll always have the poor around, but not me." {26:12} "She's prepping me for burial." {26:13} He's like, "Everywhere the gospel's preached, they'll talk about what she did." {26:14} Then Judas Iscariot, one of the twelve, goes to the chief priests {26:15} asking what they'll pay him to hand Jesus over. They agree on thirty pieces of silver. {26:16} From then on, Judas looked for his chance to sell out Jesus. {26:17} On the first day of Passover, the disciples ask Jesus where to set up. {26:18} He sends them to a guy in the city, saying it's time for Passover at his place with the crew. {26:19} They set it up as Jesus told them. {26:20} That evening, Jesus kicks back with the twelve. {26:21} During dinner, he's like, "One of you will betray me." {26:22} They're all sad, like, "Is it me?" {26:23} Jesus says, "The one sharing my dish will betray me." {26:24} He's like, "It's written, but woe to that betrayer." {26:25} Judas asks, "Is it me?" Jesus is like, "You said it." {26:26} While eating, Jesus blesses and shares bread, calling it his body. {26:27} Then he shares a cup, saying it's his blood for forgiving sins. {26:28} He's like, "I won't drink this again till we're in my Father's kingdom." {26:29-30} After singing, they head to the Mount of Olives. {26:31-32} Jesus tells them they'll all doubt him that night because the scripture says so, but he'll meet them in Galilee after rising. {26:33} Peter's like, "Even if everyone doubts you, I won't." {26:34} Jesus says, "Before the rooster crows, you'll deny me three times." {26:35} Peter's all, "Even if I die with you, I won't deny you." All the disciples say the same. {26:36} They go to Gethsemane, Jesus tells the crew to chill while he prays. {26:37} Taking Peter and Zebedee's sons, he starts feeling down. {26:38} He's like, "I'm super sad; stay with me." {26:39} Jesus prays, "If possible, let this cup pass, but your will be done." {26:40} He finds them sleeping, wakes Peter, "Couldn't you stay awake?" {26:41} "Stay alert to avoid temptation, even if your spirit's willing, your flesh is weak." {26:42} He prays the same again. {26:43} Finding them asleep, he prays a third time. {26:44-45} He tells them to rest since his betrayer's coming. {26:46} "Let's go, he's here." {26:47} Judas arrives with a mob, {26:48} and signals by kissing Jesus. {26:49} Jesus is like, "Friend, why are you here?" They arrest him. {26:50-51} One of the disciples tries to fight, cutting off a dude's ear. {26:52} Jesus stops him, saying swords lead to doom. {26:53} He could ask for angels but has to fulfill scripture. {26:54-55} He's like, "Why come at me now? I was teaching in the temple every day." {26:56} But it's to fulfill the prophets; all the disciples bail. {26:57} They take Jesus to Caiaphas with the council. {26:58} Peter follows but denies knowing Jesus. {26:59} The council looks for false witnesses to condemn Jesus. {26:60-61} They find none until two false witnesses claim Jesus boasted about destroying the temple. {26:62-63} The high priest asks if Jesus is the Son of God. {26:64} Jesus confirms, adding that they'll see him with power. {26:65} The high priest cries blasphemy, and they agree Jesus is guilty. {26:66} They mock and hit Jesus, saying, "Prophesy!" {26:67} Peter denies knowing Jesus, and the rooster crows, reminding him of Jesus's words. He weeps bitterly.

{27:1} When morning came, all the main priests and older heads plotted to take out Jesus; {27:2} they tied him up and handed him over to Governor Pontius Pilate. {27:3} Then Judas, the one who snaked him, saw Jesus was condemned, felt sorry, and took back the thirty pieces of silver to the priests and elders, {27:4} saying, "My bad, I messed up by betraying an innocent dude." They brushed him off, saying, "That's your problem." {27:5} Judas tossed the silver in the temple, split, and offed himself. {27:6} The priests took the silver but couldn't use it for the treasury since it was blood money. {27:7} They used it to buy a potter's field for burying strangers. {27:8} That's why it's called the Field of Blood. {27:9} This fulfilled what Jeremiah said about the thirty pieces of silver used to value the one they priced. {27:10} They bought the potter's field as the Lord directed. {27:11} Jesus faced Pilate, who asked, "Are you the King of the Jews?" Jesus replied, "You said it." {27:12} When accused by the priests and elders, Jesus stayed quiet. {27:13} Pilate was like, "Aren't you going to defend yourself?" {27:14} Jesus didn't say a word, leaving Pilate amazed. {27:15} During the feast, Pilate usually released a prisoner, so they had Barabbas, a notable criminal. {27:16-18} Pilate asked who they wanted freed: Barabbas or Jesus (the Christ), knowing they envied Jesus. {27:19} While judging, Pilate's wife warned him to leave Jesus alone because of a dream. {27:20} But the priests persuaded the crowd to ask for Barabbas and crucify Jesus. {27:21} Pilate asked, "Barabbas or Jesus?" They yelled, "Barabbas!" {27:22} Pilate asked what to do with Jesus. They all shouted, "Crucify him!" {27:23} Pilate questioned why, but they demanded Jesus's crucifixion louder. {27:24} Pilate, seeing the chaos, washed his hands, claiming innocence from Jesus's blood, putting it on them. {27:25} They agreed, saying, "His blood's on us and our kids." {27:26} Pilate released Barabbas, then had Jesus flogged and handed over for crucifixion. {27:27} The soldiers took Jesus to their barracks, gathering the whole squad. {27:28} They stripped him, put a scarlet robe on him, {27:29} crowned him with thorns, handed him a reed, kneeled, and mocked, "Hail, King of the Jews!" {27:30} They spit on him, hit him with the reed, and mocked more. {27:31} After mocking, they dressed him and led him to be crucified. {27:32} On the way, they forced Simon of Cyrene to carry his cross. {27:33-34} They reached Golgotha (Skull Place) and offered Jesus vinegar mixed with gall, which he refused. {27:35} They cast lots for his clothes, fulfilling the prophecy. {27:36} They sat and watched him. {27:37} They put a sign over his head: "This is Jesus, the King of the Jews." {27:38} Two thieves were crucified beside him. {27:39-40} Passersby mocked him, challenging him to save himself if he's the Son of God. {27:41-42} The priests joined in, saying, "He saved others, but he can't save himself. If he's the King of Israel, let him come down, and we'll believe." {27:43} They taunted, "If God's with him, let God save him." {27:44} Even the thieves insulted him. {27:45} Darkness fell from the sixth to ninth hour. {27:46} Around the ninth hour, Jesus cried out, feeling forsaken. {27:47} Some thought he called for Elijah. {27:48-49} They offered vinegar on a sponge, but others waited to see if Elijah would save him. {27:50} Jesus cried out again and died. {27:51} The temple veil tore, the earth quaked, and saints rose from the dead. {27:52} The centurion and crew, witnessing this, acknowledged Jesus as the Son of God. {27:53} Many women who followed Jesus from Galilee watched from afar. {27:54} A rich man named Joseph from Arimathea, a disciple, asked Pilate for Jesus's body, which Pilate granted. {27:55} Joseph wrapped Jesus in linen and placed him in a new tomb, sealing it with a stone. {27:56} Mary Magdalene and another Mary sat by the tomb.

{28:1} After the sabbath, as it started getting light on the first day of the week, Mary Magdalene and the other Mary went to check out the tomb. {28:2} Suddenly, there was a big earthquake because an angel of the Lord came down from heaven, rolled away the stone, and sat on it. {28:3-4} This angel was glowing like lightning, dressed in white like snow, scaring the guards stiff. {28:5} The angel told the women not to be scared, knowing they were looking for Jesus who was crucified. {28:6} "He's not here; he rose just like he said. Come see where he was." {28:7} "Hurry and tell his disciples he's risen and is heading to Galilee; they'll see him there. I've told you." {28:8} The women bolted from the tomb, scared but thrilled, running to tell the disciples. {28:9} On their way, Jesus met them, saying, "Hey!" They held onto his feet and worshipped him. {28:10} Jesus told them not to fear and to tell his crew to meet him in Galilee. {28:11} Meanwhile, some guards went to the chief priests, spilling everything. {28:12} The priests, elders, and guards colluded, bribing the soldiers. {28:13} They told the soldiers to lie, saying the disciples stole Jesus while they slept. {28:14} They promised to deal with the governor if word got out. {28:15} The soldiers took the bribe and spread the story, which stuck around among the Jews. {28:16} The eleven disciples headed to Galilee to the mountain Jesus picked. {28:17} When they saw him, they worshipped, although some had doubts. {28:18} Jesus approached, saying, "I've got all power in heaven and earth." {28:19} "Go out and teach all nations, baptizing in the name of the Father, Son, and Holy Ghost, teaching them to follow my commands. I'm with you always, even to the end of the world." Amen.

Mark

✚✚✚

{1:1} Here's the scoop on Jesus Christ, the Son of God, straight from the get-go. {1:2} It's like the prophets said, "Yo, I'm sending someone ahead of you to prep the scene." {1:3} Picture this: a voice in the wild yelling, "Get ready for the Lord, make his path smooth." {1:4} Then, John shows up, dunking folks in the river, preaching about fixing up their lives. {1:5} Everyone from Judaea and Jerusalem hits him up, getting baptized and owning up to their sins. {1:6} John's vibe? Rocking camel threads, snacking on locusts, and wild honey, and dropping truth bombs. {1:7} He's like, "Someone way bigger than me is on the way, I'm not even worthy to tie his kicks." {1:8} Like, I'm just using water, but he's about to hit you up with the Holy Ghost. {1:9} So, Jesus rolls up from Nazareth, gets baptized by John, and bam, the heavens open, Spirit vibes descending like a dove, and God's like, "Yo, you're my main homie, Jesus." {1:10} Jesus then dips out to the wilderness, chillin' for 40 days, getting tested by Satan, hanging with some wild animals, and getting angelic support. {1:11} After that, John gets locked up, and Jesus slides into Galilee, preaching the Kingdom of God, saying, "It's go time, repent, and get on board with the good news." {1:12} Walking by the sea, Jesus spots Simon and Andrew, fishermen dudes, and he's like, "Yo, come hang with me, and I'll turn you into fishers of people." {1:13} They ditch their nets and roll with him. {1:14} A bit later, Jesus sees James and John, fixing nets on a boat, and they're in too. {1:15} They hit up Capernaum, Jesus drops truth bombs in the synagogue, blowing everyone's minds with his authority. {1:16} Suddenly, a dude with an unclean spirit flips out, recognizing Jesus as the real deal, but Jesus shuts him down. {1:17} People are shook, asking, "Who's this dude speaking like he's in charge, even demons listen up?" {1:18} Word spreads, Jesus' fame goes viral in Galilee. {1:19} Post-synagogue, they crash at Simon and Andrew's pad, with James and John in tow. {1:20} Simon's mother-in-law's sick, they fill Jesus in, and he heals her, and she's back on her feet, serving them. {1:21} That evening, the whole town lines up at Simon's door, bringing their sick and possessed. {1:22} Jesus goes to work, healing diseases, casting out demons, and keeping them silent because they know who's boss. {1:23} Early next morning, Jesus dips out to a quiet spot to pray, Simon and the crew track him down. {1:24} They're like, "Yo, everyone's looking for you!" {1:25} Jesus is like, "Let's bounce to the next town so I can preach there too, that's my gig." {1:26} He's all over Galilee, preaching and casting out demons. {1:27} Along comes a leper, begging Jesus to heal him, and Jesus, filled with compassion, touches him and says, "Cleanse time, my dude." {1:28} Instantly, the leprosy is gone. {1:29} Jesus is like, "Keep it on the down-low, but go show the priests as proof, follow the rules Moses laid out." {1:30} The leper spills the beans everywhere, so Jesus can't roll through the city anymore, he's chilling in the desert, and folks come from all over to vibe with him.

{2:1} Jesus rolls back into Capernaum after a minute; word gets out that he's chilling at this house. {2:2} Instantly, there's a huge crowd, like packed to the max, not even space by the door, and Jesus starts dropping truth bombs. {2:3} Then these homies roll up with their buddy who's sick as, on a stretcher. {2:4} They can't get through the crowd, so they straight up lift their boy onto the roof and bust through it to lower him down to Jesus. {2:5} Jesus peeps their faith and tells the sick dude, "Bro, your sins are forgiven." {2:6} But some haters, the scribes, are there thinking, "Who does this guy think he is, forgiving sins? Only God can do that!" {2:7} Jesus, sensing their vibe, calls them out like, "Why you thinking such nonsense?" {2:8} Then he drops a question bomb on them, like, "What's easier, saying 'Your sins are forgiven' or 'Get up and walk'?" {2:9} Then he's like, "Check this out," and tells the sick dude to get up, grab his stretcher, and bounce. {2:10-12} Dude does it, everyone's mind-blown, and they're all like, "Never seen anything like this!" {2:13} After that, Jesus heads to the beach, and a massive crowd gathers, and he starts dropping knowledge. {2:14} On the way, he spots Levi, just chilling at his customs booth, and tells him, "Come roll with me." Levi's like, "Word," and starts following. {2:15} Later, at Levi's spot, Jesus and his crew are eating with a bunch of tax collectors and sinners, 'cause they're curious and tagging along. {2:16} The religious crew sees this and is like, "Why's he chilling with these folks?" {2:17} Jesus hears and says, "Healthy people don't need a doctor; I'm here for those who know they messed up and want to change." {2:18} Then some folks from John the Baptist's crew and the Pharisees are like, "Why don't your guys fast?" {2:19} Jesus schools them, "You don't fast at a wedding while the party's going; that'll come later." {2:20} He's like, "When I'm gone, they'll fast, but not now." {2:21} Then he drops wisdom, "You don't patch old clothes with new fabric; it won't work." {2:22} And new wine goes in new bottles, otherwise, you'll spill it all. {2:23} One time on a Sabbath, Jesus and the squad stroll through a cornfield, picking grain as they go. {2:24} Pharisees are like, "Yo, why break Sabbath rules?" {2:25} Jesus hits them with a story about David and the showbread. {2:26} He's like, "Sabbath's for people, not the other way around." {2:27} Then he drops the mic with, "I'm the boss of the Sabbath."

{3:1} Jesus rolls back into the synagogue, right? And there's this dude there with a messed-up hand. {3:2} And everyone's eyeballing Jesus, waiting to see if he's gonna heal the guy on the sabbath, just so they can throw shade at him. {3:3} Jesus is like, "Yo, dude with the jacked-up hand, step up." {3:4} Then he's all like, "Is it cool to do good on the sabbath or what? To save a life or to be a buzzkill?" But they're all silent. {3:5} Jesus looks around, totally cheesed off by how hard-hearted they are, and tells the guy, "Yo, stretch out that hand." And bam! Dude's hand is good as new. {3:6} Then the Pharisees bail and start scheming with the Herodians, plotting how to take down Jesus. {3:7} But Jesus peaces out with his crew to the sea, and a massive crowd from all over starts following him, amazed by his sick moves. {3:8} People from Galilee, Judea, Jerusalem, even Idumaea, and beyond Jordan, plus Tyre and Sidon, they're all there, hyped by the word on the street about Jesus. {3:9} Jesus tells his squad to prep a small boat so they don't get mobbed by the crowd. {3:10} 'Cause he's been healing mad folks, and they're all up in his space, trying to touch him for that divine vibe. {3:11} Even the demons, when they see Jesus, are like, "You're the Son of God!" {3:12} But Jesus is like, "Shh, keep it on the down-low." {3:13} Then he hits up a mountain and calls out whoever he wants, and they come running. {3:14} Jesus picks out twelve dudes, tags them to hang with him and spread the word. {3:15} They're packing power to heal and cast out demons. {3:16} Like, Simon's new name is Peter, and James and John get dubbed the "Sons of Thunder." {3:17} Then there's Andrew, Philip, Bartholomew, Matthew, Thomas, James (son of Alphaeus), Thaddaeus, and Simon the Canaanite. {3:18} And Judas Iscariot, the ultimate betrayer, is in the mix too, and they all crash at some crib. {3:19} Meanwhile, the crowd is back, so thick they can't even grab a bite. {3:20-21} And Jesus's crew hears about it and tries to haul him away, thinking he's lost it. {3:22} Then these snobby scribes from Jerusalem roll up, dissing Jesus, saying he's got powers from the devil. {3:23} Jesus calls them out, dropping parables like, "How's Satan gonna fight Satan?" {3:24} Like, if a crew's divided, they're gonna crash, right? {3:25} And if a house is at war with itself, it's toast. {3:26} Same goes for Satan—no way he can stand if he's fighting himself. {3:27} Jesus lays down the truth: You can't rob a tough guy's house unless you tie him up first. {3:28-29} Straight up, all sins can be forgiven, but dissing the Holy Ghost? No redemption, just eternal damnation. {3:30} 'Cause they're saying Jesus is possessed. {3:31} Then Jesus's fam shows up, trying to reach him. {3:32} The crowd tells Jesus, "Yo, your fam's outside looking for you." {3:33} And Jesus is like, "Who's my fam, though?" {3:34} He scans the crowd and says, "Look, my fam is whoever's down to do God's will." {3:35} If you're on that vibe, you're fam—bro, sis, whatever.

{4:1} Jesus hits up the beach to drop some knowledge, and a huge crowd gathers, so he hops in a boat and starts teaching from there while everyone chills on the shore. {4:2} He's dropping mad wisdom in his teachings, spitting truth in parables, like, "Listen up, picture a farmer sowing seeds." {4:3} Some seeds land on the path and birds swoop in and snack them up. {4:4} Other seeds land on rocky ground, shoot up fast but wither away when the sun hits. {4:5} Then there's seeds that fall among thorns, they grow but get choked by life's worries and riches. {4:6} But the real winners are the seeds that fall on good soil, they grow like crazy and bear fruit, big time. {4:7} Jesus is like, "Listen up, if you got ears, use 'em." {4:8} Later, when he's alone, his crew and the twelve are like, "Yo, what's with the farmer story?" {4:9} Jesus is like, "You guys are in on the Kingdom secrets, but outsiders won't get it, so I'm speaking in parables." {4:10} He's like, "Look, understanding this parable is key to getting all my teachings." {4:11} Then he drops the explanation: the farmer is spreading the word, but not everyone's gonna catch on. {4:12} Some hear it but Satan snatches it away, others dig it at first but bail when things get tough, and some let life's drama suffocate the message. {4:13} But those who really get it, they're like fertile soil, bringing in a huge harvest. {4:14} Then Jesus hits them with another analogy, comparing the Kingdom to a mustard seed, small but growing into something massive. {4:15} He's dropping these truth bombs in parables, keeping things on the DL for those who are ready to hear it. {4:16} But when it's just his crew, he breaks it down for them, no frills. {4:17} Later that day, he's like, "Let's bounce to the other side of the lake." {4:18} After ditching the crowd, they sail off, but a crazy storm hits, and they're freaking out, waking Jesus up like, "Don't you care if we die?" {4:19} Jesus calms the storm, and they're like, "Whoa, this dude can even control the weather?"

{5:1} So they cruise over to the other side of the sea, into Gadarenes' turf. {5:2} Soon as Jesus steps off the boat, this wild dude from the tombs, possessed and all, bolts up to him. {5:3} This guy was living in the graveyards, uncontrollable, breaking chains like it's nothing, and nobody could calm him down. {5:4} He'd been chained up multiple times, but he'd just break free; no one could handle him. {5:5} He's always in the hills and tombs, yelling and cutting himself with rocks. {5:6} But when he spots Jesus from afar, he runs up and bows down, shouting, "Why you messing with me, Jesus, Son of the Most High? I beg you, don't torture me!" {5:7} Jesus tells the unclean spirit to bounce out of the man. {5:8} Then he asks the spirit its name; it's like, "We're Legion, man, loads of us here." {5:9-10} They beg Jesus not to kick them out of the country. {5:11} Nearby there's this huge herd of pigs. {5:12} The spirits ask to go into the pigs, and Jesus lets them. {5:13} They leave the man, possess the pigs, and the pigs go nuts, rushing into the sea and drowning. {5:14} The pig farmers freak and tell everyone in town what went down. {5:15} People come and see the formerly possessed guy, now chilling, dressed, and totally sane; they're shook. {5:16} Folks who saw it spill the beans about the guy and what happened to the pigs. {5:17} They start begging Jesus to leave their area. {5:18} So Jesus heads back to the boat, and the once-possessed guy wants to go with him. {5:19} But Jesus is like, "Nah, go home, tell your friends about the amazing stuff God did for you." {5:20} Dude goes and spreads the word in Decapolis about what Jesus did, blowing everyone's minds. {5:21} Jesus hops back on a boat, and a big crowd gathers by the sea. {5:22-23} Then Jairus, a synagogue ruler, shows up, falls at Jesus' feet, and begs him to come heal his dying daughter by laying hands on her. {5:24} Jesus rolls with him, and a massive crowd tags along, all up in his space. {5:25-28} Meanwhile, a woman who'd been bleeding for twelve years, suffering and broke from doctors, hears about Jesus and sneaks up to touch his clothes in the crowd, thinking it'll heal her. {5:29} Immediately, she stops bleeding; she knows she's healed. {5:30-32} Jesus senses power go out from him, turns around in the crowd, and asks who touched him. {5:33} The woman, scared but honest, comes clean and tells Jesus everything. {5:34} Jesus says, "Your faith made you well; go in peace, free from your affliction." {5:35} While he's talking, messengers from Jairus' house arrive, saying his daughter died, so why bother Jesus anymore? {5:36} Jesus tells Jairus, "Don't sweat it; just believe." {5:37} He only lets Peter, James, and John come with him. {5:38} They get to Jairus' house, and it's chaotic with crying and wailing. {5:39-40} Jesus says, "Why all the fuss? She's not dead; she's just sleeping." {5:41} Everyone laughs, but Jesus kicks them out, takes the girl's parents and his crew, and goes to her room. {5:42} He takes her hand, says, "Get up, girl," and she does, shocking everyone. {5:43} Jesus tells them to keep it on the down-low and gives the girl something to eat.

{6:1} Jesus dips from there and heads back to his hometown, with his crew trailing behind. {6:2} When it's Sabbath, he starts spitting wisdom in the synagogue, blowing everyone's minds. They're like, "Where'd this dude get all this knowledge and power?" {6:3} They start throwing shade, like, "Isn't this just the local carpenter, Mary's kid? And ain't his siblings here with us?" They're straight up offended. {6:4} But Jesus shuts them down, saying, "Prophets get no love in their own hood, among their fam, or even in their own crib." {6:5} He couldn't flex his full power there, just healed a few sick peeps by laying hands on them. {6:6} He's shook by their lack of belief and bounces to teach in other spots. {6:7} Jesus calls his twelve homies and sends them out in pairs, giving them power over demons. {6:8} He tells them to travel light, just with a staff, no bags, no bread, no cash. {6:9} But they gotta have kicks and not rock double coats. {6:10} He's like, "Crash wherever you're welcomed till you peace out." {6:11} If they're dissed, they gotta shake off the dust and bounce, leaving a vibe of judgment. It's gonna be worse for those haters than for Sodom and Gomorrah. {6:12} So they hit the streets, preaching repentance. {6:13} Casting out demons, anointing the sick with oil, and healing them became their daily hustle. {6:14} King Herod catches wind of Jesus, thinking he's John the Baptist risen from the grave, all 'cause of the buzz about his miracles. {6:15} Others think he's Elijah or a prophet. {6:16} Herod's like, "Nah, it's definitely John, the guy I had killed." {6:17} He offed John 'cause he called him out for marrying his brother's wife, Herodias. {6:18} That ticked off Herodias, who wanted John dead but couldn't touch him 'cause Herod respected him. {6:19} Herod throws a lit birthday bash and makes a wild promise to his stepdaughter. {6:20} She asks for John the Baptist's head, and though Herod's bummed, he follows through for the sake of his word. {6:21} John's disciples lay him to rest, while Jesus and his crew share their adventures. {6:22} Jesus suggests they chill in a remote spot for a bit, 'cause the crowds are relentless. {6:23} But the peeps track them down, showing up in droves. {6:24} Seeing them, Jesus feels for them, like lost sheep needing a shepherd, and starts teaching again. {6:25} When evening hits, the disciples remind Jesus it's a desert out there and the people need food. {6:26} Jesus flips it on them, telling them to feed the crowd. They're like, "You want us to drop serious dough on food?" {6:27} He's like, "Nah, what you got?" They find five loaves and two fish. {6:28} Jesus blesses it, breaks it, and feeds thousands, with leftovers to spare. {6:29} After that miracle, they head across the sea, Jesus stays back to pray. {6:30} When night falls, Jesus walks on water, freaking out his disciples. {6:31} But he reassures them, and when he joins them in the boat, the storm calms, blowing their minds even more. {6:32} They're so shook they miss the lesson from the feeding miracle, 'cause their hearts are hard. {6:33} They hit Gennesaret, and word spreads like wildfire, with sick folk getting carried to Jesus from every corner. {6:34} Sick peeps just wanna touch his clothes, 'cause they know that's all it takes to get healed.

{7:1} So, the Pharisees and some scribes roll up from Jerusalem. {7:2} They peep Jesus' crew munchin' on bread without washing their hands, and they start hatin'. {7:3} Pharisees and Jews are all about washing hands before meals, stickin' to elders' rules and all that jazz. {7:4} They're strict about washing after market runs, even cleanin' cups, pots, and tables. {7:5} So, they're like, "Yo Jesus, why your squad not following the elder traditions, eating with dirty hands?" {7:6} Jesus hits back, like, "Isaiah was spot on about you hypocrites, all talk but no heart." {7:7} He's like, "Your worship's pointless, you're teaching human-made rules as gospel." {7:8} "You're ditching God's rules for human traditions, like washing cups." {7:9} Jesus calls them out, "You're ignoring God's commands for your own traditions." {7:10} Moses said, "Respect your parents," but y'all are like, "Screw it, just say 'Corban' and you're off the hook." {7:11} You're even stopping people from helping their parents, making God's word worthless with your traditions. {7:12} Then Jesus calls everyone over and drops some truth bombs. {7:13} He's like, "Listen up, what goes into your mouth don't defile you, only what comes out does." {7:14} If you got ears, use 'em. {7:15} Later, his squad's like, "Explain the parable, Jesus." {7:16} He's like, "Seriously? Don't you get it? Stuff from outside doesn't make you dirty." {7:17} Jesus breaks it down further when they're alone, saying what you eat goes through you, it's no biggie. {7:18} He's like, "Evil stuff comes from within, like bad thoughts, adultery, theft, and all that jazz." {7:19} It's all about what comes out that messes you up. {7:20} Jesus lays down some wisdom, saying evil stuff comes from the heart, not from outside. {7:21} He's like, "From inside, you get all the messed-up stuff, not from outside." {7:22} So, Jesus bounces to Tyre and Sidon, trying to lay low, but word spreads. {7:23} This Greek lady with a daughter possessed by a demon rolls up, begging Jesus to help. {7:24} Jesus is like, "I gotta hook up the Israelites first, not cool to throw their bread to the dogs." {7:25} She's like, "Okay, but even dogs get crumbs." {7:26} Jesus is impressed and cures her daughter remotely. {7:27} She heads home, finds her daughter demon-free, chillin' in bed. {7:28} Jesus dips from Tyre and Sidon, heads back to the Sea of Galilee through Decapolis. {7:29} They bring him a deaf guy with a speech impediment, begging for help. {7:30} Jesus takes him aside, does some weird stuff with spit, fingers, and words, and boom, the guy can hear and talk. {7:31} Jesus warns them to keep it on the down-low, but they can't help but spread the word about his miracles. {7:32} Everyone's mind-blown, saying, "This dude's legit, he's making deaf people hear and mute people talk like it's NBD."

{8:1} In those days, there was this massive crowd hanging around, starving because they'd been chilling with Jesus for three days straight with no grub. {8:2-3} Jesus feels for them, knowing they've been with him a while and need food, or they'll drop on the way home, especially those who came from far out. {8:4} The disciples are like, "How can we feed all these people out here in the middle of nowhere?" {8:5} Jesus asks them, "How much bread do we have?" They say, "Seven loaves." {8:6} So Jesus has everyone sit down, takes the seven loaves, blesses them, breaks them, and gives them to the disciples to distribute to the crowd. {8:7} They also have a few small fish, which Jesus blesses and tells them to serve as well. {8:8} Everyone eats and is full, and they collect seven baskets of leftovers. {8:9} There were about four thousand people who ate, and then Jesus sends them off. {8:10} He hops on a boat with his disciples and heads to Dalmanutha. {8:11} The Pharisees show up and start hassling Jesus, demanding a sign from heaven to test him. {8:12} Jesus sighs deeply and asks why this generation is so obsessed with signs. {8:13} He bounces, gets back on the boat, and heads to the other side. {8:14} The disciples realize they forgot to bring enough bread, having only one loaf with them. {8:15} Jesus warns them to watch out for the leaven of the Pharisees and Herod. {8:16} The disciples start worrying, thinking Jesus is talking about bread. {8:17} Jesus calls them out, asking if their hearts are still hard, even though they've seen so much. {8:18-20} He's like, "You've got eyes but don't see, and ears but don't hear? Don't you remember when we fed five thousand with five loaves and twelve baskets were left over, or four thousand with seven loaves and seven baskets were left over?" {8:21} He's like, "Why don't you get it?" {8:22} They roll up to Bethsaida, and they bring a blind guy, begging Jesus to touch him. {8:23} Jesus takes the blind man out of town, spits on his eyes, puts his hands on him, and asks if he can see anything. {8:24} The man looks up and says he sees people like trees walking around. {8:25} Jesus lays hands on him again, and suddenly the guy can see clearly. {8:26} Jesus tells him not to go back into town or tell anyone in town what happened. {8:27} They head into the towns of Caesarea Philippi, and Jesus asks his disciples who people say he is. {8:28} They say some think he's John the Baptist, others say Elijah or one of the prophets. {8:29} Jesus asks them directly, "Who do you say I am?" Peter steps up and says, "You're the Christ." {8:30} Jesus warns them not to tell anyone about him. {8:31} Then he starts teaching them about how the Son of Man must suffer, be rejected by the elders, chief priests, and scribes, be killed, and rise after three days. {8:32} He says this openly, but Peter rebukes him. {8:33} Jesus turns around, looks at his disciples, and tells Peter to get behind him, calling him out for focusing on human things, not God's things. {8:34} Jesus gathers the crowd with his disciples and tells them that anyone who wants to follow him must deny themselves, take up their cross, and follow him. {8:35} He explains that those who try to save their own lives will lose them, but those who lose their lives for his sake and the gospel's will save them. {8:36} He asks what good it does to gain the whole world but lose your soul. {8:37} Or what can you give in exchange for your soul? {8:38} Jesus warns that if anyone is ashamed of him and his words in this messed up generation, he'll be ashamed of them when he comes in his Father's glory with the holy angels.

{9:1} So, Jesus tells them straight up, "Some of you here won't kick the bucket till you've seen God's kingdom come in full power." {9:2} Six days later, Jesus rolls with Peter, James, and John up this high mountain, and bam! He's glowing like a cosmic light show. {9:3} His gear shines brighter than a snowstorm, no laundry detergent could get them that white. {9:4} Then out of nowhere, Elijah and Moses pop up, shooting the breeze with Jesus. {9:5} Peter's hyped, like, "Let's build three chill spots, one for you, one for Moses, and one for Elijah." {9:6} He's clueless and scared stiff. {9:7} Suddenly, a cloud covers them, and a voice booms out, "This is my boy, Jesus. Listen up!" {9:8} And just like that, the other dudes vanish, leaving only Jesus with the squad. {9:9} Coming down the mountain, Jesus tells them to keep it on the low until he's risen from the dead. {9:10} They're puzzled, hashing out what "rising from the dead" even means. {9:11} They're like, "Why do the scribes say Elijah's gotta show up first?" {9:12} Jesus schools them, saying Elijah will come and fix things, but he's gotta suffer a lot, as the prophecy says. {9:13} He drops a truth bomb, saying Elijah's already come, but they did him dirty, just like the prophecy said. {9:14} Back with his crew, Jesus finds a mob and scribes arguing. {9:15} Everyone's shook seeing him and rushes to greet him. {9:16} Jesus asks, "What's the debate about?" {9:17} Some dude steps up, like, "My kid's possessed, and your disciples couldn't do squat." {9:18} The kid's possessed, wild, and the dad's desperate for help. {9:19} Jesus calls them out for their lack of faith and heals the kid. {9:20} The spirit freaks, throws the kid down, but Jesus fixes him up. {9:21} Jesus asks the dad how long the kid's been messed up, and the dad's like, "Since he was a kid, man." {9:22} The spirit's been trying to wreck him since day one, but the dad's hoping for a miracle. {9:23} Jesus tells him, "If you believe, anything's possible." {9:24} The dad's in tears, admitting his doubts. {9:25} Jesus shuts down the spirit, and the kid's healed, blowing everyone's minds. {9:26} They think he's dead until Jesus lifts him up. {9:27} Back at the crib, the disciples ask Jesus why they couldn't do it. {9:28-29} Jesus tells them some demons only bounce with prayer and fasting. {9:30} They bounce, cruising through Galilee, keeping things low-key. {9:31} Jesus warns them he's gonna get nabbed and offed, but he'll bounce back in three days. {9:32} They're clueless and too scared to ask. {9:33} They hit up Capernaum, and Jesus asks what they were arguing about. {9:34} They clam up, 'cause they were squabbling about who's the top dog. {9:35} Jesus schools them, saying the last shall be first, and he even grabs a kid to prove his point. {9:36} He's like, "If you welcome a kid in my name, you're welcoming me." {9:37} John's like, "We saw this dude casting out demons in your name, but he ain't part of our squad, so we told him to chill." {9:38} Jesus is like, "Nah, if he's not against us, he's for us." {9:39} Anyone repping Jesus won't be talking smack about him. {9:40-41} If someone's just offering a drink in Jesus's name, they're getting blessed. {9:42} But if you mess with believers, it's better to sink in the ocean with a millstone around your neck. {9:43} If your hand, foot, or eye leads you to sin, chop it off, 'cause it's better to be maimed and in heaven than burning in eternal fire. {9:44} Everyone's getting tested by fire, and sacrifices gotta be seasoned with salt. {9:45} Salt's good, but if it loses its flavor, what's the point? Stay salty and chill with each other.

{10:1} Jesus bounced to the Judean side of the Jordan, and the crowd came flockin' to him like usual, and he dropped some knowledge bombs on 'em. {10:2} Then the Pharisees slid up to him, asking, "Is it cool to divorce your spouse?" trying to trip him up. {10:3} Jesus clapped back, "What did Moses tell you?" {10:4} They're like, "Moses said we could give our spouses the boot with a legal paper." {10:5} Jesus hits 'em with truth, "Moses only gave you that 'cause you're hard-headed." {10:6} He's like, "From the start, God made humans male and female." {10:7} "That's why folks leave their parents to be with their spouse." {10:8} "They become one flesh, so don't mess with that bond." {10:9} "God put them together, don't tear 'em apart." {10:10} Later, his crew's like, "Break it down again, Jesus." {10:11} He's like, "Anyone who dumps their spouse and hops to another is straight-up cheatin'." {10:12} "Same goes if a woman ditches her man for another dude." {10:13} Folks tryna bring their kids to Jesus, but his crew's like, "Nah, chill." {10:14} Jesus ain't havin' it, he's like, "Let the kids vibe with me, 'cause the kingdom's all about them." {10:15} "You gotta embrace God's kingdom like a kid, or you ain't gettin' in." {10:16} So, he scoops up the kids, blesses 'em, and keeps it movin'. {10:17} On the road, this guy runs up, kneels, and asks, "How do I score eternal life?" {10:18} Jesus is like, "Why you callin' me good? Only God's truly good." {10:19} "You know the rules: don't cheat, kill, steal, lie, or disrespect your folks." {10:20} Dude's like, "I'm good on all that since I was a kid." {10:21} Jesus peeps him, loves him, and hits him with a bombshell, "Sell your stuff, give to the poor, and roll with me." {10:22} Dude's bummed 'cause he's loaded. {10:23} Jesus tells his crew, "Rich folks strugglin' to enter God's kingdom, real talk." {10:24} They're shook, so Jesus repeats, "It's easier for a camel to squeeze through a needle than a rich dude makin' it in." {10:25-26} They're mind-blown, like, "Who can even be saved then?" {10:27} Jesus hits 'em with the truth, "Can't do it on your own, but with God, anything's possible." {10:28} Peter's like, "We left everything for you, Jesus." {10:29-30} Jesus says, "You'll get back a hundred times what you lost, plus eternal life." {10:31} "The first might be last, and the last first." {10:32} As they head to Jerusalem, Jesus predicts his death and resurrection. {10:33} James and John ask to be top dogs in Jesus' kingdom. {10:34} Jesus checks 'em, "You know what you're askin' for?" {10:35} They're like, "Yeah, we're good." {10:36} Jesus says, "That's not up to me, but those it's prepared for." {10:37} His crew's ticked at James and John. {10:38} Jesus schools them, sayin', "Real leaders serve, not boss people around." {10:39} "Even I came to serve, not be served, and to give my life for everyone." {10:40} They hit up Jericho, and this blind dude Bartimaeus begs for mercy. {10:41} When he hears it's Jesus, he shouts for help. {10:42} Folks tell him to shush, but he yells even louder for Jesus' mercy. {10:43} Jesus stops, calls him over, and folks tell him, "Cheer up, Jesus wants to see you." {10:44} Dude throws off his coat, hustles to Jesus. {10:51} Jesus asks, "What can I do for you?" Dude's like, "I wanna see again." {10:45} Jesus says, "Your faith healed you," and boom, dude can see, and he follows Jesus.

{11:1} When they were getting close to Jerusalem, near Bethphage and Bethany on the Mount of Olives, Jesus sends out two of his disciples {11:2} and tells them, "Go into the village ahead of you, and as soon as you get there, you'll see a young donkey tied up that no one has ever ridden. Untie it and bring it to me." {11:3} If anyone asks why they're taking it, Jesus tells them to say, "The Lord needs it," and they'll let them take it. {11:4} The disciples go, find the donkey tied up where two roads meet, and untie it. {11:5} Some people standing there ask them what they're doing, untying the donkey. {11:6} They reply just as Jesus instructed, and the people let them go. {11:7} They bring the donkey to Jesus, throw their cloaks on its back, and Jesus sits on it. {11:8} Many spread their cloaks on the road, while others cut branches and spread them on the road. {11:9-10} The crowd that went ahead and those following behind shouted, "Hosanna! Blessed is he who comes in the name of the Lord! Blessed is the coming kingdom of our father David! Hosanna in the highest heaven!" {11:11} Jesus enters Jerusalem and goes into the temple. After looking around at everything, since it was already late, he leaves for Bethany with the twelve. {11:12} The next day, after they come from Bethany, Jesus feels hungry. {11:13} Seeing a fig tree in the distance covered with leaves, he goes to it hoping to find something to eat. But when he gets there, he finds nothing but leaves because it wasn't the season for figs. {11:14} Jesus curses the fig tree, saying, "May no one ever eat fruit from you again!" His disciples overhear him. {11:15} They arrive in Jerusalem, and Jesus goes into the temple. He starts driving out those who were buying and selling there. He overturns the tables of the money changers and the benches of those selling doves, {11:16} and doesn't let anyone carry merchandise through the temple courts. {11:17} He teaches them, quoting Scripture: "My house will be called a house of prayer for all nations, but you have made it a den of thieves." {11:18} The scribes and chief priests hear this and start looking for a way to kill Jesus because the people were amazed at his teaching. {11:19} When evening comes, Jesus and his disciples leave the city. {11:20} The next morning as they pass by, they see the fig tree withered from the roots. {11:21} Peter points it out to Jesus, saying, "Master, look! The fig tree you cursed has withered!" {11:22} Jesus replies, "Have faith in God." {11:23} He tells them that if anyone says to a mountain, "Be lifted up and thrown into the sea," and believes it will happen without doubting, it will be done. {11:24} Jesus encourages them to pray with faith, believing they will receive what they ask for. {11:25} He also teaches them that when they stand praying, if they have anything against someone, they should forgive them so that their Father in heaven may forgive their sins. {11:26} But if they don't forgive others, their Father won't forgive them either. {11:27} They return to Jerusalem, and as Jesus is walking in the temple, the chief priests, scribes, and elders approach him {11:28} and demand, "By what authority are you doing these things? And who gave you this authority?" {11:29} Jesus responds, "Let me ask you a question, and if you answer me, I'll tell you by what authority I do these things." {11:30} He asks them about John the Baptist's baptism—was it from heaven or of human origin? {11:31} They discuss among themselves, worried about how to answer. {11:32} They're afraid to say it was merely human because the people considered John a prophet. {11:33} So, they tell Jesus they don't know, and Jesus responds that he won't tell them by what authority he acts either.

{12:1} Jesus starts spitting some parables. There's this dude who plants a vineyard, fences it up, digs out a spot for the wine, throws up a tower, then rents it out and jets off. {12:2} When it's time, he sends a servant to collect his share, but the renters beat him and send him back empty-handed. {12:3-4} He tries again with another servant, and they chuck stones at him and send him back busted up. {12:5} They straight up kill the next guy, and even more after that, beating and killing them. {12:6} Finally, he sends his son, thinking they'll respect him. {12:7} But these dudes are like, "Yo, this is the heir. Let's off him and take his inheritance." {12:8} So, they kill the son and chuck him out. {12:9} What's the landlord gonna do? He'll kick out those renters and give the vineyard to someone else. {12:10-12} Jesus is like, "Ever read that scripture? The stone the builders rejected is now the cornerstone. It's wild, right?" {12:13} Then the Pharisees and Herodians try to trip him up. {12:14} They're like, "Yo, is it cool to pay taxes to Caesar?" {12:15} Jesus ain't falling for it and tells them, "Show me a coin." {12:16} They flash the coin, and he's like, "Whose face is on this?" They're like, "Caesar's." {12:17} Jesus drops wisdom, saying, "Give Caesar what's his and give God what's His." They're shook. {12:18} Next up, the Sadducees question Jesus about the afterlife. {12:19} They're like, "Moses said if a dude dies leaving his wife without kids, his bro should marry her." {12:20-23} They spin a tale about seven brothers all marrying the same chick 'cause they all die. {12:23} They're like, "In heaven, whose wife will she be?" {12:24} Jesus schools them, saying they're clueless about the Bible and the power of God. {12:25} Ain't no marriage in heaven; it's like angels up there. {12:26} God ain't God of the dead but of the living. They're way off. {12:27-28} Then a scribe asks Jesus which commandment is tops. {12:29-30} Jesus says, "Love God with everything you've got, and love your neighbor like you love yourself." {12:31} Loving God and others is the real deal, no sacrifice can top that. {12:32} The scribe agrees, and Jesus says he's close to the kingdom. Nobody dares to question him after that. {12:33} Jesus flips the script, asking how the scribes think the Messiah is David's son. {12:34} David calls the Messiah "Lord." Crowd's loving it. {12:35} Jesus warns about scribes who love showing off in fancy clothes, hogging the best seats, and scamming widows. {12:36} He watches people donating, and a poor widow gives everything she's got. Jesus points her out, saying she gave more than the rich folks.

{13:1} Jesus is bouncin' out of the temple, and one of his homies goes, "Yo, peep these dope stones and buildings!" {13:2} Jesus is like, "Check it, all these buildings? They're gonna get wrecked, not a single stone left on top of another." {13:3} Later, Jesus is chillin' on the Mount of Olives, and Peter, James, John, and Andrew pull him aside. {13:4} They're like, "When's all this gonna go down, and what are the signs?" {13:5} Jesus lays it out, "Watch out for fakes claimin' to be me, tryna fool y'all." {13:6} "Wars, rumors, earthquakes, famines? Chill, it's just the start of the craziness." {13:7-9} "You'll get dragged to court, beaten up in synagogues, and dragged in front of rulers 'cause you're reppin' me." {13:10} "But first, gotta spread the gospel worldwide." {13:11} "When you get hauled in, don't stress about what to say. The Holy Ghost will give you the words." {13:12} "Families gonna turn on each other, hatin' 'cause of me." {13:13} "Everyone's gonna hate you for followin' me, but if you hang tight, you're good." {13:14} "When you see the 'abomination of desolation,' get outta Dodge, especially if you're in Judaea." {13:15} "Don't fall for folks sayin', 'Jesus is here or there.' They're lying, tryna deceive even the faithful." {13:16} "Watch out for fake Messiahs and prophets pullin' stunts, tryna trick even my chosen crew." {13:17} "No one knows when it's goin' down, not even me, only the big man upstairs." {13:18} "Stay woke, pray, 'cause you never know when it's game time." {13:19} "I'm like a boss leavin' town, givin' my squad jobs and tellin' 'em to stay alert." {13:20} "What I'm sayin'? Everyone, stay on guard."

{14:1} So, like two days later, it was time for the Passover and the Feast of Unleavened Bread. The chief priests and the scribes were plotting to arrest Jesus secretly and kill him. {14:2} But they were like, "Not during the festival, or there might be a riot among the people." {14:3} Meanwhile, in Bethany at Simon the leper's house, while Jesus was chilling at dinner, a woman came in with this fancy alabaster box of expensive spikenard ointment. She breaks open the box and pours it all over Jesus' head. {14:4} Some people were like, "Why this waste of expensive ointment?" {14:5} They were saying it could have been sold for a ton of money and given to the poor, and they were grumbling about it. {14:6} Jesus was like, "Leave her alone, why are you bothering her? She's done a good thing for me." {14:7} He reminds them that they'll always have the opportunity to help the poor, but he won't be around forever. {14:8} Jesus acknowledges that she did what she could, and she's anointed him in advance for his burial. {14:9} He predicts that her story will be told wherever the gospel is preached as a memorial to her. {14:10} Meanwhile, Judas Iscariot, one of the twelve disciples, goes to the chief priests to betray Jesus. {14:11} They're totally thrilled and promise to pay Judas. He starts figuring out the best way to betray Jesus. {14:12} On the first day of the Feast of Unleavened Bread, when they were preparing to celebrate the Passover, Jesus' disciples asked him where he wanted them to go to prepare for the Passover meal. {14:13} Jesus sends two of his disciples into the city, telling them they'll meet a guy carrying a water pitcher. They should follow him. {14:14} When they see him go into a house, they should tell the owner, "The Master says, 'Where is the guest room where I can eat the Passover with my disciples?'" {14:15} The owner will show them a furnished upper room—perfect for the Passover. They get everything ready there. {14:16} Later that evening, Jesus arrives with the twelve. {14:17-18} As they sit down to eat, Jesus drops a bombshell: one of them eating with him will betray him. {14:19} They start feeling sad and each one asks him, "Is it me?" {14:20} Jesus reveals it's one of the twelve who's dipping bread with him in the dish. {14:21} Jesus talks about his fate, saying it's written that he will be betrayed, but it will be terrible for the one who does it. {14:22} During the meal, Jesus takes bread, blesses it, breaks it, and gives it to them, saying, "Take this, it's my body." {14:23} Then he takes a cup, gives thanks, and they all drink from it. {14:24} He explains that the cup is his blood of the new covenant, shed for many. {14:25} Jesus adds that he won't drink wine again until he does so in the kingdom of God. {14:26} After singing a hymn, they head to the Mount of Olives. {14:27} Jesus tells them they'll all abandon him that night, fulfilling the prophecy about scattering the sheep when the shepherd is struck. {14:28} He assures them that after his resurrection, he'll meet them in Galilee. {14:29} Peter confidently declares that even if everyone else falls away, he won't. {14:30} But Jesus predicts that before the rooster crows twice that night, Peter will deny him three times. {14:31} Peter insists that he'll never deny Jesus, even if it means dying with him, and the others agree. {14:32} They arrive at Gethsemane, and Jesus tells his disciples to wait while he prays. {14:33} Taking Peter, James, and John with him, Jesus becomes deeply distressed and troubled. {14:34} He tells them his soul is overwhelmed with sorrow to the point of death and asks them to stay and keep watch. {14:35} Jesus goes a little further, falls to the ground, and prays that if possible, he can avoid his upcoming ordeal. {14:36} He submits to God's will, saying, "Father, everything is possible for you. Take this cup from me. Yet not what I will, but what you will." {14:37} Jesus returns to find his disciples sleeping and rebukes Peter for not staying awake. {14:38} He tells them to pray to avoid temptation since their spirit is willing but their flesh is weak. {14:39} Jesus prays the same words again, then returns to find them sleeping once more, too tired to respond. {14:40-41} When he comes back a third time, he tells them to rest since the time has come for him to be betrayed into the hands of sinners. {14:42} Jesus urges them to get up because the one who will betray him is approaching. {14:43} Right then, Judas arrives with a crowd armed with swords and clubs, sent by the chief priests, scribes, and elders. {14:44} Judas had agreed to identify Jesus by kissing him, and when he arrives, he does just that. {14:45-46} The guards arrest Jesus, {14:47} and one of the bystanders draws a sword, cutting off a servant's ear. {14:48} Jesus questions their use of force to arrest him like he's a criminal when he taught openly in the temple without resistance. {14:49} He points out that they could have arrested him in public, but it had to happen this way to fulfill the Scriptures. {14:50} The disciples all abandon him and run away. {14:51-52} One young man tries to follow Jesus but flees naked when they seize him. {14:53} They bring Jesus to the high priest along with the assembled chief priests, elders, and scribes. {14:54} Peter follows at a distance, even entering the high priest's courtyard to warm himself by the fire. {14:55} Inside, the chief priests and council seek false testimony against Jesus to put him to death but find none that agree. {14:56} Many give conflicting false testimonies. {14:57} Finally, some stand and falsely accuse Jesus of saying he would destroy the temple and rebuild it in three days. {14:58-59} Even these witnesses can't agree. {14:60} The high priest demands that Jesus answer the charges against him, but Jesus remains silent. {14:61-62} When the high priest asks if he's the Christ, the Son of the Blessed, Jesus affirms, "I am, and you will see the Son of Man seated at the right hand of Power and coming with the clouds of heaven." {14:63} Outraged, the high priest tears his clothes, declaring Jesus guilty of blasphemy. {14:64} They all condemn him, spitting on him, covering his face, and striking him while mocking him. {14:65} Meanwhile, Peter denies knowing Jesus when questioned by a servant girl, then again when accused by others. {14:66} The rooster crows, and Peter recalls Jesus' prediction. Overcome with regret, he weeps bitterly.

{15:1} The next morning, the big shots — the chief priests, elders, and scribes — gather up Jesus and hand him over to Pilate. {15:2} Pilate's like, "Are you the King of the Jews?" Jesus is just like, "You said it." {15:3} The priests throw all sorts of accusations at him, but he stays silent. {15:4-5} Pilate's getting annoyed, like, "You're not gonna say anything?" He's shocked Jesus isn't defending himself. {15:6} During the feast, Pilate usually sets a prisoner free, so he's like, "Who do you want this time?" {15:7-8} There's this dude Barabbas, a real troublemaker, and the crowd starts shouting for him to be released. {15:9} Pilate's like, "You want the King of the Jews or Barabbas?" He knows the priests are just jealous. {15:10} But the priests stir up the crowd to ask for Barabbas instead. {15:11} Pilate's getting desperate, like, "What do you want me to do with this guy you call the King of the Jews?" {15:12} To please the crowd, Pilate lets Barabbas go and hands Jesus over to be whipped and crucified. {15:13} The soldiers take Jesus to the Praetorium and gather their crew. {15:14} They deck him out in purple and make a crown of thorns for him, mocking him as the King of the Jews. {15:15} They beat him up, spit on him, and pretend to worship him. {15:16} After they've had their fun, they put his own clothes back on and take him to be crucified. {15:17} They force this guy Simon from Cyrene to carry Jesus's cross. {15:18} They bring him to Golgotha, which means "skull place." {15:19} They offer Jesus some wine mixed with myrrh, but he refuses. {15:20} They divide up his clothes and throw dice for them. {15:21} It's around 9 AM when they nail him to the cross. {15:22} The sign above him reads "THE KING OF THE JEWS." {15:23} They crucify two criminals with him, one on each side. {15:24} From noon to 3 PM, darkness covers the whole land. {15:25} At 3 PM, Jesus shouts, "My God, my God, why have you forsaken me?" {15:26} With a loud cry, Jesus breathes his last breath. {15:27} The temple curtain tears in two from top to bottom. {15:28} The centurion overseeing Jesus's execution sees how Jesus dies and declares, "This man was truly the Son of God." {15:29} Some women, including Mary Magdalene and Mary the mother of Joses, watch from a distance. {15:30} Joseph of Arimathea, a good dude waiting for God's kingdom, goes to Pilate and asks for Jesus's body. {15:31} Joseph wraps Jesus's body in linen and lays him in a rock tomb, rolling a stone over the entrance. {15:32} Mary Magdalene and Mary, Joses's mom, see where Jesus is laid.

{16:1} So, after the chill sabbath vibe, Mary Magdalene, Mary the homie of James, and Salome, copped some sweet spices to roll up to the spot and anoint Jesus. {16:2} Mad early on Sunday, they hit up the tomb at sunrise. {16:3} They're like, "Yo, who's gonna move this stone for us?" {16:4} But when they get there, the stone's already rolled away. It's huge, yo! {16:5} Inside, they see this dude in a fresh white fit, and they freak out. {16:6} He's like, "Chill, fam. You're lookin' for Jesus of Nazareth? He's risen, not here. Check where they laid him." {16:7} "Tell the disciples, especially Peter, he's heading to Galilee. That's the move, just like he said." {16:8} They bolt outta there, shook and speechless. They don't tell anyone 'cause they're scared stiff. {16:9} Jesus shows up first to Mary Magdalene, who he helped out before. {16:10} She spreads the word to the crew, who were straight mourning. {16:11} But they're not buying it, even after hearing she saw him alive. {16:12} Later, Jesus pops up in a different form to two others, out in the boonies. {16:13} They tell the squad, but they're still skeptical. {16:14} Then he shows up to the eleven, roasting them for their doubts and hard hearts, even after others confirmed seeing him. {16:15} He's like, "Spread the good news worldwide to everyone." {16:16} "Believe and get baptized, you're safe. Doubt, and you're out." {16:17-18} "Those who believe will do some crazy stuff in my name: casting out demons, speaking new languages, even handling snakes and drinking poison without getting hurt, healing the sick." {16:19} Then Jesus peace out, heading up to heaven, chillin' at God's right hand. {16:20} The crew spreads the word far and wide, with Jesus backing them up, dropping miracles left and right. Amen.

Luke

+++

{1:1} Yo, a lot of peeps have tried to lay out what we totally believe, based on the word of eyewitnesses and God's messengers. {1:2} They passed this down to us, straight from those who were there from the start, spreading the word. {1:3} I thought it'd be rad to write this down for you, Theophilus, so you know for sure about everything you've been taught. {1:4} I want you to be certain about what's up. {1:5} Back in Herod's days ruling Judaea, there was this priest named Zacharias from the Abia group, and his wife was from Aaron's family, named Elisabeth. {1:6} They were tight with God, keeping all His rules spot-on. {1:7} But they didn't have kids 'cause Elisabeth couldn't, and they were getting up there in age. {1:8} One day, while Zacharias was doing his priest thing, it was his turn to burn incense in the temple. {1:9} The whole crew was praying outside when boom, an angel shows up next to the incense altar. {1:10} Zacharias was shook when he saw him. {1:11-13} But the angel was like, "Chill, Zacharias, your prayers are answered—Elisabeth is gonna have a son, and you're gonna name him John. {1:14} You'll be stoked, and lots of folks will celebrate when he's born. {1:15} This kid's gonna be a big deal to God, never touching wine or strong stuff, filled with the Holy Ghost from the get-go. {1:16} He'll turn many Israelites back to God. {1:17} He's gonna be like Elijah, getting hearts right with God, bringing people ready for the Lord. {1:18} Zacharias was like, "How can this be? We're old!" {1:19} The angel's like, "Dude, I'm Gabriel, sent by God to tell you this awesome news, but since you doubted, you'll be mute till it happens." {1:21} The people were wondering why Zacharias was taking so long in the temple. {1:22} When he came out, he couldn't talk, just gestured, and they knew he'd seen something supernatural. {1:23} After his temple shift, he bounced back home. {1:24-25} Elisabeth got pregnant and laid low for five months, thanking God for taking away her shame. {1:26} In the sixth month of Elisabeth's pregnancy, Gabriel heads to Nazareth, Galilee. {1:27} He drops in on a virgin named Mary, engaged to Joseph from David's fam. {1:28-29} The angel's like, "Hey, you're awesome, favored by God. He's with you, super blessed among women." {1:30} Mary's tripped out but the angel's like, "Chill, Mary, you're chosen by God. {1:31} You'll get pregnant, have a son named Jesus. {1:32} He's gonna be epic, Son of the Most High, and reign forever over Jacob's house." {1:33-34} Mary's like, "How's this gonna happen? I haven't been with anyone." {1:35} The angel's like, "The Holy Ghost's power will make it go down. Your kid will be called the Son of God." {1:36-37} "And yo, your cousin Elisabeth is also preggo, even though she's older—six months in!" {1:38} Mary's like, "I'm down for whatever God wants." Then the angel splits. {1:39} Mary jets to the hill country, visiting Elisabeth in Juda. {1:40-41} When Elisabeth hears Mary, her baby jumps in her belly, and she's filled with the Holy Ghost. {1:42} She shouts, "Mary, you're blessed among women, and blessed is your baby." {1:43} "Why am I so lucky that the mother of my Lord's come to me?" {1:44} When I heard your voice, my baby went wild with joy in my belly. {1:45} Blessed are you for believing; what God told you will happen." {1:46} Mary's like, "My soul shouts out to God, my Savior." {1:47} "He's noticed me, even though I'm nothing special; everyone will call me blessed from now on." {1:48} "God's done amazing stuff for me; He's holy and powerful." {1:49-51} "His mercy's for those who respect Him, from generation to generation." {1:50} "He's shown strength, humbling the proud and lifting up the lowly." {1:52} "He takes down the powerful and feeds the hungry; sends the rich away empty." {1:53} "He helps Israel, keeping His promise to Abraham and his descendants forever." {1:54} Mary chills with Elisabeth for three months, then heads home. {1:55} When Elisabeth's time comes, she has her baby. {1:56} Her neighbors hear about God's mercy and celebrate. {1:57} On the eighth day, they come to circumcise the baby, naming him Zacharias after his dad. {1:58} But Elisabeth's like, "Nah, he's John." {1:59} Zacharias confirms it, and everyone's amazed. {1:60} Zacharias starts speaking again, praising God. {1:61} Everyone's amazed and talking about this in Judaea's hills. {1:62} Zacharias gets filled with the Holy Ghost and starts prophesying, praising God for visiting and redeeming His people.

{2:1} So, back in the day, Caesar Augustus issued this decree that everyone had to be taxed. {2:2} This tax thing went down when Cyrenius was governor of Syria. {2:3} Everyone had to head to their hometown to get taxed. {2:4} Joseph, from Nazareth in Galilee, had to roll to Bethlehem (David's town) 'cause he was part of David's fam. {2:5} He brought Mary, his fiancée who was preggo, along for the ride. {2:6} While they were there, Mary gave birth to her firstborn son. {2:7} She wrapped him up and laid him in a manger 'cause there was no room at the inn. {2:8} Nearby, some shepherds were chilling in the fields, watching their flock at night. {2:9} Suddenly, an angel appeared, and God's glory shone around them. They freaked out. {2:10} But the angel was like, "Chill, I've got awesome news that's gonna bring joy to everyone." {2:11} "Today, in David's city, a Savior was born—Christ the Lord." {2:12} The angel gave them a sign: they'd find the baby wrapped up in a manger. {2:13-14} Then a bunch of angels appeared, praising God and saying, "Glory to God in the highest, and peace on earth to all." {2:15} After the angels bounced back to heaven, the shepherds were like, "Let's go check out what just went down in Bethlehem." {2:16} They hurried over and found Mary, Joseph, and the baby in a manger. {2:17} After seeing it for themselves, they spread the word about what they'd heard from the shepherds. {2:18} Everyone who heard it was amazed by the shepherds' story. {2:19} Mary kept all this in her thoughts. {2:20} The shepherds bounced back, hyped up, and praising God for everything they'd seen and heard. {2:21} Eight days later, they circ'ed the baby and named him Jesus, just like the angel said before he was even born. {2:22} Then, when the time was up for Mary's purification according to the law of Moses, they took Jesus to Jerusalem to present him to the Lord. {2:23} This was the law: every firstborn male is holy to the Lord. {2:24} They also offered a sacrifice as the law prescribed—either two turtledoves or two young pigeons. {2:25} Now, there was a dude named Simeon in Jerusalem, righteous and devout, waiting for Israel's consolation. {2:26} The Holy Spirit revealed to him that he wouldn't die before seeing the Messiah. {2:27-28} So, led by the Spirit, he goes to the temple. When Mary and Joseph bring in Jesus, Simeon takes him in his arms and blesses God, saying, {2:29} "Now, Lord, you can let your servant go in peace, as you promised. {2:30} I've seen your salvation, {2:31-32} which you prepared for all people—a light for the Gentiles and glory for Israel." {2:33} Joseph and Mary were amazed at what Simeon said about Jesus. {2:34} Simeon blessed them and told Mary that Jesus was destined to cause the falling and rising of many in Israel, and be a sign that would be spoken against. {2:35} He even told Mary that a sword would pierce her soul too, revealing the thoughts of many hearts. {2:36-37} There was also a prophetess named Anna, from the tribe of Asher, who had lived many years as a widow in the temple, serving God night and day with fasting and prayers. {2:38} When she saw Jesus, she gave thanks to God and shared the news about him with others waiting for Jerusalem's redemption. {2:39} After following all the law's requirements, Mary and Joseph headed back to Nazareth in Galilee. {2:40} Jesus grew up strong in spirit, filled with wisdom, and blessed by God. {2:41} Every year, his parents went to Jerusalem for the Passover festival. {2:42} When Jesus was twelve, they went as usual for the feast. {2:43} After the festival, Jesus stayed behind in Jerusalem, and Mary and Joseph didn't know it. {2:44} Assuming he was with their group, they traveled for a day before realizing he was missing. {2:45} They went back to Jerusalem to find him. {2:46} Three days later, they found him in the temple, talking with the teachers and impressing everyone with his understanding and answers. {2:47} Everyone who heard him was blown away. {2:48} Mary was like, "Why'd you do this to us, son? Your dad and I were so worried." {2:49} Jesus was like, "Why were you looking for me? Didn't you know I'd be about my Father's business?" {2:50} They didn't get what he meant. {2:51} Jesus went back with them to Nazareth and obeyed them, but Mary kept all these things in her heart. {2:52} Jesus grew in wisdom and favor with God and people.

{3:1} Back in the day when Tiberius Caesar was ruling the place, Pontius Pilate was calling the shots in Judaea, and Herod and his bros were holding it down in Galilee and Trachonitis, and Lysanias was doing his thing in Abilene, {3:2} Annas and Caiaphas were high priests, that's when John, Zacharias' kid, got a message from God while he was chilling in the wilderness. {3:3} He rolled up around the Jordan, preaching about how you gotta get baptized to wipe away your sins, you know? {3:4} Just like that old prophecy from Isaiah, saying, "Yo, there's gonna be a voice in the wilderness, telling you to get ready for the Lord, straighten out those paths." {3:5} Talking about how every valley's gonna get filled, every mountain's gonna get leveled, and all the messed up stuff's gonna get fixed up nice and smooth. {3:6} And everyone's gonna see God's salvation, no doubt. {3:7} So, to the crowd lining up for baptism, he's like, "You snakes, who told you to run from the coming storm?" {3:8} "Show some real change in your lives, don't just say you're good because you're descended from Abraham. God could make new kids out of rocks if He wanted to." {3:9} "And let me tell you, the axe is already at the root of the trees. If you're not producing good fruit, you're gonna get chopped down and thrown into the fire." {3:10} People are like, "Okay, so what should we do then?" {3:11} And he's like, "If you got extra, share with those who don't, and if you got food, do the same." {3:12} Then even the tax collectors showed up, asking, "Hey, what's our move?" {3:13} He's like, "Don't overcharge anyone, just take what you're supposed to." {3:14} And the soldiers are like, "And us?" He says, "Don't extort anyone, don't make false accusations, and be happy with what you earn." {3:15} While everyone's thinking about John, wondering if he's the one they've been waiting for, {3:16} he's like, "Nah, I'm just dunking you in water. But there's someone way bigger coming, I'm not even worthy to tie his shoes. He's gonna baptize you with the Holy Spirit and with fire." {3:17} "He's got this winnowing fork, ready to clean out the threshing floor. He'll gather the good wheat into his barn, but he'll burn up the useless chaff with a fire that won't quit." {3:18} He kept dropping truth bombs like this on the people. {3:19} But Herod, that ruler dude, got called out by John for marrying his brother Philip's wife and all the other shady stuff he was pulling, so he threw John in jail. {3:20-21} Meanwhile, when everyone's getting baptized, Jesus joins the line. While he's praying, the heavens crack open, {3:22} and the Holy Spirit swoops down like a dove, while a voice from heaven says, "You're my beloved Son, and I'm totally feeling you." {3:23} Jesus was about thirty, or so they thought, the son of Joseph, who was the son of Heli, {3:24} and the family tree goes back through Matthat, Levi, Melchi, Janna, Joseph, Mattathias, Amos, Naum, Esli, Nagge, Maath, Mattathias, Semei, Joseph, Juda, Joanna, Rhesa, Zorobabel, Salathiel, Neri, Melchi, Addi, Cosam, Elmodam, Er, Jose, Eliezer, Jorim, Matthat, Levi, Simeon, Juda, Joseph, Jonan, Eliakim, Melea, Menan, Mattatha, Nathan, David, Jesse, Obed, Booz, Salmon, Naasson, Aminadab, Aram, Esrom, Phares, Juda, Jacob, Isaac, Abraham, Thara, Nachor, Saruch, Ragau, Phalec, Heber, and Sala, Cainan, Arphaxad, Sem, Noe, Lamech, Mathusala, Enoch, Jared, Maleleel, Cainan, Enos, Seth, Adam, and finally, God.

{4:1} Jesus, all hyped up with the Holy Ghost, comes back from Jordan, guided by the Spirit, and heads straight into the wilderness, {4:2} where he's tempted by the devil for, like, forty days. And during that time, he's fasting, so you know he's starving by the end of it. {4:3} Then the devil's like, "Yo, Jesus, if you're really God's son, turn these stones into bread." But Jesus is like, "Nah, man, we don't live on just bread, but on every word from God." {4:4} Then the devil takes him up this huge mountain, showing off all the kingdoms of the world, trying to flex. {4:5} And he's like, "All this power's mine to give, bro. Just worship me, and it's yours." But Jesus ain't having it, telling him to get lost because God's the only one worth worshipping. {4:6} Next, the devil brings Jesus to Jerusalem, sets him up on the temple roof, and tells him to jump off, saying God's angels got his back. But Jesus knows better, quoting scripture about not testing God. {4:7-13} After all these tests, the devil backs off for a bit. {4:14} Jesus, now all pumped up with the Spirit, heads back to Galilee, with everyone buzzing about him. {4:15} He starts dropping knowledge bombs in the synagogues, and everyone's in awe. {4:16} He goes back to Nazareth, his hometown, and does his usual Sabbath routine, reading from the scroll of Isaiah. {4:17} Finding the spot he's looking for, he reads about being anointed to preach good news to the poor and heal the brokenhearted, basically setting the oppressed free. {4:18} He drops the mic, hands the scroll back, and sits down, and everyone's eyes are glued to him. {4:19} He's like, "Yo, this scripture's all about me, right here, right now." {4:20} Everyone's blown away by his words, wondering how Joseph's kid got so wise. {4:21} Then Jesus drops some truth bombs about how prophets get no love in their hometown. {4:22} He reminds them of Elijah helping a widow in Sidon and Elisha healing a Syrian, not just the locals. {4:23} The crowd's not feeling it, though, and they try to chuck him off a cliff. But Jesus just walks right through them. {4:24} He rolls into Capernaum, teaching on the Sabbath, blowing minds with his wisdom. In the synagogue, there's this dude possessed by a demon, screaming about Jesus being the real deal. {4:25} Jesus shuts him up and casts the demon out, leaving everyone amazed at his power. {4:26} After that, he goes to Simon's place, where his mother-in-law's sick, but he heals her up right quick. {4:27} Word spreads, and by sunset, the whole town's bringing their sick to Jesus, and he's healing them all. {4:28} Even the demons are recognizing him as the Son of God, but Jesus ain't letting them talk, shutting them down because they know who he is. {4:29} Next day, Jesus bounces to a deserted spot, but the crowd tracks him down, begging him to stick around. {4:30} He tells them he's gotta spread the word elsewhere, 'cause that's his mission. {4:31} So, he keeps preaching in the synagogues throughout Galilee.

{5:1} So, one time, a bunch of people were crowding around Jesus by Lake Gennesaret, eager to hear God's word. {5:2} He spotted two boats by the lake, but the fishermen were out, cleaning their nets. {5:3} Jesus hopped into Simon's boat and asked him to push out a bit from the shore. Then Jesus sat down and started teaching the people from the boat. {5:4} After he finished, Jesus told Simon to go into deeper water and cast out his nets. {5:5} Simon was like, "We've been working hard all night and caught nothing, but okay, I'll do it." {5:6} When they did, they caught a massive amount of fish, and their net almost broke. {5:7} They signaled their partners in the other boat to come help, and both boats were filled to the brim, nearly sinking. {5:8} Simon Peter was blown away and fell down at Jesus' feet, saying, "Leave me, Lord, 'cause I'm a sinner." {5:9} Simon and his crew were amazed at the huge catch of fish they had just caught. {5:10} Jesus reassured Simon, saying, "Don't be afraid; from now on, you'll be catching people." {5:11} They brought the boats to land and left everything to follow Jesus. {5:12} Another time, Jesus was in a city when a man covered in leprosy approached him, fell on his face, and begged to be made clean. {5:13} Jesus reached out, touched him, and said, "I will; be clean." Immediately, the leprosy left the man. {5:14} Jesus instructed him not to tell anyone but to show himself to the priest and offer the cleansing as Moses commanded, for a testimony. {5:15} However, word spread like wildfire about Jesus, and huge crowds gathered to hear him and be healed of their ailments. {5:16} Jesus withdrew to the wilderness to pray. {5:17} Once, while he was teaching, Pharisees and law experts from all over Galilee, Judaea, and Jerusalem were present, and the power of the Lord was there to heal them. {5:18} Some dudes brought in a paralyzed man on a stretcher, trying to get him in front of Jesus. {5:19} When they couldn't reach Jesus through the crowd, they climbed onto the roof, removed some tiles, and lowered the man down with his stretcher into the middle of the room before Jesus. {5:20} Jesus saw their faith and said to the man, "Dude, your sins are forgiven." {5:21} The scribes and Pharisees started freaking out, wondering who Jesus thought he was to forgive sins, claiming only God could do that. {5:22} Jesus, knowing their thoughts, asked them why they were doubting. {5:23} He then asked them which was easier: to forgive sins or to tell the paralyzed man to get up and walk. {5:24} To demonstrate his authority, Jesus told the paralyzed man to get up, take his stretcher, and go home. {5:25} Immediately, the man got up, picked up his stretcher, and left, glorifying God. {5:26} Everyone was shocked and glorified God, filled with fear, saying, "Today we've seen some crazy stuff." {5:27} After these events, Jesus saw a tax collector named Levi at his customs booth and said, "Follow me." {5:28} Levi left everything, got up, and followed Jesus. {5:29} Levi threw a big party at his place for Jesus, with a ton of tax collectors and others. {5:30} The scribes and Pharisees complained to Jesus' disciples, asking why Jesus was hanging out with tax collectors and sinners. {5:31} Jesus responded, "Healthy people don't need a doctor; sick people do. {5:32} I'm here to call sinners to repentance, not the righteous." {5:33} The Pharisees questioned why John's disciples and theirs fasted and prayed a lot, but Jesus' crew ate and drank freely. {5:34} Jesus explained, "You don't fast while the party's happening with the bridegroom. {5:35} But the time will come when the bridegroom is gone, and then they'll fast." {5:36} Jesus also shared a parable: you don't patch an old garment with new fabric, or else it'll tear. {5:37} You don't put new wine into old bottles; it'll burst them. {5:38} New wine goes into new bottles, preserving both. {5:39} People prefer old wine over new, saying the old is better.

{6:1} So, like, one chill Saturday, Jesus and his crew were strolling through a field of corn, and they started picking some ears and munching on them. {6:2} And then, like, these Pharisees come up all like, "Um, why are you breaking the Sabbath rules?" {6:3} Jesus is like, "Haven't you read about David? When he and his crew were hungry, they went into God's crib and snacked on some holy bread, which only the priests are supposed to eat." {6:4-5} And he's like, "Yo, peeps, the Son of Man is even the boss of the Sabbath." {6:6} Another Sabbath, Jesus rolls into the synagogue and starts teaching, and there's this dude with a messed up hand. {6:7} The religious big shots are watching, hoping he'll heal the dude so they can throw shade at him. {6:8} But Jesus is on it, he knows what they're thinking. He tells the dude to stand up, and boom, his hand's all good. {6:9} Then Jesus drops this bomb on them, asking if it's cool to do good or bad on the Sabbath, to save a life or wreck it. {6:10} Then he's like, "Yo, dude, stretch out your hand," and just like that, it's fixed. {6:11} Those Pharisees were so mad, plotting what to do with Jesus. {6:12} So Jesus bounces to a mountain to pray, chilling there all night. {6:13-16} When morning comes, he calls his crew and picks out twelve homies, naming them apostles: Simon (who he also called Peter), Andrew, James, John, Philip, Bartholomew, Matthew, Thomas, James (son of Alphaeus), Simon (known as the Zealot), Judas (brother of James), and Judas Iscariot, who later betrays him. {6:17} He comes down with them, kicks it on a plain with his crew and a huge crowd from all over, trying to hear him and get healed. {6:18} He even sorts out those troubled by evil spirits, and they get healed too. {6:19} Everyone's trying to get close to him, feeling that positive vibe flowing out of him, healing them all. {6:20} Jesus looks at his crew and drops some wisdom, saying, "Blessed are the broke, 'cause they'll own the kingdom of God. {6:21} Blessed are the hungry now, 'cause they'll get filled. Blessed are those crying now, 'cause they'll be laughing later. {6:22} If people hate on you, exclude you, or talk trash about you because of me, don't sweat it, you'll be straight. {6:23} Celebrate when that happens, 'cause you'll score big in heaven, just like the OG prophets. {6:24} But yo, rich folks, you're in for a rough ride. {6:25} If you're full of yourself now, you'll be starving later. If you're laughing it up now, you'll be crying later. {6:26} And if everyone loves you, watch out, 'cause that's what they did to the fake prophets too. {6:27} But yo, listen up, love your haters, do good to those who diss you, bless those who curse you, and pray for those who treat you like trash. {6:28-29} If someone smacks you, offer them the other cheek, and if they swipe your jacket, let 'em have your shirt too. {6:30} Give to anyone who asks, and if someone takes your stuff, don't ask for it back. {6:31} Treat others how you want to be treated. {6:32} If you're only nice to those who are nice to you, what's the big deal? Even jerks do that. {6:33} And if you only do favors for those who do favors for you, big deal, even jerks do that. {6:34} And if you only lend to those who you expect to pay you back, so what? Even jerks lend to other jerks, expecting to get back the same amount. {6:35} But love your haters, do good to them, and lend to them without expecting anything in return, and you'll score big, 'cause that's how God rolls. {6:36} So be chill like God, who's all about showing mercy. {6:37} Don't judge, and you won't get judged. Don't condemn, and you won't get condemned. Forgive, and you'll be forgiven. {6:38} Give, and you'll get back, pressed down, shaken together, and overflowing. Whatever measure you use will be used to measure you. {6:39} Jesus drops a metaphor on them, asking if a blind dude can lead another blind dude without both ending up in a ditch. {6:40} A student ain't above his teacher, but when you're fully trained, you'll be just like him. {6:41} Why are you focused on the tiny speck in someone else's eye when you've got a huge log in yours? {6:42} How can you try to help someone else when you're blind to your own mess? Sort yourself out first, then you can help others. {6:43} Good people do good things, and bad people do bad things. Your words spill what's in your heart. {6:44} Why you call me "Lord, Lord" but don't do what I say? {6:45} If you follow my lead, I'll show you what you're like. {6:46} You're like a dude who builds his house on solid ground. {6:47} But if you hear me out and don't act on it, you're like someone who builds on shaky ground. When the storm hits, your house is toast.

{7:1} After dropping some knowledge on the crowd, Jesus rolls into Capernaum. {7:2} There's this centurion whose servant, like, means everything to him, and the dude's on death's door. {7:3} When he hears about Jesus, he sends some Jewish elders, begging Jesus to come and heal the servant. {7:4} They're all like, "This guy's legit, Jesus, you gotta help him out." {7:5} They mention how the centurion loves their people and even built them a synagogue. {7:6} Jesus agrees to come, but before he gets there, the centurion sends some friends, saying he's not worthy for Jesus to come to his house. {7:7} He's like, "I'm nobody, but if you just say the word, my servant will be healed." {7:8} He explains how he's got authority over soldiers, and they do what he says, so Jesus just needs to say the word. {7:9} Jesus is blown away by this and tells everyone, "Man, this guy's got more faith than anyone in Israel!" {7:10} When the messengers go back, they find the servant all better. {7:11} The next day, Jesus heads to a place called Nain, with his crew and a bunch of people. {7:12} At the city gate, they run into a funeral procession for a young guy, the only son of a widow. {7:13} Jesus feels for the mom and tells her not to cry. {7:14} Then he walks up to the coffin, tells the dead guy to get up, and bam, the dude's alive and chatting. {7:15} He hands him over to his mom, and everyone's freaking out, saying, "Whoa, this guy's a prophet, and God's definitely here!" {7:16} Word spreads like wildfire through Judea and the surrounding areas. {7:17-18} Even John the Baptist's crew hears about it. {7:19} John sends some of his followers to Jesus, asking if he's the real deal or if they should keep waiting. {7:20} They come to Jesus, repeating John's question. {7:21} Right then, Jesus starts healing people left and right, curing diseases, casting out evil spirits, and giving sight to the blind. {7:22} He tells them to go back and tell John what they've seen and heard: blind see, lame walk, sick healed, dead raised, and the poor getting good news. {7:23} And he adds, "Blessed is anyone who doesn't doubt me." {7:24} After John's messengers leave, Jesus starts talking to the crowd about John. {7:25} He's like, "What did you expect to see out in the wilderness? Some wishy-washy guy? Nah, the rich and fancy hang out in palaces." {7:26} "But John's more than a prophet, he's the dude Isaiah was talking about, paving the way for me." {7:27-28} "Seriously, John's the real deal. Greatest prophet born of women, but even the least in God's kingdom is greater than him." {7:29} The people, including tax collectors, agree, showing they're on board with God's plan through John's baptism. {7:30} But the Pharisees and lawyers? They're not feeling it, rejecting God's plan by not getting baptized by John. {7:31} Jesus is like, "What can I compare this generation to?" {7:32} "They're like kids at a market, refusing to join in the fun, no matter if we play happy or sad tunes." {7:33-34} "John came fasting, and you called him crazy. I come eating and drinking, and you call me a glutton and a lush, hanging out with the wrong crowd!" {7:35} "But, you know, wisdom's proven right by the results." {7:36} At a Pharisee's dinner party, a sinful woman shows up, knowing Jesus is there. {7:37-38} She brings fancy perfume, crying and washing Jesus' feet with her tears, drying them with her hair, and anointing them. {7:39} The Pharisee's like, "If Jesus was a prophet, he'd know what kind of woman this is!" {7:40} Jesus tells him a story about two debtors, one owing a lot more than the other, and how the one forgiven more will love more. {7:41} He points out how the woman's been super hospitable compared to the Pharisee. {7:42} Then he tells the woman her sins are forgiven. {7:43} And he sends her off, saying her faith saved her, telling her to live in peace.

{8:1-3} So, after that, Jesus went around every city and village, spreading the good news about God's kingdom, with his crew of twelve and some women who had been healed of evil spirits and sicknesses, including Mary Magdalene (who had seven devils cast out), Joanna (the wife of Herod's steward Chuza), Susanna, and many others who supported him from their own pockets. {8:4} One time, when a huge crowd gathered from all over, Jesus dropped a parable: {8:5} "A dude went out to plant his seeds. Some fell on the path and got trampled, and birds ate them up. {8:6} Some landed on rocky ground, sprouted quickly, but died out because they lacked moisture. {8:7} Others fell among thorns, got choked by worries, riches, and pleasures, and didn't produce any fruit. {8:8} But some fell on good soil, grew, and produced a hundredfold. After saying this, Jesus called out, 'If you've got ears, then listen up!' {8:9} His crew asked him what the parable meant. {8:10} Jesus said, "You guys get the secrets of God's kingdom, but others get parables so they see without understanding and hear without getting it. {8:11} Here's the deal: the seed is God's word. {8:12} People on the path hear it, but then the devil snatches it away from their hearts to prevent them from believing and being saved. {8:13} Those on rocky ground hear the word with joy but don't stick with it; they believe for a bit but bail when things get tough. {8:14} The ones among thorns hear but get caught up in worries, wealth, and pleasures, producing nothing. {8:15-18} But those on good soil, with an honest heart, hear the word, keep it, and produce fruit patiently. {8:19-20} Then Jesus' mom and brothers couldn't reach him due to the crowd, and someone told him they were outside wanting to see him. {8:21} Jesus replied, "My real fam are the ones who hear God's word and act on it." {8:22} On another day, Jesus and his squad got on a ship to cross the lake. {8:23} While sailing, Jesus crashed for a nap, and a storm hit, filling the boat with water and putting them in danger. {8:24} His crew woke him up, freaking out, "Master, we're gonna drown!" Jesus got up, rebuked the wind and water, and everything went calm. {8:25} Jesus then asked, "Where's your faith?" They were amazed, wondering, "Who is this guy? He even commands the winds and water, and they obey!" {8:26} They reached Gadarenes, and a demon-possessed man from the city, who had been naked and living in tombs, met Jesus. {8:27} The man cried out and fell before Jesus, saying, "Don't torment me, Son of God!" Jesus commanded the unclean spirits to leave, and they entered a herd of pigs, which ran into the lake and drowned. {8:28} People who saw what happened freaked out and spread the news. {8:29} They found the once-possessed man, now sitting clothed and sane at Jesus' feet, and were afraid. {8:30} Jesus told him to go home and share what God had done for him. {8:31} When Jesus returned, the people welcomed him gladly. {8:32} Then Jairus, a synagogue leader, begged Jesus to come heal his dying daughter. {8:33} On their way, a crowd surrounded Jesus. {8:34} A woman with a twelve-year issue of blood, who had spent all her money on doctors, touched Jesus' garment edge and was instantly healed. {8:35} Jesus told her, "Your faith healed you; go in peace." {8:36} While Jesus spoke, someone came and said Jairus' daughter had died. Jesus reassured Jairus, {8:37} "Don't be afraid; just believe, and she'll be fine." {8:38} Jesus took the girl's hand, told her to get up, and she came back to life. {8:39} Her parents were amazed, but Jesus told them not to spread the word.

{9:1} Jesus gathers up his squad of twelve and hooks them up with mad power and authority to kick demon butt and heal the sick. {9:2} Then he sends them out to spread the word about God's kingdom and do some healing. {9:3} And he's like, "Don't take anything with you on your journey, no walking sticks, no bags, no bread, no cash, not even an extra jacket." {9:4} He's like, "Just crash wherever you're welcome and bounce when it's time to leave." {9:5} And if someone doesn't welcome you, just shake off the dust from your shoes as a sign against them. {9:6} So they hit the road, preaching and healing everywhere they go. {9:7} Meanwhile, Herod hears about all this and starts freaking out, thinking John the Baptist came back from the dead or something. {9:8} People are buzzing, saying maybe it's Elijah or one of the old prophets making a comeback. {9:9} Herod's like, "Yo, I beheaded John, so who's this I'm hearing about?" And he's curious to meet Jesus. {9:10} When the apostles come back, they spill all the tea to Jesus about what they've been up to. So he takes them to a chill spot in the desert near Bethsaida. {9:11} But word gets out, and a crowd follows him, so he starts preaching and healing peeps in need. {9:12} As the day goes on, the twelve are like, "Send these folks off to the nearby towns to crash and grab some grub 'cause we're in the middle of nowhere." {9:13} But Jesus is like, "Nah, you feed them." And they're like, "But all we got is five loaves and two fish, unless we hit up the grocery store." {9:14} There's like 5,000 dudes there, so Jesus tells his crew to organize them into groups of fifty. {9:15-17} They do it and everyone chows down. {9:16-17} Jesus takes the loaves and fish, blesses them, breaks them, and hands them out, and everyone eats till they're stuffed. They even have twelve baskets of leftovers. {9:18} Later, when Jesus is off by himself praying, his crew is with him. He's like, "So, what's the word on the street about me?" {9:19} They're like, "Some say you're John the Baptist back from the dead, some say you're Elijah, and others think you're one of the old prophets." {9:20} Jesus is like, "What about you guys, who do you say I am?" Peter pipes up, "You're the chosen one, the Christ of God." {9:21} Jesus is like, "Keep it on the down-low, though." {9:22} Then he drops the bomb that he's gotta go through some tough stuff—rejected, killed, but then he'll rise again. {9:23} Jesus lays it out for everyone, saying if you wanna roll with him, you gotta drop your ego and be down to carry your own cross every day. {9:24} 'Cause trying to save your own life will make you lose it, but losing your life for Jesus's sake will save it. {9:25} What good is it to gain the whole world but lose yourself in the process? {9:26} If you're ashamed of Jesus and his words, he'll be ashamed of you when he comes in all his glory with his crew of angels. {9:27} And some of the folks standing there won't kick the bucket till they see God's kingdom. {9:28} About eight days later, Jesus takes Peter, John, and James up a mountain to pray. {9:29} While he's praying, his whole vibe changes, and his clothes start glowing white. {9:30} Then, bam, Moses and Elijah show up, chatting with Jesus about his upcoming gig in Jerusalem. {9:31} Peter and his crew are half asleep, but when they wake up, they see Jesus shining and chatting with these legends. {9:32} As they're leaving, Peter's like, "Yo, let's set up some tents for you guys and kick it." He's kinda clueless though. {9:33-34} While he's talking, a cloud rolls in and covers them, freaking them out. {9:35} Then a voice booms out, "This is my son, my favorite, listen to him." {9:36} When the cloud clears, it's just Jesus standing there, and they keep quiet about what went down. {9:37} The next day, they head down the mountain and bump into a big crowd. {9:38} Some dude begs Jesus to help his son possessed by a demon. {9:39} The demon messes the kid up bad, but Jesus fixes him up and hands him back to his dad. {9:40} Everyone's amazed at the power of God. {9:41} Jesus is like, "Y'all need to get it together, though." {9:42-45} Later, his crew's clueless about what he meant, but they're too scared to ask. {9:46} So they start arguing about who's the top dog among them. {9:47-48} Jesus sees what they're thinking and grabs a kid, saying whoever welcomes a kid in his name welcomes him, and whoever welcomes him welcomes God. {9:49} John's like, "Yo, we saw some dude using your name to cast out demons, but we shut him down 'cause he wasn't rolling with us." {9:50} Jesus is like, "Chill, if he's not against us, he's with us." {9:51} It's time for Jesus to head to Jerusalem, so he sets his face toward it. {9:52-53} He sends messengers ahead, but some Samaritans diss them 'cause they're heading to Jerusalem. {9:54-55} James and John are ready to bring down some heavenly fire on them, but Jesus is like, "Nah, you're missing the point." {9:56} He's all about saving lives, not wrecking them. So they bounce to another village. {9:57} On the road, some dude pledges to follow Jesus anywhere. {9:58} Jesus is like, "Look, animals have homes, but I don't even have a bed. {9:59} Another guy's like, "I'm down, but let me go bury my dad first." {9:60} Jesus is like, "Let the dead deal with the dead, you need to spread the word about God's kingdom." {9:61} Another guy's like, "I'm in, but let me say goodbye to my fam first." {9:62} Jesus is like, "Once you're on this journey, there's no turning back."

{10:1} The Lord gathers up another seventy homies and sends them out two by two ahead of him to every spot he's gonna hit up. {10:2} He's like, "Yo, the work is mad heavy, but the squad is thin. Pray to the big man upstairs to send more peeps to help out." {10:3} Then he's dropping truth bombs, saying, "I'm sending you out like lambs among wolves, so brace yourselves." {10:4} "Leave the wallets, backpacks, and kicks at home, and don't be stopping to chat with anyone on the way." {10:5} "When you hit up a crib, throw out some good vibes, man. Spread that peace around first thing." {10:6} "If the vibe there is chill, your peace sticks around. If not, it bounces back to you." {10:7} "Chow down on whatever they serve you, and don't be bouncing around from house to house. A worker deserves their chow, yo." {10:8} "And if a city's down with you, grub on what they got, and heal up any sick folks while you're there, spreading the word that God's kingdom is close at hand." {10:9-11} "But if a city ain't feeling you, shake the dust off your kicks as a sign, but make sure they know the kingdom of God was right at their doorstep." {10:12} "Let me tell you, Sodom's gonna have an easier time on judgment day than those cities." {10:13} "Chorazin and Bethsaida, you're getting called out! If the miracles done there were done in other places, they would've repented ages ago!" {10:14-15} "But those other spots will catch a break compared to you, Capernaum, acting all high and mighty, but you're headed for a fall." {10:16} "Listen up, when you hear my crew, you're hearing me. And dissing them is dissing me, and dissing me is dissing the big boss upstairs." {10:17} The seventy roll back, hyped as heck, saying, "Lord, even the demons listen up when we throw your name out!" {10:18-19} And the Lord's like, "I saw Satan take a dive like lightning. You're getting power to step on snakes and scorpions and crush the enemy, and nothing's gonna touch you." {10:20} "But don't get too hyped about controlling spirits. Be stoked that your names are written in the big book upstairs." {10:21} Jesus is feeling blessed, giving a shoutout to the big guy, thanking him for keeping the deep stuff hidden from the big shots and sharing it with the regular folk. {10:22} "Everything's in my hands, handed down by the big guy. Nobody knows the whole deal except me and the big guy, and whoever I decide to spill the beans to." {10:23-24} Then he turns to the squad and says quietly, "You guys are lucky to see what you're seeing. Prophets and kings wanted in on this action, but they never got the invite." {10:25} Just then, this lawyer dude steps up, trying to test Jesus, asking how to score eternal life. {10:26} Jesus is like, "What's the law say? How are you reading it?" {10:27} The lawyer's like, "Love God with everything you've got and love your neighbor like yourself." {10:28} Jesus is like, "Solid answer, bro. Do that, and you're set for life." {10:29} But the lawyer, trying to justify himself, asks, "Who even counts as my neighbor?" {10:30} So, Jesus drops a story about a guy getting wrecked by thieves, and who shows up to help him out. {10:31} Jesus finishes up, asking who was the real neighbor in the story, and the lawyer's like, "The dude who showed him some love." And Jesus is like, "Go do the same, man." {10:32} As they're rolling, they hit up this village, and this chick named Martha invites them in. {10:33} Her sister, Mary, kicks back with Jesus, soaking up his wisdom. {10:34} Meanwhile, Martha's running around stressing about serving up snacks and is like, "Yo, Jesus, you cool with my sister just chilling while I'm doing all the work?" {10:35} Jesus tells her, "Martha, Martha, you're sweating the small stuff. Mary's got the right idea, and that's not gonna get taken away from her."

{11:1} One day while Jesus was praying in a spot, after he finished, one of his followers asked, "Yo, teach us to pray like John taught his crew." {11:2} Jesus was like, "When you pray, keep it real and say, 'Our Father up in heaven, your name's sacred. Bring your kingdom, do your thing here and up there. {11:3-4} Give us our daily bread. Forgive our sins, just like we forgive those who owe us. And keep us away from temptations and evil.'" {11:5-7} Then Jesus told them a story, "Imagine you need bread from a friend at midnight, 'cause your homie rolled in and you got nothing to offer." {11:8} Jesus was like, "Even if the friend's being lazy, he'll still come through 'cause you won't let up." {11:9-10} Jesus added, "Ask, and it's yours; seek, and you'll find; knock, and it's open for you. {11:11} If a kid asks for bread, would you give them a rock? Or a fish, and you hand them a snake? {11:12} If even you, with your flaws, know how to give good stuff to your kids, imagine how much more your heavenly Father will give the Holy Spirit to those who ask." {11:13} Meanwhile, Jesus was casting out a demon, and when it was gone, the mute started talking, blowing people's minds. {11:14} But some haters were like, "He's only casting out demons 'cause he's tight with Beelzebub, the top demon." {11:15} Jesus was like, "If I'm casting out demons by Beelzebub, who are your crew using? They'll be the ones to judge you." {11:16} Jesus warned, "When a tough dude's guarding his turf, everything's chill; but when someone tougher steps up, they take his stuff." {11:17} He was clear, "If you ain't with me, you're against me; there's no in-between." {11:18} Then this woman in the crowd shouted, "Blessed is your mom!" But Jesus was like, "Nah, those who hear God's word and live it, they're the blessed ones." {11:19} Jesus called out the crowd, saying, "This generation's messed up, always seeking signs. The only sign they'll get is like what happened with Jonah." {11:20} Jesus told them, "You don't hide a light; you put it where everyone can see." {11:21} Later, a Pharisee invited Jesus to dinner and got hung up on him not washing first. {11:22} Jesus called them out, "You guys focus on looking good outside but inside, it's a mess." {11:23} Jesus called them out for obsessing over minor rules but neglecting love and justice. He dropped truth bombs on the Pharisees, pointing out their hypocrisy and how they burden others without lifting a finger to help.

{12:1} So, like, there's this huge crowd gathered, you know, packed so tight they're stepping on each other's kicks, and Jesus starts dropping some truth bombs to his squad, starting with, "Watch out for those Pharisees and their fake vibes, man, it's all about the hypocrisy." {12:2} He's like, "Nothing stays hidden forever, what's covered up will get exposed, what's kept secret will come out into the open." {12:3} "So, whatever you've said in the dark will be heard in the light, and what you've whispered in secret will be shouted from the rooftops." {12:4} Then he's all, "My homies, don't sweat those who can only mess with your body, worry about the one who's got the power to mess with your soul and send it to hell. Yeah, fear that guy." {12:5} "Check it, ain't five sparrows sold for next to nothing? And yet, not a single one is forgotten by God." {12:6} "And even the hairs on your head are counted, so don't trip, you're worth way more than a bunch of birds." {12:7} "So don't stress, okay? You're more important than some birds, and God's got your back." {12:8} "Listen up, if you stand up for me in front of others, I'll have your back when it counts, in front of the angels." {12:9} "But if you deny me in front of others, I'll have to deny you in front of the angels, so, like, watch your step." {12:10} "Now, dissing me might get a pass, but if you diss the Holy Ghost, that's a no-go, no forgiveness for that." {12:11} "When they haul you in front of the synagogues and the courts, don't stress about what to say, the Holy Ghost will hook you up with the right words on the spot." {12:12} "So don't sweat it, the Holy Ghost will come through for you with the words when you need 'em." {12:13} Then some dude's like, "Hey Jesus, can you tell my bro to split the inheritance with me?" {12:14} And Jesus is like, "Whoa there, I'm not a judge or a lawyer, why you bringing this to me?" {12:15} Then he's like, "Listen up, greed is wack, dude. Life's not about having tons of stuff." {12:16} "Let me break it down for you with a story: there's this rich dude whose land is blowing up with crops." {12:17} "He's like, 'What do I do with all this stuff? My stash is maxed out.'" {12:18} "So he's like, 'I'll tear down my old storage and build a bigger one, then I can chill, party, and live it up.'" {12:19} "But God's like, 'Nah, you're a fool, tonight you're outta here, then what happens to all your stuff?'" {12:20} "So, yeah, anyone who's all about hoarding for themselves and not sharing with God is missing the point." {12:22} "And check it, don't stress about what you'll eat or wear, life's about more than just that." {12:23} "Think about the birds, they don't plant or harvest, but God takes care of them. You're way more important than some birds." {12:24} "And who here can add a single inch to their height by stressing? Not you, bro." {12:25} "So, why sweat the small stuff if you can't even do that?" {12:26} "Look at the flowers, they don't hustle or bustle, yet they're decked out better than King Solomon. If God takes care of them, how much more will he take care of you, you little faith squad?" {12:27-30} "So stop stressing about what to eat or drink, or being unsure about stuff. The rest of the world's obsessed with that stuff, but God knows what you need." {12:31} "Instead, focus on God's kingdom, and all that other stuff will fall into place." {12:32} "Don't stress, little crew, God's stoked to hook you up with the kingdom." {12:33} "Sell your stuff, give to those in need, and stash your treasure in heaven where it's all good, no thieves or moths messing with it." {12:34} "Where your treasure is, that's where your heart's at." {12:35} "Keep your game tight, be ready for action, keep your lights on, be ready for when the big boss comes back from the party." {12:36} "Blessed are those who are ready and waiting for him, he'll hook them up for sure." {12:37-38} "Even if he shows up late, those who are still on point are blessed." {12:39} "So be ready, 'cause the Son of man's coming when you least expect it." {12:40-41} Then Peter's like, "Yo Jesus, is this story just for us or for everyone?" {12:42} Jesus is like, "Who's the boss who takes care of business when the master's away? That's the one who's on point." {12:43} "Blessed is that servant who's still holding it down when the master shows up." {12:44} "Trust me, that servant's gonna get promoted big time." {12:45} "But if that servant starts slacking, thinking the boss won't be back anytime soon, and starts partying it up, he's gonna get a rude awakening." {12:46} "The boss will come back when he least expects it and lay down the law, and he'll get what's coming to him with the other slackers." {12:47-48} "So, if you know what's up and still don't do it, you'll get what's coming to you. But if you didn't know any better, you'll get a lighter punishment. But hey, the more you know, the more is expected of you, you feel me?" {12:49} "I'm bringing the heat, yo, and I can't wait till it's lit. But first, I gotta go through some stuff." {12:50} "You think I came to bring peace? Nah, I'm bringing division, man." {12:51} "From now on, families will be split, some for me, some against me." {12:52} "Parents against kids, kids against parents, it's gonna be a whole vibe." {12:53} "It's gonna be a crazy time, yo, you can read the weather, but you can't read the signs of the times? Come on now." {12:54} "When you're settling things with your opponent, sort it out before you get dragged into court and locked up." {12 :55} "Trust me, you don't wanna end up in jail, paying every last cent."

{13:1} There's some folks chilling there, talking to Jesus about these Galileans who got mixed up with Pilate's drama while they were doing their sacrifices. {13:2} Jesus jumps in, like, "You think those Galileans were worse sinners 'cause that happened to them? Nah, unless y'all change your ways, you're gonna end up the same." {13:3} "And what about those eighteen folks the Siloam tower took out? You think they were the worst sinners in Jerusalem? Nah, same deal. Change your ways or you're done." {13:4} Then Jesus drops this story about a fig tree in a vineyard that ain't producing. {13:5} The dude in charge is ready to chop it down, but another guy's like, "Nah, let's give it one more shot. I'll work on it, and if it still ain't giving fruit, then we'll cut it." {13:6} Now, picture this: there's this woman, bent over for eighteen years with some bad vibes. {13:7} Jesus rolls up, tells her she's free from all that negativity, and boom, she's standing tall, giving props to God. {13:8} But the synagogue boss is mad 'cause Jesus healed her on the Sabbath, saying healing should wait for the workdays. {13:9} Jesus calls him out, like, "You'll take care of your animals on the Sabbath, but this woman, who's been tied up for years, can't get some freedom?" {13:10} His haters are speechless, but the crowd's loving it, celebrating all the good stuff Jesus is doing. {13:11} So Jesus is like, "Let me paint a picture of the kingdom of God for you." {13:12} "It's like a tiny mustard seed that grows into a big tree, giving shelter to birds." {13:13} "Or it's like yeast that a woman hides in a bunch of flour, making the whole batch rise up." {13:14} Jesus is cruising through towns and villages, spreading knowledge, heading toward Jerusalem. {13:15} Someone asks him, "Yo, Jesus, are only a few gonna make it to heaven?" {13:16} And Jesus is like, "You gotta work hard to get through the narrow gate 'cause lots of folks will try but won't make it." {13:17} "Once the party's started and the door's shut, you can't just knock and expect to get in. Sorry, but I don't know you." {13:18} "You can't claim to be part of the crew just 'cause you hung out with me and listened to my teachings." {13:19} "I'm telling you, I don't know where you're from. Get outta here, you troublemakers." {13:20} There's gonna be crying and grinding of teeth when you see Abraham, Isaac, Jacob, and the prophets partying in the kingdom, and you're left out. {13:21} People will come from all over to join the kingdom. {13:22} And hey, some who seem last now will end up first, and some who think they're first will end up last. {13:23} Later that day, some Pharisees roll up, telling Jesus to bounce 'cause Herod's out to get him. {13:24} Jesus ain't bothered, telling them to take a message to Herod, that he's busy doing his thing now and tomorrow, and on the third day, he'll be wrapping it up. {13:25} But he's gotta keep moving 'cause no prophet's gonna get taken out except in Jerusalem. {13:26} Jesus gets real, talking about how he wanted to bring the people of Jerusalem together like a mama hen gathering her chicks, but they weren't having it. {13:27} He drops a truth bomb, saying their place is gonna be empty, and they won't see him until they're ready to welcome him with open arms.

{14:1} Jesus was kicking it at a Pharisee's house for a Sabbath meal, and they were all watching him closely. {14:2} Then, bam, this guy with dropsy shows up. {14:3} Jesus throws shade at the lawyers and Pharisees, asking, "Is it cool to heal on the Sabbath?" {14:4} They stay quiet, so Jesus heals the guy and sends him on his way. {14:5} Then he's like, "If your donkey or ox falls into a pit on the Sabbath, you'd rescue it, right?" {14:6} They had no comeback. {14:7} Jesus drops some knowledge on choosing seats at a party, saying, {14:8-9} "Don't grab the best seat; you might get bumped for someone more important." {14:10} Instead, start low-key, and you might get moved up with mad respect. {14:11} 'Cause if you act all high and mighty, you'll get knocked down, but stay humble and get lifted up. {14:12} Jesus tells the host, "Don't invite your squad, family, or rich neighbors; invite the less fortunate." {14:13-14} It's all about that humble blessing, 'cause they can't repay you, but you'll get yours at the resurrection. {14:15} Some dude hears this and shouts, "Blessed are those at the kingdom feast!" {14:16-20} Jesus drops a story about a big feast where the invited guests start making excuses. So the host sends servants to bring in the poor, disabled, and needy. He tells them to fill the house with anyone they find. {14:21} 'Cause those who first got invited and turned it down won't get a taste. {14:22} Huge crowds are rolling with Jesus, so he lays down the truth: {14:23} "To be my disciple, you gotta be ready to put me above everything—family, even yourself. {14:24} Take up your cross and follow me." {14:25} He's like, "Before you start a big project, count the cost, or you'll end up looking foolish." {14:26} Same with following Jesus; it's all or nothing. {14:27} Salt's good, but if it loses its flavor, it's useless. {14:28} Don't be flavorless; listen up if you've got ears!

{15:1} So, like, all these tax collectors and party animals start vibing with Jesus, wanting to hear what he's about. {15:2} But then you got these Pharisees and scholars talking smack, like, "This dude hangs with sinners and eats with them, what's up with that?" {15:3} So Jesus drops a story on them, like, {15:4} "Imagine you got a hundred sheep, right? And you lose one. You're gonna leave the rest and go find that lost one, no doubt." {15:5} "And when you find it, you're stoked, you throw it on your shoulders, and head home, telling everyone to party 'cause you found your lost sheep." {15:6-7} "Same vibe in heaven, man, when one sinner repents, the whole squad's lit, even more than for the ninety-nine who are already good." {15:8} "Or, think about this chick with ten coins, loses one, she's turning her house upside down looking for it, you know?" {15:9} "And when she finds it, she's calling up her crew, saying, 'Let's celebrate, I found that lost coin!'" {15:10} "Same deal, man, angels are throwing a party when one sinner turns their life around." {15:11} "So then Jesus tells this story about this dude with two sons." {15:12} "The younger one's like, 'Dad, give me my share of the inheritance.' So the dad splits his stuff between them." {15:13} "The younger son takes off to live it up in some far-off place, blowing all his cash on parties and stuff." {15:14} "But then a famine hits, and he's broke, like, totally struggling." {15:15} "He ends up working in a pig pen, wishing he could eat the pig slop 'cause he's so hungry." {15:16-17} "Then he's like, 'Wait a minute, my dad's servants have food to spare, and I'm starving here.'" {15:18} "So he heads back home, ready to apologize and work as a servant." {15:19} "But while he's still far away, his dad sees him, runs to him, hugs him, and throws a party 'cause his lost son is back." {15:20} "Dad's like, 'Get him some fresh clothes, a ring, and shoes, and let's feast 'cause my son's back from the dead.'" {15:21} "Meanwhile, the older son's out in the fields, and he hears music and dancing." {15:22} "He's ticked off, won't even go inside, so his dad comes out to talk to him." {15:23} "The older son's like, 'I've been loyal all these years, never got a party, and now you're celebrating for this loser who blew his cash?'" {15:24} "Dad's like, 'Chill, everything I have is yours, but it's only right we celebrate 'cause your brother's back from the dead.'"

{16:1} Jesus is dropping some wisdom to his crew, telling them about this rich dude who had a manager. {16:2} But word got out that this manager was slacking, wasting the boss's stuff. {16:3} So the boss calls him in like, "What's up with this mess? Give me a report, 'cause you might be out of a job." {16:4} The manager's like, "Oh no, I'm in trouble now. I can't do manual labor, and I'm too embarrassed to beg." {16:5} "I know! I'll butter up the boss's debtors so they'll hook me up when I'm jobless." {16:6-8} And surprisingly, the boss pats him on the back for being smart, saying that people in the world know how to hustle better than the faithful. {16:9} Jesus drops some truth bombs, saying, "Make friends with dirty money, so when it's gone, they'll welcome you into heaven." {16:10-12} "If you can be trusted with small stuff, you'll handle the big stuff. But if you're shady with the little things, you can't be trusted with the real deal." {16:13} "You can't serve God and money at the same time. Pick one." {16:14} Even the Pharisees, who were all about the cash, heard this and laughed at Jesus. {16:15} But Jesus isn't impressed, telling them that what's cool with people is garbage to God. {16:16} He's like, "The old rules were cool until John showed up. Now everyone's trying to get into heaven." {16:17} "And let me tell you, it's easier for the sky to fall than for God's rules to change." {16:18} "Cheating on your spouse is a big no-no. Period." {16:19-21} Then Jesus tells a story about this rich dude living it up and a beggar named Lazarus chilling by his gate, begging for scraps. {16:22-23} Lazarus dies and gets VIP treatment from the angels, while the rich dude kicks the bucket and ends up in hell, seeing Lazarus chilling with Abraham. {16:24} He's like, "Yo, Father Abraham, have some pity and send Lazarus to cool me down, I'm burning up here." {16:25} But

Abraham's like, "Nah, man. You had it good in life, while Lazarus suffered. Now he's living it up, and you're in agony." {16:26} "Plus, there's no crossing over between us and you." {16:27} The rich dude's like, "Then send Lazarus to warn my family, so they don't end up here." {16:28-29} But Abraham's like, "They got the old-school prophets to listen to." {16:30} The rich dude's like, "Nah, if someone came back from the dead, they'd listen." {16:31} But Abraham's like, "If they don't listen to the prophets, they won't listen to someone coming back from the dead."

{17:1} Jesus told his crew, "Look, there's no avoiding people causing trouble, but damn, the ones doing it are in for a bad time!" {17:2} He's like, "It'd be less painful to have a millstone around your neck and be tossed in the sea than to mess with these little ones." {17:3} He drops some wisdom, saying, "If your bro does you wrong, call him out; if he's sorry, forgive him." {17:4} Even if he messes up seven times a day and asks for forgiveness each time, you gotta forgive. {17:5} The apostles are like, "Yo Jesus, we need more faith." {17:6} And Jesus is like, "Even faith as small as a mustard seed can do big things, like moving a tree into the sea." {17:7-9} Then he's like, "If you had a servant plowing or tending animals, you wouldn't let him chill right after work; he's gotta serve you first." {17:10} So when you've done all you're supposed to, don't expect a pat on the back; you've just done your duty. {17:11} While heading to Jerusalem, Jesus rolls through Samaria and Galilee. {17:12} He hits a village and meets ten lepers who keep their distance. {17:13} They yell out to Jesus for mercy. {17:14} Jesus tells them to show themselves to the priests, and as they go, they get healed. {17:15} One of them, a Samaritan, turns back, praising God loudly. {17:16-18} He bows down, thanking Jesus, and Jesus is like, "Yo, where are the other nine?" {17:19} He tells the Samaritan, "Get up and go; your faith has made you whole." {17:20-21} Pharisees ask Jesus when the kingdom of God is coming, and he's like, "You won't see it coming like a show; it's within you." {17:22} He tells the disciples, "There'll be a time when you'll wish to see the Son of Man's days, but you won't." {17:23} People will say, "Look here!" or "Look there!" but don't chase after them. {17:24} When the Son of Man comes, it'll be sudden and far-reaching like lightning. {17:25} But first, he's gotta suffer and be rejected by this generation. {17:26} Just like in Noah's time, life was normal until the flood came and wiped them out. {17:27-29} Same deal with Lot's time; everything seemed normal until destruction hit. {17:30} That's how it'll be when the Son of Man is revealed. {17:31-32} Remember Lot's wife—don't look back. {17:33} If you try to save your life, you'll lose it; lose it for Jesus, and you'll save it. {17:34} At night, two people in one bed—one taken, one left. {17:35} Two women grinding together—one taken, one left. {17:36} Two dudes in the field—one taken, one left. {17:37} They ask, "Where, Lord?" and Jesus is like, "Where the bodies are, that's where the eagles will gather."

{18:1} Jesus drops a story, you know, to show that you gotta keep praying and not give up. {18:2} He's like, "Check it, there's this judge in a city, not scared of God or people." {18:3} "Then there's this widow bugging him, like, 'Yo, make things right with my enemy!'" {18:4-5} "At first, he's like, 'Nah,' but then he's like, 'Man, this lady's persistent, I better do something.'" {18:6} "Jesus is like, 'Listen up, even this shady judge gives in eventually.'" {18:7} "So, you think God won't help out his peeps who keep asking, even if it takes a while?" {18:8} "He's gonna come through, but yo, when he returns, will he find anyone still believing?" {18:9} "Jesus lays this down for those thinking they're all that and dissing others." {18:10} "Two dudes hit up the temple to pray, a Pharisee and a tax collector." {18:11} "Pharisee's like, 'God, thanks I'm not like these losers, I'm on point.'" {18:12} "He's bragging about fasting and tithing, you know?" {18:13} "But the tax dude's like, 'Sorry God, I'm a mess, have mercy on me!'" {18:14} "Jesus is like, 'Boom, that tax guy goes home forgiven, not the Pharisee.'" {18:15} "Then they bring kids for Jesus to bless, but his crew's like, 'Nah, chill.'" {18:16} "But Jesus is like, 'Let them kids come, the kingdom's for peeps like them.'" {18:17} "He's real, saying only those who humble up like kids get in." {18:18-21} "This rich dude asks Jesus about eternal life, and Jesus is like, 'Only God's good, you know the commandments?'" {18:22} "Jesus tells him, 'Sell all you got, give to the poor, and follow me.'" {18:23} "Rich dude's bummed 'cause he's loaded." {18:24} "Jesus drops a truth bomb, saying rich dudes have a hard time getting into heaven.""People are like, 'Who can be saved then?'" {18:25} "Jesus is like, 'What's impossible for humans is possible for God.'" {18:26-28} "Peter's like, 'We gave up everything for you, man!'" {18:29-30} "Jesus is like, 'Those who leave it all for God get way more, now and later.'" {18:31} "Jesus tells his crew they're heading to Jerusalem, and everything's gonna go down like the prophets said." {18:32-33} "He's like, 'I'm gonna get beat up, killed, but I'll rise up on the third day.'" {18:34} "Now there's this blind dude begging by the road." {18:35} "They tell him, 'Jesus is passing by!'" {18:36} "He shouts, 'Jesus, have mercy on me!'" {18:37} "Jesus hears him, asks what he wants." {18:38} "He's like, 'Bam, you're healed 'cause of your faith!'" {18:39} "Dude gets his sight back, starts following Jesus, and everyone's praising God."

{19:1} Jesus rolls into Jericho. {19:2} There's this dude called Zacchaeus, big shot among the tax guys, loaded. {19:3} Zacchaeus is curious about Jesus but can't see him because he's short and the crowd's too thick. {19:4} So he hustles, climbs a tree, hoping for a view 'cause Jesus is passing by. {19:5} When Jesus spots him, he's like, "Yo, Zacchaeus, come down quick! I'm crashing at your place today." {19:6} Zacchaeus rushes down, hyped to welcome Jesus. {19:7} But the crowd starts grumbling, like, "Why's Jesus chillin' with a sinner?" {19:8} Zacchaeus steps up, saying to Jesus, "Boss, I'm donating half my stuff to the poor and paying back anyone I ripped off four times over." {19:9} Jesus is like, "Bro, today salvation hits your crib 'cause you're one of Abraham's crew." {19:10} "I'm here to rescue the lost," Jesus adds. {19:11} Then he drops a story 'cause they're close to Jerusalem, and folks think the kingdom's coming ASAP. {19:12} He's like, "This VIP goes off to snag a kingdom and return." {19:13} He hands out cash to his peeps, saying, "Make it grow while I'm gone." {19:14} But the locals hate him and send a message: "We don't want you ruling us." {19:15} When he returns with his kingdom, he checks in on his servants' profits. {19:16-17} The first doubled his cash; he gets major props. {19:18-19} The second makes a tidy sum too. {19:20} But the third just hid the cash, fearing the boss. {19:221} The boss calls him out for being lazy and gives his cash to the top earner. {19:22} The boss clarifies: "Those who have will get more, while the slackers lose everything." {19:23} The boss orders his haters executed. {19:28} Jesus heads for Jerusalem. {19:24} He sends two disciples ahead to fetch a colt. {19:25} If asked why, they're to say, "Boss needs it." {19:26} They bring it to Jesus, and he rides it into town. {19:27} His crew starts celebrating, shouting praises for all his dope miracles. {19:28} The Pharisees want Jesus to quiet them down. {19:29} Jesus snaps back, saying even rocks would cheer if his crew stayed silent. {19:30} He weeps over Jerusalem, knowing its fate. {19:31} He hits up the temple, kicking out the merchants, declaring it's a house of prayer. {19:32} He's dropping wisdom there every day, but the religious big shots want him gone. {19:33} They're plotting, but the people are all ears, so they can't touch him.

{20:1} One day Jesus is teaching and spreading the gospel in the temple, and here come the chief priests, scribes, and elders rolling up on him. {20:2} They're like, "Yo, who gave you the authority to do this stuff?" {20:3} Jesus flips it back on them, saying, "I'll ask you something: was John's baptism from heaven or just a human thing?" {20:4-6} They start whispering to themselves, "If we say 'from heaven,' he'll ask why we didn't believe John; if we say 'human,' the people will flip out 'cause they think John was a prophet." {20:7} They chicken out and say they don't know where John's baptism came from. {20:8} Jesus is like, "Cool, then I ain't telling you where my authority comes from either." {20:9} So Jesus starts spitting a parable to the crowd: a dude plants a vineyard and leases it out, then leaves for a long trip. {20:10-12} When it's harvest time, he sends a servant to get some fruit, but the tenants beat him up and send him away empty-handed. {20:13} Finally, the owner sends his son, thinking they'll respect him, but the tenants are like, "Let's kill him and take his inheritance!" {20:14} The owner will come and wreck those tenants and give the vineyard to others. {20:15} The chief priests and scribes get heated and want to arrest Jesus, but they're scared of the crowd 'cause they know the parable's about them. {20:16} They start spying on Jesus, sending undercover peeps to trap him with his words and hand him over to the authorities. {20:17} They approach Jesus like, "Yo, you speak the truth and don't play favorites; is it cool to pay taxes to Caesar or not?" {20:18} Jesus sees through their game and says, "Why you trying to trick me?" {20:19} He asks for a coin, and they show him a Caesar coin. {20:20} Jesus is like, "Give Caesar what's his and give God what's God's." {20:21} They can't say nothing back, and the crowd's amazed at his response. {20:22} Next up, some Sadducees show up, denying the resurrection, and they hit Jesus with a hypothetical. {20:23} They're like, "Moses said if a guy dies and leaves no kids, his brother should marry his widow and have kids for him. What if seven brothers marry the same woman in a row?" {20:24} Jesus schools them, saying in the afterlife, people don't marry; they're like angels and children of God. {20:25} Jesus drops the mic, reminding them that God is the God of the living, not the dead. {20:26} The scribes are like, "Well said, Jesus," and then they keep their mouths shut 'cause they can't top that. {20:27} Jesus flips it on them, asking how the Messiah can be David's son if David calls him Lord in the Psalms. {20:28} Then he warns everyone about the scribes who love showing off with long robes and fancy greetings, looking for the best seats and praying for show—they're in for a big punishment.

{21:1} Jesus peeped the rich dudes dropping their cash in the offering. {21:2} Then he noticed this poor widow tossing in two cents. {21:3} And he's like, "Real talk, she gave more than all these ballers combined!" {21:4} "They're just tossing in what they can spare, but she's putting in everything she's got." {21:5} As people were chatting about how swanky the temple looked, Jesus dropped a truth bomb. {21:6} "Check it, a day's coming when not one stone will be left standing here." {21:7} They're like, "Yo, when's that gonna happen, and how we gonna know?" {21:8} Jesus warns, "Don't get played, many will front like they're me, talking about the end times, but don't buy into it." {21:9} "When you hear about wars and chaos, stay chill, it's gotta happen before the end." {21:10} "Nations will go at it, earthquakes, famines, and crazy stuff going down." {21:11-12} "Before all that, though, they'll come for you, drag you to court and jail, just for repping my name." {21:13} "But don't stress, it's a chance to speak up for what's real." {21:14} "So, don't sweat what you'll say, I'll give you the words to shut 'em down." {21:15-16} "Even your own fam might turn on you, but don't trip, I got you." {21:17} "People will hate you because of me, but you'll be good, not even a hair on your head's gonna be touched." {21:18-19} "Keep it cool, keep your soul tight." {21:20} "When you see Jerusalem surrounded, know it's about to go down." {21:21} "Get outta there, flee to the hills, don't even look back." {21:22} "It's payback time, fulfilling all the prophecies." {21:23} "But it's gonna be rough, especially for those with kids." {21:24} "Jerusalem's gonna get trampled until the end of the non-Jewish era." {21:25} "Crazy stuff's gonna go down, signs in the sky, nations freaking out." {21:26} "People's hearts failing from fear of what's coming, 'cause the world's gonna get rocked." {21:27} "Then everyone's gonna see me rolling up in the clouds with power and glory." {21:28} "When this starts going down, look up, 'cause your redemption's close." {21:29} Jesus breaks it down with a metaphor about trees and knowing when summer's near. {21:30-31} "Same goes for y'all, when you see this stuff, know the kingdom's coming." {21:32} "No joke, this generation won't pass till it's all gone down." {21:33} "Everything might fade, but my words, they're here to stay." {21:34} "Keep your heads in check, don't get too caught up in partying and stressing about life, or that day's gonna hit you outta nowhere." {21:35-36} "Stay woke, keep praying, so you're ready when all this goes down, and you're standing before me." {21:37} "He spent the days teaching in the temple, and at night, he crashed on the Mount of Olives." {21:38} "Everyone was early to catch him in the temple, eager to hear what he had to say."

{22:1} The Passover's rolling in, right? {22:2} But the big shots, priests, and scholars are plotting Jesus' demise, scared of the public opinion. {22:3} Then boom, Satan hops into Judas Iscariot, one of the squad. {22:4} Judas is like, "Yo, let's chat," with the religious leaders, plotting Jesus' betrayal. {22:5} They're stoked and promise him cash. {22:6} Judas agrees and scouts for a chance to sell out Jesus when the crowds aren't around. {22:7} Passover Day dawns, time to slaughter the Passover lamb. {22:8} Jesus sends Peter and John to get things ready for the Passover meal. {22:9} They're like, "Where do you want us to set up?" {22:10} Jesus is like, "Chill, when you hit the city, you'll meet a dude carrying water; follow him to the spot." {22:11} "Tell the homeowner the Boss wants to know where to have the Passover meal," Jesus says. {22:12} They find the place, all set up. {22:13} They prep the Passover meal as Jesus instructed. {22:14} When it's time, Jesus and the gang sit down for the meal. {22:15} He tells them how he's been looking forward to this meal before he goes through some rough times. {22:16} He's like, "This is the last time I'm eating this until the kingdom of God is in full swing." {22:17} He takes a cup, gives thanks, and tells them to share it. {22:18} "I'm not drinking wine again until God's kingdom comes," he says. {22:19} Then he takes some bread, gives thanks, breaks it, and hands it to them, saying it's his body and they should remember him with it. {22:20} Then he hands them a cup after dinner, saying it's a new deal sealed in his blood for them. {22:21} He drops the bomb that the one who's selling him out is at the table with them. {22:22} He knows what's coming but still calls out the betrayer. {22:23} The disciples start questioning who's gonna do the dirty deed. {22:24} And they're even arguing over who's the top dog among them. {22:25} Jesus schools them, saying, "Gentile leaders play boss, but not you guys." {22:26} "The real leader is the one who serves," he adds. {22:27} "I'm here to serve, not be served," Jesus emphasizes. {22:28} He gives them props for sticking with him through the tough times. {22:29} He's like, "You're in for a kingdom ride, just like my Father promised me." {22:30} "You'll be dining with me at my table in my kingdom, calling the shots over Israel's tribes." {22:31} Then he drops a truth bomb on Simon, saying Satan wants to test him. {22:32} Jesus promises to have his back and expects Simon to help the squad after he's back on track. {22:33} Simon's like, "I'm down to roll with you, even if it means prison or worse." {22:34} But Jesus predicts Simon will deny him three times before the rooster crows. {22:35} He's like, "Remember when I sent you out with nothing? You didn't lack anything, right?" {22:36} "Well, now grab your wallet and backpack, and if you don't have a sword, sell something and buy one," Jesus instructs. {22:37} He quotes scripture, saying it's about to be fulfilled, so they better be ready. {22:38} They're like, "We've got two swords," and Jesus is like, "Cool, that's enough." {22:39} After that, they head to their usual spot on the Mount of Olives, with the crew tagging along. {22:40} Jesus tells them to pray so they don't fall into temptation. {22:41} He goes a little farther, kneels, and prays. {22:42} He's like, "God, if there's any other way, but your will, not mine," showing he's willing to do what's needed. {22:43} An angel shows up, giving him strength. {22:44} He's in such agony that he's sweating blood. {22:45} When he goes back to check on his squad, he finds them sleeping from sadness. {22:46} He's like, "Wake up and pray, or you'll get caught slipping." {22:47} Just then, Judas shows up with a mob, ready to kiss Jesus, the signal of betrayal. {22:48} Jesus calls him out on it. {22:49} His squad asks if they should fight, but Jesus shuts it down. {22:50} One of them still gets trigger happy and slices off a dude's ear. {22:51} Jesus fixes it up and asks why they're rolling on him like he's some criminal. {22:52} He's like, "I was out here teaching every day, and now you're coming after me with swords and clubs?" {22:53} He knows this is their moment, powered by darkness. {22:54} They take him to the high priest's place, with Peter following from a distance. {22:55} Peter sneaks in and sits with the crowd by the fire. {22:56} A girl recognizes him and calls him out for being Jesus' crew. {22:57} He denies it. {22:58} Then another person points him out, and again, he denies it. {22:59} People keep insisting, but Peter keeps denying until the rooster crows. {22:60} When he realizes what he's done, he's crushed. {22:61} Jesus gives him a look, and Peter remembers Jesus' warning. {22:62} He leaves and breaks down in tears. {22:63} Meanwhile, the crew holding Jesus is mocking and hitting him. {22:64} They blindfold him and dare him to guess who's hitting him. {22:65} They keep disrespecting him in every way possible. {22:66} When morning comes, the religious big shots assemble, questioning Jesus. {22:67} They're like, "Are you the Messiah? Tell us." {22:68} Jesus is like, "If I tell you, you won't believe me, and if I ask you, you won't answer or let me go." {22:69} "But soon, I'll be sitting at God's right hand in power," he adds. {22:70} They press him, asking if he's the Son of God, and Jesus is like, "You said it, not me." {22:71} They're like, "We've heard enough from you

[23:1} This huge crowd gets together and takes Jesus to Pilate. {23:2} They start accusing him, like, "We caught this dude stirring up trouble, saying he's a king and telling people not to pay taxes to Caesar." {23:3} Pilate's like, "Are you claiming to be the King of the Jews?" Jesus responds, "You said it." {23:4} Pilate tells everyone he finds no fault in Jesus. {23:5} But the crowd gets louder, saying Jesus is riling up the people from Galilee to here. {23:6-7} When Pilate hears Jesus is from Galilee, he sends him to Herod, who's also in Jerusalem at the time. {23:8} Herod's stoked to finally see Jesus 'cause he heard so much about him and hoped to see a miracle. {23:9} He bombards Jesus with questions, but Jesus stays silent. {23:10} Meanwhile, the chief priests and scribes keep accusing him. {23:11} Herod and his crew disrespect Jesus, mock him, dress him in fancy clothes, and send him back to Pilate. {23:12} Later that day, Pilate and Herod squash their beef and become friends. {23:13-15} Pilate calls together the chief priests, rulers, and people, saying, "You brought me this guy, saying he's causing trouble, but I find no fault in him." {23:16-17} Pilate decides to punish Jesus and let him go, since it's customary to release someone during the feast. {23:18-19} The crowd shouts to release Barabbas instead. {23:20} Pilate tries again, but they keep yelling, "Crucify him!" {23:21} Pilate's like, "Seriously, what did he do wrong?" {23:22} They keep demanding Jesus be crucified, and the priests' voices win. {23:23} As they lead Jesus away, they grab Simon from Cyrene to carry the cross. {23:24} A big crowd follows, with women crying and mourning. {23:25} Jesus tells them not to cry for him but for themselves and their children. {23:26} He warns them about worse times to come. {23:27} They crucify Jesus between two criminals. {23:28} Jesus prays for forgiveness for those who don't get what they're doing. {23:29} People taunt him, saying if he's the chosen one, he should save himself. {23:30} One criminal mocks Jesus, but the other defends him and asks to be remembered in Jesus' kingdom. {23:31} Jesus promises the defending criminal they'll be together in paradise. {23:32} Darkness falls over the land until Jesus dies. {23:33} Jesus cries out and dies, entrusting his spirit to God. {23:34} The centurion recognizes Jesus as righteous. {23:35} Everyone watching hits their chests and leaves. {23:36} Jesus' friends and the women from Galilee watch from a distance.

[24:1} So like, on the first day of the week, super early in the morning, they rolled up to the tomb with their spices ready, plus some others. {24:2} When they got there, the stone was already moved away from the entrance. {24:3} So they went in, but Jesus wasn't there. {24:4} And they were totally freaked out, when suddenly two dudes in shining outfits appeared. {24:5} They were scared stiff and bowed down, then these guys were like, "Why you looking for the living among the dead?" {24:6} "He's not here, man, he's risen! Remember what he told you in Galilee?" {24:7} "He said he'd be handed over to some shady folks, get crucified, then bounce back on the third day." {24:8} And then it clicked for them; they remembered his words. {24:9} They jetted back to the crew and spilled all the deets to the eleven and everyone else. {24:10} Mary Magdalene, Joanna, Mary (mother of James), and the other women were the ones who first spilled to the apostles. {24:11} But they thought it was all nonsense and didn't buy it. {24:12} So Peter jumped up and raced to the tomb, where he saw the linen clothes neatly laid out and he was shook, wondering what was up. {24:13} Later that same day, two of them headed to a village called Emmaus, about 7 miles from Jerusalem, talking over everything that went down. {24:14} While they were chatting, Jesus himself came up and joined them, but they didn't recognize him. {24:15} He was like, "What are you guys talking about? You look bummed." {24:16} They were clueless, so he kept up the act. {24:17} "What? You been living under a rock in Jerusalem?" Cleopas replied, surprised. {24:18} Jesus was like, "What's been happening?" {24:19} They spilled about Jesus of Nazareth, a powerful prophet before God and everyone, how the big shots had him arrested and nailed to a cross. {24:20} "We thought he was the one to save Israel, and today's the third day since it all went down." {24:21} "Plus, some women from our crew blew our minds, saying they saw angels and that he's alive." {24:22-24} "A few others checked it out and confirmed—just like the women said—but they didn't see him." {24:25} Then Jesus said, "Seriously? You guys are slow to believe what the prophets said!" {24:26} "Didn't the Christ have to go through all this to hit his glory?" {24:27} From there, he gave them a crash course in all the scriptures about him, starting with Moses and the prophets. {24:28} They reached Emmaus, and Jesus acted like he was moving on. {24:29} They insisted he chill, 'cause it was getting late, so he hung with them. {24:30} While they ate, he took the bread, blessed it, broke it, and handed it over. {24:31} Suddenly, their eyes popped open, and they recognized him—but then he vanished! {24:32} They were like, "Didn't our hearts catch fire while he was talking and explaining the scriptures?" {24:33} They dashed back to Jerusalem and found the crew, announcing, "The Lord is alive—Simon saw him!" {24:34-35} They shared all the tea about what went down, especially how they recognized him when he broke bread. {24:36} While they were dishing, Jesus appeared in the middle of them, saying, "Chill, guys, peace to you." {24:37} They were shook, thinking they'd seen a ghost. {24:38-39} Jesus was like, "Why are you tripping? Look, it's me, with flesh and bones—not a ghost." {24:40} Then he showed them his hands and feet. {24:41} They were stoked but still in shock, so he asked for food. {24:42} They gave him some fish and honeycomb, and he chowed down. {24:43-44} Then he dropped this: "Remember what I said while I was with you—everything the law of Moses, the prophets, and the psalms said about me had to happen." {24:45} Then he opened their minds to understand the scriptures. {24:46} He was like, "It was written: the Christ had to suffer and rise on the third day." {24:47} "And that the word should go out, calling for a change of heart and forgiveness of sins in his name, starting in Jerusalem." {24:48} "And you guys saw it all go down—you're witnesses." {24:49} "Oh, and get this—my Father's promise is coming your way, but stay put in Jerusalem until you get powered up from above." {24:50} Then he led them to Bethany, blessed them, and poof—ascended into heaven. {24:51} They worshipped him and bounced back to Jerusalem, hyped and praising God non-stop. Amen.

John

✦✦✦

{1:1} So, like, from the get-go, there was the Word, chilling with God, being God himself. {1:2} This dude was there right from the start, hanging out with God. {1:3} Everything? Yeah, he made it, like, every single thing, not one thing left out. {1:4} In him, there was life, and that life was the real deal for humans, bringing light into the dark scene. {1:5} But yo, even though the light was shining, darkness couldn't even grasp it. {1:6} Now, there's this guy, sent straight from God, named John. {1:7} His gig was to testify about the Light, so everyone could get on board. {1:8} He wasn't the Light himself, just hyping up the real deal. {1:9} That Light, though? Legit, shining on everyone who's ever entered this world. {1:10} He was right here, but the world was clueless, didn't even recognize him. {1:11} He showed up on his home turf, and his own peeps were like, "Nah, we're good." {1:12} But those who did dig him? He hooked them up, giving them the power to be part of God's fam, just by believing in his name. {1:13} They didn't score this hookup through some family tree or human hustle, but straight from God himself. {1:14} And then, yo, the Word became human and set up camp among us. We saw his glory, like he was the Father's one and only, packed with grace and truth. {1:15} John vouched for him, shouting, "This is the dude I've been talking about! He's the real deal, way ahead of me!" {1:16} And from him, we all got showered with blessings, one after another, grace stacked on top of grace. {1:17} See, back in the day, it was all about the law, but Jesus rolled through with grace and truth. {1:18} Nobody's ever seen God, but the one and only Son, who's cozy with the Father, has let us in on the deal. {1:19} So, this is how it went down with John: the Jewish crew sent some priests and Levites from Jerusalem to grill him. {1:20} John owned up, no dodging, straight-up said, "I'm not the Messiah." {1:21} They pressed him, "Are you Elijah?" He's like, "Nah." "What about the prophet?" "Nope." {1:22} So, they're like, "Who are you, then? We gotta give an answer to the bosses." "Well," he says, "I'm just the voice yelling in the desert, 'Make way for the Lord!'" Like Isaiah said. {1:23} And the crew they sent? Yeah, they were Pharisees, no doubt. {1:24} They're like, "Why are you baptizing if you're not the Messiah, Elijah, or the prophet?" {1:25} John sets them straight: "I'm all about dunking folks in water, but there's someone among you you don't even know yet. {1:26} He's the real deal, coming after me, even though I'm not even worthy to mess with his kicks." {1:27} This all went down at Bethabara, east of the Jordan River, where John was doing his dunking. {1:28} The next day, John spots Jesus rolling up and shouts, "Check it out, the Lamb of God, taking away the world's sin!" {1:29} This was the guy John had been talking about, "After me comes a dude who's way ahead of me, 'cause he's been around way longer." {1:30} Even though John didn't know him at first, he was there to show him off to Israel, that's why he was dunking folks in water. {1:31} So, John drops the scoop, "I saw the Spirit coming down from the sky like a dove and hanging out with him." {1:32} "I didn't know who he was," John admits, "but the one who sent me to dunk people told me, 'When you see the Spirit chilling and staying with someone, that's the one who's all about the Holy Spirit dunk.'" {1:33} "And yo, I saw it go down and can confirm, this dude is the Son of God." {1:34} The next day, John's chilling with two of his homies, and as Jesus walks by, he's like, "Yo, check out the Lamb of God!" {1:35} The two hear him and start following Jesus. {1:36} Jesus peeps them and asks, "What's up? What are you looking for?" They're like, "Rabbi, where you staying?" (Which means "Teacher.") {1:37} So, Jesus is like, "Come see for yourselves." They hang out with him all day, 'cause it was about ten in the morning. {1:38} One of the two who followed John is Andrew, Simon Peter's bro. {1:39} He finds his bro Simon and says, "Yo, we found the Messiah!" (Which means "Christ.") {1:40-42} Andrew brings Simon to Jesus, who checks him out and says, "You're Simon, son of John? From now on, you'll be called Cephas!" (Which means "Peter" or "Rock.") {1:43} The next day, Jesus heads to Galilee and finds Philip, saying, "Follow me." {1:44} Now, Philip's from the same town as Andrew and Peter, Bethsaida. {1:45} Philip finds Nathanael and tells him, "We found the dude Moses and the prophets wrote about, Jesus from Nazareth, Joseph's son." {1:46} Nathanael's like, "Nazareth? Can anything good come from there?" Philip's like, "Come check it out." {1:47} Jesus sees Nathanael coming and says, "Here's a true Israelite, no fakeness in this guy!" {1:48} Nathanael's like, "How do you know me?" Jesus says, "Before Philip called you, I saw you chilling under the fig tree." {1:49} Nathanael's mind is blown, and he's like, "Teacher, you're the Son of God, the King of Israel!" {1:50} Jesus is like, "Just 'cause I saw you under the fig tree, you believe? You're gonna see way crazier stuff than that." {1:51} Then he tells him, "For real, you're gonna see heaven open up, and the angels of God rolling with me, the Son of Man."

{2:1} On the third day there was this wedding in Cana of Galilee, and Jesus' mom was there too. {2:2} Jesus and his crew got invited to the party. {2:3} When they ran out of wine, Jesus' mom was like, "Yo, they're all out of wine." {2:4} Jesus was like, "Mom, why you bringing this up? It's not my time yet." {2:5} But his mom told the servants, "Just do whatever he says." {2:6} There were these six stone water jars there for Jewish purification, each holding a bunch of gallons. {2:7} Jesus told them, "Fill those jars with water," and they filled them to the brim. {2:8} Then he said, "Now draw some out and take it to the party planner." So they did. {2:9} When the party planner tasted the water turned to wine (and didn't know where it came from, but the servants did), he called the groom over. {2:10} He was like, "Most folks bring out the good wine first, then the cheap stuff later. But you saved the best for last." {2:11} This was the first miracle Jesus did in Cana, showing off his skills, and his crew started believing in him. {2:12} After that, Jesus and his peeps headed to Capernaum and kicked it there for a bit. {2:13} When the Jewish Passover was coming up, Jesus rolled into Jerusalem. {2:14} He found folks selling animals and exchanging money in the temple. {2:15} So he made a whip out of cords and went to town, clearing out the animals and flipping over the money tables. {2:16} He told those selling doves, "Get out of here! Don't turn my Dad's house into a marketplace." {2:17} His crew remembered that it's written: "Passion for your house has consumed me." {2:18} The Jews were like, "What's your deal? Show us a sign if you're gonna act like this." {2:19} Jesus was like, "Destroy this temple, and in three days I'll rebuild it." {2:20} They were like, "It took 46 years to build this temple—how you gonna rebuild it in three days?" {2:21} But he was talking about his body being the temple. {2:22} Later, when he rose from the dead, his crew remembered what he said and believed him. {2:23} While Jesus was in Jerusalem for Passover, lots of people believed in him when they saw the miracles he was pulling off. {2:24} But Jesus wasn't trusting them, 'cause he knew everyone inside out. {2:25} He didn't need anyone to tell him what people were like—he knew it all.

{3:1} There's this Pharisee dude named Nicodemus, big shot in Jewish circles. {3:2} He sneaks up to Jesus at night, all like, "Yo, Rabbi, we peep your game. No one's pulling off these miracles unless they got some divine connection." {3:3} Jesus hits him with truth, "Listen up, unless you hit the reset button and start fresh, you ain't seeing God's scene." {3:4} Nicodemus is shook, "How's a dude supposed to reboot when he's old? Jump back in the womb?" {3:5} Jesus drops more knowledge, "Nah, it's about a spiritual birth, not just a physical one." {3:6} "Flesh gives birth to flesh, but spirit births spirit, you feel me?" {3:7} "Don't trip when I say you gotta start over." {3:8} "The wind blows where it wants, you hear it but can't see it; same with everyone born of the spirit." {3:9} Nicodemus is still lost, "How's that even work?" {3:10} Jesus ain't holding back, "You're a big shot around here and don't know this stuff?" {3:11} "We're speaking facts, but you ain't feeling it." {3:12} "If you can't handle the basic stuff, how you gonna handle the heavenly knowledge?" {3:13} "No one's gone up to heaven except the one who came down – the Son of Man, repping heaven while still on Earth." {3:14} Jesus goes deep with a reference, "Just like Moses lifted up the serpent, I'm getting lifted up too." {3:15} "Whoever vibes with me won't fade out, they're in for the long haul." {3:16} "God's love for the world is wild, he sent his only Son so believers get the hook-up on eternal life." {3:17} "God didn't send his Son to hate on the world, but to save it." {3:18} "Believers are in the clear, but haters are already judged for not getting down with the Son." {3:19} "Here's the deal: people dig darkness over light 'cause they're shady." {3:20} "Anyone doing dirt hates the light, they don't want their dirty deeds exposed." {3:21} "But those living truth come into the light, showing their deeds are legit God vibes." {3:22} After that, Jesus and his squad roll into Judaea, chilling and baptizing. {3:23} Meanwhile, John's dunking folks in Aenon near Salim 'cause there's mad water there, and people are lining up to get baptized. {3:24} John's still doing his thing, not locked up yet. {3:25} Then there's some back-and-forth between John's crew and the Jews about cleansing rituals. {3:26} They hit up John, "Yo, that dude you cosigned across the Jordan? Now he's baptizing, and everyone's flocking to him." {3:27} John schools them, "Dudes only get what heaven gives 'em." {3:28} "Y'all heard me say it, I'm not the main act, just warming up for him." {3:29} "He's the groom, I'm just stoked to hear his voice." {3:30} "His shine's gotta get brighter, mine's gotta take a backseat." {3:31} "The one from above's top dog, speaking truth; the earthly ones are stuck on earthly vibes." {3:32} "I'm just sharing what I've seen and heard, but folks ain't always feeling it." {3:33} "Those who vibe with his message know God's legit." {3:34} "He's repping God's words, no holding back; God's given him the whole deal." {3:35} "The Father loves the Son and put everything in his hands." {3:36} "Believers ride the wave to eternal life, but haters miss out and catch God's wrath."

{4:1} When Jesus found out the Pharisees were gossiping about how he was pulling in more disciples than John and even dunking more peeps, {4:2} (even though he wasn't the one dunking, but his crew was), {4:3} he bounced out of Judea and headed back to Galilee. {4:4} And of course, he had to pass through Samaria. {4:5} So he rolls up to this town called Sychar in Samaria, near this piece of land Jacob gave to his boy Joseph. {4:6} There was Jacob's well there, and Jesus, tired from the journey, kicks back by the well. It was like noon. {4:7} Then this Samaritan woman shows up to draw water, and Jesus is like, "Can you hook me up with a drink?" {4:8} (His crew had gone to grab some grub from the town.) {4:9} She's like, "Um, why are you, a Jew, asking me, a Samaritan chick, for a drink? Y'all don't roll with us Samaritans." {4:10} Jesus hits her with, "If you knew what God's all about and who's talking to you, you'd be asking me for a drink of living water, and I'd hook you up." {4:11} She's like, "Hold up, you ain't got no bucket, and this well is deep. Where you gonna get this living water?" {4:12} "Are you saying you're better than our dude Jacob, who hooked us up with this well and drank from it himself, along with his fam and animals?" {4:13} Jesus lays it out, "Anyone who drinks this water will get thirsty again, but the water I give will keep them satisfied forever, like a spring bubbling up to eternal life." {4:14-15} She's like, "Yeah, I'll take that water so I don't have to keep coming here for water." {4:16} Jesus is like, "Go call your husband and come back." {4:17-18} She's like, "I ain't got no husband." Jesus is like, "You're right, you've had five husbands, and the dude you're with now ain't your hubby. You're keeping it real." {4:19} She's like, "You must be a prophet." {4:20} "Our ancestors worshipped on this mountain, but y'all say Jerusalem is the place to be for worship." {4:21} Jesus tells her, "Believe me, the time's coming when where you worship won't matter, 'cause the real worshippers will worship the Father in spirit and truth. {4:22} You Samaritans don't know what's up, but we Jews do, 'cause salvation comes from us." {4:23} "But it's already go-time for true worshippers to vibe with the Father in spirit and truth, 'cause that's what he's after." {4:24} "God's all about the spirit, so anyone who wants to worship him has gotta do it with a real spirit and realness." {4:25} She's like, "I know the Messiah's coming, the Christ, and when he does, he'll spill all the tea." {4:26} Jesus is like, "Girl, I'm him." {4:27} Just then, his crew rolls up and is like, "What's going on here?" But they don't say anything to Jesus. {4:28-30} The woman bounces, leaving her water jar, and heads back to town, telling everyone, "Come see this dude who knew all my business! Could he be the Christ?" {4:31} Meanwhile, his crew is like, "Yo, Jesus, you gotta eat something." {4:32} He's like, "I've got food y'all don't even know about." {4:33} They're all confused, like, "Did someone bring him food?" {4:34} Jesus is like, "Nah, my food is doing God's work and finishing what he sent me to do." {4:35} "Don't say the harvest is still months away. Open your eyes and check out the fields—they're ready for harvesting now." {4:36} "The one who harvests gets paid and brings in eternal life, so everyone's hyped." {4:37}

"And it's true what they say, one person plants, another person harvests." {4:38} "I sent you to harvest what you didn't even plant. Others did the hard work, and you get to reap the rewards." {4:39} A bunch of Samaritans from the town believed in him because of what the woman said: "He knew everything I've done." {4:40} So when they came to him, they begged him to stay, and he hung out there for two days. {4:41} Lots more peeps believed because of his own words, not just what the woman said. {4:42} They told the woman, "Now we believe, not 'cause of what you said, but 'cause we've heard him ourselves and know he's the real deal, the Savior of the world." {4:43} After those two days, Jesus bounces to Galilee. {4:44} He's like, "Y'all know how it is, a prophet's got no respect in his own hood." {4:45} But when he gets to Galilee, the Galileans welcome him, 'cause they saw all the crazy stuff he did in Jerusalem at the feast—they were there too. {4:46} So he's back in Cana of Galilee, where he turned water into wine. And there's this big shot, whose kid is sick in Capernaum. {4:47} When he hears Jesus is in Galilee, he hustles over and begs Jesus to come and heal his kid, who's on his deathbed. {4:48} Jesus is like, "Y'all only believe if you see signs and wonders." {4:49} The big shot's like, "Sir, just come before my kid dies." {4:50} Jesus is like, "Go, your kid's good." The guy believed Jesus's word and took off. {4:51} As he's heading home, his servants meet him and tell him his kid's alive and kicking. {4:52} He asks when his kid started feeling better, and they're like, "Yesterday, around one in the afternoon, the fever broke." {4:53} And the dad realizes, "That's the same time Jesus said, 'Your kid's good.'" And he and his whole household start believing in Jesus. {4:54} This was the second miracle Jesus pulled off when he came from Judea to Galilee.

{5:1} So, like, after this there was this big Jewish feast, and Jesus rolled up to Jerusalem. {5:2} Now, in Jerusalem near the sheep market, there's this pool called Bethesda with five covered areas. {5:3} Lots of sick and disabled people would chill there, hoping for the water to get stirred up. {5:4} They believed an angel would stir the water sometimes, and whoever got in first after that would get healed, no matter what was wrong with them. {5:5} There was this one dude who'd been sick for 38 years hanging out there. {5:6} Jesus saw him lying there and asked, "You wanna get better?" {5:7} The guy was like, "I don't have anyone to help me into the pool when the water gets stirred up. By the time I try to get in, someone else beats me to it." {5:8} Jesus told him, "Get up, pick up your mat, and walk." {5:9} Right away, the guy was healed, grabbed his mat, and started walking around—this all went down on a Sabbath. {5:10} So, the Jewish leaders were like, "Hey, it's the Sabbath! You can't be carrying your mat around." {5:11} The healed guy was like, "The dude who made me well told me to carry my mat and walk." {5:12} They asked him, "Who's this guy who told you to pick up your mat?" {5:13} But the dude didn't know who it was, 'cause Jesus had slipped away in the crowd. {5:14} Later, Jesus found him in the temple and said, "You're all better now. Stop sinning, or something worse might happen to you." {5:15} The guy went and told the Jewish leaders that it was Jesus who had healed him. {5:16} Then the Jewish leaders started going after Jesus and wanted to kill him 'cause he did this on the Sabbath. {5:17} Jesus was like, "My Father is always working, and so am I." {5:18} This just made the Jewish leaders want to kill him even more, 'cause not only did he break the Sabbath, but he also called God his Father, making himself equal to God. {5:19} So, Jesus was like, "I'm telling you the truth: the Son can't do anything by himself. He only does what he sees the Father doing. {5:20} The Father loves the Son and shows him everything he does. And he's gonna show him even greater things, so you'll be blown away. {5:21} Just like the Father raises the dead and gives them life, the Son also gives life to those he wants. {5:22} The Father judges no one but has entrusted all judgment to the Son, {5:23} so everyone should honor the Son just like they honor the Father. If you don't honor the Son, you're not honoring the Father who sent him. {5:24} If you hear my words and believe in the One who sent me, you'll have eternal life and won't face judgment. You've already moved from death to life. {5:25} I'm telling you, the time is now when the dead will hear the voice of the Son of God, and those who hear will live. {5:26} Just as the Father has life in himself, he's also given the Son life in himself. {5:27} And he's given the Son authority to judge because he's the Son of Man. {5:28} Don't be shocked by all this. The time is coming when everyone in the graves will hear his voice {5:29} and come out—those who did good things to life and those who did evil to damnation. {5:30} I can't do anything by myself. I judge as I hear, and my judgment is fair 'cause I'm not doing my own thing but following the Father's will. {5:31} If I talk about myself, my testimony isn't valid. {5:32} But there's someone else testifying about me, and I know his testimony is true. {5:33} You sent to John, and he testified to the truth. {5:34} But I'm not just saying this for myself; I want you to be saved. {5:35} John was like a shining light, and for a while, you were into it. {5:36} But I've got an even bigger witness than John—the work the Father has given me to finish. {5:37} And the Father who sent me has testified about me himself. You've never heard his voice or seen his form. {5:38} And you don't have his word living in you 'cause you don't believe the one he sent. {5:39} Check the Scriptures—they talk about having eternal life, and they're all about me. {5:40} But you won't come to me to have that life. {5:41} I'm not here for people's praise. {5:42} But I know you don't have God's love in you. {5:43} I came representing my Father, but you don't welcome me. If someone else comes in their own name, you'll welcome them. {5:44} How can you believe when you're all about getting praise from each other and don't care about the honor that comes from God alone? {5:45} Don't think I'm gonna accuse you before the Father. Moses, the one you trust, will do that. {5:46} If you believed Moses, you'd believe me, 'cause he wrote about me. {5:47} But if you don't believe what Moses wrote, how will you believe my words?

{6:1} Jesus hits up the Sea of Galilee, aka Tiberias, with his crew. {6:2} Word got out about his sick miracles, so a huge crowd rolls with him, especially those needing healing. {6:3} Jesus peaces out to a mountain, chillin' with his squad. {6:4} Passover's coming up, a big deal for the Jewish scene. {6:5} Jesus spots the crowd and hits up Philip like, "Yo, where we copping bread for all these heads?" {6:6} Jesus knew what was up, just testing the waters. {6:7} Philip's like, "Bro, even if we drop mad cash, it ain't enough for everyone to even get a snack." {6:8} Andrew pipes up, "We got a kid here with five loaves and two fish, but come on, that's nothing for this mob." {6:9} Jesus is like, "Cool, have everyone sit down." There's plenty of grass, so they all chill, about five grand deep. {6:10} Jesus blesses the loaves, hands them to his crew, and they pass them out, along with the fish. {6:11} Everyone's fed, leftovers stacked. {6:12} They gather up the extras, not wasting a crumb. {6:13} Ended up with twelve baskets of leftovers from five barley loaves. {6:14} People see the miracle and know Jesus is the real deal, the prophet they've been waiting for. {6:15} Jesus peeps the crowd getting hyped to crown him king, so he dips solo to the mountain. {6:16} When night falls, his squad hits the sea for Capernaum, but Jesus isn't with them yet. {6:17} They hop in a boat, but it's dark and Jesus is MIA. {6:18} The wind picks up, making waves. {6:19} After rowing for miles, they see Jesus walking on water, and freak out. {6:20} But he's like, "Chill, it's me." {6:21} They let him in, and boom, they're instantly at their destination. {6:22} Next day, people see Jesus' crew's boat is the only one missing, so they roll to Capernaum, Jesus-style. {6:23} Some other boats from Tiberias pull up where they had their snack after Jesus gave thanks. {6:24} When they realize Jesus and his crew aren't there, they set sail to find him. {6:25} When they track him down, they're like, "Hey, how'd you get here?" {6:26} Jesus lays down truth, "You're not chasing me for miracles, just for free grub." {6:27} He's like, "Don't chase temporary stuff; aim for that eternal life vibe I'm handing out." {6:28} They're like, "Okay, what do we do?" {6:29} Jesus keeps it real, "Believe in the one God sent." {6:30} They're like, "Prove it, show us a sign." {6:31} They throw shade, bringing up manna from back in the desert days. {6:32} Jesus schools them, "Moses didn't hook you up; God's bringing the real heavenly bread." {6:33} "This bread is God's gift, giving life to the world." {6:34} They're like, "Yeah, give us that bread forever." {6:35} Jesus drops the mic, "I'm that bread of life. Come to me, and you'll never go hungry or thirsty again." {6:36} "But y'all seen me and still don't believe." {6:37} "Everyone sent to me by the Father will come, and I won't turn them away." {6:38} "I'm not here for myself, but to do what the Father wants." {6:39} "And he wants me to keep it real with everyone he gave me, raising them up in the end." {6:40} "Everyone who sees me and believes gets that eternal life hookup, and I'll raise them up in the end." {6:41} The Jews start whispering, not feeling Jesus calling himself heavenly bread. {6:42} They're like, "Isn't he just Joseph's kid? How's he saying he came from heaven?" {6:43} Jesus shuts down the gossip. {6:44} "No one can come to me unless the Father draws them, and I'll raise them up in the end." {6:45} "Prophets said God's people would be taught by him, so everyone who hears and learns from the Father comes to me." {6:46} "No one's seen the Father except the one from God; he's seen the Father." {6:47} "Believe in me, and you'll get that eternal life vibe." {6:48} "I'm the bread of life." {6:49} "Your ancestors ate manna but still kicked the bucket." {6:50} "I'm the bread that came down from heaven; eat it, live forever." {6:51} "I'm the living bread; eat this, and you'll live forever. My flesh is the real deal, given for the world." {6:52} The Jews start debating, like, "How's he gonna give us his flesh to eat?" {6:53} Jesus lays it out, "Unless you eat my flesh and drink my blood, you're outta the life club." {6:54} "Those who munch on me get eternal life, and I'll raise them up in the end." {6:55} "My flesh and blood are the real deal." {6:56} "Those who munch on me vibe with me, and I vibe with them." {6:57} "Just like I live because of the Father, those who munch on me live because of me." {6:58} "I'm that heavenly bread; not like your ancestors who ate manna and kicked the bucket. Munch on me, live forever." {6:59} Jesus drops these truth bombs in the synagogue while teaching in Capernaum. {6:60} Many disciples are like, "Whoa, that's heavy stuff. How can we handle it?" {6:61} Jesus knows they're tripping, "Does this mess with you?" {6:62} "What if you see me ascend back to where I came from?" {6:63} "Spirit gives life; flesh ain't doing squat. My words are spirit and life." {6:64} "Some of you don't believe, and I knew from the start who'd betray me." {6:65} "I told you, no one comes unless the Father brings them." {6:66} After this, many disciples bail, no longer rolling with Jesus. {6:67} Jesus asks the twelve, "You out too?" {6:68} Peter's like, "Nah, you got the real talk, eternal life hookup." {6:69} "We believe you're the Christ, the Son of God." {6:70} Jesus reminds them, "I chose you, but one of you's a snake." {6:71} He's talking about Judas Iscariot, the betrayer among the twelve.

{7:1} Jesus was chilling in Galilee 'cause he didn't wanna roll in Judea since the Jews were gunning for him. {7:2} And then the Jews' Tabernacles fiesta was about to go down. {7:3} His bros were like, "Yo, bounce from here and head to Judea so your followers can peep your moves." {7:4} They're like, "You don't keep anything on the down-low; if you're gonna do stuff, do it out in the open. Show off to the world." {7:5} But, like, even his brothers didn't believe in him. {7:6} Jesus is like, "My time's not now, but you guys can do whatever whenever." {7:7} "The world might not have beef with you, but it's all about hating on me 'cause I call out its evil deeds." {7:8} "You guys can hit up the fiesta, but I'ma hold off for now 'cause my time hasn't come." {7:9} So after dropping these lines, Jesus stays put in Galilee. {7:10} But once his bros bounced, he dips to the fiesta too, not upfront but on the low. {7:11} At the fiesta, peeps are like, "Where's Jesus at?" {7:12} Everyone's talking about him, some saying he's legit, others calling him a fraud. {7:13} But nobody's saying anything loud 'cause they're scared of the Jews. {7:14} Around halfway through the fiesta, Jesus pops up at the temple and starts dropping knowledge. {7:15} And everyone's like, "How's this dude so wise when he didn't even go to school?" {7:16} Jesus is like, "My teachings ain't mine, they're from the one who sent me." {7:17} "If you're down to do what's right, you'll see if my teachings are from God or just me talking." {7:18} "Anyone who talks about themselves is after their own fame, but if you're all about the one who sent you, that's realness with no shady business." {7:19} "Moses gave you the law, but none of y'all are keeping it. So why are you trying to ice me?" {7:20} They're like, "You're crazy! Who's trying to off you?" {7:21} Jesus is like, "I did one thing and y'all are shook." {7:22} "Moses said circumcision was cool, even on the Sabbath. So why you hating 'cause I made someone fully whole on the Sabbath?" {7:23-24} "Don't judge by what you see; make fair judgments." {7:25} Some folks from Jerusalem are like, "Ain't this the dude they're trying to off?" {7:26} "But he's speaking bold, and they ain't doing anything. Maybe the bigwigs know he's the real deal?" {7:27} "We know where this dude's from, but when the Christ shows up, no one's gonna know where he's from." {7:28} Jesus shouts, "Y'all think you know me and where I'm from, but I'm not doing my own thing; the one who sent me is legit, even if you don't know him." {7:29} "But I know him 'cause I'm from him, and he sent me." {7:30} They try to nab him, but no one lays a finger on him 'cause it ain't his time yet. {7:31} And lots of people start believing in him, wondering if the Christ will do crazier stuff than Jesus did. {7:32} The Pharisees hear the gossip and send officers to grab him. {7:33} Jesus tells them, "I'm only here a little longer, then I'm out to the one who sent me. You'll look for me, but you won't find me, and where I'm going, you can't come." {7:34} So they're like, "Where's this dude going that we can't find him? Is he gonna teach the Gentiles?" {7:35} They're all confused about what Jesus said, like, "What's he talking about, saying we won't find him?" {7:37} Then, on the last day of the fiesta, Jesus shouts, "Anyone who's thirsty, come to me and drink!" {7:38} "If you believe in me, you'll be flowing with living water, just like the scriptures say." {7:39} He's talking about the Spirit, which believers will get, but it wasn't around yet 'cause Jesus wasn't done doing his thing. {7:40} Lots of peeps were like, "This dude's the real deal, the Prophet!" {7:41} Others are like, "Nah, he's the Christ!" But some are skeptical, like, "Can the Christ come from Galilee?" {7:42} "Isn't the script saying he's gotta be from David's crew and Bethlehem?" {7:43} So the crowd's divided 'cause of Jesus. {7:44} Some wanna grab him, but they can't get their hands on him. {7:45} The officers come back to the big shots, who are like, "Why didn't you nab him?" {7:46} The officers are like, "Man, nobody talks like this dude." {7:47-48} The big shots are like, "Are you fools too? Have any of us bought into his game?" {7:49} They're like, "Only the clueless fall for this guy." {7:50} Nicodemus, who sneaked to see Jesus at night, pipes up, {7:51} "Shouldn't we hear him out before we judge him?" {7:52} They're like, "You from Galilee too? Go check; no prophet comes from there." {7:53} And everyone heads home.

{8:1} Jesus headed up to the Mount of Olives. {8:2} Early in the morning, he rolled back into the temple, and all the people gathered around him, so he sat down and started teaching them. {8:3} Then these religious guys, the scribes and Pharisees, dragged in this woman they caught in the act of adultery and stood her right in front. {8:4} They were like, "Hey, Master, we caught this woman red-handed in adultery. The law of Moses says we should stone her, but what's your take?" {8:5-6} They were trying to trap Jesus into saying something they could use against him. But Jesus just bent down and started doodling in the dirt with his finger, ignoring them. {8:7-8} Finally, after they kept badgering him, Jesus stood up and said, "Whoever here hasn't messed up can throw the first stone at her." {8:9} When they heard that, their guilty consciences hit them hard, and they all left, starting with the oldest dudes, until it was just Jesus and the woman left standing there. {8:10} Jesus looked at her and said, "Where'd everyone go? Did no one condemn you?" {8:11} She said, "No one, Lord." And Jesus told her, "I don't condemn you either. Go, and try to avoid messing up again." {8:12} Then Jesus spoke up again, saying, "I'm like the light of the world. If you stick with me, you won't be lost in the dark; you'll have the light of life." {8:13} The Pharisees then accused him of self-promotion and said his testimony wasn't valid. {8:14} Jesus shot back, "Even if I'm talking about myself, what I say is legit 'cause I know where I came from and where I'm going. You have no clue about that." {8:15} "You guys just judge based on what you see on the outside, but I'm not here to judge anyone." {8:16} "But even if I did judge, my judgment would be fair 'cause I'm not alone—my Dad who sent me is with me." {8:17} "Your own law says the testimony of two people is valid." {8:18} "I testify about myself, and my Father who sent me also testifies about me." {8:19} They were like, "Where's your Father then?" Jesus said, "You don't know me or my Father. If you knew me, you'd know my Father too." {8:20} Jesus dropped these truth bombs in the temple treasury area while teaching, and no one laid a hand on him because it wasn't his time yet. {8:21} Then Jesus told them, "I'm outta here, and you'll look for me but won't find me; you'll die in your mess-ups. Where I'm headed, you can't come." {8:22} The Jews were puzzled, wondering if Jesus planned to off himself since he said they couldn't follow where he was going. {8:23} Jesus told them straight up, "You're from down here; I'm from up there. You belong to this world; I'm not about that." {8:24} "I told you that you'll mess up and die in your mess-ups. If you don't believe that I am who I say, you're toast." {8:25} They were like, "Who even are you?" And Jesus replied, "Exactly who I've been telling you from the start." {8:26} "I've got loads to say and judge about you, but the one who sent me is legit, and I'm just telling the world what he tells me." {8:27} They couldn't grasp that he was talking about the Father. {8:28} Jesus said, "Once you've lifted up the Son of Man, you'll get it. I don't act on my own; I speak what my Father teaches me." {8:29} "And my Father's with me; he hasn't left me alone 'cause I'm always doing what pleases him." {8:30} When Jesus dropped these truth bombs, many believed in him. {8:31} So Jesus told those who believed in him, "If you keep following my lead, you're truly my crew; {8:32} and you'll know what's real, and that reality will set you free."

{9:1} Jesus is strolling along and spots this dude who's been blind since day one. {9:2} His crew's like, "Yo, Jesus, who's at fault here? This guy or his parents?" {9:3} Jesus shuts that down, "Nah, neither of them. It's about showing off God's power." {9:4} "Gotta do God's work while it's light; night's coming when no one can work." {9:5} "While I'm around, I'm bringing that light to the world." {9:6-7} Then Jesus gets creative, spits on the ground, makes some mud, rubs it on the dude's eyes, and sends him to wash in the pool of Siloam. Dude comes back seeing like a boss. {9:8} Neighbors and folks who knew him when he was blind are like, "Isn't this the dude who used to beg?" {9:9} Some say, "Yeah, that's him," others are like, "Looks like him," but the dude's like, "Yeah, it's me." {9:10} They're like, "How'd you get your sight back?" {9:11} Dude's like, "This guy Jesus made some mud, slapped it on my eyes, and told me to wash up. Did it, and bam, sight restored." {9:12} They're like, "Where's this Jesus guy?" Dude's clueless. {9:13} They haul the formerly blind dude to the Pharisees. {9:14} But it's the Sabbath when Jesus did his mud magic. {9:15} Pharisees are curious how he got his sight. Dude's like, "Jesus put mud on my eyes, I washed up, and now I see." {9:16} Some Pharisees are like, "Jesus can't be legit; he broke Sabbath rules." Others are like, "But how can a sinner pull off miracles?" Split opinions all around. {9:17} They ask the once-blind dude, "What do you say about Jesus giving you sight?" He's like, "He's a prophet." {9:18} But the Jews are skeptical until they grill the dude's parents. {9:19} They're like, "Is this really your son? Wasn't he born blind? How's he seeing now?" {9:20} Parents confirm he's their son and was born blind but dodge the rest, afraid of getting kicked out of the synagogue for backing Jesus. {9:21} They're like, "He's old enough to speak for himself; ask him." {9:22} Parents are shook about the consequences of acknowledging Jesus as Christ. {9:23} "He's old enough; ask him," they repeat. {9:24} Pharisees call the once-blind dude again, pressuring him to give props to God, not Jesus, because they're sure Jesus is a sinner. {9:25} Dude's like, "I dunno if he's a sinner or not, but I know one thing: I was blind, now I see." {9:26} Pharisees are relentless, demanding to know how it all went down again. {9:27} Dude's like, "I told you already; why you wanna hear it again? You wanna be Jesus fans too?" {9:28} Pharisees clown him, saying he's a Jesus fan, but they're all about Moses. {9:29} They're like, "We're all about Moses; we don't know this Jesus dude." {9:30} Dude's like, "This is wild! You don't know where Jesus is from, but he hooked me up with sight." {9:31} "God doesn't listen to sinners, but if you're all about God and doing his thing, he listens." {9:32} "Nobody's ever heard of a blind dude getting his sight back, but Jesus did it, so he's gotta be from God." {9:33-34} Pharisees are salty, calling dude a sinner from birth, then kick him out. {9:35} Jesus hears they booted him and finds him, asking if he believes in the Son of God. {9:36} Dude's like, "Who is he, so I can believe?" {9:37} Jesus tells him he's seen him and is talking to him. {9:38} Dude's like, "I'm in; you're the man, Lord," and bows down. {9:39} Jesus explains he's here to open the eyes of the spiritually blind and blind those who claim to see it all. {9:40} Some Pharisees are like, "Wait, are we blind too?" {9:41} Jesus hits back, "If you were blind, you wouldn't be guilty. But since you claim to see it all, your guilt remains."

{10:1} So like, listen up, y'all. If someone doesn't come through the main door into the sheep pen but tries to sneak in some other way, they're straight-up shady, like a thief or a robber. {10:2} But the real deal, the one who rolls in through the door, that's the shepherd. {10:3} The doorkeeper lets him in, and the sheep recognize his voice; he calls them by name and leads them out. {10:4} And when he's got his crew together, he leads the way, and they follow him 'cause they know his voice. {10:5} They won't follow some random stranger; nah, they'll bounce 'cause they don't recognize that voice. {10:6} Jesus laid this story on them, but they were clueless about what he meant. {10:7} So he breaks it down for them again, saying, "I'm the door for these sheep, straight up." {10:8} "Anyone who came before me, they're just trying to pull a fast one, but my sheep ain't buying it." {10:9} "I'm the door. If anyone comes through me, they're saved, free to come and go, and find good pasture." {10:10} "The sneaky types are all about stealing, killing, and wrecking stuff. But I came so these sheep can live their best lives, overflowing with goodness." {10:11} "I'm the ultimate shepherd; I'll even lay down my life for these sheep." {10:12} "But the hired help? Nah, they ain't loyal like the real shepherd. When danger shows, they bounce, leaving the sheep to fend for themselves." {10:13} "They split 'cause they're just in it for the paycheck; they don't care about the sheep." {10:14} "I'm the legit shepherd, I know my sheep, and they know me." {10:15} "Just like the Father knows me and I know him; I'm ready to lay it all down for these sheep." {10:16} "And there are more sheep out there, not just these; I gotta bring them in too. And then it'll be one big flock, one shepherd for all." {10:17} "That's why the Father's all about me; I'm willing to give it all up just to take it back again." {10:18} "No one's snatching my life away; I'm laying it down myself. I got the power to drop it and pick it back up. This is straight from the big guy upstairs." {10:19} "This whole spiel divided the Jews again. {10:20} Some were like, 'This dude's possessed, off his rocker. Why even listen to him?'" {10:21} "But others were like, 'Nah, these words ain't coming from a crazy person. Can a nutcase heal the blind?'" {10:22} "Anyway, it was winter, and the scene was Jerusalem, where they were celebrating the dedication fiesta." {10:23} "And Jesus was just chilling in the temple, kicking it at Solomon's spot." {10:24} "Then the Jews roll up on him, like, 'How much longer you gonna keep us hanging? If you're the Christ, just say it outright.'" {10:25} "Jesus hits them with, 'I already told you, but you didn't buy it. My actions, though, they speak for themselves, repping my Father's name." {10:26-27} "But y'all don't believe 'cause you ain't part of my crew. Like I said before, my sheep hear me, and I know them, and they follow me." {10:28} "And I'm hooking them up with eternal life; they ain't ever gonna perish, and nobody's snatching them from my grip." {10:29} "My Father's got my back; he's bigger than anyone, and no one can snatch my crew from his grip." {10:30} "Me and my pops, we're tight, like two peas in a pod." {10:31} "Then the Jews start reaching for rocks again, ready to stone him." {10:32} "But Jesus throws it back at them, like, 'Yo, I've been dropping mad good deeds from my Father; which one's got you reaching for rocks?'" {10:33} "They hit back with, 'We ain't stoning you for doing good; it's 'cause you're out here claiming to be God, and you're just a regular dude!'" {10:34} "Jesus hits them with, 'Yo, ain't it written in your law that you guys are gods?'" {10:35} "If they're called gods, and the word of God came to them, and the scripture's legit, then why trip when I say I'm the Son of God?" {10:36-38} "If I'm doing what my pops sent me to do, then don't trip. But if you ain't feeling me, at least check the facts; my pops is in me, and I'm in him." {10:39} "So they try to grab him again, but he slips through their fingers." {10:40} "He dips out again, heading back across the Jordan to where John was doing his baptism thing; that's where he kicks it for a while." {10:41} "And a bunch of peeps start showing up, saying, 'John didn't do any miracles, but everything he said about this dude, it's all true.'" {10:42} "And a bunch of them start believing in him right there."

{11:1} So, there's this dude named Lazarus from Bethany, where Mary and Martha live. {11:2} Mary, the one who poured expensive oil on Jesus and wiped his feet with her hair, yeah, her brother Lazarus is sick. {11:3} So, Mary and Martha hit up Jesus, like, "Yo, our boy Lazarus, the one you love, he's sick." {11:4} Jesus hears this and is like, "Nah, this sickness ain't gonna kill him. It's all about showing off God's power and giving glory to the Son of God." {11:5} Jesus had mad love for Martha, Mary, and Lazarus. {11:6} But instead of rushing over, Jesus chills where he's at for two more days. {11:7} Then he's like, "Let's head back to Judea." {11:8} Disciples are shook, like, "But Jesus, remember how the Jews tried to stone you? You sure about this?" {11:9} Jesus drops some wisdom, like, "Ain't it daytime for twelve hours? Long as you're walking in the day, you're good. Nighttime's when you trip 'cause there's no light." {11:10} Then Jesus is like, "Our homie Lazarus is just sleeping. I'm gonna wake him up." {11:11} Disciples are like, "Sleep's good for him, right?" {11:12-13} But Jesus is talking about death, not just a nap, but they don't get it. {11:14} So Jesus spells it out, "Lazarus is dead." {11:15} Then he's like, "I'm kinda glad I wasn't there; gonna amp up your belief though. Let's roll." {11:16} Thomas pipes up, like, "Might as well join him; might as well die too." {11:17} By the time Jesus gets there, Lazarus has been dead four days. {11:18} Bethany's close to Jerusalem, like a fifteen-minute walk. {11:19} Jews start rolling in to comfort Mary and Martha. {11:20} Martha hears Jesus is coming and bolts out to meet him, but Mary stays put. {11:21} Martha's like, "Jesus, if you were here, Lazarus wouldn't have died." {11:22} But she's still hopeful, like, "I know whatever you ask God, he'll give you." {11:23} Jesus hits her with some truth, "Lazarus gonna rise again." {11:24} Martha's on about the resurrection at the last day. {11:25} Jesus lays it down, "I am the resurrection and the life. Anyone who believes in me lives, even if they die. You feelin' this?" {11:26} Martha's like, "Yeah, I'm in; you're the Christ, the Son of God, the real deal." {11:27-28} She bounces to tell Mary, like, "Jesus is here and wants you." {11:29} Mary's on it, jumps up, and heads to Jesus. {11:30} But Jesus is still outside where he met Martha, not in town yet. {11:31} Jews with Mary, trying to console her, see her take off and think she's going to the grave to cry. {11:32} Mary finds Jesus, falls at his feet, and repeats what Martha said, "If you were here, Lazarus would be alive." {11:33} Jesus sees Mary crying, plus the Jews with her, and he feels it deep, like, "Where's Lazarus buried?" {11:34} They're like, "Come, check it out." {11:35} Jesus gets emotional and sheds a tear. {11:36} Jews peep this and are like, "Dang, he really loved Lazarus." {11:37} Some wonder why Jesus, who healed the blind, didn't stop Lazarus from dying. {11:38} Jesus feels the vibe and heads to the grave, which is a cave with a stone over it. {11:39} Martha's like, "Hold up, Jesus, he's been dead four days; he's gonna stink." {11:40} Jesus reminds her, "Didn't I tell you? If you believe, you'll see God's glory." {11:41} So, they roll the stone away, and Jesus prays, thanking God for hearing him. {11:42} He does it for the people's sake, so they know God sent him. {11:43} Then, with a booming voice, Jesus calls out, "Lazarus, come out!" {11:44} And out comes Lazarus, wrapped in grave clothes. Jesus is like, "Unwrap him and set him free." {11:45} Lots of Jews see this and believe in Jesus. {11:46} But some snitch to the Pharisees about Jesus' miracle. {11:47} So, the chief priests and Pharisees call a meeting, like, "What do we do about this Jesus? He's out here doing miracles." {11:48} They're worried everyone will believe in him, and then the Romans will swoop in and ruin everything. {11:49} Caiaphas, the high priest that year, lays down some wisdom, like, "Better for one dude to die for the people than the whole nation go down." {11:50} He's not just saying this; he's predicting Jesus' sacrifice for the nation. {11:51} But it's bigger than one nation; Jesus is bringing all God's kids together. {11:52-53} From then on, they plot to off Jesus. {11:54} So Jesus lays low, bouncing to a spot near the wilderness, chilling with his squad. {11:55} Passover's coming up, so people head to Jerusalem to get holy. {11:56} They're talking about Jesus, wondering if he'll show up. {11:57} Chief priests and Pharisees order anyone who knows where Jesus is to snitch so they can nab him.

{12:1} So like, six days before Passover, Jesus rolls up to Bethany where Lazarus, the dude he raised from the dead, was chilling. {12:2} They throw a dinner party there, and Martha's doing her thing serving, while Lazarus is just kicking it at the table with Jesus. {12:3} Then Mary comes in with this fancy, expensive spikenard ointment, anoints Jesus' feet, and wipes them with her hair. The whole house smells amazing. {12:4-5} But then Judas Iscariot, one of Jesus' disciples (who was also planning to betray him), pipes up and asks why they didn't sell the ointment for three hundred bucks and give it to the poor. {12:6} He's not actually caring about the poor; he's just a thief in charge of the money bag. {12:7} Jesus shuts him down, saying to leave Mary alone because she did this in preparation for his burial. {12:8} He drops some wisdom, saying you'll always have poor folks around, but you won't always have him. {12:9} So word spreads, and not only do people come to see Jesus, but they also want to check out Lazarus, the guy Jesus brought back to life. {12:10} Now the religious big shots are plotting to off Lazarus too because his resurrection was causing people to believe in Jesus. {12:11} The next day, when a crowd shows up for the feast and hears Jesus is coming to Jerusalem, they grab palm branches, head out to meet him, and shout "Hosanna! Blessed is the King of Israel!" {12:12} Jesus finds a young donkey and rides it, fulfilling prophecy. {12:13} His disciples don't get it at first, but later on, they connect the dots after Jesus is glorified. {12:14} People who were there when Lazarus was raised from the dead testify about it. {12:15} Some Greeks show up for the feast and ask Philip if they can meet Jesus. {12:16} Jesus responds, saying it's time for him to be glorified. {12:24} He drops a truth bomb about how a seed has to die to produce much fruit. {12:17} Jesus gets real, troubled in his soul, but acknowledges it's the reason he came. {12:18} He prays for God to glorify his name, and a voice from heaven responds. {12:19} Jesus talks about being lifted up and drawing people to himself. {12:20} He warns them about the light being with them briefly, urging them to believe and walk in the light while they can. {12:21} Jesus declares that believing in him is believing in the one who sent him.

{13:1} So, before the Passover bash, Jesus knew his time was up to bounce from this world to the big guy upstairs, but he had mad love for his squad down here, straight up to the end. {13:2} After dinner, the devil put the betrayal bug in Judas Iscariot's head, Simon's kid, to throw Jesus under the bus. {13:3} Jesus, knowing he had the divine hookup from the Father and was heading back to him, gets up, strips down, and grabs a towel. {13:4} He starts washing the crew's feet, wiping them clean with the towel. {13:5} When he gets to Peter, Pete's like, "Hold up, Lord, you're not washing my feet!" {13:6} Jesus tells him, "You don't get it now, but you will later." {13:7} Pete's like, "No way, you're not touching my feet!" Jesus hits back, "If I don't clean you up, you're not rolling with me." {13:8} Pete's like, "Fine, wash all of me then!" {13:9} Jesus schools him, saying, "You're already clean; just need a foot wash." But not everyone's squeaky clean, 'cause Jesus knew one of them was playing dirty. {13:10} After foot duty, he gets real with them, asking if they understand the move he just pulled. {13:11} They call him Master and Lord, and he's like, "Yeah, that's me. So if I'm doing this, you should too." {13:12-17} He drops some truth, saying, "No servant's above their boss, and no messenger's above the one who sent them. If you get this, you're golden." {13:18} He's like, "Not all of you are on my level; I've picked my crew, but one of you's about to flip on me." {13:19} Jesus drops a hint before it goes down, so when it does, they'll know he's legit. {13:20} He lays it down, "Anyone who's cool with the peeps I send is cool with me, and anyone who's cool with me is cool with the big guy upstairs." {13:21} Jesus gets real, saying one of them's about to do him dirty, and they're all shook trying to figure out who. {13:22} They're all clueless, so one of the crew, chillin' close to Jesus, asks who's the traitor. {13:23} Laying low on Jesus' chest, he whispers, "Yo, who's the snake?" {13:24-26} Jesus calls it out, "The one I give this bread to after dipping it." And he hands it to Judas Iscariot, Simon's kid. {13:27-29} Satan hops in Judas after that. Jesus tells him, "Do what you gotta do, and do it fast." {13:30} Judas takes the hint and dips out, and it's dark outside. {13:31} Jesus drops some wisdom, saying now's the time for him to shine, and God's in on the glory too. {13:32} If God's in on it, he'll glorify Jesus in himself and boost him up pronto. {13:33} He tells the crew he's only hanging for a bit longer and they can't follow where he's going, like he told the Jews before. {13:34} He lays down a fresh rule: love each other like he loves them. {13:35} That's the ID for being on Team Jesus—mad love for each other. {13:36} Pete's like, "Where you headed, Lord?" Jesus drops the truth, "You can't roll with me right now, but you will later." {13:37} Pete's all in, "Why can't I follow you now? I'll throw down my life for you!" {13:38} Jesus hits him with reality, "You really think so? You're gonna bail on me three times before the rooster crows."

{14:1} Don't stress, fam. You believe in God, right? Believe in me too. {14:2} My Dad's place has tons of rooms; if that wasn't true, I'd tell you. I'm heading there to get things ready for you. {14:3} When I go and prepare a spot, I'll come back for you so we can chill together. {14:4} You know where I'm going and how to get there. {14:5} Thomas is like, "Yo, we have no clue where you're going, so how can we know the way?" {14:6} Jesus drops knowledge: "I'm the way, the truth, and the life. No one gets to the Father except through me." {14:7} If you knew me, you'd know my Dad too; from now on, you know him and have seen him. {14:8} Then Philip's like, "Yo, show us the Father, and we're good." {14:9} Jesus is like, "Bruh, I've been with you this whole time; seeing me is seeing the Father. How can you say that?" {14:10-11} Do you not believe I'm in the Father and the Father's in me? The words I say aren't just mine; it's the Father working through me. {14:12} Real talk, if you believe in me, you'll do what I do and even greater things because I'm going to my Father. {14:13} Ask for anything in my name, and I got you, so the Father gets the glory through me. {14:14-15} If you love me, follow my rules. {14:16} I'll ask the Father to send another Comforter, the Holy Ghost, to chill with you forever. {14:17} This Spirit of truth, the world can't vibe with, but you can 'cause he's with you and will be in you. {14:18} I won't leave you hanging; I'll come back to you. {14:19} In a bit, the world won't see me, but you will 'cause I'm alive and so will you be. {14:20} Then you'll get it: I'm in my Father, you're in me, and I'm in you. {14:21} The ones who keep my rules love me, and my Father and I will show ourselves to them. {14:22} Judas (not Iscariot) is like, "How are you gonna show yourself to us but not the world?" {14:23} Jesus says, "If you love me, you'll follow my words, and my Father and I will chill with you." {14:24-25} If you don't love me, you won't follow my words; they're my Father's, not just mine. {14:26} The Comforter, the Holy Ghost, will come and teach you everything and remind you of what I've said. {14:27} I'm leaving you peace—my peace, not the world's. Don't stress; don't be scared. {14:28} Remember when I said I'm heading out but coming back? If you loved me, you'd be happy 'cause I'm going to the Father, who's greater than me. {14:29} I'm telling you this ahead of time so when it happens, you'll believe. {14:30} I won't talk much more; the prince of this world's coming, but he's got nothing on me. {14:31} The world needs to know I love the Father, so let's bounce and do what he told me. Peace out!

{15:1} So, listen up fam, I'm like the real deal vine, and my Dad's the one tending to it all. {15:2} Any branch on me not bringing in fruit, he's cutting it off. But if you're fruitful, he's gonna trim you down so you can grow even more. {15:3} Now, y'all clean 'cause of what I've been telling you. {15:4} Stick with me, and I'm with you. Just like a branch can't fruit solo, you can't do squat without me. {15:5} I'm the vine, and y'all are the branches. If you stay connected to me and I'm in you, that's when you'll see real results. Without me, you're toast. {15:6} If you disconnect, you're toast, like a branch dried up and tossed in the fire. {15:7} Stay with me, let my words sink in, and whatever you ask, consider it done. {15:8} This is how my Dad gets his props, when you bear a ton of fruit and rep my crew. {15:9} Just like my Dad's got love for me, I'm throwing it right back at you. Keep that love train going. {15:10} Keep my rules, stay in my love, just like I'm rolling with my Dad's rules and love. {15:11} I'm dropping this knowledge so my joy sticks with you and yours is on full blast. {15:12} Here's the deal: love each other just like I love you. {15:13} There's no greater love than someone laying down their life for their homies. {15:14} You're my squad if you're down to do what I ask. {15:15} Forget calling you servants; you're my crew, in on everything my Dad told me. {15:16} You didn't choose me; I chose you. I'm sending you out to bring in fruit that lasts, and whatever you ask in my name, my Dad's got you. {15:17} I'm all about that love command; keep loving one another. {15:18} If the world's hating on you, remember, they hated me first. {15:19} If you were all about this world's vibe, they'd be all over you, but since you're not, they're giving you the cold shoulder. {15:20} Stay woke: if they dissed me, they'll diss you too; if they're down with what I'm saying, they'll vibe with you too. {15:21} But all this hate they're throwing? It's 'cause they don't know the One who sent me. {15:22} If I hadn't shown up and laid it all out, they could play dumb, but now they've got no excuse for their hate. {15:23} Hating on me? You're hating on my Dad too. {15:24} If I hadn't shown them what's up with those miracles, they wouldn't be guilty, but now they've seen it all and still hate on both of us. {15:25} But hey, it's all good; this was bound to happen to fulfill what's written, "They hated me for no reason." {15:26} But once the Comforter rolls through, the one I'm sending from my Dad, the Spirit of truth, he's gonna back me up. {15:27} And you? You're gonna back me up too 'cause you've been riding with me from the start.

{16:1} Yo, I'm dropping truth bombs on you so you don't get shook. {16:2} They're gonna kick you out of places of worship, and some fanatics will straight up think they're doing God's work by taking you out. {16:3} They're clueless about the Big Guy and me, so they're gonna pull some shady stuff. {16:4} But I'm giving you a heads up so when stuff goes down, you'll remember I called it. I didn't lay this on you earlier 'cause I was right there with you. {16:5} Now I'm bouncing back to the one who sent me, but none of you are asking where I'm headed. {16:6} I drop this bomb, and suddenly you're all in your feels. {16:7} But real talk, it's better for y'all if I bounce 'cause then I'll send in the real MVP. {16:8} When he shows up, he's gonna call out the world for its mess, starting with not believing in me. {16:9} He'll call out what's right 'cause I'm heading back to the Big Guy and you won't see me no more. {16:10-11} And he's gonna lay down the law 'cause the big boss of this world is already judged. {16:12} I got more wisdom to drop on you, but you can't handle it now. {16:13} But when the truth guru shows up, he's gonna spill all the tea 'cause he's not about himself, he's about dropping knowledge from the top. {16:14} He's all about boosting me up 'cause he's got the hookup from me to you. {16:15} Everything the Big Guy's got is mine, so I'm giving him the green light to pass it on to you. {16:16} Chill for a sec 'cause soon you won't see me, but then I'll be back 'cause I'm going back to the Big Guy. {16:17} Some of the squad is clueless, like, what's he on about with this "in a bit you won't see me, then you'll see me" vibe and bouncing to the Big Guy? {16:18} They're like, "What's he mean, 'in a bit?'" We're lost in translation here. {16:19} But Jesus knows they're curious, so he's like, "You got questions? Ask away, but get ready 'cause it's gonna get heavy." {16:20} For real, you're gonna be crying while the world parties, but then your sadness will turn to joy. {16:21} It's like a mama in labor, crying in pain, but once the baby's born, it's all joy vibes. {16:22} You're sad now, but I'll be back, and your joy will be lit, and no one's gonna kill that vibe. {16:23} And one day, you won't need to ask me anything 'cause you'll be dialed into the Big Guy direct. {16:24} Up till now, you haven't used my name for your asks, but once you do, you're gonna get the hookup and be maxed out on joy. {16:25} I've been dropping hints, but soon I'll spill all the tea about the Big Guy. {16:26} When that day comes, you'll ask in my name, and I won't need to put in a good word for you 'cause the Big Guy's already feeling the love for you. {16:27} The Big Guy's all about you 'cause you're all about me and believe I'm straight from him. {16:28} I came from the Big Guy and hit up Earth; now I'm bouncing back to him. {16:29} The squad's like, "Now you're speaking our language, no more cryptic talk." {16:30} They're convinced Jesus knows all the things and doesn't need anyone to clue him in, so they're all in. {16:31} Jesus is like, "Now you're on board?" {16:32} But real talk, the time's come, you're all gonna scatter, leaving me solo, but I'm never truly alone 'cause the Big Guy's got my back. {16:33} I'm dropping these truth bombs so you can find peace in me, even though the world's gonna throw some heavy stuff your way. But keep your head up; I've already conquered all that craziness.

{17:1} Jesus spoke up, looked to the sky, and said, "Father, it's time; make your Son shine so that your Son can shine you up too. {17:2} You gave him power over everyone, so he can give eternal life to those you've given him. {17:3} Eternal life is all about knowing you, the one true God, and Jesus Christ, the one you sent. {17:4} I've hyped you up on earth; I've finished the job you gave me. {17:5} Now, Father, give me back the glory we had before the world started. {17:6} I showed your name off to the crew you gave me; they're yours, and you gave them to me. They've kept your word. {17:7} Now they know everything you've given me comes from you. {17:8} I passed on the words you gave me, and they've received them, knowing for sure I came from you, believing you sent me. {17:9} I'm praying for them—not the world—because they're yours. {17:10} Everything I have is yours, and what's yours is mine; they bring me glory. {17:11} I'm out of here soon, but they're still in the world. Holy Father, protect them by your name so they can be one, just like us. {17:12} While I was with them, I kept them in line by your name. I've kept the ones you gave me; none of them is lost except the son of perdition, as the scripture said. {17:13} I'm heading to you now, saying these things in the world so they can have my joy in themselves. {17:14} I gave them your word, and the world hates them because they're not part of it, just like I'm not part of it. {17:15} I'm not asking you to take them out of the world, but to keep them safe from evil. {17:16} They're not of this world, just like I'm not of this world. {17:17} Make them holy through your truth; your word is truth. {17:18} Just like you sent me into the world, I'm sending them into the world too. {17:19} I'm setting myself apart for their sake so they can be set apart by the truth. {17:20} I'm not just praying for them, but for everyone who will believe in me because of them. {17:21} I want them all to be one, just like you and I are one, so the world will believe you sent me. {17:22} I've given them the same glory you gave me so they can be one, just like we are one. {17:23} I'm in them, and you're in me, making them perfect in unity, showing the world you sent me and loved them like you loved me. {17:24} Father, I want those you gave me to be with me where I am, to see my glory that you gave me because you loved me before the world began. {17:25} Righteous Father, the world doesn't know you, but I do, and they know you sent me. {17:26} I've told them about you and will keep telling them so they can have your love in them and I in them."

{18:1} After Jesus dropped these truth bombs, he bounced with his crew across the Cedron brook to this garden, where he and his homies often chilled. {18:2} Judas, the one who double-crossed him, knew the spot too well since Jesus and the squad were always there. {18:3} So, Judas rolls in with a whole posse, armed up, sent by the bigwigs, priests, and Pharisees, carrying lanterns, torches, and weapons. {18:4} Jesus, knowing what's up, steps up and asks them straight, "Who are you looking for?" {18:5} They're like, "Jesus from Nazareth." He's like, "Yeah, that's me." And Judas, the traitor, is right there with them. {18:6} Soon as he says he's the one, they all stumble back and hit the ground. {18:7} So he asks again, "Who you searching for?" They're like, "Jesus from Nazareth." {18:8} Jesus is like, "Told you already, I'm the one. If you want me, let these guys go." {18:9} He's making sure what he said comes true, "None of the crew you gave me are lost." {18:10} Then Peter, always ready for action, whips out his sword and chops off the high priest's servant's ear. The servant's name? Malchus. {18:11} Jesus tells Peter to chill, "Put the sword away. I gotta drink from the cup my Dad's given me, right?" {18:12} So, they grab Jesus, tie him up, and take him to Annas first, who's the father-in-law to Caiaphas, the big shot priest that year. {18:13} Caiaphas was the one who said it's better for one dude to die for the people. {18:14} Meanwhile, Peter's lurking around, trying to see what's going down. Another disciple, who's tight with the high priest, sneaks Peter into the palace. {18:15} But Peter's just chilling outside. So, the other disciple vouches for him, gets him in, and Peter's there, warming himself by the fire with the servants and officers. {18:16} Inside, the high priest starts grilling Jesus about his crew and his teachings. {18:17} Jesus is like, "I've been real public about it all. I've been teaching openly. Ask anyone who's heard me; they know what's up." {18:18} This officer nearby isn't feeling Jesus' response, so he slaps him and says, "Is that how you talk to the high priest?" {18:19} Jesus hits back with, "If I've done wrong, show me. But if I haven't, why are you hitting me?" {18:20} Now, Annas sends Jesus off to Caiaphas, still tied up. {18:21-25} Meanwhile, Peter's still trying to keep warm. The servants question him again, "Aren't you one of his crew?" He's like, "Nah, not me." {18:26} One of the high priest's servants, whose ear Peter sliced, says, "Yo, I saw you in the garden with him, right?" {18:27} Peter's like,

"Nah, not me." Right then, the rooster crows. {18:28} They take Jesus from Caiaphas to the big court, but they don't go in 'cause they don't wanna be ritually unclean during Passover. {18:29} Pilate comes out to them, "What's the charge against this dude?" {18:30} They're like, "If he wasn't guilty, we wouldn't have brought him to you." {18:31} Pilate's like, "You deal with him then, by your laws." They're like, "We can't execute anyone." {18:32} This is all happening so Jesus' words about his death can come true. {18:33} So Pilate brings Jesus back in, "You claiming to be King of the Jews?" {18:34} Jesus is like, "You coming up with this or did someone tell you?" {18:35} Pilate's like, "I ain't Jewish. Your people and priests handed you over to me. What'd you do?" {18:36} Jesus is like, "My kingdom ain't from this world. If it was, my squad would've fought to stop me getting handed over. But that ain't the deal here." {18:37} Pilate's like, "So you're a king?" Jesus is like, "You said it. I'm all about bringing truth to the scene. Anyone down with truth hears what I'm saying." {18:38} Pilate's like, "Truth? What's that?" Then he bounces back to the Jews, "I don't see any charge against this guy." {18:39} Pilate's trying to be cool, so he's like, "I can release someone for Passover. You want this Jesus dude or Barabbas?" {18:40} They're all shouting, "Barabbas!" Barabbas was a crook, by the way.

{19:1} Pilate snags Jesus and starts laying on the pain. {19:2-3} The soldiers whip up a makeshift crown of thorns, slap it on his head, throw a royal purple robe on him, and start clowning him like, "Yo, hail to the king, right?" Then they start smacking him around. {19:4} Pilate comes back out, trying to flex like, "Look, I can't find anything wrong with this dude." {19:5} Jesus rolls up, looking all messed up, and Pilate's like, "Check this out, dudes, look at this guy!" {19:6} But the religious big shots see him and start chanting, "Crucify him, crucify him!" Pilate's like, "Fine, do it yourselves, I'm cool with this guy." {19:7} But the Jews are like, "Nah, our law says he's gotta go down for saying he's God's son." {19:8} Pilate starts freaking out even more when he hears that. {19:9} He pulls Jesus aside like, "Where you from, dude?" But Jesus keeps quiet. {19:10} Pilate's like, "Seriously, you're not gonna say anything? I got the power to end you or let you go." {19:11} Jesus is like, "You wouldn't even have power over me if it wasn't given to you from up top. The one who handed me over is the real guilty one here." {19:12} Pilate tries even harder to let Jesus off the hook, but the Jews are like, "If you do that, you're no friend of Caesar's. Anyone who claims to be king is challenging Caesar." {19:13} Pilate's really feeling the pressure now, so he brings Jesus out and takes a seat on the judge's bench in this spot called the Pavement, or Gabbatha in Hebrew. {19:14} It's the day before Passover, around noon, and he's like, "Here's your king!" {19:15} But they're not having it, they're shouting, "Get rid of him, crucify him!" Pilate's like, "Should I crucify your king?" And the priests are like, "We ain't got no king but Caesar." {19:16} So Pilate hands Jesus over to them to get crucified, and they haul him off. {19:17} He's carrying his own cross to this place called Skull Hill, or Golgotha in Hebrew. {19:18} They nail him up there between two other dudes. {19:19} Pilate slaps up a sign on the cross that says "JESUS OF NAZARETH THE KING OF THE JEWS." {19:20} Everybody's reading it since it's close to the city and written in Hebrew, Greek, and Latin. {19:21} The religious bigwigs are like, "Nah, don't write 'King of the Jews,' write that he 'claimed' to be king." {19:22} Pilate's like, "What's written is written, deal with it." {19:23-24} So the soldiers are divvying up Jesus' clothes, but his tunic is seamless, so they're like, "Let's roll for it." That's to make good on the scripture that says, "They divided my clothes among them and cast lots for my garment." That's exactly what they did. {19:25} Meanwhile, Jesus' mom, along with her sister, Mary the wife of Cleophas, and Mary Magdalene, are standing by the cross. {19:26-27} Jesus spots his mom and his favorite disciple and says, "Mom, he's your new son now." Then he tells the disciple, "She's your new mom." From then on, the disciple takes care of her. {19:28} After that, Jesus knows it's a wrap, so he's like, "I'm thirsty." {19:29} There's a jar of vinegar nearby, so they soak a sponge in it, put it on a stick of hyssop, and give it to him to drink. {19:30} Once he's had a sip, he's like, "It's a wrap," and he bows out. {19:31} The Jews are like, "We gotta get these bodies down before sundown since it's the Sabbath." They ask Pilate to break their legs so they die quicker. {19:32-33} So the soldiers break the legs of the other two guys, but when they get to Jesus, they see he's already dead, so they don't break his. {19:34} Instead, one of them stabs him in the side with a spear, and out comes blood and water. {19:35-36} The guy who saw it all swears it's true, so you know it's legit, and he says it's to fulfill the scripture that says, "Not a bone of his will be broken." {19:37} Another scripture says, "They will look on the one they pierced." {19:38} Later, Joseph of Arimathaea, a secret follower of Jesus, asks Pilate if he can take Jesus' body. Pilate gives him the green light, so he goes and gets it. {19:39} Nicodemus, the guy who came to Jesus at night, brings a hundred pounds of myrrh and aloes. {19:40} They wrap Jesus up in linen with the spices, like they do for Jewish burial customs. {19:41} They put him in a new tomb in a nearby garden, since it was the Jews' prep day for the Sabbath, and the tomb was close by.

{20:1} Like, early in the morning on the first day of the week, Mary Magdalene goes to the tomb while it's still dark and sees that the stone has been rolled away from the entrance. {20:2} She freaks out and runs to Simon Peter and the other disciple, the one Jesus was super tight with, and tells them, "They took the Lord out of the tomb, and we don't know where they put him!" {20:3} Peter and the other disciple haul over to the tomb. {20:4} They both sprint there, but the other disciple outruns Peter and gets there first. {20:5} He looks inside and sees the burial cloths lying there, but he doesn't go in. {20:6} Then Peter shows up and goes right into the tomb; he sees the burial cloths lying there {20:7} and the cloth that had been on Jesus' head, neatly folded up in a separate place. {20:8} Then the other disciple, the one who got there first, goes in too, and he sees and believes. {20:9} They still didn't understand from Scripture that Jesus had to rise from the dead. {20:10} So, they peace out and head back home. {20:11} But Mary stays outside the tomb crying. As she's crying, she stoops down and looks into the tomb, {20:12} and sees two angels in white sitting where Jesus' body had been, one at the head and one at the feet. {20:13} They ask her, "Why are you crying?" She tells them, "They took my Lord, and I don't know where they put him." {20:14} After saying this, she turns around and sees Jesus standing there, but she doesn't recognize him. {20:15} Jesus asks her, "Why are you crying? Who are you looking for?" Thinking he's the gardener, she says, "Sir, if you've taken him away, tell me where you put him, and I'll take him." {20:16} Then Jesus says her name, "Mary." She turns and says to him, "Rabboni!" (which means "Teacher"). {20:17} Jesus tells her, "Don't hold on to me, because I haven't gone up to my Father yet. Instead, go tell my followers that I'm going up to my Father and your Father, my God and your God." {20:18} So Mary Magdalene goes and tells the disciples that she's seen the Lord and what he told her. {20:19} Later that same day, on the first day of the week, even though the doors were locked because they were scared of the Jews, Jesus shows up and stands among them and says, "Peace be with you." {20:20} After he says this, he shows them his hands and side. The disciples are stoked when they see the Lord. {20:21} Jesus says to them again, "Peace be with you. Just like the Father sent me, I'm sending you." {20:22} Then he breathes on them and says, "Receive the Holy Spirit. {20:23} If you forgive anyone's sins, their sins are forgiven; if you don't forgive them, they aren't forgiven." {20:24} Now, Thomas (also called Didymus), one of the twelve, wasn't there when Jesus came. {20:25} The other disciples tell him, "We've seen the Lord!" But Thomas says, "I won't believe it unless I see the nail marks in his hands, put my finger into the wounds from the nails, and put my hand into his side." {20:26} A week later, the disciples are inside again, and Thomas is with them. Even though the doors are locked, Jesus shows up, stands among them, and says, "Peace be with you." {20:27} Then he says to Thomas, "Put your finger here; see my hands. Reach out your hand and put it into my side. Stop doubting and believe." {20:28} Thomas responds, "My Lord and my God!" {20:29} Jesus tells him, "Because you've seen me, you believe. Blessed are those who haven't seen me but still believe." {20:30} Jesus did many other miraculous signs in front of his disciples, which aren't even written in this book. {20:31} But these things are written so that you'll believe that Jesus is the Messiah, the Son of God, and that by believing, you'll have life in his name.

{21:1} So, after all that went down, Jesus pops up again with the crew at the sea of Tiberias, showing up like this. {21:2} It's Simon Peter, Thomas (aka Didymus), Nathanael from Cana, the Zebedee bros, and a couple more disciples. {21:3} Peter's like, "I'm hitting the water for some fishing." They're like, "Cool, we're coming too." They hop on a boat right away, but catch zilch that night. {21:4} When morning hits, Jesus is chilling on the shore, but they don't recognize him. {21:5} He's like, "Any luck catching fish, guys?" They're like, "Nada." {21:6} Jesus is like, "Try the right side." They do, and boom, so many fish they can't even pull the net. {21:7} The disciple Jesus loved is like, "It's the Lord, guys!" When Peter hears this, he throws on his coat (since he's naked) and dives into the sea. {21:8} The other disciples bring the catch in another boat, about 200 cubits away, dragging the net full of fish. {21:9} Once they hit land, there's a fire with fish cooking and some bread. {21:10} Jesus is like, "Bring some of the fish you just caught." {21:11} Peter hauls in the net, bursting with fish, 153 of 'em, and the net's not even torn. {21:12} Jesus invites them to grub, but none of them ask who he is 'cause they know it's the Lord. {21:13} So, Jesus hooks them up with bread and fish. {21:14} This is the third time Jesus has shown himself after rising from the dead. {21:15} After they eat, Jesus asks Peter, "Yo, Peter, you love me more than these?" Peter's like, "For sure, you know I do." Jesus is like, "Then feed my lambs." {21:16} He asks again, "Peter, you love me?" Peter's like, "Yeah, you know I do." Jesus is like, "Then take care of my sheep." {21:17} He asks a third time, and Peter's kinda bummed, but he's like, "You know everything, Lord. You know I love you." Jesus is like, "Then feed my sheep." {21:18} Jesus drops some truth, saying Peter used to do his own thing, but when he's old, he'll face some heavy stuff. {21:19} This is Jesus hinting at how Peter's gonna die and still bring glory to God. Then he's like, "Follow me." {21:20} Peter notices the disciple Jesus loved following too, the one who was close to him at dinner and asked about the traitor. {21:21} So Peter's like, "What's up with him, Jesus?" {21:22} Jesus is like, "What's it to you? You follow me." {21:23} Word gets around that this disciple won't die, but Jesus never said that. He was just saying, "What's it to you if he sticks around till I come back?" {21:24} This disciple is the one giving the scoop and writing it down, and his word's legit. {21:25} And that's just the tip of the iceberg of what Jesus did. If we wrote it all down, the world couldn't hold the books. Amen.

Acts

✚✚✚

{1:1} I wrote this whole thing, fam, for my boy Theophilus, about everything Jesus started doing and teaching {1:2} up until the day he bounced, but not before giving the squad some last-minute instructions through the Holy Ghost. {1:3} He showed up to them after coming back from the dead, no cap, and kicked it with them for forty days, talking about God's kingdom. {1:4} Then, when they were all together, he told them to chill in Jerusalem and wait for what God promised, which he'd already mentioned. {1:5} John was all about that water baptism, but soon y'all gonna get hit up with the Holy Ghost, real soon. {1:6} They're like, "Yo Jesus, you gonna bring the kingdom back to Israel now?" {1:7} But he's like, "Nah, that's not on you to know. That's up to the big man upstairs." {1:8} But yo, once the Holy Ghost drops on y'all, you gonna get mad power and rep for me everywhere, from the block to the ends of the earth. {1:9} And just like that, while they're watching, he dips out, and a cloud scoops him up. {1:10-11} As they're still staring up, two dudes in white show up and are like, "Why you still looking? Jesus will come back just like you saw him leave." {1:12} So they head back to Jerusalem from this spot called Olivet, about a sabbath day's hike away. {1:13-14} Once they're back, they hit up this upper room, where Peter, James, John, and the rest of the crew are posted up, plus Jesus' mom, and his siblings, just vibing together. {1:15} Then Peter steps up and is like, "Yo, we got about 120 heads here, and it's time to talk about Judas." {1:16} He's dropping some wisdom about how the Holy Ghost already called Judas out through David's rhymes. {1:17} He's like, "Remember that verse from Psalms? It's about Judas, and we need to fill his spot." {1:18} So they're like, "We need someone who's been with us since day one, seen Jesus' whole hustle, from John's baptism to his send-off." {1:23} They pick two dudes, Joseph and Matthias. {1:19} They're like, "God, you know what's up, pick the right guy." {1:20} Matthias joins the apostle squad after winning a coin flip.

{2:1} When the day of Pentecost came, all the believers were chillin' together in one place. {2:2} Suddenly, there was this crazy loud sound from heaven, like a rush of wind, and it filled the whole house where they were hanging out. {2:3} Then they saw what looked like tongues of fire that split apart and rested on each of them. {2:4} They were all filled with the Holy Spirit and started speaking in different languages, as the Spirit enabled them. {2:5} Now, there were Jews in Jerusalem from every nation under heaven. {2:6} When word got out about this, a huge crowd gathered and got totally confused because everyone heard them speaking in their own language. {2:7} They were blown away, like, "Aren't all these guys Galileans? How are we hearing them in our own native languages?" {2:8} People from Parthia, Media, Elam, Mesopotamia, Judea, Cappadocia, Pontus, Asia, Phrygia, Pamphylia, Egypt, Libya near Cyrene, visitors from Rome—both Jews and converts— {2:9} Cretans and Arabs, we're all hearing them talk about God's awesome works in our own languages. {2:10-13} Everyone was amazed and wondering what was up with this. Some were like, "They must be drunk on new wine or something." {2:14} But Peter stood up with the other eleven, raised his voice, and said to the crowd, "Yo, people of Judea and all Jerusalem, listen up! {2:15} These guys aren't wasted like you think—it's only 9 in the morning!" {2:16} Peter explains that what's going down was predicted by the prophet Joel, {2:17} saying that in the last days, God would pour out His Spirit on everyone. {2:18} Peter quotes Joel about young people seeing visions and old folks dreaming dreams, {2:19} with God showing wonders in the heavens and signs on the earth. {2:20} The sun will go dark and the moon turn to blood before the Lord's big day comes. {2:21} And whoever calls on the Lord's name will be saved. {2:22} Peter continues, "Fellow Israelites, listen up! Jesus of Nazareth was approved by God among you with miracles, wonders, and signs, as you all know. {2:23} You guys took Him, and by wicked hands crucified and killed Him. {2:24} But God raised Him up, breaking the chains of death because it couldn't hold Him down. {2:25} David spoke about Him, saying he saw the Lord always at his side, {2:26} filled with joy and hope because God wouldn't abandon His soul in Hades or let His body decay. {2:27-28} God revealed the path of life to Him and filled Him with joy in His presence. {2:29} Peter speaks of David as a prophet who knew God had promised to raise up the Messiah from his descendants. {2:30} David foresaw Christ's resurrection, {2:31} saying His soul wouldn't be left in Hades, nor His body see decay. {2:32} We're all witnesses—God raised Jesus up, exalted Him to His right hand, and sent forth the Holy Spirit, which you see and hear now. {2:33} David didn't ascend to heaven, but said, 'The Lord said to my Lord, sit at my right hand {2:34-25} until I make your enemies your footstool.' {2:36} So, all Israel should know for sure that God made Jesus, whom you crucified, both Lord and Messiah. {2:37} When they heard this, they felt it in their hearts and asked Peter and the apostles, "What should we do?" {2:38} Peter tells them, "Change your ways and get baptized, each of you, in the name of Jesus Christ for the forgiveness of your sins, and you'll receive the Holy Spirit. {2:39} This promise is for you, your children, and for everyone God calls." {2:40} Peter preached more, urging them to save themselves from this corrupt generation. {2:41} Those who welcomed Peter's message got baptized, and about three thousand people joined them that day. {2:42} They kept on learning from the apostles, sharing meals, and praying together. {2:43} Fear gripped everyone, and the apostles performed many miracles and signs. {2:44} All the believers stuck together and shared everything they had. {2:45} They sold their stuff and gave to those in need, {2:46} meeting daily in the temple and having meals together with joyful and sincere hearts. {2:47} They praised God and were well-liked by everyone, and every day the Lord added to their community those who were being saved.

{3:1} Peter and John roll up to the temple for prayer time, around 3 PM. {3:2} There's this dude who's been lame since birth, always posted up at the Beautiful Gate, asking for some cash from folks heading into the temple. {3:3} When he spots Peter and John about to go in, he hits them up for some change. {3:4} Peter's like, "Look at us, man." {3:5} Dude's all ears, thinking he's about to get paid. {3:6} But Peter's like, "Sorry, no cash on me. But in the name of Jesus Christ, get up and walk." {3:7} He grabs the dude's hand, helps him up, and bam, dude's legs and ankles get strong right away. {3:8} He starts jumping around, praising God, and heads into the temple with them, walking, leaping, and giving thanks. {3:9} Everyone sees him walking and praising God, recognizing him as the guy who used to beg at the gate, and they're blown away. {3:10-11} As he clings to Peter and John, a crowd gathers, all amazed, in Solomon's Porch. {3:12} Peter's like, "Why are you so shocked? We didn't make this happen by our own power or holiness." {3:13} He reminds them about Jesus, whom they rejected, even when Pilate was ready to let him go. {3:14} Instead, they chose a murderer over the Holy One and the Just. {3:15} But God raised Jesus from the dead, and we saw it go down. {3:16} It's faith in Jesus that made this dude strong, right in front of you all. {3:17} Peter's like, "I get it, you didn't know any better, neither did your leaders." {3:18} But all this was foretold by the prophets, that Christ would suffer. {3:19} So, change your ways, get converted, and your sins will be wiped out when God brings refreshment. {3:20} He's sending Jesus back, who was already preached to you. {3:21} Jesus is chilling in heaven until it's time to fix everything, just like the prophets said. {3:22} Moses talked about a prophet coming, just like him, and you gotta listen up to what he says. {3:23} If you don't listen, you're out. {3:24} All the prophets talked about these days, starting with Samuel, and you're part of that legacy. {3:25} You're the heirs of the prophets and the covenant God made with your ancestors. {3:26} God sent Jesus to bless you by turning you away from your wrongdoing.

{4:1} While they're speaking to the crowd, the priests, temple captain, and the Sadducees roll up, bummed out that they're teaching about Jesus' resurrection, {4:2} They straight-up arrest them and lock them up till the next day 'cause it's getting late. {4:3} But yo, mad people believe the word they're dropping, like around five thousand guys. {4:4} Next day, all the big shots - rulers, elders, and scribes, plus Annas, Caiaphas, John, Alexander, and the whole high priest fam - gather in Jerusalem. {4:5} They sit them in the middle and ask, "How you pulling off this stuff? What power or name?" {4:6-8} Then Peter, hyped up on the Holy Ghost, steps up like, "Listen up, rulers and elders of Israel," {4:9} He's like, "You wanna talk about this good deed? Let's talk about Jesus, the one you crucified but God raised up. He's the reason this dude's standing here straight." {4:10-12} He's spitting facts, "Jesus, the one you builders rejected, is the main foundation now. And there's no other way to be saved except through him." {4:13} The leaders see Peter and John's confidence, and they're shook 'cause these dudes are uneducated, but they know they've been chilling with Jesus. {4:14} And they can't even front when they see the healed dude standing there. {4:15} So they're like, "Let's talk in private." {4:16-17} They're like, "We gotta shut them down, but let's just warn them not to talk about Jesus anymore." {4:18-20} But Peter and John are like, "Bruh, we gotta listen to God, not you. We can't stop talking about what we've seen and heard." {4:21} After more threats, they let them bounce 'cause they can't punish them with everyone glorifying God for the miracle. {4:22} The healed dude was over forty, so it's not like they can deny the miracle. {4:23} They go back to their crew and spill all the tea on what the priests said. {4:24} When they hear it, they start praying together, acknowledging God as the Creator of everything. {4:25} They ask for boldness to keep spreading the word, and for God to keep doing miracles in Jesus' name. {4:26} After they pray, the place shakes, they all get filled with the Holy Ghost, and start preaching with even more boldness. {4:27} The believers are all united, sharing everything they have. {4:28} The apostles are out here dropping truth bombs about Jesus' resurrection, and everyone's feeling the grace. {4:29} Ain't nobody lacking 'cause those who got land and houses are selling them and sharing the cash with everyone. {4:30} They bring the cash to the apostles, who distribute it as needed. {4:36} Like Joses, also known as Barnabas, a Levite from Cyprus, who sells his land and gives the money to the apostles.

{5:1} There's this guy named Ananias with his wife Sapphira who sold some property, {5:2} but they kept part of the money for themselves, and his wife was in on it too. They brought some of it to the apostles. {5:3} Peter calls out Ananias, like, "Dude, why did you let Satan mess with you to lie to the Holy Spirit and keep part of the money from the land sale?" {5:4} Peter's like, "You had full control over the money. Why did you plot this in your heart? You're not lying to people; you're lying to God." {5:5} Ananias drops dead after hearing this, and everyone who hears about it gets super freaked out. {5:6} Some young guys come, wrap him up, and bury him. {5:7} About three hours later, his wife shows up, unaware of what happened. {5:8} Peter asks her, "Did you sell the land for this amount?" She lies and says, "Yeah, that's what we got." {5:9} Peter's like, "Why did you two plan to test the Lord's Spirit? The guys who buried your husband are at the door and will carry you out too." {5:10} She drops dead right then, and the young guys come in, find her dead, and bury her next to her husband. {5:11} Everyone in the church is seriously scared after this. {5:12} The apostles are doing tons of miracles and signs, all while sticking together in Solomon's porch. {5:13} People are hesitant to join them, but everyone's talking about them. {5:14} More and more people, men and women, are joining the Lord. {5:15} They start bringing sick people into the streets, hoping Peter's shadow passing by might heal them. {5:16} Crowds from nearby cities bring their sick and those tormented by evil spirits to Jerusalem, and everyone gets healed. {5:17} The high priest and the Sadducees get super mad about this, {5:18} arrest the apostles, and throw them in jail. {5:19} But an angel of the Lord opens the prison doors at night and tells them to go speak in the temple about this life. {5:20-21} So they go and start teaching early in the morning. The high priest and his crew call a meeting, summon the apostles from prison, {5:22-23} but the officers find the prison doors locked, guards outside, and no one inside. {5:24} The high priest and the temple captain hear this and wonder what's next. {5:25} Someone reports that the apostles are in the temple teaching the people. {5:26} The captain brings them in without force because they're afraid of the people rioting. {5:27} The high priest questions them, {5:28} asking, "Didn't we tell you not to teach in this name? Yet you've filled Jerusalem with your teachings and are blaming us for this man's death." {5:29} Peter and the apostles reply, "We gotta obey God, not you guys. {5:30} The God of our ancestors raised up Jesus, whom you killed by hanging Him on a tree. {5:31} God exalted Him as Prince and Savior to bring repentance and forgiveness of sins to Israel. {5:32} We're witnesses of this, and so is the Holy Spirit given to those who obey God." {5:33} The council is furious, wanting to kill them. {5:34} But a Pharisee named Gamaliel steps in, tells them to chill for a bit, and warns them about past failed uprisings. {5:35} He advises, "Leave these guys alone. If their movement isn't from God, it'll flop. But if it is, you'll be fighting against God." {5:36} The council agrees, beats the apostles, orders them not to speak in Jesus' name, and lets them go. {5:37} The apostles leave, stoked to suffer for Jesus' name, and continue teaching about Him daily in the temple and in people's homes.

{6:1} Back in the day, when the crew of disciples was blowing up, there was some drama between the Greek-speaking crew and the Hebrew-speaking crew. The Greeks were beefing because their widows weren't getting looked after in the daily grind. {6:2} So, the twelve called everyone together and said, "We can't ditch preaching to wait tables." {6:3} They were like, "Look, fam, pick out seven legit dudes, full of the Holy Spirit and wisdom, to handle this. {6:4} We'll focus on praying and preaching." {6:5} The idea went down well with everyone, so they chose Stephen, a solid believer filled with the Holy Spirit, along with Philip, Prochorus, Nicanor, Timon, Parmenas, and Nicolas, a dude from Antioch who converted. {6:6} They brought these guys to the apostles, prayed over them, and laid hands on them. {6:7} The word of God kept spreading, and the disciples kept multiplying in Jerusalem, even a bunch of priests joined in. {6:8} Stephen, especially, was on fire, doing miracles and wonders among the people. {6:9} But then some haters from the Synagogue of the Freedmen, Cyrenians, Alexandrians, and others from Cilicia and Asia started arguing with Stephen. {6:10} But they couldn't match his wisdom and spirit. {6:11} So, they cooked up lies, saying Stephen was talking smack about Moses and God. {6:12} They riled up the crowd and leaders, grabbed Stephen, and dragged him to the council. {6:13} They brought in fake witnesses, saying Stephen was dissing the holy place and the law. {6:14} Claiming Stephen said Jesus would wreck the place and change Moses' rules. {6:15} Everyone in the council was staring at him, and he looked angelic.

{7:1} The head honcho priest asks, "Is this true?" {7:2} And the dude's like, "Listen up, fam, let me drop some knowledge. The OG God showed up to our main man Abraham back in the day when he was chilling in Mesopotamia, before he hit up Charran," {7:3} And God's like, "Yo, leave your hood and fam behind, come to this spot I'll show you." {7:4} So Abe dips from Chaldea and sets up shop in Charran, then later when his old man kicks the bucket, God moves him here, where we're kicking it now. {7:5} God didn't give him squat here, not even a patch of land, but promised it to him and his crew, even though he didn't have a kid yet. {7:6} And God was like, "Your descendants gonna get messed with in some foreign land, enslaved and treated like dirt for four hundred years." {7:7} But then I'm gonna drop some judgment on the nation that enslaved them, and after that, they'll bounce and worship me in this spot. {7:8} So Abe got the circumcision deal, then had Isaac, who had Jacob, who had the twelve patriarchs. {7:9} These patriarchs got jelly and sold Joseph into Egypt, but God was on his side, {7:10} He was Pharaoh's right-hand man, ruling over Egypt and his peeps. {7:11} Then a famine hit Egypt and Canaan, and our ancestors were starving. {7:12} When Jacob hears there's food in Egypt, he sends the fam there. {7:13} Second time around, Joseph reveals himself to his bros, and Pharaoh finds out about his fam. {7:14} So Joseph brings Jacob and his whole crew, seventy-five in total, to Egypt. {7:15} They chill there, then get buried in Sychem, in the tomb Abe bought from Emmor's sons. {7:16-17} But when the time's right, as God promised Abe, our people multiply in Egypt. {7:18} Until a new king who didn't know Joseph shows up and treats our peeps foul. {7:19} So they start chucking their babies, trying to wipe 'em out. {7:20} Moses pops up, a cute baby, raised in Pharaoh's crib for three months. {7:21} Then Pharaoh's daughter adopts him as her own. {7:22} Moses gets educated in all things Egyptian, slick with words and actions. {7:23} At forty, he's like, "Time to check on my Israelite homies." {7:24} He sees one getting wronged, defends him, and avenges him by knocking out an Egyptian. {7:25} He figures his bros would get it, that God would use him to save them, but they don't. {7:26-27} Next day, he tries to squash a fight, but they're like, "Who made you boss?" {7:28} They're like, "You gonna off us like you did that Egyptian?" {7:29} Moses bounces and ends up in Midian, where he has two sons. {7:30} Forty years later, God pops up to him in a burning bush. {7:31-34} God's like, "I see my people suffering, I'm gonna save them. Let's roll, I'm sending you to Egypt." {7:35} They rejected Moses, but God sent him as a leader and savior with an angelic co-sign. {7:36} He busts them out, doing miracles in Egypt, at the Red Sea, and in the wilderness for forty years. {7:37} That's the Moses who said, "God's gonna raise up a prophet like me for you Israelites." {7:38} He was with the angel in the wilderness, getting the real deal from God to pass on to us. {7:39} But our ancestors were haters, ditching Moses and wanting to head back to Egypt, {7:40} Saying to Aaron, "Make us some gods to lead us, 'cause Moses, who brought us out, is MIA." {7:41} So they make a calf, worship it, and get hyped on their own handiwork. {7:42-43} God's like, "Fine, you're into idols now," and ditches them to worship stars and stuff, just like the prophets warned. {7:44} They had the tent of witness, made as God told Moses, passed down through the generations, ending up with Joshua. {7:45} He leads them into the land of the Gentiles, God clears out for them, until David's time. {7:46-47} David wants to build God a house, but Solomon does it. {7:48} But God's bigger than buildings, like the prophets said, {7:49} "Heaven's my throne, earth's my footstool. You gonna build me a house?" {7:50-51} Stephen's like, "You stubborn, closed-off peeps, you always fight the Holy Spirit, just like your ancestors." {7:52} "Which prophet didn't your ancestors mess with? You even killed the Just One they talked about. You're just like them, backstabbers and murderers." {7:53} "You got the law from angels but didn't keep it." {7:54} They're not feeling it, gnashing their teeth at him. {7:55} But Stephen, full of the Holy Spirit, looks up, sees God's glory, and Jesus chilling at His right hand. {7:56} He's like, "Check it, I see the heavens open, and the Son of Man posted at God's right hand." {7:57} They freak out, cover their ears, and rush him. {7:58} They chuck him out of the city and stone him, while the witnesses stash their jackets at Saul's feet. {7:59} As they stone him, Stephen calls out to God, "Lord Jesus, take my spirit." {7:60} He kneels down and prays, "Don't hold this sin against them." Then he bites the dust.

{8:1} Saul was totally okay with Stephen getting taken out. After that, the church in Jerusalem faced serious persecution, and everyone scattered across Judea and Samaria, except the apostles. {8:2} Some devout dudes buried Stephen and were super sad about it. {8:3} Meanwhile, Saul was going all out against the church, busting into houses and throwing both men and women into prison. {8:4} The ones who scattered started preaching the word everywhere they went. {8:5} Philip went down to Samaria and started preaching about Christ. {8:6} The people were all ears, checking out Philip's words and witnessing the miracles he performed. {8:7} Demons were getting cast out left and right, and many who were sick or lame got healed. {8:8} The whole city was buzzing with joy. {8:9} But there was this guy named Simon, who used to practice sorcery in Samaria, fooling the people into thinking he was some big shot. {8:10} Everyone, from the least to the greatest, bought into his act, thinking he had the power of God. {8:11} They were into Simon for a long time because of his sorceries. {8:12} But when they believed Philip's preaching about God's kingdom and Jesus Christ, they got baptized, men and women alike. {8:13} Even Simon himself believed and was baptized, sticking close to Philip and amazed by the miracles and signs. {8:14} When the apostles in Jerusalem heard that Samaria accepted the word of God, they sent Peter and John. {8:15} They prayed for the believers there to receive the Holy Spirit because, up to that point, they had only been baptized in Jesus' name. {8:16} So Peter and John laid hands on them, and they received the Holy Spirit. {8:17} When Simon saw this, he tried to buy the power of the Holy Spirit from the apostles with money. {8:18} Peter shut him down, saying, "May your money go down with you because you thought you could buy God's gift with cash. {8:19} You've got no part in this; your heart's not right with God. {8:20} Repent of your wickedness and pray to God to forgive you for thinking this way." {8:21} Peter sensed that Simon was full of bitterness and bound by sin. {8:22-24} Simon asked Peter to pray for him so that none of the bad stuff Peter mentioned would happen to him. {8:25} After testifying and preaching, Peter and John returned to Jerusalem and spread the gospel in many Samaritan villages. {8:26} Then an angel told Philip to head south to the desert road from Jerusalem to Gaza. {8:27} On his way, Philip met an Ethiopian eunuch, a high-ranking official of Candace, queen of the Ethiopians, who was in charge of her treasury. {8:28} The eunuch was returning from Jerusalem and reading the prophet Isaiah in his chariot. {8:29} The Spirit told Philip to join the eunuch's chariot. {8:30} Philip ran up to him, heard him reading Isaiah, and asked if he understood what he was reading. {8:31} The eunuch was like, "How can I understand unless someone guides me?" He invited Philip to sit with him. {8:32} The passage he was reading was about someone led like a sheep to slaughter, and like a lamb before its shearer, he didn't open his mouth. {8:33} In his humiliation, his justice was taken away. Who can describe his generation? His life was taken from the earth. {8:34} The eunuch asked Philip who Isaiah was talking about—himself or someone else. {8:35} So Philip started explaining from that Scripture and preached Jesus to him. {8:36} As they traveled, they came across water, and the eunuch asked to be baptized. {8:37} Philip said, "If you believe with all your heart, you can." The eunuch said he believed Jesus Christ is the Son of God. {8:38} They stopped the chariot, and both Philip and the eunuch went down into the water, and Philip baptized him. {8:39} After they came up out of the water, the Spirit of the Lord whisked Philip away, and the eunuch went on his way rejoicing. {8:40} Philip ended up in Azotus and preached the gospel in all the cities until he reached Caesarea.

{9:1} Saul was totally on a mission to take down anyone repping for the Lord. He even hit up the high priest, asking for permission to roll into Damascus and nab anyone down with the Christian vibe, whether they were dudes or chicks, and drag them back to Jerusalem. {9:2} As he was cruising to Damascus, suddenly this crazy light beamed down from heaven, and Saul was like, whoa! {9:3} He hit the ground, and then he hears this voice like, "Saul, Saul, why you gotta be so harsh on me?" {9:4} Saul's like, "Whoa, who's talking?" And the voice is like, "I'm Jesus, the one you're coming after. It's not cool to fight against what's right." {9:5} Saul's freaking out, like, "Okay, okay, what do you want me to do?" And Jesus is like, "Get up, go into the city, and I'll tell you what's up." {9:6} Saul's shaking, like, "Uh, okay, sure." His crew is there, but they can only hear the voice and see nothing. {9:7-9} So they help Saul up, but he can't see anything. They lead him into Damascus, and for three days, he's blind and fasting. {9:10} Meanwhile, there's this disciple in Damascus named Ananias, and he's just chilling when he gets a vision from the Lord. Ananias is like, "Yo, what's up, Lord?" {9:11} And the Lord's like, "Go to Straight Street, find this dude named Saul from Tarsus. He's praying, and he had a vision about you coming to give him his sight back." {9:12} Ananias is like, "Hold up, Lord. I've heard about this Saul dude, and he's bad news for Christians. He's got the chief priests' permission to mess us up." {9:15} But the Lord's like, "Nah, it's cool. Saul's got a big mission ahead, representing me to everyone, even the non-Jews, kings, and Israelites. But he's gonna go through a lot for my name." {9:17} So Ananias goes to Saul, lays hands on him, and Saul's sight comes back, and he gets filled with the Holy Spirit. {9:18} Immediately, scales fall from Saul's eyes, and he can see again. He gets baptized and starts eating again. He hangs with the disciples in Damascus for a while. {9:20} Straightaway, Saul starts preaching about Jesus in the synagogues, telling everyone He's the Son of God. {9:21} People are shocked, like, "Wait, isn't this the guy who was hunting down Christians in Jerusalem? And now he's preaching Jesus?" {9:22} But Saul just keeps getting stronger, shutting down the Jewish arguments in Damascus, proving Jesus is the real deal. {9:23} After a while, though, the Jews are so mad, they're plotting to kill him. {9:24} Saul hears about it, so he bounces. They're even watching the gates day and night to catch him. {9:25} The disciples help him escape by lowering him down the city walls in a basket at night. {9:26} When Saul tries to join the disciples in Jerusalem, they're all scared of him, thinking it's a trick. {9:27} But Barnabas vouches for him, takes him to the apostles, and tells them how Saul had a vision of Jesus and was preaching boldly in Damascus. {9:28} Saul hangs with them, going in and out of Jerusalem. {9:29} He's not shy about speaking up for Jesus, even when the Greek-speaking Jews try to kill him. {9:30} When the disciples find out about the plot, they send Saul off to Caesarea and then Tarsus. {9:31} After that, things calm down for the churches in Judea, Galilee, and Samaria. They grow stronger, respecting the Lord and finding comfort in the Holy Spirit. {9:32} Meanwhile, Peter's making his rounds and heads over to Lydda, where some Christian peeps live. {9:33} He meets this guy named

Aeneas, who's been bedridden for eight years with palsy. {9:34} Peter's like, "Aeneas, Jesus is hooking you up. Get up and fix your bed." And Aeneas jumps up, healed. {9:35} Everyone in Lydda and Saron sees him and starts turning to Jesus. {9:36} Over in Joppa, there's this disciple named Tabitha, also called Dorcas, who's known for her good deeds and charity work. {9:37} But she gets sick and dies. They clean her up and put her in an upstairs room. {9:38} Some folks from Joppa hear that Peter's in nearby Lydda and send for him, asking him to come right away. {9:39} So Peter goes with them, and when he gets there, they take him upstairs. All the widows are there, crying and showing him the clothes Dorcas made while she was alive. {9:40} Peter kicks everyone out, kneels down, and prays. Then he turns to Dorcas and says, "Get up, Tabitha." And she opens her eyes, sees Peter, and sits up. {9:41} Peter helps her up, calls in the saints and widows, and presents her alive. {9:42} Word spreads all over Joppa, and lots of people start believing in the Lord. {9:43} Peter sticks around in Joppa for a while, crashing with a dude named Simon, who's a tanner.

{10:1} So, there's this dude in Caesarea named Cornelius, a centurion in the Italian crew. {10:2} He's legit, fears God, throws mad cash to the people, and stays praying 24/7. {10:3} One day, around 3 PM, he sees an angel rolling up to him in a vision, saying, "Cornelius!" {10:4} Dude's shook, like, "What's up, man?" The angel's like, "God's feeling your prayers and generosity." {10:5} Then the angel's like, "Send some dudes to Joppa, find this guy Simon, AKA Peter, crashing with a dude named Simon the tanner by the beach. He'll fill you in." {10:6-8} So Cornelius sends his homies to Joppa. {10:9} Next day, while Cornelius' crew heads to Joppa, Peter's up on a rooftop around noon, praying. {10:10} He's starving, but while they're cooking, he zonks out. {10:11} He sees heaven open, and this massive sheet drops down with all sorts of animals. {10:12} There's, like, everything - beasts, creepy crawlies, and birds. {10:13} Then this voice is like, "Yo, Peter, eat up!" {10:14} But Peter's like, "Nah, man, I only roll clean." {10:15} The voice is like, "Don't trip, what God cleanses, ain't unclean." {10:16} This happens three times, then the sheet's hauled back up. {10:17} While Peter's mulling over the vision, Cornelius' squad rolls up, asking for him. {10:18} They're at Simon's house, asking if Peter's around. {10:19} While Peter's still pondering, the Spirit's like, "Three dudes are looking for you." {10:20} So Peter's told to bounce and roll with them, no questions asked. {10:21} Peter links up with Cornelius' peeps and asks why they're there. {10:22} They spill the beans about how Cornelius, a stand-up guy, got a heads-up from an angel to fetch Peter and hear his words. {10:23} Peter brings them in for the night, then hits the road with them and some Joppa crew. {10:24} The next day, they hit Caesarea. Cornelius has his crew waiting, plus fam and friends. {10:25} When Peter arrives, Cornelius bows down, but Peter's like, "Chill, I'm just a regular dude." {10:26-27} They chat, then head inside where a bunch of folks are gathered. {10:28} Peter's like, "Y'all know Jews don't chill with outsiders, but God showed me everyone's cool." {10:29} So, he's there without hesitation, wondering what's up. {10:30} Cornelius spills how he was fasting and got a divine visit, told to get Peter. {10:31-32} Peter's told to go to Joppa and fetch him. {10:33} Peter's like, "No prob, glad to be here. Let's hear what God's got to say." {10:34} Peter's like, "For real, God's all about everyone, no favoritism." {10:35} "Anyone who respects God and acts right is good with Him." {10:36} "God's word, through Jesus, is all about peace." {10:37} "Y'all know about Jesus, right? He was doing big things in Galilee after John's baptisms." {10:38} "God hooked up Jesus with power, healing folks left and right." {10:39} "We saw it all go down, from the Jews' turf to Jerusalem. They offed Him, but God brought Him back." {10:40-41} "He didn't show Himself to everyone, just us who kicked it with Him after He rose." {10:42} "He told us to preach and testify that He's the real deal, appointed by God to judge everyone." {10:43} "The prophets back this up, saying whoever's down with Him gets their sins wiped clean." {10:44} While Peter's dropping these truths, the Holy Ghost vibes with everyone listening. {10:45} The Jewish believers are blown away that even the Gentiles get the Spirit. {10:46} 'Cause they're hearing them speak in tongues, praising God. Peter's like, {10:47} "Who's gonna stop them from getting baptized? They've got the Holy Ghost, just like us." {10:48} So, he orders them to get baptized in the Lord's name. They're stoked and ask Peter to hang out for a bit.

{11:1} When the apostles and crew in Judaea found out that even the Gentiles were on board with the Word of God, {11:2} they started giving Peter a hard time when he rolled back into Jerusalem, saying, "You hung out with uncircumcised dudes and ate with them." {11:3} Peter laid it all out from the beginning, explaining step by step, {11:4} "I was in Joppa praying when I had this crazy vision—a big sheet coming down from heaven with all kinds of animals on it. {11:5} I heard a voice telling me to 'get up, Peter, and eat.' {11:6} But I was like, 'Nah, Lord, I've never eaten anything common or unclean.' {11:7} The voice said back, 'Don't call unclean what God has cleaned.' {11:8} This happened three times, then the sheet went back up to heaven. {11:9} Right after that, three dudes from Caesarea showed up at the house where I was. {11:10} The Spirit told me to go with them without doubting. Six other dudes came with me, and we went to the guy's house. {11:11-14} He told us about seeing an angel who said to send for Simon Peter in Joppa to hear words that would save him and his whole house. {11:15} While I was talking, the Holy Spirit fell on them just like it did on us at the start. {11:16} Then I remembered what the Lord said about baptizing with the Holy Spirit. {11:17} If God gave them the same gift as us who believed in Jesus, who am I to argue with God?" {11:18} When they heard all this, they quieted down and praised God, saying, "God's given the Gentiles a shot at repentance and life." {11:19} Meanwhile, the ones who scattered during Stephen's persecution traveled as far as Phenice, Cyprus, and Antioch, only preaching to Jews. {11:20} But some guys from Cyprus and Cyrene, when they hit up Antioch, started preaching to the Greeks about Jesus. {11:21} God was with them, and a ton of people believed and turned to the Lord. {11:22} When news of this got back to the church in Jerusalem, they sent Barnabas to Antioch. {11:23} When he got there and saw God's grace at work, he was stoked and encouraged everyone to stay committed to the Lord. {11:24} Barnabas was a solid dude, full of the Holy Spirit and faith, and a bunch more people joined the Lord. {11:25} Barnabas took off for Tarsus to find Saul, {11:26} and when he did, brought him to Antioch. For a whole year, they hung with the church and taught a bunch of people, and that's when they started calling the disciples Christians in Antioch. {11:27} During this time, some prophets from Jerusalem showed up in Antioch.

{11:28} One of them, Agabus, stood up and predicted by the Spirit that there would be a big famine worldwide, which did happen during Claudius Caesar's reign. {11:29} So, the disciples decided to send help to the brethren in Judaea, {11:30} which they did through Barnabas and Saul.

{12:1} So, like, Herod the king was on a power trip and started messing with some of the church peeps. {12:2} He straight-up offed James, John's brother, with a sword. {12:3} Then, because he saw the crowd was vibing with it, he decided to nab Peter too. (This all went down during the feast of unleavened bread.) {12:4} So, he snatched up Peter and threw him in jail, putting him under heavy guard, planning to bring him out for the people after Easter. {12:5} Peter was locked up, but the church was going full-on prayer mode for him, non-stop. {12:6} When Herod was ready to parade Peter out, Peter was just chilling between two soldiers, snoozing, all chained up, with guards at the door. {12:7} Then, out of the blue, an angel appears, lights up the place, taps Peter, and tells him to get up, quick. Peter's chains fall off, just like that. {12:8} The angel's like, "Get dressed, put on your shoes," and Peter's like, "Cool, got it." Then the angel's like, "Wrap yourself up and follow me." {12:9} So Peter does, thinking it's all a dream. {12:10} They stroll past the guards and hit the iron gate to the city, which swings open by itself. They roll out, take a street, and poof, the angel's gone. {12:11} When Peter comes to his senses, he's like, "Whoa, God's angel just saved me from Herod and all the crazy stuff the Jews were expecting." {12:12} So he heads over to Mary's crib, John's mom, where a bunch of peeps are praying. {12:13} Peter knocks, and this chick Rhoda comes to the door. {12:14} She hears Peter's voice, freaks out, and runs back inside to spill the tea. {12:15} The others are like, "You're tripping," but Rhoda's like, "Nah, it's Peter for real." {12:16} They finally let him in, and they're shook. {12:17} Peter's like, "Shh, chill, let me tell you how God busted me out." Then he's like, "Go tell James and the crew." So Peter dips and finds another spot. {12:18} The next day, the soldiers are freaking out, wondering where Peter went. {12:19} Herod's ticked, so he checks with the guards and orders them to get axed. Then he bolts from Judea to Caesarea and kicks it there. {12:20} Herod's got beef with the folks from Tyre and Sidon, but they come together and make friends with his dude Blastus, the king's main man, begging for peace 'cause they depend on Herod's territory for survival. {12:21} On a big day, Herod's decked out in royal gear, giving a speech. {12:22} The crowd starts yelling, "He's a god, not a dude!" {12:23} But bam, just like that, an angel smacks Herod down 'cause he didn't give God props, and he gets eaten up by worms and bites it. {12:24} Meanwhile, God's word keeps spreading and multiplying. {12:25} Barnabas and Saul bounce back from Jerusalem after finishing their gig, and they take John Mark with them.

{13:1} So, in the Antioch church crew, there were some prophets and teachers - like Barnabas, Simeon (aka Niger), Lucius from Cyrene, Manaen (who hung with Herod the tetrarch), and Saul. {13:2} While they were doing their thing for the Lord, fasting and all, the Holy Ghost was like, "Yo, set aside Barnabas and Saul for my gig." {13:3} After more fasting, praying, and some laying on of hands, they sent them off. {13:4} So, guided by the Holy Ghost, they bounce to Seleucia, then hop on a boat to Cyprus. {13:5} In Salamis, they hit up Jewish synagogues, preaching God's word, with John tagging along as their sidekick. {13:6-7} They roll through the island to Paphos and find this sketchy sorcerer named Bar-jesus, hanging with the deputy, Sergius Paulus, who's keen to hear God's word. {13:8} But this sorcerer, Elymas, tries to throw shade and steer the deputy away from the faith. {13:9} So, Saul (also known as Paul), filled with the Holy Ghost, locks eyes with him. {13:10} He's like, "Bruh, you're full of tricks and wickedness, straight up evil, messing with God's path." {13:11} "Now, get ready, 'cause you're about to go blind for a bit." And bam, darkness falls over him, and he's groping around for help. {13:12} When the deputy sees this, he's shook and starts believing in the Lord's teachings. {13:13} Later, Paul and his crew sail off from Paphos and hit Perga in Pamphylia. John peaces out and heads back to Jerusalem. {13:14} They then roll into Antioch in Pisidia, hit up the synagogue on the Sabbath, and take a seat. {13:15} After the readings, the synagogue leaders are like, "If you've got something to say, spill the tea." {13:16} So, Paul stands up, throws a hand gesture, and calls out, "Listen up, Israelites and God-fearing peeps!" {13:17} He starts preaching about Israel's history, how God had their back in Egypt and brought them out, flexing His power. {13:18} Then he talks about their time in the wilderness and how God dealt with their disobedience. {13:19} He mentions wiping out seven nations in Canaan and divvying up the land. {13:20} Then he's like, "After that, God sent judges for about 450 years, until Samuel stepped in." {13:21} "Then y'all wanted a king, so God gave you Saul for 40 years." {13:22} "But then He gave you David, who was all about God's will." {13:23} "And from David's line, God sent us a Savior, Jesus, just like He promised." {13:24} "But before Jesus, John came, preaching repentance to Israel." {13:25} "When his time was up, he was like, 'I'm not the one, but someone's coming after me.'" {13:26} "So, peeps, Jews, and anyone else who respects God, this message of salvation is for you." {13:27} "But y'all in Jerusalem and your leaders didn't recognize Jesus or understand the prophets' words, even though they hear 'em every Sabbath." {13:28} "They had no legit reason to off Him, but they wanted Him gone." {13:29} "They did everything the prophets said would happen to Him, even taking Him down from the cross and laying Him in a tomb." {13:30} "But God brought Him back from the dead." {13:31} "He hung around for a while, seen by those who followed Him from Galilee to Jerusalem, spreading the word." {13:32} "And we're here to tell you the good news: God kept His promise and raised Jesus up, just like it's written in the Psalms." {13:33} "He declared, 'You're my Son; today I've become your Father.'" {13:34} "And about raising Him from the dead, God was like, 'No decay for You; I got Your back, like I promised David.'" {13:35} "In another Psalm, He's like, 'You won't see decay, Holy One.'" {13:36} "David did his thing for God, then rested with his ancestors, but Jesus didn't see decay." {13:37-38} "So, peeps, you gotta know: through Jesus, forgiveness of sins is up for grabs." {13:39} "And through Him, all believers get right with God, something the Law of Moses couldn't do." {13:40} "But watch out, 'cause what the prophets warned about might come true for you." {13:41} "Those who reject this message will be shook, even if someone spells it out for them." {13:42} "After the Jews bounced from the synagogue, the Gentiles were like, 'Yo, preach to us next Sabbath!'" {13:43} "After the crowd broke up, many Jews and converts followed Paul and Barnabas, who urged them to stick with God's grace." {13:44} "Next Sabbath, almost the whole city shows up to hear God's word." {13:45} "But when the Jews peep the massive crowd, they get jelly and start hating on Paul's message, contradicting and dissing him." {13:46} So Paul and Barnabas get bold and call them out, saying, "We had to give you the scoop first, but since you're not feeling it and don't think you deserve eternal life, we're taking this message to the Gentiles." {13:47} "The Lord told us, 'You're a light for the Gentiles, bringing salvation to the ends of the earth.'" {13:48} "When the Gentiles hear this, they're stoked and give props to God's word, and all who were destined for eternal life believe." {13:49} "And the word about the Lord spreads throughout the region." {13:50} "But the Jews start drama, getting the devout ladies and VIPs in the city to kick Paul and Barnabas out of town." {13:51} "So they shake the dust off their kicks and head to Iconium." {13:52} "And the disciples are hyped, filled with joy and the Holy Ghost."

{14:1} They rolled into Iconium and hit up the synagogue, dropping truth bombs that got a ton of Jews and Greeks on board. {14:2} But some salty Jews started stirring up trouble, turning folks against the believers. {14:3} Despite the haters, they kept it real, speaking boldly and dropping miracles left and right. {14:4} The city was split—some sided with the Jews, others with the apostles. {14:5} Things got real when both Gentiles and Jews came together to mess them up and stone them. {14:6} They peaced out to Lystra and Derbe, preaching the gospel in those spots. {14:7} That's where it went down. {14:8} In Lystra, they spotted a dude who had been crippled since birth, tuning in to Paul's message. {14:9-10} Paul could tell the guy had faith to be healed, so he told him to stand up—and boom, he walked. {14:11-12} When the crowd saw this, they went nuts, thinking Paul and Barnabas were gods in human form. {14:13} They even brought oxen and garlands for a sacrifice. {14:14} But when Paul and Barnabas caught wind of this, they freaked out, tearing their clothes and setting the record straight. {14:15} Then some troublemakers from Antioch and Iconium showed up, convincing the people to stone Paul. They thought he was toast, but the crew rallied around him, and he bounced back, heading to Derbe with Barnabas. {14:16} After preaching in Derbe, they circled back to Lystra, Iconium, and Antioch, encouraging the believers to stay strong despite the hardships on the road to God's kingdom. {14:17} They appointed elders in each church, prayed, and bounced, spreading the word to Pisidia and Pamphylia, then to Perga and Attalia. {14:18} Finally, they sailed back to Antioch, reporting back to the church about all the dope stuff God did, especially opening the door for the Gentiles to get in on the faith.

{15:1} So, like, these dudes from Judaea showed up preaching to the crew, saying, "If you ain't circumcised like Moses said, you're out of luck for salvation." {15:2} Paul and Barnabas weren't having it, so they had a big argument with them. They decided to head to Jerusalem to talk to the big shots about it. {15:3} On the way, they stopped in Phenice and Samaria, spreading the word about how the non-Jews were getting down with the faith, bringing mad joy to everyone. {15:4} When they hit Jerusalem, the church and the bigwigs welcomed them and heard all about the amazing stuff God was doing with them. {15:5} But then, some Pharisees who had converted were like, "Nah, they gotta get circumcised and follow Moses' law." {15:6} So, the bigwigs got together to talk it out. {15:7} After a bunch of back and forth, Peter got up and reminded them how God chose him to spread the gospel to the non-Jews, giving them the same Holy Spirit as the Jews. {15:8} He was like, "God knows what's up in people's hearts, and he gave the Gentiles the same deal as us, cleansing their hearts through faith." {15:9} So, why make it hard for them by making them follow all these rules? {15:10} Peter was like, "We're saved by the grace of Jesus, just like them." {15:11} Everyone was cool with that and listened to Barnabas and Paul share all the miracles they'd seen among the non-Jews. {15:12} After they finished, James spoke up, saying, "Listen up, guys." {15:13} He reminded them how God first reached out to the Gentiles to build a community for himself. {15:14} He said this lined up with what the prophets had said about rebuilding David's kingdom. {15:15} Basically, it was all about bringing everyone, Gentiles included, to the Lord. {15:16} James quoted some scripture, saying this was all part of God's plan from way back. {15:17} He wrapped it up by saying, "God's got this, and he's been planning it since forever." {15:18} So James was like, "Let's not make it hard for the non-Jews who are turning to God." {15:19} He suggested they just tell them to avoid idols, sexual stuff, strangled animals, and blood. {15:20} James pointed out that Moses' teachings are already available in every city's synagogue every Saturday. {15:21} The bigwigs agreed, along with the whole church, and decided to send some dudes to Antioch with Paul and Barnabas to spread the word. {15:22} They picked Judas and Silas to go along, both top-notch dudes. {15:23} They sent a letter with them, saying hi to the Gentile crew in Antioch, Syria, and Cilicia. {15:24} The letter was like, "We heard some people were causing trouble, so ignore them. We didn't tell them to preach circumcision and Moses' law." {15:25} The bigwigs had all agreed on this, and they were sending Judas and Silas to confirm it all in person. {15:26} They were like, "These dudes risked their lives for Jesus, so listen up." {15:27} Judas and Silas were gonna back up the letter with their own words. {15:28} They figured the Holy Spirit was cool with their decision, so they weren't gonna drop any more heavy rules on the Gentiles. {15:29} Just stick to avoiding idol worship, blood, strangled animals, and sexual stuff, and you're good. Later, dudes! {15:30} So they bounced, landed in Antioch, and handed over the letter to the crew. {15:31} Everyone was stoked when they read it. {15:32} Judas and Silas, who were also prophets, gave the crew some encouragement and confirmed everything. {15:33} After chilling for a bit, they headed out peacefully. {15:34} Silas decided to stick around, though. {15:35} Paul and Barnabas stayed in Antioch, teaching and spreading the word, along with a bunch of others. {15:36} After some time, Paul was like, "Yo, Barnabas, let's hit up all the cities we preached in and see how everyone's doing." {15:37} Barnabas was down and wanted to take John Mark with them. {15:38} But Paul wasn't feeling it 'cause Mark had bailed on them in Pamphylia and didn't want to put in the work. {15:39} They argued about it hard and split up. Barnabas took Mark and sailed to Cyprus, while Paul chose Silas and left, with the blessing of the crew. {15:40} They toured Syria and Cilicia, strengthening the churches along the way.

{16:1} Paul hits up Derbe and Lystra, and guess what? He meets this dude Timotheus, whose mom's a Jew but his dad's Greek. {16:2} Everyone's vibing with Timotheus in Lystra and Iconium. {16:3} Paul's like, "You're rolling with us, Timotheus," and even gets him circumcised because of the Jewish peeps in the area, knowing his dad's Greek. {16:4} As they roll through the cities, they pass on the rules laid down by the apostles and elders in Jerusalem. {16:5} Churches are getting lit, growing every day, staying solid in the faith. {16:6} But when they try to hit up Asia, the Holy Ghost is like, "Nah, not here." {16:7} So they're like, "Let's try Bithynia," but nope, the Spirit's not feeling it. {16:8} So they end up in Troas, cruising along. {16:9} Paul gets a vision: this dude from Macedonia is like, "Yo, come help us out!" {16:10} So, they're like, "Bet, Macedonia it is," knowing the Lord's calling them to preach there. {16:11} From Troas, they hit up Samothrace, then Neapolis, and finally, Philippi, the main spot in Macedonia, chilling there for a bit. {16:12-13} On the Sabbath, they head out by the river, where peeps pray, and they chat with the ladies. {16:14} Lydia, a boss lady from Thyatira, is feeling their vibe, and the Lord opens her heart to Paul's message. {16:15} She gets baptized, along with her fam, and invites them over to her place, insisting they crash there. {16:16} While they're heading to prayer, they run into this girl possessed by a spirit of divination, making bank for her owners with her fortune-telling skills. {16:17} She starts following Paul and the crew, shouting about them being servants of the Most High God, showing the way to salvation. {16:18} This goes on for days until Paul's had enough, and he's like, "In Jesus' name, get out!" And the spirit bounces. {16:19} But when her owners realize their cash flow's dried up, they grab Paul and Silas, dragging them to the market square before the rulers. {16:20-21} They snitch, saying these Jewish dudes are causing chaos in the city, teaching stuff that ain't kosher for Romans. {16:22} The crowd gets riled up, and the rulers strip Paul and Silas and order them to be beaten. {16:23} After taking a beating, they get thrown in the slammer, with the jailer told to keep 'em locked up tight. {16:24} Dude takes it seriously, locking them up in the deepest part of the prison and securing their feet in stocks. {16:25} At midnight, Paul and Silas start praying and singing, and the other prisoners are listening in. {16:26} Suddenly, there's a massive earthquake, shaking the prison to its core, unlocking all the doors and freeing everyone's chains. {16:27} The jailer wakes up, sees the open doors, and freaks out, thinking everyone's escaped. {16:28} But Paul's like, "Chill, we're all here." {16:29-30} The jailer, trembling, brings them out and asks, "What do I gotta do to be saved?" {16:31} They tell him, "Believe in Jesus, and you're good, you and your fam." {16:32} They preach the word to him and his household. {16:33} Dude takes them in, cleans their wounds, and gets baptized with his whole crew right then and there. {16:34} After, they head to his house, share a meal, and everyone's stoked, believing in God. {16:35} When it's morning, the magistrates are like, "Let 'em go." {16:36} The jailer tells Paul, "You're free to go, peace out." {16:37-38} But Paul's not having it, calling them out for beating them, Roman citizens, without a trial and now trying to sneakily kick them out. {16:39} The magistrates are shook when they find out they're Romans, so they come and beg them to leave. {16:40} Paul and Silas dip out of the prison, head to Lydia's house, encourage the brethren, and bounce.

{17:1} So, after hitting up Amphipolis and Apollonia, they rolled into Thessalonica, where there was a Jewish synagogue. {17:2} Paul did his thing and went in there for three Sabbaths, breaking it down with them using scripture. {17:3} He talked about how Christ had to suffer and rise again from the dead, and that this Jesus he was preaching about was the real deal. {17:4} Some bought into it and joined Paul and Silas, along with a bunch of Greek folks and even some prominent women. {17:5} But the jealous Jews who didn't believe started stirring up trouble, bringing in some shady characters and causing chaos in the city. {17:6} They couldn't find Paul and Silas, so they dragged Jason and some other believers to the city rulers, accusing them of turning the world upside down by preaching about Jesus as king. {17:7} The believers sent Paul and Silas away to Berea by night, where they hit up the synagogue again. {17:8} Meanwhile, Paul was chilling in Athens, shook by how much idol worship was going down. {17:9} He then stood up on Mars' Hill and called out the Athenians for being superstitious, pointing out their altar to the "Unknown God." {17:10} Paul broke it down that God, who made everything, doesn't dwell in temples made by human hands. {17:11} He dropped truth bombs, saying that in the past God overlooked ignorance, but now calls everyone to repentance because there's a day of judgment coming, backed up by Jesus' resurrection.

{18:1} So, like, Paul bounced from Athens and hit up Corinth; {18:2} there he met this dude Aquila, a Jew from Pontus who just rolled in from Italy with his wife Priscilla. {18:3} They were all tentmakers, so Paul crashed with them and worked together. {18:4} Every Sabbath, he'd hit up the synagogue, chatting with both Jews and Greeks, trying to convince them. {18:5} When Silas and Timothy showed up from Macedonia, Paul was all fired up, preaching to the Jews that Jesus was the real deal. {18:6} But when they started hating and dissing him, he was like, "Your loss, dudes. From now on, I'm taking this message to the Gentiles." {18:7} So he dipped and crashed at this guy Justus's crib, who was into God, and it was right next to the synagogue. {18:8} Crispus, the head honcho at the synagogue, and his whole fam believed in the Lord, along with loads of other Corinthians who got baptized. {18:9} Then one night, the Lord spoke to Paul in a dream, saying, "Don't stress, keep preaching. I've got your back, and there are heaps of believers in this city." {18:10} So Paul stuck around for a year and a half, teaching the word of God to everyone. {18:11} When Gallio was in charge of Achaia, the Jews tried to bring Paul up on charges, saying he was teaching against the law. {18:12} But just as Paul was about to speak, Gallio shut it down, saying, "If this was a real crime, I'd listen. But it's just a bunch of religious talk, so sort it out yourselves." {18:13-16} And he kicked them out. {18:17} Then the Greeks grabbed Sosthenes, the head of the synagogue, and gave him a beating in front of the court, but Gallio didn't give a damn. {18:18} After that, Paul hung around for a bit longer, said his goodbyes, and sailed to Syria with Priscilla and Aquila, cutting his hair in Cenchrea as part of a vow. {18:19} He left them in Ephesus and hit up the synagogue to chat with the Jews. {18:20-21} When they asked him to stay longer, he said nah and took off, saying he had to hit up a festival in Jerusalem, but he'd come back if it was cool with God. And off he sailed from Ephesus. {18:22} After chilling in Caesarea and giving props to the church, he went down to Antioch. {18:23} Then he hit up Galatia and Phrygia, boosting the faith of all the believers. {18:24} Meanwhile, this dude Apollos, a Jew from Alexandria, rolled into Ephesus. {18:25} He was smart and passionate about God, but only knew about John's baptism. {18:26} He started preaching boldly in the synagogue until Aquila and Priscilla schooled him on the full deal about God. {18:27} When he wanted to head to Achaia, the crew wrote to the disciples, telling them to welcome him, and he ended up helping loads of believers with his convincing arguments that Jesus was the Christ.

{19:1} So, while Apollos is chilling in Corinth, Paul rolls through the upper spots and lands in Ephesus. There, he finds some peeps who are into the vibe. {19:2} He's like, "Yo, have you guys felt the Holy Ghost since you started believing?" And they're like, "Bro, we haven't even heard of the Holy Ghost." {19:3} Paul's like, "Then what were you baptized into?" And they're like, "John's baptism, dude." {19:4} So Paul's like, "John's all about repentance, paving the way for Jesus. Get baptized in Jesus' name." {19:5-6} They're down, get baptized in the name of Jesus, and boom, Paul lays hands on them, and they're speaking in tongues and prophesying. {19:7} There are about twelve of them total. {19:8} Paul's bold, hitting up the synagogue for three months, dropping truth bombs about the kingdom of God. {19:9} But when some people start hating and spreading rumors, Paul's like, "Peace out," and starts teaching elsewhere. {19:10} This goes on for two years, and everyone in Asia, Jews and Greeks alike, hears about Jesus. {19:11-12} Paul's pulling off mad miracles, like healing folks just by touching handkerchiefs or aprons and casting out evil spirits. {19:13} Then some wannabe exorcists try using Jesus' name without really knowing Him, and it goes south real quick. {19:14-16} Seven sons of Sceva, a Jewish chief priest, get wrecked by an evil spirit, running out naked and bruised. {19:17} Word spreads, and everyone in Ephesus, Jews, and Greeks alike, start freaking out, giving mad props to Jesus. {19:18} People start confessing their wrongs and burning their witchy stuff, totaling fifty thousand pieces of silver. {19:19} After this, Paul's like, "Time to bounce," planning to hit up Macedonia and Achaia before heading to Jerusalem and eventually Rome. {19:20} But things get heated in Ephesus, especially for a dude named Demetrius, a silversmith making bank off of shrines for Diana. {19:21} The whole city gets chaotic, with Gaius and Aristarchus getting caught up, so Paul's friends are like, "Stay out of the drama, bro." {19:22} The crowd's all over the place, confused as heck about why they're even there. {19:23} Finally, the town clerk calms everyone down, reminding them how Ephesus is all about Diana worship, and they need to chill. {19:24} He's like, "Y'all better be careful, or we'll catch flak for this wild scene today." {19:25} With that, he sends everyone packing.

{20:1} After all that chaos settled down, Paul gathered up the crew, gave 'em a big hug, and bounced to Macedonia. {20:2} He did his thing there, pumped everyone up with some hype talks, then jetted off to Greece. {20:3} Chilled there for three months until the haters tried to ambush him before he set sail to Syria, so he pivoted and decided to backtrack through Macedonia. {20:4} Sopater from Berea, Aristarchus, and Secundus from Thessalonica, Gaius from Derbe, Timotheus, Tychicus, and Trophimus from Asia all rolled with him to Asia. {20:5} They went ahead and waited for us at Troas. {20:6} We sailed from Philippi after the spring festival and reached Troas in five days, then hung out there for a week. {20:7} On Sunday, when the crew gathered for grub, Paul preached a marathon sermon since he was leaving the next day, going on and on until midnight. {20:8} They lit up the place with a bunch of lights in that upper room. {20:9} Meanwhile, there's this kid Eutychus chillin' in the window, nodding off hard while Paul's still going strong. The dude nods off too far and plummets from the third floor, dead as a doornail. {20:10} Paul rushes down, hugs him, and says, "Chill, he's alive." {20:11} After that, they ate, talked all night, and Paul hit the road at daybreak. {20:12} They brought the kid back to life, and everyone was stoked. {20:13} We got on the ship and sailed to Assos, where Paul was supposed to join us on foot. {20:14} We met up with him in Assos, picked him up, and went to Mitylene. {20:15} Then we sailed off, passed by Chios the next day, hit up Samos, and stopped at Trogyllium; the day after that, we arrived at Miletus. {20:16} Paul wanted to skip Ephesus to save time in Asia 'cause he was in a rush to get to Jerusalem by Pentecost. {20:17} From Miletus, he sent for the elders in Ephesus. {20:18} When they arrived, he was like, "Y'all know how I've been rollin' since day one in Asia—humble, grindin' hard, dealing with mad drama from those haters." {20:19-21} He didn't hold back anything useful, teaching everyone publicly and house to house, spreading the word to Jews and Greeks alike about turning to God and having faith in Jesus. {20:22} Now he's feeling led to go to Jerusalem, not knowing what's in store except for what the Holy Spirit's been hinting at—trials and tribulations. {20:23-24} But none of that shakes him; he's ready to finish strong, testifying the gospel of God's grace. {20:25} Paul knows he won't see these folks again, the ones he's been preaching the kingdom to. {20:26} He's trying to make it to Jerusalem by Pentecost, so he's racing through his travels. {20:27} He's been keeping it real, not holding back any of God's wisdom. {20:28-29} He warns them to watch out for themselves and the crew, 'cause some savage wolves are gonna try to mess things up after he's gone. {20:30} Even some of them will flip and start talking nonsense, trying to snag followers for themselves. {20:31} So, stay woke and remember how Paul was on them day and night, droppin' truth with tears. {20:32} Now he's passing the baton to God and His word of grace, which can build them up and secure their inheritance. {20:33} Paul's never been about that money or material stuff—his hands have been working hard to support himself and his crew. {20:34-35} He's shown them how it's done, working hard and helping the weak, just like Jesus said—it's blessed to give, not just get. {20:36-37} After all that, he kneels down, prays with everyone, and they all start bawling, hugging Paul tight, knowing they won't see him again. {20:38} They're especially bummed about never seeing him again, seeing him off to the ship.

{21:1} So, like, after we dipped from there, we sailed straight to Coos, then the next day to Rhodes, and from there to Patara; {21:2} we found a ship headed to Phenicia, so we hopped on board and set sail. {21:3} When we spotted Cyprus, we left it on our left and sailed into Syria, landing at Tyre where the ship was unloading its cargo. {21:4} We hung out there for a week with some disciples who told Paul, through the Spirit, not to go to Jerusalem. {21:5} After that, we said our goodbyes, and they all walked us out of the city with their families, and we knelt down on the shore and prayed. {21:6} Then we boarded the ship, and they headed back home. {21:7} When we left Tyre and arrived at Ptolemais, we greeted the believers there and stayed with them for a day. {21:8} The next day, we, who were with Paul, went to Caesarea and stayed at the house of Philip the evangelist, one of the seven, and hung out with him. {21:9} This dude had four daughters who were prophets and still single. {21:10} While we were chilling there, a prophet named Agabus came down from Judea. {21:11} He took Paul's belt, tied himself up, and said, "This is what the Holy Ghost says: The Jews in Jerusalem will tie up the man who owns this belt and hand him over to the Gentiles." {21:12} When we heard this, along with the locals, we begged Paul not to go to Jerusalem. {21:13} But Paul was like, "Why you gotta make me sad? I'm ready not just to be bound but also to die in Jerusalem for Jesus' sake." {21:14} Even when we couldn't convince him, we stopped arguing, saying, "Let God's will be done." {21:15} After that, we packed up and headed to Jerusalem. {21:16} Some disciples from Caesarea came with us and brought along Mnason from Cyprus, an old disciple who offered us a place to crash. {21:17} When we got to Jerusalem, the believers there welcomed us warmly. {21:18} The next day, Paul went with us to see James, and all the elders were there too. {21:19} After greeting them, Paul gave a detailed report of what God had done among the Gentiles through his ministry. {21:20} When they heard, they praised God and said, "Bro, you see how many Jewish believers there are, and they're all super into the law. {21:21} But they've heard rumors that you're telling Jews among the Gentiles to ditch Moses, saying they shouldn't circumcise their kids or follow Jewish customs. {21:22} So what's the deal? You gotta do something to calm them down because they'll freak out when they hear you're here." {21:23} They suggested this: "We have four dudes who are under a vow. {21:24} Take them, purify yourself with them, and pay for their expenses, so it'll show that those rumors about you ain't true, and you're cool with following the law." {21:25} As for the Gentile believers, we've already written to them, saying they don't have to do any of that stuff except avoid food sacrificed to idols, blood, strangled animals, and sexual immorality. {21:26} So, the next day, Paul went along with the dudes and purified himself with them, then went to the temple to announce the end of the purification period until offerings were made for each of them. {21:27} When the seven days were almost up, some Jews from Asia saw Paul in the temple and stirred up the crowd, grabbing him and yelling, {21:28} "People of Israel, help! This is the guy who's been teaching everywhere against our people, our law, and this place. Besides, he even brought Greeks into the temple and defiled this holy place!" {21:29} (They had seen Trophimus, the Ephesian, with Paul in the city earlier and assumed Paul had brought him into the temple.) {21:30} The whole city got stirred up, and people ran together, seizing Paul and dragging him out of the temple, and immediately the doors were shut. {21:31} As they tried to kill him, word reached the commander of the Roman regiment that all Jerusalem was in chaos. {21:32} He took soldiers and officers and rushed down to the crowd, and when they saw the commander and his soldiers, they stopped beating Paul. {21:33} The commander arrested Paul, ordering him to be bound with two chains, and asked who he was and what he had done. {21:34} Some shouted one thing, some another, and since the commander couldn't get the truth because of the uproar, he ordered Paul to be taken to the barracks. {21:35} As Paul was being carried up the steps, the crowd followed, shouting, "Get rid of him!" {21:36-37} When Paul was about to be taken into the barracks, he asked the commander, "Can I talk to you?" The commander was surprised and asked, "Can you speak Greek? {21:38} Aren't you that Egyptian who stirred up trouble before and led four thousand terrorists out into the wilderness some time ago?" {21:39} But Paul said, "I'm just a Jewish guy from Tarsus, a respectable city in Cilicia. Please, let me speak to the people." {21:40} After the commander gave him permission, Paul stood on the steps and motioned to the crowd. When they were all silent, he spoke to them in their own language, Hebrew, saying,

{22:1} Yo, dudes, listen up, I gotta spill my story to y'all. {22:2} When they heard me speaking in Hebrew, they were all ears, dead quiet, you know? {22:3} So, I'm a Jewish dude from Tarsus, but I got schooled here in the city under Gamaliel, learning the law like a boss, just like you all are now. {22:4} Back then, I was hardcore against this Jesus crew, even sending peeps to jail or worse. {22:5} The high priest and all the elders can vouch for me. They even gave me letters to nab Jesus followers and drag 'em to Jerusalem. {22:6} But then, one day near Damascus, a blinding light from heaven shook me up big time. {22:7} I hit the ground, and a voice called out, "Saul, why you gotta be so anti-me?" {22:8} I'm like, "Whoa, who are you, dude?" And he's all, "I'm Jesus of Nazareth, the one you've been messing with." {22:9} My crew saw the light but didn't hear the voice, trippy, right? {22:10} I'm like, "Okay, what now?" And Jesus is like, "Get up, head to Damascus, and you'll find out what's up." {22:11} Blinded by the light, I stumble into Damascus, and this guy Ananias hooks me up with my sight again. {22:12} He's all, "God chose you to know His deal and witness for Jesus." {22:13} So, I'm like, "Cool," and boom, my sight's back. {22:14} Ananias says, "You're gonna see and hear some wild stuff and be Jesus' witness to everyone." {22:15-16} He's like, "What are you waiting for? Get baptized, wash away your sins, and call on Jesus." {22:17-18} So, I'm back in Jerusalem, praying in the temple when I get this vision, telling me to bail 'cause they won't dig my Jesus talk. {22:19-20} I'm like, "But Jesus, they know I was all about busting believers, even rocked with the Stephen execution." {22:21} Jesus is like, "Nah, time to jet, I'm sending you far out to the Gentiles." {22:22-23} They ain't feeling it, start yelling, and toss dust in the air like it's a concert gone wrong. {22:24} The boss orders me inside for interrogation, ready to whip me to figure out what's up. {22:25} I'm like, "Yo, is it even legal to beat a Roman citizen without a trial?" {22:26} The centurion's shook, spills the beans that I'm Roman. {22:27} The boss is like, "Wait, you're Roman?" And I'm all, "Yeah, dude." {22:28} He's like, "I paid big bucks for my citizenship." And I'm like, "I was born with mine, bro." {22:29} They bounce, scared I'm Roman, and the boss wants answers, so he sets me free and calls a meeting with the big shots to sort things out.

{23:1} So Paul's like, looking dead serious at the council, and he's all, "Yo, bros, I've been living right, keeping it 💯 with God up to today." {23:2} Then the high priest Ananias straight-up tells the dudes next to him to smack Paul in the face. {23:3} Paul's not having it, and he's like, "God's gonna strike you, you hypocrite! You sit there judging me by the law but order me to be hit against the law?" {23:4} The people around him are like, "Yo, you dissing God's high priest?" {23:5} Paul's like, "My bad, didn't realize he was the high priest. Scripture says not to disrespect the leader of your people." {23:6} Then Paul sees that some are Sadducees and others Pharisees, so he shouts out, "I'm a Pharisee, born and raised Pharisee, and they're grilling me over the hope of resurrection!" {23:7} This causes a huge argument between the Pharisees and Sadducees, splitting the crowd. {23:8} 'Cause the Sadducees say no resurrection, angels, or spirits, but the Pharisees are down with all that. {23:9} The Pharisee scribes are like, "We don't see anything wrong with this dude. If a spirit or angel spoke to him, let's not fight against God." {23:10} The chief captain's worried they'll tear Paul apart, so he orders soldiers to swoop in, snatch Paul, and bring him to safety. {23:11} Later that night, the Lord shows up to Paul like, "Chill, Paul. Just like you've been repping me in Jerusalem, you're gonna testify in Rome too." {23:12} When morning comes, some Jews hatch a plan to kill Paul, taking an oath not to eat or drink until they do. {23:13} There's like over forty of 'em in on this plot. {23:14} They spill the beans to the chief priests and elders, like, "We swore not to eat till we off Paul." {23:15} They tell the council to request Paul for more questioning, but they're ready to jump him before he gets there. {23:16} Paul's nephew catches wind of this and runs to the castle to spill the tea to Paul. {23:17} Paul calls over a centurion and tells him to bring the young man to the chief captain, 'cause he's got some intel. {23:18} So the centurion brings the kid to the chief captain, saying Paul wants to talk. {23:19} The chief captain takes him aside and asks what's up. {23:20} The kid spills that the Jews want Paul brought back to the council for more questioning, but they really wanna take him out. {23:21} The chief captain's like, "No way, I'm not handing him over to them." There's like over forty dudes ready to pounce, waiting on your word." {23:22} So the chief captain lets the kid go and warns him not to spill this to anyone. {23:23} Then he gets two centurions ready with a big squad—two hundred soldiers, seventy horsemen, and two hundred spearmen—to roll out at 3 AM. {23:24} They get horses for Paul, ensuring he gets safely to Governor Felix. {23:25} The chief captain writes Felix a letter, explaining how he saved Paul from the Jews who wanted him dead, knowing he's a Roman citizen. {23:26} The captain tells Felix they couldn't figure out why they were accusing Paul, so he's sending him over for more answers. {23:27-32} Then the soldiers, following orders, escort Paul to Antipatris under the cover of night. The horsemen continue with Paul, while the rest head back to the castle. {23:33} When they reach Caesarea, they hand over Paul and the letter to Governor Felix. {23:34} Felix reads the letter and asks where Paul's from. {23:35} He's like, "I'll hear you out once your accusers show up," and has Paul held in Herod's judgment hall.

{24:1} So, like, after five days, Ananias the high priest rolled up with the elders, and this dude Tertullus, who was like their speaker, to throw Paul under the bus to the governor. {24:2} When they called Paul out, Tertullus started accusing him, saying, "Hey, Governor Felix, we're all about that peace and prosperity thanks to you, and we're super grateful. {24:3} We're totally cool with you everywhere, bro. {24:4} But, like, just a quick word, if you don't mind. {24:5} 'Cause this guy Paul? He's trouble. He's stirring up drama among Jews all over, leading this Nazarene crew, and even tried to disrespect the temple. {24:6} We grabbed him, wanting to do our thing by our law, but then Captain Lysias swooped in and snatched him away, telling us to take our beef to you. {24:7} The Jews are all nodding, agreeing with us. {24:8} So, like, you gotta hear our side, man." {24:9} And the Jews were like, "Yeah, what they said." {24:10} Then Paul, when the governor motioned for him to speak, was like, "Yo, Governor, you've been in charge for a hot minute, so I'm down to talk. {24:11} Just so you know, it's only been twelve days since I hit up Jerusalem to pray. {24:12} And I wasn't causing any trouble at the temple, stirring up riots, or even preaching in the synagogues or the city. {24:13} They can't even prove their accusations against me. {24:14} But I'll own up to this: I follow what they call heresy, but it's just me being true to the God of my ancestors, believing in everything written in the law and the prophets. {24:15} And, like, I'm all about that resurrection vibe, for everyone, good or bad. {24:16} I'm all about keeping it real with God and people, you feel me? {24:17} So, after a bunch of years, I came to drop off some donations for my peeps and do some offerings. {24:18} Then these Asian Jews found me all chill at the temple, not causing a scene or anything. {24:19} They should've been here if they had anything against me. {24:20} Or let these guys speak up if they saw me doing anything wrong when I faced the council. {24:21} The only beef they have with me is preaching about the resurrection of the dead." {24:22} When Felix heard this, knowing more about this faith, he was like, "Hold up, I need more info. Let's wait for Captain Lysias to come down." {24:23} So he told a centurion to keep Paul safe but chill, and not to stop his friends from visiting him. {24:24} After a few days, when Felix and his wife Drusilla, who was Jewish, came through, he called for Paul and heard him out about the whole Jesus thing. {24:25} As Paul talked about doing the right thing, self-control, and future judgment, Felix got shook and was like, "Okay, I gotta go. I'll hit you up when I'm free." {24:26} He was hoping Paul would slip him some cash to set him free, so he kept calling him in and chatting with him. {24:27} But after two years, Porcius Festus took over Felix's job, and Felix, trying to score points with the Jews, left Paul locked up.

{25:1} So, like, when Festus rolled into the province, he chilled for three days in Caesarea, then bounced to Jerusalem. {25:2} But the high priest and the big shots from the Jewish crew started dissing Paul, begging Festus {25:3} for a favor to drag Paul to Jerusalem, planning to off him on the way. {25:4} But Festus shut it down, saying Paul stays put in Caesarea, and he's dipping out soon. {25:5} He's like, "Yo, if any of you got beef with Paul, roll with me to Caesarea and bring your accusations." {25:6} After chilling with them for over ten days, he heads back to Caesarea and the next day throws Paul in the hot seat. {25:7} When Paul shows, the Jewish crew from Jerusalem starts trash-talking, but they can't back up their claims. {25:8} Paul's like, "I didn't break no Jewish laws, disrespect the temple, or diss Caesar, you feel me?" {25:9} But Festus, wanting to score points with the Jews, asks Paul if he wants to take his case to Jerusalem. {25:10} Paul's like, "Nah, I'm cool right here at Caesar's crib. I didn't wrong the Jews, and you know it." {25:11} He's like, "If I'm guilty, I'll take the heat, but if not, nobody's handing me over to them. I'm appealing to Caesar." {25:12} So, after consulting the crew, Festus is like, "You appealed to Caesar? Caesar it is, then." {25:13} Later on, King Agrippa and Bernice roll up to Caesarea to give Festus props. {25:14} Festus spills about Paul, saying he's stuck in chains since Felix's time. {25:15} Back in Jerusalem, the priests and elders were all up on him, pushing for a verdict against Paul. {25:16} But I'm like, "Nah, Romans don't deal with executions till the accusers face off, you know?" {25:17} So, when they come through, I waste no time, throw Paul in the hot seat, ready to hear it all. {25:18} But their accusations didn't match up to what I expected, {25:19} just some weird questions about their beliefs and this dude Jesus, who Paul says rose from the dead. {25:20} Confused, I ask Paul if he wants to head to Jerusalem for trial. {25:21} But Paul's like, "Nah, I'm sticking to Caesar's court." So, I keep him in custody until I can ship him to Caesar. {25:22} Then Agrippa's like, "I gotta hear this guy myself." "Tomorrow," Festus says, "you'll get your chance." {25:23} Next day, Agrippa and Bernice, with all their entourage, strut into the hearing spot, and Paul's brought out. {25:24} Festus is like, "Check it, Agrippa, and everyone else here, peep Paul. Jews been hounding me about him, saying he shouldn't live." {25:25} But I'm like, "Dude didn't do anything worthy of death, and he appealed to Caesar, so off he goes." {25:26} But I got nothing solid to tell Caesar, so I brought Paul here, especially for you, King Agrippa, to get the scoop. {25:27} It's only right to lay out the charges before sending a prisoner, you know?

{26:1} So Agrippa's like, "Yo, Paul, you can speak up for yourself." Then Paul raises his hand and starts defending himself. {26:2} He's like, "I'm feeling good about this opportunity, King Agrippa, to explain myself today about all the accusations from the Jews." {26:3} Paul's giving props to Agrippa, knowing he's knowledgeable about Jewish customs and stuff, and asks him to listen patiently. {26:4} Paul talks about his life from way back, how all the Jews know he was a Pharisee, strict and loyal to the Jewish faith. {26:5} They know from the start that he was hardcore Pharisee vibes. {26:6-7} Now he's on trial because of God's promise to the ancestors, which the twelve tribes of Israel are waiting for, serving God day and night. That's why the Jews are coming after him. {26:8} Paul's like, "Why is it so unbelievable to you that God can raise the dead?" {26:9} He admits he used to be anti-Jesus, doing whatever he could against the name of Jesus of Nazareth. {26:10} He even locked up saints and gave the thumbs down for their executions, authorized by the chief priests. {26:11} Paul admits he was wild, punishing believers in every synagogue and forcing them to blaspheme. He was so heated against them, he chased them down to other cities. {26:12} Then on his way to Damascus with the chief priests' authority, a crazy thing happened at noon. {26:13} Paul saw this blinding light from heaven, brighter than the sun, shining on him and his crew. {26:14} They all hit the ground, and Paul hears a voice in Hebrew, calling him out for persecuting Jesus and warning him against resisting. {26:15} Paul's like, "Who are you, Lord?" The voice responds, "I'm Jesus, the one you're going after." {26:16} Jesus tells Paul to stand up because he's been chosen to be a witness to what he's seen and will see, saved from both Jews and Gentiles. {26:17-18} He's sent to open people's eyes, turn them from darkness to light, and bring them from Satan's power to God's, so they can receive forgiveness and be sanctified by faith in Jesus. {26:19} Paul's like, "So, King Agrippa, I didn't ignore that heavenly vision." {26:20} He explains how he spread this message from Damascus to Jerusalem, Judea, and to the Gentiles, telling them to repent, turn to God, and live out their changed lives. {26:21} That's why the Jews tried to off him in the temple. {26:22} Paul says God's been helping him stay strong, testifying to everyone, big and small, only preaching what the prophets and Moses said would happen. {26:23} That the Christ would suffer, rise from the dead first, and bring light to both Jews and Gentiles. {26:24} While Paul's explaining all this, Festus interrupts, shouting, "Paul, you're out of your mind! Too much learning has made you crazy." {26:25} Paul's like, "Nah, I'm not crazy, most honorable Festus. I'm speaking truth and keeping it real." {26:26} He tells Festus that King Agrippa knows all this stuff because it wasn't done in secret. {26:27} Then Paul puts it to Agrippa straight, asking if he believes the prophets. He's pretty sure Agrippa's on board with that. {26:28} Agrippa's like, "Man, you almost got me to become a Christian." {26:29} Paul's like, "I wish everyone here would be just like me, except without these chains." {26:30} After Paul drops this, everyone stands up—King Agrippa, Governor Festus, Bernice, and their crew. {26:31} They step aside and chat, agreeing that Paul didn't do anything deserving of death or chains. {26:32} Agrippa tells Festus, "This dude could've been set free if he hadn't appealed to Caesar."

{27:1} So, like, when they decided we should head to Italy, they handed Paul and a few other prisoners over to this dude Julius, a centurion from Augustus' crew. {27:2} We hopped on a ship from Adramyttium, planning to cruise along the coasts of Asia, with Aristarchus, this Macedonian dude from Thessalonica, tagging along. {27:3} The next day, we stopped at Sidon, and Julius was cool to Paul, letting him kick it with his friends to chill. {27:4} But when we set sail again, we had to go under Cyprus 'cause the winds were acting up. {27:5} After sailing through the sea of Cilicia and Pamphylia, we hit up Myra, a city in Lycia. {27:6} There, Julius found a ship from Alexandria bound for Italy, so we jumped on board. {27:7} We cruised slowly for a bunch of days, barely making it past Cnidus 'cause the wind was against us. {27:8} Eventually, we made it to this spot called The Fair Havens, near the city of Lasea, after a tough journey. {27:9} With a lot of time passed and sailing getting risky 'cause it was past the Fast, Paul warned them, {27:10} He was like, "Yo, this trip is gonna be bad news. We're gonna lose cargo, the ship, and maybe even our lives." {27:11} But the centurion trusted the ship's captain and owner more than Paul's words. {27:12} Since The Fair Havens wasn't ideal for winter, most of the crew wanted to push on to Phenice, a better port in Crete facing southwest and northwest. {27:13} When a soft south wind blew, they thought they were good to go, so they sailed close to Crete. {27:14} But then, outta nowhere, this crazy storm called Euroclydon hit us hard. {27:15} The ship couldn't handle it, so we just let it drift. {27:16} We managed to get close to an island called Clauda, but it was a struggle to secure the lifeboat. {27:17} They used ropes to reinforce the ship, fearing we'd hit quicksand, and then lowered the sails to drift. {27:18} The next day, they threw out some cargo to lighten the load. {27:19} And on the third day, they tossed out the ship's tackle with their own hands. {27:20} With no sun or stars for days and a massive storm raging, everyone lost hope of being saved. {27:21} But after fasting for a while, Paul spoke up, saying they should've listened to him and stayed in Crete to avoid the trouble. {27:22} Then he reassured them that while they might lose the ship, no one would lose their life. {27:23} 'Cause an angel of God told him that everyone on the ship would be safe. {27:24} So, he urged them to stay positive, trusting that what was told to him would happen. {27:25} Even though they'd end up on some island. {27:26} Finally, after fourteen nights of being tossed around in the Adriatic Sea, the crew sensed land nearby around midnight. {27:27} They sounded and found it twenty fathoms deep, then a little further, fifteen fathoms. {27:28} Worried about hitting rocks, they dropped four anchors from the stern and wished for daylight. {27:29} As the shipmen tried to escape in the lifeboat, pretending to drop anchors from the front, Paul warned the centurion and soldiers that if they left, they wouldn't survive. {27:30} So the soldiers cut the ropes and let the lifeboat go. {27:31} As daylight approached, Paul urged everyone to eat, reminding them they hadn't eaten in two weeks. {27:32} Then he took bread, gave thanks to God in front of them all, and started eating. {27:33} Everyone felt better and joined in eating. {27:34} In total, there were 276 people on the ship. {27:35} After they ate their fill, they lightened the ship by throwing the wheat into the sea. {27:36} When day broke, they couldn't recognize the land, but they spotted a bay with a sandy beach and decided to try to run the ship aground there. {27:37} So, they pulled up the anchors, let the ship go with the current, and hoisted the mainsail to the wind, heading toward the shore. {27:38} They hit a spot where two seas met and ran the ship aground. {27:39} The front got stuck, but the back was smashed by the waves. {27:40} The soldiers wanted to kill the prisoners to stop them from escaping, {27:41} But the centurion, wanting to save Paul, stopped them and ordered those who could swim to jump overboard and reach land. {27:42} The rest grabbed onto planks or broken pieces of the ship. {27:43} In the end, everyone made it safely to land.

{28:1} So, once they busted out, they figured out the island was called Melita. {28:2} And the locals were surprisingly chill, hooking us up with a fire and shelter from the rain and cold. {28:3} Paul's out here gathering firewood when a viper jumps out and bites him. {28:4} The locals start tripping, thinking Paul's a murderer who's finally getting what's coming to him. {28:5} But Paul just shakes off the snake into the fire and keeps it moving, no harm done. {28:6} They were waiting for him to swell up or drop dead, but when nothing happened, they switch it up and start calling him a god. {28:7} In that area, there was this big shot named Publius, who hooks us up, letting us crash for three days. {28:8} Paul rolls in and heals Publius's old man, who's sick with a fever and stomach issues. {28:9} Word gets out, and soon everyone on the island with illnesses is lining up to get healed. {28:10} These folks show us mad love, even loading us up with supplies when we bounce. {28:11} After three months, we hop on a ship from Alexandria, reppin' Castor and Pollux, and set sail. {28:12} We kick it in Syracuse for three days, then make moves to Rhegium. {28:13} After chilling for a day, a south wind picks up, and the next day we hit up Puteoli. {28:14} There, we link up with some believers who ask us to chill for a week before we head to Rome. {28:15} Word spreads, and the believers come out to meet us at Appii Forum and The Three Taverns. Paul sees them and gives thanks, feeling encouraged. {28:16} When we finally hit up Rome, the centurion hands over the prisoners, but Paul gets to stay in his own crib with a guard. {28:17} Three days later, Paul calls together the Jewish leaders and breaks it down for them, saying he's done nothing against his people or their customs but got snatched up by the Romans in Jerusalem. {28:18} They checked him out and found nothing worthy of death, but since the Jews were acting up, he appealed to Caesar. {28:19} He's like, "I'm only here to talk about the hope of Israel, not to accuse my own peeps." {28:20} They're like, "We haven't heard squat about you from Judea, but we're curious about your beliefs 'cause everyone's talking trash about them." {28:21-23} So they set a date, and a bunch of them roll up to Paul's spot. He spends all day breaking down the kingdom of God and persuading them about Jesus, quoting Moses and the prophets. {28:24} Some buy into what he's saying, others don't. {28:25} When they can't agree, they bounce, and Paul drops a line from Isaiah about their hard hearts. {28:26-28} Isaiah basically said they're stubborn and won't listen, so they're missing out on God's healing. Paul's like, "Fine, Gentiles get the good news then." {28:29} After dropping that bomb, the Jews split, leaving Paul to drop knowledge on whoever comes through. {28:30} Paul kicks it for two years, holding it down in his own crib, welcoming anyone who wants to chat. {28:31} He's out here preaching the kingdom of God and schooling folks about Jesus, no one's stopping him.

Romans

✦✦✦

{1:1} Yo, it's Paul, just doing my thing for Jesus, you know? Called to spread that gospel vibe. {1:2} Like, it's been promised since way back by the prophets, in all those holy scrolls and stuff. {1:3} It's all about Jesus, you feel? He's from David's line, in the flesh and all that. {1:4} But then, bam! He's declared the Son of God with major power when He rose from the dead, straight up. {1:5} And thanks to Him, we're out here spreading grace and being apostles, all about that faith life, worldwide. {1:6} Yeah, you guys in Rome are part of this too, called by Jesus, you know? {1:7} So, shout out to all the believers in Rome, you're loved by God, called to be saints. Blessings and peace from God and Jesus, y'all. {1:8} I gotta give a shoutout to my God through Jesus, 'cause your faith is making waves everywhere. {1:9} I'm telling you, I'm constantly talking you guys up to God, non-stop prayers and all. {1:10} I'm hoping and praying I can finally make it to you, with God's blessing, of course. {1:11} I'm itching to see you so I can share some spiritual vibes, you know, to help you grow strong. {1:12} It's like, we'll boost each other up with our faith, vibes bouncing back and forth. {1:13} Just so you know, fam, I've been wanting to visit y'all for a while now, but things kept popping up. I'm trying to get some good fruit outta you, like I have with other peeps. {1:14} I'm in debt to everyone, whether they're Greek or not, smart or clueless. {1:15} So, I'm ready to drop the gospel on y'all in Rome, no shame in my game. {1:16} 'Cause that gospel? It's God's power for salvation, for anyone who believes, starting with the Jews and then everybody else. {1:17} That's where God's righteousness is revealed, from faith to faith. It's like the scripture says, "The righteous live by faith." {1:18} But peeps who ain't living right, they're in for some heat from God, straight up. {1:19} See, God's been showing Himself to them, but they're ignoring it, playing foul with the truth. {1:20} It's like, God's power and divine nature are obvious in creation, so they can't play dumb. {1:21} But instead of giving props to God, they're out here tripping in their own thoughts, getting lost in their foolishness. {1:22} Claiming to be wise, they're straight up acting foolish, swapping the glory of God for idols. {1:23} They're trading in the true God for some cheap knock-offs, like humans and animals and all that. {1:24} So, God's like, "Fine, do your thing," and lets them get down and dirty with their sinful desires. {1:25} They start buying into lies and worshiping creation instead of the Creator, who's always blessed. Amen to that. {1:26} And that's why God's like, "Okay, have it your way," and lets them get caught up in messed up desires, like going against nature and all that. {1:27} Guys getting with guys, girls getting with girls, doing stuff that's just not right, and getting what's coming to 'em. {1:28} They're so not feeling God, so He's like, "Fine, do your thing," and lets them spiral into even more messed-up stuff. {1:29} They're full-on sinful, doing all sorts of shady stuff, hating on God, being spiteful, arrogant, and just plain nasty. {1:30} They're talking trash, haters of God, acting all high and mighty, inventing new ways to be wicked, disrespecting their parents, you name it. {1:31} They're clueless, breaking promises, heartless, unforgiving, and totally lacking compassion. {1:32} And they know deep down they're on a one-way trip to trouble, but they're all in, even cheering on others who are just as messed up.

{2:1} So, like, you can't be making judgments, man, because when you judge others, you're just condemning yourself, especially if you do the same stuff. {2:2} But we know God's judgment is based on truth against those who do wrong. {2:3} So, if you think you can judge others for their actions while doing the same, you really think you'll escape God's judgment? {2:4} Don't underestimate God's kindness, patience, and mercy; it's meant to lead you to change your ways. {2:5} But if you keep being stubborn and unrepentant, you're just storing up trouble for yourself on judgment day. {2:6} God will judge everyone based on what they've done. {2:7} Those who persist in doing good will receive glory, honor, and eternal life. {2:8} But those who are argumentative and disobedient to the truth will face God's wrath and anger. {2:9} Trouble and distress will come upon every soul that does evil, whether Jew or Gentile. {2:10} Glory, honor, and peace will come to everyone who does good, whether Jew or Gentile, because God shows no favoritism. {2:11} God judges everyone fairly. {2:12} Those who sin without knowing the law will perish without the law, and those who sin under the law will be judged by the law. {2:13} It's not just about hearing the law; it's about doing it that counts with God. {2:14} Even Gentiles who don't have the law naturally do what's right, showing they have the law written in their hearts and their conscience guiding them. {2:15} Their thoughts either accuse or excuse them. {2:16} God will judge everyone's secrets through Jesus Christ, as I teach in my gospel. {2:17} Hey, you call yourself a Jew, brag about the law, and boast in God. {2:18} You know what's right and approve what matters most, having been taught from the law. {2:19} You're confident in your knowledge, thinking you're a guide for the blind, a light in the darkness, {2:20} an instructor of the foolish, and a teacher of the simple, with all this knowledge and truth in the law. {2:21} But here's the thing: you teach others not to steal, but do you steal? {2:22} You preach against adultery, but do you commit adultery? {2:23} You condemn idols, but do you rob temples? {2:24} By breaking the law, you dishonor God, and the Gentiles see it and disrespect God because of you, just like it's written. {2:25} Circumcision is beneficial if you keep the law, but if you break it, circumcision means nothing. {2:26} So if an uncircumcised person obeys the law, won't their uncircumcision be regarded as circumcision? {2:27} The natural uncircumcised person who keeps the law will judge you who, despite having the written law and circumcision, break the law. {2:28} A true Jew isn't just outwardly, and true circumcision isn't just physical. {2:29} A real Jew is one inwardly, with a circumcised heart and spirit, praised by God, not just by people.

{3:1} What's the deal with being Jewish, and what's up with circumcision? {3:2} Well, it's actually pretty major, 'cause they're the ones who got the word of God. {3:3} But, like, even if some don't believe, does that mean God's word is worthless? Nah, not at all. {3:4} God's always true, even if everyone else is lying, as it says, "You're right, God, even when people judge you." {3:5} But if our screw-ups make God look good, does that mean God's not fair for punishing us? Nah, dude, that's ridiculous. {3:6} 'Cause if that were true, how could God judge anyone? {3:7} And if God's truth shines brighter because of my lies, then why am I still judged as a sinner? {3:8} Some people even say we preach doing evil to bring about good. They're totally wrong, and they'll get what's coming to them. {3:9} So, are we better than others? Heck no! We've already shown that everyone, Jews and non-Jews alike, are all messed up with sin. {3:10} Just like it says, nobody's good, not even one. {3:11} Nobody gets it, nobody's looking for God. {3:12} We've all gone off track, totally useless. No one's doing good, not a single soul. {3:13} Our mouths are like open graves, our tongues full of lies, and venom drips from our lips like snake bites. {3:14} We curse and speak bitterness. {3:15} We're quick to shed blood. {3:16} Everywhere we go, it's just destruction and misery. {3:17} We don't know the way of peace. {3:18} We don't fear God at all. {3:19} The law speaks to those under it, shutting everyone up and showing that the whole world's guilty before God. {3:20} So, following the law won't make anyone right with God; it just shows us where we messed up. {3:21} But now, God's way of being right with people is clear, even though it's been there all along, talked about by the law and the prophets. {3:22} It's all about believing in Jesus, 'cause everyone's messed up and falls short of God's glory. {3:23} But we can be made right with God for free, by his grace, through Jesus saving us. {3:24} God made Jesus a sacrifice to make up for our sins, through faith in his blood, to show that God is fair when he forgives. {3:25} This shows God's fairness, now and before, and that he's right to make right anyone who believes in Jesus. {3:26} So, where's the bragging now? It's gone, 'cause it's all about faith, not works. {3:27} So, we figure that God's for everyone, not just Jews, 'cause there's only one God, and he makes everyone right through faith. {3:28} So, it's not about following the law, it's about believing in Jesus. {3:29} Is God just for Jews? Nah, he's for everyone, 'cause there's only one God, and he makes Jews right by faith and non-Jews too. {3:30} So, does faith cancel out the law? Heck no! We're all about keeping the law.

{4:1} What's the deal with Abraham, right? Like, what did he figure out? {4:2} 'Cause if Abraham got right with God by doing stuff, then he could brag about it, but not in front of God, you know? {4:3} 'Cause the Bible says Abraham believed God, and that's what got him the righteousness points. {4:4} See, if you work for it, it's not a freebie, it's like you owe someone, you know? {4:5} But if you don't hustle for it, and just trust the One who makes things right for the ungodly, then you're good. Your faith is like your righteousness card. {4:6} Even David talks about this, how awesome it is when God just gives you a pass on your mess-ups, no work required. {4:7} Like, super blessed are those whose screw-ups are wiped clean, and their sins are covered up. {4:8} Blessed is the one God doesn't keep score on. {4:9} So, is this blessedness just for the religious insiders, or can anyone get in on it? 'Cause we're saying Abraham scored big time with faith, not with religious rituals. {4:10} And did he get this score while he was playing by the religious rules, or before he even got into all that? Before, definitely before. {4:11} He got the circumcision stamp, like an official seal of approval on his faith, even before he was circumcised, to show he's the OG faith father for everyone, not just the religious crowd. {4:12} He's not just the father of those who follow the religious rules, but also of those who follow his footsteps of faith, even if they're not part of the religious club. {4:13} 'Cause the promise wasn't about Abraham or his descendants getting it all through religious law, but through faith. {4:14} 'Cause if it's all about religious law, then faith doesn't even matter, and the promise is pointless. {4:15} 'Cause religious law just brings down the hammer, you know? Without the law, there's no rule-breaking. {4:16} So, it's all about faith, making sure the promise is solid for everyone, not just those who follow the religious rulebook, but also those who have the same faith as Abraham, who's like the faith father for us all. {4:17} Just like it says, "I've made you the father of many nations," in front of God, who can bring the dead to life and make things happen out of nothing. {4:18} So, even when things looked hopeless, Abraham kept on believing, like, "Yeah, I'm gonna have a ton of descendants," just like God said. {4:19} He didn't let his old age or Sarah's infertility shake his faith. {4:20} He totally trusted God's promise, giving props to God for keeping it real. {4:21} He was totally convinced that God could do what He promised. {4:22} And that's why God saw him as righteous. {4:23} But this story isn't just about Abraham; it's for all of us too, if we believe in the God who raised Jesus from the dead. {4:24} Jesus got handed over for our screw-ups and brought back to life so we could be made right with God. {4:25} So, yeah, it's all about Jesus, taking care of our mess so we can be made right with God.

{5:1} Since we're made right with God through faith, we have peace with Him through our Lord Jesus Christ. {5:2} Through Him, we also got access by faith into this grace where we stand, and we're stoked about the hope of God's glory. {5:3} And not only that, we're actually proud of our tough times too, because we know they build patience. {5:4} Patience leads to experience, and experience brings hope. {5:5} And hope doesn't let us down, because God's love has filled our hearts through the Holy Spirit He gave us. {5:6} 'Cause, you know, when we were weak, Christ died for the ungodly at just the right time. {5:7-8} Like, hardly anyone would die for a good person, right? But God showed His love by having Christ die for us while we were still sinners. {5:9} So, like, now that we're made right with God by Christ's blood, we're saved from His wrath through Him. {5:10} 'Cause if we were once enemies and got reconciled to God through His Son's death, we'll be saved through His life too. {5:11} And not only that, we're stoked about God through Jesus Christ, 'cause we've received reconciliation through Him. {5:12} So, like, sin entered the world through one dude, Adam, and death came because of sin. {5:13} Sin was around before the law, but it's only counted when there's a law. {5:14} Still, death ruled from Adam to Moses, even over those who didn't sin like Adam. {5:15} But the free gift isn't like the trespass. 'Cause if one dude's mistake caused many to die, God's grace and gift, through Jesus Christ, overflow to many. {5:16} The judgment followed one sin and brought condemnation, but the gift of grace follows many sins and leads to justification. {5:17} If death ruled through one man's mistake, how much more will those who receive God's grace and righteousness reign in life through Jesus Christ? {5:18} So, like, through one guy's offense, everyone was condemned, but through one man's righteousness, everyone's made right with God to have eternal life. {5:19} Through one man's disobedience, many became sinners, but through one man's obedience, many will be made righteous. {5:20} The law came so sin would increase, but where sin grew, grace overflowed even more. {5:21} So just as sin ruled with death, grace will rule through righteousness to eternal life by Jesus Christ our Lord.

{6:1} So, like, what's the deal? Should we just keep on sinning so that grace keeps on flowing? {6:2} Heck no! How can we, who are supposed to be done with sin, still live in it? {6:3} Don't you know that when we got baptized into Jesus, we got baptized into his death too? {6:4} So, when we went underwater in baptism, it's like we were buried with him, and just as Jesus was raised from the dead, we should live a new life too. {6:5} If we've joined him in his death, we'll also be raised to life like him. {6:6} Knowing this, our old selves, ruled by sin, got nailed to the cross with him so that sin's power over us would be destroyed, and we wouldn't be slaves to sin anymore. {6:7} 'Cause when you're dead, you're free from sin's grip. {6:8} If we died with Christ, we believe we'll also live with him. {6:9} Knowing that Christ was raised from the dead and won't die again, death doesn't control him anymore. {6:10} When he died, he died to break the power of sin once and for all, but now that he lives, he lives for God. {6:11} So, think of yourselves as dead to sin but alive for God in Jesus Christ. {6:12} Don't let sin run the show in your body, making you obey its desires. {6:13} Don't give in to sin by using your body parts as tools for doing wrong, but give yourselves to God, as people who've been brought back to life from the dead, and use your body parts as tools for doing what's right by God. {6:14} Sin can't control you anymore, 'cause you're not under the law but under grace. {6:15} So, just because you're not under the law but under grace, does that mean you should sin? No way! {6:16} Don't you know that when you give in to someone or something as your master, you become its slave—whether it's sin leading to death or obedience leading to righteousness? {6:17} But thank God! You used to be slaves to sin, but now you've obeyed the teaching that's been handed down to you. {6:18} So, now that you've been set free from sin, you've become slaves to doing what's right. {6:19} I'm speaking in everyday terms because you're weak in your human nature. Before, you used your body parts as slaves to do evil, but now use them as slaves to do what's right and make you holy. {6:20} When you were slaves to sin, you were free from doing what's right. {6:21} So, what good did you get from doing those things you're now ashamed of? They lead to death. {6:22} But now that you've been set free from sin and have become slaves to God, you get the benefit, and the result is eternal life. {6:23} Sin pays its employees with death, but God gives us the free gift of eternal life through Jesus Christ our Lord.

{7:1} Yo, fam, listen up, especially if you know the law, 'cause I'm about to drop some knowledge. The law is like the boss of a person as long as they're alive, you feel me? {7:2} Like, a married woman is bound to her husband by the law as long as he's alive. But if he kicks the bucket, she's free from that law. {7:3} So, if she hooks up with another dude while her hubby's alive, she's called an adulteress. But if he's dead, she's in the clear, even if she's married again. {7:4} So, my peeps, thanks to Jesus, we're dead to the law, so we can be all committed to someone new, and that's Jesus, who's risen from the dead. That's how we can bear fruit for God. {7:5} 'Cause back when we were living in the flesh, sin was running the show, making us do all sorts of messed up stuff that leads to death. {7:6} But now, we're free from that law that had us locked down, so we can live with a fresh attitude, not stuck in old ways of following rules to the letter. {7:7} So, what's the deal with the law, then? Is it evil? Heck no! It showed me what sin was, man. Like, I wouldn't even know what lust was if the law didn't say, "Hey, don't covet." {7:8} But sin took advantage of the law, stirring up all sorts of desires in me. Without the law, sin was just chilling, not bothering me. {7:9} I used to be cool without the law, but when it showed up, sin got a second wind, and I got screwed. {7:10} And the law, which was supposed to bring life, ended up bringing death. {7:11} 'Cause sin got crafty with the law, tricking me and using it to mess me up. {7:12} But the law itself is legit, man. It's holy, righteous, and good. {7:13} So, did the good thing become death for me? Heck no! It was sin playing dirty, using the good law to show how bad it really is. {7:14} 'Cause, like, I know the law is all spiritual and righteous, but I'm just a regular dude, stuck in sin. {7:15} Like, I end up doing stuff I hate, you know? I don't do what I want to do; I do the stuff I hate. {7:16} So, if I'm doing stuff I don't want to do, it's like I'm admitting that the law is cool. {7:17} But it's not really me doing it; it's the sin hanging out in me. {7:18} 'Cause I know there's nothing good in me, especially in my flesh. Like, I want to do good stuff, but I can't figure out how. {7:19} I want to do good, but I end up doing bad stuff instead. {7:20} So, if I'm doing stuff I don't want to do, it's like I'm not even the one doing it; it's the sin living in me. {7:21} I notice this law, like, when I want to do good, evil's right there with me. {7:22} 'Cause deep down, I'm all about God's law, you know? {7:23} But there's this other law in my body, fighting against my mind's law and making me a prisoner to the sin law inside me. {7:24} Man, I'm a wreck! Who's going to save me from this messed-up life? {7:25} Thank God for Jesus Christ, bro. So, with my mind, I'm all about God's law, but with my flesh, I'm stuck dealing with sin.

{8:1} If you're in Christ Jesus and walking in the Spirit, there's totally no condemnation. {8:2} 'Cause the law of the Spirit of life in Christ Jesus set me free from the law of sin and death. {8:3} 'Cause the law couldn't cut it, being weak through our flesh, so God sent His own Son in human form, condemning sin in the flesh. {8:4} This way, the righteousness of the law can be fulfilled in us, if we walk in the Spirit and not in the flesh. {8:5} Those who live by the flesh are all about fleshly things, but those led by the Spirit focus on spiritual things. {8:6} 'Cause a mind set on fleshly stuff leads to death, but a mind set on spiritual things brings life and peace. {8:7} 'Cause a fleshly mindset is against God—it doesn't play by God's rules. {8:8} So if you're all about the flesh, you can't please God. {8:9} But you're not about the flesh, you're about the Spirit, if God's Spirit lives in you. And if you don't have the Spirit of Christ, you don't belong to Him. {8:10} If Christ lives in you, sin's grip on your body is dead, but your spirit is alive because of righteousness. {8:11} And if the Spirit of Him who raised Jesus from the dead lives in you, He'll give life to your mortal bodies too. {8:12} So, my friends, we don't owe anything to our flesh to live according to its desires. {8:13} 'Cause if you live by the flesh, you'll die, but if by the Spirit you put to death the deeds of the body, you'll live. {8:14} 'Cause those led by God's Spirit are God's children. {8:15} You didn't receive a spirit of fear and slavery again; you received the Spirit of adoption, and we cry out, "Abba, Father!" {8:16} The Spirit Himself testifies with our spirit that we're God's children. {8:17} And if we're His children, we're heirs—heirs of God and co-heirs with Christ, if we suffer with Him so we can also be glorified together. {8:18} 'Cause I figure the suffering we go through now can't compare to the glory that'll be revealed in us. {8:19} Creation eagerly waits for God's sons to be revealed. {8:20} 'Cause creation was made subject to futility, not by choice, but by hope that it'll be set free from corruption into the freedom of God's children. {8:21} Creation will be liberated from its bondage to decay into the glorious freedom of God's children. {8:22} The whole creation groans and struggles in pain together until now. {8:23} Not just creation, but we too, who have the firstfruits of the Spirit, groan inwardly, waiting for our adoption and redemption of our bodies. {8:24} We're saved by hope, but if we hope for what we don't see, we wait for it with patience. {8:25} Likewise, the Spirit helps us in our weaknesses, 'cause we don't even know what to pray for sometimes, but the Spirit intercedes for us with inexpressible groanings. {8:26-27} The One who searches hearts knows the Spirit's mind because He intercedes for the saints according to God's will. {8:28} We know all things work together for good for those who love God and are called according to His purpose. {8:29} Those God foreknew, He predestined to be conformed to the image of His Son, so He could be the firstborn among many brothers and sisters. {8:30} Those He predestined, He also called; those He called, He also justified; those He justified, He also glorified. {8:31} So what do we say about all this? If God is for us, who can be against us? {8:32} God didn't spare His own Son but gave Him up for us all—how will He not also graciously give us all things with Him? {8:33} Who can bring any charge against God's chosen ones? It's God who justifies. {8:34} Who can condemn? Christ died and rose again, and He intercedes for us at God's right hand. {8:35} Who can separate us from Christ's love? Trouble, distress, persecution, hunger, nakedness, danger, or sword? {8:36} As it's written, "For Your sake we're killed all day long; we're regarded as sheep for slaughter." {8:37} No, in all these things we're more than conquerors through Him who loved us. {8:38} I'm convinced that neither death, life, angels, rulers, things present, things to come, height, depth, nor anything else in creation can separate us from the love of God in Christ Jesus our Lord.

{9:1} Yo, I'm spittin' straight facts in Christ, swear it's true, my conscience backed up by the Holy Ghost, {9:2} But yo, I'm feelin' mad heavy and sad all the time in my heart. {9:3} 'Cause I'd straight up wish I could take the hit for my peeps, my fam according to the flesh: {9:4} They're the Israelites, they got the adoption, the glory, the covenants, the law, the service to God, and the promises; {9:5} They're the ones with the ancestors, and from their line, Christ came—He's the one over everything, God forever praised. Amen. {9:6} But just 'cause they're Israelites don't mean they're all part of Israel, ya feel? {9:7} And just 'cause they're Abraham's seed don't mean they're all his kids—nah, it's Isaac's line that's the real deal. {9:8} So, peeps born from flesh aren't God's kids; it's the ones promised who count. {9:9} This promise was when God said, "I'm comin' through, and Sarah's gonna have a son." {9:10} And it's not just that—when Rebecca got pregnant, same deal, and this was all before they were even born or did any good or bad stuff. {9:11} It was to keep God's plan going, based on His choice, not on what they did, but on who He is. {9:12} He told her, "The older will serve the younger." {9:13} Like it says, "I loved Jacob, but I hated Esau." {9:14} So, what's the deal? Is God being unfair? No way. {9:15} He straight up told Moses, "I'll be merciful to whoever I wanna be merciful to, and I'll show compassion to whoever I wanna show compassion to." {9:16} So, it's not about what you want or do; it's about God's mercy. {9:17} And the Scripture says to Pharaoh, "I raised you up for this reason—to show my power and make my name known everywhere." {9:18} So, God has mercy on who He wants and makes peeps hard if He wants. {9:19} So, you might ask, "Why does He still blame us? Who can resist His will?" {9:20} But yo, who do you think you are, talkin' back to God? Can the thing made talk smack to the Maker, like, "Why'd you make me like this?" {9:21} Doesn't the potter have the right to make one pot for fancy stuff and another for junk? {9:22} So, what if God, wanting to show His anger and power, put up with the trashy peeps, even though He could've smashed them a long time ago? {9:23} And it's so He can show off His glory to the peeps He prepared for glory. {9:24} That's us, the ones He called—not just Jews, but Gentiles too. {9:25} Like He said in Hosea, "I'll call those not my peeps, my peeps, and the one not loved, my loved one." {9:26} And in the place where He said, "You're not my peeps," they'll be called children of the living God. {9:27} Isaiah shouts out about Israel, saying, "Even if there's tons of 'em, only a few will be saved." {9:28} 'Cause God's gonna wrap things up fast and set things straight, 'cause He's all about justice, and He's gonna do a quick job on the earth. {9:29} Isaiah already said, "If the Lord of Heaven's Armies hadn't left us some peeps, we'd be wiped out like Sodom and Gomorrah." {9:30} So, what's the deal? Gentiles who didn't chase after right living got it right, 'cause they grabbed onto the right living that comes from faith. {9:31} But Israel, tryin' to follow the law to be right with God, didn't get there. {9:32} Why? 'Cause they weren't after it by faith, but by the law, and they tripped over the stumbling block. {9:33} Like it says, "Check it, I'm putting a stumbling block and rock of offense in Zion, but whoever believes in Him won't be let down."

{10:1} Yo, fam, listen up, my heart's all about praying to God for Israel's salvation. {10:2} Like, they're all hyped about God, but they're not really getting it, you know? {10:3} 'Cause they're all clueless about God's righteousness and trying to do their own thing instead of rolling with God's plan. {10:4} But Jesus is like the end of the law game for being righteous for everyone who believes in him. {10:5} Moses was all about the law saying you gotta do stuff to live right, you feel me? {10:6} But being righteous by faith is like, don't stress about trying to bring Jesus down from heaven or pull him up from the dead. {10:7-8} It's all about the word, man. It's right there in your mouth and heart, preaching that faith vibe. {10:9} So, if you're down to shout out about Jesus and believe he rose from the dead, you're good to go for salvation. {10:10} 'Cause believing in your heart brings righteousness, and speaking it out loud leads to salvation.

{10:11} The scripture's all like, anyone who believes in Jesus won't be let down. {10:12} 'Cause there's no difference between Jews and Greeks, man. Same Lord for everyone who calls on him. {10:13} So, anyone who calls on the Lord's name is set for salvation. {10:14} But how can they call on him if they don't believe? And how can they believe if they haven't heard about him? And how can they hear without someone preaching? {10:15} And how can anyone preach unless they're sent? It's like, Isaiah's saying, "Check out those who spread the gospel, spreading peace and good news!" {10:16} But not everyone's on board with the gospel, you know? Isaiah's like, "Who's actually believing what we're saying?" {10:17} So, it's like, faith comes from hearing, and hearing comes from the word of God. {10:18} But for real, they've heard, man. The message went out everywhere. {10:19} So, like, Israel should've known, right? Moses was all like, "I'm gonna make you jealous by blessing others," and, "I'll tick you off with a nation that's not even on your radar." {10:20} Isaiah's going bold, saying, "I showed up for those who weren't even looking for me, man. I came through for those who didn't even ask." {10:21} But to Israel, it's like God's reaching out all day to a stubborn and argumentative bunch.

{11:1} Yo, has God straight up ditched His people? No way, dude. 'Cause I'm an Israelite, from the tribe of Benjamin. {11:2} God hasn't bailed on His people whom He knew beforehand. Don't you know what the scripture says about Elijah? How he pleaded with God against Israel, saying, {11:3} "Lord, they've killed your prophets, wrecked your altars, and I'm the only one left, and now they're after me." {11:4} But what did God say to him? "I've kept for myself seven thousand who haven't bowed down to Baal." {11:5} So, even now, there's a remnant chosen by grace. {11:6} And if it's by grace, it's not about works; otherwise, grace wouldn't be grace anymore. But if it were about works, then it wouldn't be grace; otherwise, work wouldn't be work. {11:7} So what's the deal? Israel hasn't achieved what it sought after, but the chosen ones did, and the rest were blinded {11:8} (Just like it's written, God gave them a spirit of slumber, eyes that don't see, and ears that don't hear), even to this day. {11:9} David said, "Let their table become a snare and a trap, a stumbling block and a recompense to them." {11:10} "Let their eyes be darkened so they can't see, and bend their backs forever." {11:11} So, did they stumble so they'd fall? No way! But because of their stumble, salvation came to the Gentiles, to make Israel jealous. {11:12} If their fall means riches for the world and their loss means riches for the Gentiles, how much more will their full inclusion mean? {11:13} So, speaking to you Gentiles—I'm an apostle to you guys, I take pride in my ministry. {11:14} I hope to provoke my own people to jealousy and save some of them. {11:15} 'Cause if their rejection means reconciliation for the world, what will their acceptance be but life from the dead? {11:16} If the first part of the batch is holy, so is the whole batch; and if the root is holy, so are the branches. {11:17} Some branches were broken off, and you, a wild olive tree, were grafted in among them, sharing in the nourishment of the olive tree. {11:18} Don't boast against the natural branches. If you boast, remember you don't support the root; the root supports you. {11:19} You might say, "Branches were broken off so I could be grafted in." {11:20} True, they were broken off due to unbelief, and you stand by faith. Don't get conceited; fear instead: {11:21} If God didn't spare the natural branches, don't think He'll spare you. {11:22} Consider both God's kindness and severity: He was severe with those who fell, but He's kind to you, if you continue in His kindness; otherwise, you'll be cut off too. {11:23} They can be grafted in again if they abandon unbelief, 'cause God can graft them back in. {11:24} If you, a wild olive tree, were grafted against nature into a cultivated olive tree, won't they, the natural branches, be grafted back into their own olive tree? {11:25} Bros, I don't want you to be clueless about this mystery, so you don't get cocky: Israel's partial blindness will end when the full number of Gentiles comes in. {11:26} Then all Israel will be saved, just like it's written: "The Deliverer will come from Zion and turn ungodliness away from Jacob." {11:27} "This is my covenant with them when I take away their sins." {11:28} Regarding the gospel, they might be enemies for your sake, but as far as election goes, they're loved because of the patriarchs. {11:29} God's gifts and calling are irrevocable. {11:30} Just as you were once disobedient but now have received mercy because of their disobedience, {11:31} so they too are now disobedient so they may receive mercy because of the mercy shown to you. {11:32} God has bound everyone in disobedience so He can have mercy on everyone. {11:33} Oh, the depth of God's wisdom and knowledge! His judgments are unsearchable, and His ways are beyond tracing out! {11:34} Who can know the Lord's mind? Who's been His counselor? {11:35} Who's given Him anything that He should repay them? {11:36} For from Him and through Him and to Him are all things. To Him be glory forever. Amen.

{12:1} Yo, listen up fam, I'm begging you in the name of God's mercy, present yourselves as a living sacrifice, all pure and good, which is only right. {12:2} Don't just blend in with the world—nah, transform yourselves by changing how you think, so you can know God's dope, perfect plan. {12:3} 'Cause let's be real, I'm speaking straight from the grace God gave me: Don't get all high and mighty, but keep it real and humble, 'cause God gave each of us faith in the right dose. {12:4} Just like we got many parts but make up one body, and each part has its own job. {12:5} We're all part of one big family in Christ, looking out for each other. {12:6} So if you got a gift, use it, whether it's speaking the truth or helping out. {12:7} And if you're all about giving advice or showing mercy, do it with all your heart. {12:8} Keep it real, love each other without faking it. Hate what's whack and stick to what's good. {12:9} Be chill with each other, like real siblings. Put others first and stay hype serving the Lord. {12:10} Stay pumped up with hope, stay strong when things get tough, and stay lit in prayer. {12:11} Help out others in need, and always be ready to welcome strangers. {12:12} Bless those who throw shade at you—bless and don't curse 'em. {12:13} Celebrate with those who are celebrating, and cry with those who are hurting. {12:14} Be on the same page with each other, don't try to act all high and mighty, but chill with anyone, no matter their status. Don't act like you know everything. {12:15} Don't pay back evil with more evil. Be legit in the eyes of everyone. {12:16} If possible, live in peace with everyone. {12:17} Don't take revenge, let God handle it, 'cause He said, "I got this, I'll handle it." {12:18} So if your enemy's hungry, feed 'em; if they're thirsty, give 'em a drink. By doing this, you'll make 'em feel the burn of shame. {12:19} Don't let evil take you down; instead, take down evil with good.

{13:1} Everyone needs to respect the government, 'cause it's all from God. {13:2} If you go against the government, you're going against God's order, and you're asking for trouble. {13:3} 'Cause rulers ain't there to trip good people up, but to keep the bad ones in check. Do good stuff, and they'll praise you. {13:4} The government's there to do good for you. But if you're all about doing wrong, watch out, 'cause they got the power to punish you. {13:5} So, you gotta follow the rules, not just 'cause you're scared of getting caught, but 'cause you know it's the right thing to do. {13:6} That's why you gotta pay taxes, 'cause the government's working for God all the time. {13:7} So, give everyone what you owe 'em: taxes, respect, honor—keep it real. {13:8} Owe no one anything except to love each other. Loving others fulfills all the rules. {13:9} 'Cause when you love others, you're living out God's law. {13:10} Love never hurts anyone, so if you're all about love, you're keeping it real with the law. {13:11} It's time to wake up, 'cause our rescue's closer than ever. {13:12} Night's almost over, day's almost here—so let's drop the shady stuff and suit up in God's light. {13:13} Let's live like it's daytime—no partying, no drunkenness, no messing around in bed, no fighting, no jealousy. {13:14} Instead, put on Jesus Christ, and don't even think about feeding your desires.

{14:1} Yo, if someone's not fully vibing with the faith, chill with them, but don't start arguments, you know? {14:2} Like, one person's all about eating anything, while another, who's not so sure, sticks to veggies. {14:3} Don't diss someone for what they eat, and don't judge the ones who eat differently; God's cool with everyone. {14:4} Who are you to judge someone else's servant? They answer to their own boss, and God's got their back, making sure they're good. {14:5} Some peeps think one day's special, others think every day's the same. Whatever you believe, own it. {14:6} If someone's all about a day, they're doing it for the Lord. If they're not, that's cool too. Whether they eat or not, it's all about giving thanks to God. {14:7} None of us are living for ourselves, and no one's dying for themselves either. {14:8} Whether we're living or dying, it's all for the Lord; we belong to him, no matter what. {14:9} Jesus did his thing, dying and coming back, so he's boss over the living and the dead. {14:10} So, why you judging your bro? We're all gonna stand before Christ's judgment seat. {14:11} It's written, "Everyone's gonna bow to God and confess to him." {14:12} So, each of us is gonna answer to God for ourselves. {14:13} So, let's not judge each other anymore; focus on not tripping up your bro. {14:14} I'm cool with Jesus; I know nothing's unclean by itself. But if someone thinks something's unclean, then for them, it's unclean. {14:15} If your bro's bummed out by what you eat, you're not showing love. Don't mess up someone Jesus died for. {14:16} Don't let your good vibes be seen as bad. {14:17} 'Cause God's kingdom isn't about food and drinks, but about doing right, having peace, and being stoked in the Holy Spirit. {14:18} If you're all about this, God's happy with you, and so are people. {14:19} Let's chase after things that bring peace and build each other up. {14:20} Don't wreck what God's building over food. Everything's cool, but it's bad if you eat and upset someone. {14:21} It's better not to eat meat or drink wine if it messes with your bro. {14:22} Got faith? Keep it between you and God. You're blessed if you're not guilty about what you're doing. {14:23} But if you're not sure and you eat anyway, that's not cool; if you're not doing it in faith, it's not right.

{15:1} Those of us who are strong should totally support those who are struggling, not just looking out for ourselves. {15:2} Let's all try to do what's good for our neighbors, building each other up. {15:3} 'Cause even Christ didn't just please Himself; like it says, "The insults hurled at you fell on me." {15:4} Everything written in the past was meant to teach us and give us hope through patience and the comfort of the Scriptures. {15:5} May the God of patience and encouragement help you all be united in Christ Jesus, {15:6} so you can glorify God with one voice. {15:7} So, accept each other, just as Christ accepted us to glorify God. {15:8} I'll tell you, Jesus Christ served the circumcised to confirm God's promises to the patriarchs. {15:9} And so the Gentiles can praise God for His mercy; like it's written, "That's why I'll praise you among the Gentiles and sing to your name." {15:10} And again, "Celebrate, O Gentiles, with His people." {15:11} And again, "Praise the Lord, all you Gentiles; let all the peoples extol Him." {15:12} And again, Isaiah says, "The root of Jesse will spring up, and he who rises to rule over the Gentiles; in him the Gentiles will hope." {15:13} May the God of hope fill you with joy and peace as you trust in Him, so you may overflow with hope by the power of the Holy Spirit. {15:14} I'm confident, my brothers and sisters, that you're full of goodness, filled with knowledge, and able to encourage one another. {15:15} But still, I've written boldly to you in some places to remind you, because of the grace God gave me {15:16} to be a minister of Christ Jesus to the Gentiles, serving the gospel of God, so that the Gentiles may be an acceptable offering, sanctified by the Holy Spirit. {15:17} So, I boast in Christ Jesus about what God has done through me in bringing the Gentiles to obedience by word and deed, {15:18-19} through mighty signs and wonders, by the power of the Spirit of God. From Jerusalem all the way to Illyricum, I've fully proclaimed the gospel of Christ. {15:20} Yeah, so I made it my goal to preach the gospel where Christ wasn't known, so I wouldn't build on someone else's foundation. {15:21} But as it's written, "Those who were not told about Him will see, and those who have not heard will understand." {15:22} This is why I've been delayed from visiting you. {15:23} But now, since I have no more work in these parts and have longed for many years to visit you, {15:24} when I go to Spain, I hope to see you and be helped on my way there by you, once I've enjoyed your company for a while. {15:25} Right now, I'm going to Jerusalem to serve the saints. {15:26} The believers in Macedonia and Achaia were happy to make a contribution for the poor among the saints in Jerusalem. {15:27} They were pleased to do it, and indeed they owe it to them. If the Gentiles have shared in the Jews' spiritual blessings, they owe it to the Jews to share with them their material blessings. {15:28} Once I've completed this task and delivered this contribution, I'll come to Spain and visit you on my way. {15:29} I know that when I come to you, I'll come in the fullness of the blessing of Christ's gospel. {15:30} So, I urge you, brothers and sisters, for the Lord Jesus Christ's sake and in the love of the Spirit, to join me in my struggle by praying to God for me. {15:31} Pray that I may be kept safe from unbelievers in Judea and that the service I'm bringing to Jerusalem may be acceptable to the saints there.

{15:32} Then, by God's will, I may come to you with joy and be refreshed in your company. {15:33} May the God of peace be with you all. Amen.

{16:1} Yo, gotta give a shoutout to Phebe, she's been holding it down for the crew over at Cenchrea, serving up some real church vibes. {16:2} So, when she rolls through, show her some love like true saints and help her out with whatever she needs—she's been a real MVP for many, including yours truly. {16:3} Big ups to Priscilla and Aquila, my partners in spreading the word about Jesus. {16:4} These two even put their lives on the line for me—mad respect! And shoutout to all the churches in the Gentile hood—they're feeling the love too. {16:5} Also, big love to the church fam chillin' at Priscilla and Aquila's crib. And shoutout to Epaenetus, the OG Achaia crew who came through for Christ. {16:6} Can't forget Mary, she's been putting in work with us. {16:7} Big shoutout to Andronicus and Junia, my fam and former cellmates, they've been repping for Jesus since way back. {16:8} Big love to Amplias, a real one in the Lord. {16:9} And Urbane, always got our backs, and Stachys, a true homie. {16:10} Props to Apelles, keeping it real in Christ. And sending love to everyone at Aristobulus' place. {16:11} Shoutout to Herodion, my fam. And greetings to the squad at Narcissus' crib, all about that Jesus life. {16:12} Much love to Tryphena and Tryphosa, hustling for the Lord. And shoutout to Persis, putting in major work. {16:13} Big love to Rufus, chosen for the Lord's squad, and his mom who's like family to me. {16:14} Shoutout to Asyncritus, Phlegon, Hermas, Patrobas, Hermes, and all the crew rolling with them. {16:15} Gotta show love to Philologus, Julia, Nereus, and their crew, and to Olympas, and all the saints with them. {16:16} Show some love with a holy kiss, from all the churches repping Christ. {16:17} Now, listen up fam, watch out for anyone causing drama and going against what we've been teaching you—stay away from that toxic vibe. {16:18} 'Cause those kind of people ain't about serving Jesus, they're all about serving themselves and tricking the innocent with smooth talk. {16:19} But yo, your dedication to Jesus is getting noticed everywhere, and that's what's up. Stay wise about what's good and keep it real when it comes to evil. {16:20} And soon enough, God's gonna shut down Satan's game, for real. Peace and blessings from our Lord Jesus Christ to all of you. Amen. {16:21} Timotheus, Lucius, Jason, and Sosipater, my crew, they're giving you a shoutout too. {16:22} Oh, and I'm Tertius, the one writing this message—I'm giving you a shoutout in the Lord too. {16:23} Gaius, the ultimate host, representing the whole church, sends his greetings. Erastus, holding it down as city treasurer, and Quartus, another homie, are saying what's up too. {16:24} Peace and blessings from our Lord Jesus Christ to all of you. Amen. {16:25} Big ups to the one with the power to keep you grounded in the truth of my gospel and the teachings of Jesus Christ, revealed now but been kept on the down-low since day one. {16:26} But now, it's out in the open, and it's all in line with what the prophets been saying, following the orders of the eternal God, spreading to all nations to bring them to faith. {16:27} All glory to God, who's the only one truly wise, through Jesus Christ forever. Amen.

1 Corinthians

✠✠✠

{1:1} Yo, it's Paul, called to rep Jesus by God's plan, with Sosthenes, our homie. {1:2} Shoutout to the Corinth church, all you Christ fam, and everyone else down with Jesus, whether near or far. {1:3} Big ups for grace and peace from God the Father and Jesus. {1:4} Massive thanks to God for hooking y'all up with Jesus's grace, always. {1:5} You're stacked with knowledge and words, all thanks to him. {1:6} You've been legit testified by Christ, no doubts. {1:7} So, you're not lagging in any gift, waiting on Jesus's comeback. {1:8} He's gonna keep you solid till the end, blameless when he rolls back. {1:9} God's legit, calling you to chill with his Son, Jesus Christ, our Lord. {1:10} So, fam, I'm begging you in Jesus's name: be on the same page, no beef, just pure unity in mind and judgment. {1:11} I've heard from Chloe's crew that there's some drama among y'all. {1:12} Seriously, some claim they're all about me, others about Apollos, Cephas, or Christ. {1:13} But come on, is Christ split? Was I crucified for y'all? Or did you get dunked in my name? {1:14} Glad I barely baptized any of you, except Crispus and Gaius, to dodge the "I'm Team Paul" vibe. {1:15} Oh, and also Stephanas's crew, but honestly, lost count after that. {1:16-17} 'Cause, yo, Christ sent me to preach, not dunk folks, so no flexing with fancy words that cheapen his cross. {1:18} 'Cause for those heading downhill, preaching Christ's crucifixion is nonsense, but for us saved peeps, it's God's power. {1:19} Just like it's written, God's gonna wreck the wisdom of the wise and squash the cleverness of the smart. {1:20} Where's the wise guy now? The hotshot thinker? God's made them all look dumb. {1:21} 'Cause even though humanity couldn't wise up to God's wisdom, he used preaching—yeah, preaching—to save believers. {1:22-23} Jews demand proof, Greeks want wisdom, but we're out here dropping Christ on 'em, which trips up Jews and seems dumb to Greeks. {1:24} But to those chosen, Jews or Greeks, Christ is God's power and wisdom. {1:25} 'Cause God's foolishness is wiser than humans, and his weakness is stronger than them. {1:26} Check it, fam: not many big shots, smart cookies, or VIPs are called. {1:27} But God chose the nobodies to school the somebodies, the weak to teach the strong. {1:28} He picked the lowly and despised to overthrow the high and mighty, making nothing out of something. {1:29} So, no bragging in front of God. {1:30} But in Jesus, God made us wise, righteous, holy, and redeemed. {1:31} So, if you gotta boast, do it about the Lord.

{2:1} Yo fam, when I rolled up to y'all, I wasn't about fancy talk or trying to sound wise when I laid down God's truth. {2:2} Nah, I was all about one thing—Jesus Christ, especially Him getting crucified. {2:3} I was keeping it real with y'all, feeling weak, scared, and shaking in my boots. {2:4} My talk and preaching wasn't about smooth words or human wisdom, but showing the Spirit's power. {2:5} I did that so your faith wouldn't rest on human wisdom, but on God's power. {2:6} We do drop wisdom for those who get it, not the world's wisdom or what those big shots are into that fades away. {2:7} Nah, we drop that God-style wisdom, the mysterious stuff God planned for our glory before the world began. {2:8} Those big shots didn't get it, 'cause if they did, they wouldn't have nailed the Lord of glory to a cross. {2:9} But like it says, no eye has seen, no ear has heard, and no mind can grasp what God's got for those who love Him. {2:10} God showed us this stuff by His Spirit 'cause the Spirit knows all of God's deep truths. {2:11} Just like only a person's spirit knows their thoughts, only God's Spirit knows His thoughts. {2:12} We got the Spirit of God, not the spirit of the world, so we can know what God freely gave us. {2:13} We ain't talking using human wisdom's words, but words the Holy Spirit teaches, comparing spiritual things with spiritual. {2:14} But people who aren't spiritual don't get God's Spirit stuff; it sounds dumb to them 'cause it's understood through the Spirit. {2:15} Spiritual people can judge all things, but no one can judge them. {2:16} 'Cause who can know the Lord's mind? But we got the mind of Christ.

{3:1} Yo, fam, I couldn't hit you up with deep spiritual stuff; I had to keep it basic like talking to babies in Christ. {3:2} I've been feeding you milk, not solid food, 'cause you ain't ready for it—still ain't. {3:3} 'Cause y'all acting all carnal with envy, strife, and divisions. Ain't that like acting just like everyone else? {3:4} You're all like, "I'm with Paul!" "I roll with Apollos!" Ain't that being all worldly and not spiritual? {3:5} Like, who's Paul, anyway? Who's Apollos? They're just servants who helped you believe, as the Lord gave to each of us. {3:6} I planted, Apollos watered, but God made it grow. {3:7} So, those who plant and those who water aren't special; it's God who makes things grow. {3:8} Planters and waterers are on the same team, and everyone gets rewarded based on their work. {3:9} We're God's co-workers; you're like God's field and building. {3:10} God gave me grace to be a smart builder; I laid the foundation, and others are building on it. But everyone should be careful how they build on it. {3:11} No one can lay a foundation other than Jesus Christ. {3:12} People can build on this foundation with gold, silver, precious stones, or with wood, hay, or straw. {3:13} The quality of each person's work will be shown on judgment day, 'cause fire will reveal it. {3:14} If someone's work survives the fire, they get a reward. {3:15} If someone's work burns up, they suffer loss, but they'll still be saved—just escaping through the flames. {3:16} Don't you know you're God's temple and His Spirit lives in you? {3:17} If anyone destroys God's temple, God will destroy them, 'cause His temple is sacred—and that's what you are. {3:18} Don't fool yourself; if anyone thinks they're wise by this world's standards, they should become fools to become truly wise. {3:19} 'Cause this world's wisdom is dumb to God. Like it says, "He traps the wise in their own cleverness." {3:20} And again, "The Lord knows the thoughts of the wise; they're useless." {3:21} So, don't boast about people. Everything belongs to you—whether it's Paul, Apollos, Cephas, the world, life, death, the present, or the future—all belong to you. {3:22} And you belong to Christ, and Christ belongs to God.

{4:1} Yo, peeps, think of us as Christ's crew, holding down the secrets of God. {4:2} And listen up, in this gig, you gotta be reliable, no flakiness allowed. {4:3} As for me, I ain't sweating your judgment or anyone else's—I leave that up to the big guy upstairs. {4:4} I might not know everything about myself, but that doesn't make me innocent. It's the Lord who's the real judge here. {4:5} So, don't go jumping to conclusions too soon. Wait for the Lord to bring everything into the light, then we'll see who gets the real props. {4:6} I'm dropping some truth bombs here, using myself and Apollos as examples, so you don't get all high and mighty over one person or another. {4:7} Seriously, who do you think you are? Everything you have, you got from somewhere else. So why act like it's all you? {4:8} You might think you're living large now, but you're nothing without us. I hope you really do reign, 'cause then we'll be reigning too. {4:9} Us apostles, we're like the last ones picked, getting all the tough gigs, putting on a show for the world, angels, and everyone else. {4:10} We're out here looking like fools for Christ, while you're strutting around like you got it all figured out. {4:11} We're struggling to make ends meet, getting no respect, while you're living it up. {4:12} We're busting our butts, taking all the hits, but still spreading love and forgiveness. {4:13} We're getting trashed by everyone, treated like trash, but still holding it down. {4:14} I'm not trying to shame you, just giving you a heads up, my beloved fam. {4:15} 'Cause even if you got a million teachers, you only got one spiritual parent—me, through the gospel of Christ. {4:16} So, take a page from my book and follow my lead. {4:17} That's why I sent Timotheus to you—he's my ride or die, and he's gonna remind you of how we do things in Christ, just like I do in every church. {4:18} Some of you think I won't show up, but trust me, I'll be there sooner than you think, checking out your actions, not just your words. {4:19} 'Cause it's not about talking the talk, it's about walking the walk, showing that kingdom of God power. {4:20} So, what's it gonna be? Am I gonna have to lay down the law with you, or can we do this with love and humility?

{5:1} Word on the street is, there's some serious scandal going down among you, stuff even the Gentiles wouldn't touch with a ten-foot pole. {5:2} And yet, you're acting all proud, instead of mourning and taking action to fix it. {5:3} Look, I might not be there in person, but I'm there in spirit, and I've already made up my mind about the one causing all this drama. {5:4} So when you all gather together, and with the power of the Lord Jesus, we're kicking this troublemaker out, handing them over to Satan so their spirit can still be saved. {5:5} Your bragging ain't doing you any favors. Don't you know a little bad behavior spreads like wildfire? {5:6} So, clean house and start fresh, like you're unleavened bread, 'cause Christ already paid the price for us. {5:7} Let's keep it real, celebrating with sincerity and truth, not holding onto bitterness and wickedness. {5:8} I told you before, don't hang with those messing around with immorality, greed, or idolatry—stay away from that toxic vibe. {5:9} But I'm not saying avoid everyone in the world like that, otherwise, you'd have to leave the planet. {5:10} Nah, I'm talking about anyone claiming to be part of the crew but living foul—don't even eat with them. {5:11} Why should I judge those outside the crew? You handle your business within, and let God handle the rest. {5:12} Those outside the crew, God's got them covered. But when it comes to your own, kick out the bad apples.

{6:1} Yo, can you believe some of you are taking your beefs to court instead of sorting it out with fellow believers? {6:2} Like, don't you know we're gonna be judging the world? If we're gonna do that, we should be able to handle smaller stuff too. {6:3} And get this: we're gonna judge angels, so sorting out earthly matters should be a piece of cake. {6:4} If you gotta deal with this stuff, at least let the least important folks in the church handle it. {6:5} I'm saying this to shame you: isn't there a single wise person among you who can settle disputes? {6:6} It's messed up when believers take each other to court in front of non-believers. {6:7} Seriously, y'all are totally missing the point. Why not just take the hit and move on? Why let yourselves get ripped off? {6:8} Nah, you're doing wrong by each other and cheating your own fam. {6:9} And don't be fooled: folks living foul won't inherit God's kingdom. Don't be out here acting like immoral, idol-worshipping, cheating, greedy, drunk, or verbally abusive jerks, thinking you're cool. {6:10-11} Like, some of you used to be like that, but now you're washed up, purified, and made right in the name of Jesus and by God's Spirit. {6:12} I get it, technically I could do anything, but not everything's a good idea. I won't let anything take control over me. {6:13} Food's for the stomach and the stomach for food, but God's gonna do away with both. Our bodies aren't meant for immorality but for the Lord, and he's for our bodies. {6:14} God brought Jesus back to life, and he's gonna do the same for us by his power. {6:15} Don't you realize your bodies are parts of Christ? So, should I take what belongs to Christ and join it to a prostitute? No way! {6:16} Think about it: when you hook up with a prostitute, you're becoming one flesh. {6:17} But if you're united with the Lord, you're one spirit with him. {6:18} Stay away from immorality. Every other sin a person commits is outside the body, but sexual sin is against your own body. {6:19} Don't you know your body is God's temple, and his Spirit lives in you? You don't even belong to yourselves. {6:20} God paid a high price for you, so honor God with your body and spirit, which belong to him.

{7:1} Now, onto what you wrote me about: it's cool if guys don't mess with girls. {7:2} But to avoid sexual sin, every dude should have his own girl, and every girl her own guy. {7:3} Husbands and wives should treat each other with love and respect. {7:4} The wife doesn't have authority over her own body, and neither does the husband; they belong to each other. {7:5} Don't withhold sex from each other, except by mutual agreement for a short time to focus on prayer. Then come together again so Satan won't tempt you because of your lack of self-control. {7:6} But I'm just giving advice here, not orders. {7:7} I wish everyone could be single like me, but everyone has their own gift from God, some one thing, some another. {7:8} I'm saying to singles and widows, it's cool if you stay single like me. {7:9} But if you can't handle it, get married; it's better than burning with desire. {7:10} To the married peeps, I say this—not me, but the Lord—don't split up. {7:11} If you do split, stay single or make up; and dudes, don't divorce your wives. {7:12} Now, this isn't the Lord speaking, it's me: if a believer has a non-believing spouse and they're cool living together, don't divorce them. {7:13} Same goes if a non-believer is cool living with a believing spouse. {7:14} 'Cause the believer sanctifies the non-believer, and the kids are sanctified too. {7:15} But if the non-believer bounces, let 'em; you're not slaves to the marriage in that case, but God's called us to peace. {7:16} Who knows if you'll save your spouse? {7:17} Everyone should live the life they're called to. {7:18} If you're circumcised, stay that way; if not, don't get circumcised. {7:19} Circumcision doesn't mean anything, and neither does being uncircumcised; what matters is obeying God's commands. {7:20} Stick with the life situation you were in when God called you. {7:21} If you're a slave, don't let it bother you too much; but if you can get free, take the chance. {7:22} 'Cause whether slave or free, we all belong to Christ. {7:23} You were bought with a price; don't become slaves of people. {7:24} Whatever your situation, stay connected with God. {7:25} Now, about the virgins, I don't have a direct word from the Lord, but I'll give my opinion, having received mercy from him to be faithful. {7:26} Considering the present crisis, it's good for a person to stay single. {7:27} If you're married, don't try to get out of it; if you're single, don't go rushing into marriage. {7:28} But if you do get married, you're not sinning; and if a virgin gets married, she's not sinning either. But marriage comes with challenges; I'm just trying to help you out. {7:29} 'Cause the time we have left is short: whether you have a spouse or not, live like you don't. {7:30 } Don't let your emotions rule you; whether you're happy or sad, buying or not buying, just don't get caught up in this world's ways, 'cause it's all passing away. {7:31} Live like you're not tied down by this world's stuff, 'cause it's all temporary. {7:32} I want you to be free from concerns. Unmarried folks can focus on pleasing the Lord, while married ones are busy pleasing their spouses. {7:33} There's a difference: single peeps are all about the Lord, body and soul, while married folks have to worry about worldly stuff too, pleasing their spouses. {7:34} I'm saying this for your benefit, not to trap you, but so you can focus on the Lord without distractions. {7:35} But if a guy thinks he's not treating his girlfriend right and she's getting older, he can go ahead and marry her; it's not a sin. {7:36} But if he's got self-control and isn't pressured, and he's decided to stay single, that's cool too. {7:37} So, if a guy decides to get married, it's cool; but if he decides not to, that's even better. {7:38} A wife is bound to her husband as long as he's alive, but if he dies, she's free to marry anyone she wants, as long as they're in the Lord. {7:39} But she's better off staying single, in my opinion; and I think I have God's Spirit too.

{8:1} Yo, about eating stuff sacrificed to idols—look, we all know stuff. Knowledge can make you full of yourself, but love builds others up. {8:2} If someone thinks they know it all, they really don't know squat yet. {8:3} But if you love God, He knows you, period. {8:4} When it comes to eating idol-offered stuff, idols are nothing—they're fake, and there's only one true God. {8:5} Sure, there are so-called gods out there, many in heaven and on earth, {8:6} But for us, there's only one God, the Father, who created everything, and we're all in Him, and one Lord Jesus Christ, who made everything, and we're made through Him. {8:7} But not everyone gets this; some eat the idol stuff with a guilty conscience because they think it's bad, and it messes them up. {8:8} Eating this meat doesn't make us closer to God, and not eating it doesn't make us worse off. {8:9} But be careful; don't let your freedom trip up those who are weak. {8:10} If someone sees you eating in an idol's temple and they're weak in faith, they might think it's cool to eat idol-offered stuff too. {8:11} Your knowledge could mess up a weak brother, someone Christ died for. {8:12} When you do that, you're sinning against them and against Christ. {8:13} So, if eating meat messes up my brother, I'll skip meat as long as I'm around, 'cause I don't want to cause anyone to stumble.

{9:1} Yo, am I not an apostle? Am I not free? Haven't I seen Jesus our Lord? Aren't y'all my work in the Lord? {9:2} Even if others doubt my apostleship, you know I'm the real deal. {9:3} When people question me, here's my answer: {9:4} Don't we have the right to eat and drink? {9:5} Don't we have the right to have a wife, like other apostles and the Lord's brothers, and Cephas? {9:6} Me and Barnabas—don't we have the right to not work for a living? {9:7} Who goes to war and pays their own way? Who plants a vineyard and doesn't eat its fruit? Who tends a flock and doesn't drink its milk? {9:8} Come on now, this isn't just me talking—ain't it in the law too? {9:9} The law says, "Don't muzzle the ox while it's treading out grain." God's not just talking about oxen here, right? {9:10} It's for us—for those who work can hope to enjoy the fruits of their labor. {9:11} If we've sown spiritual things among you, isn't it fair to reap some material things too? {9:12} Others use their authority over you, so why not us? But we haven't used our rights; we've endured everything so we don't hinder the gospel. {9:13} Don't you know those who serve in the temple get their food from the temple, and those who offer sacrifices share with the altar? {9:14} In the same way, the Lord commanded that those who preach the gospel should live from the gospel. {9:15} But I haven't used any of these rights. I'm not writing this to ask for them either; I'd rather die than lose my reason to boast. {9:16} Preaching the gospel isn't something to brag about; I'm compelled to do it. It's a calling, and woe to me if I don't preach it! {9:17} If I do it willingly, I get a reward, but even if I do it reluctantly, I'm still entrusted with a duty. {9:18} So what's my reward? Preaching the gospel for free, not abusing my authority. {9:19} Even though I'm free, I've made myself a servant to all to win more people. {9:20} To the Jews, I became like a Jew to win them over. To those under the law, I acted like I was under the law to win them over. {9:21} To those without the law, I acted like I was without the law (though I'm under Christ's law) to win them over. {9:22} I became weak to win the weak. I adapt to everyone to save some. {9:23} I do all this for the sake of the gospel, so I can share in its blessings with others. {9:24} Don't you know that everyone in a race runs, but only one gets the prize? Run to win it. {9:25} Athletes train hard for a perishable prize, but we aim for an imperishable one. {9:26} So, I don't run aimlessly; I fight with purpose, not like someone shadowboxing. {9:27} I discipline myself and bring my body into subjection so that after preaching to others, I myself won't be disqualified.

{10:1} Yo, fam, listen up! I don't want you clueless about our ancestors. They were all under that cloud, crossed the sea, you know the drill. {10:2} They got baptized into Moses through that cloud and sea vibe. {10:3} Same spiritual food, same spiritual drink, all from that rock following them, and that rock? It was straight-up Christ. {10:4} But yo, not everyone was making God happy. Some got wiped out in the wilderness, harsh, right? {10:5} Check it, their stories are like cautionary tales for us. Don't be craving evil stuff like they did. {10:6} And don't be idolizing like them either—remember the party they threw? {10:7} Or getting freaky like some did, leading to twenty-three thousand hitting rock bottom in one day. {10:8} And don't go messing with God, like those who got on His bad side and got bitten by snakes. {10:9} Or complaining like them, griping about everything and getting wiped out. {10:10} All that went down to teach us something, you feel me? It's a wake-up call for us now that we're at the end of the line. {10:11} So, if you think you're standing tall, watch out, you might just take a nasty fall. {10:12} Every temptation you face, it's common ground, nothing you can't handle. And God's got your back, giving you an out so you don't get wrecked. {10:13} So, my peeps, bounce from idolatry, no room for that vibe. {10:14} I'm talking to the wise ones here, you feel me? You know what's up. {10:15} That cup we bless? It's like we're vibing with Christ's blood. And that bread? It's like we're all part of Christ's crew. {10:16} We're all in this together, one squad, one vibe. {10:17} And yo, check out Israel after the flesh—those who eat the sacrifices, they're part of that altar scene. {10:18} But hold up, idols ain't nothing, and what they sacrifice? It's to demons, not God. So, don't get mixed up in that mess. {10:19} You can't sip from both cups, fam. You can't roll with the Lord and the demons at the same time. {10:20} Think we can outdo the Lord? Nah, He's way above us. {10:21} Sure, technically, everything's cool for me, but not everything's helpful. Not everything builds you up. {10:22} Don't be all about yourself, look out for each other's best interests. {10:23} Whatever's at the market? It's fair game, no need to stress about it. {10:24} 'Cause, yo, the earth and everything in it? It's all God's. {10:25} If non-believers invite you over, and you're down, eat whatever's on the table, no questions asked. {10:26} But if they bring up the sacrifice stuff, pass, for their sake and yours. {10:27} It's not about your conscience, it's about theirs. {10:28} If I'm sharing in something, why should I catch flak for it? {10:29} Whether you're eating, drinking, whatever, do it all for God's glory. {10:30} Don't cause problems for anyone—Jews, Gentiles, or fellow believers. {10:31} Just like me, I aim to please, not for my gain, but for the good of many, so they can find salvation.

{11:1} Yo, follow my lead like I'm following Christ. {11:2} Props to y'all for keeping it together and sticking to the rules I laid down. {11:3} Just so you know, Christ's the boss of every dude, dudes are the bosses of chicks, and God's the big boss of Christ. {11:4} If a guy's praying or preaching with his head covered, he's disrespecting his boss, Christ. {11:5} And if a chick's doing the same with her head uncovered, she's dissing her boss too; it's like having a shaved head. {11:6} If a chick doesn't want to cover up, might as well shave her head; but since that's embarrassing, she better cover up. {11:7} Guys shouldn't cover their heads 'cause they're made in God's image and reflect his glory, but chicks show off the glory of guys. {11:8} 'Cause dudes didn't come from chicks, but chicks came from dudes. {11:9} And dudes weren't made for chicks, but chicks were made for dudes. {11:10} That's why chicks should have something on their heads to show they're in charge, especially around angels. {11:11} But it's not like guys are all alone or chicks are either; we need each other in the Lord. {11:12} Chicks came from dudes, but dudes come from chicks; ultimately, it's all from God. {11:13} You decide: is it cool for a chick to pray to God without covering up? {11:14} Doesn't common sense tell you that it's embarrassing for a dude to have long hair? {11:15} But for a chick, long hair's like her crown; it's her natural covering. {11:16} And if anyone wants to argue about it, nah, that's not how we do things, not in God's crew. {11:17} But here's the thing, I'm not stoked about how you gather together; seems like it's more for the worse than the better. {11:18} 'Cause I've heard there are cliques among you when you come together, and I kinda believe it. {11:19} It's cool, though, 'cause differences gotta come out so the real deal can shine. {11:20} But when you gather, it's not just about grubbing down on the Lord's supper. {11:21} 'Cause some are scarfing down while others are left hungry, and some are getting wasted. {11:22} Seriously, can't you eat at home? Don't disrespect God's crew and shame those who have nothing. Can't say I'm impressed with this. {11:23} Here's the scoop I got from the Lord and passed on to you: the night Jesus got snaked, he grabbed some bread. {11:24} After giving thanks, he broke it and said, "Dig in; this is my body, wrecked for you. Remember me when you chow down." {11:25} Same deal with the cup after dinner: "This cup's the new deal, sealed with my blood. Drink up, and do it in memory of me." {11:26} Every time you eat this bread and drink from this cup, you're repping the Lord's death until he rolls back. {11:27} So if you munch on this bread or sip from this cup without the proper respect, you're disrespecting the Lord's body and blood. {11:28} Check yourself before you wreck yourself; then eat the bread and drink the cup. {11:29} If you disrespect the Lord's body and blood by scarfing it down without recognizing what it means, you're asking for trouble. {11:30} That's why some of you are sick or weak, and some have kicked the bucket. {11:31} If we checked ourselves, we wouldn't need to be checked by God. {11:32} But when God checks us, it's to keep us in line, so we don't get the same treatment as the rest of the world. {11:33} So, when you get together to eat, chill out and wait for everyone. {11:34} If you're hungry, eat at home so you don't end up in a bad spot when you come together. I'll sort out the rest when I'm around.

{12:1} Yo, peeps, let me drop some wisdom on you about spiritual stuff. I don't want you clueless. {12:2} Remember when y'all were into those lame idols, just going with the flow? {12:3} Here's the deal: if someone's speaking through God's Spirit, they ain't dissing Jesus. Only those touched by the Holy Ghost can truly recognize Jesus as the Lord. {12:4} There are all sorts of gifts, but they're all from the same Spirit. {12:5} Different ways to serve, but it's all under the same boss. {12:6} Different ways things get done, but it's the same God working it all out. {12:7} The Spirit gives each person their own way to shine, for the good of everyone. {12:8} One person might drop wisdom, another knowledge, another faith, healing, miracles, prophecy, discernment, speaking in tongues, interpreting tongues—yup, all from the same Spirit, just doing its thing. {12:9} Everyone gets their slice of the spiritual pie, as the Spirit sees fit. {12:10} Think of it like this: the body's one unit, but it's got mad parts, each doing its thing. Same with Christ, yo. {12:11} We're all baptized into this one crew, whether Jew, Gentile, slave, or free, all sipping from the same Spirit juice. {12:12} Imagine if the body was just one part—how lame would that be? Nah, we're many parts, but still one body. {12:13} The eye can't be dissing the hand, or the head saying it don't need the feet—nah, we all need each other, even the less flashy parts. {12:14} If the whole deal was just one part, where's the body at? Nah, we're many parts, but still one body. {12:15} Don't let any part feel left out—it's all part of the squad. {12:16} We gotta look out for each other, feel me? {12:17} If the body was all eyes, where's the hearing at? If it's all hearing, where's the smelling at? {12:18} But yo, God's got it all figured out, putting each part where it needs to be. {12:19} If it was all one part, where's the body at? Nah, we need variety, but still one body. {12:20} And yo, the eye can't be dissing the hand, nor the head saying it don't need the feet. Nah, every part's essential. {12:21} Even the weaker parts? They're crucial. {12:22} And those less flashy parts? They get extra love. {12:23} God balanced it all out, giving extra love where it's needed. {12:24} It's about keeping the unity, with each part looking out for the others. {12:25} When one part's hurting, we all feel it. When one part's killing it, we all celebrate. {12:26} We're all part of Christ's squad, with our own roles to play. {12:27} God's got a plan, putting different roles in the church—apostles, prophets, teachers, miracle workers, healers, helpers, leaders, and those who speak in tongues. {12:28} Not everyone's gonna be an apostle, prophet, or teacher, you feel me? {12:29} Not everyone's got the healing touch or speaks in tongues. {12:30} But yo, chase after the best gifts, and let me hit you with something even better. {12:31} Even if I could speak all the languages of the world and even the language of angels, without love, I'm just noise.

{13:1} Even if I could predict the future, unravel mysteries, have all knowledge, and even move mountains with my faith, without love, I'm nada. {13:2} Even if I give away everything I own to the poor or even give up my body, without love, it's all pointless. {13:3} Love's patient, love's kind, doesn't envy, doesn't boast, isn't rude or self-seeking, doesn't easily lose its temper, doesn't keep score of wrongs, doesn't delight in evil but rejoices in the truth. {13:4} Love sticks with you through thick and thin, believes the best, hopes for the best, and endures through it all. {13:5} Love never gives up, even when everything else fails. Prophecies, tongues, and knowledge will all fade away. {13:6} We only know bits and pieces for now, but one day, we'll know it all, just as we're fully known. {13:7} Now, faith, hope, and love—these three stick around. But the greatest of them all? Love, my friends.

{14:1} Yo, aim for love, and yeah, want those spiritual gifts, but especially aim for the gift of prophecy. {14:2} When someone speaks in a language nobody understands, they're talking to God, but to everyone else, it's a mystery. {14:3} But when someone prophesies, they're speaking to people to lift them up, encourage them, and bring them comfort. {14:4} Speaking in a language nobody knows might help you, but prophesying helps the whole crew. {14:5} I mean, speaking in tongues is cool and all, but prophecy is even better 'cause it helps the crew unless there's someone to translate. {14:6} So, if I show up speaking in tongues, what good does it do you unless I share something from God, some knowledge, prophecy, or teaching? {14:7} It's like musical instruments; if they don't make distinct sounds, how do you know what's being played? {14:8} Same with a bugle; if it doesn't sound clear, who's gonna get ready for battle? {14:9} So, unless you speak in a way people can understand, you're just talking into thin air. {14:10} There are all kinds of languages in the world, and they all mean something. {14:11} So, if I don't understand a language, I'm a foreigner to the speaker, and they're a foreigner to me. {14:12} So, since you're all eager for spiritual gifts, make sure they help the crew grow. {14:13} If someone speaks in tongues, they should pray for the ability to translate. {14:14} 'Cause if I pray in tongues, my spirit's praying, but my mind's not getting anything out of it. {14:15} So, what's the deal? I'll pray with my spirit and my mind, and I'll sing with my spirit and my mind too. {14:16} But if you bless in tongues, how can someone say "amen" if they don't understand what you're saying? {14:17} You might be giving thanks great, but the others don't get anything out of it. {14:18} I'm grateful I speak in tongues more than any of you, but in church, I'd rather speak five understandable words than ten thousand in tongues. {14:19} Bro, don't be a kid in understanding, but when it comes to being sneaky, sure, be innocent. {14:20} The Bible says, "I'll speak to this people in other languages, but they still won't listen to me." {14:21} So, tongues are a sign for unbelievers, not believers, but prophecy is for believers, not unbelievers. {14:22} If the whole church starts babbling in tongues and some newbies or unbelievers walk in, won't they think you're crazy? {14:23} But if everyone's prophesying and someone who doesn't believe or understand comes in, they'll get convinced and exposed, falling on their face in worship, knowing God's really among you. {14:24} So, bro, if everyone's prophesying and an unbeliever or newbie comes in, they'll get convicted and judged by everyone. {14:25} That's when the secrets of their heart get spilled, and they'll bow down to God, declaring he's really with you. {14:26} So, when you come together, everyone's got something: a song, a teaching, a tongue, a revelation, an interpretation. Make sure everything's for building each other up. {14:27} If someone speaks in tongues, let it be done by two or three at most, and someone should interpret. {14:28} But if there's no interpreter, keep quiet and talk to God. {14:29} Let the prophets speak one or two, and let the others judge. {14:30} If someone gets a revelation while someone else is speaking, the first one should hold off. {14:31} That way, everyone gets a chance to prophesy, and everyone learns and gets encouraged. {14:32-33} And the spirits of the prophets are under control; God's not about confusion but peace, just like in all the churches. {14:34} Women should keep quiet in church; they shouldn't speak but should be under their husbands' authority, as the law says. {14:35} If they wanna learn something, they should ask their husbands at home; it's embarrassing for women to speak in church. {14:36} Seriously, did God's word only come to you guys, or did it start with you? {14:37} If anyone thinks they're a prophet or spiritual, they should recognize what I'm saying as the Lord's command. {14:38} But if anyone ignores this, let them ignore it. {14:39} So, bros, aim to prophesy, and don't stop speaking in tongues. {14:40} Just make sure everything's done respectfully and in order.

{15:1} Hey fam, let me drop some truth about the gospel I've been preaching to you—the same one you've accepted and stand firm in. {15:2} This gospel saves you if you remember what I taught you, unless you believed for nothing. {15:3} First off, I passed on to you what I also received: Christ died for our sins according to the scriptures; {15:4} He was buried and rose again on the third day, just like the scriptures said. {15:5} He appeared to Cephas, then to the twelve; {15:6} After that, he appeared to over five hundred of us at once—most of them are still around, but some have passed on. {15:7} Later, he was seen by James and then by all the apostles. {15:8} Last of all, he appeared to me too, like I was born at the wrong time. {15:9} I'm the least of the apostles, not even worthy to be called one because I persecuted the church. {15:10} But by God's grace, here I am, working harder than all of them—though not me, it's the grace of God with me. {15:11} So whether it's me or them, this is what we preach, and this is what you believed. {15:12} Now if they're out here preaching Christ rose from the dead, why are some of you saying there's no resurrection of the dead? {15:13} If there's no resurrection, then Christ didn't rise. {15:14} And if Christ didn't rise, our preaching is useless, and so is your faith. {15:15} We'd be liars claiming God raised Christ if that didn't happen. {15:16} If the dead don't rise, then Christ didn't rise; {15:17} And if Christ didn't rise, your faith is pointless, and you're still in your sins. {15:18} Those who died in Christ are lost forever. {15:19} If our hope in Christ is only for this life, we're the saddest people around. {15:20} But Christ has risen from the dead, the first to be raised from death. {15:21} Death came through one man (Adam), and the resurrection of the dead comes through one man (Christ). {15:22} Just like everyone dies because of Adam, everyone will be made alive because of Christ. {15:23} But each in their own order: Christ first, then all who belong to him when he comes back. {15:24} Then the end will come when Christ hands over the kingdom to God the Father, after putting down all rule, authority, and power. {15:25} Christ must reign until all his enemies are under his feet. {15:26} The last enemy to be destroyed is death. {15:27} God has put everything under Christ's feet—except Himself. {15:28} Once everything is under Christ, then even Christ himself will be subject to God, so God will be everything to everyone. {15:29} If there's no resurrection, what's the point of those being baptized for the dead? {15:30} Why do we face danger every hour if there's no hope beyond this life? {15:31} I swear by your joy in Christ Jesus our Lord, I face death daily. {15:32} If I fought wild beasts at Ephesus, what's the point if the dead don't rise? Let's party if there's no tomorrow. {15:33} Don't let bad company mess up your good habits. {15:34} Wake up and do what's right; some of you don't even know God—I say this to shame you. {15:35} But someone will ask, "How are the dead raised? And with what kind of body do they come?" {15:36} You fool! What you sow doesn't come to life unless it dies. {15:37} When you sow, you don't plant the body that will be, but just a seed, maybe of wheat or something else. {15:38} God gives it a body as he determines, and to each seed its own body. {15:39} All flesh isn't the same: humans have one kind, animals have another, birds have another, and fish have another. {15:40} There are heavenly bodies and earthly bodies; the glory of heavenly bodies is different from earthly bodies. {15:41} The sun, moon, and stars each have their own glory; stars differ in brightness. {15:42} It's the same with the resurrection of the dead: buried in decay, raised in glory; {15:43} Buried in weakness, raised in power; {15:44} Buried as a natural body, raised as a spiritual body. There's a natural body and a spiritual body. {15:45} It's written, "The first man Adam became a living soul"; the last Adam (Christ) is a life-giving spirit. {15:46} First comes the natural, then the spiritual. {15:47} The first man is from the earth, earthly; the second man is from heaven (the Lord). {15:48} Just like the earthly, so are those who are earthly; just like the heavenly, so are those who are heavenly. {15:49} Since we've borne the image of the earthly, we'll also bear the image of the heavenly. {15:50} I'm telling you, fam, flesh and blood can't inherit God's kingdom, and decay can't inherit incorruption. {15:51} Listen up, I'll tell you a secret: not all of us will die, but we'll all be transformed— {15:52} In an instant, when the last trumpet sounds; the dead will be raised imperishable, and we'll be changed. {15:53} This perishable must put on imperishability, and this mortal must put on immortality. {15:54} When this perishable is clothed with imperishability and this mortal with immortality, then the saying will come true: "Death is swallowed up in victory." {15:55} Death, where's your sting? Grave, where's your victory? {15:56} The sting of death is sin, and the power of sin is the law. {15:57} But thanks be to God, who gives us the victory through our Lord Jesus Christ. {15:58} So, my beloved fam, stand firm and unshakeable, always giving yourselves fully to the work of the Lord, knowing that your work in the Lord isn't for nothing.

{16:1} Yo, about collecting cash for the saints, I've told the Galatian churches the deal—same goes for y'all. {16:2} Every Sunday, stash some cash, based on what you've got. That way, no last-minute scrambling when I roll through. {16:3} When I swing by, whoever you trust, send 'em with your dough to Jerusalem. {16:4} If it makes sense for me to tag along, they'll roll with me. {16:5} I'm heading your way after hitting up Macedonia. {16:6} Might chill with y'all for a bit, even crash through winter, if you're down to see me off on my next move. {16:7} Won't catch me on the road this time, but I'm hoping to chill with you, if the big guy upstairs is cool with it. {16:8} But I'll be kicking it in Ephesus until Pentecost. {16:9} Big opportunities but also plenty of haters out here. {16:10} If Timotheus shows, treat him right—dude's grinding for the Lord, just like me. {16:11} Don't diss him, send him my way in peace. Got the homies waiting for him. {16:12} About Apollos, I was hoping he'd roll with me, but he's not feeling it right now. Maybe later, when it fits his schedule. {16:13} Stay woke, stand firm in the faith, be brave, be real. {16:14} Whatever you do, do it with love. {16:15} Shout out to Stephanas' crew—they're OG saints in Achaia, fully committed to serving others. {16:16} Show them respect, and everyone else putting in work with us. {16:17} Big ups to Stephanas, Fortunatus, and Achaicus—they filled in the gaps you left empty. {16:18} They brought good vibes to me and you—give props where it's due. {16:19} Churches in Asia sending love. Aquila, Priscilla, and their home church send mad love too. {16:20} All the crew say what's up. Spread love with a holy kiss. {16:21} Signed, sealed, delivered by yours truly, Paul. {16:22} If anyone ain't down with Jesus, they out. {16:23} Peace out, Jesus' grace be with you. {16:24} Love to you all, in Christ Jesus. Amen.

2 Corinthians

✚✚✚

{1:1} Yo, it's Paul, Jesus' apostle 'cause God wanted it, with my bro Timothy, hittin' up the church in Corinth and all the holy ones in Achaia. {1:2} Yo, peace and grace from God our pops and Jesus. {1:3} Big ups to God, Jesus' dad, the one full of mercy and comfort. {1:4} He's the one who gets us through tough times so we can help others out too. {1:5} When we suffer like Jesus did, we also get his comfort. {1:6} Whether we're going through hard times for your sake or being comforted, it's all for your benefit. {1:7} We're hopeful for you 'cause you suffer like us, so you'll get the same comfort. {1:8} Bros, we gotta fill you in on the hard times we had in Asia, man, it was heavy, like way too much, we were even thinkin' we might not make it. {1:9} But that just made us rely on God, who can even raise the dead. {1:10} He saved us from certain death, and we trust he'll keep on saving us, with your help through prayer. {1:11} And when God pulls through, you can join in thanking him for us. {1:12} Our conscience is clear, we've kept it real and sincere, not relying on our own smarts but on God's grace, especially when we were with you. {1:13} We ain't writing anything you can't understand or agree with, and I know you'll keep that up till the end. {1:14} You've already shown us some love, and we'll all be rejoicing together when the Lord Jesus shows up. {1:15} I was planning to visit y'all twice, first on my way to Macedonia and then when I came back, so you'd get blessed twice. {1:16} I was gonna visit you guys first, then head to Macedonia, and afterward, you could help me on my way to Judea. {1:17} So, when I made these plans, do you think I was just blowing smoke or making promises I couldn't keep? {1:18} Nah, bro, God's true, and so are we; we don't go back on our word. {1:19} Jesus Christ, the Son of God, who we preached to you, wasn't wishy-washy; he's the real deal. {1:20} Every promise God made finds its yes in Jesus; that's why we praise him. {1:21} God's the one who makes us strong in Jesus and gives us his Spirit as a guarantee. {1:22} He's sealed us and put his Spirit in our hearts as a down payment. {1:23} I swear to God, I didn't come to Corinth to spare y'all, not 'cause I'm in charge of your faith, but to help you be happy; you stand by faith.

{2:1} I decided not to visit y'all in sadness again. {2:2} 'Cause if I make you sad, who's gonna cheer me up? {2:3} I wrote to you like this 'cause I didn't wanna be bummed out when I visited, I wanna be proud of y'all, and I'm confident that you guys bring me joy, just like I bring you joy. {2:4} I wrote to you when I was hurting, with a heavy heart and lots of tears, not to make you sad, but to show you how much I love you. {2:5} If someone's caused grief, they haven't just grieved me, but all of us, but I ain't laying it on too thick. {2:6} The punishment that dude got from the majority is enough. {2:7} So now, instead of laying into him, you gotta forgive and comfort him, or else he might get overwhelmed with sorrow. {2:8} So, I'm asking you to show him love and support. {2:9} I wrote to see if you guys are really obedient in everything, and forgiving this guy is part of that test. {2:10} If I've forgiven anything, I've done it for you, and I did it in the name of Christ. {2:11} We ain't ignorant of Satan's tricks; we don't wanna give him an inch. {2:12} When I went to Troas to spread the good news about Christ, and God opened a door for me, {2:13} I was stressed 'cause I couldn't find my bro Titus; so, I said goodbye and went to Macedonia. {2:14} Big shoutout to God, who always helps us win through Jesus, spreading the knowledge of him everywhere. {2:15} We're like a sweet smell to God, spreading the knowledge of Christ to those who are saved and to those who aren't. {2:16} To some, we're the smell of death leading to death, but to others, we're the smell of life leading to life. And who's up for handling that? {2:17} We ain't like those who twist God's word for their own gain; we're straight up, coming at you from God, in Christ's sight.

{3:1} Yo, do we really need to keep patting ourselves on the back or get letters of recommendation from others? Nah, you all are our living proof, known and read by everyone. {3:2} You're like a letter from Christ, not written with ink but with the Spirit of God on our hearts—real talk, not stone tablets. {3:3} Our confidence comes from Christ toward God, not from our own abilities; it's all from God. {3:4} He made us able to serve under the new covenant, not by the letter of the law but by the Spirit, 'cause the law kills, but the Spirit brings life. {3:5} Remember that epic time when Moses had to cover his face because it was so lit? Yeah, the old covenant was lit, but the new one with the Spirit is even more fire. {3:6} If the old covenant brought condemnation, the new one brings righteousness in even greater glory. {3:7} The Lord is the Spirit, and where the Spirit is, there's freedom. {3:8} And all of us, with unveiled faces, reflect the glory of the Lord and are being transformed into his image by the Spirit.

{4:1} So, since we've received this amazing ministry through God's mercy, we don't give up. {4:2} We've ditched the shady stuff and don't manipulate God's word; we keep it real, showing the truth to everyone's conscience before God. {4:3} If our message is hidden, it's hidden to those who are lost, blinded by the god of this world. {4:4} We're not about ourselves but about Christ Jesus the Lord, serving you for Jesus' sake. {4:5} God's light has shined in our hearts, revealing the knowledge of his glory through Jesus Christ. {4:6} We have this amazing treasure in weak vessels to show God's power, not ours. {4:7} We may face all kinds of troubles, but we're not crushed; we're confused sometimes but not in despair. {4:8} We get persecuted but not abandoned; knocked down but not destroyed. {4:9} We carry in our bodies the death of Jesus so that his life may also be seen in us. {4:10} We're always facing death for Jesus' sake, so his life is revealed in us. {4:11} Our suffering leads to life for you. {4:12} We keep the faith and speak because we believe in the one who raised the Lord Jesus, who will also raise us with Jesus and present us to God. {4:13} Everything is for your sake, so that grace might spread through more people, bringing glory to God. {4:14} So, we don't give up; even though our bodies are wasting away, our spirits are renewed every day. {4:15} Our temporary troubles are working for us a glory that will last forever, focusing on what's eternal rather than what's seen.

{5:1} So, like, we know that if this body we're in gets wrecked, we got a sick setup from God, like, a heavenly crib that's eternal. {5:2} We're all just like, ugh, can't wait to ditch this body and get decked out in our heavenly one. {5:3} Like, we don't wanna be caught naked, you know? {5:4} 'Cause we're not looking to be stripped down, but to be fully suited up, ditching mortality for life. {5:5} It's all God's plan, man. He's given us a taste of the Spirit as a down payment. {5:6} So, we're chill, knowing that while we're chilling in this body, we're not fully with the Lord. {5:7} 'Cause, you know, we walk by faith, not by what we see. {5:8} We're cool with ditching this body to be with the Lord. {5:9} We're grinding, whether we're here or not, to be accepted by Him. {5:10} 'Cause, like, we're all gonna stand before Christ's judgment seat, and it's all gonna come out, good or bad. {5:11} And knowing what's up with the Lord, we try to persuade people. But at the end of the day, God knows us, and I hope you do too. {5:12} We ain't trying to hype ourselves up to you, but we're giving you something to brag about on our behalf when you face those who only care about appearances, not the heart. {5:13} Whether we're all out there or keeping it real, it's for God's sake or yours. {5:14} Christ's love drives us, because we're convinced that if He died for everyone, then everyone was dead, right? {5:15} And He died so we'd stop living for ourselves and start living for Him, the One who died for us and came back to life. {5:16} So, from now on, we don't judge people by what they look like, not even Christ. {5:17} If you're in Christ, you're a whole new person—old stuff is gone, everything is fresh. {5:18} And it's all from God, who reconciled us to Himself through Jesus and hooked us up with the job of spreading that reconciliation. {5:19} He was all about bringing the world back to Him, not holding their mess-ups against them, and He's put us in charge of sharing that message. {5:20} So, we're like Christ's reps, begging you to make things right with God. {5:21} 'Cause He made Christ take on all our junk, even though He was sinless, so we could be made right with God through Him.

{6:1} So, since we're all in this together, we're begging you not to waste the grace God's given you. {6:2} Like, God's ready to hook you up, right here, right now. Don't sleep on it. {6:3} Don't do anything sketchy that could mess up the ministry's rep. {6:4} But in everything, show that we're legit servants of God, handling everything with patience, even when things get tough. {6:5} We've been through it all—beatings, jail time, riots, hard work, sleepless nights, fasting; {6:6} but also through being pure, knowledgeable, patient, kind, and genuinely loving. {6:7} We're spreading truth by God's power, armed with righteousness. {6:8} We've seen it all—respect and disrespect, good news and bad news; people think we're fake, but we're real. {6:9} We might seem like nobodies, but people know us; we've been beaten down but not knocked out; {6:10} we're sad sometimes, but always happy; we might look broke, but we make others rich; we might have nothing, but we got everything. {6:11} Yo, Corinthians, we're keeping it real with you. We're opening up to you, our hearts are wide open. {6:12} We're not holding back, but it seems like you are. Time to step it up, my dudes. {6:13} So, like, we're showing you love, and you should too. {6:14} Don't get tangled up with people who don't believe. Righteousness and wickedness don't mix, and neither does light with darkness. {6:15} Christ and the devil can't vibe together, and believers and unbelievers don't mix. {6:16} God lives in you, and you're His temple. He's like, "Separate yourselves and keep it clean, and I'm all yours." {6:17} So, leave that shady stuff behind, and God will welcome you in. {6:18} He'll be your Dad, and you'll be His kids. That's what the Lord Almighty says.

{7:1} So, fam, with these promises, let's scrub ourselves clean from all the junk, both in our bodies and in our souls, and let's level up in holiness, showing mad respect for God. {7:2} Yo, accept us; we haven't messed with anyone, we haven't twisted anyone up, we haven't ripped anyone off. {7:3} I ain't saying this to put you down; I've said it before, you're in our hearts, whether we're alive or dead. {7:4} I can speak my mind with you, I can boast about you; I'm feeling good, I'm super stoked even in all the hard times we're going through. {7:5} 'Cause when we hit up Macedonia, it was rough, man; battles outside, fears inside. {7:6} But God, who cheers up the downcast, cheered us up with Titus showing up; {7:7} And not just him showing up, but also with the encouragement he got from you guys, telling us how much you missed us, how sad you were, how much you wanted to see me; that made me even happier. {7:8} 'Cause even though my letter made you sad, I ain't sorry now, even though I was before, 'cause I see that it made you sad for a bit. {7:9} Now I'm happy, not 'cause you got sad, but 'cause you got sad in a good way, so you wouldn't suffer any loss because of us. {7:10} 'Cause when you're sad in a good way, it leads to changing your ways and getting saved, and that's not something you regret. But being sad about worldly stuff leads to death. {7:11} See, when you got sad in a good way, it made you careful, cleared your name, made you mad at the wrong you did, scared you straight, made you wanna make things right, got you pumped to fix things. You proved yourselves innocent in everything. {7:12} So, when I wrote to you, it wasn't because of the dude who did wrong or the dude who got wronged, but so you could see how much we care about you in God's eyes. {7:13} So, we were comforted by your comfort; and even more, we were stoked by Titus' joy, 'cause you guys cheered him up big time. {7:14} 'Cause if I talked you up to him, I ain't embarrassed; just like I told you the truth, what I said to Titus turned out to be true too. {7:15} And he's feeling the love for you even more, remembering how respectfully you treated him, with fear and trembling. {7:16} So, I'm happy I can trust you guys in everything.

{8:1} And now, fam, let me tell you about the amazing stuff God's done for the churches in Macedonia; {8:2} Even though they were going through some serious tough times, they were still super joyful, even though they were dirt poor, they gave generously. {8:3} They gave as much as they could, and even more than they could, willingly. {8:4} They begged us to take their gift and help out the saints. {8:5} And they didn't just give money; first, they gave themselves to the Lord and then to us, following God's will. {8:6} They even asked Titus to help finish what he started with you guys. {8:7} So, since you're all about faith, speaking up, knowing stuff, being diligent, and loving us, make sure you're all about this too. {8:8} I ain't giving you orders; I'm just bringing it up because of how eager other people are and to test how genuine your love is. {8:9} 'Cause you know what Jesus did for us, right? Even though he was rich, he became poor for us, so we could become rich through him. {8:10} So, here's my advice: since you were so eager to start this last year, you should finish it up now too. {8:11} So, get to it and finish what you started, just like you wanted to back then. {8:12} 'Cause as long as you're willing, it's all good, even if you can't do as much as you want to. {8:13} I ain't saying you should have it easy and others should have it hard; I'm saying everyone should have what they need, so it's fair for everyone. {8:14} 'Cause right now, you've got plenty, and others are struggling, but maybe later they'll have plenty, and you'll be the ones needing help. That's equality. {8:15} Like it says, if someone had a lot, they didn't have leftovers, and if someone had a little, they didn't run out. {8:16} Big shoutout to God for putting the same care for you in Titus' heart as he has in ours. {8:17} 'Cause he was all about it, and he went to you on his own, no pushing from us. {8:18} And we've sent with him the brother who's well known for spreading the gospel in all the churches. {8:19} And not just him; he was also chosen by the churches to travel with us and help out with this gift, to honor the Lord and show off your eager spirit. {8:20} We're trying to avoid any suspicion about how we handle all this money. {8:21} We wanna do what's right, not just in God's eyes but in everyone's eyes. {8:22} And we've sent with them our brother who's tested and proved many times over, and now even more because of how much faith we have in you guys. {8:23} If Titus or any of the other brothers ask about you, they're messengers of the churches and a credit to Christ. {8:24} So, show them and the churches how much you love us and how proud we are of you.

{9:1} Yo, I don't even need to write much about helping out the saints 'cause I know you're all about it. I've been bragging to the folks in Macedonia about how Achaia was ready a year ago, and your enthusiasm got so many hyped. {9:2} But I've sent the brothers just to make sure our bragging about you isn't for nothing; you better be ready when they show up, or we'll both be embarrassed after all that boasting. {9:3} So, I urged the brothers to go ahead of me and collect your generous gift as you planned, not out of greed but out of kindness. {9:4} Remember, sowing sparingly means you'll reap sparingly, but sow generously and you'll reap generously. {9:5} Everyone should give what they've decided in their heart, not reluctantly or under pressure, 'cause God loves a cheerful giver. {9:6} And God can make all grace overflow to you, so you'll have everything you need for every good work. {9:7} Remember, it's written that those who give to the poor will be blessed forever. {9:8} God gives us what we need and multiplies our seed for sowing. {9:9} This generosity causes thanksgiving to God and glorifies him for your commitment to the gospel and sharing with others. {9:10} Thanks be to God for his indescribable gift.

{10:1} Now, I Paul, urge you by the gentleness and humility of Christ—I might seem weak when I'm with you, but I'm bold when I'm away. {10:2} I beg you not to make me be bold when I'm with you against those who think we're just human. {10:3} Even though we live in the world, our battles aren't worldly. {10:4} Our weapons are powerful through God for tearing down strongholds, destroying false arguments, and bringing every thought into obedience to Christ. {10:5} We're ready to punish disobedience when your obedience is complete. {10:6} Don't judge by appearances; if anyone thinks they belong to Christ, they should remember that we do too. {10:7} Even though I boast about our authority, it's for building up, not tearing down. {10:8} I don't want to intimidate you by letter; some say my letters are weighty and intimidating, but in person, they say I'm weak and my words are nothing. {10:9} Let them know that my actions will match my words, whether near or far. {10:10} We're not competing with others or boasting beyond our limits; we've been assigned a measure of authority by God to reach even you. {10:11} So, whether by letter or in person, we're the real deal. {10:12} We're not comparing ourselves to others; those who do aren't wise. {10:13} We won't boast beyond our limits but stick to the work God has given us. {10:14} We're not boasting about work done by others; we hope to reach new areas with the gospel. {10:15} Let anyone who boasts do so in the Lord, not themselves. {10:16} We're eager to preach beyond you, not boasting about someone else's work. {10:17} It's not about self-commendation; it's about being approved by the Lord.

{11:1} Yo, I wish you could just chill with me for a bit, even though I'm gonna sound kinda silly, so, like, just hear me out, okay? {11:2} I'm totally protective of you, like, in a godly way, 'cause I'm committed to hooking you up with Christ, like presenting you as this pure, loyal homie to Him. {11:3} But I'm legit worried that, just like Eve got played by that snake, you might get led astray from the simple truths of Jesus. {11:4} 'Cause, like, if some dude rolls in preaching a different Jesus, or if you start buying into some other vibe, or even a different gospel, I'm like, "Bro, really?" {11:5} Just so you know, I'm not lagging behind those top apostles. {11:6} Even if I'm not the smoothest talker, I know my stuff, and you've seen that firsthand. {11:7} Did I mess up by, like, not asking for money when I could've, just so you'd feel important 'cause I gave you the scoop on God for free? {11:8} I didn't hustle other churches for cash to serve you. {11:9} When I was broke and chilling with you, I didn't sponge off anyone. The crew from Macedonia hooked me up, and I made sure not to be a burden to you, and I'll keep it that way. {11:10} You can trust me, like, the real deal about Christ is in me, and no one's gonna shut me down when I boast about it in Achaia. {11:11} Why? 'Cause I don't love you? God knows that's not true. {11:12} But what I'm doing, I'm doing to shut down those haters who love to talk smack; I want them to get exposed just like us. {11:13} 'Cause those fake apostles are, like, total phonies, acting like they're all about Christ. {11:14} But that's no shocker, 'cause even Satan can front as an angel of light. {11:15} So, it's no biggie if his crew acts like they're all about righteousness; in the end, they'll get what's coming based on their actions. {11:16} Lemme say it again: don't think I'm stupid. But even if you do, just roll with it for a bit, so I can flex a little.

{11:17} What I'm saying isn't, like, straight from the Lord, but I'm just being a bit silly here, boasting with confidence. {11:18} Since so many brag about worldly stuff, I'll join in too. {11:19} You're cool with putting up with fools, thinking you're wise and all. {11:20} But seriously, you're letting people walk all over you, even if they're treating you like trash, taking advantage, or straight-up disrespecting you. {11:21} I'm saying this like you're looking down on us 'cause we seem weak. But however bold these other guys are (and yeah, I'm talking crazy now), I'm just as bold. {11:22} Are they Hebrews? So am I. Israelites? Same. Descendants of Abraham? Yup, that's me. {11:23} They're preaching Christ? Well, I'm going all out, working harder, getting beat up more, thrown in jail more often, and staring death in the face way too many times. {11:24} I've been whipped by the Jews five times, just shy of forty lashes each time. {11:25} Beaten with rods three times, stoned once, shipwrecked three times, spent a night and a day in the deep. {11:26} I've traveled a lot, been in danger from rivers, robbers, my own people, foreigners, in cities, in the wild, at sea, and with fake believers. {11:27} I've been tired, in pain, stayed up late, hungry, thirsty, gone without food, cold, and naked. {11:28} On top of all that, I deal with the daily stress of looking after all these churches. {11:29} If someone's struggling, I'm right there with them. If someone's hurt, it hurts me too. {11:30} If I gotta brag, I'll brag about how I handle my weaknesses. {11:31} God, who's blessed forever, knows I ain't lying. {11:32} When I was in Damascus, the governor was after me, but I got away by sneaking out through a window in a basket.

{12:1} Yo, it's not really my thing to boast, but let's get real and talk about the visions and revelations from the Lord. {12:2} So, there was this dude I knew in Christ about fourteen years back, don't know if he was in his body or out of it, only God knows that, but he got caught up to the third heaven, no joke. {12:3} And I knew this same dude, still not sure if he was in or out of his body, only God knows that, {12:4} But he got taken up to paradise and heard some wild stuff, stuff that's not even cool to talk about. {12:5} I could brag about that dude, but I won't brag about myself, just my weaknesses. {12:6} 'Cause even if I wanted to brag, I wouldn't be dumb about it 'cause I'd tell the truth. But for now, I'll chill, so nobody thinks I'm more than what they see or hear from me. {12:7} And just to keep me from getting a big head because of all the dope stuff I've seen, I got this thorn in my flesh, this pain in my side, sent by Satan to mess with me and keep me humble. {12:8} I begged the Lord three times to take it away, but he told me, "Nah, my grace is all you need; my power works best in weakness." So, I'm cool with being weak, 'cause then Christ's power can kick it with me. {12:9} That's why I'm cool with all the hard stuff, insults, tough times, persecution, and suffering I go through for Christ's sake; 'cause when I'm weak, that's when I'm really strong. {12:11} Yo, I feel stupid bragging like this, but you guys forced me into it. I should've got props from you, 'cause I'm not any less legit than those super apostles, even though I'm nothing special. {12:12} You saw the signs of a true apostle when I was with you, all the patience, miracles, and powerful stuff. {12:13} So, what were you missing out on compared to other churches, huh? Only thing is, I didn't burden you with my needs. My bad for that. {12:14} This is the third time I'm coming to you, and I won't be a burden; I ain't after your stuff, I'm after you. Parents should be saving up for their kids, not the other way around. {12:15} I'll gladly spend everything I have and even wear myself out for you, even if you don't love me as much. {12:16} I didn't trick you when I sent Titus and the bro with him, did I? We were on the same page, right? {12:17} Did I use any of the guys I sent to make a profit off you? Nah, we all worked together in the same spirit and walked the same path. {12:18} So, when I wanted Titus to come, I sent the bro with him. Did Titus take advantage of you? Didn't we both do things the same way and with the same spirit? {12:19} You think we've been making excuses this whole time? Nah, we've been talking straight with God in Christ, and everything we do, fam, is for your growth. {12:20} I'm kinda worried, though, that when I come, you won't be who I hoped you'd be, and you'll find me to be someone you don't like, and then we'll end up with all kinds of drama: arguments, jealousy, anger, fights, gossip, arrogance, chaos. {12:21} And then when I come back again, God might humble me among you, and I'll be grieving for all those who've been sinning and haven't turned from their messed-up ways.

{13:1} This is the third time I'm coming to you. Every word needs to be confirmed by at least two or three witnesses. {13:2} I've warned you before, and I'm warning you again, even though I'm not there in person this time, but writing to all who've messed up before and to everyone else: if I come again, I won't go easy on you. {13:3} You're looking for proof that Christ is speaking through me? You're gonna find it, all right, 'cause he's powerful in you, not weak. {13:4} Yeah, even though he got crucified 'cause he seemed weak, he's all about that God-power now. And we might seem weak, but we'll live with him 'cause of God's power for you. {13:5} Check yourselves, see if you're really in the faith. Test yourselves. Don't you know yourselves, if Jesus Christ is really in you? Unless you're, like, totally fake. {13:6} But I trust that you'll see we're not fake. {13:7} I'm praying to God that you don't do anything wrong, not so we look good, but so you do the right thing, even if it makes us look bad. {13:8} We can't do anything against the truth, only for it. {13:9} We're happy when we're weak, and you're strong; and what we really want is for you to be perfect. {13:10} That's why I'm writing this while I'm away, 'cause when I come, I might have to come down hard on you, according to the authority the Lord gave me to help you grow, not to tear you down. {13:11} So, yeah, fam, peace out. Be dope, be chill, be united, live in peace, and the God who's all about love and peace will kick it with you. {13:12} Greet each other with a holy kiss. {13:13} All the saints say what's up to you. {13:14} May the Lord Jesus Christ's grace, God's love, and the Holy Spirit's presence be with all of you. Amen.

Galatians

✚✚✚

{1:1} Yo, it's Paul, an apostle, not 'cause of people or anything, but 'cause Jesus Christ and God the Father, who raised him from the dead, said so. {1:2} Shoutout to all my homies with me, hitting up the churches in Galatia. {1:3-5} Yo, may you all get that grace and peace from God the Father and our Lord Jesus Christ, who straight up sacrificed himself for our sins, freeing us from this messed-up world, just like God and our Father wanted. All the glory to them forever. Amen. {1:6} Yo, I'm buggin' out that you're already jumping ship from the one who called you to roll with Christ's grace to some other gospel. {1:7} But let's get it straight, there ain't no other gospel, just some people trying to stir up trouble and twist Christ's message. {1:8} And let me tell you, even if we, or some angel from heaven, starts preaching anything different than what we've told you, they can take a hike. {1:9} I've said it before, I'm saying it again: If anyone preaches a different gospel, they're cursed. {1:10} Am I trying to win over people, or God? Am I trying to please people? Nah, if I was, I wouldn't be serving Christ. {1:11} But let me make it clear, the gospel I'm preaching ain't something I got from humans; it's straight from Jesus Christ himself. {1:12} I didn't learn this stuff from any human teacher; I got it through a revelation from Jesus Christ. {1:13} Remember how I used to be all about the Jewish tradition, hardcore persecuting the church? {1:14} I was way ahead in the Jewish game, more zealous than anyone else, all about my ancestors' traditions. {1:15} But then God stepped in, set me apart since birth, and called me by his grace. {1:16} He showed his Son in me, so I could preach him to the non-Jews, and I didn't need any human help for that. {1:17} I didn't even roll with the other apostles in Jerusalem; I headed straight to Arabia and then back to Damascus. {1:18} Three years later, I finally made it to Jerusalem to see Peter, and kicked it with him for fifteen days. {1:19} Only other apostle I saw was James, the Lord's brother. {1:20} And let me swear before God, I ain't lying about any of this. {1:21-23} After that, I hit up Syria and Cilicia, still a total unknown to the churches in Judea, except for hearing about how the dude who used to wreck us is now preaching the faith he once tried to destroy. {1:24} And they were praising God 'cause of me.

{2:1} Fourteen years later, I went back to Jerusalem with Barnabas and brought Titus along too. {2:2} I went because of a revelation and shared the gospel I preach to the non-Jews, but only with those who seemed legit, so my work wouldn't be for nothing. {2:3} And yo, even Titus, who's Greek, didn't have to get circumcised. {2:4} But some sneaky fakes tried to bring us back under the law, spying on our freedom in Christ, trying to drag us back into slavery. {2:5} But we didn't let them win, not even for a minute, so the truth of the gospel would stay with you. {2:6} And those who seemed important didn't add anything to me. {2:7} On the flip side, when they saw that preaching to the non-Jews was my thing, just like preaching to the Jews was Peter's thing, {2:8} the same God who worked through Peter for the Jews worked through me for the non-Jews. {2:9} And when James, Peter, and John, who seemed like big shots, recognized the grace given to me, they shook hands with me and Barnabas, agreeing we should hit up the non-Jews while they dealt with the Jews. {2:10} They just asked us to remember the poor, which I was already down for. {2:11} But when Peter came to Antioch, I called him out to his face 'cause he messed up. {2:12} Before some guys from James showed up, he was cool with eating with non-Jews, but then he chickened out and separated himself when they came, scared of the circumcision crew. {2:13} And even the other Jewish believers joined in the act, even Barnabas got carried away. {2:14} But when I saw they weren't being straight about the truth of the gospel, I told Peter in front of everyone, "If you, a Jew, can live like a non-Jew, why force the non-Jews to live like Jews?" {2:15} We may be Jewish by birth, but we ain't sinners like the non-Jews. {2:16} We know we ain't made right with God by following the law, but by believing in Jesus Christ. And we believed in Christ so we could be made right with God through faith, not by doing what the law says, 'cause that ain't how anyone gets right with God. {2:17} But if we're trying to be made right with God through Christ and we still end up being sinners, does that mean Christ's promoting sin? Heck no. {2:18} If I start rebuilding what I tore down, then I'm showing I'm a lawbreaker. {2:19} I've died to the law, so I can live for God. {2:20} I've been crucified with Christ, so now I'm living, but it ain't really me, it's Christ living in me. And the life I live now, I'm living by trusting in the Son of God, who loved me and gave himself for me. {2:21} I ain't gonna mess up God's grace, 'cause if following the law could make us right with God, then Jesus died for nothing.

{3:1} Yo, Galatians, what's up with you? Who put a spell on you, making you ditch the truth? Like, you saw Jesus get crucified, right in front of you! {3:2} Let me ask you something: Did you get the Spirit by following rules or by just hearing and believing? {3:3} Seriously, are you that clueless? You started off all spiritual, and now you're trying to be perfect by following rules? {3:4} Did you go through all that hardship for nothing? I hope not. {3:5} The one who gives you the Spirit and does miracles among you, does he do it because you follow rules or because you believe? {3:6} Remember how Abraham believed God, and it was counted as righteousness? {3:7} So, if you're all about faith, you're basically Abraham's crew. {3:8} The scripture knew way back that through faith, God would make non-Jewish peeps righteous. It told Abraham, "Everyone's gonna be blessed because of you." {3:9} So, those who have faith get the same blessings as Abraham. {3:10} But if you're all about following rules, you're under a curse, 'cause you gotta do every single thing in the rulebook. {3:11} It's obvious that no one gets right with God by following rules; it's all about faith. {3:12} Rules and faith don't mix; if you're all about rules, you gotta live by them, but faith is different. {3:13} Jesus took away the curse of following rules by becoming a curse for us, just like it says, "Cursed is anyone who hangs on a tree." {3:14} That way, Abraham's blessing could spread to everyone through Jesus, and we could get the Spirit through faith. {3:15} Look, even when it's just a regular human agreement, once it's made official, no one can change it or add stuff to it. {3:16} When God made promises to Abraham and his descendants, He didn't say "descendants" like there were many; He said "descendant," as in one, who is Christ. {3:17} The covenant with Abraham, which came way before the law, can't be canceled out by the law that came much later. {3:18} So, if the inheritance is based on rules, it's not based on promises anymore. But God gave it to Abraham as a promise. {3:19} So why did God even give the law? It was added because of sin until the promised descendant came. It was handed down by angels through a mediator. {3:20} Now, a mediator represents more than one party, but God is just one. {3:21} So, is the law against God's promises? Heck no! If following rules could give life, then yeah, they'd be legit. {3:22} But the scripture says everyone's messed up, so the promise given through faith in Jesus Christ could be given to those who believe. {3:23} Before faith came, we were kept under lock and key by the law, until faith showed up. {3:24} The law was like our strict teacher leading us to Christ, so we could be made right with God through faith. {3:25} But now that faith is here, we don't need that strict teacher anymore. {3:26} 'Cause y'all are God's children through faith in Christ Jesus. {3:27} If you've been baptized into Christ, you've put on Christ like a fresh outfit. {3:28} There's no more labels; we're all one crew in Christ Jesus, whether Jew or non-Jew, slave or free, male or female. {3:29} And if you belong to Christ, then you're Abraham's squad and get in on the promise.

{4:1} So, here's the deal: Even though you're the heir, as long as you're a kid, you're no different than a servant, even though you own everything. {4:2} You gotta follow rules and listen to the adults until the time your dad says you're grown up. {4:3} Same goes for us; when we were kids, we were stuck following the basic rules of the world. {4:4} But when the time was right, God sent His Son, born of a woman and living under the rules, to redeem those under the rules so we could become His adopted children. {4:5} And since you're His kids, God sent the Spirit of His Son into your hearts, so now you can call out to Him like a loving dad. {4:6-7} So, you're not just servants anymore; you're His kids, and if you're His kid, then you're an heir through Christ. {4:8} But back when you didn't know God, you were all about serving things that aren't even gods. {4:9} But now that you know God, or more like, now that God knows you, why would you go back to those weak, useless rules and get stuck all over again? {4:10} You're going all out with your religious observances, tracking days, months, seasons, and years. {4:11} I'm scared I might've wasted my time with you. {4:12} Brothers and sisters, I'm begging you, be like me, 'cause I'm like you. You've never done me wrong. {4:13} Remember how, even though I was sick, I still preached to you at first. {4:14} You didn't treat me like garbage; you welcomed me like you'd welcome an angel or even Christ himself. {4:15} So, where's all that happiness you had back then? I'll tell you, if you could, you would've given me your own eyes! {4:16} Am I your enemy now 'cause I'm telling you the truth? {4:17} Those guys are all over you, but not for the right reasons; they wanna cut you off so they can feel important. {4:18} It's good to be passionate, but make sure it's for the right things, not just when I'm around. {4:19} My dear children, I'm going through labor pains all over again until Christ is fully developed in you. {4:20} I wish I could be with you right now; I'm really unsure about you. {4:21} Let me ask you something: You wanna go back to following the law, but do you even know what the law says? {4:22} Listen up: Abraham had two sons, one from a slave woman and the other from a free woman. {4:23} The slave woman's son was born in the usual way, but the free woman's son was born because of God's promise. {4:24} Now, think about it: These two women represent two covenants. The one from Mount Sinai leads to slavery; that's Hagar. {4:25} And Hagar represents Mount Sinai in Arabia and is like present-day Jerusalem, because it and its kids are slaves. {4:26} But the Jerusalem above is free and is our mom. {4:27} As it says in scripture, "Be happy, woman who can't have kids. Shout and cry out loud, woman who couldn't have labor pains. The woman who is alone has more kids than the woman with a husband." {4:28} So, my brothers and sisters, you're like Isaac, children of the promise. {4:29} But just like back then, the kid born in the usual way bullied the kid born by the power of the Spirit. That's still happening now. {4:30} But what does scripture say? "Get rid of the slave woman and her son, because the slave woman's son will never share the family's inheritance with the free woman's son." {4:31} So, my friends, we're not the children of the slave woman; we're the children of the free.

{5:1} So, stand strong in the freedom Christ has given us and don't get caught up again in the chains of old rules. {5:2} Listen up—I'm telling you, if you go down the route of circumcision, Christ's work means nothing to you. {5:3} Let me make this clear: if you get circumcised, you're obligated to follow the entire law. {5:4} Trusting in the law makes Christ pointless to you; you've fallen from grace. {5:5} We're waiting for righteousness through the Spirit, not by following rules. {5:6} In Christ, neither circumcision nor uncircumcision matters; it's faith working through love that counts. {5:7} You were doing so well; who's tripped you up and made you turn away from the truth? {5:8} This persuasion didn't come from the One who called you. {5:9} A little leaven spreads throughout the whole dough. {5:10} I trust that you won't be swayed, but whoever's causing trouble will face the consequences. {5:11} If I were preaching circumcision, why am I still persecuted? If that were the case, the offense of the cross would be gone. {5:12} I wish those causing you trouble would just cut themselves off. {5:13} Brothers and sisters, you've been called to freedom; just don't abuse it to satisfy your desires, but serve one another in love. {5:14} The entire law is fulfilled in one command: love your neighbor as yourself. {5:15} But if you keep tearing each other apart, watch out or you'll destroy each other. {5:16} Here's the deal: live by the Spirit, and you won't give in to sinful desires. {5:17} The flesh and the Spirit are at odds with each other; you can't always do what you want. {5:18} If you follow the Spirit, you're not bound by the law. {5:19} The acts of the flesh are obvious: adultery, sexual immorality, impurity, debauchery, {5:20} idolatry, witchcraft, hatred, discord, jealousy, fits of rage, selfish ambition, dissensions, factions, {5:21} envy, drunkenness, orgies, and the like. Those who live like this won't inherit the kingdom of God. {5:22} But the fruit of the Spirit is love, joy, peace, forbearance, kindness, goodness, faithfulness, {5:23} gentleness, and self-control. Against these, there is no law. {5:24} Those who belong to Christ have crucified the flesh with its passions and desires. {5:25} If we live by the Spirit, let's also walk in step with the Spirit. {5:26} Let's not strive for empty glory, provoking and envying each other.

{6:1} Brothers and sisters, if someone messes up, those of you who are more mature should help them get back on track with gentleness, being mindful of your own weaknesses. {6:2} Support each other; that's how we live out Christ's law. {6:3} Don't get cocky; if you think you're something when you're not, you're fooling yourself. {6:4} Let each person be responsible for their own actions and take pride in their own work, not someone else's. {6:5} Everyone has to carry their own load. {6:6} Those who are taught should share with their teachers in all good things. {6:7} Don't fool yourselves; God can't be mocked. Whatever you sow, you'll reap. {6:8} Sowing to please your flesh leads to corruption, but sowing to please the Spirit leads to eternal life. {6:9} Keep doing good; you'll reap the rewards if you don't give up. {6:10} Whenever you can, do good to everyone, especially fellow believers. {6:11} Look at how long this letter is; I wrote it myself. {6:12} Those trying to look good in the flesh are pressuring you to get circumcised, just to avoid persecution because of the cross of Christ. {6:13} Those who insist on circumcision don't even keep the law themselves; they just want to boast about what they've done to you. {6:14} But I only boast in the cross of Jesus Christ, through whom the world is dead to me, and I to the world. {6:15} In Christ Jesus, neither circumcision nor uncircumcision matters; what counts is being a new creation. {6:16} Peace and mercy to all who follow this rule, and especially to God's people. {6:17} From now on, don't let anyone cause trouble for me; I bear the marks of Jesus on my body. {6:18} Brothers and sisters, may the grace of our Lord Jesus Christ be with your spirit. Amen.

Ephesians

✦✦✦

{1:1} Yo, it's Paul, doing apostle things for Jesus Christ by God's plan, sending shoutouts to the saints in Ephesus and the faithful in Christ Jesus. {1:2} Yo, may grace and peace come your way from God our Father and the Lord Jesus Christ. {1:3} Big ups to the God and Father of our Lord Jesus Christ, who hooked us up with all the spiritual blessings up in heaven through Christ. {1:4} He picked us out before the world even started, so we could be blameless and holy in his eyes, all filled up with love. {1:5} He already decided we're gonna be adopted as his children through Jesus Christ, just 'cause he felt like it. {1:6} So we can sing praises about how awesome his grace is, since he made us cool in his eyes through Christ. {1:7} 'Cause of Jesus, we get redeemed by his blood, forgiven for all the messed-up stuff we did, all because of his crazy rich grace. {1:8} He's been super generous with us, giving us all this wisdom and insight. {1:9} He let us in on the secret plan he had, 'cause that's what he felt like doing. {1:10} And here's the deal: when the time's right, he's gonna bring everything together in Christ, both the stuff up in heaven and down here on earth. {1:11} Through Christ, we got this inheritance, 'cause that's what he wanted. {1:12} And we're here to brag about how awesome he is, us who were the first to believe in Christ. {1:13} And you guys, after hearing the truth about salvation and believing in Christ, you got stamped with the Holy Spirit, just like we did. {1:14} That Spirit's like a down payment on our inheritance, until we get it in full and praise God for it. {1:15} So when I heard about your faith in Jesus and love for all the saints, I couldn't stop thanking God for you, mentioning you in my prayers. {1:16} I'm asking God, who's the Father of glory, to give you wisdom and revelation so you can know him better. {1:17} I want the eyes of your heart to see clearly, so you can know the hope he's calling you to and how rich and glorious his inheritance is for his holy people. {1:18} I want you to understand how incredibly great his power is for us who believe, the same power that raised Christ from the dead and put him in charge of everything, not just now but forever. {1:19} Everything's under his control, and the church is his body, filled with him who fills everything everywhere.

{2:1} And you, yeah you, you were dead because of your sins, just following the crowd and doing whatever the ruler of the spiritual powers in the air wanted. {2:2} You used to live just like everyone else, driven by your desires and thoughts. You were like everyone else, just doing whatever felt good at the time and disobeying God. {2:3} We all used to be like that, living by our selfish desires, following our own ideas, and heading straight for God's anger, just like everyone else. {2:4} But God's got mad love for us, and because of his crazy love, he gave us new life when we were dead in sin. {2:5} Even when we were dead because of our sins, he made us alive together with Christ. (Yeah, you heard me right, by grace you're saved.) {2:6} He raised us up with Christ and made us sit with him in the heavenly realms, where he is, all because we're down with Christ Jesus. {2:7} And he did all this to show off his crazy rich grace for all eternity, treating us with kindness through Christ Jesus. {2:8} 'Cause let me tell you, it's by God's grace that you're saved through believing in him. You didn't earn it yourselves; it's a gift from God. {2:9} It's not about doing good deeds, 'cause then you'd be bragging about it, and that ain't the deal here. {2:10} We're God's masterpiece, created in Christ Jesus to do good stuff he planned for us to do way ahead of time. {2:11} So, don't forget where you came from: you used to be non-Jewish by birth, called "the Uncircumcised" by those who call themselves "the Circumcised." {2:12} At that time, you were separated from Christ, excluded from citizenship in Israel, and foreigners to the covenants of the promise, without hope and without God in the world. {2:13} But now, because of Christ Jesus, you who were far away from God have been brought near by the blood of Christ. {2:14} He's our peace, the one who broke down the barrier that divided us, the wall of hostility. {2:15} By his body on the cross, he put an end to the hostility and the law that commanded us to obey its rules. He made peace between Jews and non-Jews by creating in himself one new people from the two groups. {2:16} Together as one body, Christ reconciled both groups to God by means of his death on the cross, and our hostility toward each other was put to death. {2:17} He came and preached peace to you non-Jews who were far away from him and peace to us Jews who were near him. {2:18} And now, through Christ, we can all come to the Father by the same Holy Spirit. {2:19} So, you're not outsiders or strangers anymore. You're citizens together with God's people. You belong to God's family. {2:20} You're like a building that's been built on the foundation of the apostles and prophets, with Christ Jesus himself as the cornerstone. {2:21} In him, the whole building is joined together and rises to become a holy temple in the Lord. {2:22} And in him, you're being built together to become a place where God lives through the Spirit.

{3:1} So, like, I'm Paul, stuck in jail for Jesus 'cause of y'all non-Jews. {3:2} If you've heard about how God's grace has been given to me for y'all, then you know what's up. {3:3} God let me in on a secret by revelation, like I mentioned before in a nutshell, {3:4} so when you read, you can understand what I know about Christ's secret plan. {3:5} This secret wasn't known in the past but is revealed now to God's holy crew, the apostles and prophets, by the Spirit. {3:6} It's that non-Jews get to share everything with Jews and be part of God's promise through the gospel. {3:7} And I got picked to be the one to spread this message, thanks to God's grace and power. {3:8} Even though I'm the least of all the saints, God gave me this grace to preach to non-Jews about Christ's endless blessings. {3:9} My gig is to show everyone this secret fellowship that's been hidden since day one, created by Jesus. {3:10} This way, even the big shots up in heaven can peep the wisdom of God through us. {3:11} It's all part of God's master plan in Jesus. {3:12} And because of Jesus, we can boldly approach God with confidence through faith. {3:13} So, don't freak out 'cause I'm going through stuff for you; it's all good for your rep. {3:14} That's why I get down on my knees before God, the Father of Jesus, {3:15} who's like the dad of the whole crew, both in heaven and on earth. {3:16} My wish is that you get pumped up with inner strength through God's Spirit, {3:17} so Christ can chill in your hearts through faith, grounding you in love. {3:18} That way, you and all the saints can fully grasp the endless dimensions of Christ's love, {3:19} and know a love that's way beyond what you can understand, so you can be filled with all of God's goodness. {3:20} Shoutout to the one who can do way more than we could ever ask or think, by His power at work in us! {3:21} Praise be to him, through Christ Jesus, forever. Amen.

{4:1} Now, peeps, since I'm also in lockdown for Jesus, I'm begging you to live up to the calling you got, {4:2} with all humility, gentleness, patience, and love, {4:3} doing your best to keep the peace and unity of the Spirit. {4:4} 'Cause there's only one body, one Spirit, one hope, {4:5} one Lord, one faith, one baptism, {4:6} one God and Father of all, who's over everything, through everything, and in all of us. {4:7} But God gives each of us grace based on what Christ gives us. {4:8} That's why it says, "When He went up, He led a bunch of prisoners with Him and gave gifts to people." {4:9} (Now, when it says He went up, it means He also went down to the lower parts of the earth. {4:10} The same dude who went down is the one who went way up above all the heavens to fill everything.) {4:11} And He gave some to be apostles, some to be prophets, some to be evangelists, and some to be pastors and teachers, {4:12} to train God's peeps for the work of serving, to build up Christ's body, {4:13} until we all get it together in our faith and knowledge of God's Son, growing up to be like Christ in every way. {4:14} Then we won't be like kids, all tossed around and tricked by slick talkers and their deceitful schemes. {4:15} Instead, we'll speak the truth with love and grow up in every way into Christ, who's the head. {4:16} And the whole body, joined and held together by every supporting ligament, grows and builds itself up in love. {4:17} So, I'm telling you, from now on, don't live like other non-Jewish peeps, all caught up in their pointless thoughts, {4:18} with their minds all dark and separated from God's life because they don't know any better, thanks to their stubborn hearts. {4:19} They've gone so far down that road they don't even feel it anymore and just do whatever feels good. {4:20} But that's not how you learned about Christ, {4:21} if you really heard Him and were taught the truth in Him. {4:22} That's when you took off your old self, corrupted by lustful desires, {4:23-24} and got a fresh start in your mind and put on the new self, created to be like God in true righteousness and holiness. {4:25} So, put away lying and speak truthfully to each other, 'cause we're all part of one crew. {4:26} It's cool to be angry, but don't let it lead to sin; don't let the day end with your anger still burning. {4:27} And don't give the devil a chance to mess with you. {4:28} If you used to steal, stop it and start working instead, doing something useful with your hands, so you can share with those in need. {4:29} Watch your mouth and only say stuff that's helpful, building others up and giving them what they need to hear. {4:30} And don't hurt God's Spirit, who marked you as His own, keeping you safe until the day of redemption. {4:31} Get rid of all bitterness, rage, anger, harsh words, and slander, as well as all types of evil behavior. {4:32} Instead, be kind to each other, tenderhearted, forgiving one another, just as God forgave you because of what Christ has done.

{5:1} So, be imitators of God, like beloved kids. {5:2} Live in love, just as Christ loved us and gave Himself up for us, a sweet-smelling sacrifice to God. {5:3} But don't let fornication, uncleanness, or greed even be mentioned among you—this isn't how saints behave. {5:4} No dirty talk, foolishness, or joking around that's inappropriate; instead, be grateful. {5:5} Understand this: no immoral, impure, or greedy person (who is an idolater) has any place in the kingdom of Christ and God. {5:6} Don't be fooled by empty words; God's wrath comes because of such things upon disobedient people. {5:7} So, don't join in with them. {5:8} You used to be in darkness, but now you're light in the Lord; live like children of light. {5:9} The fruit of the Spirit is all goodness, righteousness, and truth. {5:10} Find out what pleases the Lord. {5:11} Don't associate with the deeds of darkness; instead, expose them. {5:12} It's shameful even to talk about what's done in secret by them. {5:13} But everything exposed by the light becomes visible. {5:14} That's why it says, "Wake up, sleeper! Rise from the dead, and Christ will shine on you." {5:15} Be careful how you live—don't be foolish, but wise. {5:16} Make the most of every opportunity, because these are evil times. {5:17} So, understand what the Lord's will is; don't be foolish. {5:18} Don't get drunk on wine, which leads to reckless behavior. Instead, be filled with the Spirit. {5:19} Speak to one another with psalms, hymns, and spiritual songs; sing and make music in your heart to the Lord. {5:20} Always give thanks to God the Father for everything, in the name of our Lord Jesus Christ. {5:21} Submit to one another out of reverence for Christ. {5:22} Wives, submit yourselves to your own husbands as you do to the Lord. {5:23} For the husband is the head of the wife as Christ is the head of the church, his body, of which he is the Savior. {5:24} Now as the church submits to Christ, so also wives should submit to their husbands in everything. {5:25} Husbands, love your wives, just as Christ loved the church and gave himself up for her {5:26} to make her holy, cleansing her by the washing with water through the word, {5:27} and to present her to himself as a radiant church, without stain or wrinkle or any other blemish, but holy and blameless. {5:28} In this same way, husbands ought to love their wives as their own bodies. He who loves his wife loves himself. {5:29} After all, no one ever hated their own body, but they feed and care for their body, just as Christ does the church— {5:30} for we are members of his body. {5:31} "For this reason, a man will leave his father and mother and be united to his wife, and the two will become one flesh." {5:32} This is a profound mystery—but I am talking about Christ and the church. {5:33} However, each one of you also must love his wife as he loves himself, and the wife must respect her husband.

{6:1} Children, obey your parents in the Lord, for this is right. {6:2} Honor your father and mother—which is the first commandment with a promise— {6:3} so that it may go well with you and that you may enjoy long life on the earth. {6:4} Fathers, do not exasperate your children; instead, bring them up in the training and instruction of the Lord. {6:5} Slaves, obey your earthly masters with respect and fear, and with sincerity of heart, just as you would obey Christ. {6:6} Don't work only while being watched, to please men; work with sincerity of heart, fearing the Lord. {6:7} Serve wholeheartedly, as if you were serving the Lord, not men, {6:8} because you know that the Lord will reward each one for whatever good they do, whether they are slaves or free. {6:9} And masters, treat your slaves in the same way. Do not threaten them, since you know that he who is both their Master and yours is in heaven, and there is no favoritism with him. {6:10} Finally, be strong in the Lord and in his mighty power. {6:11} Put on the full armor of God, so that you can take your stand against the devil's schemes. {6:12} For our struggle is not against flesh and blood, but against the rulers, against the authorities, against the powers of this dark world and against the spiritual forces of evil in the heavenly realms. {6:13} Therefore put on the full armor of God, so that when the day of evil comes, you may be able to stand your ground, and after you have done everything, to stand. {6:14} Stand firm then, with the belt of truth buckled around your waist, with the breastplate of righteousness in place, {6:15} and with your feet fitted with the readiness that comes from the gospel of peace. {6:16} In addition to all this, take up the shield of faith, with which you can extinguish all the flaming arrows of the evil one. {6:17} Take the helmet of salvation and the sword of the Spirit, which is the word of God. {6:18} And pray in the Spirit on all occasions with all kinds of prayers and requests. With this in mind, be alert and always keep on praying for all the Lord's people. {6:19} Pray also for me, that whenever I speak, words may be given me so that I will fearlessly make known the mystery of the gospel, {6:20} for which I am an ambassador in chains. Pray that I may declare it fearlessly, as I should. {6:21} Tychicus, the dear brother and faithful servant in the Lord, will tell you everything, so that you also may know how I am and what I am doing. {6:22} I am sending him to you for this very purpose, that you may know how we are, and that he may encourage you. {6:23} Peace to the brothers and sisters, and love with faith from God the Father and the Lord Jesus Christ. {6:24} Grace to all who love our Lord Jesus Christ with an undying love.

Philippians

✠✠✠

{1:1} Yo, it's Paul and Timotheus, doing servant gigs for Jesus Christ, sending mad love to all the saints in Christ Jesus at Philippi, including the bishops and deacons. {1:2} Yo, may grace and peace be with you, coming straight from God our Father and the Lord Jesus Christ. {1:3} I'm thanking my God every time I think about you, fam. {1:4} Every time I pray for y'all, it's with joy, straight up. {1:5} I'm hyped about how we've been rolling together in the gospel since day one. {1:6} I'm totally sure that God, who started this dope work in you, will keep it going until Jesus comes back. {1:7} I'm feeling this way about y'all 'cause you're always in my heart. Whether I'm locked up or defending the gospel, we're all in this together, sharing God's grace. {1:8} God knows I miss y'all like crazy, with a love that's all Jesus. {1:9} And here's my prayer: I'm asking that your love just keeps growing, along with your knowledge and wisdom. {1:10} So you can figure out what's best and stay true to Jesus until he comes back, living a life that's real and free from messing up. {1:11} I'm hoping you'll be filled up with the good stuff that comes from doing what's right, all thanks to Jesus, and that'll give glory and praise to God. {1:12} Check it, fam, I want you to know that what's been happening to me has actually helped spread the gospel. {1:13} My situation's made it clear that I'm in this for Jesus, and it's got everyone talking, even in the palace and everywhere else. {1:14} And because of what's happening to me, a lot of believers are getting bold and speaking out about Jesus without holding back. {1:15} Some are doing it out of jealousy and competition, but others are doing it out of love. {1:16} There are those who preach about Jesus because they want to stir up trouble for me while I'm locked up, thinking it'll make things worse for me. {1:17} But others preach about Jesus out of love, knowing that I'm here to defend the gospel. {1:18} So, what's the deal? Whether they're real or just fronting, Jesus is getting preached, and that's what's up. I'm stoked, and I'll keep on being stoked. {1:19} 'Cause I know this whole situation is gonna turn out all right for me, thanks to your prayers and the help of the Spirit of Jesus Christ. {1:20} I'm expecting and hoping that nothing will make me ashamed, but I'll keep on being bold, just like always, and Jesus will be lifted up, whether I'm living or dying. {1:21} 'Cause for me, living is all about Jesus, and dying means getting the ultimate win. {1:22} But if I keep on living in this body, it means I get to keep on working for Jesus. But to be honest, I can't decide which one I'd rather do. {1:23} I'm torn between the two, wanting to leave this life and be with Christ, which would be way better. {1:24} But for your sake, it's better that I stick around in this body. {1:25} And because I'm sure of this, I know I'll stay and be with you all, helping you grow and be happy in your faith. {1:26} So you can be even happier about Jesus because of me when I come back to see you again. {1:27} Just make sure you live in a way that's worthy of the gospel of Christ. Whether I'm there or not, I want to hear that you're standing firm, united in one spirit and fighting together for the faith of the gospel. {1:28} And don't let your enemies scare you. This'll show them that they're doomed, but you're saved, and that's all because of God. {1:29} 'Cause you've been given the privilege of not only believing in Jesus but also suffering for him. {1:30} You're in the same fight I'm in, and now that you've seen me fighting, you're hearing about me fighting.

{2:1} So, if you find any encouragement in Christ, any comfort from his love, any connection with the Spirit, any feelings of compassion and mercy, {2:2} make my day by being on the same page, having the same love, being totally down with each other, and being on the same vibe. {2:3} Don't let selfishness or pride get in the way. Instead, be humble and think of others as better than yourselves. {2:4} Don't only think about your own interests, but look out for the interests of others too. {2:5} Have the same attitude that Jesus had. {2:6} Even though he was God, he didn't think that being equal with God was something to hold onto. {2:7} Instead, he gave up his divine privileges; he took the humble position of a servant and was born as a human being. {2:8} When he appeared in human form, he humbled himself in obedience to God and died a criminal's death on a cross. {2:9} That's why God raised him up to the highest place and gave him the name that's above every name, {2:10} so that at the name of Jesus, everyone will bow down—those in heaven, on earth, and under the earth. {2:11} And everyone will confess that Jesus Christ is Lord, bringing glory to God the Father. {2:12} So, my dear friends, you've always obeyed God, not only when I was with you, but even more now that I'm not there. Keep working out your salvation with a sense of awe and responsibility. {2:13} 'Cause it's God who's working in you, giving you the desire and the power to do what pleases him. {2:14} Do everything without complaining or arguing, {2:15} so you can be blameless and pure, children of God without any fault. Shine like stars in a dark world {2:16} as you hold firmly to the word of life. And then I can boast about you on the day of Christ, knowing that I didn't run or work for nothing. {2:17} Even if I have to sacrifice myself for your faith, I'm stoked about it and want to share my joy with all of you. {2:18} You should be stoked too and share in my joy. {2:19} I trust in the Lord Jesus to send Timotheus to you soon, so I can feel better when I know how you're doing. {2:20} I don't have anyone else like him who genuinely cares about you. {2:21} Most people are only looking out for themselves, not for what matters to Jesus Christ . {2:22} But you know what's up with Timotheus. He's proven himself like a son who works with his father to spread the gospel. {2:23} So I hope to send him as soon as I see how things are gonna turn out for me. {2:24} And I trust in the Lord that I'll be able to come to you myself before long. {2:25} But for now, I thought it was necessary to send Epaphroditus to you. He's like a brother to me, a coworker, and a soldier who's fought alongside me. And he's been your messenger too, taking care of my needs. {2:26} He's been missing you all and worrying because you heard he was sick. {2:27} And he really was sick—almost died! But God showed him mercy, and not just him, but me too. I would've been bummed out big time if he had died. {2:28} So I'm sending him back to you with even more love, so you can be happy to see him again, and I can be less bummed out. {2:29} Welcome him with open arms, as a follower of the Lord, and give him the respect that people like him deserve. {2:30} He risked his life for the work of Christ, so he could make up for the help you couldn't give me.

{3:1} Alright fam, time to vibe in the Lord. Writing this stuff to you isn't a drag for me, but it's all about keeping you safe. {3:2} Watch out for those shady characters, the ones causing drama. They're not about the real deal. {3:3} We're the ones who are truly connected to God, doing our thing in the Spirit, stoked about Jesus, and not trusting in our own hype. {3:4} I could flex about my background too. If anyone could brag about their past, it's me. {3:5} I was legit born into this, part of Israel's crew, a Pharisee, all about the law. {3:6} I was all in, even going after those who didn't agree, thinking I was blameless. {3:7} But all that stuff I used to think was important? Total garbage now because of Jesus. {3:8} Seriously, knowing Jesus is worth more than anything, even if it means losing everything else. {3:9} It's not about my own righteousness anymore, but about rocking Jesus' vibe, the kind of goodness that comes from God and is received by faith. {3:10} I'm all about getting to know Jesus better, feeling His power, sharing in His struggles, even if it means facing death. {3:11} I'm not claiming to have it all figured out yet; I'm still on the journey, chasing after what Jesus wants from me. {3:12} I haven't made it to the finish line, but I'm pushing forward, leaving the past behind and reaching for what's ahead. {3:13} So, I'm not dwelling on past mistakes; I'm reaching for the prize, aiming for the high calling that Jesus offers. {3:14} I'm focused on that goal, pushing ahead for the win that God's calling me to in Jesus. {3:15} If you're on the same wavelength, cool. And if you're not, God will help you get there too. {3:16} For now, let's keep following the path we're on, staying focused on the same mission. {3:17} Take notes from me and others who walk the walk we talk. {3:18} 'Cause there are plenty out there who talk a big game but are actually enemies of what Jesus stands for. {3:19} They're all about themselves, living for their own desires and glorifying things that don't matter. {3:20} But we're all about that heavenly vibe, waiting for Jesus to come back and transform us. {3:21} He's gonna upgrade our bodies to match His, using His power to make everything right.

{4:1} So, fam, stand strong in the Lord, my dear ones. {4:2} Shoutout to Euodias and Syntyche, get on the same page, y'all. {4:3} And to my homie who's got my back, help out those ladies who've been grinding with me for the gospel, along with Clement and the rest of the crew whose names are in the book of life. {4:4} Keep the party going, always vibing in the Lord. Yeah, I said it twice. {4:5} Keep it chill, everyone's watching. The Lord's coming soon. {4:6} Don't stress about anything; just pray about everything and be thankful. {4:7} God's chill vibes, beyond what we can even get, will keep you in check through Jesus. {4:8} Finally, fam, whatever's true, honorable, fair, pure, lovely, and worthy of praise, think about that stuff. {4:9} Do what I've taught you, seen you do, heard from me, and the God of peace will be right there with you. {4:10} I'm super stoked, you've come through for me once again, showing you care. You were always down, just didn't always have the chance. {4:11} I'm not saying this 'cause I need anything; I've learned to be cool no matter what. {4:12} I've been through the highs and lows, and I'm good with whatever 'cause Jesus gives me strength. {4:13} I can handle anything 'cause of Jesus. {4:14} You've been awesome, hooking me up when I needed it. {4:15} And you Philippians know the deal; you were the only ones who had my back when I dipped from Macedonia. {4:16} Even in Thessalonica, you came through for me more than once. {4:17} It's not about the stuff you give me; it's about the fruit that grows from it and adds to your account. {4:18} But honestly, I'm good. Your gifts are like a sweet smell to God, totally legit. {4:19} And God's got your back too, filling your needs from His riches through Jesus. {4:20} So, all props to God, now and forever. Amen. {4:21} Say what's up to all the saints in Jesus. The crew with me says hi too. {4:22} Shoutout to all the saints, especially those repping in Caesar's crib.

Colossians

✝✝✝

{1:1} Yo, it's Paul, repping Jesus Christ, 'cause that's what God wants, and Timotheus, my bro, {1:2} Sending love to the crew in Colosse: Grace and peace from God and Jesus. {1:3} Big ups to God, the Father of Jesus, always praying for y'all, {1:4} Ever since we heard about your faith in Jesus and love for all the crew. {1:5} Props for keeping the hope alive, stashed up in heaven, straight from the gospel truth. {1:6} The same vibe's spreading everywhere, including you, since you got the scoop on God's grace. {1:7} Shoutout to Epaphras, keeping it real for you, a solid servant of Christ, {1:8} Spreading the word about your love vibe. {1:9} That's why we're always praying for you, hoping you'll get the full scoop on God's plan. {1:10} So you can walk the walk, pleasing the Lord, being productive, and leveling up in knowing God. {1:11} Powered up with all that strength, rocking patience and joy. {1:12} Mad props to the Father, hooking us up with a piece of that heavenly inheritance, {1:13} Pulling us outta darkness into the kingdom of Jesus, where we're forgiven and redeemed. {1:14} Jesus, the image of the invisible God, the real OG, making everything and ruling it all. {1:15} He's the head of the crew, the church, leading the way, first to rise from the dead, taking the top spot in everything. {1:16} God's all about Jesus, making peace through His blood, bringing everything together. {1:17} Once you were off track, but now you're back on, all thanks to Jesus. {1:18} He's the reason you're blameless, holy, and approved in God's eyes. {1:19} God's all about Jesus, putting His fullness in Him, {1:20} And making peace through His blood, bringing everything together, on earth and in heaven. {1:21} You used to be lost, but now you're found, made right with God through Jesus, {1:22} 'Cause of Jesus, you're presented as perfect before God, as long as you stay true to the gospel. {1:23} That's why I'm cool with suffering for you, to fill in the gaps of what's left of Jesus' struggles, for the sake of His crew, the church. {1:24} God's given me a mission for you, to share the good news. {1:25} The mystery's out, revealed to God's people, especially the Gentiles: Jesus in you, the hope of glory. {1:26} So we're out here, preaching Jesus, teaching everyone to be top-notch in Him. {1:27} I'm all in, going hard, powered up by God's strength at work in me.

{2:1} I'm in a serious battle for you and the crew in Laodicea, and for anyone I haven't met in person, {2:2} Hoping your hearts stay chill, connected in love, and fully understanding God's mystery, the Father, and Jesus. {2:3} 'Cause all the wisdom and knowledge you need is in Jesus. {2:4} Watch out for smooth talkers trying to trick you. {2:5} Even though I'm not there in person, I'm with you in spirit, hyped about your order and solid faith in Jesus. {2:6} So, if you've accepted Jesus, walk the walk. {2:7} Stay rooted and grounded in Him, keeping it real in your faith, and always giving thanks. {2:8} Don't get sidetracked by empty philosophies or fake traditions; stick with Jesus. {2:9} 'Cause Jesus is the full package, everything you need, ruling over all. {2:10} You're set with Jesus, the head of all power and authority. {2:11} In Jesus, you've got a spiritual circumcision, not a physical one, cutting off sin's power over you. {2:12} You've been buried with Jesus in baptism and raised up with Him through faith in God's power. {2:13} Once you were dead in your sins, but now you're alive in Jesus, forgiven for everything. {2:14} Jesus canceled out all the charges against you, nailed them to the cross, {2:15} And put the powers of darkness in their place, triumphing over them openly. {2:16} Don't let anyone judge you based on what you eat or drink or on religious festivals; that stuff's just a preview of what's to come, but Jesus is the real deal. {2:17} So don't let anyone trip you up with false humility or angel worship, getting caught up in stuff they don't understand, all puffed up by their own thinking, {2:18} Not keeping it real with Jesus, the head of the crew, who's making the whole crew grow. {2:19} So, if you're all about Jesus and not the world's ways, why play by their rules? {2:20} Rules like "Don't touch, don't taste, don't handle," which all just fade away. {2:21} Those rules might look wise with their self-imposed worship and fake humility, but they don't do anything to help you live right. {2:22} It's not about satisfying your own desires but honoring Jesus.

{3:1} Yo, if you're all about that risen life with Christ, focus on what's up above, where Christ is kicking it next to God. {3:2} Keep your vibe on heavenly stuff, not on earthly junk. {3:3} 'Cause you're dead to all that earthy noise, but your real life is hidden with Christ in God. {3:4} And when Christ, who's our real deal, shows up, you'll be right there with him, shining in glory. {3:5} So, kill off all that earthy stuff in you—sexual immorality, impurity, lust, evil desires, and greed. That stuff just messes you up and makes God mad. {3:6} And you used to be all about that life, but not anymore. {3:7} Now, ditch all that anger, rage, malice, slander, and filthy language. {3:8} Don't lie to each other either, 'cause you've stripped off the old self with its nasty habits. {3:9} Instead, put on the new self, which is being renewed in knowledge in the image of its Creator. {3:10} Where labels like Greek or Jew, circumcised or uncircumcised, barbarian, Scythian, slave or free don't mean squat. Christ is all that matters, and he's in all of us. {3:11} So, as God's chosen ones, holy and dearly loved, clothe yourselves with compassion, kindness, humility, gentleness, and patience. {3:12} Bear with each other and forgive one another if any of you has a grievance against someone. Forgive as the Lord forgave you. {3:13} And over all these virtues, put on love, which binds them all together in perfect unity. {3:14} And let the peace of Christ rule in your hearts, since as members of one body you were called to peace. And be thankful. {3:15} Let the message of Christ dwell among you richly as you teach and admonish one another with all wisdom through psalms, hymns, and songs from the Spirit, singing to God with gratitude in your hearts. {3:16-17} And whatever you do, whether in word or deed, do it all in the name of the Lord Jesus, giving thanks to God the Father through him. {3:18} Wives, submit yourselves to your husbands, because it's the right thing to do as followers of the Lord. {3:19} Husbands, love your wives and don't be harsh with them. {3:20} Kids, obey your parents in everything, 'cause that's what pleases the

Lord. {3:21} Dads, don't push your kids' buttons, or you'll crush their spirits. {3:22} Slaves, obey your earthly masters in everything, not only when their eye is on you and to curry their favor, but with sincerity of heart and reverence for the Lord. {3:23} Whatever you do, work at it with all your heart, as working for the Lord, not for human masters, {3:24} since you know that you'll receive an inheritance from the Lord as a reward. It's the Lord Christ you're serving. {3:25} Anyone who does wrong will be repaid for their wrongs, and there is no favoritism.

{4:1} Masters, treat your slaves justly and fairly, knowing that you also have a Master in heaven. {4:2} Keep praying and stay alert, with a heart full of thanks. {4:3} And pray for us too, that God may open a door for our message, so that we may proclaim the mystery of Christ, for which I'm in chains. {4:4} Pray that I may proclaim it clearly, as I should. {4:5} Make the most of every opportunity, 'cause time's ticking. {4:6} Let your conversation be always full of grace, seasoned with salt, so you know how to answer everyone. {4:7} Tychicus, my homie and fellow servant in the Lord, will tell you all the news about me. {4:8} I'm sending him to comfort your hearts, 'cause he's got your back. {4:9} With him is Onesimus, our faithful and beloved brother, who's one of you. They'll fill you in on everything happening here. {4:10} Aristarchus, my fellow prisoner, sends you his greetings, along with Mark, the cousin of Barnabas. (You received instructions about him; if he comes to you, welcome him.) {4:11} And Jesus, who's called Justus, sends his greetings. These are the only Jews among my co-workers for the kingdom of God, and they've been a comfort to me. {4:12} Epaphras, who's one of you and a servant of Christ Jesus, sends his greetings. He's always wrestling in prayer for you, that you may stand firm in all the will of God, mature and fully assured. {4:13} I vouch for him that he's working hard for you and for those at Laodicea and Hierapolis. {4:14} Luke, the doctor, and Demas send greetings. {4:15} Give my greetings to the brothers and sisters at Laodicea, and to Nympha and the church in her house. {4:16} After this letter has been read to you, see that it's also read in the church of the Laodiceans and that you in turn read the letter from Laodicea. {4:17} Tell Archippus: "See to it that you complete the ministry you've received in the Lord." {4:18} This greeting is in my own hand—Paul. Remember my chains. Grace be with you.

1 Thessalonians

✦✦✦

{1:1} Yo, it's Paul, Silvanus, and Timotheus hittin' up the Thessalonian crew, chillin' in God the Father and the Lord Jesus Christ. Big shoutout to y'all, wishin' you grace and peace from God our Father and the Lord Jesus Christ. {1:2} We always shout out to God for y'all in our prayers, never forgettin' your faith hustle and patience in Jesus Christ. {1:3} You're always on our minds, grindin' for the Lord, and we see it, fam. {1:4} We know you're chosen by God, fam. {1:5} Our message wasn't just talk, it came with power and the Holy Spirit, and you know we were real with you. {1:6} Y'all followed our lead and the Lord's, even when it got tough, you stayed joyful in the Holy Spirit. {1:7} Word got out about you all over, how you held it down for Jesus. {1:8} The word about y'all's faith has spread like wildfire, no need for us to say anything. {1:9} People talk about how you turned to God from idols, and now you're all about serving the true God and waiting for Jesus to come back. {1:10} He's the one who saved us from the wrath to come.

{2:1} You know our trip to you wasn't for nothin', fam. {2:2} Even after getting beat up in Philippi, we still came at you with the gospel, no holding back. {2:3} We weren't out here to deceive or be shady; God trusted us with the gospel, so we kept it real. {2:4} We ain't tryna please people, just God, who knows our hearts. {2:5} We didn't come with fancy words or tryna get rich; God knows. {2:6} We weren't after fame, not from you or anyone else, even though we could've thrown that weight around as Christ's reps. {2:7} Nah, we were gentle with y'all, like a mom with her kids. {2:8} We were real about wanting to share not just the gospel but our lives with you, 'cause you mean something to us. {2:9} Remember how we worked night and day not to be a burden while we preached the gospel to you. {2:10} Y'all and God saw how we lived among you, keeping it pure and righteous, no blame. {2:11-12} Like a dad, we encouraged, comforted, and urged each one of you to live worthy of God, who called you into his kingdom and glory. {2:13} We thank God 'cause when you heard the word from us, you didn't take it as just words from people, but as the real deal from God, and it's changing you. {2:14} You're following the lead of other churches in Judea who are in Jesus, even though you're catching the same heat from your own people that they did from the Jews. {2:15} Those same folks who killed Jesus and the prophets and are persecuting us ain't making God happy and are against everyone. {2:16} They're tryna stop us from saving the Gentiles, just addin' to their sin and sealing their fate with God's wrath. {2:17} Even though we had to bounce for a bit, we never stopped wanting to see you, fam. {2:18} We wanted to come back, but Satan was throwin' roadblocks. {2:19} 'Cause what's our hope, joy, and crown of boasting? Ain't it y'all when Jesus comes back? {2:20} Y'all are our pride and joy.

{3:1} So, we couldn't hold back anymore and decided it was best for me to chill solo in Athens; {3:2} Sent Timotheus, our bro and God's worker, to boost you up and reassure you about your faith: {3:3} So you wouldn't be shaken by these tough times, 'cause you know we signed up for this. {3:4} We warned you when we were with you that we'd face hard times, and yup, it happened, and you remember. {3:5} That's why I had to check in on your faith, just to make sure the tempter hadn't messed with you, and our hard work hadn't gone to waste. {3:6} But when Timotheus brought back good news about your faith and love, and how you're always thinking of us, wanting to see us as much as we want to see you, {3:7} Man, we felt so much better knowing you're holding it down in your faith, even with all our struggles. {3:8} 'Cause if you're staying strong in the Lord, then we're living life to the fullest. {3:9} Seriously, what can we even do to thank God enough for you? We're stoked about you, and it's all because of God. {3:10} We're praying day and night to see you, and to help you grow in your faith. {3:11} We're hoping God himself and Jesus clear the way for us to see you. {3:12} And may the Lord make your love for each other and for everyone else grow and overflow, just like ours does for you. {3:13} So you can stand strong and blameless before God when Jesus comes back with all His crew.

{4:1} Yo, we're urging you, fam, and asking you in the name of the Lord Jesus, to keep living the way we taught you, and to step it up even more. {4:2} You know the rules we laid down in the name of the Lord Jesus. {4:3} God wants you to live clean, avoiding any kind of sexual immorality. {4:4} Treat your bodies with respect and honor, not giving in to lust like those who don't know God. {4:5} Don't take advantage of others or cheat them, 'cause the Lord doesn't play when it comes to that stuff, and we've warned you before. {4:6} God didn't call us to live in sin but to live holy lives. {4:7} So anyone who rejects this ain't dissing us but dissing God, who gave us His Holy Spirit. {4:8} But y'all already know about loving each other, 'cause God's already taught you that. {4:9} And you're showing love to all the fam in Macedonia, but keep leveling up. {4:10} And make it your goal to live a peaceful life, handling your own business and working hard, just like we told you. {4:11-12} So you can live right in front of everyone, without needing anything from them. {4:13} But I don't want you to be clueless, fam, about those who've died, so you don't grieve like those who have no hope. {4:14} 'Cause if we believe Jesus died and rose again, then we know God will bring those who died with Jesus back with Him. {4:15} We're telling you this straight from the Lord: when Jesus comes back, those of us still alive won't get there before those who've died. {4:16} 'Cause Jesus Himself will come down from heaven with a shout, with the voice of the archangel, and with God's trumpet. And the ones who died believing in Jesus will rise first. {4:17} Then those of us who are still alive will be caught up together with them in the clouds to meet the Lord in the air. And we'll be with the Lord forever. {4:18} So encourage each other with these words.

{5:1} Yo, fam, I ain't gotta spell out the times and seasons to you. {5:2} Y'all know the deal—the day of the Lord rolls in like a thief in the night. {5:3} When they start shouting "peace and safety," that's when destruction hits like birth pains, and they won't escape it. {5:4} But y'all ain't in the dark; that day won't catch you off guard like a thief. {5:5} We're all about that light life, not the night or darkness. {5:6} So, let's stay woke, unlike others; be alert and clear-headed. {5:7} Those who sleep, do it at night; those who get wasted, do it at night. {5:8} But we, we're day people—stay clear-headed, with faith and love as our armor, and salvation as our helmet. {5:9} God didn't set us up for wrath but to score salvation through Jesus. {5:10} He died for us so whether we're awake or asleep, we're living together with Him. {5:11} So, keep each other encouraged and build each other up, just like you're already doing. {5:12} Shoutout to those who work hard among you, leading and guiding—respect them and live in peace. {5:13} Show mad love for their hustle. {5:14} And yo, keep it real—call out the troublemakers, comfort the down-and-outs, support the weak, and be chill with everyone. {5:15} Don't play tit-for-tat; always bring the good vibes, to each other and to everyone else. {5:16} Stay joyful, no matter what. {5:17} Keep the prayers flowing nonstop. {5:18} Thank God in all situations; that's what's up in Christ Jesus for y'all. {5:19} Don't shut down the Spirit. {5:20} Don't hate on prophecy. {5:21} Test everything; hold tight to what's legit. {5:22} Steer clear of anything that looks sketchy. {5:23} May the God of peace make you totally legit; may your whole being—spirit, soul, and body—be blameless when our Lord Jesus Christ rolls through. {5:24} God's faithful—he's got your back, and he'll pull through. {5:25} Fam, keep us in your prayers. {5:26} Greet all the fam with a holy vibe. {5:27} I'm telling you, spread this letter to all the holy crew.

2 Thessalonians

+++

{1:1} Hey fam, it's Paul, Silvanus, and Timotheus shoutin' out to the Thessalonian crew, kickin' it with God our Father and the Lord Jesus Christ. {1:2} Sending you all grace and peace from God our Father and the Lord Jesus Christ. {1:3} Yo, we gotta give props to God all the time for y'all, fam, 'cause your faith game is strong and the love you show each other is off the charts; {1:4} We're straight up proud of you in all the churches for your patience and faith, even when you're going through it. {1:5} It's clear evidence of God's righteous judgment that you're worthy of his kingdom, even though you're dealing with tough stuff; {1:6} God's gonna pay back those who trouble you, just watch. {1:7} And you'll get some rest along with us when the Lord Jesus comes back with his squad of angels, straight fire. {1:8} He's gonna deal with those who don't know God and ain't down with the gospel; {1:9} They're gonna get hit with eternal destruction, far from the Lord's presence and his power; {1:10} But when he comes back, he'll be glorified in his crew and admired by all who believe, 'cause you believed our message. {1:11} So we're always praying for you, that God will make you worthy of his call and fulfill all his good plans for you, pumpin' up your faith with power; {1:12} 'Cause we wanna see Jesus glorified in you and you shining in him, all thanks to God's grace and the Lord Jesus Christ.

{2:1} Now, we're askin' you, fam, by the time Jesus comes back and we're all together with him, {2:2} Don't let nobody mess with your heads, sayin' the day of Christ is already here, whether by spirit, word, or fake letter from us; {2:3} Don't let nobody fool you; before that day comes, there's gotta be a major fallin' away and the man of sin has to be revealed, the ultimate troublemaker; {2:4} He's gonna set himself up as God, even chillin' in God's house, actin' like he's God himself. {2:5} Remember when I was with you and told you all this? {2:6} Now you know what's holdin' him back, waitin' for the right time to show up; {2:7} 'Cause the forces of evil are already at work, but there's someone holdin' them back for now, until they're outta the picture. {2:8} Then the real troublemaker will show himself, but Jesus will shut him down with just a word and his brightness when he shows up; {2:9} He's gonna come with all the power and tricks of Satan, deceivin' those who ain't down with the truth, 'cause they'd rather live in lies. {2:10} They're gonna get what's comin' to 'em 'cause they rejected the truth and chose wickedness. {2:11} And 'cause they ain't down with the truth, God's gonna let 'em believe lies and be condemned; {2:12} So they'll pay the price for not believin' the truth and lovin' what's right. {2:13} But we gotta keep givin' thanks to God for y'all, fam, 'cause you're loved by the Lord and he chose you from the jump for salvation through the Spirit and believin' the truth; {2:14} He called you through our message to share in the glory of our Lord Jesus Christ. {2:15} So, fam, stand firm and keep holdin' onto the teachings you've learned, whether from our words or letters. {2:16} Now may our Lord Jesus Christ himself and God our Father, who loves us and gives us eternal comfort and good hope through grace, {2:17} Encourage your hearts and strengthen you in every good word and work.

{3:1} Yo, fam, pray for us that the message of the Lord keeps spreading and gets the respect it deserves, just like it does with y'all. {3:2} And pray we steer clear of sketchy and wicked people 'cause not everyone's down with the faith. {3:3} But trust, the Lord's got our back, He'll make sure you stay strong and safe from evil. {3:4} We're confident in the Lord that you'll keep following our teachings, both now and in the future. {3:5} And may the Lord guide your hearts to love God more and to patiently wait for Christ. {3:6} Listen up, fam, in the name of Jesus, we're telling you to cut ties with anyone living messy lives, not following the path we laid out. {3:7} You know how we rolled when we were with you; we didn't act all crazy. {3:8} We didn't freeload off anyone; we worked hard day and night so we wouldn't be a burden to you. {3:9} Not 'cause we couldn't, but to set an example for you to follow. {3:10} Remember, we told you even when we were there: if someone's not willing to work, they shouldn't expect a free meal. {3:11} We've heard about some of y'all being lazy and gossiping instead of working. {3:12} So we're telling those folks, in the name of Jesus, to chill out, work quietly, and earn their own keep. {3:13} But you, fam, don't get tired of doing good. {3:14} And if someone ain't following our rules in this letter, take note of them and don't hang out with them, so they realize their mistake. {3:15} But don't treat them like enemies; remind them they're still part of the fam. {3:16} May the Lord of peace give you peace always, no matter what. May the Lord be with all of you. {3:17} This shoutout from Paul is legit; you know it's me 'cause I'm signing off. {3:18} May the grace of our Lord Jesus Christ be with all of you. Amen.

1 Timothy

✚✚✚

{1:1} Yo, it's Paul, reppin' as an apostle of Jesus Christ 'cause God our Savior and Lord Jesus Christ are our hope; {1:2} Shoutout to Timothy, my homie in the faith: grace, mercy, and peace from God our Father and Jesus Christ our Lord. {1:3} When I was chillin' in Macedonia, I hit you up to stay in Ephesus and make sure folks ain't preachin' no other stuff; {1:4} Don't be listenin' to all them crazy stories and never-ending family trees that just stir up arguments instead of buildin' people up in faith. {1:5} 'Cause the whole point of these commands is to spread love from a genuine heart, with a clean conscience, and real faith; {1:6} But some people veer off course and get caught up in useless talkin'. {1:7} They wanna act like they know it all about the law, but they ain't got a clue what they're talkin' about. {1:8} But we know the law is legit if you use it right; {1:9} The law ain't for those who are already doin' right but for the lawbreakers, disobedient folks, and all kinds of sinners. {1:10} It's for those into all sorts of shady stuff, like sex outside marriage, human trafficking, lyin', and anything else that goes against sound teachings; {1:11} This all lines up with the dope news about our blessed God, which I've been entrusted with. {1:12} Big ups to Christ Jesus our Lord for givin' me the strength and trust to serve in this ministry; {1:13} I used to be all about dissin' Jesus and messin' with his peeps, but I got mercy 'cause I was ignorant and didn't know better. {1:14} But Jesus hooked me up with mad grace, and now I'm all about faith and love in him. {1:15} This truth ain't no joke: Jesus came into the world to save sinners, and I'm the prime example of that. {1:16} But I got shown mercy so others could see how patient Jesus is, leading them to eternal life. {1:17} So shoutout to the eternal King, immortal and invisible, the only wise God, for all the honor and glory, now and forever. Amen. {1:18} Timothy, my dude, I'm passin' on this mission to you, based on the prophecies spoken over you, so you can fight the good fight; {1:19} Holdin' on tight to faith and a clear conscience, 'cause some folks out there ditched their faith and wrecked their lives, like Hymenaeus and Alexander, who I had to hand over to Satan so they'd learn not to diss God.

{2:1} So here's the deal: prayin' should be priority number one, with all kinds of prayers and thanks for everyone, {2:2} Especially for leaders and those in charge, so we can live chill lives, focused on God and keepin' it real. {2:3} God's all about this, diggin' it when people get saved and find the truth. {2:4} 'Cause he wants everyone to be saved and know what's up. {2:5} 'Cause there's only one God and one go-between for God and us—Jesus, the ultimate homie; {2:6} He gave himself up to save everyone, and that's the real talk. {2:7} I'm all about preachin' and teachin' this truth, swearin' by Christ, not messin' around; I'm all about bringin' this to the Gentiles, keepin' it real. {2:8} So I'm down for prayer sessions everywhere, with pure intentions and no doubts. {2:9} And girls, keep it classy with modest clothes, no flashy jewelry or fancy hairstyles; {2:10} Instead, let your godly actions do the talkin'. {2:11} Stay quiet in church and respect authority; {2:12} I ain't lettin' girls take charge or teach; they should keep it chill and listen. {2:13} 'Cause Adam came first, then Eve, no cap. {2:14} And Adam wasn't fooled, but Eve fell for it and messed up. {2:15} But she'll be alright through childbearing, if she keeps it real with faith, love, and holiness.

{3:1} Yo, here's the real deal: if someone's aiming to be a bishop, that's a solid gig they're after. {3:2} A bishop's gotta be on point—faithful to one spouse, always alert and chill, well-behaved, hospitable, and good at teaching. {3:3} No drinking, no fighting, no love for money—just patience, no drama, and no greed. {3:4} He's gotta run his own house well, with respectful kids. {3:5} 'Cause if he can't handle his own fam, how's he gonna run God's crew? {3:6} And he can't be a newbie, 'cause he might get cocky and fall into the devil's trap. {3:7} Plus, he needs a good rep even outside the crew, so he doesn't get caught up in scandal. {3:8} Deacons gotta be serious too—no double-talk, not heavy on the drinks, and definitely not into shady money. {3:9} They gotta keep the faith tight with a clear conscience. {3:10} First, test 'em out; if they're solid, then let 'em do the deacon thing without any issues. {3:11} Oh, and their wives? Gotta be classy—no gossip, level-headed, faithful. {3:12} Deacons also gotta stick to one spouse and keep their family in line. {3:13} If they do well as deacons, they're leveling up in the faith game big time. {3:14} I'm writing this hoping to visit you soon, but if I'm delayed, you gotta know how to act in God's house—the church is where it's at, the truth's foundation. {3:15} And no doubt, the mystery of godliness is huge: God came in human form, approved by the Spirit, seen by angels, preached to the Gentiles, believed in worldwide, and taken up in glory.

{4:1} Listen up, the Spirit's saying it straight: in the future, some will bail on the faith, falling for deceitful spirits and messed-up teachings. {4:2} They'll be fakin' it, their consciences burnt out. {4:3} They'll try to ban marriage and certain foods, but that's not the vibe for believers who know what's up. {4:4} Everything God made is good, nothing's off-limits if you're thankful. {4:5} The word of God and prayer make it legit. {4:6} Remind the crew of this stuff, and you'll be a solid minister of Jesus, nourished in faith and good teachings. {4:7} Leave behind those wild stories; focus on living a godly life. {4:8} Physical workouts are cool, but being godly pays off now and later, guaranteeing a lit life. {4:9} This truth is rock solid and worth embracing. {4:10} We hustle and take heat 'cause we trust the living God, the Savior of everyone, especially believers. {4:11} Teach this stuff like it's the real deal. {4:12} Don't let anyone doubt you 'cause you're young; set an example in how you talk, act, love, and live out your faith. {4:13} Until I come, focus on reading, encouraging, and teaching. {4:14} Don't ignore the gift you've been given; it came through prophecy and laying on of hands. {4:15}

Dive deep into these things; give yourself fully to them, and everyone will see your growth. {4:16} Stay true to yourself and the teachings; stick with it 'cause it's not just about you—it's about saving yourself and those who listen to you.

{5:1} Yo, don't diss an older person; treat 'em like you would your pops, and treat younger dudes like your bros; {5:2} Respect older ladies like your moms, and younger ones like your sisters, keeping it pure. {5:3} Look out for widows who really need help. {5:4} But if a widow's got family, they gotta step up and take care of 'em first, showing love and respect, 'cause that's what God's about. {5:5} A real widow trusts in God and stays devoted in prayer day and night. {5:6} But if a widow's all about that party life, she's spiritually dead. {5:7} Spread this word so they can't pin no blame on us. {5:8} But anyone who doesn't take care of their own fam, especially those in their own house, is worse than someone who don't even believe. {5:9} Don't put young widows on the support list; they'll end up wanting to get married again and turn away from God, breaking their first commitment. {5:10} Only put older widows on the list who've been faithful to their husband, known for their good deeds, like raising kids, taking care of strangers, washing feet, helping the needy, and doing good in general. {5:11} Younger widows, though, should marry again, have kids, run their households well, and not give the haters any reason to talk trash. {5:12} Some have already fallen for Satan's tricks. {5:13} If anyone's got believing relatives who are widows, they should step up and help them out, so the church isn't left with the whole burden. {5:14} Show double respect to those elders who lead well, especially those who work hard at preaching and teaching. {5:15} Don't jump to conclusions about elders; make sure there are witnesses before you start accusing them of anything. {5:16} Call out those who are sinning in front of everyone, so others learn from it. {5:17} I swear by God, Jesus, and the angels, stick to these rules without playing favorites. {5:18} Don't lay hands on anyone too quickly, and don't get caught up in other people's sins; keep yourself clean. {5:19} Drink a little wine instead of just water; it's good for your stomach and helps with other health issues. {5:20} Some people's sins are obvious, leading to judgment, while others follow later. {5:21} The same goes for good deeds; some are obvious, while others are hidden.

{6:1} Slaves who believe should respect their masters so God's teachings aren't disrespected. {6:2} Even if your boss is a believer, don't slack off; do your job well 'cause they're family and you're benefitting from them. Spread this message around. {6:3} Anyone teaching differently and not sticking to the words of Jesus and godly teachings is arrogant and ignorant, causing arguments and envy. {6:4-5} They're all about arguing and stirring up trouble, thinking that being religious means making money. Stay away from people like that. {6:6} True godliness with contentment is where it's at. {6:7} We came into this world with nothing, and we'll leave with nothing. {6:8} So as long as we got food and clothes, we're good. {6:9} But those chasing after wealth fall into traps and get messed up with foolish desires that lead to ruin. {6:10} Money's the root of all evil; some folks want it so bad they lose their faith and end up miserable. {6:11} But you, man of God, stay away from all that and focus on doing what's right, living for God, and being patient, loving, and humble. {6:12} Fight the good fight of faith, grab hold of eternal life, and stay true to your faith in front of everyone. {6:13} I charge you in front of God and Jesus, who stayed true to their faith even when faced with death. {6:14} Keep these commandments clean and blameless until Jesus shows up. {6:15-16} He'll come when the time's right, the only one with true power, the King of kings and Lord of lords, dwelling in light no one can approach. To Him be all honor and power forever. Amen. {6:17} Tell rich folks not to get too cocky or trust in their money, but in God, who blesses us with everything to enjoy. {6:18} Encourage them to do good, be generous, and share what they have, building up a good future and holding onto eternal life. {6:19} Timothy, stay true to your calling, avoiding worthless arguments and false teachings. {6:20} Some people claiming to be wise have strayed from the faith because of it. Grace be with you. Amen.

2 Timothy

✦✦✦

{1:1} Yo, it's Paul, an apostle of Jesus Christ, doin' my thing 'cause that's what God wants, spreadin' that promise of life in Christ Jesus; {1:2} Big shoutout to Timothy, my boy, much love and blessings from God the Father and Christ Jesus our Lord. {1:3} I gotta give props to God, keepin' it real like my ancestors, always keepin' you in my prayers, day and night; {1:4} Can't wait to see you, rememberin' those tears, but I know we'll be straight-up stoked when we chill; {1:5} Thinkin' back on that real faith you got, first from your grandma Lois and your mom Eunice, and I know you got it too. {1:6} So, don't forget to keep that gift God gave you, through me layin' hands on you. {1:7} 'Cause God didn't bless us with fear, but with power, love, and a clear mind. {1:8} Don't trip about preachin' the truth or about me bein' locked up; embrace the struggles that come with the gospel, trustin' in God's power; {1:9} He saved us and called us with a holy purpose, not 'cause of our deeds, but 'cause of his own plan and grace, way back before the world started; {1:10} And now, it's all out in the open with Jesus bustin' death and bringin' life and immortality to light through the gospel. {1:11} That's why I'm out here as a preacher, apostle, and teacher, especially for the Gentiles. {1:12} Even though I'm goin' through some stuff for it, I ain't ashamed 'cause I know who I'm rockin' with and I trust him to hold it down for me till the end. {1:13} Hold onto those solid teachings you got from me, keepin' the faith and love in Christ Jesus. {1:14} Guard that good stuff you got through the Holy Spirit livin' in us. {1:15} You know how it is, everyone in Asia turned their backs on me, even dudes like Phygellus and Hermogenes. {1:16} But shoutout to Onesiphorus and his fam for always havin' my back, even when I was locked up; {1:17} When he was in Rome, he went outta his way to find me and kick it, no shame in his game; {1:18} Hope God gives him some mad mercy on judgment day, 'cause he straight-up blessed me when I was in Ephesus, and you know it.

{2:1} So, my dude, stay strong in that grace you got from Christ Jesus. {2:2} Pass on the stuff you learned from me to reliable peeps who can teach others too. {2:3} Brace yourself for some tough times like a soldier for Jesus Christ. {2:4} Don't get caught up in the day-to-day stuff of life, focus on pleasin' the one who enlisted you; {2:5} And if you're gonna compete, make sure you play by the rules if you wanna win. {2:6} The farmer who works hard deserves to enjoy the first fruits of his labor. {2:7} Think about what I'm sayin', and may the Lord give you insight in everything. {2:8} Remember, Jesus Christ, from the line of David, rose from the dead, just like I've been preachin'. {2:9} Yeah, I'm locked up, but God's word ain't locked down. {2:10} So, I put up with all this for the sake of the chosen ones, so they can also get in on that salvation in Christ Jesus with eternal glory. {2:11} It's like a slogan we can trust: If we die with him, we'll live with him; {2:12} If we tough it out, we'll reign with him; if we bail, he'll bail too; {2:13} Even if we doubt, he stays true to himself; he can't disown who he is. {2:14} Keep remindin' folks of this stuff, warning them not to get caught up in pointless arguments that mess people up. {2:15} Do your best to show God you're legit, a worker who ain't gotta be ashamed, rightly dividing up the truth. {2:16} But steer clear of trash talk and useless debates 'cause they only lead to more ungodliness. {2:17} That kinda talk spreads like a disease, just ask Hymenaeus and Philetus; {2:18} They straight-up missed the truth, sayin' the resurrection already went down, messin' with people's faith. {2:19} But don't trip, God's foundation stands strong with his seal: he knows who's his, and anyone who claims to follow Jesus gotta bounce from evil. {2:20} In God's house, there's all kinds of peeps—some honorable, some not so much. {2:21} If you wanna be one of the honorable ones, cleanse yourself from the garbage and be ready for whatever the Master wants, ready to do good deeds. {2:22} Stay away from those young-person temptations and chase after what's right, showin' love, faith, and peace with those who call on the Lord from a pure heart. {2:23} Don't get caught up in dumb arguments; you know they only lead to drama. {2:24} God's servants ain't here to argue but to teach with kindness, even to those who disagree, hopin' God will lead 'em to the truth and they'll come to their senses and escape the devil's trap, 'cause he's got 'em locked up tight.

{3:1} Yo, peep this—when we're in the end times, things are gonna get sketchy. {3:2} People will be all about themselves, greedy, bragging, full of pride, disrespecting parents, ungrateful, and unholy. {3:3} They won't show love, break promises, lie, be uncontrollable, fierce, and hate anyone who's good. {3:4} They'll be straight up traitors, cocky, and care more about fun than God. {3:5} They'll act all religious but reject its power—stay away from those types. {3:6} These are the ones sneaking into homes, fooling weak women loaded with sins and all kinds of desires. {3:7} They're always learning but never getting to the truth. {3:8} Remember how Jannes and Jambres messed with Moses? These guys are just like that—twisted minds, rejected when it comes to real faith. {3:9} But they won't get far; their foolishness will be obvious to everyone, just like it was with those two. {3:10} You've seen how I roll—my teachings, life, goals, faith, patience, and love, even through tough times. {3:11} I've been through it all—persecution in Antioch, Iconium, and Lystra—but God came through. {3:12} Anyone aiming to live godly in Christ is in for some tough times. {3:13} Evil people and deceivers will only get worse, fooling and getting fooled. {3:14} Stick with what you've learned and who taught you—it's legit. {3:15} Since you were young, you've known the Scriptures, which lead to salvation through faith in Christ Jesus. {3:16} All Scripture is inspired by God and helps with teaching, correcting, and training in what's right, so God's people can be fully equipped for good deeds.

{4:1} So listen up—I'm putting you on blast before God and Jesus Christ, who's gonna judge everyone, living and dead, when he appears. {4:2} Preach the word in and out of season; correct, rebuke, and encourage with patience and solid teaching. {4:3} 'Cause people will ditch sound doctrine, chasing their desires and piling up teachers who tell them what they want to hear. {4:4} They'll turn away from truth and go after made-up stories. {4:5} Stay alert, endure hard times, do the work of spreading the good news, and prove you're all in with your ministry. {4:6} I'm ready to go; my time's almost up. {4:7} I've fought the good fight, finished the race, and kept the faith. {4:8} Now, I'm looking forward to a righteous crown from the Lord, the ultimate judge, and not just for me but for all who love his appearing. {4:9} Hurry up and come see me. {4:10} Demas bounced 'cause he loved this world too much; Crescens went to Galatia, Titus to Dalmatia. {4:11} Only Luke's chilling with me; bring Mark—he's been a huge help in ministry. {4:12} Tychicus is holding it down in Ephesus. {4:13} Bring my cloak and books from Troas, especially the parchments. {4:14} Alexander the coppersmith did me dirty; may the Lord give him what he deserves. {4:15} Watch out for him—he's been a real pain. {4:16} No one stood by me at first, but God had my back, spreading the message to the Gentiles and saving me from danger. {4:17} The Lord will keep me safe and bring me to his heavenly kingdom—praise him forever. {4:18} Amen. {4:19} Shout out to Prisca, Aquila, and Onesiphorus' crew. {4:20} Erastus is posted up in Corinth; Trophimus is sick in Miletum. {4:21} Try to visit before winter. Eubulus, Pudens, Linus, Claudia, and all the crew send their regards. {4:22} May the Lord Jesus Christ be with your spirit. Grace be with you. Amen.

Titus

✝✝✝

{1:1} Yo, I'm Paul, doing my thing as a servant of God and an apostle of Jesus Christ, because of the faith of God's chosen peeps and the truth that leads to godliness. {1:2} I'm all about that eternal life God promised long ago, 'cause you know He never lies. {1:3} God revealed His plan at the right time through preaching, a gig He put me on by His command. {1:4} Shoutout to Titus, my homie in the faith: grace, mercy, and peace from God the Father and Jesus Christ our Savior. {1:5} I left you in Crete to get things sorted and appoint elders in every city, like I told you. {1:6} Elders gotta be legit—married once, with well-behaved kids, not out there causing chaos. {1:7} A bishop's gotta be blameless, managing God's business—not stubborn, hot-tempered, or into partying. {1:8} They should be hospitable, loving what's good, and keeping it real. {1:9} They gotta hold tight to solid teaching, so they can encourage and shut down the haters with the truth. {1:10} There are lots of troublemakers out there, especially those from the Jewish crew. {1:11} Shut 'em down—they're ruining whole households for money's sake. {1:12} One of their own prophets even called them out for being liars and lazy gluttons. {1:13} It's true—rebuke them hard so they get back on track, instead of falling for made-up stories and human rules. {1:14} To the pure, everything's cool, but those who are messed up inside can't see that; their minds and consciences are all messed up. {1:15} They claim to know God, but their actions show otherwise—they're a mess and reject anything good.

{2:1} Let's talk about what's real and right. {2:2} Older dudes should be chill, serious, and rock-solid in faith, love, and patience. {2:3} Older women should keep it classy—holy behavior, no gossip, and not partying too hard. {2:4} They should teach the younger women to be level-headed, love their husbands and kids, and handle things at home. {2:5} Young guys, stay on point and be responsible. {2:6} Show everyone how it's done with good deeds, solid teaching, and sincerity. {2:7} Speak truth that can't be argued with, so haters have nothing on you. {2:8} Encourage workers to be respectful and dependable—make God's teachings look good in everything. {2:9} Don't steal; be trustworthy—this way, you represent God's truth well. {2:10-12} God's grace brings salvation to everyone, teaching us to say no to ungodliness and worldly desires, living righteously and godly in this world. {2:13} We're waiting for that blessed hope—Jesus' glorious return. {2:14} He gave Himself to redeem us from sin and make us passionate about doing good. {2:15} Speak up and lead with authority; don't let anyone disrespect you.

{3:1} Yo, remind 'em to respect authority, obey the law, and be down for doing good deeds; {3:2} Don't be out here talking smack about nobody, no fighting, just keep it chill and show kindness to everyone. {3:3} 'Cause let's be real, we used to be fools too, acting all disobedient, getting played, chasing after whatever felt good, living in hate and envy, just a mess; {3:4} But then, bam, God's love and kindness showed up, saving us, not 'cause we did anything great, but 'cause he's merciful, giving us a fresh start through the Holy Spirit; {3:5} He poured it out on us big time through Jesus Christ, hooking us up; {3:6} So now, we're all good, made right with God by his grace, and we're in line for that eternal life vibe. {3:7} And check it, this is some solid truth: keep preaching this stuff so those who believe in God stay on point with doing good stuff. That's what's up and it helps everyone out. {3:8} But don't waste time on dumb arguments, family trees, or legal debates; they're a waste of time. {3:9} If someone keeps causing drama after you've warned them twice, peace out on 'em; {3:10} 'Cause they're messing themselves up, no need to mess with that. {3:11} When Artemas or Tychicus roll through, make sure you come kick it with me in Nicopolis; I'm planning on chilling there for the winter. {3:12} Hook up Zenas the lawyer and Apollos, make sure they got everything they need for their trip. {3:13} And tell our crew to keep doing good stuff for those who need it, so we ain't just sitting around being useless. {3:14} Shoutout to everyone with me, big love to all who ride with us in the faith. Grace to you all. Amen.

Philemon

✦✦✦

{1:1} Yo, it's Paul, locked up for Jesus, shoutout to my bro Timothy. This one's for Philemon, our homie and partner, {1:2} Also big ups to Apphia and Archippus, our crew, and the church at your place. {1:3} Sending you grace and peace from God the Father and Jesus Christ. {1:4} I'm always thanking God for you in my prayers, {1:5} I've heard about your love and faith, how you're all about Jesus and the saints. {1:6} Keep sharing your faith—it's making a difference in Christ Jesus. {1:7} Your love brings us joy, refreshing all the saints. {1:8} I could be bold and tell you what's up, {1:9} But I'm asking you as Paul the old-timer and Jesus' prisoner, out of love. {1:10} I'm asking for Onesimus, my boy I raised while I was locked up. {1:11} He used to be no good, but now he's valuable to both of us. {1:12} I'm sending him back—take him in like you'd take me in. {1:13} I wanted to keep him with me, helping me out, {1:14} But I didn't wanna force it; I want your kindness to be genuine. {1:15} Maybe he left for a bit so you could have him back forever. {1:16} Treat him like family, not just a servant—a beloved brother. {1:17} If you see me as a partner, treat him like you'd treat me. {1:18} If he owes you anything, charge it to me. {1:19} I, Paul, will take care of it—I won't mention how much you owe me. {1:20} Let's bring joy to each other in the Lord. {1:21} I trust you'll go above and beyond what I'm asking. {1:22} And hey, get a place ready for me; I believe your prayers will bring me to you soon. {1:23} Shoutout to Epaphras, my fellow prisoner in Jesus, {1:24} And to Marcus, Aristarchus, Demas, and Luke, my crew. {1:25} Grace of our Lord Jesus Christ be with you. Amen.

Hebrews

✚✚✚

{1:1} Yo, God used to drop knowledge in mad different ways to our ancestors through prophets back in the day, {1:2} But nowadays, he's speaking straight to us through his Son, who's like the heir of everything and even made the whole universe happen; {1:3} This dude shines with God's glory, he's the exact image of God, and he's holding everything together just by his word, and get this, he cleared our sins by himself and then kicked it on God's right side; {1:4} And he's way above the angels, like he scored a way better name than them just by being him. {1:5} 'Cause like, when did God ever say to any angel, "You're my Son, today's your birthday"? Or, "I'm your Dad, and you're my kid"? {1:6} Or when he introduced his Son to the world, he was like, "All angels, bow down and show respect." {1:7} But when it comes to angels, he's like, "Y'all are just spirits doing your thing, and flames of fire serving me." {1:8} But to his Son, he straight-up says, "You're God, and your rule's gonna last forever; you're all about righteousness." {1:9} And 'cause you're all about doing what's right and hating what's wrong, God's hooked you up with mad joy more than anyone else. {1:10} And he's like, "You, Lord, laid down the foundation of the earth from the jump; the heavens are your handiwork; {1:11} They're gonna fade away, but you're staying strong, and they're all gonna wear out like old clothes. {1:12} But you'll be chilling, staying the same, never getting old." {1:13} But he never said to an angel, "Sit by my side while I take care of your enemies." {1:14} Aren't angels just servants sent out to help those who are gonna inherit salvation?

{2:1} So, we gotta be seriously paying attention to what we've been hearing, 'cause we can't let it slip away. {2:2} 'Cause if the word spoken by angels was legit and every time someone messed up, they got what was coming to them, {2:3} Then how can we escape messing up big time if we ignore this super dope salvation deal that the Lord started talking about and confirmed to us by the ones who heard him? {2:4} God was backing them up, showing signs, doing miracles, and giving out gifts through the Holy Spirit, all according to his plan. {2:5} 'Cause he didn't put the future world under angel control, and that's what we're talking about here. {2:6} Instead, someone else said, "What's up with humans? Why you even care about us? Why you coming to check us out?" {2:7} You made us a little less than angels but hooked us up with honor and made us rulers over your stuff; {2:8} You put everything under our feet. But we don't see everything under our control yet. {2:9} But we see Jesus, who went through some rough times, got crowned with glory and honor, all 'cause of God's grace, taking death for every person. {2:10} 'Cause it made sense for God to make the dude who's in charge of everything to go through tough times to bring a bunch of people to glory; it was like the perfect training. {2:11} 'Cause he's the one who makes us holy, and we're all connected in that. That's why he's not ashamed to call us family; {2:12} He's like, "I'm gonna tell everyone about you, God, and in the middle of the crew, I'm gonna give you props." {2:13} And he's like, "I'm putting my trust in him," and, "Check it out, me and all the people God gave me." {2:14} 'Cause now that we're part of this flesh and blood deal, he got in on it too, taking on the same stuff so he could take down the one who had the power over death, the devil; {2:15} And free up those who were scared of dying and living in fear their whole lives. {2:16} 'Cause he didn't come to help out angels, but he came to help out Abraham's descendants. {2:17} So, he had to be like us in every way to be a compassionate and faithful high priest, taking care of our connection to God and fixing things up between us and God 'cause of our mess-ups. {2:18} 'Cause since he went through tough times and got tempted, he knows how to help out when we're dealing with tough times too.

{3:1} Yo, fam, let's recognize Jesus as our main Apostle and High Priest. {3:2} He stayed loyal to God who appointed him, just like Moses held it down in his time. {3:3} Jesus gets even more props than Moses 'cause he built the whole house, and the builder gets more respect than the house itself. {3:4} Every house is built by someone, but God built everything. {3:5} Moses was faithful too, like a servant, setting the stage for what was to come. {3:6} But Jesus runs his own house—we're his crew if we stay confident and hopeful till the end. {3:7} So listen up, when you hear God's voice today, don't harden your hearts like they did in the wilderness. {3:8} Don't be stubborn like back in the day when they tested God's patience. {3:9} Remember when your ancestors tested God for forty years? {3:10} God was fed up with that generation; they didn't know his ways. {3:11} So he swore they wouldn't enter his rest. {3:12} Be careful, fam, don't let unbelief mess you up and turn you away from God. {3:13} Encourage each other every day, so sin doesn't deceive and harden your hearts. {3:14} We're with Christ if we stay confident from start to finish. {3:15} Don't harden your hearts like they did in the past. {3:16} Some heard but still rebelled—not everyone who left Egypt with Moses made it. {3:17} God was fed up for forty years with those who sinned and died in the wilderness. {3:18} They missed out on God's rest because they didn't believe. {3:19} So learn from that—they couldn't enter because of unbelief.

{4:1} Let's be careful not to miss out on God's promise of rest. {4:2} The gospel was preached to us just like to them, but it didn't help them because they didn't believe what they heard. {4:3} We who believe are the ones entering into that rest promised by God. {4:4} God rested on the seventh day from his work, and he talks about entering his rest. {4:5} He still offers that rest, and those who were first offered it didn't enter because of unbelief. {4:6} So there's still a rest for God's people to enter. {4:7} God sets a specific day, saying, "Today, if you hear his voice, don't harden your hearts." {4:8} If Joshua had given them rest, God wouldn't talk about another day. {4:9} There's still a rest waiting for God's people. {4:10} Those who enter God's rest stop working, just like God did. {4:11} Let's work to enter that rest, so we don't fall like they did because of unbelief. {4:12} God's word is alive and powerful, sharper than any sword, revealing our thoughts and intentions. {4:13} Everything is laid bare before him; nothing is hidden from his sight. {4:14} We have a great high priest, Jesus the Son of God, who's gone into heaven. {4:15} He understands our struggles and temptations but never sinned. {4:16} So let's come boldly to God's throne of grace to find help when we need it most.

{5:1} Yo, check it: every high priest picked from the crew is set up for the people when it comes to God stuff, to make offerings and sacrifices for sins. {5:2} They can feel for the clueless and those who've lost their way 'cause they're dealing with their own struggles. {5:3} So they gotta offer sacrifices not just for the people but also for themselves. {5:4} No one just grabs this gig; it's a call from God, like it was for Aaron. {5:5} Same goes for Christ; He didn't take on the high priest role himself but got appointed by God, who said, "You're my Son; today I've become your Dad." {5:6} And in another spot, God says, "You're a priest forever, just like Melchisedec." {5:7} When Jesus was doing His thing on Earth, He prayed hard with tears to the One who could save Him from death, and He was heard 'cause He was reverent. {5:8} Even though He was God's Son, He learned obedience from what He suffered. {5:9} And once He was perfect, He became the source of eternal salvation for all who obey Him, chosen by God to be a high priest like Melchisedec. {5:10} There's a lot more to say about this, but it's hard to explain since y'all are slow to catch on. {5:11-12} By now, you should be teaching, but you still need someone to teach you the basics all over again—like you're babies needing milk, not solid food. {5:13} Anyone still on milk is clueless about what's right; they're still babies. {5:14} But solid food is for the mature, who've trained themselves to know the difference between good and evil.

{6:1} So let's move on from the basic stuff about Christ and aim for deeper understanding, not going back to repenting from dead deeds or just having faith in God. {6:2} We're talking about diving into deeper stuff like baptisms, laying on hands, resurrection from the dead, and eternal judgment. {6:3} We'll do that if God allows. {6:4-5} 'Cause once you've tasted the heavenly gift, shared in the Holy Spirit, tasted God's good word, and felt the power of the future age, {6:6} then turned your back, it's impossible to bring you back to repentance. You'd be crucifying the Son of God all over again and making a public spectacle of Him. {6:7} Just like how the earth drinks up rain and produces crops, but if it produces thorns and weeds, it's useless and in for burning. {6:8-9} But we're confident better things await you—things that come with salvation, even though we're talking like this. {6:10} God won't forget how you've served and are still serving His peeps out of love for Him. {6:11} Keep up the same diligence so you can have full assurance of hope until the end, {6:12} not slacking off, but following the footsteps of those who inherited God's promises through faith and patience. {6:13} When God made a promise to Abraham, since He couldn't swear by anyone greater, He swore by Himself, {6:14} saying, "I will surely bless you and give you many descendants." {6:15} So after Abraham patiently endured, he received what was promised. {6:16} People swear by someone greater than themselves, and an oath confirms what they say and ends all argument. {6:17} So when God wanted to make the unchanging nature of His purpose very clear to the heirs of what was promised, He confirmed it with an oath. {6:18} This hope is a strong and trustworthy anchor for our souls. It leads us through the curtain into God's inner sanctuary. {6:19} Jesus has already entered there for us. He has become our eternal High Priest in the order of Melchisedec.

{7:1} So, like, there's this dude Melchisedec, right? He's like king of Salem, totally a priest of the most high God. He's hanging with Abraham after he totally kicks some kings' butts, and he's all blessing him and stuff. {7:2} And get this, Abraham gives him like a tenth of everything, 'cause Melchisedec is king of righteousness and then peace, yo. {7:3} And check it, this dude's got no dad, no mom, no beginning or end, just like Son of God vibes, you know? And he's rocking that priest gig forever. {7:4} Seriously, Abraham gave him the tenth, like showing mad respect. {7:5} And then there's the sons of Levi, doing their priestly thing, taking tithes and all, as per the law, even though they're like Abraham's fam. {7:6} But Melchisedec, he ain't even from that crew, yet he's getting tithes from Abe and blessing him like he's got the power. {7:7} No doubt, the lesser gets blessed by the greater. {7:8} And check it, people are giving tithes to dudes who kick the bucket, but Melchisedec? Nah, he's living large, still getting his. {7:9} And Levi, he's still in his dad's loins when Melchisedec is doing his thing, so he's technically tithing too. {7:10} Like, if the Levitical crew were all about perfection, why the need for another priest like Melchisedec, not following the Aaron crew? {7:11} Switch up the priesthood, you gotta switch up the law, man. {7:12} 'Cause this dude, he's from another tribe, no one's ever seen his face at the altar. {7:13} And get this, Jesus, he's from the tribe of Judah, and Moses never said anything about priests from there. {7:14} It's crystal clear, a priest like Melchisedec means a new game, not bound by old-school rules but rocking that eternal life vibe. {7:15} He's like the OG, setting the stage for another priest to step up, not following the old-school laws but bringing that endless life energy. {7:16} He's not about some outdated commandments but rocking that eternal power, you feel me? {7:17} Because he's got that stamp of approval, "You're a priest forever, Melchisedec style." {7:18} Old rules? Yeah, they're out, 'cause they were weak and useless anyway. {7:19} Those laws? They couldn't make anyone perfect, but now we got a better hope to get close to God. {7:20} And since Melchisedec got that oath, he's in a league of his own, no random priest vibes here. {7:21} Unlike those other priests, he's got God's oath backing him up, making him the ultimate priest, Melchisedec style. {7:22} Jesus, he's like the guarantor of this new deal, a covenant that's way better. {7:23} Back in the day, priests were dropping like flies, but not this guy, he's here for the long haul. {7:24} Unlike those other priests, he's in it for life, no changing his game. {7:25} So yeah, he can save anyone, totally bring them close to God, 'cause he's always there, making moves for them. {7:26} He's the high priest we need, pure, blameless, undefiled, and way above any earthly stuff. {7:27} No need for daily sacrifices, he did it once, for everyone, offering himself up. {7:28} The old law? Yeah, it had some flaws, making imperfect men priests, but this new deal? It's all about the Son, consecrated forevermore.

{8:1} Summing it up, we got this high priest, chilling at God's right hand in the heavenly throne room. {8:2} He's all about the sanctuary, the real deal tabernacle, not some human-made stuff. {8:3} Every high priest? Yeah, they're all about offering sacrifices, so this guy's got something to bring to the table too. {8:4} But if he was on Earth, he wouldn't even qualify, 'cause there are already priests doing their thing according to the law. {8:5} They're just copying the heavenly setup, like Moses was told when he was building the tabernacle, following the heavenly blueprint to a T. {8:6} But this guy? He's got a way better gig, 'cause he's the mediator of a better deal, a covenant based on way better promises. {8:7} If the old covenant was perfect, there'd be no need for a new one, right? {8:8} But there were issues with the old crew, so God's like, "Time for a new covenant, with Israel and Judah." {8:9} Not like the old one when they bailed on me, says the Lord. {8:10} This new deal? It's all about getting those laws inside their heads and hearts, being their God, and them being my people, no teaching needed, 'cause they'll all know me from top to bottom. {8:11} I'll be forgiving their mess-ups, forgetting all their junk, making the old covenant obsolete. {8:12} That old covenant? It's dying out, ready to vanish, 'cause something way better's coming. {8:13} So there you have it, old stuff making way for the new, getting ready to fade into history.

{9:1} So, the first covenant had rules for worship and a physical sanctuary. {9:2} There was a tabernacle with the candlestick, table, and showbread, known as the sanctuary. {9:3} Behind the second veil was the Holiest of all, {9:4} containing the golden censer, the ark of the covenant with manna, Aaron's rod, and the covenant tablets. {9:5} Above it were the cherubim overshadowing the mercy seat, too deep to explain fully here. {9:6} The priests regularly entered the first tabernacle to serve God. {9:7} But the high priest entered the second part alone once a year, with blood for his sins and those of the people. {9:8} The Holy Spirit was showing that the way into the holiest place wasn't clear while the first tabernacle stood. {9:9} This setup was symbolic for that time, with gifts and sacrifices that couldn't perfect the conscience. {9:10} It focused on external rituals until a better way came. {9:11} Jesus arrived as a high priest of greater things through a perfect tabernacle not made by human hands. {9:12} He entered the holy place with his own blood, securing eternal redemption. {9:13} If animal blood could purify, how much more can Christ's blood cleanse us to serve the living God? {9:14} Christ's sacrifice purges our consciences from dead works. {9:15} He's the mediator of a new covenant, bringing redemption for sins under the old covenant, so believers receive eternal inheritance. {9:16} A covenant needs a testator's death to take effect. {9:17} It's only valid after the testator dies. {9:18} The first covenant was established with blood. {9:19} Moses used blood to seal the covenant with the people and the tabernacle. {9:20} He said, "This is the blood of the covenant God commands for you." {9:21} Moses also sprinkled blood on the tabernacle and its vessels. {9:22} Almost everything is purified by blood under the law, and without shedding blood, there's no forgiveness. {9:23} It was necessary for heavenly things to be purified with better sacrifices. {9:24} Christ entered heaven itself, appearing before God for us. {9:25} He doesn't need to offer himself repeatedly like the high priest; {9:26} he appeared once to remove sin by sacrificing himself. {9:27} People die once, then face judgment; {9:28} Christ was offered once to bear many sins, and he'll return for salvation without sin for those waiting for him.

{10:1} Yo, peeps, peep this: the old law was like a sneak peek of good stuff that was coming, but it couldn't fully deliver the goods like the real deal. Those sacrifices they kept offering year after year couldn't make people perfect. {10:2} If they did, they would've stopped, right? Once you've been cleansed, you shouldn't feel guilty for your sins anymore. {10:3} But those sacrifices just kept reminding people of their sins every year. {10:4} 'Cause let's face it, the blood of bulls and goats can't erase sins. {10:5} So, when Jesus stepped onto the scene, He was like, "No more sacrifices and offerings for me, thanks. You've prepared me a body to do your will." {10:6} God wasn't really into burnt offerings and sacrifices for sin. {10:7} Jesus was like, "Here I am, ready to do your will, God," as it's written in the scriptures. {10:8} See, God wasn't into all those sacrifices offered under the old law. {10:9} So Jesus was like, "I'm here to do your will, God," and He replaced the old system with the new. {10:10} And by following God's will, we're made holy through Jesus Christ's sacrifice once and for all. {10:11} Meanwhile, the priests are still at it, offering the same sacrifices every day, but they can't really wipe out sins. {10:12} But Jesus, after offering one sacrifice for sins forever, took a seat at God's right hand. {10:13} Now He's just waiting until His enemies become His footstool. {10:14} And by that one offering, He's made us perfect forever. {10:15-18} The Holy Ghost backs this up, and God's new covenant is all about putting His laws in our hearts and minds and forgiving our sins for good. {10:19} So, peeps, now that we have Jesus's blood, we can boldly step into God's presence. {10:20} He's set up a new and better way for us through His flesh, like a fresh path through the veil. {10:21} And with Jesus as our high priest, we can come close to God. {10:22} Let's come with pure hearts, fully believing, with our consciences cleared by Jesus's blood and our bodies washed clean. {10:23} Hold on tight to your faith without wavering 'cause God keeps His promises. {10:24} Let's motivate each other to love and do good deeds. {10:25} Don't ditch the gatherings like some do, especially now that the end times are coming closer. {10:26-27} If we keep sinning after knowing the truth, there's no more sacrifice for our sins—just a scary expectation of judgment. {10:28-29} Think about it: under Moses's law, anyone who disrespected it got punished hard, so imagine the consequences for dissing the Son of God and treating His blood like trash. {10:30-34} God's gonna serve up some serious justice. But remember the tough times you faced when you first believed. {10:35} So, keep your confidence strong; it comes with a huge reward. {10:36} You gotta be patient and keep doing God's will to get the promise. {10:37} 'Cause Jesus is coming back real soon, no doubt about it. {10:38} Those who live right with faith will thrive, but if you bail on faith, that's a major bummer for me. {10:39} But we're not about that quitting life; we're all about believing and saving souls.

{11:1} Yo, faith be like the real deal when you're all about hoping for stuff you can't even see. It's like the receipts for things that are totally invisible. {11:2} Elders got mad props for it, you know? {11:3} Faith's got us vibin' on how God straight up spoke the universe into existence, like, things we see weren't made from stuff we can peep. {11:4} Abel, by faith, dropped a way better sacrifice than Cain, and even though he's gone, his righteousness still speaks volumes. {11:5} Enoch skipped death 'cause God was like, "Nah, we out," before he vanished, pleasing God big time. {11:6} You can't please God without faith, yo. Gotta believe He's there and that He's got mad rewards for those who chase after Him. {11:7} Noah, movin' on a word from God about stuff nobody's seen, built an ark and saved his fam, calling out the world's nonsense, and snagged some righteous cred. {11:8} Abraham, by faith, bounced to a place he didn't even know, trusting he'd get some sweet inheritance down the line. {11:9} He lived like a nomad in the land God promised, chillin' with Isaac and Jacob, sharing the same faith. {11:10} He was all about that heavenly city God's building, not some earthly nonsense. {11:11} Sara, by faith, got the strength to pop out a kid way past her prime 'cause she knew God wouldn't flake on His promises. {11:12} From one dude who was as good as dead, a whole army of descendants came out, countless as the stars. {11:13} These homies died still trusting in the promises, even though they only saw them from a distance, declaring they were just passing through this earth. {11:14} They were straight up like, "Yo, we're looking for a better place," not hung up on where they came from. {11:15} If they wanted to go back, they could've, but nah, they were after that heavenly spot. {11:16} God's not ashamed to claim them 'cause He's got a dope city ready for them. {11:17} Abraham, when put to the test, was ready to offer up his son Isaac, knowing God could raise him up from the dead if needed. {11:18} 'Cause God said Isaac's the one through whom Abraham's descendants would come. {11:19} Abraham figured God could bring Isaac back from the dead, 'cause in a way, He already did. {11:20} Isaac, by faith, blessed Jacob and Esau, talkin' about stuff that hadn't even happened yet. {11:21} Jacob, on his deathbed, blessed Joseph's sons and straight up worshipped, leanin' on his staff. {11:22} Joseph, when he was dying, mentioned the Israelites bouncin' from Egypt and gave orders about his bones. {11:23} Moses' parents hid him as a baby 'cause they saw he was legit and weren't scared of the king's orders. {11:24} Moses, when he grew up, ditched the royal fam, choosin' to suffer with God's people instead of chillin' in sin's pleasures. {11:25} He thought gettin' shade for Christ was way better than all the riches in Egypt, 'cause he was focused on the big reward. {11:26} Moses peaced out of Egypt, not sweatin' the king's anger, 'cause he was all about the invisible God. {11:27} By faith, he kept it real with the passover and blood sprinkle, so death would pass over them Egyptians. {11:28} By faith, they straight up walked through the Red Sea like it was dry land, while the Egyptians got dunked tryin' to do the same. {11:29} By faith, Jericho's walls straight up crumbled after some circling for seven days. {11:30} Rahab, the former lady of the night, didn't get wrecked with the non-believers 'cause she welcomed the spies with peace. {11:31} And yo, what more can I say? Time's short to talk about Gideon, Barak, Samson, Jephthah, David, Samuel, and the prophets. {11:32} They straight up conquered kingdoms, did righteous stuff, got promises fulfilled, shut lions' mouths, {11:33} Put out fires, dodged swords, got strong when they were weak, fought hard, and made enemy armies run for the hills. {11:34} Women saw their dead peeps come back to life, while others got tortured but didn't bail so they could snag a better resurrection. {11:35} Some got laughed at, whipped, locked up, {11:36} Stoned, sawn in half, tempted, killed with swords, and lived rough in animal skins, homeless, poor, and tormented. {11:37} These peeps were too good for this world, wandering through deserts, mountains, caves, and hideouts. {11:38} They were the real deal, getting props for their faith, even though they didn't see everything promised. {11:39} God's got something better for us, so they ain't perfect without us. {11:40} He's got us covered, makin' sure we all get there together.

{12:1} Alright, since we're surrounded by a bunch of witnesses, let's drop all our baggage and the sins that trip us up, and let's run this race with patience, okay? {12:2} Keep your eyes on Jesus, the one who started our faith journey and will finish it. He endured the cross, ignoring the shame, and now he's chilling at God's right hand. {12:3} Think about what he went through dealing with sinners so you don't get worn out and lose heart. {12:4} You haven't shed blood fighting against sin yet. {12:5} Remember when God disciplines you, don't take it lightly; don't lose heart when he corrects you. {12:6} The Lord disciplines those he loves and accepts as his children. {12:7} If you endure discipline, that's how God treats you as his child. {12:8} If you're never disciplined, then you're not really his child, you know? {12:9} Our earthly parents disciplined us, and we respected them. Shouldn't we respect God even more and live? {12:10} Earthly parents disciplined us for a short time for their own pleasure, but God disciplines us for our own good, so we can share in his holiness. {12:11} Discipline isn't fun at the time, but it yields good results for those who learn from it. {12:12} So, lift up those droopy hands and weak knees. {12:13} Keep on the straight path so no one gets lost or hurt. {12:14} Strive for peace and holiness, because without holiness, no one will see the Lord. {12:15} Watch out so you don't miss God's grace or let bitterness mess things up for you and others. {12:16} Avoid being immoral or godless like Esau, who traded his birthright for a meal. {12:17} You know what happened to him later; he couldn't get the blessing back, no matter how hard he tried with tears. {12:18} We're not coming to a mountain that can be touched and is full of fire, darkness, and storms. {12:19-23} We're coming to Mount Zion, the heavenly Jerusalem, with countless angels, the assembly of the firstborn, God the Judge of all, and the spirits of righteous people made perfect. {12:24} We also come to Jesus, the mediator of the new covenant, and his blood that speaks better things than Abel's. {12:25} Don't ignore the one speaking to you, because if people didn't escape when they ignored the one speaking on earth, we won't either if we turn away from the one speaking from heaven. {12:26} God shook the earth before, but now he's promised to shake not only the earth but also heaven. {12:27} This means everything that can be shaken will be removed, leaving what can't be shaken. {12:28} So, let's be grateful for the kingdom we're receiving, and serve God with reverence and godly fear, because our God is like a consuming fire.

{13:1} Yo, keep spreading that love among your squad. {13:2} Don't forget to show hospitality to strangers; you never know, you might just be chillin' with angels without even knowing it. {13:3} Remember those who are locked up, like you're right there with them, and those going through tough times, like it's hitting you personally. {13:4} Marriage is legit, and the bedroom is meant to be kept pure, but God's gonna call out the players and cheaters. {13:5} Keep your convo real, without being all greedy; be cool with what you got 'cause God's got your back, always. {13:6} So, don't sweat it; with the Lord on your side, who cares what anyone else thinks or does to you? {13:7} Show respect to those leading you, especially if they're laying down the Word of God for you; follow their faith and peep the endgame of their lifestyle. {13:8} Jesus Christ is the same yesterday, today, and forever; no changes, no flip-flopping. {13:9} Don't get swayed by all sorts of crazy teachings; it's way better to be grounded in grace than in some dietary rules that don't do squat for your soul. {13:10} We got our own altar, and those who stick to the old tabernacle don't get to chow down at our table. {13:11} The animals whose blood the high priest brings into the holy place as a sacrifice for sin are burned outside the camp. {13:12} Similarly, Jesus suffered outside the city gate to make us holy through His own blood. {13:13} So, let's join Him outside the camp, bearing the shame that comes with it. {13:14} 'Cause, yo, we ain't got no permanent city here; we're all about that eternal vibe. {13:15} Through Jesus, let's keep offering up praise to God, giving thanks from our lips for His name. {13:16} And don't forget to do good and share what you have; that's the kind of stuff God's all about. {13:17} Listen to and respect those who lead you; they're looking out for your spiritual well-being and will have to give an account for it, so don't make their job harder. {13:18} Hold it down with prayers for us; we're trying to keep it real and live honorably in every way. {13:19} And, yo, make it happen sooner rather than later, so I can be back in the mix with y'all. {13:20-21} Shoutout to the God of peace who brought back Jesus, the ultimate shepherd, through His everlasting covenant blood, making us all about that good work to please Him, through Jesus; all glory to Him, now and forever. Amen. {13:22} Oh, and take this word of encouragement to heart; I kept this letter short and sweet for y'all. {13:23} Just so you know, our boy Timothy's out of lockdown; if he rolls through soon, I'll catch y'all then. {13:24} Big ups to all the leaders and saints holding it down. Much love from the crew in Italy.

James

✚✚✚

{1:1} Yo, James here, just a servant of God and Jesus, hittin' up the twelve tribes scattered around, yo, what's good? {1:2} A'ight fam, when life throws you mad curveballs, be happy 'cause it's building up your patience game. {1:3} Peep this: testing your faith makes you patient AF. {1:4} So, let patience do its thing, 'cause when it's done, you'll be all complete, no missing pieces. {1:5} Need wisdom? Ask God, yo, He's handing it out like candy, no questions asked. {1:6} But ask with faith, none of that wishy-washy vibe. Doubters are like waves in a storm, tossed everywhere. {1:7} Don't expect anything from the Lord if you're double-minded, that's a no-go. {1:8} Can't be wishy-washy, fam, it's like trying to stand on a slippery slope. {1:9} If you're low-key, be happy when life gets you high. {1:10} But if you're living large, stay humble 'cause your time's ticking like a wilting flower. {1:11} The rich may shine, but they're fading fast like grass in the scorching sun. {1:12} Props to those who ride out the trials; they get the crown of life, a big promise for those who love God. {1:13} Don't blame God for your temptations; that's on you, chasing after your own cravings. {1:14} Craving leads to sin, and sin's endgame? Death, no questions asked. {1:15} Don't play yourself, fam. {1:16} Every lit gift comes straight from God, no changing His vibe, no shady moves. {1:17} God's all about consistency, like the OG Father of Lights, no shadows in sight. {1:18} He chose us, using His truth to make us His top-tier crew. {1:19} So, fam, be quick to listen, slow to chat, and chill with the anger, 'cause that's not bringing any righteous vibes. {1:20} Lose the dirt and bad vibes, and be open to God's truth that can save your soul. {1:21} Don't just hear the word; live it out, or you're just frontin' on yourself. {1:22} If you're all talk and no action, it's like looking in a mirror and forgetting what you look like. {1:23} But if you're all about that freedom law and stay true, you'll be blessed in what you do. {1:24} Fake religiosity? Nah, don't even. If you can't control your mouth, your faith's a joke. {1:25} Real religion's about helping the helpless and staying clean in a messed-up world.

{2:1} Fam, don't play favorites with your faith, Jesus don't roll like that. {2:2} If some bougie dude and a broke homie show up, don't be kissing up to the rich one, dissing the poor; that's some shady vibes, yo. {2:3} God's all about the underdogs, rich in faith and heirs to His kingdom, straight up. {2:4} So, peep this: if you're showing favoritism, you're judging people wrong, and that's not cool. {2:5} God's squad? They're often the underdogs; rich dudes just drag you into court. {2:6} They disrespect God's name, the same one you're repping. {2:7} If you're all about that royal law, loving your neighbor as yourself, you're on point. {2:8} But if you're playing favorites, you're breaking the law, straight up. {2:9} Mess up once, you mess up the whole deal, yo. {2:10} Break one, break 'em all, no exceptions. {2:11} 'Cause if you're all about not cheating on your girl but then you kill someone, you're still breaking the law. {2:12} So, speak and act like you're facing the freedom law's judgment 'cause that's the real deal. {2:13} No mercy for those who show no mercy; mercy's got the upper hand on judgment day. {2:14} So, fam, what's the point if you say you've got faith but don't back it up? Faith alone ain't cutting it. {2:15} If your bro's starving and you're like, "Peace out, stay warm and full," but don't lift a finger to help, what's the deal? {2:16} Faith without action is dead, end of story. {2:17} Someone's like, "I got faith," and another's like, "I got works." Prove your faith through your actions, fam, that's the real deal. {2:18} You believe in God? Cool, even demons do that, and they're shook. {2:19} But check it, faith without works is dead, plain and simple. {2:20} Abraham wasn't just talkin' faith; he showed it when he almost sacrificed his son Isaac. {2:21} Faith and works? They're a tag team, making each other better. {2:22} Abraham's faith got a workout, and his actions made his faith complete. {2:23} God called him righteous, his faith was the real deal. {2:24} So, peep this: faith and works? They're a package deal, not just one or the other. {2:25} Rahab, the ex-homie, was legit 'cause she helped out the spies and got them out safe. {2:26} Dead faith? It's like a body without a soul, no use at all.

{3:1} Yo, fam, don't be all about being the big boss; remember, those in charge get judged harder. {3:2} 'Cause let's be real, we all mess up sometimes. If you can keep a lid on your mouth, you're a total legend and can handle anything. {3:3} Check it, we put bits in horses' mouths to control them, and that tiny rudder on a ship directs the whole beast; same deal with your tongue, small but mighty, sparking major drama. {3:4} Look at ships, massive as they are, they're steered by a tiny rudder wherever the captain wants; that's how powerful words are, yo. {3:5} The tongue might be small, but it talks big game; it can cause a huge mess with just a spark. {3:6} It's like a flame, starting all sorts of trouble, corrupting the whole crew; it's straight-up lit by hell itself. {3:7} Humans have tamed all sorts of wild beasts, but that tongue? Untamable, a straight-up evil, full of toxic vibes. {3:8} With it, we praise God and trash-talk others who are made in His image; straight-up two-faced. {3:9} Yo, it's whack how we bless God and diss our fellow humans; that ain't right, fam. {3:10} How you gonna bless and curse from the same mouth? That's not how we roll, peeps. {3:11} Think about it, a fountain doesn't gush out both fresh and salty water, right? {3:12} A fig tree doesn't bear olives, and a vine doesn't produce figs; same deal, a mouth can't talk blessings and curses. {3:13} If you're smart and chill, show it with your actions, not your ego. {3:14} But if you're all about jealousy and drama, don't front like you're all that; that's not wisdom, it's straight-up toxic. {3:15} That kind of "wisdom" ain't from above; it's earthly, selfish, and straight-up devilish. {3:16} 'Cause where you find jealousy and drama, you find chaos and all kinds of messed-up behavior. {3:17} Real wisdom, though? It's pure, peaceful, and easy to vibe with, full of mercy and good deeds, no faking or favoritism. {3:18} And those who spread that vibe of peace reap the fruits of righteousness.

{4:1} Yo, why you beefin' and brawlin' all the time? Ain't that just your own desires messing you up? {4:2} You want stuff, but you ain't getting it, so you start beefin' and brawlin'; but guess what? You ain't got it 'cause you ain't askin' for it. {4:3} And when you do ask, it's all about satisfying your own selfish cravings; that ain't the vibe, peeps. {4:4} Don't you know being all buddy-buddy with the world means you're like enemies with God? Yeah, that's real talk. {4:5} The Spirit within us ain't all about jealousy, is it? {4:6} But guess what? God's all about grace, especially for those who stay humble; He's all about shutting down the proud. {4:7} So, bow down to God, flip off the devil, and watch him run for the hills. {4:8} Get close to God, and He'll roll up on you; but first, clean up your act, you double-minded peeps. {4:9} When things get rough, don't front; let your vibe be real, even if it means getting heavy with it. {4:10} Humble yourselves before the Lord, and He'll boost you up; that's how we roll. {4:11} Don't be talking smack about each other, fam; dissing your bro is straight-up disrespecting the law; you ain't no judge, so don't act like it. {4:12} There's only one judge who can dish out life or death; who do you think you are to judge someone else? {4:13} Listen up, peeps, all you big talkers making plans for tomorrow and beyond; but you ain't got a clue what's coming next; your life? It's like a puff of smoke, here one sec, gone the next. {4:14-15} You gotta get real, fam; you don't know what tomorrow holds, so it's all about saying, "If the Lord wants it, we'll do it." {4:16} But don't be boasting about your plans; that's just shady. {4:17} If you know what's good but don't do it, that's on you, fam; you're straight-up sinning.

{5:1} Hey, you rich folks, better start crying and screaming 'cause hard times are coming your way. {5:2} Your cash flow's rotting, your designer threads are falling apart. {5:3} Your bling's rusted, and it's gonna call you out big time; all that wealth you hoarded? It's gonna rot away. {5:4} You stiffed the workers who brought in your cash crop, and now they're crying out to God; He's hearing them loud and clear. {5:5} You've been living it up, partying hard while others suffer; you're like sheep headed for slaughter. {5:6} You're straight-up condemning the innocent, and they ain't even putting up a fight. {5:7} So, chill, fam, and wait it out for the Lord's return; just like a farmer waits for that sweet harvest, be patient. {5:8} Keep it cool, fam, and stay strong; the Lord's coming soon. {5:9} Don't be holding grudges, fam; the Judge is already at the door. {5:10} Take notes from the prophets who stayed true to the Lord, even when life got tough; that's how it's done. {5:11} Those who stay strong through the trials? They're the real MVPs; just look at Job and how it all worked out for him. {5:12} And above all, fam, keep it real; don't be throwing around oaths left and right; let your word be your bond, or you'll be in for a world of hurt. {5:13} If you're down and out, pray; if you're feeling good, sing some praises. {5:14} If you're sick, call on the elders of the church to pray for you and anoint you with oil; that prayer of faith can do wonders. {5:15-16} Confess your mess-ups to each other and pray for one another; that's how you find healing. A righteous person's prayers pack a punch. {5:17} Elijah was just a regular dude like us, but his prayers stopped the rain for three and a half years. {5 :18} And when he prayed again, the rain came down, and the earth sprouted new life. {5:19} If someone's lost their way, and you bring them back? You just saved a soul from death and covered over a whole lot of mess-ups.

1 Peter

✝✝✝

{1:1} Yo, it's Peter, dropping a line as Jesus' crew member, shoutout to all the fam scattered around Pontus, Galatia, Cappadocia, Asia, and Bithynia. {1:2} Chosen by God the Father, set apart by the Spirit, and washed in Jesus' blood - y'all got that grace and peace, multiplied like crazy. {1:3} Big ups to God and Jesus for that mad mercy, hooking us up with a fresh start through Jesus rising from the dead. {1:4} Our inheritance? It's straight-up legit, locked in heaven, untouched and eternal. {1:5} God's got our backs, keeping us safe through faith 'til the final showdown. {1:6} So, even though life's hitting hard right now, know it's building up your faith game, worth more than gold when Jesus shows up. {1:7} And speaking of Jesus, even though you haven't seen Him, you're all about that love, trust, and hype for His return. {1:8} That faith? It's the real deal, leading to the ultimate prize: saving your souls. {1:9} Prophets were all up in it, searching and digging deep into the grace coming your way. {1:10} They were all about that grace that's now here, thanks to those preaching the gospel with the Holy Ghost backing them up. {1:11} They were all about that prophetic vibe, pointing to Jesus' suffering and glory to come. {1:12} It's lit 'cause angels wanna know what's up with this good news. {1:13} So, gear up mentally, stay sharp, and keep hope alive for that grace coming your way when Jesus drops in. {1:14} Act like the obedient squad, leaving behind your old ways of ignorance. {1:15} Be holy 'cause God's holy, keeping it 100 in all your dealings. {1:16} Remember, it's written: "Be holy 'cause I'm holy." {1:17} And if you're calling on the Father, know He's checking your actions, so live this life with respect and awe. {1:18} You ain't bought with cash; it's Jesus' blood that got you out of that messed-up lifestyle your ancestors handed down. {1:19} His blood's the real deal, spotless and pure, straight-up valuable. {1:20} Jesus was the plan from way back, now revealed for your time. {1:21} Through Jesus, you're all about that faith and hope vibe in God. {1:22} Your souls got a makeover through truth and love, so keep that love flowing, no fake vibes. {1:23} You're reborn, not from some weak stuff but from the eternal Word of God. {1:24} 'Cause let's face it, life's temporary, but God's Word? It's forever. {1:25} And that's the word being preached to you through the gospel.

{2:1} So, drop the negativity, the fake vibes, and all that gossip. {2:2} Be like newborns, craving that pure spiritual milk to grow strong. {2:3} If you've tasted God's goodness, you know what's up. {2:4} Jesus, the living stone, rejected by people but chosen by God, that's the real MVP. {2:5} And you? You're like living stones, building up a spiritual house where God's down for your offerings through Jesus. {2:6} It's written: "Check out this cornerstone in Zion, chosen and legit. Believe in Him, and you won't be disappointed." {2:7} For those who believe, Jesus is the real deal, but for those who don't, He's a stumbling block. {2:8} Some trip up on Jesus' words, but that's on them; it's all part of the plan. {2:9} But you? You're chosen, royal, holy, and unique, showing off God's goodness to the world. {2:10} Once you were nobody, now you're God's crew, full of mercy. {2:11} So, as strangers in this world, steer clear of those lusts that mess with your soul. {2:12} Keep it real among non-believers, so when they talk trash, they'll see your good deeds and give props to God. {2:13} Respect the authorities, whether it's the king or the governors, 'cause that's what God's about. {2:14} They're there to keep the peace and reward the good, so be part of making that happen. {2:15} Doing good shuts down the haters' ignorance, so use your freedom wisely, repping God's crew. {2:16} Show respect to all, love your crew, fear God, and honor those in charge. {2:17} If you're a worker, respect your boss, not just the chill ones but even the tough ones. {2:18} It's all good if you're suffering for doing what's right 'cause that's commendable in God's eyes. {2:19} What's the big deal if you take a hit for doing wrong? But if you take it for doing good, that's what's up with God. {2:20} Jesus went through it, setting the example for you to follow. {2:21} He never did anything wrong, never talked smack, even when he was dissed; He trusted God to handle it all. {2:22} He took on all our sins, so we could live right; His wounds got us healed. {2:23} Y'all were lost, but now you're back in the Shepherd's care, safe and sound.

{3:1} Yo, wives, listen up: respect your husbands, even if they ain't all about the faith; your behavior might just win them over without you even saying a word, especially if they see you keeping it real and living right. {3:2} Keep it classy and low-key, not all about that flashy stuff like fancy hairdos or bling; nah, it's all about that inner vibe, that chill and humble spirit that's priceless in God's eyes. {3:3} Back in the day, even the holy women kept it real, trusting in God and showing respect to their husbands; take Sarah, for example, she straight-up obeyed Abraham, no questions asked, setting the vibe for all y'all wives. {3:4} Fellas, take notes too; treat your wives with respect, showing them love and honoring their vibe, recognizing they might be physically weaker but equal partners in God's grace, so your prayers ain't blocked. {3:8} And yo, finally, peeps, get on the same page, show some love and empathy to each other, like you're family, compassionate and kind-hearted, never trying to pay back evil with more evil, but straight-up blessing each other, 'cause that's what you're called to do, securing that blessing vibe. {3:9} 'Cause let's face it, if you wanna live your best life and see those good days, you gotta keep your tongue in check, no lies or trash talk; instead, choose good, seek peace, and chase after it, 'cause the Lord's eyes are watching the righteous, and He's listening to their prayers, but He's giving the side-eye to those on the wrong path. {3:13} And seriously, who's gonna mess with you if you're all about that good life? {3:14} But even if you catch flak for doing what's right, count yourself blessed and don't sweat their hate; just keep repping the Lord in your heart, always ready to share the hope within you, but with humility and respect. {3:18} 'Cause it's better to catch heat for doing good than for doing dirt; take Jesus, for example, suffering once for all our mess, bringing us closer to God, though He was put to death in the flesh, He was made alive in the Spirit. {3:20} And yo, peeps, back in Noah's day, when God's patience was running thin, He sent Christ to preach even to those disobedient spirits locked up, 'cause back then, only eight souls got saved through the flood, showing baptism ain't just about washing away dirt but about being right with God, all thanks to Jesus rising up. {3:22} Now, Jesus is up in heaven, chilling at God's right hand, with angels, authorities, and powers all bowing down to Him.

{4:1} So, since Christ suffered in the flesh, you gotta arm yourselves with the same mindset, 'cause anyone who's suffered like Him has said goodbye to sin. {4:2} From now on, it's all about doing God's will, not living for your own desires like you did in the past, partying hard and acting wild; nah, that's so last season. {4:3} 'Cause you've had enough of that old lifestyle, living it up in all sorts of wild ways, but now you're on a different vibe, and those still stuck in the party scene think you're weird for not joining in, dissing you for being different; but they'll have to answer to God, who's ready to judge the living and the dead. {4:6} Yeah, even the dead heard the gospel, giving them a shot at living right with God in the spirit, even though they got judged like everyone else when they were alive. {4:7} But yo, peeps, time's running out, so keep it real and stay woke, staying on your grind with prayer. {4:8} And above all, show mad love to each other, 'cause love covers a multitude of screw-ups. {4:9} Be hospitable to each other, no grudging allowed; share what you got, serving each other with the gifts God gave you, being good stewards of His grace. {4:11} Whether you're speaking or serving, do it like it's straight from God, 'cause in the end, it's all about giving glory to Jesus, who deserves all the praise and power forever and ever. Amen. {4:12} Beloved, don't trip when life gets rough, like it's some crazy surprise; nah, embrace it, 'cause sharing in Christ's sufferings means sharing in His glory too, and when He shows up, you'll be stoked beyond measure. {4:14} If you catch heat for repping Christ, count yourself blessed, 'cause the Spirit of God's glory rests on you, even if they diss you, 'cause on your part, you're straight-up glorifying God. {4:15} But don't suffer for being a criminal or a gossip; nah, if you're gonna catch heat, make sure it's for repping Christ, and when you do, don't be ashamed, but keep it real, giving props to God. {4:17} 'Cause it's time for judgment to start with the fam of God, and if it starts with us, imagine what it'll be like for those who ain't down with the gospel? {4:19} So, if you're catching heat for doing what's right, commit your soul to God and keep doing good, trusting in Him as your faithful Creator.

{5:1} Listen up, elders—I'm right there with you, having seen and shared in Christ's sufferings and the future glory to come. {5:2} Take care of God's crew among you, not because you have to, but because you want to, and definitely not for money, but with a willing heart. {5:3} Don't boss around God's people; instead, lead by example. {5:4} When the head honcho Shepherd shows up, you'll score an eternal crown of glory. {5:5} Younger folks, respect your elders. Everyone, treat each other with humility, 'cause God's not into pride, but He loves showing grace to the humble. {5:6} So, humble yourselves under God's mighty hand, and He'll lift you up at the right time. {5:7} Give all your worries to Him because He cares about you. {5:8} Stay alert and clear-headed because the devil's out there like a roaring lion trying to mess with whoever he can. {5:9} Stand firm against him, knowing you're not alone in facing these challenges. {5:10} After you've suffered a bit, the God of all grace, who called you to eternal glory through Christ, will make you strong, steady, and settled. {5:11} All glory and power to Him forever and ever. Amen. {5:12} Silvanus passed this message along—I'm pretty sure he's a solid bro—just a quick note to encourage and confirm that this is the real deal, God's grace that you're standing in. {5:13} The church in Babylon, along with Marcus, sends their greetings to you. {5:14} Show some love to each other with a kiss. Peace to all of you who belong to Christ Jesus. Amen.

2 Peter

✦✦✦

{1:1} Yo, it's Simon Peter, just your boy servin' up Jesus vibes, shoutin' out to all y'all who got that same dope faith as us, all thanks to God's righteousness and our homie Jesus Christ. {1:2} Yo, may grace and peace flow to you like crazy as you get to know God and Jesus our main man. {1:3} 'Cause check it, God's divine power hooked us up with all we need for life and living right, all through knowing Him who called us to be epic and virtuous. {1:4} And get this, He hooked us up with some sick promises, so we could be part of His divine crew, escaping the messed-up stuff in the world 'cause of lust. {1:5} And yo, on top of all that, add some hustle to your faith, stackin' up that virtue and knowledge. {1:6} Then throw in some self-control, patience, and godliness, keepin' it real with your crew. {1:7} And don't forget to show love to your peeps and everyone else, 'cause love's the ultimate vibe. {1:8} 'Cause if you're all about that life and it's flowin' in you, you'll never be dry or unproductive in knowing Jesus. {1:9} But if you ain't got these vibes, you're blind to what's up, forgettin' you got cleaned up from your past mess. {1:10} So, fam, make sure you're on point with your callin' and chosen status, 'cause if you do, you won't ever fall off. {1:11} That's how you get that VIP access into Jesus' everlasting kingdom. {1:12} And yo, I ain't gonna sleep on reminding you of all this, even though you already know it and got it down; it's all about keepin' it fresh in your minds. {1:13} 'Cause while I'm still kickin' it in this body, I'm gonna keep pumpin' you up with these reminders. {1:14} But yo, I know my time's comin' to bounce, just like Jesus showed me. {1:15} So, I'm gonna make sure you still remember this stuff even after I'm gone. {1:16} 'Cause let's keep it real, we ain't spittin' some made-up stories when we told you about Jesus; nah, we saw His power and glory with our own eyes. {1:17} Like when God the Father gave Jesus major props, sayin' He's His main dude, well pleased and all. {1:18} And we straight-up heard that voice from heaven when we were rollin' with Jesus up on that holy mountain. {1:19} Plus, we got that solid word from the prophets, so you better pay attention, 'cause it's like a light in a dark room, guiding you until the dawn breaks and Jesus lights up your heart. {1:20} And check it, ain't no prophecy in the Bible just some private interpretation; nah, it's all straight from God through His holy crew. {1:21} 'Cause back in the day, it wasn't some human idea that drove the prophets to speak; nah, it was the Holy Spirit movin' them.

{2:1} But yo, don't sleep on this, there were fake prophets back in the day, and there's gonna be fake teachers among you too, sneakin' in with some whack teachings, even denyin' Jesus who bought them, and they're bringin' on their own destruction. {2:2} And believe me, a bunch of people are gonna follow their messed-up ways, dissin' the truth left and right because of them. {2:3} And they're gonna hustle you with smooth talk 'cause they're all about that cash, but trust me, their judgment's been in the works for a while, and they ain't gettin' off easy. {2:4-5} Remember, if God didn't hold back on punishin' angels who messed up, they're locked up tight, waitin' for judgment day; same goes for the old world, 'cept Noah got saved 'cause he was preachin' righteousness while the world got washed away. {2:6-8} And don't forget Sodom and Gomorrah, turned to ash as a warnin' to anyone livin' foul; but God saved Lot, even though he was surrounded by wickedness, it messed with his soul seein' and hearin' all that dirt every day. {2:9} So, God knows how to rescue the righteous and hold the wicked for judgment day, especially those who live for their own desires and diss authority. {2:10-12} But these fakes, they're like dumb animals, just doin' what comes naturally, talkin' trash about stuff they don't understand, and they're gonna pay for it big time. {2:13} They're gonna get what they deserve, livin' it up in the daytime with their sinful pleasures, corrupt to the core, messin' with people's heads while they party with you. {2:14} Their eyes are full of lust, they can't stop sinning, luring in those who ain't steady, they're doomed, cursed kids. {2:15} They've ditched the right path and gone astray, followin' in the footsteps of Balaam, lovin' the cash he got for his evil deeds. {2:16} But he got called out for his mess, even a donkey had to shut him down. {2:17} These fakes are like dry wells, clouds blown away by the wind, headed for total darkness. {2:18} They talk big, offerin' all sorts of stuff to satisfy your desires, they're just tryna trap those who barely escaped from their messed-up ways. {2:19} They promise freedom, but they're slaves to their own corruption; whoever gets caught up with them ends up in bondage. {2:20} 'Cause if you know Jesus and then go back to your old messed-up ways, you're worse off than when you started. {2:21} It would've been better if they never knew about doin' right in the first place, 'cause once you know and turn away, you're in deep trouble. {2:22} It's like that saying, a dog goes back to its own vomit, and a washed pig goes back to rollin' in the mud.

{3:1} Hey again, fam. Gotta remind you to stay sharp. {3:2} Hold tight to the old-school teachings and commands. Stay woke. {3:3} Last days gonna be rough, haters gonna hate, ignoring truth for their own desires. {3:4} Asking where's Jesus, like everything's been chill forever. {3:5-6} Truth is, God's word made everything, and it'll all get washed away. {3:7} But chill, judgment day's coming, heavens and earth held for that fire. {3:8} Time's different for God, patience ain't slacking on promises. {3:9} He's patient, wants everyone to turn around. {3:10} Judgment day gonna sneak up, everything burns. {3:11} So, live holy and godly lives. {3:12} Eyes on the prize, new heavens and earth. {3:13} Keep grinding, chill in peace, spotless and blameless. {3:14} God's patience means salvation, like Paul said. {3:15} Some stuff's hard to get, don't twist it up. {3:16} Watch out for fakes, don't lose your ground. {3:17} Grow in grace and knowledge. {3:18} All glory to Jesus, forever. Amen.

1 John

+ + +

{1:1} Yo, from the jump, we heard it, saw it with our own eyes, and even touched it - the Word of life, fam. {1:2} Life showed up, we saw it, and we're telling you about that eternal life vibe, chilling with the Father, and now, with us. {1:3} What we've seen and heard, we're dropping it here so you can vibe with us, connecting with the Father and His boy Jesus. {1:4} We're hitting you up with this so your joy can be maxed out. {1:5} Here's the deal we got from Him and are passing on: God's all about light, no darkness in His game. {1:6} If we're claiming to be tight with Him but living shady, we're faking it - straight up. {1:7} But if we're living in the light, rolling like Jesus, we're tight with each other, and Jesus' blood keeps us clean from all that dirt. {1:8} Saying we're sin-free? Nah, that's self-deception, and the truth ain't in us. {1:9} But own up to your wrongs, and He's there to wipe the slate clean, making us squeaky clean. {1:10} Denying we've sinned? Man, that's calling God a liar, and we're not about that life.

{2:1} Listen up, my squad, I'm dropping this so you can stay on point. But if you slip up, Jesus has your back with the Father, keeping it real. {2:2} He's the deal-breaker for our sins, not just ours but for everyone worldwide. {2:3} How do we know we're tight with Him? By keeping it real with His rules. {2:4} Fronting like you're down with Him but not following His lead? That's fake, and you ain't got the truth in you. {2:5} But those who stay true to His word? They're dripping with God's love, showing they're in the zone with Him. {2:6} Claiming you're down with Him? Then you gotta walk the walk like He did. {2:7} Fam, I'm not laying down new rules, just reminding you of the OG ones from the start. {2:8} But here's the scoop: the new rule is legit 'cause the darkness is out, and the real light's shining bright. {2:9} If you claim to be in the light but hate on your bro, you're still in the dark, no doubt. {2:10} Loving your crew keeps you in the light, no stumbling blocks in sight. {2:11} But if you're hating, you're walking blind, lost in the dark, not knowing where you're headed. {2:12} I'm dropping this for you, squad, 'cause your slate's clean, thanks to Jesus. {2:13} Shoutout to the OGs, 'cause you've been down with Him from the jump. And to you, young bloods, you've beaten the evil one. And to my little homies, you know the Father. {2:14} To the OGs again, you've been there from the start. To the young guns, you're tough, with God's word deep in you, defeating the evil one. {2:15} Don't get caught up in this world's vibe or its stuff. If you're all about it, you're not feeling the Father's love. {2:16} 'Cause all that worldly stuff - chasing pleasure, craving stuff, and flexing - ain't from the Father but from this world's scene. {2:17} This world's scene? It's fading fast, along with its desires. But those who do God's will? They're in it for the long haul. {2:18} Squad, it's the final countdown, and you've heard about the antichrist coming? Well, there are already many imposters, so you know it's game time. {2:19} They bounced from us 'cause they weren't one of us; if they were, they'd still be rolling with us. But their exit just proved they weren't legit. {2:20} But you? You're anointed by the Holy One, knowing what's up. {2:21} I'm not telling you 'cause you're clueless but 'cause you're woke, and truth ain't about lying. {2:22} Who's lying? Anyone who's denying Jesus as the Christ - they're antichrist, denying the Father and the Son. {2:23} Denying the Son means you're not vibing with the Father, but if you're down with the Son, you're rolling with the Father too. {2:24} Stick with what you heard from the start; if you do, you're sticking with the Son and the Father. {2:25} And that promise? It's eternal life. {2:26} I'm dropping this to school you on those trying to lead you astray. {2:27} But that anointing you got? It's got you covered; you don't need anyone else to teach you 'cause it's all truth, no lies, and it's got you dialed in. {2:28} So, my little homies, stay tight with Him, so when He pops up, you'll be confident, not embarrassed. {2:29} If you know He's legit, you know anyone living right is tight with Him.

{3:1} Yo, peep this: God's love for us is next level, makin' us His own fam, even though the world ain't got a clue 'cause it never knew Him. {3:2} Fam, we're God's squad now, and even though we don't know exactly what's up next, we do know that when Jesus shows up, we're gonna be on His level, seein' Him for who He really is. {3:3} Anyone who's holdin' onto this hope is all about keepin' it pure, just like Jesus is pure. {3:4} And yeah, whoever's out there sinning is breakin' the rules, 'cause sin's just that, breakin' the rules. {3:5} And you know why Jesus showed up? To wipe out our sins, and He's all clean, no sin in Him. {3:6} If you're stickin' with Jesus, you ain't out there sinning; but if you're sinning, you ain't really seen or known Jesus. {3:7} Listen up, fam, don't let nobody fool you; anyone who's livin' right is right with God, just like Jesus is right. {3:8} But anyone who's out there sinning is rollin' with the devil, 'cause he's been at it since day one. Jesus showed up to wreck his game. {3:9} Anyone born of God ain't out there sinning, 'cause God's spirit's in them, keepin' them straight. {3:10} So, it's pretty clear who's reppin' God and who's rollin' with the devil: if you ain't doin' right, you ain't on God's team, and if you ain't lovin' your bro, you ain't with God either. {3:11} This is the deal from the start: love each other. {3:12} Not like Cain, who was straight evil and offed his bro 'cause his own deal was shady and his bro was righteous. {3:13} Don't trip if the world's hatin' on you, fam. {3:14} We know we've moved from death to life 'cause we love our crew; if you ain't lovin', you're still stuck in death. {3:15} If you're hatin' on your bro, you're like a murderer, and you know a murderer ain't got no eternal life. {3:16} Check it, this is love: Jesus laid down His life for us, so we gotta be down to lay ours down for our crew. {3:17} If you're sittin' on this world's riches and see your bro strugglin' but don't help out, God's love ain't in you. {3:18} My fam, don't just talk about love; show it for real. {3:19} 'Cause that's how we know we're livin' right, and it gives us peace with God. {3:20} If our heart's makin' us feel guilty, God knows what's up better than we do. {3:21} But if our heart ain't guilt-trippin', we got confidence with God. {3:22} And when we ask for stuff, we get it 'cause we're keepin' His rules and doin' what He likes. {3:23} And here's the deal: believe in Jesus and love each other, like He told us. {3:24} Stickin' to His rules means we're hangin' with Him, and He's hangin' with us, and we know that 'cause of His Spirit with us.

{4:1} Fam, don't just believe everything you hear; test it to see if it's really from God, 'cause there's a bunch of fake prophets out there. {4:2-3} You can tell if it's from God if it's all about Jesus bein' human and divine; if it ain't, it's just some anti-Jesus vibe, and that's been around and messin' with folks already. {4:4} Y'all are God's crew, and you've already beat those fake vibes, 'cause God's power in you is way stronger than anything in the world. {4:5} Those fakes are all about the world, so that's what they talk about, and the world's all ears for 'em. {4:6} But we're all about God, so anyone who's down with God hears us out; if they ain't, they ain't rollin' with God. That's how you know what's real and what's fake. {4:7} Fam, let's love each other 'cause love comes from God, and anyone who's lovin' is connected with God and knows what's up. {4:8} If you ain't lovin', you don't know God 'cause God is love. {4:9} This is how we know God loves us: He sent His Son to give us life. {4:10} That's love right there: not that we loved God, but that He loved us and sent His Son to take the hit for our mess. {4:11} If God loved us like that, we gotta love each other too. {4:12} Nah, nobody's seen God, but if we love each other, God's right there with us, and His love's all complete in us. {4:13} So, if we're all about lovin' each other, God's chillin' with us, and we know 'cause He gave us His Spirit. {4:14} And we've seen it, we're testifying: God sent His Son to save the world. {4:15} Anyone who says Jesus is God's Son, God's right there with them, and they're with Him. {4:16} And we've got that love God's got for us; if we're all about love, we're all about God, and God's all about us. {4:17} That's how we know we're all set for judgment day; we're all about love like Jesus is in this world. {4:18} Love crushes fear; if you're scared, your love ain't complete. {4:19} We love God 'cause He loved us first. {4:20} If you say you love God but hate your bro, you're straight up lyin'; if you can't love someone you see, you can't love God you can't see. {4:21} And this is what God's laid down for us: if you're lovin' God, you gotta love your bro too.

{5:1} Anyone who's all about Jesus bein' the real deal is on God's team; and if you're all about lovin' God, you're all about lovin' His crew too. {5:2} If you're down with God, you're down with His squad and His rules. {5:3} Lovin' God means keepin' His rules, and they ain't no hassle. {5:4} Anyone who's God's got what it takes to beat the world, and our faith is what's got us the win. {5:5} Who's got what it takes to beat the world? Anyone who's all in for Jesus bein' God's Son. {5:6} Jesus showed up with water and blood; not just water, but water and blood. And the Spirit's co-signin' 'cause the Spirit's all about truth. {5:7} Three in heaven got the record straight: the Father, the Word, and the Holy Ghost; and they're all one. {5:8} Three on earth back that up too: the spirit, the water, and the blood; and they're all on the same page. {5:9} If you believe people's word, God's word's way bigger; and He's sayin' Jesus is His Son. {5:10} If you're all about Jesus, you're on the right track; but if you ain't believin' God's word about His Son, you're callin' God a liar. {5:11} This is the deal: God's given us eternal life through His Son. {5:12} If you've got the Son, you've got life; if you ain't got the Son, you ain't got life. {5:13} I wrote all this for you who believe in Jesus, so you know you've got eternal life and you keep believin' in Him. {5:14} And here's the deal: if we're all about Jesus, He's all about us, and we know He hears us when we ask for stuff. {5:15} And if we know He hears us, we know we've got what we asked for. {5:16} If you see someone messin' up but it ain't the end of the line for 'em, pray for 'em and they'll get back on track; but there's some mess you don't need to bother prayin' about. {5:17} All sin's bad, but not all of it's deadly. {5:18} Anyone born of God don't mess with sin; God's got 'em covered, and the devil can't touch 'em. {5:19} We know we're with God, and the whole world's off doin' its own thing. {5:20} Jesus showed up and gave us the lowdown, so we know what's what, and we're all in with Him, in His Son Jesus Christ. That's the real deal, and it's eternal life. {5:21} Little homies, stay away from idols. Amen.

2 John

✦✦✦

{1:1} Yo, writing to a dope lady and her crew, whom I totally dig because they're all about the truth. And it's not just me—everyone who's in the know loves you too. {1:2} 'Cause truth's where it's at, chilling with us forever. {1:3} Peace and love from God the Father and Jesus Christ, the Son of the Father, all in truth and love. {1:4} I was stoked to find your kids walking in truth, just like we've been told by the Father. {1:5} Yo, lady, I'm not dropping some new command on you, but just reminding us all to love one another like we've known from the start. {1:6} Love is all about keeping His commandments. Remember, stick to what you've been taught. {1:7} Watch out for all those deceivers out there who won't confess Jesus Christ in the flesh—they're deceivers and anti-Christ. {1:8} Keep your guard up so we don't lose what we've worked for, but bag that full reward. {1:9} Anyone who goes against Christ's teachings isn't with God. Stick with Christ's doctrine, and you've got the Father and Son. {1:10} If someone rolls up not packing this doctrine, don't let 'em crash at your place or give 'em any props. {1:11} Supporting them means you're down with their shady business. {1:12} I've got loads to share, but I'll save it for when we can chat face to face and max out our joy. {1:13} Greetings from your sister's crew. Peace out.

3 John

✢ ✢ ✢

{1:1} Yo, shoutout to my homie Gaius, much love to you for keeping it real. {1:2} Bro, I hope everything's going great for you and that you're healthy and thriving spiritually just like you are in every other way. {1:3} I was super stoked when the crew came through and confirmed how solid you are in the truth, staying true to yourself. {1:4} Nothing makes me happier than hearing that my peeps are staying true to the path. {1:5} Gaius, you're always looking out for the fam, whether they're friends or strangers. {1:6} They've all testified to your kindness, and if you keep supporting them on their journeys in a righteous way, you're doing it right. {1:7} They do this for the name's sake, not for personal gain. {1:8} We should definitely support them too, helping spread the truth. {1:9} I tried reaching out to the church, but Diotrephes, who's all about that top spot, shut us down. {1:10} When I come through, I won't forget how he's been talking trash about us and even kicking out those who want to help. That's not cool. {1:11} Gaius, stick with what's good and avoid what's shady. Doing good shows you're walking with God, but doing wrong means you're off track. {1:12} Demetrius is solid, everyone knows it's true. We've got nothing but good things to say about him. {1:13} I've got more to share, but we'll save it for when we link up in person. {1:14} Peace out, looking forward to catching up soon. Friends say what's up. Give my regards to everyone personally.

Jude

✦✦✦

{1:1} Yo, it's Jude, down with Jesus Christ, and brother of James, hitting up all the sanctified crew by God the Father, chillin' in Jesus Christ, and called out for this: {1:2} Peace, love, and mad mercy to y'all, cranked up to the max. {1:3} Fam, I was all about droppin' a line about our shared salvation, but I had to hit you up and say: hold it down for the faith we've had from way back when, the OG saints laid it out for us. {1:4} 'Cause there's some shady characters slidin' in unnoticed, long marked out for this gig—total godless types, twisting God's grace into a free pass for bad choices, dissing the real deal, our only Lord God, and Jesus Christ. {1:5} Gotta remind you of how the Lord saved Egypt's crew but took out the ones who didn't vibe with him. {1:6} Also, peep the angels who ditched their home turf; they're on lockdown till judgment day in heavy chains. {1:7} Sodom and Gomorrah? Same deal—gave into wild desires, chasing after whatever they fancied, and ended up in eternal blaze. {1:8} These dreamers? Nothin' but filth—disrespectin' authority, throwin' shade at those in charge. {1:9} Even Michael, the top angel, didn't throw down with the devil; he just hit him with "The Lord put you in your place." {1:10} But these clowns talk trash about stuff they don't get, actin' all wild and end up messin' themselves up. {1:11} Big trouble for them—trippin' like Cain, chasin' money like Balaam, and getting wrecked like Core. {1:12} They're like stains at your get-togethers, grubbin' without a care, empty clouds gettin' tossed around, fruitless trees—twice dead, ripped out at the roots. {1:13} They're like wild waves, embarrassing themselves, lost stars headin' straight for eternal darkness. {1:14} Enoch, way back in the day, was on it—called out how the Lord's rollin' in with thousands of saints, layin' down the law on all the godless deeds and talk. {1:15-16} These folks? Always complaining, doing what they want, buttering people up for personal gain. {1:17} But yo, remember what the apostles said about these clowns showin' up in the end times, just doin' their own thing? {1:18-19} They're the ones who cut themselves off, all about the physical, without any spiritual game. {1:20} But you, keep buildin' up your faith, prayin' in the Holy Ghost, {1:21} Stay locked in with God's love, waiting for Jesus Christ to bring that eternal life vibe. {1:22-23} Show compassion to some, keep others in check, snatching 'em from the flames, hatin' the dirty ways. {1:24} Big ups to the one who's got our backs, keepin' us on track, flawless in front of his glory, with mad joy. {1:25} To the only wise God our Savior—big shouts for the glory, the power, now and forever. Amen.

Revelation

✠✠✠

{1:1} So, peep this: it's the Revelation of Jesus Christ, straight from God to him, to drop some knowledge on his crew about what's gonna go down soon. He sent it through his angel to his homie John: {1:2} John's here to spill the tea on God's word and what he's seen about Jesus Christ. {1:3} You're blessed if you read and hear this prophecy and actually keep what's written, 'cause time's ticking. {1:4} John's shoutout to the seven churches in Asia: Grace and peace from the OG—the Almighty who is, was, and is to come—and from the seven Spirits before his throne; {1:5} Also from Jesus Christ, the real deal, the first one to rise from the dead, and the top dog over all rulers. He loved us, washed us clean with his own blood, {1:6} and made us kings and priests for God. All glory and power to him forever. Amen. {1:7} Get ready, 'cause he's coming back in style, everyone's gonna see him—even those who did him dirty—and the whole earth's gonna feel it. Amen. {1:8} He's the beginning and the end, the Lord who is, was, and is to come—the Almighty, no less. {1:9} John here, just like you—a brother in the struggle, hangin' in there for Jesus Christ, on lockdown in Patmos for speaking the word of God and testifying about Jesus. {1:10} I was in the Spirit on the Lord's day, vibing, when I heard this crazy voice behind me, loud like a trumpet, {1:11} saying, "I'm the beginning and the end—write down what you see and send it to the seven churches in Asia: Ephesus, Smyrna, Pergamos, Thyatira, Sardis, Philadelphia, and Laodicea." {1:12} So I turned around to see who's talking, and I see seven golden lampstands; {1:13} and in the middle, someone like the Son of Man, dressed up, with a golden belt. {1:14} Hair as white as snow, eyes like flames, {1:15} feet like shiny brass, and a voice like thunder. {1:16} He's holding seven stars in his hand, and his words are sharp as a double-edged sword; his face is as bright as the sun in full force. {1:17} When I saw him, I hit the floor like I was out cold. But he touched me, saying, "Chill, I'm the real deal—the first and the last. {1:18} I was dead, but now I'm alive forever, and I got the keys to hell and death. {1:19} Write down everything you've seen, what's happening now, and what's coming next; {1:20} The seven stars you saw in my hand and the seven golden lampstands? The stars are the angels of the seven churches, and the lampstands are the seven churches themselves.

{2:1-3} Yo, gotta drop a message to the Ephesus crew, straight up. The one holding those seven stars and walking the scene with the seven golden candlesticks says this: I peep your hustle, your grind, and your patience. You're not vibing with evil, and you've called out the fakes who claim to be apostles but ain't. You've been holding it down, staying patient, putting in work in my name, and not backing down. {2:4} But, fam, I gotta call you out on one thing: you've lost that fire you had at the start. {2:5} Remember where you came from, turn it around, get back to what you were about before, or else I'm coming through quick, and your spot's getting snatched, unless you change course. {2:6} But, big props for hating on the Nicolaitanes' shady moves - I'm feeling that too. {2:7} Whoever's got ears, listen up to what the Spirit's saying to the crew. Whoever sticks it out and overcomes, I'm hooking them up with a taste of that tree of life, chilling in God's paradise. {2:8-9} Now onto the Smyrna squad: The OG, the first and the last, the one who's been there, done that with death and came back to life, drops this: I see your grind, your struggles, your hustle, (even though you're broke, you're rich), and I see through the lies of those who claim to be legit Jews but ain't nothing but fakes for Satan. {2:10} Don't stress about the tough times ahead; Satan might throw some of you in lockdown to test you, but stick it out, stay loyal till the end, and I'll hook you up with that crown of life. {2:11} Whoever's got ears, listen up to what the Spirit's saying to the crew. Whoever overcomes won't get messed up by that second death. {2:12-13} Now, shoutout to the Pergamos crew: The one with the sharp double-edged sword drops this: I peep your scene, where you're at, even Satan's HQ, and I see you holding it down for my name, not backing down even when Antipas got taken out for sticking with me. {2:14-15} But, I gotta call you out for letting those Balaam followers and Nicolaitanes slide in, spreading their messed-up teachings. {2:16} Change your ways, or I'm rolling up fast, ready to throw down with the truth. {2:17} Whoever's got ears, listen up to what the Spirit's saying to the crew. Whoever overcomes gets a taste of that hidden manna and a fresh name on a white stone - only they know what's up with that. {2:18-19} Now, onto the Thyatira crew: The Son of God, with eyes blazing like fire and feet solid like brass, drops this: I peep your scene, your love, your service, your faith, your grind, and your hustle - you're leveling up. {2:20} But, gotta call you out for letting Jezebel do her thing, spreading lies, seducing my peeps into shady stuff. {2:21-22} She had her chance to change, but she's sticking to her ways. {2:23} She and her crew? They're gonna face some serious consequences, and everyone's gonna see that I'm about justice. {2:24} But to the rest of you in Thyatira who ain't about that life, I ain't dropping any more burdens on you. {2:25} Just hold onto what you got until I roll through. {2:26-27} Whoever overcomes, staying true to my deal till the end, I'm giving them power over nations, ruling with an iron fist, just like I got from my old man. {2:28} And they'll get that morning star. {2:29} Whoever's got ears, listen up to what the Spirit's saying to the crew.

{3:1} Yo, to the angel chillin' in Sardis, check it: I'm the one rockin' the seven Spirits of God and the seven stars. I peep your hustle, but let's be real, you're frontin'; you got a rep for bein' alive, but you're straight up dead. {3:2} Wake up, bro, and fix what's left before it flatlines; your game ain't on point with God yet. {3:3} Remember what you've been told and tighten up, or else I'm droppin' in like a stealth ninja, and you won't see it comin'. {3:4} Props to the few in Sardis keepin' it clean; they're rollin' with me, rockin' white threads 'cause they're legit. {3:5} Whoever keeps it real gets the white fit and a spot in the big book; I ain't crossin' their name out, but I'm shoutin' it out to the big man upstairs and his crew. {3:6} If you're catchin' my vibe, then listen up; the Spirit's droppin' truth bombs on the reg. {3:7-8} Now, to the angel holdin' it down in Philadelphia, peep this: I'm the holy one, the true OG with the keys to the kingdom. Your hustle's on point; I opened a door for you that nobody can close 'cause you've been keepin' it real, stayin' true to my word, and reppin' my name. {3:9} I'll make those fakers who say they're down but ain't, come bow down to you, showin' that I got mad love for your crew. {3:10} 'Cause you stuck with me when things got rough, I got your back when temptation hits the scene, testin' everyone on the block. {3:11} I'm comin' in hot, so hold on tight to what you got, and don't let anyone snatch your crown. {3:12} For those who keep grindin', I'll make 'em solid as a rock in my squad's temple, reppin' my God's name and the fresh city vibes from heaven, along with my new handle. {3:13} If you're vibin' with this, then listen up; the Spirit's got more to say to the whole crew. {3:14} Now, to the angel reppin' the Laodiceans, here's the deal: I'm the real deal, the truth talker, and the start of God's creation. {3:15} I peep your hustle, and let's just say, you're neither hot nor cold; you're just lukewarm, and that's not cool with me. {3:16} So, since you're playin' it safe, I'm spittin' you out like bad takeout; you think you're livin' large, but you're really just clueless, broke, and blind. {3:17-18} Here's some real talk: cop some real riches from me, rock some fresh threads to cover up that shame, and get some clarity with my vision drops. {3:19} I'm droppin' truth 'cause I got love for you; so get hype and change your ways. {3:20} I'm knockin' at your door; if you hear me, open up, and we'll kick it together, me and you. {3:21} Those who keep grindin', I'm givin' 'em a spot with me on my throne, just like I scored with my pops. {3:22} If you're vibin' with this, then listen up; the Spirit's got more to say to the whole crew.

{4:1} After that, I checked out what was up, and boom, there's a door wide open up in heaven; this voice was like a hype trumpet tellin' me to come check out what's next. {4:2} So, I'm zonin' out, and bam, I'm in the spirit, and there's a throne front and center, with someone holdin' it down. {4:3} This dude's glowin' like precious stones, with a rainbow backdrop like an emerald party. {4:4} Around the throne, there's twenty-four VIP seats, with twenty-four elders rockin' gold crowns on their heads. {4:5} And from the throne, there's all sorts of lightnin' and thunderin', plus seven fire lamps representin' the seven Spirits of God. {4:6} There's this crystal clear sea in front of the throne, with four beasts all eyes on deck, front and back. {4:7} The first beast's like a lion, the second's like a calf, the third's got a human face, and the fourth's like an eagle on the fly. {4:8} These beasts are decked out with six wings each, and they're covered in eyes inside and out, never takin' a break from shoutin' out, "Holy, holy, holy, Lord God Almighty, who's been, is, and is to come." {4:9} And when these beasts give props to the big boss on the throne, who's livin' it up forever and ever, {4:10} the elders straight up drop to their knees, givin' mad respect to the one who's always livin' it up, chuckin' their crowns at the throne, sayin', "You're the real MVP, worthy of all glory, honor, and power 'cause you made everything, and it's all for your pleasure."

{5:1} So, I peeped this crazy vision: there's this dude on a throne holding a book, sealed up tight with seven seals. {5:2} Then this loud angel pipes up, asking who's worthy to crack open the book and unleash its secrets. {5:3} But nobody—like, literally nobody in heaven, on earth, or under the earth—can even peek inside. {5:4} That's when I started bawling my eyes out, 'cause no one was up to the task. {5:5} But hold up! One of the elders tells me to chill. The Lion of Judah, the real deal from David's line, steps up and unlocks the book. {5:6} I look over, and there's a Lamb—looking all sacrificed, with seven horns and eyes, symbolizing the seven Spirits of God sent everywhere. {5:7} The Lamb grabs the book from the dude on the throne's hand. {5:8} When this goes down, the four crazy beasts and twenty-four elders bow down with their harps and golden bowls filled with prayers. {5:9} They start jamming a new tune, praising the Lamb for redeeming us all with his blood, from every tribe, language, nation—making us kings and priests destined to rule on earth. {5:10-12} Then I see and hear this insane number of angels, like, too many to count, shouting that the Lamb is totally worthy of power, riches, wisdom, strength, honor, glory, and blessings. {5:13} All creation joins in, shouting praises to the One on the throne and the Lamb forever. {5:14} The four beasts say "Amen," and the elders bow down and worship the eternal One.

{6:1} After all that, I see the Lamb pop open one of the seals, and it's like thunder. {6:2} I see a white horse, and its rider's got a bow and crown, going out to conquer. {6:3} The second seal gets cracked, and out comes a fiery red horse, bringing war and death to the earth. {6:4} The third seal opens, and a black horse appears, with its rider holding scales. {6:6} I hear a voice saying food's gonna be expensive, but don't mess with the oil and wine. {6:7} Next, the fourth seal opens, and a pale horse shows up—Death riding it, with Hell tagging along. They've got power over a quarter of the earth, bringing death by sword, hunger, and wild beasts. {6:9} The fifth seal reveals the souls of those slain for God's word and testimony, crying out for justice. {6:12} Then, the sixth seal breaks, and there's a massive earthquake; the sun goes dark, and the moon turns blood-red. {6:13} Stars fall from the sky like figs in a storm. {6:14} The sky rolls up like a scroll, and mountains and islands shift. {6:15-16} Everyone—leaders, the rich, soldiers, slaves—tries to hide from the Lamb's wrath. {6:17} 'Cause judgment day's here, and who's gonna stand?

{7:1} So, after all that, I peeped four angels posted up on the four corners of the earth, holding back the wind so it wouldn't wreck everything - no blowing on the earth, sea, or trees. {7:2} Then, I spot another angel coming from the east, rockin' the seal of the living God. He shouts at the four angels, telling them to chill before they mess up the earth and sea, {7:3} saying, "Hold up, don't wreck the place yet. We gotta seal up the crew serving our God first." {7:4-8} I heard the count: 144,000 sealed up tight, representing all the tribes of Israel. {7:9} But then, check this out, I see this massive crowd, too many to count, from all over the globe, standing before the throne and the Lamb, dressed in white, waving palm branches, {7:10} shouting, "Salvation belongs to our God and the Lamb on the throne!" {7:11} All the angels, elders, and those four badass creatures around the throne hit the floor, worshipping God, {7:12} saying, "Amen! Blessing, glory, wisdom, thanks, honor, power, and might belong to our God forever. Amen." {7:13} One of the elders hits me with a question, asking who these people in white are and where they came from. {7:14} I'm like, "Yo, you're the wise one, you tell me." And he's like, "These are the ones who went through the grind, washed their robes clean with the Lamb's blood." {7:15} They're chilling before God's throne, serving Him day and night, and He's right there with them. {7:16} No more hunger, thirst, or scorching sun - the Lamb's got them covered, leading them to fresh water. {7:17} He wipes away all their tears, too.

{8:1} Now, when the seventh seal got popped open, heaven went dead silent for about half an hour. {8:2} I saw those seven angels in God's spot, and they got handed seven trumpets. {8:3} Another angel rolls up to the altar with a golden censer, getting a bunch of incense and the saints' prayers ready, offering them up on the golden altar in front of the throne. {8:4} The smoke from the incense, mixed with the saints' prayers, goes up to God from the angel's hand. {8:5} Then, the angel fills the censer with fire from the altar and throws it down to earth, causing thunder, lightning, and an earthquake. {8:6} The seven angels with the trumpets get ready to blow. {8:7} The first angel blows, and bam, hail and fire mixed with blood rain down, burning up a third of the trees and all the green grass. {8:8-9} The second angel blows, and it's like a fiery mountain gets chucked into the sea, turning a third of it into blood, killing a third of sea life and wrecking a third of the ships. {8:10} The third angel blows, and this huge star falls from the sky, lighting up the rivers and water fountains. {8:11} It's called Wormwood, and it turns a third of the water bitter, killing many. {8:12} The fourth angel blows, and a third of the sun, moon, and stars go dark - no light for a third of the day or night. {8:13} Then, I hear this angel flying through the sky, shouting, "Woe, woe, woe to everyone on earth because of what's coming with the last three trumpet blasts!"

{9:1} Yo, when the fifth angel dropped his beat, I peeped a star straight fallin' from the sky, and homeboy got the key to the abyss. {9:2} He popped that pit open, and out came this smoke, thick like it just came out of a lit furnace, blockin' out the sun and the air. {9:3} Then out of that smoke, locusts swarmed the scene, packin' a sting like earth's scorpions. {9:4} But they got orders: don't mess with the greenery, just target those without God's seal on their forehead. {9:5} These locusts ain't killin', just tormentin' for five months, stingin' like a scorpion's worst. {9:6} It gets dark, man; folks wantin' to check out, but death's ghostin' them. {9:7} These locusts? They look like battle-ready horses, rockin' golden crowns and human faces. {9:8} They got flowin' hair like women and teeth like lions. {9:9} Their armor's like iron, wings soundin' like a stampede of chariots. {9:10} With scorpion tails, they sting for five months, led by the angel king of the abyss, known in Hebrew as Abaddon and Greek as Apollyon. {9:11-12} First woe's over; brace yourself 'cause there's two more on deck. {9:13-14} Then the sixth angel brings the noise, shoutin' from the golden altar horns, tellin' the sixth angel with the trumpet to set free four angels chillin' by the Euphrates. {9:15} These four are armed and ready for a day, a month, a year, geared up to take out a third of humanity. {9:16-17} The cavalry? Two hundred million strong, with lion-like heads, fiery breastplates, and fire, smoke, and brimstone breath. {9:18} With fire, smoke, and brimstone, they drop a third of humanity. {9:19} Their power's in their mouths and tails, laced with serpent-like heads, causin' havoc. {9:20} Even after all this chaos, the rest of humanity still ain't changin' their ways, stuck on idol worship and all sorts of foul play. {9:21} They won't give up their wickedness, even after all that destruction.

{10:1} Then this other big-time angel comes down from the heavens, rockin' a cloud cloak with a rainbow crown, his face like the sun, and fiery feet. {10:2} He's got a poppin' open book in hand, standin' on the sea and earth like he owns the joint. {10:3} He roars like a lion, makin' seven thunders speak up. {10:4} Just when I'm 'bout to jot it all down, a voice from heaven's like, "Nah, keep those thunders on the down-low." {10:5-6} This angel throws up a hand to heaven, swearin' by the eternal Creator, sayin' time's up. {10:7} But when the seventh angel busts out his tune, God's mystery's gonna be revealed, just like he told his prophets. {10:8} Then I hear the voice from heaven again, tellin' me to grab that open book from the sea-and-earth angel. {10:9} So, I roll up to him and ask for the book; he's like, "Take it, eat it up; it'll taste sweet but leave a bitter aftertaste." {10:10} I chow down on that book, and it's sweet as honey in my mouth, but it straight sours my stomach. {10:11} And the angel's like, "You gotta spit out more prophecies, to everyone and their mom, worldwide."

{11:1} So, like, I get this rod-like reed from an angel, and he's all, "Yo, go measure up the temple of God, the altar, and the peeps worshipping there." {11:2} But he's like, "Don't bother with the outside court, that's for the non-believers. They'll trample the holy city for forty-two months." {11:3} Then, these two witnesses get power and prophesy for twelve hundred and sixty days, all dressed in sackcloth. {11:4} They're like the two olive trees and candlesticks chilling with the God of the earth. {11:5} And if anyone messes with them, fire comes out of their mouths and fries their enemies. Like, if you try to mess with them, you're toast. {11:6} They can shut up the sky so it won't rain, turn water into blood, and hit the earth with plagues whenever they want. {11:7} But when they're done, this beast from the bottomless pit starts a fight, beats them, and kills them. {11:8} Their dead bodies lay in the street of this huge city, which is like Sodom and Egypt, where our Lord was crucified. {11:9} People from all over see their bodies for three and a half days and won't let them be buried. {11:10} The earthlings throw a party when they're dead because these two prophets were a pain in their butts. {11:11} But after three and a half days, God's spirit brings them back to life, and everyone freaks out. {11:12} Then, a voice from heaven calls them up, and they ascend in a cloud while their enemies watch. {11:13} Right after that, there's a massive earthquake, and a tenth of the city falls. Seven thousand people bite it, and the rest are terrified, giving glory to God. {11:14} The second woe is over, but brace yourselves, the third one's coming real soon. {11:15} Then the seventh angel blows his horn, and everyone in heaven shouts, "Our Lord and his Christ now rule over all the kingdoms forever!" {11:16} The elders bow down and worship God, saying, "Thanks, Almighty, for flexing your power and taking charge." {11:17-18} The nations are mad, your wrath is here, it's judgment time for the dead, and you're rewarding your faithful servants, prophets, and saints while taking out those who messed up the earth. {11:19} The temple in heaven opens up, revealing the ark of the covenant, and there's lightning, voices, thunder, an earthquake, and big hail.

{12:1} Then, this wild scene goes down in heaven - a woman decked out in the sun, the moon at her feet, and twelve stars crowning her head. {12:2} She's pregnant and in pain, ready to give birth. {12:3} And there's this massive red dragon with seven heads, ten horns, and seven crowns, ready to pounce as soon as the baby pops out. {12:4-5} When she has the baby - this dude meant to rule the world - he gets snatched up to God and his throne. {12:6} Then, the woman peaces out to the wilderness, where she's taken care of for twelve hundred and sixty days. {12:7-8} Up in heaven, Michael and his crew throw down with the dragon and his posse, but they lose and get kicked out for good. {12:9} The dragon - aka, the Devil and Satan - gets the boot, along with his crew, and they're tossed to earth. {12:10} There's this big celebration in heaven because Satan's out of there, and salvation, strength, and God's kingdom are on the scene. {12:11} They beat him with the Lamb's blood and their testimonies, not even afraid to die. {12:12} So, heaven's stoked, but earth's in for a rough ride because the devil's ticked and knows his time's short. {12:13} The dragon starts messing with the woman who had the baby, but she gets wings and flies to safety in the wilderness, where she's taken care of for a while. {12:14} The dragon tries to flood her out, but the earth helps her out, swallowing up the flood. {12:15} Now, the dragon's furious and goes after the rest of her kids who keep God's commandments and follow Jesus.

{13:1} So, I'm posted up by the beach, peepin' this beast poppin' out of the sea, rockin' seven heads, ten horns, and ten crowns, all with blasphemous names. {13:2} This beast? Picture a leopard with bear feet and a lion's mouth, but the dragon hooked him up with mad power and authority. {13:3} One of his heads looked like it got wrecked, but then it bounced back, blowin' everyone's minds. {13:4} People start bowin' down to the dragon and the beast, gassin' them up like, "Who's as fly as the beast? Who can even try to step to him?" {13:5} He starts talkin' big and blasphemous, rockin' the mic for forty-two months straight. {13:6} He's straight up dissin' God, dissin' His name, His crib, and all His homies up in heaven. {13:7} Homeboy's got the green light to go after the saints and take 'em down, with power over every tribe, tongue, and nation. {13:8} Everybody on earth who's not in the Lamb's VIP club is bowin' down to him. {13:9} Yo, if you're tuned in, listen up. {13:10} Those who take others captive will be taken captive, and those who slay with the sword will get sliced right back. Saints, hold steady; this is where your faith gets real. {13:11} Then I peep this other beast risin' from the ground, rockin' two horns like a lamb but speakin' straight dragon talk. {13:12} He's got all the first beast's power and gets everyone to worship him, the one with the crazy comeback from a fatal blow. {13:13} He's droppin' miracles left and right, even summonin' fire down from the sky, makin' everyone go, "Whoa." {13:14} He's playin' mind games, convincin' people to make an image of the first beast, the one who got shanked but lived. {13:15} This beast has the power to bring that image to life, talkin' and makin' anyone who won't bow down get taken out. {13:16} He's got everyone, big or small, rich or broke, gettin' a mark on their hand or forehead, no buyin' or sellin' without it, or without pledgin' allegiance to the beast. {13:17} No one's gettin' around this; it's gonna be a wild ride. {13:18} You gotta be wise, count the number of the beast, it's some next-level stuff, six hundred and sixty-six.

{14:1} Then I see this Lamb chillin' on Mount Zion, with a crew of a hundred and forty-four thousand, reppin' His dad's name. {14:2} I hear this voice, like thunder mixed with ocean waves, and these harpers throwin' down heavenly jams. {14:3} They're vibin' with a new song, exclusive to the Lamb's crew, the ones redeemed from the earth. {14:4} These are the ones keepin' it pure, stayin' true to the Lamb no matter where He goes, the firstfruits of God and the Lamb. {14:5} No cap, they're speakin' straight facts, standin' flawless before God's throne. {14:6} Then this angel slides in the scene, holdin' the eternal gospel for everyone on earth, from every nation and tongue. {14:7} He's loud and clear, sayin', "Respect God, give Him props, 'cause judgment day's here, and bow down to the One who made it all." {14:8} Another angel follows up, announcin' Babylon's fall, that big city that got everyone sippin' on her wrath-filled wine. {14:9} Then another angel drops some truth bombs, warnin' anyone thinkin' of bowin' down to the beast and his image or takin' his mark. {14:10} They're in for a world of hurt, with God's wrath straight-up poured out on them, no mixers, just straight fire and brimstone, with the Lamb and His squad watchin'. {14:11} It's gonna be a nightmare, with no rest for those who worship the beast and his image, or anyone who gets tagged with his mark. {14:12} This is where the saints gotta stand firm, keepin' God's commands and holdin' tight to Jesus. {14:13} Then I hear a voice from heaven, sayin', "Those who die for the Lord are blessed, they get to kick back and rest, and their good deeds follow 'em." {14:14} I peep a white cloud, and on it sits someone like the Son of Man, rockin' a golden crown and a sharp sickle. {14:15} Another angel rolls up, hollerin' to the dude on the cloud, "Time to harvest, reap that crop; the earth's ripe for pickin'!" {14:16} So, the guy on the cloud swings down his sickle, and the earth's harvest gets snatched up. {14:17} Then another angel steps out of heaven's temple, also holdin' a sharp sickle. {14:18} And yet another angel steps out from the altar, with power over fire, shoutin' to the sickle-holder, "Start gatherin' those grapes; they're ripe for the crushin'!" {14:19} So, the sickle goes in, collectin' those grapes, and they get tossed into God's wrathful winepress, outside the city. {14:20} The press gets stomped, and blood flows deep, like a river, for about twelve hundred miles.

{15:1} So, I peeped this insane scene up in heaven: seven angels with the final plagues, holding God's wrath all locked and loaded. {15:2} There's this sea of glass mixed with fire, and those who beat the beast, his image, and his mark, chillin' there with God's harps. {15:3} They start singing the songs of Moses and the Lamb, giving props to God Almighty for His epic works and righteous ways. {15:4} Who wouldn't fear and honor the Lord? All nations will worship Him, 'cause His judgments are crystal clear. {15:5-6} Then I see the heavenly temple open up, and the seven angels step out, ready to bring on the plagues, dressed in pure white with golden belts.

{15:7} One of the beasts hands them golden vials filled with God's wrath. The temple fills with smoke from God's glory and power, and no one can go in until those seven plagues do their thing.

{16:1} Then I hear a booming voice from the temple, telling the seven angels to go pour out God's wrath on the earth. {16:2} The first angel does it, causing nasty sores on those with the beast's mark and worshippers of his image. {16:3} The second angel pours out on the sea, turning it into blood, and everything in it dies. {16:4} The third angel hits up the rivers and springs, turning them to blood too. {16:5} The reason? These folks shed the blood of saints, and now they get blood to drink—fair play. {16:6} The fourth angel scorches people with intense heat from the sun, and instead of repenting, they curse God. {16:7} The fifth angel makes the beast's kingdom go dark, causing immense pain. {16:8} The sixth angel dries up the Euphrates to prep the way for eastern kings. {16:9} Then I see three nasty spirits like frogs come from the dragon, the beast, and the false prophet, spewing evil and gathering world leaders for a big showdown. {16:10} Jesus warns, saying, "I'm coming when you least expect it. Stay woke, keep it clean, so you don't get caught out." {16:11} They all get herded to Armageddon. {16:12} The seventh angel empties his vial in the air, and a voice from heaven declares, "It's done." {16:13} There's thunder, lightning, and a mega earthquake like never before. {16:14} Cities crumble, and Babylon's time's up, getting the full force of God's wrath. {16:15} Islands and mountains vanish. {16:16} Hailstorms drop, and people curse God for the chaos.

{17:1} So, like, one of the seven angels with those seven vials comes up to me and is all, "Yo, come check this out. I'm gonna spill the tea on this huge scandal with that big-time ho sitting on tons of water." {17:2} Turns out, she's been getting it on with all the kings, and the whole earth is wasted on her sleazy vibes. {17:3} Then he whisks me away in spirit, and I see this chick sitting on a red beast, full of blasphemous names, with seven heads and ten horns. {17:4} She's decked out in purple and scarlet, blinged up with gold, jewels, and pearls, holding this golden cup full of nasty stuff from her hookups. {17:5} She's got "MYSTERY, BABYLON THE GREAT, THE MOTHER OF HARLOTS AND ABOMINATIONS OF THE EARTH" written on her forehead. {17:6} And get this, she's wasted on the blood of saints and martyrs of Jesus. When I saw her, I was shook. {17:7} The angel's like, "Why you so surprised? Let me spill the tea on this woman and the beast she's riding - the one with seven heads and ten horns." {17:8} This beast you saw? Used to be, then wasn't, and now it's back, about to head into destruction. Those whose names ain't in the book of life will be shook when they see it. {17:9} Here's the scoop: the seven heads are seven mountains where this woman chills. {17:10} Plus, there are seven kings: five are out, one's in, and one's on the way, but won't stick around long. {17:11} The beast you saw, used to be, then wasn't, but now it's the eighth, from the seven, and it's headed for destruction. {17:12} And those ten horns? They're ten kings who haven't had their kingdoms yet but will reign with the beast for a hot minute. {17:13-14} They're all in on this, giving their power to the beast, ready to battle the Lamb. But guess what? The Lamb wins because he's the boss of bosses and the king of kings. Those who roll with him are chosen and faithful. {17:15} The waters where the ho's sitting? That's peeps from all over - different nations, tongues, and tribes. {17:16} And those ten horns on the beast? They'll turn on the ho, strip her down, tear her up, and burn her. {17:17} God's put it in their hearts to do his bidding until everything he said goes down. {17:18} That woman you saw? She's that big city calling the shots over all the kings.

{18:1} Then, I see another angel coming down, shining bright, lighting up the whole earth with his glow. {18:2} He's yelling at the top of his lungs, "Babylon the great's fallen! It's become the hangout for devils, foul spirits, and all sorts of gross stuff." {18:3} Every nation's drunk on her junk, and the kings are getting it on with her while merchants are raking in the cash from her luxuries. {18:4} Another voice from heaven's like, "Get out of there, my peeps, so you don't get caught up in her mess and end up with her punishment." {18:5} Her sins are sky-high, and God's taking note of every dirty deed. {18:6} Pay her back double for what she did, give her twice the trouble she gave you. Fill up her cup with double the nastiness she dished out. {18:7} She's all high and mighty, but she's in for a world of hurt. She thinks she's queen bee, never gonna see sorrow, but she's dead wrong. {18:8} Her doom's coming in one day: death, mourning, famine, and she'll be burned up big time. 'Cause the Lord God's the real deal, judging her. {18:9} Even the kings who partied with her will cry when they see her burn. {18:10} They'll stand back in fear, watching her downfall happen in a flash. {18:11} The merchants will bawl their eyes out too since no one's buying their stuff anymore. {18:12} All the fancy goods they sold? Gone. No more bling, no more fancy threads, no more of anything they used to flaunt. {18:13} Her treasures? They're all gone too, and no one's buying them anymore. No more fancy parties, no more luxury, no more getting rich off her hustle. {18:14} The things they lusted after are gone, and they won't find them anywhere. {18:15} Those who got rich off her will watch from afar, crying and wailing over her torment. {18:16} They'll mourn the loss of that once-great city, decked out in the finest threads and jewels. {18:17} All that wealth gone in an instant. Even the sailors and merchants at sea will stand back, shocked at her downfall. {18:18} They'll cry out when they see her burn, wondering if any city could compare to her greatness. {18:19} They'll throw dust on their heads, wailing and crying, mourning the loss of that once-great city that made them rich. {18:20} But heaven and the holy crew - they'll be celebrating 'cause God's finally avenged them on her. {18:21} Then this mighty angel grabs a massive stone and chucks it into the sea, saying, "This is how Babylon the great's going down - never to be seen again." {18:22} No more music, no more crafts, no more business in that city. {18:23} No more light, no more weddings - all gone 'cause her merchants were the big shots, and they fooled all the nations with their tricks. {18:24} And in her? They found the blood of prophets, saints, and everyone who got offed on earth.

{19:1} So, there's this massive crowd up in heaven, shouting "Alleluia!" They're giving props to God for salvation, glory, honor, and power. {19:2} They're all hyped because God's judgments are spot-on, especially on that shady figure corrupting the earth. Justice served! {19:3} They keep shouting "Alleluia!" as the smoke rises from her downfall. {19:4} The elders and beasts bow down, praising God on the throne with an "Amen, Alleluia!" {19:5} Then a voice from the throne calls on everyone, big or small, who fears God to praise Him. {19:6} A massive crowd roars like thunder, shouting "Alleluia!" because the Almighty God reigns supreme. {19:7} They're all stoked and celebrating because the Lamb's marriage is happening, and His wife is ready. {19:8} She's decked out in clean, white linen, representing the righteousness of saints. {19:9} Then I'm told to write down that those invited to the Lamb's wedding feast are truly blessed—God's word, no cap. {19:10} I start to worship, but I'm told to chill and worship God instead, 'cause Jesus' testimony is where it's at. {19:11} Suddenly, heaven opens, and I see a white horse with a rider known as Faithful and True, ready to bring righteous judgment and war. {19:12} His eyes blaze like fire, with many crowns on his head and a name known only to him. {19:13} He's draped in a blood-dipped garment, known as The Word of God. {19:14} Heavenly armies roll with him on white horses, dressed in clean, white linen. {19:15} He wields a sharp sword from his mouth to smite nations and rule with an iron rod, bringing God's fierce wrath. {19:16} His clothes and thigh bear the title "KING OF KINGS, AND LORD OF LORDS." {19:17} Next, an angel in the sun calls out to all birds to gather for a feast, devouring the flesh of kings, captains, mighty men, and all kinds of people. {19:18-19} Then I see the beast, kings, and their armies gearing up for war against the rider on the white horse and his crew. {19:20} The beast and false prophet get nabbed and tossed into a lake of fire, still kicking. {19:21} The rest get taken out by the rider's sword, and birds feast on their flesh.

{20:1} I spot an angel coming down from heaven with a key to the abyss and a huge chain. {20:2-3} He grabs the dragon, that old serpent—the Devil and Satan—and locks him up for a thousand years, sealing him away to stop his deception. {20:4} Then I see thrones with judges, and souls of those martyred for Jesus and God's word, who never worshipped the beast or took his mark—they're alive and ruling with Christ for a thousand years. {20:5} Others don't come back to life until after those thousand years. This is the first resurrection. {20:6} Blessed are those in the first resurrection—death has no power over them, and they serve as priests of God and Christ, reigning for a thousand years. {20:7} Once the thousand years wrap up, Satan gets released to deceive the nations for one last hurrah. {20:8-9} He rallies Gog and Magog for a massive battle, but God rains fire down on them. {20:10} Finally, the devil joins the beast and false prophet in eternal torment. {20:11} I see a great white throne and the Judge sitting on it, and the earth and heaven flee from His presence—nowhere to hide. {20:12} Small or great, the dead stand before God, and the books are opened, including the Book of Life. {20:13} Sea, death, and hell give up their dead for judgment according to their deeds. {20:14} Death and hell get tossed into the lake of fire—this is the second death. {20:15} Anyone not found in the Book of Life gets thrown into the lake of fire.

{21:1} So, peep this, I spot a whole new heaven and earth; the old ones got replaced, and there's no more ocean vibes. {21:2} Yours truly, John, catches sight of this lit city, New Jerusalem, sliding down from God's crib, decked out like a bride for her groom. {21:3} Then I hear this booming voice from heaven, talking about how God's setting up shop with us, chilling together as His crew, with Him as our main homie. {21:4} God's on tear patrol, wiping away all tears, shutting down death, sorrow, crying, and pain; that old stuff's history. {21:5} The big boss on the throne declares, "Check it, I'm giving everything a fresh start." And He tells me to jot it down, 'cause it's straight facts. {21:6} He's like, "Done deal. I'm the A to Z, the start and finish. Anyone thirsty? I got that living water on tap, no charge." {21:7} Those who rise above get the keys to the kingdom; I'll be their God, and they'll be my squad. {21:8} But those who punk out, disbelieve, and do all sorts of shady stuff end up in a fiery lake, second death vibes. {21:9} Then one of the seven angels with the final plagues comes over, talking to me like, "Yo, come peep the Lamb's wifey." {21:10} He whisks me off in spirit mode to this massive mountain and shows me New Jerusalem, straight outta heaven, shining with God's glory. {21:11} This city's lit up like a gem, glowing bright, clear as crystal. {21:12} It's got this huge wall, twelve gates, and each gate's got an angel guard with the names of Israel's tribes on 'em. {21:13} Three gates on each side, all locked and loaded. {21:14} The city's foundation's stacked with the apostles' names, solid as a rock. {21:15} The angel dude busts out a golden ruler, measuring the city, gates, and walls. {21:16} It's a perfect cube, twelve thousand furlongs on all sides. {21:17} The wall's about a hundred and forty-four cubits high, angel-standard size. {21:18} It's decked out in jasper, with streets of pure gold, crystal-clear vibes. {21:19} The foundation's blinged out with all kinds of precious stones, from jasper to amethyst. {21:20} The gates? Each one's a giant pearl, and the streets? Pure gold, like see-through glass. {21:21} No temple vibes in this city; God and the Lamb are the hotspot. {21:22} No need for sun or moon; God and the Lamb light it up with their glory. {21:23} The saved nations stroll in its eternal glow, bringing their best to the table. {21:24} The gates stay open 24/7; no need for night lights in this town. {21:25} The nations keep bringing their honor and glory into the mix. {21:26} Only the real deal gets in; no fakers or sinners allowed, just those with their names in the Lamb's VIP list.

{22:1} So, peep this, I got a glimpse of this totally pure river, straight-up life water, clear as crystal, flowing from God and the Lamb's throne. {22:2} In the middle of its streets and along the riverbanks stood the tree of life, serving up twelve different kinds of fruit, fresh every month, with its leaves bringing healing vibes to all the nations.{22:3} No more curses, just God and the Lamb reigning supreme, with their crew serving them up. {22:4} They're straight-up seeing God's face, with His name stamped on their foreheads. {22:5} No darkness vibes; God's got the light hookup, and they're reigning for eternity. {22:6} The scoop's legit and true; God sent His angel to spill the beans to His peeps. {22:7} "I'm sliding in real soon," He says. Blessed is anyone who keeps it real with the prophecy of this book. {22:8} Yours truly, John, sees and hears it all, ready to worship the angel giving the lowdown. {22:9} But the angel's like, "Nah, don't bow down to me; I'm just another servant like you, keeping it real with the prophecy. Only God gets the worship." {22:10} "Don't keep this prophecy on lockdown," he adds. "Time's ticking." {22:11} Those who do wrong keep doing wrong; those who keep it clean stay clean; God's bringing the rewards soon. {22:12} "I'm the start and finish," He says, "the A to Z, and I'm dishing out rewards based on what people bring to the table." {22:13} He's the OG, the first and last. {22:14} Blessed are those who keep it real, scoring access to the tree of life and VIP entry into the city. {22:15} Outside are the fakes, the sorcerers, the shady players, and the liars. {22:16} I, Jesus, sent my angel to spill the beans to you church folk. I'm the real deal, the root of David, and the morning star. {22:17} The Spirit and the bride are calling out, inviting anyone who's thirsty to come get some living water, no strings attached. {22:18} Don't mess with the words of this prophecy; adding or subtracting brings some serious plagues. {22:19} Mess with the prophecy, and you're outta the Lamb's VIP list and outta the holy city. {22:20} I'm coming real soon; amen. Come through, Lord Jesus.

Made in United States
Orlando, FL
05 November 2024

53506171R00230